Reunion Association Wisconsin Soldiers

Wisconsin soldiers and sailors reunion roster

Containing the postoffice address

Reunion Association Wisconsin Soldiers

Wisconsin soldiers and sailors reunion roster
Containing the postoffice address

ISBN/EAN: 9783337135331

Printed in Europe, USA, Canada, Australia, Japan

Cover: Foto ©ninafisch / pixelio.de

More available books at **www.hansebooks.com**

WISCONSIN
SOLDIERS AND SAILORS
REUNION ROSTER

—·—∗—·>CONTAINING THE<—∗—·—

Postoffice Address, Occupation and Name of every Wisconsin Soldier and Sailor, now living in any part of the World, and every other Soldier, now in the State, who responded to the Reunion Call. Also the Name of every Wisconsin Soldier who perished in the War—giving the Battle in which he was killed, or place where he died, with date; each class arranged by Companies and Regiments.
Also a Complete Roster of Wisconsin's Armed Military Organizations, The State National Guard, taking part in the Grand Inter-State Military Display and Contest, during Reunion Week, with the only

COMPLETE PROGRAMME OF THE REUNION EXERCISES,

—·—∗—·>TOGETHER WITH<—∗—·—

A Vast Collection of Instructive, Entertaining, and Amusing Historical Sketches, Personal Reminiscences and Anecdotes of

WISCONSIN MEN IN THE WAR.

—·—∗—·>CONTRIBUTED BY<—∗—·—

GEN. J. A. KELLOGG,	COL. ED. E. BRYANT,	COL. AMASA COBB,
GEN. E. S. BRAGG,	COL. J. A. WATROUS,	COL. G. W. CARTER,
GEN. JOHN GIBBON,	COL. JOHN HANCOCK,	COL. E. A. CALKINS,
GEN. H. C. HOBART,	COL. GEO. B. GOODWIN,	COL. O. C. JOHNSON,
GEN. LUCIUS FAIRCHILD,	COL. H. B. HARSHAW,	HON. H. B. WARNER,
GEN. T. S. ALLEN,	MAJ. L.U. DRURY,	MAJ. J. H. HAUSER,
GEN. JAMES BINTLIFF,	"GRAYSON",	CAPT. GRIFF J. THOMAS,
LIEUT. H. B. EASTMAN,	CAPT. D. N. KASSON,	LIEUT. D. L. JONES,
SERGT. O. B. CHESTER,	LIEUT. JOHN A. OWENS,	LIEUT. D. C. PAVEY,
MRS. SARAH D. HOBART,	MRS. H. N. SMITH.	MISS ADDIE L. BALLOU,	KATIE PIER,

And many others not above named.

Compiled under the Supervision of the President of the Wisconsin Soldiers Reunion Association.

FOND DU LAC, WIS.
STAR STEAM JOB AND BOOK PRINTING HOUSE.
1880.

NORTHWESTERN MUTUAL LIFE INSURANCE COMPANY

MILWAUKEE, WISCONSIN.

DIVIDENDS

Payable in 1879 and 1880, less State tax where such is imposed, on life policies (all cash, no dividend additions) issued at age 35 for $10,000.

Year of Issue	Premium	Dividend 1879	Dividend 1880
1879	264 90	—	74 80
1877	264 90	73 30	77 60
1876	264 90	77 60	81 50
1875	264 90	81 50	85 70
1874	264 90	85 50	89 70
1873	264 90	89 70	94 00
1872	264 90	94 00	98 40
1871	264 90	98 40	103 00
1870	264 90	103 00	107 80
1869	268 70	111 30	116 30
1868	268 70	116 00	122 10
1867	268 70	122 10	127 40
1866	268 70	127 40	132 80
1865	268 70	132 80	138 50
1864	268 70	138 50	144 20
1863	268 70	144 20	150 00
1862	268 70	150 00	155 90
1861	268 70	155 90	162 00
1860	268 70	162 00	168 10
1859	268 70	168 14	174 30
1858	268 70	171 30	180 00

The only company which has in recent years printed its current dividends for the information of the public. The **Northwestern** has done this for eight consecutive years.

Assets, over **$18,000,000.00**.

For the past six years (1874, 1875, 1876, 1877, 1878, and 1879,) its interest receipts have exceeded its entire death losses, and working expenses by

$7,000,000.

This showing is unparalleled in the history of Life Insurance.

Ask any person carrying policies in this or other companies how Company ranks in his perience.

Obtain from the nearest Agent, or send direct to Company for any information desired.

Surplus, over 4 per ct. Reserve, $3,028,158.

The reader is requested to compare the accompanying figures, with corresponding idends, with those of any other company.

H. L. PALMER, President. **MATTHEW KEENAN, Vice-President.**
EMORY McCLINTOCK, Actuary **WILLARD MERRILL, S**

WISCONSIN COMRADES:

A little more than a year ago, suddenly and unexpectedly, the "Wisconsin Soldiers Reunion Association" was born into existence.

Unheralded, lacking ancestry, without dowery, no father, no mother, or even respectable claim to *bona fide* orphanage, it appeared before us.

If there be among you those who think the charge of this foundling, should have been placed with an older, abler, and more worthy soldier, the sentiment meets my most hearty concurrence.

Except for the kind and continuous aid, extended from all sides, by soldier hands and veteran hearts, the child could scarcely have survived its infancy.

But it had friends—friends by the tens of thousands, scattered here and there all over the world, where Wisconsin comrades might be.

Yet—how to find them?

The *newspapers*—the patriotic, enterprising publishers, threw wide open their columns—free as the air we breathe; and no absent soldier was so far away, or so secluded, but they found him and told him of this new born waif, claiming recognition.

Did the soldiers deny the relationship? No! from the entire circuit of this big world came the ringing response:

"*I am proud to say I was a Wisconsin Soldier.*"

In this volume all are gathered. Without the aid of newspaper ink, years of toil and thousands of money could not have produced this roster.

But after they had come, these letters and cards, by the bushels and baskets full! think of it! the cost of time, labor, money. To assort, arrange, copy, compare, and recopy, and the expense of publication, would have placed the volume beyond the reach of many.

To prevent this—loyal, enterprising, liberal, BUSINESS MEN, the leading firms and corporations, opened their purses.

Don't forget them. When you are in need of anything, from a Threshing Machine to an Insurance Policy, look within and patronize those who patronized you.

SOLDIERS:

In the near future, one by one, we shall be called to join those of our former associates, who on the field of battle, in hospital or in prison, gave up *their* lives "that the nation might live."

Ere another roll-call, the ranks of surviving Wisconsin veterans, now numbering less than one-quarter their original strength, will surely and rapidly be still further depleted. May we not hope—soldier comrades —these reunions are not confined to those in this life alone: but that as we gather to-day in social greetings, those long since gone—the departed ones—the brave, the true, the kind and generous boys, we knew so well—*also* come: are with us, around and about us——

"Even they.
The dead, though dead so dear,
Fond Memory to her duty true,
Brings back each manly form to view.
We see them as in times long past,
From each to each, kind looks are cast.
We hear their words, their smiles behold—
They are with us, as they were of old."

COMRADES AND FRIENDS:

For countless favors received at your hands, accept sentiments of keenest appreciation and gratitude from me; and in this life, and the life to come may Heaven's choicest blessings rest upon you, and yours, time without end.
C. K. PIER.

June 7, 1880.

THE WISCONSIN SOLDIERS REUNION ASSOCIATION.

HOW IT COMMENCED—WITH A STORY.

CAPT. C——, of Janesville, was one of the nicest men who ever lived, but his age alone placed him among the counsellors, rather than the warriors, of his country; and beside, although brave as the bravest, he was nervous to such an extent that in cases of sudden emergency he was apt to "go off his feet" and give orders to his company which would baffle Hardee himself to either duplicate or execute.

During Grant's rapid and tedious flank movement from Cold Harbor to Petersburg, in 1864, the men became extremely exhausted and footsore. As the inevitable result, intervals were extended and stragglers multiplied, until a company occupied space sufficient to execute brigade evolutions. Now and then, as firing in the advance became sharper or more continuous, a staff officer or orderly would come galloping down the line with "compliments of the commanding general who directs your men be well closed up, ready to go into battle at a moment's notice."

These orders interpreted and passed along, served for a while to keep the men closer together, but repeated false alarms soon made them heedless and they quickly relapsed back into former, or even worse, disorder. At one time when the firing had been unusually heavy and prolonged, and the orders to keep men well in hand, came more frequent and positive, the colonel of Capt. C's regiment drew out from the column, and, as the various companies passed, he called the attention of respective captains to [the necessity of complying with the order, as the enemy were liable to engage us at any moment. Capt. C. came along at the head of his company, begrimed with dust and half staggering under his load of knapsacks and muskets which the kindness of his heart prompted him to carry for some of his sick and blistered soldiers. The colonel said rather sharply, "Captain, did you know we are both liable to court martial, for disobedience to orders, in not keeping the men closed up?" This, of course, operated as a complete upset. Dropping his load, with sword in one hand and hat in the other, he turned and shouted: "Company H, for G-o-d's s-a-k-e, c-l-o-s-e u-p," and then as he comprehended the immense distance over which the men were spread he added: "Great H-e-a-v-

e-n-s! if the rebels were to suddenly fire upon you, scattered as you are, they couldn't hit a d-a-m-n-e-d one of you."

JANUARY 1ST, 1880.

Nearly fifteen years after the close of the war, the surviving soldiers and sailors of Wisconsin scattered in every clime and latitude were very much in the condition of company H, as stated by Captain C.

If, for social, business, or other reasons, a comrade desired to find another who had moved from his former residence, the chances strongly were he couldn't find a b-l-e-s-s-e-d one of them. This fact, together with the strong sentiment of fellowship which every good soldier feels toward another good one, even though they never met, and the disinclination on part of the soldiers to allow the union sentiment to die out, or certainly not until they, too, were dead, prompted action as shown by the following card, which was very generally and freely published by leading and local newspapers throughout the United States and territories:

WISCONSIN SOLDIERS.

SOLDIERS:—At a meeting of old comrades, held at Berlin, Jan. 1, there was organized the Wisconsin Reunion Association. Every surviving soldier or sailor who enlisted from Wisconsin and was honorably discharged from the United States military or naval service is earnestly requested to write upon a postal card his name, occupation, P. O. address, letter of company or companies, number of regiment or regiments, in which he served, and send it to Grifl. J. Thomas, Secretary of the Wisconsin Reunion Association, Berlin, Wis., who will arrange a complete roster, in alphabetical order by company and regiment, for record and publication. Sailors will give name of boat or boats on which they served.
Comrades! Attend to this at once, or we shall not know whether you are dead, proud, or gone to Texas. C. K. PIER, President.
FOND DU LAC, Wis., Jan. 1, 1879.

The result is simply marvelous. The war itself, the material of the immense armies contending, their defeats and victories, and their final disbandment, are each historic wonders. But the subsequent histories of the survivors of that war form an equal, if not greater and more entertaining, subject of investigation and study.

To the surviving soldier there is nothing which more promptly calls and holds his attention. Into the grand army of the Union, Wisconsin sent 91,379 of her sons. Of these, 74,891 were honorably discharged and returned to their homes. It is probable (an estimate of course) that not more than 30,000 are still living.

Where are they all? What are they doing? What standard of citizens are they making? In short, "how are the boys getting on, anyway?" To answer these questions this little card invoked the aid of American newspa-

pers. Right grandly was that aid extended, and right soldierly have the returns responded "here." From every state and territory, from Mexico, South America, Europe and the Islands of the sea, in every style of language and expression, with endless inquiries, and every variety of information, the soldiers send back their ringing responses.

IN THIS VOLUME

You have the names alphabetically arranged by regiments and companies, with occupation, when given, and post-office addresses.

In the very nature of things there are errors. There was no way to avoid them. We have done the best we could. In many instances the writing was almost illegible. Others stated they were in "Captain Smith's Company," and there being numerous Capt. Smiths, we had to make the best guess possible under the surrounding circumstances. Others have given their regiment as the First, Second, Third, or Fourth, without specifying whether infantry or cavalry, and we have to guess again.

In other ways it may be expected errors have crept in. These should be reported as fast as discovered, in order that correction be made. Names not reported should be sent in, and changes of P. O. address, or death ot a soldier, sent to the secretary.

THE ADVANTAGES

Already inuring to members of the Association, guarantees its continuance so long as there remain two surviving Wisconsin soldiers or sailors. Brief as has been its life, hundreds of comrades have already received incalculable benefit therefrom.

In another place an able article invites your attention to the "Future of our Society," and offers suggestions prompted by patriotic principles—the best basis of true statesmanship.

Still another comrade gives excellent views as to "Membership Duties," which show thought and earnestness in the good cause, and if followed, the Association will leave a monument to coming generations to which posterity will over refer with pride.

1880.
LaBELLE WAGON WORKS,
FOND DU LAC, WIS.

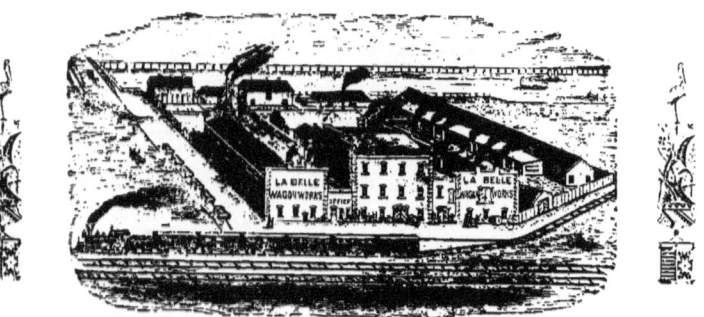

MANUFACTURERS OF THE CELEBRATED

LaBELLE WAGON

For Farm, Freight and Plantation Use.

THESE WAGONS ARE MANUFACTURED FROM

The Best and Most Thoroughly Seasoned Timber.

They are WELL and STRONGLY IRONED, FINELY PAINTED, and the GENERAL WORKMANSHIP CANNOT BE EXCELLED.

THESE WAGONS ARE NOTED FOR THEIR

VERY LIGHT DRAUGHT,

And for Durability they have no Superior. They have NEVER failed of giving the

BEST SATISFACTION.

WISCONSIN SOLDIERS AND SAILORS
REGIMENTAL REUNION ROSTER.

EXPLANATIONS TO THE READER:

Regiments are in their numerical order commencing with the Infantry; then Cavalry, Heavy Artillery, Batteries, Sharp Shooters, Soldiers of other States, State National Guard, Reunion Programme, and Sketches interspersed.
Commissioned officers' names with rank are at head of their respective commands.
The soldier's surname comes first followed by his christian name or initials.
If known, his occupation comes next, and last his P. O. address. When state is omitted *Wisconsin* is understood. When soldier's name is followed by a + it shows he was killed in action at the place and date then given. When the name is succeeded by a ± it shows the man died of wounds at place and date given. When neither * nor ± is given, but the line ends with a date it shows he died of disease while in the army at such place and date. Any soldier's name not appearing, shows either he has died *since* the war or has failed to respond to the Reunion call.
In the Appendix will be included names received after the Regimental Roster went to press.

ABBREVIATIONS:

ar—Artist. a—Attorney. b—Banker. bk—Bookkeeper. c—Carpenter. d—Druggist. cl—Clergyman. e—Engineer. ed—Editor. f—Farmer. h Hotel. l—Laborer. m—Merchant. mf—Manufacturer. me—Mechanic. p—Printer. pr—Publisher. pa—Painter. ph—Physician.

FIRST INFANTRY.

(Three months. Organized in April 1861.
Campaigns in Maryland and Virginia.)
Three years. Organized Oct. 19th, 1861. Original strength, 945; gain by recruits, etc., 563. Total, 1,508. Death loss, 238—killed in action, 91, died of wounds, 41, of disease, 103. Other losses, 402—missing 0, desertion, 57, transfer, 47, discharge, 298. Campaigns in Tenn., Ky., Ala., and Ga.

REGIMENTAL ROSTER.

Col J C Starkweather, a Washington, D C
Col G B Bingham, f Cozzens Grove, Kansas
Lt Col D H Lane Robestown, Neb
Lt Col Henry A Mitchell
Maj. D C McVean Benton Barracks, Mo
Maj. T H Green, architect Fond du Lac
Adj H L Franklin Milwaukee
Adj W W Watkins Milwaukee
Q M Henry Bingham
Q M Nathaniel Bingham
Q M Chas H Benton, h'dware Fond du Lac
Surg L J Dixon Montpelier, Vt.
1st A Surg James Crugon Milwaukee
1st A Surg Egbert Jamieson Racine
1st A Surg Fred Cofe Mt. Sterling
2d A Surg D B Davendorf Delavan
2d A Surg Joseph Green Hudson
2d A Surg John R McCullough, d Jefferson
Chaplain, John McNamara Des Moines, Iowa

COMPANY ROSTER.

A

Capt G B Bingham, f Cozzens Grove, Kansas
Capt J C Goodrich, m 56 W Randolph st, Chi'go
Lt S Babcock Chicago, Ills
Lt W W Watkins Milwaukee
Lt H P Schuyler Amsterdam, Holland
Lieut Edward Mehle
Lt H S Lee Milwaukee
Allen, G P, sergt Murfreesboro, Feb 11—63
Anderson, N Warrensburg, Illinois
Andrews, M G Cedarburg
Anderson, J * Dallas, May 26—64
Allard, Wm, f Pine Grove
Anderson, N * Chaplin Hills, Oct. 8—62
Buckhoff, Geo H Oshkosh
Buxton, Chas P Eldorado, Iowa
Buzzell, D P * Chaplin Hills, Oct 8—63

Bowen, K M Big Rapids, Mich
Bridges, M L Hubbardstown, West Va
Clark, Henry Lenox, Mass
Carroll, J J Louisville, Jan 31—62
Chase, G M, corp Andersonville, Sept 7—67
Chase, W E Nashville, March 4—62
Cunneen, M * Chaplin Hills, Oct. 8 - 62
Carlton, B F Nashville, Nov 2- 62
Clarkson, Ben Benton, Kansas
Crayson, I. C Chattanooga, Feb 19—64
Davendorf, D B Delavan
Drake, G G * Falling Waters, July 2—61
Drewson, Isaac Fond du Lac
F Farman, e Stevensville
Grey, J, m Menominee Falls
Grigg, A Nashville, April 14—62
Greeley, Peter, m Mukwanago
Hammers, H + Chaplin Hills, Oct 15—62
Haus, Geo A Milwaukee
Ferguson, Ed, Pension, Agt Milwaukee
Heywood, Geo Milwaukee
Johnson, J * Chaplin Hills, Oct 8—62
Keyes, W H Beaver Dam
Keyes, D W Milwaukee
La Poin, E* Chaplin Hills, Oct 8—62
Luther, P J M. dison
La Trune, L S A * Chaplin Hills, Oct 8—62
Lerett, N, e Mastersville
Morterns, E * Chaplin Hills, Oct 8 - 62
McCracken, L J St Louis, Mo
McCall, Irwin Omro
Nilson, N J, sergt+ Chaplin Hills, Oct 20—64
Newman, J, corp* Chaplin Hills, Oct 8—63
Newerman, J, l Harrison
Peteram, August Binghamton
Proronsha, Peter, f Stoneville
Roche, Julius Tess Corners
Smith, J A * Chaplin Hills, Oct 8—62
Trowbridge, H, f Waupun
Thyfault, C Chattanooga, March 12—62
Wheelock, A B, Post Master Eden, Dakota

B

Capt Henry A Mitchell
Capt John M Cosgrove
Capt Henry O Montague Topeka, Ka
Lt Jas S White, ed Milwaukee
Lt Thomas Caliger, salesman Chicago
Bockloee, Henry Chippewa Falls
Bloom, John Wauwatosa

Carpenter, W F Fond du Lac
Cathcart, H Louisville, Nov.—62
Davis, J Andersonville, Oct. 10—64
Diercks, -- Soldiers' Home, Milwaukee
Ehlers, J P J- Chattanooga, Oct. 20—63
Ermentenger, J Nashville, Feb. 5—64
Fitzgerald, John Soldiers' Home, Milwaukee
Geisman, W D Milwaukee
Gould, Levi, me Chicago
Graham, W M, serg't !- Falling Waters, Aug.28—61
Greenly, J W * Nashville, March 5—63
Hauker, Charles West Bend
Hansan, M Andersonville, Nov 8—64
Hendricks, Wm Cleveland, Ohio
Hewett, L F Ishpeming, Mich
James, Charles, f Waterford
Knox, John Council Bluffs, Iowa
La Roche, Battise Rice Lake
Lumb, William, f Adams
Lyon, C G, serg't Madison, Nov 19—63
Martin, Henry, serg't Milwaukee
Mulligan, J Andersonville, June 15—64
McCann, Stephen S Eau Claire
McAfee, John Oregon
Palmer, C B Lincoln, Neb
Post, C J on G B & M R R, Green Bay
Relyea, L, corp Nashville, Sept 13—62
Sanders, Edward Chicago
Smith, H F, corp Nashville, March 15—62
Stuart, E H Hamilton
Swan, J Murfreesboro, Feb 15—63
Walker, A V Nashville, March 17—62
Walsen, F J, h East Saginaw, Mich
Weber, N Nashville, Oct 5—62
Whilden, J B Nashville, May 4—62
Zanders, A T Nashville, April 14—62

C

Capt Robert Hill
Capt Hiram A Sheldon Racine
Lieut Wm E Gibbons
Lieut Robert J Niekles* Sept 11—63
Lieut Albert M Dyer
Lieut Edward Ferguson, pension agt Milwaukee
Lieut Jacob Weyrough
Addison, P + Bridgeport, Ala, Sept 24—63
Aderson J * Chickamauga, Sept 19—64
Austin, E P + Bridgeport, Ala, Sept 24—63
Bouchoiz, W Murfreesboro, June 5—63
Brainard, J Nashville, July 1—63

DUTCHER, COLLINS & SMITH,

IMPORTERS AND JOBBERS OF

TEAS,

MILWAUKEE, WISCONSIN.

ALSO JOBBERS OF

TOBACCOS,
FINE CUT, SMOKING AND PLUG

SEGARS AND SYRUPS,

Orders by Mail will receive Prompt Attention.

JOHN A. DUTCHER.   WILLIAM A. COLLINS.   EVERETT A. SMITH.

WISCONSIN SOLDIERS AND SAILORS REUNION ROSTER

Briggs, J L — Colby
Coleman, Henry — Sergeants' Bluff, Iowa
Cosmer, W W — Richland Centre
Crawford, N * — Chickamauga, Sept 19—63
Emmett, J E — Perkinsville, Pa
Everst, John I — Neosho
Evon, Evonson — Caldwell's Prairie
Fabien, C * — Chickamauga, Sept 18—63
Fields, C A * — Chaplin Hills, Oct 8—62
Fisher, C E — Nashville, Dec 5—61
Grout, J — Nashville, Jan 30—62
Hamilton, Walter — Rich City, Idaho
Hill, D, * — Chaplin Hills, Oct 8—62
Hunt, J M, corp * — Chaplin Hills, Oct 8—62
Kendall, Albert — Troy, N. Y
Kewes, E S — Neosho, Missouri
Luck, J * — Chaplin Hills, Oct 8—62
McKisson, A J, corp* — Chaplin Hills, Oct 8—62
Monroe, J H — Camp Scott, Wis, June 8—61
Norris, Alex, pa — Milwaukee
Norton, H J — Vickersville, Mich
Palmer, H * — Chickamauga, Sept 14—63
Parkins, J G — Brandon
Parmerton, G * — Chickamauga, Sept 19—63
Peake, Wm — Nashville, Feb 5—62
Perry, W W — Beaver Dam
Perry, H H — Kenosha
Pierce, James C, a — Memphis, Tenn
Reynolds, John, justice — Burlington
Sheldon, H A — Racine
Smith, R C, c — Milwaukee
Sutton, A — Nashville, Nov 27—61
Sutton, E * — Chaplin Hills, Oct 8—62
Tewes, A * — Kenesaw, June 22—64
Thele, John, f — Geneva, Iowa
Wallace, C C — Annapolis, Feb 1—63
Webber, Geo P — Independence, Iowa
Weinborn, J* — Chaplin Hills, Oct—62
Wells, A E — Racine
Wild, J, sergt — Madison, Nov 19—63
Williams, L — Columbus
Wilson, W, corp * — Chickamauga, Sept 19—63
Winter, O G — Pine Hill
Wolcott, S * — Jonesboro, Sept 1—64
Wood, C W — Racine

D

Capt Henry A Starr
Capt Wm S Mitchell* — Sept 19—63
Capt Charles H Messenger
Lieut Howard H Chandler
Lieut George Lund
Lieut Wm K Hughes — Milwaukee
Brooker, H — Louisville, Jan 21—62
Brown, W, serg't * — Chaplin Hills, Oct 8 - 62
Carpenter P — Nashville, April 14—62
Elliot, S * — Chickamauga, Sept 9—63
Gutch, H — Andersonville, July 11—64
Guthrie, D T — Chattanooga, Oct 20—63
Howard, S — Oakfield
Hughes, Wm R — Milwaukee
Hupp, J A — Atlanta, Georgia
Joice, O * — Chaplin Hills, Oct 8 - 62
Kirst, Joseph — West Bend
Littlefield, A — Chickamauga, Sept 19—62
Mob, Christian — Maple Works
Peck, C E, corp — Dec 1—61
Post, C — G B & M R R
Schlegel, Christian, shoemaker — Westfield
Spears, N B, corp — Stevenson, Nov 1—63
Stephens, C * — Chaplin Hills, Oct 8—62
Sweetster, S M — Chattanooga, June
Wechselberg, R, corp* — Chickamauga, Sept 19—63
Wechselberg, W * — Chaplin Hills, Oct 8—62
Wicker, Wm H H — Neillsville
Wicker, W H — Unity
Wood, Geo, Serg't — Chattanooga, Aug 31—64

Young, D * — Chaplin Hills, Oct 8 62

E

Capt Donald C McVean — Jefferson Barracks, Mo
Capt Benjamin F Tevis
Lieut Geo E Scott
Lieut Richard F Hambrook
Lieut Collins C McVean* — June 23—64
Lieut Edward Healey
Bates, C H — Fulton
Boyler, Chas H C, janitor — Madison
Bryant, Geo E — Madison
Chapel C — Andersonville, July 31—64
Christop erson, H — Rome, July 5—64
Colter, Wm, shoemaker — Racine
Dauntz, W * — Aug 12—64
Dimmich, Russell F — Milwaukee
Gray, Albert — Osceola
Greenwood, H, in the field † — June 2—64
Griffin, G B — Murfreesboro, June 3—63
Harkin, John — Kenosha
Harmon, W * — Chaplin Hills, Oct 8—62
Haskins, J — Andersonville, July 3 —64
Herman, C * — Chickamauga, Sept 19—63
Herrick, T W * — Chaplin Hills, Oct 8—62
Holmes, T — Feb 23—62
Jefferson, B, bus line — Madison
Langworthy, S A, serg + Chaplin Hills, Oct 12—62
Loomis, L, in the field + — July 10 64
Meacle, W K — Feb 17—62
Mellor, S — Chaplin Hills, Oct 9—63
Munger, M W — Nashville, July 28—64
Myrick, Seth B — Briston, Iowa
Orvis, C H — April 16—62
Osmondson, O, in the field— — Aug 11—64
Palmer, Joseph — Osceola
Palmer, Wm — Osceola
Radtke, W* — Chaplin Hills, Oct 8—62
Seaton, C S* — Chattanooga, Jan 13—64
Spencer, J C* — Chickamauga, Sep 19—63
Spencer, Jno W C, sergt+ — Chaplin Hills, Nov 5—62
Stoddard, H* — Chickamauga, Sep. 19—63
Stokin, E H+ — Chaplin Hills, Oct 11—62
Thayer, Chauncey R — Clay Bank
Krumble, W * — Chaplin Hills, Oct 8—62
VanAbstine, G H — Nashville, Oct 14—62
Vantassel, H W — Eden
Wicks, O * — Chaplin Hills, Oct 8—62

F

Capt Maurice M Samuels
Lieut Wm J Vincent
Lieut Pembroke V Wise
Lieut Seth W Button
Lieut Junius A Bartlett
Lieut F T Starkweather
Bennett, H* — Chickamauga, Sept 19—63
Buell, S, Sergt * — Chickamauga, Sept 19—63
Cowels, H, sergt* — Chaplin Hills, Oct 8—62
Davis, M L * — Chaplin Hills, Oct 8—62
Ellis, J * — Chaplin Hills, Oct 8—62
Kaylor, H * — Chaplin Hills, Oct 8—62
Lovel, P, corp * — Chaplin Hills, Oct 8—62
Maloney, R* — Chaplin Hills, Oct 8—62
McKenzie, J* — Andersonville, July 7—64
Nichols, J N, sergt * — Chaplin Hills, Oct 8 - 62
Peabody, J P, * — Chaplin Hills, Oct 8—62
Phillips, J, — Murfreesboro, April 4—64
Pollard, A, corp * — Chaplin Hills, Oct 8 - 62
Pickett, T B, corp — Chaplin Hills, Oct 8 - 62
Sauberly, Henry — Janesville
Schemerhorn, S — Janesville
See, Alexander F — Rollo, Mo
Sireasey, S + — Chaplin Hills, Oct 24—62
Turner, D H — Bowling Green, Oct 18—62
Warrendorph, Ed — Albert Lea, Minn

Webster, N + — Chaplin Hills, Oct 16—62
Wing, G W, corp * — Chaplin Hills, Oct 8—62

G

Capt Edward Bloodgood
Capt Wm H Wilson
Lieut Edward J Watkins
Lieut Chas A Searles * — Sept 19—63
Lieut Zerah P Clark
Lieut Charles H Benton — Fond du Lac
Lieut Addison S Gardiner
Lieut Chas J Robinson
Lieut Geo W Lawton
Andrews, J — Chattanooga, June—64
Ashby, H — Louisville, Jan 28—62
Austin, S — Murfreesboro, March 11—63
Baker, Chas W — Soldiers Grove
Baker, H J — March 3—62
Baker, J B — Louisville, Jan 24—62
Bergaman, A+ — Nashville, July 11—64
Boardman, O, corp — Murfreesboro, Mar 13—63
Bremmer, J A, Enuseryman — Stevens Point
Brooks, W S* — Dallas, May 30—64
Bruemmer, Louis — Kewaunee
Burke, G,+ in the field — June—64
Burns, W — Louisville, Dec 5—62
Christman, H, f — Menominee Falls
Clement, C* — Chaplin Hills, Oct 8—62
Cille, Jr, J — Nashville, Sept 5—64
Cory, John — Madison
Dent, A B* — Chaplin Hills, Oct 8—62
Fletcher, Arthur — Badger
Fogg, T W* — Chaplin Hills, Oct 8—62
Gibson, F A — Racine
Greenge, J C, sergt, f — Menominee Falls
Gretzer, John — Hastings, Neb
Ham, John, D — Clemensville
Howland, A — Fort Howard
Humphrey, J+ — Nashville, July 11—64
Irwin, Jesse, f — Ontario
Johnson, A* — Dallas, May 27—62
Knight, A R — Nov 27—61
Laine, J H, pil — Sacramento, Cal
Lamark, F — Chaplin Hills, Oct 8—62
Lee, D H, corp* — Chickamauga, Sept 20—63
Lewis, A H * — Chickamauga, Sept 19—63
Marlan, J W — Louisville, Jan 18—62
McKenzie, C, corp* — Chaplin Hills, Oct 24—62
McMahon, J+ — Chattanooga, June—64
Miller, M P, sergt* — Chickamauga, Sept 20—63
Minor, J G* — Chaplin Hills, Oct 8—62
Mulkins, Wm — Plover
Pelton, F — Aug 26—62
Phelon, J* — Chaplin Hills, Oct 8—62
Rose, John, I — Kendall
Ruby, B* — Chaplin Hills, Oct 8 - 62
Searles, C A, 1st lt* — Chickamauga, Sept 19—63
Smier, G* — Dallas, May 30—63
Steadman, C H — Feb 24—62
Sweeney, E — Nov 15—61
Taple, Wm B, ed — Peru, Ill
Thayer, Chauncey R — Clay Bank
Whalee, J — Nashville, Feb 1—64
Williams, L — Columbus

H

Capt Henry Requay
Capt A F Adams
Capt Eugene Carey
Capt John C McMullen
Lieut Gilbert B Bingham — Cozzens' Grove, Kan
Lieut Lewis C Trowbridge
Lieut J S Richardson — Oct 5, 63
Lieut Horace E Wood
Baker, P — Nashville, July 18—64
Breed, J H, corp* — Chaplin Hills, Oct 8—62
Carver, W H* — Chaplin Hills, Oct 8—62

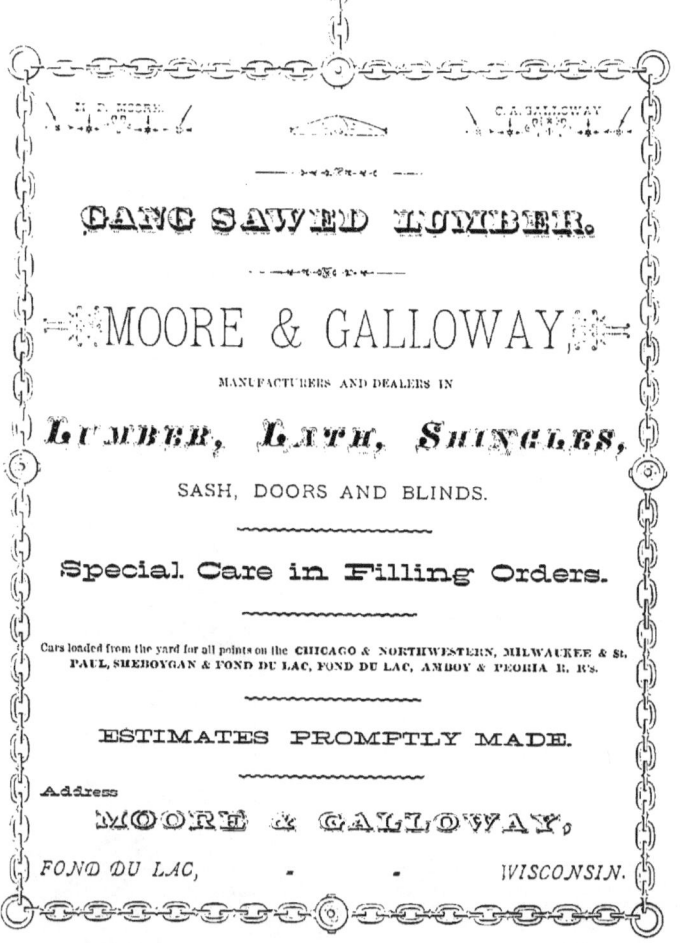

WISCONSIN SOLDIERS AND SAILORS REUNION ROSTER.

Name	Location/Date
Chapel, C H*	Chattanooga, Aug 16—64
Dieterle, J	Sauk City
Darkee, C+	Chaplin Hills, Oct 10—62
Farron, W	Andersonville, Aug 20— 64
George, W	Nashville, Feb 6—63
Grimm, L	March 17—62
Henricks, Wm	Cleveland, Ohio
Holcomb, A	Nashville, Aug 19—64
Koohell, A	Murfreesboro, March 7—63
Kummelt, J	Andersonville, May 16—64
Littlefield, A	Feb 27—62
Littlefield, M	March 2—62
Lymun, W B+	Louisville, Jan 10—63
Moore, R	Jan 21—62
Morgan, Phineas	Menomonie
Nichols, J *	Chaplin Hills,Oct 8 62
Peter, A *	Kenesaw, June 12—63
Richardson, J S 1st lt +	Chattanooga,Oct 6—62
Sawyer, J H	Murfreesboro, Feb 22 63
Still, D	April 27 62
Stroub, A	Jan 14—63
Stutz, Peter, postmaster	Plain
Tucker, W H	March 24—62
Uphum, M +	Chaplin Hills, Oct 9—62
Wagnor, F	Murfreesboro, Feb. 23 - 63
Wilson, G J	Feb 3—62
Woodworth, W B	Andersonville, Sept 21—61

I

Name	Location/Date
Capt Oran Rogers	
Capt Abner O Heald *	Sept 19 - 3
Capt George W Huffum	
Lt Sylvester Colwell	
Lt Jerome F Brooks	
Lt Charles C White	
Abers, H V	Nashville, Feb 2—62
Annis, A, l	Fond du Lac
Arnold, E	March 5—62
Arnold, H +	Nashville, Jan 23—63
Babcock, D, a	Fond du Lac
Batcheider, J	Andersonville, Sept 12—64
Brown, C W+;	Chaplin Hills, Oct 15—62
Churchill, D	Murfreesboro, March 27—63
Clark, J E *	Chaplin Hills, Oct 8—62
Cuffeen, Moses	Taycheedah
Coleman, S	Chicago
Craig, Ezekiel L	Tomah
Deetsh, J *	Chaplin Hills, Oct 8—62
Duncan, Albert, f	Boltonville
Everdell, L B. a	Wahpeton, Dakota
Ferris, Ed J	Eagle Rock, Idaho
Green, T H, architect	Fond du Lac
Greizer, Jno	Hastings, Neb
Hauer, A +	Chickamauga, Sept 19- 63
Hart. Lewis	Waupun
Harvey, D M	Andersonville, June 6—64
Hayford, Wm T	Taycheedah
Henry, C S, m	Fond du Lac
Johnson, H L	Waldo
Laveox, R *	Chaplin Hills, Oct 8—62
Littlefield, A D *	Chickamauga, Sept 19—63
Magensen. Thomas	Taycheedah
McIntosh, C M	Murfreesboro, March 4—63
McNewson, T, l	Fond du Lac
Meach, N W	Taycheedah
Mentinek, H	Chickamauga, Sept 19 - 63
Norton, H J	Vickeryville, Mich
Ogle, F C *	Chaplin Hills, Oct 8—62
Pier, C K, b	Fond du Lac
Preston, C	April 10—62
Root, A E	Wisconsin, Dec 20—63
Rot, S E +	Chaplin Hills, Oct 10—62
Row, John	Boltonville
Row, William	Boltonville
Swann, W H,' corp *	Chaplin Hills, Oct 8—62
Strong, Jr T F	Fond du Lac
Swann, W H, corp *	Chaplin Hills, Oct 8-62
Tibbetts, W, sergt *	Nashville, Jan 3—63

K

Name	Location/Date
Capt T H Green, Architect.	Fond du Lac
Capt Chris Kluck, stock. gr, Mastersville, Texas	
Lt W S Burrows, marble cutter,	Lyons, Mich
Lt R M Sawyer+	Nashville, Oct 1—62
Lt Henry Stone	
Lt D F Morgan, sheriff	Oshkosh
Lt F G Rice,	Benton Harbor, Mich
Lt H G Leonard, p	Fond du Lac
Arnold, Geo	Chickamauga, Sep 17—63
Atkinson, A, me	Omaha, Neb
Bryant, G E, f	Madison
Baer, Henry	Fond du Lac
Bryant, Thos, loan agent	Omaha, Neb
Baker, F N+	Chaplin Hills, Oct 14 - 62
Baker, C H	Nashville, April 11—62
Brainard, C S	Nashville, Feb. 10—62
Crites, Isaac	Minnesota
Crites, Paul	Minnesota
Contin, James	Raymond
Coffeen, M J*	Chaplin Hills, Oct 8—62
Compte, Henry	Raymond
Cooper, Wm	Oakfield
Dashing, E B*	Chickamauga, Sept 19—63
Driess, H -	Chaplin Hills, Oct 17—62
Buell, Strabo	Lamartine
Delong, Chas	Lamartine
Durby, Ed	Oakfield
Foster, Geo	Oakfield
Foster, W M *	Chaplin Hills, Oct 8—62
George, Samuel	Raymond
Hill, Joseph	Lamartine
Huuser, James	Raymond
Herring, Theo, f	Fond du Lac
Hide, Wolcott	Lamartine
Keiser, H,	Chattanooga, July 18—64
Kellogg. C P, corp	Mitchellville, Nov 18—
Longstreet, R K	Osceola
Laddar, John,	Oakfield
Leonard, H G, pr	Fond du Lac
Love, W W, sergt+	Chaplin Hills, Oct 8—62
LeClare, J	Danville, Va. Jan 8—62
McCall, Irwin	Ouro
McArthur, W*	Chaplin Hills, Oct 8—62
Morley, H O R	Nashville, Sep 11—62
Mahaffey, Alex	Raymond
McLaughlin, K, e	Stevens Pt
Mathson, Cyrenus	Lamartine
Namas, R*	Chaplin Hills, Oct 8—62
Navens, Robert	Oakfield
Owen, Fred	Oakfield
Prosser, J	Lamartine
Palmer, C S, corp	Jan 4—62
Pells, J,	Colonia
Post, C J	G B & M R R, Green Bay
Randall, P P ;	Andersonville, Dec 8—64
Rapier, P,	Oakfield
Ruth, F M*	Chickamauga, Sept 19—63
Rowrke, M+	Chaplin Hills, O t 20—62
Russel, G J+	Chattanooga, Oct 15—62
Reed, E, on the march +	July 22—61
Stone, Geo	Lamartine
St John, F R, c	Fond du Lac
Smith, A P*	Chaplin Hills, Oct 8—62
Strong, T F, Jr, pr	Fond du Lac
Scott, G A	Nashville, Sep 11—62
Thele, Henry	Geneva, Iowa
Thompson, Wm	Oakfield
Wiley, J *	Chaplin Hills, Oct 8—62

UNASSIGNED.

| Bridges, M L | Hubbard City |

SECOND INFANTRY.

Three years, organized June 11th, 1861. Original strength, 1051 ; gain by recruits, etc., 315 ; total, 1366. Death loss, 261—killed in action, 48, died of wounds 60, of disease, 53. Other losses, 945—missing, d, desertions, 65, transfers, 134, discharged, 4o 6. Strength at muster out, July 2d 1864, 348. Campaigns in Virginia, with the old, "Iron Brigade."

REGIMENTAL ROSTER.

Name	Location
Col S Park Coon a	Chicago
Col Edgar O Conner*	Gainesville, Aug 28—62
Col Lucius Fairchild	Madrid, Spain
Col John Mansfield, senator	Los Angeles, Cal
Lt Col H W Peck	Monroe
Lt Col D McDonald	Sioux City, Iowa
Lt Col T S Allen, ed	Oshkosh
Lt Col G H Stevens+	Gettysburg, July 5—63
Lt Col W L Parsons	Racine
Maj G H Otis	McGregor, Iowa
Adj E M Hunter	Milwaukee
Adj C K Dean	Busonbet
Adj G M Woodward	LaCrosse
Q M H F Paine	Washington, D. C
Q M J D Ruggles	Lincoln, Neb
Q M J G MacCormac	
Surg J M Lewis	Oconomowoc
A Surg T P Russell	Oshkosh
Surg A J Ward	Madison
A Surg P S Arndt	Kenosha
A Surg P Fox	Madison
A Surg S Tucker	Homer, Iowa
A Surg H Babcock	Gowanda, N Y
A Surg J C Richmond	

A

Name	Location/Date
Capt G H Stevens +	Gettysburg July 5- 63
Capt H B Converse	Randolph,
Capt W W Jones	Madison
Capt Alfred Larke	Ft. Kenneth, Texas
Capt D B Dally	Council Bluffs, Ia
Lt E B Mann	
Lt A T Morgan	Washington, DC
Lt H Naegely	Macomanie
Lt S N Bond, conductor	
Lt J M Chappel	Kingston
Adams, John B	City Point, June 27 64
Bennett, Silas *	Gainesville, Aug 8 62
Bennett, H D, harness maker	Milwaukee
Bennett, A D, 1st sergt *	Wilderness, May 5—64
Brandsletter, Chas +	Gettysburg, July 12—64
Buondon, Robert	R R C on St L & Mon Ry
Burton, Daniel	Oak Hill
Carhart, J M, corp*	Bull Run, July 21—61
Chappel, J M	Kingston
Converse, H B	Randolph
Cook, Samuel	Randolph
Dexter, Frank	Madison, Nov - 63
Downs, Thomas *	Gainesville Aug 28—62
Fletcher, Chas	Fredericksburg, May 21 62
Gallette, N G, railroading	Toledo, Ohio
Gorum, Harvey *	Hatcher's Run, Oct 27—64
Gould, James H	Washington, April 19 62
Hanson, Charles, miller	Manston
Hayne, Charles I	Chapin, Iowa
Hill, George, marble cutter	Fox Lake
Horn, Gustavus *	Antietam, Sept 17 62

Insurance on Business Principles.

PROVIDENT SAVINGS
LIFE INSURANCE
SOCIETY OF NEW YORK.

SHEPPARD HOMANS, President and Actuary.

❈SAFETY, SIMPLICITY, AND DURABILITY❈

OF THIS POLICY IS ADMITTED BY THE MOST EMINENT INSURANCE EXPERTS TO BE THE VERY BEST PLAN YET ADOPTED. SEE THE FOLLOWING EXTRACTS:

[From Philip L. Spooner, Insurance Commissioner of Wisconsin.]

"The plan of life insurance presented by the "Provident Savings" is one the want of which has long been felt as being within the comprehension of the ordinary mind. It might well be called the common-sense system of life insurance, for while the indemnity is as unquestioned as that of the old system, yet, unlike the latter, it is not so inextricably connected with fine spun theories as to mystify the assured, if not the Actuary himself."

[From the Report of Hon. Stephen H. Rhodes, Insurance Commissioner of Massachusetts.]

"It is becoming more apparent every day that a radical change in the plans of life insurance is demanded. Of the various schemes or plans for insurance adapted to the wants of the masses, that of Sheppard Homans, known as "Life Insurance Without Large Accumulations of Reserves," is the most prominent."

[From Report of Hon. Oliver Pillsbury, Insurance Commissioner of New Hampshire.]

"No substantial reason has been adduced why a person should not pay and renew insurance on his life annually, as he does on his property. Life insurance conducted somewhat after the manner of fire insurance would largely do away with the necessity of heavy "reserve" accumulations, already the subject of deep concern among business men."

NEW YORK, May 20, 1878.

SHEPPARD HOMANS, *Actuary:*—DEAR SIR: We have carefully considered the theory and proposed application of your "Plan for Life Insurance Without Reserves," and I believe that for insurance companies it will be fully as secure as the present system, and, for a large portion of the insuring public, more satisfactory. If it receives the appreciation it deserves, it will inaugurate a new era in life insurance.

Yours Truly,
D. P. FACKLER, Actuary.
ELIZUR WRIGHT, Actuary and Com'r.
BEN. GRIFFIN, Actuary Mutual Life N. Y.
HENRY F. HOMES, Actuary.
JAS. C. WATSON, Actuary Mich. Mut. Life Ins. Co.

BOSTON, March 22, 1875.

MY DEAR MR. HOMANS: I am exceedingly obliged by your letter of yesterday. To *you* I hardly need say that I fully approve the circular of the "Provident Savings" enclosed in your letter. I should be happy to say it to everybody. Your institution really leaves nothing to be desired as to equity, safety and convenience in life insurance.

Yours Truly,
ELIZUR WRIGHT.

BOARD OF DIRECTORS:

ABRAHAM AVERY, Rand, Avery & Co., Printers, Boston.
ALFRED S. BARNES, Publisher, 3 Williams street.
CHAS. K. BINGHAM, Westfield, Mass.
E. A. BRINCKERHOFF, Brinckerhoff, Turner & Co., 109 Duane.
ADDISON BROWN, Counselor at Law.
WILLIAM A. CAMP, Manager New York Clearing House.
STEPHEN G. CLARKE, Counselor at Law.
ALONZO B CORNELL, Vice-Pres. West'n Union Telegraph Co.
FRANCIS O. FRENCH, First National Bank
TRACY R. EDSON, Late President American Note Co.
PARKE GODWIN, Editor Evening Post.

BENJAMIN GRIFFEN, D. A. Van Horne & Co., 25 Park Place.
DANIEL A. HEALD, Vice-President Home Insurance Co.
SHEPPARD HOMANS, President and Actuary.
JOSEPH H. PARSONS, Manufacturer, Cohoes, N. Y.
EDWARDS PIERREPONT, Late U. S. Minister to England.
TIMOTHY H. PORTER, Banker, (Soutter & Co.)
GEORGE S. SCOTT, Vice-Pres't Pacific Mail S. S. Co.
JOHN R. SMITH, Vice-Pres't Gebhard Fire Insurance Co.
WILLIAM STANLEY, Counselor. (Stanley, Brown & Clarke.)
CHARLES TAYLOR, Treasurer Domestic Sewing Machine Co.
A. F. WILLMARTH, Vice-President Home Insurance Co.

H. C. HOPKINS, Manager.

420 MILWAUKEE STREET, - - MILWAUKEE, WIS.

WISCONSIN SOLDIERS AND SAILORS REUNION ROSTER.

Jones, W W, in land office — Madison
Knoble, Henry — City Point, June 20—64
Lewis, H door-k'p house rep, Washington, D C
Lord, Austin aI * — Antietam, Sept 17—62
Luhn, William * — Gainesville, Aug 28—62
Mann, E B — Milwaukee
Marden, Joseph W * — Gettysburg, July 1—63
Maynard, Geo A — Neilsville
Marshall, Judd — Chicago
McDonald, John, corp+ — Gettysburg, July 2—61
Morgan, Albert T — Fox Lake
Morrow, Peter * — Gainesville, Aug 28 -62
Mulroy, P — New London
Nichols, T A, corp+ — Gettysburg, July 2—63
Ogden, Alexander * — Antietam, Sept 17—62
Pardee, Marcus * — Antietam, Sept 17—62
Phillips, F L, R R agt — Fox Lake
Pomroy, Cady — Chicago
Quinn, Thomas, f — Fox Lake
Robbins, L — Blue Earth, Minn
Sharpe, John W * — Gainesville, Aug 28—62
Stafford, Edgar * — Bull Run, July 21—61
Welch, Robert * — Wilderness, May 5—64
Wing, Jesse f — Rozellville

B

Capt Wilson Colwell* — S Mountain, Sept 14—52
Capt B H Hughes* — Laurel Hill, May 10—64
Capt H E Morgan — Washington
Lt Frank Hatch — LaCrosse
Lt G M Woodward — LaCrosse
Lt J D Wood — St Paul, Minn
Lt Thomas Kelby — Racine
Andres, Ignatius* — Antietam, Sept 17—62
Braudford, Oscar M* — Gettysburg, July 1—63
Brennan, Michael* — Gettysburg, July 1—63
Brewster, Edwin O* — Gainesville, Aug 28—62
Burton, Daniel — Oak Hill
Bushee, C C, corp — Andersonville, Sept 12—61
Castor, Silas+ — Gettysburg, July 5—63
Colwell, William* capt S Mountain Sept 14—62
Dailey, Dennis B — Council Bluffs, Ia
Fox, George, — Gettysburg, July 2—63
Gardner, Myron* Blackburn's Ford, July 18—61
Gillies, George, l — Madison
Hatch, Frank, chief of police — La Crosse
Higgins, Eli, com traveler — St Joseph, Mo
Hughes, Robert, capt* — Laurel Hill, May 10—64
Knolbauck, Anton+ — Richmond, July 21—61
Knox, David W* — Bull Run, July 21—61
Marvin, Lee — Fredericksburg, Jan 9—63
McClintock, Robert — Fredericksburg, Nov 21—62
McHardy, Harmon+ — Antietam, March 30—63
McIntosh, William P — Algona, Iowa
Olin, Urell P+ — Antietam, Sept 17—62
Potter, Edward* — Gainesville, Aug 28—62
Rackoma, Klaus+ — Washington, Jan 9—63
Ratejin, Hans I- — City Point, June 23—61
Reibs, Ferdinand* — Antietam, Sept 17—62
Stael, William, gunboat — Mound City
Symes, G C — Denver, Col
Van Cott, C H, f — Adair, Iowa
Washburn, Chas C — Adair, Iowa
Wencen, Godihelp, — Bangor
Woodward, Gilbert M, a — LaCrosse
White, Henry+ — Washington, June 29—14

C

Capt D McKee +
Capt G W Gibson, — Boscobel
Lt C K Dean, — Boscobel
Lt Wm Booth, — Potosi
Lt F H Lascom, — Lancaster
Lt E P Kellogg * — Gainesville, Va, Oct 9—62
Lt Levi Showalter, — Berlown
Barnhersel, Martin J — Gainesville, Aug 28—63
Beasley, George * — Antietam, Sept 17—62
Belknap, S, corp — Aug 18 - 61

Booth, William — Potosi
Brown, Joseph * — Gainesville, Aug 28—62
Burgess, John H — July 22—62
Burton, Daniel — Oak Hill
Burton, Daniel * — Gettysburg July 1—63
Carter, Richard, a — Dodgeville
Cook, Michael, corp + — Gainesville, Sept 16—62
Cox, Thomas D * — Bull Run, July 21—61
Crossley, W T, sergt — Washington, July 1—63
Curtis, A J, m — Lowell, Mass
Dean, C K, ed — Boscobel
Ewing, Wm A + — Gettysburg, Aug 12—63
Gow, James — Gettysburg, July 2—63
Gudger, D, corp* — Gettysburg, July 1—63
Gibson, Geo W — Boscobel
Halloway, Geo W * — Antietam, Sept 17—62
Heasley, Ephraim K — May 16- 62
Hyde, Geo B + — Gainesville, Sept 10—62
Hyde, James W
Kellogg, O I*, 2d lt + — Gainesville, Oct 9—62
La Font, — July 9—62
Ludwig, Otto W * — Gettysburg, July 1—63
Luscom, Frank H — Lancaster
McKenzie, R H + — Antietam, Sept 64
Neaville, F, 1st sergt * — Gainesville, Aug 28—63
Neaville, H B — Antietam, Sept 17—62
Nevins, Geo W, Postmaster, — Bloomington, Ill
Pottinger, R S * — Gainesville, Aug 28—62
Schmidt, John * — Gainesville, Aug 28—62
Simpson, R J — Antietam, Sept 17- 62
Spease, Albert W — April 25—63
Stevenson, R S * — Antietam, Sept 17—62
St. John, John + — Oct 8—62
Train, Spencer M + — Gettysburg, Aug 25—63
Waldorf, Albert + — Gainesville, Nov 25—62
Waldorf, Francis M — Dec 19—62
Weible, Wieland
Wilcox, Newton * — Gainesville, Aug 28—62

D

Capt G B Ely
Capt James D Wood — St Paul, Minn
Capt E P Perry — New London
Lt A B McLean
Lt D D Dodge
Lt G F Sanders
Lt W A Jameson+ — Gettysburg, July 5—63
Lt A F Lee
Atchinson, Edwin — Carroll City, Iowa
Bell, John — Stoughton
Bachu, Henry — Berlin
Batchelder, Geo+ — Gettysburg, July 1—63
Bean, Andres * — S Mountain, Sept 14—62
Bressler, Miles D* — S Mountain, Sept 14—62
Brown, Charles C* — Bull Run, July 21—61
Brown, Jasou* — Bull Run, July 21—61
Eble, John M, surgeon gen's office — Washington
Eble, Chauncy, corp — Nov—62
Fagan, Bartley* — Fredericksburg, Dec 13—62
Foote, W H, miller — Watertown
Gage, Ashel* — S Mountain, Sept 14—62
Hamilton, J, corp — Richmond
Hughes, Wm K — Milwaukee
Knell, Thomas H — Beloit
Martin, Stewart* — S Mountain, Sept 14—63
Monker, Gottleib — Dodgeville
Peacock, J, corp* — Gainesville, Aug 28—62
Perry, Hugh D* — Bull Run, July 21—61
Sacket, John * — June 24—63
Scott, John W+ — Gettysburg, Aug—63
Seymoure, Geo W — Dec 3—63
Smith, William, corp — Nov—63
Tra nblic Joseph* — Gainesville, Aug 28—62
Wilcox, Oramel — Janesville
Wilcox, P, corp+ — Gettysburg, July 1—63

E

Capt Gabriel Bouck — Oshkosh

Capt L H Smith — Oshkosh
Capt M R Baldwin — Oshkosh
Lt John Hancock — Oshkosh
Lt A M Thornes — Oshkosh
Lt Reuben Ash — Oshkosh
Lt H B Jackson — Oshkosh
Lt Jas N Ruby — Oshkosh
Lt H B Harshaw — Oshkosh
Abrams, G* — Mound City
Adams, Henry C, me — Oshkosh
Ash, Reuben, m — Oshkosh
Baldwin, M R, agt G T ine, — Minneapolis Minn
Baldwin, Melvin R — Oshkosh
Barton, John* — Bull Run, July 21—61
Bartlett, J C corp+ — Gainesville, Aug 28—62
Bauderob, Jno — Oshkosh
Bedient, Geo W — Jan 22—62
Birch, John — Winneconne
Bouck, Gabriel, a — Oshkosh
Boyd, Wm R — Oshkosh
Bridge, W* — S Mountain, Sept 14—62
Carpenter, G* — Mound City
Carwardime, G, corp* — Gettysburg, July 1—63
Conner, Timothy* — Antietam, Sept 17—62
Cooper, Edwin+ — Gainesville, Dec 15—62
Crary, Oscar F — Oshkosh
Davids, John B, surveyor — Vancouver, Oregon
Davis, Wm L* — Gainesville, Aug 28—62
Davis, O M — Beaver Dam
Dillon, William* — Gainesville, Aug 28—62
Dougherty, James* — Mound City
Ellsworth, Edwin — Oshkosh
Firman, L+ — Sept 8—61
Finney, Ed E — Oshkosh
Flanagan, Vincent* — Antietam, Sept 17—62
Graham, Stephen — Feb 11—63
Graves, Charles
Hackett, Samuel T* — Gettysburg, July 2—63
Hamer, James, bk — Oshkosh
Hancock, John, a — Oshkosh
Harshaw, Henry B, a — Oshkosh
Hirch, Henry — Sept 7—63
Jackson, H B, a — Oshkosh
Lester, Richard, a — Appleton
Mackerson, E H — Andersonville, Sept 5—64
McIntosh, L L* — Antietam, Sept 17—62
Montgomery, Charles
Nutter, Geo* — S Mountain, Sept 14—62
Perry, Ebenezer P, a — New London
Rouse, W S, 1st sergt+ — Gettysburg, July 1—63
Robert, J W, col office — Michigammie, Mich
Ruby, James N, me — Oshkosh
Schintz, Louis, abst office — Appleton
Scoville, Henry — April 11—62
Smith Lyman H — Oshkosh
Smith, L H, col of customs — Island Pond, Vt
Smith, Geo E, — Racine
Smith, Joseph W* — Gainesville, Aug 28—62
Sprague, J G, elk — Oshkosh
Stever, Wells — Gainesville, Sept 30—62
Strand, Horace, traveling salesman — Oshkosh
Strong, Wm E — 370 Ohio st, Chicago
Taplin, Osman B+ — Antietam, Sept 34—62
Thomas, Alanson M, lumberman — Oshkosh
Thornes, A M — Oshkosh
Torrence, Elmer* — Mound City
Waite, Joseph M — Chicago
Ward, Lawson* — Gettysburg, July 1—63
Whiting, W C — Stillwater, Minn
Whiting, Benj* — Gainesville, Aug 28—62
Wing, Edwin B — Southern, Ill

F

Capt Wm E Strong — Racine
Capt Wm L Parsons — Racine
Capt Martin L Gorman — Racine
Lt A O Doolittle — Racine
Lt A F Sexton — Racine

J. Q. HAAS. F. F. HAAS.

HAAS BROS.'

REPRESENT THE FOLLOWING | **INSURANCE** | REPRESENT THE FOLLOWING

OLD and RELIABLE COMPANIES: | | OLD and RELIABLE COMPANIES:

CONTINENTAL!
OF NEW YORK.

LANCASHIRE,
OF ENGLAND.

CONNECTICUT
OF HARTFORD.

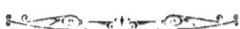

NORTHERN,
OF NEW YORK.

GERMAN,
OF BALTIMORE.

BOYLSTON,
OF BOSTON.

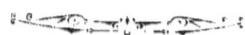

—AND—

REAL ESTATE AGENCY.

These Companies combine Age, Experience, and Wise Management, which has been shown by large fires through which they have passed.

Business Inquiries by Mail Receive Prompt Attention.

Office, Savings Bank Block,   -   -   Corner Forest and Macy Streets,

FOND DU LAC, WISCONSIN.

WISCONSIN SOLDIERS AND SAILORS REUNION ROSTER.

Lt F L Graham — Burlington
Lt Henry Hurlburt — Racine
Lt Martin Rodman — Darien
Adams, Alexander — Racine
Beauman, George — Oshkosh
Benson, Henry E * — Bull Run, July 21 -61
Burns, Peter — Racine
Chrystie, John T + — Gettysburg, July 5 -63
Christy, Hans P * — Gainesville, Aug 28 62
Cole, A C — Nebraska, City, Neb
Cole, Frank D * — Gainesville, Aug 28 62
Coombs, L D — Colorado Springs, Col
Doolittle, A O — Charles City, Iowa
Doolittle, A — Racine
Field, N J — Racine
Flor, Chas * — Bull Run, July 21—61
Fuller, William — Racine
Gorman, Martin — Racine
Gorman, Mark — Racine
Graham, Frank — Chicago, Ill
Graham, Francis L — Burlington
Gregory, Walter * — Gainesville, Aug 24 -62
Higgins, John C — Racine
Hinton, John E + — Antietam, Oct 14—62
Humes, Marion F * — Bull Run, July 21- 61
Hurlburt, Charles — Racine
Hurlburt, Henry — Racine
Ives, Charles — Racine
Jewett, Charles — Bakersfield, Cal
Jones, Thomas — Alexandria, Nov 12- 62
Judson, Shel — Washington, D C
Kelly, Thomas — Chicago, Ill
Liedy, John B * — Gettysburg, July 1 -63
Lincoln, G P, corp * — Gainesville, Aug 28—62
Manderson, Samuel — Racine
Mann, Jas M * — Gainesville, Aug 28—62
Mead, Sid — Chicago, Ill
Meigs, Nath'l* — Gainesville, Aug 28—62
Packard, E — Racine
Parsons, Lou — Kansas
Parsons, William — Racine
Pitcher, S D — Oshkosh,
Powels, Henry G, stone mason — Union Grove
Price, William, corp + — Gainesville, Sept 62
Rangott, A O * — Fredericksburg, Dec 14—62
Rodman, Martin — Darien
Rogan, James * — Wilderness, May 6—64
Ruby, J N. me — Oshkosh
Sanford, Henry — Manitowoc
Seaman, Samuel * — Gainesville, Aug 28— 2
Sexton, A J — New Orleans, La
Sexton, Andrew F — Racine
Small, Adam, corp * — Gainesville, Aug 28—62
Smith, D C * — Spottsylvania C H, May 10—64
St George, Thomas — Racine
Stickney, E B, corp* — Gainesville, Aug 28—62
Stone, Walter — Deadwood, D T
Strong, Wm F, Sturgeon Bay Canal Co Chicago
Sapling, O W, mf — Racine
Upham, William — Marshfield
Warrington, H, sergt * — Gettysburg, July 1—63
Weber, Peter * — Gainesville, Aug 28—62
Yates, John * — Antietam, Sept 17—63

G

Capt A S Hill — Portage City
Capt John Mansfield — Los Angeles, Cal
Capt C C Dow — Minneapolis, Minn
Lt S H Morrison
Lt S K Vaughan — Portage City
Lt W S M Abbott — Dodgeville
Allen, G H, — Andersonville, Aug 12—64
Bentley, Van R+ — Antietam, Sept 20—62
Bloom, Chas* — Gainesville, Aug 26—64
Brittett, Geo W, magistrate — Wenona, Ill
Chapman, J — Andersonville, June 29—64
Christy, John* — Bull Run, July 21—61
Coffin, Henry R* — Bull Run, July 21—61

Costley, Joseph G
Cowring, T F, m — Alexandria, Minn
Davis, O W corp* — Gainesville, Aug 28—62
Dean, Wm* — Gainesville, Aug 28 —62
Dow, Charles C, a — Minneapolis, Minn
Elterman, Gustav* — Antietam, Sept 17—62
Fletcher, Theod- — S Mountain, Oct 13—62
Follusby, Geo — Minneiska, Minn
Font, Edward, — Delafield
Ford, John — Madison, Feb 14—62
Hill, A S — Portage City
Hoesley, Henry, mf — New Glarus
Holbridge, S A, blacksmith — Lodi
Jackson, Edwin* — Gainesville, Aug 28—62
Kent, J G, sergt* — Gainesville, Aug 28—62
Leclear, Gustav, corp* — Gainesville, Aug 24—62
Lestor, John* — Gainesville, Aug 28- 62
Loomer, Judah T* — Gettysburg, July 1—63
Mansfield, John, a — Los Angeles, Cal
Mack, Geo W* — Gainesville, Aug 28—62
Mahoney, Patrick* — Gettysburg, July 1 -63
McDonald, Randall* — Gainesville, Aug 28- 62
McHugh, Stephen — Milwaukee
Noonan, John — Bull Run, July 21—61
Pardee, Andrew T* — Gainesville, Aug 28—62
Parker, Orson* — Gainesville, Aug 28- 62
Phillios, M L* — Gainesville, Aug 28— 62
Plumstead, W C* — Gainesville Aug 28—62
Ransacier, H — Andersonville, July 20 –64
Reynold, Charles — Milwaukee
Schilden, John P* — Gainesville Aug 26—62
Sharpe, J H — Andersonville, July 30—64
Sherwood, Guy* — Gainesville, Aug 28 62
Shumway, D J. — Castle Rock, Minn
Sines, James G — May 2—62
Slatey, T J* — Gainesville, Aug 28 -62
Snyder, Jas A* — Gainesville, Aug 28 62
Siffany, Alonzo P — Nov 2 63
Tupper, Hanford* — Gettysburg, July 1—63
Vaughn, S K — Portage City
Williams, Wm H* — Bull Run, July 21—63

H

Capt Julius F Randolph *Gainesville, Aug 28—62
Capt Nathaniel Rollins — Leadville, Col
Lt Aaron A Meredith — Madison
Lt G M Humphrey — Pawnee City, Neb
Lt Wm S Winegar* — Gettysburg, July 1—63
Allyn, Henry A + — Antietam, Sept 26—62
Bacon, Chas T* — Gainesville, Sept 10- 62
Beaver, Thomas + — Gainesville, Sept 62
Bohanan, G W — Racine
Brayton, Chas H + — Gainesville, Sept 62
Britton, Francis M + — Gettysburg, July 4—63
Bryan, J K * — Gettysburg, July 1—63
Burdick, Amos G — Wisconsin, April 64
Catlin, William * — Gainesville, Aug 28—62
Chilcote, Benj T * — Gainesville, Aug 28—62
Davidson, R E J — Algona, Iowa
Doty, Joseph W * — Gettysburg, July 1—63
Edmunds, E L + — Gainesville, Aug 29- 62
Erickson, Chas * — South Mountain, Sept 14—62
Eskew, Jas M + — Gainesville, Aug 28—62
Grover, J H, f — Algona, Iowa
Hamilton, A T+ — Antietam, Sept 26—62
Heath, Edwin, corp * — Gettysburg, July 1—63
Heise, Fred + — Antietam, Sept 26—62
Kelly, T H F, corp — Feb 21—64
Kelly, John, miller — Okee
Knulson, Isaac — Oct 10—62
Knulson, Thomas, corp * — Antietam, Sept 17- 62
McCollom, H R * — Gettysburg, July 1- 63
Moore, Wm R * — Lodi
Moore, James E — Gainesville. Aug 28—62
Northup, James E — Newton, Iowa
Packard, Eldridge + — June 64
Randolph, J F, capt * — Gainesville, Aug 28—62
Reed E B, janitor — Madison
Smith, H A — Algona, Iowa

Storm, Henry* — Antietam, Sept 17—62
Sutphen, Shead* — Gainesville, Aug 28—62
Thompson, John A — Wisconsin, March 64
Tule, John, butcher — Lodi
Watkins, James* — Gainesville, Aug 28—62
Weatherbee, A* — Gainesville, Aug 28- 62
Wells, Sidney, f — Okee
Wilbur, Geo W — Nov 62
Winegar, W S, 2d lt* — Gettysburg, July 1—63
Wyatt, Hiram C — April 62
Young, James, corp* — Gainesville, Aug 28—62
Yule, John — Lodi

I

Capt Thos S Allen — Oshkosh
Capt Wm La Fleische — Neillsville
Capt Geo H Otis — McGregor, Iowa
Lt Edw Devlin — Mineral Point
Lt Alonzo Bell — McGregor, Iowa
Lt T W Bishop
Lt Wm Noble* — Wilderness, May 5—64
Lt C Wheeler* — Milwaukee
Lt O W Sanford* — Gainesville, Sept 17—62
Avery, Luke* — Gettysburg, July 1—63
Chappell, R — Arlington Heights, March 7- 62
Curry, H P corp* — Gainesville, Aug 28- 62
Belknap, F A, f — Goldfield, Iowa
Bell, Alonzo — McGregor, Iowa
Devlin, Edward — Mineral Point
Dew, William H f — Weyauwega
Geib, Neik — Mineral Point
Genk, George — Mineral Point
Gilbert, Geo* — South Mountain
Hanson, Charles, miller — Mauston
Hesse, Mortz* — Gettysburg, July 1—63
Kay, Isaac* — Gainesville, Aug 28—62
Kesler, C — Dodgeville
Labouch, Peter — Milwaukee
Lawrence Phillips — Elkador, Iowa
Le Flaish, — Bellmout
Maloney, Thomas — Des Moines, Iowa
Meiser William — Dubuque, Iowa
Moffat, David W * — Gettysburg, July 1—62
Nelson, Wm A, corp+ — South Mountain, Oct 16—62
Noble, William, 1st lt * — Wilderness, May 5—64
Otis, George H, ed — McGregor, Iowa
Owens, Wm A, miner — Dodgeville
Perrine, Jos C L — Gettysburg, July 10—63
Sanford, O W, 2d lt + — Antietam, Oct 13—62
Tregea, Leonard, ed — Des Moines, Iowa
Tregea, John F* — Gainesville, Aug 28—62
Wheeler, C Ins agt — Milwaukee
Williams, J O, corp* — Gettysburg, July 1—63
Winne, O F — East Troy

K

Capt John Stahel, — Mazomanie
Capt J R Spoerri * — Wilderness, May 5—64
Lt C G Esslinger — Manitowoc
Lt H T Spoerri
Lt H Naegely — Mazomanie
Baumgartner, B — Andersonville, June 20- 64
Beckwith, Ed S — Elkhorn
Blasser, Ulrich* — Gainesville, Aug 28—62
Blum, John* — Gainesville, Aug 28—62
B and, Fritz — Richmond, Dec 70—63
Durland, Thos* — Gainesville, Aug 28—62
Esslinger, C G — Manitowoc
Folmsbey, George — Minneiska, Minn
Geiser, T, sergt* — Gettysburg, July 1—63
Gemender, B — Arlington Heights, Jan 16—62
Haltman, John — Arena
Huppe, H + — Spotsylvania C H, May 2—64
Klucsi Fridolin — Luni, Iowa
Korrapp, John* — Gainesville, Aug 28—62
Langworthy, A J, ed — Milwaukee
Lathrop, Wm R — Washington, Dec 28—62
Leonel, George, me — St Killians

WISCONSIN SOLDIERS AND SAILORS REUNION ROSTER.

Tuchsinger, M* — Fredericksburg, June 29--62
Marden, W H — Neillsville
Meudlick, Rodolph + — Gainesville, Sept 11--62
Milch, Chas* — Wilderness, May 5--64
Mulroy, P — New London
Munster, Anton + — Gainesville, Oct 26--62
Naegely Henry — Mazomanie
Nokes W H — Unity
Oswald, John + — South Mountain, Sept 14--62
Paschke, John corp* — Gettysburg, July 8--63
Plott, Conrad + — Gainesville, Aug 28--62
Ramthen, Wm + — Gettysburg, July 30--63
Remington, Wm N — Mauston
Roth, John + — Gainesville, Oct 19--62
Rose, Eugene P — Mauston
Shuchart, E corp + — Gettysburg, July 4--63
Sem, John + — Oct 20--62
Smith, Eustus — Mauston
Stahl, John — Mazomanie
Tarehoow, John — Falls Church, Aug 12--62
Vam Wie, William H — Mauston
Zerua, Adolph + — Gainesville Sept 27--62
Zeirnet, Peter + — Gainesville. Sept 11--62

UNASSIGNED.

Tompson, John D — Longmont, Col
Bogbee, Alvin N — Grantsburg
Briene, Wm — La Crosse
Billings, Edward L — Peach Grove, Kan
Bedient, Horace — Oshkosh
Briggs, Lewis A — Appleton
Cary, John — Oshkosh
Cusick, Hiram — Owatonna, Minn
Defoe Lewis — Oshkosh
Ellenwood, David J — Stevens Point
Encking, John — Fond du Lac
Ford, Elisha — New London
Ford, Alsworth — Oshkosh
Hart, Benjamin D — Waupaca
Holland, John — Oshkosh
Hasbrouck, George M — Oshkosh
Hays, Luther M — New York City
Hugento, Chester M — Clintonville
Hamlin, John M — Kansas City, Mo
Howe, Charles — Shawano
Miller, John L — Oshkosh
Murty, Patrick — Oshkosh
Bryant, William C — Cedar Falls, Iowa
Swings, Hiram,
Ostering, Sebastian — Oshkosh
Oleson, Ole — Oshkosh
Oatman, Isaac — Spencer
Pitcher, Sylvester D — Oshkosh
Stroud, Horace — Oshkosh
Steevers, Robert — New London
Stinson, Prosper — New London
Weed, H C — Oshkosh
Zahn, Fred O — Cincinnati, Ohio
Rodger, Geo W — Ladoga
Hutchinson, John A — Raymond
Hart, John — Escanaba
Holden, Charles N — Mauston
Hart, J H, musician — Escanaba, Mich
Smith, Waldo G — Madison
Hart, John — Appleton

THIRD INFANTRY.

Three years. Organized June 29th, 1861. Original strength, 979, gain by recruits, etc., 1177, total, 2156, death loss, 247--killed in action, 97, died of wounds, 82, of disease, 68. Other losses 1346--missing, 5, desertion, 51, transfer, 98, discharged, 945. Strength at muster out, July 19th, 1865, 810. Campaigns in Virginia, Georgia, North and South Carolina.

REGIMENTAL ROSTER.

Col Chas S Hamilton — Milwaukee
Col Thos H Ruger — Atlanta, Ga

Wm Hawley — Flint, Mich
Lt Col Bertine Pinckney — Peabody, Kan
Lt Col L H D Crane* Cedar Mountain, Aug 9--62
Lt Col J W Scott* — Chancellorsville, May 1--63
Lt Col Martin Flood
Lt Col G W Stevenson — Wiota
Maj E I. Hubbard — Cimarron, New Mexico
Maj Warham Parks — Oconomowoc
Adj Henry G Bertram — Juneau
Adj E E Bryant — Madison
Adj Jasper Woodford
Adj A C Taylor
Q M J G Knight
Q M E J Meeker — Kinsley, Kan
Q M J T Marvin
Surg Don A Raymond — Fond du Lac
Surg O F Bartlett — Meridian, N Y
Surg J G Conley
Surg G E Conant — Neosho, Mo
Surg Wilson Torrey — Sleepy Eye, Minn
Surg Thos Kopff — Beaver Dam
A Surg J B G Baxter, p bureau Washington D C
A Surg E J Farr — Eau Claire
Chap Wm L Mather — Fond du Lac
Chap J M Springer † — Murfreesboro May 28--64
Chap Isaac A Springer

A

Capt D S Gibbs
Capt H Bertram — Juneau
Lt Jno Forsyth — McGregor, Ia
Lt E E Bryant — Madison
Lt Jas W Linder
Lt Seth Raymond
Lt J D Babcock — David City, Neb
La Orin S Howard — Detroit, Mich
Lt E L Blanchard
Lt Abner Wood* — Chancellorsville, May 3 65
Lt J M Schweers — Shawano
Lt E F Proctor
Lt Geo H Cook
Glasur, Fred, 1st sergt + — Antietam, Oct 26--62
Putney, 2d, 1st sergt + — Aug 8--64
Brainard, G W, sergt — Nashville, June 28--64
Tuttle, D A, corp* — Chancellorsville, May 17--63
Wales, Anson, corp* Fairfax Station, Dec 24--63
Woodruff, H, corp* Chancellorsville, May 3 63
Allison, Alex — Frederick, Md, March 17--62
Ambrose, Austin
Brown, A L.* — Dallas, May 25--64
Buchterkirchen, D* Cedar Mountain, Aug 9--62
Bragg, John — Sandy Hook, Md. Sept 26--62
Clement, Henry* — Bolivar Heights, Oct 16--61
Cook, Lyman* — Dallas, May 25--64
Comley, Jacob, mr — McGregor, Ia
Collius, Joseph E, f — Oak Centre
Dunn, John* — Bentonville, N C
Dutcher, John* — Alexandria, June 24--63
Donward, Alexander — Neosho
Donnovan, J F — Lomira
Davids, Henry, f — Brothertown
Eull, Simon, f — McGregor, Ia
Fowler, Isaac* — Chancellorsville, May 3--63
Fidler, Jefferson* — Dallas, May 25--64
Gould, Abner p — May 15--64
Haswell, Jos — Hustisford, Aug 7--64
Hagerman, Charles — Mauston
Hubbard, O W — Sparta
Lord, Chas T, e — Adrian, Mich
Littlejohn, John — Madison, Jan 22--65
Meadows, W H — Glasgow, Minn
Nettleton, N B* — Antietam, Sept 17--62
Narraceung, Davis S* — Dallas, May 25--64
Poor, Chas H* — Dallas, May 25 64
Rathert, Henry A, f — Brothertown
Riener, Reuben T — Brookside
Stabenfelt, Ernest — Watertown
Super, Thos J* — Dallas, May 25--64
Sphon, A W — Murfreesboro, May 29--64
Shelly, Elias, f — Brothertown

Tuttle, I F* — Bolivar Heights, Oct 16--61
Turner, Delos P — Northfield
Thayer, Frank B — Atlanta, Aug 22--64
Tanner, G W W, a — Lowell
Tanner, Chas G, f — Rockville, Ia

B

Capt John W Scott* — Chancellorsville, May--63
Capt G W Stevenson — Wiota
Capt Wm M Snow — Boston, Mass
Capt S Buck — Fort Wayne, Ind
Capt J E Kleven — Culbertson, Neb
Lt Wm S Moscrip
Lt G W Rollins
Lt W H Dick
Lt C I, Dering — Columbus
Lt O A Hegg — Independence
Lt B W Clark
Lt Thos Slagg
Lt H C Spencer — July 3--62
Lt Jas E Crane — Milwaukee
Lt J R Amidon — Cedar Rapids, Ia
Leach, Wm, sergt — Lynchburg, July 8--62
Blake, Colburn, sergt* — Antietam, Sept 17--62
Beeman, J P, sergt* Chancellorsville, May 3 63
Dibble, Cyrus, corp — Fayetteville, March 31--64
Steigman, John, corp — Frederick, Md, Oct 28--61
Alling, Jas A + — Averysboro, March 17--65
Burns, Charles — Shboeton
Berschbacher, Jno N — Kewasknm
Curwell, Adam — Murfreesboro, June 26--64
Collins, J E — Oak Centre
Dean, Jesse P — Frederick, Md, Feb 5 63
Eddy, Fred* — Cedar Mountain, Aug 9--62
Eamer, Wm H — Baltimore, Sept 26--61
Evans, G D, f — Wild Rose
First, Henrich — Green Bay
Harmon, Edward P, a — Hustisford
Hinman, David* — Chancellorsville, May 3--63
Jarvis, G J — Richland Centre
Jones, Christopher W — Wankau
Larrimore, J C* — Cedar Mountain, Aug 9--62
Lovelace, A W* — Cedar Mountain, Aug 9--62
Liebenstein, William — Scott
Mason, Wm T* — Antietam, Sept 17--62
McFarlane, Edward P, f — Racine
Maxwell, Geo I* — Cedar Mountain, Aug 9--62
Magloskey, Fred* — Antietam, July 4--62
Mericle, Arnold — Tullahoma, April 30--64
Premo, A, mf — Warren's Mills
Pasco, Robert — Tullahoma, May 5--64
Roundy, Albert B, mason — Fond du Lac
Simpson, Simon + — Chancellorsville, May 3--63
Strapher, Jno — Oshkosh
Thompson, Ole, f — Otronto, Iowa
Wright, W W, f — Oshkosh
Warren, Wm B r — Dallas, May 25--64
Ward, J M — Oshkosh
Wright, Jeff — Stevens Point

C

Capt Martin Flood
Capt S E Gardiner
Lt M O'Brien
Lt W Parks — Oconomowoc
Lt T Slagg
Lt J Collins — Plainfield
Lt Abner Hubbell
Lt C C Smith
Lt G W Rollins
Lt J T Marvin
Lt S I Thompson — Johnson's Creek
Guy, George, corp* — Antietam, Sept 17--62
Kimberly, W, corp* Chancellorsville, May 3--63
Rorke, David, corp* Cedar Mountain, Aug 9--62
Becker, John* — Dallas, May 25--64
Bemis, J W — Frederick, Md, Dec 21--61
Clark, Owen, f — Stevens Point
Crawford, Alonzo, m — Hartwellville, Mich

WISCONSIN SOLDIERS AND SAILORS REUNION ROSTER.

Clark, Austin — Frederick, Md
Coates, I C — Neillsville
Crane, Moses — Wilmington, N C, March 26—65
Dunn, M H — Woodman
Fuller, H — Neillsville
Green, John M — Fayetteville, April 18—61
Loveland, Franklin — Monticello
Mosier, S F* — Bolivar Heights, Oct. 16—61
Northrup, Horace — Frederick, Nov 30—61
Oseveson, Torger — Washington, May 29—65
Roger, Fred* — Cedar Mountain, Aug 9—62
Roberts, Wm, f — Magnolia
Raymond, Henry* — Bolivar Heights, Oct 16—61
Ross Edgar* — Bolivar Heights, Oct 16—61
Sheffield, Seymour J* — Antietam, Sept 17—62
Thurlow Isaac* — Antietam, Sept 17—62
Trow, Wm G+ — Resaca, May 15—61
Underwood, Josiah — Baltimore, Sept 1—61
Winans, Isaac W* — Cedar Mountain, Aug 9—62
Wolf, Wm — Pella
Webb, Daniel — Vinings, Ga, July 21—61
Yarger, Perry L — Frederick, Nov 20—61

D

Capt Andrew Clark — Wabasha, Minn
Capt L B Balcom — Waupun
Capt C R Barrager — Crete, Neb
Lt Edw S Case — Hutchinson, Minn
Lt Oren S Howard, — Detroit, Mich
Lt Asher C Taylor
Lt Algie S Hill — Hastings, Neb
Lt J W Hinkley — Indianapolis, Ind
Lt C H Lindsley — Waupun
Lt Wilber Hanghowout
Lt John H Meigs, — May 7—65
Anderson, And — Atlanta, Ga, Oct 29—64
Amadon, W P, f — Waupun
Butts, Wesley J* — Cedar Mountain, Aug 9—62
Baldwin, J S — Vernon
Biedieman, W H+ — Vining's Station, Aug 27—61
Cornell, C* — Peach Tree Creek, July 20—64
Clark, Job, c — Fond du Lac
Close, Richard — Fond du Lac
Close, Levi — Jan 25—62
Gee, John W+ — Antietam, Oct 28—62
Gee, J G, ph — Brandon
Gruson, Peter, f — Riceville
Hawley. F — Andersonville, Aug 28—61
Jacobs, Curtis* — Cedar Mountain, Aug 9—62
Last, Ferdinand* — Antietam, Sept 17—62
Ludwigson, Christian, — Madison, Jan 22—65
Miles, Wm, f — Oak Centre
Myers, John — Nov 17—61
Norton, Geo W, m — Atlantic, Iowa
Neal, Oliver* — Chancellorsville, May 2—63
Oliver, Andrew* — Peach Tree Creek, July 20—64
Page, Clinton W — Waupun
Robinson, A W — Vinings, Ga, Aug 30—61
Smith, Samuel — Fond du Lac
Smith, Wm, f — Oakfield
Snyder, Edwin R+ — Antietam, Sept 17—62
Temple, J L* — Antietam, Sept 17—62
Washburn, Dennis* — Chancellorsville, May 3—63
Wright, John S — Nashville, July 2—64
Wait, Lewis — Savannah, Feb 13—65

E

Capt Gustave Hammer — Beaver Dam
Capt J W Hinckley
Lt Nahum Daniels
Lt W M Snow — Boston, Mass
Lt A D Haskins
Lt J M Schweers — Shawano
Lt J B Dubois
Lt W B Dick
Lt David Clark — Waupun
Raymond, C, M corp*Chancellorsville, May 3—63
Arms, J H — Loyal
Brockett, Geo W* — Antietam, Sept 17—62

Brown, William A — Racine
Bergnau, Enfried+ — Antietam, Sept 17—62
Bergman, Ernest+ — Washington, July 4—64
Clark, David — Waupun
Ehlers, Henry — Louisville, Aug 2—61
Elliot, Robert, mason — Dodgeville
Emory, George — Chattanooga, Aug 15—61
Foreman, Geo — Oconto
Fry, Fred* — Chancellorsville, May 3—63
Furlong, John* — Argyle Island, Ga, Dec 16—61
Hellur, Wm, f — Minnesota Lake, Minn
Jones, Edward, f — Mineral Point
Jones, A Sheridan, o — Visalia, Cal
Krause, Magnus+ — Kingston, Aug 7—61
Kinyon, Wilson B — Brownsville
Leavenworth, G W — Tullahoma, April 11—64
Matte, Charles+ — Frederick, July 6—62
Miller, Erhard — Brandon
Myer, Peter — Manitowoc Rapids
Nelson, Thos — Cambridge
Owen, G B, t — Waupun
Odekirk, Ed, f — Eden
Paukow, Fred+ — Chattanooga, May 23, 64
Parrott, Lewis — Chattanooga, June 13—61
Reynolds, Alvin P — Lewerne, Minn
Reynold, Ira B, f — Eagle Lake, Minn
Reese, August — York, Pa, Dec 1—62
Steffen, Wm+ — Kingston, June 1—61
Thurn, Frederick — June 30—61
Taylor, Silas D. f — Retreat
Van Norman, G W* — Antietam, Sept 17—62
Weber, George+ — Antietam, Nov 2—62
Werth, Frank — Carlton
Whalen, David — Fayetteville, March 15—61
Wile, J, mason — Menominee Falls
Wirth, Ludwig — Theresa
Wallace, William — Kekoskee

F

Capt G W Linbocker — Platteville
Capt E J Bentley
Capt Jas Hunter+ — Chattanooga, June 8—61
Capt C R Barrager — Crete, Neb
Capt Jasper Woodford
Lt E J Meeker — Kinsley, Kansas
Lt Chauncey Field
Lt E L Blanchard
Lt G G H Cutter — Lexington, Mass
Lt A S Hill — Hastings, Neb
Lt Herman Buchner — Lancaster
Sortley, F M, 1st sergt+ — Resaca, May 2—61
Gaston, John F, corp Frederick, Md. Oct 8—61
Nottom, R, corp+ — Savannah, Jan 21—63
A ten, Robert S — N Y Harbor, Apr 9—65
Allen, Henry — Lone Rock
Andrews, Geo — Alexandria, May 20—65
Butler, Eaton W* — Cedar Mountain, Aug 9—62
Beckwith, Alfred — Richland City
Barton, Thos* — Gettysburg, July 3—63
Craigs, Andrew* — Cedar Mountain, Aug 9—62
Dowd, F J, m — Harvard, Neb
Duncan, Thos F* — Antietam, Sept 17—62
Darlin, Frank+ — Alexandria, Aug 17—62
Elliot, B F, f — Fond du Lac
Gallopy, Henry — Frederick, Feb 16—62
Henderson, W A — Whitewater
Haag, Craft — Cascade
Hopkins, C B — Homer
Keil, L E, f — Lynd, Minn
Marlson, John — Chattanooga, June 28—61
Mekker, E J, — Kinsley, Kan
McKinnee, Richard — Beaufort, May 31—65
Meissner, Geo H, f — Webster City, Iowa
Murphy, James — Cincinnati, Ohio
Oleson, John* — Antietam, Oct 12—62
Onsun, Christian — Alexandria, Sept 17—62
Purine, Henry, f — Wisner, Neb
Retzow, John, f — Sandy Bay
Sinnett, Geo R + — Atlanta, Aug 2—61
Stone, Charles C — Wooster

Schnee, Theodore — Fayetteville, March 21—61
Vandervort, F — Princeton
Wagner, Wm+ — Gettysburg, July 3—63

G

Capt E L Hubbard
Capt Ephriam Giddings — Neenah
Lt A J Cady — Chippewa Falls
Lt J P Shepard+ — Antietam, Nov 10—62
Lt J Woodford
Lt E F Proctor
Lt P D Walker
Lt Seth Raymond — David City, Neb
Lt E V Moran
Rabe, C S, sergt — Nashville, June 16—61
Allen, Richard — Antietam, Sept 17—62
Billing, Jonathan — Fayetteville, April 16 -61
Blake, W W, f — Parsons, Kansas
Brown, Wm A, pa — Racine
Christian, Rasmus — Alexandria, June 7—62
Christian, Johannes — Frederick, April 25—62
Coates, H E — Neenah
Edwards, A A* — Bueton Station, May 22—62
Farnum, P P — Little Prairie
Freeman, W W, post master
Giddings, Ira+ — Washington, June 29—63
Gerry, B T — Appleton,
Giddings, E — Neenah
Howland, Christian* — Dallas, May 25—61
Hubbard, John+ — Kingston, June 5—61
Holman, Andrew — Harpers Ferry, Oct—62
King, Edw B, hospital steward — Green Bay
Langstaff, Robert M — Fond du Lac
Liddle, Harvey — Savannah, Dec 30—61
Litton, Philander — Louisville, June 15—64
Lee, Frank — Neenah
Mason, Wm H — Chancellorsville, May 3—63
Martin, Francis H* — Dallas, May 25—61
Martin, Henry E+ — Chattanooga, July 1—61
Nichols, Lewis B, bk — Fond du Lac
Nugent, John B, f — Sherwood
Noricung, J M — Frederick, Dec 16—61
Oleson, Eagle — Bridgeport, Feb 2—65
Oleson, Olans C — Albaton, Iowa
Phetteplace, L A, ma — Menasha
Raymond, Israel — Nashville, Oct 1—61
Rush, Wm — Washington, June 7—65
Rader, Frederick, f — Komira
Roble, Benjamin F — Waupona
Roble, B F — Waterman, Iowa
Simonds, A H* — Chancellorsville, May 3—63
Soule, Chas P, p — Russell, Kansas
Shelby, John* — Chancellorsville, May 3—63
Stoker, Peter T — Maple Grove
Stansbury, Wm — Frederick, Jan 16—62
Tait, Henry H+ — Antietam, Sept 30—62
Van Duzen, Cyrus B+ — Winchester, May 30—62
Whitenack, A J — Neenah
Whitney, James, c — Fort Atkinson

H

Capt G J Whitman — Cambridge
Capt Thos Shagg
Capt J M Schweers — Shawano
Lt G W Stevenson — Wiota
Lt Joseph Marvin
Lt E J Meeker — Kinsley, Kan
Lt J E Kleven
Lt W W Freeman — Menasha
Lt J G Knight
Lt Chauncey Field
Lt E G Biers
Anderson, Ole* — Dallas, May 25—61
Bush, Henry L* — Winchester, May 25—62
Cushby, W H, f — Shullsburg
Blair, R T clerk — Monroe
Blankenhorn, John, f — Shullsburg
Cutler, Geo M, m — Lexington, Mass
Cherry, Wm, f — Strongsburg, Neb
Gear, John H* — Dallas, May 25—61

PECK'S  SUN.

PUBLISHED AT MILWAUKEE, EVERY SATURDAY.

This is a paper that always tries to

LOOK ON THE BRIGHEST SIDE.

Its success is attested by its

CIRCULATION,

NOW 9,000 COPIES.

TERMS: $2.50 PER ANNUM, IN ADVANCE.	*About 3,000 of which have been added within the past five months.*	**ADVERTISING REASONABLE.**

Predicting the future by the past it is safe to expect an edition of

15,000 COPIES

BY THE FIRST OF JANUARY NEXT.

—AS AN—

ADVERTISING MEDIUM

Its excellence is apparent, as there is scarcely a town in the state where it is not taken, and there is little doubt it is read thoroughly by fully 60,000 people, if not more.

GEORGE W. PECK,
EDITOR AND PROPRIETOR,
MILWAUKEE, WIS.

WISCONSIN SOLDIERS AND SAILORS REUNION ROSTER.

Gussette, Benj — Savannah, Jan 21—65
Groff, Freeman G — Dalton, Feb 14—65
Hanson, John L — Chattanooga, July 9—64
Hamilton, Wm S — Chattanooga, July 24—64
Johns, Josua P* — Antietam, Sep 17–62
Longstaff, Robert M, pa — Fond du Lac
Meffert, W C — Arena
McMurty, Lee — Richland Centre
Mason, Wm* — Cedar Mountain Aug 9—62
March, Nelson — Beaufort April 20—65
Osborn, H W ph — Mineral Point
Shriver, Joshua M — Tullahoma May 4—64
Shuerman, Herman, I — Lane Station
Sales, Wm — Savannah Jan 21—65
Slagg, Thomas m — Cambridge
Stubbs, Wm — Beaufort, April 12—65
Schaubs, Peter — Dalton March 26—65
Thiesen, Mathew, I — St Michaels
Thoms, James — Chattanooga, Feb 15—65
Tracy, Albert S — Pontiac, Ill
Thompson, Never — Annapolis, April 2—65
Wilcox, Wm* — Antietam, Sep 17—62
Watts, Daniel B ar — Chamois, Mo
Watts, Wm H + — Lost Mountain, June 22—64
Weckersburger, A — Washington, June 14–65
West, George — Neillsville

I

Capt Howard Vandagrift
Capt Moses O'Brien+ — Cedar Mt, Va, Aug 12—62
Capt Nahum Daniels
Lt J E Ross
Lt A N Reed+ — Antietam, Md, Sept 18—62
Lt Wm Freeborn
Lt Jno Agnew
Lt Chas L Dering — Columbus
Lt Wilson S Buck — Fort Wayne, Ind
Lt Geo N Faucett — Canyonville, Oregon
Bonlen, E — Neillsville
Kirkpatrick, J, corp* Chancellorsville, May 3—63
Sullivan, M, corp* Chancellorsville, May 3—63
White, W, corp* — Averysboro, March 16–65
Anderson, Peter — Murfreesboro, May 11—65
Buxton, Geo+ — Bolivar Heights, Oct 18—61
Benton, Jas — Nov 30—61
Bright, Thos H — Shullsburg
Brooks, George — Neillsville
Bryant, Perry — Dalton, Ga, Feb 15—64
Collender, Daniel* — Beverly Ford, June 9—63
Christian, Hans* Averysboro, N C, March 15—65
Deming, Demas V* — Antietam, Sept 17—62
Dudley, John* — Kenesaw, June 21—61
Danks, W H — Fond du Lac
Dibble, Chas H* — Averysboro, March 16—65
Dougherty, John — Winchester, May 3—63
Fay, Sylvester + — Dallas, May 36—64
Foits, F C — Platteville
Folts, Volts, Robert, Sept 19—62
Harrison, Giles L* — Dallas, May 25—64
Hoage, Lewis S — Frederick, Jan 12—62
Hill, Dallas A — Antietam, Sept 6—64
Jones, Wm — Bell Plaine
Knickerbocker, Geo* — Dallas, May 25—64
Lewis, Wm G — Fayetteville, March 16—64
Looney, James* — Artula
Leslie, John W — Benton Harbor, Mich
Pattan John + — Dallas, June 23, 64
Ruter, August+ — Winchester, May 27—62
Thomas, Wm* — Antietam, Sept 17–62
Thoen, Hanson F — Atlanta, Oct 8—64
Townsend, A, Ins Agent, — Shullsburg
Wallace, Nichols+ Cedar Mountain, Aug 11—62
Wescott, Charles+ — Antietam, Sept 24—62
Wood, Hiram T — Waupun
Ware, Edward* — Antietam, Sept 17—62
Wiley, Alex* — Antietam, Sept 17—62
White, Thos* — Antietam, Sept 17—62

K

Capt Wm Hawley — Flint, Mich

Capt Warham Parks — Oconomowoc
Capt T E Orton — July 25—64
Capt A D Haskins
Lt T J Widvey — La Crosse
Lt J M Schweers — Shawano
Lt J D Goodrich — 6 La Salle st, Chicago
Lt F C Merrill
Lt Thos Slagg
Lt Jens Moe
Lt Lewis Colby — South Haven, Mich
Johnson, F C 1st sgt+ — Dallas May 26—64
Jones, W R 1st sgt+ — Atlanta, Aug 10—64
Kiel, Amos A, sgt — Frederick, Oct 26—62
Condite, J E, corp* — Antietam, Sep 17—62
Johnson, E J, corp+ — Antietam, Sept 17—63
Lyman, J Q, corp+ — Cedar Mount'n Aug 9—62
Curtis, C S, corp+ — Cedar Mountain, Aug 9—62
Colby, A C, corp+ — Resaca, May 15—64
Allison, C, corp+ — Resaca, June 1—64
Baker, J H — Neillsville
Buxter, Wm+ — Resaca, June 19—64
Burg, Martin, I — Brothertown
Borge, Chris — Atlanta, Nov 1—64
Daily, Geo F, I — Colby
Emery, John — West Middleton
Glimsdahl, John E* — Antietam, Sep 17—62
Graves, Alonzo M* — Averysboro, March 16—65
Hubbell, Wm H* — Cedar Mountain, Aug 9—62
Halverson, S — Neenah
Halverson, Allen — Goldsboro, April 20—65
Johnson, Andrew* — Winchester, May 26—62
Janson, Peter* — Cedar Mountain, Aug 9—62
Karlis, Gabriel* — Chancellorsville, May 3–63
Minton, Wm+ — Resaca, May 15—64
Monson, Knud — Stafford, March 4—63
Mattson, Andrew — Madison, Sept 14—64
Osmundson, Ole — Frederick, Oct 17—61
Oleson, Ole T — Chattanooga, Nov 19–64
Polly, Edwin E* — Cedar Mountain, Aug 9—62
Phun, Stephen* — Lost Mountain, June 11—64
Remmele, John — Frederick, Oct 24—61
Roscoe, Boardman
Severson, Sever L — Cambridge
Stillwell, B — Chattanooga, Sept 1—64
Thomas, Andrew — Harpers Ferry, Jan 1—63
Waterhouse, M J+ — Antietam, Sept 17—62
Watkins, Wm+ — Resaca, May 15—64
Wagner, Anthony — Winchester, May 25—62

UNASSIGNED.

Burklin, B M — Janesville
Brigham, C W — Campbellsport
Brineison, Thos — Taylor
Cherry, Wm — Stromsburg
Hart, Dudley M, dep sheriff — Belmont
Jenkins, Henry — Dresden, Mo
Lansing, Wm — Neenah
Mead, Mathias — Lincoln, Neb
Nobles, C D — Algona, Iowa
Olson, Ole — Cylon
Olesson, H P — Rush River
Riekeman, G A — Racine
Ruger, Thomas J — Atlanta, Ga
Small, Robert — Vineland
Stone, J N — Neenah
Snow, Wm M — Boston
Stevenson, Geo W — Wiota
Watts, D B — Chamois, Mo
Walsh, Francis, I — Darlington
Wells, Wilbur — Neenah
Whitenack, A — Neenah
Whitenack, Samuel — Neenah

FOURTH INFANTRY.

[Reorganized as Cavalry Sept. 1, 1863 in pursuance of special order No. 375 from the War Department, approved by the Governor of Wis-

consin in general order No. 16. See Fourth Wisconsin Cavalry.]

FIFTH INFANTRY.

Three years, organized July 13th, 1861. Original strength, 1058; gain by recruits, etc., 1198. Total, 2256. Death loss, 285–killed in action, 98, died of wounds, 71, of disease, 116. Other losses, 547—missing, 4, desertions, 165, transfer, 33, discharged, 405. Strength at muster out, June 20th, and July 11th, 1865, 1124. Campaigns in Virginia, from Yorktown to Appomattox Court House.

REGIMENTAL ROSTER.

Col Amasa Cobb — Lincoln, Neb
Col Thos S Allen — Oshkosh
Lt Col H W Emery — Lisbon, N H, Oct 13—62
Lt Col W F Behres
Lt Col T B Catlin, — Green Bay
Maj C H Larrabee — Seattle, Wash Ter
Maj H M Wheeler+ — Washington, Nov 19—63
Maj Enoch Totten — Washington, D C
Adj T S West — Philadelphia, Pa
Q M J G Clark — Lancaster
Q M Alex Samuels — Beaver Dam
Surg C E Crane — Green Bay
A Surg G D Wilbur — Mineral Point
A Surg J W Davis
Chap A A Drown — Baraboo
Chap A H Reid — Des Moines, Iowa

INDEPENDENT BATTALION.

Capt C W Knapp — Milwaukee
Capt J B Doughty* — Petersburg, April 2—65
Capt J H Cook — Unity
Capt Miles L Butterfield — Waukesha
Lt C H Mayer
Lt Eben Reifenback
Lt H H Linnell, — Sacramento, Cal

REORGANIZED.

Col Thos S Allen — Oshkosh
Lt Col A S Bennett
Lt Col G M Sabin — Eureka, Nev
Lt Col J M Bull — Bismarck, Dakota
Maj C W Kempf — Milwaukee
Adj W B Sturges
Q M Alex Samuels — Beaver Dam
Surg C E Crane — Green Bay
Surg G D Wilbur — Mineral Point
A Surg Ambrose Jones
Chap B C Hammond — Waverly, Iowa

A

Capt Temple Clarke — Hyde Park, Ill
Capt H Walker* Brandy Station, Va, Nov 7–63
Capt W S Goodwin — Black Hills
Lt A B Gibson — Robinson, Kan
Lt Peter Scherfius — Sauk Centre, Minn
Lt Henry Rhohr
Lt Jas Malcom ber
Lt Julius Ebert — Chicago, Ill

REORGANIZED.

Capt J B Doughty* — Petersburg, April 2—65
Capt E R Jones
Lt C H Mayer+ — Petersburg, April 21—65
Lt Thos Blair — Lochiel
Lt Henry Curren — Stevens Point
Lt Francis Kelly — Menominee
J R Strong, serg maj* Fredericksburg, May 15—62
Goodwin, J, sgt* — Rappahannock, Nov 7—63
Cotherns, J, corp+ — Williamsburg, May—82
Stick, John, corp — Philadelphia, Sept 11—62
Adams, G W* — Fredericksburg, May 3—63
Anderson, J L, a — Manitowoc
Bosorth, Aubert* — Fredericksburg, May 3—63
Barth, J* — Rappahannock, Nov 7—63

R. A. BAKER, Pres.   G. M. MIHILLS, Supt.   C. K PIER, Treas.

Capital Stock, Paid in, $200,000.

The Mihills Manufacturing Co.,

—MANUFACTURERS OF—

Doors, Sash, Blinds,

LUMBER, LATH, SHINGLES, ETC.

Dealers, Contractors, and Builders,

Will find it to their advantage to obtain estimates from this company as their manufacturing facilities enable them to make

CLOSE FIGURES ON GOOD GOODS

———CORRESPONDENCE SOLICITED.———

FOND DU LAC,   • •   WISCONSIN.

WISCONSIN SOLDIERS AND SAILORS REUNION ROSTER.

Bride, Robert+ Fredericksburg, May 23—63
Buboltz, T Belle Plaine, Feb 23—63
Bride, Jas* Fredericksburg, May 3—63
Buboltz, Daniel Reedsville
Borcherd, Fred W Chicago, Ill
Borland, Jno Menominee
Craussant, G H Corps Hospital, April 3—63
Cox, Joseph L Milwaukee
Cadwell, Anthony Manitowoc
Davis, Chas Philadelphia, Dec 8—62
Dexter, Sam B Detroit, Mich
Davidson, Wm H Clarks Mills
Dlack, Archie B Detroit, Mich
Eddy, B C+ Williamsburg, May—62
Eagle, Geo B, Jr ag't Burlington, Ia
Enert, Julius, pa Chicago, Ill
Eargood, John C Menominee
Erickson, Christopher Menominee
Fossner, Wm California, Mo
Galvin, Martin Washington, April 9–62
Gibbon, A B, f Robinson, Kan
Gilbert, John Clarks Mills
Goodwin, W S Black Hills
Gibson, A B Robinson, Kan
Harlick, Francis* Fredericksburg, May 3—63
Henrich, G Liberty Hall Hospital, June 19—62
Hubbard, H A Frederick, Oct—62
Jackson, Julius, m Red Cloud, Neb
Kent, Depuey, Winchester, Sept 19–64
Kelly, Frank, mf Menominee
Kaiser, Frank Clarks Mills
Loeller, C* Petersburg, April 2—65
Leyder, Peter Belle Plaine, Jan 29—63
Linnell, Henry, m Sacramento, Cal
Landoldt W H, b Port Washington
Leonard, James H Stevens Point
Leykorn, John R, pr Chicago, Ill
Langress, Fred Cincinnati, O
Lindeman, Guido, Madison
Liudman, E G, Clerk Madison
LaConut, Louis B, ph Shawano
Linuell, Henry H Sacramento, Cal
Lindman, E G Madison
Leonard, J H Green Bay
Mill, John Canterville
Mallet, John Manistee, Mich
Ninneman, Gottleb, Milwaukee
Olcott, Thos* Fredericksburg, May 3—63
Oleson, Ole Liberty Hall Hospital, June 17—62
Poebl Henry+ Winchester, Sept 19—61
Poleha, Michael* Wilderness, May 5—64
Perry, S W Detroit, Mich
Riley, Abraham Fredericksburg, May 3—63
Rath, C Hagerstown, Nov 8–61
Rickaby, Willard Niels
Stick, Henry+ Fredericksburg, May 3—63
Schissel, William Milwaukee
Skinner, J H Gen Hosp, Dec 4—61
Steele, Albert B Charlevoix, Mich
Sheridan, Patrick Soldiers' Home, Milwaukee
Stroff, Jos Green Bay
Stahlie, John Toronto
Stirn, Frank Manitowoc
Schlinoler, Edward Manitowoc
Schissel, Wm, pa Milwaukee
Severson, Sever Menominee
Turpin, Wm St Martin's Island
Woodcock, David+ Williamsburg, May—62
Whalling, S Fredericksburg, May 12—63
Weidner, Charles Green Bay
Wagner, Arnold Sturgeon Bay
Waguer, Thomas Sturgeon Bay

B

Capt Elisha C Hibbard Milwaukee
Capt Robt Ross
Capt J B Oliver Milwaukee
Capt G W Madison
Lt A N Nichols Milwaukee
Lt G E Bissell

Lt C T Hutchinson Jefferson, N Y
Lt L W Rossiter La Crosse
Lt S H Burrell
Lt Henry Frayser Milwaukee

REORGANIZED.

Capt J H Cook Unity
Capt C D Moore Menominee
Lt Eben Reifenbach
Lt T B Marcos Fond du Lac
Lt Benj Smith Oshkosh
Lt Alex Q Smith
Cavanaugh, C, sgt* Fredericksburg, May 3—63
Mosher, S H, sgt* Spottsylvania, May 10—64
Lord, P W, sgt* Petersburg, April 2—65
Prevo, Dodge, corp+ Washington, July 25—63
Hayward, J, corp Harpers Ferry, Aug 15—64
Thompson, J W, corp Baltimore, Aug 8—64
Allen, Jas W I Williamsburg, May 62
Atherholt, W D Lib Hall Hosp, June 11–62
Allen, T S Eau Claire
Andrews, John Menominee
Baily, M* Rappahannock, Nov 7—63
Buel, John, ph Taycheedah
Ball, Ezra, c Lamartine
Billings, Wm, e Calumet
Brown, C E Janesville
Creasser, Wm Belle Plaine, May 1–63
Colvin, Oscar W Corps Hospital, May 1 63
Cook, J H, d Unity
Conlon, Jas Beaver Dam
Duggan, Walter T Milwaukee
Foley, Michael Annapolis, Oct 9 –63
Gee, C H—
Huffald, Hugh* Cold Harbor, June 1- 64
Hastings, Thos Hospital
Johnson, Oscar, f Brothertown
Kelly, Wm N* Fredericksburg, May 3—63
Keyes, Geo E, f Fond du Lac
Kyle, John, f Downsville
Keyes, Geo E. f Taycheedah
Keyes, Geo H Fond du Lac
Lowe, H B, Register of Deeds Hartford
McKittrick, Thos* Fredericksburg, May 3—63
McLaughlin, J+ Washington, June 16—63
Millore, F Whitewater
Morris, F B July 31—61
Moore, Chas D, Sheriff Menominee
Mc Farland, W H, m Eau Claire
McFarland, W H Eau Claire
McFarland, W H Chippewa Falls
Marcoe, T B, m Fond du Lac
Marcoe, Theodore B Stetsonville
Mead, Wm, f Fond du Lac
Nichols, Elias H* Winchester, Sept 19—64
O'Brien, Edw. me Milwaukee
Parkinson, J J+ Fredericksburg, May 4—63
Potter, A T+ Winchester, Sept 19—64
Perrigo, Mayron H, bk Merrimac
Pigg, Henry Merrimac
Parkins, Robert Merrimac
Porter, Fred, f Lamartine
Pflelger, Geo Taycheedah
Rierton, John* Sailors Creek, April 6—65
Rossiter, L, R B Contractor La Crosse
Salesman, S W* Federicksburg, May 3—63
Smith, Benj, Salesman Oshkosh
Spencer, David J, f Berlin
Schlieger, Andrew Milwaukee
Summer, Albert* Fredericksburg, May 3—63
Smith, John+ Washington, June 4—63
Spencer, Geo Dec 14—61
Starkey, B F Rebel Prison, Sep 4—64
Tiffany, P B, c Taycheedah
Walt, J H+
Walker, W B, Miller Bowen's Mills
Zimmerman, Wm, f Lamartine

C

Capt W F Behrens

Capt Chas F Herman
Capt Chaw W Kempf Milwaukee
Lt J C Schroeling Port Washington
Lt Chas Pizzala* Chancellorsville, Va
Lt Fritz von Baumbach Milwaukee
Lt L F Muller* May 10– 64
Lt Hans Boebel Milwaukee
Lt C H Mayer

REORGANIZED.

Capt M L Butterfield Waukesha
Lt H H Linnell Sacramento, Cal
Lt E R Jones
Lt Angus Cameron Washington, D C
Wissman, Jacob, sergt—Washington, May 26—64
Hall, Wm, sergt Virginia, March 25—65
Kisshiger, C, sergt Fort Monroe, May 31—62
Heiberlig, J S, corp* Sailors' Creek, Apr 6—65
Johnson, A, corp* Sailors' Creek, Apr 7—65
Zeigler, Philip, corp+ Williamsburg, May- 62
Langhoff, T, corp L H Hospital, June 20—61
Bilg, Levis* Wilderness, May 5—64
Brown, H Alexandria, Apr 8—65
Burroughs, Wm Philadelphia, Aug 31—62
Bean, J M Milwaukee
Demuth, Franz, New York City, Nov 28– 62
Folkman, Fred A Milwaukee
Geisel, John Hagerstown, July 5—62
Herzog, Golfried New York City, June 28—62
Harshman, Samuel Waukau
Hesketh, Jos Chippewa Falls
Jolie, Geo B Rinner
Kaiser, Frank Clarks Mills
Kissinger, J W Philadelphia, Feb 6—63
Landolt, W H, b Port Washington
Linderman, E G, clerk Madison
Linnell, H H, m Sacramento, Cal
Mahler, G Lib Hall Hosp, June 14—62
Mulhauser, A Lib Hall Hosp, June 14—62
Menzer, Henry+ Alexandria, May 30—64
Parker, Thomas Menominee
Reengans, P H Washington, Nov 9—62
Rice, G W Milwaukee
Rossiter, L, R B contractor La Crosse
Sheriner, A A+ Williamsburg, May 5—62
Stuck, Wm+ Washington, Nov 29—63
Volkman, Fred A Milwaukee
Weidner, Chas Green Bay
Wertenhagen, Erick, m Milwaukee

D

Capt T B Catlin Green Bay
Capt Jas Ordway* Brandy Station, Nov 1—62
Capt S White+ May 30—64
Lt D E Tilden Texas
Lt H H Linnell Sacramento, Cal
Lt T R Spafford
Lt J H Douglas Rochester, Minn
Lt A Turnbull Grand Rapids

REORGANIZED.

Capt Jno W Van Meyers St Louis, Mo
Lt Jas La Count Kansas
Lt C T Wyman Milwaukee
Lt Jas Young Wausau
Honey, S H, sgt* Spottsylvania, May 10—6
Purdy, John, _l* Sailors Creek, April 6—65
Hera, H ¨ Williamsburg, May —62
Adams, John Q, me Rochester, Minn
Ashton, Wm, m* Beaver Dam
Berninger, Chas Beaver Dam
Blanchard, H B Stevens Point
Buffum, G W* Sailors Creek, April 23—65
Buck, Marens D L Dexterville
Blodgett, Philip Stevens Point
Bancroft, Jerome, m Amherst
Buck, LaFayette Port Edward
Callin, Theodore Green Bay
Canterbury, James B La Crosse
Crane, E A Beaver Dam
Channock, Charles Parkersburg, Iowa

National Bell Telephone Company.

EXCLUSIVE OWNERS OF ALL ELECTRIC TELEPHONE PATENTS.

Lines Built and Telephones Rented.

ESTIMATES GIVEN.

Address

C. H. HASKINS, GENERAL AGENT.

MILWAUKEE, WISCONSIN.

ELECTRIC LIGHTING

THE

WESTON DYNAMO MACHINE CO.

This Light is the Cheapest, Whitest, and most Brilliant, ever known for

Streets, Churches, Factories, Stores, Theatres, Halls,

AND PUBLIC GARDENS.

Address

C. H. HASKINS, GENERAL AGENT,

MILWAUKEE, WISCONSIN.

WISCONSIN SOLDIERS AND SAILORS REUNION ROSTER.

Name	Location/Battle, Date
Channock, Edward	Los Angeles Cal
Coly, Lewis*	Spottsylvania, May 10—64
Curran, John D	Stevens Point
Cartwright, Wm	Colby
Douglas, H A	Philadelphia, Sep 20—62
Douglas, Jeremiah H	Rochester, Minn
Deleut, L	Beaver Dam
Evans, A E	
Evans, Jno J	Rochester, Minn
Farrar, M J	Philadelphia, Sep 18 —62
Fox, H D	Appleton
Foster, Wm*	Spottsylvania, May 10—64
Galligher, John*	Sailors Creek, April 6 —65
Gibbs, Zeno	Dec 23—11
Hutchins, W N	Lib Hall Hosp, June 10—62
Houle, Ephraim	Phillips
Hardy, Geo H	Clarion, Iowa
Hecox, Horace, f	Donelsville
Hadley, Benjamin	Mosinee
Hencox, Horace H	Randolph
Hecox, Horace H	Beaver Dam
Hall, Geo	Beaver Dam
Kirby, Marion	Cumberland
Kinnesley, Chas	Washington, March 1—64
Lyon, Wm D	Washington, Dec 19—62
Lindgues, Peter	Washington, Territory
Lawley, A	Annapolis, Aug 13—61
Lavigne, Frank, m	Grand Rapids
Longstaff, Lewis, mc	Fond du Lac
Louden, Mayhew	Janesville
Linnell, H H, m	Sacramento, Cal
Longstaff, e	Fond du Lac
Miller, Louis	Beaver Dam
Martin, Edw*	Sailors Creek, April 6—65
McCoy, Charles	Oshkosh
Muzzy, L M°	Sailors Creek, April 6—65
Macler, Eli, f	Ripon
Moffitt, W T+	Washington, April 6—65
Millard, Geo	Beaver Dam
Naylor, Wm B	Tomah
Purnville, Paul*	Wilderness, May 5—64
Page, G W	Oct 1—61
Pringle, Robert	Washington, Ter
Parker, S C	Madison, April —64
Powers, James, f	Sparta
Riley, J L	May—62
Rinzler, Jno	Menominee
Redfield, A B	Stevens Point
Samuels, Alex, com traveller	Beaver Dam
Sloan, Henry, c a	Appleton
Smith, Benj	Oshkosh
Samuels, David	Beaver Dam
Samuels, Alex	Portland, Oregon
Smith, Edward, Restaurant	Valparaiso, Ind
Stultz, Geo L, pa	Beaver Dam
Thoilke, Henry+	Washington, June 6—61
Turnbull, Andrew	Grand Rapids
White, Harry+	Wilderness, May 6—64
Wilmot, Asel	Stevens Point
Watson, James	Beaver Dam
Worthington, Brainard	Colorado Springs, Col
Young, Herbert P	Beaver Dam
Young, Elijah	Beaver Dam
Yetter, Jno, t	Beaver Dam
Young, James	Wausau

E

Name	Location/Battle, Date
Capt H M Wheeler	
Capt H P Clum	
Capt A W Hathaway	
Lt E P Miles+	May 5—64
Lt Jas McDaniels	
Lt Jas Mills	
Lt H K Johnson	

REORGANIZED.

Name	Location
Capt Chas R Nevitt	Oshkosh
Lt Jno McCabe	
Lt P B Smith	
Lt Fred W Smith	

Name	Location/Battle, Date
Walker, R W, sgt*	Wilderness, May 5—64
Verbeck, C, sergt+	Spottsylvania, May 12—64
Cntis, A L, sergt	Fairfax, March 8—62
Augur, A K*	Sailor's Creek, April 6—65
Arnett, W W*	Petersburg, April 2—65
Anderson, Leslie	Towsley
Bussell, John B*	Rappahannock, Nov 7—63
Beach, H+	Washington, Nov 25—63
Braithwaite, W	Hagerstown, Oct 26—62
Batchen, Eli	Cumberland, Dec 11—64
Bly, Edwin P, me	Janesville
Blion, Jas H, c	Superior, Neb
Bilvou, Jas H	Superior, Neb
Buck, Thos F	Sinwano
Courtright, Brazil,	Camp Griffin, Oct 22—61
Curran, Henry	Stevens Point
Coonan, J W	Baltimore, Dec 18—62
Crandal, A	Wilson Station, May 11—65
Graham, James A	Shellrock, Ia
Foule, Wm H	Western Flotilla
Fisher, J A, f	Taycheedah
Glover, S C*	Wilderness, May 5—64
Gurnae, J D*	Sailor's Creek, April 6 —65
Gilmau, Ira*	Petersburg, April 2 65
Hale, Geo W	Washington, Sept 24—62
Howard, A M	Springfield
Hutzell, G E	Hospital, May 4—65
Hursh, E G, a	Roseburg, Oregon
Jarvin, Henry	Janesville
Lelm, John+	Spottsylvania, May 12—64
Lindeman, F G	Madison
Morgan, Edw	Wilderness, May 5—64
Main, G S	Shioeton
Parks, John	Shioeton
Pierson, Jos*	Wilderness, May 5—64
Pitts, Royal	Fredericksburg, May 3—63
Peterson, G+	Cold Harbor, June 3—64
Platts, R K	Lib Hall Hosp, June 18—62
Parker, Frank	Janesville
Raymond, P G	Spottsylvania, May 12—64
Russell, L A, f	Madley
Rhodes, Martin	Rockford, Ill
Simons, J C	Baltimore, Sept 26—62
Southmayd, J S	Division Hosp, Jan 24—65
Williams, Whitney*	Spottsylvania, May 10—64
Valentine, John D	Fredericksburg, May 3· 63
Vaughn, A N	May —62
Valentine, C L, Register of Deeds	Janesville
Walker, F E, clk	Stevens Point

F

Name	Location
Capt I M Bean	Milwaukee
Capt Enoch Totten	Washington, D C
Capt M L Butterfield	Waukesha
Lt B F Crain	Madison
Lt A J Bennett	

REORGANIZED.

Name	Location
Capt Wm Bremmer	
Lt C D Richmond	
Lt C D Moore	Menominee
Lt Wm J Baker	Waseca, Minn
Wright, Wm, sgt*	Spottsylvania, May 10—64
Doghue, J, sgt, f	Menominee Falls
Welty, Geo, corp*	Sailor's Creek, April 6—65
Geo, V B, corp+	Washington, July 23—63
Davidson, E F, corp	Camp Griffin, Nov 30—61
Ackhert, Wm*	Fredericksburg, May 3—63
Aber, E L	Petersburg, April 2—65
Aber, John F, f	Grant
Aber, John T	Grand Rapids
Beggs, Albert A*	Petersburg, April 2—65
Bagley, C W	Baltimore, Dec 11—62
Baker, Henry, m	Albany, N Y
Baker, W J	Waseca, Minn
Becker, Henry	Albany, N Y
Bouge, J, f	Menominee
Cote, C J	Williamsburg, May—62
Culver, J F	Whitehall, Mich
Darling, H, f	Portsmouth Grove, Oct 17—62

Name	Location/Battle, Date
Dwinell, A B	Stevens Point
Dwinell, C H	Amherst
Echman, Jos-	Washington, April 17—65
Frost, Chauncey*	Wilderness, May 5—64
Gower, Samuel	Baltimore, Oct 5—62
Hall, Lucius+	Baltimore, July 27—62
Horton, D	Bell Plaine, March 17—62
Hasketh, Jos, m	Chippewa Falls
Holbrook, Arthur, Dentist	Milwaukee
Klusnerr, F	Washington, May 29—64
Lisner, H*	Petersburg, April 2—65
Marlatt, E*	Washington, April 17—65
Magnus, J M+	City Point, March 15—65
Phelps, W M+	Washington, April 13—65
Pooler, Dwight, f	Colfax
Powrie, Robt, mf	Fond du Lac
Rattery, J	Rappahannock, Nov 11—63
Richmond, Calvin D	Plover
Rice, Geo W, c	Milwaukee
Stickles, Wm	Mukwonago
Thompson, W D	Acquia, Nov 28—62
Thompson, J C, me	Grand Junction
Valentine, C L, Register of Deeds	Janesville
West, A J, Post Master	Shenandoah
Wyman, C F, me	Milwaukee
Worden, Geo A, f	Amherst
Wroith, Wetzel*	Sailor's Creek, April 6—65
Wood, Isaac T	Transport, Aug 26—62

G

Name	Location/Battle, Date
Capt W A Bugh	
Capt L G Strong*	May 3—63
Capt G E Hilton*	May 10—64
Capt W H Kees	Oshkosh
Lt H K W Ayres	
Lt S Y Naylor	Bloomington, Ill

REORGANIZED.

Name	Location
Capt H L Walker	
Capt Henry Curran	Stevens Point
Lt H D Squires	Black River Falls
Lt W B Sturges	
Lt C J Bracken	Mineral Point
VanNorman, H S, sgt*	Spottsylvania, May 10—64
Williams, J R, corp+	Spottsylvania, May 12—64
Santora, M I, corp	Philadelphia, Aug 25—62
Smith, S J	Philadelphia, Feb 26—62
Livermore, A H, corp	Philadelphia Aug 12—62
Billington, Hiram*	Petersburg, April 2—65
Bates, Jas	Rappahannock, Nov 9—63
Beal, Whitney A, f	Geneva Lake
Brown, B J, f	Winneoke
Brown, B J	Neillsville
Brown, B F	Neillsville
Conlin, Jas*	Sailor's Creek, April 6—65
Chamberlain, Geo M	Waupaca
Cantwell, K+	Washington, Nov 14—63
Carbonneau, Alexander	Wausau
Clark, C C, f	Winneoke
Curran, Henry	Stevens Point
Cam, Jos M	Fort Howard
Chandler, C W	Neillsville
Cammi, M B	Fort Howard
Dean, J	Neillsville
Denu, James	Spencer
Day, A B	Neillsville
Flyn, Wm+	April 18—65
Forsyth, Andrew	Green Bay
Gruniu, Todd+	Washington, May 27—64
Hinson, O P+	Wilderness, May 6—61
Hommel, R S	Neillsville
Hulott, Benjamin, f	Norfolkeld
Irving, Robert*	Fredericksburg, May 3—63
Jordan, N D+	Cold Harbor, June 8—64
Keys, W H, m	Oshkosh
Keyes, W H, Route agt	Oshkosh
Knutson, C, me	Menominee
Knusten, Charles	Menominee
Lachapelle, Jno, f	Neillsville
La Chappel J	Neillsville

WISCONSIN SOLDIERS AND SAILORS REUNION ROSTER.

Millard, Burton+ — Williamsburg, May–62
Maclosh, Jas, m — Berlin
McGowan, R J O, m — Iowa Falls, Ia
Mevvy, Frank — Waupaca
Naylor, Sam Y, Amer Express, Bloomington, Ill
Olesou, E — Neillsville
Osborn, Chas D — Hagerstown, Nov 24–62
Perkins, Hiram — Remington
Raymond, G E+ — Fredericksburg, May 6–63
Smith, Stephen* — Sailor's Creek, April 6–65
Super, Peter H — Oshkosh
Smith, Wm* — Fredericksburg, May 3–63
Smoley, Henry+ — Wilderness, May 6–64
Smith, Hugh B — Belle Plaine, April 12–63
Sanborn, Henry M — Springfield, Mass
Sullivan, John — City Point
Tanner, Vera W — Dec 9–61
Tanner, Ira — Washington, Dec 15–62
VanAlstine, C A+ — April 7–65
Wright, Marshal+ — Washington, May 21–64
Wait, J — Harrisons Landing, July 19–62
Walt, Geo — Orangeville, O., June 4–63
Wanzer, A J, m — Unity
Welsh, Chas, Rauchman — Oder, Dakota

H

Capt R C Hawkins — Swan Lake, Dakota
Capt J J Turner* — Mary's Heights, May 3–63
Ca-t J Mc Murtry+ Fredericksburg, May 30–64
Capt C E B sseli
Lt Annan Hoskin
Lt G W Bell
Lt J B Doughty
Lt A H Robinson* — Mary's Heights, May 3–63
Lt T J Edwards — Ash Ridge

REORGANIZED.

Capt Chas T Wyman — Milwaukee
Lt H S Kribb — Moline, Ill
Lt H L Furr
Turner, J J, capt* — Mary's Heights, May 3–63
McMurray, Jno, capt+ — Washington, May 30–63
Robinson, A H, 2d lt* Mary's Heights, May 3–63
Hungerford, E C,1st sgt*Fredericksbur'g, May 3–63
Hoyt, W F, sergt* — Fredericksburg, May 2–63
Tompkins, Wm, corp — Oct 5–64
Austin, Edwin+ — Williamsburg, May–62
Bigford, Edw* — Sailors Creek, April 6–65
Blodgett, F J — Alexandria, Oct 31, 64
Chismore, A — Nov 10–61
Cummings, R C, m — Hampton, Oregon
Church, C B — Oakfield
Church, O B — Oakfield
Cerosgrow, Jos — Brothertown
Downs, R E — Harrison's Landing, July 3–62
Dick, David — Brothertown
Francisco, T B W — Belle Plaine, Dec 2–61
Gluston, John, e — Richland Center
Graham, Allen* — Petersburg, April 2–65
Holencamp, Henry, f — Wheatland
Hoke, E — Washington, Sept 16–61
Hoener, William — Downsville
Jarvis, George, m — Richland Center
Johnson, Henry+ — Williamsburg, May–62
Kribs, William, f — Trempeleau
Kimitt, James, mc — Richland Center
Kuygar, H C — Knapp Creek
Kribs, Wm — Trempeleau
Kyger, C C, f — Knapp Creek
Lebnske, John, t — St Killan
Moore, G W + Chesapeake Hospital, 37–64
McCourt, D O — Livingston
McPheten, W H — Belle Plaine, Feb 18–62
Miller, John — Philadelphia, May 6–62
Moon, Jno R, f — Richland Centre
Nicks, W A — Savage Station, July 5–62
Older, W H, mo — Packwaukee
Pratt, E C — Beaver Dam
Reilly, M C, l — In Zulu war
Shoemaker, W — Baltimore, July 5–63

Stalker, C L — Newark, Sept 6–62
Stoddard, W H — Washington, May 23
Tripp, Byron* — Fredericksburg, May 3–63
Towley, John* — Fredericksburg, May 5–63
Thomas, A L — Dec 1–61
Walker, Henry+ — Williamsburg, May–62
Wyman, C T — Milwaukee
Wright, A M — C & N W Railway, Ft Howard

I

Capt R H Emerson
Capt J H Cook — Unity
Lt Chas F Wyman — Milwaukee
Lt Wm Berry — Fond du Lac
Lt Richard Carter
Lt Eben Beifeuback
Lt G S Davis
Lt Chas Langridge — Lancaster
Lt J F Dwilley — Washington Territory

REORGANIZED.

Capt Thos Flint — Albany
Lt Lars E Johnson
Lt Nelson E Allen
Lt H B Mason
Norton, Wm, sgt+ — Washington, June 28–63
Norton, A, sgt+ — Spottsylvania, May 12–64
Bennett, Geo R, corp* Fredericksburg, May 3–63
Reid, Wm A, corp+ — Williamsburg, May –63
Tiffany, J W, corp — Camp Griffin, Nov 28–61
Allen, Geo S, ed — Oshkosh
Barstead, Andrew* — Fredericksburg, May 3–63
Bragg, John* — Petersburg, April 2–65
Brewster, Jas M* — Spottsylvania, May 10–64
Busel, Jno D, f — Taycheedah
Breed, E — Camp Griffin, Nov 22–61
Berry, Wm, f — Fond du Lac
Billings, Wm — Calumet
Bizzelle, Frank — Calumet
Brown, Wm Preston — Shenandoah, Ia
Cook, J H — Neillsville
Case, Aaron — Alexandria, Nov 1–62
Carter, Richard, a — Dodgeville
Day, J C C* — Wilderness. May 5–64
Daniels, John — Eden
Drake, J P — Neillsville
Eastman, J R — Philadelphia, Sep 14–62
Fuller, Ben — Calumet
Fuller, B, l — Taycheedah
Flint, Thos, f — Albany
Gray, Wm+ — Cold Harbor, June 3–64
Gilbert, Franklin* — Petersburg, April 2–65
Gibson, Charles, f — Taycheedah
Green, Alfred, l — Fond du Lac
Hayes, Robert+ — Wilderness, May 5–64
Harvey, Benj* — Spottsylvania, May 10–64
Heggegar, Peter Warren's Station, March 22–65
Hart, David — Calumet
Johnson, Isaac* — Rappahannock, Nov 7–63
Mansfield. T — Camp Griffin, Nov 16–61
Morton, Thomas — Calumet
McCrystal, Thos A — Cottage Grove
Marcus, Theodore D — Stetsonville
Metzpuker, James, f — Atlanta, Ia
Noble, John, mc — Grathot
Pedley, Bidwell* — Fredericksburg, May 3–63
Reed, J — Alexandria, Dec 5–64
Reed, Wm — Calumet
Shoemaker, E* — Fredericksburg, May 3– 63
Shoemaker, E R* — Fredericksburg, May 3–63
Simons, Jno, f — Bayville, Mich
Sanders, H O — Alexandria, Nov 2–62
Sargent, Wm B — Atlantic, Ia
Salpman, Ellek — Byron
Smith, Jonathan — Yankeetown
Sable, Peter, f — Taycheedah
Schimian, Joseph — Eau Claire
Tiffany, F W, f — Taycheedah
Thomas, Geo B* — Fredericksburg, May 3–63
Tallmadge, Butler — Calumet

White, Wm T* — Fredericksburg, May 3–63
Wheelock, T H+ — Williamsburg, May –62
Wheelock, Sanders — Calumet
Wood, Ichabod — Calumet

K

Capt Wm Evans+ — Aug 1–62
Capt J M Mott — July 26–63
Lt C R Bayard — Washington, D C
Lt Jas Decivy — Rice Lake
Lt Thos Blair — Lochiel
Lt J A Hill — Menominee
Lt L S West
Lt C S Bundy — Washington, D C
Lt M H Wilson — Menominee
Lt H H Stout* — May 10–64

REORGANIZED.

Capt S A Hall
Lt L A Day — Le Claire, Iowa
Lt A T Fleetwood
Lt P R Tiffany — Taycheedah
Evans, Wm, capt — Philadelphia, Aug 1–62
Mott, John M, capt Fredericksburg, July 26–63
Stout, H H, 2nd lt* — Spottsylvania, May 10–64
Green, John, corp* — Rappahannock, Nov 7–63
Miller, Jas, corp* — Spottsylvania, May 12–64
Stovy, J H, corp — Alexandria, April 11–64
Apel, Michael — Petersburg, Feb 5–65
Bolton, J K+ — Spottsylvania, May 14–64
Burlingame, H — Camp Griffin, Oct 20–61
Bruen, Ernest — Belle Plaine, Feb 24–63
Barpe, C E — Corps Hospital, Jan 20–64
Babcock, Henry, l — Waukau
Crasley, John* — Wilderness, May 5–64
Crouch, Jas — Chippewa Falls
Christmau, Henry
Carpenter, B W — City Point, April 9–65
Dutcher, Platt — U S Hosp, Md, Oct 9–63
Fillmore, John A — Hortonville
Fraker, John — Washington, 3–61
Himmelsbach, Barney, H — Chippewa Falls
Holmes, P C — Menominee
Knoll, Wm B, f — Omro
Larson, G, — U S Hosp, Md
Langdell, Niles — Philadelphia
McCray, Andrew* — Fredericksburg, May 3–63
Messer, F — Andersonville, Aug 21–64
Moore, A B — Harrison's Landing, Aug 14–62
Nolte, Frederick* — Washington, May 21–64
Orban, Ludw.g, f — Wheatland
Pelengs, Aug* — Fredericksburg, May 3–63
Phillips, Wm* — Rappahannock, Nov 7–63
Pavell, M H* — April 15–65
Robinson, Thos+ — Spottsylvania, May 12–64
Riley, J E, f — Berlin
Squires, H C — May –61
Tiffany, P B — Taycheedah
Wood, Harrison — Belle Plaine, March 10–63
Wales, S S, m — Burlington, Ia
Wright, Geo — Badger Mills
Williams, Charles D — Knapp

UNASSIGNED.

Berry, Wm, Sr, f — Taycheedah
Baldwin, B B, c — Waupun
Brand, Robert — Oshkosh
Campbell, Charles — Hammond
Craig, Joseph, dentist — Mount Vernon, O
Catlin, Thos B — Green Bay
Fulton, F S, d — Beloit
Fenton, F G, d — Beloit
Franz, August — La Crosse
Gilson, N S, a — Fond du Lac
Gregg, Jno, c — La Crosse
Graham, Wallace, f — Iowa
Hammond, E C — Waverly, Iowa
Harrison, John, jeweler — Lone Rock
Harrison, A J — Lone Rock
Jesse, August, f — Eau Galle
Knapp, Frank — Menominee

COMMERCIAL FIRE INSURANCE COMPANY

OF NEW YORK CITY.

Organized 1850.

M. V. B. FOWLER, Pres't.   DAVIE QUACKINBUSH, Sec'y

Cash Capital, paid up,	$200,000.00
Net Surplus to Policy Holders,	312,401.30
Net Surplus to Stock Holders,	112,401.30
Cash Assets,	$513,544.39
Of which U. S. Bonds,	294,155.50
Liabilities,	$137,590.59
Re-Insurance Reserve,	163,552.60
Losses Paid since organization over	$2,000,000.00
Dividends Paid since organization,	800,000.00
Book par value of Stock,	156.20

Insure in the Solid Old Commercial.

An Experience of 30 Years.
    Its Directors among the Foremost Business Men of the United States.
        Conservative in its Selection of Risks.
            Honorable in its Adjustment of Losses.
                Prompt in its Settlements.

ITS ASSETS AVAILABLE AT AN HOUR'S NOTICE.

Western Department for the States of

Illinois, Indiana, Michigan, Iowa, Wisconsin, Minnesota and Missouri.

JOHN NAGHTEN,
GENERAL AGENT AT CHICAGO.

All Losses in this Department Adjusted and Payable at our Agencies.

AGENTS WANTED AT DESIRABLE POINTS.

WISCONSIN SOLDIERS AND SAILORS REUNION ROSTER. 29

Lenden, James	Janesville	Blake, Wm P*	Antietam, Sept 17 -62	Goggins, Wm I	Hatcher's Run, Feb 8—65
Louden, Matthew	Janesville	Brunzel, Frederick*	Gravelly Run, March 31—65	Gilbertson, Wm	City Point, April 17—65
Linnett, Henry H	Sacramento, Cal	Baur, Frederick*	Gravelly Run, March 31—65	Gunderson, Ole	St Croix
Louden, James W	Janesville	Bodecker, H*	Hatcher's Run, Feb 7—65	Haie, Frank	Galesville
Miller, Chas H, cl'k	Minneapolis, Minn	Gales, Ashbury +	June 25 -64	Hale, J F	Washington, Oct 27- 62
Palmer, Frank C	Northfield, Minn	Brecker, John	Tomah	Harvey, B W	One
Peckham, Geo G	Ottawa, Ill	Clay, Harvey, clerk	Waupun	Kinne, Darwin W	Trumbull
Smith, Edward,	Valparaiso, Ind	Cheek, Phil, n	Baraboo	Keeler, A D	Smokytown, Md Oct 7- 62
Slater, Jno, band teacher	Belvidere, Ill	Copeland, W H*	Antietam, Sept 17 62	Lowell, H	La Crosse
Schimmelphennig, John	Oconomowoc	Crandall, Frank M	July 6—64	McCawdron, M*	Antietam, Sept 17—62
Voger, L E	Saginaw City, Mich	Dawley, Ebenezer	Baraboo	Murphy, Jere, lumber inspector	Eau Claire
Windecker, Sidney, f	Fond du Lac	Fort, S*	Antietam, Sept 17—62	Mallony, A*	Hatcher's Run. Feb 6—65
Winn A B	Beloit	Garlaugh, F	Antietam, Sept 17—62	McLaughlin, J H	Trumbull
Winn, G B	Beloit	Hodgeden, J*	Wilderness, May 5- 64	Richardson, Jas*	Wilderness, May 5—64
Ward, Wm E	Ottawa, Ill	Hodgen, J G	Maine	Sutter, N*	Antietam, Sept 17 62
Wright, E G	Washington, D C	Hill, James	Sept 18—61	Streiff, M*	Laurel Hill, May 10—64
Winn, George, Sr	Beloit	Harp, Geo A f	Baraboo	Smith, A C*	Spottsylvania, May 8—64
Winn, George	Beloit	Huntington, A J	Green Bay	Steensrud,	Black Earth
Young, James	Wausau	Inman, I	Annapolis, Dec 27- 62	Thompson, John*	Wilderness, May 5—64
Zassder, Halmuth, m	Larrabee	Jones, B M*	Gettysburg, July 1 63	Tomlinson, R	Andersonville, June 28—64
		Jones, F A		Winkler, I	Gravelly Run, March 31—65
		Johnson, 7 C, f	Baraboo		
		Johnson, D W	Petersburg, Feb, 15- 65		C

SIXTH INFANTRY.

Three years, organized July 16th, 1861. Original strength, 1106, gain by recruits, etc., 1035. Total, 2143. Death loss, 321—killed in action, 163, died of wounds, 71, of disease, 84, of accidents, 3. Other losses, 684—missing, 7, desertions, 79, transfers 75, discharged, 513. Strength at muster out, July 14th, 1865, 1148. Campaigns in Virginia with the old "Iron Brigade."

REGIMENTAL ROSTER.

Col Lysander Cutler	Milwaukee	Jenkins, John J, a	Chippewa Falls		
Col Edw S Bragg	Fond du Lac	Keys, J O*	Antietam, Sept 17- 62	Capt Alex B Hove	Prairie du Chien
Col Rufus R Dawes	Marinette, O	Kitner, W J	Petersburg, Aug 19—64	Capt T W Plummer	Prairie du Chien
Col Jno A Kellogg	Wausau	Kline, Wm	Kernsville, Md, Sept 24—62	Capt Edw A Whaley	Prairie du Chien
Lt Col J P Atwood	Leadville, Dakota	Kellogg, C *	Lt Wm Partridge		
Lt Col Thos Kerr	Milwaukee	Keys, Wm E*	May 7—62	1J J L G Harris	St Louis, Mo
Maj Jno F Hauser	Prussia	Langhart, J E*	South Mountain, Sept 14—62	Lt Harley L Sprague	Beetown
Maj D B Dailey	Council Bluffs, Ia	Miles, Geo*	South Mountain, Sept 14- 62	Lt O D Chapman*	Gettysburg, July 1—63
Adj Edw P Brooks,	Cork, Ireland	Pierson, Wm*	Gettysburg, July 1 63	Lt N S Bull	Washington, Sept 17—63
Adj J A Watrous	Fond du Lac	Palmer, Wm	Neillsville	Adams, G G, sgt	Frederick, Jan 23—63
Adj W H Church	Charles City, Iowa	Pierson, J*	Petersburg, June 18 -64	Chestnut, J N, sgt	Gettysburg, July 1—63
Q M Otto Schorse	Milwaukee	Palmer, Uriah	Gettysburg, July 1 -63	Armstrong, W B*	Gettysburg, July 1—63
Q M L B Upham	Friendship	Pierson, S*	July 21 -64	Amman, F*	Petersburg, Aug 18—64
Q M L A Roberts	Prescott	Rice, Geo -	Washington, Oct 13—62	Boyd, A*	Petersburg, Aug 18—64
Q M Sol B Holman	Prescott	Stults Henry	Baltimore, Feb 19- 65	Brown, M H	May 23—65
Surg J C Hall	Monroe	Saare, Wm	St Joseph, Mo	Brewer, Simpson	Port Byron, Ill
A Surg O F Bartlett	Meridian, N Y	Smalley, P J	Green Bay	Beeman, John	Andersonville
A Surg A D Andrews	River Falls	Tilden, Geo f	Milwaukee	Berkenhagen, Wilhelm	Adell
A Surg L G Armstrong	Boscobel, April 25—65	Voss, John	Jeffersonville, Ind, July 1 - 65	Cottrell, A D	June 13- 65
A Surg Wm Lay	Almaton	Whitman, J C*	South Mountain, Sept 14—62	Cladayn, Austin	Andersonville
Chap W Cochran	Oshkosh	Whittaker, H*	Antietam, Sept 17—62	Drysdale, John	March 29—65
Chap John Berk		Williams, Harvey	March 5- 62	Day, William	Fond du Lac
J A McDonnell, gen	Chicago, Ill	Whittle, James, no	Baraboo	Fisker, W*	Laurel Hill, May 12—64
Wm H Allen, lt col				Fisk, A L	Arlington, Feb 1—62
P J Plummer, maj*	Wilderness, May 5—64			Green, G	Prairie du Chien, Feb 1—65
C Babcock, sergt maj*	Petersburg, Aug 19—64		B	Hickock, Wm*	Jericho Ford, May 23- 64
Lynus, John, asst serg	April 25- 65			Harris, Lloyd G	St Louis, Mo
		Capt D J Dill	Prescott	Hewitt, E P	Sharpsburg, Sept 17—62
	A	Capt K P Converse*	Wilderness, May 5—64	Johnson, Alex	Bloomington
		Capt W W Hutchins*	Yellow House, Aug 19 -64	Jordon, T	Mendota, Ill
		Capt H E Sawyer		Klumb, Nicholas, f	Kohlville
		Lt J F Marsh	New Hampshire	Koenig, George, f	Greenville
Capt A G Malloy	Jefferson, Texas	Lt Henry Sevill		Lillie, H t	Fredericksburg, June 20—62
Capt D K Noyes, postmaster	Baraboo	Lt Arthur C Ellis	Eau Claire	Marston, P*	Gettysburg, July 1—63
Capt L A Kent	Denver, Col	Lt Sol B Holman	Prescott	Mc Coy, J*	Hatcher's Run, Feb 6—65
Lt T C Thomas	Baraboo	Lt D W Kinney	Prescott	McAdams, Melvin	Osceola Mills
Lt J A Congdon		Lt Harry Lowell		Petitt, Henry E	Tomah
Lt H J Huntington	Green Bay	Sargeant, O, serg	Arlington, March 7 - 62	Petitt, H C*	Bull Run, Ind, Aug 30—62
Lt Malr Polston	Canby, Minn	Young, D Z, corp*	Antietam, Sept 17—62	Paine-, C H, U S Gov employe	Yankton, D T
Lt Nelson Moore	Woodstock, Minn	Evans, W E, corp	Gettysburg, July 1—63	Powell, J*	Fredericksburg, April 27—63
Pruyn, D P, 1st lt*	Laurel, May 8—64	Kelley, J, corp f	Gettysburg, July 1—63	Russell, S	Washington, Dec 8—61
Fowler, A, sgt*	Hatcher's Run, Feb 6—65	Anderson, H*	Gettysburg, July 1—63	Roddeck, Frederick T	Platteville
Alexander, J, corp f	Antietam, Sept 17 62	Alverson, F W,	May -64	Rose, S	Richland Centre
Johnson, A P, corp, m	Baraboo	Anderson, A	Washington, May 19—65	Schroeder, John, M	Barton
Dawler, E, corp, f	Baraboo	Brown, L*	South Mountain, Sept 14—62	Sheldon, L W+	Washington, Nov 5—62
Fenton, S D, corp*	Cold Harbor, June 2—64	Barrett, G C*	Jericho Ford, May 23—64	Steinmetz, Mathias, f	Cedar Creek
Artridge, R, corp f	Frederick, Sept 14—62	Bruce, C H, f	Warren	Tooley, A*	Wilderness, May 5—64
Ames, A D	Jan 2—62	Cassady, Geo	Alexandria, Dec 8— 62	Vespers, S S	Bull Run 2nd, Aug 30- 62
		Cole, V A*	Antietam, Sept 17- 62	Vanderwalker, S	Maryland, March 30—65
		Casparas, W J	Antietam, Sept 17- 62	Whaley, Ed, postmaster	Prairie du Chien
		Clark, C	Washington, Sept 11—61	Young, F*	Bull Run 2nd, Aug 30—62
		Conrad, Henry	Scott	Young, Frank	Chicago, Ill
		Faust, W*	Gettysburg, July 1—63		
		Fulton, B A*	Gainesville, Aug 28 -64		D
		Francis, C H +	Alexandria, Oct 6—64		
		Fort Isaac	Merrimac	Capt Jno O'Rourke	
		Gluth, F*	Antietam, Sept 17—62	Capt Jno F Marsh	

THE
Fond du Lac, Amboy & Peoria Railway

[NARROW GAUGE]

Runs from Fond du Lac, Wis., to Iron Ridge, connecting with the

MILWAUKEE & St. PAUL R'Y

(The Largest Railway in the United States) making close connections with their trains, East and West, twice each day.

BAGGAGE CHECKED AND PASSENGERS TICKETED TO ALL IMPORTANT POINTS.

THIS IS THE SHORTEST AND BEST ROUTE FROM

Fond du Lac to St. Paul, Minneapolis, Manitoba, La Crosse, Winona, Sioux City, Yankton, the Black Hills, and Northern Nebraska, also via.

Racine and Southwestern Division of Milwaukee and St. Paul Railway, the Direct Route to

Rock Island, Davenport, Cedar Rapids, Des Moines and all Points in

KANSAS AND MISSOURI.

Standard Gauge Cars Brought though by Change of Trucks at Iron Mountain

Making it a safe and convenient route.

For Through Rates, Bills of Lading or Any other Information, Apply at

GENERAL OFFICES, FOREST STREET,
FOND DU LAC, WIS.

WISCONSIN SOLDIERS AND SAILORS REUNION ROSTER. 31

Name	Battle/Date	Name	Battle/Date	Name	Battle/Date
Capt Sam'l Burdsall Jr		Jones, E J*	Petersburg, Feb 6—65	Lt Geo I. Montague	Whitewater
Capt Thos Kerr	Milwaukee	Johnson, J B	Fond du Lac	Lt Wm A Reader	Fond du Lac
Capt J R Launney+	Feb 15—'5	King, F	Gettysburg, July 1—63	Lt H H Carpenter	Brownsville
Capt H C Matraw	Holland, Mich	Leaman, E*	Gettysburg, July 1—63	Lt Jas I. Converse*	Wilderness, May 5—64
Lt M H Fitch	Denver, Col	Lambert, F	White Oak, Nov 2—61	Lt H C Matraw	Holland Mich, May 5—64
Lt E P Brooks	Cork, Ireland	McKinnon, C+	Chambersburg, Dec—67	Lt Sam'l M Bond	Milton
Lt Jno Davidson	Prairie du Chien	Marston, J, m	Appleton	Lt Wm H Allen	
Lt Patrick McCawlrey		Martin, Judas*	Petersburg, Feb 6—65	Lt Wm H Church	Charles City, Ia
Lt H B McIntosh	Milwaukee	Miller, Henry	Fairfax, June 5—65	Hyatt, J A, sgt*	Gainesville, Aug 28—62
Boehm, Joseph	Lucas	Noyce, Geo	Merrimac	Barnes, W H H, sgt*	Gettysburg, July 1—63
Campbell, D. 1st sgt	Baltimore, Aug 3—61	Parkhurst, J A	Neillsville	Cowan, J H, corp*	Antietam, Sept 17—62
Gallup, W, serg't*	Gettysburg, July 1—63	Peters, Theodore	March, 20—65	Mead, Chas corp*	Gettysburg, July 1 63
Montgomery, E, corp*	S Mountain, Sept 14—62	Rouch, David*	Petersburg, Feb 6—65	Moore, J M, corp+	Boonsboro, 2nd Oct, 18—62
Simmons, D, corp*	Gettysburg July 1—63	Rost, A*	Petersburg, Feb 5—61	Jenks, C M corp+	City Point, Nov 25—64
Spear, D, corp*	Petersburg, Aug 18—64	Rowell, John	Chilton	Mason, J, corp—	March 31—65
Odell, M, corp*	Hatcher's Run, Feb 6—65	Shay, John*	Gainesville, Aug 28—62	Bedford, W m*	Gainesville, Aug 28—62
Arnold, F*	South Mountain, Sept 14—62	Smith, Wm	Campbellsport	Brooder, J	Philadelphia, Aug 14—63
Ancy, J J, f	Norwalk	Smith, Guilford	Neillsville	Burbank, D-C—	Middletown, Oct—62
Charlesworth, O*	Gettysburg, July 1—63	Thorn, P C	Andersonville, Aug 26—64	Burch, Perry	Point Lookout, Dec 13—63
Cook, Jno H	Chippewa Falls	Van Dorstan, F	May 11—64	Ballweg, Andrew	Dane Station
Covey, John H	Englewood, Ill	West, James	City Point, May 1—65	Burr, H M	Beloit
Cook, John H	Englewood Ill	Walker, W H	Fond du Lac	Cole, E W+	April 16—63
Dunning, H M*	Bull Run 2nd, Aug 30—62	Watrous, J A	Fond du Lac	Corey, V W+	April 2—65
Davidson, W R	Mazomanie	Zipp, Phil	Fond du Lac	Cannon, Barney+	Rebel Prison
Daily, Dennis B	La Crosse			Clark, Alonzo+	Rebel Prison
Eversoll, F*	Gainesville, Aug 28—62	**F**		Dahl, K J	March 17—62
Eagan, J+	Frederick, Oct 10—62	Capt Frederick Schumacher*	Perryville	Emmons, R K	Washington, Dec 30—62
Geary, Francis*	Antietam, Sept 17—62	Capt W Von Bachell|,	Antietam, Sept 17—62	Frodine, J W+	Frederick, Oct 15—62
Gallup, Warren*	Antietam, Sept 17—62	Capt Otto Schorse	Milwaukee	Green. Frank*	Antietam, Sept 17—62
Hansburg, F*	Hatcher's Run, Feb 7—65	Capt Oscar Graetz*	May 10—61	Gramble, Richard*	Gettysburg, July 1—63
Haydem, A.+	Gettysburg, Aug 5—63	Capt Henry Schildt,	Mazomanie	Haley, M*	Gainesville, Aug 28—62
Hall, George	Milwaukee	Lt Wm F Bode*	Antietam, Sept 17—62	Holland, Wm	Washington, Dec 14—62
Hall, George	Soldiers Home, Milwaukee	Lt Wm Golterman	Mequon River	Hanson, John A	Rockford, Ill Feb 5 63
Jorves, Jus+	Baltimore, Feb 2—65	Lt Edw P Brooks		Hubbard, C R, stock raiser	Tallorville, Texas
Klabenow, J+	April 22—65	Lt D O Davis		Losel, Geo. me	St Killians
Lavitt, M	April 8—5	Lt Chas Bertram		Manning, P*	Gettysburg, July 1—63
Miller, G W+	Washington, June 13—61	Lt A J Barberich		Mogler, W*	Hatchers Run, Feb 7—65
Metlee, Thomas	Hingham	Gratz, Oscar, 1st lt*	Laurel Hill, May 10—61	Maun, C*	Gainesville, Aug 28—62
Perkius, A M*	South Mountain, Sept 24—62	Lampe, C, 1st segt*	Bull Run 2nd, Aug 30—62	Mainwold, R	Washington, April 24—64
Powers, M J+	Hatcher's Run, Feb 8—65	S uge, M, sgt*	Petersburg, June 18—64	Naegly, Henry	Mazomanie
Rosenberg. H	Tess Corners	Hagenow, F, sgt	May 21—54	Purfield Henry L	Cairo, Ill Dec 11—62
Sprague, C*	Gettysburg, July 1—63	Islep, Geo, corp*	Antietam, Sept 17—62	Powers, H C, me	Fond du Lac
Siebenthall, F*	Gettysburg, July 1—63	Dunby, C+	Washington, June 11—64	Reader, W A, m	
Shields, P J+	Washington, June 1—64	Beckelhaust, Wm	Washington, Oct 22—62	Michal, Allen	Shetek
Schneider, John+	April 4—65	Bush, Jacob	Milwaukee	Schnider, J S+	Washington, June 6—64
Stewart, Jas	Mazomanie	Celig, Conrad	Spring Green	Wrinch, Gottfried*	Sailors Creek, June 6, 65
Wilson, A B*	South Mountain, Sept 14—62	Downey, C H	Baltimore	Wright, R O*	Antietam, Sep 17—62
		Duck, A	Annapolis, April 8—65	Wilson, O C	Washington, D C Oct 1 62
		Emley, Frederick	Scott	Wallin, W H	East Saginaw, Mich
E		Goetsch, Leo	Washington, Dec 10—63	Young, S*	Antietam, Sept 17—62
Capt Edw S Bragg	Fond du Lac	Goelsch, Leo	Painesville	Zeueir, F	Alexandria, June 9—65
Capt E A Brown*	Antietam, sept 17—62	Harre, C*	Gettysburg, July 1—63		
Capt Chas P Hyatt*	Philadelphia, Sept 22—64	Hang J*	Hatcherl's Run, Feb 7—65	**H**	
Capt H L Garfield		Hermann, Christopher, f	Riceville		
Lt Jas T Conklin	London, Ont	Hohenstein, H	Washington, April 12—65	Capt Jno F Hauser	Prussia
Lt J B Johnson	Fond du Lac	Henning, Franz	Fillmore	Capt Albert T Morgan	Washington, D C
Lt A O Deacon	Jeffersonville, Mo	Ivers, Neils	Washington, June 3—63	Lt John D Lewis	
Lt Michael Mangan	Fond du Lac	Klokow, C*	Antietam, Sept 17—62	Lt Jno A Lester	Alma
Lt Geo D Eggleston	Appleton	Keuchenmeister, Fred	Fillmore	Lt Jno Bealey	Fountain City
Burns, J H, sergt+	Wilderness, May 7—64	Marsh, Wm L.	Pontiac, Mich	Lt Thos Kelley	Racine
Smith, B C, sergt	Dec 18—61	Maertz, August	Whittlesey	Lt H B Merchant	St Louis. Mo
Hart J P, corp*	Spottsylvania, May 8—64	Maoeh, Wm	Pontiac, Mich	Snyder, N, 1st sergt*	Laurel Hill, May 12—64
Webb, S P, corp	Arlington, Oct 23—61	Rader, J+	Germantown, Pa, Aug 2—65	Polleys, F, sergt+	Alexandria, June 30—64
Boweis, J T	City Point, Jan 2—65	Spengler, Philip*	Gettysburg, July 1—63	Baily, Wm, corp*	Antietam, Sept 17—62
Bragg, E S, a	Fond du Lac	Schulster, H*	Petersburg, July 1—61	Many, John, corp*	Gettysburg, July 1—63
Campbell, J+	April 28—64	Sulzer. Adolph	Milwaukee	Doyle, John, corp*	Hatcher's Run, Feb 6—65
Diener, J *	Petersburg	Schorer, Otto	Milwaukee	Kelly, D, corp*	
Dennis, A	Neillsville	Thesmier, A*	Bull Run 2nd, Aug 30—62	Blake, Thos*	Laurel Hill, May 12—64
Durant, J W+	July 3—63	Vetter, J	Andersonville, July 9—64	Butler, E W+	Washington, April 8—65
Dilamater, N	Harrisburg, Aug 2—61	Wellhausen, H*	Bull Run 2nd, Aug 30—62	Cottrell. S	Washington, March 4—64
Elliott, C D, ed	Fond du Lac	Zrociiel, Jost, dairyman	Milwaukee	Canon, J F	Neillsville
Flood, J, l	Fond du Lac			Eggleston, L W+	Gettysburg, July 26—63
Fenner, Jacob	Lone Rock	**G**		Fry, Jas*	Petersburg, June 19—64
Garfield, E	Nov 27—61	Capt M A Northrup	Beloit, Wis	Fuch, John	City Point, Jan 21—65
Garfield, M A	Washington, Sept 2—63	Capt Lewis A Kent	Denver. Col	Fisher, F	Belle Plain, Jan 18—62
Gaffney, A	Campbellsport	Capt Jno Simmons*	Yellow House. Aug 19—64	Haffner, John	Andersonville, Oct 2—64
Gaffney, Nick	Osceola	Capt D B Daliey	Council Bluffs b.	Johnson, W L	Andersonville, Oct 2—44
Hardy, E S	Andersonville, Feb 6—65	Capt Heury Snegely	Mazomanie	Johnson, John O	Stevens Point
Havilbud, E	Scott			Kufuer, Jos*	Antietam, Sept 17—62

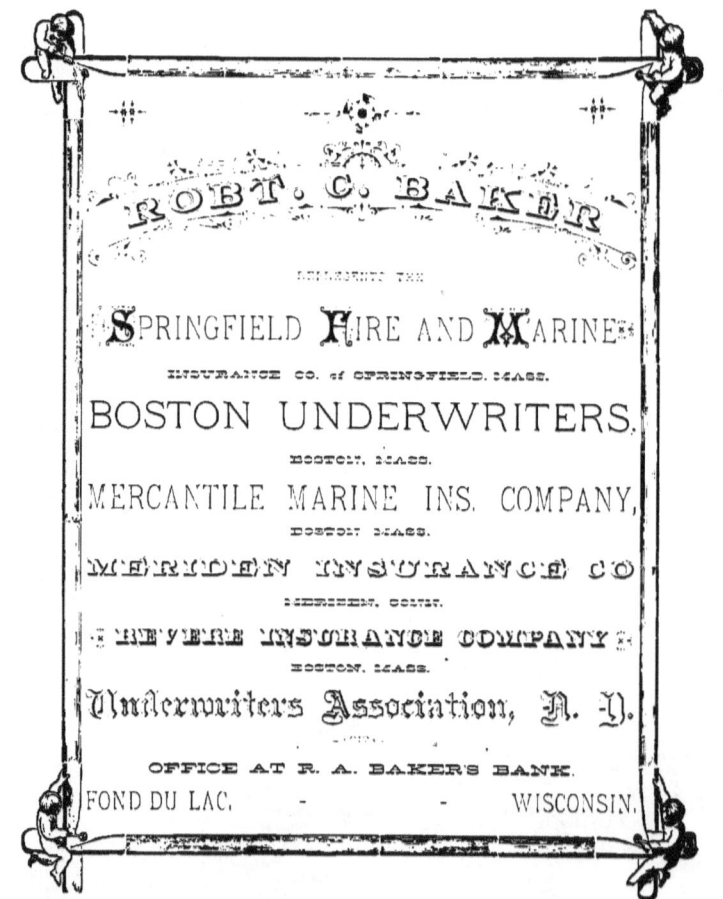

WISCONSIN SOLDIERS AND SAILORS REUNION ROSTER.

Kumley, Uris	Washington, Nov 11—64	White, Thos	Sept 14—64	Gibson, John	St Paul, Minn
Martin, N*	Gettysburg, July 1—63	Wareham, R A, m	Plymouth, Ia	Hill, "Doc"	Hillsborough
May, J*	Laurel Hill, May 12—64	Walker, Samuel	Ontario	Hart, Louis, f	Ontario
Muller, Paul+	Washington	Wallace, Jas S	Viroqua	Hockabout, W H, f	Readstown
Nettleton, S*	Antietam, Sept 17—62	Zwarink, A*	Gravelly Run, March 31—65	Kauouse, Thos D, musician	Watertown
Philbrick, P H	March 5—65			Kuehenmeister, Ferdinand	Kewaskum
Poor, C P	Jenny	**K**		Lind, Charley, f	Hillsborough
Parkin, Kirby	Coloma			Law, R	Chicago, Ill
Read, Uris	Barton	Capt Rufus R Dawes,	Marietta, Ohio	Lind, Ed,	Sydney, Neb
Schlorenbocker, E*	Gettysburg, July 1—63	Capt David L Quaw	Wausau	Lyms, Jim	Glendale
Smith F*	Laurel Hill, May 12—64	Capt Jno Ticknor*	Gettysburg, July 1—63	Morgan, Albert T	Fox Lake
Schinoe, O	Barton	Capt Wm N Remington	Mauston	Mangan, M E, m	Fond du Lac
Taylor, Samuel—		Capt Andrew Gallup		Mathews, G	Cylon
Troutman, Anton	Andersonville, Sept 12—64	Lt Jno A Kellogg	Wausau	Moody, Jim	LaCrosse
Webber, Peter+	Frederick, Oct 23—62	Lt Wm S Campbell		Moore, Billy	Green Bay
White, H M+	Washington, June 2—64	Lt Israel Hendricks+	Feb 12—65	Minchell, W E, p	Chicago, Ill
Walters, Henry H	Dodgeville	Lt Wm H Van Wie	Mauston	McClure, T W	Hillsborough
Witherell, Halle	Fond du Lac	Lt Jno Crane		Nutting, Dan	
		Lt Lyman B Plumb		Newton, Thos	
		Lt Samuel F Gordon		Neagely, Henry	Nazomanle
I		Tarbox, A E, sgt *	Gettysburg, July 1—63	Nelson, Frederick	Canton, Dakota
Capt Leonard S Johnson	Glendale	Fletcher, A, corp*	Gettysburg, July 1—65	Patton, W H	Oshkosh
Capt Jno A Kellogg	Wausau	Revels, W J, corp*	Weldon, R R, Aug 19—64	Page, Chas	Desota
Capt Earl M Rogers	Viroqua	Abbott, Chas A*	Antietam, Sept 17—62	Richardson, Mart, f	Chippewa
Lt Milo M Baker		Chamberlain, G C*	South Mountain, Sept 14—62	Riley, Bill, e	Geneva
Lt Clayton E Rogers	Chippewa Falls	Cleveland, T J	St Croix	Somerly, John, p	N Y Tribune office
Lt Francis A Waller	De Sota	Cummings, Daniel*	Antietam, Sept 17—62	Soerl, f	Hillsborough
Lt Jno C Goodwin,	Wonewoc	Coppernall, C E—	Aug 15—64	Schuett, J O	Tess Corners
Miller, A, 1st sgt*	Gettysburg, July 1—63	Dufour, William	Washington, Dec 21—62	Schuler, Gottlieb, f	Greenwood
Green, C A, sgt*	Petersburg, June 18—64	Edward H H	New Lisbon	Shreve, Caleb, f	Greenwood
Fox, Wm, sgt*	Keedysville, Sept 21—62	Harrison, W P*	Arlington, Nov 25—61	Smith, Neill	Clinton In
Ruby, G A, corp*	Fredericksburg, Aug 29—64	Freudwyn, A*	Five Forks, April 1—65	Sweet, Bill, f	Chippewa
Nicholas, W H, corp*	Laurel Hill, May 10—64	Folmsbey, Geo	Minneska, Minn	Southwick, Milton	Franklin
Thompson, H, corp+	Washington, June 27—64	Gardner, L S*	Bull Run 2nd, Aug 30—62	Thuber, Geo W, f	Hillsborough
Atwood, G W*	Antietam, Sept 17 62	Gile, C M	Washington, May 12—65	Tongue, Le Grand, f	Desota
Burnham, Chas*	Gainesville, Aug 28—62	Gordon, S P, f	Wadena, Minn	Warham, Dick, m	Iowa
Boughton S M*	Gettysburg, July 1—63	Hustley, R*	South Mountain, Sept 14—62	Wyman, Chester	Hillsborough
Benedict, L S	Laurel Hill, May 10-64	Harrison, W P*	Antietam, Sept 17—62	Williams, Isaiah	Nebraska
Bishop, H W	Salisbury, N C, Nov 6—61	Hancock, W P*	Petersburg, June 18—61	Wallace, James	Viroqua
Crane, W R*	Laurel Hill, May 10—64	Hancock, W D*	Salisbury Prison, Nov 16—64	Wood, L L	Chicago, Ill
Conklin, C A—	Stafford C H, May 9—63	Hahn, Geo	Petersburg, Feb 13—65	Wilcox, Franklin	Mauston
Collins, W M+		Hills, L B, f	Mauston	Waller, T A, f	Desota
Carter, M D+	Feb 11—63	Johnson, L	Glendale		
Campbell, Daniel	Albanville	Kellogg, J A, a	Wausau		
Didiot, L*	Gainesville, Aug 28—62	Lowery, A	LaCrosse		
Douglas, Geo*	Antietam, Sept 17—62	Patersen, Wm*	Gainesville, Aug 28—62	**SEVENTH INFANTRY.**	
Dibble, C P	Wilderness, May 5—64	Patterson, W M, f	Mauston		
Darrow, Wm H	Point Bluff	Pratt, Lorenzo	Mauston	Three years. Organized Sept. 18th, 1861.	
Ellsworth, F*	Gainesville, Aug 28—62	Rogers, E M	La Crosse	Original strength, 1029; gain by recruits, etc.,	
Ellis, C C*	Hatcher's Run, Feb 6—65	Rose, Eugene	Hillsboro, Dec 2—64	903, total, 1932, death loss, 301—killed in action,	
Emmons, A,	Hillsboro, Dec 2—64	Scoville, J*	Gettysburg, July 1—63	172, died of wounds, 95, of disease, 124. Other	
Fine, R*	Bull Run 2nd, Aug 30—62	Scott, John+	City Point, April 1—65	losses, 629—missing, 6, desertions, 44, transfers,	
Fenton, D C+		Sweet, Geo N	Hunter, N Y	166, discharges, 473. Strength at muster out,	
Fox, Abijah	Belle Plaine, March 6—63	Trumbull, H W*	Fredericksburg, April 29—63	July 32, 1865, 912. Campaign in Virginia with	
Fosdick, H A	Washington, Sept 21—63	Thompson, Jas H+	City Point, Feb 13—65	the old "Iron Brigade."	
Gray, Richard+		Wescott, L*	Petersburg, June 18—64		
Grant, A C	Washington, April 6—65	Williams, J P+	Baltimore, March 9—65	**REGIMENTAL ROSTER.**	
Hasland, J*	Gettysburg, July 1—63	Yates, A I,	Laurel Hill, May 12—64		
Hopps, C*	Petersburg, June 18—64	UNASSIGNED.		Col Joseph Van Dor	Prussia
Harding, J+	Boonsboro, Md, Nov 18—62			Col W W Robinson	Madagascar
Johnson, J A*	Petersburg, Aug 19—64	Allen, Thos W f	Hillsborough	Col Mark Finnecum	Michigan
Johnson, J P*	Wilderness, May 5—64	Allen, G L, f	Valley Red River of the North	Col Hollon Richardson	Chippewa Falls
Lawrence, Wm*	South Mountain, Sept 14—62	Bohn, Charley, f	Hillsborough	Lt Col Chas A Hamilton	Milwaukee
Longmire, John	Oct 28—61	Burdett, O C	Ontario	Lt Col Jno B Callis	Nuscoda
Lind, Henry J, f	Hillsborough	Burchell, N	Greenwood	Lt Col Martin C Hobart	Fall River
Lewis, F L, ph	Arcadia	Baveus, Tom, f	Iowa	Maj Geo Bill	
Markle, Peter S—		Briggs, Ed	Decorah, Ia	Maj Geo S Hoyt	Regular Army
McClure, H F	Washington, Jan 14—64	Clawster, Wm, f	Liberty Pole	Adjt Chas W Cook	Wilmington, Ill
Moody, Jas C	North La Crosse	Campbell, Dan	Ontario	Adjt Robt Monteith	Madison
McDill, Geo M, a	Osceola Mills	Cushing, Shep	Desota	Adjt S J Phillips*	Petersburg, Va, June 21—64
Phillips, Richard H	Oct 20—64	Cobb, Amasa	Lincoln, Neb	Adjt E A Campbell	
Robbins, Geo+	Georgetown, Sept 21—62	Driggs, John, f	Nebraska	Adjt R L Moore	
Reeves, Selah	Empire	Davis, Lawson	Hillsborough	Q M David Shirrell	198 Niagara St, Buffalo
Rogers, Earl M, m	Viroqua	Dawes, R R	Marietta, Ohio	Q M LaTour M Christ	Lancaster
Sutler, G W*	Gettysburg, July 1—63	Durlin, Walter	Pittsfield, Penn	Q M Fred'k Dunham	
Salts, A	Five Forks, April 1—65	Everest, Chas	Barton	Surg Henry Palmer	Janesville
Smith, Clark+		Fern, Sargeant, f	Kansas	Surg D C Ayres	Green Bay
Siedman, Levi	July 2—65	Goodwin, Joe M, f	Wonewoc	A Surg E F Spaulding	East Boston, Mass
Southwick, Milton, f	Viroqua	Grupe, Ferdinand	Hika	A Surg L B Brainard	Waupaca
Thompson, G W	Washington, Nov 15—62				
Wright, Caleb C+					

H. F. ATKINSON, Pres. JAS. F. ATKINSON, Sec'y.

Appleton Chair and Bedstead
FACTORY.
APPLETON, - WISCONSIN.

—MANUFACTURERS OF—

CHAMBER SUITS SIDEBOARDS

BUREAUS, CANE AND WOOD SEAT CHAIRS, WALNUT, ASH AND MAPLE

BEDSTEADS, BOOK CASES,

SECRETARIES, LIBRARY AND CENTRE TABLES.

OTTOMAN FRAMES MADE TO ORDER.

Designs and estimate Furnished for all kinds of Cabinet work.

Store Fitting and Office Furnishing a Specialty

Cogs, Mill Flights, Framing Pins, Newel Posts and Ballusters Furnished on Short Notice.

Orders Promptly Filled. All Work Guaranteed.

YOUR PATRONAGE RESPECTFULLY SOLICITED.

WISCONSIN SOLDIERS AND SAILORS REUNION ROSTER.

A

A Surg F J Despieres — Wausau
A Surg Ernest Kramer — Milwaukee
Chap S L Brown
Chap S W Eaton — Lancaster

Capt Geo Bill
Capt Hollon Richardson — Chippewa Falls
Capt Jas Johnson
Lt M B Misner
Lt W W Ryan — Okee
Lt Jas Holmes* — Wilderness, May 6–64
Lt T J T Buchanan
Lt Conrad Gunkel — Chippewa Falls
Lt Richard Lindsay
Agan, John — Andersonville, Aug 10–64
Ball, Henry — Andersonville, June 16–64
Bartholomew, J M* — Gainesville, Aug 28–62
Bartholomew, M — Lodi
Bartholomew, Jos M, Express Agt — Lodi
Bascom, John — Madison, Nov 19–64
Bascom, L+ — Middleton, Md, Dec 1–62
Beauregard, F H — Andersonville
Brown, J* — Wilderness, May 5–64
Buck, H M — May 10–64
Burke, M* — South Mountain, Sept 14–62
Byron, Henry — Iron Ridge
Carrow, Joseph+ — Petersburg, July 3–64
Carter, W P — Washington, Oct 14–64
Carter, Bissell — Washington, Oct 28–63
Charles, J N+ — Washington, July 9–64
Chase, M* — Gettysburg, July 1–63
Cleveland, James* — Gainesville, Aug 28–62
Cleveland, Wm, I — Lodi
Clune, Patrick+ — April 11–68
Cole, Otis N — Rebel Prison
Collins, Wm* — Laurel Hill, May 10–64
Crandall, W W, County Clerk — Chippewa Falls
Douglass, A F* — Gainesville, Aug 28–62
Eithorp, C — Columbus
Evaus, G W+ — Petersburg, July–64
Faith, John+ — Petersburg, July 31–64
Fowler, Francis A — Andersonville, Sept–64
Fragrer, Philip — Annapolis, Oct 1–63
Hall, Alexander — Philadelphia, Sept 6–62
Hart, C* — Petersburg, June 18–64
Hawks, Milo — Dorchester
Hawks, M — Neillsville
Hicks, Edwin M — April 7–65
Hinton, W+ — Washington, Dec 22–62
Hobart, O B* — Laurel Hill, May 9–64
Holmes, L P* — Cold Harbor, June 2–64
Holmes, J* — Wilderness, May 4–64
Johnson, L* — Wilderness, May 6–64
Kalb, Jacob* — Wilderness, May 5–64
Kurst, Wm* — Wilderness, May 5–64
Luck, Peter — Andersonville, July 7–64
Lasky, Wm F+ — Alexandria, Oct 3–62
Leban, Alonzo* — Wilderness, May 6–64
McCabe, James, pa — Columbus
McCalvary, A T* — Petersburg, June 18–64
McCalvary, T+ — Philadelphia, July 23–61
Mead, J H* — Gettysburg, July 1–63
Mills, C E* — Gainesville, Aug 28–63
Moor, John* — Wilderness, May 5–63
Osborne, S J — Washington, March 31–63
Philips, R* — Gainesville, Aug 28–62
Pierce, Hiram+ — Middleton, Oct 7–62
Rafferty, Peter* — Wilderness, May 5–64
Ruspel, Seraphim* — Gainesville, Aug 28–62
Ryan, W W — Okee
Sanderson, J W* — Wilderness, May 5–64
Sawyer, J D* — Antietam, Sept 17–62
Sayre, E P — Washington, Nov 15–61
Sheehann, M* — Gainesville, Aug 28–62
Simmers, B* — Petersburg, July 31–64
Stevers, D E* — Wilderness, May 6–64
Stilson, Thos H+ — Petersburg, July 31–64
Stone Albert — Arlington, Va, Dec 14–62

B

Strangeway, F W — Lodi
Townley, W J, I — Warren Mills
Zinger, Jacob* — Wilderness, May 5–64

Capt Jas H Huntington
Capt Geo H Brayton* — Gainesville, Aug 28–62
Capt M C Hobart — Fall River
Capt C E Weeks — Marshall
Lt Jno Walter
Lt S L Bachelder
Lt Herb D Dyer — Durand
Lt Sam'l H Shields
Lt E A Campbell
Lt C C Spaulding — Rio
Acres, W D, sergt — Philadelphia, Aug 6–63
Batteau, P A, corp* — Laurel Hill, May 10–64
Brayton, Geo H, capt* — Gainesville, Aug 28–62
Brownson, M P, sergt — Belle Plain, Mar 26–63
Brown, James — Kalorama, Dec 16–62
Brunson, E* — Antietam, Sept 17–62
Bush, Geo E — Rio
Carney, P — Balls Cross Roads, May 26–63
Caseney, Peter — Washington, May 26–65
Casson, Alfred — Madison, Sept 9–61
Cole, Rufus+ — Middleton, Oct 7–62
Cromwell, Orrin D — Falmouth, May 14–62
Frost, A — Andersonville, Feb 5–63
Frost, S — Gainesville, June 28–62
Graham, B F — Gettysburg, July 1–63
Hancock, E R, corp* — Middleton, Sept 20–61
Hatfield, Silas+ — Hospital, June 18–64
Hawes, G H — Gettysburg, July 25–63
Hein, T, sergt* — Wilderness, May 5–64
Hillicker, John T — Washington, Nov 19–61
Hobart, M C, I — Fall River
Hughes, Alexander — Elk Pond, D T
Hulbert, O A, corp* — Wilderness, May 6–64
Kippen C* — Laurel Hill, May 10–64
Lewis, Julian* — Gainesville, Aug 28–62
Maxfield, J H* — Wilderness, May 6–64
Miller, Azel — Georgetown, June 28–62
Miller, J H, sergt* — Petersburg, June 19–64
Monroe, M C, sergt+ — Gettysburg, Oct 7–63
Myers, Wm* — Gettysburg, July 1–63
Newell, Homer — Wisconsin, Aug 18–64
Pelts, J A, corp — Washington, Sept 10–62
Plummer, C E, corp* — S Mountain, Sept 14–62
Provost, Louis* — Laurel Hill, May 10–64
Richardson, W* — Wilderness, May 5–64
Salesburg, J K — Grand Meadow, Minn
Sickler, W H — Elroy
Spaulding, C C — Rio
Van Walker, Allen — Baltimore, Dec 20–63
Walker, Charles — Rio
Weeks, C E, I — Columbus
Wheeler, Edwin* — Antietam, Sept 17–62
Wilcox, Daniel — Middleton, Oct 28–62
Wilkinson, A J — Washington, July 7–64

C

Capt A R Bushnell — Lancaster
Capt J Neumann* — Wilderness, Va, May 5–64
Capt E A Andrews
Lt J H Holcomb
Lt D C Ashmore
Lt Wielan Oswald
Lt Wm O Topping+ Fitz Hugh Cross, April 29–63
Lt Geo W Davis
Armstrong, J* — Wilderness, May 5–64
Bryant, D H+ — Washington, July 4–64
Burkholder, David, I — Scott
Calvert, Wm — Rebel Prison, Oct 16–64
Carpenter, Wm — Wilderness, May 5–64
Collins, Alonzo — Dubuque, Ia
Cox, William, mu — Platteville
Daggett, A E+ — Feb 26–65
Danner, John — Fredericksburg, July 22–64

Eason, Edward — Feb 26 –65
Eastman, J L+ — Washington, Oct 1–62
Fordney, John W — Andersonville, May 12–64
Hodges, James, I — Kingsbury, Cal
Holmes, W* — South Mountain, Sept 14–62
Howarth, Wm* — Washington, July 29–63
Hull, Wm* — Gettysburg, July 1–63
Hurst, L D* — Laurel Hill, May 12–64
Inman, H — Arlington, Nov 22–61
Lameck, John* — Gravelly Run, March 31–64
Link, David H — Oct 78–62
McKinney, W G+ — Antietam, Sept 23–63
Mitchell, G* — Wilderness, May 5–64
Newcomb, W B– — Frederick, March 5–63
Palmer, J — Andersonville, May 12–64
Parker, Ezekiel — Wilderness, May 5–64
Ray, Madison — Middleton, Oct –64
Rice, Jacob — Andersonville, Sept 27–64
Russell, Alonzo — Washington, Feb 28–63
Sain, Geo W+ — Gettysburg, July 10–63
Sanders, J — Andersonville, Sept 26–64
Sperry, Enoch S — New York City, Nov 3–62
Stout, Albert* — Antietam, Sept 17–62
Sutton, T B* — Bull Run, Aug 30–62
Will Geo+ — New York, July 9–64

D

Capt E F Giles — Stoughton
Capt Alex W Bean — Stoughton
Capt Fred B Dearborn — Troy, Kan
Capt Wm W Machen, Jr — Adel, Iowa
Lt C W Cook — Wilmington, Ill
Lt H P Colton — West Grove, Ia
Lt J Compton — Adel, Ia
Lt G W Shumpner — Rutland
Lt Bon L Estis — Bay View
Lt Chas Campbell — Waupun
Best, James — Stoughton
Burnett, George — Stoughton
Brigham, E P — Burr
Buckman, P C* — Gainesville, Aug 28–62
Buckman, B G+ — May 24–64
Bull, F M+ — Gettysburg, July 9–63
Compton, Wm H — Washington, Nov 13–61
Cook, W H+ — May 36–64
Coon, A D+ — Washington, Sept 3–62
Crane, Edward+ — Washington, Sept 3–62
Crocker, J M+ — May 2–64
Cummings, James — Arlington, Jan 26–62
Edwards, John A — Washington, Nov 28–62
Emery, W H* — Gainesville, Aug 28–62
Emmas, Henry — Washington, Sept 21–62
Estes, E A J, I — Virginia, Dakota
Evans, James* — Gainesville, Aug 28–62
Farnham, L C* — Gainesville, Aug 28–62
Guernsey, Otis — Stoughton
Haines, M V — Stoughton
Hunt, John — Richmond, Oct 12–63
Isham, L S* — Stoughton
Isham, L S* — Wilderness, May 5–64
Kluefelter, H G — Nora
Little, O S* — Gainesville, Aug 28–62
Main, E E — Stoughton
Murphy, J+ — Transport, April 11–65
O'Connor, J C, I — Frederick, Oct 3–62
Ordway, B P+ — Five Forks, April 1–65
Ortley, Godfried* — May 15–64
Parrish, Geo+ — Yankton, D T
Powers, W M, mu
Renbeiger, J* — Gettysburg, July 1–63
Richmond, S B — Arlington, Jan 5–62
Shampern, Geo — Stoughton
Sherfelt, Sidney — Omro
Shelter, Henry — Stoughton
Sherman, Wm H — Oct 24–62
Simmons, Elmore — Stoughton
Markweather, M M+ — May 24–64
Stillman, B H — Albert Lea, Minn

GALLOWAY FLOURING MILLS.

T. S. HENRY & CO.,

MANUFACTURERS, DEALERS AND SHIPPERS OF THE CHOICE BRANDS OF

PATENT FLOURS

THE BEST IN THE MARKET.

GRAHAM, BUCKWHEAT, OAT MEAL, BOLTED CORN MEAL

AND CRACKED WHEAT.

GROUND FEED.

MILL, *Corner Arndt and Packer Streets.*

SALES ROOM, *443 Main Street.*

FOND DU LAC, WISCONSIN.

WISCONSIN SOLDIERS AND SAILORS REUNION ROSTER.

Sylvester, Wm — Stoughton
Taylor, Geo* — Gravelly Run, March 31—65
Thomas, John+ — Washington, May 16—64
Thompson, R* — Gettysburg, July 1—63
Tippee, O F — Stoughton
Treat, James M* — Alexandria, Sept 21—62
Walker, L A* — Gettysburg, July 1—63
Walker, W — Stoughton
Wheeler, A A — Washington D C, Nov 10—64
Wright, J E — Stoughton

Smith, Chas A — Arlington, Feb 11—62
Smith, James M+ — Washington, June 2—64
Spooner, E J — Arlington, March 4—62
Straight, J B+ — Gettysburg, July 1—63
Thalacker, Henry — Montello
Thurston A R* — Wilderness, May 5—64
Tomlinson, Chas R — Arlington, March 3—62
Wall J J D — Annapolis, Dec 28—64
Webster, A R, sergt — Andersonville, May 7—64
Wheeler, Arch — Alexandria, April 29—65
Wheeler, James — Washington, Nov 10—64
Wheelock, W H H — Wilderness, May 5—64
Worcester, W, corp+ — Washington, Oct 9—62
Worden, G H, sergt— Locust Grove, May 12—64

Lt Lemuel Kramer — Grand Rapids
Lt Hugh Evans
Armstrong, W J — Neillsville
Atwood, A M — Grand Rapids
Barker, Chauncey — Oct 6—64
Bean, Solomon — Arlington, Dec 7—62
Bennett, Moses— Washington, June 16—64
Buck, John M — April 8—65
Burt, F W — Grand Rapids
Burns, Z S* — Gettysburg, July 1—63
Cally, Hamilton N, f — Scotia, Neb
Campbell, J H* — Gainesville, Aug 28—62
Carpenter, L* — Petersburg, June 18—64
Coffin, R W — Gainesville, Aug 28—62
Crandall, Seely E, f — Plainfield
Creavey, D* — Antietam, Sept 17—62
Divine, Mitchell+ — City Point, April 22—65
Durkee, Stephen, f — Sheffield
Durkee, S — Schofield
Dyer, H D, mu — Durand
Everest, Juel, f — Pine River
Gould, A G, f — Oregon
Gray, A R — Fredericksburg, May 27—64
Ingraham, Jas E — Grand Rapids
James, Joseph — Sherwood
Johnson, W* — Laurel Hill, May 10—64
Jones, Obadiah — Arlington, Jan 24—62
Lever, Peter* — Bull Run, Aug 30—62
Lynh, M H, — Grand Rapids
Lynn, T J* — South Mountain, Sept 14—62
Lytle, G* — Laurel Hill, May 10—64
McAuliff, M— — Alexandria, June 18—61
McCaskey, Alex, f — Homewood
Moe, Alna O* — Gravelly Run, March 31—65
Olvson, P M* — Gettysburg, July 1—63
Parker, Henry — Madison, Oct 1—61
Partridge, G N* — Gettysburg, July 1—63
Priest, James E — Arlington, Dec 28—61
Razor, Joseph* — Laurel Hill, May 13—64
Richards, W* — Gravelly Run, March 31—65
Rogers, Franklin — Philadelphia, Dec 1—62
Shaw, Frank+ — Washington, May 25—64
Shortell, M* — Jericho Ford, May 23—64
Singoy, John+ — Washington, June 18—64
Sparks, Stephen — Rebel Prison
Tapping, John — Antietam, Sept 17—62
Tennant, Ed — Grand Rapids
Verinder, Robert J — Rebel Prison
Wardwell S B* — Gettysburg, July 1—63
Warner, Fred, m — Randolph
Weatherby, David — Alexandria, April—62
Wing, Noah, f — Roseville
Withroog, Adolphus — Rebel Prison
Work, Robt M — Elroy

E

Capt Levi E Pond — Westfield
Capt Wm H Gildersleeve
Lt E J Buck — Westfield
Lt W F Bailey — Portage City
Lt W B Mauning — Chicago, Ill
Lt David Shirrell — Buffalo, N Y
Lt Henry Gibson — Westfield
Lt Jno H Hopper — Coloma
Lt Aug M Hubbard+ — Five Forks, April 2—65
Lt Jno Harrison
Baldwin, C L+ — Gettysburg, July 1—63
Blackburn, E G, clerk — Berlin
Boles, Geo E — Hancock
Boller, Geo J, drover — Brookville, Kansas
Bowen, Jos E — Fredericksburg, June 22—62
Bradshaw, Wm — Arlington, March 22—62
Bradshaw, M W+ — Fredericksburg, May 18—64
Briggs, Jas+ — near Antietam, Sept 18—62
Bristol, Henry O — Belle Plaine, March 16—63
Cassey, D E — Wilderness, May 8—64
Case, David — Cincinnati, April 19—63
Casey, J F — Alexandria, June 15—62
Craudall, H J, sergt* — Gainesville, Aug 28—62
Dewey, G J, corp* — Laurel Hill, Sept 17—62
Eddy, Geo W+ — Washington, Sept 9—62
Eubanks, Jno* — Jericho Ford, May 28—62
Figger, Geo+ — Washington, June 1—64
Flagg, E H+ — Hospital, April 23—65
Fonda, Martin — Baltimore, March 26—64
Fuller, C W, corp — Andersonville, May 21—64
Gathers, Henry — Hancock
Gathers, H — Coloma
Ghering, Aug+ — Gettysburg, July 1—63
Gibson, Henry — Westfield
Gupill, F A* — Wilderness, May 5—64
Harrison, Jno — Friendship
Hoffman, Herman A, f — Amherst
Holcomb, W L+ — Gettysburg, July 1—63
Holcombe, Henry — Hancock
Hopper, J H — Coloma
Hopwood, Geo — Dansville, June 25—65
Huggabome, L* — Gainesville, Aug 28—62
Hutchinson, Geo — Hancock
Jump, William — Hancock
Lackey, C S+ — Washington, May 22—64
Luther, Justus P, mu — Berlin
Marsh, Samuel B — Brookside
Marsh, C H* — Wilderness, May 5—64
Marshall, Alanson — Arlington, Jan 20—62
Millen, Henry M — Harrisonville
Mills, Elijah, corp — Andersonville, Oct 1—64
Mills S S — Hancock
Montgomery, Chas — Culpepper, April 17—64
Mussey, J C, sergt* — Wilderness, May 5—64
Narcester, W F, corp+ — Washington, Oct 9—65
Orvis G A, corp* — Wilderness, May 5—64
Orvis, N — Westfield
Osborne, C A, sergt* — Hatcher's Run, Feb 6—65
Pattingill, James+ — Antietam, Sept 17—62
Pease, Silas W* — Gettysburg, July 1—63
Pond, L E, m — Westfield
Robinson, W W — Fort Totten, Dakota
Rou, Louis, f — Scott
Rose, J J, corp+ — Washington, Sept 11—62
Sargent, G, corp* — Antietam, Sept 17—62
Sharpe, E W, sergt + — Petersburg, June 8—64

F

Capt Jno B Callis — Muscoda
Capt H F Young — Patch Grove
Capt Francis A Boynton
Lt Sam'l Woodhouse
Lt W E Sloat — Mount Hope
Lt Jesse M Roberts — Plainfield, Ia
Lt Wm E Stout
Lt J W McKenzie
Lt Bruce Bryan
Atwood, Orlando W — Arlington, Nov 24—61
Bennett, Philip+ — Gettysburg, July 4—63
Blakely, Robert — Andersonville, Nov 15—64
Blunt, T+ — Gravelly Run, March 31—65
Calvert, M* — Petersburg, June 18—64
Clark, J A* — South Mountain, Sept 14—62
Cooley, G W* — South Mountain, Sept 14—62
Cormick, Geo f — Washington, May 23—64
Craig, W F* — Antietam, Sept 17—62
Darnell, T H B — Gettysburg, July 5—63
Drew, J A — Muscoda
Ellis, J H — Frederick, April 7—62
Eugle, George — Madison, March 22—64
Evans, James H — March 2—65
Francis, Peter* — Wilderness, May 5—64
Geneava, F* — Gravelly Run, March 31—65
Gilligan, James — Arlington, March 9—62
Halbert, G F— — Middleton, Sept 29—63
Kaump, H A* — South Mountain, Sept 14—62
Kentner, H* — Gainesville, Aug 28—62
Kuntz, I* — Antietam, Sept 17—61
Leppa, John—
Limkins, J A+ — Frederick, Oct 8—62
Marks, J L* — South Mountain, Sept 14—62
Marks, Fred — Dakota
McDonald, R S* — Gainesville, Aug 38—62
McPhail+ — Newton
Miles, W N* — Gainesville, Aug 28—62
Nehten, John — Charlesburg
Parker, C G* — Petersburg, June 18—65
Pauley, W B* — Petersburg, June 18—64
Reamer, J* — Gravelly Run, March 31—65
Roberts, H* — Gettysburg, July 4—63
Ross, Wm+ — Fredericksburg, April 30—63
Runnion, J R — Gainesville, Aug 28—62
Salm, William S, f — Burlington
Schlosser, J F — Andersonville, March 10—64
Sprague, Henry S— — Washington, July 7—64
Staley, Albert — Bell Plaine, March 31—63
Stevens, L W* — Gainesville, Aug 28—62
Weber, Mathias — July 28—64
Weymouth, Orin — July 26—61
Whitney, W W — Frederick, Dec 18—64
Wilkinson, Jos* — Gravelly Run, March 31—65
Young, H F, f — Patch Grove

G

Capt Fred L Warner — Randolph
Capt Walter B Peck
Lt Sam'l J Miller
Lt Burns Newman* — Jericho Ford Va, May 25—64
Lt Onesime Rondeau

H

Capt Mark Finnicum — Mich
Capt Robt C Palmer — LaClede, Minn
Capt Robt Monteith — Madison
Capt Chas Falks
Lt C M H Meyer
Lt Thos C Alexander
Lt Tanner Thomas* — Petersburg June 18—64
Lt Jos Heathcock — Linden
Adams, Thos f — May 25—64
Allen, Robert — Indianapolis, Dec 16—64
Andrews, J* — Laurel Hill, May 12—64
Bishop, J* — Petersburg, June 18—64
Burton, B* — South Mountain, Sept 14—62
Carver, E— — Alexandria, June 18—64
Church, Alfred — Andersonville, July 12—64
Costly, William — Arapahoe, Neb
Cutts, R J* — Laurel Hill, May 9—64
Dillon, George — Washington, Jan 23—63
Eastman, Lucius— — Gainesville, Aug 26—64
Fulks, James+ — April 23—74
Gillotte, Jerome — Andersonville, July 16—64
Hichcock, S* — Laurel Hill, May 16—64
Hitchcock, Eli — Potomac Creek, May 16—62

THE WISCONSIN CENTRAL RAILROAD

THE SHORT LINE
BETWEEN
CHICAGO AND MILWAUKEE

Green Bay
  Fort Howard,
    Menasha,
      Neenah,
        Appleton,
          Stevens Point,
            Ashland,

AND THE
Great Lumber Regions of the Northwest.

The Branch to APPLETON has just been completed, and THROUGH COACHES are now run between that point, [via Milwaukee and Chicago.]

To the Sportsman, Tourist and Pleasure Seeker, this route, better known as

"THE LAKE SUPERIOR LINE,"

offers peculiar advantages. The numerous streams and lakes along the line are teeming with fish and the forests abound with game.

The hotels offer every comfort; that at Ashland, "The Chequamegyon, owned by the company," has recently been enlarged and refitted and is kept in regal style.

WISCONSIN SOLDIERS AND SAILORS REUNION ROSTER.

Johnson, J+ April 3–65
Kellebre, T* Laurel Hill, May 9–64
Kemey, H* Laurel Hill, May 12–64
Marchall, Lucius Westfield
Mathews, J R Fredericksburg, Oct 18–62
Monroe, Wm C Bull Run 2nd Aug 30–62
Miller, Wm City Point
Mitchner, F Gettysburg, July 1–62
Monteith, S* Antietam, Sept 17–62
Monroe, W G Bull Run, Aug 30–62
Moore, Martin Washington, Sept 14–62
Murden, Frederick Laurel Hill, Aug 12–61
Page, G* Petersburg, June 18–64
Picket, J J Jan 26–65
Pryor, Joseph Fredericksburg, July 4–62
Rogers, Adam C Hopkins, Mo
Salesbury, James K Grand Meadow, Minn
Schnee, L* Gainesville Aug 28–62
Scott, Wm G M+ Bull Run, Aug 30–62
Smith, G A* Wilderness, May 6–64
Steers, J M Gettysburg, July 1–63
Turnbee, John Washington, Oct 23–63
Wanyack, John* Hatcher's Run, Feb 6–65
West, Sumter Washington, April 30–61
Wright, John* Wilderness, May 5–64

I

Capt Theo S West
Capt Augustus S. Rogers
Capt Geo H Walther Milwaukee
Capt Jos N P Bird Wautoma
Capt Edson Terrill, Terrill's Corners
Lt Chris F Lefior
Lt Chr'o M Putnam Tioga, Pa
Lt Edwin Terrill
Lt W W Walrath* Wilderness, May 5–64
Lt S E Waterman Plainfield
Bird, J L P Wautoma
Borden, J E, m Colby
Buck, S F Mazomanie
Casey, J E* Wilderness, May 5–64
Corry, L* Wilderness, May 5–64
Crandall, Thos B+ Wilderness, May 5–64
Currin, Horace, corp Annapolis, Aug 15–63
Curry, T* Gainesville, Aug 28–64
Dawes, N D* Laurel Hill, May 9–64
Dawes, F L, corp* Petersburg, July 30–64
Deagan, James Richmond prison, March 21–61
Fleming R* Wilderness, May 5–64
Gouchen, Adolph Casco
Hay, William Fond du Lac
Hayes, William, corp Berlin, March 12–64
Kill, J O Plainfield
Hued, Jos* Gainesville, Aug 28–62
Hursh, C W Richmond prison, March 24–64
Johnson, H B Plainfield
Kelly, Patrick, f Philadelphia, Pa
Miller, William, l Big Suamico
Moore, George* Wilderness, May 5–64
Perkins, Hugh Neillsville
Phillips, J J Plainfield
Powers, Jno* Oct 15–61
Ramsey, Edwin* Laurel Hill, May 12–64
Riley, J D* Petersburg, June 18–64
Rozell, James Plainfield
Seely, William Plainfield
Seely Fillmore Culpepper, April 21–64
Shrolls, Lewis* Laurel Hill, May 12–64
Terrill, C, corp* Gravelly Run, March 31–65
Thorngate, David Alexandria, July 19–62
Toplin, Oscar M Alexandria, April 5–62
Updike, B, corp* Wilderness, May 5–64
Waterman, W W* Wilderness, May 5–64
Waterman, A W Plainfield
White, John* Laurel Hill, May 12–64
Whitcomb, F E, corp* Hatchers Run, Feb 6–65
Williams, Wm D* Gainesville, Aug 28–63
Williams, J W Richmond prison, Feb 11–64

K

Capt A Gordon Jr* FitzHugh Cross., April 29–63
Capt Geo S Hoyt Regular Army
Capt Jno M Hoyt Beloit
Lt Frank W Oakley Madison
Lt A D Rood Milwaukee
Lt Washington Stever
Lt David Shirrell, Buffalo, N Y
Lt Sam'l Morse Washington D C
Lt Jno W Bruce Clinton
Lt David McDermit
Allen, N S Gravelly Run, March 31–65
Baldwin, O M+ Washington, July 7–64
Barnum, W H+ Gettysburg, July 16–63
Beard, J H* Gainesville, Aug 28–62
Bloom, Wm* Gravelly Run, March 31–65
Brace, John W, m Clinton
Cochran, M L* Gainesville, Aug 28–62
Crawford, James M Washington, Nov 7–62
Davis, J B May 21–62
Dunham, Joseph* Arkansas
Eddy, Nahum Washington, Sept 7–62
Fuller, Levi Brillion
Garner, F J* South Mountain, Sept 14–62
Galner, C K+ Sept 11–62
Keibl, Charles Tomah
Kinman, Phineas+ Gettysburg, July 26–63
Kirsher, Wond Francis Creek
Knapp, J H* Gettysburg, July 1–63
Livingstone, John A Libby Prison, Sept 12–64
Lombard, A A+ Philadelphia, Aug 14–64
Lord, David Arlington, Feb 23–62
McFarland, L J Washington, Dec 19–62
McKinney W D Gettysburg, July 18–63
Miller, C* Gettysburg, July 1–63
Moriarty, Daniel+ Aug 21–61
Noack, David+ Washington, July 6–64
Norton, C B Gainesville, Aug 28–62
Norton, N H* Fredericksburg, Dec 13–63
O'Ryan, M H, pr Milwaukee
Ovlatt, E H+ Sept 20–62
Ramsay, Edwin* Laurel Hill, May 12–64
Rubin, F L+ Fairfax Va
Sebring, Nathan+ Washington, Sept 19–62
Sedgewick, G H+ Washington, Sept 19–62
Shoemaker, Geo W Washington, Oct 21–62
Simons, Geo* Gettysburg, July 1–63
Stever, W R R c Gettysburg, July 1–63
Thompson, Louis Philadelphia, Pa, Aug 14–61
Tibbetts, Robert Libby Prison, Feb 17–64
Tichauser, Andrew May 27–65
Tower, J F* Gettysburg, July 1–63
Van Orman, Theo Richmond, Va, Aug 19–62
Watson, G F Washington, July 24–64
Wilson, Wm S* South Mountain, Sept 14–62
Youngs, Joseph C Tunnel City

UNASSIGNED.

Babcock, C W Packwaukee
Brainard, L B, pb Waupaca
Bruce, J W Clinton
Clough, W Oshkosh
Colby, H F Scotia, Neb
Despiere, F J Wausau
Despina, J F, pb Wausau
Hinman, W H Hutchinson, Kan
Kline, Carl Belmont, N J
Milone, H A Westfield
Orvis, Orson Westfield
Peters, S W Montello
Prentice, H B Dakota
Roberts, J M, 1st lt Plainfield, Minn
Robinson, W W consul at Jamatava, Madagascar
Sontag, John Wautoma
Thompkins, Harrison Westfield
Wyman, Cyrus* Wilderness, May 5–64

EIGHTH INFANTRY.

(Three years. Organized September 13th 1861. Original strength,973 ;gained by recruits, etc. 670. Total,1,843. Death loss, 255—killed in action, 38, died of wounds,14, of disease,201, of accidents 8, Other losses, 424, missing 3, desertion, 60, transfer 41, discharged, 320. Strength at muster out, Sept 5th, 1865, 964. Campaigns in Mo., Tenn., Miss., Ala., La., Ark.,

REGIMENTAL ROSTER.

Col Robt C Murphy
Col Geo W Robbins
Col Jno W Jefferson Memphis, Tenn
Col Wm B Brittan Janesville
Maj Wm C Young
Maj Duncan A Kennedy Island Lake, Minn
Adj Ezra L Sprague S. H Lake City
Adj Wm H Sargent* Nashville, Dec 16–64
Adj Henry L Bull Cincinnati, O
Q M H O Clark
Q M Pascal&M Hovey
Q M Hugh McAulay
Surg Jos E Murta La Grange, Tenn
A Serg Wm Robbins Madison
A Surg L G Armstrong
A Surg H M Murdock New Richmond
A Surg Reuben Wilson Mantorville, Minn
A Surg Jas A Jackson Madison
Chap Wm McKinley Winona, Minn
Chap Jno Hobart Chicago, Ill

A

Capt J B Redfield Omaha, Neb
Capt Chas Christenson St Louis, Mo
Capt Benj D Gauo
Lt Melvin Patchin
Lt A L Hungerford
Lt Jason S Jones Rural, Jan 15–65
Lt Thos Farll
Lt R J Baker
Lt Jno Jardine Waupaca
Allen, Augustave Cal.o, Jan 29–64
Allen, George Waupaca
Bacon, L O New Madrid, May 11–65
Barker, W I* Hurricane Cr. Aug 12–64
Bougle, C A Fort Gaines, May 1–65
Beers, Alonzo J Cairo, Feb 28–62
Bennett, Jos Farmington, July 2–63
Brown, Henry E Memphis, Aug 18–64
Bockman, Moses Freemont
Bumpus, Orson* Vicksburg, May 22–63
Burbank, A J La Grange, Jan 23–63
Christian, Charles St Louis, Mo
Clemons, Hiram R Memphis, Aug 31–64
Collur, Charles Madison, July 16–64
Copperlie, A Jefferson Barracks, Nov 20–64
Davis, Alfred Memphis, Sept —64
Dake, R P Colby
Downer, David, cl Arkansaw
Droin, A L Wisconsin, Oct 22–62
Friday, G C Memphis, July 31–64
Gardiner, Schyler, l Madison
Hartwigson, Thos Farmington, May 26–62
Horsefield, Wm H New Orleans, April 24–65
J .udine, John, ml Waupaca
Jones, Jason I Wisconsin, Jan 15–65
Letmolieu, Lavol Farmington, May 29–62
Minton, Henry Selma, Aug 15–65
Mitchel, James Plainsfield
Owen, William Turtle, Ia
Perkins, Hugh C Sherwood
Phillips, Bradford Corinth, Oct 19–82
Pope, Henry Farmington, July 16–62
Redfield, T B Omaha
Redfield, Charles E Omaha, Neb
Redfield, J B Omaha, Neb

WHOLESALE
GROCER AND JOBBER OF TEAS,
234 EAST WATER STREET,
Letter Box 106. MILWAUKEE, WIS.

USE JACOB MORAWETZ'
CHAMPION SOAP,
THE PUREST SOAP IN USE.

USE JACOB MORAWETZ'
BEST SALERATUS.
IT IS THE BEST.

USE JACOB MORAWETZ'
Magic Baking Powder.
NONE BETTER MADE.

USE JACOB MORAWETZ'
GOLD LEAF, NEW TAX,
REVOLUTION, SURE SHOT
Chewing Tobaccos, the Best in Use.

USE JACOB MORAWETZ'
Centennial Smoking Tobacco,
THE FINEST MADE.

USE JACOB MORAWETZ'
BEST SYRUP,
Will be found the best and purest Goods in Market.

USE JACOB MORAWETZ'
TONY CIGARS,
THE FINEST SMOKE OUT.

USE JACOB MORAWETZ'
Minnehaha Chewing Tobacco
Seldom Equaled. Never Excelled.

LARGEST AND FINEST STOCK OF
Coffees, Teas, Spices and Fancy Groceries
IN TOWN.

WISCONSIN SOLDIERS AND SAILORS REUNION ROSTER. 41

Reed, George L. — Memphis, Feb 16–63
Seabright, Archable — Arkansaw
Spaulding, J — Farmington, June 11–62
Speers, Jacob — Memphis, Oct 7–64
Thorstenson, Thos* — Corinth, Oct 3–62
Wood, Austin — Sulphur Springs, Jan 3–62

B

Capt D R Conger, — Grand Haven, Mich
Capt Albert E Smith — Denver, Col
Capt Chas P Stewart — Pine River
Lt Jno A Smith — Greenbush
Lt Levi H Mead — Waverly, Iowa
Lt C D Stevens — Pilot Knob, Mo, Nov 6–61
Lt Emerson Webster — Greenbush
Lt Ephraim Miller — St Gilman, Iowa
Arnold, James W — Vicksburg, July 22–63
Baldwin, T R — Greenbush
Benjamin, Herbert — Vicksburg, July 15–63
Butler, C M — April 6–65
Butler, Jno — Ironton, Mo, Dec 3–61
Chase, O F, county clerk — Oshkosh
Conger, D B — Grand Haven, Mich
Conger, David, Clerk — Milwaukee
Corbett, Charles — Greenbush
Crandall, A B — St Louis, May 23–63
Dobbins, Solomon — Dec 25–61
Dobbins, Wm H — Memphis, Sept 3–64
Durkee, W F, corp — Germantown, Feb 26–63
Elmore, Sylvanus — Bear Creek, Aug 8–63
Esterling, John* — Lake Chicot, June 6–64
Goodnough, J N — Neosho
Gorman, C D, collector — Olivet
Hodges, T — La Grange, Tenn, Nov 16–61
Hogue, J M, corp+ — Corinth, Oct 5–62
Hull, David* — Nashville, Dec 16–64
Jepson, W M — Waverly, Iowa
Johnson, Geo A — Louisville, Sept 2–65
Mead, Levi, — Waverly, Iowa
Mellon, A A — Waldo
Mellon, Bert — Plymouth
Miller, J W, corp* — Lake Chicot, June 10–64
Monk, Silas — Mound City, May 14–62
Odell, Thos M — March 15–62
Pettet, Joe A, m — Campbellsport
Pettit, Jasper A, m — Campbellsport
Pettit, Joseph A — Unity
Pettit, J A — Neillsville
Rogers, Timothy G — Clear Lake
Root, Augustus — Jan 29–63
Shaw, Joseph — March 12–62
Smith, John A — Greenbush
Stagg, William* — Corinth, Oct 3–63
Stevens, S E — Elkhart Lake
Tometty, John, f — Plymouth
Underhill, A, corp — Bear Creek, Aug 5–63
Underhill, — — Plymouth
Weissert, A G, a — Milwaukee

C

Capt J E Perkins* — Farmington, Miss, May 9–62
Capt Victor Wolf — Eau Claire
Capt Thos G Butler — Eau Claire
Lt Burnett Demarest — Eau Claire
Lt Frank McGuire —
Lt Seth Pierce —
Lt Jno Woodworth — Elgin, Ill
Lt Christian Scholkopf —
Atwater, James — May 28–63
Benian, Alphonzo — Ironton, Mo, Dec 4–61
Brown, George A — March 22–62
Butler, Charles — Eau Claire
Butler, T G — Eau Claire
Canfield, Daniel — June 9–62
Coon, Thomas B — Kilbourne City
Curtis, C H* — Corinth, Oct 3–62
Delapp, Wm — Bear Creek, Miss, Aug 38–63
Demorest, J D — Eau Claire

Farley, David — Youngs Point, La, July 11–63
Fuller, Solomon — Pepin, Kan
Hausseome, N+ — Corinth, Oct 11–02
Hooper, James W — Memphis, Nov 19–63
Metlord, W F, bk — Chicago, Ill
Miles, J T* — Corinth, Oct 4–64
Miller, C W — Eau Claire
Muth, C* — Corinth, Oct 3–63
Parker, F N — Young's Point, La, July 8–63
Quick, Walter — Iron Ridge
Reigar, A — Young's Point, La, June 29–63
Riley, G W, corp, f — Eau Claire
Roberts, Edwin — March 9–62
Russell, Charles — St Louis, Dec 16–63
Sargent, C A — Germantown, Tenn, March 4–63
Stewksbury, U A* — Waterford, Miss, Aug 7–64
Swinson, D — Bear Creek, Miss, Sept 3–63
Wilcox, Jr, Ephraim — Trempeleau
Wolf, Victor — Eau Claire
Woodsworth, John — Elgin, Ill
Worth, Max — Bear Creek, Miss, Aug 7–63

D

Capt Wm J Dawes — Fox Lake
Capt Benj S Williams — Yankton, D T
Lt Sam'l C McDowell — Fox Lake
Lt Corydon Houghton — Upper Grove, Iowa
Lt Geo S Newbury — Stillwater, Iowa
Adams, A — Jeffersonville, Ind, Jan 20–65
Adams, Ernest — May 30–62
Avey, James D — Yankton, D T
Armitage, Ambrose, f — Neosho
Armitage, Sykes P — Logansville
Armitage, Thomas — Seymore
Badgers, Wm W — Vicksburg, Nov 9–63
Burt, Calvin W — Cairo, April 6–63
Chamberlain, H C* — Nashville, Dec 16–64
Cryderman, Jos — Cairo, Feb 19–62
Day, William — Dakota
Fletcher, Elisha — Ironton, Mo, Dec 19–62
Green, James B — March 10–62
Halsey, Silas — Farmington, July 10–62
Hanshaw, Joshua — St Louis, May 4–62
Haskell, Seth+ — Vicksburg, May 23–63
Hasse, August — Clinton
Hill, Augustus — May 31–62
Jones, Charles — Nashville, Jan 4–65
Learned, Osgood — May 28–62
Maxwell, John — Memphis, Sept 9–63
McDowell, Samuel — Fox Lake
Noteman, I C, f — Fall City
Osborn, W H — New Orleans, Mar 6–65
Owen, Wm, b — Fertile, Iowa
Palmer, C W — Lyons
Parker, Adelbert, f — Parker, Fraction, Iowa
Plank, G I. — Uniontown, Ala, Aug 22–65
Richards, Geo W — Spanish Fort, March 30–66
Robinson, Avery — Memphis, July 1–64
Robinson, H — Bear Creek, Miss, Aug 9–63
Welch, Patrick, f — Grafton, O
Whirry, Geo W — St Louis, May 1–62
Williams, B S, m — Yankton, D T
Wilson, J* — Corinth, Oct 3–63
Wines, Charles — April 14–62
Wisner, Frank O, p — Kilbourne City
Woodward, Gen T, serg — Memphis, Jan 31–64

E

Capt Wm C Young —
Capt Jacob Leffler — Garnett, Kan
Lt James L Gilbert —
Lt M H Helms —
Lt Chas A Smith — Loyal
Lt Geo Murphy —
Ames, Laban A, f — Fall City
Anderson, James — Milwaukee
Blackledge, Clarkson* — Corinth, Oct 3–62
Currie, Phil — Milwaukee

Day, Ellis — Farmington, Miss, July 5–63
Douglas, W H — Eau Claire
Denson, O F — Spencer
Gifford, Myron S — Vicksburg, Dec 11–63
Gilbert, F J, serg* — Spanish Fort, March 27–65
Hastings, Seth — Cairo, March 9–62
Hogan, Michael — Madison
Host, A J — Lyons
Myhart, Wm H — Farmington, June 18–62
McPherson, W B — Spencer
Miles, C C — Spencer
Palmer, E N — Fitchburg
Payne, Chauncey+ — Louisville, Dec 29–64
Pinceek, John, serg* — Corinth, Miss, Oct 3–62
Sayles, H, f — Middleton
Sayles, Mordecai — St Louis, Aug 24–62
Silver, Monroe |- — Corinth, Oct 27–62
Spears, Jos F — Duval's Bluff, Ark, Sept 12–64
Story, Wm+) — Keokuk, Ia, Nov 12–62
Watson P — Tiptonville, Tenn, April 5–62

F

Capt Jas H Green — Massillon, Ohio
Capt Jno W Greenman — Salt Lake City
Lt Zenas Beach — Eastman
Lt J T McClure+ — Bayou Glaize, May 18–64
Lt Geo M Robbins —
Lt Bowdish Bailey — Centre, Kansas
Lt Jas Berry —
Lt W D Chapman* — Vicksburg, May 22–63
Lt F X Waggoner —
Baily, Boltish — Centre, Kansas
Belrechard, Charles — July 8–62
Bush, B — Wauzeka
Clark, John — Madison, Nov 25–61
Cummings, S M — Jackson, Oct 2–62
Dawson, Stephen — Sulphur Springs, Jan 7–62
Drum, G M — Point Pleasant, April 10–62
Ellis, Edward, serg — Chicago, April 19–64
Fallender, Wm — Vicksburg, July 22–63
Forshay, W K, serg — Andersonville, Aug 8–64
Fox, Samuel — Memphis, June 11–64
Green, Charles H — Seneca, April 10–65
Greenman, Jno W — Salt Lake City, Utah
Griffin, Adna H — Farmington, June 12–62
Groves, Benj F — Farmington, June 12–62
Groves, Eli M — Bear Creek, Aug 7–63
Groves, W C — New Madrid, April 11–62
Hamilton, James — New Madrid, April 18–62
Henderson, Alex — St Louis, July 15–62
Henry, Joseph* — Nashville, Dec 15–64
Irwin, C I — Sulphur Springs, Jan 18–62
Joseph, John P — Farmington, July 9–62
Lang, Fred — Batavia, Oct 1–63
Maloy, A — Batavia, Aug 1–62
Marston, C A* — Baynotilit, June 5–61
McColoch, S, serg — Young's Point, July 9–63
McQueen, E — St Louis
Munn, Charles, — Hamburg, May 27–62
Nyland, Martin — April 10–62
Ostrander, Edwin — May 10–62
Parker, C W, c — Little Grant
Petrey, John* — Corinth, Oct 8–62
Shaw, A P — Ellistown, July 17–61
Shell, John W, corp* — Corinth, Oct 3–62
Shumway, F — Farmington, June 12–62
Smith, John L, corp — Black River, July 24–63
Thomas, John — Ironton, Nov 17–61
Wilder T A — Memphis, Jan 6–64
Wolford, Wm — Ironton, Nov 25–61

G

Capt W R Britton — Janesville
Capt Chas P King — Glenwood, Ia
Capt M H Doty — Stoughton
Lt Wm H Sargent — Nashville, Dec 14–64
Lt Chas H Lee — Janesville
Lt R D Beamish* — Farmington, Miss, May 9–62

TWENTY-TWO YEARS   *SATISFACTION.*

B. WILD & CO.,
Excelsior Steam Bakery

MAKES AND SELLS

CHOICE CRACKERS, CONFECTIONERY

CIGARS,

CREAMS & CRACKNELS

CALL AND SEE OR CORRESPOND.

ORDERS BY MAIL RECEIVE PROMPT ATTENTION.

32 EAST FIRST ST. AND 509 MAIN STREET,

FOND DU LAC, WISCONSIN.

WISCONSIN SOLDIERS AND SAILORS REUNION ROSTER.

Lt J B Huggins
Bear, J L — Janesville
Bryan, Chas K — Cairo, Jan 29—62
Carney, John — Pilot Knob, Mo, Oct—64
Conroy, Wm — Memphis, Jan 5—64
Dave, John — Black River, Oct 7—63
Doty, J M H — Stoughton
Fisher, Fred — Bear Creek, Miss, Aug 7—63
Franklin, Julius — Sandwich, Ill
Graves, E L, dentist — Chicago, Ill
Holloway, Andrew — Cairo, Jan 24—62
Johnson, Amego — Farmington, May 31—63
Kelly, Thomas T, corp* Spanish Ft, March 29—65
King, C K — Glenwood, Ia
Lee C H — Janesville
Paul, Alexander, corp Germantown, Mar 10—63
Peters, Robert — Janesville
Runge, Fritz — Memphis, July 16—64
Slosson, D H — Queen City, Mo
Smith, J B Sulphur Springs, Mo, Jan 16—62
Thompson, S — Mound City, Aug —63
Tramble, Julius — Sand ish, Ill
Tramble, Jonas — Janesville
White, J A, corp* Farmington, Miss, May 9—62
Whittier, H H, sergt — Vicksburg, July 15—63
Williamson, M, sergt — Iuka, Aug—62
Wilson, Martin T — March 4—62
Wood, Charles — Janesville

H

Capt Stephen Estee+ — Sept 26—63
Capt P B Willoughby
Lt La Fayette Mansell
Lt S K Ellsworth — Madison
Lt Patrick McFarland
Barnes, W E — Milliken's Bend July 9—63
Bennett, J L — Cairo, March 5—62
Brownell, Russell — Sparta
Chamberlain, C J — Farmington, July 3—63
Corbin, Jacob — Blancherdsville
Corbin, C C, corp — Cairo, Jan 18—62
Corse, Charles — Vicksburg, Nov 14—3
Dean, James T — Memphis, Aug 28—63
Devine, Albert — Sulphur Springs, Dec 30—61
Devine, Clark — St Louis, May 17—62
Ellsworth, Sherman — Madison
Ellsworth, D R, Serg't — Ironton, Nov 25—61
Entrikin, E P — Clarion, Iowa
Flinn, James — Memphis, Aug 5—64
Gould P H — Corinth, Oct 26—62
Green, Thomas — Dayton
Ham, Jerry — Dayton
Heal, Walter — Dayton
Heal, Alfred — Dayton
Illingsworth, John P* — Corinth, Oct 5—62
Illingsworth, W P — Corinth, Oct 3—63
Illingsworth, D T — Fredericktown, Oct 23—61
Judd, C A — La Grange, Jan 2—63
Long, Jacob — Memphis, Aug 22 64
Loomis, O R — Sulphur Springs, Jan 21—63
Lovejoy, Wm — Nashville, Dec 18—61
Lucy, Daniel — Mazomanie
Mansur, Michael, corp* Nashville, Nov 16—64
Milen, Robert — Feb 8—63
Oleson, Nels — Keokuk, Aug 4—63
Oliver, W J — Jeff Barracks, Oct 10—63
Palmer, Edwin — Wisconsin, Dec 6—64
Perry, Geo — Eastport, Jan 28—63
Powell, H J — Jeff Barracks, Aug 12—63
Severson, Ole — Tupelo, July 15—61
Shaw, Frank — Columbia, Dec 26—63
Thornton, J W — Germantown, March 15—63
Thornton, Wm M — Jeffersonville, March — 63
Van Norman, Geo P — Milwaukee
Waldo, J — Corinth, Oct 6—62

I

Capt Milo M Baker

Capt A D Hickok
Capt D A Kennedy — Walla Walla, W T
Capt S J Sargent
Lt H S Phillips — Mindoro
Lt H M Lathrop
Lt Daniel A Kennedy, — New Richmond
Allen, Alvin K — Young's Point, La, June 17—63
Allen, John — Farmington, Miss, June 30—63
Andre, Wm* — Nashville, Dec 16—64
Aney, J N, f — Norwalk
Anderson, S — LaCrosse
Ashbury, Samuel — Bear Creek, Sept 16—63
Bassett, Martin — Iuka, Sept 13—62
Beardsley, Benj P, corp — Iuka, Sept 4—62
Cinnamon, W H — Bear Creek, Sept 2—63
Clover, F D — LaCrosse
Conboy, Isaac — Young's Point, La, June 20—63
Croton, E — La Crosse
Dormer, Rev David — Arkansas
Downer, Anthony — Memphis, Sept 11—63
Dyers, Benjamin — New Orleans, April 14—65
Edgar, James C — New Orleans, Sept 12—64
Erickson, Paul* — Corinth, May 28—62
Frederickson, Ole — Stevenstown
Garmon, Geo L, sergt — Cairo, Feb 16—62
Gladsen, Andrew, serg — Memphis, Nov 22—64
Goodnough, Jerome B — Wilton
Hewitt, W E — LaCrosse
Hewitt, J C — La Crosse
Holbrook, Lera* — Corinth, Oct 3—63
Jansen, Christian — Keokuk, Jan 1—65
Johnson A J — Nashua, La
Johnson, Zebulon — June 6—62
Kennedy, D A — New Richmond
Kindall, James — July 30—63
Lucia, H V — LaCrosse
Larson, Ole* — Corinth, Oct 3—62
Maller, James+ — Louisville, Jan 2—62
McNiel, Hiram A — Vicksburg, July 18—63
Nash, Abraham F — March 31—64
Nash, Jonathan W — Farmington, June 9—62
Newton, John — Vicksburg, June 4—64
Northrop, Manley — Vicksburg, June 4—64
Oleson, Ever* — Racine
Oleson, John — Farmington, June 30—63
Phillips, H S — LaCrosse
Plunges, P — LaCrosse
Pinkerton, John — LaCrosse
Pinkerton, Joseph — LaCrosse
Queggle, N M — Farmington, Feb 16—63
Rogers, Robert — Selma, July 6—65
Sanders, Nelson N — April 12—62
Schenck, M — LaCrosse
Thorp, John W* — Corinth, Oct 3—62
Trainer, Barney — Corinth, Oct 3—62
Toed, D — Baton Rouge, April 25—65
Van Loon A — La Crosse
Vernon, E J — Bolivar, Tenn, Jan 1—63
Warden, Henry D — Tomah

K

Capt Wm P Lyon — Madison
Capt Theo A Fellows, — Leadville, Col
Lt A E Smith, — Denver, Col
Lt Chas Palmetier — Geneva
Lt Jas A Cary, — Racine
Baker, Horace — Clinton
Benedict, Henry — Kenosha
Billings, Levi — Green Bay
Bull, Henry L — Cincinnati, Ohio
Burke, Myron — Vicksburg, June 1—64
Cadwell, W S — Prairie du Chien, Dec 10—64
Cary, J A — Racine
Collins, Henry — Young's Point, July 15—63
Coon, C W — Badger Mills
Coon, Ralph M* — Corinth, May 28—62
Dickenson, Charles D — Elgin, Ill

Evens, A E — Corinth, Sept 17—62
Fulkner, John — Genoa
Farley, Edwin — Paducah, Ky
Felch, I N — Racine
Fellows, T F. — Leadville, Col
Fernald, Clarence — Vermillion, D T
Fernald, Fred — Genoa
Finch A B — Racine
Forsley, Wm R — Andersonville, Aug 8—64
Hall, Timothy — Elkhorn
Harrison, Wm H — Genoa
Hatch, U W, m — Whitewater
Henderson, Alfred H — Barrington, Ill
Hernes, Joseph — Neosho, Mo
Hickox, Wm E — Central Lake, Mich
Holmes, Geo S — Lyons
Humphrey J B, corp — May 22—64
Hutchinson J J — Racine
Jones, George A — Racine, Aug 28—64
Janson, Neil* — Nashville, Dec 16—64
Lathrop, Edwin — Vermillion, Dakota
Lathrop, Lucas B — Racine
Losser, Geo — Jeffersonville, Ind, Dec 30—64
Loss, Leonard — Racine
Lowe, John H — April 26—62
Lyons, Wm P — Madison
Maive, Albert E — May 17—62
Manning, C B Sulphur Springs, Mo, Dec 23—61
Mason, Edward + — Nashville, Dec 24—61
Massey, John — Oct 2—62
McPherson, W D — Racine
McPherson, Robt — Thompsonville
Meredith, John — Racine
Miller, Amos J — Geneva
Mott, Josiah — May 12—62
Murphy, Daniel — Memphis, April 13—63
Nobes, Robert — Western Union Junction
Noyes, Charles A — Geneva
Olp, Henry — Springfield
Off, Henry — Mt Carroll, Ill
Paddock, Herbert — April 27—62
Palmetier Chas — Geneva
Peterson, L — Jeffersonville, Ind, Dec 28—84
Phillips, John — Racine
Pritchard, Hugh — Racine
Putney, Jos — Spring Valley, Minn
Rowell, Frank — Geneva
Shaughnessy, Pat — Racine
Smith, A E — Denver, Col
Smith, W G, f — Racine
Thompson, Jos — New Orleans, April 15—65
Torre, Thomas — Owatonna, Minn
Van Ness, Edwin — Nov 22—62
Wadworth, Geo — Racine
Walker, Mosley — Racine
Walker, Wm H — Chicago, Ill
Weed, J L — Three Oaks, Mich
Weeks, Levi — Springfield
Wentworth, Sid T — Racine
White, Andrew — St Louis, Nov 27—64
Wynnann, G — Germantown, Tenn, Feb 13—63

UNASSIGNED.

"Old Abe"
Barrows, Jacob J — Keokuk, Aug 14—62
Britton, Wm B, — Janesville
Co e, Jesse, cl — Branden
Cronan, Edward, agt — La Crosse
Doty, M H — Janesville
Ebert, M J — Chilton
Graves E C — Chicago, Ill
Hobart, John, — Chicago, Ill
Jefferson, J W — Memphis
Lawler, Iowa
McGinnis, J n — Jackson, Sept 19—62
Murdock, H M, ph — New Richmond
Marta, J E — La Grange, Tenn
Oleson, Christian — Cairo, June 17—64
Overen, Simon — St Louis, June 30—62
Quick, W — Campbellsport

A. K. HAMILTON,

MANUFACTURER AND DEALER IN

LUMBER, LATH, SHINGLES,

SASH, DOORS, BLINDS, MOULDINGS, TIMBER, ETC.

DEALERS AND CONSUMERS

ON ANY OF THE

PRINCIPAL RAILWAY LINES OF WISCONSIN,

Will find it to their advantage to secure

Quotations on Large or Small Lots,

AS THE FACILITIES OF THE

MILL AND YARD,

IN SUPPLYING ALL DEMANDS, ARE

UNSURPASSED IN THE STATE.

Mill on Luco Harbor,   *Office and Yard 355 Main Street,*

FOND DU LAC, WISCONSIN.

WISCONSIN SOLDIERS AND SAILORS REUNION ROSTER. 45

Sprague, E T	Salt Lake City, Utah	
Thompson, A, com sgt	Grand Gulf, May 10—63	
Upson, Hezekiah	Memphis, Feb 25—65	
Volts, Henry L, f	Parkers Prairie, Minn	
Viney, Charles		Janesville
Weissert, A G		Milwaukee
Zuñil, Franklin	Ironton, Dec 9—61	
Hutchins, Charles R, musician	Macon City, Mo	
Hutchins, S	do	Herman, Dakota
Hutchins, James D	do	Sioux Falls, Dakota
Hutchins, C M	do	Fond du Lac
Douty, C M		St Croix

NINTH INFANTRY.

(Three years. Organized October 26th, 1861. Original strength 870; gain by recruits etc, 852 Total, 1,422. Death loss, 175—Killed in action, 51 died of wounds, 24, of disease, 96, of accidents 4, Other losses, 223, missing, 0, desertions, 25, transfers 7, discharged 131, by muster out, Nov. 1st 1864—730. Strength at muster out, January 30, 1866, 265. Campaigns in Mo., Kans., and Ark.,

REGIMENTAL ROSTER.

Col Fred'k Salomon U S Surveyor, Salt Lake
Col Chas E Salomon St Louis, Mo
Col Arthur Jacobi Green Bay
Lt Col Henry Orff Milwaukee
Maj H Schlueter Chicago, R :: Mail Agt
Maj Geo Eckhart Milwaukee
Adj B Hartfield
Surj H Naumann Milwaukee
Surg Louis Lochr Germany
A Surg Chas Ottilie La Crosse
A Surg H E Haase Milwaukee
A Surg Theo Haering Bloomington, Ill
Chap Jno Hently Foreston, Ill

VETERAN VOLUNTEERS.

Lt Col Arthur Jacobi Green Bay
Surg Chas Ottilie La Crosse

A

Capt Fred'k Aude Milwaukee
Capt H Storks Milwaukee
Lt Chas Franz Kenosha
Lt Edw Ruegger Monroe
Lt Adam Knies Sheboygan
Lt August Krueger Sheboygan
Lt Edw Bischoff Milwaukee
Lt Louis Schnetze Monroe
Lt M A Miller Chicago, Ill

REORGANIZED.

Capt Geo Eckhart Milwaukee
Lt Geo Graemer
Lt Wm Doerner
Lt Jno Ludwig Winona, Minn
Kaiser, C, corp* Jenkins Ferry, April 30—64
Blum, Wm Little Rock, Sep 4—65
Brewery, Louis Kiel
Doll, Jacob Camden, July 2—65
Fuchs, Sebastian Plymouth
Guthul, Louis Kiel
Groth, Carl Howards Grove
Gochring, Frederick Silver Creek
Henkel, H Fort Scott, Sept 21—62
Keiser, Frederick Silver Creek
Klohe, Joseph+ Camden, April 17—64
Kirst, Wm. nuf Franklin
Luethge, Robert Fort Scott, Sept 12—64
Lindon, Wm Franklin
Miller, A C, m Milwaukee
Petri, Jacob Little Rock, March 30—64
Riesen, Wm Little Rock, Oct 13—65
Rossman, John, b Berlin
Rossman, F Pulaski, Feb 1—64
Spann, C Little Rock, Jan 26—64

B

Schmidt, Charles
Schilling, J+ Jenkins Ferry, April 30—64
Scheller, August A Plymouth
Voigt, Albert Meeme
Welchlein, John M Milwaukee

Capt Fred's E cker Manitowoc
Capt A F Dunkee Manitowoc
Lt Jacob Bohn Sauk City
Lt Wm Schulten New Cassel
Lt Gisbert Guetzloe Manitowoc
Lt Hugo Koch Manitowoc
Lt B Hartfield
Lt H J Lorenizen New Holstein
Lt Gustavus Clement Chicago, Ill

REORGANIZED.

Lt P Weibel Winona, Minn
Lt Jacob Barge near Winona, Minn
Bollar, K, sgt Little Rock, April 3—65
Miller, J F, sergt Little Rock, Oct 23—65
Berger, Wm, corp* Spoonville, Ark. April 2—65
Beadler, C Little Rock. Nov 23—64
Brunner, Frank J New Glarus
Burkhard, Anton* Jenkins Ferry, April 30—64
Damsner, Joseph Little Rock, March 15—65
Escher, C Springfield, Mo, Feb 18—63
Egger, M St Louis, Nov 11—64
Howard, John Leavenworth, Feb 15—62
Ibsch, Carl Little Rock, Oct 9—65
Kirsh, L LaCrosse
Krundick, John+ Princeton, May 31—64
Lutien, John Kewaunee
Mueller, John Little Rock, Sept 28—62
Myers, G LaCrosse
Ottilie, C LaCrosse
Ristowsky, F* Spoonville, April 2—64
Stelmes, Jones Camden, Sept 6—64
Stole, H Two Rivers
Sigglekow, Wm Little Rock, Oct 18—65
Spoher, Frederick Shiorton
Tagmire, Frederick Omro
Wakerhansen, W* Spoonville, April 2—64
Wirth, J Theresa
Wolkampt, J Little Rock, Sept 21—64

C

Capt Geo Eckhart Milwaukee
Lt Jno Arentson
Lt Chas Franz Kenosha
Lt Jno Van Ells Milwaukee
Lt Jacob Blecher Milwaukee
Lt A E Chladek Chicago
Lt Aloys Klaus Green Bay
Lt Wm Doerner

REORGANIZED.

Capt Chas Franz Kenosha
Capt H J Lorentzen New Holstein
Lt Daniel Goetz
Lt Julius Ulrich Oshkosh
Lt Edw Haug
Ljervers, Theo, sgt Milwaukee, Aug 17—63
Binhanmer, F St Louis, Sept 11—63
Bedorko D Little Rock, Jan 21—64
Bicknell, Lansing, f Waukau
Buellersbach, J Princeton, Sept 5—64
Doebald, Franz Fort Scott
Fleishman, John Little Rock, June 26—61
Frederick, F Little Rock, July 18—64
Gnssisberg, C Fayetteville, Dec 17—62
Groth, W F Madison, Nov 16—64
Hicks, J Camp Ford, Texas
Kuhn, Geo Fort Scott, Dec 15—61
Kasdorff, August Little Rock, Sept 22—64
Miller, Gottfried Little Rock, Sept 22—64
Reitumann, M Little Rock, June 1—64
Ramel, Caspar Little Rock, Sept 13—64
Schneider, Peter Little Rock, July 12—64

D

Leopold s
Schmidt, Ernst Feb 22—61
Tschabold, D Princeton, March 30—61
Follmer, C Little Rock, Oct 26. 64
Wellems, J Little Rock, Oct 25—64
Zeiger, Lorenz Little Rock, Sept 27—64

Lt Jno Gerber, Madison
Lt Jacob Bohn, Sauk City
Lt Herbert Pfotenhauer, Green Bay
Lt Wm Schulten, New Cassel
Lt Hugo Koch,
Lt Louis Schnetze Monroe
Lt Richard Kempter, Alma
Lt Gerhardt Tucker, Chicago, Ill
Lt Anton Fischer, Baraboo
Capt Wm Schulten, formerly of New Cassel
Lt Albert Schroeder
Lt Herman Schurman
Dobczensky, J, sgt* Newtonia, Mo, Sept 30—62
Buol, Casper, corp* Sarcoxie, Mo, Sept 30—62
Cruse, Arthur, corp* Newtonia, Mo, Sept 30—62
Crasher, Max, corp* Newtonia, Mo, Sept 30—62
Preissner, N Princeton, Ark
Anderson, B* Jenkins Ferry, April 30—64
Accola, Geo Little Rock, Oct 24—64
Buol, John Little Rock, Aug 3—64
Bettler, Peter Camden, June 2—64
Baphardt, Gottfried Owatonna, Minn
Baumgarth, Gustav* Newtonia, Sept 30—62
Baumgarth, C* Newtonia, Sept 30—62
Bieneck, E* Jenkins Ferry, April 30—64
Bildenstein, F Jenkins Ferry, March 14—64
Dischler, E Little Rock, Feb 20—65
Durisch, J P Mazomanie
Ferber, Geo Prairie du Sac
Fiedemann, Christian Kiel
Fischer, Anton Baraboo
Grossmeyer, J Madison, Aug 5—64
Haidle, C Little Rock, Sept 13—65
Jesse, Franz Fayetteville, Jan 17—63
Jung, Gottfried Port Washington
Kingsley, Lovein Little Rock, July 27—64
Kuom, C, f Sauk City
Kuntz, Jacob Ft Scott, Oct 23—62
Kohn, Julius Springfield, March 10—62
Keller, Ferdinand
Keuhne, C Spoonville, June 1—64
Lohr, John* Jenkins Ferry, April 30—64
Langemak, Wm Brillion
Lambrecht, C* Newtonia, Sept 30—62
Lehmann, Carl Sauk City
Pingo, M Little Rock, March 30—64
Roediger H* Newtonia, Sept 30—62
Haedel, Julius Leavenworth, July 18—62
Rufe, John Little Rock, Feb 6—65
Santer, A* Jenkins Ferry, April 30—64
Schlenke, F* Jenkins Ferry, April 30—64
Sigglekow, Jno J McFarland
Suffer, V Waseca
Thadinn, Fred Ravine
Young, Christopher Bell Centre

E

Capt Henry Orff Milwaukee
Capt Herman Schlueter Chicago
Capt Edw Ruegger Monroe
Lt Conrad Branke
Lt Wm Markhoff Milwaukee
Lt Louis Schnetze Monroe
Lt Erhard Weber
Lt Edw Klabbatt Milwaukee
Lt Albert Schroeder
Lt A F Chladek Chicago
Lt M Wehr
Farpagel, Julius, f Burlington
Flimmer, J, orderly sgt Burlington
Hart, J, sgt Burlington

A. T. PERKINS.   J. L. CLEMENT.

SPRING WAGON CO.,
OF FOND DU LAC.

EVERY CLASS OF

SPRING WAGON

PERFECT AND COMPLETE, MANUFACTURED

FOR THE TRADE,
AND ON

SPECIAL ORDERS.

All work done under the personal supervision of the Prop's.

Universal Satisfaction Always Given.

ADDRESS

PERKINS & CLEMENT,
FOND DU LAC,   -   -   WIS.

Host, August, sgt	Springfield, Mo, April 21—63	Erion, Mathes	Willon
Krakrassky, Chas, sgt	Burlington	Fenstermacher, H+	Princeton, May 28 -64
Stroh, John, corp	Carrollton, Ark, April 5—63	Geiger, Simon*	Sarcoxie, Sept 30— 62
Wilhaft, Fred, corp	Burlington	Gamke, Carl	Leavenworth, March 1— 62
Kargls, Fred, corp,f	Burlington	Heym, Adam	Fort Scott, Oct 16—62
Richard, J, corp	St Louis, Sept 27- 63	Kundert, Randolph	Camden, July 8 64
Miller, Jos, corp*	Newtonia, Sept 30—62	Kuns, Jno, f	Danville, Mina
Gruener, H, corp+	Princeton, Ark, May 18—64	Manteufel, A*	Sarcoxie, Sept 30 — 62
Breitung, Henry*	Jenkins Ferry, April 30—64	Muller, Jno F W, f	Milwaukee
Becker, F	Fort Scott, Sept 1—62	Maas, C*	Sarcoxie, Sept 30—62
Dobratz, C	St Louis, Feb 14—63	Schmid, U+	Jenkins Ferry, May 1—64
Drais, Joseph*	Jenkins Ferry, April 30—64	Tekintrups, fl	Fort Scott, March 30— 62
Friese, Carl F*	Newtonia, Sept 30—62	Vetter H*	Spoonville, April 2—64
Farpagel, Fred, f	Burlington	Vetter, C*	Spoonville, April 2 -64
Glaeser, P	Sager's Spring, Ark, Nov 14—64	Wagner H*	Newtonia, Sept 30—62
Onett, John, f	Burlington	Waguer, M*	Spoonville, April 2—64
Herman, John	Babcock, Nov 24—62	Wernderlich, Franz	Jefferson
Hefenbeneck, Louis, f	Burlington	Winterhalter, Leo	Little Rock, Aug 9—64
Heblein, G	Little Rock, July 19—61	Zech, Jacob	Little Rock, Oct 5—64
Kitzman, G*	Sarcoxie, Sept 30—62		
Laske, Wm, saloon-keeper	Burlington	**H**	
Martin, Geo*	Jenkins Ferry, April 30—64		
Medge, August	Little Rock, Feb 17—63	Capt Jno Gerber	Madison
Pudelwitz F+	Ft Scott, Kan, Nov 7—62	Lt Fred Molzner	
Huntzler, Fred, mo	Burlington	Lt Hugo Koch	
Seiger, Mathias	Helena, Ark, Feb 16—64	Lt Philip Kruer	Milwaukee
Shuman, Geo, saloon-keeper	Burlington	Lt H J Lorentzen	New Holstein
Schultz, C, f	Burlington	Lt Edw Bischoff	Milwaukee
Schritter, Jno, dealer in live stock	Burlington	Lt Gustavus Clemen	Chicago, Ill
Scheller, Fred, f	Burlington	Lt Edw Klaubatz	
Scheller, Julius, f	Burlington	Lt Julius Ulrich	Oshkosh
Withman, Chris	Quincy	Burkel, Nicholas*	Jenkins Ferry, April 29 63
		Aul, Wallis	Milwaukee, Jan 30—61
F		Duerkopp, Henry+	Princeton, Ark
		Feddler, V	St Louis, Aug 5—63
Capt Martin Voegele	St Louis	Fingerlee, J A+	Princeton
Capt Carl H Schmidt	Manitowoc	Feldtrappe, R*	Newtonia, Sept 30 —62
Lt Philip Kruer	Milwaukee	Haredh, Ernst+	Princeton
Lt Jno Gerber	Madison	Horn, Charles*	Sarcoxie, Mo, Sept 30—62
Lt A Schroeder		Helmeritz, D*	Newtonia, Sept 30—62
Lt Jacob Blecher	Milwaukee	Haak, V	Newtonia, Sept 30—62
Lt Geo Graemer		Jacob, Marx, gardener	Milwaukee
Lt Peter Weibel	Winona, Minn	Kirchner, Wm	Leavenworth, May 7—62
Huber, H, corp	Fort Scott, Aug 14—62	Krause, F	Little Rock, Nov 17—63
Chaney, Petrol	Little Rock, Sept 22—64	Kuhn, Jacob+	Princeton, Ark
Moy, Frederick	Little Rock, Sept 22—64	Lothwesen, H*	Sarcoxie, Sept 30—62
Melbor, Frederick	Grand Rapids	Mohwinkel, Ernest	Madison
Neuhoff, Wm*	Pine Bluff, April 23—64	Rahn, Wm, f	Green Bay
Pyloud, J M	Milwaukee	Schulz, August*	Jenkins Ferry, April 30—64
Reuser, Jacob*	Camden Road, April 17—64	Schulz, F	Little Rock, July 19—64
Selwedel, L	Baxter Springs, June 17—62	Zylensky, M*	Sarcoxie, Sept 30—62
Scheck, G	Little Rock, Oct 8—64		
Welgen, H	Fort Scott, Aug 20—62	**I**	
		Capt Peter Spehn	Port Washington
G		Capt Philip Kruer	Milwaukee
		Lt Wm Markhoff	Milwaukee
Capt J C G Hartlest		Lt Edw Ruegger	Monroe
Capt Fred Molzner		Lt Huge Koch	
Capt Chas Franz	Kenosha	Lt Wm Schulten	New Cassel
Lt Wm Melsner		Lt Herbert Pfotenhauer	Green Bay
Lt Otto Leissring	Washington, D C	Lt Jacob Blecher	Milwaukee
Lt Dominie Klutch		Englebrecht, C, corp+	Princeton, Ark
Lt Bernhard Hartfeil		Adelfang, Peter	Little Rock
Lt Albert Schroeder	Manitowoc	Borgena, H	Leavenworth, Jan 22—63
Lt Chas H Schmidt		Baden, Wm +	Little Rock, May 29—64
Lt Hans J Lorentzen	New Holstein	Burgaud, Wm+	Princeton, Ark
Lt Geo Reinhard		Fisher, Geo*	Camden Road, Ap.ll 16—64
Stevens, C A,	Shakopee, Minn	Kempter, R R	Alma
Lobenstein, Carl, sergt*	Newtonia, Sept 30—62	Kruer, Philip	Milwaukee
Ashling, H, corp*	Newtonia, Sept 30—62	Moh, O	Nellisville
Brehlen, H, corp*	Spoonville, April 2—64	Oswald, Peter	Paw Paw, Kan, Aug 6—62
Stumpf, John, corp*	Spoonville, April 2—64	Schmidt, J	Sarcoxie, Mo, Oct 8—62
Zubldorf, A, corp*	Spoonville, April 2—64	Stelner, Joseph	Milwaukee
Handikon, C+	Elkins Ferry, April 30—64	Seifert, Wm*	Jenkins Ferry, April 30—64
Brosserald, S	Little Rock, Jan 8—61	Schmidt, John M	Milwaukee
Becker, M+	Princeton, June 7—64	Tobias, M	Grand River, Ark, July 19—62
Berger, Christian, mo	Waterford	Weber, Anton+	Princeton, Ark
Commenstroht, U	Clarendon, Oct 8—63		
Diedrich, Felix	Waterford		
Enders, Stephen*	Spoonville, April 2—64		

Willhoft, F		Racine
	K	
Capt Jno Gerber		Madison
Lt Edw Ruegger		Monroe
Lt Jacob Blecher		Milwaukee
Lt Otto Leissring		Washington, D C
Lt Bernhard Hartfeil		
Lt H Pfotenhauer		Green Bay
Lt Reinhard Schliehting		Chilton
Birnschein, Trangott		Little Rock, Sept 10—61
Daumau, D+		Princeton, May 27—61
Feige, B		Fayetteville, Dec 27—62
Gloor, Jacob		Little Rock, Sept 21—64
Linnert, Simon		Little Rock, Sept 16—64
Legler, Geo+		Princeton, June 3—64
Retelsen, Nicholas		New Holstein
Stubb, H		Fort Scott, Sept 2—62
Stussey, Fredoline		Sussex
Stussey, Peter		Sussex
UNASSIGNED.		
Bantly, John		Foreston, Ill
Bauberger, Mathews		Plymouth
Jenger, H*		Newtonia, Sept 30—62
Jendick, C		Little Road, July 8—64
Heuschmidt, Anton		Little Rock, Nov 3—61
Rausner, Henry		Little Rock, Sept 10—61
Meier, Conrad		Fort Scott, Feb 7—61
Moeller, Carl		Fort Scott, Aug 17—62
Rupstral, Adolph		Little Rock, J 30—61
Sturm, Chas, musician		Milwaukee

TENTH INFANTRY.

(Three years. Organized October 14th, 1861. Original strength,916, gained by recruits, etc. 118, Total, 1,034. Death loss, 213—killed in action, 66 died of wounds, 27, of disease, 120. Other losses, 366—missing 0, desertion, 21, transfer 23, discharged,316. Strength at muster out, about Oct. 28th, 1861, 445. Campaigns in Ala., Ky., Tenn., and Georgia.

REGIMENTAL ROSTER.

Col J G McMynn	Racine
Col D McKercher	
Lt Col J J Guppey	Portage
Lt Col Jno J Ely+	Richmond, Va, Oct +—63
Lt Col J W Roby	Horicon
Ma) H O Johnson*	Chaplin Hills, Oct 8—62
Maj Robt Harkness	Salt Lake City
Adj Wm A Collins	Milwaukee
Adj Jas M Goff	Walnut, Kan
Q M Benton McConnell	Horseellsville, N Y
Q M Elliott H Benton	
Surg Solon Marks	Milwaukee
A Surg Robt Mitchell	Moundville
A Surg Robt G James	Appleton
A Surg Jas T Reeve	
A Surg Wm A Gordon	
Chaplain Jas S Coffin	Troy
Chaplain Harmon H Benson,	Richland Centre

A

Capt H O Johnson*	Perryville, Ky
Capt Robt Harkness	Salt Lake City
Lt J Harrington	Jefferson, Ia
Lt C A Burdick+	Charleston Prison
Lt W B Ellenwood	
Hooper, J H sgt	Dowling Green, March 5—62
Bell, Wm J, corp*	Chaplin Hills, Oct 8—62
Manning, F E, corp*	Chaplin Hills, Oct 8—62
Wilson, J S, corp	Nashville, Sept 8—64
Tucker, C P, corp	Andersonville, July 16—64

D. C. & J. H. LANG,

MANUFACTURERS, DEALERS AND SHIPPERS

TRUNKS,

WHOLESALE AND RETAIL.

TWENTY YEARS CONTINUOUS EXPERIENCE,

Warrants us in the belief that the wants of the American traveling community can be

Amply Supplied on Satisfactory Terms, on Short Notice.

ORDERS FOR THE TRADE SOLICITED

FIRST STREET NEAR MAIN

FOND DU LAC,   WISCONSIN.

WISCONSIN SOLDIERS AND SAILORS REUNION ROSTER.

Adams, M — Cincinnati, May 26—64
Adams, A — Andersonville, Oct 12—64
Adams, Daniel* — Chaplin Hills, Oct 8—62
Brown, S — Murfreesboro, April 5—62
Bradt, W T — Elkhorn
Bovee, A D — July 11—64
Conklin, J H* — Chaplin Hills, Oct 8—62
Coburn, W — Andersonville, Oct 15—64
Carver, E W, hardware — Beloit
Consant, Shumway — Clinton Junction
Dugan, Walter P, a — Milwaukee
Devor, James — Delavan
Frost, F M — Bowling Green, April 5—62
Fountain, N H — Andersonville, June 28—64
Griffin, DeWitt — Murfreesboro, Jan 15—63
Helm, Peter* — Chaplin Hills, Oct 8—62
Hunt, G W+ — Chaplin Hills, Oct 9—62
Harkness, Robt — Salt Lake City, Utah
Hay, Washington — Odebolt, Ia
Hoyt, Wm R — Chippewa
Jones, T — Elizabethtown, Feb 2—62
Kimberly, Benj, f — Hudson
Long, J H* — Stone River, Tenn, Dec 31—62
Lee, L — Paint Rock, Ala, May 19—62
Lansing, G — Andersonville, Aug 24—64
McCan, J — Bowling Green, April 2—62
Matteson, W* — Chickamauga, Sept 13—63
Montague, H — Troy
Molville, Martin, Postmaster — Delavan
Moffatt, W B — Delavan
Nicole, Theo — Elkhorn
Osborn, W — Andersonville
Pillery, Richard — Elkhorn
Pellintz, R — Spring Prairie
Roctor, H A — Murfreesboro, April 18—63
Ronevlek, H — Nashville, Aug 10—63
Snell, Chas* — Chaplin Hills, Oct 8—62
Sach, J — Delavan, Feb 22—62
Spurr, Geo — Milwaukee
Sheldon, Josiah, f — Durand
Turner, W — Sugar Creek, July 26—62
Weed, E J, f — Mapleton

B

Capt J W Roby — Horicon
Lt S W Herrick
Lt Dan'l A Steele
Minnick, S E+ — Perryville, Oct 15—62
French, M A, corp — Nashville, Feb 2—63
Bennett, J I+ — Perryville, Oct 25—62
Brezee, G H — Bowling Green, March 14—62
Cowles, D — Andersonville, July 6—64
Cowles, R R+ — Murfreesboro, Jan 11—63
Cotton, N, Jr+ — Huntsville, June 28—62
Debar, B+ — Perryville, Nov 10—62
Griest O E — Wellington, Ill
Haswell, John C* — Altoona, June 2—64
Herrick, G — Murfreesboro, April 10—62
Hewick, N — Andersonville, Aug 2—64
Hoffman, H J — Nellisville
Jiggen, J+ — Chattanooga, Sept 20—63
Martin, A S — Nashville, Nov 10—62
Miles, William — Oak Centre
Nimes, S E — Chaplin Hills, Oct 8—62
Ryle, Chester, H, f — Smith Hill, Minn
Sedgwick, D P — Bacon Creek, Dec 30—64
Soule, J B — June 30—61
Smith, W H — Andersonville, July 31—64
Sutton, J — Andersonville, July 19—64
Turner, F — Nashville, Dec 19—62
Tyler, J H — June 30 - 64

C

Capt A W Richardson — Milwaukee
Capt Jas C Adams
Lt C A Burdick+ — Charleston prison
Lt S L Hart — Menasha
Lt S M Noxon

Wright, H C, sergt — Chickamauga, Sept 19—63
Jewett, J H, sergt* — Chickamauga, Sept 19—63
Nugent, W H, sergt — Nashville, March 28—62
Ellenwood, S, sergt — Andersonville, Sept 12—62
Elliot, P B, corp* — Chaplin Hills, Oct 8—62
Ferris, J, corp — Perryville, Nov 4—62
Hill, E, corp — Bowling Green, Feb 28—63
Robinson, W M, corp — Andersonville, Aug 18—64
Bemis, H — Andersonville, Aug 9—64
Ballow, A — Nellisville
Coose, P — Murfreesboro, April 7—62
Cotten, Wm — Winneconne
Dowde, P — Chattanooga, March 2—61
Douglass, P A* — Resaca, Ga, May 16—64
Frank, D P — Huntsville, May 10—62
Freeman, P M — Andersonville, Oct 16—64
France, E — Webster City, Iowa
France, Augusta, f — Wallerman, Iowa
Goodwin, H M* — Chickamauga, Sept 19—63
Locker, T S* — Chaplin Hills, Oct 8—62
Linch, Joseph — Menasha
McKillop, John* —
Pratt, E H — Sherwood
Phelps, Allen J — Kokoskee
Robinson, A* — Chaplin Hills, Oct 8—62
Rifenburg, John K, f — Oakfield
Witcher, W H* — Chaplin Hills, Oct 8—62
Wheeler, Wm E — Menasha
Wheeler, C — Dobbston
Zuchlke, Julus — Hortonville

D

Capt Jas L Coffin — Troy
Capt O B Twogood
Capt Wm A Collins — Milwaukee
Lt Thos L Kennan — Portage
Lt Chas H Ford — New York City
Lt A A Patchin — Wyocena
Lt G W Marsh — Portage
Lt E P Stowell — Iron Ridge
Forsythe, C, sgt* — Chaplin Hills, Oct 8—62
Dixon, J, sgt* — Chaplin Hills, Oct 8—62
Crouch, S, corp — Nashville, March 7—62
Sweet, E, corp — Larkinsville, Aug 3—62
Buell, A A+ — Perryville, Oct 10—62
Beach, F — Murfreesboro, April 18—62
Bannister, J D — Shepherdsville, Nov 25—61
Clark, J* — Stone River, Dec 31—62
Conlon, M* — Stone River, Dec 31—62
Clark, Geo C — Delavan
Ellis, C — Nashville, April 17—62
Farnham, A* — Chaplin Hills, Oct 8—62
Hunt, E — Chickamauga, Sept 20—63
Hand, G — Andersonville, Jan—65
Jones, A+ — Perryville, Nov 1—62
Luthar, J C* — Chickamauga, Sept 20—63
Morey, H* — Chickamauga, Sept 20—63
Moore, G W — Eliz. Jonhtown, March 21—62
Merril, C C — Nashville, March—63
Morties, N — Andersonville, Aug 7—64
Mason, Hiram, f — Grand Marsh
Parmenter, M M — Louisville, June 1—62
Parmenter, A H* — Chaplin Hills, Oct 8—62
Rosebaugh, A* — Chickamauga, Sept 20—63
Rouse, G W* — Chickamauga, Sept 20—63
Smoke, O M — Louisville, Feb 8—62
Wiltse, A — Louisville, Feb 14—62

E

Capt J H Ely
Capt Geo M West* — Chickamauga, Ga, Sept 20—63
Lt Robt Kohlsdorf — West Bend
Lt Norman Thatcher — Menasha
Lt Robt Rennie — Chickamauga, Sept 14—63
Lt Robt Roach
Trimble, A, sergt* — Chaplin Hills, Oct 8—62
Frater, Joun, sergt* — Chickamauga, Sept 19—63
Easton, W H, Jr, sergt* — Chickamauga, Sept 19—63

Dunning, S, corp — Chickamauga, Sept 19—63
Austin, J M — Louisville, Feb 27—62
Burke, J — Andersonville, Aug 30—64
Bodwell, W+ — Chattanooga, Oct 20—63
Cayer, J* — Chaplin Hills, Oct 8—62
Crowfoot, J — Nashville, Jan 11—63
Clark, W E — Andersonville, Nov 1—64
Chapman, W W — Hartford
Daniels, Elon M* — Chickamauga, Sept 19—63
Ewey, G E — Nashville, Nov 4—62
Fuller, Levi — Brillion
Howell, A, Jr — Elizabethtown, Feb 2—62
King, A F — Nellisville
Lansing, John — Rock Elm Centre
McComb, R A — Hartford
O'Brien, Patrick — Berlin
Phillips, J C* — Chaplin Hills, Oct 8—62
Purdy, M — Andersonville, July 30—61
Rogers, G W — Louisville, Feb 12—62
Straw S — Nashville, Nov 19—62
Voltz, F — Andersonville, Oct 25—64
Warner, C H — Murfreesboro, April 15—62
Wycott, J T — Murfreesboro, June 24—62
White, H+ — Larkinsville, Ala, Aug 22—62

F

Lt Robt Harkness — Salt Lake City
Lt Robt Rennie* — Chickamauga, Ga, Sept 19—63
Lt A A V Knapp — Platteville
Northy, R H, sgt* — Chickamauga, Sept 19—63
Rohan, H A, sgt — Andersonville, June 18—64
Painter, H, sgt — Andersonville Sept 16—64
Glover, P L* — Chaplin Hills, Oct 8—62
Dodge, A M, corp* — Chaplin Hills, Oct 8—62
Brown, C — New Albany, Nov 1—62
Castley, Jos D — Arapahoe, Neb
Crodey, Reuben, J — Beetown
Bayers, W A* — Chaplin Hills, Oct 8—62
Gleason, M L* — Chaplin Hills, Oct 8—62
Goram, A — Louisville, Jan 5—63
Hilgers, T — Larkinsville, Ala, Aug 30—61
Jarrett, Robert* — Chaplin Hills, Oct 8—62
Jewell, T M* — Chickamauga, Sept 19—63
Lumpkins, David C* — Chaplin Hills, Oct 8—62
Leroy, W W — Huntsville, April 28—62
McDonald, E — Jan 16—64
Owen, M C* — Chaplin Hills, Oct 8—62
Parker, W H — Bacon Creek, Ky, Jan 5—62
Shoemaker, F M* — Chaplin Hills, Oct 8—62
Tyler, E D — Andersonville, Oct 22—64

G

Capt Wm Moore+ — Bellfonte, July 4—62
Capt A W Richardson — Milwaukee
Capt N Thatcher — Menasha
Lt L B Brewer — Black River Falls
Lt B F Johnson
Lt J C Hassey
Lt S A Wilcox — Lynn
Lt Thos C O'Neal
Schemerhorn, J G corp* — Chaplin Hills, Oct 8—62
Fish, Wm M, corp* — Chaplin Hills, Oct 8—62
O'Flaherty, E, corp+ — Murfreesboro, April 1—63
Marsh, W — Elizabethtown, March 21—62
Anderson, L* — Perryville, Nov 3—62
Anger, A J+ — Nashville, March 19—62
Amidon, G W — Elizabeth, March 15—62
Babcock, T J — Tomah
Babcock, John H — Nashville, Jan 9—63
Christopherson, H — Perryville, Oct 16—62
Campbell, W R+ — Tyrone Station, May 9—61
Carmichell, H — Oct 16—62
Court, John H+ — Bowling Green, March 8—62
Douglas, E — Nellisville
Dimmick, L L — Nellisville
Enhelder, J — Alma Centre
Eldredge, Timothy P — City Point
Felt, C J

G. W. LUSK,

PINE LUMBER, TIMBER

SASH, DOORS, BLINDS,

AND USUAL MILL MERCHANDISE.

Straight Business Orders given best rates and satisfactory terms.

OFFICE AND MILL NEAR C. & N W. R. R. DEPOT.

FOND DU LAC, - - WISCONSIN.

WISCONSIN SOLDIERS AND SAILORS REUNION ROSTER.

Franz, Charles — Neillsville
Grober, Nicholas — Black River Falls
Hulet, H+ — Perryville, Oct 13—62
Hoffman, H J — Neillsville
Hoffman, E L — Neillsville
Jacobson, N — Rochester, April 6—62
Lane, Job — Murfreesboro, April 9—63
Marsh, J B — Murfreesboro, April 5—62
Nelson, L* — Chaplin Hills, Oct 8—62
Oleson, Ole* — Chaplin Hills, Oct 8—62
O'Connor, Thomas — Cataract
Root, M J — Louisville, Feb 12—62
Reitz, Fred — Neillsville,
Reitz, Charles — Neillsville
Stafford, S S — Nashville, Sept 16—62
Sargent, P H
Schrigley, H — Andersonville, April 8—64
Tiffany, John* — Chaplin Hills, Oct 8—62

H

Capt Duncan McKercher
Capt Robt H Spencer
Lt O E Foote
Lt Ingersoll George
Lt Aug H Makimson — Poney Hollow, N Y
Curey, P, 1st sgt. — New Albany, March 17—63
Mitchell, W P, sgt* — Chaplin Hills, Oct 8—62
Anthony, Premo H — Warrens Mills
Baker, G M — Wartrace, Tenn, Sept 14—62
Curry, G W — Cowan, Tenn. Aug 3—63
Chester, O B, m — New Lisbon
Inzotello, J — Bacon Creek, Ky, Feb 23—62
Gorman, A H — Bowling Green, March 31—62
Hloman, H M* — Chaplin Hills, Oct 8—62
Hogue, C P — Neillsville
Haywood, Joel* — Chaplin Hills, Oct 8—62
Johnson, Ole — Bowling Green, Ky April, 1—62
Landon, J — Prisoner of War
McClure, Samuel — Tomah
O'Larry, D* — Chaplin Hills, Oct 8—62
Spooner, C W — Annapolis, Md
Schoettbaus, A — Nolin, Ky, Dec 26—61
Spaulding, Henry — Tomah
Svilender, Fred, l — Beloit
Thompson, Dwight — Tomah
Weaver, H — Andersonville, July 4—64

I

Capt C I Overton
Capt S W Herrick
Lt H H Fairchild
Lt John Small
Lt Wm O Butler
Schaffer, G A, sgt — Nashville, Oct 7—63
Bonner, H F, corp — Andersonville, June 25—64
Bryant, Andrew — Nashua, Iowa
Bryant, L A, me — Nashua, Iowa
Barnes, A M, ms — Beaver Dam
Durlan, T P* — Mud Creek, Aug 23—62
Grash, F — Andersonville, June 24—62
Holmes, J B+ — Aug 23—63
Kielder, F — Cincinnati, Oct 15—62
McClure, A — Andersonville, Aug 20—64
Moore, O W — Louisville, Dec 31—62
Miller, Johann Jacob — Dorinda Centre, Ill
Nichols, W — Andersonville, Aug 18—64
Piddington, E+ — Stevenson, Oct 27—63
Purdee, J — Andersonville, Sept 1—64
Reed, Henry* — Mud Creek, Aug 23—62
Ray, A — Nashville, Aug 6—62
Reed, Morgan — Burton
Ray, James J, l — Platteville
Shaffer, F L — Nashville, April 15—63
Taenzier, Jacob B — Annaton
Winebrenner, D — Bowling Green, Sept 29—62
Waster, J T — Nashville, Feb 19—63
Woods, J — Nashville, Feb 19—63
White, B+ — Mud Creek, 23—62

K

Capt Edwin Hillyer — Waupun
Capt Robert Kohlsdorf — West Bend
Capt Chas H Ford — New York
Lt L B Hills — Madison
Lt L Dwight Hinkley — Waupun
Lt Jno K Relfenburgh — Oakfield
Comstock, C M, sergt — Murfreesboro, Nov 4—62
Gilbert, O, sergt — Andersonville, Jun 1—64
Watson, C A, corp* — Chaplin Hills, Oct 8—62
Gibbs, A, corp* — Chaplin Hills, Oct 8—62
Babbitt, J G, corp — Elizabethtown, March 21—62
Haugle, D F, corp — Andersonville, June 27—64
Alkins, E+ — Chattanooga, Sept 30—63
Butler, M — Andersonville, Nov—64
Bishop, George — Platteville
Cole, John B, l — Oxford
Calhoun, John, l — Byron
Dean, M — Louisville, Jan 15—63
Dilley, E A — Elizabethtown, Ky, May 6—62
Hudson, C — Beacon Creek, Ky, Jan 27—62
Howard, F W — Andersonville, Aug 11—64
Hinkley, Dwight — Waupun
Hills, L B — Madison
Hatch, Delos, l — Oakfield
Ingram, J — Andersonville, Sept 15—64
Judson, J — Louisville, Dec—62
Lathrop, W W — Neillsville
Little, A A — Sept—61
Miles, H+ — Huntsville, Ala, July 22—63
Marks, Solon — Milwaukee
Mitchell, R — Moundville
Rambough, J — Macon, Ga
Reynolds, P S — Andersonville, July 20—64
Rockwell, Horace — Neillsville
Shaw, A+ — Cincinnati, Nov 25—62
UNASSIGNED.
Padgham, E A, sgt — Waupun
Benson, H H — Richland Centre
Beebe, P S — Cylon
Cornell, P — Whitewater
Deverel, W J, l — Delavan
Eaton, J S J — Paris, France
Hancock, G W* — Mud Creek, Aug 22—62
Hudson, J T — Huntsville, May 29—62
Nelson, Christ — Blair
Oleson, Christ — Blair
Turcott, A+ — Chattanooga, Oct 12—63
Walton, Mark — Star Prairie
Wood, Abraham+ — Perryville, Oct 15—62

ELEVENTH INFANTRY.

Three years. Organized Oct. 18th, 1861. Original strength, 1020; gain by recruits, etc., 936. Total, 1956. Death loss, 348—killed in action, 36, died of wounds, 45, of disease, 262, of accidents, 5. Other losses, 353—missing, 6, desertions, 25, transfers, 9, discharges, 319. Strength at muster out Sept 4,1865, 1204. Campaign in Missouri, Arkansas, Mississippi, Louisiana, Texas, Tenn., Ala.

REGIMENTAL ROSTER.

Col Chas L Harris
Lt Col Chas A Wood
Lt Col L H Whittelsey
Maj Arthur Platt
'Maj Jesse S Miller — Kekoskee
Maj Otis Remick
Adj Daniel Lincoln
Adj Ira W Hunt — Hudson
Adj Jno F Spencer
Q M G M Subin
Q M Chas d Mayers — Madison
Surg H P Strong — Beloit
Surg Edw Everitt

A Surg Jos Green — Whitewater
A Surg Jno T Wilson
A Surg E A Woodward
A Surg C C Barnes
A Surg S L Bennett
A Surg H W Boyce
Chap Jas B Brittan
Chap Geo W Wells — Whitewater

A

Capt D E Hough+ — Black River, June 3—63
Capt Wm L Freeman+ — Mazomanie, June 7—64
Capt L T Park
Lt P W Jones
Lt A R MacDonald
Lt J T Hillyer
Lt T H Brainard — Mazomanie
Ellis, T G, corp, l — Sparta
Wheeler, J F, corp* — Ft Blakely, April 9—65
Turk, W, corp+ — Ft Blakely, April 10—65
Haney, M, corp+ — Ft Blakely
Enderly, H K, corp Reeves' Station, April 10—62
Arland, C H — Cross Plains
Austin, John — Arena
Bowman, R* — Black River, Miss, May 17—63
Boardman, J — St Louis, Oct 12—62
Borroughs, John — Sparta
Brainard, T H — Mazomanie
Blynn, E — Mazomanie
Beardsley, J E — Black Earth
Beardsley, James, me — Helena, Oct 3—62
Begrdsley, James, me — Black Earth
Barrett, J — Brashear City, Sept 18—64
Banhart, R — Brashear City, Sept 8—64
Campbell, S W — Camp Randall, Oct 5—61
Coola, Milo — Van Buren, Mo, Jan 11—63
Cammach. John — Mazomanie
Campbell, A B — Prairie du Chien
Charlesworth, W — Mobile, Aug 8—65
Carpenter, B — Alexandria, La, May 17—64
Knright, B+ — Vicksburg, June 11—63
Ellis Geo H — Mazomanie
Ellis, tieo H — Mineral Point
Ford, W A — Alton, Mo, Jan 13—63
Ford. John A — Mazomanie
Fox, John — Hospital Boat, Oct 9—62
Fox, Abijah — Madison, May 1—64
Fagler, L H — Ironton, Jan 26—63
Hazeltine, J E+ — Vicksburg, May 28—63
Haller, J — Oldtown, Ark, Aug 18—64
Hademan, J — Aug 25—63
Ison, R — New Orleans, Oct 1—64
Johnson, H W — Ironton, Jan 21—63
Kerr, David — Ironton, Oct 17—62
Kullsch, Peter, me — Berlin
Logerson, J — Jefferson Barracks, Aug 2—64
Learnard, H W — Montgomery, June 8—45
Learnard, H R, me
Lungun, A — Madison, Oct 5—62
Millard, E A — Brashear City, Aug 1—64
Merrill, J C — Mazomanie
Perry, T A — Ironton, Oct 24—62
Prichard, Jas — Mazomanie
Prich. D J — New Orleans, Dec 17—64
Queenan, Michae — Nashua, Ia
Reeves, C+ — Memphis, Dec 8—3
Roundy, Heltis — St Louis, Oct 15—63
Rice, T — Ironton, Jan 6—63
Robinson, C H — New Orleans, Oct 8—63
Roberts, L A — Black Earth
Roberts, L H — Brashear City, Aug 31—64
Ray, Jas — Madison, April 30—64
Stevens, F T — Port Gibson, Miss, May 1—63
Swift, Myron — Batesville, Sept 1—64
Slater, John — Brashear City, Sept 10—64
Shrew, T H — New Orleans, May 1—64
Skinner, W — Moscow, Dec 16—64
Tinker, A A — Black Earth

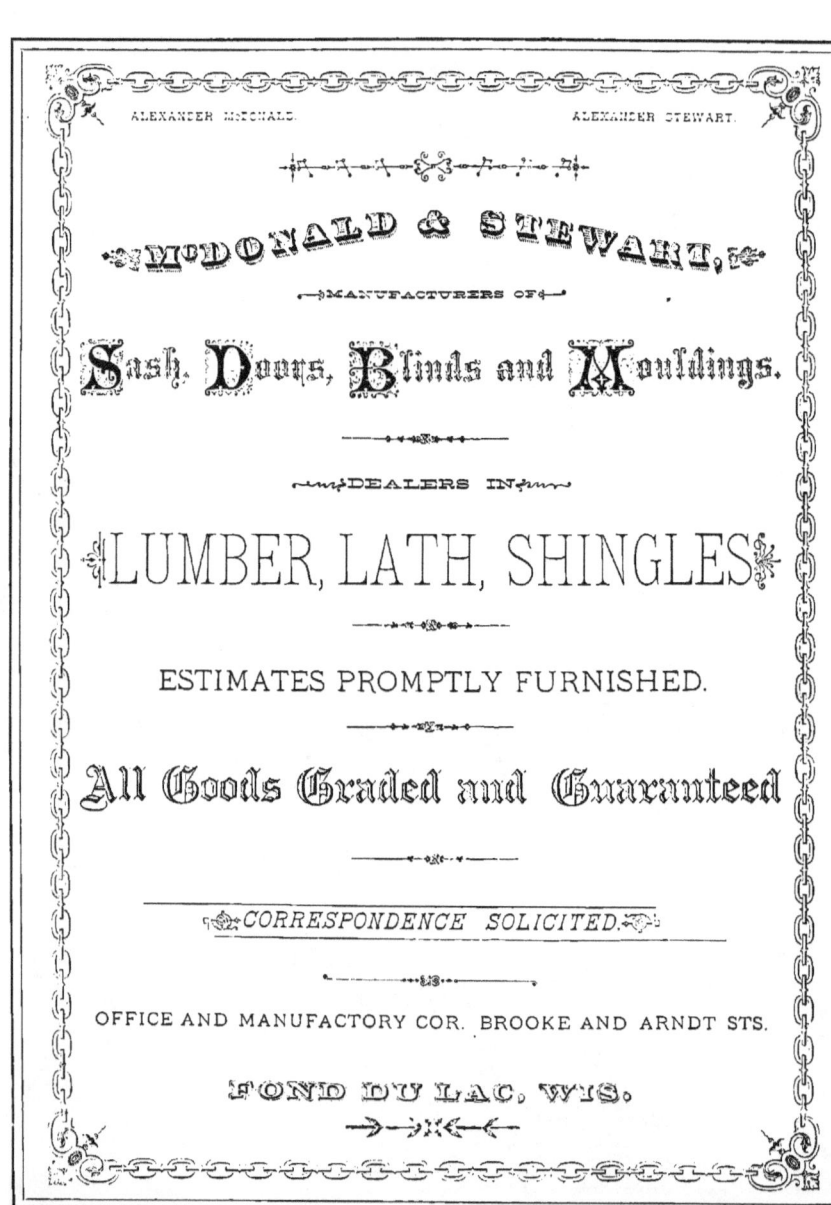

WISCONSIN SOLDIERS AND SAILORS REUNION ROSTER.

Turk, Alfred E — Vicksburg, Aug 4–63
Wells, H N — Union Hill, Ark, July 8–62
Winkler, A A — Black Earth
Webster, J H — Clarendon, Ark, July 10–62
Walker, L D, hardware — Plymouth, Ia
Yeager Leonard — Sauk City
Yagen, L — Sauk City
Zirbel, John — Brashear City, Aug 6–64

B

Capt J H Hubbard
Capt E S Oakley
Capt Otis Remick — Kekoskee
Capt Wm Charlton
Lt W W Day
Lt Jas M Bull
Lt H D Smith — Clarendon, July 10–62
Lt Marvin Colby
Lt H J Luneburg
Grout, A A, 1st sgt Sulphur Springs, Mar 12–62
Rogers, Lyman, sat — Madison
Richardson, W, corp* — Jackson, July 11–63
Anderson, C — Oldtown, Sep 9–62
Allen, J H, — New Iberia, Oct 8–63
Arpin, Charles — Carlton
Bentley, S R — Arena
Baumann, A* — Ft Blakely, April 9–65
Barry, Samuel — Madison
Brossard, G W — New Orleans, Sept 25–64
Beers, David — Colby
Buck, J W — New Orleans, 5 pt 29–64
Beers, Frederick, — Colby
Cross T+
Daggett, M — Reeve's Station, April 25–62
Darrow, E — St Louis, Oct 27–62
Dengel, J — Perkins, April 26–63
Drake, S — Brashear City, Dec 5–61
Fountain, A — Montgomery, July 13–65
Glidden, L — St Louis, Nov 10–62
Gilbert, J H — New Orleans, Dec 9–63
Glidden, J N — New Orleans, Dec 24–63
Hunt, E S — East Middleton
Howard, R — Ironton, Nov –2 62
Landon, F* — Vicksburg, May 22–63
Lindsley, C — Old Mills, Nov 1–62
McGowan, J* — Ft Blakely, April 9–65
Mullenwog, F* — Ft Blakely, April 9–65
Miles, Layton B, f — Madison
Millen, J — Montgomery, June 5–65
Noble, B F — Sioux Falls, D T
Norton, Henry J — Vickeryville, Mich
Plackett, H — New York, June 10–64
Rhenehard, Geo W — Helena, Oct 7–63
Rogers, F — Oldtown, Sep 1–62
Smith, C F* — Jackson, July 11–63
Sheldon, D — Reeves Station, April 20–63
Stetsman, F — Pocahontas, May 27–62
Smith, W — Jacksonport, June 27–63
Stowell, Israel — Vicksburg, July 16–63
Taylor, W W — Brashear City, Oct 27–64
Vannasse, Joseph — Mobile, Aug 17–65
Widner, W V — Milwaukee
Williams, W M — Ironton, April 4–62
White, C J, R R Conductor — Madison

C

Capt Chas Perry
Capt Jas Lang
Lt H V S Hutchinson
Lt Axel Grover
Lt Jno Sewright
Lt O F Mattice
Lt H E Smith* — Vicksburg, May 22–63
Lt Jas H Roach — Menomonee
Knapp, H P, sgt — Brashear City, Aug 14–64
Smith, H E, sgt* — Vicksburg, May 22–63
Wilber, F, sgt+ — Fort Blakely, April 11–65
Weed, T, sgt — Cairo, Nov 25–64
Ingamells, G R, corp* — Ft Blakely, April 9–65

Roache, N, corp — Montgomery, July 22–65
Pixley, B F, corp — Brashear City, Dec 6–64
Krogh, B J, corp, f — Cambridge
Alexander, William — Valley Junction
Alexander, Obediah — Valley Junction
Anderson, J — Brashear City, July 17–64
Burnett, J A — Bayou Deview, July 8–62
Brown, Si....., 4, pb — Madison
Behm, W — Mobile, Aug 22–65
Fryer, H — Augusta, July 4–62
Griffith, O — Bayou Cache, July 8–62
Huckbert, F — New Orleans
Hoyt, N, m — Yazatou, D T
Hitchcock, W — St Louis, Nov 14–62
Ingamels, C+ — Memphis, June, 16–63
King, W C — Ironton, April 27–62
Lusted, John — Brashear City, Sept 15–64
Roach, James H — Menomonee
Robinson, N A — Ironton, April 27–62
Roach, Ross — Menomonee
Smith, Wm — St Louis, Dec 29–62
Sickles, W H — Waterloo, May 12–65
Sickles, Chas E — Sun Prairie
Swift, F H, e.a — Clinton
Thompson, Martin V — St Louis, June 8–62
Trapp, Andrew — Waterloo
Twining, John O — Pilot Knob, March 24–62
Twining, Aaron — Oldtown, Aug 25–64
Wilcox, E+ — Memphis, June 25–63
Wise, T — Sulphur Springs,June 7–62
Whittelsoe, Wm — Jackson, Feb 10–62
Williams, S A — Waterloo
Wood, Ira A — Batesville, June 29–62
Wright, Geo — Brashear City, Aug 2–64

D

Capt J S Miller
Capt Henry Toms — Richland Centre
Lt Wm Hill — Richland Centre
Lt A A Chamberlain
Lt G W Dale
Lt W H Dawson
Lt Hiram Freeman
Lt Rich'd Caddell* — Ft Blakely, Ala, April 9–65
Lt Jas 8 Robinson
Hoyt, N, sergt* — Bayou Cache, July 7–62
Carleton, A, sergt — Victoria, Mo, Jan 20–62
Titus, A, sergt — Brashear City, April 5–64
White, G C, corp* — Bayou Cache, April 7–62
Altbough, G, corp* — Ft Blakely, Ala, April 9–65
Magill, G P, corp — Pocahontas, May 26–62
Amery, R — Ft Blakely, Ala, April 9–65
Aylesworth, D — Richland, Aug 17–64
Brace, J+ — Jeff Barracks, Mo, April 7–62
Burke, J — St Louis, Dec 11–64
Beigley, J D — Black River, Mo, Dec 15–62
Braunon, J — Jeff Barracks, July 22–63
Bond, F — St Louis, Nov 16–62
Bennet, W — Greenville, La, April 20–65
Cooper, J — Oldtown, Ark, Aug 1–62
Creekpan, J — Madison, March 31–64
Campbell, W — Madison, March 17–64
Campbell, A — New Orleans, June 20–64
Core W M — Brashear City, Feb 14–65
Coates, F — Neillsville
Dillingham, C L — Victoria, Mo, Oct 24–63
Fife, Charles — Ironton, Nov 8–62
Huffman, D W — Ironton, May 7–62
Hill, Wm — Richland Centre
Haukins, M D — Richland Centre
Hill, W — Brashear City, July 7–62
Hennan, W — New Orleans, Sept 16–64
Hively, M B — Madison, March 24–64
Hook, John — Madison, March 8–64
Johnson, W — Brashear City, Sept 5–64
Kennedy, J W* — Ft Blakely, Ala, April 9–65
Kennedy J W — Madison, March 1–64
Kinney, A J — Richland Centre

Karnes, Adam — Brashear City, Sept 5–64
Lyons, C D — Victoria, Mo, Jan 20–62
Nickel, G N — Richland Centre
Marsh, T — Brashear City, Oct 16–64
Miller, James L — Orion
Noble, Angus — Ironton, Nov 28–62
Owen, E,f — Boaz
Reinhart, G W — Black River, Mo, Dec 15–62
Robinson, J M — Ft Blakely, Ala, April 9–65
Robinson, B F* — Batesville, Ark, June 22–62
Sullivan, Wm — Ironton, Oct 31–62
Smith, M V — Black River, Mo, Dec 31–62
Smalley, Daniel — New Orleans, May 17–64
Smaller, R — Madison, March 17–64
Shaw, D W — Brashear City, Nov 8–61
Sharp, Wm A — Van Buren, Mo, Jan 24–63
Southein, H D — Iron Mt R R, Mo, Nov 28–62
Toms, Henry — Richland Centre
Thompson, B F — Orion
Walker, C C — Paterson, Mo, Nov 12–62
Widner, H — St Genevieve, Mo, March 16–63
While, E G — Rapps, Ark, Oct 3–62
Ward, Peter — Van Buren, Mo, Jan 4–63
Wilson, R J — Richland Centro
Wildermouth, E E — Loyd
Widner, Matthias — Brashear City, Nov 25–64
Walbridge, Edwin — Brashear City, Nov 21–64
York, Peter — Blakely, Ala, April 7–65

E

Capt L H Whittelsey
Capt Abner Powell
Lt S E Shepard
Jones, U R, sgt+ — Vicksburg, May 25–63
Prisk, R T W, sgt — Mineral Point, July, 3–65
Phelps, W H, sgt* — Ft Blakely, April 9–65
Shen, M, corp* — Ft Blakely, April 9–65
Andrews, G+ — Vicksburg, July 3–63
Allen, A — Oldtown, Aug 21–62
Beuder, M — Sulphur Springs, Dec 7–61
Brinnon, J — Brashear City, July 29–64
Bennett, W H, ed — Mineral Point
Chaney, E — Memphis, Sept 11–63
Curry, T W — Black River, Dec 14–62
Davis R T+ — Grand Gulf, May 11–63
Davis, T T — Pitmans Ferry, May 22–62
Dain, J M — Nashville, April 16–63
Fouster, David — Mobile, Aug 2–65
Gibson, M D — Sulphur Springs, June 22–62
Gingerty, W A — Brashear City, July 15–64
Hendrickson, A — Aug 26–63
Knudson, P — July 24–65
Kreager, Carl — Mobile, July 26–64
McElhatteu, D* — Ft Blakely, April 9–65
Newton, Isaac+ — Vicksburg, May 24–63
Phelps, O W* — Vicksburg, June 23–63
Powell, T — Brashear City, Oct 23–64
Priestly, Thomas — Mineral Point
Palmer, P M — Nov 27–64
Scott, J* — Vicksburg, May 22–63
Shannon, A* — Ft Blakely, April 9–65
Smith, J — Millikens Bend, July 20–63
Scoggins, J S — Oldtown, July 10–62
Swift, P H, ed — Clinton
Stevens, John+ — Vicksburg, July 2–63
Satterley, T M+ — Vicksburg, July 2–63
Scott, R+ — Vicksburg, June 16–63
Thomas, Daniel — Oldtown, Aug 27–62
Walbridge, Edwin D — Brashear City, Nov 21–64

F

Capt E R Chase
Capt F D Stone
Capt R E Jackson
Lt Wm R McConnell
Lt C A Northrop — Sept 3–63
Lt L T Locke
Flannagan, M, corp — Brashear City, Aug 23–64

J. Q. GRIFFITH & SONS,

Logs, Lumber, Lath,

SHINGLES, SASH, DOORS, MOULDINGS PICKETS,

PLANING AND RE-SAWING.

Cars loaded in the Yard for all points connected with the principal Railways of the State.

A Fair Share of Public Patronage Solicited.

Our Grades are Well Assorted and Prices Advantageous to Purchasers.

Office Mill and Planing Shop, Division Street.

Between C. & N. W. and F. du L, A. & P. Ry's.

WISCONSIN SOLDIERS AND SAILORS REUNION ROSTER.

Alexandria, P — M...phis, May 6--65
Butler, J* — Vicksburg, May 22--63
Butler, F — Mobile, Aug 10--65
Brennan, M+ — Port Gibson, May 5--63
Bryant, H — Helena
Brill, M — Sulphur Springs, Jan 11--62
Billings, M F, com tray — McGregor, Iowa
Black, E — Lake Providence, March 26--63
Costello, J+ — Carrollton, March 16--63
Davis W M* — Vicksburg, May 23--63
Dahl, Burke — Ironton, Dec 25--62
Donnelson, Ole — Oldtown, Sept 18--62
Doryea, G W — Batesville, June 25--62
Freeman, C — Sept 13--62
Fleck, C B — Neillsville
Griffith, S — Batesville, May 28--62
Goudy, J A — Jacksonport, June 30--92
Hesford, D A — Mound City, Nov 2--62
Hodget, A — Rapps, Sept 21--62
Inman, W R — Madison, March 6--65
Jones, Obed K — Platteville
Kinzley, G W+ — Milliken's Bend, Aug 6--63
Lips, J W — Willow Springs, Feb 11--63
Lester, Edward — Spring Green
Leston, Geo — Mazomanie
Mather, O S+ — Vicksburg, May 27--63
McCormick, J M — Orion
Mather, Jesse — Prairie du Sac
Morton, David C — Warrens Mills
Newell, C L — Jefferson Barracks, Aug 15--62
Paul, C A — Keokuk, Sept 14--63
Robotham, A — Pocahontas, May 8--62
Rohn, Evans — Montgomery, July 26--64
Rowley, A A — Middleton
Reding, Martin — Verona
Stearnes, W E — Memphis, June 15--63
Spencer, Jas F, b — Hudson
Thomas, Chas — Clarendon, July 1--64
Thompson, Ole — Mobile, Aug 3--65
Welch, A* — Ft Blakely, April 9--65
Williams, Herman — Brashear City, Oct 18--64

G

Capt W F Felton
Capt E D Partridge
Capt Jno A Peaslee* — Vicksburg, Miss, May 23--63
Capt D C Wymann
Capt W S McCready
Lt Nathan Downs — Mazomanie
Lt A R Winn
Lt Geo Farwell
Lt Henry Blake
Lt Jas Law+ — On the march, June 8--63
Hayden, U, corp* — Bayou Cache, July 7--62
Tiernan, F, corp+ — Memphis, June 22--63
Masterman, W, corp — Van Buren, Feb 3--63
Anderson, J W — Arena
Bywater, John — Mazomanie
Borwell, Ed — Hamlin
Baker, Geo H — Chilton
Cleveland, C B — Clarendon, Ark, July 11--62
Dally, F* — Vicksburg, May 23--63
Dodge, Jacob M — Round Lake, Minn
Denens, N H, f — Mazomanie
Downs, N H — New Chester
Gilbertson, T G — St Louis, Nov 9--62
Gibson, E D — Ironton, Nov 17--62
Hodgen, C Z — St Louis, April 13--64
Holcomb, D — Arena
Kocker, D+ — Memphis, July 1--63
Logenhart, J* — Vicksburg, May 22--63
Michael, J A* — Vicksburg, May 22--63
Marquardt, J+ — Memphis, June 16--63
May, H M+ — Memphis, June 26--63
McGeen, D+ — Ft Blakely, April 10--64
Mabbott, E J — Arena
Mallory, J — Ironton, Oct 30--62
Mallon, W H — St Louis, Nov 21--63
Murphy, M — Wisconsin, April 8--64
Partlow, S+ — New Orleans, La, June 16--65

Platt, A B — Mazomanie
Rood, Calvin — Oldtown, Ark, Aug 22--62
Richards, Wm — Mobile, Aug 9--65
Stroud, G W+ — St Louis, Aug 11--65
Stewart, Hugh — Mazomanie
Shay, Jeremiah
Sanders, Henry — Arena
Small, Wm — Wisconsin, Nov 7--63
Stewart, Hugh, pa — Mazomanie
Shusta, Jacob — Montgomery, June 27--65
Stickle, Sam — Waterloo
Tollard, R A — Sulphur Springs, Dec 13--63
Wells, Chas H — St Louis, Nov 9--62
Wolf, A — Lone Rock
Wolf, C — Mobile, Aug 6--65
Wingad, David — Hamlin

H

Capt Alex Christie
Capt Jas O'Neal
Lt E H Mix
La Chas Allen
Lt C A Johnson — Montgomery, Ala, July 5--65
Lt Jno E Lyon
Lt I J Wright
Lt Wm N Gates
Bacon, C A, 1st sgt* — Bayou Cache, July 7--62
Jacobus, W H, 1st sgt* — Vicksburg, May 23--63
Brunuller, C, sgt* — Vicksburg, May 22--61
Parsons, G, sgt — Ironton, Mo, Dec 1--62
Phillips, R C, sgt — Dec 10--62
Henson, B P, corp+ — St Louis, July 20--62
Fay, W N, corp+ — Vicksburg, May 28--63
Hughbanks, J, corp+ — Vicksburg, May 11--63
Washburn, D S, corp — Ironton, Mo, Nov 13--62
Ackerman, E — Oldtown, Ark, Sept 13--62
Alusy, S — Ironton, Dec 13--62
Bilke, Wm, f — Seneca, Alo
Baker, H C — Black Creek
Bacon, R+ — Ft Blakely, April 12--65
Baker, H C — Black Creek
Bidwell, E W — Patterson, Mo, Nov 25--62
Bauer, Frederick — Webster City, Ia
Colburn, A — Cole's Bridge, Feb 1--62
Cox, C A — Troy
Delap, Wm A — Brashear, La, Sept 14--64
Dickenson, Jas S — Brownton, Minn
Faith, John — Arcadia, Mo, Oct 31--62
Faith, G W — Jeff Barracks, Mo, Sept 27--62
Hartson, F N* — Port Gibson, Miss, May 1--63
Holzinger, Frederick — Baraboo
Hornby, R — Mound City, Nov 4--62
Jones, John E — Oldtown, Ark, Aug 12--63
Johnson, Benajah — Alton
Kent, Wm+ — June 11--63
Langdon, F — Pickett's, Ark, July 2--63
Lum, J K — Loyal
Miller, A C — St Louis, Aug 10--62
Mather, W — Ironton, Nov 8--62
McElory, W — Van Buren, Mo, Jan 26--3
Newman, Wm P — Arkansas, July 1--62
Olmsted, D H — Brashear City, Oct 9--64
Perkins, J W — New Chester
Powderly, W H+ — Clarendon, Ark, July 7--62
Porter, Hiram — Oldtown, Ark, Aug 30--62
Quaw, S M — Wausau
Robinson, O S+ — Vicksburg, May 23--63
Richards, Wm L, f — Republican City, Neb
Richardson, G — Cairo, July 31--62
Risk, Wm — Easton
Richardson, P — Loyal
Sheldon, Horace — Grand Gulf, May 31--63
Spaulding, J F — Coloma
Sawyer, Reuben G — New York, April 27--65
Washburn, Orison — Ironton, Nov 9--62
Walters, W H — Richland Centre
Wheelock, E C — Brashear City, Nov 29--64

I

Capt A J Whittler
Capt N B Dean
Lt De Witt C Benham
Lt Jerome Cheebro, — Grand Gulf, May 3--62
Lt H C Welcome
Lt H H Hopkins — Nashua, Iowa
Whitcher, L, corp — Plot Knob, March 4--62
Boalen, C W — Sulphur Springs, Feb 17--65
Bailey, H W, — Ironton, Feb 22--3
Bedient, J S — Oldtown, Aug 15--64
Cheeebro, Mason — Markesan
Dickason, J H — Milwaukee
Dixon, Thomas C — Heron Lake, Minn
Gorden, George H — Tomah
Halverson, Ole+ — Vicksburg, May 22--63
Hamer, Geo T, me — Princeton
Hobbs, H C — Ironton, Nov 3--62
Hopkins, A C — Nashua, Iowa
Hopkins, H H, m — Nashua, Iowa
Haskins, L D — Sulphur Springs, Nov 3--62
Hamer, N W — Oconto
Johnson, J C — St Louis, Aug 17--62
Larrabee, F — Jefferson Barracks, Aug 2--62
Lumke, John, f — Muscoda
Laughlin, L D — St Louis Aug 17--62
Mitchell, J H, m — Nashua
Myres, Nicholas — Feb 28--3
Morse, E S, me — Nashua
Ostrander, C — Oldtown, Aug 32--62
Parker, F — Ironton, Dec 7--62
Pierce, Edwin — Montello
Rhylander, E — Montgomery, July 30--64
Reilley, Daniel T — Berlin
Stedman, Hollis — Berlin
Sergeant, Marshall — Elkmound
Stowe, Martin — Ironton, Oct 30--62
Walker I M* — Vicksburg, May 16--63
Washburn, Datus E — Pitman's April 24 - 62
Whitney, Daniel — Mound City, Sept 16--62
Willis, Wm H — St Louis, Dec 7--62
Weller, H H — Vicksburg, June 17--63

K

Capt C J Wheeler
Capt H J Lewis
Lt Wm Chariton
Capt Alvin Abell
Lt Ira W Hunt
Lt Artemus Adams
Lt C S Gilbert
Lt Robt P House
Rollee, W F, sgt+ — Vicksburg, May 28--63
Nelson, C C, sgt — New Orleans, Oct 10--64
Brockway, A, corp — Ironton, Nov 17--62
Conley, J corp — Brashear City, Sept 25--64
Pohlman, H A, corp — Brashear City, July 14--65
Anderson, J — Brashear City, Sept 12--64
Bashford, R — New Orleans, June 14--64
Brandes, J C — Brashear City, Sept 12--64
Brisbane, W H — Arena
Bainson, Ole — Brashear City, Oct 3--64
Burkey, L — Sulphur Springs, Jan 16--62
Couley, N — Helena, Sept 21--62
Doughey, S — Ironton, Nov 11--62
Edwards, Henry H — Ironton, March 1--63
Giebel, J+ — Ft Blakely, April 10--65
Hayden, A — Ironton, Nov 27--62
Houman, Albert — St Louis
Hanson, Ole — Brashear City, Sept 16--64
Klampe, Gottliebo — Jacksonport, May 17--63
Kleiber, Andrew — Lathrop, Mich
Koppel, A M — Ironton, Jan 14-- 3
Lloyd, Elias W — Vicksburg, July 3--63
Moyer, James T — Batesville, July 28--2
Sturgeon J+ — Vicksburg, May 26--6
Small, Robert, f — Vinland
Secor, James T — Van Buren, Jan 1--63

⁂FARGO'S⁂
PATENT
Solid Steel V-Shaped Harrow Tooth,

MAKES THE BEST

HARROW

IN THE WORLD.

And is made in the following regular
SIZES:

8 bars	2 Section's	48 Teeth.
10 "	2 "	60 "
12 "	3 "	72 "
15 "	3 "	90 "
18 "	3 "	108 "

And for a working capacity of 17 ft. breadth.

WHAT PRACTICAL FARMERS SAY.

[From all over the Northwestern Grain Growing States and Territories, have come to us the voluntary, unsolicited expression of practical farmers, whose life-long experience and disinterested opinions are of the highest value to those who contemplate making a choice from the thousands of patent harrows offered on every hand. Limited space prevents the publication of only a fraction of these testimonials, and indeed, only a line or so of letters we should be glad to publish in full. We have added to each signature the P. O. address, and invite correspondence direct with the parties.]

Fond du Lac Harrow Co.,
GENTS:—We beg leave to add our testimonial to the many in favor of the justly celebrated Fargo Steel-tooth Harrow. We hear from all we have sold, nothing but praise. Parties buying them say that they more than come up to their expectations, and that they can do doubly more work with them than with any other make. Yours, etc.,
FORT WAYNE STEEL PLOUGH WORKS, Fort Wayne, Ind.

Fond du Lac Harrow Co.,
GENTS:—We take pleasure in recommending your Fargo Improved V-toothed Harrow to the general public as a first class farm implement. We have given it a thorough and extensive trial, on old and new land, having harrowed in *Forty five hundred acres* of small grain this season with them. We have several other makes of harrows on our place, but we give yours the decided preference. Yours etc., E. F. WARNER, Manager Rock County Farm Co., St. Paul Minn.

WHAT ONE OF THE LARGEST FARMERS OF MINNESOTA SAYS.

Fond du Lac Harrow Co.,
GENTS:—Your letter of inquiry as to working of your harrow, is at hand. In reply will say that I have given your harrow a thorough trial, and was much pleased with the result. It is the best harrow and does the most thorough work of any that I have tried. Yours, D. H. VALENTINE, St. Paul, Minn.

ONE BETTER THAN THREE.

"The harrow gives more than good satisfaction. Once over the ground with it, is better than three times with other harrows." S. V. R. BROCKWAY, Clyman Wis.

CLEANEST AND EASIEST DRAFT.

"It is easier draft, cleaner, and does better work than any of my neighbors or I have ever used before. I recommend it without reserve." W. H. ANGELL, Sun Prairie, Wis.

THREE TO ONE AND SOME TO SPARE.

"I consider it the best harrow ever used, and will do more work in going over ground once, than with a common harrow three times, and do it much better." O. W. STILLMAN, Milwaukee, Wis.

IT IS ALL CLAIMED FOR IT.

"Fargo's V-shaped Solid Steel Tooth Harrow is all claimed for it. It is the best we ever used, and is of great value to farmers." R. E. LEWIS, C. P. THURSTON, N. E. NELSON, J. M. SLASSEN, A. C. WALKER, Northwood, Ia.

When not on sale in your immediate vicinity, or you desire further information. Address

FOND DU LAC HARROW CO.,
FOND DU LAC. - - WISCONSIN.
[SEE PAGE 4.]

WISCONSIN SOLDIERS AND SAILORS REUNION ROSTER.   57

Torrence, W E — St Louis, Dec 3—62
Thompson, C O — St Louis, Feb 13—62
Wooledge, Galus S — Ironton, Nov 16—62
Warner, Reuben — Rolla, Jan 16—62
Wescott, Carver D — St Louis

UNASSIGNED.
Moore, Daniel B, capt — Chicago, Ill
Barrett, J A — Brashear City, Sept 18—61
Carpenter, R A — Alexandria, May 17—61
Cobbett, H C — Sulphur Springs, Jan 16—62
Douglas J H — La Valle
Hendricks, H H — Wrightstown
Kline Charles — Menomonee
Lindsley, John C — Old Mills, Nov 1—62
Linn, J K, surg — Loyal
Logue, John — Montgomery, June 16—65
Marsh, L Y — Black Earth
Matze, Fred — Mazomanie
Mayers, Chas Geo — Madison
Moore, D B — Chicago, Ill
Norton, H J — Vickeryville, Mich
Strong, H P, ph — Beloit
Wright, J P — Oxford

TWELFTH INFANTRY.

Three years. Organized October, 1861. Original strength 1045; gain by recruits etc, 1141 Total, 2186. Death loss, 201—Killed in action, 59, died of wounds, 32, of disease, 202. Other losses, 420, missing, 0, desertions, 26. transfers 61, discharged 536. Strength at muster out, July 16th, 1865, 1162. Campaigns in Mo., Kans., Tenn., Miss., La., Ala., Ga., S C., N C.

REGIMENTAL ROSTER.
Col Geo E Bryant — Madison
Col Jas K Proudfit — Wyandotte, Kan
Lt Col De W C Poole — Ft Clark, Texas
Lt Col Wm E Strong — Chicago, Ill
Maj John M Price — Savannah, Dec 20—61
Maj C B Wheelock
Adj Levi M Bevare — Madison
Q M Andrew Sexton — Madison
Q M Frank B Bryant — Omaha, Neb
Surg Luther Cary — Oakland, Cal
Surg Ezra M Rogers — Hartford
A Surg E A Woodward — Sun Prairie
A Surg A B Cary — Fond du Lac, Sept 14—62
A Surg S L, Morrison — New Cassel
A Surg A F St sdre Lindsfelt — Sheboygan
A Surg De W C Bennett
A Surg J B Cooper
A Surg N E Seeley
A Surg H J Walker — Cottonwood Falls, Kan

A
Capt Norman McLeod
Capt Orin T Maxson — Waukegan, Ill
Capt Chas Reynolds — Jacksonport
Lt Jas W Lusk — Reedsburg
Lt Wallace Kelsey
Lt Francis Hoyt
Lt Gordon Allen — Vicksburg, Aug 4—63
Lt Alva McKee
Metlcarge, J, corp — Natchez, Oct 12—63
Anderson, Sovan — Hammond
Arrington, Gibson, sergt — New Richmond
Askenette, Peter* — Atlanta, Ga, July 21—61
Bowers, Henry* — Atlanta, Ga, July 21—61
Beebe, C A — Natchez, Oct 1—61
Houghton, E — Natchez, Jan 24—64
Barlow, Henry — St Louis, Feb 16—64
Barrett, A J — Trimbelle
Connelly, W F — Weston, Mo, March 15—62
Comstock, B B — Humboldt, Tenn, July 17—62
Colgan, J M — Neaville Station, Feb 24—63
Chadwick, Albert — New Richmond

Degarmond, C
Dresser, D S*
Davis, L D
Duey, J* — Bentonville, N C March 21—65
Gibbs, James — St Louis, Oct 1—63
Gibson, el — New Richmond
Gilstead, H C — Cylon
Hampel, G C — Cylon
Hodgers, Wm H* — Atlanta, July 21—61
Humphrey, B I* — Atlanta, July 21—61
Hope, George W* — Atlanta, July 21—61
Holman, J H+ — Marietta, Sept 1—61
Huntington, C F, ar — New Richmond
Huntington, Charles — New Richmond
Jewell, P B — St Croix
Johnson, J H — Columbus, Ky, June 22—62
Kelsey, Wallace, f — Cottage Grove, Minn
Loring, Horace C — St Louis, Oct 1—62
Law, Harvey, Jr, me — New Richmond
Miley, James* — Vicksburg, June 2—63
McIntyre, Dougal — Natchez, Aug 25—63
Maxon, O T, ph — Waukegan
Nelson, Peter — Bolivar, Tenn, Jan 27—63
Nichols J G — Aug 28—63
Northrop, D D — St Louis, July 21—63
Oleson, J* — Atlanta, July 2—64
Otis, John A — Rome, Ga, June 16—64
Patterson, Jacob B — Weston, Mo, April 1—62
Prescott, G W — Bolivar, Tenn, Nov 8—62
Pumplin, W L H — Vicksburg, July 6—63
Quirk, John — St Louis, Aug 11—64
Russell, Solomon M — Vicksburg, June 16—63
Schuyler, T — Louisville, June 26 65
Severance, Joseph — Beldenville
Trigg, Robert* — Atlanta, July 21—63
Taylor, J H — Madison, Feb 16—64
Tubman, Edward — Hammond
Wilson, Robert — Natchez, Aug 29—63
Womack, Wm — Platteville
Womack, J H — Platteville
Young, J F, ph — New Richmond

B
Capt Giles Stevens — Reedsburg
Capt C G Higbee — St Paul, Minn
Capt J W Root
Lt B F Blackman — Ironton
Lt H P Ballard
Lt J W Lusk — Reedsburg
Lt T J Davis
Miles, S S, sgt — Marietta, Aug 10—64
Henry, T W, sgt* — Atlanta, July 25—61
Richards, Wm, corp* — Atlanta, July 25—61
Bell, G W, corp+ — Marietta, Aug 4—64
Allen, J F — Savannah, Dec 13—61
Bailey, G W — St Croix
Baldwin Rathburn — Reedsburg
Bundy, W F — Sauk City
Bemis, Levi D, f — Spring Creek
Donward, Abey W — Neosho
Cornwell, L B* — Atlanta, July 21—61
Camp, N+ — Kenesaw, July 14—64
Campbell, C S — Weston, March 1—62
Curtis, Horace — Vicksburg, June 29—63
Conklin, M — Vicksburg, Aug 29—63
Curtis, George — Holly Springs, Dec 11—62
Crouch, Horace — Reedsburg
Dowden, A* — Atlanta, July 22—64
Dearholt, Henry — Ft Riley, May 6—63
Duddleston, H — Coilierville, Feb 7—63
Elliot, J W* — Atlanta, July 28 64
Ford, Amos* — Atlanta, July 20 64
Ford, George* — Atlanta, July 20—64
Fosbinder, Charles W — Mauston
Gulliford, Chas W — Logansville
Hagaman, E H* — Atlanta, July 22—63
Hoyt, Ralph+ — Rome, Aug 15—64
Hobart, Alvis — Weston, Mar 7—62
Hagaman, Jehiel D — Natchez, Aug 7—63
Hobart, Anderson — Memphis, June 17—63

Higbee, C G, ph — St Paul, Minn
Long, M B+ — Chattanooga, Nov 23—64
Lane, O — Neville Station, Feb 16—63
Lusk, J W — Reedsburg
Lane, Philo — Reedsburg
Mason, James D — Cairo, Ap 13—64
Meade, James B — Atlanta, Oct 1—64
Miles, James — Reedsburg
Osborn, W C — Natchez, Aug 28—63
Pollock, C T — Bolivar, Nov 20—64
Palmer, James — Chattanooga, Feb 10—65
Purcell, James K — Port Andrew
Richmuth, C — Kenesaw, June 27—61
Rogers, Wm H — Hopkins, Mo
Rogers, H H — Hopkins, Mo
Rathbun, Baldy — Reedsburg
Sebastian, B — Racine
Sammons, J — July 3—63
Settle, Thos — Leavenworth, March 7—62
Seymour, E — Jackson, March 5—63
Stark, Edgar, d — Amherst
Stevens, G — Reedsburg
Spicer, D G — Reedsburg
Scoon, Alfred F — Logansville
Sweetzer, Joe — Racine
Wickersham, J E* — Atlanta, July 18—63
Wool, F C — July 18—64

C
Capt C G Locher
Capt David G Jones — Arena
Lt M J Cantwell — Madison
Lt Wm C Stevens — Utica
Lt Jas F Sampson
Lt Edw S Whiting
Lt Jas Sexton — Nashkora
Rowe, J H D, 1st sgt — La Grange, Nov 17—62
Paul, Edward, sgt — July 15—63
Wood, E P, sgt* — Atlanta, July 5—61
Hinkle, John, corp+ — Atlanta, July 4 64
Loyd, T P, corp — Humboldt, Sept 13—62
Wood, D C, corp — Vicksburg, July 5—63
Powers, R, corp — Memphis, Jan 17—64
Baker, G, corp — Savannah
Baxter, Charles — Linden
Chestleson, F — St Louis, July 27—63
Coggin, L — Vicksburg, July 1—63
Chestleson, Aslak — Vicksburg July 30—63
Darberne, Elzeard — West Depere
Eddy, Thomas R — July 15 —63
Fish, Charles — Rome, Aug 7—64
Fuller, George W — Denison
Gear, Elmore — Wisconsin, May 7—64
Henson, John Jr* — Atlanta, July 21—61
James, C J — Oxford, Dec 22—63
Level, Jonas — La Grange, Nov 18—62
Morris, W E — Paw Paw Island, June 2—63
Niggins, R — Neillsville
Orcutt, Cyrus — Vicksburg, Jan 10—64
Parker, Levi W — Pulaski, June 7—64
Rawdon, P* — Atlanta, July 21—61
Ralson, S* — Atlanta, July 21—61
Rich, Henry — Lawrence, April 25—62
Reed, Otis — Lawrence, April 25—62
Swanson, A* — Atlanta, July 21—61
Tamby, Peter — Okonee, Nov 20—61
Walker, Niel — Flandreau, D T
Wilson, Joe — Mazomanie

D
Capt Wm Nungesser
Lt Thos Farmer — Hartford
Lt Wm J Norton
Lt D J Sullivan
Lt H M Waller — Hiawatha, Kan
Lt Geo T Wescott
Wheeler, T B, sgt — Memphis, March 15—53
Prestice, F E, corp* — Atlanta, July 21—61

WINDOW BLINDS

⁕FOR THE MILLION⁕

Comfort, Utility, Economy and Beauty Combined.

THE ADVANTAGES of having a dwelling house furnished with window blinds are so apparent that reasons therefor seem unnecessary and out of place.

That they are an absolute and never-failing protection against the violent storms of wind and hail so frequent and destructive to window glass, has been demonstrated time and time again.

That they keep out cold in winter, and thereby save fuel, is the universal testimony of everybody who has used or tried them.

That they protect the rooms of the house from the hot rays of summer's sun, is equally well established.

Nothing can be more pleasant, in warm weather, than to sit or work in a room protected from the sun, and yet with a breeze wafting through the house. Window Blinds afford this comfort every time.

For a sick room, or children's nursery, Blinds are almost indispensable. The light may be toned down to any grade, permitting sleep in the day-time, which otherwise would be impossible, or at best uneasy and broken.

It also often occurs that a person out of health cannot bear the strong light of mid-day sun, and how frequently do we meet those whose eyes have been ruined by carelessness in this particular.

Again there are some people to whom sharp lightning is very unpleasant, and whose rest at night is disturbed by a thunder shower. To such, closing the Window blinds gives immediate relief.

Blinds, to a limited extent, are protection against tramps and petty thieves. Ordinary windows are easily raised from the outside, but it requires skilled practice and expertness to unlock a fastened window blind.

Besides these and many other advantages, the improved appearance of a residence when furnished with Window Blinds, more than compensates the cost of improvement.

In looks alone, to say nothing of comfort and protection, blinds pay for themselves each and every year.

All inquiries cheerfully and promptly answered, and when desired a competent person will be sent to view, measure and estimate on work, without expense to the party purchasing.

Address the

FOND DU LAC BUILDING ASSOCIATION,
C. W. MIHILLS, Manager,

FOND DU LAC, WISCONSIN.

WISCONSIN SOLDIERS AND SAILORS REUNION ROSTER.

Smith, E P, corp*   Atlanta, July 21-64
Bally, C H   Memphis, March 24—64
Bullard, A J   Neillsville
Brackley, K   Burton, Dec 1—64
Cawan, Hugh   Racine, Nov 28—63
Cep, C   Toonsboro, Nov 21—61
Dutcher, N   Natchez, Nov 27—63
Fisheo   Campbellsport
Goldner, Henry+   Atlanta, Aug 10—64
Green, Harrison J   St Louis, Aug 7—63
Hookman, Wm*   Atlanta, July 21—61
Holt, John M   Rome, Oct 11—64
Harris, Nicholas   Andersonville, Nov 24—64
Jackel, Victor   Two Rivers
Jones, J B   Neillsville
Lampert, Matthias*   Atlanta, July 21—64
Lampert, John*   Atlanta, July 21—64
Meyers, Wm G   Decatur, Feb 12—64
Melter, F   Quincy, March 23—62
McLaughlin, J   Union City, July 13—62
McDonald, W W   Holly Springs, Dec 15—62
Martin, H   July 19—63
Miller, Nelson   Newbern, May 6—65
Munger, James E
Nash, Edward M
Porter, W H, ar   Myra
Roohr, H F L   Vicksburg, July 21—63
Robbins, A D   La Grange, Feb 13—63
Roberts, R   Campbellsport
Smith, C+   Atlanta, July 23—64
Southwick, W P   La Grange, Nov 8—2
Stannard, H R   St Louis, Aug 22—63
Smith, C   Neillsville
St John, S D   Washington, May 10—65
Smith, A   Neillsville
Stahl, Charles, Police Milwaukee
Taylor, H H, pa   Burton
Warren, H H
Wispel, Henry   Leavenworth, Mar 14—62
Weber, N   Goldsboro, April 1—65
Waller, David M   Andersonville, Sept 20—64
Wolf, Frank, sgt, me   West Bend
Whalen, Moses   Andersonville, Nov 21—64
Wells, James O   Onro
Wescott, W R, ar   Burton

E

Capt Abram Vanderpoel
Capt A E Kinney
Lt R Cronk
Lt L T Linnell   Cobden, Ill
Lt Michael Griffin   Eau Claire
Lt Jas H Thayer*   Marietta, Ga, Oct 8—64
Lt H H Dyer
Shultz, John, corp*   Atlanta, Ga, July 21—64
Fields, Chas, corp*   Atlanta, July 21—64
Lowman, J J, corp   Troy, Tenn, June 27—62
Houghton, C A+   Atlanta, Ga, July 23—64
Briggs, Chas B, me   Baraboo
Boyd, J L+   Davids Island, N Y, April 9—65
Barton, E W   Washington, May 23—65
Bailey, G W   Delton, May 20—65
Clement, J H   Atlanta, Aug 5—61
Camp, James, f   Baraboo
Cole, Eddy, f   Mauston
Edmunds, J C   Natchez, Aug 30—63
Elghmy, O W, f   Shetek
Pluno, H A+   Nickajack, Ga, July 6—64
Fisher, W H   Humboldt, Tenn, Sept 14—62
Freeman, Joel M   Rome, Ga, July 9—64
Griffin, A T, me   Baraboo
Gloyd, Charles L   Kenesaw Mt, June 8—64
Harbaugh, Wesley   Memphis, Nov 19—63
Johnston, Enos   Humboldt, Tenn, Aug 27—62
Knapp, A   Milton, Ga, Nov 8—64
Marshall, G W   Vicksburg, Sept 22—63
Montague, G C   Kenesaw Mt, June 25—64
Ostrander, Horace   Hebron, Miss, Feb 25—64
Rockwell, H   La Grange, Tenn, Feb 23—63
Rolison, Millan   Baldwin

F

Stowell, W+   Atlanta, July 21—63
Smith, Ladero S   Lawrence, April 17—62
Squires, Harlan A   Vicksburg, July 28—63
Titus, D A*   Atlanta, July 28—64
Truell, Edwin M   Washington
Truell, Ferdinand   Waverly, Neb
Velviek, J W   Madison, March 4—64
Walker, H, me   Baraboo
Wright, Orson, f   Mauston
Wilson, Warren   Spring Bluff

Capt F J Bartels   Peshtigo
Lt Levi Odell   Galesville
Lt Levi N Turner
Lt Jas W Loughrey   Marinette
Lt Henry Tourtillotte
Lt David Jones
Lt G R Brooks
Libby, I, 1st sgt*   Atlanta, July 21—61
Rennel, F, corp+   Atlanta, Jan 15—64
Foster, N L, corp   La Grange, Jan 15—63
Amundson, A   Savannah, Feb 1—65
Ames, Hiram   Villenow, Oct 17—61
Bruelle, Geo   Atlanta, July 21—64
Bundy, James   Brockside
Covarts, F   Kenesaw, June 19—64
Delann, Moses   Leavenworth, April 10—62
Dumme, Acedor   Natchez, Sept 10—65
Dyer, Samuel J   Keokuk, Oct 13—63
Egan, Michael   Osman
Garland James   Memphis, April 4—61
Goddard, Jno   Pensaukee
Hale, Edgar W*   Atlanta, July 21—64
Haggett, B   Rome, Nov 8—61
Hamlan, L L   Rutland
Kanaly, John   Madison, Jan 10—62
Lyon, Abner   Rome, July 16—61
Lathrop, Elias   Aug 1—63
Leonard, Henry L   Marble Works
Leach, Hiram   St Louis, Aug 10—61
Lawe, Joseph, m   Oconto
Leake, Edward   Los Angeles, Cal
Murry, Wm*   Atlanta, July 21—64
McCollum, A   Vicksburg, Aug 10—63
Norton, C   May 8—62
Peuvee, Leonard   Natchez, Sept 9—63
Perry, Wm, f   Big Suamico
Pleasure, Octave+   Marietta, Sept 3—61
Plush, Davis+   Atlanta, Aug 20—64
Shappy, Louis   Vicksburg, Jan 22—64
Thomas, David*   Atlanta, July 21—64
Wilson, E H+   Chattanooga, Jan 13—64
Whitney, A   La Grange, Jan 4—64
Williams, John   Vicksburg, July 16—63
Whitcomb, W W   West Pensaukee

G

Capt Daniel Howell   Waukesha
Capt W W Botkius   Deer Lodge, W T
Capt W P Langworthy,   Princeton, Ill
Lt C M Webb   Grand Rapids
Lt H P Bird   Menomimee, Mich
Lt F H Putney   Waukesha
Oleson, Ole O, corp*   Nickajack, Ga, July 8—64
Arvidson, L P   Troy, Tenn, June 26—62
Baker, Girard*   Atlanta, July 21—64
Benson, Jacob   Lawrence, Kan, April 20—62
Bangs, S W   Collierville, Tenn, March 15—63
Crampton, Oscar   Lawrence, Kan, April 6—62
Carpenter, Wm M   Stevens Point
Ellington, Ira   Clifton, Dakota
Fritchie, George   Chattanooga, Dec 19—62
Fontain, Henry   Newbern N C, April 30—65
Gitguon, Ignace   Necedah
Green, Chas W   Wilton
Harkness, Francis   Vicksburg, Aug 0—63
Howell, D   Waukesha

King, John   Memphis, March 23—63
Newton, B B*   Atlanta, July 21—64
Oleson, Ole   Natchez, Oct 2—63
Olzan, Andrew   Nelsonville
Price, George   Menominee
Robarge, J*   Atlanta, Aug 12—64
Roberts, Eugene, janitor   Madison
Ruckstadt, Ole C   St Louis, Aug 10—63
Smith, Edward A   Vicksburg, July 4—63
Smith, E P   Madison, March 21—64
Shaughnessy, G   Kenesaw, Mt, June 25—61
Sullivan, Thomas   Savannah, Dec 30—64
Scott, Jacob   Emmetsburg, Ia
Scott, William   Emmetsburg, Ia
Simenson, Martin   Albon
Taylor, R M   Natchez, Oct 17—63
Thompson, Louis M   May 7—65
Waldo, O   Virginia, June 5—65
Whipple, E E   Racine
Webb, C H, a   Grand Rapids
Warren, C S, me   Grand Rapids

H

Capt C B Wheelock
Capt Ephraim Blakeslee   Ironton
Lt N A C Smith   Washington, D C
Lt Wm R Bouton
Lt C C Loritt
Lt James Lemon   Green Bay
Smith, H, corp   Suamico
Krouse, P, 2d corp, m   Big Suamico
Allen, C H   Newbero, N C, May 6—65
Adams, Alexander, f   Big Suamico
Brown, Daniel   Natchez, Oct 23—64
Beaulieu, H*   Chattahoochee, Ga, July 15—64
Brailliard, Peter,   Lawrence, Kan, May 2—62
Bersell, Thomas   Flintville
Bilderback, E J   Minneiska, Minn
Blakeslee, E.   Ironton
Brumley, V B, a   Green Bay
Buckmaster, William   La Crosse
Coates, John   Natchez, Jan 24—61
Campbell, Selon   Nashville, Feb 8—66
Codington, Levi, m   Big Suamico
Forsyth, Jerome   Leavenworth, March 30—62
Gunn, John   Marietta Sept 26—64
Gribner, Henry   July 23—63
Jepson, Joseph   St L uis, July 30—63
Keeler, H A*   Atlanta, July 25—64
Krause, Peter   Big Suamico
Lusha, Charles G   Big Suamico
Mitchell, James   Neaville Station, March 5—63
Mack, Leroy   Clintonville
Neilson, H N   Troy, Tenn, June 26—62
Ping, John*   Atlanta, July 21—64
Peterson, Peter   Sturgeon Bay
Rogers, Jacob   Nashville, April 20—65
Roe, James   Peshtigo
Staddaker, C*   Lovejoy, Ga, Sept 4—64
Sherwood, A H   Sturgeon Bay
Solway, O'e   Sturgeon Bay
Solway, Jno   Sturgeon Bay
Tonard, J
Watkins, S   Humboldt, Tenn, Aug 30—62
Wright, R M   Fish Creek
Warren, Julius   Sturgeon Bay

I

Capt H L Turner
Capt Van S Bennett   Buckbridge
Capt Francis Hoyt
Lt Eli McVey
Lt Jerome S Tinker
Lt L M Bresee
Lt Salma Rogers
Lt Irwin Gribbell
Dascey, G, corp   Andersonville, Sept 24—61
Baldwin, E*   Bakers Creek, Feb 4—64

Western Steam Tobacco Works.

ATTENTION, WISCONSIN SOLDIERS AND SAILORS.

B. LEIDERSDORF & CO.,

ARE MANUFACTURERS OF THE CELEBRATED

"OLD ABE"

FINE CUT CHEWING

AND

SMOKING TOBACCOS.

The most Popular and consequently the most Patriotic Brand of Tobaccos now before a Discriminating Public.

FOR SALE EVERYWHERE.

B. LEIDERSDORF.   **HENRY M. MENDAL.**

MILWAUKEE, WISCONSIN,

WISCONSIN SOLDIERS AND SAILORS REUNION ROSTER. 61

Bryant, Thomas, f	Ontario	Bennett, H H, ar	Kilbourn City	Johnson, Wm	Lawrence, Apr 23—62
Cook, Wm C	Savannah, Dec 16—61	Briggs, W S, m	Kilbourn City	Jackson, J L	Stevensville, May '93—61
Dean, Thomas*	Atlanta, July 21—61	Bryant, Geo E, f	Madison	Johnson, J B	Darlen
Dearnell, Elias	Humboldt, Aug 22—62	Cadman, W F	Stevens Point	Miller, Ernest	San Antonia, Sept 21—65
Dobson, Wm T	Quincy, Feb 21—62	Ford, Amos*	Atlanta, July 21—64	Madison, Neels	Wall Lake, Iowa
Dupee, Henry+	Marietta, Aug 16—61	Gaylord, Josiah W, musician	Elkhorn	Nichols, Lewis J, mf	
Degarmo, C	Rome, Sept 20—64	Grimmer, Fred E	Mauston	Nohr, Herman	Wayside
Dewitt, Eliphaz	Savannah, Jan 3— 65	Hay, John T, fifer	Rush River	Randolph, I A T	Lawrence, Apr 23—62
Eno, Edgar, f	Valley	Latham, Edward M, musician	Elkhorn	Rice, Albert	Edgerton
Foster, B F*	Atlanta, Aug 17—61	Letson, A H	Rush River	Ring, Jno	Janesville
Hays, Alexander	Madison, Mar 4—61	Marston, H, teamster	Kilbourn City	Ruger, Edward	Janesville
Henthorn, John	Marietta, Oct 6—61	Peterson, P	Post Lowenville	Smith, E S	Lawrence, May 5—62
Jordan, T S, f	West Lima	Robinson, Ed, f	Kilbourn City	Smith, Charles H	Janesville
Keepers, Lewis M+	Marietta, Aug 9—61	Stannard, W*	Atlanta, July 21—64	Terch, Jno	West Mitchell, Iowa
Lind, Ove*	Bakers Creek, Feb 4—61	Sexton, A J, m	Kilbourn City	Valentine, R B+	Waverly, Jan 13 - 64
Leavitt, Nathan	W Savannah, Feb 14—62	Strong, Wm E	Racine	Warren, N	Columbus, Aug 2 - 62
Murry, W H*	Bakers Cr, Feb 4—61	Strong, Wm E	Chicago, Ill	Wilbor, Frank M, f	Milton
Moon, L F	Atlanta, July 21—64	Sullivan J D	Chicago, Ill	Weaver, H M	Janesville
Marshall, G S	Bolivar, May 25—62			Wood, D A	Janesville
Mc Clug, Seth	Madison, Jan 28—63				
Moore J	Sun Prairie, April 4—61			**B**	
Munyon, John	Vicksburg, Apr 5- 61	**THIRTEENTH INFAN-**		Capt E E Woodman, ed	Baraboo
Murray, Jno A, f	Delta			Capt Jason W Hall	Winona, Minn
Murray, Lewis E, f	Olivet	**TRY.**		Lt Jas L Murray	
Ostrander, C	Bristol, Aug 16—63			Lt D H Cheney	
Osmer, William D	Maple Spring	(Three years. Organized October 17th, 1861.		Lt Geo C Brown	
Pettygrove, Neal, f	New Era, Neb	Original strength, 920, gained by recruits, etc. 961.		Lt Fred k C Buten	
Richards, George C	Vicksburg, July 3—63	Total, 1,931. Death loss, 181--killed in action, 3,		Burns, W M, 1st sergt	Stevenson, Oct 30—63
Sample, M*	Kenesaw, July 1—64	died of wounds, 2, of disease, 176. Other		Hulse, G W, corp*	Whitesburg, July 5—61
Sanford, David	Fayetteville, Mar 11—65	losses, 1197--missing 3, desertion, 71, transfer		Leaven, J E, corp	Jeffersonville, Nov 25—64
Thorpe, Abner	Cairo, Apr 16—61	6, muster out, Nov 1st 1864—797, discharged 320.		Alverson, John	Ft Henry, Jan 4—63
Topline, J T	Quincy, May 6—62	Strength at muster out, Nov. 24th, 1864, 530.		Auris, Adam	Lawrence, April 18—62
Thompson, C H	Marietta, Aug 20— 61	Campaigns in Mo., Kan., Ky., Tenn., Miss., Ala..		Butts, Charles M	Ft Henry, Nov 10—61
Tenny, David	Humboldt, Aug 1 - 62	La., and Texas.		Baker, Charles I	Ft Donelson, April 21—63
Tyler, A B	Vicksburg, July 12—63			Beecher, Joseph A	Donelson, July 3—63
Thurpe, John A	Bolivar			Crouc, John	Nashville, June 6—65
Wempner, A*	Rome, June 5—64	**REGIMENTAL ROSTER.**		Campbell, Wm	Victoria, Texas, Sept 5—65
West, A W+	Atlanta, July 21—64	Col Maurice Maloney		Carter, Charles A, m	Johnstown
Wempner, A C	Marietta, Aug 1—61	Col Wm P Lyon		Carter, C A	Janesville
Yakey, 8 D	St Louis, Sept 27—63	Col A H Kummel		Ferchingeo, J	Nashville, May 29—65
	Fredericksburg, May 17—65	Lt Col J F Chapman		Harvey, Nathan	Nashville, May 17—65
		Lt Col Thos O Bigney		Hulett, Milo	Aug 11—65
		Lt Col C S Noyes		Horn, J R	Wheatland, Neb
K		Maj 8 C Cobb	Janesville	Koucher, Anton	Charlesburg
Capt D R Sylvester	Boscobel	Adj Wm Ruger		Miller, Amos S	Fort Scott, March 16—62
Capt A N Chandler*	Pocotaligo, 8 C, Jan 14—65	Adj Wm M Scott	Chicago, Ill	Mills, Peter	Fort Henry, Dec 16—62
Capt Geo R Pyle		Adj A W Lounsbury		Miller, S C J	Whitewater
Lt Franklin Philbrick		Q M P Eyelesheimer		Richardson, Lyman A	Johnstown Centre
Lt Isaac Walker	Hickory Grove, Sept 17—63	Q M Ira B Dutton	Louisville, Ky	Stevens, D E	Milton
Lt G D Clark		Surg Jno Evans		Stearnes, G R	Milwaukee
Lt Geo Brown		Surg Schlen Cady		Vanderwerker, C H	Nashville, Nov 15— 67
Close, A F, sgt	Pearl River, Feb 27—64	A Serg E G Horton	Whitewater	Woodman, Edwin E, ed	Baraboo
Peckham, 8 C, corp	Vicksburg, Oct 12—63	A Sarg J T McClure			
Bonney, E A	Colliervile, Tenn, F, b 12—62	A Sarg C D Woodruff			
Blanchard, W W	Natchez, Sept 26—62	A Surg 8 L Lord		**C**	
Blandin, N	Jan 16—61	A Sarg C M Smith		Capt A H Kummel	
Brunemer, Jno T	Fennimore	Chap H C Titton		Capt Jno T Fish	
Clark, Caleb B*	Atlanta, July 22—64	Chap J 1 Foot		Lt D R Lamoreau	
Erickson, Andrew	Cairo, March 24—64			Lt H G Bardwell	
Ewing, J M	Beaufort, 8 C, April 25—65	**A**		Lt Wm Loucks	
Hooverson, Hover	Soldiers Grove			Lt H N Moulton	
Kast, James W	Madison, Oct 27—63	Capt Edw Ruger	Janesville	Boyce, L D F, corp	Sharon, March 26—64
Knudson, Halger	Dalton, Ga. Jan 27—65	Capt 8 C Cobb	Janesville	Ruch, Peter, corp	Victoria, Oct 18— 65
Killion, John	Nashville, Feb 17—65	Capt Jno Auld	Berlin	Brown, Wm J	Fort Riley, May 8—62
Larson, Lewis	Madison, March 31—65	Lt L T Nichols		Burton, Harlow	Lawrence, Kan, May 21—64
Munns, Henry R+	Atlanta, July 21—64	Lt M Bowerman		Bowman, E M	Fort Henry, Nov 16—62
Miller, L	Lumpkin.'s Mill, Dec 26—64	Lt O G Gibbs		Boss, Benj, f	Sharon
Munson, W	Rome, Ga, Sept 29—64	Lt Wm Ruger		Boyce, Volney	Sharon
Newcomb, Elon	Weston, Mo, March 26—62	Lt D B Wond	Janesville	Bradwell, Henry	Sharon
Palmer, Andrew	Vicksburg, June 28—63	Whatlesey, D H, sgt	Lawrence, Apr 20—62	Bush, William H	Sharon
Rounds, C W	Vicksburg, Aug 24—63	Bently, M L, corp	Leavenworth, Feb 11—62	Carpenter, J H	Ft Donelson. Aug 24—63
Sellerland, John G	Natchez, Aug 20—64	Ackerman, Milo	Lawrence, May 4—62	Carpenter, Joseph O	Nashville. Dec 9—63
Stevens, G A	Vicksburg, Aug 19—64	Butts, A T	Leavenworth, May 16—62	Craik, Wm M	Nashville, Nov 18—64
Thompson, C H	Humboldt, Tenn, Aug 1—62	Butler John T	Ft Henry, Nov 6 — 2	Clark, A S	Green Lake, Texas, Sept 16—65
Taylor, C L	Vicksburg, April 12—64	Babcock, Elorus W	Spart	Carey, C H	Leavenworth, Feb 2 —62
Vaughan, A	Jeff Barracks, Jan 22—65	Capelle, August	Scott	Cleary, Henry, f	Springville
Walker, S	Lawrence, Kan, May 24—62	Denening. A C	Janesville	Cline, C	Sharon
Wood, Isaiah	Vicksburg, April 22— 64	Goveael, Joseph	Ft Scott, Apr 30—62	Cole, Frank	Sharon
UNASSIGNED.		Gibbs, Jenson	Janesville	Dennis, Wm	Cairo, Oct 18—62
Bartels, Henry+	Atlanta, Sept 10—64	Hastings, Geo, f	Wachita, Iowa		

O. C. STEENBURG,

MANUFACTURER FIRST CLASS

White Pine Doors,

GLAZED SASH,

Window Blinds and Mouldings.

Will be pleased to Quote Customers, Dealers and Consumers in these goods, Inside Prices for

Best Quality of All Grades.

Office, Factory and Warehouse near Cor. McWilliams and Juneau Streets,

FOND DU LAC,   =   =   WISCONSIN.

WISCONSIN SOLDIERS AND SAILORS REUNION ROSTER.

Name	Location
Dougal, F H	Sharon
Eckerson, Willis D	Sharon
Hollister, H A	Sharon
Holt, Henry	Sharon
Johnson, Warren W	Sharon, July 18—62
Kammerer, John A	San Antonio, Oct 18—64
Knaub, W H	Sharon
Marreouss, J B*	Ft Donelson, Aug 22—63
McCannon, Hugh	Darien
Markel, William H	Sharon
Markel, Charles	Sharon
Moulton, Henry	Sharon
Merrill, Henry	Sharon
Mc Ginnis, Patrick	Baraboo
Priadle, F	Leavenworth, Feb 17—62
Rice, Seymour	Leavenworth, Feb 17—61
Renne, L	Ft Henry, Jan 23—63
Schroder, M	Ft Scott, Mar 6—62
Schermelhorn, B B	Leavenworth, Feb 16—62
Sebring, I D P	Paoli, Apr 27—62
Stupfel, Chas	Sharon
Totten, Lyman, f	Sharon
Woodworth, N	Nashville, Oct 30—64
Wilson, Chas A	Sharon

D

Name	Location
Capt E W Blake	
Capt C E Patchin	
Lt S A Couch	
Lt D Everest	
Lt N D Walters	
Lt D B Lovejoy	
Witham, John, corp	Janesville, Dec 4—61
Buntrock, E, corp	Watertown, Feb 16—64
Bubolz, Carl	Victoria, Texas, Sept 3—65
Condon, R C	Lawrence, Kan, May 23—62
Cotton, Owen	Magnolia, Feb 16—64
Christian, H	Huntsville, June 16—65
Earl, Isaac	New Madrid, June 26—63
Eastman, A	Nashville, Oct 30—63
Ellis, Joseph J	New Albany, Dec 3—63
Frung, Ed, f	Plymouth
Geevin, D	Columbus, Ky, Sept 29—62
Hall, Frank	Nashville, Nov 6—63
Hunt, Henry C	Delavan
McCormick, Edward	Janesville
Patchin, H	Claysville, Ala, June 19—61
Patchin, David	Nashville, Nov 10—61
Robinson, H R	Edgefield, Tenn, Dec 19—63
Roller, D	Green Lake, Texas, Aug 5—65
Strobel, Matthew	Victoria, Texas, Sept 26—65
Schuman, C	Columbus, Ky, Dec 7—62
Vanderburg, John	Lawrence, April 23—62
Williams, John H	Claysville, Ala, June 16—61
Witherell, Geo, f	Racine

E

Name	Location
Capt R H Hewitt	
Capt Lemuel Parker	
Capt Simeon Taylor	
Lt E F Warren	
Lt A C Smith	
Lt S S Rockwood	Whitewater
Lt E R Dunbar	
Babcock, Henry, sgt	Columbus, June 23—62
Abbey, James	Nashville, Mar 15—64
Adams, A W	Stevenson, Oct 15—61
Burnum, C E	Lawrence, June 4—62
Botsford, James M	Humbird
Chasse, A C	Kildon
Chase, A C	Pedee
Dunekleburg, John H, m	Versailles, Ill
Erickson Colben	Keokuk, Mar 30—65
Fellbaum, A	Nashville, May 19—65
Hafes, Charles	New Orleans, June 25—65
Hyde, E A	St Louis, July 28—65
Huyok, Edgar	Columbus, Aug 1—62
Horn, J A, m	Kasson

Name	Location
Johnson, Wm M	Huntsville, Feb 21—63
Kreiger, L	Aug 14—65
Lawless, Thomas	Nashville, Mar 1—61
Murphy, John	Columbus, Aug 1—62
McCreedy, G W	Paducah, Apr 15—63
Meighells, E J	St evenson, Oct 10—61
Orr H, George D	Jeffersonville, Nov 29—61
Patrick, J B	Monticello
Post, Isaac, f	Bloomingdale
Roll, Wm M	Nashville, June 8—65
Rockwood, B D, f	Janesville
Redner, John, f	Delton
Starkweather, E A	Ft Donelson, Mar 28—63
Sherman, Geo S	Nashville, Mar 15—61
Wagner, Peter	Nashville, June 9—65
Warren, E F, me	Waukesha

F

Name	Location
Capt F F Stevens	Janesville
Capt S S Hart	
Capt J W Briggs	
Lt N Crotzenburg,	Janesville
Lt Jas L Fowle	
Lt A L Ford	
Culver, C, corp	Huntsville, Aug 5—61
Anderson, H A	Clinton
Bliss, J H	Janesville
Butler, Wm	Edgerton
Burdick, Bradford	Edgerton
Cartwright, Alex, f	Unionville, Mich
Carter, G A	Janesville
Chamberlain, Nelson	Edgerton
Crotzenburg, N	Janesville
Collins, Patrick	Edgerton
Donlen, Sidney	Johnson Centre
Duily, James, f	Edgerton
Finney, Alvin T	Lawrence, May 10—62
Harrison, Henry, f	Depere
Krouse, Carl, f	Big Suamico
Nanwaluttle, L	Green Lake, Sept 24—65
Percy, Geo A	Nashville, Apr 13—61
Rolfe, R C	Ft Riley, May 18—62
Rice, E H	Lawrence, Apr 26—62
Shurrack, W B	Stevenson, May 23—61
Stevens, F F	Janesville
Shultz, August	West Mitchell, Iowa
Tiller, Hiram	Nashville, June 2—65
Tuttle, E H	Ft Riley, May 11—62

G

Name	Location
Capt T O Biguey	
Capt A N Randall	
Capt Wm A Kallaus	Delavan
Lt H M Balls	
Lt C R Matson	
Lt K W Taylor	
Lt S C Wagoner	
Anderson, Lars C	St Louis, May 6—65
Ballis, Luther	Claysville, Ala, June 16—64
Benjamin, Ole	Cairo, July 15—65
Benjamin, Jason D	Vicksburg, March 26—65
Balls, Abraham Day	Red Bluff, Cal
Cass, Geo W	Madison, Aug 27—65
Decker, Isaac	Vicksburg—65
Erickson, Truels	Ft Donelson, May 11—65
Fuller, Wm A	Vicksburg, April 1—65
Gauseil, Peter	Janesville, Dec 22—61
Gould, Lemuel	Cahawba, Ala Feb 22—65
Johnson, A	Fort Donelson, May 2—63
Kinney, C W	Lawrence, Kan, April 25—62
Moran, James	Ft Riley, May 12—62
Minor, W S	Ft Henry, Nov 25—62
Martin, John V*	Madison, Feb 17—65
Mulle, M E	St Louis, April 27—65
Martin, Joseph W	Victoria, Sept 13—65
Marsh, C H	Ft Atkinson
Nelson, Lars P	Huntsville, Nov 21—64
Pomeroy, J M	Lawrence, Kan, May 6—62

Name	Location
Pryor, Geo S	Nashville, Feb 28—61
Penn, John	Nashville, June 4—66
Purdy, John F	Cairo, July 4—65
Rhodes, James D	Paducah, April 17—63
Rossiter, Edmund S	Orfordville
Shaffner, Peter	St Louis, May 24—65
Shaffer, Alex, f	Janesville
Shurrum, Geo D	Milwaukee
Taylor, R B	Paducah, April 17—63
Wenright, G	Ft Donelson, Aug 17—63

H

Name	Location
Capt Jos L Pratt	
Capt C N Noyes	
Capt E J Pratt	
Capt G H Beckwith	
Lt Robt Glover	
Lt A J Smith	
Lt C E Graham	
Lt Ole Jacobson	
Markey, Wm, sgt	Moscow July 1—62
Munning, G N, sgt	Columbus, Aug 19—62
Patterson, J, sgt	Fort Donelson, June 28—63
Dobie, John C, corp	Columbus, Aug 23—62
Ammon, Joo	Fort Atkinson
Burnham, J M, f	Hebron
Bullock, Ferdinand	Madison, Jan 14—64
Codding, Geo, f	Whitewater
Dwight, Richard, m	Cohoes, N Y
Horton, M D	Huntsville, Oct 14—64
Hanson, Halver	Victoria, Oct 8—65
Hall, W H, f	Eagle
Hall, W H	Troy Centre
Herrington, Charles L	Whitewater
Haley, Andrew	Granville Centre
Kestleson, Jesse	Fort Donelson, June 10—62
Kliiske, C F, f	Hebron
McDonald, Adam	Leavenworth, Mar 2—62
McCarthy, M L	Palmyra
McDonald, Geo W	Troy Mills, Iowa
Marsden, William	Janesville
Marston, Jno	Fall River
Samuelson, Ole	Ft Henry, Oct 31—62
Palmer, Laman	Huntsville, Jan 14—65
Porter, Hezekiah, f	Ft Atkinson
Rolof, Wm	Nashville, Aug 8—65
Salsbury, Albert	Whitewater
Shields, Louis	Lawrence, Apr 28—62
Smith, E H	Edgerton
Seely, David	Lawrence, June 26—62
Wilds, Geo W	Victoria, Oct 1—65
Weed, Nathaniel	Mapleton, Minn

I

Name	Location
Capt J H Lauderdale	
Capt N H Kingman	
Capt Geo H Cameron	Nov 11—65
Lt W A Kullaus	Delavan
Lt I B Dutton	Louisville, Ky
Lt A Carroll	
Lt H H Knox	
Niblick, John, corp	Ft Donelson, Aug 1—63
Baldwin, R K	Huntsville, Oct 13—64
Babcock, H, f	Little Prairie
Bull, John	Mullison
Battrell, R	Eagle
Chipman, S D	Smithland, Ky, Nov 5—62
Chatfield, D, f	Little Prairie
Clemons, Harvey	Madison, Dec 16—64
Clemons, John	Huntsville, Oct 13—64
Christianson, O	Green Lake Texas, July 27—65
Christopherson, E	San Antonio, Oct 10—65
Dane, David	Nov 19—65
Dibble, Virgil M	Columbus, Ky, Aug 31—62
Edmundson, S D	Green Lake, Tex, Sept 6—65
Finch, L D	Huntsville, March 29—65
Hamilton, G	Ft Donelson, July 11—63

1350.      1880.

THE

INSURANCE COMPANY OF NEW YORK.

W. A BREWER, Jr., President.

Assets,	$5,500,000.00,
Surplus,	$942,000.00.

Reasons Why I Insure in the Washington Life:

1.—*Because*, Its investments are the very best that can be obtained;—none of them are even questionable.
2.—*Because*, During all the recent financial depression, it continued to increase its assets and surplus.
3.—*Because*, Ff its unusually large surplus.
4.—*Because*, Whatever advantages may be claimed under the New York State law of 1879, in favor of policy holders, they have in the Washington the additional protection of its non-forfeiting dividends. It is the only company that allows its dividends to hold its policies in force when premium is unpaid.
5.—*Because*, Its new form of policy expresses a very liberal contract in plain, concise language, contains fewer restrictions than any other policy, and leaves no hooks on which to hang legal quibbles.

Secure a Policy in the Washington Life
AT ONCE WHILE YOU ARE IN GOOD HEALTH.

A. H. HAWES,	DR. S. L. FULLER,
State Agent for Wisconsin,	General Agent for Wisconsin and Michigan,
Milwaukee, Wisconsin.	Detroit, Michigan.

WISCONSIN SOLDIERS AND SAILORS REUNION ROSTER. 65

Hodkis, Jerd	Adams	losses, 540—missing, 13, desertions, 97, transfers,		St John, F R, mc		Fond du Lac
Hooper, John	Madison, March 30—64	23, discharges, 467. Strength at muster out		St John, F		Fond du Lac
Jaquith, Ambrose	Madison, Feb 18—64	Oct. 9th,1865, 1355. Campaigns in Tenn., Missis-		Spence, James, m		Fond du Lac
James, Wm, f	Little Prairie	sippi, Louisiana, Arkansas, Missouri, Ala. Ga.		Steady, F, me		Fond du Lac
Kingman, T R	Stevenson, Nov 30—64			Titus, Wm, f		Eden
Mills, John V	Madison, March 17—64	**REGIMENTAL ROSTER.**		Titus, George		Campbellsport
Murdock, Alex	East Troy			Titus, J B		Farley, Minn
McCart, A	Columbus, Ky, July 6—62	Col D E Wood	Fond du Lac, June 14—62	White, S S		Nashville, Sept 24—64
McMaster, Charles H	Victoria, Sept 6—65	Col Jno Hancock	Oshkosh	Wederman, Jacob*		Vicksburg, May 19—63
Olds, W, f	Little Prairie	Col L M Ward	Benton Harbor, Mich	Wiley, W		Ripon
Pitcher, T F	Ft Donelson, June 3—63	Lt Col I E Messmore	Grand Rapids, Mich	Warner, Jno		Ripon
Parrish B	Millard	Lt Col Jas M Polleys	La Crosse	Wilcox, Orin		Ripon
Roper, Ernest	Madison, Jan 14- 65	Lt Col E F Ferris	Ogden, U tah	Wilcox, W W, f		Omro
Salisbury, S	Quincy, July 4—65	Maj Asa Worden	Oshkosh	Wilcox, Wm, f		Fond du Lac
Waters, J	Brownsboro, Ala, Nov 5—61	Maj Wm J Henry		Warner, John, m		Fond du Lac
Wilkins, Alden	Huntsville, March 3—65	Adj Wm H Landor				
		Adj B E Brower				
	K	Adj Van Epps Young	Grand Rapids, Mich		**B**	
		Adj Jno M Reed	Kewaunee			
Capt Pliny Norcross. a	Janesville	Q M J T Conklin	London, Ont	Capt Asa Worden		Oshkosh
Capt Jno H Wemple		Q M Newton Clark		Capt S B Carpenter		Plover
Capt U S Hollister, m	St Paul, Minn	Surg Wm H Walker	Fond du Lac	Lt W F Eldridge		Yankton, D T
Capt G W Steele,	Fertile	Surg Harmon Benson		Lt Royal L Potter		
Lt W P Clark	Milton	Lt Francis McGuire		Lt F T Wilmot		
Lt A D Burdick. pa	Milton	A Surg D LaCount	Chilton	Lt A B Chambers		Aug 28—65
Lt H C Curtis		A Surg H E Zielley	Chilton	Chambers, A B, sgt		Weyauwega, Aug 25—65
Sweet, J sgt	Ft Donelson, Apr 26—63	A Surg G E Talbert		Drake, C, sgt+		St,Louis, Apr 20—62
Savage, John A, corp	Cookville, Nov 17—63	A Surg H T Fowler		Hill, Phelps E, corp*		Corinth, Oct 3 62
Fuller, S, corp	Ft Atkinson, May 17—64	A Surg Wm Wiley	Fond du Lac	Alston, M		Andersonville, Nov 8—64
Norcross, F, corp	Nashville, May 17—65	A Surg E C Strangeland		Boyden, F H		Sherman, D T
Burdict, A Delos, m	Milwaukee	Chaplain Geo D Engle		Brummer, A		Vicksburg, Oct 22—63
Burdict, A DeLone. pa	Milton	H F Newland, prin mus Cave Spring, Oct 31—64		Beach, Jas D		Plover
Clark, Frank, m	Naragansett Pier, R 1	Stephen Benedict, drum major	Oshkosh	Baker, C G		Montgomery, Aug 19—65
Colt, S T, f	Milton			Beach, Jno F		Plover
Clark, W P, d	Milton			Beadleston, J J +		Corinth, Dec 10—62
Carnes, Jed, f	Hebron	**A**		Deadleston, John		Waupaca
Church, Jacob	Fertile			Barker, Wm H		Wausau
Deering, N W	Osceola			Blair, Robt		Amherst Junction
Early, U	Nashville, May 6—65	Capt L M Ward	Benton Harbor, Mich	Benedict, Wm H		Omaha, Neb
Flint, David B	Huntsville, Aug 31—64	Capt C L Kimball		Bruce, W		La Crosse
Hencock, James O	Nashville, June 17—65	Capt John V Frost		Crysler, James H		Rome, Sept 9—64
Hollister, C S, m	St Paul	Lt W H Durand	Ogden, Utah	Cornell, Jas		Dalw
Keeter, Wm	Lawrence, Ap 18—62	Lt Geo C Denniston	Fond du Lac	Chambers, J		Marietta, Sept 20—74
Morrison, B H	Madison, May 5—64	Hendricks, J, sgt*	Campbellsport	Clark, Jno		Waupaca
Maxon, B F	Tustin City, Cal	Witters, B F, sgt	Vicksburg, May 12—62	Daniels, D W		Brownsville, Oct 3—64
Neym, John	Leavenworth, Mar 21—62	Kings, Joseph, corp*	Vicksburg, M-y 22—63	Denny, Jackson		Weyauwega
Norton, E H	Wetherfield, Sept 22—63	Krake, Nelson, corp*	Vicksburg, May 22—63	Deland, Stephen*		Vicksburg, May 22—63
Norcross, P, a	Janesville	Abbey, Charles*	Vicksburg, May 22—63	Dewey, Horace Jr		Amherst Junction
Noyes, Sylvester+	Leavenworth, June 30—62	Badger, Conrad	Memphis, Oct 2—63	Dwinell, A B		Stevens Point
Plantz, John	Lawrence, Apr 29—62	Baumgarden, J	Montgomery Aug, 9- 65	Eastwood, John*		Shiloh, Ap 7—62
Robinson, C B	Nashville, Sept 21- 64	Bradford, A A, f	. Sheboygan Falls	Everling, Jno		Wausau
Stannard, M B	Ft Donelson, Mar 20—63	Bassett, E B	Milwaukee	Eldridge, Wm, bk		Yankton D T
Sharda, A F	Nashville, Nov 16—64	Basset, E B	Loyal	Flte, John R		Memphis, Feb 15—65
Smith, Lewis	Madison	Connish, A	Lake Providence, March 2—62	Fairbanks, Chas		Weyhauwega
Steele, Geo W	Fertile	Coon, Jno D	Fond du Lac	Fife, Amos		New Orleans, Mar 27—65
Scott, W M, m	Chicago, Ill	Coon, Jno, mf	Fond du Lac	Fortner, Isaac H		New Orleans, Mar 18—65
Swan, John, p m	Juda	Cornish, Adin	Hortonville	Glorie, B		Jeffersonville, Dec 10—64
Wisegar, Geo W, f	Clinton	Chapin, James, t	Fond du Lac	Gillson, S H		Weyauwega
Wyse, W A, a	Reedsburg	Carste, Charles, m	Fond du Lac	Herrington, H		Newburg, June 28—2
		Durand, P	Campbellsport	Hardy, Chas M		Weyauwega
UNASSIGNED.		Durand, H W, m	Fond du Lac	Hearn, Wm		Vicksburg, Jan 3—64
Balls, Abraham D, f	Red Bluff, Cal	Davis, Clark, e	Fond du Lac	Healey, Mike		Weyauwega
Curry, E	Black Earth	Fiel, Michael	New Orleans, Mar 33—65	Harkness, H*		Vicksburg, May 22—63
Cotton, H T	Palmyra	Hall, John, f	Fond du Lac	Hearne, Wm		Waupaca
Clemens, S B	Janesville	Kider, F J	Oxford, Neb	Hogle, Washington		Berlin
Forester, Robt	Delavan	Laduke, L P	Fond du Lac, Apr 1—65	Jones, Wm D		Atlanta July 24—64
Kinlaus, W A, I	Delavan	Lafavre, D V	Rome, Ga, Nov 30—61	King, Wm H		Chicago, Ill
Loomer, Chas E	Tomah	Leonard, O S	Fond du Lac	Lichterman, Theodore		Kewaunee
Miner, R S	Delavan	Morgan, T +	Pittsburg, Landing, Apr 7 - 62	Lilley, A E		Madison, March 18—64
Morris, A B, f	Whitewater	Older, Charles	Vicksburg, Feb 15—65	Lamere, Frances H		Plover
Webster, E A	Neillsville	Oleson, J A, f	Fond du Lac	Messinger, Westly		Weyauwega
Vaughn, William. f	Kendall	Pomerene, Robert	West Bloomfield	Mason, F	Pittsburg Landing, May 21—62	
		Powers, W H	Oshkosh	Mack, Holmes		Weyauwega
		Rand, M W	St Louis, May 21—62	Myers, Theo		Plover
FOURTEENTH INFAN-		Reed, Otis L	St Louis, June 1—63	Mason, Francis		Weyauwega
TRY.		Ryarson, M	June 21—62	Marshall, Francis		Weyauwega
Three years. Organized Jan. 30th, 1862.		Russell, W S, m	Oakfield	McEwen, Lorenzo		Waupaca
Original strength, 970; gain by recruits, etc.,		Spafford, E D	Pittsburg Landing, Apr 6—62	McCroplin, Tom		Waupaca
1212. Total, 2182. Death loss, 267—killed in action.		Simpson, Wm A	Vicksburg, June 29—63	Misper, Henry G		Harlan, Ia
61, died of wounds, 34, of disease, 192. Other		Summers, John*	Vicksburg, May 22—63	Noll, Joo		Weyauwega
				Noll, Jno, e		Fond du Lac

GENERAL INSURANCE AGENCY

P. C. HALE,

13 MITCHELL BUILDING,
MILWAUKEE, :: WISCONSIN.

Insurance Company of North America, Philadelphia.

LONDON ASSURANCE CORPORATION, LONDON.

Union Insurance Company, Philadelphia.

COMMONWEALTH INSURANCE COMPANY, Boston.

AMERICAN FIRE INSURANCE COMPANY, NEW YORK.

Citizens' Insurance Company, New York.

NATIONAL FIRE INSURANCE COMPANY, NEW YORK.

HOWARD INSURANCE CO., N. Y.

DETROIT F. & M. INSURANCE COMPANY, DETROIT.

MERCANTILE INSURANCE COMPANY, CLEVELAND.

WISCONSIN SOLDIERS AND SAILORS REUNION ROSTER.

Name	Location/Date	Name	Location/Date
Otis, John*	Vicksburg, May 22—63	Reed, Royal W	Omro
Otis, Jno	Weyauwega	Stone, J W	Pittsburg Landing, May 19—62
Pelton, Jno C	Weyauwega	Statler, Jas	Fairbault, Minn
Quimby, C	Lovejoy, Sept 3—64	Statler, S	Omro, Feb 26—65
Quimby, Chas	Weyauwega	Statler, Jas L	Fairbault, Minn
Quimby, Moses	Weyauwega	Stevens, Julius	Omro
Rur, Hiram	Stevens Point	Stemiller, Frederick	Scott
Robinson, Jno	Weyauwega	Taylor, Truman	Omro
Stauby, G	St Louis' May 4—62	Tasquin, John B	Mobile, Sept 1—63
Sweet, W A, c	La Crosse	Worden, W J	Chattanooga, June 22—64
Starks, Chas	Atlanta, Oct 22—64	White, Wm	Oshkosh
Smith, Albert	Weyauwega	White, John B	Cairo, May 20—64
Starks, Chas	Weyauwega	West, Chas	Minneapolis, Minn
Swan, Jno W	Badger	Winchester, S	Marietta, Sept 22—61
Smith, M M	Jeff Barracks, Aug 2?—62	Winchester, Perry	Omro
Smith, G L	Jackson, Jan 16—63	Wanio, John A	Jefferson Barracks, June 23—62
Trunir, D N	Montgomery, Aug 14—63		
Teal, Peter	Weyauwega	**D**	
Thompson, J A*	Corinth, Oct 3—64		
Teal, Geo W	Weyauwega	Capt J W Polleys	La Crosse
Vincent, Edw	Weyauwega	Capt David Law	La Crosse
Warner, B C	Lind	Capt S A Harrison	
Worden, W H	Amherst Junction	Capt C P Shepherd	Worthington, Minn
Whittaker, E L	St Louis, May 9—62	Lt Geo Staley	
Wood, S M	Manawa	Lt A M Watson	La Crosse
Wilson, John	Huntsville, July 8—64	Lt Edw Elkins	
Wilson, G	Madison, Apr 11—64	Lt Tim O'Brien	La Crosse
Waite, Geo S	Weyauwega	Lt H Runge	
Whitney, S	Wanpaca	S A Harrison	La Crosse
Young, Louis	Almond	Ed Howard	La Crosse
		E Hollgren	La Crosse
C		J Hainer	La Crosse
		Woodcock	L Crosse
Capt W W Wilcox	Omro	A M Watson	La Crosse
Capt A S Childs,	Beaver Dam	H K Vincent	La Crosse
Lt Colin Miller*	Vicksburg, May 23—63	Wm Tucker	La Crosse
Lt M L Drake		Wm Taylor	La Crosse
Lt Alfred Corfee	New London	G Stalcer	La Crosse
Lt P N Cro-s	Lodi, D T	A Dunham	La Crosse
Wells, J P, sgt*	Vicksburg, May 22—63	A Brooks	La Crosse
Putnam, R, corp*	Corinth, Oct 3—62	J Evans	La Crosse
Alley, J+	Pittsburg Landing, Ap 9—69	B Brawer	La Crosse
Anderson, Wm M+	Corinth, Nov 21—64	J Foster	La Crosse
Bicknell, L	Waukau	S Childers	La Crosse
Boynton, O L+	New Orleans, Ap 9—65	D Fern	La Crosse
Bishop, Jas	Waukau	T Carrelton	La Crosse
Barron, Robert	Corinth, Oct 18—62	J Flush	La Crosse
Benedict, Stephen	Oshkosh	J Carrol	La Crosse
Bicknell, Lansing	Waukau	E Glen	La Crosse
Carter, James	Omro	E F Doane	La Crosse
Clark, G S*	Corinth, Oct 3—62	Sam Guertin	La Crosse
Cross, P N	Lodi, Dakota Territory	Wm Dolan	La Crosse
Campbell, Thos J	Omro	D Davis	La Crosse
Ditty, Wm	Worthington, Minn	G Strobridge	La Crosse
Franklin, Jas	Omro	J Snodgrass	La Crosse
Galleger, P	Omro	C Shefard	La Crosse
Howe, Daniel	Keokuk, Dec 2—63	G Orthans	La Crosse
Hebron, Pat	Omro	R E Osborne	La Crosse
Harling, A	Montgomery, July 15—65	T O'Brien	La Crosse
Hunter, Robert	Omro	S H Moody	La Crosse
Harter, David M	Hartford	S Lambert	La Crosse
Judson, Lucius	St Louis, Mar 12—63	C Jenks	La Crosse
Johnson, John	Omro	L Harrison	La Crosse
Johnson, Chas		Allen, O P	Pittsburg Landing, May 22—63
Miller, Ira P	Pittsburg Landing, May 2—62	Atkinson, W	La Crosse
Miller, Alonzo	Utica	Allen, G	La Crosse
Maxon, Geo	Yankton, D T	Barkley, W	La Crosse
Maxon, D S		Collins, Alfred*	Vicksburg, May 22—63
Marston, S	Jefferson Barracks, May 15—62	Cram, C L	Pittsburg Landing, June 7—62
McMahon, Jno	Weyauwega	Crawford, Henry	Memphis, Aug 25—64
Melcher, Lewis, f	Charles City, Iowa	Calkins, G W	Baldwin
Noyes, Geo H+	Memphis, June 16—63	Crippen, Amos, corp	New Orleans, March 21—65
O'Conner, M	Pittsburg Landing, June 6—62	Duval, Wm*	Lovejoy, Sept 3—64
Porter, Elry+	Corinth, Oct 16—62	Farrand, D E	Gary, Dakota
Pierce, Jeremiah, f	Omro	Glen, John B*	Shiloh, April 7—62
Ridout, E	Jefferson Barracks, June 20—62	Gerymas, Tella	Mound City, Sept 30—64
Romain, B P	Loyal	Glenn, Cyrus H	St Louis, May 16—62
Romain, E W	Neillsville	Hamlin, H	New London
Reed, Ed	Omro	Hans, J	La Crosse
Reed, Rieb, Jr	Omro	Hill, G	La Crosse
Jackson, C	Apr 4—65		
Koch, F W C*	Vicksburg, May 22—63		
Lowell, M	Lake Providence, May 7—63		
Lee, Robt	Fond du Lac		
Mason, Thomas*	Corinth, Oct 3—62		
McPherson, N	Memphis, Jan 11—63		
Mason, S	Galesville, July 31—61		
O'Halloron, Pat	Freeport, Ill		
O'Brien, Timothy	La Crosse		
Pease, S	Memphis, July 12—64		
Sprague, C A	Pittsburg Landing, June 7—62		
Swineson, C	May 27—64		
Shirley, H L	Nov 21—64		
Taylor, Wm	La Crosse		
Tucker, John E*	Corinth, Oct 3—62		
Thomas, R J	Chattanooga, Nov—64		
Washburne, G W	Vicksburg, June 3—64		
Woodhouse, H B	Evansville		

E

Name	Location/Date
Capt W J Henry	
Capt Jos Smith	
Lt Don A Shove	Manitowoc
Lt B F Goodwin	
Lt W J Ramsdell	
Lt F E Engle	
Austin, E B+	Pittsburg Landing, Apr 16—62
Badett, H	Forestville
Brieger, Nie	Kewaunee
Bregger, Nick	Kewaunee
Collius, C E	Alexandria, May 20—64
Clark, W M	Pittsburg Landing, June 6—62
Day, B D, f	Larrabee
Dill, Orsemus	Glenmore
Dunn, H	La Crosse
Dill, Myron*	Vicksburg, May 22—63
Eldridge, William, b k	Yankton, D T
Eveland, A C	Ahnapee
Kidder, James A	Pittsburg Landing, Apr 30—62
Eveland, D S	Lake City, Minn
Eveland, Andras	Minneapolis, Minn
Fay, Mark G	Memphis, Feb 3—63
Fagg, Wm	Ahnapee
Fuetson, F	Clay Banks
Grogan, F	Pittsburg Landing, Apr 25—62
Green, Michael	Pittsburg Landing, June 7—62
Hallum, H	Ahnapee
Hier, F	Ahnapee
Johnson, H	Fond du Lac
Killiher, John	Ryan
Lovel, John	Ahnapee
Lee, Jacob	Fond du Lac
Monroe, Geo A*	Vicksburg, June 21—63
Murphy, Jas	Memphis, July 14—63
McDonald, M	Ahnapee
Moore, Joseph	Kewaunee
McAllister, C	Keokuk, Oct 3—63
Perry, Wm	Ahnapee
Perry, Rich	Forestville
Perry, Matt	Forestville
Rouse, O G	Ahnapee
Sweet, Reeder	Stevensville
Sweet Wm	Fond du Lac
Sabine, M	Pittsburg Landing, Apr 25—62
Schmilling,	Ahnapee
Stone, S A	Twin Rivers
Stoneman, Wm	New Albany, Sept 1—64
Stacier, Peter	Manitowoc
Tufts, Albert	Clay Banks
Tufts, Albert	Horns Pier
Thayer, W P	Kewaunee, Aug 17—63
Tyler, J M	Fond du Lac
Tyler, C M	Fond du Lac
Vanduzer, Morris*	Corinth, Oct 3—63
Whitcomb, M	Mill Creek, June 3—64
Whitcomb, Wm	St Louis, May 4—62
Wheeler, W C	Oshkosh
Whitcomb, Joel	Manitowoc
Williams, Jacob	Manitowoc

THE SENTINEL COMPANY

OF MILWAUKEE,

PUBLISHES FOUR EDITIONS.

Daily, Tri-Weekly, Weekly and Sunday.

Daily by Mail, per Year — — $11.00.
Tri-Weekly by Mail, per Year — — 5.50.
Weekly by Mail per Year — — 1.00.
Sunday, by Mail, per Year — — 2.00.

JOB DEPARTMENT.

THE JOB DEPARTMENT OF THE SENTINEL COMPANY TURNS OUT THE

FINEST OF WORK IN ALL LINES.

BINDERY.

THE SENTINEL COMPANY HAS NO SUPERIOR IN THE EXCELLENCE OF ITS

BLANK BOOK AND MISCELLANEOUS WORK.

WISCONSIN SOLDIERS AND SAILORS REUNION ROSTER.

F

Name	Location	Date
Capt J J Lawton	Depere	
Capt Samuel Harrison †	Corinth, Oct 26—62	
Capt Delos A Ward	Fond du Lac	
Capt Jno P Ryan	Milwaukee	
Lt Geo W Bowers		
Lt Jas Camm	Ft Howard	
Lt O F Cooley	Depere	
Lt Chas Beattie	Ft Howard	
Lt Reuben Wheeler	Depere	
Lt Jas K Newton	Oberlin, O	
McFarland, J C, 1st sgt †	Mlks Bend, June 18—63	
Cady, H J, corp	Millikins Bend, July 1—63	
Cavill, Wm, corp	Jeff Barracks, June 21—63	
Antonine, Abram	Vicksburg, June 11—64	
Balduck, Louis, 1	Red River	
Bergman, G*	Vicksburg, May 22—63	
Brighton, Rich	Depere	
Baird, T	Big Shanty, Ga., June 16—64	
Casey, M	Depere	
Coord, O T	Depere	
Camm, James	Ft Howard	
Cramer, Jas T	Montgomery, July 27—65	
Camuer, M B	Ft Howard	
Covil, R	Depere	
Danforth, C	St Charles, Ark, Aug 24—64	
Dallard, Jno	Glenmore	
Fields, Isaac	Neillsville	
Foster, H, f	Menomonee Falls	
Garrow, Isaac	Millikens Bend, June 5—63	
Gibson, Byron	Taycheedah	
Jonrow, Edw	Stevens Point	
King, Simon*	Atlanta, July 22—64	
LaCoutal, A	Atlanta, Oct 14—64	
LeDuc	Fond du Lac	
Manger, John L*	Vicksburg, June 18—63	
Morrison, Samuel*	Corinth, Oct 3—62	
Michelis, Chas	Depere	
Murphy, D A F	Glenmore	
Morrison, S E	Apr 30—62	
Mayrel, Peter	Depere	
McNeal, Thos	New Albany, May 9—64	
Nisham, James	Keokuk, Feb 9—63	
O'Neal, Thos	Suamico	
Putnam, John D	Shiloh, Apr 7—62	
Peep, John	Depere	
Ryan, Patrick	Milwaukee	
Rochwood D F	Jeff Barracks, Jan 9—63	
Ryan, Thos	Milwaukee	
Ryan, Jno P	Milwaukee	
Steel, Thos	Depere	
Silver, Frank	Glenmore	
Stewart, Thos	Fond du Lac	
Steady, F	Fond du Lac	
Tidd, A	Keokuk, Sept 30—62	
Thetro, Hamilton	Fond du Lac	
Thomas, T	Brownsville, Ark, Oct 4—64	
Tariff, Thos	Depere	
Talcott, Jesse	Suamico	
Vertz, A	Hamburg, Tenn, July 26—63	
Vincents, Chas	Depere	
Vieaw, A J	Pulaski, Tenn, July 26—62	
Wright, Wm J	Depere	
Westcott, Matthew	Stevens Point	
Woodward, Geo	Depere	
Westcott, Henry	West Depere	
Zoehler, Alvis	Suamico	

G

Capt F H Magdeburg	Milwaukee
Capt C R Potter	Potters Mills
Capt M S Lake	
Lt Jas La Count	Denver, Col
Lt Edw J Kennedy	Merrillan
Lt Schuyler Powell	Brillion
Potter, L C, corp †	Corinth, Oct 6—62
Anthony, T	Montgomery, June 26—65
Auhart, J H	Duvals Bluff, Sept 5—64
Barker, Lucius*	Shiloh, Apr 7–62
Bump, Samuel*	Shiloh, Apr 7—62
Berge, A C*	Corinth, Oct 3–62
Batcheldor, C R +	Holly Springs, Nov 31—62
Baker, John	Columbus, Jan 20—63
Burton, C	Pulaski, Tenn Aug 18—63
Carney, Patric* *	Corinth, Oct 3—62
Crawford, Andrew	Chilton
Crawford, Lucius	Hilbert
Chicks, James	Corinth, Nov 6—62
Delane, Hatzil*	Corinth, Oct 3—62
Dascom, Ed	Brillion
Dixon, John	Hilbert
Doxtater, Paul	Cairo, May 3—64
Duchow, Albert	Potters Mills
Gutt, Ulrich	Keokuk, Nov 19—64
Gassink, G W	June 28 65
Herring, John	Memphis, Feb 25 65
Knudson, Iver	Keokuk, July 30—62
Lake, B	St Louis, May 12 62
Lalton, W	Fond du Lac, July 23—64
Moser, John*	Shiloh, Apr 7—62
Mosee, Michael	Kassou
Morgan, Wm	Wausau
McCorkle, J A	Newburg, May 28—63
McCalvy, —	Loyal
McCalvey, B	Neillsville
Newton, E*	Shiloh, Apr 7—62
O'Brien, Edw	Concord
Owen, K*	Spanish Ft, Apr 8—65
Oliver, John	Fond du Lac
O'Brien, Henry	Concord
Packard, J *	Pittsburg Landing, May 20—62
Packard, Henry	Niles
Powell, Schuyler	Brillion
Peters, C	New Orleans, Mar 15—65
Pratt, Stephen G	Colby
Ransom, S	Neillsville
Raub, L*	Corinth, Oct 3—62
Ransom, S	Christee
Rasmussen, Fritz	Denmark
Scott, A	Alexandria, May 16—66
Stanton, Cato	Chilton
Siegrist Henry	Colby
Sherman, Elias	Huntsville, Dec 15—64
Siscoe, E, 1	Mukwonago
Tolleyson, Knud*	Vicksburg, May 22 63
Terry, A O	Chilton
Tenluer, Frank, ar	Berlin
Turner, A L*	Atlanta, Aug 13—64
Vine, T R	Greenland
Whalen, Abel	Neillsville
Westcott, G P	Hilbert
Yule, Harvey	Dorchester

H

Capt Wm D Ghostin	
Capt C M G Mansfield	Greenbush
Capt Jno H Kennealy	Fond du Lac
Lt V E Young	Grand Rapids, Mich
Lt J F Rosser	Colby
Lt Chas W Gibson	Forest
Lt Wm Gardner	
Lt M K Barnes	Sheboygan, July 12—63
Lt E N Moore	Irving
Lt Wm A Bratt	Loyal
Gibson, W B, corp	Pittsburg Landing, June 29—62
Burch, P C	Pittsburg Landing, June 15—62
Burrows, J M	Pittsburg Landing, June 21—62
Butler, John	May 4—62
Boomhouer, B	Plymouth, Feb 10—64
Bleyer, J	Duval's Bluff, Ark, Sept 15—64
Beram, Frank	Cairo, Jan 30—65
Carig, Geo W*	Vicksburg, May 22—63
Crownhart, N C	Pittsburg Landing, June 20—62
Cleveland, A	Pittsburg Landing, June 20—62
Cornier, C	New Orleans, March 11—65
Eastwood, I G*	Corinth, Oct 3—63
Gilson, Edward	St Cloud
Garrow, Peter †	Memphis, Sept 5—65
Gates, Albert	Berlin
Gibson C W	Forest
Galligen, S C	Armstrong Corners
Hannnon, D D †	May 26—62
Hinman, Philo	Brookville
Hodge, Joshua	St Louis, May 31 62
Howe, Geo W	Marietta, Ga, Sept 17 64
Keuhn, Ludwig	Montgomery, Aug 12 65
Lewis, J P	Lake Providence, March 2 63
Lockwood, C A	Menomonee
Ledingwell, M J	St Louis, July 25—64
Mansfield, E M G	Greenbush
Nuns, Frank	Nashville, Dec 16 64
Owens, F, Jr	Memphis, Aug 10 63
Prosser, J S, m	Oakfield
Peeler, Henry*	Shiloh, April 7 62
Prosser, Jas	Colby
Prosser, J P	Oakfield
Pease, Sylvester	Neillsville
Pergua, John S	St Louis, May 19 62
Prosser, Jno F	Colby
Prosser, Frank	Colby
Rodgers, C	Lake Providence, Mar 1 63
Rogers, D R	Loyal
Rogers, D R	Neillsville
Reimer, T	Lake Providence, May 31 63
Steinmetzger, A	Vicksburg, May 22—63
Stevens, Wm	St Louis, May 3—62
Sears, Albert W	Cairo, Dec 1 64
Speekman, John	Montgomery, May 26—65
Schmidt, John	Montgomery, July 22 65
Vosburg, H	Jeff Barracks, May 6—62
Van Valkenburg, R B	Oasis
Van Alstein, W E	New Orleans, April 7 65
Williams Geo*	Corinth, Oct 3—62
Wright, H G	Jeff Barracks, May 9 62
Walker, O F	Chilton
Ward, Hiram	Rome, Ga, July, 42 64
Ward, E G	Rome, Ga, July, 22—64

I

Capt C R Johnson	Black River Falls
Capt M Crawley	Black River Falls
Lt Jno Kittinger	
Lt C Blakesley	Neillsville
Lt A J Mauley	Clear Lake, Iowa
Lt C D Sturgeon	Truckee, Cal
Lt Jos Clancey	Black River Falls
Lt W Foster	
Lt Wm Nevermann	Neillsville
Colville, A J, sgt †	Corinth, Oct 6—62
Cullen, F A, corp*	Shiloh, Apr 7—62
Lisherness, W R, corp*	Jeff Barrcks, May 9 62
Rider, C W, corp †	Vicksburg, May 24—63
Parker, S D, corp	Aug 3 65
Ayers, G R	Pittsburg Landing, May 2—62
Ayers, G R	Humbird
Bone, C F	Rice Lake
Blakeslee, C	Neillsville
Bacon, Charles G	St Louis, May 7—62
Clancey, Jos	Black River Falls
Clapp, N M	Black River Falls
Crawley, N	Irving
Canon, H	Loyal
Clapp, N M	Neillsville
Colville, W S	Neillsville
Chamberlain, H G	Neillsville
Clark, J H	Merrillan
Covell, W S	Neillsville
Denmark, J J	Pittsburg Landing, May 22—62
Ehrke, Joachim	June 20—63
Erickson, Peter	Mobile, Sept 19—65
Ferguson, J W	Neillsville
Ferguson, Jas	Neillsville
Frost, Harvey E*	Shiloh, Apr 7—62
Fuller, H	Bixton
Font, Chas	Neillsville

THE MASSACHUSETTS
MUTUAL
LIFE INSURANCE COMPANY
— OF —
SPRINGFIELD, MASS.

INCORPORATED 1851

E. W. BOND,	President.
HENRY FULLER, Jr.,	Vice-President.
AVERY J. SMITH,	Secretary.
OSCAR B. IRELAND,	Actuary.
DAVID P. SMITH, M. D.,	Med. Examiner.
F. W. CHAPIN, M. D.,	Asst. Med. Examiner.
JOHN A. HALL,	Superintendent of Agencies.

Assets, Dec. 31, 1879,	$6,639,727.39.
Liabilities, "	5,975,289.38.

Issues Liberal Policies at Established rates of Premium.

SEND FOR CIRCULARS.

Is Economical in its Management,
    Conservative in its Plans,
        Fair and Honest in its Dealings,
            Prompt to Pay its Obligations,
                Accommodating to its Policy Holders.

It offers Perfect Security at reasonable cost and guarantees all Policies the benefits of

The Massachusetts Non-Forfeiture Law.

WISCONSIN SOLDIERS AND SAILORS REUNION ROSTER.

Name	Location/Date
Green, A	Milwaukee, Apr 30 –65
Green, Alex	Neillsville
Green, Chester	Irving
Graham, John	Montgomery Aug 17–65
Houghton, D J	Jeff Barracks, May 14—62
Houghton, E P, f	Humbird
Hide, Joel	Memphis, Jan 9—64*
Houghton, E P	Neillsville
Harvessetter, Leonard	Colby
Ives, Jas	Sacramento, Cal
Johnson, C R, a	Black River Falls
Johnson, C R	Neillsville
Jones, O E	Sparta
King, J F	Neillsville
King, Geo P	Humbird
Lewison, A	Memphis June 4–64
Lynch, Lewis	Rome, Ga, July 29—64
Markey, E H	Neillsville
Meek, Geo	Alma Centre
Meek, Jos	Alma Centre
Markey, Edw	Neillsville
Mattice, F B+	Spanish Ft, Ala, Apr 4—65
McCready, Jas	Black River Falls
McCarty, David	Soldiers Home, Milwaukee
Nichols, Jno	Neillsville
Nettleton, Cyrus	Humbird
Neverman, Wm	Neillsville
O'Neill, Jno	Paducah, March 15—65
Olm, Martin F	Vicksburg, Feb 16—65
Owen, Peter F	Mobile, June 29—65
Paulley, Ira	St Louis, May 13 –62
Preston, John	Merrillan
Pratt, Stephen G	Colby
Powers, Jno B	Vicksburg, May 22—63
Page, D C	Mobile, Apr 30—62
Rumpff, Frederick	Merne
Rayson, Thos*	Shiloh, Apr 7—62
Relyea, Adam	Taylors Station
Reader, Geo	Soldiers Home, Milwaukee
Rockwood, Jno J*	Shiloh, Apr 7—62
Rutherford, Geo	Alma Centre
Ross, Henry	Mound City, Apr 18—62
Rickaby, Robt	Cato Corners
Schlinsog, G*	Shiloh, Apr 7—62
Sturtevant, R F	Dayton, W T
Sturtevant, J R	Neillsville
Storkwell, Elisha	Taylors Station
Steinberg, A R	St Louis, May 14—62
Sturgeon, Cyrus O	Truckee, Cal
Salisbury, James K	Grand Meadow, Minn
Short, W	Memphis, June 19—64
Sturdevant, J R	Neillsville
Titz, Wm	Montgomery, Aug 2—65
Voight, T L	Madelia, Minn
Vins, Tom B	Greenwood
Vine, T R	Neillsville
White, Henry	St Louis, March 28—62
Wilson, J B	Eau Claire
Wage, F C	Neillsville
Withman	Quinney
Youkey, F	Keokuk, Aug 14—62
Youkey, Fred'k	Neillsville

K

Name	Location/Date
Capt E W Cornes	
Capt O W Fox	
Capt J N Price	
Capt J T Postel	
Lt H Blackett	Lawler, Iowa
Lt J W Pettit	
Lt M W Hurlburt	
Lt Newton Clark	
Cowles, C, corp	Duvals Bluff, Sept 2—64
Underwood, I, corp—	Corinth, Oct 7—62
St John, R E, corp+	Corinth, Oct 10—62
Bach, C, corp +	Vicksburg, June 28–63
Lyman, H F, corp+	Mound City, Apr 19—62
Arman, H J*	Clifton, July 5—65
Ankerbrand, J	Pittsburg Landing, May 24—62
Ankerbrand, M	
Brown, Wm*	Corinth, Oct 3—62
Bright, Jesse	Chippewa Falls
Blake, Henry A	Madison
Billings, Rufus*	Corinth, Oct 3—62
Blackett, H S	Lawler, Iowa
Briar, C A+	Mound City, Apr 26—62
Begood, John+	Memphis, June 8—62
Covenstance, J+	Corinth, Oct 6 - 62
Collins, Wm	Marietta, Sept—64
Dunten, H+	Tupelo, June 13—64
Dean, J K, ar	Kansas
Dawley, Ebenezer	Baraboo
Edson, R L+	Corinth, Oct 11—62
Gibson, H M	Beaver Dam
Harper, Robert*	Corinth, Oct 3—62
Hill, Ed C	Baraboo
Hill, John F	St Louis, May 7—6..
Horn, Herman	Cairo, Feb 9—65
Jenness, R	Jefferson Barracks May 23—6..
Johnson, L B	Florenceville, Iowa
Johnson, James, f	Battle Creek, Iowa
Keller, C	New Orleans, Mar 7—65
Lee, W W+	Spanish Ft, Apr 1—65
Looker, E E	Marietta, Aug 28—64
Mott, E L	Pittsburg Landing, June 27—62
McGrath, Thos	Mobile, Aug 24—65
Pemainasatoo, John	Cairo, Mar 27—65
Palmetoes, Abner	Rome, Sept 9 –65
Segrage, E	Montgomery, Aug 14—65
Shaw, H W	Battle Creek, Iowa
Swain, J B	Union, Iowa
Theele, Ernst	Muscoda
Wilson, J F	Pittsburg Landing, June 6—62
UNASSIGNED.	
Baker, C W	Janesville
Duir, Philip	Leopolis
Duns, J	Tomah
Fulmer, Peter	Oconomowoc
Gates, II M, f	Beaver Dam
Gibson, Byron, f	Taycheedah
Helmstreet, F B	Janesville
Hancock, John, a	Oshkosh
Hill, Ed K	Baraboo
Keneally, J H, mt	Fond du Lac
McCann, J S	Montevideo, Minn
McCart, Jno	Cato
Oleson, J A A	Fond du Lac
Ruby, J N, mc	Oshkosh
Thiele, Earnest, f	Muscoda
Terry, Albert O	Chilton
Woodcock, Thos	Chicago
Wentermeyer, Julius C	Chicago, Ill
Wiley, W, ph	Fond du Lac
Yound, D M	North Bend

FIFTEENTH INFANTRY.

Three years organized February 14th, 1862. Original strength, 801, gain by recruits, etc., 105. Total, 906. Death loss, 287—killed in action 49, died of wounds, 33, of disease, 165. Other losses, 319—missing, 46, desertions, 46, transfers, 47, discharges, 204. Strength at muster out, February, 13th, 1865, 320. Campaigns in Ky, Tenn, Miss. Ala, Ga.

REGIMENTAL ROSTER.

Name	Location/Date
Col Hans C Heg*	Chickamauga, Sept 26—63
Col Ole C Johnson	Beloit
Lt Col O McKee*	Stone River, Dec 31—62
Maj C M Reese	
Maj Geo Wilson	Rochester, Minn
Adj H Borchsenius	Baldwin
Adj Henry Hauff	
Adj L G Nelson	Kasson, Minn
Adj O A Risum	Pulcifer
Q M Ole Heg	
Q M Selah Matthews	
Surg S O Himoe	
Surg A E Lindsfelt	
A Surg S J Hauser	
A Surg G Trenkler	
A Surg C P Garlick	
A Surg J F Meithom	Oct—63
A Surg G F Newell	
A Surg A H Whipple	
A Surg D P Wooster	
A Surg Sam'l Bell	
Chap C I, Clausen	
Chap J H Johnson	

A

Name	Location/Date
Capt A Torkildsen	
Capt J N Johnson*	Chickamauga, Sept 26—63
Capt H Siegel	
Lt Engelsted	
Lt N I Gilbert	Baldwin
Lt O Thompson*	Altoona, Sept 20—63
Black, Ole, sgt+	Murfreesboro, Jan 16—63
Georgeson, G, sgt	Chattanooga, Oct 5—64
Brunstead, G O, sgt	Andersonville, Aug 6—64
Johnson, K, corp	Louisville, Nov 9—62
Arneson, Nels	Chicago, Ill
Branstead, Ole*	Chickamauga, Sep 20—63
Bretelson, F	Louisville, Nov 7—62
Christiansen, T	Andersonville, Oct 18—64
Ellinger, A+	Murfreesboro, Feb 21—63
Ellielson, A, f	Albert Lea, Minn
Edson, E	Chattanooga, Feb 4—64
Geuber, Peter	Hortonville
Gilbert, N J, m	Baldwin
Halvorsen, O	Corinth, Sep 6—62
Johnson, Pedro	Chattanooga, Dec 17—62
Johnson, C A, m	Chicago, Ill
Johnson, Lars	Chicago, Ill
Johnson, Christian, m	Chicago, Ill
Johnson, E	Nashville, Nov 13—62
Johnson, E	Nashville, Dec 2—62
Johnson, C	Nashville, Feb 7—62
Johnson, A	Iuka, Aug 24—62
Larsen, Ole+	Murfreesboro, Mar 26—63
Lawrence, Jno	Chicago, Ill
Loraas, A	Mound City, April 10—62
odgnard, E	Andersonville, Sep 1—64
Norman, P	Bowling Green, Nov 22—62
Olsen, Michael	Chicago, July 28—62
Oleson, Almond, f	Curry, Minn
Olson, Nile	Coon Prairie
O'Connor, William	Lowell
Olsen, Amund	Nashville, July 27—63
Peterson, Knud+	Nashville, Apr 13—63
Syversen, J*	Altoona, May 27—64
Sowenson, A	Coon Prairie
Sampson, T	Island No 10 May 25—62
Sampson, S	Island No 10 May 30—62
Thompson, L	Island No 10 May 7—62
Tompson, Jonas, mc	Omaha, Neb

B

Name	Location/Date
Capt O C Johnson	Beloit
Capt Jos Mathieson	Madison
Lt Ole G Thompson	Chicago, Ill
Lt Ole R Dahl	Chippewa Falls
Lt Geo Wilson	Rochester, Minn
Lt O P Olson	New Richmond
Lt C Heyer	
Syvorsten, B, sgt+	Chattanooga, July 6—64
Britton, R, sgt	Andersonville, Oct 10—64
Mikkelson, T, corp*	Stone River, Dec 31—62
Larsen, Erick, corp+	Chattanooga, July 1—64
Larson, J, corp	Nashville, Nov 12—62
Aspenheim, A*	Resaca, Ga, May 15—62
Bus,s, Ole O	Andersonville, June 11—64

PINE LANDS FOR SALE!

V. R. WILLARD,

ATTORNEY at LAW,

REAL ESTATE, TAX PAYING

AND ABSTRACT OFFICE.

JENNY, LINCOLN CO., WISCONSIN.

WISCONSIN SOLDIERS AND SAILORS REUNION ROSTER.

Erager, O E — Black Earth
Dahl, C O — Murfreesboro, July 2-63
Dahl, O R — Chippewa Falls
Erickson, C — Andersonville, Aug—19—64
Fasted, John H — Nashville, Nov 25—62
Halvorsen, L — Island No 10, May 25-62
Hoff, Christopher — Christiana
Hoff, Christopher, f — Cambridge
Halvorsen, H — Cincinnati, Oct 22—62
Hanson, L — Andersonville, Sept 1—64
Johnson, John* — Chickamauga, Sept 19-63
Johnson, Engle, f — Otronto, Ia
Johnson, J H — Island No 10, July 3—62
Knudsen, O* — Altoona, May 27—64
Lasseson, R — Murfreesboro, Apr 3 -63
Larsen, M — Andersonville, Sept 1-64
Moe, J O — Island No 10, May 19—62
Mjeld, R, f — Black Earth
Mikkelsen, O — Jacinto, Miss, Aug 10=62
Nelson, L* — Kenesaw Mt, June 28—64
Nelson, A — Winchester, Tenn, Aug 4 - 62
Oleson, L J* — Stone River, Jan 3- 63
Olaes, Nells — Greenville
Oleson, G* — Chickamauga, Sept 19-63
Opdahl, J S — Richmond, Va, Mar 15—61
Oleson, Ole M — Andersonville, July 11—64
Oleson, Michael — Andersonville, Nov 9-64
Olson, O P, me — New Richland
Peterson, H — Chattanooga, June 11—64
Skjelde, O N — Island No 10, May 14—62
Starkson, Nelse, f — Adams, Minn
Thompson, O G — Chicago
Urnas, Peter — Bowling Green, Oct 19—62

C

Capt F R Berg
Capt Hans Hansen+
Capt Jno T Rice — Atlanta, Oct 13—63
Nt Jas Larcom
Gibson, O W, corp — Richmond, Feb 2—64
Armson, Arne — Madison, Feb 1   2
Brown, J P+ — Racine, June 15—64
Danielsen, P — Racine, Oct 15—63
Emonson, T — Stevenson, Oct 20—61
Finkelsen, Knud* — Murfreesboro, Dec 31—62
Hanson, G E* — Murfreesboro, Dec 30 62
Hanson, T — Richmond, Jan 27—61
Iversen, E — Bowling Green, Dec 1—62
Jensen, R — Richmond, Feb 2—61
Johnson, H — Bowling Green, Feb 25—63
Johnsrn, John — Andersonville, Ga
Larsen, O — Nashville, Dec 15—63
Mathiasen, M* — Murfreesboro, Dec 31—62
Nellson, J — Island No 10 June 23 -62
Nellson, L G, m — Kasson, Minn
Nellson, Jacob — Canton, D T
Nielsen, — Iuka, Aug 31—62
Nielson, L — Chattanooga, Dec 3—63
Peterson, O — Murfreesboro, Apr 14—62
Steensen, Lars — Louisville, Nov 9—62
Sorensen, P — Nashville, Nov 17—63
Swenson, E — Chattanooga, Nov 29—63

D

Capt Chas Campbell
Capt A Skofstadt
Capt L G Nelson — Kasson, Minn
Lt E Tanberg
Lt N G Tufte
Freidstad, N, sgt — Bowling Green, Nov 18—62
Turguson, F, corp — Bowling Green, Jan 1—63
Jacobson, A L, corp — Chattanooga, Nov 5—63
Jacobson, Ole, corp — Andersonville, June 15—64
Hovland, J B, corp — St Louis, Mar 17—62
Annnerson, Rolof — Colby
Bendixon, Ole M, f — Lewiston
Dahl, A A, f — Cutril, Minn
Delap, — Ontario
Dsivorson, H* — Chickamauga, Sept 19—63

Halvorsen, John — Cincinnati, Oct 22—62
Halvorsen, H — Richmond, Va, Feb 2—64
Ingebretsen, C — Madison, Feb 18—62
Johnson, Peter — Corinth, July 21—62
Joasen, I — Jackson, Tenn, Oct 4- 62
Johnsen, I — Nashville, Dec 2- 62
Jacobson, H L — Pine Lake, Feb 3—62
Lee, Ole A* — Murfreesboro, Dec, 31—62
Nelson, N* — Murfreesboro, Dec 31—62
Nelson, L G, d — Kasson, Minn
Olson, Nels — Jackson, Tenn, May 22—62
Olson, Ole, Jr — Jackson, Tenn, Sept 28—62
Olsen, Knud — Chattanooga, Feb 1—64
Pederson, P. — Portage City, June 10—62
Pederson, H — Columbus, Ky, Sept 21—63
Pederson, Peder — Nashville, Dec 8—62
Sorensen, O — Danville, Ky, Oct 24 - 62
Tolagsen, L — Chattanooga, Dec 4 —63

E

Capt J Ingmundsen*Stone River,Tenn,Dec30—62
Capt Henry Hauff* Chickamauga,Ga,Sept 19—63
Capt T A Rossing
Lt Win Tjentland
Lt T P Sloan- Big Shanty, Ga, June 28—64
Lt Rollin Olson
Lt J M Johnson
Lt J N Brown
Lt P W Chantland
Lenvig, Ole, sgt* — Allatoona, May 27—64
Hulley, E, corp* — Allatoona, May 27—64
Lokke, G, corp* — Allatoona, May 27—64
Johnson, A, corp+ — New Albany, Mar 18—63
Amundsen, S, corp+ — Richmond, Va
Peterson, A, corp — Bardstown, Ky, Nov 6—62
Erickson, Ole, corp — Nashville, Feb 14—64
Anderson, J* — Allatoona, Ga, May 27—64
Arneson, L+ — Atlanta, June 22—64
Anderson, Peter — Washington, Sept 5—61
Burgerson, Wm — Nashville, Nov 19—63
Christopher, Ole — Cincinnati, Sept 5—62
Dahl, Ole E — Island No 10, April 30—62
Ericksen, Ole* — Allatoona, Ga, May 27—64
Ericksen, Ole* — Allatoona, May 27—64
Ericksen, Peter — Richmond, Va, May 27—64
Ericksen, T — Edgefield Junc, Nov 15—62
Gmilus, C — York, Aug 4—62
Homlebeck, P — Bowling Green, Oct 12—62
Houson, Liri — Black River Falls
Halvorsen, P — Bowling Green, Sept 14—62
Hanson, H — Chattanooga, Dec 21—63
Ingebretsen, L — Chattanooga, Dec 21—63
Johnson, G — Cairo, Oct 3—62
Johnson, Peter — Bowling Green, Jan 11—63
Jenson, Halvor, — Nashville, Jan 12—63
Julsen, E — Chattanooga, Jan 2—64
Lemvig, H* — Rocky Face Ridge, May 15—64
Lee, C H+ — Murfreesboro, Jan 17—63
Lindloe, O — Nashville, May 27—62
Milesteen, O H* — Chickamauga, Sept 20—63
Nielson, John — Iuka, Miss, Aug 30—62
Oleson, Peter — Allatoona, May 27—64
Olson, K — Stevenson, Ala, Oct 10—63
Olsen, C — Nashville, Jan 14—63
Peterson, B — Louisville, May 10—64
Rossum, Mads+ —
Rusto, C — Island No 10, May 2—62
Roosmas, I — Chattanooga, Dec 1—63
Thompson, C* — Chickamauga, Sept 19—63
Thomaset, L — Jackson, Tenn, Sept 11—62
Tjerans, Job — Murfreesboro, May 15—63

F

Capt C Gustaveson — Manitowoc
Lt T Simonson
Lt S Samuelson
Oberg, John, sgt — St Louis, Aug 2—63

Larson, C I, sgt — Louisville, Nov 24 - 62
Thompson, A, corp* — Kenesaw Mt, June 27—64
Marshall, G W, corp* — Kenesaw Mt, May 27—64
Knudson, Erick, corp — Cincinnati, Aug 2—62
Hultman, C, corp — Chattanooga, Sept 23—63
Oleson, Albert, corp — Knoxville, Mar 17—64
Paulson, G, corp — Danville, Va, Apr 6—61
Anderson, Gilbert — Moscow
Christenson, H* — Rocky Face Ridge, May 14-64
Christensen, Ole — Baldwin
Christiansen, Ole I — Island No 10, May 29—62
Dahl, A — Moscow
Flack, John* — Murfreesboro, Dec 30 -62
Grell, John — Island No 10, Apr 15 -62
Holn, H — Jacksonville, Tenn, Sept 27—62
Hanson, H — Nashville, Oct 1—62
Halvorsen, B — Chattanooga, Dec 16—63
Haldorsen, O — Andersonville, July 21—64
Iverson, K — Murfreesboro, Dec 31 62
Jorgeson, G — Island No 10, May 1—62
Knudson, O N — Murfreesboro, Dec 30—62
Mekison, Albert, f — Albert Lea, Minn
Oppen, T O — Columbus, Ky, Sept 2—62
Oleson, Knud — Milwaukee
Olson, T — Murfreesboro, Mar 10—63
Rundberg, O — Madison, Feb 26—62
Rundberg, O — Louisville, Oct 4—62
Siler, Jacob — Nashville, Nov 30—62
Severson, Dryngel — Moscow
Syversou, K — Island No 10, Apr 10—62
Spickerman, W — Island No 10, Apr 21—63
Steffes, R — Andersonville, July 3—61
Forgeson, T — Murfreesboro, Apr 3—63
Tallacksen T — Iuka, Miss, Apr 25—62
Torstenson, C — Louisville, Nov 15—62
Voigt, Christian, book-binder — Watertown

G

Capt J A Gordon
Lt H Hauff
Lt W A Montgomery — Chicago, Ill
Lt C B Nelson
Lt Jno N Brown
Torgenson, T, sgt — Andersonville, Sep 24—64
Thosten, G, corp — Island No 10, Oct 3—62
Gordon, corp — Omaha, Neb
Sandall, S C, corp — Chattanooga, Nov 27—63
Andresen, Anton — Island No 10, May 1—62
Andersen, C — Island No 10, May 18—62
Anderson, Haus — Island No 10, June 4—62
Donnua, John+ — Chattanooga, June 24—64
Benjamine, A S — Island No 10, May 31—62
Bronus, O — Andersonville, June 30—61
Christiansen, M — Island No 10, May 24—62
Christiansen, J — Columbus, Sept 28—62
Erikseu, C+ — Atlanta, July 12—64
Greenwood, Alfred, mf — Belleville
Johnson, Geo — Resaca, May 14 -64
Jones, D W — Belvidere
Lindell, H O — Island No 10, Oct 18—62
Merchant, A — Island No 10, June 21—62
Murphy, M — Cairo, Sep 7—62
Nielson, — Island No 10, June 9—62
Asgood, J P — Island No 10, June 25—62
Olufson, H — Columbus, Apr 2—63
Setter, J I, — Island No 10, June 19—62
Thompson, O* — Allatoona, May 27—62
Tonneson, Jens — St Croix
Torgenson, And — Island No 10, May 17 -62

H

Capt K J Sime
Capt Geo Wilson — Rochester, Minn
Capt A A Brown
Lt C E Williams — Chicago
Lt J I Johnson
Lt M Erickson — Eau Claire

THE TRAVELERS
OF HARTFORD, CONN.

The Oldest and Largest Accident Company in America.

One of the Strongest and Best Life Companies in the World.

FURNISHES EVERYTHING SAFE AND DESIRABLE

IN PERSONAL INSURANCE.

Paid-up Cash Capital,	$600,000.
Solid Cash Assets,	$4,955,000.
Surplus to Policy Holders,	1,296,000.
No. Accident Policies Written,	585,000.
No. Accident Claims Paid,	45,000.
Amount Accident Losses paid,	$3,600,000.

LIFE AND ENDOWMENT POLICIES,
Of all well approved forms, on the low rate, all cash, stock plan. Ample security, definite contract, and policies non-forfeiting. No "dividends," and no disappointed expectation, but cash Insurance payable promptly at maturity.

GENERAL ACCIDENT POLICIES,
By the year or month, written by Agents at small cost and short notice. Principal sum payable in case of death by accident, or weekly indemnity for wholly disabling injury. They cover accidents in all lawful occupations, traveling or not.

LIFE AND ACCIDENT POLICY COMBINED,
Being a regular life policy with weekly indemnity attached, giving the insured complete protection for life and limb under one contract. The cost is about the same as the ordinary mutual premium for a life policy alone.

REGISTERED GENERAL ACCIDENT TICKETS,
Insuring $3,000 against death by accidents, or $15 per week for total disability, at 25 cents a day, or $4.30 for thirty days. They are much used by travelers, and may be obtained at the Company's local agencies or at railway stations.

THE TRAVELERS is relatively one of the strongest companies in the world. Its resources are estimated at actual market value. Its investments are made in the most conservative manner. Its surplus above all liabilities is twenty-six per cent of the gross assets. Its management is proverbially energetic and honest, and its record is clean. Upon such a basis it confidently offers THE BEST in all forms of Personal Insurance.

JAMES G. BATTERSON, President,	GEORGE ELLIS, Actuary,
RODNEY DENNIS, Secretary,	EDWARD V. PRESTON, Sup't. of Agencies,
JOHN E. MORRIS, Assistant Secretary,	G. P. DAVIS, M. D., Medical Examiner,

J. B. LEWIS, M. D., Surgeon and Adjuster.

M. N. McLAREN, Jr., State Agent for Wisconsin and Minnesota,
82 MICHIGAN STREET, MILWAUKEE, WIS.

AGENCIES.

BELDEN & McLAREN, Milwaukee,	DANIEL & GILE, Oshkosh,
WM. M. McDERMOTT, Fond du Lac,	NATHAN COLE, Sheboygan,
KIMBALL & LIBBEY, Green Bay,	ALEX. MAIN, Madison,

S. C. YOUT, Racine.

And in the Principal Cities and Towns of the United States and Canada.

WISCONSIN SOLDIERS AND SAILORS REUNION ROSTER. 75

Bristud, S E, 1st sgt, f	Cambridge	Holland, H H, sgt	Andersonville, June 4 -64	Capt Geo A Spur		New London
Johnson, M, sgt	Corinth, July 22—62	Damness, O N, corp*	Chickamauga, Sept 19—63	Capt Jno W Cotaugh		
Tortouron, Ole, sgt, f	Cambridge	Sander, Brent, corp	Jacinto, sept 27—64	Capt A Gallagher		Vicksburg, Aug 12—63
Thompson, A T, sgt	Island No 10, May 22—62	Peterson, N	Edgefield Junc, Nov 16—62	Capt Jno L Vidal		
Berg, Lars N, corp	Island No 10, May 22—62	Peterson, Axel, corp	Andersonville, July 3—64	Capt Jas A Biggert		Berlin
Olson, Tobias, corp	Nashville, March 8—63	Olson, C, corp	Chattanooga, Nov 12—63	Lt Oscar P Silver		Berlin
Fosse, A L, corp*	Nashville, Dec 31—62	Amundson, I	Island No 10, Nov 12- 63	Lt Cooly Smith+		Shiloh, May 6—62
Johnson, W, corp*	Murfreesboro, June, 27—62	Aslaksen, T	Island No 10, June 2- 62	Lt A C Lathrop		
Ager, G	Jeff Barracks Aug 28—62	Aslaksen, O	Nashville, Nov 11- 62	Lt G W Graves		Berlin
Bjornson, K +	Whiteside, Tenn, Dec 4—64	Aneson, B	Camp Dennison, Aug 23 62	Lt J H Tower		
Brown, A A	Alexandria, Mh,u	Dahl, I	Danville, Mar 16- 64	Lt D D LaBar		
Christiansen, G	Atlanta, Aug 3—64	Erickson, H	Jackson, Sept 26- 62	Lt Edw C Waring		Oshkosh
Chrisopherson, F	Island No 10, April 9—63	Erickson, E	Bowling Green Dec 1—62	McNeely, S, sgt*		July 24—64
Dokken, Lars O +	Nashville, April 1—62	Enger, Jens	Andersonville, June 24—64	Williams, J H, sgt		Shiloh, Apr 6—62
Dokken, K O	Island No 10, May 7—62	Helgeron, Hans I	Island No 10, Apr 30—62	Graves, C, sgt *		Atlanta, July 22—64
Fasse, Stephen D	Chicago, Ill	Hanson, J	Andersonville, June 23—64	Marsh, Fred, corp+		Atlanta, Oct 21—64
Fusse, Ole L	Yorkville, Ill	Johnson, John*	Altoona, May 27—64	Durgin, J G, corp		Vicksburg, Aug 26—63
Gulbranelson, Hans*	Murfreesboro, Dec 30—62	Janson, Jens, f	Albert Lea, Minn	Derry, J C		St Louis, May 12—64
Gjerde, A P +	Andersonville, Jan 18—65	Jenson, O	Chattanooga, Jan 2—64	Bowers, H G		Keokuk, Aug 5—62
Hounes, Ole L +	Andersonville, Jan 18—65	Jacobson, J	Richmond, Feb 16—64	Bagg, H M		Providence, June 10—62
Johnson, I	Nashville, Dec 23—62	Knudsen, C	Andersonville, June 25—64	Biggert, James A		Berlin
Johnson, J L, judge	Eau Claire	Lenfsou, L*	Altoona, May 27- 64	Crouk, A*		Atlanta, July 24—64
Knudsen, E	Island No 10, May 14—62	Larson, O	Island No 10, May 22—62	Camp, G M+		Shiloh, Apr 10—62
Kingland, T T, f	Cambridge	Martinson, J*	Murfreesboro, June 30—62	Charter, Schartier J+		Marietta, Aug 19—64
Knudsen, K	Louisville, Oct 16—63	Nilson, S	Edgefield Junc, Nov 15—63	Crook, John		Corinth, June 17—62
Larson, Knud+	Nashville, Jan 18—63	Nelson, Erick	Louisville, Apr 6—64	Conrick, W F		Providence, July 3—63
Larson, O	Nashville, Dec 10—64	Nilson, I	Sept 16—63	Carter, John		Rome, July 9—64
Nilsen, Larz	Nashville, Feb 25—63	Olsen, Chas, I	Madison	Cook, Geo W		
Olene, E P*	Allatoona, May 26—64	Paulsen, P M, l	Richmond, March—64	Coates, Edmund		Springwater
Olesen, Ole+	Chattanooga, Aug 20—61	Peterson, S	Andersonville, May 5—64	Chaplin, H H		Nashua, Ia
Olson, I	Columbus, Ky, Sept 2—62	Rasmussen, A	Jefferson Barracks, Aug 6—62	Eldredge, J+		Mound City, Apr 16—62
Shutten, N N	Nashville, Feb 11—63	Thompson, C	Jackson, Oct 23—62	Easbes, Walter J		Alexandria, May 19—65
Sime, Elder P	Madison			Fell, G R		Providence, July 8—63
Tinan, H G	Bowling Green, Oct 5—62	UNASSIGNED.		Florida, Edward		Deadwood, D T
Thostensen, f	Christiana	Johnson, John	New Albany, July 1—63	Fratzke, John		Alma City, Minn
Torgerson, Stephen	Moorhead, Minn	Anderson, H, f	Bass Wood	Geuder, John		Eau Claire
Thomasson, L	Columbus, Ky, Nov 3—62	Erridge, B	Oconomowoc	Graver, Geo W, ex agt		Berlin
		Gilbert, N T, m	Baldwin	Gray Orvin		Vespers
		Irgens, S J, sec of state of Minnesota		Gray, Orvin		West Fork, Ark
I		Johnson, G J, mc	Kasson, Minn	Howe, Cyrus B*		Shiloh, April 6—62
Capt A Gasman		Josslyn, F S	Oshkosh	Hawley, Bodine		Red Boue, Nov 19—63
Capt R Cook		Johnson, Christian M	Chicago	Halsey, G		Lynch Creek, Feb 27—65
Capt W A Montgomery	Chicago, Ill	Krestensen, —	Coon Prairie	Hampton, J		Corinth, Aug 15—62
Lt T M Ginsman		Overson, James	Blair	Holick, Frank		Kewaunee
Lt M Russell		Wickler, C, f	Larrabee	Jones, John E, l		Berlin
Lt C Oleson				Kilbourne, C		Corinth, June 8—62
Steenson, N, sgt +	Chattanooga, July 8—64			Lureh, John+		May 3—62
Gunderson, H, sgt	Andersonville, Oct 11—64	SIXTEENTH INFANTRY.		Moseley, John		Shiloh, Apr 21—65
Haarstad, P O, corp+	Resaca, Ga, June 8—64			Mc Leod, J N		Monterey, May 10—64
Myhre, S A, corp	Andersonville, Oct 3 - 64	Three years. Organized January 31st, 1862.		Moore, John		Tupelo, July 7—62
Peterson, S, corp	Andersonville, July 31—62	Original strength 1066 ; gain by recruits etc, 1131		McLond, M		St Louis, May 27—62
Anderson, Erick	Louisville, Sept 22- 63	Total, 2200. Death loss, 563—Killed in action, 75,		Milliken, J E		St Louis, Aug 6—62
Arneson, Dreug	Knoxville, Apr 4—64	died of wounds, 56, of disease, 232. Other		Patterson, James +		May 4—62
Alderson, Herman	Bass Wood	losses, 665, missing, 46, desertions, 115, trans-		Silver, O F, a		Berlin
Amundson, O.e	Chattanooga, July 22—64	fers 38, discharged 36 Strength at muster out,		Spencer, Wallace, f		Sibley, Ia
Bjornson, K	Andersonville, Oct 14—64	July 12th, 1865, 1482 Campaigns in Tenn., Miss.,		Canterwort, J H		Tomah
Clausen, Peter	Chattanooga, Sept 23—63	La., Ala., Ga., S. C., N. C.		Wright, F W		Atlanta, July 22—64
Fagan, R	Andersonville, Oct 2—64			Wakeman R*		Atlanta, Aug 28—64
Grund, Lars	Andersonville, Aug 31—64	REGIMENTAL ROSTER.		Walbridge, W P+		St Louis, Apr 21—62
Grum, N P, f	Stockholm	Lt Col Thos Reynolds	Madison	Wakeman, L		Marrietta, Aug 17—64
Johnson, Soren*	Resaca, Ga, May 15—64	Maj Wm S Dawes	Neeedah	Warren, T T		Dayton, Aug 23—62
Knudsen, T	Mound City, Oct 26—62	Maj Jno H Wheeler	Dunlap, Ia	Waring, Ed G, p		Oshkosh
Lorenson, E	Bird's Point, Mo, Apr 7 - 62	Maj Jos Craigg	Canton, Ohio			
Nelson, Ren	Sand Creek	Adj Geo M Sabin				
Olson, K*	Altoona, May 27—64	Adj D L Jones	Stevens Point			
Oleson, Iver+	Chattanooga, July 2—64	Q M Jno F Jones		**B**		
Oleson, A	Island No 10, May 24—62	Q M W L Scribner	Chicago, Ill	Lt S B Tuller		
Peterson, Ole	Andersonville, Sept 21—64	Surg Geo W Eastman	Platteville	Lt Jas O Hazelton		
Peterson, P	Kenesaw Mt, June 22—64	A Surg J C Rogers	New York	Lt W D Winship		
		A Surg W S Schermerhorn		REORGANIZED.		
		A Surg Otto Manrer	Corinth, June 25—62	Capt Jno Taylor		
		Chap L S Livermore	Iowa	Capt Jno Kelly		Eau Claire
K		A Surg Wm Meacher	Portage	Lt A P Noyes		
Capt M Gringer	Worthington, Minn	A Surg S W Dunn		Lt Wm E Trowbridge		
Lt Ole Peterson		A Surg Geo A Lamb		Hoisington, W F, sgt		Corinth, June 5—62
Lt Andrew Clement	Briggsville, Sept 27—64	A Surg Jas McCallum		Morris, T H, corp*		Shiloh, Apr 5—62
Lt E Erickson				Purdie, P S, corp*		Atlanta, July 21—64
Lt O Solberg		**A**		Rice, Edgar, corp		Pittsburg, Tenn, Apr 11—62
Lt J E Irgins	Minnesota			Slattery, A H,		In Field, Miss, May 9—62
Lt J P Struomer		Capt Edw Laye	Shiloh, Apr 6—62	Bunker, W W		Keokuk, Sept 20—63
Olson, K R, sgt+	Murfreesboro, Jan 3—63					

⁂ SURVIVAL OF THE FITTEST. ⁂

JOHN L. MARTIN,
PHŒNIX INSURANCE AGENT,
FOND DU LAC,   □   WISCONSIN.

A record of brilliant success and financial prosperity indicates soundness of managaement, conservative practice and legitimate Underwriting.

ARE YOU INSURED?

Discharge at once this duty which YOU KNOW you owe your family. The feeling that your family is provided for, no matter what may happen, will afford you comfort which an equal amount of money laid out in any other way could not purchase.

This Question Claims Your Consideration NOW.

TIME TRIED & FIRE TESTED COMPANIES

North German,
Mercantile,
Rhode Island,
Equitable Star,
North German,
Phœnix,

La Confiance,
American Central,
Equitable Life,
Hamburg Magdeburg,
North German,

Equitable Life Assurance Society of the U. S.

WISCONSIN SOLDIERS AND SAILORS REUNION ROSTER.

Name	Location/Date
Bolson, W H	Stone Bank
Baliyel, L H	East Troy
Collins, Patrick	Corinth, May 3–62
Cross, J H	Madison, Jan 14 63
Clement, Ira	Waupun
Coates, Lester	Springwater
Chapin, H H	Nashua, Ia
Dart, Charles	Mound City, Apr 26–62
Davis, John	Keokuk, Apr 22–62
Dally, Wm	Chattanooga, June 24–64
Drake, S H	Rome, Ga, Aug 1–64
Dupee, Francis	Beaufort. S C, Dec 27–64
Eusign, U A*	Atlanta, July 22–64
Evenson, E S+	St Louis, Apr 23–62
Eastman, George W	Mound City–62
Fuller, E U*	Atlanta, July 22–64
Furguson, C	Madison, Jan 20–62
Flemming, John G, f	Grantsburg
Hoover, John+	Corinth, Oct 7–62
Hastings, O+	Atlanta, July 24–64
Kizer, N H	Savannah, Ga, Jan 11 65
Lawton, B	Marietta, Ga, Sept 19–64
Lockerby, C R	Wautoma Nov 22–61
Mantaney, George	St Louis, May 30–62
Mantaney, N G	In the field, May 30–62
Pringle, Andrew*	Atlanta, July 22–64
Powers, Henry+	May 14–62
Quiner, J C	Savannah, Apr 28–02
Robbins, James*	Atlanta, July 22–61
Severson, L	Beaufort, May 1–65
Smith, V W	Neillsville
Tullon, Sydney B	East Troy
Van Cott, S	Rome, Aug 27–64
Warren, A V+	Marietta, Jnly 24–64
Yale, Henry, mo	Janesville

C

Name	Location/Date
Capt HJD Patch	Corinth, Miss, June 22–62
Capt;P M Hovey	Marietta, Ga, Aug 4–64
Capt I J Hibbard,	Beaver Dam
Capt KrossPPeifert	
Lt Jno G Daily	Hustisford
Lt D Lloyd Jones	Stevens Point
Lt Chas Baxton	Beaver Dam
Wilsen, J P, sgt*	Shiloh, April 6–64
Hewes, David*	Corinth, Oct 3–62
Douglas, R A, sgt	Vicksburg, Aug 22–63
Teed, T, corp+	Providence, July 6–63
Rex. F, corp	Keokuk, July 15–62
Jones, Henry, corp	Corinth, Oct 10–62
Adams, W+	Atlanta, July 22–64
Adams, Geo W, a	Medford
Armstrong, Chas W, f	Marshfield
Bowman, L W	Pittsburg Landing, May 15–62
Burten, Aron	Pittsburg Landing, May 6–62
Butterfield, B S	Memphis. June 20–63
Bagley, Ralph,f	Stevens Point
Cummings, N C	Corinth, June 13–62
Clark, David	Corinth, June 9–62
Duckworth, Joseph*	Atlanta, July 22–64
Everet, Francis, In the field Miss, May 8–62	
Evans, Wm H	Marshfield, Minn
Foster, T+	Marietta, Ga, Aug 8–64
Filke, A W	Mound City, Apr 23–62
Fowler, B	Pocotaligo, S C, Jan 18–65
Fairbanks, W, a	Charles City, Iowa
Fisher, William N	Quincy
Griffin, Lewis	Corinth, June 29–02
Gould, C H	Lincoln, Neb
Holton, Henry*	Shiloh, April 6–62
Harrington, W J +	Rome, Ga, July 21–64
Hauchett, H J	Corinth, June 2–62
Jones, Wm J, messenger	Madison
Jamas, D G	Richland Centre
Jameson, Geo, f	Millburn, Ill
Knowles, D	Pittsburg Landing, May 31–62
Knapp, W O	Providence, La, July 7–63
Lyman, J	Vicksburg, Aug 10–63
McMillan, M +	Cincinnati, May 11–62

D

Name	Location/Date
Mather, M R	Savannah, Ga. Jan 4–65
Newton, Alva E	St Louis, Mo, May 26–62
Nauerity, Nicholas	Manston
Oliver, N B	Pittsburg Landing, May 31–62
Post, Garrett O*	Apr 6–62
Parker, Wm E	Shiloh, Apr 23–63
Price, Edward	Paducah, Aug 6–62
Perry, Winn, m	Marshfield, Minn
Roberts, Robert D*	Corinth, Oct 3–62
Roselle, John	New York, June 15–65
Richer, Wm P	Brookside
Rehfeld, C H, m	Harrison
Swinger, G C	Corinth, Oct 3 62
Waruer, Lyman	St Louis, May 22–62
Capt O D Pease+	Shiloh Apr 11–62
Capt E B Reys	Columbus
Capt W F Gibbs	Clarion, Iowa
Capt J Leroy Bennett	Chicago, Ill
Lt Wm A Green	
Lt Milton Grover	
Lt S V Potter	
Lt Jno Hazen	
Lt Samuel Armstrong	
Taylor, W M corp*	Shiloh, Apr 6 62
Johnson, H, corp	Savannah, Feb 16–65
Anthony, R	Corinth, Aug 9–62
Broadhead, J S	Chilton
Barber, J L	Dayton
Cone L D	
Chesebro,	Gravesville
Demouth, James	Gravesville
Fuller, H	Milford, May 16–62
Fuller, Lyman	Corinth, June 20–62
Farrington, M+	St Louis
Forkin, Martin	Chilton
Fiddler, —	Brothertown
Fayville, Wm, f	Nashua
Gibbs, W F, m	Clarion, Iowa
Goll, E R	Chilton
Goff, G R	Chilton
Giffs, W F	Clarion, Iowa
Harrington, A*	Apr 6–62
Holt, T P	Columbus
Hammer, John	Hayton
Kinney, A P	Quincy, Jan 24–62
Merrell, B F	Poctaligo, Jan 21– 65
Moorr, A A	Bentonville, Mar 21–65
Marflu, Geo F	Stockbridge
Meiner, Anthony	Milwaukee
Nichols, Thomas	Keokuk, July 5–62
Nicholson, Geo	Hayton
Otis, A A	Goldsboro, Apr 20–65
Otis, Isaac	Stockbridge
Portman, Joseph	Stockbridge
Rice, Brister, c	Stockbridge
Robinson, Joel, f	Stockbridge
Reif, Wm	Stockbridge
Reader, J H	Stockbridge
Reader, G A	Stockbridge
Shrampe, Joseph	Savannah, Dec 26–64
Sparks, G W	Beaufort, Dec 26–64
Scott, John H, f	Brothertown
Shipman E D	Wrightstown
Smith, L B	Gravesville
Stanton, Wm	Chilton
Turner, Orville	Corinth, Apr 6–62
Tonsley, N R	Waterloo
Tousley R S, p m	Tousley
Terry, Geo W	Chilton
Terry, Geo H	Chilton
Tracy, H T	Hillsborough
Wollem, August*	Shiloh, Apr 6–62
Warren, Isaac	Corinth, June 13–64
Wing, Ebenezer, f	Brothertown
Welch, Horace	Brothertown

E

Name	Location/Date
Capt W F Dawes	Necedah
Capt R C Rowe	Ohio
Capt C H Bassett	Strongs Prairie
Lt Chas Weite	
Lt H P Pierce	
Lt W S Scribner	Chicago, Ill
Lt J R Martin	Necedah
Lt W D Niles	
Lt C B Curtis	Chicago
Wills, J P, sgt*	Shiloh, Apr 6–62
Holcomb, J L, sgt*	Shiloh, Apr 6–62
Webster, A;sgt+	Keokuk, Apr 20–64
Stone, H L, sgt	Atlanta, July 28–64
Sands, I P, sgt+	Marietta, Sept 18–64
Williamson, G, sgt	Lake Prov., July 31–63
Dunbar, B A, sgt	Petersburg, May 8–63
Caldwell, A, corp*	Shiloh,Apr26–62
Sheldon, G J, corp*	Corinth, Oct 3–62
Hugoboom, O, corp*	Atlanta, July 22–64
Visger, C H, corp	Providence, July 11–63
Dayton, H, corp	Vicksburg, Aug 12–63
Furgeson, R, corp	Wisconsin, Jan 8–64
Beck, Jacob+	Jackson, Jan 28–63
Bronson, Alfred O	Paducah, Apr 7–62
Becker, E F	June 26–62
Bassett, D A	Corinth, Oct 24–62
Bernardy, N	Providence, July 26–63
Chapman, E I.*	Atlanta, July 22–64
Crawford, T B	St Louis, May 14–62
Chamberlain, H W	St Louis,3May 21–62
Crawford, Wm	Westfield, July 22–62
Craig, E	Providence, July 1–63
Casler, C A	Vicksburg, Aug 9–63
Crist, Geo, c	Jefferson
Dimick, Ira*	Corinth, Oct 3–62
Dow, Wentworth	Nasonville
Drake, Martin	Corinth, Oct 30–62
Dawes, James, f	Strongs,Prairie
Bischen, Adam	New Albany, May 29–64
Edwards, James	Waupun
Ely, Henry D, f	Spring Green
Fisk, S B	Pittsburg Landing, May 12–62
Freiman, Peter	Vicksburg, Aug 6–63
Gundlack, F*	Atlanta, July 21–62
Gates, Albert	Corinth, Sept 3–62
Grary, R	Providence, July 7–63
Hastings, Wm	Shiloh, Apr 6–62
Hastings, Henry C	Shiloh, Apr 20–62
Harwood, J W	In the field, May 6–62
Holt, J	Providence, July 6–63
Hottina, H	Providence, Aug 5–63
Hopper, Wm	Coloma
Kelly, D O	Providence, Feb 18–63
Keyes, J B	Strongs,Prairie
Lambsoo, H G*	Atlanta,July 22–64
Lloyd, Silas+	Lovejoy, Sept 5–64
Lyons, J M	Wisconsin, Oct 10–63
Lioinger,	Menominee
McConnell, W	Providence, Aug 2–63
Mel'heeters, T J	Corinth, June 12–62
Maloney, M	Providence, Apr 15–63
Northrop, Wm C	St Louis, May 2— 62
Newcomb, C R	Corinth, June 10–62
Newcomb, J A, f	Unity
Older, Delos	Wisconsin ;July 2—62
Perrp, N A*	Shiloh, Apr 6–62
Phillips, Jason	Nasonville
Pretz, A	Providence, June 21–63
Proper, P B	Davis
Raggs, Henry	Tomah
Ryan, N +	Marietta, July 22–64
Rider, Erwin*	Shiloh, Apr 6–64
Smith, A	Wisconsin, Aug 20–63
Smith, Joseph	Port Washington
Schuerbach, J B	Port Washington
Smith, James J	Vicksburg, Apr 17–64
Smith, T B	Pilot Knob
Thomas, Henry L*	Shiloh, Apr 6 2
Tracy, Hiram T	Hillsborough
Van Kusan, E H	Shiloh, May 27–62
Wolf, F	Marietta, Aug 13–64

1864 — ESTABLISHED SIXTEEN YEARS — 1880

BOYLAN & CO.,

EXCLUSIVE MANUFACTURERS OF

MILITARY CLOTHING!

ARMY,
NATIONAL GUARDS,
BANDS, SCHOOLS,
Police, and Fire Departments.

CONTRACTS

For the complete Equipping and Fitting Out of Regiments, Companies, and Bands' Uniforms---Hats with ornaments, Belts with accoutrements, and Fatigue Caps---will be taken and goods furnished on Short Notice at Low Rates.

Especial Care Given to Adaption of Colors and Style of Dress.

— SEND FOR CIRCULARS. —

135 GRAND STREET,   -   -   NEW YORK CITY.

WISCONSIN SOLDIERS AND SAILORS REUNION ROSTER.

Wright, E — Atlanta, July 27—64
Wood, C J — Vicksburg

F

Capt H V Train — Mauston
Capt B E Stevens — Minneapolis, Minn
Capt Jos Craig — Canton, Ohio
Capt Geo W Roberts
Lt Jno Limburu — Camp Dennison, Apr 28—62
Lt A T Northrup* — Corinth, Oct 3—62
Lt Alfred Taggart — Rockford, Ill
Lt Jas R West, p m — Evansville
Lt Julius 8 Comstock
Harroun, A F, 1st sgt* — Atlanta, July 22—64
Potter, D M, corp — Turtle, Sept 8—62
Vosburg, W M, corp — Newark, May 8—65
Allen, Chas B — Mound City, Apr 28—64
Bader, Wm — St Louis, May 14—62
Birdsall, Geo — Corinth, July 1—62
Brink, F E — Corinth, July 15—62
Burdick, Oscar — Louisville, June 18—65
Bly, F P — Janesville
Brownell, A — Mauston
Carey, H E* — Shiloh, Apr 6—62
Clark, G A — Mound City, May 4—64
Chilson, Newton — Napouee
Cass, Henry H, f — Beloit
Corvin, W E — Watertown
Huggins, Hiram+ — Keokuk, May 7—62
Hows, W F — Madison, Apr 30—64
Heard, Wm C — Madison, Jan 10—65
King, R — New York, Apr 6—65
Long, A — Cincinnati, —62
Lawrence, S H — Keokuk, July 29—62
Love, John — Atlanta, Oct 28—64
Morse, A — Shiloh, Apr 6—62
McNown, John* — Shiloh, Apr 6—62
Miller, Wm S — Vicksburg, Mar 16—61
McMaster, Joseph, m — Windom, Minn
Naurty, Nicholas — Mauston
Provey, F* — Shiloh, Apr 6—62
Preston, Samuel — Chattanooga, Nov 12—64
Phillips, N N — Elroy
Pleasy, Charles — Mauston
Pray, D — Madison, Jan 27—65
Pearsall, Samuel — Dekora
Rowin, Robert — Stevens Point
Rushford, John — Deansville
Stilson, Lyman* — Shiloh, Apr 6—62
Starr, E+ — Andersonville, Aug 28—64
Schofield, E — New Albany, May 30—64
Filliotson, Patrick P D — St Louis, May 21—65
Train, H V — Mauston
White, Edwin — Corinth, July 13—62
Winegor, Wm — Keokuk, July 30—62
Woods, A J — Cairo, Apr 22—74
West, James B, p m — Evansville
Wray, James — Janesville

G

Capt Jno R Wheeler — Dunlap, Iowa
Capt H M Culbertson — Eau Claire
Lt Wm H Pond — Eau Claire
Lt C A Allen
Lt M E O'Connell — Eau Claire
Lt T W M McCauley — Durville
Lt. Wm J Marks — Missouri
Price, F, sgt — Providence, July 19—63
Walker, J V, corp* — Shiloh, Apr 6—64
Barnum, N, corp+ — Cincinnati, May 3—62
Archer, Wm* — Shiloh, Apr 6—62
Browning O H* — Shiloh, Apr 6—61
Bleknap, E P — Atlanta, Aug 17—64
Bartlett, W W* — Vicksburg, Aug 12—63
Burge, John B — Vicksburg, Aug 14—63
Beard, John — Marietta, Sept 6—64
Brunner, M — Atlanta, July 21—64
Coleman, R A*

Craig, Darius — St Louis, May 26—62
Cooper, G D — Providence, July 25—62
Catheart, S — Memphis, Feb 1—64
Davis, James, f — Redwood Falls, Minn
Francisco, C H*
Franklin, V — Providence, Feb 15—63
Gardner, Thos — Corinth, Aug 1—62
Gatfield, Isreal — Providence, July 19—63
Golather, Stephen — Vicksburg, Aug 21—63
Hannogan, J L* — Shiloh, Apr 6 - 62
Miley, M+ — Marietta, Oct 20—64
Mauck, C+ — Denmark, Apr 30 - 62
Moore, E B — Goodrich, June 20—63
McVicar, J D — Oct 19—62
Macauley, T W M — Menomine
O'Hara, J — Providence, July 13—63
O'Connell, M E, bk — Eau Claire
Potts, I — Hilton Head, Feb 18—65
Roley, Z C — Atlanta, July 22—64
Redmond, Patrick — Providence, July 22—63
Stock, R — Vicksburg, Aug 22—63
Smith, Horace H, f — Hardin, Iowa
Shiney, Lewis — Sioux City, Iowa
Thomas, C* — Atlanta, July 21—64
Tuttle, S* — Goodrich, Sept 30 - 61
Tuttle, S — Memphis, Feb 9—64
Welse, E — Providence, July 21—63
Wildermuth, H — Beaufort, Jan 27—65
Wilderness, J C, me — Eureka

H

Capt H G Webb — Fort Scott, Kansas
Capt A D Gray — Pepin
Capt Jno Coomer
Capt Darwin C Whipple — Eau Claire
Lt H M Decoroft
Lt Jno Lewis
Lt Wm H Monroe — Wautoma
Lt Jno T Tinker — Eau Claire
Lt Milton Grover
Lt Edw W Allen — Eau Claire
Babcock, H, sgt* — Shiloh, Apr 20—62
Thompson, A D+ — Mound City, Apr 29—62
Rashaw, G J, corp+ — St Louis, Apr 16 - 62
Kellog, D M, corp — St Louis, July 10—62
Lawton, M W, corp — St Louis, May 18—64
Allen, Edward W, m — Eau Claire
Beach, G T — New York, Feb 28 - 65
Brown, John W — Memphis, Mar 23—61
Benjamine, H N — Rome, Sept 22—64
Beebe, W H H — Eau Claire
Carroll, Charles — Shiloh, Apr 6—62
Chreslnger, M L — Philadelphia, May 1—64
Cromwell, Peter — Washington, May 27—65
Crawford, Riley, f — River Falls
Dean, Samuel C — Chicago, Aug 9 - 61
Drew, Isaiah — Oliver, Dec 9—64
Eldridge, John, l — Berlin
Firmin, B W — May 8—62
Horrick, O* — Shiloh, Apr 6 - 62
Haskins, G H* — Shiloh, Apr 6—62
Hodge, C* — Shiloh, Apr 6—62
Hennesey, John* — Shiloh, Apr 6—62
Hoskins, R — St Louis
Host, A B — Savannah, Jan 19—65
Heasley, J W — Shiloh, Feb 12—65
Hill, R — Eau Claire
Hall B B — Madison, Jan 9—62
Horton, Wm — Madison, Feb 10—62
Hennin, George* — Shiloh, Apr 6—62
Leigh, R+ — Cincinnati —62
Morgan, E J+ — Rome, July 2—64
Munroe, W H, ed — Wautoma
Nooney, Patrick — Vicksburg, Mar 14—63
Nesbitt, Noble — Marietta, Aug 25—64
Newkirk, Chas, N, f — Canton, Mich
Peabody, Wm H, corp — Baldwin
Peabody, John B — Baldwin

Raymond, L+ — Savannah, Apr 18—62
Robbins, Livingston, f — Stevens Point
Stilman, George E* — Atlanta, July 21—64
Skeels, George+ — Cincinnati, May 6—62
Welcome, F A* — Atlanta, July 21—61
Weston, James L — Wisconsin
Wicks, F E — Corinth, July 31—62
Weston, John C — Evansville, Ind
Wilcox, M S — Rome, Aug 28—64
Whipple, Darwin C, inf — Eau Claire
Young, Wm C — St Louis

I

Capt S W Osborn — Darlington
Capt B E Stevens — Minneapolis, Minn
Capt W S Monroe — Wautoma
Lt Chas H Vali+ — Shiloh, Apr 7—62
Lt D G Turman — Washington, D C
Lt Jesse Collins — Vautoma
Lt R J Cone
Lt S C Johnson — Hudson
Lt W H H Townsend
Lt A B Wilkins
O'Brien, T, sgt* — Atlanta, July 22—05
Winchester, E F, sgt* — Corinth, Nov 20—63
Long, J C, corp — Keokuk, Oct 18—62
Brewer, Wm, corp — Providence, July 31—63
Munroe, J W, corp — Wautoma, Aug 15—63
Austin, W S* — Shiloh, Apr 6—62
Brainard, L E* — Aug 10—61
Bacerhill, George — Keokuk, May 12—62
Bliss, Edmond A — St Louis
Baker, Joseph — Vicksburg, Aug 17—63
Clifford, A* — Shiloh, April 6—62
Cole, Myron — St Louis, July 16—62
Dennison, E W — Corinth, July 1—61
Dick, A C, sgt — Warren, Ill
Dunsphy, W W — Providence, July 7—63
Evanson, Abram — St Louis
Franklin, H — Savannah, Jan 19—65
Frost, Fle'ker — Savannah, Jan 25—65
Goodwin, Jas — Rome, July 21—64
Gautner, Nicholas — Wautousta
Howard, H C+ — Hazel Green, May 10—73
Hall, O D — Davenport, June 10—62
Jones, D L — Stevens Point
Keithley, E M — Pittsburg Landing, May 8—62
Lincoln, I — Providence, July 27—63
Osborn, S W — Darlington
Penn, Carl — Savannah, Apr 18—62
Potter, Wm H — Farmington
Pool, Geo — St Louis, May 14—63
Parks, Henry — Vicksburg, Aug 15—03
Perrle, T — Redbone, Nov 23—64
Robinson, H M — Providence, Aug 6—63
Solomon, John+ — St Louis, May 17—62
Saunders, John+ — Providence, June 18—63
Smith, M J, f — Jamestown
Wooding, M F+ — Shiloh, Apr 6—62
Williams, James — Dalton, Dec 12—64

K

Capt R P Derickson — Chicago, Ill
Capt Jas Norris
Lt Isaac T Carr — Jefferson
Lt Geo Richmond
Lt Dan'l F Vall — Evanston, Ill
Lt Jno Gough — Chicago, Ill
Lt H G Cleveland — Monroe
Lt Jno S Steadman
Bradford, E D, surg+ — Corinth, Oct 8—62
Cooper, E, co:p* — Shiloh, Apr 8—62
Valentine, O J, corp+ — Shiloh, Apr 18—62
Gunther, S, corp — St Louis, Aug 21—62
Wildman, T, corp — St Louis, Jun 29—64
Cline, John W, corp — Nashville, June 28—64
Ennis, John W, corp — Hilton Head, Dec 23—64
Ayres, Charles A — Corinth, July 2—62
Clark, W A* — Shiloh, Apr 8—62

THE
WESTERN ASSURANCE COMPANY!
OF TORONTO, CANADA.
INCORPORATED 1851.

Capital, full paid,	$400,000.
Gross Assets,	1,334,149.
Gross Liabilities,	631,634
Net Surplus,	302,515.

Northwestern Department,

ESTABLISHED JUNE 1st, 1879.

GEORGE W. HAYES
General Agent.
82 MICHIGAN STREET, MILWAUKEE, WISCONSIN.

R. M. WEIL, Local Agent.

WISCONSIN SOLDIERS AND SAILORS REUNION ROSTER. 81

Name	Info	Name	Info	Name	Info
Cooper, Wm	June 13—62	Q M John Geo			
Chapman, Chas W	Corinth, July 20—62	Q M C E Furlong		**C**	
Chapman, Lyman	Miss, Apr 18—62	Q M Richard Phalen			
Carr, J T, cu	Jefferson	Surg H McKennan		Capt P O'Connor	
Colling, Nic	Port Washington	Surg Benj C Britt		Capt Samuel Rea	
Divan, W	Lovejoy, Sept 3—64	Surg Geo St Sure	Sheboygan	Lt Martin Currau	Fond du Lac
Donahue, R	Chattanooga, July 2—64	A Surg Chas D Davis		Lt Simon O'Kane	Milwaukee
Deveraux, D M	Rome, Nov 15—64	A Surg Eben Jackson		Lt Alex McKenna	
Evanson, C	Madison, Jan 3—62	Chap G T Riordan		Lt N Berigan	
Glass, John K*	Atlanta, July 22—61	Chap N Mignault		Lt Jno Holland	
Gleason, G W +	Marietta, Aug 3—61	Chap Francis Fusseder	Beaver Dam	Lynch, Michael, sgt	St Louis, May 7—63
Goggin, Wm	Monterey, June 2—62			Mc Fatler, J, corp,	Goldsboro, Apr 6—65
Garrett, Jacob, f	Fall City			Anderson, Ole, +	Atlanta, Aug 19—64
Hurlbut, J C*	Atlanta, July 22—61	**A**		Ablen J C,	Oakdale
Hyde, A	Camp Prentice, Apr 23—62			Bullman, John,	Corinth, Aug 16—62
Haven, A S D, m	Hopkins, Mo	Capt P H McCaulay	Milwaukee	Berend, Joseph,	Barton
Kann, H C	Port Washington	Capt P McGrath	Chicago, Ill	Carberry, Chas,	Fond du Lac
Lampman, O	Vicksburg, Aug 10—63	Capt Jno Delahunt		Cronan, C,+	Atlanta, Aug 9—64
Manning, Thomas*	Shiloh, Apr 6—62	Lt Jno Crane		Cain, John,	Fond du Lac
Murphy, John*	Keokuk, May 13—62	Lt Thos Conan	Jefferson	Curran, M C, m	Fond du Lac
Pierce, Wm K	May 24—62	Lt M Sullivan		Corbett, John,	Fond du Lac
Powers, R J	Corloth, July 9-62	Lt Jas Brazell		Cushla, Pat,	Fond du Lac
Raynor, David P	Kenosha	Ambruster, V*	Big Shanty, Sept 5—64	Dougherty, C,	St Louis, Apr 2—5
Stewart, J	Nashville, Feb 28—65	Aldrich, A L	New York, Sept 16—64	Drum, Patrick,	Vicksburg, Dec 20—6
Tousley, S A*	Shiloh, Apr 6—62	Benson, John, janitor	Madison	Donnelly, Pierce, f	Lomira
Tousley, W H*	Shiloh, Apr 6—62	Corbett, James	Savannah, Jan 11—65	Donnelly, Pierce,	Fond du Lac
Townsend, C H	St Louis, May 17—62	Dick, S H	Lake Providence, Apr 3—63	Engenhart, F,	Madison, March 02
Turner, John W	Cairo, May 5—61	Daniels, Jno	Beaver Dam	Eastman, F, Atlanta,	July 20—64
Trogner, Joseph D	Rome, June 15—64	Hastings, Edward	Corinth, July 12—62	Gallagher, James,	Fond du Lac
Whipple, P	May 23—62	Harrington, P	Fayetteville, March 15—65	Gill, Mike,	Fond du Lac
Wilson, James	Madison, Jan 15—62	Howe, J A	Beaver Dam	Gibbs, S S, mc	Byron
Wildman, S H	Goldsboro, Mar 21—65	Hudson, W	Goldsboro, Apr 3—65	Harkins, Barney,	Fond du Lac
White, J A		Murphy, John*	Atlanta, July 28—64	Keenan, John, l	Whitewater
		McCarty, Jas	Mauston	Krueger, Christian,	Ridgeway
UNASSIGNED.		McCarty, Jus	Andersonville Association	Leahey, Michael,	Armstrong Corners
Alexander, Chas, ph	Eau Claire	McNeil, J H	Corinth, June 14-62	McKenna, Edw,	Madison, June 4—62
Bennett, J F+	May 30—62	Payne, J	Pocotaligo, Jan 27—65	McDermott, Jas,	Corinth, June 25—62
Bennett, Leroy J	Chicago, Ill	Riley, P	Beaufort, Jan 13—65	Maloney, Pat, f	Lomira
Russell, Geo F	Chicago, Ill	Ridgeway, W	Goldsboro, March 23-65	Murray, Frank,	Fond du Lac
Cheny, Fred A, f	Wiota	Storm, John*	St Louis, Jan 16—63	Murray, John,	Fond du Lac
Dudley, O L	Chicago, Ill	Stainforth, Thos	Mississippi, May 30—62	McDermott, Wm,	Corinth, June 30—62
Eargoal, John C	Menominee	Seymour, John	Corinth, July 19—62	McCulloch, Dan,	Vicksburg, Feb 10—64
Haines, Hiram	Oronto	Smith, DeWitt C	Vicksburg, Nov 3—63	O'Connell, John, f	Montecello
James, D A	Richland	Tibbitts, Hiram	Corinth, July 23—62	O'Donnel, John, f	Montecello
Knopsie, C	Evansville, Apr 18—62	Thiel, Christ, me	Beaver Dam	O'Brien, A*	Corinth, Oct 3—62
Kimble, David	Chicago, Ill	Wannamaker, P P	Savannah, Jan 3—65	Pesh, Chris,	Mazomanie
McLoud, A	Monterey, Tenn, May 1—62			Perrigo, H,	Rome, Oct 27—64
Norton, Jas D	Chicago, Ill			Pearson, Jas,	Mississippi, May 16—62
Parker, J R	New York City, Apr 1—65	**B**		Render, Wm,	Fond du Lac
Richard, G E	Keokuk, July 22—62			Ramer, John,	Fond du Lac
Robinson, Charles	Nellisville	Capt Hugh McDermott	Kenosha	Rossiter, James,	April 18—63
Reese, David, J	Marietta, Aug 26—64	Capt Jno McKenna		Smith, August,	Taycheedah
Shaw, Myron A	Cambria	Lt Jno E Mahoney		Wells, Bernard,	Corinth, June 30—62
Wilcox, W A	Corinth, June 2—62	Lt Martin Schulte		Welch, Thos,	Corinth, June 30—62
Woodworth, E W	Eastpoint, Sept 21—61	Lt G B Walsh		Welsh, Lawrence,	Waupun
		Lt Bernard Myer	Sheboygan		
		Finley, J, sgt*	Vicksburg, May 19—63	**D**	
SEVENTEENTH INFAN-		Dempsey, J, sgt*	Corinth, Oct 3—62		
TRY.		Toner, Joseph, sgt	May 22—62		
		Guide, John, corp	Rome, Ga, July 7—64	Capt D D Scott	Watertown
Three years organized March 15th, 1862,		Atkinson, D*	Lovejoy, Ga, Sept 5—64	Capt Jno C Maass	Milwaukee
Original strength, 941, gain by recruits, etc., 1023,		Brandhorst, A	Memphis, Jan 21—65	Lt Jas O Kelly	
Total, 1964. Death loss, 221—killed in action, 22,		Boese, H Lake Providence, La, March 8—63		Lt Jno Little	
died of wounds, 15, of disease, 178, of accidents 6.		Campbell, John	Beloit	Lt Florian Ries	Milwaukee
Other losses, 642—missing, 5, desertions, 107,		Clagg, Hosfield	Rome, Ga, July 27—64	Lt H H Carito	
transfers, 32, discharges, 448. Strength at muster		Daniels, Hiram*	Vicksburg, June 3—63	Lt Jas E Walker	Kewaskum
out, July 14th, 1865, 1101. Campaigns in Tenn.,		Danville, John	New York, Nov 8—64	Black, Carl	Watertown, June 8—62
Miss., La., Ala., Ga., S. C., and N. C.		Finck, C	Andersonville, Sept 22—64	Cawley, John	
		Gallagher, Hugh	Chicago	Carrigan, John	Corinth, July 22—62
REGIMENTAL ROSTER.		Gaffney, Thos	Madison, Apr 5—64	Davis, Hugh	
		Harding, Wm	Medville, Iowa	Dennison, H C	La Crosse
Col Jno L Doran		Johnson, Edwin	Mississippi, May 21—62	Frandler, Joseph	Corinth, June 22—62
Col A O Malloy	Jefferson, Texas	Lannie, Hugh	Vicksburg, May 19—63	Frahm, John	Corinth, June 21—62
Lt Col Thos McMahon		Maguire, Timothy	Vicksburg, April 28—63	Gross, Julius	Mississippi, June 1—62
Lt Col D D Scott	Watertown	Meyer, Emanuel,	Omaha, Neb	Gratany, G W	Springfield
Maj Wm H Plunkett		Mekenna, Wm	Sept 6—61	Haus, August*	Vicksburg, June 15—63
Maj P H McCaulay	Milwaukee	Kiesto, Daniel	Georgia, Nov 27—64	Hansburg, F	Cairo, Mar 19—64
Adj Jno Crane		Schulte, Anton	Sparta	Halling, Delos T	Cairo, May 21—64
Adj Hardy Denniston	LaCrosse	Stelshoff, Henry	Sparta	Happe, Jacob	Newbern, N C, Apr 12—65
Q M Thos Reynolds		Thomas, Otta+	Vicksburg, May 19—63	Keyes, Marcus	Corinth, Aug 6—62
		Wulf, Wm	St Louis, June 5—62		

GOOD REASONS WHY THE INSURED SHOULD PREFER THE

"SPRINGFIELD."

1st. *IT IS AN OLD COMPANY*, having been chartered in 1849.

2d. *IT IS A STRONG COMPANY*, having a Cash Capital of $750,000, and total Assets of $1,858,477.34. The reserve for all liabilities, *including re-insurance*, amounts to $664,143.00, leaving a net surplus over capital of $444,334.34. The surplus as regards Policy-Holders, $1,194,334.34,—one of the best tests of a company's strength,—is a large as that of many companies having larger assets. It is the largest and oldest Fire Insurance Company in Massachusetts. It does no Marine business.

3d. *IT IS NOT EXPOSED TO FAILURE FROM A SWEEPING FIRE IN LARGE CITIES.* It was represented at Troy in 1862, losing $50,000 ; at Portland in 1866, losing $100,000 ; at Chicago in 1871, losing $525,000; at Boston in 1872, losing $250,000. All its losses have been paid promptly, and in full. *Its lines are limited in all cities to a point of perfect safety.*

4th. *THE SPRINGFIELD HAS AN EXCELLENT REPUTATION*, as becomes a good old Massachusetts Company, for fair dealing with its patrons. It is organized under the laws of Massachusetts, which are noted for their liberality to policy-holders, and for their stringent requirements for the maintenance of the solvency of Companies. Those who have best known the company locally, are its best friends.

5th. *IT IS AN AMERICAN AGENCY COMPANY.* It cannot withdraw from the country, and will not from the West, as it is as well able to bear losses as any company can be, and has over 1,000 agents in the West. It has been doing business in Chicago since 1858. Among the stock-holders in Chicago, a.. Field, of Field, Leiter & Co., and Edson Keith, of Keith Brothers ; the former being a d...

The list following, contains the names of some of those to whom the Spr...

DRY GOODS.
Cooley, Farwell & Co., Field, Leiter & Co., Stettauers & Wineman, Carson, Pirie & Co., J.V. Farwell & Co., Bowen, Hunt & Winslow.

CLOTHING.
C. P. Kellogg & Co., Clement, Morton & Co., Clayburgh, Einstein & Co., Leopold, Kuh & Co., H. A. Kohn & Bros., Tuttle, Thompson & Wetmore, Calm, Wampold & Co.

BOOTS AND SHOES.
M. D. Wells & Co., C. M. Henderson & Co., C. B. Sawyer & Co., C. H. Fargo & Co., Farnum, Flagg & Co., Kirtland, Ordway & Co., Greensfelder, Rosenthal & Co.

HARDWARE.
H. W. Austin, Coleman & Co., Hibbard & Spencer, C. L. Rice & Co., W. E. Spencer.

GROCERIES AND CROCKERY.
Sprague, Warner & Co., G. C. Cook & Co., Stearns & Forsythe, Burley & Tyrell, A Liebenstein

STATIONERY AND PAPER.
Hadley Bros., Western News Co, J. W. Middleton, Western Methodist Book Concern, Oglesby, Barnitz & Co., McCann, Fitch & Converse, Braduer, Smith & Co., Culver, Page & Hoyne.

Walsh & Hutchinson & Co.

HOTELS.
Tremont, Sherman, Briggs, Massasoit'

MISCELLANEOUS.
Arthur Farrar, Gen'l Agt Wheeler & Wilson Sewing Machine Co.; Mutual Security Ins. Co.; Home Ins. Co., of New York; Chicago & Alton Railroad; Cayuga Chief Manufacturing Co., Reapers ; Western Bank Note Engraving Co.; American Clock Co.; "Post" Printing Co.; American Sunday School Union ; "Evening Journal," C. L. Wilson.

The SPRINGFIELD is represented at every important point throughout the West. The Company's Statement, and all other information, will be freely furnished by its Agent at your place.

APPLICATIONS FOR AGENCIES MAY BE MADE TO THE WESTERN DEPARTMENT,
118 LA SALLE STREET, CHICAGO, ILL

A. J. HARDING,   **C. E. MANTZ,**
General Agent.   Ass't General Agent.

WISCONSIN SOLDIERS AND SAILORS REUNION ROSTER.

Little, Wm — Savannah, Ga, Jan 12—65
McElory, T* — Corinth, Oct 3—62
Murphy, M* — Marietta, Ga
Murray, John — Milwaukee
McGee, Thomas — Vicksburg, Aug 27—62
Paddleford, S S — Corinth, June 3—62
Quick, J — St Louis, Apr 2—62
Ringwood, James — St Louis, June 26—62
Rodgers, Michael — Natchez, Sept 9—63
Voss, Chas+ — Marietta, Aug 20—61
Weigler, Andrew — Corinth, May 26—62
Wayne, A
Wahner, Fred Anton — Dodgeville
Wright, James — Vicksburg, Jan 11—64
Yarm, Wm — Corinth, June 22—62

Capt Jno McGowrin
Capt J Mc D Roe
Capt Peter Fargan — Sheboygan
Capt Patrick Croghan
O'Connor, B, sgt — Vicksburg, Oct 14—63
Sullivan, M, corp+ — Marietta, Sept 27—64
Cain, Thos, corp — Mississippi, May 25—62
Bailey, Ench L — Corinth, June 25—62
Betaw, Wm — Savannah, Jan 24—65
Buss, F — Savannah, March 15 - 65
Callagan, Thos, Sr — Corinth, July 22—62
Costello, Patrick — St Louis—62
Chute, Thos — Natchez, Aug 2—61
Dumpyrope, Henry — Corinth, June 23—62
Flynn, John E — Fond du Lac
Flynn, John, mc — Dundee
Flannagan, Thos — St Louis—62
Gilroy, Wm, f — Mitchel
Holcomb, Henry+ — St Louis, March 8—63
Hineblil, Thos, m — Monroe
Holcomb, Andrew — St Louis, Feb 27—63
Kayser, Jos — Mitchell
Lambert, John K — Preston, Ia
McLean, Daniel+ — Vicksburg, May 25—64
Murray, Michael — Mitchel
McKinley, Gilbert J — Mitchell
McGranville, Daniel — Corinth, July 7- 62
Milke, Gottfried — Newbern, Apr 1—65
O'Brien, Terence — Corinth, June 24 62
O'Mally, John, f — Mitchell
Pattek, B+ — Vicksburg, June 7—63
Phelan, Richard — Mitchell
Porter, Geo W — Corinth, June 27—62
Rief, J — Averysboro, March 17—65
Reagen, Michael — Fond du Lac
Steffesan, Herman — Corinth, May 22—62
Short, Peter, m — Alma
Sherwood, Allen J — Seymour
Sherwood, C L, p — Birmingham, Ia
Toomey, Timothy — Bear Creek

F

Capt P Gernaughty
Lt Chas K Furlong
Lt Peter Smith
Lt Allan McDonald
Lt Thos McKinlry
Lt Jno F Whalen
Lt Patrick Delany
McCormick, P, sgt+ — Marietta, Sept 6—64
Gallagher, P, sgt — I. Providence, Jan -63
Mooney, Michael, corp — Memphis, Jan 16—63
Bray, Jas, — Vicksburg, Aug 6—63
Carroll, Jas, — Corinth, July 22—62
Dener, Oliver* — Vicksburg, June 27—63
Delaney, John, — Delevan
Dixon, Wm, — New York, Apr 29—65
Fairbanks, Cyrus, — New York, Apr 26—65
Howley, W W, — Corinth, July 5—62
Hubbell, David T. — Marietta

Heiling, Henry, f — Racine
Howe, Edmund, — Corinth, July 8—62
Hazelius, Erick, — Memphis, Aug 24—63
Harrington, Jno, — Janesville, Mch 25—61
Hartman, Jacob, — Fort Monroe, May 14—65
Joyce, Jas, — Mazomanie
Laneviene, Jos, — Mississippi, May 17—62
Lane, D, — New York, Jan 10—63
Lenk, Chas, — New York, Apr 28—65
McBride, J, l — Whitewater
Mangen, Jas, — Carlton
Osberg, Paul, — Corinth, June 30—62
Plumteanz, S, — 62
Purvis, T, — Andersonville, Aug 22—64
Reardon, Patrick, — Keokuk
Smith, Thos, — Corinth, June 15—62
Sullivan, Pat, — Delevan
Stokes, Conly, — Delevan
Sullivan, J, — Vicksburg, Jan 13—64
Tappan, Geo, — Corinth, June 30—62

G

Capt Wm Southward
Capt Wm Bopre — Wausau
Capt Simon O'Kane — Milwaukee
Lt J G Moreau — Menominee
Lt Theo Roehe
Lt M L Rousseau
Lt August Cautin
Jameson, O M, sgt* — Atlanta, Aug 8—64
Bronyette, A — Mississippi, May 20—62
Bouching, Joseph — Menomine
Briesman, A — Mound City, Oct 13—62
Couvillon, Frank — Savannah, Feb 9 -65
Deshalerid, D — July 30—62
Dehgne, Joseph
Deruck, V J — Vicksburg, July 8—63
Duhel, Silas — Natchez, Sept 11—63
Detrit, Amand — Natchez, Sept 17—63
Forvilly, Maximillian — Menominee
Greenwood, Lewis — April—64
Golden, Wm — Escanaba
Lafanl, Frank — Two Rivers
Lafonl, Godfrey — Two Rivers
Moran, L — Menomonee
Nells, John B, f — Red Rivers
O'Kane, Simon, notary public — Milwaukee
Oilert, Collis — Menominer
Pastil, Joseph — Nashville, Nov 25—63
Rousseau, A — Mississippi, May 22—62
Reilly, John+ — Atlanta, Sept 4 - 64
Reando, Louis — Menominee
Rouleau, Henry — Hancock, Mich
Raich, Oliver — Cairo, Aug 19—63
Schant, John — Vicksburg, Aug 13- 62
Steward, Wm — Vicksburg, Nov 16—63
St Peter, T — Chicago, Ill
St Peter, Frank — Two Rivers
Simons, Edw — Fond du Lac
Simmons, Edw, f — Fond du Lac
Tetro, Octave — Menominee
Theriauld J N — Menominee

H

Capt Chas Armstrong — Chicago
Capt Sam'l R Apker
Lt Darius E Palmer
Lt Henry A Nolf
Lt Miles Joyce
Lt Jas B Fowler
Ames, Ira L — Corinth, June 15—62
Burgess, N A — Madison, Apr 6 - 62
Babutting, G — Raleigh, Apr 15—65
Carmichael, D — Lake Providence, May 6—63
Flanders, Jas F+ — Marietta, Sept 27—64
Griffin, John* — Atlanta, Aug 26—64
Gorman, Jas — Milwaukee
Herman, Jos — Corinth, July 6—62

Hamblin, Joel — Corinth, July 9—62
Lourence, Tennis O — Mulsino
McMahon, John+ — St Louis, July 21—63
McNuity, John — St Louis, Apr 10—62
McCiute, John — Corinth, July 2—62
Nelson, Thomas — Corinth, July 5—62
Noyes, H C — Baraboo
Ordman, F — Mar 4—65
Power, John — Madison, Apr 4—62
Plum, Chas — Corinth, July 8—62
Scott, Walter P — Rome, Oct 10—64
Watson, James P — St Louis, July 4—64
Weber, Henry — Kildare

I

Capt Alex McDonald
Capt J G Nordman
Capt O A Austin — Waupun
Capt Thos H Reilley
Lt Chas Pitcher
Lt Geo H Fisler
Lt Goodloe Gage
Lt Dan'l S Thurston
Lt Jno Kane
Bates, A L, corp — Mississippi, May 23—63
Bennine, C, corp — Corinth, Sept 15—62
Austin, O — Nederland, Col
Anderson, Joseph — Fond du Lac
Brown, L — Corinth, May 9—62
Briggs, S — Corinth, May 1—62
Brown, J — Grand Junction, Nov 24—62
Boyer, Alfred S — Vicksburg, Nov 18 - 63
Barwick, S — Andersonville, Aug 19—64
Close, Jonathan — Mississippi, May 14 - 62
Corn, Peter — Mississippi, May 24—62
Clark, Warren P — Vicksburg, June 17—63
Conners, John — Vicksburg, July 11—63
Crane, Rowell — Rome, July 11—64
Carter, C A — Marietta, Sept 17—64
Drake, L W - — Wateree River, Feb 23—65
Drake, Geo L — Rome, July 28—64
Evans, Jno M — Corinth, July 7—62
Higgins, M W — Corinth, May 7—62
Hammons, W M — Corinth, July 14—62
Hyer, A — Alexandria, May 26—65
Holbrook, J W — Corinth, May 23—65
Haskell, A B, b — Sparta
Hanse, Amos P — Kerssaw Mt, June 17—64
James E F — Brownsville, Sept 23—63
Kiele, Chas — Grand Junction, Nov 14—62
Kafla, M — Alexandria, June 25—65
Lewis, Jno — Corinth, July 31—62
Lane, M — Milwaukee
Miller, N — Atlanta, Aug 30—64
Miller, Vitalis — Kewaunee
McCrory, Hiram — St Louis, May 1—62
Metcalf, Z — Madison, March 27—64
McClung, James — New York, May 19—65
Nash, Albert — Corinth, May 24—62
Otto, Albert — Atlanta, July 24—64
Oliver, N — Madison, Apr 18—64
Owery, Henry — New York, Apr 18—65
Payne, Samuel — St Louis, May 6—62
Phillips, J B, ms — Dansville
Stantz, Jos — Savannah, Dec 27—64
Smith, P E — Nashville, March 2—65
Smith, G A — Soldiers Grove
Sutherland, Jas T — Marietta, July 15—64
Williams, J C* — Kenesaw Mt, June 13—64
Winn, C J — Jackson, Sept 28—63

K

Capt Welcome Hyde
Capt Rollin H Crane
Lt Dand S Bishop
Lt Jno Nichol
Lt Jno Henderson
Lt Jas E Richards
Lt E W Bradbury

THE MUTUAL LIFE INSURANCE
COMPANY OF NEW YORK.
V. S. WINSTON, President.

☞ GET THE BEST. ☜

REDUCED RATES FOR $1,000 LIFE INSURANCE IN THE MUTUAL LIFE Insurance Co. OF NEW YORK. Annual Premium Ordinary Life.		PREMIUM RATES FOR $1,000 LIFE INSURANCE IN OTHER COMPANIES. Annual Premium Ordinary Life.
AGE. AM'T		AGE. AM'T
25..........16.01	The best is always the cheapest in the end, and doubly so when it can be purchased for less money than an inferior article. In life insurance.	25..........19.89
26..........17.34		26..........20.40
27..........17.79		27..........20.93
28..........18.26	**THE MUTAL LIFE INSURANCE CO. OF N. Y.**	28..........21.48
29..........18.76	furnishes the very best indemnity, and at lower rates than any other company in the world. It is the largest company in the world; Its policies, now in force, numbering more than 90,000.	29..........22.07
30..........19.30		30..........22.70
31..........19.85		31..........23.35
32..........20.41		32..........24.05
33..........21.06	It is the strongest financial institution in the world, its assets amounting to $90,000,000.	33..........24.78
34..........21.73		34..........25.56
35..........22.42		35..........26.38
36..........23.16	It is the safest company in which to insure, its surplus alone as computed by the New York *Standard*, of four and one half per cent. interest, amounting to more than $11,000,000.	36..........27.25
37..........23.94		37..........28.17
38..........24.78		38..........29.15
39..........25.66		39..........30.19
40..........26.61	(*This is over and above all liabilities, and is of itself, much more than the total assets of many of our American Companies.*)	40..........31.30
41..........27.60		41..........32.47
42..........28.66		42..........33.72
43..........29.79	This company has issued since its organization, more than 210,000 policies.	43..........35.05
44..........30.99		44..........36.46
45..........32.27	It has returned to its policy-holders in dividends $50,000,000.	45..........37.97
46..........33.64	It has returned in surrender values, $40,000,000.	46..........39.58
47..........35.11	It has distributed among its beneficiaries, in payment of death claims, endowments and annuities, $60,000,000.	47..........41.30
48..........36.66		48..........43.13
49..........38.33	Total returned to policy holders, $150,000,000.	49..........45.08
50..........40.10		50..........47.18
51..........41.99	And it now holds as a guarantee for the payment of future claims, cash assets of $90,000,000.	51..........49.40
52..........44.01		52..........51.78
53..........46.16	This company does a strictly Life insurance business. It has no speculative feature. It issues no Tontine Policies, at the expense of the many and for the benefit of the few. It has no stock holders. The assets and surplus all belong to the insured.	53..........54.31
54..........48.47		54..........57.02
55..........50.92		55..........59.91
56..........53.55		56..........63.00
57..........56.35		57..........66.29
58..........59.35	Its ratio of expenses to receipts is less than that of any other company. Its dividends to policy holders are greater than those in any other company.	58..........69.82
59..........62.56		59..........73.60
60..........65.99	The cost to the insured is therefore less than in any other Company.	60..........77.63
61..........69.67		61..........81.96
62..........73.59		62..........86.58
63..........77.81	If, then, you wish insurance, and what prudent man can afford to be without it, buy the very best, where it can be obtained at the lowest rates.	63..........91.54
64..........82.31		64..........96.86
65..........87.17		65.........102.55
66..........92.35		66.........108.65
67..........97.91	If you are not acquainted with an agent of this company in your vicinity, blanks and full instructions for obtaining a policy can be obtained by addressing	67.........115.19
68.........103.87		68.........122.20
69.........110.25		69.........129.71
70.........117.09		70.........137.75

MERRILL & FERGUSON,
General Agents,
DETROIT, MICHIGAN.

For Mich., Ind., Ills., Wis., Iowa and Minn.

WISCONSIN SOLDIERS AND SAILORS REUNION ROSTER. 85

Name	Location/Date	Name	Location/Date	Name	Location/Date
Antoine, Peter*	Vicksburg, July 1—63	Maj J W Crane	Shiloh, Apr 6—62	Boynton, S B	Oshkosh
Boyer, W H.	Blairs Landing,	Maj Jos W Roberts	Michigamic, Mich	Barber, N B, m	Warrens Mills
Bell, Jos.	Bear Creek	Adj G L Park	Stevens Point	Carpenter, J M	Vicksburg, May 24—61
Bergemann, Wm.	Eau Galle	Adj Edw Colman	Fond du Lac	Conklin, John	Memphis, Jan 22 63
Charron, Jos.	Athens, May 16—64	Adj A J Welton	Plover	Davis, B S*	Jackson, May 14—63
Danks, A H, mc	Beavertown, Oregon	Adj H J Coykendall		Death, Michael J	Memphis, Nov 11—63
Forman, W H.	Neillsville	Q M J D Rogers	Plover	Davis, G W, f	Oakley
Forvilly, Frank.	Menominee	Q M Fred'k A Brewer		Farmer, John A	Vicksburg, July 31—63
Grignon, C.	New Albany, May 25—64	Surg Geo F Huntington		Goff, John	Nashville, Mar 19—65
Isabell, Chas.	Bear Creek	Surg Erastus J Buck		Hall, J	Pittsburg Landing, May 25 62
Johnson, Solomon.	Mississippi, May 27—52	A Surg J J Whitney	Emmetsburgh, Ia	Hall, Henry	Huntsville, Mar 31 61
Jordan, Thos	Corinth, July 15—62	A Surg Larkin J Mead		Hunt, John L	Broadhead
Kitson, J.	Columbia, Feb 18—65	A Surg Geo H Briggs		Knapp, R C	St Louis, Dec 16—63
Knoke, Aug.	Bear Creek	Chap Jas Delaney		Post, Ezra W	Corinth, May 30—62
Kanasha, Jno.	Huntsville, Aug 11—64	Chap Geo Stokes		Perkins, N C	Corinth, June 19—62
Lloyd, Jos.	Corinth, Aug 16 62			Price, P	Providence, Mar 2—63
Lawe, Jno.	Menominee			Schuiter, John	Louisville, June 15—65
Lusha, Geo H.	Little Rapids	A		Teis, Fred, f	Pedee
McMahon, T*	Kenesaw, June 27—61	Capt Jas P Millard		Voelker, Andrew	Kendall
McHugh, Jas.	Corinth, June 15—62	Lt Edw Colman	Fond du Lac	Worley, V	Pittsburg Landing, Apr 16—62
O'Hara, Pat.	Corinth, July 3—62	Lt Wm T Lyons	Crete, Neb	Young, Isaac	Broadhead
Page, Harrison.	Corinth, July 6—62	Lt Jos W Hubbard			
Rhoades, Edw.	Marshfield	Hitchcock, H	Nashville, Jan 17—65	C	
Rector, Chas.	Corinth, July 16—62	Knox Erastus, sgt	St Louis	Capt Robt S McMichael	Viroqua
Raesler, Gottleibe.	Bear Creek	Farrell, John, sgt	Vicksburg, Sept 12—63	Lt Wm N Carter, Jr	
Stine, Sam.	Corinth, June 15—62	Gimmee, M, corp	Shiloh Apr 6—62	Lt Chas W Pitcher	
Schaepke, A F.	Bear Creek	Bowden, Wm	Corinth, Miss	Lt Jno H Graham	
Stephens, Jno.	Corinth, July 13—62	Benedict, Adelman, f	Cozenoria	Lt Thos J Deeker	Viroqua
Sleeger, Jacob.	Bear Creek	Beaden, N U	Gravesville	Lt Jno Goode	
Selgnooth, Alvis.	Bear Creek	Beaden, Norman U	Gravesville	Lt Allen A Burnell	
Schoepke, A F.	Feb 25—65	Chase, Wm E	July 11—62	Lt R J Chase	Madison
Seifer, Martin.		Carpenter, H	Carlton	Lt Gould Hickok	
Templeton, L C.	St Louis, May 27 62	Daniels, Suman	Cincinnati	Swan, Samuel, sgt	Feb 27—63
Waupano, Jos.	Kenesaw Mt, June 25—64	Dows, Wm	Neillsville	Fredwell, T, sgt	George
Wiskens, John.	Vicksburg, Apr 9—64	Goodall, Henry J	July 6—62	McMickeal, S, corp	Macon, June 27— 62
		Howe, H F*	Champion Hills, May 16—63	Merrill, J B, corp	Nashville, July 24—64
UNASSIGNED.		Hart, E G	Gravesville	Allen, Levi R	Evansville, Ind
Donegan, Jno, sgt	Chicago	Hart, Perry A	Bentou Harbor, Mich	Chadvayne, George	Cairo, Feb 27—64
Bolton, E L, sgt-maj, teacher.	Topan	Jenner, J.*	Vicksburg, May 26—63	Downle, Wm	St Louis, Nov 30—62
Beaupre, Wm, oculist.	Wausau	Kisner, John	St Louis	Day, T Travers	Keokuk, June 28—62
Bell, Jos.	Bear Creek	Lawrence, Ira J	St Louis	Forsyth, Elijah	Keokuk, June 21—62
Crawford, Jno N.	Madison, Apr 20—61	Lyons, W F, me	Crete, Neb	Gander, Jos	Macon, July 21—62
Cowan, Thos.	Jefferson	Lalend, E, I	Stockbridge	Gray, Jno S	Macon, Ga
Fink, Henry.	Cylon	Losa, A	New Holstein	Garratt, N	Millikens Bend, July 27—63
Hollands, Geo.	Eldorado Mills	Losa, J	Gravesville	Hunter, Wm	May 21—62
Isbell, Chas.	Fremont	Mack, F, f	Taycheedah	Johnston, B W	Newbern, Mar 3—65
Kesheua, J.	Kingston, Aug 27—64	Minster, Ernest	Dayton	Lowth, Jno*	Shiloh, Apr 6—62
Knoke, Aug.	Fremont	Norris, O R, f	Stockbridge	McClellund, Jas	Washington, Nov 30—62
Lodou, Jno B*	Atlanta, July 9—64	Pitcher, Dan, I	Fond du Lac	Moore, S N	Chaseburg
Murray, Frank, f	Van Dyne	Smith, Paxon	Corinth, Miss	Page, S	May 4 62
Phillips, N H.	Bear Creek	Scott, Chas F	Memphis	Ross, Jno J	Okeo
Quinney, P W.	Marietta, Oct 27—61	Smith, L	Gravesville	Saxton, N W	Shiloh, Apr 9—62
Reddleon, Jno.	Tomah	Stearnes, Smith	Nashua, Iowa	Singles, J H	Altoona, Oct 5—64
Raisler, Gottliebe.	Bear Creek	Swift, Jackson	Cairo, Jan 20—61	Starbuck, Wm P	Shiloh, Apr 6—62
Steger, Jacob.	Fremont	Tiffany, Levi		Shepherd, N	Alexandria June 13—65
Schmalaw, Jas.	Vicksburg, May 22—63	Tubbs, L D	Bridgeport, Aug 11—63	Thompson, Wm H	Corinth, July 6—62
Seigworth, Alois.	Little Wolf	Town, Ira, I	Fond du Lac	Tooker, Orin	Huntsville, Ala
Sullivan, J T.	Vicksburg, Jan 13—64	Vandergan, Jno	Gravesville	Taylor, Isaac	Louisville, June 26—65
Schuepher, Chas.	Bear Creek	Whitmore, C A*	Shiloh, Apr 6—62	Tiffany, P R, f	Taycheedah
		Whitford, D W	Corinth, May 23—62		
		Werner, Fred	Carlton	D	

EIGHTEENTH INFANTRY.

Three years. Organized February 1862. Original strength. 902, gained by recruits, etc. 675. Total, 1,637. Death loss, 220 — killed in action, 37, died of wounds, 14, of disease, 169. Other losses, 514—missing 78, desertion, 206, transfer 27, muster out, Nov 1st 1864—797, discharged,265. Strength at muster out, July 18th, 1865, #13. Campaigns in Tenn., Miss., Ga., La., Ark., N. C. Ala..

REGIMENTAL ROSTER.

Col Jas S Alban*	Shiloh, Apr 6—62
Col Gabriel Bouck	Oshkosh
Col Chas H Jackson	St Louis, Mo
Lt Jas P Millard	

| Wilkinson, C, I | Brant |
| Wilbur | Brant |

B

Capt Chas H Jackson	
Capt Sam'l B Boynton	Oshkosh
Capt Thos A Jackson	Juda
Capt Sam'l S Frowe	
Capt Henderson Farmer	
Lt Jacob Walkey	
Lt Rich'd C Laird	
Lt Fred'k Teis	Pedee
Slow, Jno L, corp	Juda, Oct 21—63
Adair, E	Madison, Feb 21—64
Bryant, Jno P*	Corinth, Oct 3—62
Baily, Hiram E	St Louis, May 26—62
Barber, Oscar B, m	Warrine Mills
Bussey, M J	Juda

Capt Geo A Fisk	Sparta
Capt Peter Sloggy	Fargo, Minn
Capt Moulton De Forest	
Lt W C Wilson	Sparta
Lt Thos H Dolan	
Lt Nathan Hale	
Andrews, John	Vicksburg, Oct 9—63
Bugby, Lanson L*	Vicksburg, May 22—63
Brown, Jesse	Vicksburg, Sept 20—63
Campbell, George*	Corinth, May 23—62
Comstock, A L	Corinth, Aug 11—62
Crocker, Ephraim	Sparta
Dustin, John P	May—62
Getler, F, Jr	Larkinsville, Jan 5—63
Getman, David	Tomah
Gary, Jno	Neil'sville
Herrick, S C, me	Sparta
Hicks, George*	Shiloh, Apr 6—62

ESTABLISHED 1850.

NO. 393 BROADWAY, MILWAUKEE, WIS.

Royal Insurance Company	Liverpool, England
Queen Insurance Company	Liverpool, England
London & Lancashire Insurance Company	England
Standard Insurance Company	New York
Star Insurance Company	New York
Lorrillard Insurance Company	New York
Hoffman Insurance Company	New York
Williamsburgh City Insurance Company	New York
Boston Underwriters	Boston, Mass

Policies Issued, and Losses Promptly Adjusted and Paid.

WISCONSIN SOLDIERS AND SAILORS REUNION ROSTER.

Hornby, Geo J — Milwaukee, Apr 24—62
Hill, Oscar — St Louis, Dec 20—62
Merriam, E S — Grand Junction, Dec 4—62
Melvin, Geo P — Memphis, Dec 3—63
Mitchell, Lucius W — Huntsville, Apr 8—64
Mooney, Jas — Oil City
Wright, Wm — St Louis, Dec 18—62
Wood, Chas S — Berlin
Winters, Jno, t — Sparta

Capt Gilbert J. Park — Stevens Point
Capt Jos L Cotey — Grand Rapids
Lt Jas R Scott — Memphis
Lt John A Albou — June 1—63
Lt Jno Snyder
Lt Peter Tennyson — Portage City
Vican, Paul, corp — Apr 27—62
Webster, F E, corp — Chattanooga, Nov 12—62
Arneson, Arne — Louisville, June 24—85
Bullis, C J — May 22—62
Babcock, F — Providence, Mar 2—64
Conn, Alvin M — Apr 17—64
Creasy, Wm — Plover
Elderkin, N S — Memphis, June 5—63
Gilson, Samuel — Memphis, Oct 19—63
Hingley, Samuel A
Halk, Henry W — Milwaukee
Jackson, Henry W — Macon, Ga
Larson, Christian — Apr 26—62
Mathewson, Asa E, t — Stevens Point
Pitts Thomas W
Powers, Lanman
Park, G S, a — Stevens Point
Puarica, Moses — Plover
Parkhurst, Irad D, t — Doudville
Stevens, Titus
Thurston, Albert P
Taylor, John K, t — Packwankee
Waterman, D — Mar 23—62
Whitman, Peter T

E

Capt L N Carpenter
Capt Geo Collier — Colby
Lt Geo R Walbridge — Washington, D C
Lt W W Campbell
Lt Orrin Clough — Shiloh, Apr 6—62
Field, J E* corp — St Louis, May 10—62
Atwood, Lowell — Huntsville, Apr 27—64
Butterfield, S W — Appleton
Bedell, Jas W — Plover
Berry, John — Plover
Bremmer, S C
Carpenter, Allen
Dwyer, Jas
Dark, Geo — Portsmouth, Nov 28—62
Fiske, Geo P — April 27—62
Hess, Wm C — Wisconsin
Hill, Caleb — Annapolis, April 19—63
Merril, C O* — Shiloh, April 6—62
McHenry, R J — Washington, June 25—65
McMillian, Peter — Plover
Powers, Chester E — Nov 18—62
Randall, E A — May 29—62
Rand, Aaron E — Montgomery, June 9—64
Rice, Truman, c — Meboil
Tucker, Orin S — July 24—62
Whittaker S — Plover

F

Capt Jos W Roberts — Michigaumie, Mich
Lt Geo Stokes
Lt Wm A Pope
Lt Geo A Topliff
Lt Francis M Carpenter
Plumme, C N, sgt* — Nov 30—62
Anderson, A
Beckman, B E — Nashville, Apr 1—64
Cotton, Otis A* — Wheeling Mar 9—65
Cole, Henry H — Shiloh, Apr 6—62
Cooley, C H — May 16—62
Comstock, Wm — July 15—62
Crocker, Ephraim — Annapolis, Md
Doty, Henry M — Sparta
Felton, Ambrose — Madison
Felton, Willard — May 16—62
Gillman, Jacob — Sept 30—62
Hartung, F+ — Baltimore, Jan 28—65
Hull, Ezra — Vicksburg, July 2—63
Hartwell, S A — June 23—62
Hyatt, Frank H — July 26—62
Hamm, Eugene — Pittsburg
Johnson, C E — Columbus, Mar 10—65
Koller, Jno — Altoona, Oct 8—64
Loper, Lorenzo C — Indiana
Lang, Eugene W — May 26—62
McWilliams, R N* — Shiloh, Apr 6—62
Matthews, C F — Hamburg, May 11—62
Mueklor, Levi — June 16—62
Piugree, Gilman B — Sept 28—62
Pearson, Jno — Sept 26—62
Rextord, C F — Sept 11—62
Shiney, Lewis — Sioux City, Ia
Teany, H M — Wheeling, Mar 9—65
Termant, Robt, me — Embarrass
Woodruff, Perry — Marshalltown, Ia
Woodruff, W P, m — Marshalltown, Ia

G

Capt Fred'k B Case — Grand Rapids

H

Capt David A Saxton
Capt Riley P Colt — Poysippi
Lt S D Woodworth — Berlin
Lt Maurice Gay
Lt Thos H Wallace — June 7—62
Lt E T Chamberlain — Berlin
Tolman, F M, sgt t — Jackson, May 16—63
Goodwin, T D, sgt — May—62
Thomas, Alfred H, corp — May 26—62
Gay, Eugene, corp — Mound City, July 10—62
Ballou, Edward P* — Shiloh, April 6—62
Baker, Nathan R — Mar 9—62
Bess, Henry H, m — Amherst
Cottrell, W S — Oct 11—62
Carey, Wm — Allatoona, July 18—64
Chamberlain, H D, m — Berlin
Chapman, Geo H, m — Richfield, Maine
Card, H T, t — Amity, Kan
Daniels, Lewis — Fayetteville, Mar 7—63
Devoe, Peter
Diederick, P — Providence, Mar 7—63
Ely, Henry D, t — Spring Creek
Fuster, Enoch — May 29—62
Field, Stephen
Garlap, Joseph H* — Shiloh, Apr 6—62
Green, Wesley* — Vicksburg, May 22—63
Gates, A A, mo — Berlin
Halsted, Orlando J
Hesring, Andrew J — Tomah
Hill, J — Providence, Mar 26—63
Mansfield, S — Shiloh, Apr 6—62
Milton, James — Delavan
Newcomb, Joseph — Unity
Newcomb, J A — Neillsville
Ppcket, Wm A
Phillips, Burt S
Remington, M — Keokuk, Aug 2—62
Sawyer, James O — [Newburg
Simmonds, G W — Sept 2—64
Shead, Wm, t — Nashville
Swert, Ralph
Walker, C P* — Shiloh, Apr 6—62
Woodworth, R P — May 21—62
Wertney, J J — July 7—62
Walker, C C
Winans, J A — St Louis
White, Darwin B

I

Capt Wm A Colman
Capt Ira H Ford
Capt Peter McIntyre
Lt Oscar Todd
Lt Jas Mittler
Lt O A Southmayd — Columbus
Crouk, R, sgt* — Shiloh, April 6—62
Laskey, T, corp* — Shiloh, Apr 6—62
Anderson, Lewis* — Corinth, Oct 3—62
Benta, F+ — Corinth, Oct 3—62
Boyce, A — Allatoona, Oct 27—63
Beunet, Sabens — Vicksburg, Sept 18—63
Cook, Maurice C* — Shiloh, Apr 6—62
Dale, Sam C — Louisville, July 5—62
Everson, Chas — May 19—62
Ehlinger, Jno A — Corinth, Aug 11—62
Ford, Ira, t — Columbus
Hillman, G W* — Shiloh, Apr 9—62
Husaman, J — Newburo, Meh 12—66
James, H D, ass't P M — Columbus
Kettle, Wm* — Shiloh, Apr 6—62
Kurth, Geo, mo — Independence
Shaver, H W* — Shiloh, Apr 6—62
Smith, Wm, steamer McDongal, Nov 27—63
Southmayd, O A — Columbus
Smith, S W M — Cobesburg
Tucker, Alf, City Clerk — Berlin
Weist, Melvin — Aug 9—62

K

Capt Wm J Kershaw — Milwaukee
Capt Malcolm Bruner
Lt Alex Jackson
Lt Jno S Field
Lt E A Sanders
Lt P A Bennett
Lt Jno Stumpf — Stevens Point
Lt J W Baldock — Brant
Brockway, O H+ — Vicksburg
Baldock, J W — June 14—64
Crittenden, Thos — St Louis, Feb 25—62
Caldwell, B C — Jefferson
Church, A J
Dutcher, Adam — Vicksburg, May 17—63
Finley, T — July 28—62
Fallou, Jno, t — Cherry Valley, Ill
Fallon, Jno, t — Cherry Valley, Ill
Fuller, Chas D, t — Jefferson
Gray, Geo E — Jackson, May 14—63
Gerald, Jas S — Vicksburg, June 2—63
Gautier, Antoine — Carlton
Hoag, R F — Apr 7—62
Hopkins, H H — July 7 62
Herricks, B F, t — Fond du Lac
Ingersoll, N G, ed — Plover
Kelly, Jno — Jackson, May 20—63
Robert, Martin — North Bend
Lennan, Michael — Dec 21—62
Morey, Willard B — May 17—62
Morey, Gustavus — May 25—62
Marsh, S J — Madison, Mar 12—65
Pritcheri, Jno — Fillmore
Prothero, D — Providence, Mar 5—62
Sagar, Peter F — June 5—62
Stuart, E H — Hamilton, Ill
Tinpen, Jno — Bridgeport, Dec 8—63
Walker, J H* — Vicksburg, May 22—63
Weisham, M — Washington, May 29—65

UNASSIGNED.

Alexander, J A, t — Fond du Lac
Darahouse, Wm — Keokuk, June 20—62
Houck, Gabe M — Oshkosh
Franklin, Win A — Washington, Oct 21—62
Goodwin, T D — St Louis, May 16—62
Onderdonk, H W* — Shiloh, Apr 8—62
Smith, Alvin M* — Vicksburg, May 22—63
Wisnorn, Henry — Humboldt, Pa

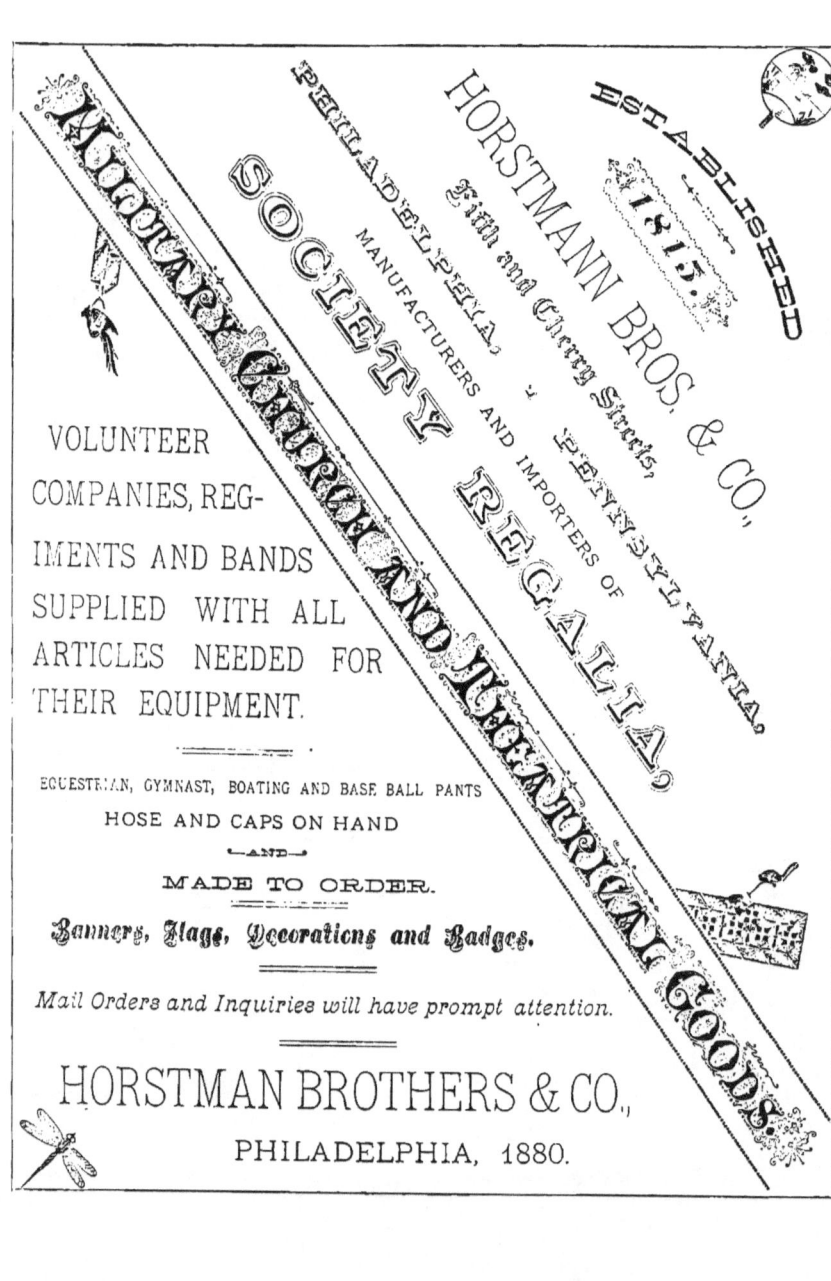

NINETEENTH INFANTRY.

Three years. Organized Apr. 30th, 1862. Original strength, 973; gain by recruits, etc., 511 Total, 1484. Death loss, 146—killed in action, 29, died of wounds, 12, of disease, 107. Other losses, 531—missing, 0, desertions, 46, transfers, 140, discharges, 345. Strength at muster out Aug. 9th, 1865, 863. Campaigns in Va., N.C.

REGIMENTAL ROSTER.

Col Rollin M Strong	Baraboo
Maj Alvin E Bovay	Ripon
Adj Lorenzo Van Slyke	Hastings, Minn
Surg Dan'l B Devendorf	Delavan
A Surg Edward F Dodge	Fond du Lac
A Surg Thomas J Linton	Portsmouth, Sept 26—62
Chap Jos H Nichols	Washington, Jan —63

A

Capt Rollin M Strong	Baraboo
Lt Chas A Chandler	Windom, Minn

REORGANIZED.

Capt Chas A Chandler	Windom Minn
Lt Alex P Ellinwood	
Lt Lewis F Caboon	
Lt Wm Swett and	
Palmer, F B, sgt*	Fair Oaks, Oct 27 –64
Smith, Jas. sgt	Wisconsin, June 14—65
Stiese, A P, sgt	July 20– 64
Rathbun, A, corp ╞	Fort Monroe, Nov 5 -64
Cheek, R*	Petersburg, Aug 7—64
Chandler, C A	Windom, Minn
Casey, John	Portsmouth, Feb 26 –63
Day, Chas*	Hampton, June 16—64
Fowler, H, d	Lroy
Hanes, E†	Portsmouth, July 5—61
Hobby, Wm D	Yorktown, July 31– 63
Horseh, Wm	Hampton, July 29–64
Miller, Wm*	Richmond, Nov 1.–64
Mallon, Jesse	Hampton, Apr 4—64
Markee, James	Portsmouth, Oct 12—62
Pitts, N W	Salisbury, Jan 16- 62
Redfield, R	Riceville, Iowa
Searles, Sylvester*	Petersburg, June 29—61
Sanburn Daniel, Jr+	Annapolis, Mar 20—65
Street, Samuel	July 2 - 64
Tuttle, A C	Kilbourn City
Waltenberger, Geo	Tomah

B

Capt Wm H Tucker	
Capt Albert A York	
Lt Jonathan S Patten	
Lt Wallace W Gordon	

REORGANIZED.

Capt Jonathan S Patten	
Lt Wm J Truesdale	
Lewis, Jos, corp	Portsmouth, Oct 3—62
Houghton, D, corp	Madison, Apr 4—64
Hauser, Jens, corp	Salisbury, N C
Anderson, O,	Norfolk, July 16–62
Blancharg, F D*	Fair Oaks, Oct 27—64
Black, W E,	Baltimore, July 22—65
Cheney, Alf D	Yorktown, July 16—63
Chrissen, D	Racine—62
Giles, S A	Fort Monroe, Aug 21—63
Holsey, Frank	Hart, Nov 22—64
Halvorsen, J	Neillsville
Johnson, Ole M	Norfolk, July 29—62
Johnson, Nieb	Norfolk—62
Kribs, Chas C, mc	Trempealeau
McPheders. J H*	Fair Oaks, Oct 27—64
Muurue, Ira	Richand Centre
Osborn, Gilbert	Richmond, Va
Pulver, W B	Portsmouth, Sept 1—62

C

Capt Jno A Chandler	
Capt Charles Case	
Capt Henry P Nichols	
Lt Wm R V Frisby	
Lt Alonzo H Russell	
Lt Eben B Hill	

REORGANIZED.

Capt Alonzo H Russell	
Lt James H Lynn	
Lt John Mulhise	
Murray, C, corp*	Fair Oaks, Oct 27—64
Whiteley, G M, corp	Newburn, Feb 13—64
Austin, W G	Galesville
Blowers, B S,	Point Lookout, July 29–64
Bauer, J,	Fredericksburg, July 27—65
Decemer, Chas,	Tomah
Blyton, Thomas	Mooneys Mills
Hutchins, S	Alexandria, July 17—62
Kottinger, John	Salisbury, Jan 24—65
Kerrigan, Wm, m	Sparta
Lovell, John	Galesville
McPheter, A	Portsmouth, Oct 3—62
McDonond, Alexander F	Warrens Mills
Moore, H J, f	Glendale
Munz, Wm, b	Norwalk
Premo, Lewis	Warrens Mills
Premo, Lewis Jr, f	Warrens Mil s
Quackenbosh, John	Pine Hill
Racherd, Peter*	Fair Oaks, Oct 27—64
Smith, C	La Crosse
Stewart, James*	Fair Oakes, Oct, 27—61
Stiles, Chas S*	Fair Oaks, Oct 27—64
Steinke, G.*	Fair Oakes, Oct 27—64
Schwalbe, Simon*	Fair Oakes, Oct 27—64
Stevans, M ,.	Point Lookout, June 12- 64
Savage, Thomas	Hampton, Feb 1—64
Sanderlin, John	Galesville
Smith, Chas	LaCrosse
Sheppard, Wm, f	Sparta
Sheppard, Geo, f	Sparta
Utter, Benj P	Sparta
Wrak, Andrew*	Fair Oaks, Oct 27—64
Witting, John	Salisbury, Jan 19—64
Woodliff, John	Norwalk
Wright, W D	Menominee

D

Capt Sam'l K Vaughan	
Lt Edward O Emerson	
Lt Jas G Lowry	

REORGANIZED.

Capt Jas G Lowery	
Lt Adam Christie	
Lt Austin B Wattles	
Richmond, S, corp*	Drury's Bluff, May 16—64
Waldref, A, corp*	Drury's Bluff, May 16—61
Daniels, B S, corp	Portsmouth, Sept 10—62
Allen, Chas*	Seven Pines, Oct 27 —64
Alvarson, Wm	Racine, March—62
Conger, J	Salisbury, Jan 19—65
Cooper, A S	
Day, Girard	Norfolk, Aug 7—62
Dempsie, Geo M	Clayton City, Ia
Gilson, C	Point of Rocks, Feb 8—65
Hall, Daniel	Hampton, Aug 21—63
Kline, A	Hampton, Sept 7—63
Lord, Jas	Yorktown, Aug 1—63
Redmond, P	Salisbury, Jan 19—65
Robinson, Jas W	Soldiers' Home, Milwaukee
Sherwin, B*	Seven Pines, Oct 27—64
Shandt, N*	Seven Pines, Oct 27—64
Smith, George R	Newburn, Nov 21—63
Sullivan, Wm H, f	Hancock
Whittaker, J S	Wilton

E

Capt Patrick Bennett*	Oct 27 -64
Capt Chas D Willard	
Lt Thomas Borns	Troy Centre
Lt S Carey Tuckman	
Lt Revill N Noffitt	

REORGANIZED.

Capt Alex P Ellinwood	
Lt Revillo Noffitt	
Lt Benj Hutchinson	
Nolan, Michael, sgt*	Seven Pines, Oct 27—64
Elliot, Thomas, sgt–	Petersburg, Aug 11—64
Merrill, Wm, sgt	Milwaukee, Feb 4—64
Clark, Hugh, sgt	David's Island, Sept 27—64
Harris, Chas G, corp	Wisconsin, Oct 25—64
Short, Richard, corp	Richmond, Mar 7—65
Ackerman, Traman	White Creek
Coffin, Amasa*	Drurys Bluff, May 14—64
Cassell, Andrew*	Fair Oaks, Oct 27—64
Callery, Hugh	Newbern, Dec 4—62
Edwards, David	Springfield
Frost, William	Point of Rocks, Jan 19—65
Franey, Thomas	Milwaukee
Johnson, T I.	Baraboo
Knowles, Jonathan	Richmond, Dec 18—64
McDermott, Michael*	Drurys Bluff, May 14—64
Ready, Jno	Edgerton
Shattuek, John*	Fair Oakes, Oct 27—64
Sly, Henry*	Fair Oakes, Oct 27—64
Sears, Franklin	Portsmouth, Dec 16—62
Scanlon, John	Newburn, Jan 15—64
Smales, Benj	Cresco, Ia
Tuttle, Ezra	Ontario
Webber, Chas L	Walnut Grove, Minn
Van Wie, James*	Fair Oaks, Oct 27- 64
Van Wie, Revillo	White Creek, Apr 4— 65

F

Capt Martin Scherff	
Lt Wolf A Rapps	
Lt Wm Springelberg	Zoar
Lt Jos Stautneraus	
La Geo W Newman	
Lt Theo Jager	
Miller, Henry, sgt	Norfolk, Jan 31—61
Senser, Peter, sgt	Hampton, Dec 10—63
Selberlick, Julius, corp	Ft Monroe, Oct 8—64
Arnold, A G	Ft Howard
Bohland, Fr	Morehead City, Jan 1—61
Balser, Wm	Annapolis, Mar 19—64
Beinert, Fred'k	Zoar
Neigenfind, Hiram	Point of Rocks, Oct 15—64
Stein, C Fred'k+	Point Lookout, Oct 5—64
Spiegelberg, Wilhelm	Zoar
Stautnereus, J	Oshkosh
Waismann, Jos	Ft Monroe, Oct 16—64
Worbes, Julius	Norfolk, Aug 20—62
Wendehoff, Sander	Madison
Weynhoff, Theo	Alexandria, June 19—62
Zurwes, Jacob	Yorktown, Aug 12—63

G

Capt Jno N Stone, ed	Neenah
Capt Henry W Kingsbury	Neenah
Capt Otto Pahlman	
Capt Austin B Wattles	
Lt Chas G Perkins, p m	Onawa, Ia
Lt Jno S Harris	
Vaughn, Irad W, corp	Ft Monroe, Nov 16—63
Austin, James T	Melrose
Andrews, Richard	Brothertown
Butler, Wells	Point of Rocks, July 23—64
Brown, Charles	Ripon
Berkner, Wm	Lomira
Builts, Ed, f	Platteville
Connell, Jno J, letter carrier	Milwaukee

Facts and Figures for 1880.

IN RELATION TO THE
NORTHWESTERN MUTUAL LIFE
INSURANCE COMPANY.

Date of Issue of First Policy, - - - Nov. 25, 1858.

No. of Policies in Force, Jan. 1, 1880, - 33,056
Amount Insured, Jan. 1, 1880, - - $61,913,846

	Jan. 1, 1870.	Jan. 1, 1875.	Jan. 1, 1880.
Assets,	$6,787,532	$15,927,532	$18,902,142
Liabilities	6,414,401	13,467,822	14,973,983
Surplus	313,131	2,080,710	3,028,159

The Liabilities are calculated according to the highest standard of reserve employed by American companies (Actuaries' four per cent.) If calculated according to the legal standard of Wisconsin, New York, and most of the other states, the liabilities on Jan. 1, 1880, would be $13,907,571, and the surplus correspondingly increased to $4,994,571.

With the record of the past as a criterion for the future, this Company furnishes reliable indemnity at the lowest rates consistent with safety.

The Company commenced business in 1858, without a dollar of capital (it being purely mutual in all respects), sustained only by its inherent strength, springing from the mutual confidence of its members.

During the past twenty years it has paid to representatives of deceased policy holders, and to living members, TWENTY-THREE MILLIONS OF DOLLARS.

The Northwestern stands at the head of the ten largest life companies of the country in strength and security, as shown by the ratio of Surplus to Liabilities.

It Invests Its Funds upon improved real estate security, at western rates of interest, and it has now thus placed over TEN MILLIONS OF DOLLARS.

Its Location enables it to select the choicest securities, and to command the highest rates of interest.

The Interest Receipts of the Company since organization have more than equalled its losses by death, and 1879 was the sixth year in succession in which its interest receipts exceeded its combined disbursements for death claims and expenses.

Interest Receipts, 1879....................$1,317,507 18
Death Losses and Expenses...........1,232,015 75

Excess of Interest Receipts........ $85,551 43
Interest Receipts since organization. $11,481,373 68
Death Losses paid since organization. 8,013,592 23

Excess of Interest Receipts.... $3,467,781 45
This is a showing that can be made by no other company.

Policies are Issued upon all approved plans which have stood the test of time, speculative policies of every kind being avoided. Documents giving detailed history of the Company, its standing, etc., can be obtained of any agent, or by addressing the office at Milwaukee, Wisconsin.

The Northwestern is the only Company which has in recent years printed its current dividends for the information of the public. The NORTHWESTERN has done this for nine consecutive years.

The reader is requested to compare the following figures with corresponding dividends of any other company.

Dividends payable in 1879 and 1880, less state tax where such is imposed, on life policies (all cash, no dividend additions) issued at age 35 for $10,000.

Year of Issue.	Prem.	Div. 1879.	Div'dend 1880.
1875.....................	264 90	....	73 80
1877.....................	264 90	77 80	77 00
1876.....................	264 90	77 60	81 50
1875.....................	264 90	81 50	85 50
1874.....................	264 90	85 50	89 70
1873.....................	264 90	89 70	94 00
1872.....................	264 90	94 00	98 40
1871.....................	264 90	98 40	103 00
1870.....................	264 90	103 00	107 60
1869.....................	268 70	111 50	116 90
1868.....................	268 70	116 90	122 10
1867.....................	268 70	122 10	127 40
1866.....................	268 70	127 40	133 80
1865.....................	268 70	133 80	138 50
1864.....................	268 70	138 50	144 20
1863.....................	268 70	144 20	150 00
1862.....................	268 70	150 00	155 90
1861.....................	268 70	155 90	162 00
1860.....................	268 70	162 00	168 50
1859.....................	268 70	168 50	174 30
1858.....................	268 70	174 30	180 60

No Other Company can equal these results, which are not exceptional—that is, such as would be produced either by an unusually prosperous year or by recklessness in making unwarrantably large dividends.

The Company has been paying large dividends for years, but its undivided surplus steadily increases.

Undiv'd Sur., Jan 1, 1873.....$1,524,086
" " " 1874.....1,779,731
" " " 1875..... 2,030,710
" " " 1876..... 2,527,558
" " " 1877..... 2,706,317
" " " 1878..... 2,789,237
" " " 1879..... 2,913,132
" " " 1880..... 3,028,159

WISCONSIN SOLDIERS AND SAILORS REUNION ROSTER. 01

Dignin, James F — Brothertown
Dignin, Wm F — Brothertown
Fowler, Geo M — Elroy
Forbush, Chebar, f — New Chester
Forbush, Chebar, f — Grand Marsh
Green, Dexter — Seven Pines, Oct 27—64
Guyer, J J, f — Kill Creek, Kan
Hollenbeck, W J, f — Sergeant Bluff, Ia
Hoskins, M B, f — Minnesota
Kenyon, Wm R — New Chester
Kinyon, Robert, f — New Chester
Keller, Ed F — Grand Marsh
Lamphere, Silas, l — Milton Junction
Miller, Holden — Madison, May 4—64
Meehann, Mike f — Brothertown
Perkins, C G, — Onona, Ia
Perry, S L — Sergeant Bluff, Ia
Pohlman, Otto — Plymouth
Sanborn, Chas H — Kenosha
Spencer, John — Ft Munroe May 4—64
Schleber, Lawrence, f — Grand Marsh
Stone, J N, ed — Neenah
Vaughn, Geo W — Yorktown, Aug 14—63
Wilson, Addison — Racine, May 16—62
Wing, Andrew, f — Clark Co
Wines, John E, f — Easton
Wattles, A B — Kenosha
Wieko, Warren S, me — Waupun

H
Capt Albert Grant
Lt Jno Wright*
Lt Theophilus Charroin* — Richmond, Apr 30—65
Lt Cromwell Lathe
Lt David R Hindman
Maxwell, Wm, sgt — Yorktown, Aug 1—63
Adams, Edward P, sgt — Hampton, Dec 11—61
Phillips, Adam — Newbern, N C
Butler, Barney — Ft Monroe, Aug 17—61
Brown, Oliver, — Baltimore, Apr 20—65
Boland, Thos, r r man — Milwaukee
Clause, J stus — Portsmouth, Nov 29—62
Duppel, Frank
Ferris, Ralph H — Portsmouth, July 29—63
Fitkins, Stephen — Baltimore, Apr 13—65
Goodnough, Wm — Salisbury, Jan 9—65
Harris, H, ed — Marinette
Krashane, Anton — New Fane
Mathewson, Wm — Salisbury, Jan 29—65
Polk, Jas R — Hampton, Oct 6—63
Phelapps, Adam — Newbern, N C
Robicheu, Wm — Menominee
Sprague, Jas — Norfolk, July 3—62
Shimer, Myron D — Point of Rocks, Feb 25—65
Smales, Benj — Cresco, Ia
Smalley, R J — Appleton

I
Capt Amos O Rowley
Lt Chipman A Holley
Lt Calvin M Wood
Lt Henry R Heward
Lt Leo Welden
Lt Wm J Trousdale
Fuguary, Aaron A, sgt — Yorktown, Sept 7—63
Ewing, Edward* — Seven Pines, Oct 27—64
Ashley, Bush — Avoca
Banks, Ed — Shetek
Camel, John — Avoca, Nov 15—64
Carver, Geo — Avoca
Fayerwether, I, D — Point of Rocks, Feb 9—65
Havens, Silas — Hampton, Aug 22—63
Jones, Jno A — Millin, June 25 - 61
Knapp, W C — Richland, City
McMullan, Oliver — Yorktown, Aug 4—63
McNurlin, John T — Norfolk, Aug 7—62
Oakes, F — Avoca
Richardson, J — Avoca

K
Shockley, Aaron — Ft Monroe, June 6—64
Salmon, Samuel — Yorktown, Aug 16—63
Sharp, Newton — Portsmouth, Aug 25—61
Sturdivant, Marcus — Avoca
Taylor, A — Avoca
Waddell, John H — Annapolis, Mar 15—65

Capt Wm W Bates
Capt Henry Myers
Capt Harmon Wentworth
Lt Silas C Seaman
Lt Albert Earthman
Lt Jas D Carmody
Moscrip, Wm S, sgt+
Poland, Solon, sgt — Fort Monroe, Va
Hendricks, L A, corp — Newport News, Sept 21—63
Bidwell, Richard — Hampton, Sept 3—63
Cook, Chas E — Point of Rocks, Va
Englehart, Jacob — Madison, May 15—62
Garry, Michael — Fort Monroe, Oct—63
Hood, Walter — Hampton, Sept 15—63
Miller, Peter — Madison
Nixon, Albert — Hampton, Oct 7—63
Rogers, Andrew — Portsmouth, Mar 26—63
Vanderhoof, Sam E — Easton
Van Cott, Jno M — Wisconsin, May 25—62
Wessenberg, Albert — Fort Monroe, June—64
                    — Newbern, Nov 28—63

UNASSIGNED.
Elliot, Win — Tess Corners
Elliot, Mathew — Tess Corners
Harrington, Jno
Kupper, Jacob — Ahnapee
Kluszing, Jno H, f — Ahnapee
Nelson, Peter — Delavan
Perkins, Lew S — Friendship
Roberts, Thos — Oxford

TWENTIETH INFANTRY.

Three years. Organized August 23d, 1862. Original strength 950; gain by recruits etc, 139. Total, 1129. Death loss, 227—Killed in action, 67, died of wounds, 36, of disease, 134. Other losses. 378, missing, 0, desertions, 41, transfers 115, discharged 222. Strength at muster out, July 14th, 1865, 524. Campaigns in Mo., Ark., Miss., La., Texas, Ala.

REGIMENTAL ROSTER.
Col Bertine Pinkney — Peabody, Kan
Lt Col Henry A Starr — Chicago
Maj Aug H Pettibone — Ohio
Maj Atherin Gillett — Olympia, Kan
Adj H V Morris
Adj Chas A Wenges — Milwaukee
Q M Jno A Douglas — Milwaukee, Oct 14—62
Q M Wm H York — Prescott
Surg C B Chapman — Olympia, Kan
Surg Orin Peak — Oak Park, Ill
A Surg Emanuel Munk — Milwaukee
A Surg Mark A Mosher — Berlin
Chap Wm H Marble
Chap A H Walters — Buffalo, N Y

A
Capt A H Pettibone
Lt Wm H York — Prescott
Lt Jas M Brackett
Lt Phineas J Clauson — Monroe
Crawford, Jas, sgt+, — Prairie Grove, Dec 7—62
Teeley, Lindsey E, sgt — Prairie Grove, Dec 7—62
Frame, Jos, sgt* — Dec 22—62
Bowen, Stephen L* — Prairie Grove, Dec 7—62
Brackett, Geo N — St Louis, Sept 24—62
Brackett, J M, ed — Eau Claire
Brunkee, Wm, f — Stockton

Chandler, Jeremiah* — Prairie Grove, Dec 7—62
Crosby, Jno H — New Orleans, Mar 7—64
Cole, Sardius F — Springfield, Nov 9—62
Dowse, Geo W* — Springfield, Jan 8—63
Davis, Geo — Ono
Fletcher, Austin — St Louis, Mo
Flint, Geo W — Springfield, May 12—63
Freeman, Orin — Memphis, Aug 28—63
Gray, Decatur — Springfield, Feb 27—63
Gray, Wilson T — Nov 3—63
Gordon, Alonzo I — Springfield, Nov 10—62
Huntsinger, Peter — Prairie Grove, Dec 7—62
Ives, Wm — Springfield, Nov 22—62
Kinney, Warren O — Crane Creek, Nov 9—62
Lawton, Wesley D — Springfield, Nov 22—62
McLaughlin E — Ross Fork, Idaho
Pierzfall, Xavier T* — Prairie Grove, Dec 7—62
Paine, M T, real estate sgt — Ellsworth
Parr, Jno B* — Prairie Grove, Dec 7—62
Pierce, S N — Waukeska
Posey, Jas B+ — Fayetteville, Dec 11—62
Rice, Frank* — Prairie Grove, Dec 7—62
Riley, Wm* — Prairie Grove, Dec 7—62
Randall, Thos — Benton Barracks, Mar 30—63
Turnby, Wm — Springfield, Mo
Thomas, Palmer — Ono
Taylor, Robt E* — Prairie Grove, Dec 7—62
Van Wormer, E, f — Lyndville
Weston, Jno B* — Prairie Grove, Dec 7—62
Welshonce, Robt L* — Prairie Grove, Dec 7—62
Williams, Jno B* — Spanish Ft, Mar 28—65

B
Capt E F Stone+ — New Orleans, Apr 1—65
Capt A S Bush — Sun Prairie
Capt Fred'k A Bird — Sun Prairie
Lt Jos Blackstone — New Diggings
Sexton, Maurice E, sgt* — Prairie Grove Dec 7—62
Curtis, Samuel F, sgt* — Prairie Grove Dec 7—62
Fozel, Henry, corp+ — Fayetteville, Dec 24—62
Williams, James, corp, f — Oconomowoc
Bingham, Augustus — New Orleans, Aug 31—63
Chilcote, Alfred, m — Washington, Ia
Cooper, Jacob W — Springfield, Mar 43—61
Frint, John — Rolla, Sept 16—62
Gayman, Eleazer — Springfield, Nov 19—62
Hineman, John — Fayetteville, Jan 20—63
Jacks, K M, r r man — Winona, Minn
Martin, S C, f — Utica, Dakota
Moon, Jos — Madison, Sept—62
March, Samuel+ — Fayetteville, Dec 11—62
Nerer, Solomon J — Madison, Sept 12—62
Pool, David — Fayetteville, Jan 9—63
Pelterplace, Delos — Springqueen
Peters, John* — Prairie Grove, Dec 7—62
Smith, James R+ — Fayetteville Dec 16—62
Standish, Nathaniel L+ — Fayetteville Dec 17—62
Stevens, James — Rolla, May 9—63
Turner, Payne — Springfield, Feb 7—63
Yakely, Wm A* — Prairie Grove Dec 7—62

C
Capt John McDermott* — Prairie Grove Dec 7—62
Capt Chas E Stevens+ — New Orleans
Capt Chas Boyle — Kansas
Lt Jacob McLaughlin — Boscobel
Lt Moritz F Eversz — Ripon
Lt Jasper W Newton — Texas
Lt B B Sanbourn — Lake Mills
Williams, Geo J, sgt — Brazos Santiago, Aug 7—64
Robinson, Geo, sgt — Springfield, Sep 2—62
Graham, Robt, corp — Springfield, Oct 18—62
Shipley, Wm H, corp — Springfield, Nov 7—62
Watkins, Jefferson, corp — Carrollton, Sept 8—63
Brown, Hiram — Rolla Sep 2—62
Craig, Henry — Brownsville, Dec 27—63
Claro, Norman B+ — Fayetteville, Dec 27—62
Farley, Benj F — Galveston, July 3—65
Fritz, John — Springfield, Oct 12—62
Kellogg, Lewis, f — Marine, Ia

The Fond du Lac, Amboy & Peoria R'y,

[Narrow Gauge,] runs from Fond du Lac, Wis, to Iron Ridge, connecting with the

CHICAGO, MILWAUKEE & St. PAUL R'Y,

(The Largest Railway in the United States) making close connections with their trains, East and West twice each day.

BAGGAGE CHECKED AND PASSENGERS TICKETED THROUGH TO ALL IMPORTANT POINTS.

Fond du Lac to St. Paul, Minneapolis, Manitoba, La Crosse, Winona, Sioux City, Yankton, the Black Hills, and Northern Nebraska, also

———◆VIA◆———

Racine and Southwestern Division of Chicago, Milwaukee & St. Paul Railway, the Direct Route to Rock Island, Davenport, Cedar Rapids, Des Moines and all Points in Southern Iowa, Kansas and Missouri.

Standard Gauge Cars Brought through by Change of Trucks at Iron Mountain, making it a Safe and Convenient Route.

For Through Rates, Bills of Lading or any other Information, Apply at

GENERAL OFFICES, FOREST STREET, FOND DU LAC, WIS.

[SEE PAGE 40.]

F. J. DIXON,
CASH GROCER,
WHOLESALE AND RETAIL

232 & 234 West Water Street, Corner Cedar,

MILWAUKEE, - WIS.
(SEE FULL PAGE AD.)

THE MERCHANTS' INSURANCE CO., NEWARK, N. J.

776 & 778 BROAD ST.

WISCONSIN SOLDIERS AND SAILORS REUNION ROSTER.

Lowers, Elias+ — Prairie Grove, Dec 5–62
Lyon, Geo — Rolla, Sep 27–62
Lull, Walter K — Springfield, Dec 11–62
Lyon, Gilbert — New Orleans, Jan 25–64
McDonald, Andrew J — Carrollton, Oct 3–63
Norton, Reuben — Prairie Grove, Dec 18–62
Powell, John — Vicksburg, Aug 18–63
Root, Alonzo N — Rolla, Sep 27–62
Smith, Geo W+ — Fayetteville, Dec 20–62
Sanborn, B.D — Lake Mills
Smith, Dunyon — Springfield, Dec 19–62
Tyler, John G — Rolla, Sep 30–62
Wright, Ephriam N — Carrollton, Sep 3–63
Ward, Madison — Carrollton, Sep 29–63
Watkins, Noah — New Orleans, Dec 1–63

D

Capt Almerin Gillett — Olympia, Kan
Capt E E Ellis — Cleveland, O
Lt Geo W Barter — Freeport, Ill
Lt Wm H Farnsworth — Joliet, Ill
Lt Chas D Butler — Bloomington, Ill
Lt Wm Young
Binkert, Jos — St Louis, Meh 17–63
Baff, Moses — Neillsville
Butts, Chas W — Cairo, Sept 20–64
Barter, A J, conductor — Freeport, Ill
Conroe, G C, m — Racine
Corlis, Jonathan S* — Prairie Grove, Dec 7–62
Chambers, Abraham — Racine
Callaghan, Dennis — Prairie Grove, Dec 7–62
Carroll, John — Mobile Point, Nov 11–64
Delano, Ed C — Mobile Point, Sept 16–64
Hogan, Jas — Springfield, Apr 5–63
Hancock, Wesley J+ — Mobile, Mch 28–65
Jenkins, John+ — Fayetteville, Dec 20–62
Johnson, Edw — Springfield, Oct 8–62
Kalg, E — Elkhorn
Ketchpaw, M W — Elkhorn
O'Connor, P J — 1312 Wentworth av, Chicago
Remington, Henry S+ — Fayetteville, Dec 12–62
Rice, Jos W+ — Fayetteville, Dec 13–64
Romain, Jno B — Vicksburg, July 28–63
Reynolds, Robt — Rolla, Sept 25–62
Wettroth, Herman — Vicksburg, Aug 11–63

E

Capt Jno Weber+ — Fayetteville, Dec 15–62
Capt Fred'k Kusel — Watertown
Capt Alfred F Bachr — Oshkosh
Lt Chas A Menges — Milwaukee
Lt Maximilin Gebhardt — Cleveland, Ohio
Lt Geo Henze — Watertown
Weber, Frederick, corp — Springfield, Nov 3–62
Brown, E — Neillsville
Button, August* — Prairie Grove, Dec 7–62
Ballow, Henry — Mauston
Berg, Jno — Brazor Santiago, Aug 30–64
Boten, Albert — New Orleans Sept 6–63
Fischer, Louis+ — Springfield, Feb 7–63
Hogan, James — Springfield, Apr 3–63
Kluge, August+ — Fayetteville, Dec 25–62
Meuster, Gottfried* — Prairie Grove, Dec 7–62
Mueller, Wm — July 26–64
Ramsey, Jno N* — Prairie Grove, Dec 7–62
Schuasse, Ernest+ — Fayetteville, Apr 20–63
Schneider, Frank+ — Fayetteville, Dec 18–62
Steindorf, Julius — Port Hudson, July 31–63
Volker, Fred'k+ — New Orleans, May 14–63
Volker, Ferdinaud — Springfield, Feb 7–63
Wurm, Jno — Prairie Grove, Dec 7–62
Weight, Julius* — Prairie Grove, Dec 7–62
Welrich, Julius* — Prairie Grove, Dec 7–62
Zauntner, Louis — Nov 3–63

F

Capt N Nelson Whitman
Lt Albert H Blake — Leadville, Col

Lt C C Rice
Lt D W Horton
Kay. Levi R, 1st sgt — Springfield, Nov 19–62
Hicks, Addison G, corp* — Prairie Grove, Nov 7–62
Cady, Albert A, corp* — Prairie Grove, Dec 7–62
Bell, Jno, corp — Wingville, Aug 31–62
Hart, Garvie W, corp — Springfield, Oct 21–62
Gaston, Jos, corp — Rolla, Nov 15–62
Harris, Christian, corp — Memphis, Aug 28–63
Brown, David+ — Fayetteville, Dec 12–62
Bacon, Jus, f — Ledgeville
Cady, Orvis+ — Fayetteville, Feb 25–63
Chappell, Orin D — Springfield, Nov 13–62
Harper, Abel+ — Fayetteville, Dec 16–62
Hooper, Jno, me — Platteville
Holmes, Emanuel T — Pt Hudson, July 30–63
Hackmau, Henry — Brazor Santiago, July 30–63
Kuner, Jos — Fayetteville, Dec 10–62
Lightner, Jas+ — Fayetteville, Dec 10–62
Lafond, Peter + — Moblie, Apr 24–65
Lamb, G L — Tomah
Nolle, Bernard — Pt Hudson, Aug 11–63
Snow, Geo W — Bon Homme, D T
Thomas, D C — Prospect, N Y
Vincery, Fred'k — Tomah
Washburn, Horace R — Rolla, Oct 25–63
Washburn, Benj F — Fayetteville, Feb 25–63
Ware, Wm — Ft Morgan, Sept 6–64
Zedekie, Lewis — Vicksburg Aug 15,–63

G

Capt Edw G Miller — Minnesota
Lt Albert J Ruckwell — Oconomowoc
Lt C C Rice
Lt Jos P Plandle — Milwaukee
Reed, Amasa T, sgt — Lebanon, Sep 29–62
Dondan, Benj S, corp* — Prairie Grove, Dec 7–62
Warne, Wm R, corp* — Prairie Grove, Dec 7–62
Allen, Alfred — Brownville, May 2–62
Allen, Wm H — Rolla, Oct 3–62
Baker, Willis — Prairie Grove, Dec 7–62
Crumpney, Elliot J — Vicksburg, July 23–63
Downing, Preston S* — Prairie Grove, Dec 7–62
Dwyer, Michael — Springfield, Mar 27–63
Doty, Levi — Springfield, Feb 4–63
Emerick, Peter F* — Prairie Grove, Dec 7–63
Gardner, Barnet — Springfield, Mar 7–63
Herring, Chas+ — Fayetteville, Dec 26–62
Johnson, Geo — Prairie Grove, Dec 7–62
Johnson, Lyman — Springfield, Dec 14–62
Lindsley, Benj B — Port Hudson, July 26–63
Lawton, Edward, T — New Auburn, Minn
Merrill, Melvin E* — Prairie Grove, Dec 7–62
McVean, J — Neillsville
Martin, Edward T — Cassville, Oct 31–67
Madare, Frank — Springfield, Dec 8–62
Murray, John — Springfield, Feb 26–63
Oertel, Geo, f — Oakdale
Orendorf, S J — Hebrou
Oertil, Geo — Hoeser Mills
Phelps, Wesley — Springfield, Dec 7–62
Poole, Alvaro D — Brownsville, Dec 13–63
Rickemian, Geo M* — Prairie Grove, Dec 7–62
Strong, S — 300 S Water st, Chicago, Ill

H

Capt H E Strong, P r agt — Baraboo
Capt Geo W Miller
Lt Geo W Hoot+ — Ripon, Feb 3–63
Lt A E Cheeney
Lt Moritz Eversz — Ripon
Lt E P Norton
Dawes, Edmund, 1st sgt* — Prairie Grove, Dec 7–62
Hinkley, Jessie, corp* — Prairie Grove, Dec 7–62
Nicholas, Jno G, corp* — Prairie Grove, Dec 7–62
Sargeant, Jno P, corp — Fayetteville, Sept 9–63
Burt, Alfred, corp — Springfield, Feb 25–63
Avert, Fredericks — New Orleans, Aug 18–63
Bradway, Edward — Springfield, Apr 6–63

Caylor, David H — Springfield, Oct 28–62
Cheney, A E, m — Fond du Lac
Christian, C W — Neillsville
Eversz Herman, m — Ripon
Forbes, Lorenze J — Ripon
Fulton, Merritt B — Delta, N Y
Hill, Jno, m — Ripon
Howard, Jas — Prairie Grove, Dec 7–62
Hartsberg, August — Lake Springs, Apr 15–63
Howard, Lorenzo — New Orleans, Aug 19–64
Hendrickson, Jno — New Orleans, Nov 3–63
Johnson, Nell, me — Berlin
Kirby, N C, f — Fairmont, Minn
La Fountain, Anthony+ — Fayetteville, Dec 11–62
Lyon, Martin — New Orleans, Aug 31–63
Markham, Chas — Springfield, Jan 13–63
Smith, S S — Fairmont, Minn
Shute, Dexter B* — Prairie Grove, Dec 7–62
Sabalka, Jno — Springfield, Aug 29–63
Warwick, Geo
Wales, Thomas H — Port Hudson, Aug 3–63
Weller, Wm H+ — Dec 31–62
Wilson, Gilbert — Ripon
Young, Richard m — Fayetteville, Jan 30–63

I

Capt Wm Harlocker — Grant
Lt Thos Bentliff* — Prairie Grove, Dec 7–62
Lt Albert P Hall
Lt David B Arthur — Grant
Lt Jno Stack
Sprague, Egbert A — Navy Cove, Oct 5–64
Beidler, Jno H — Rolla, Oct 5–62
Caylor, David H — Springfield, Nov 13–62
Cliek, Thos — Carrollton, Sept 4–63
Dewing, Thos — Pt Hudson, July 31–63
DeHart, Ira B — Cairo, Mar 26–64
Huey, Jos — Fayetteville, Jan 14–63
Helm, Lyman B — Ft Gaines, Nov 26–64
Nye, Mellen — New Orleans, Aug 16–64
Parker, D A, f — Mount Hope
Peyton, Stephen W+ — Fayetteville, Dec 11–62
Parland, Alex* — Prairie Grove, Dec 7–62
Vesper, Cyrus W* — Prairie Grove, Dec 7–62
Van Ausdell, Cornelius — New Orleans, Jan 2–64
Weaver, Geo W — Brownsville, Dec 11–63
Woodhouse, Jas, m — Lancaster
Wagner, Lester — Vicksburg, July 19–63
Zimmerman, Henry — Vicksburg, Aug 8–63

K

Lt Nathan Cole — Sheboygan
Lt Sam'l B Jackson — Oshkosh
Lt Chas Proctor
Boyd, Edgar C, sgt — Fayetteville, Jan 17–63
Jacobs, Willard, corp* — Prairie Grove, Dec 7–62
Washburn, Frank H* — Prairie Grove, Dec 7–62
Johnson, Robt, corp* — Prairie Grove, Dec 7–62
Blackburn, Jesse+ — Fayetteville, Dec 18–62
Bradley, Bigelow — Fayetteville, Jan 4–63
Cornes, Calvin — Springfield, Feb 12–63
Diestler, Wm — Wayside
Dumprope, Wm+ — Fayetteville, Dec 15–62
Dobbret, Chas* — Fayetteville, Dec 28–62
Edler, Henry — Springfield Mar 22–63
Freese, Jno W — Rolla, Feb 8–63
Gillis, Jno — Springfield, Feb 8–63
Hall, Lucius B* — Prairie Grove, Dec 7–62
Hathaway, Dan'l T — Springfield, Nov 7–62
Hager, Edward — Ft Gaines, Jan 29–65
Harkins, Eli — Springfield, Feb 7–63
Jackson, S B — Oshkosh
Lahey, Thos — Two Creeks
Leisinger, Chas* — Prairie Grove, Dec 7–63
Moon, Wm — Springfield, Jan 3–63
Olmsted, Stephen M — New Orleans, Nov 28–64
O'Kelly, Perry* — Prairie Grove, Dec 7–64
Otto, Gottlieb — Oconomowoc
Sullivan, Dennis* — Prairie Grove, Dec 7–62

MANUFACTURERS OF
FARM FREIGHT AND SPRING WAGONS
OF EVERY DESCRIPTION.

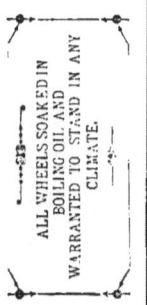

OUR CELEBRATED FARM WARGON.

THE BEST WAGON ON WHEELS.

It is the Strongest and Best Proportioned, Best Made, Best Ironed, and Best Painted Wagon in the Market.

It is the Lightest Running Farm Wagon in the World and the only Wagon having the Celebrated Holmes Patent Self Oiling Skein.

WISCONSIN SOLDIERS AND SAILORS REUNION ROSTER.   95

Struthers, Robt*   Prairie Grove, Dec 7—62
Sayles, Darius, Jr   Springfield, Dec 17—62
Schmidt, Jno C   St Louis, Jan 3—63
Truesdell, Geo*   Prairie Grove, Dec 7—62
Warden, Gardiner B*   Prairie Grove, Dec 7—62
Warden, Alpheus J   Springfield, Dec 29—62

UNASSIGNED.

Blake, E W   Rush River
Dyer, Jno, f   Eden
Dewey, E, prin high school   Delavan
Hine, Jos H, musician   Oshkosh
John, Henry   N S postoffice, Chicago, Ill
Knust, Lewis, m   Burlington
Krause, John   Oconomowoc
Nelson, L   Rush River
Schwandt, August   New Orleans, May 27—64
Shilberne, Andrew J   Springfield, Oct 13—62

TWENTY-FIRST INFANTRY.

Three years. Organized September 5th, 1862.
Original strength, 1002; gain by recruits, etc.,
169; total, 1171. Death loss, 288, killed in action,
67, died of wounds, 47, of disease, 174. Other
losses, 400, missing, 0, desertions, 40 transfers,
99, discharges, 261. Strength at muster-out,
July 8th, 1865, 483. Campaign in Ky., Tenn.,
Ga., S. C., N. C.

REGIMENTAL ROSTER.

Col Benj J Sweet
Col Harison C Hobart
Lt Michael H Fitch
Maj Fred K Schumacher   Oct 8—62
Maj Chas H Walker
Adj Jas H Jenkins   Oshkosh
Q M Henry C Hamilton
Q M B J Van Valkenburg
Q M Sam'l H Fernandez
Surg Sam'l J Carolin+   Nov 4—62
Surg Jas P Reeve
A Surg Sidney S Fuller
A Surg Wm M Hoyt
A Surg Benj C Britt
A Surg Wm R Reynolds
A Surg G W Merrill
A Surg Henry L Barnes
Chap Orson P Clinton

A

Capt Alex White
Capt Hiram K Edwards
Lt Nathan Leavitt
Lt Kelsey M Adams
Lt Watson H Cook
Lt Henry C Taylor+   Dec 12—64
Lt Samuel Dotalling
Peacock, Rich A, sgt   Murfreesboro, Feb 9—63
Hubbell, Henry W, sgt+ Perryville, Oct 14—62
Sherwood, Aaron, corp+ Perryville, Oct 16—62
Brannum, W H, corp   Murfreesboro, Mar 19—63
Armstrong, Henry H   Philadelphia, May 24—64
Austin, John F   Andersonville, Jan 18—64
Bowles, Jas A+   Perryville, Oct 9—62
Briggs, Abner   Murfreesboro, May 16—63
Blair, Leon
Book, W H   Stockbridge
Craw, Fred M+   Danville, Nov 5—62
Corey, John B   Richmond, Feb 3—63
Cummings, Solomon   Andersonville, July 14—64
Dunn, John*   Chaplin Hills, Oct 8—62
Dolan, Oliver   Murfreesboro, Feb 18—63
Depas, Anthony   Andersonville, Sept 12—64
Daroche Edw, f   Fond du Lac

Durosba, Edw   Fond du Lac
Denniston C W   Fond du Lac
Davis, Leonard F   Sahula, Ia
Fink, Henry*   Atlanta, Aug 23—64
Ford, Chas M   Taycheedah, Nov 19—65
Hilton, Harlow W*   Resaca, May 14—64
Hoteling, S, m   Fond du Lac
Jewell, Henry, e   San Francisco, Cal
Kerby, Robt W, f   Leroy
Kally, R W   Fond du Lac
McKennan, Francis*   Resaca, May 14—64
McDonald, Duncan+   Perryville, Oct 9—64
Mountian, A   Ft Howard
Marcoe, Francis, m   Fond du Lac
Orando, Moses   Andersonville, Nov 8—64
Patterson, Jacob   Andersonville, Sep 13—64
Russell, Roland F   Louisville, Jan 18—65
Rinds, M O   Andersonville, Sept 9—64
Smith, Thos   Louisville, Feb 4—63
Washburn, Ed C*   Chaplin Hills, Oct 8—62

B

Capt Chas N Paine   Oshkosh
Capt Jas E Stuart   Oshkosh
Lt Edgar Vledenburg   Winneconne
Lt Jas H Jenkins   Oshkosh
Lt Edward Donao   Oshkosh
Lt Alek Peterson   Oshkosh
Jordan, John A, sgt   Richmond, Feb 24—64
Kellet, John B, corp   Andersonville, July 27 -64
Avery, Amos, corp   Nashville, Oct 17—63
Blinn, Noble A, corp   Bowling Green Nov 12—62
Sherburne, Wm G, corp   Nashville, Feb 2—63
Brooks, Alden S   Nashville, Dec 23—62
Benn, Edgar   Escanaba
Barrett, John W   Nashville, Feb 12—63
Brun, Edgar   Oshkosh
Burns, A   Tomah
Clausen, Andrew*   Resaca, May 14—64
Cornley, Jno   Murfreesboro, Mar 23—63
Crittenden, Aretus   Bowling Green, Ky
Cowan, Geo B   Louisville, Mar 21—64
Clark, Jas   Danville, Mar 7—64
Carpenter, J D   Shiocton
Dudley, Loren*   Chaplin Hills, Oct 8—62
Grignon, Andrew, f   Winneconne
Ham, Robert B   Bowling Green, Nov 22—62
Jackman Mo..roe+   May 30—64
Krosskor, Reuben M   Louisville, Nov 16—62
Kraggs, Chas   Nashville, Oct 11—64
Miller, Nelson   Mitchellsville, Nov 24—62
Mularkey, Chas   Andersonville, Nov 8—64
Pillar, Jas*   Chaplin Hills, Oct 8—62
Raymond, Sidney   Nov 18—62
Ryan, Patrick   Nashville, Aug 6—63
Ripley, Smith   Nashville, Jan 5—63
Russell, Willard A   Murfreesboro, Feb 27—63
Russell, Hiram   Oshkosh
Showers, Elisha B*   Chaplin Hills, Oct 8—62
Stacey, Dwight   Dallas, June 14—64
Smothers, St Clair F   Savannah, June 17—65
Tipper, Jno   Camp Chase, Feb 6—63
Thompson, Harvey   Bowling Green, Ky
Vanderburg, B   Winneconne
Worden, Geo O+   Chickamauga, Sept 20—63
Walker, Luke   Murfreesboro, Jan 17—63
White, Mitchell   Lookout Mt, March 25—64

C

Capt Alphonso S Godfry   Oshkosh
Capt William Wall   Oshkosh
Lt Robert W Jackson   Oshkosh
Lt David W Mitchell*   Oct 8—62
Lt Julius P Bissell   Oshkosh
Lt Chas W Hubbard   Oshkosh
Harding, Witson H, sgt Andersonville, Aug 14—64
Britton, Henry T, sgt   Perryville, Oct 12—62
Millard, Willington H, corp* C Hills, Oct 8—62

Killbourne, Geo A, corp Murfreesboro, Mar 4—63
Baldwin, Reuben*   Chaplin Hills, Oct 8—62
Bingham, Alfred+   Perryville, Oct 17—62
Blaisier, David   Bowling Green, Nov 9—62
Bacheldor, Jas   Andersonville, Sep 12—64
Dowson. Elijah   Oshkosh
Baker, John S, f   Oshkosh
Coulson, Geo W*   Chaplin Hills, Oct 8—62
Coffin, W T   Oshkosh
Dean, W J, e   Oshkosh
Ellsworth, Nelson H*   Chaplin Hills, Oct 8—62
Hughes, John W   Murfreesboro, Apr 3—63
Kelsey, U N   Oshkosh
Lake, Levi+   Nov 5—62
Luck, Fred, f   Winchester
McCord, Thos+   Perryville, Oct 15—62
Mann, Edw+   Chickamauga Sep 19—63
Mulaney, Thos+   Resaca, May 23—64
Morris, Benj J   Murfreesboro, Mar 15—63
Owen, William*   Chaplin Hills, Oct 8—62
Ralph, Geo W*   Chaplin Hills, Oct 8—62
Rodgers, Francis M   Nolinsville, Dec 30—63
Roberts, Robert   Madison, Dec 8—64
Robert, Edgar G   Bowling Green, Dec 5—62
Stever, Wm R   Chattanooga, May 23—64
Turner, Charles H   Bowling Green, Dec 1—62
Williams, Thomas E*   Chaplin Hills, Oct 8—62
Williams, David J   Mitchellsville, Nov 19—62
Wright, W W, f   Oshkosh

D

Capt John Jewett Jr+   Nov 21—62
Capt Henry Turner
Capt John H Otto
Lt Fred W Blreherdt
A Lyman C Waite
Scott, Egbert, 1st sgt Andersonville, Aug 14—64
Clark, Theo, sgt   Murfreesboro, Mar 4—63
Seaman, Mead H, sgt   Andersonville, Sept 23—64
Nye, Geo H, corp   Covington, Dec 31—62
Abbott, Alfred   Andersonville, Aug 9—64
Baker, Richard*   Chaplin Hills, Oct 8—62
Baker, Walton   Mitchellsville, Dec 11—62
Buck, Chas, m   Hortonville
Draper, Nelson B   Stevensville
Dey, Jno, f   Greenville
Harz, Herman*   Bentonville, Mar 19—65
Hoskins, Miles+   Atlanta, Aug 9—64
Hilbert, C H   Appleton
Johns, Andrew   Vining's Station, Aug 6—64
Knowles, Henry   Andersonville, Oct 11—64
Madder, Chas   Keokuk, Oct 18—61
Manser, George   Murfreesboro, Feb 16—63
Miller, Fred'k   Nashville, Sept 14—64
Newell, Bryton   Mitchellsville, Nov 19—62
Nye, Wm B   Murfreesboro, Feb 4—63
Peebles, David W   Nashville—63
Pearson, Foster   Murfreesboro, Mar 15—63
Pearse, Richard A   Mitchellsville, Nov 22—62
Rexford, S W   Shiocton
Rawson, M C, l   Whitewater
Sykes, Lewis H*   Resaca, May 14—64
Simpson, Thos   Nashville, Jan 19—63
Somerset, Peter   Madison, Jan 19—64
Sweetser, Jno W   Nashville, Feb 14—64
Shultz, Herman   Milwaukee
Turner, Benj L*   Stone River, Dec 30—62
Van De Bogart, Henry   Murfreesboro, 21—63

E

Capt Hiram M Gibbs   Oct 16—62
Capt Ferdinand Osteufeld
Capt R J Weistrod   Oshkosh
Capt Fred W Burcherdt
Lt Jasen W Newell
Lt Chas F Weston   Oshkosh
Lt August Hansen
Lloyd, Jerome B, sgt+   Annapolis, Feb 4—64
Thurston, Danl, sgt*   Chaplin Hills, Oct 8—62

ESTABLISHED 1847.

BAKER & McKENNEY,

Manufacturers of and Dealers in

MILITARY GOODS

141 GRANT STREET, NEAR BROADWAY, NEW YORK.

AN EXPERIENCE OF

33 YEARS IN THE MANUFACTURE OF UNIFORMS,

JUSTIFIES US IN ASSERTING THAT WE CAN GIVE

Unsurpassed Advantages to Our Patrons.

SEND FOR ILLUSTRATED SHEET OF UNIFORMS AND PRICE LIST.

VOLUNTEER COMPANIES, REGIMENTS AND BANDS

Supplied With All Articles Needed For Their Equipment.

Regalia, Jewels, and other Properties for Masonic Blue Lodges, Chapters, Commanderies and Scottish Rite.

Knights Templar Uniforms a Specialty.

Odd Fellow's Lodges and Encampments, Sons of Temperance, American Protestant Associations, Knights of Pythias, Harugari, Good Templars, American Mechanics, and others, Fitted out at Short Notice.

A LARGE ASSORTMENT OF SILK, BUNTING AND MUSLIN FLAGS,

ON HAND AND MADE TO ORDER.

Also, Banner Silks, Bunting, Staffs, Eagles, Ornaments, Balls, Cords and Tassels, Fringes, Covers, Belts, and all Articles Needed for Flag and Banner Trimming.

BANNERS MADE TO ORDER.

WISCONSIN SOLDIERS AND SAILORS REUNION ROSTER.

Fowler, Wm, sgt+ — Sulphur Springs, Ky
Blount, Cornelius, sgt — Nashville, Feb 14—63
Jenson, Chas R, corp* — Chaplin Hills, Oct 8—62
Holt, Elias L, corp+ — Perryville, Oct 10—62
Kock, Helmhold, corp — Nashville, Mar 11—63
Sampson, Geo F, corp — Brothertown, Mar 11—65
Bawdrof, Henry* — Chaplin Hills, Oct 8—62
Bart, James — Stockbridge
Barlow, Amos — Stockbridge
Beach, E, — Chicago, Ill
Bremmer, J A — Stevens Point
Conoe, Worthington — Richmond, Feb 1—63
Christiansou, Dethlof — New Holstein Apr 25—63
Carey, Jas — Flambeau Station
Dillet, Wm* — Bentonville, Mar 19—65
Drake, F — Stockbridge
Drake, Phineas S — Stockbridge
Demouth, J — Neillsville
Flood, John* — Chaplin Hills, Oct 8—62
Geater, Geo — Nashville, Dec 30—62
Hitchcock, John C — Lebanon, Nov 6—62
Howe, Geo W — Stockbridge
Howey, J A — Stockbridge
Holt, Warren — Stockbridge
Johnson, Henry C+ — Perryville, Nov 6—62
Kuder, Chas* — Chaplin Hills, Oct 8—62
Kuhl, Bendix+ — Perryville, Nov 2—62
Koelsch, Frederick — Murfreesboro, Mar 13—63
Loewenluger, Lorenz — Marietta, July 18—61
Lawrence, H A — Neillsville
Ledden, J W — Stockbridge
Munster, John — Murfreesboro, Mar 7—62
Miller, Henry — Madison, Feb 6—64
Puffer, John W* — Chaplin Hills, Oct 8—62
Reader, William* — Chaplin Hills, Oct 8—62
Remon, Asmus — Murfreesboro, Jan 19—63
Sanford, Geo G — Shiocton
Stanton, Cato — Chilton
Togan, Rugus — Murfreesboro, Feb 19—63
Tams, Jordan — Murfreesboro, Jan 22—63
Wiggins, Leander E* — Chaplin Hills, Oct 8—62
Wiggins, Martin — Murfreesboro, Jan 29—63
Woolet, Thos — Murfersboro, Feb 7—63
Wewton, C F, me — Webster City, Ia

F

Capt Edgar Conklin
Capt Milton Ewen — Fond du Lac
Lt Chas H Morgan
Lt Edward Dorian — Oshkosh
Lt Martin L Clark
Lt Ambrose S Delaware
Killips, Richmond C, sgt* — Nashville, Aug 31—64
Tuolson, Cornelius, corp* Chaplin Hills, Oct 8-62
Ebgerly, Chas, corp* — Chickamauga, Sep 20—63
Petrie, Jacob, corp — Atlanta, Aug 8—64
Corrier, Cyrus C, corp — Andersonville, Sep 21—64
Allen, Delos, f — Byron
Brown, Chas F — Murfreesboro, Mar 7—63
Brown, J C, ph — Fond du Lac
Beede, L F, f — Byron
Bell, John, f — South Byron
Clark, Jasper — Mitchellsville, Dec 2—62
Dougherty, Christop — Chattanooga, June 8—64
Dillon Thomas — Stevenson, Sep 3—63
Gebson, J H, me — Oakfield
Hobbs, Alfred E* — Resaca, May 14—64
Hammond, Chas — Danville, Feb 26—64
Hunting, John — Blairs Landing, Mar 8—63
Hatch, Martin — Murfreesboro, Feb 14—63
Hale, Daniel — Bowling Green, Nov 11—62
Hale, E A, f — Lamarine
Holland, Lot, f — Byron
Kennedy, Timothy* — Kenesaw, June 18—64
Kirby, R W, f — Oakfield
Leechman, Fred'k* — Chaplin Hills, Oct 8—62
Lewis, Edw G — Chattanooga, Oct 11—63
Mc Night, Walter — New Albany, Dec 1—62
Morgan, Merrick — Chaplin Hills, Jan 11—63

G

Capt Milan H Sessions, a — Lincoln, Neb
Capt Jas M Randall
Lt Juo C Watson — New York City
Lt Juo C Crawford
Lt David D Burnham
Lt Alfred H A Harding
Ware, Oscar B, corp+ — Feb 23—63
Smith, Albert M, corp — Andersonville, Oct 10—64
Amenson, Goodwin, me — Amherst
Houghton, Myron* — Chaplin Hills, Oct 8—62
Bates, Wm H* — Kenesaw Mt, June 21—64
Beadleston, Jas — Louisville, Dec 27 62
Boyden, Henry — Chattahoochee, July 16—64
Barton, Dan'l A — Amherst
Beavers, Jno, f — Platteville
Cartwright, Alvin S+ — Perryville, Oct 10—62
Cass, Chas R+ — Chickamauga, Oct 15—63
Carr, Warner — Waupaca
Chady, W, m — Waupaca
Corulean, A B, m — Waupaca
Chandler, S S — Nashville, Jan 11—63
Dunham, Jno M — Nashville, Jan 11—63
Douglas, Chas A — Rural, Apr 12—63
Dickson, Wm — Argyle
Day, C F — Waupaca
Evans, Jno — Louisville, Feb 3—65
Gluty, Thos* — Resaca, May 14—64
Ganoe, Jas W — Chickamauga, Sept 19—63
Ganoe, Jas W — Crystal Lake
Gurley, Jason — Waupaca
Hanson, Hans Carl+ — Perryville, Oct 11—62
Hitchcock, Jas — Mitchellsville, Dec 18—62
Hall, D F — Waupaca
Ham, P A, f — Crystal Lake
Hoffer, C, h — Ogdensburg
Jones, Marcus — Danville, Jan 14—64
Johnson, Lewis E — Murfreesboro, Mar 19—63
King, Silas — Murfreesboro, Feb 26—63
Kelogher, Patrick — Menominee
Munger, Amos D* — Chaplin Hills, Oct 8—62
Manchester, D L, ph — Waupaca
Miner, Wesley, f — Rural
Noyes, Chas H+ — Nashville, Aug, 15—64
Niles, Simon B — Mitchellsville, Nov 14—62
Noyes, Alvah H — Murfreesboro, Jan 25—63
Pickle, Matt — Waupaca
Ranny, Chas H* — Resaca, May 14—64
Robertson, Finley O — Nashville, Feb 1—63
Staufield, Wm* — Resaca, May 14—64
Smith, Jerome — Springfield, Nov 2—62
Stratten, W — Crystal Lake
Sanborn, S P — Janesville
Sessions, M H — Lincoln, Neb
Thompson, E B — Waupaca
Van Duzer, Amos O* — Chattahoochee, July 6—64
Van Vort, Asa — Nashville, Jan 21—63
Winkler, Jas — Chickamauga, Sept 19—63
Watson, Isaac T — Nashville, Apr 9—64
Walter, Sam'l B — Andersonville, June 7—64
Woodnorth, Joe H — Waupaca
Weisenbon, W T — Waupaca

H

Capt Geo Bentley* — Chaplin Hills, Oct 8—62

Capt Fred'k L Clark
Capt William A Fargo — Fond du Lac
Capt Chas H Morgan
Lt Tim F Strong, Jr — Fond du Lac
Lt Edward S Midgley* — Bentonville, Mar 19—65
Lt Benj F Fuller — Memphis—79
Lt Henry N Hanson
Kirkland, Edw T, sgt* — Chaplin Hills, Oct 8—62
Thompson, Edw, sgt+ — Chattanooga, Sep 23—63
Alden, C J — Oakdale
Bergen, C C — Fond du Lac
Cook, Jno W — Savannah, Feb 24—65
Carr, Jas B — Clear Lake, Ia
Fugleberg, John* — Chaplin Hills 8—62
Fargo, W A, m — Fond du Lac
Galland, G, c — Fond du Lac
Hilts, Geo A* — Chaplin Hills, Oct 8—62
Hough, Nathan — Nashville, Dec 1—62
Hungerford, Dan'l — Murfreesboro, Mar 2—63
Hall, E P, m — Hillsboro, Ia
Johnson, John* — Chaplin Hills, Oct 8—62
Ley, Jno, f — Rantoul
Oram, John — Murfreesboro, Apr 23—63
Peters, Wm* — Dallas, June 20—64
Powell, Benj — Bowling Green, Nov 10—62
Perkins, Geo, a — Fond du Lac
Richards, Chas — Fond du Lac
Subra, John* — Dallas, June 20—64
Salverson, Hans — Goldsboro, Apr 5—65
Weber, John — Fond du Lac

I

Capt Simeon B Nelson — Menasha
Capt Abner B Smith — Cleveland, O
Capt Albert B Bradish — Atchinson, Kan
Lt Chas B Clark — Neenah
Lt Edward Delany — Fond du Lac
Lt Gustavus Jaeger
Trudell, Jas, sgt — Stevenson, Sep 24—63
Littlefield, L D, sgt — Mitchellsville, Nov 21—62
Bradish, Cyrus, Jr, sgt — Oct 15—62
Dana, Josiah H, corp* — Chaplin Hills, Oct 8—62
Forest, John W, corp — Nashville, Dec 30—62
Hale, Amos W, corp — Andersonville, Aug 22—64
Robinson, Cyrus D, corp — Nashville, Feb 17—63
Bell, Lewis N* — Resaca, June 18—64
Barns, Wm R — Danville, Feb 22—64
Bradish, A D — Atchison, Kansas
Clinton, Lanman W* — Chaplin Hills, Oct 8—62
Chamberlain, Jas A — Andersonville, Oct 25—64
Clark, C B — Neenah
Dunn, Henry S — Oct 24—62
Densiow, Abner M — Dec 5—64
Delany, E, City Clerk — Fond du Lac
Foster, Franklin F — Nashville, Dec 27—62
Hamilton, Wm — Murfreesboro, Mar 3—63
Harris, Peter — Danville, Feb 24—64
Hale, Channing A — Andersonville, Apr 22—64
Johnson, Wm W* — Chaplin Hills, Oct 8—62
Kellogg, Hollis W+ — Nashville, June 22—64
Knapp, Chas — Bowling Green, Nov 25—62
Kohnke, John — Nashville, May 7—63
Klinke, H T — Neenah
Ladd, Malcolm B — Louisville, Nov 29—62
Miller, J W — Neenah
Myot, Joseph — Warrens Mills
Nugent, Alfred A, a — Chilton, Ia
O'Drien, Edward — Nashville, Dec 6—63
Pendleton, Jerome+ — New Albany, Jan 29—63
Prouty, Wm — Nashville, Feb 14—63
Robinson, John* — Allatoona, May 31—64
Ramey, Homer C — Lebanon, Nov 12—62
Reed, Geo — Andersonville, July 25—64
Shultz, Christian — Louisville, Nov 29—62
Trudell, Oliver F — Oconto
Vinning, Thos F — Camp Chase, Feb 6—63
Wineman, Christian+ — Springfield, Nov 9—62
Webb, Lemuel W+ — Perryville, Oct 12—62

NEW YORK PRICES.

GOODYEAR RUBBER COMPANY

Afghan Hooks,	Carriage Cloth,	Pipe Combs,	Inhalers,	Pencil Heads,	Sponge Bags,
Air Beds,	Carriage Oil Cloth,	Finger Cots,	Ink Erasers,	Pencils,	Steam Hose,
Alaskas,	Cement,	Fire Buckets,	Interfering Straps,	Penholders,	Suction Hose,
Angle Worms,	Chair Cushions,	Fire Hose,	Invalid Cushions,	Pessaries,	Syphons,
Arctics,	Chair Tips,	Firemens' Coats,	Lace Cutters,	Piano Covers,	Syphon Exhausts,
Atomizer Bulbs,	Checker Boards,	Fishing Stockings,	Ladies' Cloaks,	Pipe Pipes,	Syringes,
Atomizers,	Check Lines,	Floor Matting,	Ladies' Leggins,	Pillows,	Syringe Bulbs,
Babies,	Cigar Cases,	Folding Pails,	Ladies' Ulsters,	Pipes,	Syringe Valves,
Back Combs,	Cloaks,	Foot Balls,	Laundry Sprinklers,	Pipe Stems,	Table Oil Cloths,
Balls,	Clogs,	Force Cups,	Lawn Sprinklers,	Picture Mats,	Tatting Shuttles,
Bandage Gum,	Clothes Wringers,	Fruit Jar Rings,	Leather Belting,	Plant Sprays,	Teething Pads,
Baptismal Pants,	Coats,	Funnels,	Leggins,	Pocket Combs,	Teething Rings,
Bat Balls,	Colored Balls,	Furniture Fenders,	Life Preservers,	Pocket Flasks,	Thimbles,
Bath Mats,	Combs,	Garden Hose,	Linen Hose,	Pocket Ink Stands,	Tobacco Pouches,
Bath Tubs,	Copy Press Sheets,	Gas Bags,	Lockets,	Pocket Tumblers,	Toilet Combs,
Bed Pans,	Corks,	Gas Tubing,	Lumbermens' Overs,	Pouches,	Toys,
Bellows Cloth,	Crack Proof Boots,	Gloves,	Martingale Rings,	Probangs,	Trotting Boilers,
Belt Hooks,	Crochet Hooks,	Guard Chains,	Match Boxes,	Rattles,	Tubing,
Belting,	Crude Rubber,	Gun Covers,	Merchandise Covers,	Rivets and Burrs,	Tumblers,
Belt Lacing,	Crying Dolls,	Gutta Percha,	Mirrors,	Round Combs,	Twist Combs,
Bibs,	Cuff Pins,	Gymnasiums,	Mittens,	Rubber Cement,	Ulsters,
Blankets,	Cupping Cups,	Hair Pins,	Musical Balls,	Rulers,	Urinals,
Boots,	Curry Combs,	Hat Covers,	Napkin Rings,	Scoops,	Valve Balls,
Bougies,	Dentist Rubber Dam,	Hats,	Nipples,	Scrubs,	Vest Chains,
Boys' Coats,	Desk Inkstands,	Health Lift,	Nipple Shields,	Shaft Rubbers,	Wading Pants,
Brushes,	Diapers,	Horse Boots,	Nursery Sheeting,	Shawl Pins,	Wagon Aprons,
Bracelets,	Dolls,	Horse Covers,	Nursing Bottles,	Sheeting,	Wagon Covers,
Breast Pumps,	Door Mats,	Hose Couplings,	Nursery Tubing,	Shoes,	Wagon Springs,
Drawers Hose,	Door Springs,	Hose Pipes,	Organ Covers,	Sleeve Buttons,	Water Bags,
Drawers Tubing,	Dressing Cases,	Hose Reels,	Overalls,	Slippers,	Water Beds,
Suspenders,	Dressing Combs,	Hospital Cushions,	Overshoes,	Slop Jars,	Water Bottles,
Capes,	Dress Shields,	Hot Water Bags,	Packing,	Soap Trays,	Weather Strips,
Caps,	Ear Rings,	Hunting Boots,	Pails,	Souwesters,	Webbing,
Cambrics,	Elastic Bands,	Hydrant Hose,	Pantaloons,	Spine Bags,	Window Cleaners,
Caoutchouc,	Elastic Stockings,	Ice Bags,	Pant Protectors	Spittoons,	Wire Brushes,
Cape Ann Clothing,	Elevator Buckets,	Ice Caps,	Pant Straps,	Sponge Bags,	Wringer Rolls,
Cape Coats,	Exercising Tubes,	Imperial Combs,	Pencil Erasers,		

NEW YORK—BUFFALO—CHICAGO—MILWAUKEE—ST. LOUIS—SAN FRANCISCO.

JAMES SUYDAM, Agent.   370 East Water St., MILWAUKEE.

THE ONLY STORE IN WISCONSIN AND MINNESOTA

CONNECTED WITH THE

GOODYEAR RUBBER Co.,

NEW YORK.

WISCONSIN SOLDIERS AND SAILORS REUNION ROSTER.

Winchester, Geo+   Andersonville, June 26—64

K

Lt Wyman Murphy
Lt Jno E Davies   Madison
Greenman, David, sgt   Andersonville July 13—61
Holmes, Mead, sgt   Apr 12—64
Mosier, Warren, corp*   Chaplin Hills, Oct 8—62
Borden, Eugene, corp   Andersonville, Sept 4—64
Smith, Chas, corp   Camp Chase, Nov 15—62
Sullivan, Timothy, corp   Nashville, Jan 28—63
Artridge, Thos*   Dallas, May 14—61
Boden, Jas*   Chaplin Hills, Oct 8—62
Babcock, Edwin   Lookout Mt, Feb 15—64
Burns, Geo T   Two Rivers
Campbell, Geo*   Chaplin Hills, Oct 8—62
Davis, Dan'l H, f   Mills Centre
Doolan, Jno   Manitowoc
Eslinger, Peter   Andersonville, Oct 30—64
Erickson, Alick   Baldwin
Fitch, Jno F   Nashville, Oct 24—61
Fowler, Benj   Alnapee
Hume, Wm   Lebanon, Nov 8—62
Hopkins, Chas   Louisville, Dec 28—62
Hickok, Chas C   Louisville, Dec 28—62
Houghton, Jas G   Murfreesboro, Feb 11—63
Hamblett, Atwell J   Murfreesboro, Apr 7—63
Harris, Wm H   Lookout Mt, May 2—64
Henry, Jas   Parkersburg, Mar 29—65
Hay, Jas S, m   Alnapee
Jones, Geo   Casco
Kuane, Gustav*   Resaca, May 11—64
Kellner, Michael   Nashville, Nov 10—62
Londo, Manuel +   Oct 29—62
Louerville, Geo   Burnt Hickory, June 1—64
Lyn, Jas   Sheboygan Falls
Landon, Fred'k   Jacksonville
McCorkle, Noah A+   Mar 21—65
Morris, Wm   Savannah, Jan 20—65
Moulton, Aaron   Nasewaupee
Pearson, Thos H ;   May 16—61
Powell, Jno   Murfreesboro, Mar 24—63
Reardon, J F, police   Manitowoc
Stallman, Jno*   Chaplin Hills, Oct 8—62
Smith, Jno+   June 1—64
Sand, Jno   Mitchellsville, Nov 25—62
Bartell, Jno D   Bowling Green, Jan 20—63
Soper, Amos J   Andersonville, July 13—64
Swift, J B, me   Hampton
Simon, Peter M, me   Alnapee
Smith, Jas   Warren's Mills
Wright, Wm A*   Chaplin Hills, Oct 8—62
Willard, Milo*   Chaplin Hills, Oct 8—62
Weaver, Peter S, f   Mancelona
Wintwen, J P   Baraboo
Warner, Geo   Alnapee

UNASSIGNED.

Burns, Geo T   Escanaba
Duroche, Edward   Fond du Lac
Fenno, G W   Lodi
Gibson, Jerry   Oakfield
Hart, Edward   Neenah
Miller, Jno   Neenah
Wright, W H   Oshkosh

TWENTY-SECOND INFANTRY.

Three years. Organized September 2d, 1862. Original strength, 1009, gain by recruits, etc., 496 Total, 1505. Death loss, 220—killed in action, 75, died of wounds, 32, of disease, 150. Other losses, 275—missing, 9, desertions, 46, transfers, 31, discharges, 196. Strength at muster out, June 12th, 1865, 1064.] Campaigns in Ky., Tenn,, Ga., S. C., and N. C.

REGIMENTAL ROSTER.

Col Wm L Utley   Racine
Col Edw Bloodgood   Waukesha
Lt Col Chas W Smith   Geneva Lake
Maj Edw D Murray   Chicago, Ill
Maj A G Kellam
Adjt J O Conrick
Adjt J C Dargin   Chicago, Ill
Q M Jno E Holmes   Annapolis, June 4—63
Q M Jesse L Berch   Chicago, Ill
Surg Thos Hatehard   Milwaukee
A Surg C S Blanchard   East Troy
A Surg Jerome Burbank   Waverly, Ia
A Surg Jas E Coakley
Chap C D Pillsbury   Ripon

A

Capt Geo R Williamson
Capt Francis Mead   Racine
Lt Geo Bauman   Oshkosh
Lt Lewis Dickinson   Racine
Lt F P Lawrence
Lt Chas L White   Cresco, Ia
Rose, Edward C+   Resaca, May 28—64
Braithwaite, C B+   Chattanooga, Jan 28—64
Butterfield, Albert   Nashville, Apr 6—64
Cadwell, E D   Chattanooga, June 2—64
Clark, D P, sgt   Nicholasville, Dec 15—62
Clark, J E   Nicholasville, Dec 2 62
Connell, Henry   Nicholasville, Dec 17 62
Crouch, Frank   Racine
Dickenson, Lewis   Racine
Dufour, Peter   Racine
Deal, John   Racine
De Garris, T   Columbus, Apr 4—63
Dickinson, G V*   Resaca, May '6—64
Dufore, Peter B, me   Racine
Gibson, Frank   Racine
Ginty, James   Racine
Grieve, Henry, me   Casey, Ia
Gregory, James   Racine
Glass, Alonzo H   Racine
Griffiths, John   Racine
Herron, Peter,f   Burlington, Mich
Hilton, Peter, me   Racine
Horton, Milton,   Sumico
Hilton, P H   Racine
Harris John   Racine
Hoyt, Chas   Racine
Halpin, Patrick   Racine
Jennings, Buel   Nicholasville, Dec 8—63
Kliese, L E
Lane, Theo, me   Racine
Lunn, John C   Racine
Lunn, John   Racine
Miller, Jno G   Danville, Dec 30—62
Malone, Jno M   Racine
Morris, Geo S, me   Racine
Miller, John   Racine
Northway, C L+   Aug 1—64
Pierce, Marshall   Cincinnati, Oct 9—62
Reid, Harvey   Sabula, Ia
Bennie, Robert   Chattanooga, Oct 26—64
Roberts, Wm M   Chattanooga, July 26—64
Roberts, Jno   Racine
Schafer, Christian   Brentwood, Feb 28—65
Scott, Jno M   Racine
Steadman, H K   Nicholasville, Dec 12—62
Teal, Jno G, me   Racine
Tessin, F+   Aug 12—64
White, C J   Cresco, Iowa
Woolsey, F E   Cincinnati, Oct 9—62
Walls, George   Racine
Walls, Thomas   Racine
Yout, Geo W*   Resaca, May 15—64

B

Capt T P Northrop   Beloit
Lt Ira P Nye   Eureka, Kan
Lt Wm H Calvert   Beloit
Lt Jas N Crandall   Wisconsin
Lt C H Bullock   Beloit
Anderson, A, sgt+   Mar 28—63
Bibbins, Adney F   Danville, Jan 2—63
Cullen, Martin   Lexington, Jan 1—63
Fairbanks, F S, r r   Atlanta, Ga
Hackett, Jas   Annapolis, Apr 23—68
Harwood, Geo W   Danvile, Jan 20—63
Haskell, J   Nicholasville, Jan 22—63
Herrick, S S   Beloit
Jackson, John*   Peach Tree Creek, July 20—64
Minot, W H H   Marshall, Mich
Oleson, Jno   Danville, Jan 30—63
Olmstead, C S, sgt   Bronis Grove, Kan
Ribbins, S L   Neillsville
Smith, A E   Arcadia
Teagne, John   Beloit, May 20—63
Wachter, J   Cumberland River, Feb 2—63
Wagen, Jacob   Milwaukee

C

Capt Chas W Smith   Geneva Lake
Capt D R May   Milwaukee
Capt Chas E Buell   Geneva
Lt I W Kingman   Louisville, Ky
Lt Stephen Knowles   Winthrop, N C
Lt J J Holcomb
Aiken, Jas   Murfreesboro, Feb 21—61
Aiken, Theron, corp+   Chattanooga, May 30—64
Allen Dwight S, f   Geneva Lake
Allen, D T   Jeffersonville, Nov 8—61
Burns, Michael*   Kenesaw Mt, June 28—64
Bullen, Robt   Elba, Minn
Babcom, Wm R   New Orleans, Neb
Core, Jno G, e   Manitowoc
Corune, Albert   Lexington, Jan 26—63
Crane, F S   Danville, Jan 15—64
Dayton, Jno S*   Atlanta, Aug 13—64
Denning, Wm H   Nicholasville, Dec 7—62
Dinsmore, E   East Troy
Ellis, Carlin G   Nashville, Mar 8—63
Eiiler, Adam   Racine
Fellows, Amos C+   Kingston, June 19—64
Fellows, F, sgt   Murfreesboro, Aug 19—63
Ingham, Hamilton   Nashville, Mar 7—63
McMillen, K G, sgt   Burkeville, Apr 7—63
Millard, Muxon P   Chattanooga, July 22—64
Morgan, R F   Nashville, Mar 17—63
Pierce, Franklin S   Nashville, June 20—64
Reed, F B   Madison
Redford, Robt, e   Oshkosh
Rogers, Joshua F   Danville, Jan 19—63
Ross, Martin F   Danville, Feb 1—63
Rouse, Anthony D   Nashville, Aug 15—63
Rust, Jno F+   Chattanooga, July 3—64
Spoor, Wallace   Nashville, Feb 19—61
Streeter, T E, f   Maple Springs
Stork, J K   Gage Valley, Neb
Wait, J P   Darien
Walton, Jno C   Nicholasville, Dec 23—62

D

Capt A G, Kellam
Capt Chas, E Dudley   Geneva
Lt G W Beach
Lt J O Conrick
Lt R M Williams
Lt W W Barlow
Avery, Y   Nicholasville, Nov —63
Ayers, W S   Danville, Feb 11—63
Clark, Geo R   Danville, Jan 5—62
Colurn, Geo   Nashville, Mar 10—64
Congdon, John R   Kenesaw Mt, June 22—64

MUTUAL BENEFIT
Life Insurance Company,
NEWARK, N. J.

INCORPORATED 1845.   PURELY MUTUAL.

LEWIS C. GROVER, Pres't.
   JAMES B. PEARSON, Vice-Pres't.
     EDWARD L. DOBBINS, Sec.
        THEODORE MACKNET, Treas.

Assets, Jan. 1, 1880, [par values]..........$33,804,261.13
Liabilities, [Mass. Standard]............ 31,418,746.03

Surplus, including dividends of 1880..... $2,355,515.10
Surplus on New York Standard. }
Market Value of Assets .... } $6,012,528.64

H. NICHOLS, State Agent,
412 MILWAUKEE ST.,
MILWAUKEE, - WIS.

READ WHAT
T. A. CHAPMAN & CO.,
SAY TO THE
Soldiers and their Friends
ON ANOTHER PAGE.

NORTHWESTERN
NATIONAL INSURANCE CO.,
MILWAUKEE, WIS.

CASH CAPITAL, $600,000.

ALEX. MITCHELL, President.
ALFRED JAMES, Vice-Prest.
JOHN P. McGREGOR, Secretary.

This Company writes Mercantile Risks, Buildings, Dwellings, and their Contents, and all the better Classes of Risks.

SEE PAGES 40 and 60.

WISCONSIN SOLDIERS AND SAILORS REUNION ROSTER.

Davis, Edwin F — Louisville, July 21—64
Fuhr, W* — Peach Tree Creek, July 20—64
Goodwin, Edwin — Independence, la
Gregary, M L — Davenport, la
Guernsey, H H — Janesville
Hall, Willeard M — Danville, Jan 8—63
Jacobs, Geo W* — Tullahoma, Dec 25—63
Johnson, H R, f — Millard
Kolians, Geo — Richmond
Kenney, Stephen — Delavan
Maynard, Abner — Waupun
Morrison, L — Peach Tree Creek, July 20—64
Mosher, Thos, o — Delavau
Owens, W A — Millard
Parker, H — Brentwood, Feb 25—63
Rowley, Jno D+ — Franklin, Mar 31—63
Russell, Robt — Annapolis, Apr 20—63
Sipperly, Jno R, e — Delavan
Weiskoff, Peter* — Peach Tree Creek, July 20—64
Whilden, Robt — Annapolis, May 3—63
Wood, Henry — Danville, Nov—62
Wood, Geo W — Annapolis, May 7—63

E

Capt Isaac Miles — Janesville
Capt H R Stetson
Lt Calvin Reeves
Lt F N Keely
Lt P P Bump
Alcott, Burlit — Nashville, May 12—63
Alden, Ed — Janesville
Adams, A R — Racine
Classett, Peter J — Danville, Mar 2—63
Crawford, Sam'l — Nashville, Feb 13—63
Culp, Aaron — Oregon
Downs, F E — Brentwood, Mar 1—63
Fitch, H W — Danville, Jan 4—63
Foley, Jas — Atlanta, Oct 2—64
Harper, R W — Nashville, Mar 9—63
Harvey, I D, corp* — Kenesaw Mt, June 18—64
Hill, B R — Janesville
Jones, Jos A — Nicholasville, Dec 26—62
King, Solomon R — Resaca, May 16—64
King, R W — Janesville
Knight, Paul — Danville, Feb 13—63
Lindsay, A — Murfreesboro, July 20—63
Macomber, C H — Nicholasville, Jan 9—63
McCoy, G W — Sandersville, Nov 18—62
Mersen, Martin+ — Chattanooga, July 12—64
Miles, Isaac — Janesville
Moore, A C, sgt — Nashville, Feb 15—63
Osburn, Chauncey, Jr — Atlanta, Oct 20—64
Patterson, Wm, Jr — Nashville, Mar 5—63
Reynolds Eber — Annapolis, Apr 12—63
Smith, Walter — Dallas, May 26—64
Thompson, Wm — New York City
Walker, A, corp* — Peach Tree Creek, July 20—64
Warner, Oscar W — Danville, Feb 7—63
Warner, A O, sgt* — Atlanta, Aug 20—64
Young, R P — Janesville

F

Capt Owen Griffiths — Whitesboro N Y
Capt Robt T Pugh — Racine
Lt Nelson Darling
Lt Jno Bowen — Racine
Lt Wm H Hughes — Racine
Baker, Richard T — Nashville, Feb 16—63
Bowen, Jno, m — Racine
Baird, David — Racine
Daniels, Harrison — Nashville, Mar 16—64
Davis, Edward L — Golgotha, June 16—64
Edwards, W H — Berlin
Evans, David, f — Berlin
Float, Jacob H — Waterford
Foat, Samuel, m — Genesee
Foreman, J B, Sr+ — Resaca, May 19—64

Hanson, Theo+ — Chattanooga Aug 31—64
Hayburn, Chris — Racine
Horton, Ezra S — Annapolis, Apr 18—63
Howard, H D — Murfreesboro, Feb 3—63
James, Morris — Racine
James, M B — Racine
Jones, Hugo R — Racine
Jackson, Jno C — Nashville, July 29—63
Jones, R Blair — Racine
Jones, E O — Racine
Jones, Owen R — Lynchburg, Apr 6—63
Jones, Samuel — Danville, Jan 15—63
James, J M — Racine
Morgan, Jno D, sgt+ — Nashville, Mar 25—63
Northrup, A L, corp — Nashville, Feb 24—63
Ord, C L, corp* — Resaca, May 15—64
Pearson, H B — Milwaukee
Pritchard, Elias, — Racine
Pugh, R J — Racine
Roberts, B G+ — Big Shanty, June 24—64
Ready, Jno — Racine
Rowlands, David — Racine
Smith, A E — Arcadia
Thomas, T W — Chattanooga, June 4—64
Tapling, Chas W — Racine
Williams, Richard Jr — Danville, Jan 1—63

G

Capt Jas Bintliff — Darlington
Capt Fenette Abnis — Brodhead
Lt Thos H Eaton
Lt Chas D Booth — Monroe
Lt Stephen F Ball
Adair, Mathias — Danville, Jan 21—63
Aldinger, E, corp — Lexington, Dec 28—02
Allen, Gideon G — Danville, Jan 20—63
Anderson, G — Peach Tree Creek, July 20—64
Booth, Chas A, ed — Monroe
Canfield, W — Danville, Dec 27—02
Cunningham, M L, corp+ — Chattanooga, June 7 64
Damon, Sam'l — Danville, Jan 12—63
Divan, Wm A — Danville, Jan 17—63
Darling, A — Neillsville
Enderson, Ole — Nicholasville, Dec 24—62
Erickson, Ole+ — Nashville July 14—64
Fleck, H M, corp* — Mar 5—63
Gould, Nathan C* — Kenesaw Mt, June 22—64
Grudell, Dan'l — Danville, Jan 9—63
Gray, Timothy* — Resaca, May 15—64
Helmer, August — Louisville, July 4—64
Jackson, Jesse H — Nashville, Mar 15—64
King, Wm H, m — Darlington
Moore, Jas S — Louisville, July 2—63
Nelson, Edward — Nashville, June 15—64
Ransom, Geo C — Louisville, Feb 23—64
Reima, Michael — Resaca, May 15—64
Seitzier, L — Monroe
Sowles, Lucius M — Danville, Mar 10—63
Sue, Dan'l M — Chattanooga, July 14—64
Watt, Farhn E — Atlanta, Aug 4—64
Worley, Aaron — Danville, Dec 21—02

H

Capt C Goodrich — Caledonia, Apr 15—63
Capt H H Jennings
Capt A S Cole
Lt J R Bones — Racine
Lt J J J Peterson — Chattanooga, May 27—64
Allen, Wm J — Raymond
Bones, Jas R — Covington, Feb 8—65
Coole, Henry — Danville
Crouch, Walter — Racine
Drought, J W* — Tullahoma, July 12—64
Goodwin, Thos — Chattanooga, July 12—64
Grimm, A — Nicholasville, Apr 5—63
Ingersoll, J N* — Peach Tree Creek, July 20—63
Irish, T T — Danville, Jan 2—63

Kelly N T — Sparta
Law, Jonathan — Annapolis, Apr 26—63
Landsgard, A — Nicholasville, Dec 15—62
Lytle, Abram — Danville, Jan 17—63
Madama, Wm* — Peach Tree Creek, July 20—64
Madison, Peter — Annapolis, Apr 11—63
McCaulcss, Wm* — Resaca, May 15—64
McCouncil, Jno C — Danville, Jan 8—63
McIluron, G — Mount Pleasant, Aug 28—63
Murphy, J B, corp — Danville, Feb 4—63
Muth, Geo — Hebron, Neb
Nelson, P, corp+ — Jeffersonville, June 14—61
Nobles, M — Sandersville, Nov 16—62
Peterson, J J — Raymond
Phelps, Geo — Murfreesboro, Feb 22—24
Reed, J L* — Lost Mountain, June 16—64
Reed, T W — Racine
Salvorsen, Peter — Annapolis, May 2—63
Schritzmeyer, Jno — Nashville Apr 20—63
Schlagheck, H — Annapolis, Apr 18—63
Shuck, N — Nicholasville, Dec 2—62
Sipperly, Reuben — Danville, Feb 11—63
Slater, Wm — Danville, Jan 16—63
Smith, Phillip — Nicholasville, Dec 16—62
Smiley, J A — Lexington, Nov 14—62
Stacks, Moses A — Nashville, Mar 9—63
Stewart, Hugh — Danville, Dec 22—62
Vanderhill, Frank — Racine
Wood, B S — Danville, June 9—63
Wright, J D H* — Resaca, May 16—64
Wyatt, Wm — Nicholasville, Dec 22—62
Young, John C — Almond

I

Capt P W Tracy — Brooklyn, N Y
Capt M W Patton* — Resaca, May 18—64
Capt Jno W Parker — Chicago, Ill
Lt L C Morgan
Barry, Ed — Janesville
Bullis, Arnd+ — Kingston, June 26—64
Cadman, Wm F — Danville, Feb 25—63
Carpenter, Sam'l — Danville, Jan 14—64
Dond, C F — Danville, Feb 7—63
Doud, Milo P — Danville, Jan 12—63
Everett, Wm — Danville, Jan 8—63
Goddard, E A, corp — Lexington, Feb 10—63
Hanson, Christian — Nashville, Mar 8—63
House, Jas E, sgt — Danville, Jan 15—63
Jenson, Carl — St Louis, Mar 23—62
Lapp, Chas+ — Chattanooga, Aug 11—61
Lee, Hugo Jr, f — Beloit
Lund, Jacob+ — Columbia, Mar 11—63
Merical, J — Turner's Ferry, Aug 30—64
Mills, Chas — Superior, Minn
Nicholas, Albert — Annapolis, Apr 28—63
Parker, Wm F — Danville, Dec 24—63
Rambault, G r — Columbia, Mar 25—63
Rombault, V — Danville, Feb 8—63
Rice, H — Neillsville
Secrest, Geo — Danville, Dec 21—62
Sherman, F — Nashville, Feb 16—63
Smith, Albert C — Nashville, Apr 23—63
Taltman, Alexis W+ — Lost Mountain, June 16—4
Willett, Jno — Annapolis, Apr 16—63

K

Capt Lester Perkins
Capt G E Bingham
Lt Jno Stewart
Lt Van B S Newman
Lt B F Raymond
Lt Wm C Penn
Austin, E W — Nashville, May 2—63
Austin, Seth — Louisville
Baker, F — Annapolis, Apr 20—63
Berry, Jno H, corp — Apr 8—63
Boyer, Andrew — Brandon

FISH BROTHERS & CO.,
MANUFACTURERS OF
OPEN AND TOP BUGGIES
PHAETONS AND CARRIAGES.

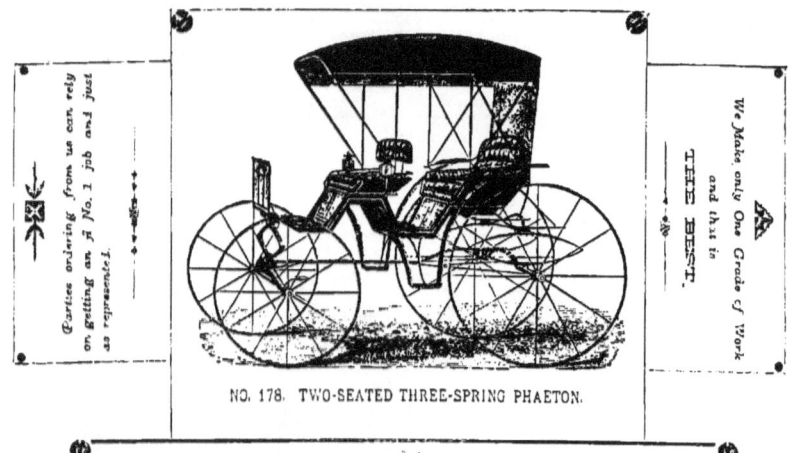

NO. 178. TWO-SEATED THREE-SPRING PHAETON.

Parties ordering from us can rely on getting an A No. 1 job and just as represented.

We Make only One Grade of Work and that is THE BEST.

Fine English broadcloth or fancy colored leather trimmings. Side lamps and wet weather top.

Makes a very handsome, durable and comfortable Family Carriage.

SEND FOR ILLUSTRATED CATALOGUE.

RACINE, - - WISCONSIN.

See Page 94.

Bradshaw, C W Annapolis, Apr 25—63
Churchill, Urias* Resaca, May 15—64
Conert, J M, f Brodhead
Cramer, Jno G Kenesaw Mt, July 1—64
Danabaugh, C St Louis, May 5—63
Davis, Z P, corp* Resaca, May 18—64
Debolt, Jno, corp* Mar 5—63
Gould, S Indianapolis, Oct 19—64
Hale, F M Resaca, June 2—64
Harrington, M Pedee
Harrington, Wm Kildore
Howard, H J, f Albion, Neb
Jones, Wm C Annapolis, Apr 24—63
Kildow, J P, f Brodhead
Lindsley, Wm E, f Neosho
Lindsley, Chas C, l Montana
Meldon, J P Oakley
Morris, Rubt Paducah, Feb 14—63
Roby, Hazzard* Resaca, May 10—64
Smith, Jas, l Warren's Mills
Stablnicker, Jas W Lexington, Ky
Swan, Richard Louisville, Jan 2—63
Warner, Wm H Nashville, Mar 16—63
Wooding, Levi S+ Resaca, May 19—64
Young, Henry Danville, Jan 5—63

UNASSIGNED.

Hines, Jas, sgt maj+ Mar 16—63
Babcock, Leonard H, me Murfreesboro, Mar 7—64
Bellows, Leonard H, me Delavan
Davis, H N, b Beloit
Davison, Thos J Danville, Feb 15—63
Decker, Henry, pa Delavan
Edwards, Evon Delavan
Halverson, H Danville, Feb 9—63
Hazelton, W B Madison
Hunt, Wm J Lexington—63
Jones, Evan, b Delavan
Kavanaugh, T P, corp May 5—65
Kittinger, F Murfreesboro, Sept 23—63
Morris, David Nashville, Mar 2—64
Noyes, Wm Janesville
Purdy, Geo Nicholasville, Nov 13—63
Stewart, Arthur Columbus, May 6—63
Smith, C W Geneva Lake
Thayer, C R Clay Bank
Wells, P B Racine

TWENTY-THIRD INFANTRY

Three years. Organized August 26th, 1862. Original strength, 994, gain by recruits, etc, 123. Total 1117. Death loss, 289—killed in action, 22, died of wounds, 16, of disease, 249, accidents, 2. Other losses, 412—missing, 1 desertions, 6 transfers, 124, discharges, 281. Strength at muster out, July 4th, 1865, 416. Campaigns in Ky, Tenn, Miss, La, Ark, Texas, Ala.

REGIMENTAL ROSTER.

Col J J Guppey Portage
Lt Col Edmund Jassen Chicago
Lt Col Wm F Vilas Madison
Lt Col E P Hill N Y City
Maj O H Williams Baraboo
Adj W G Pitman Madison
Adj Geo Gibson
Adj Carl Jussen N Y City
Q M F L Hicks Muscoda
Q M J C Tredway St Louis, Mo
Q M H L Gray Baraboo
Surg Jas Prentice Portage
Surg Jno Groening
Jno H Angell
A Surg O H Woods
A Surg E H Irwin Lodi
A Surg M G Todd

A

Capt Wm F Vilas Madison
Capt S W Botkin Madison
Lt Alex Atkinson Omaha, Neb
Lt Jas E Karn Madison
Adams, Harvey Baton Rouge, June 27—64
Atkinson, A, m Omaha, Neb
Beyler, Charles H Madison
Brooks, W L Millikens Bend, Apr 23—63
Daniels, Wm Louisville, Nov 15—62
Eaton, C O Millikens Bend, Mar 10—62
Ellickson, Jno New Orleans, Oct 26—64
Gudinausen, Lewis New Orleans, Oct 13—63
Giosanlis, Jno Memphis, Dec—62
Hill Jos A, corp Millikens Bend, Apr 4—63
Hoffstetter, J June 12—63
Jack, A G* Carrion Crow, Nov 3—63
Jacobson, C Youngs Point, Feb 5—63
Johnson, Reler, corp Millikens Bend, Apr 2—62
Lelhimer, Matthew May 4—63
Lynch, J W Yankton, D T
Lyon, D P Louisville, May 25—63
Lyon, Benton Youngs Point, Mar 4—63
Musier, James New Orleans, Aug 27—64
Pearsons, S E, corp, me Madison
Pierce, Q June 29—63
Rivers, Thomas Millikens Bend, Apr 7—63
Roy, F I Nashville, Apr 1—63
Sutton, John E Memphis, March 14—63
Vanatta, Levi+ St Louis, Mar 5—63
Van Buren, R B Memphis, Dec 2—62
Vroman, D Millikens Bend, Apr 2—63
Waltz, Geo Memphis, Mar 10—63
Wells, Jas A Tomah
Wharnby, Thomas+ New Orleans, Nov 18—63

B

Capt Jno E Duncan Eldora, Ia
Lt Jno N Sumner Madison
Lt F O Marsh
Lt Warren Gray
Beer, Taylor Young's Point, Feb 22—63
Bennett, Jas, sgt Madison
Berteashaw, W+ Vicksburg, May 26—63
Bray, Thos N Yankton, D T
Buss, Jas Young's Point, Feb 14—63
Buss, Richard Mar 9—63
Case, LaFayette Vicksburg, Aug 12—63
Cullen, Simon Memphis, Aug 31—63
DeGroff, Watson Memphis, Apr 4—63
Dunlap, Jno W Memphis, July 3—63
Duncan, J E, ed Eldorado, Ia
Evans, Jesse T St Louis, Mar 21—63
Garrison, J M Manchester, Ia
Hanford, Geo E St Louis, Mar 21—63
Hickey, Patrick Calamine
Hill, Oscar Vicksburg, May 20—63
Hughes, Henry O Memphis, Apr 4—63
Judkins, Orin, corp Apr 10—63
Knause, John Memphis, Oct 3—63
May, Orlando U St Louis, Apr 4—63
McCoy, Philip H Apr 18—63
Norton, Willis* Sabine Cross Roads, Apr 8—64
Ray, G B* Arkansas Post, Jan 11—63
Van Hook, F Memphis—63
Woodbury, N St Louis, Aug 23—63

C

Capt E P Hill
Capt O H Sorenson Portage
Lt Jno Shoemaker Green Bay
Lt S F Salisbury
Lt Jos E Bull
Lt Jno V Richardson
Lt J L Jolley
Anderson, H Young's Point, Feb—63
Becker, G W Helena, Nov 8—64
Blood, I P Sand Creek

Cobb, L, sgt* Marcellon, Aug 13—63
Cook, Martin* Jackson, Oct 5—64
Crosby, Jno Frankfort, Apr 24—63
Dempsey, J, sgt White River, Dec 22—63
Eastman, W New Orleans, June 11—64
Edgarton, Jno L Keokuk, July—63
Flower, C H Youngs Point, Feb—63
Fitts, Jas F Memphis, Jan 25—63
Glasgow, P, corp Jan 22—63
Halsey, T E, 1st sgt Millikens Bend, Mar 30—63
Hewitt, Jos, Jr Millikens Bend, June 1—63
Hosford, Jno W Jan 22—63
Johnson, Jno P Chicago, Ill
Jones, Wm F Youngs Point, May 31—63
Lewis, J A, sgt* Vicksburg, May 26—63
Mason, Matthew T Moundville
Morrison, Nelson Feb—63
Northrup, S H Feb 18—63
Parmenter, G G Vicksburg, July 31—63
Pulver, J H Youngs Point, Feb—63
Repler, F, f Kildare
Ressler, Frank Kildare
Roberts, Wm M Millikens Bend, May—63
Rosecrans, Frank New Orleans, June 9—64
Shoemaker, J M Green Bay
Smith, Jno Feb—63
Spicer, A D Wilton
Van Zandt, S E, corp St Louis, Feb 11—73
Whitney, Jas Norwalk
Williams, J D Millikens Bend—63
Wilson, N D Millikens Bend, Apr 5—63

D

Capt Jno N Sumner Madison
Lt J W Tolford Nellsville
Lt Jas L Baker St Louis, Mo
Lt F A Stoltze Madison
Lt B AlTaft Whitewater
Lt Wm Drink
Andell, Jas Jan 16—63
Anderson, Jas Jan 16—63
Arneson, Arno Millikens Bend, Apr 6—63
Baker, Wm H Oshkosh
Bakke, Ole O Millikens Bend, May 22—63
Braun, A G Millikens Bend, June 1—63
Cole, A B Vicksburg, Dec 16—64
Crooks, Jas Millikens Bend, May 25—64
Davidson, A Memphis, May 25—64
Elder, D, sgt Vicksburg, May 22—63
Ellis, N H Sparta
Finch, T Millikens Bend, May 26—63
Haveland, N A Millikens Bend, Apr 1—63
Holcomb, H H Helena
Jura, A K Youngs Point, Jan 26—63
Larson, Evan Millikens Bend, Mar 13—63
Lee, Alaek A Mar 16—63
Lepley, Isaac April 25—63
Lewison, Ole* Carrion Crow, Nov 3—63
Marsh, Eli E St Louis, June 29—63
Moon, Ole G Millikens Bend, June 9—63
Morton, Henry Northfield, Minn
North, David Millikens Bend, Mar 20—63
Noti, C B Lake Providence, Apr 7—63
Oleson, Tosten Youngs Point, Feb 4—63
Palmeter, E S Dec 27—62
Rall, Herman Vicksburg, Aug 27—64
Salsbury, N H May 11—63
Sanderson, Jas+ Vicksburg, Aug 3—64
Slagg, A Millikens Bend, Mar 23—63
Slagg, E E Cambridge, Mar 22—64

E

Capt Jas M Bull, el Minn
Lt Jas E Bull Washington, Kan
Lt Robt M Addison
Lt Henry Vilas Nov—72
Lt Jas Hays March 23—62
Lt O D Tredway St Louis, Mo

THE APPEAL.

A LIVE

TEMPERANCE PAPER,

Largely in the Interest of

THE TEMPLE OF HONOR.

THE APPEAL gives more temperance news than any other paper published in the northwest, and is furnished at the low price of

FIFTY CENTS A YEAR

It also contains a large amount of choice literary matter, and much other matter not pertaining to the temperance question. It is the largest, best and cheapest paper of the kind published in the West. Temperance people can in no way help their cause more substantially than by extending its circulation.

J. A. WATROUS'
EDITOR AND PROPRIETOR,
MILWAUKEE, WIS.

WISCONSIN SOLDIERS AND SAILORS REUNION ROSTER. 105

Lt Carl Jassen — N Y City
Lt Wm Suden
Harden, Hiram
Borwell, J C — Youngs Point, Mar 5—63
Bull, E C — Frankfort, Jan 27—62
Bull, John A — Washington, Kan
Casey, Jas — Millikens Bend, Jan 21—63
Courtin, P — Youngs Point, Mar 8—63
Crandall, John A — July 9—63
Dejean, Harrison — Youngs Point, Jan 27—63
Dodge, A — Millikens Bend, Mar 15—63
Drake, Allen — Memphis, July 17—63
Durin, T D — Youngs Point, Feb 1—63
Harris, G T — Vicksburg, Nov 30—64
Hayes, Jacob E — St Louis, Apr 12—64
Hayes, I, sgt — Millikens Bend, Mar 23—63
Hoke, Chas — Millikens Bend, Mar 22—63
Holcombe, W — Youngs Point, Feb 13—63
Ivory, J J — Arkansas Post, Jan 12—63
Laughlin, J L — Millikens Bend, Mar 15—63
Lawrence, N I. — Youngs Point, Feb 22—63
Melville, T — Youngs Point, Mar 9—63
Meyer, Carl H — Columbus, Jan 23—63
Netherwood, C W, p m — Oregon
Newman, C T — Millikens Bend, Mar 8—63
Norton, J E — Millikens Bend, Apr 20—63
Palman, J E — Youngs Point, Mar 6—63
Phelps, Jno — Millikens Bend, Apr 3—63
Porter, Jno F — Tyler, Sept 12—64
Powers, H C, corp — Jeff D Tracks, July 6—63
Richardson, D F — St Louis, Apr 12—63
Robinson, T — Memphis, July 1—63
Schultz, Ernst* — Vicksburg, May 20—63
Spears, Jno D — Napoleon, Jan 1—63
Tyler, O — Memphis, Apr 2—63

F

Capt C H Williams — Baraboo
Capt J A Schlick — Bennington, N Y
Lt E L Walbridge — La Crosse, May 31—63
Lt D C Stanley — Baraboo
Lt Robt E Crandall — Baraboo
Baley, I, J — Millikens Bend, Apr 14—63
Bailey, Z E — Nicholasville, Nov 21—62
Bates, Chas — Millikens Bend, May 15—63
Blivins, Calvio E — St Louis, Mar 9—63
Case, E W — Youngs Point, Mar 9—63
Cline, Jacob — Baraboo
Delap, Edw — Memphis, Mar 14—63
Densmore, J M — Youngs Point, Feb 19—63
Freeman, E R — Millikens Bend, Mar 20—63
Hamilton, W H, corp — Youngs Point, Feb 11—63
Hague, Jno F* — Sabine Cross Roads, Apr 8—64
Kezartee, Jno W+ — St Louis, Aug 30—63
Kipp, Peter H — Memphis, Mar 28—63
Knowles, Peter — Millikens Bend, Mar 19—63
Lippett, Wm — Youngs Point, Mar 5—63
Mason, Jas W — Memphis, July 15—63
Miller, Erastus D* — Blakely, Apr 8—65
Miles, Andrew J — Jan 20—63
Newhall, Cephas K — Millikens Bend, Mar 21—63
Platt, Jacob — July 9—63
Pollock, Wm — Youngs Point, Jan 24—63
Porter, Jno F — Tyler, Sept 12—64
Remmington, M — Memphis, Feb 16—63
Roberts, Jus D — Millikens Bend, Apr 1—63
Savage, Jno — Baraboo
Savage, J N — Baraboo
Seamans, E G, sgt — Logansville, Feb 29—63
Shearer, Jno — Youngs Point, Mar 9—63
Spear, Elijah C — Cincinnati, Oct 22—62
Spooner, B B — Decrows Point, Jan 1—64
Smith, G H — Youngs Point, Mar 27—63
Staley, Jno — Memphis, Apr 4—63
Stoner, C L — Millikens Bend, May 15—63
Stowell, Geo — Youngs Point, Feb 4—63
Thomas, O W, sgt — Memphis, Jan 1—63
Van Orman, M — St Louis, Feb 1—63
Waltz, Jno — Memphis, Mar 9—63

G

Capt Jas F Hazelton
Capt J W Tolford — Neillsville
Lt C W Tuttle
Lt Wm H Dunham
Lt F H Lull
Lt L F Warner
Lt G S Campbell
Bently, E
Cowes, F S — New Orleans, Mar 31—61
Dedish, Nicholas* — Memphis, Dec 18—62
Easson, E E, sgt — Vicksburg, June 26—63
Edwards, Jos S — Memphis, Mar 21—63
Fuller, Alfred E — Bangalls
Johnson, M L+ — Millikens Bend, Mar 27—63
Jones, StClaire — Feb 5—63
Jones, John G, corp* — Hamlin
Kehler, Lewis — Sandy Bayou, Oct 5—64
Keifer, Francis D — Memphis, Mar 15—63
Kelley, John, corp — Memphis, Mar 15—61
Moore, J M, corp — New Orleans, Dec 23—63
Nelson, F — Youngs Point, Feb 17—63
Nickerson, Nelson H — Jackson, July 10—63
Page, Q A — Transport, Jan 22—63
Parry, E, corp — Baton Rouge, July 20—64
Thum, L F — Youngs Point, Feb 2—63
Quinn, Charles E+ — Keokuk, Jan 25—63
Rogers, Manfred — Vicksburg, June 22—63
Task, Seth — Youngs Point, Feb 7—63
Tolford, J W — Morganzia, Aug 1—64
Warner, Daniel C — Neillsville
Whiting, W J — Transport, Jan 24—63
Williams, R R — Youngs Point, Feb 14—64
Williams, Jabez* — St Louis, May 22—63
Carrion Crow, Nov 3—63

H

Capt E H Irwin — Lodi
Capt D C Holdridge
Lt Robt Steele — Dane
Lt J R Duncan — Eldora, Ia
Lt A W Baker
Bates, Jno* — Vicksburg, June 23—63
Brown, C L* — Vicksburg, May 22—63
Brown, J C, f — Lodi
Bromfield, Edwin+ — Memphis, June 13—63
Bunker, T — Madison, Nov 20—63
Collins, J R, f — Lodi
Bowden, Thos J — Youngs Point, Mar 2—63
Duel, Alonzo F — Memphis, Mar 23—63
Eaton, F A G — St Louis, Aug 5—63
Ellington, Ole — Feb 8—63
Grindell, Wm — Mound City, Feb 5—63
Harmley, Jno — Memphis, Apr 5—63
Holcomb, O E — Youngs Point, Apr 8—63
Jones, Wm J — Jeff Barracks, June 28—63
Kenworthy, Jno — Vicksburg, June 28—63
Kingsley, G W — Millikens Bend, Dec 26—62
Kyle, A J — Chicago, Ill
Oleson, Lars — Morganzia, July 20—63
Paul, Jno W, f — Lodi
Pettit, Jas — Millikens Bend, July 22—63
Richmond, Edgar — Lodi
Riddle, Edwin C — New Orleans, Sept 14—61
Ring, Wm — Memphis, Jan 31—63
Rood, Wm H — Youngs Point, Feb 29—63
Shaw, Jason W+ — Vicksburg, May 26—63
Shurtliff, Wm T, sgt — Vicksburg, June 7—63
Stacker, C F, sgt — Jan 30—63
Stahl, J F, corp+ — Vicksburg, May 26—63
Stroud, J D* — Sabine Cross Road, Apr 8—64
Varrender, G H — Jan 26—63
Waffle, Harvey — Kendall
Warriner, L C — Jan 23—63
Waterbury, E O, t — Augusta
Weber, V — Kildare

I

Capt A R Jones — Madison
Capt W G Pittman — Madison
Capt S F Salisbury
Capt Jno Shoemaker — Green Bay
Lt L D Frost — Chicago, Ill
Lt Jno M Shumer — Madison
Lt J G Norton — Viroqua
Bonner, R A — Mississippi River, Aug 21—63
Conliard, J A — Millikens Bend, Apr 7—63
Clark, Wm G — Merrimac
Duignon Winced — Footville
Durfey, Chas — Mar 11—64
Edgley, Jerome — Millikens Bend, Apr 1—64
Felhand, A — Memphis Apr 13—63
Ford, Robt E* — Vicksburg, May 19—63
Hayden, L F — Millikens Bend, Mar 28—63
Hoffman, Philip — Door Creek
Inskeep, P S — Youngs Point, Feb 25—63
Jenkins, Amos F — St Louis, July 10—63
Killer, W J — Clay Centre, Neb
Kessenich, C A* — Sabine Cross Road, Nov 3—63
Kinsman, Jerome — Covington, Oct 7—62
Malts, Wm L — Verona
Mayhew, F W — Millikens Bend, Apr 1—63
Meyers, Jesse — Verona
Mithun, O L — Youngs Point Feb 19—63
Moore, L H — Jan 3—63
Nerison, T — Jan 20—63
Newell, J H — Millikens Bend, Apr 18—63
Nichols, G E — Mound City, Jan 2—63
Nye, Josiah — Verona, Sept 5—63
Park, R J — Helena, Nov 25—64
Pierce, Sam'l S — New Orleans, Oct 8—62
Plackett, Edwin, — St Louis, July 2—63
Pritchard, E — Feb 11—63
Sherman, J F — New Orleans, July 18—64
Sweep, C R — Youngs Point Feb 20—63
Torgerson, Ole — Youngs Point, Jan 22—63
Tubbs, Daniel — Memphis, Apr 1—63
Tyler, Ezra — May 8—63
Williams, E T, corp — Mississippi River, Aug 24—63
Wood, Wm H — St Louis, Apr 7—63
Young, D B, corp — Vicksburg, Oct 16—64

K

Capt N S Frost — Memphis, Dec 19—62
Capt E S Fletcher
Lt A J McFarland+ — Portage, July 4—63
Lt Jos W Richardson
Lt Jno D Malloy
Lt Basil Smout
A'drick, N B — Vicksburg, Aug 8—63
Amhler, Washington — Hannibal, Mo
Ballard, W M+ — Carrion Crow, Nov 4—63
Baxter, H J — Prairie du Sac
Blakely, R — Youngs Point, Mar 8—63
Buroham, Jas — Youngs Point, Feb 12—63
Campbell, Jool — Jan 7—63
Clements, Henry — Apr 6—63
Dewey, Moses — Mound City, Jan 19—63
Douglas, D M — Dec 27—62
Getty, Jno W — Memphis, Dec 4—63
Hardy, Thos, corp — Tyler, Sept 17—64
Henry, Jacob — White Mound
Hilliard, Jno G, sgt* — Carrion Crow, Nov 3—63
Hines, Nelson — Jan 30—63
Hines, S — Youngs Point, Mar 4—63
Hughes, Hugh — Millikens Bend, Apr 28—63
Jacobs, Henry, corp — Jan 28—63
James, D C — May 2—63
Johnson, G W — Odevalt, Ia
Johnson, Merrill — Prairie du Sac
Jones, W, corp* — Vicksburg, July 17—63
Lindley, B F* — Ft Hindman, Jan 11—63
Little, W H — Independence, Ia
Mather, Henry — Youngs Point, Feb 17—63

GODFREY & CRANDALL
COMMERCIAL, BOOK AND
JOB PRINTERS

114 MICHIGAN STREET
MILWAUKEE,   WISCONSIN.

We would respectfully inform our citizens and the public in general, that we have greatly increased our facilities by the purchase of new material, for the prompt execution of every description of

LETTER PRESS, BOOK and COMMERCIAL

PRINTING!
AT GREATLY REDUCED RATES.

KIRBY HOUSE

ONE OF THE LARGEST AND BEST.

In the very centre of the City.

RATES REDUCED,
$1.00 to $2.00 per Day,
As to Length of Time You Stay.

ABNER KIRBY,
Proprietor.

G. A. TILDEN.
MANUFACTURING
JEWELER & ENGRAVER

Diamond Setting a Specialty.

107 WISCONSIN STREET.
MILWAUKEE,   -   -   WIS.
FIRST FLOOR OVER RICH & SILBER.

HOMESTEAD
SUPERPHOSPHATE,

A Pure Bone Black

FERTILIZER,

Which is not a Simple Stimulant, but contains the necessary

Food For Plant Life!

MANUFACTURED BY THE

MICHIGAN CARBON WORKS,
DETROIT, MICHIGAN.

FRANK WHITNAL,
AGENT.
428 MILWAUKEE STREET.
MILWAUKEE.   -   WISCONSIN.

TWENTY-FOURTH INFANTRY.

Three years. Organized August 15th, 1862. Original strength, 1003; gain by recruits, etc., 14; total, 1017. Death loss, 175—Killed in action, 61, died of wounds, 35, of disease, 77. Other losses, 498, missing, 0, desertions, 71, transfers, 138, discharges, 289. Strength at muster-out, June 10th, 1865, 406. Campaigns in Ky., Tenn., Ala., Ga.

REGIMENTAL ROSTER.

Col C H Larrabee	Seattle, W T
Col Theo S West	Philadelphia, Penn
Col Arthur McArthur, Jr	Little Rock, Ark
Lt Col E L Buttrick	Kanania, N Y
Lt Col E C Hibbard	Milwaukee
Maj C Von Baumbach	Milwaukee
Maj Alra Philbrook*	Franklin, Nov 30—64
Maj Wm Kennedy	Milwaukee
Adj H Buchanan	Little Falls, N Y
Q M G E Starkweather	Minneapolis, Minn
Q M F W Kid lle	Detroit, Mich
Surg H E Knapp	Milwaukee
A Surg Chas Muller+	Covington, Ky
A Surg J P Wheeler	Brighton, N Y
Chap Francis Fasseder	Beaver Dam
Chap Jno F Roe	Omaha, Neb

A

Capt E C Hibbard	Milwaukee
Capt R H Austin	Chicago, Ill
Lt T E Balding	Milwaukee
Lt Benj Hickox	New York City, N Y
Lt Geo F Eddy	Milwaukee
Lt W H Coburn	
Lt Geo Dieyer*	Stone River, Jan 31—63
Lt H F Drake	Milwaukee, Jan 24—3
Adams, A K	Milwaukee
Axtell, W B, corp+	Chattanooga, Oct 4—63
Barrows, W C L	Richland Centre
Bate, T S	Vining Station, Aug 30—64
Buckley, J	Manistee, Mich
Buckley, Ed	Manistee, Mich
Boone, Jno	Pensauke
Bullard, H D	Delavan
Case, L B	Murfreesboro, Jan 15—63
Cheeney, F W	Louisville, July 11—63

May, P S	Youngs Point, Mar 1—6
McCready, Sam'l*	Ft Hindman, Jan 11—63
McKeever, Jas*	Carrion Crow, Nov 3—63
Murray, A	Youngs Point, Feb 26—63
Nichols, Jno F	Youngs Point, Feb 21—63
Oakley, Jas	St Louis, Aug 11—63
Olson, L	Ft Hindman, Jan 12—63
Parker, Morris S	Youngs Point, Feb 17—63
Patchin, O, sgt	Nov 25—62
Phegley, T	Millikens Bend, Mar 16—63
Rouse, Chas	Youngs Point, May 25—63
Schluckenbier, F	Covington, Sept 30—62
Thompson, A M	June 12—63
Thornburgh, A D	Memphis, Feb 5—63
Thornton, E R	Dec 25—62
Thomas, Jno W	Memphis, Dec 15—62
Waffenschmidt, F	Youngs Point, Mar 3—63
Wanzee, L	Memphis, Feb 14—63

UNASSIGNED.

Axtell, J, A Surg	Covington, Oct 18—62
Calentyre, Geo	Andersonville, Sept 18—64
Crawford, F M	Feb 2,—63
Pruyn, B W	Portage
Rufult, F	Neillsville
Stehn, Henry D	Black River Falls
Towsley, C	Algiers, July 9—64
Young, D M	North Bend

B

Capt Wm H Eldred	Milwaukee
Capt Howard Green*	Mission Ridge, Nov 25—63
Capt C D Morris	Milwaukee
Capt Geo Allanson	Milwaukee
Lt Geo H Cole	
Lt Henry G Rogers	Milwaukee
Alexander, John H	Annapolis, Mar 6—62
Bantly, Bart	Milwaukee
Broderick, Michael	Milwaukee
Bardick, Norman L	Milwaukee
Childs, W	Nashville, Jan 5—63
Christian, August	Milwaukee
Clayton, David	Murfreesboro, Feb 3—63
Cochran, B*	Stone River, Dec 31—62
Cor, G A	Annapolis, Feb 18—63
Comstock, Eugene	Chicago, Ill
Elimaker, Chas	Jefferson, Ind
Farel, Berkley	Milwaukee
Griswold, N	Murfreesboro, Feb 7—63
Haydon, Geo R	Milwaukee
Heth, Jas, Jr	Shakopee, Minn
Heth, Chas B, sgt	Milwaukee
James, C L	Bowling Green, Nov 16—62
Joyce, N*	Stone River, Dec 31—62
Kendrick, Thos	Milwaukee
Kingsland, Alfred	Murfreesboro, May 44—63
Kissam, O C	Nashville, Nov 26—62
Kussim, S	Murfreesboro, Feb 11—63
Leienitz, August F	Milwaukee
Loveland, Chas, Ins Agt	Milwaukee
Maustield J S	Milwaukee

Church, Wm P	Nashville, Feb 27—63
Clark, J H	Lancaster
Cook, I S	Bowling Green, Nov 29—62
Cookson, C I*	Stone River, Dec 31—62
Cooley, Geo A, sgt	Milwaukee
Cooley, H H*	Kenesaw Mt, June 22—64
Conway, Thos A	Milwaukee
Corgun, R*	Chickamauga, Sept 20—63
Corneille, P C+	Milwaukee, June 13—63
Crocker, Asa D	Sheboygan
Dewey, Jno S+	Dallas, May 25—64
Eddy, Geo T, sgt	Milwaukee
Fellows, L	Bardstown, Oct 9—62
Flemming, Wm, mc	Milwaukee
Groneuger, L C	Murfreesboro, Jan 6—61
Hockley, L D	Milwaukee
Hubband, S D	Mendota
Hunter, David	Caldwells Prairie
Kline, Sidney	Negaunee, Mich
Logan, Geo M	Nashville, Oct 14—63
Mahoney, Jno	Milwaukee
Macaroy, Wm	Kilbourn City
Marsh, Geo	Valley City, D T
Mallory, J L	Sheboygan
McAvery, Wm	Kansas City, Mo
McCarthy, Jno	Milwaukee
McDonald, W H	Richmond, Nov 4—63
Meyer, C G	Madison
Parsons, Jno	West Salem
Parsons, Silas B*	Chickamauga, Sept 20—63
Puhlman, Otto	Plymouth
Reynolds, T	Madison
Schwarzburg, Wm	Milwaukee
Sherman, Wm	Colorado Springs, Col
Sherman, Lewis N	Milwaukee
Silsby, A+	Chattanooga, July 3 —64
Singer, J F	Milwaukee
Smith, Chas A	Milwaukee
Staff, Geo C, sgt, me	Milwaukee
Story, Isaac M	Buffalo, N Y
Snyder, M L	Waukesha
Syder, Matt	Waukesha
Tuirek, Thos T	Chicago, Ill
Thomas, W H	Pewaukee
Woodward, C I*	Chickamauga, Sept 20—63
Yesson, A	Andersonville, Aug 20—64

Mason, H W, corp+	Nashville, Dec 23—64
Maxfield, W H	Milwaukee
McIntyre, Jno	Harrisville
Merrill, David L	Union City, Mich
Merrick, Geo W	Milwaukee
Miller, John	Milwaukee
Morrison, J C	La Crosse
Niedma, Conrad	Milwaukee
Ogden, John G	Milwaukee
Partridge, Henry, sgt	Milwaukee
Ransom, Lewis, sgt	Milwaukee
Rockwell, G, sgt*	Stone River, Dec 31—62
Shurr, Levi	Chicago, Ill
Siran, Chas H, sgt	Milwaukee
Smyth, Joseph+	Nashville, Jan 17—63
Trentlage, H A+	Chattanooga, Nov 26—63
Ward, Philip+	Nashville, Jan 16—62
Warnikee, John	Milwaukee
Vibber, Orville	Milwaukee
White, J L	Brookfield Junction
Williams, Chas	La Crosse
Williams, S J	Milwaukee
Wilson, Jas J	Lake View, Ill
Wisson, Wm	Milwaukee

C

Capt C Von Baumbach	Milwaukee
Capt Chas Hartung	Green Bay
Lt Peter Strack	Milwaukee
Lt C Grede	Chicago
Lt F Schleustedt*	Jonesboro, Sept 1—64
Lt C C Mayer	
Lt Fred'k Wolgram	West Bend
Lt John Zettler	Milwaukee
Albert, Lewis H	Oconomowoc
Armbruster, H	Knoxville, June 24—64
Beck, G+	Nashville, Mar 19—63
Ballman, Jerry, f	Eau Claire
Davitz, Wm	Milwaukee
Doerfler, J	Knoxville, May 1—63
Eckhardt, B*	Stone River, Dec 31—62
Fox, Frank N	Fond du Lac
Goll, Jacob	Marietta, Oct 23—64
Gathrle, Bernhardt	Kiel
Hegelmeyer, John	Milwaukee
Hermann, Mich, t	West Bend
Iserhot, H+	Ackworth, June 22—63
Jensen, Fritz O	Milwaukee
Kahler, F	Chattanooga, July 1—64
Kaul, Andrew	Scott
Klumb, C B	Kenesaw Mt, June 17—64
Krieger, Ferdinand	Kiel
Kruger, Fred	Kiel
Kull, L	Andersonville, July 31—64
Lang, Andreas	Louisville, Apr—63
Lauterbach,	Cedarburg
Leubben, D, corp*	Franklin, Nov 30—64
Mayer, L F, corp*	Resaca, May 14—64
Mueller, A E, corp+	Resaca, May 14—64
Mueller, Henry	St Louis
Nockerman, G, corp*	Stone River, Dec 31—62
Pankow, Carl*	Stone River, Dec 31—62
Porth, Wm	Milwaukee
Rosenbaum, A+	Atlanta, July 4—64
Rupert, G	Murfreesboro, Apr 27—63
Santee, J	Nashville, Dec 25—63
Serberlich, J*	Resaca, May 14—64
Seifert, A	Andersonville, July 9—64
Spann, H	Nashville, Dec 4—62
Unzer, Martin	Milwaukee
Vetter, Chas, corp	Richmond, Dec 7—63
Zahl, Jno, sgt*	Franklin, Nov 30—64
Zettler, Fred F	Oconomowoc

D

Capt Alra Philbrook*	Franklin, Tenn
Capt L T Battell	Milwaukee
Lt T T Keith*	Adansville, May 17—64

A. W. RICH.   ESTABLISHED SINCE 1864   LEWIS SILBER.

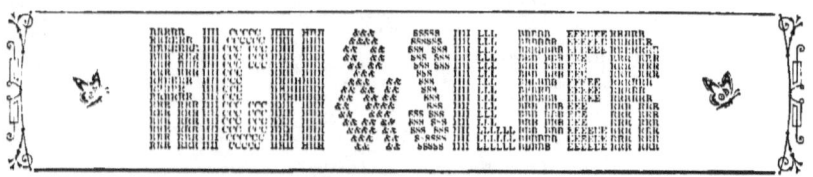

103, 105 AND 107 WISCONSIN STREET,
MILWAUKEE, WISCONSIN.

Manufacturers and Jobbers and Retail Dealers of

LADIES AND CHILDREN'S
CLOAKS AND SUITS
AND
Ladies and Gents' Furnishing Goods.

HEADQUARTERS FOR THE CELEBRATED

"Foster," "Seamless" and "Princess of Wales" Kid Gloves

Corsets and Dress Trimmings a Specialty.

WISCONSIN SOLDIERS AND SAILORS REUNION ROSTER.

Lt D D Goodrich — Ottumwa, Ia
Lt Christian, Nox* — Stone River, Dec 31—62
Booth, R* — Chickamauga, Sept 20—63
Brewster, Henry — Wesley, Ia
Campion, T* — Pleasant Hill, May 17—64
Coleman, P+ — Louisville, Aug 29—64
Curtis, L N* — Chickamauga, Sept 20—63
Dolan, Chas, me — Milwaukee
Gendner, Jno B — Stevens Point
Gregg, Geo* — Stone River, Dec 31—62
Hanuy, L B — Nashville, Dec 23—63
Hazel, J W* — Chaplin Hills, Oct 8—62
Hennessy, S* — Stone River, Dec 31—62
Jeffers, R M* — Stone River, Dec 31—62
Lane, Geo — Milwaukee
Malouey, M — Jeffersonville, June 19—64
McMullen, A — Murfreesboro, Feb 9—63
Meehan, Jno — Milwaukee
Morgau, E S, sgt — Madison, Dec 16—64
Moore, Edwin, l — Fond du Lac
Ryne, P — Chattanooga, Sept 2—64
Shanahan, Jno* — Pleasant Hill, May 16—65
White, D — Nashville, Nov 26—62
Wilson, M. f — Hebron

E

Capt D C Reed — Milwaukee
Capt D Y Horning — New Hampton, Ia
Lt J L Mitchell — Milwaukee
Lt Byron D L Abert — Milwaukee
Lt R P Elmore — Rock Falls, Ia
Alroynes, Jno — Andersonville, June 16—61
Barber, E R, sgt — New Albany, May 6—63
Barnice, Fred — Wauwatosa
Barritt, J D* — Peach Tree Creek, July 20—64
Berngen, Jno H* — Dallas, May 28—64
Bessenger, Chris — Wauwatosa
Bardwell, Irinead — Chicago, Ill
Breen, John H — Nashville, Dec 3—62
Brownell, Chas — Milwaukee
Brownell, David — Milwaukee
Bryant, Geo — Milwaukee
Buckley, Daniel — Milwaukee
Cleaveland, A W — Nashville, Dec 22—62
Cook Frank — McGregor, Ia
Doran, Chas — Milwaukee
Dunch, Garrett — Milwaukee
Eschenbaugh, A, l — Menominee Falls, Mo
Evert Fred's — Prairie du Chien
Everett, Fred — Prairie du Chien
Fingado, Chas — Wauwatosa
Fishback, John — Chicago, Ill
Ferris, William — Smithville
Hartmann, L — Bowling Green, Nov 2—62
Harvey, James — Baraboo
Hinds, Geo — Fond du Lac
Hinds, Wm — Fond du Lac
Hinds, Jno M — Nashville, Dec 7—62
Hoft, F* — Resaca, May 14—64
Hutchinson, Daniel — Wauwatosa
Karpenstien, Garrett — Milwaukee
Kitchell, Jno — Chattanooga, Dec 23—63
Kramer, Jos — Grafton
Krause, Geo+ — Nashville, Jan 25—63
Kusse, Wm — Milwaukee
Leister, Chas — Milwaukee
Lewis, Jno — Granville
Lyons, Moses, — Elm Grove
Mitchell, Albert
Mitchell, Geo — St Paul, Minn
Montgomery, J H — Richmond, Jan 26—63
Moore, Geo. — Wauwatosa
Moore, Wm — Wauwatosa
Moore, Martin — Beaver Dam
Moore, M P — La Crosse
Muth, Phillips — Wauwatosa
Noyes, Fanning — Briggsville
Phillips, Eugene — Butler
Poertner, Adam — Milwaukee

Putney, R M M+ — Chattanooga, Jan 23—64
Queenan, A* — Stone River, Dec 31—62
Queenan, Wm — Milwaukee
Reuter, Frank — Milwaukee
Rorentann, Wm — Milwaukee
Sackett, E H, corp — Nashville, Nov 22—62
Schirure, Adam — Butternut Colony
Seifert, Fred — Marsey
Shallock, Wm — Milwaukee
Singer, Joseph — Milwaukee
Snickel, Dodbel — Bowling Green, Nov 12—62
Springstead, D H — Stone River, Dec 31—62
Todhunter, J+ — Chickamauga, Sept 20—63
Trller, G P — St Louis, Apr 7—65
Tyler, J H, sgt — Milwaukee, Jan 7—63
Walter, A W, corp* — Dallas, May 28—64
Watson, C D — Butler
Worth, D* — Nashville, Dec 16—64

F

Capt Jno W Clark — Bowling Green, Ky
Capt Julius W Clark — Kankakee, Ill
Lt F C Lusk — Elgin, Ill
Lt C P Huntington — Milwaukee
Lt Patrick Dunn — Milwaukee
Allen, Albert — Milwaukee
Anderson, John — Milwaukee
Anderson, Jas — Austin, Minn
Buchanan, Horace — Little Falls, N Y
Coleman, J B* — Stone River, Dec 31—62
Damon, A A — Nashville, Jan 8—65
Dolan, Wm — Kenesaw Mt, June 30—63
Downer, Chas T — Milwaukee
Downer, Tim — Milwaukee
Dunn, Jno — Milwaukee
Dunn, Patrick — Appleton
Fental, Bernard — Milwaukee
Ferriter, P — Madison
Flemming, Jas — Chattanooga, July 17—64
Frowleiter, E — Madison
Gilligan, Jno — Milwaukee
Heckman, J H, me — Atlanta, Oct 1—63
Hoffman, Jno — Chicago, Ill
Holt, Norman — Milwaukee
Hollister, J W — Mission Ridge, Nov 25—63
Hunt, D* — Minneapolis, Minn
Johnson, John — Milwaukee
Kehoe Patrick — Milwaukee
Keeley, Geo — Beaver Dam
Koyes, N — Resaca, May 14—64
Kinsley, DeWitt C* — Milwaukee
Lawrence, Nat — Portage City
Little, Thos — Kenosha
Maher, Thos — Milwaukee
Mellingh, Jas — Manlius, N Y
McClenthen, Jno B, corp — Milwaukee
McKay, Jno — Murfreesboro, May 11—62
McKillips, M M, corp — Milwaukee
McLaughlin, P — Portage City
McLorley, Fellx — Portage City
McLorley, Jno — Milwaukee
Moffatt, Wolf — La Crosse
Morrison, Jno — Milwaukee
New, Jos — Murfreesboro, June 29—63
Presbrey, C — Nashville, Jan 27—63
Riley, Wm — Portage City
Sargent, Jno — Milwaukee
Seulley, Jno — Milwaukee
Shaw, Geo — Delavan
Smith, Henry — Stevenson, Nov 5—63
Sullivan, C T — Chickamauga, Sep 20—63
Tebbenbam, A J, sgt* — Eau Claire
Thompson, Geo — Milwaukee
Tighe, Thos — St Louis
Toohey, Thos — La Crosse
Whittaker, Geo — La Crosse
Williams, C

G

Capt Wm Kennedy — Milwaukee

Capt Jno W Plummer — Plummersville, N C
Lt E K Holton — St Louis M
Lt D N Kasson — Milwaukee
Lt H L Cage — Milwaukee
Anderson, Albert — Milwaukee
Anderson, Jno — Milwaukee
Bacon, Fred — Milwaukee
Baxter, A* — Kenesaw Mt, June 27—64
Connelly, Morris — Wauwatosa
Davis, R H, sgt+ — Resaca, May 24—64
Davis, Geo, sgt — Milwaukee
DeLury, Dennis — Nashville, May 27—63
Dooley, J — Andersonville, Aug 5—63
Foley, Jas — Wauwatosa
Gage, Henry L. — Milwaukee
Gage, Henry, e — St Paul, Minn
Hale, Frank A, corp* — Stone River, Dec 31—62
Kasson, D N — Milwaukee
Lewis, W B, drummer — Evanston, Ill
Long, Jno — Andersonville, Oct—61
McShane, Mike — Milwaukee
Ormond, Wm M — Milwaukee
Rourke, T* — Kenesaw Mt, June 22—64
Smile, Philip+ — Pleasant Hill, Sept 2—64
Syrreh, R B — Washington
Thompson, Edward — Milwaukee
Thorsen, P — Andersonville, Oct 5—64
Tichr, Thos, sgt — Milwaukee
Webber, F G — Milwaukee, June 26—64
Whitney, Jas — Madison
Wood, Henry — Milwaukee
Wood, Harvey — Milwaukee

H

Capt H W Gunnison — Dayton, Ky
Capt Gustav Goldsmith*—Chickamauga, Oct 4—63
Capt J G Tannatt — Washington, D C
Capt Julius W Clark — Kankakee, Ill
Capt J N Kiefer — Sheboygan Falls
Lt Geo Coote
Lt Edw A R Blake — Port Washington
Lt C P Larkin — Milwaukee
Aurehammer, C* — Stone River, Dec 31—62
Baker, F L* — Chickamauga, Sept 20—63
Berlandl, Wm — St Paul, Minn
Blake, E R — Port Washington
Beckler, Henry — Port Washington
Bisch, Chas — Port Washington
Bold, Wm V — Milwaukee
Bredfelt, Geo W — Wenona, Ill
Brichler, Geo — Louisville, Sept 7—62
Bruce, Il — Andersonville, July 20—64
Buehler, Henry — Port Washington
Burns, Thos — Chattanooga, Jan 8—61
Cline, Chas — Port Washington
Douglas, Geo H — Milwaukee
Eder, Jno* — Stone River, Dec 31—62
Ehrenbecker, Frauk* — Pleasant Hill, May 16—64
Ford, Thos J — Towanda, Ill
Frisch, Charley — Port Washington
Fuller, C — Nashville, March—63
Geary, Jas — Milwaukee
George, Sam? — Milwaukee
Gielzier, Jos — Port Ashington
Howerd, Jno+ — Chattanooga, July 2—64
Keopp, Jno B — Milwaukee
Kiefer, J H — Port Washington
Klein, Thos — Port Washington
Mangan, Jas, corp — Andersonville, July 10—64
McCullough, Jno — Janesville
McElroy, Thos — Milwaukee
McQuirken, Thos — Milwaukee
Meyer, Leopold — Alhatee
Mohrlansen, L T — Manitowoc
Neustadtl, N E* — Chickamauga, Sept 20—63
Parker, T C+ — Milwaukee
Rauschenberger, J+ — Kenesaw Mt, June 22—6
Reilley, Morris — Milwaukee
Sexton, T — Cleveland, Apr 26—64

MILWAUKEE SUNDAY TELEGRAPH

Is true, in spite of our natural and acquired modesty, we are compelled to admit it is

THE LARGEST, THE CHEAPEST AND THE BEST

FAMILY JOURNAL PUBLISHED.

Write to us for Specimen Copy and Judge for Yourself.

In its columns the reader will find All The News, Ample Variety of Editorial, Poetry, Literary Articles, Stories and Sketches, Tales of Travel, Society Gossip, Interviews with Prominent Men, Financial Reports, Dramatic Criticism, Religious Tidings, Agricultural and Domestic Articles, and every other feature that can make a paper valuable. The miscellany of spirited writings, covering every variety and range of subject and thought will be maintained as of old by contributors who stand at the head of their specialties.

A Special Feature will be the Continuation of

THE SOLDIER CHAPTERS,

GRAPHICALLY WRITTEN BY SOLDIERS.

Descriptive of scenes and events in which they took an active part, one chapter of which will appear in each number. Giving Soldier readers a

Weekly Reunion with Comrades all over the World

An Eight-Page Seven-Column Newspaper, Furnishing 56 Columns of Reading Matter, and Printed at Daylight Every Sunday Morning.

E. A. CALKINS, 3d Wis. Cavalry,   J. A. WATROUS, 6th Wis. Infantry

EDITORS AND PUBLISHERS.

OFFICE AT 88 MASON STREET.

MILWAUKEE,   □   □   WISCONSIN.

WISCONSIN SOLDIERS AND SAILORS REUNION ROSTER.

Shenan, Jno, corp
Turner, A A
Ulbricht, Theo
Watchtman, A+
Wanderer, C
Weiskopf, G*

Capt F A Root
Capt Wm H Sibley
Lt K J Chivas*
Lt Jno Borth
Lt H A Reed
Lt J L Mitchell
Lt F W Riddle
Bough, Caro
Cameron, G+
Casey, W C
Conkilu, S J
Curley, E+
Davis, Dan'l B
Devine, Pat
Dunck, Garrett H
Fehrenkamp, M
Fetter, Jacob
Frattinger, Peter
French, John
Habn, H
Heywood, Geo, sgt
Hollander, Adam
Jones, Richard
Jones, Owen
Lawrence, J
Ormsby, Wm E
Pritchard, T
Ryan, Wm*
Scott, Thos
Sholes, Chas L
Smith, Wm J
Stott, Thos G
Sullivan, Jno
Thompson, C G
Usigen. Louis
Vose, Wm
Ward, Wm
Wehe, C L
Welrick, C L

Capt E B Parsons
Capt Thos E Balding
Lt Louis T Battell
Lt Jno E Armitage
Lt Thos W C Moore
Baldwin, Horace
Bersch. Nicholas
Brooks, N B*
Coles, Jue*
Covalt, B C, corp*
Day, Luke K
Disch, Wm
Gage, Augustus*
Gallagher, S
Gillaert, Jas*
Grover, Sanford
Harman, E
Kassner, L*
Keithur, D
Lamb, Ed
Link, Jno T
Moore, Juo* .
Nicholson, Guy
Platt, Henry*
Place, Charles
Puffenroth, Jno
Putz, Wm
Saddler, Jno
Spear, Philip+

Audersonville, July 30—64
Nashua, Ia
Milwaukee
Nashville, Sept 30—63
Aluapee
Stone River, Dec 31—62

Chattanooga, Dec 2—63
Milwaukee
Mission Ridge, Nov 25—63
Milwaukee
West Point, N Y
Milwaukee
Detroit, Mich
Milwaukee
Nashville, Jan 18—63
La Crosse
East Troy
Nashville, Jan 18—63
Milwaukee
Milwaukee
Milwaukee
Chattanooga, Dec 31—63
Fond du Lac
Milwaukee
Milwaukee
Nashville, Jan 23—63
Milwaukee
Milwaukee
Milwaukee
Chicago, Ill
Murfreesboro, Dec 10—63
Milwaukee
Chickamauga, Sept 28—63
Stone River, Dec 31—62
Milwaukee
Milwaukee
Chicago, Ill
Milwaukee
Milwaukee
Ripon
Milwaukee
Waterford
Chicago, Ill
Chicago, Ill
St Louis, Mo

Milwaukee
Milwaukee
Milwaukee
Milwaukee
Jacksonville Florida
Oak Creek
Winneconne
Stone River, Dec 31—63
Chickamauga, Sept 30—63
Franklin, Nov 30—63
Oak Creek
Bay View
Stone River, Dec 31—62
Louisville, Feb 10—64
Stone River, Dec 31—62
Oak Creek
Milwaukee
Adairsville, May 17—61
New Albany, Dec 14—63
Chicago, Ill
Nashville, Dec 19—62
Resaca, May 4—64
Oak Creek
Stone River, Dec 31—62
New Lisbon
Madison, Dec 20—64
St Francis Station
Mukwanago
Chattanooga, May—64

I

Spence, T
Stearns, F+
Suhr, F
Thompson, F L
Thompson, Wm
Wyre, Wm .
Yochum, G

Bowling Green, Dec 17—62
Chattanooga, Mar 16—64
Murfreesboro, July 20—63
Chicago, Ill
St Francis Station
Oak Creek
Chickamauga, Sept 20—63

UNASSIGNED.

Barnes, F J, sgt+
Cheever, Anson E
Comstock, Eugene E
Flemming, James S
Hoiton, Ed K, f
Langhoff. Henry
McKintrick, Robt
Mullen, O
Place, Geo, Q M sgt
Rubenstein, C
Strong, Isaac M
Wehe, Chas L
Weison, Jas J

Nashville, Mar 27—64
Covington, Ky
Chicago, Ill
Madison
St Louis, Mo
Mischicott
St Paul, Minn
Covington, Sept 11—62
Milwaukee
Atlanta, July 20—63
Buffalo, N Y
Chicago, Ill
Chicago, Ill

TWENTY-FIFTH INFANTRY.

Three years. Organized Sept. 14th, 1862. Original strength, 1018, gain by recruits, etc., 426 Total, 1444. Death loss, 423—killed in action, 26, died of wounds, 16. of disease, 376, of accidents, 4. Other losses, 230—missing, 0, desertions, 20, transfers, 65, discharges, 165. Strength at muster out June 7th, 1865, 772. Campaigns in Minn., Ky., Tenn., Miss., La., Ark., Ala., Ga., S. C., N. C.

REGIMENTAL ROSTER.

Col'Milton Montgomery
Lt Sam'l J Nasmith
Lt Jeremiah M Rusk
Maj Wm H Joslyn
Adj Geo G Symes
Adj Jno Fitzgerald
Q M W H Downs
Q M David C Hope
Surg Martin R Gage
Surg Wm A Gott
A surg Jacob McCreary
A Surg Wm H Borden
A Surg C C Olmstead
A Surg J Copp Noyes
A Surg Dan'l L Downs
A Surg A Young
A Surg Chas A Dalgairns
Chap Thos C Golden
Chap Thos Harwood

Platteville, Aug 17—63
Viroqua
Madison

Helena, Aug 3—63

Oshkosh

A

Capt Jas Berry
Capt Cyrus M Butt
Capt Jno H Casson
Lt Warren G Davis
Lt Jno Williams
Ferrill, Isaiah, sgt
Miller, Jas, sgt
Furguson, Jno A, corp
Jonas, Wm, corp
Mason, Jas, corp
Smith, Justus, corp
Adams, Jonathan
Ashbury, Alex M
Baldwin, Jason
Baker, Christopher C
Barstow, Chas
Beau, Abraham
Biddison, Amon
Guard, Wm F O

Beaufort, Mar 7—65
Memphis, Aug 31—63
Memphis, Sept 11—63
Madison, Dec 21—62
Viroqua, Oct 16—63
Marietta, Sept 4—64
Viroqua, Oct 5—63
Memphis, Sept 11—63
Washington, May 25—64
Helena, Aug 23—63
Helena, Aug 21—63
Viroqua, Feb 24—64
Mound City, Sept 4—63
Memphis, Sept 7—3
Memphis, Sept 13—63

Casson, Jno R
Cummings, Geo W
Crago, Lewis
Douglas, Jas A
Delap, Chas W
Dunlap, Josiah
Foreaker, Wm H
Gill, Arthur
Grubb, Purley B*
Garrett, Jno
Giller, B L.l
Gebser, Phillip
Green, Geo F
Graham, Jno
Griffin, Sam'l L
Hadley, Moses E
Hope, Geo W
Huoter, Wm B H
Huntington, Edward F
Marshall, Jno
McClurg, Manassah
Moore, Peter S
Pideock, Wm
Pierce, Geo J
Ranger, Franklin
Rogers, Jas A
Reed, Wm C
Richard, V B
Rhee, Jas F
Sewell, Harvey
Sharp, Nicholas V
Smith, Finley
Smith, Nathaniel H
Sayne, Jas H, Jr
Steadman, Hiram
Strieker, Silas H
Sutton, Freeman
Kilbaugh, Philip
Swanton, J S, m
Tenney. Gilman
Vance, Sampson A
Wisel, Ira
Wood, Joe

Viroqua
St Louis, Dec 19—63
Soldiers Grove
Helena, Sept 21—63
Viroqua, Feb 18—64
Newbern, Apr 5—63
Helena, Aug 20—63
Paducah, Aug 27—63
Resaca, May 14—64
Weisser, Jan 8—64
Warrens, Mills
Snyders Bluff, July 6—63
Snyders Bluff. July 9—63
Memphis, Sept 6—3
Madison, Feb 24—63
Madison, Feb 5—63
Memphis, Sept 21—63
Columbus, Apr 14—63
Memphis, Sept 12—63
Jeff Barracks, Sept 26—63
Helena, Aug 21—63
Memphis, Sept 17—63
Madison, Feb 5—63
Snyders Bluff, July 18—63
Memphis, Sept 6—63
. Desoto
Madison, Jan 8—63
Viola
Helena, Aug'11—63
Bishopville, Oct 9—63
Alexandria, Feb 1—63
Madison, Feb 5—63
Helena, Dec 18—63
Viroqua
Madison, Jan 13—64
Snyders Bluff, July 9—63
Viroqua, Oct 20—63
Newbern, May 5—65
Leon
Desota, Oct 1—63
Boscobel, Apr 29—64
Helena, Aug 14—63
Willetts Point, May 12—66

B

Capt Wm H Joslyn
Capt Wm H Bennett
Capt Warren C S Barron
Lt Wm Roush
Lt Edw E Honstain
Lt Edwin B Waggoner
Albaugh, Adam, sgt
Clark, Ethan A, sgt
Mark, Juo A, sgt
Trousdale. Alfred N, sgt
Gault, Wm W, sgt
Breese, Wm S, corp*
Higgins, Chas C, corp
McMahon, Jas R, corp
Wallace. Ensley
Bolenbaugh, Jno
Blake, Simon S
Barton, W C S
Runell, Jesse G
Bayse, Jno W
Bolenbaugh, Peter
Brown, Wm D
Crandall, Wm
Crandall, Jno G
Creigo, Lewis, f
Craig, Stephen V
Core, Juo
Christopherson, Ole
Craig, Lewis
Dodge, Kibridge
Dosch, Edmund
Dickanson, Jacob
David, Marquis

Richland Centre
Macon. Aug 10—64
Richland Centre

Paducah, Aug 16—63
Memphis, July 31—63
Memphis, Aug 21—63
Helena, Dec 25—63
Helena, Dec 13—63
Decatur. July 22—64
Vicksburg, Oct 18—63
Bloom, Oct 11—63
Paducah, Aug 3—63
Snyders Bluff, July 6—63
Richland Centre
Richland Centre
Richland Centre
Decatur, Feb 21—64
Richland Centre
Cairo, Apr 29—64
Memphis, Sept 21—63
Richland, Oct 6—63
Yankeetown
Madison, Apr 10—64
Benz
Madison, Aug 27—64
Port Andrew
Columbus, May 1—63
Masenia
Marietta, Aug 31—61
Blue River

TO THE SOLDIERS!

All in want of New Garments should bear in mind that

WOOD & NOTBOHM,

---KEEP THE---

ARCADE CLOTHING HOUSE.

A Splendid Stock of Suitings of the most Fashionable designs. OUR TAILORING DEPARTMENT is in charge of SAMUEL D. JOHNSON, a cutter who has been all through the war, and yet challenges any of the fraternity for fine fitting and reliable work. Call at Headquarters,

68 & 70 WISCONSIN ST., MILWAUKEE, WIS.

COMRADES TRY

FLINT'S

MAY QUEEN

CHEWING TOBACCO.

A NEW DEAL.

As the Demand is constantly increasing for

DRAPERIES, CURTAINS

Lambrequins and Shades,

MESSRS. MATTHEWS BROS. & CO.

Have added that branch of business to the

FURNITURE TRADE

And they have employed a first class Curtain Man to superintend that department. They have in stock a very large and

New Line of Goods,

And hope to please the public in styles and prices.

BOOTS & SHOES.

NEW STYLES

For the Spring Trade. My stock was never before so complete, comprising all the leading makes and styles at less price than the same quality can be bought elsewhere. Agent in Milwaukee for

BURT'S CELEBRATED

FINE

BOOTS & SHOES,

The best goods made; also sole agent for Fargo's Sole Leather Tip School Shoes for boys and girls. Will give a new pair for any pair wearing through at the toe. All Goods Warranted.

W. G. CAMPBELL,

113 WISCONSIN STREET, SIGN RED BOOT,

MILWAUKEE,   —   **WIS.**

WISCONSIN SOLDIERS AND SAILORS REUNION ROSTER. 113

Fish, Isaac — Columbus, May 21—63
Fosmer, Wm — Calif ania, Mo
Freeman, Geo W — Helena, Nov 21—63
Fitzgerald, Jno — Ironton
Gher, Henry+ — Marietta, Aug 10—64
Graham, David — Madison, Mar 15—64
Gray, Benj — Ackworth, June 12—64
Hulbert, Ansel, f — Richland
Hough, Wm — Memphis, Oct 20—63
Houston, Ed E — Muscoda
Hurd, Robt F — Helena, Aug 27—63
Hulbut, Ansel — Muscoda
Hoyt, Geo T L — Atlanta, Aug 23—64
Hoyt, Albert J — Muscoda
Jones, Alex S — Madison, Feb 11—63
Jones, Jesse — Snyders Bluff, July 20—63
Joslyn, Wm H — Richland Centre
James, Thos D — Bloom, Oct 8—65
Jewell, Benj B — Memphis, Nov 19—63
Johnson, Jno — Port Andrew
Jenks, Julius C — Decatur, May 1—51
Justin, Jas W — Port Andrew
Kilogler, Arlow — Richland Centre
Logue, Geo J — Muscoda
Logue, Jno A — Muscoda
Lewis, Sam'l L — Paducah, Aug 30—63
Lewis, Juo M — Orion
Lyons, Franklin E — Louisville, Mar 8—65
McNally, Jno — Memphis, Sept 26—63
Mayfield, Green — Richland Centre
Miller, Abram — Richland Centre
Moody, Jos — Westford
Morris, Edw — Richland Centre
Munson, Christian — Rome, Aug 7—64
McKey, Jno — Richland Centre
Myres, Geo* — Resaca, May 14—64
Marshall, Sam'l — Fancy Creek
Miles, Chas — Orion
Miller, Geo — Orion
Nimock, Robt — LaCrosse
Nicks, Jno D — Viroqua
Neal, Pettygrove — New Era, Neb
Oleson, Ole* — Resaca, May 14—64
Oleson, Andrew E — Marrietta, Oct 4—64
Paulson, Ole — Vicksburg, Aug 9—63
Peekham, Chas W — West Branch
Peekham, W R — West Branch
Perkins, Geo E — Memphis, Aug 28—63
Pearson, Edw — Excelsior
Reeves, Jno — Richland, Dec 21—63
Robinson, R D — Chicago, Ill
Rose, W F — Richland Centre
Sutton, Jas — Savannah, Apr 4—64
Seeley, Franklin E — West Lima
Stockton, Albert W — Faribault Minn
Wallace, Dan'l — Snyders Bluff, July 11—63
Waddell, Wm A — Richland
Wallace, Hiram — Memphis, Nov 14—63
Waggoner, Ed B — White Hall
Wallace, Stephen J — Helena, Aug 20—63
Wood, De Witt C — Mill Creek
Wildermuth, Jno — Decatur, May 7—64
Welton, Mill J — Vicksburg, Sept 6—63
Young, Jno, f — West Lima
Yoder, Jacob — Memphis, Nov 11—63

C

Capt Hival D Farquharson
Lt Lyman S Mason
Lt Chas Barrett
Lt Joel Adon Barker
Lt Pleasant S Pritchett
Knight, Jno, sgt — Vicksburg, Aug 14—63
Simpkins, Silas P, sgt — Mound City, Apr 12—64
Arnold, Jno — Helena, Aug 25—63
Barnhelsel, Geo — New Albany, Feb 17—65
Bishop, Marshall B — Vicksburg, Aug 11—63
Breithaupt, L H — Lancaster
Bradley, Jas — Vicksburg, Mar 16—65

Craig, Wm E — Lake Providence, Aug 9—63
Dougherty, Jno II — Memphis, Sept 2—63
Ewer, Rene! — Helena, Aug 9—63
Flaherty, David — Sauk Centre, Dec 8—62
Fenel, Allen — Louisville, July 8—64
Farquharson, H D — Boscobel
Greeby, Henry — Vicksburg, Aug 12—63
Groesser, Thos — Sandtown, July 5—64
Halferty, Jno — Memphis, Sept 10—63
Hayden, Henry J — Helena, Oct 26—63
Henderson, Wm — Helena, Aug 20—63
Irwin, Alexander — Andersonville, Sept 26—64
Irwin, Robt — Chattanooga, Nov 8—61
Julius, Chas — Snyders Bluff, June 30—63
Kretzer, Wm — Paducah, Aug 18—63
Latham, Lorenzo — Providence, Aug 1—63
Lick, Jas — Vicksburg, Feb 2—64
Laurence, Thos — Memphis, Dec 2—63
Maner, Jno — Memphis, Aug 20—63
Parce, Lucien — Memphis, Aug 27—63
Pierce, Dan'l F — Vicksburg, Aug 6—53
Pritchett, Jas M — Helena, Nov 16—63
Potter, Chas R — Marietta, Aug 17—61
Roberts, Jas W — Ellenboro, July 24—64
Rouse, Benj — Willetts Point, Mar 21—65
Rays, I. M, f — Harlan, Ia
Sehmitz, Peter — Cassville, Oct 17—63
Schreiner, David — Lancaster
St John, Edwin G — Memphis, Sept 17—63
Seitz, Blazius* — Resara, May 14—64
Tobler, Jno B — Paducah, Aug 17—63
Twining, Quincy — Aug 14—63
Weiss, Peter — Memphis, Oct 12—63
Wellestumph, Jno H — Memphis, Aug 19—63
Wurden, Wm R — Rome, Sept 7—64

D

Capt Jas D Condit — Sparta
Capt Mortimer E Leonard — Sparta
Lt Chas S Farnham
Lt Andrew J High
Justis, Jno, sgt — Helena, Aug 19—63
Denimon, Ira P, corp — Cheraw, Mar 2—65
Harmon, Jno A, corp — Helena, Sept 30—63
Ahles, Henry A — Helena, Aug 26—63
Alger, Thos — Helena, Dec 18—63
Boyle, Peter — Andersonville, Sept 4—64
Boughton, M T, ph — Northwood, Ia
Branlan, R E — Tunnel City
Brid, H R — Mifflin
Broman, R E — Warrens Mills
Campbell, David H — Snyders Bluff, July 1—63
Chatterson, Jeff — St Louis, Jan 1—64
Cleveland, D F — St Croix
Conger, Lewis B — July 23—63
Cressy, Warren P — Cairo, Sept 6—62
Cressey, Henry W+ — Decatur, July 24—64
Day, Henry — Mankato, Nov 22—62
Depew, Wiley — Dallas, June 1—64
Dorwin, S N, f — Decatur, July 23—64
Dunlevy, Thos+ — Greenfield, Dec 1—63
Edgerton, Henry L — Helena, Aug 19—63
Edgerton, Chas L — Chattanooga, Sept 7—63
Ellis, Richard — Helena, Mar 10—64
Gleason, Geo — Emery
Goff, Spence S — Tomah
Goff, Spencer S — Tomah
Groser, Eleazer H — Decatur, July 22—64
Huntley, Jabez L* — Atlanta, Aug 7—64
House, Philemon P+ — Ashland
Howes, D S, cl — Winslow Furnace, June 6—64
Harp, Geo F — Wilton
Houghteling, Henry — Memphis, Sept 15—63
Hyde, Alf — Snyders Bluff, June 15—63
Holgate, Francis — Andersonville, Aug 4—64
Hollenbeck, Amos J — Vicksburg, Feb 23—64
Kinney, Wm H — Helena, Dec 27—63
Landon, Orin

Morrison, Wm A — Goldsboro, Apr 1—65
Minor, Wm H — Paducah, Oct 9—63
Manley, Henry — Pelican Rapids, Minn
Mills, Elias — Paducah, Aug 18—63
Matchel, Jas — Tomah
Mills, Eli — July 26—63
McLeon, Wm — Tomah
Miller, Alex — Oct 16—64
Musgrave, Wm P — Snyders Bluff, July 23—63
Owens, Louis E — Helena, Sept 10—64
Quackenbush, Ernest, f — Lancaster
Rathbun, Oliver J — Chattanooga, Feb 10—65
Randles, J, jo — Andersonville, Nov 4—64
Rottenstetter, Simeon — Helena, Nov 15—63
Shaw, Wm F — Memphis, Sept 17—63
Sawyer, Peter E — Helena, Oct—63
Stull, Lewis — Sparta, Feb 18—65
Slike, Jno J — Tomah
Spooner, Dan'l H — Tomah
Snow, Geo M+ — Louisville, June 9—64
Thompson, Jas W — Paducah, Aug 26—63
Thompson, Allen — St Louis, Oct 15—63
Ustick, Jacob Y — Paducah, Aug 30—63
Worden, Sam'l H — Marietta, Sept 17—64
Watson, Geo E — Tomah
Wolcott, Geo L — Memphis, Oct 11—63
Youmans, Wm H — Memphis, Sept 17—63

E

Capt Jno G Scott — Mound City, Apr 14—64
Capt Jno M Shaw
Lt Jno W Smelker
Lt Jas McCoy
Lt Wm H Gribble*
Lt Benj F Saltzman — Decatur, July 22—64
Bailey, Wm H, corp+ — Andersonville Aug 13—64
Bailey, Jonathan, corp — Helena, Aug 24—63
Barstow, Myron, corp — Helena, Sept 10—63
Armstrong, Jno D — Madison, Jan 8—63
Basye, Sam'l — Paducah, Sept 28—63
Bartle, Ransom J* — Decatur, July 22—64
Basye, Isaac N — Bowling Green, Jan 21—64
Batchelor, Fred T — Atlanta, Sept 23—64
Beazley, Pearl — Dunleith, Nov 6—63
Beckwith, Nelson J — Platteville, July 10—63
Block, Jno C — Atlanta, Oct 23—64
Black, J L, ja — Charles City, Ia
Blanchard, Elijah — Helena, Aug 10—63
Chambers, Hiram — Snyders Bluff, June 30—63
Clifton, Isaac N, f — Washburne
Clifton, DeWitt C — Rome, Aug 11—64
Cloud, Nathaniel — Jeff Barracks, July 8—64
Dougherty, Thos C* — Decatur, July 22—64
Yoskett, Elizur H+ — Kenesaw Mt, June 27—64
Grover, Jno* — Decatur, July 22—64
Heigh Marion+ — Andersonville, Sept 12—64
Hall, Warren — Memphis Sept 12—63
Haney, Dan'l — Vicksburg, Mar 3—64
Kamup, Jno F — Snyders Bluff, June 27—63
Kiel, Jno C — Snyders Bluff, July 12—63
Kiel, Chas B — Platteville, Feb 5—64
Lalolet, Geo* — Decatur, July 22—64
Mero, Fred'k — Helena, July 25—63
Morrison, Geo — July 27—63
Phillips, Wm B — Platteville, Sept 17—63
Richey, Chas* — Decatur, July 23—64
Schuster, Jacob — Paducah, Aug 9—62
Shiner, Abraham — Snyders Bluff, July 21—63
Stone, Sam'l — St Louis, Oct 8—63
Stone, Sylvanus — Mound City, Sept 27—63
Stevens, Leonard — Helena, Aug 16—63
Simpkins, Jos — Paris, June 2—64
Stant, Andrew — Sylvan Corners
S mpkins, Jno — Memphis, Apr 2—64
Taylor, Albert R — Andersonville, Aug 1—64
Vanatta, Morgan B H — Helena, Dec 6—63

STARK BROTHERS,

129 and 131 WISCONSIN STREET,

Have now in Store and are daily receiving the Latest Spring Styles of

CARPETS,

—NOVELTIES IN—

Curtain Goods and Fancy Articles,

Lace Curtains in sets or by the Yard; the largest Stock in the City.

TABLE AND TOILET LINENS,

TIDIES, TABLE AND PIANO SPREADS.

CHINTZES, CASHMERES,

RAW SILK AND JUTE TAPESTRIES,

Imberline, Brilliantes, Belgique,

And other Novelties in Drapery Curtain Goods, which we can make up in Drapery Curtains in the most approved styles.

All kinds of Curtain Trimmings and Cornice Fixtures,

WISCONSIN SOLDIERS AND SAILORS REUNION ROSTER.

F

Name	Location, Date
Capt Jas C Farrand	
Capt Geo G Symes	
Capt Rob Roy McGregor	
Lt Parker C Dunn	
Lt Whiting A Woolbiser	
Lt Oscar E Foote	Helena, Aug 9–63
Lt Alf H Lamb	
Brewer, Hiram M, sgt	Snyders Bluff, July 26–63
Hickock, Oscar K, sgt	LaCrosse, Dec 10–63
Williams, Wm S, sgt	Snyders Bluff, July 22–63
Brown, Jas E, corp	Helena, Nov 4–63
Chadwick, Jas, corp	Rome, Sept 3–61
Taylor, Pratt M, corp	Mound City, Aug 18–2
Alley, Leonard	Helena, Aug 14–83
Artus, Fred	LaCrosse
Aiken, Jos	Vicksburg, Aug 11–63
Bedford, Jno	Helena, Aug 22–63
Bell, W D	LaCrosse
Boardman, Geo	LaCrosse
Cheeney, Walt R	Paducah, Aug 17–63
Davis, Henry C	Irving
Davis, Theron	Memphis, Sept 9–63
Dell, Edw	Jeffersonville, Dec 26–64
Echner, Phileman	Vicksburg, May 9–64
Forsythe, Abe	Helena, Aug 18–63
Fleming, Jas F	Madison
Farwell, Edwin P	Memphis, Sept 5–63
Gregory, Geo D	Helena, Aug 14–63
Gregory, Jno H	Snyders Bluff, July 18–63
Germaine, Walt	Irving, May 20–63
Germaine, Wm	Mankato, Dec 12–62
Getts, Jno	LaCrosse
Germaine, Fred'ck,	Millikens Bend, July 6–63
Gedney, Seth M	Helena, Dec 31–63
Goodrich, Chas	Vicksburg, Mar 24–64
Godbold, David	Rome, Aug 27–61
Harswell, Jno	Helena, Aug 22–63
Hendrickson, Ole	LaCrosse
Jewett, Henry L	Woodstock, Dec 16–63
Jones, Milt	Rome, Sept 21–64
Lewis, Timothy A, me	LaCrosse
Lincoln, Jas H	Providence, July 23–63
Lauterbeek, David	Aug 9–63
Lamb, A J	LaCrosse
Lewis, Jno	Chattanooga, Nov 5–64
Lewis, Sam'l C	Tomah-va
Lockman, E	LaCrosse
Lamb, A H	LaCrosse
Morthuy, Alf	Memphis, Sept 9–63
Miller, Paul	St Louis, Mar 7–64
Molitor, Paul	Louisville, June 22–61
Morey, Wm	Savannah, Feb 14–65
Mellott, Simeon	Sparta, Feb 21–64
Nichols, Hudson	Helena, Sept 16–63
Nichols, Jno C*	Decatur, July 22–64
Oleson, Knud	Rome, July 30–61
Pfaff, Geo	LaCrosse
Rausenberger, Geo F	Marietta, Sept 1–64
Samerer, E	Somerset
Smith, Jesse F	Memphis, Sept 10–63
Sutton, Aaron	Memphis, Aug 20–63
Shaffer, Jos	Memphis, Sept 25–63
Schwanz, Henry	Athens, Apr 15–61
Sherman, Norman C	July 31–63
Shepherd, Geo F	New York, May 7–65
Staley, Jno	Savannah, Feb 9–65
Stanford, Leroy	Pole Greve, Jan 19–64
Skelis, Wm	LaCrosse
Schroder, Henry	LaCrosse
Skinner, Alva*	Dallas, May 30–64
Shoemaker, Nathan+	Big Shanty, June 16–61
Thorp, Lewis F	Snyders Bluff, July 17–63
Thorp, Wm H	Island 67, Aug 16–63
Thomas, Geo H	Mound City, Aug 7–63
Tjostleson, Erick	Rome, Aug 2–61
Van Ostrand, Wm J	Memphis, Sept 8–63
Walker, Chas M	Columbus, July 4–63

Name	Location, Date
Wolgeford, C	LaCrosse
Woodman, Chas W	Memphis, Aug 30–63
Wells, Jas H	Memphis, Sept 1–63

G

Name	Location, Date
Capt Virus W Dorwin	
Capt Robt J Whittleton	
Capt Benj B Gurley	
Lt Jos W Brackett	
Lt Julius A Parr	
Lt Jno W, McKay	
Allen, Delos F, corp	Stoughton, Aug 11–63
Webb, Orlando V, corp	Corfu, Oct 18–63
Dickason, Sam'l L, corp	N Y Harbor, Apr 8–65
Adams, Orlando D	Grant, June 10–63
Ainsworth, Marvel	Helena, Nov 9–63
Anderson, Wm E	Cairo, Dec 7–63
Ausiin, Isaac	Andersonville, Aug 1–64
Bump, G O	Mondovi
Bammert, Jno B	Menominee
Barnum, J W	Mondovi
Bribst, Jno	Mondovi
Brill, Geo	Rock Falls
Bishop, A	Weston
Bump, W R	Rock Falls
Christian, Jno W*	Decatur, July 22–64
Coleman, Ed C	Rice Lake
Cook, C H, f	Gilmanton
Cook, C H	Mondovi
Crandall, Albert	Arcadia
Dehms, Aas C	St Louis, Oct 10–63
Dediroff, J W	Alma
Enger, Nathaniel	Memphis, Sept 11–63
Eddington, Jno	Helena, Dec 3–63
Fitzgerald, Jno T	Paducah, July 21–63
Graham, Horace	Vicksburg, Apr 1–64
Gillham, Ransom	Greeu, La
Grippen, A Judson	Nashville, June 6–64
Hill, W E, musiclau	Durand
Hervey, Alex	Mondovi
Herman, Joel	Mondovi
Hillard, O W	Mondovi
Hadley, D R	Mondovi
Ide, Geo W	Dallas, June 2–64
Joyner, Judson N	St Cloud, Oct 25–63
Kidder, Ruben A	Memphis, Apr 20–64
Kelley, Vincent+	Resaca, May 20–64
Mann, Nathan	Columbus, Apr 13–63
McKay, J W	Minersink, Minn
Morse, Henry L	Goldsboro, Apr 6–65
Miller, Lorenzo	Portage City
Richmond, Philip	Waumandee, Oct 10–62
Sanborn, Azro E	Keokuk, Oct 15–63
Silvernail, Calvin C	Menominee
Smith, Wm H	Dane, Feb 10–62
Thompson, Ira E	Memphis, Oct 2–63
Thompson, Wm P	Memphis, Aug 20–63
Wilson, Robt	Vicksburg, Mar 4–64

H

Name	Location, Date
Capt Ziba S Swan	
Lt Chas F Olmsted	Memphis, Aug 6–63
Lt Henry C Wise	Helena, Oct 27–63
Lt Eugene B Wise	
Lt Robt H Kendrick	
Lt Jas Frawley	
Lt Thomas H Wellock	
Clarke, Thos Y, sgt+	Resaca, May 16–64
Curtius, Fred'k	Paducah, Sept 19–65
Allinson, John, sgt	Athens, Apr 11–64
Brown, Jeremiah, sgt	Snyders Bluffs, July 20–63
Aldrich, John J	Savannah, Dec 11–64
Buchacker, Louis*	Minersink, Minn
Bilderback, E J	Snyders Bluffs, July 20–63
Beldon, Theodore	Helena, Aug 11–63
Bilderback, Chas H	Menphis, Sep 11–63
Bilderback, Friend B	

Name	Location, Date
Botts, Wm	Memphis, Sep 10–63
Bradbury, Jno	Memphis, Apr 2–61
Chester, Jas H	Marietta, July 8–64
Foster, Jno A	Vicksburg, Aug 13–63
Finley, Howard*	Decatur, July 22–64
Groshong, Walter M	Lincoln, Aug 17–63
Haney, Alva	Rome, Aug 3–64
Hudsmith, Jas	Madison, Nov 7–63
Hurst, Michael	Paducah, Aug 15–63
Jackson, Andrew	Columbus, Apr 18–63
Kaempfer, Anton	Rock Ridge
Lasherness, Austin	Memphis, Sep 25–63
Lowry, Sam'l W	Memphis, Sep 0–63
Meir, Michael	Helena, Aug 13–63
McDonnel, Thos	Memphis, Sep 25–63
McPhail, Allen	Patoui, July 31–63
Richardson, Jas	Helena, Dec 12–63
Schmitz, John K	Paducah, Sep 17–63
Sprague, Jas	Memphis, Sep 6–63
Shepton, Jesse	Paducah, Dec 3–63
Turner, Jasper	Jeff Barracks, Dec 15–64
Walker, Wm	Helena, Aug 4–63
Webb, Jno	Paducah, Sep 20–63
Wise, Daniel	Memphis, Aug 21–63
Woodruff, Wm	Memphis, Aug 28–13

I

Name	Location, Date
Capt Robt Nash	Memphis, Aug 21–63
Capt Daniel N Smalley	
Lt Jno T Richards	
Lt Chas B Blanchard	
Tomlinson, Wm S, sgt*	Salkehatchie, Feb 2–68
Wayne, Thos T, sgt	Helena, Oct 24–63
McReynolds, Robt, sgt	Helena, Jan 7–64
Osborn, Robt, sgt	Decatur, May 3–64
McDaniel, Bazzel B, corp	Helena, Aug 23–63
Nelson, Jos, corp+	Kenesaw Mt, June 15–64
Barnes, Thos	Helena, Aug 14–63
Crouse, W F	Greene, Ia
Cabanis, Jasper N	Wilton, Dec 8–62
Carroll, Albert	Memphis, Sept 8–63
Cook, Sam'l H	Columbus, June 14–63
Darlin, Jos C	Paducah, Aug 6–63
Fouley, Jno H	Paducah, Aug 24–63
Fenley, Mordecai	Indianapolis, Nov 8–64
Lauterman, Jno L	Memphis, Oct 24–63
Leaser, Wm	Jamestown, Oct 3–64
Louthain, Geo W	Decatur, July 22–64
McPherson, Jas D	New Ulm, Nov 10–62
Mitts, Morgan V	Memphis, Sept 21–63
Murrish, Moses	Helena, Aug 25–63
Percell, Jas H	Port Andrew
Relfstack, Fred'k	Memphis, Sept 13–63
Richards, Chas	St Louis, Nov 28–63
Sadler, Wm H	Marietta, Sept 24–64
Serens, Jno W	Columbus, Apr 18–63
Shuee, Lewis	Paris, Feb 5–64
Shoemaker, Theo	Columbus, June 11–63
Sincox, Wm H	Memphis, Sept 17–63
Sisson, Philo F	Memphis, Sept 21–63
Sneatpoch, Lawrence	Helena, Aug 18–63
Stillwell, Martin	Columbus, Sept 2–63
Thurtell, Edward	Paducah, Aug 30–63
Taylor, Sam'l A*	Dallas, May 27–64
Tenney, Eber J	Tomah
Vonderan, Jno	Helena, Nov 3–63
Wilkenson, Jno B	Memphis, Sept 16–63

K

Name	Location, Date
Capt Robt M Gorden	
Capt Chas A Hunt	
Lt Jno R Cannon	
Lt Lewis F Grow*	Decatur, July 22–64
Lt Oliver M York	
Bennell, Aaron H, corp*	Atlanta, Aug 1–64
Reistad, Simon C, corp*	Decatur, July 22–64
Wakefield, Thos S, corp	Andersonville Aug 4–64
Parshell, Alexis M, corp	Helena, Aug 11–63

GOLDSMITH & CO.

— WHOLESALE AND RETAIL —

CARPETS,

OIL CLOTHS, MATTINGS,

CURTAINS, SHADES,

UPHOLSTERY MATERIALS,

HOUSE FURNISHING LINEN

BEDDING, ETC.,

Wood Carpets and Parquette Floors.

355 and 357 EAST WATER STREET.

MILWAUKEE,   -   WIS.

WISCONSIN SOLDIERS AND SAILORS REUNION ROSTER. 117

Anderson, Chas H	Quincy	Maj Henry Baetz	Milwaukee	Lingsch, Henry	Murfreesboro, Jan 20—64
Andrew, Lunderville	Gilmantown	Maj Jno W Fuchs		Meyer, B C	Reshalto, Ill
Anderson, Erick	Cairo, Mar 22—63	Adj Philip J Schlosser		Pagenkopf, Hermann	Annapolis, Dec 7—63
Ashley, Willis	Paducah, Aug 6—63	Adj Albert Wallber		Sasse, Wm*	Peach Tree Creek, July 20—64
Anderson, Matthias	Memphis, Mar 11—64	Adj Geo P Traeumer		Shaffer, A E, e	Fond du Lac
Armstrong, Henry	Mound City, July 20—63	Adj Geo W Jones		Schultz, Herman, f	Milwaukee
Bartholomew, Benj J	Menominee	Q M Fred W Hundhausen		Shape, A E	Fond du Lac
Cummings, Sam'l	Snyders Bluff, July 8—63	Q M Adolph Heusel		Tolzmann, Aug*	Chancellorsville, May 2—63
Cary, Daniel E	Grand Rapids	Surg Francis Huebschman		Thiele, Henry	Stafford C H, Mar 1—63
Cook, Alonzo H	Snyders Bluff, July 20—63	Surg S Vandervaart		Vondran, Chas+	Chancellorsville, May 23—63
Canon, J R	Neillsville	A Surg Theo Fricke		Wendorff, Fred'ck+	Nashville, July 1—64
Chase, David R*	Salkehatchie, Feb 2—65	A Surg Carl Georgii		Weifenback, Jno	Chattanooga, June 3 - 64
Campbell, H W, me	Extra	Chap Wm Vette		Will, Fred	Oconomowoc
Campbell, S A,l	Extra	Chap Joe Killian		Juchisdorff, Fred'ck*	Gettysburg, July 1—63
Caraley, Jonathan C	Paducah, Aug 29—63				
Clark, Orvill	Paducah, Aug 22—63	**A**		**C**	
Draper, Jno A	Memphis, Sept 2—63				
Diegle, Martin*	Decatur, July 22—64	Capt Wm George		Capt Robt Mueller*	Peach Tree Cr, July 20—64
Erickson, Simon	Memphis, Sept 7—63	Capt Jno W Fuchs		Capt Henry Rauth	
Evensou, Jas	Louisville, June 18—64	Lt Christian Sarnow		Lt John Wm Fuchs	
Finch, Henry,f	Hazleton, Ia	Lt August F Mueller		Lt Bernhard Domschke	
Guttenger, J, f	Buffalo	Lt Martin Young*	Gettysburg, July 1—63	Lt Rudolph Klein*	Averysboro, Mar 8—65
Green, Geo B	Helena, Sept 14—63	Lt Conrad Grude		Lt Julius Mueller	
Higbee, Sylvester M	Paducah, Aug 27—63	Lt Sigismund Juenger		Michel, Jacob, sgt+	Chattanooga, July 12—64
Hunt, C A	Melvina	Lt Frank M Fless		Kruegar, Christian, sgt+	June 24—64
Harris, Milo,f	White Creek	Carstenjen, Hugo, sgt maj*	Chan'sville, May 2-63	Berlandi, Philip, corp+	Gettysburg, July 1—63
Howell, Franklin M	Adams, June—64	Metzel, Alex, sgt maj+	Washington, July 26—63	Muelhaupt, A, corp+	Washington, Jan 1—64
Henry, Chas H	Phillips	Fless, Stephen, sgt*	Peach Tree Creek, July 20-64	Schaeffner, T, corp+	Chattanooga, June 20—61
Hatch, E R	Neillsville	Krauss, Jno, corp*	Gettysburg, July 1—63	Balmes, Jacob+	July 10—63
Johnson, Ole, Jr	Cairo, Aug 1—63	Illigen, Jacob, corp*	Averysboro, Mar 16—65	Dallmann, John*	Chancellorsville, May 2—63
Judd, Arya	Helena, Aug 6—63	Felter, Frank	Milwaukee	Ehlert, Theo, me	
Johnson, Gilbert L	Vicksburg, Apr 25—14	Geuman, Christian*	Gettysburg, July 1—63	Hermann, Hermann	Washington, June 17—63
Knudson, Peter*	Salkehatchie, Feb 2—65	Gutbmann, Andreas	Atlanta, Aug 5—64	Holtz, Asmus	Andersonville, Aug 10—64
Lindall, Peter A	Helena, Aug 16 - 63	Hanptman, Jacob	Stafford, Jan 20—63	Koch, Jos*	Gettysburg, July 1—63
Leesch Nicholas	Helena, Aug 24—63	Jeager, Henry	Centreville, Nov 30—62	Kreuscher, Peter+	July 8—63
Larimer, Jno H	Memphis, Apr 9—64	Koenig, Theo	Nashville, July 3—64	Langer, Edw*	Burnt Hickory, May 25—64
Nelson, Ole A	Columbus, Mar 17—63	Luscha, Fred'k	Northern Junction	Leken, Henry*	Gettysburg, July 1—63
Probst, Urst	Madison, Aug 1—64	Mueller, Wm	Arqula, Feb 2—63	Lauer, Jno+	Chattanooga, July 14—64
Peterson, Ole	Helena, Aug 13—63	Nemitz, Reinhold*	Atlanta, Aug 6—64	Muenzenberger, Adam	Richmond, Dec 3—63
Sult, John+	Marietta, Aug 22—64	Ollig, Jno	Lookout Valley, Dec 10 - 63	Nenmann, Jos*	Gettysburg, July 1—63
Slyer, Peter	La Crosse	Paul, Jno	Kenesaw Mt, June 24—64	Perry, Franklin	Kenosha
Sweet, Wm	Paducah, Sept 2—63	Rost, August*	Chancellorsville, May 2—63	Perry, Chr	Kenosha
Stiles, Chas	Omro	Semicli, Julius, f	Fall Creek	Rinke, Anton+	Dallas, June 2—61
Tuttman, Ell M	Paducah, Aug 17—63	Stamm, Leonhard*	Gettysburg, July 2—63	Rosenthal, Wm, f	Fond du Lac
Walker Geo	Savannah, Dec 28—64	Spangenberg, Wm	Stafford, May 21—63	Snettinger, Julius	Resaca, May 15—64
Woolsey, Sam'l	Madison, Feb 23—63	Schmitt, Christ, me	Milwaukee	Stoltz, Geo	Richmond, Feb 5—61
York, Wm A	Helena, June—64	Werner, Wm		Springling, Andrew	Milwaukee
UNASSIGNED.		Wade, F	Neillsville	Steinle, C D, m	Kenosha
Allen, Jno	Warrens Mills	Vetter, Gustav, me	Milwaukee	Volmer, Chas	Milwaukee
Joslin, W H	Madison			Webber, Math, me	Milwaukee
Kirby, Morris	Cumberland	**B**		Weller, Chas	Kenosha
Logus, Jno L	Muscoda				
Privett, J C	Orion	Capt Fred C Winkler, a	Milwaukee	**D**	
Purcell, Jas K	Port Andrew	Capt Chas Schmidt*	Averysboro, Mar 6—65		
Ronison, S J	Richland Centre	Capt Peter Guttman		Capt August Ligowsky	
Salmon, Cutler	Muscoda	Lt Wm E Huttman		Capt Jos Marschauer	
Wilsey, Geo W	Muscoda	Lt Francis C Lackner		Lt August Schueler	
Willoughby, Wm	Boscobel	Lt Adolph Hensel		Lt Edward Carl	
		Lt Chas H Doerflinger		Lt August Bartsch	

TWENTY-SIXTH INFANTRY.

		Lt Wm Steinmeyer	Lt Leopold Melchior
		Ehlert, Freder'k, sgt*	Gettysburg, July 1—63	Lt Peter Guttman
Three years. Organized, Sept. 16th, 1862. Original strength, 1002, gain by recruits, etc., 87 Total, 1089. Death loss, 264—killed in action, 128, died of wounds, 56, of disease, 68, of accidents, 2. Other losses, 368—missing, 0, desertions, 31, transfers, 125, discharges, 272. Strength at muster out June 13th, 1865, 447. Campaigns in Va., Pa., Ala., Tenn., Ga., S. C. N. C.		Brantz, Aug+	Gettysburg, Aug 1—63	Lt Henry Elsner
		Backhaus, Wm, corp*	Gettysburg, July 1—63	Lt H Furstenberg
		Brunnschweig, Fred*	Gettysburg, July 1—63	Warver, Franz J, sgt+	Nashville, Oct 14—64
		Busse, Chas*	Averysboro, Mar 16—65	Gross, Jos, corp*	Chancellorsville, May 2—63
		Caspar, Carl*	Chancellorsville, May 2—63	Chalaupka, Geo, corp*	Gettysburg, July 1—63

REGIMENTAL ROSTER.

Col Wm H Jacobs		Distelhorst, Henry*	Chancellorsville, May 2—63	Held, Jno, corp*	Peach Tree Creek, July 20—64
Col Fred C Winkler, a	Milwaukee	Duehring, Ferdinand	Richmond, May 11—64	Dross, Louis*	Chancellorsville, May 2—63
Lt Chas Lehman		Damback, Mathew	Fountain City	Dronkers, Dirgenius*	Gettysburg, July 1—63
Lt Hans Boebel		Eberhard, Jacob*	Gettysburg, July 1—63	Gerhauser, Jno	
Lt Francis C Lackner		Entz, Christian	Chattanooga, Jan 8—64	Hoffranz, Peter	Stafford, Feb 26—63
Maj Philip Horwitz		Feistel, Edw*	Gettysburg, July 1—63	Huntz, Michael, l	Chilton
		Gessner, Henry*	Kenesaw Mt, June 19—61	Koerner, Carl+	Goldsboro, Apr 27—65
		Hartmann, Wm	Milwaukee	Kwapli, Frank	Racine
		Hensel, Adolph, agt	Milwaukee	Lersch, Peter	Atlanta, Aug 7—64
		Johns, Albert*	Resaca, May 15—64	Milke, Wm+	Gettysburg, July 1—63
		Jaeger, Aug	Lookout Valley, Nov 8—63	Pfau, Andreas*	Racine
		Kuhlmann, Chas	Nashville, May 19—64	Rasmussen, Neils	
		Kuhlke, Aug	Brooks Station, May 10—63	Solms, Chas*	Kenesaw Mt, June 22—64
		Lauer, Wm	Washington, July 16—63	Stoppels, Francis*	Gettysburg, July 1—63

DRY GOODS EMPORIUM.

121 AND 123 WISCONSIN STREET, MILWAUKEE. WIS.

The Acknowledged Headquarters in Wisconsin for

BLACK SILKS AND BLACK CASHMERES!

BLACK SILKS,
At 75c; 1.00; 1.12½; 1.25; 1.40; 1.50; 1.65; 1.75; 1.85; 2.00; 2.25; 2.50; 2.75; 3.00; 3.25; 3.50;

COLORED SILKS,
75c; 1.00; 1.25; 1.50; 1.75; 2.00.

BLACK SATINS,
75c; 1.00; 1.12½; 1.25; 1.50; 1.75; 2.00; 2.25 2.50; 2.75; 3.00.

COLORED SATINS,
75c; 1.00; 1.25; 1.50; 1.75; 2.00.

BLACK VELVETS,
1.25; 1.50; 1.75; 2.00; 2.25; 2.50; 2.75; 3.00 up to 15.00.

COLORED VELVETS,
Same.

NEW SPRING DRESS GOODS,
Arriving Every Day.

COLORED BUNTINGS,
In all the new spring shades and colors.

VELVETEENS,
From 40 cents upward.

FANCY VELVETS,
In elegant shades and combinations.

BLACK CASHMERES,
At 37½c; 40c; 45c; 50c; 55; 65c; 75c; 87½c; 1.00.

BLACK BUNTINGS,
25c; 30c; 35c; 37½c; 40c; 45c; up to $3.75.

TAMISE HENRIETTAS, &c.,
And other Black Fancy Goods usually found in a black goods stock.

MOMIE CLOTH,
1.00; 1.15; 1.25.

ALPACAS,
20c; 25c; 30c; 35c; 37½c; 40c to 1.00.

KID GLOVES,
(Every pair warranted.)
2 buttons, — $1.00   4 buttons, — $1.50
3 buttons, — 1.25   6 buttons, — 2.00
New novelties in

LACE TOP GLOVES,

Strangers Visiting Milwaukee are cordially invited to our stores whether they wish to purchase or not.

WHITE & VAN PELT,

Wisconsin Street, Opposite Post Office.

WISCONSIN SOLDIERS AND SAILORS REUNION ROSTER.   119

Schwartz, Henrich+Chancellorsville, May 19—63
Schuberger, Jacob   Racine
Schneider, Jno A   Racine
Schelt, Henry   Racine
Thiele, Fred'k*   Chancellorsville, May 2—63
Westhoff, August*   Kenesaw Mt, June 22—64
Weborn, Jacob*   Peach Tree Creek, July 20—64
Wildhagen, Jno +   Annapolis, Sept 3—63
Weinmert, Jno   Racine
Zollowsky, Jos+   New York City, Sept 3—63

E

Capt Anton Kettles   Byron
Capt C W Neukirch+   Washington, May 12—63
Capt Peter Ferneckes
Capt Wm Stehnmeyer
Lt Henry Greve
Lt Casper Buechner, mf   Fond du Lac
Lt John F Hagen
Lt Anton Vogt   Fond du Lac
Lt Jos Arnold   Oshkosh
Zipp, Philip, sgt   Fond du Lac
Herrmann, Chas, sgt   Fond du Lac
Meyer, Chas J, sgt   Milwaukee
Hagemann, Christian, sgt   New Holstein
Braun, Jno, sgt   Colorado
Stier, Chas, sgt   Oshkosh
Reichert, Chas, sgt   Watertown
Fuchs, M, corp*   Chancellorsville, May 2—63
Winkelmann, C, corp*   Chan'ville, May 2—63
Thurwaechter, M corp*   Chan'ville, May 2—63
Lindenmuth, H corp+   Averysboro, Mar 17—65
Diener, Henry corp   Mound City, Oct 1—64
Knein, Francols, corp   Andersonville, Oct 8—64
Schneider, M, corp   Andersonville, Sept 24—64
Knoble, A, corp, mf   Menominee Falls
Kefer, Ferdinand, corp
Wagner, Heinrich, corp   Granville
Krueger, Carl, c rp   Milwaukee
Schmidt, Carl, corp   Lomira
Leisgang, Geo, corp
Rietz, Ernest, corp   New Holstein
Altmann, Alois
Arndt, Carl   Gilbert Station
Braun, Xavier*   Peach Tree Cr, July 20—64
Burg, Lorenz*   Chancellorsville, May 2—63
Behling, Carl+   Baltimore, Aug 8—63
Behling, Frederick   Granville
Beimel, Carl
Borge, Rudolph   Fond du Lac
Burggraff, Wm   Lamartine
Doessel, Wm   Milwaukee
Drebiab, Edw   Fond du Lac
Elchmeler, Adolph   Richmond, Dec 9—64
Evens, Anton   Milwaukee
Fuhrmann, John   Princeton
Fischer, Wm
Flammang, Henry
Gruhlke, Johann*   Averysboro, Mar 16—63
Glazel, Paul P, h   Milwaukee
Grass, Wm E   Granville
Grass, Jno Ludwig   Granville
Gaulaitz, Reinhardt   Stockbridge
Hammaug, Paul   Stafford C H, Jan 28—63
Hageman, C, m   New Holstein
Haertley, Mathias   Mayville
Hanyen, Fredrick   Fond du Lac
Herzag, Heinrich   Granville
Hilgert, Jacob   Granville
Hubatzcheck, Robt   Fond du Lac
Jenny, John   Richmond
John, Fred'ck   Granville
Krause, Reinhold*   Dallas, May 27—64
Kuehn, August+   Resaca, June 10—64
Krause, Geo+   Dallas, May 26—64
Kroll, Fritz
Klefes, Nickolaus   Dakota
Krause, A E
Knolle, Albin   Menominee Falls

Kumneri, Carl   Princeton
Lunkow, Frederick+   Chattanooga, June 4—64
Luedke   Wausau
Lange, Wm   Princeton
Lechelt, Johan
Meler, Hehnrich*   Gettysburg, July 1—63
Ostering, Jno   Chattanooga, May 2—64
Oehlke, Franz   Andersonville, Oct 27—64
Parbs, Carl   Atlanta, Sep 13—64
Pammerich, John   Lake Superior
Proechel, Sam'l   Minnesota
Konnig, Henry*   Kenesaw Mt, June 22—63
Reichardt, Jno   Watertown
Reinecke, Frederick   Milwaukee
Rumpel, Christian   Minnesota
Ruppelt, Oswald   Princeton
Rosenthal, Wm   Friendship
Rossman, Hans   New Holstein
Ruchsamen, Carl   Milwaukee
Schleustedt, Herman*   Gettysburg, July 1—63
Schneider, Nicholas*   Kenesaw Mt, June 22—61
Schwister, Mathias+   Gettysburg, July 5—63
Stange, Wm   Washington, Jan 4—63
Stauber, Jos   Alexandria, Oct 18—63
Soll, Fred, 1   Fond du Lac
Saak, Fred W   Wacousta
Schmidt, Wm
Schneller, Jno   Michigan
Schaefert, Carl   Doryville
Stark, Jno   Granville
Strule, Jno
Schmitz, Jos   Taycheedah
Sall, Fredrick   Fond du Lac
Stengel, August   Green Bay
Sanck, Fred'k Wm   Wacousta
Tomke, Fritz   Nashville, July 6—64
Urban, Johann   Princeton
Weetzci, Chas*   Chancellorsville, May 2—63
Woller, Ferdinand   Atlanta, Aug 16—64
Walz, Michael   Granville
Witzel, Frederick   Plymouth
Wells, Christian   Milwaukee
Zreiluger, Gotlub   Milwaukee
Zirbel, Frederick   Green Bay
Zech, Jos A   New Holstein
Zappe, August   Green Bay
Zellger, David   Milwaukee
Zerger, Gottleib, f   West Bend

F

Capt Henry Baetz   Milwaukee
Capt Francis C Lackner
Capt Andrew J Fullerton
Lt Bernhard Domschke
Lt Otto Proemel
Lt Christian Phillip*   Resaca, May 15—61
Lt Carl W Karsten, m   West Bend
Lt Albert Walliser
Lt Adolph Cordier
Lt Peter Hook*   Gettysburg, July 1—63
Schmidt, Christ, sgt*Chancellorsville, May 2—63
Hess, Wm, sgt*   Gettysburg, July 1—63
Lippman, Henry, sgt   Chattahoochee, Oct 2—64
Oestreich, Chas, corp*   Averysboro, Mar 16—65
Arnn, Wm*   Peach Tree Creek, July 20—64
Arndt, Gottfred   Rika
Benda, Franz+   Gettysburg, Aug 8—63
Dietericks, Carl   Two Rivers
Hacker, Henry*   Resaca, May 15—61
Heidenreich, Joseph   Stafford C H, Feb 5—63
Krueger, Gottlieb*   Kenesaw Mt, June 22—61
Krueger, Julius   Chattanooga, Dec 31—63
Kaufmann, Conrad   Chattanooga, May 6—64
Koetzdinger, Alois   Rappahanock, Sept 17—63
Lindloge, Wm   Madison, July 3—64
Neiphaus, Gerhard*   Peach Tree Cr, July 20—61
Pickeruhn, August*   Chancellorsville, May 2—63
Pleuss, Diederick   Evansville, Dec 31—64

Pailter, Jos, me   Kewaunee
Reisenberger, Mathias*   Bentonville, Mar 19—65
Roehr, Hermann*   Chancellorsville, May 2—63
Raatz, Herman   Alexandria, Jan 31—63
Roeder, Nicholas   Chattanooga, Dec 28—63
Schmidt, Leopold*   Gettysburg, July 1—63
Schara, Franz*   Gettysburg, July 1—63
Schmidt, Jno*   Averysboro, Mar 16—65
Stier, Christian+   July 14—63
Tiedemann, Ehlert   Nashville, Feb 17—64
Traeumer, Geo P   Milwaukee
Voss, Frederick*   Chancellorsville, May 2—63
Wagner, Michael   Resaca, May 15—64
Winter, Fred'k+   Chattanooga, Aug 16—64

G

Capt Jacob E Mann
Capt Chas Pizzala*   Chancellorsville, May 2—63
Capt H Furstenberg
Capt August Bartsch
Lt Wm Smith
Lt Bernhard Domschke
Lt Adolph Cordier
Lt Nicholas Vollner+ Jeffersonville, Aug 24—64
Lt Lambert Weiss
Lt Julius Meiswinkel   Milwaukee
Lt Jno Orth
Lt Sigismund, Juenger
Crowley, Jno, 1st sgt   Stafford, June 5—63
Frenze, Chr's, sgt, me   Kohlville
Weimand, Jacob, corp*   Chan'ville, May 2—63
Guenther, Henry, corp*   Chan'ville, May 2—63
Husen, Geo W, corp* Chancellorsville, May 2—63
Koehler, Geo, corp*   Gettysburg, July 1—63
Ritger, Jno, corp*   Gettysburg, July 1—63
Templeton, Robt H, corp*   Dallas, May 25—64
Cassell, Alfred H, corp   Stafford, Mar 25—63
Johnston, Sam'l, corp   Murfreesboro, Feb 22—64
Wagner, Jacob, corp, f
Trentel, Henry, corp, me   Aurora
Dexhelmer, Jacob*   Chancellorsville, May 2—63
Daily, Richard*   Chancellorsville, May 2—63
Distler, Fred'k+   Andersonville, Aug 16—61
Dellenbach, Geo+   Kingston, July 2—64
Emmett Geo   Myra
Fritz, Ferdinand*   Gettysburg, July 1—63
Finks, Wm, pa   Kohlville
Hafeman, Chas   Wayside
Jewison, Julius*   Gettysburg, July 1—63
Jones Geo W, f   West Bend
Kuhn, Peter*   Gettysburg, July 1—63
Lauerimann, Jacob* Chancellorsville, May 2—63
Mack, Conrad   Stafford C H, Dec 23—62
Metzner, Gotlieb, me   Kohlville
Remmel, Jno   Kewaskum
Smith, Emerson L*   Dallas, May 25—64
Schnepf, Killan*   Chancellorsville, May 2—63
Steinmetz, Jos*   Chancellorsville, May 2—63
Schmidt, Jno*   Chancellorsville, May 2—63
Stoffel, Peter*   Chattanooga, June 10—61
Schnorrenberg, Peter   Stafford C H, Feb 2—3
Strupp, Jacob   Jeffersonville, Apr 4—64
Stubanus, Andreas   Washington, Aug 23—63
Salter, Robt   Sherman
Steuerwald, Daniel   West Bend
Storey, A, f
Vetter, Jno C+   Chancellorsville, May 8—63
Wolf, Albert*   Chattanooga, June 17—64
Young, Nicholas*   Gettysburg, July 1—63
Zihlsdorf, Fritz*   Gettysburg, July 1—63
Zih'sdorf, Franz*   Gettysburg, July 1—63
Zoger, Mathias+   Washington, June 24—63

H

Capt Hans Boebel
Capt Bernhard Domschke*
Lt Jos Wedig

STRANGER!

IF YOU ARE BUYING A

PIANO OR ORGAN,

CALL ON

JAMES B. BRADFORD,

422 BROADWAY,

And select from the largest assortment in the Northwest, of the BEST MAKES, and at

Special Low Prices for the Holidays.

CHICKERING
ERNEST GABLER
DUNHAM & SONS
FONCHARD & CO.
MARSHALL & SMITH

AND
Loring & Blake "Palace" Organs.

JAMES A. HOSCH,

HATTER,

404 EAST WATER STREET.

THE LATEST STYLES OF

HATS

RECEIVED DAILY.

ALSO ON HAND A LARGE STOCK OF

Caps, Gloves and Umbrellas,

Which I am selling cheaper than any house in the city.

Manufacturing of Furs A Specialty.

ELEGANT
DIAMOND JEWELRY,
BEAUTIFUL
Pearl and Onyx Jewelry

Massive Silverware,
French Clocks,
Opera Glasses,
Ladies Watches,
Waltham Watches,
Elgin Watches,
Howard Watches,
Tiffany Watches,

In all the Latest Styles of Cases. All the Latest Novelties in our Line at Reasonable Prices.

O. L. ROSENKRANS & CO.,
100 Wisconsin Street.

MACHINERY

AND SUPPLIES,

For IRON and WOOD WORKERS

ENGINES, BOILERS & STEAM PUMPS,

Blacksmith's Tools, Etc.

O. L. PACKARD,
No. 87 West Water Street.

WISCONSIN SOLDIERS AND SAILORS REUNION ROSTER. 121

Lt Chas Vocke
Lt Chas Schmidt
Lt Jos Marschauer
Lt Christian Crusius
Weckersberg, Chas, sgt* Resaca, May 15—64
Mohr, Henry, corp* Gettysburg, July 1—63
Diefenthaler, Phil, corp* Gettysburg, July 1—63
Reuter, Franz, corp* P'ch Tree Cr'k, July 20—64
Mathes, Phil, corp* Gettysburg, July 1—63
Nell, Phil, corp+ Louisville, July 20—64
Conrad, Aug+ Louisville, Aug 2—61
Gottfried, Wenzel* Chancellorsville, May 2—63
Gropp, Henry Marshfield
Hartmann, Jno* Gettysburg, July 1—63
Held, Carl Andersonville, Apr 1—64
Kapmos, Wenzel Mazomanie
Mueller, Valentine+ Kingston, Aug 17—64
Meyer, Jno G* Gettysburg, July 1—63
Roth, Jno C, c Madison
Strutz, Gottleb* Averysboro, Mar 16—65
Sprauger, Fred'ck+ Resaca, May 16—61
Stamp, Phil Washington, Oct 26—62
Sommer, Gottleb Fairfax, Nov 17—62
Schaefer, Geo Berea Church, Feb 2—63
Schwenecke, Aug Bridgeport, Dec 2 63
Siblist, Wm, c Milwaukee
Welsch, Henry, m Colby
Werner, Fred'ck* Chancellorsville, May 2—63
Wappler, H, me Milwaukee
Zinke, Juo A* Chancellorsville, May 2—63

I

Capt Franz Landa
Capt William Smith* Gettysburg, July 1—63
Capt Jno P Beeman* P'ch Tree Cr'k, July 20—64
Capt Wm H Henschemeyer
Lt Henry J Berninger
Lt Albert Walther
Lt Oswald Schubert
Lt Jno Orth
Lt Peter Fernekes
Lt Geo P Traeumer
Lt Chas Brueckert* Gettysburg, July 1—63
Brueckert, Chas, sgt* Gettysburg, July 1—64
Waldorf, Phil, sgt. Resaca, May 18—64
Ferge, Gottleb, corp* Gettysburg, July 1—63
Neusser, Paulus, corp* Gettysburg, July 1—63
Braun, Ferdinand Stafford C H, Feb 19—63
Behnke, Henry Brooks Station, June 10—63
Domkoeller, Ernest Andersonville, June 26—64
Feldman, Phil+ Warrenton, Aug 2—63
Fisher, Henry A Volga City, Ia
Giljohann, Fred'ck+ Atlanta, Aug 13—64
Jenkens, Michael Belle Islei, Oct 8—63
Koepnick, Jno* Kenesaw Mt, June 22—64
Kristaky, Rudolph Kenosha
Kruse, Fred'ck* Vicksburg, July 1—63
Kowall, Jos Milwaukee, Sept 19—62
Lau, Jno* Chancellorsville, May 2—63
Lang, Lorenz Nashville, Nov 5—61
Marquardt, — Chattanooga, June 27—64
Nero, Fred'ck+ Washington, June 11—63
Pfeiffer, Anton Alexandria, Oct 10—63
Sadler, Jos Kewaunee
Style, Jno* Kenesaw Mt, June 23—64
Stollenwerk, Jos* Chancellorsville, May 2—63
Stolberg, Fred'ck* Gettysburg, July 1—63
Stark, Jno, f Lake City, Mich
Schrieber, Jono Sherman
Stolberg, Chas, m Milwaukee
Stollberg, Fred, m Milwaukee

K

Capt Louis Pelosi
Capt August Schueler* Chan'sville, May 2—63
Capt Edward Carl
Capt Fred'k Koerner
Capt Casper Buechner mf Fond du Lac
Lt Jacob Help

Lt H J Berninger
Lt Chas H Doerflinger
Lt Henry Greve
Lt Christian Phillip
Otto, Benhard, sgt* Peach Tree Creek, July 20—64
Laich, Fritz, sgt Andersonville, Sept 30—64
Regenbrecht, Geo, corp* Gettysburg, July 1—63
Fleck, August, corp* Chancellorsville, May 2—63
Balk, Fred'k Atlanta, Sept 30—64
Becker, Robt, teacher Horns Corners
Frank, Gotthardt Chattanooga, Dec 23 - 63
Fuchs, Theopold Spring Green
Hermann, Jno* Gettysburg, July 1—63
Heldslab, Christian Rice Lake
Indermauer, Jacob* Chancellorsville, May 2—63
Klinke, Jacob* Burnt Hickory, May 25—64
Kremer, William Lone Rock
Lehmann, August Sauk City
Mengeld, Martin* Chancellorsville, May 2—63
Mueller, Jno Stafford C H, Apr 15—63
Phillip, Lucius Sauk City
Roell, Fred'k* Burnt Hickory, May 25—64
Rausch, Michael* Chancellorsville, May 2—63
Roehrig, Fred'k* Gettysburg, July 1—63
Rothacker, David* Gettysburg, July 1—63
Steinhoff, Fred'k+ Chancellorsville, May 7—63
Sonnenschein, Fred'k—Philadelphia, May 25—63
Van Wald, Leonhard, f Sauk City

UNASSIGNED.

Huebner, Fred Oconomowoc
Labouch, Peter Milwaukee
Michiel, Leonhard Monroe, Mich
Orth, Mathias, f Larabee
Wendert, Jno Oconomowoc
Schroeder, August Kenosha
Limpert, Geo C Kenosha
Wirshum, Peter Kenosha
Stemm, Fred Kenosha
Yoernelt, Fred Kenosha
Radatz, Fred Kenosha
Bentz, Jno Kenosha

TWENTY-SEVENTH INFANTRY.

Three years.   Organized March 7th, 1863. Original strength, 805, gain by recruits, etc, 291. Total 1196. Death loss, 248—killed in action, 15, died of wounds, 8, of disease, 222, of accidents, 3. Other losses, 363—missing, 2, desertions, 56, transfers, 87, discharges, 248. Strength at muster out, Aug. 29th, 1865, 585. Campaigns in Ky., Ark., Ala., La.

REGIMENTAL ROSTER.

Col Conrad Krez, a Sheboygan
Lt Col Jno J Brown
Lt Col P E G Olmstead
Maj Chas H Cunningham
Adj Chas Meyer
Adj D Leprelette Moore
Q M Wm N Schaefer
Q M Jos F Kent
Surg Chr Krack
Surg Robt Mitchell
A Surg Geo H Hitchinson
A Surg Jerome C Saltzman
A Surg Jas B Cooper
A Surg Franz Simon
Capt Wm P Stowe

A

Capt Chas H Cunningham
Capt Jno J Borland
Lt Jerome C Saltzman
Lt Ewd Bach
Lt Wm Stone

A Surg J L Chapel Kewaunee
Roberts, Thos R Carlton, Nov 6—62
Arnold, Conrad Jeff Barracks, Dec 19—64
Bunker, Jos Little Rock, Sept 27—63
Brenninger, Henry Little Rock, Dec 11—64
Bodecker, August Little Rock, June 17—64
Clark, Chas Memphis, Sept 13—63
Cory, Reuben A Poet
Cory, Aaron Mansfield, Oregon
Dalziel, Robt Memphis, Oct 3—63
Dalzid, Wm Carlton
Doleusky, Frank Kewaunee
Dickenshort, L* Jenkins Ferry, Apr 30—64
Dishmaker, Jno Casco
Grover, Thos Milwaukee, Mar 21—63
Harlow, Albia A Little Rock, July 30—64
Hoffman, Valentine Kewaunee
Hughes, Jno, f Flintville
Jadin, Maximilian Kewaunee
Lonergan, David Little Rock, Sept 15—63
Lutz, Lorenz Kewaunee
Mathiessen, Jes Little Rock, Aug 24—64
Meister, Julius Kewaunee
Nehels, August Kewaunee
Olewon, Tiron Mobile, Apr 27—65
O Hara, Ewd Casco
Osborn, Walter Jenkins Ferry, Apr 30—64
Plinke, Conrade+ Oct 17—64
Priest, Timothy St Louis, Oct 22—63
Pronto, Jno Chicago, Feb 18—61
Rosey, Pierre A St Louis, Oct 7—63
Rooney, Patrick J Kewaunee
Schneider, Jno Kewaunee
Seammon, Ignatius Kewaunee, Oct 7—63
Stoffels, Peter Kewaunee
Smith, Seth Poet
Trearnaur, Jno July 30—63
Torrey, E N, c Larabee
Trindel, Frank+ New Orleans, Apr 8—65
Trudell, Aleck Kewaunee
Trudel, Jos Paducah, Aug 18—65
Villet, Safra Okotona, Apr 3—64
Vibber, Alfred Kewaunee
Whipple, J P, ar Whitewater
Wickham, Nathaniel B Madison, May 6—64
Whittaker, Jno Kewaunee
Wrabetz, Jno Kewaunee

B

Capt Erastus W Stannard June 8—63
Capt Aaron Hobart Nov 5—63
Capt Julius Schlaich
Lt Josiah Plant
Lt Roswell H Tripp
Lt Oscar H Silver Aug 29—63
Lt Anthony Ortmayer
Wilson, Biel, corp Madison, Dec 8—63
Barrager, Sidney Memphis, Sep 6—63
Becker, Chas Little Rock, Nov 20—63
Hauberger, Mat Plymouth
Beflinger, Henry Little Rock, May 29—64
Doetimer, Chas F Little Rock, Jan 30—65
Burton, Geo F Menomonee
Copley, Selah Snyders Bluffs, July 20—63
Couch, H W Olivet
Couch, Win A Little Rock, Nov 5—63
Delmart, Derrick Little Rock, Nov 20—63
Dufert, Fred Little Rock, Nov 21—63
Fletcher, Lewis Mound City, Oct 12—63
Glassow, Fred Sep 2—63
Gilman, Chester, M Helena, Aug 23—63
Johnson, John* Spanish Fi, Apr 2—65
Knowles, Jno S Greenbush, Oct 24—63
Kiffey, Geo Mound City, Apr 22—65
Lawrence, Harvey O Plymouth, July 17—63
Lampe, August Memphis, Sep 1—63
Monk, Wm Little Rock, Jan 16—64
Muth, Phil Little Rock, Nov 4—61
Pruessler, August Helena, Aug 6—63

DRESS GOODS.

JAS. MORGAN,

HAS THE BEST ASSORTMENT OF FINE

DRESS GOODS

EVER SHOWN BY HIM IN THIS MARKET.

LADIES WILL FIND GOODS

In Every Department in keeping with the

VAST IMPROVEMENTS

Being Made throghout the entire Establishment.

An Inspection of Goods and Prices Solicited.

386 AND 388 EAST WATER STREET,

MILWAUKEE, - WIS.

WISCONSIN SOLDIERS AND SAILORS REUNION ROSTER.

Name	Location, Date
Prieder, Ch s	Snyders Bluff, July 14—63
Patterson, Geo H	Little Rock, Sep 21—64
Rogers, Jas H, s	Baldwin
Scherrer, Peter	Little Rock, May 12—65
Stagg, Wesley H*	Jenkins Ferry, Apr 30—64
Smith, Jas	Hingham
Steinfeldt, Jno	Sheboygan Falls
Stantee, Wm G	Yankton
Toplin, Wm L	Ft Gaines, Mar 16—65
Tripp, H H	Hingham
Wright, Josiah A	Helena, Aug 13—63
Willis, Horace	Rhine, Nov 8—63

C

Name	Location, Date
Capt Fred'k Schnellen	
Capt Conrad F Smith	
Lt David Schretack	
Lt Carl E W Struve	
Lt Jno Gehring	
Lt Julius Bolenstab	
Lt Philip C Enders	
Theiss, Phil, sgt	Princeton, May 8—64
Gosse, Fred'k, corp	Little Rock, Dec 3—63
Buchholz, Aug	Milwaukee, Feb 1—63
Buchholz, Wilhelm	Milwaukee, Feb 4 - 63
Bramstendt, Jno	Memphis, Sept 9—63
Dengen, Peter	Little Rock, Nov 8—63
Diedrichvandam, Geo	Little Rock, June 8—61
Fischer, Jno H	Two Rivers
Frisky, Jno	
Goedeke, Fred'k	Duvals Bluff, Sept 23—63
Herninghaus, Wm	Little Rock, Oct 11 - 64
Joos, Matt	Mobile, Apr 22—65
Jaksch, Leuold	St Louis, Aug 31—63
Kohl, Geo	Milwaukee, Nov 26—62
Koelmer, Fred	Franklin
Kups, Jno	Kewaunee, Nov 18—63
Lemke, Wm	Memphis, Sept 4—63
Lempke, Aug	Little Rock, Aug 27—64
Linden, Jos, ms	Menomines
Linden, Jno	New Orleans, May 26—65
Martiozen, Fritz	Little Rock, Feb 3—64
Matthies, Fred'k	Milwaukee, Nov 6—62
McDonald, Jas	Waupun
Nuffer, Jacob F	Memphis, Sept 5—63
Petzold, C J	Two Rivers
Pfrenger, Ernst A	Milwaukee, Feb 1—63
Schaefer, Fred'k	Little Rock, Sept 14—63
Selberg, Fred'k	Little Rock, Dec 2—63
Witte, Chas*	Jenkins Ferry, Apr 30—64
Wehrmann, Simon	Snyders Bluff, July 22—63
Zottels, Jno	Little Rock, Nov 14—63
Zindel, Peter	Jefferson Barracks, Oct 13—63
Zech, Frank	Little Rock, Nov 16—61

D

Name	Location, Date
Capt Ten Eyck G Olmstead	Chicago, Ill
Capt Jos Bankin	Manitowoc
Lt Peter Mulholland	
Lt Thomas McMillan	
Lt Nicholas Hansen	
Lt Wm Henry	
Barnard, Geo P, corp	Memphis, Sept 12—63
Allen, A A	Mountaindale, Cal
Aldridge, H A, f	Cooperstown
Bart, Peter*	Jenkins Ferry, Apr 30—64
Burt, Geo, f	Larrabee
Bailey, Gilbert	St Louis, July 17—63
Burt, Milo, f	Larrabee
Courter, J W	Neillsville
Criton, Justen f	East Gibson
Cayn, Alfred	Two Rivers, Dec 23—63
Chaterton, Jno	Larrabee
Chase, E, f	Larrabee
Ehrensberger, Jno	Little Rock, Dec 6—63
Everson, Christopher, f	Larrabee
Ellis, Cyrus	Brownsville, Sept 6—63
Edwards, Edward A, p	Yankton, D T
Gillis, Wm H	Little Rock, July 28 - 63
Henike, Henry	Two Rivers
Huss, Geo	Duvals Bluff, Sept 24—63
Hurst, Wm	Two Rivers
Hill, Edw	Milwaukee, Jan 17- 63
Johnson, Ephraim, f	Mishicott
Kingsland, Isaac W	Camden, Nov 12—64
Knudson, Ole, f	Larrabee
King, Clifford, f	Cooperstown
Leger, Edmond	Cato, Oct 15—63
Lovel, W D	
Lyon, Edw W	Little Rock, Sept 13—63
Mandel, Helbrick -	Jenkins Ferry, Apr 30—64
Oemichen, Reinold	Columbus, Apr 14—63
Piper, Jonas	Snyders Bluff, July 14—63
Roberts, Jno	Little Rock, Nov 27—63
Sullivan, Cornelius	Helena, Aug 13—63
Sutherland, Jno J	Memphis, Sept 23—63
Snekson,	Little Rock, Nov 2—63
Sotan, Peter	Little Rock, Aug 2—63
Schroeder, Fred	Kewaunee
Tisch, Henry	Kewaunee
Welch, David	Helena, Aug 3—63
Walker, Wm H	La Porte City, Ia
Wulf, Christian	Snyders Bluff, July 22—63
Wagner, Michael, f	Larrabee
Wulf, Fritz	Snyders Bluff, July 23—63
Wood, Alex, m	Two Rivers
Whitcomb, Jno, f	Grimms P O

E

Name	Location, Date
Capt Alfred Marschner	
Capt Carl Witt	
Lt Jno A S Verdier	
Lt Chas W Walther	
Lt Irving V Bliss	
Schmidt, Geo, corp*	Pine Bluff, May 25—64
Desloch, Jacob, corp	Little Rock, Sept 22—64
Arve, Fred'k	Duvals Bluff, Aug 21—63
Altenhofen, Jno	Kewaskum, Sept 26—63
Barnes, Jno J	Helena, Aug 21—63
Dentrupp, Florence H	Snyders Bluff, July 5—63
Bohm, Wm H	Memphis, Sep 9—63
Buhl, Jos	Mobile, May 6—65
Cane, Alf	Cairo, Sept 1—64
Demmler, Jno	Helena, Aug 13—63
Ehren, Jno	Little Rock, Oct 22—63
Feiten, Jno	Snyders Bluff, July 24—63
Hautz, Tobias	Kewaskum, Nov 11—62
Hoberg, Henry	Snyders Bluff, Aug 26—63
Hockmuth, Sebastian	Madison, May 4—63
Heiman, Jos	Clarksville, June 13—65
Janke, Carl	Snyders Bluff, July 23 63
Klug, Herman, m	Milwaukee
Lahey, Jno	Two Creeks
Lussender, Jno	Milwaukee, Nov 12—62
Lawrence, Horace A, f	Millsville
Large, Chris	Memphis, Sept 16—63
Lund, Jno	Charles City
Roehrborn, Jno C	Little Rock, Sept 23—63
Weiner, A	Mazomanie
Wright Harvey L	Madison, Apr 5—64
Wilks, Wm	Sheboygan Falls
Ziebarth, Aug*	Spanish Ft, Mar 28—65

F

Name	Location, Date
Capt Samuel D Hubbard	
Capt Josiah Platt	
Lt Edward W Robbins	
Lt Peter Danne, Jr	
Lt Wm F Mitchell	
Lt Clayton Stevens	
Hazelton, Herman, sgt	Memphis, Sept 1—63
Robinson, Elisah J, sgt	Duvals Bluff, Sep 16—63
Bates, Eller H, corp*	Prairie d'Ane, Ap. 10—64
Akin, Jos E, corp	Mitchell, Oct 4—63
Allen, J	Neillsville
Busmaster, Fred	Chicago, Sep 14—63
Brown, Ephriam, f	Boltonville
Baum, Geo, f	Scott
Bult, Elijah	New Orleans, May 31—65
Buchanan, Daniel M	Springdale, Neb
Cole, Geo W*	Jenkins Ferry, Apr 30—64
Drake, Jno	Memphis, Sep 12—63
Eernisse, Jacob	Helena, Aug 17—63
Furguson, Ozias	Duvals Bluff, Sep 10—63
Gasnal, Chas	Helena, Aug 17—63
Godard, Jos	Little Rock, Sep 20—63
Gerriets, Jno F	Little Rock, Oct 20—63
Gersdorf, Jus, f	York Neb
Graf, Geo	New Orleans, Mar 3—65
Graf, Mathew, f	Helena, Sep 27—63
Hart, Levi	Helena, Sep 27—63
Heise, August	Scott
Hicken, H J, f	Beechwood
Jackson, Andrew	Memphis, Sep 7—63
Kommers, Abraham J	St Louis, Aug 19—63
Kroutkromer, Jno, f	Scott
Krictzinger, Henry	Beechwood
Lieffroer, Jas*	Smiths Landing, May 21—64
Lafever, T H, f	Boltonville
Loomis, Alonzo	Helena, Aug 7—63
Minick, David	Milwaukee, Nov 6—64
Misner, J P, me	Fond du Lac
Miller, Edw	New Orleans, Mar 8—65
Munger, A R, f	Boltonville
McCormack, Henry	Boltonville
McMullen, Alex J	Hingham, Mass
Naumon, Frank	Scott
Pettis, S W, f	York, Neb
Pond, Simeon	Helena, Aug 14—63
Potter, W W	Hingham
Phillips, Chauncey	Mobile Point, Mar 3—65
Row, Samuel, f	Boltonville
Rohrbacker, Chas	Scott
Smith, Victory J	Memphis, Sep 23—63
Smith, Chas	Oakfield
TeMaat, Anthony	Columbus, June 4—63
TeMaat, Jan H	Memphis, Oct 3—63
Te Cump, Gerrett J	Memphis, Aug 3?—63
TeSlaa, Gerrett J	Aug 30—61
Voskuil, Anthony	Helena, Aug 1—63
Winklehorst, Gerret H	Little Rock, Oct 7—63
Wiersig, Julius	Sept 22—63
Wescott, Tim	Jenkins Ferry, May 4—64
Weingordner, Nicholas	Boltonville

G

Name	Location, Date
Capt Wm Wigham	
Capt Jas Gund	
Lt Amanzer Strong	
Lt Robt Horner	Jan 6—63
Lt Jno C Brooker	
Brennan, Thos, corp	Memphis, Sept 12—63
Ford, Patrick, corp	Milwaukee, Jan 9—63
Norris, Luke, corp	Blue River, Nov 6—63
Nolan, Ewd, corp	Pine Bluff, Dec 28—64
Ambling, Wm*	Okoloma, Apr 8—65
Ald, Jno	Milwaukee, Nov 2—62
Brooker, J C	Racine
Booth, Jno A	Rock, Ia
Bremer, Wm	Avoca
Buthoim, Wenzel	Highland, Nov 12—63
Conley, Michael	In the Field, Aug 15—63
Braves, Wm	Muscoda
Downey, Jno	Duvals Bluff, Sept 8—63
Fassel, Anton	Little Rock, Nov 8—63
Goerke, Chas	Two Rivers
Helmich, Fred'k	Memphis, Aug 27—63
Heigerson, Henry	Little Rock, Nov 1—63
Kassebaum, Chas	Little Rock, Feb 21—64
Kurtz, Adam	Avoca
Morgans, Wm	Little Rock, Nov 23—63
Nolan, Wm	Milwaukee, Mar 16—63
O'Donnel, Ewd	Duvals Bluff, Aug 31—63
Stewart, Alex	Little Rock, Nov 11—63

WALL PAPER HOUSE
| IN THE CITY. |

MUELLER & ILHARDT,

465 East Water St., MILWAUKEE.

H L. LAWSON'S.
Insurance
AND
LOAN AGENCY.

Hermann's Block 90 Main Street.

The following old and reliable companies represented.

WESTERN ASSURANCE CO., of Toronto, organized 1851
NORTH GERMAN INS. CO., of Hamburg.
CONNECTICUT FIRE INS. CO., of Hartford, organized 1850.
LYCOMING FIRE INS. CO., of Pennsylvania; organized 1840.
GIRARD FIRE INSURANCE CO., of Philadelphia; organized 1853.
NORWICH UNION. of England; organized in 1797.
TRADERS, of Chicago, organized 1850.
ÆTNA LIFE INS. CO., of Hartford; organized in 1850.

All Losses Equitably adjusted and promptly paid

Brilliant Diamond Jewelry.

Latest Novelties in all Kinds of

Gold and Silver Ware

Newest Styles. Most Fashionable Patterns.

Wm. C. Stanley, Jr.   Arthur K. Camp.

STANLEY & COMPANY,
108 WISCONSIN STREET,   -   -   MILWAUKEE. WIS

FRENCH CLOCKS, GORHAM SILVER WARE, REED
& BARTON'S PLATED WARE, ETC., ETC.

WISCONSIN SOLDIERS AND SAILORS REUNION ROSTER. 125

Sallenger, Jno, f — Calumira
Schrader, Aug — Avoca
Scheavle, Jno — Highland, Ia
Snyder, H J, f — Oak Center
Whalen, Jno — Little Rock, Dec 5—63

H

Capt Chas Cornelliusen — Memphis, Sept 10—63
Capt Jno A S Verdier
Lt Ole Jackson
Lt Geo L Hartwell
Lt Ole Nelson
Lt Albert L Lund
Lt Jno S Isaacsou
Thompson, Wm, corp Snyders Bluff, July 26—63
Nordhoe, Jacob J, corp — Helena, Aug 16—63
Oleson, Matthias, corp — Christiana, Nov 21—63
Anderson, Kjel A — Aug 1—63
Amunn, G A, me — Whitewater
Anderson, Marius — Little Rock, Nov 15—63
Anderson, Andrew — Little Rock, Mar 4 64
Abrahansen, Knud — Little Rock, Aug 21—64
Bryngelden, Asbjorn — Helena, Aug 13—63
Falks, O N — Stoughton
Groven, Ole Nelson — Duvals Bluff, Sept 4—63
Gundersen, Knud — Helena, Sept 15—63
Guttomsen, Tolof — Little Rock, Jan 14—64
Hareldsen, Arne — Little Rock, Feb 8—64
Hagen, Ole O — Blue Mounds
Halvorsel, Lars M — Gulf of Mexico, June 5—65
Johansen, Ole — Paducah, Oct 30—63
Jorde, Kettel A — Helena, Aug 9—63
Johnsen, Jeus — Little Rock, Sept 23—64
Jameson, Silvert — Little Rock, July 29—64
Jackson, Henry — Little Rock, Jan 22—65
Knudsen, Knud — Helena, Aug 11—63
Knudsen, Lewis — Christiana, Oct 9—63
Larsen, Nels H — Helena, Aug 11—63
Lintved, Ole Nelson — Memphis, Sept 16—63
Monssen, Ingebrigt — Little Rock, Nov 4—63
Nelson, Ellen — Mound City, Aug 9—63
Olsen, Soren — Memphis, Sept 22—63
O'Brien, Michael — Milwaukee, June 5—63
Paulsen, Jacob — Little Rock, Oct 18—63
Rader, Jno Geo — Memphis, Aug 29—63
Siversten, Tosten — St Louis, Sept 28—63
Skeple, Ole Aruesen — Paducah, Aug 3; —63
Steusou, Henry — Belleville, July 25—64
Siensen, Ole — Paducah, Sept 10—63
Syvertsen, Amund — Little Rock, Jan 23—64
Stevenson, Hans — Jeff Barracks Nov 12—64
Thompson, Ole — Memphis, Sept 26—63
Turonsen, Ole — St Louis, Nov 16—63
Ulnrud, Jno A — Mound City, Aug 11—63
Wiig, L Larson — Little Rock, Aug 18—64
Williamsen, Knud — Jeff Barracks, Dec 17—63
Wilson, Geo, f — Mishicott
Wilson, Chas, me — Mishicott

I

Capt Jas C Barnes
Lt Chas H Raymer
Lt Julius Bodenstab
Lt Wm T Cole
Lt August Hinard
Dricken, Peter, corp — St Nichoels
Bruss, Aug+ — New Orleans, Apr 2—4,5
Bullard, Geo — Neillsville
Bruck, Jacob +— Jenkins Ferry—61
Jewett, Priny, ass't p'm — Chilton
Mynderse, Reuben — Little Rock, Apr 12—65
McCarthy, Geo W, f — West Bend
Perry, J E — Sparta
Pierce, A C — Manitowoc Rapids
Rudley, Ewd 8+ — Spanish Ft, Apr 5—65
Ruethlisberger, Ulrich — Helena, Aug 6—63
Raabgrund, Louis — Paducah, Oct 4—63

K

Schmitt, Peter — Little Rock, Dec 2—63
Taylor, Thos — Oct 17—64
Taylor, J W — Fairfield, Neb
Van Epps, Evert — Little Rock, July 13—64

Capt Peter Mulholland
Lt Chas H Raymer
Lt Michael Mullen
Lt Chas F Folger
Lt Michael Maguire
Williams, Wm N, 1st sgt Duvals Bluff, Aug 29—63
Ruch, Wm, sgt — Little Rock, Oct 20—63
Aadncsen, Thore — July 28—63
Burk, Martin — Orleans, Neb
Cox, Jeremiah — Manitowoc
Classon, Andrew D — Manitowoc, Sept 10—63
Davis, Jno — Springfield
Ellingbo, Helgo, f — Larrabee
Ferguu, Zachariah — New Orleans, May 8—66
Horrigan, Michael — Little Rock, Dec 1—63
Hudson, Adolph — Mishicott
Hamilton, Wm — Memphis, Aug 4—63
Jones, Dan'l — June 9—63
Knudsen, Ole — Mobile, May 16—65
Lotseh, Fred'k — Little Rock, Nov 24—63
Lawrence, Lemuel — Millikens Bend, July 23—63
Nolan, Michael — Memphis, Oct 5—63
Pierce, Joshua H — Little Rock, Oct 7—63
Ravey, Hiram — Milwaukee, Aug 15—63
Smith, Oscar — July 28—63
Sullivan, Dennis — Kewaunee
Wilson, Henry — Milwaukee, Apr 3—63
Neber, Mathias — Milwaukee

UNASSIGNED.

Adams, K M — Fond du Lac
Beeson, Peter — Kaukauna
Brown, J J, ph — Sheboygan
Gaertner, Henry — Chicago
Johnson, Jno P — Chicago
Krez, Conrad, a — Sheboygan
Makee, W H — Lafort, Ia
Shroeder, Henry — Kewaunee

TWENTY-EIGHTH IN-FANTRY.

Three years. Organized September 13th, 1862. Original strength 961; gain by recruits, etc, 176 Total, 1137. Death loss, 225—Killed in action, 3, died of wounds, 2, of disease, 222. Other losses, 332, missing, 0, desertions, 31, transfers 81, discharged 220. Strength at muster-out, August 23d, 1865, 573. Campaigns in Ky., Ark., Miss., Ala., Texas.

REGIMENTAL ROSTER.

Col Jas M Lewis
Col Edmund B Gray
Lt Chas Whittaker
Lt Calvert C White
Maj Jno A Williams
Adj Jno A Savage Jr
Adj Albert S Kendrick
Adj Jerome P Magill
Q M Geo W Wylie
Q M Chas J Coltier
Surg Wm H Smith
A Surg Lewis K Hawes
A Surg Dan'l M Miller
A Surg Chas W Frisbie
Chap Ebenezer S Peake

A

Capt Jno A Williams

Capt Wm E Coates
Lt Arthur Holbrook — Milwaukee
Lt Wm E Coates
Lt Rulif F Hopper
Lt Ethan A Gage
Lt Lauren Barker
Hannah, Jos, corp — Helena, Feb 10—63
Wildish, Chas W, corp — Helena, Aug 21—63
Tack, Chas, corp — Little Rock, Apr 19—64
Alexander, Geo T — Pine Bluff, Apr 27—64
Alexander, Chas E — Pine Bluff, Aug 13—64
Baines, Henry — Memphis, Mar 30—63
Bully, Anson E — Helena, Feb 26—63
Barker, Jno, me — Milwaukee
Bulman, Henry — Tomah
Bradley, Elisha, a — Granville, Mich
Barker, L, f — Brookfield Junction
Berg, F C — Owatonna, Minn
Berg, Fred — Owatonna
Berg, Peter, me — Oconomowoc
Churchill, Chas H — Helena, May 8—63
Churchill, Francis — Waukesha, Sept 11—63
Carver, Sam'l — Helena, Apr 8—63
Carrier, Jno S, me — Milwaukee
Carlson, Oscar W, pb — Milwaukee
Cook, G, f — Menominee Falls
Carver, Jas — Brookfield Junc
Cootes, Wm E, m — Milwaukee
Carlton, Wm, c — River Falls
Campton, Wm, f — Hammond
Crossman, Lewis, e — Brookfield Junc
Currier, Jno A, me — Bay View
Dapkins, Wm H, m — Appleton
Daubner, Geo, f — Brookfield Junc
Enders, Nicholas — Fort Gaines, Mar 23—65
Elliott, Rubt C — Chicago, Ill
Fuller, Zack T, m — Cedar Falls, Ia
Gillet, Peter V D — Milwaukee, Nov 30—62
Gripps, Fred'k — Helena, Apr 19—63
Goodwin, Geo, m — Hartland
Gower, Thos, me — Beaver Dam
Howard, Albert — Helena, May 17—63
Harrison, Jacob — Memphis, Sept 20—63
Hurgen, Chas, m — Delafield
Hawley, W, agt — Reedsburg
Haward, Hiram, l — Menominee Falls
Hopper, Rulif F, m — Eatontown, N J
Holbrook, Arthur, pb — Milwaukee
Jeffrey, Geo C — Helena, Mar 6—63
Judson, Noah, f — Waukesha
Keeler, Ell, painter — Menominee Falls
Lansdale, Henry M — Oct 19—64
Lobdell, Emmett L — Mobile, Apr 13—65
Luce, Chas D — Pine Bluff, Aug 28—64
Luther, Chas — Gravesville
Maynard, Wm A, m — Muskota, Kan
Martin, E, l — Menominee Falls
Pickle, Jas F — Mobile, May 4—65
Pickle, Dewitt — Horicon
Reed, Jas J — Memphis, Sept, 11—63
Reise, Herman R — Memphis, Apr 20—63
Rowe, Sylvester, c — Menominee Falls
Rowe, R S, c — Menominee Falls
Ridgeway, Alonzo, f — Menominee Falls
Swac, Wm W — New London
Shaffer, Jno, f — Memphis, Oct 31—63
Sawyer, Geo S — Tryberg, la
Short, Geo, f — Mt Pulaski, Ill
Stanhope, C D, ph — Waukesha
Swan, Polez, me — Milwaukee
Smith, Wright W, f — Brookfield June
Taylor, Schuyler, photo — Spring Lake, Mich
Wilson, Orin M — Berlin
Woodcock, Ira — Pine Bluff, Aug 8—64
Williams, Jno — Pine Bluff, Aug 3—61
Wilkins, Ed, f — Helena, Ap 11—63
Williams, Jno A, a — Wausau
Wardrobe, Fr, d — Pine Bluff
Williams, Wm — Milwaukee
Ward, Albert, pa — Manistee, Mich
— Milwaukee

INSURANCE AGENTS,

FRAKER BLOCK,
OSHKOSH - WISCONSIN.

Represent the strongest and most reliable insurance companies,

Fire, Life and Accident,
IN THE UNITED STATES.

CALL AND SEE US.

DANIEL & GILE.

MISS M. CONNER,

FASHIONABLE

 MILLINERY

FULL ASSORTMENT OF

SPRING HATS

JUST RECEIVED.

NO. 430 MILWAUKEE STREET,

MILWAUKEE, WIS.

 BADGER STATE

TOBACCO WORKS

Established, A. D. 1847.

F. F. ADAMS & CO.,
PROPRIETORS.

Nos. 1, 3, and 5, Clybourne Street,

MILWAUKEE, - WIS.

→✕←

HENRY REILLY,

MERCHANT TAILOR,

AND DEALER IN

GENTS' FURNISHING GOODS,

434 Milwaukee St., Between Mason and Wisconsin.

MILWAUKEE, - WIS.

Stock Complete. Prices for first-class work the lowest in the city.

WISCONSIN SOLDIERS AND SAILORS REUNION ROSTER. 127

B

Capt M G Townsend* — Marks Mills, Apr 25—64
Capt Chas B Stawson
Lt Cushman K Davis
Lt Franklin A Bennett
Lt Chesley B Tuttar
McCall, Martin, corp — Pine Bluff, Aug 8—61
Steen, Ephraim, corp — St Louis, Apr 30—63
Arnold, Isaac — Little Rock, Oct 21—63
Baker, Wester, — Little Rock, May 7—5
Bennett, F A — Janesville
Bennett, Frank, m — Janesville
Cook, Edwin B — Helena, Jan 23—63
Crall, Hugh — Helena, Apr 19—63
Cross, August — Little Rock, Dec 18 63
Church, Daniel A — Prospect Hills
Cumming, Jno — Ottawa
Carpenter, Jno — Mukwonago
Damuth, William — St Louis, May 6—63
Duncan, John — Greenwood, Mar 30—63
Davis, C K, a — St Paul, Minn
Deidrich, Ezra — Milwaukee
Fletcher, Andrew — Memphis, Mar 17—63
Finnegan, Peter — St Louis, Oct 9—63
Foster, Albert, d — Denver, Col
Gault, Thos, a — Chicago, Ill
Helder, John P — Helena, Apr 18—63
Howie, John — St Louis, Apr 11—63
Hill, David, e — Milwaukee
Hogg, Sam'l W+ — Spanish Ft, Mar 28—65
Jones, Jabez — Pine Bluff, Aug 17—64
Jones, Richard — Ottawa
Killip, Robt — Helena, June 2—63
Munroe, Alonzo, f — Prospect Hills
Mullen, Anthony, p m — Portland, Ia
Mullan, A G, m — Portland, Ia
Patterson, Geo, h — Milwaukee
Stickels, Jacob I. — Keokuk, June 15—63
Tesch, Fred, m — Manistee
Vanderhoof, Orlin — Helena, Feb 5—63
Voght, Albert — Pine Bluff, Nov 9—61
Vanderpool, Geo J, f — Vernon
Vanderpool, Geo J — Mukwonago
Wehaud, Fred — St Louis, Oct 26—63
Watkins, Chas W — North Prairie, Aug 21—64
Watson, Jno — Knapp

C

Capt Thomas N Stevens
Lt Daniel S Cnitis
Lt Andrew Gilmore — Milwaukee, July 30—63
Lt Lowell I. Alvord
Lt Joseph G Robinson
Lt Fred'k B Brown, Jr
Plympton, F W, sgt — Duvals Bluff, Aug 24—62
Alvord, J M — Oconomowoc
Ballard, Willard — Helena, Feb 26—63
Brown, F B, Jr — Spirit Lake, Ia
Bogart, A — Monterey
Brown, F B — Storm Lake, Ia
Berg, P C — Oconomowoc
Clausen, Seaman G — Helena, Mar 1—63
Christy, Leander G — Helena, June 22—63
Chafler, V W — Oconomowoc
Coal, Geo — Oconomowoc
Decker, Wm E — Pine Bluff, Aug 1—64
Fritsinger, Levi D — Pine Bluff, July 16—64
Graper, Wm — Helena, July 5—63
Haight, Morris P — Helena, Feb 26—63
Hauso, Amund
Harshaw, Albert K — Helena, May 21—63
Holcomb, Hiram C — Pine Bluff, May 28—64
Hardell, Jno W — Pine Bluff, Sept 11—61
Hall, Jas J — Oconomowoc
Johnson, Andrew E — Helena, Mar 10—63
Jacobson, Julius — Oconomowoc
Jacobson, Andrew — Albaton, Ia
Knudson, Halver — Helena, Apr 12—63

Lillie, Geo
Lewis, Horatio S
Mellwain, David
Muckey, Myron, f
Nelson, O:e
Nelson, Marshall
Osborn, Geo A
Rendal, Job A
Rugg, Chas A
Robinson, Jas W
Smalley, Alexander C
Smalley, Theon M
Stein, Hans A
Stinson, Ebridge,
Ludington, Frank
Tucker, P K
Witherill, Milton J — Pine Bluff, Oct 20—61
Watson, Abraham, — Pine Bluff, Sept 19—64
Zimmerman, Jno — Monterey

D

Capt Edw S Redington
Lt Hiram N Hayes
Lt Jas B Schrom
Lt Henry H Watts
Lt Jas M Mead — Helena, Feb 13—63
Lt Wm G Palmer
Hodge, Jas A, sgt — Milwaukee, Dec 9—62
Amundson, Barney — Pine Bluff, Sep 23—64
Busch, Henry — Milwaukee
Bowen, Jos R, f — Eau Galle
Clark, Melvin J — Pine Bluff, June 19—64
Carpenter, Lewis — Whitewater
DeGroat, Geo — Pine Bluff, Nov 26—64
Daucey, T J, mf — Palmyra
Dann, E F, ph — Berlin
Earley, Juo, me — Whitewater
Feiss, Benedict — Pine Bluff, Aug 8—61
Foust, Frank, b — Whitewater
Fero, Sile, l — Whitewater
Goodrich, D N — Whitewater
Grant, Jno, mf — Whitewater
Henderson, Donald — Milwaukee, Dec 7—62
Hare, Jesse — Helena, Apr 29—63
Hills, Geo — Sep 7—63
Holmes, Chas. l — Whitewater
Kuhn, Chas — Pine Bluff, Sep 20—61
Keenan, Patrick, l — Whitewater
Kershaw, Jos — Whitewater
Kinney, Francis, e — Whitewater
Miller, Isaac — Pine Bluff, Nov 22—64
Nickerson, G E — Whitewater
Patten, Franklin — Pine Bluff, Sep 2—64
Prichard, Jas F — Pine Bluff, July 6—61
Palmer, Wm H, f — Hebron
Robbin, Chas E — Duvals Bluff, Sept 25—63
Rockwell, C W, mf — Whitewater
Smith, Henry F — Jeff Barracks, Oct 20—64
Simpson, Chas H — Pine Bluff, Aug 23—64
Scholl, Chas, me — Whitewater
Schrobel, Chas, f — Whitewater
Smith, Oscar, e — Whitewater
Torrey, Julius H — Ft Pemberton, Mar 29—63
Taylor, James — Lime Rock
Trausman, Geo — Whitewater
Thomas, Jacob — New London
Warker, Jacob — St Louis, July 18—63

E

Capt Jas R Kenyon
Lt Wm E Bingham
Lt Chas J Collier
Lt Asa W Hibbard
Althaus, Henri — Pine Bluff, Dec 13—64
Arwood, Andrew W, f — Hearts Prairie
Bingham, Chas K — Helena, Aug 27—63
Bromley, Jno — Madison
Brain, J — Eagle

Brown, Chas C, f — Hebron
Bigelow, A — Millard
Davis, Jno C — Wautoma
Feder, Wilhelm — Pine Bluff, Mar 10—64
Henderson, Sylvester — Tallaha'chie R, Apr 3—63
Hunter, Wm — Pine Bluff, Feb 27—64
Heinze, Jno — Boca Chica, J'y 29—65
Hax l, W P — Hebron
Kohler, Jacob — Helena, Aug 18—63
Krotz, Jo. — Pine Bluff, July 10—64
Loomer, Wm E — Paola, Kan
Means, Jno W — Helena, May 28—63
Robinson, Jno B — White River, Feb 11—65
Smith, Lyman D — Helena, Feb 13—63
Snow, D'bert — Helena, June 1—63
Sullivan, Michael — Pine Bluff, July 26—64
Taylor, J B, f — Millard
Velhau, Andrew* — Helena, July 4—63
Welch, Hiram J — Helena, Feb 6—63
Wilford, Hardy — Little Rock, Oct 20—63
Webster, W B, me — Delevan

F

Capt Calvert C White
Capt Jeremiah Noon — Aug 10—62
Capt Archie D Monteith
Lt Hiram F Syke
Lt Jas Northman
Lt Walker I. Dean — Columbus, Dec 29—62
Lt Geo W Higgins
Styler, Wm T, sgt — Helena, July 15—63
Taylor, Wahlon, sgt — Pine Bluff, Sept 21—64
Jenson, Lars, corp — Pine Bluff, Nov 28—64
Parker, Chas J, corp — Pine Bluff, Aug 26—64
Tillson, Henry H, corp — Pine Bluff, June 4—61
Andrews, L G — Mukwonago
Bell, Sydney C — Pine Bluff, July 4—61
Caldwell, Cassius M — Helena, Feb 22—63
Caldwell, James N — Little Rock, Dec 31—64
Darrah, Jos — Helena, Mar 2—63
Fielder, Geo — Jeff Barracks, Oct 30—61
Foster, Edwin — Yazoo, Mar 2—63
Freeman, Wm H — Memphis, Oct 25—63
Gray, Gabriel — Pine Bluff, July 1—64
Holt, Ed, f — Rock Elm Centre
Howard, Nathaniel — Pine Bluff, Aug 13—64
Hubbard, Monroe — Helena, Feb 18—63
Lyke, Julius G — Yazoo, Mar 14—63
Lyke, H F, m — Oconomowoc
McGill, Chas N — Pine Bluff, Sept 2—61
Melendy, Cephas J — Mar 24—63
Moffitt, Orin D — Pine Bluff, Aug 26—64
Mason, Jno W — Stone Bank
McDonough, Jas — East Troy
Noon, Jeremiah, Jr — Pine Bluff, Mar 12—64
Rankin, Wm — Sussex
Taylor, Jno — Memphis, Sept 6—63
Warv, Austin C — Apr 9—63
Webster, Henry C — Milwaukee, Dec 12—62
Whitney, Ephraim G — Little Rock, Sept 21—63
Wilde, Jno — Duvals Bluff, Sept 3—63
Williams, Ewd F — Jan 13—63

G

Capt Ellin Enos, D m — Waukesha
Capt Willis V Ticheuor
Lt David Turner
Lt Seymour Gilbert
Lt Albert Foster
Lt Andrew McKee
Danelson, Thos, sgt — Yazoo Pass, Apr 6—63
Johnson, Thos J, sgt — Helena, May 25—63
Howard, Geo W, corp — Helena, Feb 22—63
Smith Jno H, corp — St Louis, June 26—63
Abain, Peter — Rock Elm Centre
Becker, Phil — Helena, May 17—63
Blanchard, Jos C — Pine Bluff, Oct 15—61
Brown, Jas B — Helena, June 9—63
Brain, Clement J — St Louis, July 29—63

HEMPSTED'S
TEMPLE OF MUSIC.

SHEET MUSIC & MUSICAL GOODS OF EVERY DESCRIPTION

STEINWAY,
Kranich & Bach,
Emerson,
M'Cammon,
The "Arion,"
And Hempsted

 PIANOS.

THE BEST INSTRUMENTS IN THE WORLD, AND THE LOWEST PRICES.

TERMS TO SUIT ALL PURCHASERS.

Call and Examine this Immense Stock of Musical Instruments Before Purchasing.

YOU WILL BE SURE TO FIND SOMETHING TO PLEASE YOU.

WISCONSIN SOLDIERS AND SAILORS REUNION ROSTER.

Beardsley, Sam'l B — East Troy
Bowers, Luluir L — Peshtigo
Christisan, Geo — May 17-63
Cullen, Chris — Yazoo Pass, Mar 30-63
Decker, Wm E — Pine Bluff, Aug 1-61
Donaldson, W D, f — East Troy
Enos, Elihu, p m — Waukesha
Fritsinger, Levi B — Pine Bluff, July 16-64
Green, Thos* — Mt Elba, Mar 30-64
Hartwell, Geo W — Helena, Feb 18-63
Hipes, Isaiah B J — Memphis, Dec 4-63
Howie, Jno R — Memphis, July 22-63
Jones, Wm — Brazos Santiago, June 17-65
King, Leon, h — Pewaukee
McKinstry, Jerome E* — Helena, July 4-63
Malloy, Jas — Little Rock, Feb 12-65
McKawen, Wm, m — Greenfield
Peck, Allen P — Duvals Bluff, Aug 28-62
Rehmer, Frank E — East Troy
Saffard, LeGrand D — Pine Bluff, July 31-64
Schneider, Jacob — Milwaukee, Dec 17-62
Sears, B C — Waukesha
Thornton, Jno — Pine Bluff, July 6-64
Tichenor, W V, a — Mason City, Ia
Zeloff, Jno M — Helena, Mar 8-63

H

Capt Herman A Meyer
Capt Jas Murray
Lt Thos Chandler
Lt Jonathan L O'Brien
Lt Jno W Lowry
Lt Wallace Goff
Lt Jno A Hurtgen
Budde, Jno G, sgt — Helena, Feb 13-63
Kieselbuck, Geo, sgt — Pine Bluff, July 28-64
Yager, Nicholas, sgt — Pine Bluff, July 14-64
Flood, Philip, corp* — Spanish Ft, Mar 31-64
Feely, Patrick, corp — Pine Bluff, Aug 24-64
Malcom, McTag, corp — Waukesha, July 26-63
Nattisheim, Jus, corp — Helena, May 23-63
Carney, Jno B — Milwaukee, Oct 27-63
Felton, Jno — Columbus, Apr 5-63
Greutzmacher, Carl — Helena, May 2-63
Gannon, Jno — Helena, June 24-63
Gebmann, Louis — Memphis, Sept 6-63
Hamlin, Jas H — Brownsville, Sept 5-63
Hunt, Michael — Pine Bluff, July 25-64
Hurtgen, Peter Jos — Tyler, Jan 5-65
Hollis, Nyron — Whitewater
Holzer, N — Hartland
Larsen, Jens — Delafield, Oct 7-63
Launon, Thos — Pine Bluff, Aug 6-64
Ludwig, Christian — Pine Bluff, Oct 8-64
Meier, Siegfried — Norway
Oberlander, Jos — Pine Bluff, Sept 14-64
Oberbilling, Matvias, f — Dorchester
Peter, Heinrich — Helena, Apr 12-63
Peters, Rudolph — Brookfield, Jan 5-65
Reinhard, Chas — Memphis, Oct 1-63
Ross, Nathaniel — Helena, Aug 15-63
Stanfield, Louis — Clarksville, Aug 8-65
Stark, August — Vernon
Taske, Albert — Kewaunee
Whitford, Samuel — Helena, Apr30-63

I

Capt Horace B Crandall
Capt Andrew F Shlverick — Apr 22-65
Capt Lindsay J Smith
Lt Alex F Seymour
Lt Smith A Hartwell
Capp, Elli, sgt — Helena, May 4-63
Weeks, Spencer J, corp* — Spanish Ft, Apr 4-65
Short, Geo W, corp — Helena, Apr 21-62
Allen, Fayette L, corp — Little Rock, Jan 25-65
Adams, H A — East Troy
Bentley, Sam'l — Pine Bluff, Aug 24-64

Baman, W H — East Troy
Bell, S R — Milwaukee
Cowles, Asa S — Helena, Feb 24-63
Coulter, W Jas — Helena, Apr 12-63
Dingman, Chas — Troy Centre
DuPuy, E M — Plymouth
Edwards, Ed — Troy Centre
Frank, Hiram P — St Louis, June 27-62
Fichler, Augustus — Little Rock, Feb 9-65
Gleason, Burnan Tallahatchie River, Mar 10-61
Gaskell, Jno — Helena, May 31-63
King, Earl — East Troy
Murray, Jas — Little Rock, Feb 12-65
Mathewson, Donald — East Troy
Mathesen, Jno — Mayhew
Molton, Michael — Wilton
O'Ragan, Wm — Helena, Apr 21-63
O'Brien, Patrick, Jr* — Mt Elba, Mar 30-61
Peak, Gilbert — Helena, June 12-63
Patterson, Alfred — Mukwonago
Smith, Delos C — Helena Apr 17-63
Sullivan, Jeremiah — Pine Bluff, Aug 22-64
Thomas, Francis — East Troy, July 13-63
Vaughn, Jno — Little Rock, Nov 11-63
Waters, Isaac E — Helena, Apr 9-63
Whitton, Jno — Helena, June 22-61

K

Capt Ira H Morton — Little Rock, Sept 1x-63
Capt Levi J Billings
Capt Geo F Cowling
Lt Wm J Briggs
Lt Wm H Chase
Lt Gordon Conant
Russell, Edw, corp — Helena, Apr 22-63
Aslakson, Knud — Greenwood, Apr 5-63
Ambler, Wm — Helena, Apr 5-63
Austin, Chauncey — White Creek
Bauer, Louis — Memphis, Sept 1-63
Buetow, Henry, f — Eldorado
Buruick, Geo J — St Louis, Dec 27-62
Billings, Levi J, a — Green Bay
Carle, Abram — Helena, Feb 5-63
Cretty, Dan'l — Pine Bluff, July 14-64
Dort, Amos — Greenwood, Apr 5-63
DuPuy, Edw M — Plymouth
Dupuy, E M, f — East Troy
Douglass, O W — Walworth
Farley, Jno A — Pine Bluff, Nov 15-61
Gordon, Tolliff O — Helena, Feb 15-63
Gould, Alvin — Greenwood, Mar 14-63
Grunwold, Jno — East Troy
Grenewold, Jno, f — Pine Bluff, July 15-64
Henry, Jos — Pine Bluff, July 15-64
Harroll, Lewis J — Racine
Kellogg, Sam'l S — Pine Bluff, Aug 12-61
Kilbow, Wm — Painesville
Larsen, Nils — Mar 25-63
Peck, Jno F — Helena, Feb 5-63
Phelps, Arthur — Pine Bluff, May 28-64
Rice, Griffith T — Memphis, Mar 18-63
Steverson, Gunder — Dane Co, June 26-63
Stacy, Pete — Sussex

UNASSIGNED.

Berg, L C, musician — Owatonna, Minn
Bowers, Frank — Tess Corners
Catlin, Jno — Chicago, Ill
Deveraux, Nicholas — Mukwonago
Donaldson, Wm — Elkhorn
Finley, Chas — Tess Corners
Flynn, Jno — Tess Corners
Frisby, Chas F — Milwaukee
Holmes, Chas — Whitewater
Hawks, A D, bk — San Francisco, Cal
Huttou, Wm — Merton
Kendrick, Albert, m — St Louis, Mo
Kinderman, Jacob, f — Wauwatosa
Lewis, Jas M — Oconomowoc

Lonckey, Jas B — Tess Corners
Muckey, Myron — Tess Corners
Miller, Mc L, ph — Oconomowoc
Perkins, Clark, f — Mukwonago
Roe, Thos — Merton
Rogers, Jno, l — Whitewater
Times, Edw — Merton
Welchmar, Chas — Oconomowoc

TWENTY-NINTH INFANTRY.

Three years. Organized September 27th, 1862 Original strength, 961; gain by recruits, etc., 128 total, 1089. Death loss, 296—Killed in action, 40, died of wounds, 37, of disease, 210, of accidents, 9, Other losses, 326, missing, 0, desertions, 29, transfers, 193, discharges, 184, Strength at muster-out, June 22d, 1865, 467. Campaigns in Ark., La., Miss., Texas., Ala.,

REGIMENTAL ROSTER.

Col Chas R Gill — Madison
Col Wm A Greene
Col Bradford Hancock — Chicago, Ill
Lt Col G T Thorn — Nebraska City, Neb
Lt Col H F Coudltt, a — Fond du Lac
Maj G H Bryant, f — Tecone, Ia
Adj Valentine Sweeney — Watertown, Apr 21-63
Adj Jno W Blake
Adj Geo W Blake
Adj H C Hadley — Janesville
Q M Sam'l Baird
Q M Jno P DeMerritt — Williamstown, Vt
Surg Wm C Spalding — Watertown
Surg Darwin Dubols
Surg Jacob L Potter
A Surg Robt Addison
A Surg Geo D Winch
A Surg W W Reed
A Surg W S Schermerhorn
A Surg W H Hipolite
A Surg Geo W Harber
A Surg J F McClure
A Surg W H Summerfeldt
A Surg B F Rolfe
Chap Jno I Herrick

A

Capt Bradford Hancock — Chicago, Ill
Capt O F Mattice — New Orleans, June 3-64
Capt O L Ray
Lt Geo Works
Lt Jno N Davis
Robbins, Lionel E, sgt* — Memphis, June 24-63
Matthews, C F, corp* — Champion Hills, May16-63
Andrews, Chas B — May 10-63
Agnew, John — Carrolton, Sep 4-63
Bridges, Jno S — May 8-63
Bleeker, Wm J + — Vicksburg, June 13-63
Halcom, Geo — Millikens Band, Apr 29-63
Butler, Nelson — St Louis, Aug 8-63
Blasky, Wm — Cherokee
Carter, N H* — Champion Hills May 16-63
Coughlin, Richard* — Champion Hills, May 16-63
Cruger, Jefferson — New Orleans, Apr 23-64
Drangerson, Toller — White River, Sep 4-63
Gaskins, Geo K — Helena, Apr 4-63
Griffin, Fernando D — Memphis, Sep 14-63
Gregg, Lucius B — St Charles, Sep 23-64
King, Jno* — Champion Hills, May 16-63
Kimball, J A — Neillsville
Listner, Chas B — Vicksburg, July 26-63
Levere, Thos — Thibodeaux, Aug 1-63
Nelson, Jno — Chicago, Oct 9-64
Peschack, Wenel* — Port Gibson, May 1-63

ESTABLISHED IN 1842.

H. BOSWORTH & SONS,
WHOLESALE DRUGGISTS,

JOBBERS IN

Drugs, Paints, Oils, White Lead, Turpentine and Putty,

WINDOW GLASS, GLASSWARE, VARNISHES AND GLUES, PAINTS,

Horse, Shoe, Scrub and Whitewash Brushes.

Druggists Sundries and Toilet Articles a Specialty.

LARGEST HOLDERS OF

FINE OLD KENTUCKY WHISKIES,

CHAMPAGNES,

IMPORTED BRANDIES, WINES AND GIN.

ALL GOODS WARRANTED AS REPRESENTED AND PRICES GUARANTEED.

339 EAST WATER STREET.

WISCONSIN SOLDIERS AND SAILORS REUNION ROSTER. 131

Parks, Wm H — Vicksburg, July 3—63
Smith, Fred — Vicksburg, June 26—63
Spooner, Jno — New Orleans, Oct 23—63
Thompson, Henry — Carrolton, Aug 23—63
Wilsey, Abraham — Helena, Mar 18—63
Wetmore, Warner — Franklin, Dec 7—93
Weeks, Geo — Columbus
Yeryea, Louis — Franklin, Mar—64

B

Capt Thos R Mott
Capt D S Gibbs
Lt Chas Wood — Watertown
M Norman Humphrey
Lt F B Northrop
Lt Royal P Branson
Lt C B Scott
Lt Jno N Reed
Craudall, Alonzo C, sgt — Texas, Dec 5—61
Phelps, Wm, corp — Vicksburg, July 7—63
Barrett, Calvin* — Sabine Cross Road, Apr 8—44
Burke, Jas* — Sabine Cross Road, Apr 8—64
Blanchard, Sargent J — Helena, Feb 18—63
Bolser, Jas S — Helena, Feb 11—63
Bennett, Henry — Helena, Feb 28—63
Bartlett, J Marcellus — Vicksburg, June 12—63
Bartz, Jno — New Orleans, July 3—64
Frank, Peter — St Charles, Sept 26—61
Griffeth, David — Helena, Mar 11—63
Grifley, Ashbel D — Vicksburg, June 19—63
Grafley, Cyrus M — Memphis, Apr 8—65
Hawes, Ewd B* — Pt Gibson, May 1—63
Hungerford, Henry — Youngs Point, June 13—63
Holcomb, Geo — Texas, Nov 15—61
Irvin, Jas S — Helena, Jan 11—63
Karr, Jos — Helena, Jan 11—63
Keyes, J H, ed — Watertown
King, W T — Grand Rapids
Marshall, Matthew* — Pt Gibson, May 1—61
Mead, Ransom — Helena, Feb 20—13
Middlestates, Wm — New Orleans, May 24—64
William, Wm — New Orleans, Feb 8—65
Norton, Amiel — Vicksburg, July 24—63
Parker, Geo H+ — Grand Gulf, May 20—61
Ringer, Robt H* — Pt Gibson, May 1—63
Richards, Bradley — Millikens Bend, May 1—63
Roberts, Jno — New Orleans, Oct 11—63
Thompson, Hiram S — Mansfield, June 7—64
Visgar, Albert P — Emmett, Nov 27—63
Welton, Orin E — Vicksburg, July 29—63
Wright, Williston H — Natchez, Aug 10—13
Wollensack, Andrew J — Natchez, Aug 15—67
Wood, Chas — Watertown
Webb, E K — Leoni, Mich
Young, Cyprian B — Texas, Sept 27—64

C

Capt H E Connitt, a — Fond du Lac
Capt Jno F Parsons — Kalamazoo, Mich
Lt Jas O Pierce — Memphis, Tenn
Lt L F Willard — Horicon, Jan 10—61
Lt Oscar Lawrence
Hanff, Jno A, sgt* — Champion Hills, May 16—63
Graham, B, sgt+ — Champion Hills May 17—63
Deming, DeForest 8+ — Alexandria, May 9—64
Norton, Jno B, corp* — Spanish Fort, Mar 27—65
Netzer, Franz E, corp — Vicksburg, May 28—63
Pompe, Chas, corp — Shreveport, June 16—65
Anderson, Nat C, — New Orleans, July 1—64
Brandt, Jno H+ — Champion Hills, May 27—63
Blanchad, Merit A — St Louis, Feb 23—63
Benz, Chas — Helena, Feb 22—63
Baum, Geo — Millikens Bend, May 22—63
Beter, Julius — Burnette Station
Bunrue, O H P — Neillsville
Barett, Eugene, me — Mayville
Cody, Wm — Helena, Mar 21—61
Duke, Gilbert+ — Champion Hills, May 17—63

Deisley, Geo
Daly, Robt
Fritz, Lawrence
Galtey, Paul F
Humphrey, Horace
Hollister, Sam'l B
Kruschke, Julius
Linbucker, Jno W
Morrison, Andrew A — Millikens Bend, Apr 19—63
Montieth, Robt
Minnick, Levi
McFate, Wm
Page, H C
Pierce, Jas O, a
Parsons, W F
Rhodes, Jno A
Smith, Thos
Spommaus, Christian
Seitz, Wm
Veon, Joshua G — Millikens Bend, Apr 28—63
Wellnitz, Ernst — Helena, Ark, Mar 25—63
Ward, David — Helena, Ark, Apr 11—63
Woudland, Jno — Memphis, April 5—63
Ward, Wm — Aug 8—53

D

Capt G H Bryant — Ticonic, Ia
Lt D W Curtis — Ft Atkinson
Lt Edw N Potter — Cambridge
Lt Chas Townsend — Macomb City, Miss
Potter, E N, 1st sgt, f — Cambridge
Piper, H Delos. sgt* — Pt. Hudson, May 1—63
Bryant, Spencer A, sgt+ — Memphis, June 2—61
Millard, Walter, sgt — Carrolton, Aug 24—63
Ludtke, C, corp* — Sabine Cross Road, Apr 8—64
Bower, Henry A, corp — Vicksburg, May 28—63
Hall, Arlando R, corp — Helena, Apr 16—63
Matson, Sylvester, corp — Lake Mills, Nov 3—64
Butler, Thos H — Champion Hills, May 16—63
Brainard, Harlow D — Escanaba
Backus, Cyrus — Helena, Feb 8—63
Bryant, G H, f — Ticonic, Ia
Brewer, Jno, I — Baraboo
Bemis, A T
Culver, J M, me — Willford
Cabell, Albert — Kenosha
Curtis, D W — Lake Mills
Conuitt, Wm E, a
Dietsch, Carl — Vicksburg, July 10—63
Dyke, Fred'k A — Millikens Bend, June 7—63
Donley, Jos — St Louis, July 5—63
Damuth, Sam'l — Mobile, May 14—65
De Forest, Francis — Memphis, Apr 16—64
Damuth, D S — Ft Atkinson
Drager, Chas — Lake Mills
Drake, Hiram — Ft Atkinson
Foat, Alfred J — Fox Lake, Jan 9—61
Fillable, Wm, f — Cambridge
Flanuagan, Isaiah — Vicksburg, Aug 16—63
Felbell, Wm, f — Ft Atkinson
Ford, H, me — Beloit
Felbell, Wm J — Oakland Centre
Goodrich, Jerome — Atchafalaya, July 28—64
Griffin, Nelson T — Helena, Feb 7—63
Green, W A — Hubbleton
Gill, C B, a — Madison
Hume, Walter — Helena, Mar 17—63
Hurlburt, Wallace — Jeff Barracks, May 22—63
Hanson, J W — Ft Atkinson
Hadley, H C, bk — Janesville
Hadley, Henry — Janesville
Johnson, D C — Ft Atkinson
Kline, Geo A — Aug 7—61
Koser, f — Jefferson
Kusten, Wm — Keokuk, Aug 36—61
Kover, Ignatius — Ft Atkinson
Krogh, Albert — Cambridge
Krough, Albert, me — Cambridge
Ludtke, Ferd* — Sabine Cross Road, Apr 8—64

Lengner, Herman — Ft Atkinson
Meise, Jno B+ — Champion Hills, May 28—63
Mack, Jacob — Carrolton, Sept 4—63
Major, Thos P — New Orleans, Jan 1—64
Millard, Walter, f — Lake Mills
Miller, Christian, f — Lake Mills
Nimmo, Richard — Memphis, Mar 16—65
Nelson, J I, f — Ft Atkinson
Nelson, Willis, me — Ft Atkinson
Overbeck, Wm — St Louis, Aug 15—63
Packard, E J — Santa Barbara, Cal
Pohlman, C F W, f — Lake Mills
Ringer, J Wilson* — Champion Hills, May 16—63
Rockwood, Jason — Helena, Feb 1—63
Rhoda, Carl, f — Jefferson
Reese, August, f — Ft Atkinson
Rose, Wm, f — Ft Atkinson
Spoor, Fred'k* — Sabine Cross Road, Apr 8—64
Spoor, J, l — Ft Atkinson
Shott, G — Neillsville
Shorl J — Neillsville
Seuley, D W, me — Cambridge
Sontag, f — Neillsville
Schmitz, Wm — Whitehall
Short, Jas+ — Pt Gibson, May 1—63
Skinner, Edwin+ — Black River, June 12—63
Smith, Moses M I — Ft Atkinson
Selgmann, Carl — Pleasant Hill, Apr 10—64
Smith, Emery, l — Ft Atkinson
Smith, Jesse — Helena, Feb 20—63
Skud, T F, me — Sioux City, Ia
Spear, Carlos C — Memphis. Mar 17—63
Smith, M M — Ft Atkinson
Stanley, Daniel — Kansas
Scobie, David W — Cambridge
Thorn, G L, a — Appleton
Townsend, C H, ed — McComb City, Miss
Tiffany, Henry, f — Ft Atkinson
Wheeler, Addison — Black River, July 22—63
Weeks, Wunzer — Houston, Sept 30—64

E

Capt H Dunham
Capt D J Wells
Capt Jos A Stark
Lt G W Dale
Lt C H Eggleston
Lt Jas Armstrong
Ketchum, Delazon S, sgt Port Gibson, May 1—63
Alexander, Geo W, sgt — Port Gibson, May 1—63
Bennett, Jas W, corp — Jeff Barracks, Mar 27—63
Powers, N, corp — Millikens Bend, July 30—63
Jackson, Richard, corp — Carrolton, Sep 4—63
Bryant, Chas — Westford, Oct 9—63
Barrett, Sam'l — Camp Salmon, Dec 14—62
Burchard, Geo M, a — Fort Atkinson
Carlisle, Newman — Mobile, May 20—65
Derawan, Patrick — Fox Lake, July 16—63
Dorwood, S S — Belvidere, Il
Dutte, Chss A, a — Chicago, Ill
Evans, Henry H — Carrolton, Aug 26—63
Fendon, Richard D+ — Grand Gulf, May 1—63
Floyd, Albert J+ — Memphis, July 7—63
Follet, Wilbor — St Louis, Jun 30—63
Grosse, Chris+ — Magnolia, May 3—63
Gray, Alfred D — Jeff Barracks, Feb 12—63
Herrick, Wm H+ — Magnolia, May 3—63
Hugget, Geo — Worrenton, June 1—61
Jackson, Jno — Champion Hills, May 16—63
Lodin, Jno W, m — Oshkosh
Mead, Sam'l — Memphis, Aug 11—63
Oliver, Sam'l B — Jeff Barracks, Mar 20—63
O'Rirey, Jno — New Orleans, May 18—65
Ragow, Gottfried — St Louis, Feb 4—63
Sawistaskie, A* — Sabine Cross Road, Apr 8—64
Sering, Herman J+ — Grand Gulf, May 14—63
Wilber, Benj W — New Orleans, Oct 20—63
Wood, Chas — Watertown

DRY GOODS.

~AN IMMENSE STOCK OF~
DRY GOODS OF ALL KINDS,
AT THE LOWEST PRICES.

Silks,
    Shawls,
        Dress Goods,
            Cloaks,
                Hosiery,
                      Millinery Goods.
                        Cloths.
GENTS FURNISHING GOODS,
        KID GLOVES,
            CORSETS.
                LACES.
                    EMBROIDERIES, ETC.

T. A. CHAPMAN & CO.
125, 127, 133, AND 135 WISCONSIN STREET,

WISCONSIN SOLDIERS AND SAILORS REUNION ROSTER.

F

Capt C A Holmes, a   Jefferson
Lt Emil Stoppenbach
Lt Jno B Scott
Lt D M Inman
Lt L W Ostrander
Parker, Benj, sgt⸺   Champion Hills, June 6—63
Poe, Isaac, sgt   Helena, Mar 6-63
Kaltenborn, P, corp* Champ'n Hills, May 16—63
Lang, Paul, corp* Sabine Cross Roads, Apr 8—64
Green, Hiram, corp+   St Louis, Aug 20—63
Alden, Henry   White River, Nov 9 + 64
Bradford, Thos S   Nashua, Ia
Bradford, Albert   Nashua, Ia
Bisset, Jno   Milford
Capen, Geo A   Helena, Mar 31—63
Capen, Jas M   May 31— 63
Cox, Jno   Mauston
Donner, Aug   Natchez, Aug 6—63
Dunham, Jed G   Aztalan, Oct 24—63
Filmore, Jno E   Milford
Farnerock, Henry   Concord
Hager, Jno H   Jackson, July 17—63
Hoseling, Jas E   St Louis, Sept 9- 63
Holmes, Chas A, a   Jefferson
Healy, Somon   Knapp
Jennings, Azar N   Helena, Feb 21—63
Korbendorfer, Jno*   Port Gibson, May 1—63
Krankle, Jno G   Carrollton, June 14—64
Mattis, Jno   Helena, Feb 9—63
Mueller, Henry   Jefferson
Mushelman, Chris   Jefferson
Prefontain, Anthony*   Port Gibson, May 1—63
Phillips, Elijah   Memphis, Mar 29- 63
Phillips, Chas   Milford
Queman, H   Concord
Robish, Gerhard*   Port Gibson, May 1—63
Riggle, Jesse   Friars Point, Dec 19—62
Streich, Aug   Helena, Jan 11- 63
S.hwitzer, Jno   Madison, Oct 13—62
Sawin, Albert   St Louis, June 10—63
Seyfferett, Chris E   Vicksburg, July 3—63
Smith, Andrew   Millikens Bend, Aug 15- 63
Schultz, Jno   New Orleans, Oct 25—64
Schmidt, J M   Helensville
Scribner, Porter, 1   Milford
Sanborn, Wm   Clyde, Kan
Shoop, A   Neillsville
Trump, Jno*   Vicksburg, June 6—63
Tilden, Bradley   Helena, Mar 31—63
Thorn, Jno G   Helena, Feb 21—63
Wolf, Jno, h   Ft Atkinson
Wright, Andrew J   Blakely, Apr 12—65

G

Capt F C Festner
Capt Oscar Mohr
Lt Alba M Kent
Lt Julius Schroeder
O'Brien, Patrick, corp+New Orleans, Apr 18—64
Birk, Mathias+   Champion Hills, May 17—63
Becker, Peter   Memphis, Sept 10—63
Barrett, Jas W   Vermilion Bayou, Nov 14—63
Devoe, Amos   Vicksburg, June 25—63
Fisk, Chas M G*   Champion Hills, May 16—63
Hinds, Michael*   Champion Hills, May 16—63
Hemerly, Fred   Black Earth
Hartman, Wm   May 25—65
Jocham, Jno   Helena, Nov 9—63
Lips, Henry   Millikens Bend, Aug 8—63
Mathews, All A+   Chic'saw Bayou, June 12—63
Marks, Geo S   Helena, Feb 6- 63
Mortenson Hans   May 11- 63
Menden, Christian   Nov 17—63
Martin, Wm   Nov 20—63
McFlory, Hugh   Jan 8—65
R ed, Fred'k   Memphis, Aug 16—63

H

Reich, Chas F W   Helena, Mar 7—63
Ritterbuch, J   Nelson, Neb
Shachte, Hubert   Carrollton, Aug 28 - 63
Schollhausen, Peter   Bon Homme, D T
Utecht, Anton   Sabine Cross Road, Apr 8—64
Worringen, Jno   Memphis, July 29—63
Wheeler, M C   Windsor
Wheeler, Ld G   Windsor

Capt C C Ammack
Capt Jno W Blake
Capt Wm Carroll
Lt Thos DeLaney
Lt Wm Wilson   Watertown
Lt Almon D Gibbs+ New Orleans, Oct 26—63
Updike, Lyman H, 1st sgt   Jan 27 + 63
McMullen, Leslie, sgt   Helena, Mar 7—63
Armstrong, Joel H, sgt   St Louis Jan 30—63
Stark, Robt, sgt   James Plantation May 17—63
Lewis, Fayette, corp   Helena, Feb 23—63
Coyle, Jas, corp   Opelousas, Oct 19—63
Halstead,Albert M, corp New Iberia, Nov 11—63
Noble, Fred'k, corp   New Orleans, Oct 15—63
Bowden, Felix   Helena, Feb 5—63
Bundy, Christian   Cairo, Oct 6—64
Bray, Plummer   Tayler, Oct 20—64
Baker, Israel, me
Cooper, Michael +   Mansfield, Apr 22—64
Cross, Thom   Helena, Feb 5—63
Deverean John   St Charles, Oct 5—64
Delaney, Thom   Milwaukee
Ford, Daniel*   Champion Hills, May 16—63
Fick, Geo   Helena, Mar 4- 63
Ferris, W H   Waupun
Gagon, Michael+   Grand Gulf, May 19—63
Greendeaf, David, O   Vicksburg, July 4—63
Gilan, Mathias   Mobile, May 15—65
Gibson, Geo H   Fox Lake
Hollingsworth, Jesse   Helena, Mar 7—63
Hemingsway, F S   Vernon Centre, Minn
Hewett, Clark   Wampun
Johnson, Chas*   Sabine Cross R, Apr 8—64
Menges, Henry*   Port Gibson, May 1—63
Murry, Jno   Champion Hills, May 23—63
McAviley, Thom+   Grand Gulf, May 28—63
McDonough, Thom+   Memphis, Aug 2—63
Preston, Peter H   Helena, Feb 10—63
Rathburn, Davis,   Memphis, Feb 25—63
Shaffer, Fred'k + Chic'saw Bayou, June 12 63
Tupper, Chas M   New Orleans, Oct 12- 63
Tubbs, Peter, F   Seymour
Wexsung, August
Wicks, A A   Webster City, Ia
Wilson, Wm   Watertown

I

Capt O C Bissell, m   Fond du Lac
Capt W K Barney
Lt E H Cole
Lt H Niederker, J
Cole, Ewd, sgt   Memphis, Mar 8—63
Burney, Juo J, corp*Champion Hills, May 16—63
Anderson, Albert B   Vicksburg, Aug 10—63
Adams, Ewd P   Carrollton, Oct 16—63
Allen, Aaron   New Orleans, June 78—64
Allen, J N   Loyal
Anderson, Albert   Seymour
Allen, Isaac N   Plum City
Baker, Jno W, f   Vicksburg, June 25—63
Benedict, Oscar F*   St Louis, Jan 5—63
Burdick, Harrison A   St Louis, Jan 5—63
Biptil, Oliver C, m   Fond du Lac
Brewster, Harvey, bk   Waupun
Chapman, Orange H   Grand Rapids Mich
Crofut, Jno, f   Rubicon
Cole, Chester R R   Cedar Falls, Ia

Goodall, Ewd   Helena, Mar 16—63
Harter, David M   Hartford
Herrick, Alma, f   Independence, Ia
King, Ewn H   Helena, Mar 16—63
Kern, Sylvester J   Tyler, Nov 24—64
Kern, Geo I   Lebanon
Koller, Konrad, me   Fond du Lac
Lee, Jacob I   St Louis, July 20—63
Lukers, Mathias   Nov 22—63
Leonard, Francis   Lebanon
Martin, Emery   Menominee Falls
McDuffie, Chas   St Louis, Jan 20—63
Miner, J H, peddler   Fond du Lac
Mulholland, Cyrus   Memphis, Mar 9—63
Merrill, Alfred, f   Lebanon
Nansawewn, I   Visalia, Cal
Persons, Francis -   Champion Hills, May 16—63
Peterson, Isaac   New Orleans, Oct 30—63
Persons, Jas H   Plum City
Peterson, Andrew   Alderly
Philpot, E B   Neillsville
Page, Warren   Waupun
Philpot, Tom, me   Loyal
Peterson, Andrew, f   Alderly
Rector, Jas H   Neosho
Mitto, Geo, f   Black Creek
Spaulding, Dennison   June 20—63
Swanton, Jas   Chicago, Aug 6—63
Sayles, James C, m f   Rubicon
Smith, Jno   Alderly
Torbut, Sam'l   Memphis, Mar 3—63
Thayer, Harris R   Madison, Oct 19—62
Thomas, Geo W, el   Blue Earth, Minn
Tubbs, Peter   Seymour
Wiley, Thompson M   Helena, Feb 4—63
Wiley, Wm A   Cairo, Sept 7—63
Whipple, W B   Oshkosh
Welsh, Henry   Loyal
Wood, Geo P, f   California

K

Capt W A Delamatyr
Capt Edwin Marsh
Lt Robt C Gray
Lt Wm V Perry
Lt J G Douglas
Rt J P DeMerritt   Williamstown, Vt
Morrison, Wm A, corp   Helena, Jan 18—63
Walker, Stephen P   Memphis, Aug 7—63
Farlow, Perry C, corp   Feb 5—63
Learn, Jacob J, corp   Carrollton, Aug 19—63
Arnold, Franklin D   Memphis, Feb 13—63
Ascherin, August   St Louis, Apr 29—63
Brown, Wm H +   June 20—63
Burns, Conrad C   New Orleans, June 26—64
Colburn, Norman   Helena, Jan 1—63
Chapman, J F   Neillsville
Dewey, Francis   Helena, Dec 27—62
David, Thos P   Helena, Feb 13—63
Eggert, Julius | Champion Hills, May 21—6
Ellis, M J   Fenuimore
Elkins, J H   Waupun
Forward, Marshall   Apr 27—63
Francis Oscar   Sauk City, Ia
Gilbert, Lyman B   Helena, Mar 8—63
Gillet, Leander M   Helena, Dec 26—62
Hart, Benj H   Helena, Jan 4—63
Hamilton, Alvin W   Helena, Jan 16—63
Hodge, Sam'l J   Helena, Jan 17—63
Hamilton, Avery G   Helena, Dec 25—62
Hales, B F, d   Hancock
Hyde, E B   Retreat
Mick, Philip   New Orleans, Oct 16—63
Nash, Jno   Friars Point, Dec 6—62
Owen, Peter+   Champion Hills, May 20—63
Page, Warner   Helena, Jan 14—63
Peterson, Peter   St Charles, Sept 14—64
Page, Warren   Waupun
Page, W V   Beaver Dam

FOND DU LAC COUNTY ABSTRACT OFFICE,

GREENE & NEWTON, Prop's.

INSURANCE AND LOAN AGENCY,

CORNER COURT AND MACY STREETS, OPPOSITE REGISTER'S OFFICE,

FOND DU LAC, - - WIS.

Resident Agents of the Following Well Known Insurance Companies:

LIVERPOOL AND LONDON AND GLOBE.

UNDERWRITERS AGENCY, N. Y.

NATIONAL OF HARTFORD.

JAMES T. GREENE,	HORACE W. NEWTON,
NOTARY PUBLIC	CITY ENGINEER,
AND CONVEYANCER.	ALL ORDERS FOR
Loans Negotiated, Titles Perfected	Surveying in City and County,
And all business pertaining to Real Estate	PROMPTLY ATTEND'D TO.
GIVEN PROMPT ATTENTION.	

WISCONSIN SOLDIERS AND SAILORS REUNION ROSTER.

Rogers, Franklin D — Carrollton, Oct 6—63
Streeter, Benj — Island 63, Nov 2—64
Smith, Ira H — Helena, Apr 16—63
Spaulding, Jno — Helena, Mar 25—63
Smith, Newton S — June 24—63
Schwartz, Chas — Williamstown, Oct 7—65
Tripp, Jas P — Friars Point, Dec 12—64
Thele, Henry — Geneva, Ia
Thede, Henry — Geneva, Ia

UNASSIGNED.

Brisben, S f — Palmyra
Buckingham, J O — Fort Atkinson
Bighow, W — Eagle
Chase, T W — Jefferson
Chase, S — Jefferson
Demeritt, Jno P, cl — Williamstown, Vt
Fose, Z, f — Janesville
Hulbart, G, f — East Troy
Harnton, W H, f — Madison
Judson, S — Rome
Krouse, R, m — Hebron
Leaver, F, f — Eagle
More, H, m — Fort Atkinson
Malthrop, W C — Rome
McKinnon, R M, m — East Troy
McMarkley, N — Eagle
Peck, W, f — Sun Prairi
Prell, W — Rome
Purkins, E T — Jefferson
Ray, J, f — Palmyra
Reeves, A J — Jefferson
Reeves, S — Jefferson
Stevenson, J S — Eagle
Spurbeck, R, f — Palmyra
Smith, H A — Fort Atkinson
Sears, L G — Rome, Ga
Tubbs, L C — Whitewater
Vaulone, F, f — Hebron
Weener, A O — Watertown

THIRTIETH INFANTRY.

Three years. Organized, October 21st, 1862. Original strength, 906, gain by recruits, etc., 313. Total, 1219. Death loss, 63—killed in action, 1, died of wounds, 1, of disease, 67. Other losses, 439—missing, 0, desertions, 62, transfers, 46, discharges, 340. Strength at muster-out, September 20th, 1865, 712. Campaigns in D. T., Lake Superior, Wis., Ky.

REGIMENTAL ROSTER.

Col Dan'l J Dill — Prescott
Lt Col Ed M Bartlett — Eau Claire
Maj Jno Clowney — Mineral Point
Adj T C Spencer
Q M S S Starr — Hudson
Q M F A Dresser — Osceola
Surg Otis Hoyt — Hudson
A Surg Wm Robbins
A Surg Ed O Baker — Menomine
A Surg Ed J Farr — Eau Claire
A Surg H B Jaggar — Hudson

A

Capt Sam'l Harriman — Somerset
Capt Arthur L Cox — Santa Rosa, Cal
Lt Henry A Wilson — St Paul, Minn
Lt Jas H Van Meter — Hudson
Smith, F J, sgt-maj — Richmond
Sherburne, A J, sgt — Troy
Martin, Herrich, sgt — Hudson
Martin, Geo, sgt — Madison, Jan 15—63
Young, Rufus R, sgt — Troy
Goodwin, Jack, corp, m — River Falls
Phillips, Thos B, corp — Richmond
Vanmeter, Abe, corp, ed — New Richmond

Wade, Henry, corp, f — Kansas
Young, Rufus, corp — Hudson
Lamp's on, Lew, corp, d — Roberts
Goodwin, A J, corp — Troy
Porter, Thos, corp — Richmond
Ammeren, Peter, f — New Richmond
All, Win, m — Stillwater, Minn
Ammerman, P S — Richmond
Bushnell, Al W — Ft Rice, Sept 23—61
Buckwheat, David, m — Hudson
Bishop, W R — Hammond
Chambers, David S — Madison, Jan 8—63
Crawford, Arch, d — New Richmond
Currier, Geo W — Bowling Green, Dec 18—64
Dinsmore, H F, asst p m — Hudson
Dawley, L W — Richmond
Day, E W — Troy
Dean, Jas W — Black Brook
Dolly, Ephriam, c — New Richmond
Dinsmore, Harry, f — Clayton
Dinsmore, D F — St Croix
Ensign, W S — River Falls
Egbert, W J — Hammond
Godfry, Geo W — Louisville, Aug 14—65
Godfrey, Arthur, f — Osceola
Goodnoe, M — Warren
Healey, Ezra, f — River Falls
Hoddkiss, Serant, f — River Falls
Huddkiss, Wm — Ellsworth
Hotchkiss, A J — Warren
Herrick, M — Hudson
Jones, Jno C — St Croix
Law, Frank — Richmond
Marshall, W P — Troy
Nash, Jno M — St Croix
Nye, Stephen — River Falls
Phillips, Aaron — Richmond
Phillips, Thos B — New Richmond
Phillips, Aaron, f — Boardman
Peabody, A G, f — Hammond
Patterson, Al, f — Hammond
Plumb, Chas, f — Hammond
Starkweather, S D — Clear Lake
Sanford, O D, f — Roberts

B

Sanford, O P — Warren
Taylor, Benj — Madison, Jan 10—63
Taft, Leonard, expressman — New Richmond
Vassaw, Jos — Star Prairie
Watson, Geo — Louisville, Feb 22—65
Willis, Cyrus, f — Bangor

C

Capt Thom Priestly — Mineral Point
Lt Wm H Gill — Nebraska
Lt Thos O Kent — Mineral Point
Burton, Lewis S, capt — Mineral Pt, Nov 6—64
Carter, Sheldon W, corp — Mineral Pt Apr 30—63
Bowes, Jno — Mifflin
David, Luther O — Milwaukee, Mar 7—64
Dixon, L C, me — Darlington
Delap, Robt M — Madison, Jan 17—64
Priestley, Thos — Mineral Point
Sands, Wm — Dodgeville
Watkins, Christopher C — Uklah City, Col

Capt Alex A Arnold — Galesville
Lt D D Chappell — Galesville
Lt C K Turner
Lt Jno McMaster
Lt H A Towner
Betts, Oscar B — Madison, Jan 26—63
Beardsley, Henry D — Ft Rice, Aug 2—64
Case, Geo F — St Joseph, Nov 21—61
Gilbrutson, Andrew — Ft Rice, Sept 26—62
Lein, Jno — Quincy, Dec 14—64
Olson, Edrat+ — New Lisbon, Sept 10—63
Patt, A C — Neillsville

Shaw, Wm — Madison, Jan 18—63
Shafer, Chester — Oxfordville
Simpson, Jas W — Cross Plains
VanSiyke, David O — Galesville
Wilcox, Thos D — Trempeleau

D

Capt D C Fulton — Hudson
Capt L O Marshall — River Falls
Lt C E Darling — Hudson
Lt W A Robinson — Nashua, N H
Lt W H McDiarmid — Hudson
Kilpher, Peter, sgt — St Croix
Adam, C — Lyon
Briggs, B A — Baldwin
Carsley, D O — Baldwin
Casey, Jno — Richmond
Day, Lucius — Cherry Valley W T
Frayzer, Geo — Cherry Valley, W T
Goff, G M — Tiffany
Getchel, Prescott — Ft Sully, D T, Apr 27—64
Johnson, Jos — Richmond
Johnson, Eugene — Madison, Apr 30—63
Kinne, Jno D — Richmond
Keech, G W — St Croix
Kaufman, Jno — St Croix
Longworth, J — Warren
Longfellow, Geo W — Madison, Apr 7—63
LaFlore, L — Warren
Link, Jas — Richmond
Little, Daniel — Somerset
McDoffin, C — Warren
McNamara, Michael — Ft Sully, D T Apr 16—64
Marshall, S O — River Falls
Narey, Philip — Erie Prairie
O'Rourke, Jno — Troy
Parant, E — Somerset
Smith, J A — Cylon
Stoddard, Washington — Lorhue l
Tarkelson, Tonla — Ft Rice, D T, July 27—64

E

Capt Edw Derlio — Mineral Point
Lt S W Smith
Capt D D Chappell — Galesville
Lt Edw C Foster
Lt Jno T Jones — Mineral Point
Lt Walter Evans
Deitzman, David — Mifflin
Deizman Jno H — Washburn
Davis, Jno E — Sparta
Dolphin, Jno, f — Rock Falls, Ia
Devlin, Ewd — Mineral Point
Hutson, J C — Spring Green
James, Jno T — Dodgeville
Jones, Peter — Mifflin
Jones, Jno T — Dodgeville
Laud, A H a — Clarion, Ia
Martin, Sam'l — Madison, Jan 5—63
Prisk, Paul — Mineral Point, Oct 27—63
Streeter, H R — Fennimore

F

Capt E A Meacham — Prescott
Lt E B Strong
Lt L Boud Gunn
Lt C H Grant — Drummond Bluff
Danforth, Chas W, corp — Madison, Jan 13—64
Brown, C W, corp — Ellsworth
Brown, C W — Ellsworth
Bickford, Lyman — Louisville, Feb 25—65
Cross, F A — Fergus Falls, Min
Cornelison, Jno W — Trimbebe
Craven, Leno — July 3—64
Flagg, Jno A — Ft Rice, Oct 1—64
Gregory, Corwin — Madison, Dec 1— 2
Loomis, Ewd — Hales Corners
Messer, J T — Troy

WISCONSIN SOLDIERS AND SAILORS REUNION ROSTER.

Miller, Jno M	Madison, Nov 24—62	Capt E B Strong		Newton, Geo W	Lynville
Stewart, Jonas B	Louisville, Feb 18—65	Lt Geo E Dinsmore	New Richmond	Strong, Milo G	Seneca
Stowell, Ambrose	Jan 26—64	Lt M F Hubbard	La Crosse	Vaughn, A P E	Columbus, Mar 24—63
Sechell, Geo E	Ft Sully, June 7—64	Lt Sam'l Casmer		Wallin, A C	Prairie du Chien
Sherman, Sam'l	Dartford	Stilson, Leonard F, 2orp	Madison, Jan 22—63	Washington, G	Atlanta, Aug 2—61
Truesdale, Jno D	Louisville, Apr 27—65	Adkins, Henry B	Elkhorn	Welch, J D	Columbus, Sept 1—63
White, J G	Fond du Lac	Ashley, Abram, f	River Falls		
Winter, Chas W	Crow Creek, May 8—64	Burnett, Chas E	River Falls		
West, Nelson M	Madison, Apr 6—63	Dinsmore, G F	New Richmond	**B**	

G

		Fitch, Truman	Appleton	Capt R B Stephenson	
		Tidler, Louis	Louisville, Aug 18- 65	Capt Nathaniel B Treat	
		Hubbard, M F	La Crosse	Lt Thos Beattie	
Capt Asa B Swain		Michael, Manuel M	Burlington, Ia	Lt Jno T McKnight	
Capt H J Curtice		Marshall, W P	River Falls	Lt Allen J Canfield	
Lt Jno E Tilton		Paddock, Wm	Chippewa Falls	Babson, J E, m	Mormontown, Ia
Lt B C Hugoboom	Louisville, Aug 1—65	Servis, G	La Crosse	Biniside'l, C E	In the field N C, Mar 18—65
Lt H F Treadwell		Stanton, James	Bowling Green, Jan 7—65	Hesley, Yost	Madison, Dec 9- 63
Lt P J Haskins		Tubman, Noble, f	Baldwin	Knobel, C	New York City, Mar 27 -46
Cuyswell, Jno J, 1st sgt	Lona, May 28—65	Winter, Chas H	Louisville, Feb 27—65	Willman, F C	Monroe, Mar 24—64
Burbank, Lester, me	Oakland, Cal	**UNASSIGNED.**		Norder, F	Columbus, Sept 29—64
Burk, J	Mazomanie			Schober, S	Chattanooga, Sept 19—64
Bruce, Augustus J	Davenport, Feb 8—64	Star, Sidney, capt	Hudson	Sierd, E -	Goldsboro, Mar 16- 65
Cornwell, Leroy	Plainfield	Armstrong, L P	Clarion, Ia	Virtue, T	Monroe, Dec 6—63
Coon, Alfred M	Ft Snelling, Nov 10—64	Gleason, Arthur.	Chicago	Webster, E C	Argyle, Dec 28 —62
Gould, Jonas	Davenport, Mar 24—64	Jagger, H E	Hudson		
Gamble, Alex, me	Fargo, D T	Knudteson, Knudte	Blair		
Hirst, Thos, f	Hancock	Packard, M W, m	Snohomich, Wash Ter	**C**	
Keilerson, Peter	Davenport, Apr 15—61	Packard, Jno W	Snohomieh, Wash Ter	Capt Ira D Burdick	
McNabb, Jno	Springfield	Starr, S S	Hudson	Capt Wm Williamson	
O'Connell, Jno	Madison			Lt Paul Jerneau	
Parkin, Jos	Coloma			Lt Sam'l Dunstan	
Rozell, W H	Vesper	### THIRTY-FIRST INFANTRY.		Anderson, Ole, f	Dodgeville
Sherman, Henry	Berlin			Beaumont, G H	Hyde's Mill
Sprat, Geo M	Dearfield, June 28—61			Bliss, N S	Nashville, Dec 29—61
Spear, Samuel M	Louisville, July 16—65			Bliss, F R	Chattahoochie River, Sept 1—64
Trabern, Knos F	Davenport, Mar 4—64	Three years. Organized January 13th, 1863.		Bliss, H C	Hart, Mich
Warden, Chester	Madison, Apr 7—66	Original strength, 678, gained by recruits, etc. 200.		Brunner, Casper	Hyde Mills
		Total, 1078. Death loss, 114—killed in action, 13.		Butler, Louis H	Columbus, July 24—63
		died of wounds, 9, of disease, 92. Other		Carter, Henry, f	Dodgeville
H		losses, 254—missing 2, desertion, 52, transfers		Collinwood, N H, f	Dodgeville
Capt Andrew Bedal		53, discharges, 167. Strength at muster out, July		Cowen, D A	Columbus, Apr 4—63
Lt Geo Marshall		8th, 1865, 70. Campaigns in Ky., Tenn., Ala.,		Crook, Peter Jr, f	Dodgeville
Lt Jos Matthews	Nebraska	Ga., S. C., N. C.		Davis, Thos, m	Dodgeville
Lt Wm H Hews	Kansas			Dielmuhl, Jno	Dodgeville
Lt Chester Clark		### REGIMENTAL ROSTER.		Enoch, M	Murfreesboro, Jan 16—61
Aiken, Granville	Chaseburg	Col Isaac E Messmore		Haskins, A W	Crawford Co, Nov 19—62
Brush, J W	Brushville	Col Francis H West	Milwaukee	Holdsworth, Jno	Columbus, June 22— 3
Baxter, H D	Berlin	Col Geo D Rogers		Hubbard, P A	Hyde's Mill
Bronson, Addison	Oct 19—31	Maj Jno Clowney		Jones, E D, f	Dodgeville
Carpenter, Wm J	Leon, Jan 22—3	Maj Wm J Gibson	Ft Halleck, Sep 9—63	Jones, R B	Madison, Dec 7—63
Corbitt, Wm H	Ft Rice, Oct 8—64	Maj E B Stephenson		Latham, J L	Madison, Dec 20—61
Crouch, Jas	Louisville, Feb 5—65	Maj Farlin Q Ball	Chicago, Ill	Lovell, Jas, f	Dodgeville
Dudley, Geo	Madison, Feb 12—63	Adj Jas F Suddath		Mabbott, J R	Helena
Ingraham, Clement	Berlin	Q M Rufus King		Mabbott, J T	Bentonville, Nov 19—63
Larson, Peter	Madison, Feb 21—63	Q M Wm F Benson		McMahon, J	Chattanooga, Nov 28 - 64
Marshall, Wm	Madison, Jun 31—63	Q M Jas E Owens		Richards, H	New Albany, Oct 1—63
Richardson, Daniel	Madison, Dec 11—64	Surg Geo D Wilber		Rydards, Jno*	Bentonville, Mar 19—65
		Surg Darius Mason		Ryall, Jno	Murfreesboro, Dec 17—63
		Surg Peter S Arndt		Smith, W H	Ridgeway, July 25—63
I		Surg Wm M Thomas		Stundart, J L, f	Lecmore, Cal
Capt N B Greer		A Surg Jos B Galier		Stevens, P T, county surveyor	Dodgeville
Lt Chas Buckman		A Surg H S Bascom		Thomas Benj W, e	Dodgeville
Lt Benj Cowin		A Surg Jas M Ball		Villemonte, F G	Arena
Hall, Orin C, sgt	Ft Union, Apr 27—65	Chap Alfred Drinson		Wickham, D, sgt*	Bentonville, Mar 19—63
Anderson, Peter	Eau Claire	Chap Nathan Woodworth		Williams, S	Chattanooga, Jan 2—65
Boynton, David A	Ft Union, Apr 4—65				
Buck, Norman L	Eau Claire				
Crockett, E W, f	Augusta	**A**		**D**	
Howard, Henry W	Sussex				
Koethe, Berthold	Ft Union, Mar 16—65			Capt Ormsby B Thomas	
Masters, Richard	Milwaukee, Apr 5—61	Capt Henry A Chase		Capt Nathaniel C Denio	
Perry, Phil	Madison June 3—3	Lt Geo F Lewis		Lt Chas M Lockwood	
Pritchard, Sam'l	Ft Union, Apr 5- 65	Lt Henry C Anderson		Lt David VanWirt	
Rolf, Wm H	D T, July 3—63	Lt Geo Lyman		Coleman, Nathan	Columbus, July 9—63
Schilling, Chas	Racine	Haley, Wm L	Madison	Coleman, D V, f	Bell Centre
Way, Henry J	Ft Union, Apr 24—65	Hill, Geo B	Savannah, Jun 2—62	Coleman, Jno	Bell Centre
Weirick, Wm	Ft Union, May 7—65	Johnson, Isaac	Wauzeka, Jun 19—65	Copper, M T C	Murfreesboro, June 29—64
		Johnson, W *	Bentonville, Mar 19—65	Kast, J N	Bell Centre
		La Point, Luke	Racine, Jan 3—63	Lemons, David	Atlanta, Sep 17—64
K		Michaels, J	Lynville	Lenox, Wesley	Bell Centre
Capt Jno Klatt		Montgomery, A	Soldiers Grove	Mars, Jos	Columbus, Aug 7—63

North Side of Public Square,

LANT WOOD, PROP.,

Co. I. 32d Wisconsin Infantry.

JAMES L. CLARK,

Manufacturer of

THE  MATCHES!

The celebrated "STAR MATCHES" are the best and most economical in use. Orders for matches filled with promptness and dispatch. Address

JAMES L. CLARK,

P. O. Drawer 1693, OSHKOSH, WIS.

HOME
INSURANCE COMPANY OF N. Y.

OFFICE, NO. 119 BROADWAY.

Fifty-Third Semi-Annual Statement,

Showing the Condition of the Company on the First day of

JANUARY, 1880.

CASH CAPITAL,	$3,000,000.00
Reserve for Re-Insurance,	1,841,438.00
Reserve for Unpaid Losses,	248,764.81
Net Surplus,	1,320,785.30
CASH ASSETS,	$6,410,988.11

J. H. WASHBURN, Secretary,   CHAS. J. MARTIN, President.
T. B. GREENE, } Ass't Sec's.   A. F. WILLMARTH, Vice-Pres't.
EDW. H. AHERN,   D. A. HEALD, 2d Vice-Pres't.

A Dividend of Five per cent. has been declared payable on demand.

WEAR RESISTING

At "Resistless Prices" made at

GLUCK'S
TEMPLE
OF
FASHION.

NOBBY BUSINESS SUIT.

Made to order for $20 and upward.   NO FIT, NO PAY.

INSPECTION KINDLY SOLICITED.

Gluck's Temple of Fashion,   7 Grand Avenue.

P. S. To accommodate out of town customers we will send, on application, samples of goods, fashion plate, and our rules of self measurement and forward all orders by express C. O. D.

THIRTY-SECOND INFANTRY.

Three years. Organized Sept. 25th, 1862. Original strength, 950, gain by recruits, etc, 481. Total 1474. Death loss, 275–killed in action, 17, died of wounds, 10, of disease, 244, of accidents, 4. Other losses, 274–missing, 0, desertions, 58, transfers, 27, discharges, 189. Strength at muster out, July 12th, 1865, 925. Campaigns in Tenn., Miss., Ala., Ga., N. C. and S. C.

REGIMENTAL ROSTER.

Col Jas H Howe	Kenosha
Col C H DeGroat	Fond du Lac
Lt Col W A Bugh	Berlin
Lt Col A B Smedley	Cresco, Ia
Lt Col J H Carleton	Kenosha
Maj W S Burrows	Michigan
Adj H M Beckwith	Plattsburg, N Y
Adj J S Styles	Minneapolis, Minn
Q M G P Farnsworth	Green Bay
Q M W A Tanner	Memphis
Q M S L Brasted, a	Fond du Lac
Surg Geo D Wilbur	Mineral Point
Surg Simon L Ford	Edgerton
Srg Geo W Fay	Menasha
Surg J Copp Noyes	Oshkosh
A Surg Jas LeBow	
A Surg S W Dunn	
A Surg Solomon Blood	
A Surg J L Sheppard	Sheboygan Falls
Chap S Fallows	
Chap J B Buchman	Chicago, Ill

A

Capt C H DeGroat	Fond du Lac
Capt Geo W Woodruff	Otero, New Mexico
Lt H C Glendinning	Minnesota
Lt E B Crofoot	Fond du Lac
Lt H D Carter	
Clark, H A, f	Fond du Lac
Clark, James, f	Fond du Lac
Clark, J P	Decatur, Apr 10–64
Clement, A	Decatur, July 17–64
Colbert, J H	Alexandria, May 23–65
Cowles, M T	Nashville, Sept 17–64
Crofoot, E B, f	Fond du Lac
Cruzin, R P	Atlanta, Oct 23–64
DeGroat, C H, mf	Fond du Lac
Drayers, G H	Memphis, Feb 17–63
Frost, W H+	Beaufort, Feb 20–65
Frost, J W	Memphis, Apr 16–63
Gaylord, R A	Memphis Sept 7–63
Gowin, S J	Decatur, Aug 16–64
Grace, E T	Memphis, Jan 29–64
Graham, A G	Madison, Nov 20–63
Grant, Chas H	Wilton
Grapp, Wm	Gordon, Nov 12–64
Hart, Daniel S	Merrimac
Kaern, P	Goldsboro, Mar 23–65
Korschot, D J	Decatur, June 4–64
Leroy, Beardsley	Waupun
Landry, Christopher	Milwaukee
Marshall, B H	Fond du Lac, Oct 11–64
McClain, O	Pocotaligo, Jan 5–65
Mentor, R H, corp	Decatur, June 21–64
Mitchell, T	Memphis, Dec 20–63
Miller, Maritz A, f	Langlade
Oliver, J W, ed	Waupun
Palmer, J G H, me	Fond du Lac
Pedix, Jas	Fond du Lac
Preston, W	Jackson, Feb 2–63
Rourdink, G W	Memphis, Sept 27–63
Russell, R	Decatur, May 12–64
Smith, D	Memphis, Mar 13–63
Terbeest, J	Memphis, June 11–63

Matthews, J P, corp	Savannah, Jan 20–65
Murphy, Patrick	Soldiers Grove
Price, R	Nashville, June 19–64
Sherwood, N*	Atlanta, Aug 1–64
St German, D	Neillsville
Turk, E H	Bell Centre
Twining, D M	Bell Centre
Wooborn, B D	Towerville

E

Capt Jas B Mason	Nashville, Oct 17–63
Capt Daniel B Dipple	
Lt Hiram Stevens	
Lt Chas R Bridgman	
Anderson, E	Columbus, May 16–63
Bayley, C H G, sgt*	Atlanta, July 23–64
Black, L P D	Gratiot, June 8–63
Burritt, D M	Nashville, Apr 20–64
Collins, P, sgt	Wiota, July 23–63
Greidenwise, Peter	Murfreesboro, Dec 18–63
Hanson, Lewis	Columbus, July 27–63
Harker, J, sgt	Murfreesboro, Dec 16–63
Kinsman, Thos, f	Fayette
Lath, H B	Columbus, Oct 9–63
Letkin, Seth H, f	Doniphan, Neb
O'Connell, Timothy	St Croix
Rood, Ole C	Jeff Barracks, Feb 7–65
Taylor, T J*	Bentonville, Mar 20–65

F

Capt Chas W Burns	
Lt Chas L Fayette	
Lt Jas Raynor	
Lt Oliver S Putnam	
Aldrich, W C	Racine, Dec 19–63
Church, Wm	Murfreesboro, Nov 29–63
Davis, A L	Chattanooga, Nov 8–64
Dunn, Wm N	Albany, Aug 27–63
Farmer, W D*	Savannah, Dec 9–64
Klaesy, G	Winona, Sept 12–63
Laird, J	Murfreesboro, Jan 9–64
Lewis, Alfred	Racine, Feb 22–63
Martin, Patrick	St Joseph, Mo
Shaw, Adney N	Chicago, Sep 25–63
Whipple, Jno W	Attica

G

Capt Geo D Rogers	Atlanta, Aug 12–64
Capt Farlin Q Ball	Chicago, Ill
Lt Jas P Corbin	
Lt Gilleri N Rogers	Aug 12–64
Lt Edwin E Cunnni	
Hanson, Henry	Argyle, Sep 25–63
Hecr, F	Nashville, Jan 13–64
Jackson, C*	Atlanta, July 28–64
Layton, John	Monroe, May 8–64
Manson, Wm*	Bentonville, Mar 19–65
McDonald, Jas	
Mudgett, W H	Columbus, Sep 4–63
Mozzey, P D	Murfreesboro, Sep 2–61
Smith, G+	Kingston, Aug 9–64
Stuller, U	Columbus, Mar 7–63
Tuttle, Wm H	Murfreesboro, Mar 9–64

H

Capt Edw K Buttrick	
Capt Byron Hewitt	
Lt Jno P Willard	
Lt Sam'l J Hooker	
Lt Alex F Cook	
Downs, J, corp+	Nashville, Aug 29–64
Hall, David	Murfreesboro, Nov 20–63
Lattin, C C	Madison, Oct 28–63
Magrane, J, sgt	Dodgeville, July 27–64

I

Malamphy, G	
Manly, R	Murfreesboro, Dec 19–63
McGinnis, M	Racine, Jan 30–64
Moshier, H	Alexandria, May 18–65
Murray, M	Cairo, Sept 27–63
Porter, C	Madison, Apr 9–63
Putman, Oliver S	Brodhead
Richards, J	Monroe, April 28–65
Ruskirk, Jno	Chattanooga, Sept 27–63
Schletter, C	New York City, Apr 20–65
Strader, D	Columbus, July 23–63
Weeks, Steve	Neillsville

I

Capt Jno B Vliet	
Capt Martin C Short, ed	Brandon
Lt Elvin H Smith	Chicago, Ill
Lt Edwin Turner	
Bancroft, R L, ar	Menominee
Barnes, Wm	Murfreesboro, Dec 28–63
Beecher, Philip	Jeffersonville, Dec 16–64
Bevens, Eli	Chesterfield, Mar 8–65
Callender, Richard	Raymond
Cromwell, G F+	Goldsboro, Mar 23–65
Dent, Thos W, c	Mason City, Ia
Dent, Jno T	Nashville, Sept 7–64
Holloway, L W+	Nashville, Aug 31–64
Keen, Wm	Racine, Dec 24–63
Overton, G W	Chattanooga, July 31–64
Peat, T	Columbus, Oct 15–63
Sawley, W F*	Bentonville, Mar 19–65
Schuoley, S	Atlanta, Oct 1–64
Scott, Walter	Racine
Walther, F, corp	Atlanta, July 27–64
Wilcox, J P	Newbern, Apr 9–65
Williams, Fred H L	Dartford

K

Capt Edwin A Bottum	
Capt Geo R Peek	Topeka, Kan
Lt Leonard A Looney	
Lt T B Bronson	
Lt Alex F Cook	
Lt Orville Strong	
Bacon, E N	Milwaukee
Carpenter, O T	Adairsville, July 17–64
Cook, Lyman	North Star
Cook, Fox	Milwaukee
Dresal, Phil, f	Kenosha
Farrell, Pat	Murfreesboro, May 25–64
Gilmes, Dan'l	Nashville
Hope, Robt	Wisconsin, July 21–63
McClure, J A	Columbus, Oct 1–63
McCullick, D J	Columbus, May 9–63
Peek, Geo R	Topeka, Kan
Porter, C W	Arena
Rogers, Geo D	Minneapolis, Minn
Smith, Jno F+	Atlanta, July 31–64
Smith, J J	Murfreesboro, Apr 1–64
Thomas, R M+	Bentonville, Mar 20–65
Van Ellen, Stephen	Oregon
West, F H	Milwaukee
Wilsey, J	Columbus, July 31–63
Wright, Z, corp+	Savannah, Feb 21–63

UNASSIGNED.

Harrington, S L*	Averysboro, Mar 16–65
Campbell, M	Oshkosh
Dean, Geo	Seneca
Dibble, Jno*	Atlanta, July 22–61
Hall, Levi N	Racine, Jan 16–63
Hoyt, Erastus C	Albany, Aug 27–63
Lewis, Al T	Chicago, Ill
Russell, Thos P, ph	Oshkosh
Strong, Orville	Dodgeville
Wiley, Jas	East Troy

J. H. MARSTON.   ESTABLISHED IN 1869.   C. A. BEVERIDGE.

MARSTON & BEVERIDGE,

PROPRIETORS OF

APPLETON HUB AND SPOKE
FACTORY.

AGRICULTURAL IMPLEMENT STOCK.
ALSO DEALERS IN ALL KINDS OF

WAGON STOCK.

APPLETON,   WISCONSIN.

WEBSTER & LAWSON,
PROPRIETORS

Menasha Hub, Spoke & Bending

WORKS,

DEALERS IN ALL KINDS OF

Wagon and Carriage Material,

AND HARD AND SOFT LUMBER.

MENASHA,   -   WISCONSIN.

UNITED STATES BRANCH
OF THE

QUEEN

Fire Insurance Company
OF

LIVERPOOL AND LONDON.

TRUSTEES IN NEW YORK.
SAMUEL D. BABCOCK,   WILLIAM H. MACY,
Babcock Brothers & Co.   Pres. Seaman's Savings Bank
JAMES M. MORRISON,
Pres. Manhattan Bank.

DIRECTORS IN NEW YORK.
ALL OF WHOM ARE STOCKHOLDERS.
SAMUEL D. BABCOCK,   F. H. N. WHITING,
HENRY F. SPAULDING,   J. BOORMAN JOHNSTON,
MARTIN BATES,   DAVID BINGHAM,
H. B. CLAFLIN,   JOSIAH M. FISKE.

Wm. H. ROSS,
Manager.

GEO. A. DRESSER,   J. A. HOYT,
General Agent.   Sup't of Agencies

37 & 39 WALL STREET. NEW YORK.

WISCONSIN SOLDIERS AND SAILORS REUNION ROSTER.

Town, J G — Memphis, Oct 16 –63
Vanderbeck, A — Memphis, Nov 15—62
Ward, Wm — Wonewoc
Wooden, J — La Grange, Feb 2—63
Woodward, A* — Atlanta, Aug 14—64
Young, Byron T — Belvidere, Feb

B

Capt Wm R Hodges — St Louis, Mo
Capt A S Bixby — Illinois
Lt Geo Patten —
Lt A M Bly — Brandon
Lt Aug C Gregory —
Lt Luther Spalding — Troy
Alexander, J C — Memphis, Nov 26—62
Andrews, R — Memphis, July 1—63
Bennett, H — Memphis, Aug 7—63
Bentley, Geo — Lomira
Bly, A M, f — Brandon
Churchill, C J — Alexandria, May 19—65
Comstock, O — Memphis, Jan 8—63
Craig, R — Decatur, Aug 2—64
Curtis, G — Memphis, Dec 9–62
Elliott, C — Memphis, Mar 7—63
Everhard, A B, corp — Memphis, May 24—63
Ferguson, L, m — Brandon
Frelinghuysen, H* — Salkahatchie, Feb 3—65
Gee, T A* — Salkahatchie, Feb 3—65
Haste, A, corp+ — Rome, Aug 21—64
Heminway, Aaron — Berlin
Hickey, D — Rosendale, Sep 27—63
Jackson, G W — Decatur, July 6—64
Johnson, S D — Lafayette, Jan 22—61
Johnson, O F — Savannah, Jan 3—46
Kinney, F L — Oshkosh, Oct 29—62
Kinney, E L — St Louis, Apr 6—63
Marsh, W C — Port Aurelin, Ja
Moor, T W — Atlanta, Oct 27—61
Mossin, Elisha B — Mather
Ormond, T — Memphis, Apr 22—63
Palmer, J — Memphis, Apr 8—61
Pease, D H, corp — Keokuk, June 23—61
Powers, L J — Chicago, June 30—61
Reilly, Thos — Mauston
Rheborse, J B — Jackson, Jan 25—63
Schofield, Henry M — Zumbrota, Minn
Sheldon, B F, corp + — Hilton Head, Feb 7—63
Sherwood, O — Memphis, July 2—63
Smith, A R H+ — Beaufort, Mar 1—65
Smith, J* — Salkahatchie, Feb 3—63
Stoner, Wm — Merrimac
Sumner, J A — La Grange, Jan 24—63
Taylor, J — Valley
Thorn, G, corp — Lomira, Aug 13—63
Webster, G — Metomen, Sept 24—63

C

Capt Jas H Carleton — Kenosha
Capt W D Arnold — Milwaukee
Lt Jas H Hubbard — *Princeton
Lt A S Tucker — Berlin
Lt Josiah Brown — Minnesota
Lt L S Knox — Markesan
Anglum, Wm, f — Green Lake
Arnold, Wiley B, pa — Milwaukee
Avery, L F — Rochester, Minn
Bates, G H — Memphis, June 17—63
Chaplin, L — Holly Springs, Dec 29 –62
Casily, N — Memphis, Feb 27—63
Daniels, W H — Jeffersonville, July 8 –61
Davis, H, f — Redwood Falls, Minn
Deidrich, Jno, f — Berlin
Duncan, E H, f — Berlin
Dyer, J+ — Rome, Aug 28—61
Evans, Wm — Decatur, July 23—61
Frink, J E — Cairo, Apr 9–61
Genung, P — Memphis, Aug 10—63
Green, A G — Brownsville, Feb 29—61

Gr.df, Thos, p m — Berlin
Griffeth, Wm — Berlin
Griffith, W, f — Dodge Centre, Minn
Hadley, L H — Memphis, Dec 1—63
Herman, A J* — Courtland, July 27—61
Steward, C — Vicksburg, May 14—64
Huntress, M P — Williams, Mar 31 –63
Henke, Wm — Vicksburg, May 14—64
Lowe, W P, sgt* — Atlanta, Aug 15—64
Noble, C V — Memphis, Dec 30—62
Lee, Richard, — Sand Creek
Sharp, Jas M, f — Hooks Point, Ia
Sherwood, J A, f — Green Lake
Shiner, Chas — Memphis, July 30—63
Shiney, Lewis — Sioux City, Ia
Simmons, Stephen — Berlin
Smith, J E — Memphis, Mar 31—63
Smith, C W — Memphis, Sep 2–63
Steward, C — Memphis, Mar 29—63
Stoddard, H — Beaufort, Feb 21—65
Tucker, Alfred, city clerk — Berlin
Utley, W H — Decatur, July 12—61
VanDusen, T — Jonesboro, Sept 3 –61
Walker, R R — Oxford, Dec 17—64
White, G H — Decatur, July 12—64
Williams, C — Memphis, June 21—63
Wright, J E — La Grange, Jan 12—63

D

Capt Jas Freeman — Oshkosh
Lt W A Tanner — Memphis, Tenn
Lt B L Cornish — Oshkosh
Lt A J Lapham —
Armstrong, G — Decatur, July 12—61
Barlow, Geo — Sun Prairie
Barnett, J — St Louis, Jan 8—62
Bradley, W — Jackson, Jan 13—63
Campbell, Mason — Oshkosh
Cameron, J F — Oct 5—63
Carpenter, C M — Memphis, Mar 18—61
Cleveland, C — Decatur, Apr 12—61
Cranmer, A — Memphis, Nov 7—63
Fay, C B — Jackson, Jan 9—63
Fish, G W — Mar 11—61
Goodrich, J J — Decatur, July 18—61
Hawkins, D — Cairo, Apr 4—61
Hinman, J L — Memphis, Feb 2—64
Hoxie, F — Wisconsin, July 10—63
Kopskie, A — Rome, Aug 31—64
Kruger, H G — Memphis, Mar 8—65
Norton, Chas — Oshkosh
Oleson, Ole B — Memphis, July 10—63
Pendall, I, — St Louis, June 15—63
Phelps, P J — Decatur—64
Priebo, E — Beaufort, Apr 28—65
Richards, Wm L — Republican City, Neb
Stedman, Hiram M — Berlin
St John, R — Memphis, Mar 13—63
Tennant, Jas — Decatur, Apr 26—61
Towle, H M — Memphis, Nov 10–63
Trible, C — Beaufort, Apr 28—65
Waterman, Chas F — New London
Waterman, J F — Marrietta, Sept 19—61
Wheeler, A P — Goldsboro, Mar 27 –61
Williams, E J — Jackson, Jan 16—63

E

Capt Irvin Eckels* — Rivers Bridge, Feb 3—65
Capt F M Guernsey — Clintonville
Lt C D Richmond — Stevens Point
Lt Amos M Ball —
Lt Lemuel H Wells — Portage
Lt Orrin A Phillips — Nov 25—61
Lt Franklin Phillips —
Ainsworth, G W — Memphis, June 22—61
Ainsworth, W W — Decatur, June 22—61
Amy, L C — Memphis, Mar 28—61
Baker, F M — Decatur, July 22 –61
Baldwin, Nat W, pa — Amherst
Bass, Thos H, m — Amherst

Brown, G H — Berlin
Ciperlie, P —
Chaffin, A — Fish Creek, June 7—61
Crandall, D G —
Cross, A T — Memphis, Feb 16—63
Dame, G —
Darling, A — Chattanooga, Nov 6—61
Drake, C H — Memphis, Mar 15—63
Frost, A H, sgt —
Guernsey, F M, a — Clintonville
Harrington, A S — Memphis, Sep 13—63
Helmer, M K — Campbellsport
Hicks, Jno* — South Edisto, Feb 9—65
Horton, H — Memphis, June 5—65
Horton, T — Jackson, Jan 12—63
Huntingdon, K — Oshkosh, Oct 6—62
Jenkins, J — College Hill, Dec 8—62
Jenner, L W — Vicksburg, Mar 7—64
Lee, Jesse, f — Amherst
Lehner, J — Marietta, Sep 28—61
Mitcham, U O — Amherst, Nov 1—63
Norton, A — Memphis, Sep 13—63
Phillips, O A — Madison, Nov 28—61
Phillips, Franklin, f — Amherst
Powell, R* — Hillsboro, Feb 24—64
Roe, Benj L, m — Stevens Point
Simpson, T — Marietta, Sep 10—64
Springsteen, C D, sgt — Memphis, May 30—63
Steel, Jno — Memphis, Feb 15—63
Vanskerer, Jno, f — Amherst
VanValkenberg, B — Memphis, Aug 13—63
Van Vleet, Wm — Savannah, Feb 16—65
Vasblader, F M+ — Blairs Landing, Feb 5—65
Warriner, W N, sgt — Memphis, Mar 25—63
Webster, Jno N, f — Amherst
Whittaker, P — Memphis, Mar 11—64
Wood, Jos — Neillsville

F

Capt M J Mead — Green Bay
Capt H C Graham — Fish Creek
Lt M P Kalmbach — Green Bay
Lt H L Wells —
Lt Paul Dakin — Memphis, July 12—63
Lt Oscar B Smith — Emporia, Kan
Adams, L P, c — Janesville
Anslis, D D — St Louis, Oct 14—61
Beaulin, P H — Buchanan, Oct 13—63
Cannon, S — Beotonville, Mar 20—65
Deckars, J — Memphis, July 1—63
Dequin, E — Decatur, June 7—61
Edson, A — Ft Schuyler, Feb 14—65
Fairbanks, J W, f — Waupun
Ferguson, R M — Memphis, Nov 1—64
Griffith, Jno C — Memphis, Mar 26—63
Haines, D G — Jackson, Feb 20—63
Jerdon, M — Decatur, July 7—64
Johns, Wm — Decatur, July 18—64
Kalmbach, M F — Ft Howard
Olen, A — Memphis, Oct 30—63
Paige, David, Jr — Green Bay, Dec 3—62
Smith, S W, corp+ — Memphis, Feb 10–63
Stevenson, I — Newbern, Apr 16—65
Teller, Wm — Memphis, Mar 30—64
Vaughn, Daniel — Atlanta Sept 2—64
Wending, J — Atlanta, Aug 15—61
Whidden, J G, sgt* — Atlanta, Aug 10—61
Williams, J C, mo — Eureka

G

Capt Wm G Manning — Chicago, Ill
Capt W F D Bailey — Portage
Lt Jas L Jones — Portage
Lt D B Johnston — Montello
Lt S D Forbes —
Lt H H Markham — Milwaukee
Andrews, J F — Memphis, Feb 22—63
Babcock, G W — Trenton, Jan 25—63

FASHIONABLE SHOE DEALER TO

Their Majesties, The People,

ANNOUNCES THE DAILY ARRIVAL OF NEW SPRING GOODS.

Beautiful and Attractive Styles in

Shoes and Slippers for
Ladies, Gents and Children.

The attention of the ladies is called to the fact that he is the Only Dealer in the city who makes a specialty of strictly Genuine Hand Sewed Work for Ladies' wear. These goods continue to grow in favor as their merits become more widely known. His stock of Medium Priced Goods far surpasses any preceding season in style and cheapness. Novelties in Fancy and Medium Priced Slippers.

Something New Every Day.

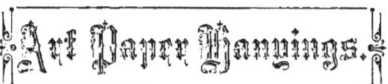

THE LARGEST ASSORTMENT AT

Mueller & Ilhardt's,

465 East Water St, MILWAUKEE.

The MacKinnon Pen

Constructed on an Entirely New and Philosophical Plan.

It writes like an ordinary lead pencil, but with ink instead of lead, at once giving the combined advantages of pen and pencil. Each pen is put up in a handsome morocco case, and mailed on receipt of price. Prices:

Long 18 kt. Gold Mounted $5.00
Short 18 kt. Gold Mounted 4.50
Long plain, ... 4.50
Short plain 4.00

DES FORGES & CO.

Sole Agents for Milwaukee. 92 Wisconsin St. & 409 Broadway

MILWAUKEE

EYE AND EAR
INFIRMARY.

Located at 220 Wisconsin Street.

DIRECTORS—

Hon. P. V. Deuster,
Hon. Satterlee Clark,
Hon. E. W. Keyes,
Hon. George Hoskinson.

For terms and a new treatise on the Eye, Ear and Catarrh, address

DR. HOUGHMAN,

STATE OCULIST, BOX 60, MILWAUKEE, WIS.

WISCONSIN SOLDIERS AND SAILORS REUNION ROSTER. 143

Name	Location
Bedell, S E	Manitowoc Rapids
Borner, F	Cahawba, Aug 14—64
Brooks, W L	Memphis, Aug 2—63
Buttles, L C, corp	College Hill, Dec 17—62
Chipman, A R*	Salkahatchie, Feb 3—65
Conklin, G	Cairo, March 31—64
Crafts, C	Nashville, June 9—64
Cramer, W S	Nashville, Sept 3—64
Dau, D, sgt	Memphis, Mar 20—63
Delong, M C	Decatur, Apr 16—64
Doucy, J	Chattanooga, Nov 2—64
Eunis, M	Jackson, Jan 13—63
Fansler, W H	Berlin, May 6—64
Farrington, W A	Decatur, June 11—64
Fleck, Peter	St Mary's
Forbes, S D, ed	Westfield
French, Homar	Cedar Falls
Gifford, H C	La Grange, Jan 21—63
Granger, A+	Pocotaligo, Feb 5 —65
Holley, W H	College Pill, Dec 16—62
Harding, A	Memphis, Feb 13—63
Heath, Thos,	Memphis, Mar 20—63
Kendall, Wm	Andersonville, Sep 12—64
Koch, L	Memphis, Apr 6—61
Leonard, J J	La Grange, Jan 9—63
Loveland, Urial, f	Montello
Lytle, E G	Memphis, Dec 20—63
Nichols, A J	Beaufort, Jan 27—65
Norracong, C M, corp	Jackson, Jan 14—63
Rowland, D G	Memphis, May 12—63
Simonds, C K	Jackson, Mar 9—64
Stebbins, Engene	Arkansas
Stowe, Jno D	La Grange. Jan 13—63
Sutfen, P	Jackson, Feb 20—63
Symes, Sam'l	Chicago, Ill
Thomas, C C	Chattanooga, Nov 7—64
Thomas, S*	Salkahatchie, Feb 3—63
Vader, C L	Kingsbridge
Werner, C W	Holly Springs, Jan 1—63

H

Name	Location
Capt Wm S Burrows	Michigan
Capt Thos Bryant	Omaha, Neb
Lt Jas H Farnsworth	Fond du Lac
Lt Jas K Pompelly	Fond du Lac
Lt Geo W King	Oakfield
Lt S L Brasted	Fond du Lac
Anthony, C H	Marietta, Sept 3—64
Bartell, P, corp*	Bentonville, Mar 21—65
Burnett, J A	Memphis, Nov 1—63
Chase, C W	La Grange, Apr 5—63
Cowhan, J M	Memphis, June 28—63
Cumniskey, F	Memphis, Dec 15—63
Davis, R	Atlanta, Aug 20—64
Everson, D H	Philadelphia, May 9—65
Fancher, J H, corp	Jackson, Jan 26—63
Gemmar, Moses	Memphis, Apr 8—63
Hayes, Jas	Memphis, Mar 26—63
Heathcote, G	Jackson, Jan 26—63
Henke, Albert	St Louis, Apr 19—61
Hill, G H	Paducah, Mar 27—64
Hutchinson, A B	St Louis, July 24—64
Kendall, Lorenzo	Memphis, Feb 21—63
Kenyon, Clark, f	Rosendale
King, Geo W	Oakfield
Lefevre, Edw, l	Green Bay
May, H D	Marietta, Sept 3—64
Miller, D E	Memphis, Feb 27—63
Pasko, S	Ripon, Feb 28—64
Pierce, T	Memphis, Mar 16—64
Pompelly, J K	Fond du Lac
Purdy, J	Cairo, Apr 13—61
Pygoll, T W	Memphis, Nov 1—62
Redman, Patrick, f	Eden
Reynolds, Chas	Oakfield
Schultz, N	Annapolis, May 17—65
Treleven, Daniel	Memphis, Aug 25—63
Walter, J	La Grange, Jan 12—63
Weddeman, Wm, f	Lamartine

I

Name	Location
Weddeman, Chancey	Lamartine
Williams, D	Memphis, Sept 14—63
Capt Geo R Wood	Milwaukee
Lt Wm Young	Youngs Corners
Lt D J Brothers	Kaukauna
Lt D J Quimby	
Lt J S Styles	Minneapolis, Minn
Lt Richard Bottrell	Appleton
Burns, Jos	Ehlueton
Cornelius, W	St Louis, July 11—65
Dalton, R C	Decatur, July 15—61
Darling, S	Memphis, Feb 8—63
Elsner, A	Memphis, Jan 28—65
Farnham, J H	Fayetteville, Mar 11—65
Glass, S*	Memphis, Mar 29—63
Grignon, D B	Memphis, Mar 29—63
Groenfeld, S	LaGrange, Mar 20—63
Hammond, Dan'l M, h	Black Creek
Hicks, H	Memphis, Nov 11—62
Hodkins, N	Memphis, July 30—63
Hughs, O	Memphis, July 11—63
Knight, L	Jackson, Jan 30—63
McClelland, C B	Fremont, Apr 2—64
McLeser, N	Jackson, Apr 26—63
McMurdo, Jno, f	Outagamie
Quadlin, S	Memphis, Aug 2—63
Rhodes, H	Memphis, Sept 1—63
Snider, Thos L, m	Sarpey Centre, Neb
Steflin, J	Vicksburg, Mar 5—64
Steffen, Francis	Madison
VanAlsteine, Wm A	Milwaukee
Wieldschien, F	St Louis

K

Name	Location
Capt Jno E Grout	Lowville
Lt Edw H Bronson, cl	
Lt Jno Walton	
Lt S L Batchelder	
Babcock, T C	Courtland, Nov 18—62
Baker, Amos	Cairo, Mar 21—64
Bissett, L	Bennettsville, Mar 5—65
Bissett, J*	Bentonville, Mar 21—65
Brasted, Sumner L, a	Fond du Lac
Carman, J	Jackson, Jan 15—63
Davis, R F	Decatur, July 10—64
Dumbleton, S	Paducah, Mar 26—64
Eichle, C	St Louis, Mar 20—63
Esterbrook, C	Decatur, Aug 9—64
Esterbrook, E, f	Fond du Lac
Frondel, B J	Vicksburg, Mar 3—64
Gillson, T	Memphis, Sept 23—63
Gunderson, M+	Hilton Head, Feb 18—65
Hoffman, Aug, l	Columbus
Hunting, f Jr, corp	Atlanta, Nov 1—64
Hunting, N W	Fall River, Nov 26—64
Leis, Bernard	St Marys
Lovejoy, Harry W	Madison
Mason, D+	Goldsboro, Mar 27—65
Morgan, R W	Memphis, Oct 4—63
Oleson, A	Keokuk, Dec 14—63
Oney, Asa	Menominee
Prevot, D	Oshkosh, Oct 20—62
Simmonson, A	Memphis, Mar 26—63
Strong, Orville, agt	Dodgeville
Tannt, S*	Atlanta, Aug 19—64
Thompson, P	Memphis, Apr 1—63
Wait, Fred'k	Cedar Falls
Walt, F	Vancerburg
Walton, Jno	Easton
Warner, R E	Memphis, Apr 17—64
Watson, J N	Bennettsville, Mar 5—65
Watson, B F	Jefferson
White, A+	Atlanta, Aug 20—64
Whitehead, A	Empline, Mar 11—65
Wright, A W	Decatur, May 9—64

UNASSIGNED.

Name	Location
Bellows, C	Decatur, Apr 25—64

Name	Location
Berge, Fred	Sturgeon Bay
Bessey, Wesley, f	Fond du Lac
Briggs, Ed F, mf	Waukesha
Carlton, J D, uf	Kenosha
Danes, Peabody, f	Big Suamico
Day, H J	Memphis, Mar 11—63
De Groat, Henry	Deadwood, Col
Gulleson, Ole	Horns Pier
Hartshorn, M	Memphis, Feb 15—63
Hitchcock, D P	Clinton, Feb 22—61
Hughes, H W	Memphis, Feb 9—64
Larson, Gunder, f	Winchester
Mann, Horace E, ph	Marinette
McCann, Jno, f	Lowville
Priebe, Emil, me	Oshkosh
Rossigue, J	Nashville, Sept 2—61

THIRTY-THIRD INFANTRY.

Three years. Organized October, 18th, 1862. Original strength, 892, gain by recruits, etc., 174. Total, 1066. Death loss, 199—killed in action 10, died of wounds, 11, of disease, 109. Other losses, 233—missing, 4, desertions, 22, transfers, 37, discharges, 170. Strength at musterout, Aug, 8th, 1865, 637. Campaigns in Tenn., Miss., La., Ark., Mo., Ala., Ky., Ga.,

REGIMENTAL ROSTER.

Rank/Name	Location
Col J B Moore	Muscoda
Lt Col H H Virgin	Platteville
Maj Geo R Frank	Boscobel
Adj Wm Warner	Kansas City, Mo
Adj A H Fitch	
Adj Dan'l E Shea	Missouri
Q M J W Nichols	
Q M A McCarn	Muscoda
Surg J B Whiting	Janesville
Surg Jerome Durbank	
A Surg C R Blackall	Chicago, Ill
A Surg M H Hanks	
A Surg D W Carley	Boscobel
Chap A A Overton	

A

Name	Location
Capt J C Moore	Avoca, July 19—63
Capt Geo B Carter	
Lt O C Denney	Platteville
Lt Frank Ward	
Lt Hudson Thomas	
Calvin, H W	Natchez, Sep 7—63
Elson, L A+	New Orleans, June 5—65
Ferry, Jno. corp	Moscow, Feb 11—63
Joiner, F S, corp	Natchez, Sep 21—63
King, David, corp	Natchez, Sept 4—63
Hannaman, F	Youngs Point, July 2—63
Hodgson, T R	Vicksburg, June 29—63
Holmes, D O	Memphis, Oct 1—64
Love, H T	Natchez, Oct 21—63
Love, L	Campti, Apr 12—64
Mctiowan, R J O, m	Iowa Fal's, Ia
Norris, P H	Moscow, Mar 1—63
Parr, W L	Wyoming
Purdy, D H	Vicksburg, Aug 3—64
Randall, C	Natchez, Oct 16—63
Reep, Chas, m	Falks Store, Idaho
Richards, G C	Montgomery, June 11—65
Frost, Jacob	Mound City, May 1—64
Vaughn, F F, corp+	St Louis, Aug 26—64
Waflle, Byron, S, f	Lodi
Wells, Isaiah, corp+	Memphis, Aug 2—64

B

Name	Location
Capt Geo R Frank	Boscobel
Capt Matthew Birchard	
Lt Geo Haw	
Lt T S Richards	

INSURANCE

COMPANIES REPRESENTED BY

JAS. BASS & CO.

GIRARD,
PHILADELPHIA, PA.

NEWARK,
NEWARK, N. J.

WESTCHESTER,
NEW YORK

LYCOMING,
MUNCY, PA.

COMMONWEALTH,
BOSTON, MASS. ALSO

ÆTNA LIFE INSURANCE

A Fair Share of Your Patronage Solicited

JAMES BASS.   R. W. BASS.

FOND DU LAC.

WISCONSIN SOLDIERS AND SAILORS REUNION ROSTER. 145

Lt Chas G Rouse
Allen, A D — Moscow, Feb 12—63
Barger, A* — Vicksburg, June 22—64
Brock, W B — Hickory Grove, Jan 24—65
Cape, J — Moscow, Jan 19—63
Catlin, J S — New Orleans, May—64
Coyer, J — Eastport, Jan 21—65
Davis, J E — Mound City, Apr 28—64
Emory, W H — Wauzeka, —62
Hough, E F — Madison, May 30—64
McClyman, E — Memphis, Aug 4—64
Mead, A — Memphis, June 18—63
Quigley, Wm — Little Grant
Quigley, T* — Yellow Bayou, May 18—64
Reeves, S — Cairo, June 7—64
Sanborn, J — Moscow, Mar 3—63
Shields, J — Vicksburg, Oct 25—63
Stewart, Henry — Christina
Tuckwood, G — Memphis, Oct 12—61
Van Allen, J — Vicksburg, June 26—64
Whales, W — Vicksburg, Aug 16—63
Wood, E F — Casper Creek, Oct 4 -64
Young, C B — Bell Centre

C

Capt Wm Weir
Lt Wm Warner — Portage
Lt D H Budlong — Kansas City, Mo
Lt U S Piekard — Carthage, Mo
Lt Jeptha Hopkins — Chicago, Ill
Arnold, J K — La Grange, Mar 12—63
Aufdeheide, J H F — St Louis, Aug 11 -64
Carter, C J — Natchez, Sept 18—63
Cline, D — Paoli, Aug 15—64
Day, G C — Evansville, Dec 3—64
Dearth, H — Holly Springs, Jan 5—63
Denson, J R, sgt — La Grange, Mar 8—63
Dunbar, Jas — Darlington
Foval, G W — Natchez, Jan 10—64
Geihi, L — Little Rock, Sept 20 -64
Harris, A J — Youngs Point, June 3 —63
Heinman, J H — Tuskegeo, June 27—66
Hillary, G — Nashville, Feb 6- 65
Hughes, W H+ — New Orleans, Apr 30—65
Morgan, P — Shullsburg, June 18 -64
Oats, Thos H, m — Shullsburg
Pepper, D H, f — Alvia, In
Ryckman, B — St Louis, May 6—63
Sonneman, W, corp* — Cane River, Apr 24—64
Tayne, Thos — Shullsburg
Viviers, R F — Shullsburg, July 6—64

D

Capt W S Earnhart
Capt Wm Warner — Kansas City, Mo
Capt A H Fitch — Chicago, Ill
Lt Amos Eubank
Lt N O Calkins, b — Elm Creek, Neb
Lt N L Baruer
Lt J T Delaware — Grant Co
Lt H B Andrews
Barnes, A J — Memphis, Mar 6—63
Barr, Wm — Glen Haven, Jan 17—65
Beer, Jacob M — Hazelton
Billings, L — Memphis, Jan 2—63
Billings, T C, corp — Tatton, May 16—63
Bingham, C L — Memphis, Mar 31—63
Blake, J H — Aug 26—63
Calkins, N O, f — Elm Creek, Neb
Cranston, E, corp — Moscow, Feb 28—63
Engle, J — Moscow, Feb 2—63
Fitch, M E — Oxford, Dec 2—63
Flint, J — Moscow, Feb 5—63
Garside, W B, corp — Vicksburg, Aug 10—63
Helm, W M — Memphis, Oct 21—64
Hollis, Geo — Memphis, Nov 8—64
Hutchcrost, T — Atlanta, Oct 20—61
Jackson, H C — Hazelton

Lard, Jonas
Lard, D H
Largeot, J W
Leighton, J, sgt +
Orr, Jno H
Pember, M C, corp +
Scott, W J
Scott, W H
Sifford, J M, sgt
Smith, E
Sutter, I.
Tracy, I W

Capt P H Swift
Capt C W Stark
Lt Henry S Swift*
Lt H B Cornell
Lt Edw Cook
Babcock, A
Bowers, Wm J
Buner, J P
Byrnes, T, f
Callender, S H
Cornell, Wm
Flint, Jno A
Freeman, J
Knudson, J
Medgorden, H H
Olsen, Ole
Olsen, S
Olsen, H
Robinson, E, c
Stafford, N
Steele, F A
Stewart, R B
Swift, P H
Swift, Adrian, c
Thuman, Wm, f

Capt A L Wemple
Capt Wm L Scott
Lt C W Stark
Lt Jos H Stickel
Lt E A Gardner
Adams, L P
Burnham, E W, sgt
Burdick, E J
Campbell, S M*
Carr, H +
Crall, Matthias, corp, f
Emmonds, W H
Fisher, Luban
Fliot, A, f
Hanan, L L, s
Hawley, R A
Hetrick, J C
Hickle, Jos
Hoyt, N R*
Jones, A E
Lyon, S E, corp
Maloy, Delbert
Maxwell, A
Merry, G
Morrell, H H
Newkirk, Jno
Nuss, Jno
Phelps, D
Pitzrick, A, corp
Pay, Jno
Reed, H*
Root, E
Seri, S E, corp
Smith, A*
Stern, C+
Thompson, J, corp
Tile, W

Memphis, Feb 4—63
Vicksburg, June 27—63
Natchez, Sept 7—63
New Orleans, Apr 15—63
Memphis, Jan 25—63
New Orleans, Apr 11—65
Moscow, Feb 7—63
Memphis Feb 1—63
Memphis, Apr 17—63
Natchez, May 22 —64
New Albany, J in 11—64
Montgomery, May 2—63

Clinton
Shopiere
Coldwater River, Apr 19—63
Lime Centre
Iowa
Memphis, Dec 4 62
Milwaukee
Vicksburg, July 7—63
Ft Atkinson
Vicksburg, Aug 21—63
Moscow, Jan 21- 63
Natchez, Dec 3—63
Vicksburg, July 6—63
Moscow, Jan 31—63
Oxfordville
Memphis, Apr 30—61
Moscow, Feb 12—63
Moscow, Feb 10—63
Whitewater
Moscow, Feb 1—63
Natchez, Oct 25—63
St Charles, Aug 14—64
Clinton
Granby, Mo
Lime Centre

Memphis, Mar 9—63
Alabama
Shopiere

Janesville
Youngs Point, May 31—63
Davis Junction, Ill
Tupelo, July 14—64
New Orleans, Apr 19—63
Centre
Memphis, Jan 23—63
Belvidere, Neb
Emerald Grove
Rutland
Sutton, Neb
LaGrange, Mar 17—63
Belvidere
Tupelo, July 14—64
Cane River, Apr 10—64
Holly Springs, Dec 22—62
Delavan
Moscow, Feb 26—63
Moscow, Mar 13—63
Lime Centre
Shopiere
Milwaukee
Memphis, June 23—64
Duvals Bluff, Sept 5—1
Belvidere, Neb
Spanish Ft, June 20—65
Eastport, Jan 20—65
Cairo, Aug 5—64
Camargo Cross Roads, July 13—61
Memphis, July 2—64
Andersonville, July 14—64

West, M S
Wright, M

Capt F B Burdick
Lt G K Harrington
Lt Louis Schneider
Lt Jos A Birchard
Lt E F Liscan
Lt Theo Shelver
Anderson, E
Berry, B
Cheeve, A W
Coleman, J—
Connolly, J B
Everson, Ole
Gebbe, H
Hurlburt, H
Kast, C D
Kast, H C
Owen, H C
Rice, H E
Ross, J B
Searle, J H
Vau Amberg, I K
Van Valen, C L
Ward, T
Woods, J
Wood, E
Young, J B

Capt Franklin Newell
Capt J E Linsley*
Capt C H Thayer
Capt Nicholas Smith
Capt Jno W Nichols
Lt E L Coburn
Lt Geo Hale
Lt H J Traber
Coburn, Wm H, sgt
Collett, S W*
Dunbar, Wm
Eddy, Jas W
Ellsworth, J
Graggert, Wm
Gray, Jno
Harris, Asa
Hill, Silas
Jacobson, Carl
Johnson, N
Kidder, Julius
Klass, H
Larson, C
Leiber, W
McCletchy, A
McCoy, C*
Nobles, Richard R, ph
Owen, C M
Rector, J G
Smith, Jno
Taylor, F B+
Thayer, C B
Thomas, H, corp
Tinkham, F L+
Van Camp, J A
Waldo, G H, corp

Capt Walter Cook
Capt C G Stetson*
Capt Chas I. Fay
Lt Wm E Roberts
Lt F W Bashford
Lt A J McKissou*
Lt G H Nichols
Lt D E Pierce

Memphis, July 1—61
Natchez, Sept 4—63

G

Boscobel
Boscobel
Prairie du Chien
Cairo, Nov 2—61
St Louis, Mar 18—63
St Louis, Mar 12—63
Tupelo, July 17 64
Vicksburg, Mar 2—63
Memphis, Jan 13—64
Youngs Point July 16—63
St Louis, Apr 19—63
New Orleans, May 18—64
St Charles, Aug 4—64
Memphis, Jan 21—63
Madison, Apr 25—64
Goodwin, D T
Red River Landing, May 22—64
Brownsville, Sept 22—63
Moscow, Mar 6—63
Natchez, Oct 12—63
Moscow, Feb 22—63
St Louis, Sept 1—64
Memphis, May 18—63

H

Kenosha
Platteville
Wisconsin, Oct 5—63
Tupelo, July 14—64
Darlington
Woodworth
Vicksburg, Aug 6—64
Moscow, D T
Memphis, Mar 25—63
Vicksburg, Oct 16—63
Darlington
Nashville, Dec 29—64
Memphis, Mar 19—63
Geneva Lake
Vicksburg, June 2—64
Natchez, Nov 9—63
Kenosha, Sept 22—64
Moscow, Jan 17—63
Tupelo, July 14—64
Vicksburg, Aug 6—64
Apr 14—63
Vicksburg, Aug 6—64
Moscow, Feb 28—63
Vicksburg, June 30—63
Clay Banks
Natchez, Sept 19—63
Bayou Cotile, Apr 25 - 64
Atlanta, Aug 9—64
Memphis, Apr 4 63

I

Neosho
Spanish Ft, Apr 2—65
Madison

Chaplin Hills, Oct 8—62

CASH GROCER,

280, 282 & 284 West Water, Cor. Cedar Sts., MILWAUKEE.

ALWAYS AT THE FRONT!

If you are coming to Milwaukee and are interested in finding out where you can buy

CHOICE, STAPLE & FANCY GROCERIES

At retail, at wholesale prices and save from 10 to 25 per cent. I would be pleased to have you call and see my

Mammoth Store and Immense Stock,

Before you buy a cent's worth, or even if you do not wish to buy, as I want all to see the great bargains that I offer. I have the disposition, the goods, and the prices to beat all competition.

A COMPLETE PRICE LIST

Quoting the price on all goods, issued semi-monthly, given to all that call or send for it, free.

ALL GOODS WARRANTED

Fresh and first-class. All goods purchased, or ordered from any part of the NORTH-WEST, in large or small lots, packed and delivered free at any Depot or Steamboat Dock in the city.

Do not Fail to call or send for the Price-List.

WISCONSIN SOLDIERS AND SAILORS REUNION ROSTER.

Allen, S K, corp — Memphis, Apr 15—63
Clark, H E — Memphis, Apr 3—63
Curtis, M S — St Louis, Aug 25—64
Dowse, J — Memphis, Dec 19—63
Fay, N H, sgt — Moscow, Feb 13—63
Fogg C M — Eastport, Jan 17—65
Groat, C F — Wiscousin, Aug 29—63
Harrington, H C — Eastport, Jan 31—65
Knopker, G — St Louis, July 9—63
Locke, Horace B — Piana, Ill
Loomis, J R — Memphis, Oct 16—63
Newton, W* — Spanish Ft, M r 31—65
Neff, Wm — Andersonville, Oct 5—64
Pierce, T — Alexandria, Apr 4—64
Reynolds, M D C — Vicksburg, Oct 18—63
Roberts, A R, sgt — Memphis, Feb 12—63
Sauils, S J — Racine, June 26—63
Stevenson, W — St Louis, Aug 1—63
Stout, W H — La Grange, Jan 14—63
Stowe, D B — St Louis, Dec 7—63
Vincent, T G — Moscow, Mar 4—63
Wells, Wm — Kenosha, May 21—65

K

Capt A Whitcher
Capt A S Sampson
Lt Dan'l E Shea — New Mexico, Mo
Lt A D Goodrich
Lt Hellonis Heath
Atkinson, E J — Black River, July 22—63
Balch, Y M — Moscow, Mar 11—63
Bartholomew, A — Moscow, Feb 2—63
Billings, Lewis, f — South Haven, Mich
Cahill, Jeremiah — East Elkport, Ia
Calbert, C H — Vicksburg, Oct 7—63
Clyne, Jno — Racine
Coffey, M — New Orleans, Apr 9—63
Deubner, J P — Nashville, Dec 4—64
Dodge, J H, f — South Haven, Mich
Freeman, Jno — Moscow, Feb 23—63
Goodrich, H W — Moscow, Mar 8—63
Heath, V, f — Lewis, Ia
Hicks, W — Oct 10—64
Hill, Jno — Cairo, Oct 31—64
Howery, W H — Elvers
Jones, Obed K — Platteville
Malobot, W R — Moscow, June 1—63
Odell, J E, corp — St Louis, Sept 1—63
Owrey, T — Campli, Apr 12—61
Peterson, Rasmus — New Denmark
Peterson, Niels P — Fontnay
Porter, C C — Racine, Oct 20—62
Smith, A* — Camargo Cross Roads, July 13—64
Tifft, J W* — Spanish Ft, Mar 30—65

UNASSIGNED.

Fuller, J W — Apr 10—64
Noble, O W — Wakefield, Mass
Wiegand, Jno — Hamlin
Wright, W H — Chicago

THIRTY-FOURTH INFANTRY.

(Drafted). Nine months. Organized December 31st, 1862. Original strength, 961, gain by recruits, etc., 0, total, 961. Death loss, 20—killed in action o, died of wounds, 0, of disease, 20. Other losses, 409—missing, 0, desertions, 283, transfers, 0, discharges, 186. Strength at muster-out September 8th, 1863, 472. Campaigns in Ky.

REGIMENTAL ROSTER.

Col Fritz Anneke
Lt Col Henry Orff
Maj Theo S West
Maj Geo H Walther

A

Adj Herman Hesse
Q M Jno A Becker
Surg Jno E Weinern
1st Surg Wm Gudden
1st Surg Theo Kopi
1st Surg Jno S Kelso
1st Surg Jno F Mehlhorn
Chap Fred'k A Beckel

A

Capt W Eugene Ferslow
Lt Henry T Calkins
Lt Michael A Leahy
Duncan, J R — Nellsville
Chapman, A B — Potosi
Lackey, Philo — Westfield
Mason, Matthew T — Moundville
Mattchee, C — Columbus, June 8—63
Perry, J C, b — Fond du Lac
Schroeder, Johann — Sussex
Sinder, C G, sgt — Columbus, July 6—63
Woodworth, A B — Milwaukee

B

Capt Jas N Ruby — Oshkosh
Lt Henry B Fox
Lt Dennis J A Murphy
Goolman, A — Madison, June 3—63
Knudson, A — Memphis, May 30—64
Liddy, J — Madison, Jan 3—63
Matthews, A C — Baraboo

C

Capt Julius G Wilmot
Lt Frank H J Oblanden
Lt Jno W Johann
Ruppert, M G — Ozaukee

D

Capt Noble W Smith
Lt Elliott M Scribner
Lt Wm H Pettit
Adamsson, Martin — Kenosha
Dunkirk, Jno — Memphis, Aug 5—63
Harper, Hugh — Neenah
Maley, Thos C — Hopkins, Mo

E

Capt Cornelius Cuntz
Lt Chas F Bauer
Lt Chas F Lachmund
Lt Chas F Blumenstein

F

Capt Henrick Keukel
Lt Jas Lonergan
Lt Rudolph Kirchner
Lt August Beecher
Dunlap, Jas — Milwaukee
Kelsey, Wm, sgt — Columbus, Apr '4—63
Rothwinkler, S — Columbus, May 10—63
Vandersander, F — Milwaukee, Dec 25—62

G

Capt Chas A Lang
Lt Robt Strohman
Lt Chas F Blumenstein
Lt Chas F Lachmund
Brasser, M — Columbus, Apr 9—63
Brethowner, H — Columbus, Apr 29—63
Dunn, Dominick — Hingham
Hartwig, Jno — Milwaukee, Mar 27—63
Hoff, C — Cairo, May 20—63
Lammers, A — Columbus, July 7—63
McCride, B — Columbus, Apr 25—63

H

Capt Isidore de St Ange
Lt Wm B Barclay
Lt Leonard La Plante
Tricot, Jno, corp — Memphis, July 16—63
Lamal, A — Memphis, July 15—63
White, Frank, f — Red River, Mo

I

Capt Fred'k A B Becker
Lt Edw J Kelly
Lt Gottlieb C Neumeister
Gust, Milton G, f — Rock Elm Centre
Gust, Lewis — Rock Elm Centre
Lorenzen, T, sgt — Columbus, Apr 10—63
Wiley, Jno M — Hartford

K

Capt Wm Walther
Lt Erhard Weber
Lt David H Dexter — Mar 25—63
Lt August Beecher
Lt Rudolph Kirchner
Jansen, Jno — Columbus, Apr 15—63

UNASSIGNED.

J Douglass, Jr — Rush River

THIRTY-FIFTH INFANTRY.

Three years. Organized February 27th, 1864. Original strength, 1000; gain by recruits, etc., 2; total, 1008. Death loss, 265—Killed in action, 1, died of wounds, 4, of disease, 250, of accidents, 4. Other losses, 203, missing, 0, desertions, 29, transfers, 11, discharges, 164. Strength at muster-out, March 15th, 1866, 615. Campaigns in La., Ark., Ala., Texas.

REGIMENTAL ROSTER.

Col Henry Orff
Col Geo H Walther
Lt Chas A Smith
Lt Robert Strohman
Maj Fred Von Baumbach — Milwaukee
Adj Herman Hesse
Adj David Hunter — Caldwells Prairie
Adj Bernard S Schoeffel
Q M Adolph J Cramer
Q M Wm H Williams
Surg Chas Krak
Surg Jno Groening
A Surg Adolph Jacobi
A Surg Jas Verbryk — Pt Hudson, July 8—64
A Surg Carmi P Garlick
A Surg D F Schwaiger
A Surg Otto Kuehn
Chap Ira W Bowen — Fond du Lac—64
Chap Alfred H Waters

A

Capt Robt Strohman
Capt Edwin Sturtevant
Capt Henry Peckham
Capt Wm Tyler
Lt Anthony C Kuhn
Lt Albert F Stein — Nov 17—65
Lt Jos Oryall
Lt Herman Schaub
Lt Paul Kiel
Albrecht, Jno C — Morganzia, Sept 4—64
Addler, Philip — Memphis, Aug 14—64
Brazelton, Oliver — New Orleans, July 13—64
Brasted, Daniel W — New Orleans, Aug 12—64
Beach, Jas H — Baldwin
Bringolf, Jno F — Natchez, Oct 12—64

PHILIPP BEST BREWING CO.

EMPIRE BREWERY.

FRED PABST,
President.
E. SCHANDEIN,
Vice President.
CHAS. BEST, JR.
Secretary.

SOUTH SIDE BREWERY.

MANUFACTURERS OF
LAGER BEER,
MILWAUKEE, WIS.

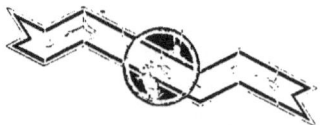

WISCONSIN SOLDIERS AND SAILORS REUNION ROSTER. 149

Brodhagen, Chas — Natchez, Sept 28–61
Caunel, Wm H+ — Mobile, Apr 8–85
Cruther, Arthur L — Morganzia, Nov 16–61
Doxtater, Jno — New Orleans, Oct 10–64
Dieter, Lyman — Brownsville, Nov 22–64
Duvigneaud, Jos — Vicksburg, Oct 20–64
Evert, Chas W — Morganzia, Aug 15–64
Early, Jas W — Pt Hudson, Aug 18–61
Ehnke, Wm — Duvals Bluff, Dec 26–64
Falling, Robt — Memphis, July 25–64
Henrichs, Geo — Pt Hudson, June 10–64
Hachne, Gottlieb — Sept 26–64
Jansen, Claus — Vicksburg, Oct 18–61
Loeb, Fred'k — Vicksburg, Oct 25–61
Moore, Henry P — Milwaukee, May 4–61
Norton, Jno E — Sept 26–64
Oleson, Ole — Christiana, Mar 25–64
Pfeiffer, Fred'k — Ossineke, Mich
Rosenow, Chas — New Orleans–64
Schaner, Michael — Pt Hudson, June 17–64
Sayre, Chas — Pt Hudson, Sept 7–64
Schmidt, Christopher — New Orleans, Sept 7–61
Stafford, Jos — Sept 26–64
Sprang, Herman — Two Rivers
Schmidt, Herman — Vicksburg, Oct 22–64
S-bulk, Jno — Duvals Bluff, Dec 5–64
Terrill, Elliott — Duvals Bluff, Dec 10–64
Wieglob, Fred'k — Morganzia, July 9–64
Weber, Herman — St Charles, Aug 4–64
Wood, Chas H — New Orleans, Sept 26–65

B

Capt Fritz Von Baunbach — Milwaukee
Capt Jasper Vosburg
Lt Frank R St John
Lt Sylvester S Barton
Lt Jno Mc Maulmin
Baether, Wm, corp — Morganzia, Aug 21–64
Fischer, Adam, corp — Sep 1–64
Dewick, Thos, corp — Marion, Mar 4–65
Anderson, Andrew C — Madison, Oct 21–61
Adams, Lewis — Clarksville, Jan 25–65
Bartlett, Levi H — New Orleans, July 22–61
Bowles, R, m — Fond du Lac
Bywater, Jas — Chicago, Sep 27–64
Baldwin, Marvin M — Vicksburg, Oct 20–61
Donovan, Jno H — White River, July 19–64
Davis, Clark — Vicksburg, Nov 5–64
Elliot, Isaac D — July 22–61
Esterbrooks, Elisha — Vicksburg, Sep 1–64
Fischer, Herman — Brownville, Feb 8–65
Gebrande, August — New Orleans, Aug 11–64
Granger, Zachariah — New Orleans, Oct 2–64
Grof, Jacob — New Orleans, Oct 22–64
Hendericks, Benj F — Port Hudson, June 19–64
Harst, Abrm — Aug 26–64
Hunger, Wm F — Vicksburg, Oct 19–61
Jung, Jno Jacob — Port Hudson, June 9–64
Johnson, Merrill — Prairie du Sac
Lee, L H — Janesville
McNalus, Jas — St Charles, Aug 4–61
Masson, Matthew T — Moundville
Morris, Jno — St Charles, Aug 20–61
Odekirk, Jos A — New Orleans, Aug 15–61
Parkin, Jno — Merrimack
Perkins, D C — Neillsville
Packlo, Robert — Merrimack
Schulte, Peter — Chicago, Sep 21–64
St John, F, c — Pond du Lac
Schultz, Frederick — Vicksburg, Oct 22–61
Senft, Fritz, f — New Cassel
Sherwood, Jas — Duvals Bluff, Feb 21–65
Toedtle, Ulrich — Brownsville, Nov 21–64
Williams, Evan — Madison, Oct 14–61
Warner, Silas — Morganzia, Aug 14–64
Wilcox, Orville — New Orleans, Sep 9–64

C

Capt W Eugene Ferslew

Capt Jno E Leahy
Capt Newton A Oleson
Lt Henry Fox
Lt Geo Broslus
Lt Adolph Reuter
Lt Robt F Martine
Stratton Geo O, sgt — Vicksburg, Nov 18–61
Peterson, Gammell, corp — Morganzia, Sep 4–64
Ballweg, Martin, corp, f — Arcadia, Ia
Buzzell, Thos — Morganzia, Oct 5–64
Clark, Samuel — Port Hudson, May 32–61
Campton, Robt — Milwaukee, Feb 8–64
Deshen, Jacob — Morganzia, Aug 26–64
Daniels, Peter F — New Orleans, Sep 22–64
Davis, Thos D — Port Hudson, July 30–64
Graff, Wm — Transport, July 16–61
Graham, Jas — New Orleans, Sep 20–61
Hall, Chas — New Orleans, Sep 4–64
Holdenburg, Carl H — Clarksville, Jan 21–65
Haskin, Enoch — New Orleans, Sep 18–64
Johnson, Jno — New Orleans, Aug 1–64
Johnson, Robert — Memphis, Aug 5–64
Knapp, Alonzo B — New Orleans, Sep 29–64
Korth, Ferd — Port Hudson, July 14–61
Murphy, Cornelius — Milwaukee, Mar 6–64
May, Nicholas — Port Hudson, June 22–6,
Morgan, Robt H — Morganzia, Sep 4–61
McCurdy, Jas — New Orleans, July 28–64
McCullow, Michael H — New Orleans, Sep 30–61
Newman, Adelbert — New Orleans, Sep 26–61
Panke, Wm — Port Hudson, May 26–64
Pugh, David H — Memphis, July 24–64
Proctor, Wm — Nov 27–61
Richards, Jno — Sep 2–64
Rugg, Sam'l — Morganzia, Oct 1–64
Stroud, Sam'l T — Morganzia, July 16–64
Schultz, Ernst — New Orleans, Aug 9–64
Steady, H, c — Fond du Lac
Shumway, Jno P — New Orleans, Sep 28–64
Stang, Fred — Vicksburg, Oct 18–64
Thompson, Christian — St Charles, Aug 2–64
Thompson, Marlon — Morganzia, Aug 1–64
Wilcox, Dwight — St Charles, July 27–64

D

Capt Michael A Leahy
Lt Aug Beecher
Lt Chas McCormick
Lt Oswald H Norris
Lt Geo Besemann
Lt Jno Goggin
Brushel, Geo U — Pt Hudson, June 11–64
Bohmert, Franz — Pt Hudson, June 7–61
Bendinger, Philip — Wauwatosa, Nov 18–64
Cofrin, Chas B — Morganzia, Aug 21–64
Chappell, Jno W — Natchez, Aug 29–64
Clifford, Jno C — Vicksburg, Aug 25–64
Cronise, Timothy — New Orleans, July 28–64
Dick, Franklin M — Vicksburg, July 22–64
Frank, Matthew — New Orleans, Sept 21–64
Fulks, Samuel — Ripley, Ia
Groves, Elias — Pt Hudson, Jan 21–64
Hayes, Wm, corp — Woodland
Jones, Horatio — Pt Hudson, June 28–64
Landsley, Whiting S — Morganzia, Sept 14–64
Loomis, Eugene — Watertown, Feb 6–64
Ilhody, Julius H — St Charles, Aug 8–64
Skeesicks, Jas — Pt Hudson, May 22–64
Swan, David — Morganzia, Aug 5–64
Simpson, Chas — New Orleans, Aug 25–61
Scott, Jonathan — Memphis, Sept 4–64
View, Michael — New Orleans, July 15–64
Vaughan, Leslie — Natchez, Sept 2–61
Veley, Gilbert C — Morganzia, Oct 1–64
Wrangham, Michael — Pt Hudson, Jan 7–64
Wauby, Aaron — Morganzia, Aug 14–64
Walker, B F, m — Colby
Yonog, Wm C — Clarksville, Aug 8–65

E

Capt Henry Fox
Lt Henry C Miles
Lt Jno Smsil — Independence, Ia
Lt Rudolph Kirchner
Lt Wm Tyler
Lt Jno L Derickson
Lewis, Homer M, corp — Duvals Bluff, Dec 16–64
Bailey, Geo W — New Orleans, Aug 2–64
Best, Hezekiah — New Orleans, Sept 18–64
Bacon, Jno M — Natchez, July 23–64
Blakely, Jno — Natchez, Sept 19–64
Cobb, Edwin — New Orleans, Oct 12–64
Dimick, Ed A — Baton Rouge, Aug 27–64
Fuessing, Henry — Port Hudson, June 8–64
Gibson, Dan J — St Charles, Aug 2–64
Huelsmann, Frank — Memphis, Sept 4–64
Ingersoll, Frank — Milwaukee, Jan 21–64
Ingersoll, Robt H — Chicago, Oct 2–64
Jewell, Jno — Milwaukee, Jan 20–65
Lord, Wm — Morganzia, Jan 21–64
Liddle, Thos — Brazos Santiago, Sept 3–65
Meyerhofer, Michael — Port Hudson, June 16–64
Pohlmann, Fred — Port Hudson, June 20–64
Palmer, Stephen — Morganzia, June 25–64
Riley, Jno — St Charles, Aug 8–61
Ructon, Anton — Memphis, Sept 1–64
Stoner, Edgarton — Port Hudson, June 22–64
Small, Jno — Independence, Ia
Terrill, Jno N — Duvals Bluff, Nov 21–64
Vannetta, Thos H — New Orleans, Sept 14–64
Verker, Theodore — Vicksburg, Oct 14–64

F

Capt Henry C Miles
Capt Jno W Johann
Lt Jas H C Drew
Lt Gideon E Newman
Lt Paul Dinner
Lt Chas N Elliott
Lt Willis Nash
Alton, L K, corp, ed — Burlington
Groat, Wm H, corp — Vicksburg, Oct 17–64
Atkins, W R — Neillsville
Atkinson, Jr, f — Green Dale, Neb
Atkinson, Sam'l, me — Greenwood, Neb
Banks, W M, i — Plum Creek, Neb
Bimer, Sam'l — Milwaukee
Claber, Philip — Milwaukee
Dickson, Orville — Morganzia, Aug 26–64
Fowler, Geo — Cairo, Oct 10–64
Gower, Chas — New Orleans, Aug 24–64
Hayden, Jno — Pt Hudson, May 26–64
Hnse, Jas H — Morganzia, Oct 2–64
Haveland, Nathan — Vicksburg, Oct 18–64
Kerwer, Matthias — Milwaukee, Jan 5–65
Langford, Jno — Pt Hudson, July 7–64
Luke, Jno — Memphis, Aug 26–64
Rogers, Isaac — New Orleans, Sept 22–64
Schammel, Nicholas — Natchez, July 14–64
Scott, Robt — Janesville
Taylor, Wm A L — New Orleans, July 31–64
Todd, Wm — Vicksburg, Oct 20–64

G

Capt Oliver C Smith
Capt Albert C Matthews
Lt Anderson F Smith
Lt Martin E Stevens
Lt Leonard Preger, m — Des Moines, Ia
Gardner, Jno J, sgt — Natchez, Sept 2–64
Banten, Henry — Vicksburg, Sept 24–64
Connelly, Wm H — New Orleans, Sept 6–64
Fisk, Hiram T — Port Hudson, June 8–64
Farrell, Jas — Duvals Bluff, July 9–64
Gates, Geo W — Aug 27–64
Hook, Sidney S — Morganzia, Sept 23–64
Hastings, W T — Waldo

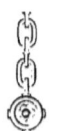

Fire and Life! INSURANCE.

REPRESENTS:

NEW YORK ALLIANCE,

WESTCHESTER FIRE.

ST. PAUL FIRE AND M.

HEKLA FIRE, WIS.

MUTUAL BENEFIT LIFE INSURANCE CO.

ALL FIRST CLASS.

FOND DU LAC, - WISCONSIN.

Notary Public.

LOANS NEGOTIATED.

REAL ESTATE BOUGHT AND SOLD.

RENTS COLLECTED.

TAXES PAID FOR NON-RESIDENTS.

CONVEYANCING DONE WITH CARE.

OFFICE.

FOND DU LAC, - WIS.

Yours Truly,

ED. L. MALONEY.

WISCONSIN SOLDIERS AND SAILORS REUNION ROSTER.

Keller, Chas	Duvals Bluff, Jan 18—65	Condit, Chas H	Rock Elm Centre	
Loehrer, Henry	Port Hudson, June 19—64	Carey, Wm	Morganzia, Aug 23—64	**THIRTY-SIXTH INFAN-**
Lawton, David E	Boyceville	Cornwell, Edwin	Aug 28—61	**TRY.**
Leuzen, Franz	St Charles, Aug 4—61	Dunham, Willis H	Morganzia, Aug 15 61	
Miller, Herman	Morganzia, Sept 16—64	Evan, Jacob	Milwaukee, Oct 14—61	Three years., Organized, March 23d, 1864.
Mathews, A C, me	Baraboo	Ferguson, Silas	Natchez, Aug 10—64	Original strength, 996, gain by recruits, etc.,
Miller, Wm	Wonewoc	French, Henry	Ironton, Oct 8—64	24. Total, 1014. Death loss, 210—killed in action,
Odrich, Fred'k	New Orleans, July 16-64	Graber, Wm T	Port Hudson, June 14—64	79, died of wounds, 47, of disease, 170. Other
Purkis, Sam'l	Sept 2—64	Gilbert, Jas	Milwaukee, Apr 10—64	losses, 273—missing, 6, desertions, 21, transfers,
Perkins, Daniel C	Sherwood	Helm, Michael	July 12—64	38, discharges, 214. Strength at muster-out,
Rakutz, Franz	Memphis, Sept 9—64	Ingham, Sam'l	Milwaukee, Mar 2—64	July 12th, 1865, 445. Campaign in Virginia.
Rechhoff, E, p	Milwaukee	Johnson, Fred, f	Burlington	
Steneraagle, Chas	New Orleans, July 15—64	Kelly, Edwin	Milwaukee, Nov 22—64	**REGIMENTAL ROSTER.**
Small, Jas	New Orleans, Sept 22—64	Martin, David B	Memphis, Sept 6—4	Col F A Haskell* Cold Harbor, June 3—64
Small, Jno H	Natchez, Sept 8—64	Nicolay, Henry	St Charles, Aug 15—64	Col Jno A Savage, Jr Washington, July 1—64
Thompson, Ole	Morganzia, Aug 14—64	Nohls, P A, me	Burlington	Col Harvey M Brown Columbus
Tragen, Leonard, cd	Des Moines, Ia	Penhallow, Ruben	Morganzia, Sept 21—64	Col C E Warner Windsor
Warne, Jas	New Orleans, Sept 12—64	Pettit, D F	Ironton	Lt Col Wm H Hamilton Sun Prairie
		Robinson, Melvin C	New Orleans, Aug 31—64	Maj Geo A Fisk Sparta
H		Robble, G	Ironton	Adj Benj D Atwell
		Slater, Fred'k	Morganzia, June 30—64	Q M Chas B Peck
Capt Cornelius Cuntz		Snelzer, Jonathan	Brazos Santiago, July 26—65	Q M F S Capron
Capt Chas Wegemann		Sweet, Julius	Racine	Surg Clarkson Miller Geneva, Dec 30—64
Lt Henry Hayden		Schubring, —	Black Hawk	Surg E A Woodward
Lt Chas H Wareham		Tuttle, Harris	St Charles, Aug 12—64	Surg L F H Bunnell
Lt David Hunter	Caldwell's Prairie	West, Isaac H	Natchez, Aug 8—64	A Surg Geo D Winch
Lt David O'Connell				A Surg Jno H Benedict
Gergen, Wm	Neillsville			A Surg C S Knapp
Gerhardt, Jno, corp	New Orleans, July 16—64	**K**		A Surg Geo W Jenkins
Sutter, Jno F, corp	New Orleans, Sep 3—64			Chap Peter S Van Nist
Birchler, Martin	Port Hudson, July 17—64			Chap B C Hammond
Baldauf, Jno	New Orleans, July 17—64	Capt August Beecher		
Black, Chas	Sep 25—64	Capt Archibald H Adams		**A**
Brown, Millard F	Morganzia, Sep 30—64	Lt Hermann Schaul		
Carley, Geo R	St Louis, June 18—64	Lt Chas J Walther		Capt W H Hamilton Sun Prairie
Carroll, K A	Grafton, Ia	Lt Jno C Pink		Capt Chas E Griffin
Crosier, Robert	New Orleans, Aug 11—64	Schilling, Sebastian, sgt	Addison, Oct 30—64	Lt Chas L Sholes Milwaukee
Drussen, Bartholomew	Port Hudson, July 18—64	Echternach, Jno, sgt	Port Hudson, July 4—64	Lt A S Ripley
Devin, Jno	Whitewater, Oct 9—64	Florey, Geo A, corp	Chicago, Oct 8—64	Lt Jas F Linn
Frana, Jos	Vicksburg, Aug 10—64	Allen, Jacob	Reedsburg, Aug 16—65	Lewis, Wm T, sgt Salisbury, Oct 27—64
Fusshoeller, Max	New Orleans, Sep 14—64	Becker, Jno C	Brownsville, Nov 16—64	Ferris, Geo W, corp+ Washington, June 17—64
Gokey, Eugene	Cairo, Oct 3—64	Burdick, Erastus P	Morganzia, Nov 5—64	Walling, Walter, corp Petersburg, July 19—64
Goebel, Henry	New Orleans, Oct 25—64	Cullen, Dempster	Morganzia, Sept 3—64	Boulton, Jas Madison, Mar 16—64
Huntley, Delos W	New Orleans, Aug 9—64	Dobberfuhl, Carl	Zoar	Bills, Wm H City Point, June 11—64
Hangaruier, Jacob	Morganzia, Oct 11—64	Giffin, Abraham	Ironton	Brown, Edward Transport, Sept 29—64
Hunter, David	Caldwell's Prairie	Gautner, Matthias	Memphis, Sept 7—64	Bitting, Chas Salisbury, Dec 29—64
Konrad, Mathias	Cairo, Oct 4 64	Harrington, Thos B	Port Hudson, May 29—64	Bailey, Ezra S Washington, June 4—65
Kretzschmar, August	New Orleans, Oct 8—64	Hanke, Christian	Port Hudson, Sept 4—64	Beaver, Peter, f Spring Green
Landgraf, Jno	New Orleans, Sep 17—64	Huhn, Jos	Morganzia, Sept 5—64	Dewey, Fred'k, f Poyslppi
Lehner, Jno	Cairo, Oct 21—64	Hacket, Michael	Rock Elm Centre	Coon, David Salisbury, Nov 2—64
Maguire, Sam'l	St Charles, Aug 17—64	Hippach, Franz Jos	Menominee, Neb	Cattin, Jos M Salisbury, Jan 3—65
Markham, Alfred P	Eagle	Johnson, H C	Waldo	Claridge, Thos W White Mound
Nickless, Jos	Natchez, Nov 15—64	Jargle, Bertram, f	Ashford	Claridge, Geo White Mound
Paar, Illiger	Morganzia, July 14—64	Lambert, Frank	Port Hudson, May 16—64	Dibol, Daniel A* May 27—64
Schneider, Jos	Sep 29—64	Leiser, Boniface	July 18—64	Davis, David W Salisbury, Dec 6—64
Smith, Jas	Morganzia, Sep 16—64	Lumby, Jos	Port Hudson, July 17—64	Dyball, Jas Salisbury, Dec 5—64
Smith, Henry	Morganzia, Sep 28—64	Lyons, Jas	New Orleans, Aug 25—64	Fazel, J D, f Orion
Tuttle, Harris	St Charles, Aug 12—64	Lehmann, Aug	Theresa	Haydon, Henry J Petersburg, June 19—64
Vanslyke, Barnett	Natchez, Aug 20—64	Mathus, Geo*	Spanish Fort, Mar 30—65	Hand, Geo G Salisbury, Nov 10—64
Willis, Peter	Morganzia, Sep 16—64	Maxfield, Chas	Morganzia, Aug 25—64	Hahn, B C Richland Centre
Wind, Chas	Natchez, Aug 8—64	Mead, Luther	Vicksburg, Oct 18—64	Jacobs, Jno Salisbury, Nov 6—64
		Newkirk, Tunis D	Vicksburg, Aug 30—64	Moore, Alonzo M Madison, Apr 4—64
I		Norton, Levi R	Morganzia, Sept 3—64	Moon, Wm W Madison, Apr 5—64
		Pugh, David F	Morganzia, Sept 21—64	McIntyre, Jas C* May 27—64
		Schuh, Jno	New Orleans, July 7—64	McNartin, Andrew J Salisbury, Jan 17—65
Capt Erhard Weber		Simon, Anton, l	Milwaukee	Mead, Ezekiel Washington, July 5—64
Capt Lyman B Everdell		Sorith, E	Tomah	Norris, Benj B Madison, May 7—64
Lt Henry E Ray		Taft, Daniel M	St Charles, May 24 61	Reason, Reanard White Mound
Lt Henry Martynson		Vesey, Jas M	Port Hudson, June 27—64	Retnard, Benson, f Plain
Lt Julius Lueck		Wilson		Reeley, G G Spring Green
Klabbatz, Edw, sgt	New Orleans, Sept 10—64			Scheble, A C Spring Green
Detyoch, Andrew, sgt, f	Burlington	**UNASSIGNED.**		Slaughter, Jno C Madison, Mar 22—64
Haas, Jno, sgt, m	Burlington			Smith, Chas F Salisbury, Feb 19—65
Eastman, Chas E, corp	Vicksburg, Oct 16—64	Bischoff, Wm	Tess Corners	Sheble, A C Spring Green
Ricketts, Edw H, corp	Port Hudson, July 30—64	Chambers, Abraham	Racine	Upwright, Wm City Point, June 22—64
Longstreet, Henry L, corp	Eden, Nov 19—64	Mathews, J B, inf	Fond du Lac	Vergir, Wm W Salisbury, Nov 29—64
Ackerman, Abraham	New Orleans, Sept 10—64	McKinley, Gilbert J	Mitchell	Wells, Henry W Madison, Mar 18—64
Barnum, Jno E	Morganzia, Sept 22—64	Martin, Daniel P	Marlo Centre, Kan	Wood, Andrew J Madison, Apr 17—64
Beller, Jno, f	Burlington	Schmidt, Chris	Tess Corners	Wright, Geo M Madison, Apr 26—64
Bennett, Jno H	New Orleans, Sept 30—64	Tess, Wm	Tess Corners	Wood, Jno G Madison, Apr 27—64
Cameron, Henderson	Morganzia, Aug 11—64	Tess, Fred	Tess Corners	

E. C. HIBBARD.   DAVID VANCE.

HIBBARD & VANCE,
Insurance and Vessel Agents

366 & 368 BROADWAY, MILWAUKEE, WISCONSIN.

REPRESENTING THE FOLLOWING COMPANIES.

FIRE.

IMPERIAL INSURANCE CO.,	London
NORTHERN ASSURANCE CO.,	London
COMMERCIAL UNION ASSURANCE CO.,	London
AMERICAN FIRE INSURANCE CO.,	Philadelphia
FIRE ASSOCIATION	Philadelphia
INS. CO. STATE PENNSYLVANIA	Philadelphia
BUFFALO INSURANCE CO.,	Buffalo, N. Y
TOLEDO FIRE INSURANCE CO.,	Toledo, Ohio
LA CONFIANCE,	Paris, Franc

MARINE.

PACIFIC MUTUAL,	New York
GREAT WESTERN,	New York
LAMAR,	New York
TOLEDO,	Toledo

We Solicit the Patronage of the Insuring Community.
Chicago Office, 150 Madison Street.

O. H. PATTERSON, City Agent.

WOLCOTT & GREGG.

GENERAL AGENTS FOR

Domestic & Dauntless

SEWING MACHINES.

Also Dealers in Attachments, Parts, Oils and Needles for ndard Machine.

124 GRAND AVENUE, MILWAUKEE.

JAS. S. PERKINS,
DENTIST,

130 & 132 GRAND AVENUE.

MILWAUKEE,   -   WISCONSIN.

West Side Hair Store.

Misses M. & A. Reinhard,

HAIR DRESSING

EMPORIUM,

27 Grand Avenue,   MILWAUKEE.

Ladies Hair Dressing for Balls and Weddings a Specialty.

WISCONSIN SOLDIERS AND SAILORS REUNION ROSTER.

B

Capt C E Warner — Windsor
Capt Geo Weeks — Columbus
Lt A P Warren
Lt Wm H Parker
Lt Wm H Lamberton* — June 3—64
Lt L C Jacobs
Lt P Lyman Brown
Haney, Anthony,sgt+
Older, Adelbert, corp+ — Richmond, June 15—64
Sholts, Calvin, corp+ — Richmond, June 13—64
Arnold, Lewis H* — Tolopotomoy, June 1—64
Barber, W A, m — Tolopotomoy, June 1—64
Baker, Chas W — Warrens Mills
Corey, Geo — Soldiers Grove
Courtier, Hezekiah — Washington, July 20—64
Cassiday, Jno — Annapolis, Oct 26—64
Duffy, Patrick* — Vernon
Du Bouine, Jno H* — Tolopotomoy, June 1—64
Davis, Jno F — Tolopotomoy, June 1—64
DuBoils, Jacob V — Andersonville, Sept 1—63
Fritz, Jas E* — Salisbury, Feb 28—65
Friday, Henry t* — Tolopotomoy, June 1—64
Finnell, Geo W+ — Tolopotomoy, June 1—64
Gunnell, Thomas — Washington, July 10—64
Grout, Ferd — Deep Bottom, Aug 14—64
Guest, Wilton C — Madison, Apr 4—64
Hundley, Geo — Rock Elm Centre
Hopkins, Jas H — Richmond, June 28—64
Harper, Geo* — Salisbury, Dec 4—64
Hawes, Milener — Tolopotomoy, June 1—64
Jayne, Edw L — Reams Station, Aug 25—64
Kite, Geo — Washington, Apr 5—64
Larson, Lauretz — Eagle Corners
Large, A T — Madison, Apr 1—64
McKveney, Wash'n D — Omaha, Neb
Mathien, Hubert — Blackwells Is, hep 18—64
McGinnis, P A — Dec 1—64
Newell, Whitfield S* — Concord
Older, Wallace* — Tolopotomoy, June 1—64
Priest, Gilbert S — Tolopotomoy, June 1—64
Pultz, Abraham — Excelsior, Apr 13—64
Petley, Hiram — Madison, Apr 18—64
Perkins, Andrew E — Richmond, July 2—64
Parker, Wm H — Richmond, July 6—64
Quinaby, Jno — Lawler, Ie
Smith, Jno L — Weyauwega
Tarr, Johnson — Andersonville, Oct 15—64
Thompson, Robt W* — Weyauwega
Thompson, Darwin D — Tolopotomoy, June 1—64
Titus, Jas — Andersonville, July 9—64
Williams, Hugh — Campbellsport
Weeks, Geo — Alexandria, Oct 6—64
Wiley, Jno M — Columbus
Hartford

C

Capt Geo A Fisk — Sparta
Capt Stephen C Miles — Prairie Farm
Lt L B Noyes — Marinette
Lt C E Bullard — Eau Claire
Lt G W Johnson — Cataract
Lt Holt Tompkins
Lt Arch Carnahan — Cataract
Cross, Geo C, sgt — Madison, May 13—64
Gallagher, Thos W, sgt — Petersburg, June 23—64
Cleaves, Cordon L, sgt* — Petersburg, June 18—64
Snyder, Willard B, corp — Petersburg, May 18—64
Amidon, Elijah H+ — Annapolis, July 9—64
Aylesworth, Leslie — Toniah
Balcom, Russel D+ — Petersburg, July 31—64
Brown, Houston+ — Deep Bottom, Aug 24—64
Barnes, John C — Madison, Apr 10—64
Butts, Martin A — Salisbury, Nov 20—64
Britton, Dan A — Annapolis, Mar 26—65
Cole, Darwin* — Petersburg, June 18—64
Casner, Thos+ — Deep Bottom, Aug 26—64
Douglas, David* — Petersburg, June 18—64
Dayton, Wm — Washington, June 26—64

Dawes, Robt A
Dunbar, Alf, bill poster
Farr, Phidelus
Graves, Nathan
Hudson, Harvey W+
Hopwood, Jno F
Hathaway, Henry
Hubbell, Jas
Ingols, Augustus B+
McClure, Chas L*
Nichols, Edw
Noyes, Lute B
Potter, Jos W, m
Printz, Jno
Rathbone, Eldridge+
Sour, Cyrus
Smith, Sam'l
Stevens, Jno E
Van Burst, Lawrence
Van Vickle, Walter
Walker, Perry C*
Wilkinson, Jno
Wdeott, Jerome B
Willsey, J J, f
Witzheb, Chas, l
Young, Chas

Cataract
Sparta
Salisbury, Dec 12—64
Salisbury, Dec 14—64
Petersburg, July 28—64
Petersburg, Aug 20—64
Salisbury, Dec 18—64
Salisbury, Jan 14—65
Petersburg, June 18—64
Cold Harbor, June 3—64
Salisbury, Nov 27—64
Marinette
Sparta
Salisbury, Jan 14—65
Washington, June 7—64
Madison, Apr 10—64
Madison, May 23—64
Salisbury, Nov 28—64
Salisbury, Jan 16—65
Salisbury, Feb 2—65
Petersburg, June 18—64
Annapolis, June 30—64
Madison, Apr 6—64
Leon
Riceville
Salisbury, Feb 25—65

D

Capt Jacob Walkey
Capt Wesley S Potter
Capt Jas P Vance
Lt A P Lockerby
Lt Daniel Whalen
Lt Jas B Taylor, f
Lt O L Baldwin
Lt E D Faucher
Patton, Wesley W, sgt*
Vandyck, Henry, corp*
Adams, Nathaniel*
Beckman, Michael
Crale, David H*
Dyson, David*
Dennis, Wm H*
Dickerson, Geo
Frost, Geo W*
Fuller, Colby, E*
Flemmer, Ford'g
Haffner, Jacob
Kruger, Wm
Mills, Chas A+
McLain, Geo
McJanklin, Jno S
O'Connor, Chas H*
Potter, Stafford D
Peterson, Nelson
Thompson, Simon
Utiger, Godfroy*
Vanderhilt, Jno W H
Wright, Milan C*

Millard
Sept 19—64

Cold Harbor, June 5—64
Cold Harbor, June 3—64
Annapolis, June 30—64
Salisbury, Nov 15—64
Petersburg, June 18—64
Reams Station, Aug 25—64
Petersburg, June 18—64
Salisbury, Dec 3—64
Petersburg, June 18—64
Petersburg, June 13—64
Madison, June 10—64
Muscoda
Salisbury, Dec 10—64
James River, Aug 14—64
Madison, May 8—64
Washington, Sept 3—64
Deep Bottom, Aug 14—64
Petersburg, Jan 28—64
Salisbury, Nov 20—64
Salisbury, Nov 12—64
Cold Harbor, June 5—64
Andersonville, Sept 19—64
Reams Station, Aug 25—64

E

Capt Jerome F Brooks
Lt Chas W Dipple
Lt Jas Greeley
Lt Porter Jones
Lt H B Ginty — Reams Station, Aug 26—64
Lt Jno Payne
Paddock, Edw R, sgt — Aug 23—64
Davidson, Henry F* — Tolopotomoy, June 1—64
Abel, Christian* — Tolopotomoy, June 1—64
Blackman, Martin, f — West Bend
Bower, Geo* — Tolopotomoy, June 1—64
Barber, Ephraim H* — Tolopotomoy, June 1—64
Bradford, Richard* — Tolopotomoy, June 1—64
Barker, Geo M* — Tolopotomoy, June 1—64
Baker, Inman* — Chickahominy, June 13—64
Bacon, Jno W* — Reams Station, Aug 25—64
Boyer, Wm — Washington, Aug 30—64
Bradford, Ira A, f — Sheboygan Falls

Bradford, David A — Sheboygan
Carter, Wm H* — Tolopotomoy, June 1—64
Conklin, Austin* — Tolopotomoy, June 1—64
Chipman, Joshua F+ — Washington, Oct 17—64
Corwin, Jas — Richmond, June 6—64
Chaplin, Wm — Plymouth
Douglas, S — Waldo
Emmery, Nathan, sgt — West Bend
Griggs, Jno A — Salisbury, Jan—65
Hoag, Philip — Washington, July 21—64
Hardee, Edw — Washington, Nov 4—64
Huber, Jos, l — West Bend
Justin, Jay P — Petersburg, Sept 27—64
Johnson, Geo — Osceola
Knoche, Henry — Madison, Mar 30-64
Kelsey, Wm, m — Columbia, Ind
Kircker, Jas D, l — West Bend
Loclis, Louis — Washington, Oct 5—64
Mack, Nelcour — Richmond, Dec 4—64
Mitchell, Henry B — Madison, Apr 1—64
Miller, Myron L — Plymouth, Sept 6—64
McGinnis, P A, f — Concord
Martich, Peter — Cascade
Prey, Edw W — Philadelphia, July 15—64
Richmond, Seymour* — Tolopotomoy, June 1—64
Reek, Herbert — Cold Harbor, June 3—64
Rood, Wm — Philadelphia, July 1—64
Root, M V, f — Plymouth
Shepard, Robert* — Tolopotomoy, June 1—64
Stagg, Chas N — Salisbury, Oct 27—64
Santer, Fred'k, f — Scott
Tiffany, Sam'l W* — Tolopotomoy, June 1—64
Tom-ity, Wm, f — Plymouth
Wilson, Geo — Richmond, June 12—64

F

Capt P D Burwell — Richmond, June 28—64
Capt O N Russell — Milwaukee
Lt Geo E Albee
Lt N J Kellogg — Warrens Mills
Twining, P E, sgt+ — Philadelphia, Oct 11—64
Daily, Jos L, sgt — Washington, Aug 10—64
Frank, Chas H, corp — Belle Island, June 28—64
Atkins, Dewitt C+ — Sun Prairie, Aug 1—64
Brazee, Martin — Salisbury, Nov 24—64
Cassiday, Frank* — Cold Harbor, June 3—64
Chapin, Marvin J — Leeds, Mar 30—65
Foster, Jno E — Madison, Apr 28—64
Hamer, Geo T, contractor — Princeton
Johnson, Leonard H — Dayton, July 8—64
Knapp, J D, liveryman — Nashua, Ia
Marr, Jno B — Philadelphia, Oct 20—64
Main, Henry — Andersonville, Oct 20—64
Magill, Wm, me — Princeton
Moe, Jno, agent — Princeton
McElroy, Chas, f — Adel
McIntyre, W N, drummer — Princeton
O'Neil, Torrence, f — Leon
Pilisbury, Granville — Salisbury, Nov 20—64
Soper, Sherman H — Salisbury, Nov 10—64
Wicks, Clarence+ — Richmond, July 18—64

G

Capt R Lindley* — Deep Bottom, Aug 14—64
Capt Wm R Newton — Friendship
Capt Wm H Lane
Lt Jas S Frisbie
Lt W S Leach
Lt Jas Aubery — Chicago, Ill
Couch, Reuben C, sgt — Salisbury, Jan 18—65
Durr, Fred'k, corp — Richmond, June 30—64
Thurber, Daniel, corp — Andersonville, Oct 21—64
Austin, Jno — Andersonville, Oct 27—64
Adams, Arthur F — Andersonville, Sept 2—64
Bartlett, Wm R+ — Washington, June 22—64
Bergen, Chas — Richmond, June 18—64
Bowe, Jno — Andersonville, Sept—64
Crites Jonas — Salisbury, Jan 25—65
Dick, Benjamin — Andersonville, Aug 25—64

MONITOR FORCE FEED GRAIN DRILL,
MANUFACTURED BY
VAN BRUNT & DAVIS CO., HORICON.

Many New and Important Features. Warranted to do Perfect Work.

We manufacture the Monitor Broadcast Seeder and Cultivator. Which has the largest sale of any made.

WHEELS THAT WILL NOT WOBBLE BY USE.

CONSTRUCTED OF THE BEST MATERIAL.

We know they are better than any made. No bearing on horses necks. No gearing in end of boxes to fill with mud. Will out wear any other.

FARMERS SAY THEY ARE THE BEST.

THE SIMPLEST AND MOST PERFECT DRILL MADE.

Feed That Gets Away With All Competition. It will seed Grass Seeds, Wheat, Oats, Corn, Peas and Beans. No Bunching or Lost Motion.

SEND FOR CIRCULARS.

WISCONSIN SOLDIERS AND SAILORS REUNION ROSTER.

Endranger, Peter* — Tolopotomoy, June 1–64
Elui, Isaac — Tolopotomoy, June 1–64
Engelhardt, Henry — Andersonville, Dec 14–64
Fenner, Gottlieb* — Tolopotomoy, June 1–64
Feteridge, Robt, l — Oshkosh
Gannon, Jno* — Tolopotomoy, June 1–64
Graudte, Henry S — Tolopotomoy, June 1–64
Goon, Jno — Andersonville, Aug 22–64
Goon, Thos E — Salisbury, Dec 9–64
Hart Orvil A, f — Brothertown
Hanford, Henry* — Cold Harbor, June 6–64
Hall, Jno — Salisbury, Jan 19–65
Kroeniz, Fred'k — Salisbury, Jan 20–65
Kruger, Wm — Andersonville, Sept 17–64
Larrabee, Geo — Washington, July 19–64
Malthouse, Jas — Salisbury, Jan 30–65
Manderschield, Louis, m — Calumet
Newton, W R — Friendship
Ormond, M M, ph — Milwaukee
Peck, Truman — Madison, Apr 12–64
Stratton, Israel D — Tolopotomoy, June 1–64
Skinner, Henry A — Madison, Mar 22–64
Sweeting, Theodore, f — Plymouth
Willis, David* — Tolopotomoy, June 1–64
Wortman, Theo V* — Tolopotomoy, June 1–64

H

Lt Cyrus Peck
Lt Geo S Morris — Carpentersville, Ill
Lt Jas G Merrill
Howell, Jno K, sgt+ — Alexandria, Aug 1–64
Tichenur, E D, sgt — Andersonville, Aug 18–64
Hill, Somon W, corp+ — Petersburg, June 19–64
Jacobs, Lester C, corp — Richmond, Oct–04
Oleson, Sam, corp — Salisbury, Nov 26–64
Lull, Marcus S, corp — Salisbury, Dec 1–64
Acken, Fred* — Cold Harbor, June 6–64
Brennan, Jno — Salisbury, Dec 10–64
Bush, A N — Ithaca
Daggett, Alanson — Salisbury, Nov 27–64
Dunstan, Thos A — Annapolis, Sep 12–64
Dargan, Pat — Salisbury, Dec 2–64
Earl, Geo W+ — City Point, June 26–64
Ertel, Daniel — Salisbury Dec 11–64
Fisher, Fred — Alexandria, Sept 3–64
Fazel, J H — Orion
Grotavant, Jesse F — Reams Station, Aug 20–64
Hale, Timothy O — Salisbury, Nov 19–64
Hayes, Sam'l H — Salisbury, Feb 3–65
Jennings, Fred — Blue Earth City, Minn
Kohler, Joshua — Washington, Aug 14–64
Lee, Jno — City Point, July 13–64
Morris, Thos* — North Anna R, May 20–64
McDonald, Geo W — Salisbury, Dec 31–64
Mettick, Matthias — Soldiers Grove
Passmore, Richard J* — Petersburg, June 18–61
Pease, Sam'l A — Richmond, Oct–61
Parker, Richard — Salisbury, Jan 16–65
Pritchard, Jno O, c — Iowa City, Ia
Popp, Jno,f — Boaz
Randall, Reuben H — Salisbury, Nov 20–64
Ripley, Sam'l D — Salisbury, Dec 2–64
Tisdale, Milan* — North Anna R, May 26–61
Thompson, Peter — Salisbury, Nov 30–64
Thomulll, A W, f — Grand Meadow, Minn
Van Dusen, Morgan* — Alexandria, July 1–64
Van Etten, Wm C — Louisville, Mar 4–65
Williams, Lewis — Madison, Apr 9–64
Welcher, Lorenzo — Madison, Apr 29–64
Wright, Albert — Salisbury, Feb 25–65

I

Capt D F Farrand — Gary, D T
Capt E W Haydon
Capt M T Matthews — Trempeleau
Lt C W Skinner
Lt Jas Smith — LaCrosse
Lt Jno J McDonald — LaCrosse

Ball, Truman P, agt+ — Deep Bottom, Aug 14–64
Grant, Benj F, corp* — Petersburg, June 18–64
Bryant, Frank M* — Petersburg, June 18–64
Brice, Milt* — Cold Harbor, June 3–64
Burns, Wm C — Madison, Apr 14–64
Brown, Geo — Madison, July 10–61
Bagley, Jas — Andersonville, Aug 26–64
Bugley, Alvah — Salisbury, Nov 23–64
Branton, Thos N, — Rocky Run
Crannn, Nat* — Cold Harbor, June 3–64
Calkins, Riley — Washington, June 10–64
Dougherty, Terence — Salisbury, Dec 11–64
Farrand, D F — Gary, D T
Gough, Wm — Salisbury, Nov 5–64
Howe, Leonard V — Salisbury, Dec 1–64
Lathrop, Wm W — Madison, Mar 25–65
McLaulln, Chas — Andersonville, June 24–64
Mills, Tim Jr — Salisbury, Nov 13–61
Martin, Wm — Madison, Apr 16–64
McDonald, J J — LaCrosse
Nash, Jno E — Washington, June 17–65
Odell, Cassius M* — Cold Harbor, June 3–64
Reynolds, Oscar* — Petersburg, Sept 30–64
Skilton, Jno* — Washington, Sept 17–64
Sherwood, C A, f — Whitehall
Tebay, Jno W — Davids Island, Aug 3–61
White, Geo E — Cold Harbor, June 3–64
Wilcox, Andrew J, f — Clyde, Kan

K

Capt Warren Graves — Aug 29–64
Capt Jos Harris
Capt Jos R Ellis
Lt Elias A Galloway* — Petersburg, June 19–64
Lt H D Schaefer
Lt Lyman C Jacobs
Davis, Jas, corp — City Point, July 11–64
Adams, Albert B+ — June 12–64
Butterfield, Wm F* — Petersburg, June 18–61
Bittles, Matthew+ — Petersburg, June 21–64
Biesecker, Reuben+ — LaCrosse, Aug 25–64
Benner, Nathaniel H — Whitehouse, June 10–64
Bradshaw, Jas D
Bowers, R — Hamlin
Campbell, Geo W — June 27–61
Cable, Marvin J — Salisbury, Oct 25–64
Coleman, Jordan — Salisbury, Oct 16–61
Crosby, Orson T — Salisbury, N C
Christopherson, Bernt — Elk Mound
Crandall, David — Rusk
Curtis, Alonzo A, sgt — Menominee
Ermalinger, Chas+ — Petersburg, June 22–64
Fairweather, David C — Belle Isle, Sept 22–64
Foss, Anton — Rocks Falls
Graham, Johnson — Annapolis, Oct 9–61
Hobbs, Walter L* — Cold Harbor, June 3–61
Hill, Jno+ — City Point, June 8–64
Houn, Jno B — Madison, Apr 26–64
Hoyt, Henry J
Howe, Martin L — Elk Mound
Johnson, Lars — Cold Harbor, June 3–64
Johnson, Oliver* — Petersburg, June 18–64
Johnson, Jno W — Menominee
Lee, Philip+ — Washington, June 11–64
Laforge, Jno T — Madison, Mar 29–64
Nelson, Samuel L — Salisbury, N C
Appelt, Martin L — Washington, June 11–64
Peterson, Lars+ — Washington, June 11–64
Pratt, Lewis+ — Alexandria, Aug 31–64
Pyle, Amos M
Reed, Edw — Salisbury, N C
Rains, Jno S — Washington, June 26–65
Swan, C H — Rock Falls
Tillesou, Harold T E — Elk Mound
Wright, Henry* — Petersburg, June 16–64

UNASSIGNED.

Brice, G W — LaCrosse
Brice, C — LaCrosse
Markham, Andrew J, sgt maj — Fremont

McIntyre, Warren — Princeton
Miller, Columbus, l — Chippewa City
Rogers, Jno, l — Whitewater
Smith, Jas — LaCrosse
Wilson, S — LaCrosse
Welch, W H — Blair

THIRTY-SEVENTH INFANTRY.

One, Two and Three Years. Organized February, 1864. Original strength, 708; gain by recruits, etc., 436. Total, 1144. Death loss, 217—Killed in action, 95, died of wounds, 40, of disease, 76. Other losses, 283—missing, 0, desertions, 29, transfers, 29, discharges, 195. Strength at muster-out, July 27th, 1865, 649. Campaigns in Virginia.

REGIMENTAL ROSTER.

Col Sam'l Harriman — Somerset
Lt Col A O Doolittle
Lt Col Jno J Kershaw — Milwaukee
Lt Robt C Eden — Kent, England
Maj Alva Nash — Waushara Co
Adj C I Miltimore — Janesville
Q M Wm C Webb — Kansas
Q M N B Prentice — Dakota
Serg Dan'l C Roundy — Davenport, Ia
A Surg Geo H Calkins — Waupaca
A Surg H J Young
A Surg Emery Sherman — Palmyra
Chap L M Howes

A

Capt Sam'l Stevens* — Petersburg, June 18–64
Capt Sanford Jones — Washington, Aug 18–64
Capt Dan'l A Lowber — Wampun
Lt H W Belden — Milwaukee
Lt Geo Hurst
Lt Theo Hobby
Lt S M Steel
Lt Geo W Teal
Hunt Oliver H, sgt — Alexandria, Dec 11–64
Wheeler, Benj F, corp* — Petersburg, June 17–64
Wade, Tim E, corp — Alexandria, Nov 7–64
Allen, L, f — Mauston
Anderson, Benj — Spring Green
Black, Wm J Jr — Alexandria, July 12–64
Beecher, Leroy — Virginia, July 7–65
Davis, Jno — Spring Green
Frit, Z C, a — Steel City, Neb
Greenhalgh, Jno E* — Petersburg, June 18–64
Hacker, T L, clerk — Madison
Lane, Jesse+ — Washington, July 7–64
Oleson, Amund — Ft Schuyler, Sept 19–64
Odell, Jno A — Richmond
Peake, Jno — Washington, July 7–64
Page, Martin — Chippewa Falls
Ruener, Jno — Madison, Nov 14–64
Rensiner, Jos — Un ly
Ransom, J C — Neillsville
Scott, Walter — Petersburg, June 24–64
Smith, Wm B* — Petersburg, June 18–64
Sanford, Munson B* — Petersburg, June 18–61
Thatcher, T J — Clear Lake
VanDusen, Edw N* — Petersburg, July 30–64
Warner, Jas L* — Petersburg, June 18–64
Whitney, Almeron* — Petersburg, June 18–64

B

Capt Robt C Eden — Kent, England
Capt N S Davison
Capt L D Harmon
Lt Wm H Earl+ — Washington, July 4–64
Lt Jno E Williamson

T. G. FISH.   E. D. FISH, 12th Wis. Battery.   J. C. HUGGINS, 2nd Wis. Vols.

FISH BROTHERS & CO.,
RACINE, MANUFACTURERS OF WISCONSIN,

Farm, Freight and Spring Wagons!

OF EVERY DESCRIPTION.

Open and Top Buggies, Phaetons and Carriages!

The material used in the construction of Our Vehicles is carefully Selected and of the Very Best Quality.

All Wheels Soaked in Boiling Oil Warranted to Stand in any Climate.

THE BEST WAGON ON WHEELS.

It is the STRONGEST and BEST PROPORTIONED, BEST MADE, BEST IRONED and BEST PAINTED Wagon in the market. It is the lightest running Farm wagon in the world, and the only wagon having the celebrated Holmes Patent Self-Oiling Skein.

We make only one grade of work and that is the Best.

Parties Ordering from us can rely on getting an A No. 1 job and just as represented.

No 178. TWO-SEATED THREE-SPRING PHAETON.

Fine English Broadcloth, or fancy colored leather trimming, Side Lamps and Best Leather Top. Makes a very Handsome, Durable and Comfortable Family Carriage. Send for a copy of our Illustrated Catalogue.

WISCONSIN SOLDIERS AND SAILORS REUNION ROSTER.   167

Lt F D Powers — Grand Rapids
Bennett, Jas, sgt — Madison
Rice, Orson E, sgt+ — Aug 14 –64
Brown, Henry G, corp+ — Washington, Aug 3—64
Barber, W A, m — Warrens Mills
Barber, Wm, m — Warrens Mills
Barnes, Wm E — City Point, Nov 10—64
Bartell, David — Sylvan Corners
Barnes, Hollis J — Berks, Jan 17—65
Cross, Otis* — Petersburg, July 30—64
Casier, E S, me — Rutland
Duley, Jno M — Sept 28 –64
Dutcher, H — Neillsville
Eaton, Cyrus R — Alexandria, Aug 3—64
Finly, Hugh* — Petersburg, June 18—64
France, Augusta, f — Waterman, Ia
Fuller, Napoleon* — Petersburg, July 9—64
Holton, Jno C — Madison, Apr 27—64
Hall, Jno* — Petersburg, June 17—64
Lee, Hugh — Washington, June 24—64
Luhm, Fred'k — Washington, Nov 18—64
Lattin, Sylvester — Olivet, D T
Lockirby, Mathew L — Grapeland, Minn
Lulu, W C — Black River Falls
Lockhart, Thos A — E o
Millard, D R — Kearney, Neb
Nelly, Jas B — Fremont
O'Reilly, Michael* — Petersburg, July 26—64
Powers, F D — Oregon
Rily, Michael* — Petersburg, June 18—64
Scoville, Leonard D* — Petersburg, June 18—64
Scott, Stephen — Fremont
Scoville, A H — Washington, July 15—64
Smith, Fred R — Rush Centre, Kan
Shoemaker, J P — Fremont
Tuttle, Peter II* — Petersburg, June 17—64
Wajahn, Wilhelm* — Petersburg, June 18—64
Young, Aaron* — Petersburg, June 17—64

C

Capt H W Belden — Milwaukee
Lt A J Parker
Lt Philip Lawrence — Kansas
Lt Wm Green
Lt F B Riddle* — Petersburg, June 27—64
Lt D A Sherwood — Alexandria, Neb
Green, Wm H, sgt+ — July 30—64
Clark, Chas, corp* — Petersburg, July 13—65
Estee, Jno W, corp* — Petersburg, Apr 2—64
Wheelock, Eugene, corp* — July 30—64
Argue, Thos — Alexandria, —64
Baker, Bryant
Baker, J — Neillsville
Crocker, Andrew E+ — Washington, Ju 1 - 64
Calgrove, Webster — Washington, July 17—64
Cooper, Frank — Black River Falls
Cooper Francis, ed — Black River Falls
Domey, Henry* — Petersburg, Apr 2—65
Evans, Boo Devine
Fuller, Joshua P* — Petersburg, July 30—64
Foster, J — Menominee
Hogness, Mathias G — Sep 11—64
Harrison, J S — Lone Rock
Lulke, Adolph, me — West Bend
Fergay, Nathaniel* — Petersburg, July 30—64
Rasey, Francis* — Petersburg, June 18—64
Ross, Otis* — Petersburg, June 18—64
Scott, Aaron — Washington, May 29 -64
Schrrer, Nicholas — Newbury
Sherwood, David, me — Alexandria, Neb
Thatcher, T J — Cylon
Woods, Ben
Williams, Thos R — July 13–64
Webster, Francis — July 19—64
Walker, Peter+ — Petersburg, Aug 23—64
Wood, Chas* — July 19—64
Weed, Ed — Mapleton, Minn

D

Capt Alva Nash — Waushara
Capt F J Munger
Lt Jas E Ramsbottom
Lt Webster C Pope — Apr 30—64
Lt David Frutsman* — Petersburg, June 28—64
Lt Geo Hurst
Lt Jno W Joslyn
Lt J A Schofield
Gustin, Geo W, sgt — City Point, Jan 3—65
Shumway, Geo B, corp* — Petersburg, June 17—64
Hayward, F, corp — Willards Point, Oct 5—64
Westbrook, Zachariah, corp — Danville, Nov 7—64
Bahren, Fred — Orihula
Duell, Joel, corp* — Petersburg, July 28—64
Eager, Dan'l C, corp* — Washington, July 14—64
Eager, Thos* — Petersburg, July 30—64
Eagan, Michael — Marion, Sept 26—64
Eagan, John, t — Spring Lake
Gillet, Elihu R — Alexandria, Aug 10—64
Gifford, J M — Jefferson
Hortz, Jno* — Ft Mahone, Apr 2—65
Harmon, Albion — Alexandria, July 5—64
Hildebrand, Jos — Orihula
Hills, Eber H — Madison, May 7—64
Hurst, Chas — Ft Schuyler, Sept 29—64
King, Jas — Washington, May 17—65
Lane, David R — Oasis
Mills, Noah — Washington, Aug 5—64
Robinson, F B — Mauston
Putnam, Lyman — City Point, Aug 12—64
Schmidt, Jos — Orihula
Shower, J A J — Mazomanie
Spect, Fred'k — Danville, Nov 3—64
Sigher, Jno — Orihula
Wagner, Marcus+ — Washington, July 8—64

E

Capt F A Cole+ — Washington, Oct 4—64
Lt Lewis U Beall — Foud du Lac—78
Cap: Wm W Buck
Lt Thos Earl
Lt M A Barry — Lodi
Lt J W Shadbolt
Douglas, Arch, 1st sgt+ — Petersburg, Aug 2—64
Meluser, Wm, corp* — July 30—64
Briggs, Robert L — Danville, Va
Brightman, Wendell D* — July 30—64
Boyer, Moses* — June 18—64
Combs, Jas W — Davids Island, N Y
Comstock, Marinus — Madison, Apr 24—64
Campbell, A L, ed — Exira, Ia
Ecke, Herman — Hilbert
Eagan, Michael — Marion, Sept 26—64
Ferry, Albert O, pa — Chilton
Fuller, Levi — Brillion
Green, Wm* — Petersburg, June 18—64
Gillett, Cyrus B — Madison, June 3—64
Gunter, Wm — Alexandria, Apr 16—65
Huntsinger, C — Warrens Mills
Laukins, Jas+ — Aug 17—64
Marshall, Jno S* — Petersburg, June 18—61
Merchant, Alex — Dewittville, N Y
Osier, Jos — July 16- 64
Partridge, Edw B* — Petersburg, June 18 -01
Speckt, Fred'k — Danville, Nov 3—64
Thompson, Jno* — Petersburg, June 17—64
Thompson, Chas B* — Petersburg, June 17—64
Whipple, Wm W, f — Avoca, Ia

F

Capt Ellsworth Burnett — River Falls
Lt Jas C Spencer — Baraboo
Lt Wm Hasson
Lt Wm H Dodge — Augusta
Lt H W Belden — Milwaukee
Lt J W Winchester — River Falls

Howes, Walter M, sgt* — Petersburg, Apr 2—65
Biss, Morris W, sgt* — Petersburg, July 30—64
Chinnock, G W, sgt — Troy
Butcher, Jno, sgt+ — Petersburg, June 26—64
Huntsinger, J V, sgt — Springfield
Cline, Geo, corp* — Petersburg, Apr 2—64
Little, Jas, corp* — Petersburg, July 30—64
Adams, L T — Clarksville, Cal
Burdick, Oscar* — Petersburg, June 17—64
Bagley, Truman — Washington, Feb 8—64
Bard, Edwin — Soldiers Grove
Conaant, Wallace* — Petersburg, June 18—64
Casa, Geo* — Petersburg, July 30—64
Carlton, Hollis D — Washington, Sep 17—64
Cox, Edw — Sturgeon Bay
Dodge, Wm H — Augusta
Dunn, Payson — Hollenburg, Kansas
Forsyth, Chas A* — Petersburg, June 17—64
Gordon, Gardener S — City Point, Sep 7—64
Graham, Sam'l
Houson, Geo* — Petersburg, June 28—64
Holt, R A, f — Fryburg, Ia
Hillebert, Jno W* — Petersburg, June 18—64
Hoefner, Jno+ — Washington, Apr 20—65
Hills, Wm H
Hill, D K — Menominee
Hoey, Geo F
Jones, Evan W+ — June 21—65
Lynn, Jno — Washington, Apr 5—65
Laphain, Chas — Cylon
Oleson, Lars
Patterson, Robt — Mauston
Powell, Wm* — Petersburg, June 17—64
Ruppo, Jno F — Weyauwega
Rhodes, Henry, f — Hingham
Selleck, Isaac* — Petersburg, June 18—64
Sanders, L, f — Barton
Saxton, Norris W — Madison, May 18—64
VanHosen, Norris W* — Petersburg, July 23—64
Walden, Elisha H* — Petersburg, July 30—64
Wood, Albert G — Philadelphia, Feb 9—65

G

Capt M W Keller — Rice Lake
Capt W P Atwell — In Regular Army
Capt Jas C Spencer — Baraboo
Capt Geo Graham — Tomah
Lt Edw L Doolittle — Menominee
Lt A J Holmes
Lt H A Babcock
Hussey, Wm E, corp+ — Petersburg, Apr 3—65
Arnor, Robt A — New York, Oct 22—64
Bergemann, Christian* — Petersburg, July 30—64
Bigelow, Franklin* — Petersburg, July 30—64
Burdick, O A — Pelican, Lake, Minn
Curtin, Thos* — Petersburg, July 30—64
Daggett, Geo — Alexandria, Aug 13—64
Draper, T S — Eagle
Doolittle, E L, sgt — Menominee
Farnsworth, Jno — Danville, Nov—64
Illiou, Fred'k, f — Scott
Long, Edmund* — Petersburg, July 24—64
Lolbl, Jno — Eagle
Lee, Thos H* — Petersburg, July 30—64
Lang Nicholas H* — Petersburg, July 30—64
Lincoln, Orange M* — Petersburg, July 30—64
Nell, Chas J* — Petersburg, July 30—64
Nickell, Chas* — Beverly, Oct 22—64
Palmer, Miner+ — Petersburg, June 28—64
Powers, C L — Hartford
Page, Adolphus* — Petersburg, July 30—64
Perry, Mortimer* — Petersburg, Apr 2—65
Pero, Marius* — Petersburg, Dec 22—64
Rose, R B — Kilbourne
Schilling, Wm, f — Eau Claire
Spencer, J C — Baraboo
Schofield, Francis — Madison, May 18—64
Skinner, W H — Whitewater
Sprague, Henry R — Danville, Nov—64

SELF-OPERATING WHEEL RAKE!

Is a perfect Self-discharging Sulky Rake. The self-discharging device has no lost motion, dumps from both wheels, will work equally as well with horse going at a fast gait as at a slow one, and which rakes using gears, ratchets, etc., cannot do.

IT CAN BE OPERATED BY THE FOOT ALONE.

Leaving both hands free for driving. Yet it is a complete Hand-Dumping Rake, at the will of the driver. CAN BE OPERATED EASILY BY ANY BOY OR GIRL that can drive a horse. Solid wrought iron axle arms. It rakes clean in any kind of hay. The more it is used the better it is liked.

SEE IT! TRY IT! BUY IT!

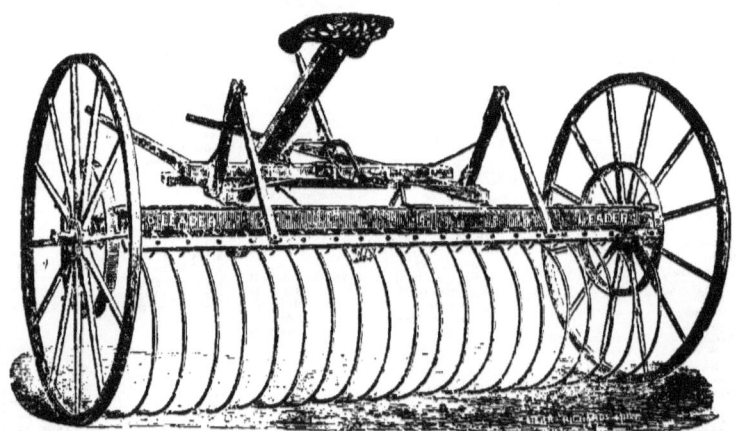

We Manufacture Three Sizes of Seeders and Cultivators

Machines with Twelve Cultivator Teeth and Five Scatterers. These are the Standard Machines, and are best adapted for general use. Machines with Ten Cultivator Teeth and Four Scatterers. Suitable for small teams and hilly farms. Machines with Fourteen Cultivator Teeth and Six Scatterers.

ALSO THE

SCOTCH PULVERIZING HARROW

In addition to the above, we manufacture seeders of any width desired without the cultivating apparatus. These machines are peculiarly adapted to farms with large acreage. Before purchasing send for our full descriptions and illustrated circulars with name of nearest agent. Address,

VAN BRUNT & BARBER,
Horicon, Wis.

WISCONSIN SOLDIERS AND SAILORS REUNION ROSTER.

Saulsbury, C, f — Little Prairie
Thatcher, Wm — Clear Lake
Thatcher, W — Cylon
Upwright, Theo T* — Petersburg, July 30—64
Wells, Wm — Petersburg, Oct 14—64
Warner, Hans D — Madison

H

Capt Frank T Hobbs — Prairie du Chien
Lt Thos Carmichael
Lt Edw I Grumley
Lt Jos H Brightman
Lt Jos Baudel
Lt Jno M Wells
Cole, David L, sgt* — Petersburg, June 18—64
Endicott, Wm A, sgt* — Petersburg, Apr 2—65
Bossack, Wm* — Petersburg, Apr 2—65
Bendrick, Jno* — Petersburg, June 18—64
Crabtree, Jno+ — Washington, Nov 8—64
Clinkhammer, Peter+ — Washington, Aug 3—64
Gault, Henry A* — Petersburg, July 30—64
Gould, Chas H* — Petersburg, June 18—61
Gillett, Marcus G+ — July 20—64
Kaselley, Wm* — Petersburg, June 18— 4
Kreinke, Carl — Orihula
Long, Thos+ — Washington, July 6—64
Leutterland, Ernest+ — Washington, July 3—64
McCloud, Dudley* — Petersburg, June 18—64
Mallow, Fred* — Petersburg, Apr 2—65
Peck, Carroll M* — Petersburg, June 18—64
Schroeder, Chas, sgt+ — Annapolis, July 6—64
Short, Thos E — Custer
Slonager, Fred — Sept 12—64
Soper, Foster M — Washington, Aug 22—64
Treigel, Herbart* — Petersburg, July 30—61
Troxill, Chas C — Mazeppa, Minn
Wood, Alexel* — Petersburg, July 30—64
Willoughby, Jno R — Sept 12—64

I

Capt Geo A Beck
Lt Edw Hanson
Lt Jas W Hitchcock — New Richmond
Lt Newell G Rowley
Lt J O Chilson
Lt Wesley Riley
Lt Geo L Cruss
Stockhardt, John, corp* — Petersburg, July 30—64
Applebee, Gilbert* — Petersburg, June 18—64
Bates, Aaron G+ — Portsmouth Grove, Aug 6—64
Brown, Chas P — City Point, Nov 28—64
Cook, Wm H — City Point, Sept 27—64
Callahan, Matthew* — Petersburg, July 30—64
Caldwell, Wm A* — Petersburg, July 30—64
Dippel, Conrad — Watertown
Fidell, Jacob* — Petersburg, July 30—64
Goodnow, Austin — Davids Island, July 30—64
Hatch, L M — Loyd
Kimball, Nathaniel+ — Davids Island, July 3—64
Lease, Wm A* — Petersburg, June 18—64
Lapham, Chas — Cylon
Mayville, E B — Neillsville
Myers, Jacob H — Oct 8—64
Pulk, Chas — Davids Island, July 24—64
Rappold, Henry* — Petersburg, July 30—64
Schons, Henry — Philadelphia, Sept 26—64
Wilcox, Seth — City Point, Oct 4—64

K

Capt Allen A Burnett+ — Washington, Aug 18—64
Capt Geo D McDill — Osceola Mills
Capt Jas W Hitchcock — New Richmond
Lt Edw I Grumley
Lt M M Willtz* — Ft Mahone, Apr 2—65
Lt A J Holmes
Lt Clark Thomas
Lt Noyes B Smith

Gaillaine, Jno, sgt*Weldon Railroad, Aug 19—64
Hahpahtakwahnoquetic, Seymour, corp*
— [Petersburg, July 30—64
McGowan, Patrick, corp — Danville, Mar 29—65
Bishop, Chester* — Petersburg, Aug 21—64
Cox, Chas — Troy Centre
Dane, Henry+ — Petersburg, Apr 6—65
Hammond, Lewis P — Cincinnati, Mar 21—64
Moshsheussh, D* — Weldon Railroad, Aug 19—64
Musser, L L — Troy
Nahwahquah, Jos* — Petersburg, July 30—64
Nelson, Gonder
Pishwahsha, Augustus — Danville, Mar 20—63
Papoupuieu, Peter — Danville, Mar 20—61
Pahpopnien, Jos* Weldon Railroad, Aug 19—64
Puller, Benj+ — Washington, Aug 8—64
Reinhard, Wm — Fort Washington
Smith, B N — Ashridge
Stevens, Chas — Menominee
Wahsahwequon, Jos — Cumberland, Apr 7—65

UNASSIGNED.

Behleng, Geo W O — Beaver Dam
Baldwin, Frank — Troy Centre
Doolittle, A O — Racine
Mc Dill, Geo D, a — Osceola Mills
Prentice, N B — Dakota

THIRTY-EIGHTH INFANTRY.

One, two and three years. Organized April 15th, 1864. Original strength, 913, gain by recruits, etc., 119. Total, 1032. Death loss, 107—Killed in action, 31, died of wounds, 25, of disease, 50. Other losses, 286—missing, 2. desertions, 55, transfers, 21, discharges, 208. Strength at muster-out July 26th, 1865, 610. Campaigns in Virginia.

REGIMENTAL ROSTER.

Col Jas Bintliff, ed — Darlington
Col Colwert K Pier, b — Fond du Lac
Lt Chas L Ballard
Maj Courtland P Larkin — Milwaukee
Maj Robt N Roberts, m — Waupaca
Maj Frank A Hayward — Waupaca
Adj Aaron H McCracken
Q M Auson Rood
Q M Jasper N Lockhart
Surg Henry L Butterfield — Waupun
A Surg Hugh Russell
A Surg Chas Cowles
A Surg C B Pierson
A Surg Chris Tochterman
Chap Jos M Walker

A

Capt Chas T Carpenter — Ithaca, Sept 3—64
Capt Chas L Ballard
Capt Jas M Searles
Lt Egbert H Little, m — Fond du Lac
Lt Geo M Pier, mf — Fond du Lac
Lt Al A Dye — Missouri
Adams, Hackley, corp*Cold Harbor, June 12—64
Weber, Wm, corp — Philadelphia, June 22—61
Albert, Chas+ — Petersburg, June 21—64
Bradford, Wm H — Washington, June 26—64
Brant, Wm — Petersburg, June 18—64
Currier, Geo W* — Petersburg, June 18—64
Cummings, Nelson* — Petersburg, July 30—64
Dana, Chas O+ — Petersburg, June 18—64
Ellenbecker, N G — Pt Washington
Foley, Jno — Madison, June 8—64
Green, Jno C — Kaukauna
Harvey, Horace E — Washington, May 12—64
Hall, Robt — Brillion
Hillard, Jas — Washington, Nov 3—64

Lake, W W, c — Oshkosh
Little, E H, m — Fond du Lac
Pier, G M, mf — Fond du Lac
Robbins, Jas, drayman — Waupun
Rappert, M G — Pt Washington
Schaffer, Conrad — Petersburg, Aug 18—64
Sackett, F W — Phillips
Sears, Chas E — Washington, Sept 25—64
Soper, H M, ar — Fond du Lac
Thomas, L D — Kenosha
Wright, Jno T — City Point, Oct 8—64

B

Capt Robt N Roberts, m — Waupaca
Capt Francis A Hayward — Waupaca
Capt Gen H Nichols
Lt L B Waddington
Lt Abraham Rude — Ft Howard
Lt Simon C Strickland
Lt Thos Parks
Burnham, Jos S, 1st sgt* — Petersburg, July 30—64
Buck, A P — Waupaca
Chandler, Henry, corp — Aug—64
Adams, Augustus* — Petersburg, June 21—64
Alderman, Jas — Madison, May 18—64
Bailey, Frank — Washington, Aug 13—64
Cannaday, Jno — Petersburg, Apr 2—65
Colburn, Judson G — Washington, June 29—64
Conway, Jno — Nov 25—64
Dickey, Joshua W* — Petersburg, June 17—64
Evans, G D, f — Wild Rose
Foss, Daniel+ — Willetts Point, Aug 2—64
Gregory, Jas S* — Petersburg, July 30—64
Hunter, Matthew* — Petersburg, July 30—61
Morse, Sam'l S — —61
Mulkins, A E — Waupaca
Mitchum, Oscar U — Dec 29—64
Parks, Sam'l E B* — Petersburg, June 17—64
Perkins, J B — Waupaca
Pierce, Chas W — Farmington, Nov 7—64
Richardson, Wm H* — Petersburg, Apr 2—65
Rice, Arthur D — Waupaca
Rule, A — Ft Howard
Raynor, David B — Milwaukee
Smith, Wm A — Napa City, Cal
Spencer, Ira — Waupaca
Sel eek, Geo A — Baltimore, Feb 18—65
Taylor, C F, l — Barton
Thomas, Francis J — Washington, June—64
Weston, Edgar D + — Petersburg, June 21—64
Welland, Henry — Washington, July 26—64

C

Capt S D Woodworth — New London
Capt L B Waddington
Lt Wm N Wright
Lt Jno D Milton
Lt Abraham A Devor
Sleeper, Hiram H, sd.
Whitcomb, S E, corp — Washington, June 13—64
Brown, Thos — Petersburg, Oct 30—64
Baldwin, Geo — Quinney
Blair, Henry — Washington, Dec 28—64
Bentliff, G — Minneapolis, Minn
Bunker, Marion F — Washington, May 22—65
Coghls, Jno B* — Petersburg, Apr 2—65
Carlton, Henry, m — Minneapolis, Minn
Cline, Adim D+ — Petersburg, June 21—64
Chapman, Geo H — Litchfield, Minn
David, Dan'l — Shawano
Evans, Wm, f — Phillips
Fowler, Jas D, musician — Brothertown
Gates, A A, mc — Berlin
Hanson, Nichols+ — Washington, June 20—64
Hicks, Robt — Petersburg, July 11—64
Hess, Steph G — Aug 30—64
Kindness, Jas, f — Brothertown
Mosher, Frank E — Washington, Nov 5—64
Musher, J Dallas — Philadelphia, Sept 18—64

THE
Fond du Lac Harrow
COMPANY.

Ask the Farmer Soldiers and Their Friends to Read Pages 4 and 56.

SEND FOR CIRCULARS BEFORE PURCHASING ELSEWHERE

C. K. PIER, 1st & 38th Wis, Vols.,   W. A. KNAPP,
       President.   Secretary.

FOND DU LAC,   -   WISCONSIN.

WISCONSIN SOLDIERS AND SAILORS REUNION ROSTER.   161

Niles, Solomon, f — Brothertown
Pendleton, Jno — Quinney
Perry, Jerome R, t — Berlin
Parmalee, David B — Washington, July 25—64
Pishery, J H — Beaver Dam
Proctor, Wm — Alexandria, Sept 13—64
Perry, G W — Elroy
Reed, Warren — Washington, June 1—61
Rivers, Alf+ — Portsmouth, July 6—61
Sears, Jno, f — Brothertown
Stevens, Wm H — Washington, Sept 28—64
Thompson, Thos G* — Petersburg, June 17—64
Welch, Lewis, f — Brothertown
Welch, Chas, f — Brothertown
Whipple, Wm, f — Otisville, Ia
Welch, Hira — Quinney
Welch, Cyrus — Depere
Wright, C B, photo — Argyle
Willmarth, A W — Embarrass
Wood, Chas S, pa — Berlin

D

Capt Jas Woodford
Capt Wm H Foster
Capt Benj S Kerr
Lt Chauncey W Hyatt
Lt Jas P Nichols
Lt Franklin Wilcox
Wyatt, Jno, sgt+ — Alexandria, Apr 18—05
Stephenson, Jno S, sgt+ — Washington, June 28—64
Snyder, Finley, corp — Baltimore, May 12—64
Carr, Jas R — Clear Lake, Ia
Carr, Amos — Washington, Oct 10—61
Campbell, Dan'l D — Oxford
Feathers, Jefferson — June—64
Haskins, Chas, l — Delton
Hyde, Thos — East Owls
Hart, Jas M — Merrimac
Martz, Wm — Washington, July—61
McCarthy, P H — Rock Bridge
Osborn, Geo W — Washington, Aug 10—64
Parks, Franklin* — Cold Harbor, June 12—61
Haynes, Jno J* — Petersburg, Jan 8—65
Squires, Jos W+ — Washington, July—64
Steese, W — Winneconne
Vaughan, Geo R, f — Palmyra
Whipple, Wm — Otisville, Ia
Wing, A — Neillsville
Wilcox, Franklin — Mauston

E

Capt Newton S Ferris* — Petersburg, July 30—64
Capt Frank G Hulton — Milwaukee
Lt Frank M Phelps
Lt Eli A Bentley
Lt Eric Erickson
Smith, Chas A, 1st sgt+ — Washington, Sept 22—61
Brant, S — Pedee
Bentley, E A, f — West Fork, Ark
Benedict, Oscar A — Buena Vista
Bonnell, David — Point Bluff
Clews, Jno* — Weldon Railroad, Aug 21—64
Calwell, S — Pedee
Donyes, Jno — Alexandria, Apr 20—65
Erieson, E — Beaver Falls, Minn
Friesburg, Hans H+ — Petersburg,—64
Hill, Wallard F — City Point, Sept 17—64
Johnson, Wm L* — Petersburg, July 30—61
Kelwine, P — Brodhead
Keller, J — Pedee
Misler, Antoine+ — City Point, Apr 7—65
Munger, Cyrus A — Pop Grove Church, Oct 5—61
Newcomer, Geo — City Point, Jan 13—65
Shesue, Simon* — Petersburg, July 30—61
Stearns, Erasmus D* — Petersburg, Apr 2—61
Siepnike, Gottlieb+ — Washington, Aug 31—61
Stanley, Jethro — Str Baltic, Sept 10—71
Smith, Frank J — Racine

F

Taylor, Henry
Taylor, W
Thompson, Wm
Thompson, W H, mc
Wess, Jno E
Wiegand, Wm

Capt Andrew A Kelly
Capt Erasmus W Pride
Lt Wm H Foster
Lt Jas W Parker
Lt Frank Glover
Arclush, Frank*
Dwyer, Jno*
Plum, E E
Foster, W H
Henderson, Wm A
James, Thos*
Joslin, Thos P
Kauer, Henry
Kelly, A A
Leonard, Peter
Lawrence, Robt A
Moska, Gazick+
Munger, Henry, f
Peaches, Nipple+
Scott, Jno+
Traux, Chas*
Yorke, Benj

G

Capt Reuben F Beckwith
Lt Wm P Mason
Lt Chas Wood
Dunn, Wm, corp*
Alyhymn, Jas
Beyer, Albert
Buntlin, G, f
Brown, Wm
Butts, J F
Camp, Sam'l J
Coonrad, J
Cheesebrough, H
Courtwright, A
Compton, B F
Crocker, Homer
Deland, Marens
Haynes, Wm+
Perrigo, Sanford*
Prothero, Wm
Thwing, Horace
Wolf, A

H

Capt Dan'l W Corey
Capt Benj M Frees
Lt Jas Heth, Jr
Lt Wm Adams
Hawkins, Wm R, corp*
Snyder, Jos, corp
Dunn, Nelson+
Heth, Jas, Jr, h
Kellogg, Josiah
Lindley, Oliver W
Lindsley, Oliver W
Trogner, G W

Churchill, Chas H, sgt
Ballinger, Asa A*
Blaisdell, Andrew
Cooney, Patrick
Cruse, Jno
Foster, W H
Hillard, Ever A*
Henry, Lewis
ann, Jno

Willetts Point, Oct 18—65
Pedee
Milwaukee
Milwaukee
Watertown, D T
La Crosse

Hudson
Ripon
Neosho

Petersburg, Apr 2—65
Petersburg, Apr 2—65
West Depere
Neosho, Mo
Whitewater
Petersburg, Apr 2—65
Jefferson
Petersburg, Dec 21—64
Hudson
Moscow
Bell Centre
Petersburg, Dec 15—64
Palmyra
Petersburg, Jan 31—65
Petersburg, Jan 8—65
Petersburg, Apr 2—64
Cataract

Petersburg, Feb 16—65
Oconto
Alexandria, Apr 15—65
Monroe
City Point, Feb 19—65
Stoughton
Madison, Oct 2—61
Edgerton
Edgerton
Fulton
Stoughton
Inwan, Minn
Brookside
Washington, May 1—65
Petersburg, Apr 2—65
City Point, Nov 23—61
Whitewater
Lone Rock

Petersburg, Apr 2—65
City Point, Dec 15—61
Washington, May 5—65
Shapspee, Minn
Onoro
Neosho
Montana
Neillsville

Petersburg, Dec 17—64
Petersburg, Apr 2—65
Elk Mound
East Port, Ia
Edgerton
Neosho, Mo
Petersburg, Dec 27—61
Richland Centre
Quinney

Mooney, Patrick — Edgerton
Rooney, Edw — Edgerton
Setzer, Michael* — Petersburg, Jan 7—65
Sisco, L — Neillsville
Tuttle, A — Neillsville
Terpening, Jos A — Athens, Ala
Tuttle, Albert — Weston
Wolf, Abraham — Lone Rock

K

Capt Henry H Coleman
Lt Joel M Straight
Lt Chas O Hoyt
Capt Thos P Marsden
Lt Solon W Pierce
Lt Fred T Zetteler, Jr — Oconomowoc
Burdick, Joel G — Ft Schuyler, Nov 12—63
Canning, Wm — Strongs Prairie
Colburn, Sherman — Point Bluff
Freeman, Thos R — Olin
Fahyer, Lorenz — Oxford
Hatch, Jas — Neillsville
Hakes, Byron — Washington, Nov 1—64
Haskins, Daniel — Coloma
Jenks, F M — White Creek
Johnson, Clarkson — Olin
Litchfield, Jas, ph — Easton
Marble, Nathan J — Adams Centre
Mix, F R — Coloma
Millard, C F — Star Prairie
O'Neill, Thos — Oregon
Polis, David+ — Petersburg, Oct 14—01
Quaw, W H — Wausau
Simpson, Philip+ — Petersburg, Oct 14—61
Thompson, Ruben — White Creek, Sept 3—61
Wintersteen, Jacob — White Creek

UNASSIGNED.

Bell, N C — Waupun
Burch, Isaac — Fond du Lac
Carr, W S — Waupaca
Dain, J M — Argyle
Mason, Leo — Marshall, Minn
Powell, Jno — Argyle
Pride, E W — Appleton
Stoner, Jno — Waupaca
Vail, H S — Chicago
Weber, Leopold — Kildare
Wright, Geo C, me — Fargo, D T

THIRTY-NINTH INFANTRY.

One Hundred Days. Organized June, 1864. Original strength, 780; gained by recruits, etc., 0. Total, 780. Death loss, 0—Killed in action, 0; died of wounds, 0, of disease, 0. Other losses,0—missing,0, desertions, 0, transfers, 0, discharges,0 Strength at muster-out, Sept 1864, 780. Campaign, in Tenn.

REGIMENTAL ROSTER.

Col E L Buttrick — Kanawha C H, W Va
Lt Col Jacob S Crane — Burlington
Maj Martin Throup — Racine
Maj Geo U Giuty — Eau Claire
Adj Arthur Holbrook — Milwaukee
Q M Sewall W Smith
A Surg Jno H Benedict
Chap J Hutchins

A

Capt Geo W Madison — St Louis, Mo
Lt Frank M Clements — Milwaukee
Lt Jas Sawyer — Milwaukee
VanMeter, Abe C, sgt — Richmond

ELECTRIC BELTS

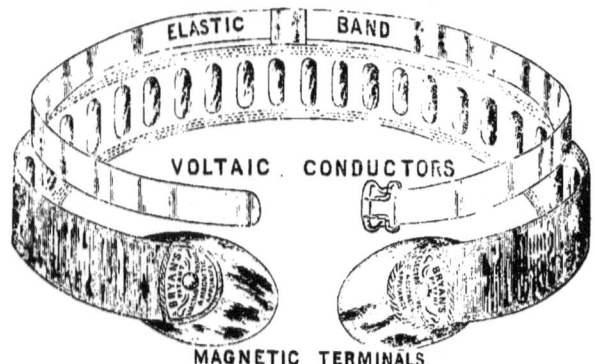

FOR SELF CURE.
THE ONLY GENUINE, PATENTED.
BEWARE OF FRAUDS.
DR. BRYAN'S ELECTRIC BELTS

Restore the Nervous and Debilitated and impart new life and strength to the waning organism. They are worn round the body in the form of Belts and Bands, highly charged with Electric and Magnetic influence; are of different degrees of intensity, suitable to all cases and conditions, and imbue the system with a constant vitalizing current; for

Electricity is Nature's Power.

Dr. Bryan's Electric Belts are a self applicable Physical curative, perfectly harmless, and a Sovereign Balm to the system exhausted by Nervous Debility and Mental anxiety. Without Medicine they cure some of the most formidable chronic ailments, and may be relied on as the last resort in all cases that arise from a loss of vital force. They increase the circulation, promote assimilation, remove pain and strengthen the nervous system. A continuous Electric Current is evolved by the moisture and heat of the body, without the aid of acids or washes, and they have the endorsements of the leading physicians of the city of New York and elsewhere. The Belts can be worn without experiencing shocks or any inconvenience whatever and never fail to benefit those who wear them. The American Institute of New York last year awarded a diploma for this invention, after having been thoroughly examined and tested by the eminent physicians and Electricians appointed for the purpose by the Directors of the Institution. Some of the most eminent physicians of the city have certified to the merits of this therapeutic agent.

Read the following from Dr. Guernsey, No. 18 West Twenty-third street: "I have used Bryan's Electric Voltaic Belts with very decided benefit. In all cases where continued action is required, they give very decided satisfaction. Their construction is thoroughly scientific, and physicians will find them of great aid in cases that resist every other form of treatment. EGBERT GUERNSEY, M. D."

Electricity will cure when all other means fail; and immediate benefit is derived. The Electric Belt will effect a speedy cure of all cases of Nervous Debility, Premature Decay, Physical Prostration, Organic Weakness, Kidney Complaints, Paralysis, Dyspepsia and all nervous derangements arising from a debilitated system.

READ THE TESTIMONY.

Dwight King, Esq., Albany, N. Y., says: "I feel that it has saved my life."
Geo. A. Preston, Esq., Binghamton, N. Y., says: "It has stopped the principal trouble."
Edward Wilkins, Esq., Newark, N. J., says: "It acted soothingly and removed the debility."
Wm. F Gilchrist, Esq., Union, N. Y., says: It has made a new man of me."
W. S. Smith, Esq., Toronto, says: "It has had a good effect already."
Norman Barnes, Esq., Quebec, says: "It has done me more good than medicine."
E. McCloud, Esq., Halifax, says: "I shall recommend it to my friends."
Miss M. J. Parker, Oswego, N. Y., says: "It has done me a great deal of good; I have gained eight pounds of flesh, and my dyspepsia is removed."

The belt is unequaled for restoring the procreative powers when injured by imprudent habits, sickness, or old age. For illustrated pamphlets address. H. M MALOY, 2 Bond Street, New York City.

WISCONSIN SOLDIERS AND SAILORS REUNION ROSTER.

Austin, Jas R .... New York City
Adams, G H .... San Isabel, Col
Housman, Jno P .... Michigamme, Mich
Meyer, Paul, m .... Sparta
Yale, J H .... Dryden, Neb

B

Capt Henry Shears .... North Lake
Lt Chas Blackwell .... July 21—64
Lt Geo Klock .... Waukesha
Lt Orlando Culver .... Waukesha
Lorieberg, Hugo .... Oconomowoc
Wood, G W .... Onawa City, Ia

C

Capt Robt Graham .... Oshkosh
Lt Jos V Quarles .... Kenosha
Lt Horace A Gaylord .... Sheboygan
Buddle, J G .... Kenosha

D

Capt Geo W Hoyt .... Rochester
Lt Amasa Hardin .... Waterford
Lt F H Trowbridge .... Negley, Neb
Brainard, Harlow D .... Racine
Cole, S G .... Shiocton
Kelsey, B F .... Madison
Kelsey, A F, ar .... Elgin, Ill

F

Capt F P Lawrence .... Kansas
Lt Chas E Jewett .... Havilah, Cal
Lt W W Clough .... California
Foster, Isaac H .... Racine
Tapley, W B .... Fern, Ill

G

Capt A J Patchen
Lt Jno G Meserve .... Manitowoc
Lt Geo Soule .... Sparta
Edington, E E .... Janesville
Kellogg, T N, corp .... Kankauna
Okey, Leroy .... Rock Valley, Ia
Thirston, Isaac .... Mishicott
Walts, Robt .... Manitowoc

H

Capt H Tourtillotte .... Oconto
Lt E V Wilson .... Chicago, Ill
Lt Geo Beyer
Chase, Nehemiah .... Brookside

I

Lt Geo H Wright .... Ft Snelling, Minn
Lt C J Sackett .... Milwaukee
McKenna, Maurice, a .... Fond du Lac
Smith, H J .... Racine

K

Capt S E Tyler .... Davenport, Ia
Lt I C Sergeant .... Randolph Station
Lt A J Smith .... Beaver Dam
Bowman, E D .... Neillsville
Cole, Alson .... Vesper
Loomis, N T .... Richmond
Manson, A G .... Beaver Dam
Nourse, S D .... Marshfield
Stackpool, Marshal .... Plymouth
Stillman, Dwight .... Beaver, Minn

UNASSIGNED.
Volmer, John .... Kenosha

FORTIETH INFANTRY.

One hundred days. Organized June 1864. Original strength, 776, gain by recruits, etc., 0. Total, 776. Death loss, 15—killed in action, 0, died

of wounds, 0, of disease, 13. Other Losses, 0—missing, 0, desertions, 0, transfers, 0, discharges, 0. Strength at muster out, September, 1864, 763. Campaign in Tennessee.

REGIMENTAL ROSTER.

Col W A Ray .... Chicago, Ill
Lt Col Sam'l Fallows .... Chicago, Ill
Maj Jas M Bingham .... Chippewa Falls
Q M A L Field
A Surg Amos S Jones .... Janesville
A Surg Geo A Lamb .... Green Bay
Chap J J Blaisdell .... Beloit

A

Capt S T Lockwood .... Chicago, Ill
Lt Gage Turgess .... Janesville
Lt Moses T DeWitt
Hinebaugh, Wm H, sgt .... Memphis, Aug 6—64
Burnham, S C .... Janesville
Howell, Harister .... Memphis, Aug 30—64
Playtor, Geo .... Memphis, Aug 15—64
Roberts, A J .... Janesville
Southerland, J H .... Janesville
Traubllle, L .... Janesville

B

Capt S M Allen
Lt H A Northup
Lt B H Smith
Bushnell, Clovius V .... Memphis, Aug 11—64
Schomaker, Wm H .... Memphis, Aug 14—64
Simmons, Henry C, cl .... Marshall, Minn
Wood, F M, pa .... Berlin
Wright, A O .... Fox Lake

C

Capt N C Twinning
Lt A B Crandall
Lt B A Warehain
Bennett, Noridan S .... Sacramento, Cal
Gibbs, C C, f .... Whitewater
Hauser, J H, a .... Fond du Lac
Lee, Jno .... Jefferson
Powers, J A .... Waupun
Sherid, E A .... Memphis, Aug 1—64
Van Vleck, J M .... Memphis, July 16—64

D

Capt Chas H Allen
Lt Sam'l H Sabin
Lt Geo W Bird
Blanchard, H B .... Stevens Point
Ferris Isaac S .... Elkhorn
Lewis, H A, a .... Madison

E

Capt Jno H Hauser .... Fond du Lac
Lt Edw F Hobart
Lt Mason D Sampson
Aiken, W H, a .... San Francisco, Cal
Bailey, Francis A .... Memphis, Aug 9—64
Melen, Henry W .... Aug 20—64

F

Capt A J Cheney
Lt Chas H Gilbert
Lt S F Bennett
Moody, David N, corp .... Memphis, July 24—64
Barker, C W .... Millard
Carswell, Orland .... Elkhorn
Clark, Horace L .... Delavan
Cochrane, W A .... Delavan
McCoy, B M .... Sharon
Mallory, Henry L
Small, Henry J .... Memphis July 9—64
Trxun, H F .... Sharon

G

Capt F J Phelps
Lt Jno K Purdy

Lt Hannibal Tower
Alter, Fred .... La Crosse
Bentley, E E .... LaCrosse
Edwards, B E .... LaCrosse
Harrison, D .... LaCrosse
Osborn, W S .... LaCrosse
Powers, H C, mo .... Beloit
Rogers, Ed W, l .... Whitewater
Rogers, Chas H, e .... Fond du Lac
Seeley, Jas .... LaCrosse
Strout, Clark .... LaCrosse
Scott, W J .... LaCrosse

I

Capt K N Hollister
Lt A P McNitt
Lt H F Spooner
Gilson, Wm E .... Warrens Mills
Jefford, S T, Jr, l .... Whitewater
Smith, Chas .... Memphis, Aug 4—64
Shafer, Jno .... Newberg

K

Capt Chas H Barton
Lt Chas E Hall
Lt N H Downs
Blake, H A .... Madison
Donens, N H, f .... Mazomanie
Dement, G F .... Mazomanie
Foster, Solomon W .... Mazomanie, July 11—64
Greening, J H .... Mazomanie
Moulton, H Z .... Mazomanie
Preston, J F .... Mazomanie
Schleuch. M .... Mazomanie
Tubman, Noble .... Hammond
Cravath, Phit, ed .... Whitewater
Hutchas, F W .... Bradford
Shilling, Geo F .... Delavan

FORTY-FIRST INFANTRY.

One hundred days. Organized June, 1864. Original strength, 578, gain by recruits, etc., 0. Total, 578. Death loss, 6—killed in action, 0, died of wounds, 0, of disease, 6. Other losses, 2—missing, 0, desertions, 2, transfers, 0, discharges, 0. Strength at muster out, September, 1865, 570. Campaign in Tennessee.

REGIMENTAL ROSTER.

Col G B Goodwin .... Milwaukee
Lt Col D G Purman .... Washington
Maj Jesse D Wheelock .... Hartford
Adj Amasa Hoskin
Q M B S Miller .... Dane
A Surg Jno D Wood .... Yankton, D T
Chap W D Ames .... Fond du Lac

A

Capt P J Seldnesser
Lt Jno Grindell
Lt Geo L Hyde
Beck, Jno C, me .... Stanton, Mich
Stein, Sam'l Isador .... Belmont

B

Capt Wm T Whiting
Lt W H H Valentine
Lt Geo Perkins .... Fond du Lac
Birmingham, Eugene, me ...... Sturgeon Bay
Byrne, Wm .... Memphis, July 23—64
Bowerman Nelson .... Chicago, Ill
Carrington, P, me .... Waupun
Ferguson, Drysdale, m .... Waupun
Halsey, S, cl .... Fond du Lac

ESTABLISHED 1873.

NELSON J. DAVIS.   WILLIAM H. DAVIS.   ROLLAND L. PORTER.

NORTHWESTERN OIL COMPANY,
WHOLESALE

MACHINERY AND BURNING OILS,
*Paints, Colors, Varnishes, Brushes,
Glues, Oil Tanks,*

Gasoline, Naphtha, Benzine, &c.

253 EAST WATER STREET.

MILWAUKEE ◻ WIS.

NORTHWESTERN AGENTS FOR

Arctic Lubricating Compound,
BEST GREASE IN THE WORLD.

OUR AGENT.

If he does not call on you, when you are needing Goods in our line, drop us a line for quotations.

L. ALBERT SMITH'S
HOOF LIQUID.

SOFTENS, PRESERVES AND PROMOTES THE GROWTH & HEALTH OF

HORSES AND CATTLE'S HOOFS.

It is a reliable remedy for Gravel, Quarter Cracks, Toe Cracks, Pumiced Feet, Foot Rot, Bruises of the Sole, Thrush, Acute Inflammation, Contraction of the Hoof, and all Sprains of the Joints, Tendons, and Ligaments of the Legs and Feet, Cuts, Corks, and all Skin Diseases, such as Mud Fever, Scratches, &c., &c.

NOTICE THE TRADE MARK.

NONE

Truly Genuine

WITHOUT IT.

TRY THIS REMEDY,
And be Convinced of its Usefulness.

IT PENETRATES,
SOFTENS
AND REVIVIFIES.

TAKE PARTICULAR NOTICE OF THE DIRECTIONS BEFORE USING.   PRICE, $1.00.

FOR SALE BY ALL WHOLESALE AND RETAIL DRUGGISTS.

WISCONSIN SOLDIERS AND SAILORS REUNION ROSTER. 165

A

July 23–64	Chap Jno W Johnson	
Waupun		
d du Lac		
'est Bend		
Waupun	Capt Duncan McGregor	
Vermont	Lt Warren G Bancroft	Oshkosh
	Lt Chas E Redfield	Omaha, Neb
	Oleson, Geo, corp	Cairo, May 12–65
Berlin	Bower, Jno	Cairo, Feb 16–65
	Bradley, Chas S	Cairo, Jan 4–65
	Bemis, W S	Waupaca
July 21–64	Emerson, Robt	Waupaca
Berlin	Martinson, Andrew	Cairo, May 20–65
Berlin	Matson, Jeffrey	Cairo, Mar 12–65
Spencer	Nelson, Jas J, m	Amherst
Olivet	Omiti, Mels	Iola
Oshkosh	Olsen, Johonas	Iola
icago, Ill	Richards, V G	Viola
Oshkosh	Stroobridge, Oliver	Cairo, Nov 2–64
Neillsville	VanNostrand, Wm H	Cairo, Feb 23–65
Berlin		

B

geles, Cal	Capt Ransom J Chase	
Marinette	Lt Chauncy J Austin	
Menasha	Lt Harvey R Coleman	
Sherwood	Bryant, Henry M, corp	Springfield, Nov 16–64
Marloette	Bump, Levi	Springfield, Dec 9–4
Oshkosh	Bradley, Smith	Lind
	Dean, Merrit W	Springfield, Dec 25–64
	Hill, Anthony	Springfield, Dec 15–64
	Myers, C H	Baldwin
Mauston	Robinson, Pryor, B	Springfield, Mar 2–65
	Tewalt, Wm	Springfield, Dec 22–64
Neillsville	Vance, Thos	Springfield, Dec 23–44
July 20–64	Wakefield, LaFayette	Springfield, Dec 12–64
Aug 16–64	Wheeler, E B, f	Lone Rock
Merrillan		

C

	Capt Geo W Humphry	
July 24–64	Lt Robt Steele	
nd Centre	Lt Cassius M Bush	
Dodgeville	Krough, P G, corp, mf	Cambridge
	Brown, Richard K, f	Lodi
	Baker, Robt H	Paducah, Mar 28–65
't Howard	Clement, Stephen, me	Lodi
ettlement	Gordon, Jas C	Ontario
't Howard	Hinds, L P	Lodi
Neillsville	Koch, Henry	Cairo, Mar 2–65
	Pigg, Chas	Merrimac
	Richman, Edgar, clerk	Lodi
Neillsville	West, Walter S	Cairo, May 27–65
terling, Ill		

D

	Capt Jno H Barnett	
IN-	Lt Fletcher S Kidd	
	Lt Andrew Jackson	
	Gillet, Geo. f	Lancaster
	Head, Nathaniel	Cairo, Mar 16–65
7th, 1864.	Jewell, Horace	Cairo, Apr 17–65
'uits, etc.,	Richardson, Jacob O	Madison, Sept 16–64
in action,	Roddick, Fernando, f	Platteville
7. Other	Stone, Geo	Cairo, May 3–65
transfers,	Shepherd, Jno N	Cairo, Mar 28–65
uster-out,	Schmidt, Conrad	Muscoda
linois.	Thompson, Thos A	Cairo, Mar 12–65
	Wamsley, Jeremiah	Cairo, May 27–65

E

	Capt Augustus Haight	Oshkosh
	Lt Bartlett M Low	
	Lt Jos Curtis	
	Allen, E B	Kildow
	Benson, Lewis W	Springfield, Jan 14–65
	Belknap, G D, s	Omro
	Cherwick, Christian	Springfield, Jan 19–65
	Chapel, J H	Kildow
	Crane, Henry	Weyauwega

F

Fowler, R D		Kildow
Grignon, Jno B		Winneconne
Hart, Wm M		Harts Mills
Howlett, Jas B		Cairo, Feb 22–65
Hampton, Benj		Cairo, Apr 9–65
Hass, J		Kildow
Hass, Jas		Pedee
Lewis, Ira M		Cairo, Mar 22–65
Moore, Wm		Springfield, Jan 11–65
McCauley, Benj F		Mauston
McKerlie, Jno		Weyanwega
Outland, Isam		Springfield, Jan 9–65
Smith, Henry		Springfield, Jan 16–65
Saddoris, Fred'k A		Cairo, Apr 17–65
Whitenack, S J		Neenah
Waterhouse, Henry		Weyauwega
Zimmerman, H		Kildow
Zimmerman, H		Pedee

Capt Ezzan H Benson		
Lt Henry E Crandall		
Lt Jno E Wheeler		
Benway, Myron J		Cairo, Apr 10–65
Colton, E P		Springfield
Harris, Jas		Elkhorn
Kniffin, Geo		Cairo, Nov 14–64
McCarty, Freeman		Delavan
Sawyer, Adna		Delavan
Spencer, D M, f		Skiddy, Kan

G

Capt Acors S Porter		
Lt Wm J Brown		
Lt Wm Faville		
Lt Chas A Keyes		
Antweiler, Phil		Palmyra
Alexander, G W		LaGrange
Allen, G W		Palmyra
Bradway, Chas		Palmyra, May 23–65
Baker, Z G		Floyd, Ia
Babcock, Rufus		Little Prairie
Bradway, B O		Palmyra
Beery, E E		Kenosha
Clark, Orlando		Apr 9–65
Chambers, W F		Palm ra
Cantbell, Dan'l, pa		Palmyra
Goodson, J		Menomonee
Hollenbeck, Robt		Springfield, Apr 5–65
Harris, B F, l		Palmyra
Lawton, Sam'l, f		LaGrange
Lawton, Jas H, f		LaGrange
McArthur, J A, clk		Palmyra
McCarty, M, l		Palmyra
Phillippa, Geo		Bear Creek
Powers, C H, f		Palmyra
Smith, E A, m		Milwaukee
Wiles, Jas, l		Palmyra

H

Capt Amasa F Parker		
Capt Josiah Thompson		
Lt Robt H Henry		
Lt Wm F Akin		
Clark, Ira A, corp		Springfield, Dec 2–64
Cramer, Christopher		Olney, Apr 19–65
Fuller, J W		Neillsville
Kebstrup, Peter C		Mound City, May 1–65
Lent, W H		Jefferson
McKee, Alexander		Springfield, Nov 12–64
McGowan, Jas		Fairfield, Jan 15–65
McCoys, C F		Magnolia
Stevens, Geo W		Aplington, Ia
Shambaugh, Jno T		Olney, Mar 1,–65

I

Capt Marshall C Nichols

PAINTS AND BUILDING MATERIAL

— TO —

CONSUMERS AND DEALERS

— AT —

WHOLESALE PRICES.

WRITE FOR ESTIMATES, PRICE LISTS, and BOTTOM FIGURES

— TO —

The Fond du Lac Building Association.

WE HAVE AGENTS EVERYWHERE.

See Pages 16 and 58.

C. K. PIER, 1st & 38th Wis.,   C. W. MIHILLS,
    President.   *Manager.*

WISCONSIN SOLDIERS AND SAILORS REUNION ROSTER.

Name	Location
Lt David G Bass	
Lt Chas E Bowles	Janesville
Aubu't, Henry	Black Earth
Coon, Wm	Cairo, Feb 24—95
Dunham, J L, f	Delavan
Holcomb, Wm	Cairo, Apr 17—65
Lowry, Jno J	Cairo, Mar 9—65
Johnson, Henry	Black Earth
McKenzie, W A	Helena
Palmer, Sam'l C	Liberty, Apr 19—65
Steadman, Alfred	Cairo, June 13 -62
Stillwell, Z B	Mazomanie
Tyler, Leonard	Janesville
Vance, Jno M, f	Liberty Pole
Widner, W Y	Milwaukee
Young, Wm	Cairo, Nov 22—64

K

Name	Location
Capt Lafayette M Rice	
Lt Elijah Rich	
Lt Chas J Hubbell	
Lt Geo W Case	
Berg, Hezekiah	Chicago, Mar 16—65
Buck, Artemas	Cairo, May 23—65
Evans, Jacob C, f	New Haven
Kitchen, Wm	Olin
Landt, Jeremiah	Big Springs, Jan 9—65
Moore, G F	Essex, N J
Nye, Edwin	Appleton
Nye, J J	Reedsburg
Parker, Ellis S	Cairo, Dec 28—65
Quigley, Jno	Verona
Ramsey, Thos M	Cairo, Nov 2—64
Waterman, A S	Olin
UNASSIGNED.	
Crosby, L E	Arlington, Ia
Wheeler, J E, me	Sturgeon Bay

FORTY-THIRD INFANTRY.

One year. Organized October 9th, 1864. Original strength, 867; gain by recruits, etc., 46. Total, 913. Death loss, 72—killed in action, 2, died of wounds, 0, of disease, 70. Other losses, 78—missing, 0, desertions, 38, transfers, 1, discharges, 39. Strength at muster-out, June 24th, 1865, 763. Campaigns in Ala., Tenn.

REGIMENTAL ROSTER.

Name	Location
Col Amasa Cobb	Lincoln, Neb
Lt Col N B Brightman	Leonard, Kan
Maj Geo R Shaw	Michigan
Adj Jno E Davis	LaCrosse
Surg Andrew J Ward	Madison
Surg Chas C Hayes	Hyde Park, Mass
A Surg H H Ruger	
A Surg Thos Beach	Dodgeville, Mar 2—65
A Surg W H Searles	
Chap Jno Walworth	Walworth Co

A

Name	Location
Capt Edw D Lowry	June 2 65
Capt Wm Partridge	
Lt Jas H McHenry	
Lt Chas M Day	
Lt T G Bronson	Prairie du Chien
Hatch, Nat H, corp	Johnsonville, Nov 15—64
Allen, Edw, corp	Clarksville, Jan 14—65
Atwood, Jared	Milwaukee, Sept 16—64
Becker, Jacob	Clarksville, May 22—65
Conklin, Jno J	Johnsonville, Nov 7—64
David, Jno W	Johnsonville, Oct 20—64
DuBois, Wm S	Forestburg, D T
Springsted, Aug J	Clarksville, Feb 8—65
Smith, Audrew F	Nashville, Mar 22—65
Skelton, N C, showman	Lodi

B

Name	Location
Capt Geo K Spaw	
Capt H H Lockwood	Madison
Lt Lewis A Williams	
Lt L V Nauseawen Visalia	California
Melvin, Frank, corp	Decherd, Mar 26—65
Barrett, Jas	Nashville, Apr 10—65
Estabrook, C E, a	Manitowoc
Haw, Thos	Nashville, Jan 8—65
Hudson, Andrew*	Johnsonville, Nov 5 -64
Lillie, Dudley	Nashville, Dec 7—64
Taylor, Richard N	Jeffersonville, Dec 17—64
Wilkenson, Wm B	Decherd, Jan 24—65

C

Name	Location
Capt Geo Campbell	Portage
Lt Levi Welden	
Lt Jno Brandon	
Nye, Austin, sgt	Nashville, Dec 10- 64
Barker, Marquis	Johnsonville, Nov 18—64
Cleary, Henry	Springfield
Ellis, Jos A	Clarksville, Dec 24—64
Harvell, Thos B*	Johnsonville, Dec 3- 64
McQueen, Thos	Keokuk, Dec 26—64
Metcalf, Jno E	Waterloo
Zellhoeffer, Michael	Louisville, Jan 6—65

D

Name	Location
Capt Josiah Hinman	Chicago, Ill
Lt Morgan O'Flaherty	
Lt Francis A Smith	
Gibson, Jno A, corp	Decherd, Oct 25—64
Bowers, R, f	Mauston
Deerhammer, Jno H	Clarksville, Dec 25—64
Garity, Bernard	Erfurt
Harrelsen, Seibert	Nashville, Feb 3—65
Olesen, Peter	Milwaukee, Oct 11 –64
Panzer, Wm	Racine
Spike, Chas	Clarksville, Mar 28—65
Warren, Gilbert W	Clarksville, Dec 31—64

E

Name	Location
Capt Isaac Stockwell	Kansas
Lt C J Wadsworth	Darlington
Lt G W Witter	
Lt H A Beckwith	
Hugabloom, Wm, sgt	Elk Riv Bridge, Jan 11—65
Emmerson, Ole	Jeff Barracks, Dec 14—64
Horsley, Henry, J	Johnsonville, Nov 20—64
Kellogg, Wm	Orleans, Neb
Parsons, Marion	Spafford
Quirk, Julius	Harrison
Ray, Sam'l O	Johnsonville, Oct 25—64
Stockwell, J, mf	Yankton, D T
Tenney, Nelson M	Nashville, Nov 27—64
Thorp, A D	Sturgeon Bay
Woodworth, Jerome B	Milwaukee, Dec 5—64
White, Richard	Clarksville, Jan 7—65

F

Name	Location
Capt Jno B Wilson	
Lt Alvin F Clark	
Lt Henry Harris	Marinette
Everts, Jos B	Luverne, Minn
Pulver, Jno N, sgt	Madison, Jan 12—65
Morgan, Evan, corp	Louisville, Dec 25—64
Rinehart, Jno, corp, of	Hortonville
Hough, H E, corp, f	Hortonville
Bryson, Wm	Clarksville, Jan 4—65
Bartholomew, Geo W	Clarksville, Jan 6—76
Brill, Wm E	Floyd, Ia
Collins, Chas M	Clarksville, Jan 6—65
Farl, Jno	Johnsonville, Jan 2—65
Fieldstadt, Andrew	Johnsonville, Oct 23—64
Garter, Christopher	Clarksville, Dec 28—64
Gibson, Jno	Centreville

G

Name	Location
Gurnee, B M	Stevensville
Hough, Horatio	Stevensville
Harris, H, ed	Marinette
Logan, Anthony	Stevensville
Larson, Anthony, f	Hortonville
Manley, H H	Stevensville
Nash, W H	Stevensville
Nye, F J	Stevensville
Nye, Freeman J	Hortonville
Odekirk, Jirah P	Clarksville, Feb 26—65
Rideout, W K, c	Hortonville
Rideout, W K	Stevensville
Rogers, Edwin, m	Hortonville
Rogers, Edw	Stevensville
Reinhart, Jno	Stevensville
Sundlin, Jas	Jeffersonville, Dec 13—64
Smith, Reinhardt	Orleans, Neb
True, Jos E	Clarksville, Feb 11 –65
Thomas, Elijah	Hortonville
Thomas, Elijah	Stevensville
Wilson, Jno S	Lawrence, Kan
Capt Bruce E McCoy	Sparta
Lt Arthur T Morse	St Louis, Mo
Lt Henry A Head	
Lt Chas W Allen	
Lt Geo P Bennett	
Seymour, E A, corp	Jeffersonville, Dec 29—64
Brunson, Stephen	Jeffersonville, Dec 23—64
Cross, W C	Raymond
Cooper, W S	Hammond
Dean, Chas	Decherd, Mar 13 65
DeGroat, Chas	Nashville, Dec 15—64
Gilbert, Geo	Madison, Jan 1—65
Hamilton, Jno I,	Johnsonville, Jan 8—65
Hale, Fred L	Keokuk, Jan 8—65
Harrison, Wm	Salton, Neb
Jones, Chas	Racine
Jacobs, J F	Neenah
Richards, Jos	Racine
Stebbins, C H	Johnsonville, Nov 19—64
West, David A	Boone, Ia

H

Name	Location
Capt Wm W Likens	
Lt Elijah Lyon	
Lt Thos O Russell	
Gammon, J no A, sgt	Clarksville, Feb 21—65
Likens, Geo W, corp	Johnsonville, Nov 20—64
Bushwell, Sam'l	Kendall
Canfield, Z A	Okee
Davis, Isaac	Clarksville, Jan 2—65
Dolan, Thos	Decherd, Apr 31—65
Henry, Philip	Prairie du Chien
Lewis, Andrew	Johnsonville, Nov 22—64
Mickenham	Decherd, Jan 31—65
Riggs, Benj F	Prairie du Chien, Dec 18—64
Reynolds, Abel	Elk River, Apr 1—65
Rider, Geo	Waupeka
Storm, F D	Ft Atkinson

I

Name	Location
Capt Geo Jackson	Madison
Lt Anthony D Miller	
Lt Orrin L Ingman	
Gallagher, M, sgt	Jeff'son Barracks, Dec 17—64
Elliott, Thos	Nashville, Dec 22—64
Bjorge, Ole Nelson	Jeffersonville, Nov 22—64
Carmody, Thos, Jr, f	Egg Harbor
Dietz, H	Neenah
Edwards, Allen	Johnsonville, Nov 24—64
Eyre, Geo M	Decherd, Feb 7—65
Gould, Thos R	Clarksville, Jan 15—65
Helmholtz, Wm, f	Clay Banks
McQuacker, Jas, f	Hartford
Reed, B O, conductor	LaCrosse
Seubert, Geo	Marshfield
Spencer, Arch	Johnsonville, Nov 12—64

✻THE BEST BUSINESS MEN INSURE.✻

WM. McDERMOTT

———❧ REPRESENTS THE FOLLOWING ❧———

Experienced and Reliable Companies:

Hartford	Hartford
North British and Mercantile	London and Edinburgh
Royal	Liverpool
Queen	Liverpool
Commercial Union	London
Imperial and Northern	London
Fire Association	Philadelphia
American	Philadelphia
Merchants	Newark, N. J.
Manhattan	New York
British America	Toronto
Orient	Hartford
Commercial	New York
Northwestern National	Milwaukee
Travelers Life and Accidental Insurance Co.	Hartford

Money Loaned on Long Time

FARMS FOR SALE.

RENTS COLLECTED.

HOUSES TO LET

DESIRABLE LOCATIONS.

✻TAXES PAID.✻

REAL ESTATE SOLD.

ADDRESS OR APPLY IN PERSON TO

WM. McDERMOTT,

Smith, Dan'l, house mover — Berlin
Slover, Jas, f — Neenah
Sheerin, Thad — Neenah
Steenrud, O A — Black Earth
Tenney, Henry — Ft Wood, Feb 25—65
Torgerson, Chester — Mount Vernon
Wade, Benj — Clarksville, Jan 17—65
Wing, Rufus L — Kewaunee
Ward, Wm — Neenah
Wilson, J D — Deansville

K

Capt Robt A Gillett — Milwaukee
Lt Jno W Howard
Lt Chas Lemke
Hader, Fred — Mazomanie
Monod, Edward — Mazomanie
Roach, Emil — Mazomanie

UNASSIGNED.

Crabten, Edmund — Williams
Hamlet, Thos — Raymond
Jones, Orlando S, f — Platteville
Patterson, David
Plunket, Wm — Tomah
Reynold, Ira B, f — Eagle Lake, Minn
Skirving, Jas — Denison, Ia
Wilson, Alexander — Raymond

FORTY-FOURTH INFANTRY.

One year. Organized October and November 1864. Original strength, 877, gain by recruits, etc., 237, total, 1114 Death loss 57–killed in action 0, died of wounds, 0, of disease, 57. Other losses, 261—missing, 0, desertions, 48, transfers, 121, discharges, 92. Strength at muster-out August 28th, 1865, 706. Campaigns in Tenn., and Ky.

REGIMENTAL ROSTER.

Col G G Symes — Denver, Col
Lt Col O C Bissell — Waupun
Maj Wm Warner, a — Kansas City, Mo
Adj Chas O Tichenor, a — Kansas City, Mo
Q M Jno N Brundage, ed — Grand Rapids
Surg P E Barber
Surg Jas M Ball
A Surg Thos Harkins
A Surg W S Kimball
Chap E W Stevens — Madison

A

Capt O F Brown
Jacobs, E H, sgt — Hammond
Thayer, A F, corp — Hammond
Young, Theo F, corp — Troy
Andrews, Jas A — St Croix
Bishop, Richard — St Croix
Brown, Henry C — Nashville, Jan 29—65
Bixbe, A — Hammond
Bowen, Gilbert — Nashville, Jan 25—65
Boardman, N C — Cylon
Bennett, A F — Jessee
Barnhart, Jas — Star Prairie
Chandler, K T — Waupaca
Caldwell, Geo — St Croix
Dillon, M — Hammond
Flanders, L — Hammond
Fitzgerald, Richard — Nashville, Feb 5—65
Gravatte, Simeon — Nashville, Dec 9—64
Hughes, Patrick — Mitchell, Ia
Hill, Chas — Nashville, Nov 7—64
Hamlin, J B — St Croix
Hays, E B — Rich'and Centre
Johnson, W P — Hammond

Jewell, T, me
Joyce, Patrick
Ruffel, Geo
Keys, Z
Mettill, John, corp
Marion, Leon, f
Meerdink, Jno M
McDonald, Hugh
Mason, C
Mansfield, W J
Nelson, Jno
Nary, Dennis
Noyes, J L
Patterson, M H
Palmer, Jno S
Plumb, F N
Price, J F
Street, G M
Searle, Robt
Trickey, Jos M

B

Capt Wm Roush
Capt Jay B Bigford
Lt Cyrus R Hinton
Lt Geo L Weymouth
Lt Porter H Campbell
Gibson, D A, sgt, bk
Magic, Jno, corp
Marenus, Nelson, corp
Soles, Jeduther, corp
Aiken, Wm H, a
Battkol, Geo
Bottkol, Geo, me
Bobb, Jno
Childs, Seth H
Child, Seth
Crane, Wilder W
Davis, Thos
Dills, Julius C
Elthrop, Nate
Fraker, Chas
Goff, Dorr
Hays, E B
Kebo, Geo W
Kling, Wm, f
Lammle, Thos
Lassig, E, f
Reas, Wm H
Riter, Jno
Teasdale, Jos
Thumbrey, Karl, f
Williams, Wm P

C

Capt O D Vaughn
Lt Earl C DeMoe
Lt Cyrus E Dering
Lt Jno B Jones, bk
Anderson, Hans C
Anderson, Christian
Christopherson, Ole
Erikson, Knud
Eggert, Chas A
Follett, Lute M
Fox, Jesse
Gregorson, Gregor
Gregorson, Peter
Gunderson, Claus
Howell, Hans
Hatch, Harland P
Jacobson, Erik
Knudson, Ole
Knudson, Knud
Larson, Ole
Miller, J R
Mason, Rufus
Paulson, Ole
Peterson, Arthur, f

Star Prairie
Erin Prairie
Hammond
Hammond
Beaver Dam
Black Brook
Nashville, Feb 13—65
Star Prairie
Hammond
Hammond
Hammond
Nashville, Mar 26—65
Troy
Hammond
St Croix
Hammond
Hammond
Hammond
Hammond
Columbus, Nov 17—64

Minnesota
Apr 22—65

Red River
Nashville, Jan 11—65
Nashville Apr 11—65
Nashville, Jan 7—65
San Francisco, Cal
Lincoln
Karin
Paducah, May 4—65
Wrightstown
Kaukauna
Weyauwega
Paducah, May 6—65
Kaukauna
Columbus
Paducah, May 3—65
Nashville, Feb 16—65
Richland Centre
Kaukauna
Mason City, Ia
Nashville, Mar 25—65
Harrison
Weyauwega
Kaukauna
Nashville, Oct 30—64
Luot, Minn
Nashville, Jan 17—65

Madison
Homer, O
Neillsville
Iola
Iola
Iola
Iola
Jeffersonville, June 26—65
Richlord
Iola
Iola
Iola
Iola
Iola
Iola
Iola
Iola
Iola
Berlin
Nashville, Mar 16—65
Iola
Amherst

Sorenson, As'ack — Iola
Schroder, Aug — Weyauwega
Tollifson, Bjorn — Iola
Towne, Sylvester — Nashville, Feb 4—65
Tranlon, Jacob — Iola
Tubas, Ole — Nashville, Apr 2—65
Tanton, Thos — Iola
Tubaas Haiver — Iola
Wipf, Jacob — Iola
Wipf, Conrad — Iola

D

Capt Dan'l G Bush, f — Pensaukee
Lt Hiram seffens, me — Columbus
Rogers, Edw, sgt — Paducah, Aug 5 65
Arnold, Jno E — Jeffersonville, May 28—64
Bishop, Wm — Nashville, Jan 27—65
Dorsino, Jean B — Nashville, Jan 4—64
Gray, Seymour — Nashville, Dec 28—64
Hodges, Wm — Neillsville
Milm, H — La Crosse
Outwaite, Henry — Janesville
Phelps, Chas J — Nashville
Pope, Henry — Lind
Patton, David — Paducah, Apr 18—65

E

Capt Jno W Moore
Lt Leonidas Lombard
Lt Edwin Hill
Bristol, E R — Madison
Collins, A G — La Crosse
David, Jos C — Louisville, Jan 15—65
Eastwood, Jno K — Nashville, Feb 18—65
Hughes, B C — Cordova, Mann
McFarlin, Wm — Westfield
McPherson, Peter — Nashville, Jan 21—65
Shipnal, B — La Crosse
Tellor, Tusan, me — Big Suantico

F

Capt Carlton W Briggs, a — Princeton
Lt Wm N Perry, m — Delavan
Lt Herman P Briggs, m — New London
Cartwright, W F — Nashville, Jan 20—65
Gonterson, Tennis — Paducah, July 8—65
Retzlaff, Wilhelm — Belle Plaine
Simerson, DuBois — Nashville, Feb 15—64

G

Capt Dan'l Harshman, f — Fall River
Lt Geo F White — Homer, O
Lt Cyrus F Dering
Lt Jno B Jones
Andrews, Wm H — Paducah, Aug 10—85
Bradley, Wm — Louisville, June 17—65
Cregg, Michael — Jeffersonville, June 17—65
Dodge, Phil — Madison, Apr 9—65
Lederer, Jos — Paducah, Aug 2—65

H

Capt Levi Houts
Capt E E Dickerson
Lt L J D Parish
Bloyer, Thos — Nashville, Mar 5—65
Blair, Wm H, f — Excelsior
Crandall, Abe W — Paducah, Apr 19—65
Cooker, Jory — Burton
Davis, Henry H — Nashville, Mar 14—65
Hardly, Eli — Nashville, Mar 28—65
Key, Chas — Nashville, Mar 25—65
McFarlin, Alex — Nashville, Apr 5—65
Morgan, Jno G, f — Langdon
McDonnough, Jno — Paducah, Aug 15—66
Sawyer, Jos — Paducah, July 3—65
Seward, Jno — Beaver Dam
Tompson, J M — Orion

JOS. SCHLITZ'
BREWING ✦ COMPANY,
Corner Third and Walnut Streets,
MILWAUKEE, - WIS.

SEE PAGE 16.

Wilson, J C — Orion
Wilson, Henry — Nashville, Apr 4—65
Warren, Geo S — Garden City, Minn
Young, Jno — Muscoda

I

Capt Leonard House, me — Janesville
Lt Jno L Waldo
Lt Jos M Hensley
Lt Wm F Crawford — Green Bay
Allen, Henry — Janesville
Corey, A G, f — Blue Valley, Neb
Curler, David — Janesville
Coty, Joseph — Janesville
Culver, E J — Belmond, Ia
Foster, Jas — Janesville
Gillispie, Nell — Janesville
Holley, Riley — Janesville
House, L — Janesville
Keyes, Jno D — Paducah, June 20—65
Muldenhauer, Aug, l — Harrison
Smith, d W — Richland Centre
Skelly, Richard — Janesville
Tooley, Solomon — Paducah, Apr 25—65

K

Capt Wm H Beebe, a — Platteville
Lt Jos M Hensbee

Lt Arch W Bell, a — Platteville
Lt Wm H Peckham — San Diego, Cal
Barnes, A M, pa — Beaver Dam
Folts, D B — Platteville
Graves, Benj, l — Platteville
Hinman, Chas H — Jeffersonville, June 10—65
Kaump, Geo C — Jeffersonville, June 6—65
UNASSIGNED.
Brott, Joseph L — Barton
Hill, E R — Rush River
Johnson, Ole — Black Earth
McCartney, M — Rush River
Spencer, Ira — Lind
Bynes, G C — Denver, Col
Underwood, Jas E, c — Oakdale

FORTY-FIFTH INFANTRY.

One Year. Organized December 1864. Original strength, 859, gain by recruits, etc., 142 Total, 1,001. Death loss, 26 —killed in action, 0, died of wounds, 0, of disease, 26. Other losses, 173—missing, 0, desertions, 8, transfers, 85, discharges, 80, Strength at muster out, July 17th, 1865, 802. Campaign in Tenn.

REGIMENTAL ROSTER.

Maj Chas A Menges — Milwaukee
Maj R Schlichting — Clinton
Q M Albert Becker — Fond du Lac
A Surg Wm Fischer
A Surg Allen S Barndt — Menominee Falls
A Surg Emil J Dahm — Madison

A

Capt R Schlichting — Chilton
Capt Henry Hoehn — Monroe
Lt H G Bulse,
Lt P Ruppenthal
Lt Chas Wittig
Altman, Jacob — Le Roy
Bellard, Reuben — Nashville, Jan 18—65
Enderle, Jacob — Theresa
Geidel, Jno, f — Fillmore
Goldammer, T, f — Fillmore
Grubec, Chas — Nashville, Jan 14—65
Helzel, Xavier, l — Barton

B

Happierlos, Geo — Boltonville
Kaes, Jacob — Nashville, July 13—65
Kuchenmeister, G — Neillsvil e
Merkins, Edw — Scott
Schoetz, Michael, me — Boltonville
Wittig, Carl, e — Fillmore

Capt Jacob Leisen — Menominee, Mich
Lt C H Beyler — Madison
Lt Jno P Surges — Milwaukee
Bertram, Lewis, sgt, f
Royler Chas H — Madison
Chugeld, Gus, l — Barton
Degintz, Carl, f — Fillmore
Doney, Wellington — Nashville, Jan 29—65
Laupp, Jno, sgt, me — Harrison
Licht, F — Neillsville
Nelson, Helge — Nashville, May 23—65
Reutter, Peter, sgt — Brillion
Selig, Ludwig — Dotyville

C

Capt Bernard Schlichting — Milwaukee
Lt A H Scheffer — St Paul, Minn
Lt Chas May
Lt Gus A Walter
Annusen, Halvor — Winchester
Cremer, Hubert L — Nashville, June 2—65
Eberhardt, Jacob — Nashville, Apr 6—65
Millett, Geo J, Jr — Utica, N T
Torgensen, Edw — Winchester

D

Capt H VanEvreyk — Milwaukee
Lt S Karbach
Lt A Lintelmann
Lt Chas Korten
Barber, Lute — Nashville, Mar 19—65
Conrad, Frank, f — Nasewaupee
Hise, Jno — Nashville, June 28—65
Kappell, M, sgt — Nashville, June 17—65
Gravos, M — Neillsville
Hamilton, Robt — Flintville
Heupp, Phil, sgt, m — West Bend
Leonard, Chas, corp — Nashville, May 3—65
Luke, Carl — Nashville, May 15—65
Rosenberg, L — Milwaukee
Schwandes, Aug — Nashville, July 2—66
Wieman, Henry — Two Rivers
Zaemer, Chas — Ellisville

E

Capt E E Schmidt — Milwaukee
Lt H VanEvreyk — Milwaukee
Lt Thos Nelson, f — Cambridge
Lt Fred Messerlin
Lt Geo Neumueller — Milwaukee
Lt Jno A Fleischer
Gessener, G, l — Harrison
Nelson, Thos — Cambridge
Peters, Fred — New Holstein
Voegeli, Balthaza — Johnsonville, May 10—65

F

Capt Ignatz Rimmele — Milwaukee
Lt Fred Siebald — Stillwater, Minn
Lt Wm F Groth — Nov 18—64
Lt Henry Hoehn — Monroe
Lt Thos Nelson
Lt Victor E Kohn
Cime, Aden — Nashville, June 25—65
Emmett, Jno, f — Barton
Fellber, J A, corp — Nashville, July 12—5
Diff, Frank — Mazomanie
Matthes, F, f — Warrens Mills
Webser, Al, f — Nasewaupee

Capt Matthias Bauer — Milwaukee
Lt B Schlichting — Milwaukee
Lt Chas White — Manitowoc
Lt Herman Rohw
Bayer, Franz, m — Milwaukee
Czarlsko, Chas — Nashville, June 2—65
Generich, Fritz — Menominee
Harsta l, Lake, bk — Madison
Johann, L — Nashville, May 19—65

H

Capt Jno D Johnson — Stevens Point
Lt Theo C Karel
Lt Vincent Heck
Lt G Schweitzer
Berner, Wm, me — Milwaukee
Buchanan, T, corp — Nashville, May 25—65
Hochauser, L, me — Milwaukee
Birchner, Henry — Nashville, May 20—65
Nichusen, Fred — New Coeln
Schalluck, Julius, express — Milwaukee
Seibley, August — Waukesha
Schmidt, Jno — Fond du Lac
Schmidt, Carl A, f — Cheney, Neb
Schalluck, Julius, me — Milwaukee
Shine, Jno — Milwaukee
VanAlstein, Albert — Nashville, Feb 13—65
Wunderlick, Jno, m — Milwaukee

I

Capt J P Nytes — Sheboygan
Lt Geo Ippel
Lt Wm Noack — Dodge Co
Albert, J B, me — Milwaukee
Benton, C H, m — Fond du Lac
Craft, J, f — Harrison
Gifford, Edw, corp — West Bend
Hardt, Conrad, me — Mayfield
Kluever, Fred, sgt, f — Barton
Kunz, Abraham — Marshfield
McQuaker, Jas — Hartford
Uthmeire, H — Nashville, July 14—65

K

Capt Robt Lasche — Milwaukee
Lt Vincent Heck
Lt Fred'k Helmbolt
Lt Max Nonweiler — Milwaukee
Albertus, A F — Nashville, July 4—65
Clement, Mathias — Nashville, June 4—65
Gnadlack, F — Menominee
Hoffman, P — Mazomanie
Huber, Heinrich — Nashville, June 19—65
Johnson, Geo — Chicago, Apr 7—65
Kahl, Fred — Mazomanie
Saemann, Louis — Cross Plains
UNASSIGNED.
Boettcher, Chas, Q M sgt — Eaton
Nebel, Ernst — Green Bay
Ruppenthal, Peter — Brillion

FORTY-SIX INFANTRY.

One year. Organized March 1st, 1865. Original strength, 914, gain by recruits, etc., 33. Total, 947. Death loss, 13—killed in action, 0. died of wounds, 0, of disease, 13. Other losses, 80, missing, 0, desertions, 8, transfers, 3, discharges, 9. Strength at muster out, September 25th, 1865, 854. Campaigns in Ala., Tenn.

REGIMENTAL ROSTER.

Lt Col Leonard Martin
Lt Col A B Smedley
Adj Wm G Ritch, See of New Mexico

C. E. ANDREWS & CO.,

MANUFACTURERS OF

COFFEE, PURE SPICES

FRENCH MUSTARD, ETC.,

AND THE CELEBRATED

PEARL BAKING POWDER.

$1,000 GIVEN
If any ALUM or any injurious substances can be found in this Powder.

PURE CREAM TARTAR.

MAKING A RAISE WITH PEARL BAKING POWDER

Largest Cans in the WORLD!
MOST FOR THE MONEY. TRY IT.
ALSO OUR
PURE SPICES, FRENCH MUSTARD and COFFEES.
C. E. ANDREWS & CO.
Milwaukee, Wis.

THE CANS CONTAINING THE PEARL ARE SO LARGE THAT IT IS EVIDENT

PEARL BAKING POWDER

That in 16 oz. (or one pound) of the

There are more teaspoonfuls of Powder than in 16 oz. (or one pound) of any other, therefore most

ECONOMICAL TO USE. TRY IT.

Try The "PEARL" A Western Powder,

Equal in Every Respect to that of any Foreign Make.

And notice the SIZE of the CANS, and our Spices. A trial will convince you that we mean what we say about their goods.

Patronize Western Manufactures,

All things being equal, especially if on trial they are found to be

ALSO OUR PURE SPICES,

IN 1-4 lb. FULL WEIGHT CANS

WISCONSIN SOLDIERS AND SAILORS REUNION ROSTER. 173

Name	Location
Q M Norman Stewart	Baraboo
Surg Danvin DuBois	Lake Mills
A Surg D L Downs	Richland Centre
A Surg G R Turner	Mazomanie
Chap Chas Anderson	

A

Name	Location
Capt I T Carr, ed	Jefferson
Lt H I Johns	
Lt M L Fairservice	
Howard, Henry C, f	Albion, Neb
McLain, Dan M	Athens, May 29—65
Thompson, Chas	Waverly, Ia

B

Name	Location
Lt Jas Macnish	
Lt Leander Ferguson	Brandon
Burrows, C A	Plainfield
Cordett, J D	Neillsville
Ford, Jno, e	Berlin
Gardner, Coryelle, f	Berlin
Macnish, Jas	Berlin
Slaker, W R,	Berlin
Slogg, Harrison	Ontario
Whitman, Frank V, l	Berlin

C

Name	Location
Capt Wm R Kennedy	Oshkosh
Lt M C Wilson	Nebraska
Lt Jno N Hoaglin	Oshkosh
Anderson, Ole	Winchester
Carmody, Jas	Bleucoe, Ia
Dagle, Alex	Athens, May 28—65
King, Chas	Palmyra
Hall, E	Oshkosh
Ham, Geo	Elo
Hawley, A W	Elo
Keufield, Alonzo	Oshkosh
Kusche, J G S	Oshkosh
Lamore, Amos	Fremont
Pierce, Halvan	Oshkosh
Sherill, J	Winneconne
Stover, G H	Oshkosh

D

Name	Location
Capt Jno E Grout	Fall River
Lt Gilson Hinton	Fall River
Lt Gilbert H Hinton	Fall River
Blacklay, Boyd, me	Baraboo
Blackley, Jas, m	New Freedom
Bower, Geo,	Baraboo
Brown, Warren A	Athens, Aug 24—65
Delapp, R, mc	Baraboo
Etchels, Thos, f	Baraboo
Henton, C P, corp	Athens, Apr 26—63
Johnson, Thos, f	Baraboo
Kingman, Wm, f	Baraboo
O'Connor, Thos	Mill Creek, Mar 18—65
Palmer, Chas, f	Baraboo
Potter, Henry	Baraboo
Woolcott, W W, c	Baraboo

E

Name	Location
Capt Jas M Lee	
Capt Hannibal Tower	
Lt Abel Bradway	
Lt Jno Agnew	
Lt Edw C Foster	
Bailey, Geo H	Colby
Bannister, Chas	Troy Centre
Draper, M, corp	Huntsville, Aug 29—63
Holt, M A	Madison
Holt, G W	Madison
Mell, Thos	Little Prairie
Reeves, Julius	Eagle
Towers, Hannibal	Ft Atkinson, Ia
Whelden, Eliaz	Bangor

F

Name	Location
Capt H B Williams	Janesville
Lt Jas A Rea	Minnesota

G

Name	Location
Lt C A Leake	
Hegner, Ernst	Madison, May 7—65
Sutherland, Orian	Janesville
Tipple, Benj C	Madison, July 1—65
Wettrugel, Frank	Milwaukee
Capt Thos H Hughes	Darlington
Lt E W Doty	Darlington
Lt H W Foss	
Brownell, Geo W, f	Strawberry Point, Ia
Peck, D S	Darlington

H

Name	Location
Capt Amasa Hoskin	Richland Centre
Lt Steplien Norris	
Lt Nels Anderson	
Lt Jno I Bovee	
Benton, Jos, Jr	Richland Centre
Devenport, Benon	Soldiers Grove
Jaquish, E	Chicago, Mar 12—65
Lynch, Michael	Athens, May 29—65
McCarty, T	Richland Centre
Ray, A C	Walnut, Ia
Capt S M Sherman	
Lt Elam Bailey	
Lt Jno S Dickson	
Anderson, M	Huntsville, Aug 29—65
Tricker, E	Mound City, Kansas

I

K

Name	Location
Capt E F Wade	Minnesota
Lt G W Webb	
Lt O F Chase	Oshkosh
Hopp, Anton	Athens, Aug 1—65
Lash, D W, f	Sparta
Mulleuberg, Andrew	St Marys
Newton, C H	Bangor
Oleson, G	New Albany, Mar 14—65
Roudorf, K	St Marys
Steffes, A S	Milwaukee
Underwood, L	Windom, Minn
Wade, E F	Cedarville, Minn

UNASSIGNED.

Name	Location
Anderson, Aug	Palmyra
Agathen, Aug	Eagle
Bagley, Isaac	LaCrosse
Bailey, Nathan	LaCrosse
Bailey, Hiram	Baraboo
Baker, Abner	Rome
Baker, Abraham	Troy
Bannister, Chas	Eagle
Baxter, Jno	LaCrosse
Bingham, Chester	LaCrosse
Blanchard, Rodolph	LaGrange
Broker, Theo	LaGrange
Burnton, Ed	Palmyra
Carpenter, Silas	Palmyra
Case, W W	Rutland
Clark, Jno H	Portage City
Davis, Jno	Madison
Delap, Joshua	Baraboo
Deval, Chas	Rutland
Downey, Matthias	Janesville
Ellis, A	Portage City
Erickson, Nelson	Palmyra
Garfield, Jno	Madison
Grace, Jos	Portage City
Hanson, Julanus	Whitewater
Hauser, Carl	Eagle
Heath, Cyrus	Palmyra
Henry, Wm H	Eagle
Henry, Geo	Eagle
Hinkley, Albert	Eagle
Holsington, Geo	Baraboo
Hotchkiss, Moses	Palmyra
Hull, Joshua	Madison
Kayser, Mat	Palmyra
King, Rollin	Madison
Knettle, Henry I	Baraboo
Kosher, Wm H	Madison
Larsson, Lafo	Palmyra
Legett, Dan'l	Baraboo
Logan, Wm A	Eagle
Man, Thos	Palmyra
Marsh, Henry	Rutland
McCord, Leo	Milwaukee
Moore, Jos	Palmyra
Morrison, Luke	Palmyra
Murphy, Jno	Eagle
Nelson, Gilbert	Palmyra
Noble, Geo	Madison
Nooks, Chas	Palmyra
O'Brien, Michael	Palmyra
Oleson, Ole	Palmyra
Oleson, Lewis	Palmyra
Parsons, Fred'k	Eagle
Patter, Gad H	Palmyra
Pickett, Geo	Palmyra
Prisco, H	Baraboo
Randell, Harmon	Palmyra
Rice, Dan'l	Madison
Richmond, Henry	Madison
Rood, Wm	Portage City
Scott, Thos	Baraboo
Sherman, David	Madison
Spencer, Edw	Madison
Stewart, Jno E	Windom, Minn
Stout, Jas	Eagle
Street, Jas	Baraboo
Saggart, Geo	Madison
Thayre, Ruel	Palmyra
Thiel, Anton	Eagle
Wall, Thos	Palmyra
May, Hiram	Eagle
Webster, C E, f	Madison
Wells, Eli	LaCrosse
Wells, Norman	Baraboo
Whelden, Elias	LaCrosse
Wilkinson, Geo	Palmyra
Williams, Albert	Eagle
Willis, Adelbert	LaCrosse
Wisbart, Yeoman	Palmyra

FORTY-SEVENTH INFANTRY.

One year. Organized February, 1865. Original strength, 927; gain by recruits, etc., 58; total, 985. Death loss, 34—killed in action, 0, died of wounds, 0, of disease, 31. Other losses, 135, missing, 0, desertions, 23, transfers, 22, discharges, 87. Strength at muster-out, September, 4th, 1865, 812. Campaigns in Tenn.

REGIMENTAL ROSTER.

Name	Location
Col Geo C Ginty	Eau Claire
Lt Robt H Spencer	Madison
Maj Kelsey M Adams	Fond du Lac
Adj Arthur W Delany	Rutland
Q M Edw T Kearney	
Surg Henry J Young	Waseca, Minn
A Surg Wm Saxton	
A Surg Jonathan G Pelton	Spring Green
A Surg Lyman D McIntosh	Waseca, Minn
Chap Rufus Cooley, Jr	

A

Name	Location
Capt Wm Young	
Lt Thos Brayton	
Lt Luke C Redfield	Omaha, Neb
Lt Geo W Bird	
Lt Robt Tompkins	
Lt Jno M Estes	

MOHOLS MANUFACTURING CO.

MANUFACTURERS, WHOLESALERS AND DEALERS IN

LUMBER,

TIMBER,

DOORS,

WINDOWS,

SASH,

MOULDINGS,

BLINDS.

Write for Prices, Circulars and Estimates.

FOND DU LAC, WISCONSIN.

SEE PAGE 22.

WISCONSIN SOLDIERS AND SAILORS REUNION ROSTER. 175

Annunsen, Helve	Winchester	
Annunsen, Kettel	Winchester	
Buck, H F, m	Hortonville	
Johnson, Jno	Winchester	
Johnson, Ole B	Winchester	
Johnson, Halvor	Winchester	
Larson, Lars	Winchester	
Muller, Mat, f	Hortonville	
Nelson, Nels	Tullahoma, Mar 29—65	
Oleson, Englebret	Winchester	
Rearick, Rube	Tullahoma, Aug 10—45	
Shuh, A, f	Outagamie Co	
Torrisen, Ole	Winchester	
Zelner, Dan'l	Winchester	
Uvaas, Ole H	Winchester	

B

Capt Robt J O McGowan	Iowa Falls, Ia	
Lt Chas W Conklin		
Lt Jas M Goff		
Lt Wm Lockerby		
Lt Edw Duggan		
Barnett, Aaron, f	Komo	
Harrington, Coleman		
Maloney, Chas, me	Berlin	
McGee, Sam'l, f	Black River Falls	
McGowan, R J O, m	Iowa Falls, Ia	
Odvns, Michael	Wilton	
Perry, Jeff B, f	Berlin	
Saxton, W	Chicago, Mar 27—65	
White, W H	Prairie du Chien, Aug 18—65	
Wilklus, Geo	Eagle	
Witchcraft, Arch	Tullahoma, July 9—65	
Wood, J R	East Troy	

C

Capt Perry R Briggs	Mauston	
Lt Chas F Suydam		
Lt Leonard LaPlante		
Lt Jas P Hulliham		
Briggs, R R	Mauston	
Campbell, Geo F, f	Strawberry, Kan	
Clark, Silas, f	Plover	
Devans, Erastus A, m	Mauston	
Leuch, Lyman	Tomah	
Lemon, Addison	Madison, Mar 18—65	
Lind, Henry J, f	Hillsborough	
Masse, Jno, m	Sturgeon Bay	
McCauley, L G	Nashville, Apr 8—65	
Phillips, Norris A, f	Elroy	
Veeder, Fred S	Mauston	

D

Capt Adolph Sorrenson		
Lt Nelse Anderson		
Lt Joseph K Howes		
Lt Julius A Jones		
Anderson, Andrew, me	Amherst	
Anderson, Christopher, f	Amherst	
Drake, R P	Colby	
Dutton, M D, musician	Waupaca	
Ebert, Adam,	Amherst	
Hood, Isaac	Tullahoma, July 28—65	
Jacobson, S	Tullahoma, Apr 12—65	

E

Capt Wm Wallace Bird		
Capt Chas A Spencer		
Lt Adelbert E Fronbridge		
Lt David J Scrampton		
Clayton, Thos E	Madison	
Felton, B R, musician	Spring Green	
Geer, Joel L	Madison, Feb 15—65	
Hamilton, Ed C	Whitewater	
Hungerford, A M	Spring Green	
Ketchum, G P	Madison, Feb 26—65	
Kimmel, Jno	Madison, Feb 23—65	

McClary, L C	Madison, Mar 6—65	
Nickey, J J	Spring Green	

F

Capt Geo R Wright		
Lt Jno P Dousman	Michigamme, Mich	
Lt Jno Dean		
Adams, G H	San Isabel, Col	
French, Chas B	Port Washington	
Lindeur, Geo	Waukesha	
Long, Elias	Madison, Mar 29—65	
Shirt, Conrad	Waukesha	
Schrt, Henry	Waukesha	
Snarley, S J	Baldwin	
Thompson, Edgar	Madison, Mar 6—65	

G

Capt Robt P Clyde		
Lt Thos Braylon		
Lt J O McGowan		
Lt Silas F Rice		
Lt Jno M Norris		
Harlocker,	Cayulle City, Oregon	
Emmons, Eli, f	Boscobel	
Haze, Jas D	Madison, Feb 23—65	
Hildreth, J W	Madison, Mar 11—65	
Hottman, 1 D	Madison, Mar 21—65	
Hurlburt, S C	Madison, Mar 20—65	
Kelly, Lloye	Bell Centre	
Manley, Wm H	Madison, Mar 9—65	
Merrel, Jno L	Tullahoma, June 30—65	
Pittsley, Chas W	Tullahoma, June 10—65	
Polley, W B	Madison, Mar 1—65	
Richardson, Jno G	Bell Centre	
Steel, Chauncey H, f	Boscobel	
Withington, Wm M	Madison, Apr 4—65	
Wood, Sam'l	Madison, Mar 11—65	

H

Capt Chas B Nelson		
Lt Wm A Field		
Lt Jas Ginty		
Lt Martin Dewey		
Lt Sam'l W Barr		
Blanchard, Hebert E	Milwaukee	
Chapman, E W, ph	Concord	
Davidson, D I,	Madison	
Freeman, Chas	Nashville, May 5—65	
Hodge, Jno M, me	Beloit	
Hausler, Wm	Madison, Mar 5—65	
Lorey, C M	Nashville, Aug 14—65	
Petrie, Adam, m	Unity	
Petrie, A	Neillsville	
Ranson, M C	Unity	
Ransom, M	Neillsville	
Webb, Jno H	Weyauwega	

I

Capt Jesse D Wheelock		
Lt Wm T Whiting, m	Waupun	
Lt Wesley G Curtis		
Lt Thomas Seaman		
Lt Chas S Chipman		
Chase, Henry A, sgt	Tullahoma, Aug 1—65	
Ellis, Lyman E	Nashville, Mar 11—65	
McFarland, Alex	Aug 14—65	
Sweat, D S, me	Elo	
	Coloma	

K

Capt Chas H Baxter		
Lt Jno Grindell		
Lt Edwin Bliss		
Fitzgerald, R D, sgt	Tullahoma, Aug 1—65	
Hale, Robt B, f	Fairfield Neb	
Heasley, Geo W	Nashville, Mar 29—65	
Knapp, R S, f	Rockford, Ill	

Bemis, Jesse	Lind	
Collar, Dan'l N	Kansasville	
Hayden, Pinkey	Tallahoma, July 2—65	
Nice, F S	Tomah	
Perkins, Anson A, f	Wamari, D T	
Stone, Chas	Wooster	
Winn, Geo P	Beloit	

UNASSIGNED.

FORTY-EIGHTH INFANTRY.

One year. Organized Feb. and March, 1865. Original strength, 826 ; gain by recruits, etc., 4 ; total, 832. Death loss, 16—killed in action, 0, died of wounds, 0, of disease, 16. Other losses, 103—missing, 0, desertions, 67, transfers, 0, discharges, 36. Strength at muster-out, Dec. 30th, 1865 and March 28th, 1865, 713. Campaigns in Mo., Kan.

REGIMENTAL ROSTER.

Col Uri B Pearsall	
Lt Col Henry Shears	
Lt Col Cyrus M Butt	
Maj Nathan Cole	
Maj Jno B Vosburgh	
Adj Alonzo B Cady	
Q M Chas Smith	
Q M Sylvester J Conklin	
Surg Leroy G Armstrong	
A Surg Jno A Rice	
A Surg Henry E Zielley	
A Surg Jas P Squires	
A Surg Horace Pratt	
Chap Truman F Allen	

A

Capt Chas W Felker	Oshkosh	
Lt Henry Felker		
Lt Edwin A Bottom		
Lt M J Briggs		
Barton, Alonzo	Omro	
Bronson, J C	Winneconne	
Disbro, Erastus	Omro	
Cross, W	Winneconne	
Fowler, Wm	Omro	
Heath, Marvin, mf	Waupun	
Heath, J, mf	Waupun	
Ingleson, Nels	Ft Scott, Aug 13—65	
Lake, David	Ft Scott, July 3—65	
Leidenburg, W	Winneconne	
Raymond, Al	Milwaukee, Feb 28—65	
Scofield, Jas	Ft Larned, Nov 1—65	

B

Capt Jno B Vosburgh		
Capt Jno J Roberts		
Lt Jno R Smith		
Lt Jno L Dale		
Lt Orlando Culver	Waukesha	
Burrow, A D, f	Kewaunee	
Edmonds, Wm	Shelton, Neb	
Hoff, R S	St Louis, Mo, 15—65	
Nourse, S D	Gilman, Ia	
Pinnau, Chas	Marshfield	
	Baldwin	

C

Capt Edwin A Bottom		
Capt Luman D Olm		
Lt Jno S Kerdall		
Lt A G Rockwell		
Lt Orin F Waller		
Burgoyne, Thos E	Milwaukee, Mar 16—65	

The Mississippi Valley Manufacturers Mutual Ins. Co.

ROCK ISLAND, ILLINOIS.

Incorporators and Directors.

J. S. KEATOR .... J. S. Keator & Son, Moline, Ill
J. M. GOULD .... President First National Bank, Moline, Ill
S. H. VELIE .... Deere & Co., Plow Works, Moline, Ill
H. A. AINSWORTH .... Williams, White & Co., Iron Works, Moline, Ill
E. H. ANAWALT, ... Rock Island Lumber and Mfg. Co., Rock Island, Ill
BENJ. HERSHEY .... Hershey Lumber Co. Muscatine, Io
R. P. DART .... Secretary Consolidated Paper Co., Chicago, Ill

E. D. RAND .... Burlington, Iowa
SILAS W. GARDINER .... Gardiner, Batchelder & Co., Lyons, Iowa
A. LAMB .... Lamb & Sons, Clinton, Iowa
C. H. SHOVE .... Underwriter, Minneapolis, Minn
WM. B. FERGUSON .... Underwriter, Rockford, Ill
WM. E. SMITH .... Underwriter, Rock Island, Ill

Officers.

E. D. RAND, President.   H. A. AINSWORTH Vice President.
            J. M. GOULD, Treasurer.   WM. B. FERGUSON, Secretary.
                          WM. E. SMITH, Manager.

Executive Committee.

E. D. RAND,   S. H. VELIE.   J. S. KEATOR.
         E. H. ANAWALT.   SILAS W. GARDINER.

Northwestern Office: Minneapolis, Minn.

C. H. SHOVE, Assistant Manager.

The extravagant cost of Insurance is a reason why manufacturers should combine for mutual protection against fire.

That such combination can be effected with the most satisfactory results is demonstrated by the experience of others.

That the manufacturers of the North-west may avail themselves of the benefits of The New England Manufacturers Mutual System, The Mississippi Valley Manufacturers Mutual Insurance Company is being organized upon that plan.

The declaration has been filed, a charter adopted in accordance with the Illinois Laws, and the books are now open for the reception of applications. As soon as one hundred applicants have united, with the requisite amount of premiums, a license will be secured and policies issued.

We ask a careful examination of our statements of facts, compiled from the experience of others. Having considered them, we ask your co-operation in this most important enterprise. Send for information.

ROCK ISLAND, ILL., MARCH, 1880.

WISCONSIN SOLDIERS AND SAILORS REUNION ROSTER.

Washer, Ira J — Ft Lyon C T, Nov 13–65
Shetfield, Jos, f — Wauzeka

Capt Adolph Wittman
Lt Franklin Davis
Lt Clayton E Rogers
Lt Jas E Brown
Busjaeger, Carl
Lesle, Wm — Washara
Liest, Paul, f — Grant City, Ia
Panth, Nicholas — Nasewaupee
Patzer, Edw — Dale
Ft Scott, Apr 29–65

Capt M V B Hutchinson
Lt David W Briggs
Lt Hobart M Stocking
Lt Don A Winchell
Cowper, Aaron — Deansville
Gregg, Rufus — Deansville
Hepp, Philip — Waukesha
Hinman, F, corp — Ft Scott, Apr 28–65
Koester, Jno, f — West Bend
Laman, Pat — Milwaukee, Mar 18–65
Muzzy, Andrew — Deansville
Tobin, Wm H — Leavenworth, Sept 11–65
Vogt, Peper — Waukesha
Voight, Fred, c — Cedar Creek
Weisner, Jacob, f — West Bend
Wood, W G — Onawa City, Ia

Capt Alex J Lumsden
Lt Geo S Rogers
Lt Mark H Sherman
Lt Adolph Wittmen
Lt Christian Amman
Lt Chas E Pratt

Capt Hobart M Stocking
Lt Mark H Sherman
Lt Jos Harrington
Lt Melville B Cowles
Lt Aaron V Bradt
Davis, Stewart — Falls City
McCumber, Sylvester — Hunnebird
Milkinson, Jno — Falls City
Sanborn, O J — Kenosha

Capt Orin F Walker
Capt Peter Prudell — Chilton
Lt Job S Driggs
Lt Dan'l O Fisher
Lt Chas B Fowler
Brackett, S D — Chilton
Breed, Geo T — Chilton
Bule, Jno — Chilton
Cheesbro, Nicholas — Chilton
Fadner, Martin, Jr — Chilton
Fields, Lem — Chilton
Flansburg, A W — Gravesville
Gasser, Ben — Watertown
Granger, Eph E — Brant
Grasser, Benj — Watertown
Healey, Stephen D — Chilton
Heintenmaler, Jacob — Chilton
Holden, F M — Neillsville
Hutchinson, A — Neillsville
Hyatt, G, corp — Ft Larned, Nov 29–65
Kelley, E — Warrensburg, Apr 29–65
Lehner, Mathias — Chilton
Mantey, Louis — Elm Grove
Oakley, C H — Chilton
Pellot, Geo, f — Chilton

Planz, Jno — Chilton
Purcell, Jno — City Point
Stanley, F H — Gravesville
Steer, Silas — Chilton
Sumner, Z M — Winneconne
Toddhunter, Isaac — Neillsville
Yule, Jr o, f — Chilton

I

Capt Lindley M Andrews
Lt Henry C Sloan
Lt C Ardel Rogers
Lt Dolphus Danuth
Lt Wm H Robinson
Arnold, Walter S, f
Barhold, H
Bassett, A A, musician — Beaver Dam
Beuchner, Jno, f — West, Bend
Brooks, L S — Beaver Dam
Cuardople, Chas — St Louis, May 3–65
Hompton, Abe — Beaver Dam
Johnson, Ed — Beaver Dam
Nicholson, T W — Gravesville
Normile, Thos — Beaver Dam
Parker, Jas L — Beaver Dam
Slaver, Chas, f — Sparta
Schurier, Jno — Gravesville
Thompson, Chas R, sgt — Beaver Dam
Tomlinson, Jos — Cottage Grove
Winebrauner, H — Beaver Dam

K

Capt Jno D Lewis
Lt Aaron Carver
Lt Merton Herrick — Hudson
Lt Silas A Wilcox
Lt Peter Mullenger
Ganz, Arnold — Ft Scott, Aug 19–65
Hang, J — Ft Leavenworth, Mar 21–65
Monteith, Wm P — Comorsville

UNASSIGNED.

Buell, L N, sgt maj — Lenox, Neb
Gibson, Hollis — Lind
Roberts, J J, R, m — Waupun
Schmidt, Albert — Fond du Lac

FORTY-NINTH INFANTRY.

One year. Organized March, 1865. Original strength, 986, gain by recruits, etc., 16. Total, 1002. Death loss, 48—Killed in action, 0, died of wounds, 1, of disease, 47. Other losses, 179—missing, 0, desertions, 6, transfers, 0, discharges, 173. Strength at muster out November 10th, 1865, 775. Campaign in Missouri.

REGIMENTAL ROSTER.

Col Sam'l Fallows, cl — Chicago, Ill
Col Edw Colman — Fond du Lac
Lt Col D T Noyes — Baraboo
Maj A J Cheney — Chicago, Ill
Adj W C Whitford — Milton
Adj Jas L Heigh — Chicago, Ill
Q M Dennis A Heed — Sturgeon Bay
Q M E T Mars
A Surg Jonathan Gibbs — Omro
A Surg Pliny W Blanchard — Sharon
Chap Jas J McIntyre — Kansas
Chap R M Beach — St Louis, Mo

A

Capt Chas E Hall — Chicago
Lt L S Benedict
Lt Elisha Whittelsey
Lt Eri Silsbee

Lt Wm M Colby
Arneson, Andrew — Baraboo
Blynn, A — Mazomanie
Boardman, W T — Mazomanie
Broughton, A S — Red Willow, Neb
Bundy, Jas — St Louis, Sept 9–65
Capron, C A — Wausau
Carr, Melancthon — Ironton, Feb 6–65
Dillingham, W M — Waseca, Minn
Freer, Eugene, inf — Rushford, Minn
Hall, J A — Crystal Lake, Ill
Hawley, S — Mazomanie
Hawley, Wm — Mazomanie
Higbee, Henry — Rolla, Mar 30–65
Olney, F A — Park City, Utah
Pradt, G A — Laguna, New Mexico
Richardson, W — St Louis, Sept 12–65
Roberts, Robt — Hyden Mills
Sines, Henry W — St Louis, Oct 25–65
Sines, Wm J — Hartman
Stanford, J E — Black Earth
Stowell, Jno A — Big Springs
Stuart, J Q — Black Earth
Stubley, Chas — Black Earth
Treuer, W — Mazomanie
Warner, Geo E — St Louis, Sept 27–65
Wolf, Gustof — Black Earth

B

Capt A G Dinsmore — Berlin
Lt Jno A Hall
Lt Jno A Bull
Lt G A Stausbury — Milwaukee
Banta, Jno — Madison, Mar 8–65
Cornwell, E B, corp — Rolla, July 28–65
Dinsmore, A D, mf — Berlin
Evans, David, Jr, f — Berlin
Gray, Francis — Rolla, July 3–65
Hildom, G M D — Madison, May 9–65
Johnson, il H — Winchester
Johnson, P O — Winchester
Mather, Jno D — Rolla, Aug 2–65
Mills, Amos — Black Earth
Nelson, Neil — St Louis, Sept 30–62
Rice, R C, e — Oshkosh
Smith, W H, f — Sparta
Smilt, Wm H — Sparta
Thomas, David — St Louis, Aug 1–65
Thomas, Jas — Rolla, Aug 3–65
Thron, A — Deansville

C

Capt Francis Down, a — New Mexico
Capt R A Wareham — Plymouth, Ia
Lt E S Watkinson
Beal, Alex, corp — Richmond
Byrns, Phil — Neillsville
Bywater, T — Mazomanie
McCarty, J A — Neillsville
McFetridge Wm — Richmond
Sundberg, J — St Louis, Oct 30–65
Thomas, Frank — St Ansgar, Ia
Wareham, R A, m — Plymouth, Ia
Wells, Thos, f — Sparta

D

Capt Jno D Hauser — Fond du Lac
Lt H M Himelaugh — Appleton
Lt C H Stevens — Appleton
Charnley, Chas — Winchester
Cole, Geo B — Shiocton
Cross, Jno, Jr — Winchester
Emerson, M — Winneconne
Hauser, J H, a — Fond du Lac
Hauser, Robt B — Solomon Rapids, Kan
Hough, Job — Winchester
Lee, R — Winneconne
McGiffin, Jas — Edgerton, Sept 26–65
Mott, Wesley — Winchester

B. LEIDERSDORF.   HENRY M. MENDAL.

B. LEIDERSDORF & CO.,

Are Manufacturers of the Celebrated

"OLD ABE"

FINE CUT CHEWING
—AND—
SMOKING TOBACCOS.

MILWAUKEE, - - WIS.

WISCONSIN SOLDIERS AND SAILORS REUNION ROSTER.

Name	Location
Meville, Jesse	Winchester
Rogers, S N	Winchester
Snyder, Jas. a	Manchester, Ia
Wood, N P, f	Franklin

E

Name	Location
Capt H M Childs	
Lt C W Farrington	
Lt W B Thomas	
Lt Jno A Martin	
Lt D E Davies	
Capt J H Hauser, a	Fond du Lac
Andersonville, A'ned	Baraboo
Ayers, Royal	Baraboo
Bust, Milton A	Reedsburg
Hildreth, A B, corp	St Louis, Aug 9—65
Hortvet, Morton	St Louis, Sept 11—65
Hudson, Jas N	Rolla, Aug 2—65
Hurlbert, Oscar	Baraboo
Jones, Chas R	St Louis, Sept 16—65
McIlvaine, Jno	Reedsburg, Mar 3—65
Pettoplace, Stephen	Spring Green
Raynor, J B	Mazomanie
Saxe, Jno	Baraboo
Schneller, Jacob	St Louis, Mar 27—65
Seeley, Lewis P	Rolla, May 18—65
Terrill, Edward	Rolla, Aug 9—65
Thayer, Geo W	Baraboo
Tirrell, Frank, c	Lodi
Wiswall, A, sgt	Rolla, Apr 3—65

F

Name	Location
Capt E H Liscum	
Capt Wm R Taylor	
Lt E B Wise	
Lt W F Bouldin	
Lt Elam Bailey	
Lt L G Wilson	
Lt Henry Green	
Campbell, Patrick, f	Richmond
Carles, F M	Neillsville
Chapman, A B	Potosi
Eick, Fred	Rolla, Aug 6—65
McElwain	Rolla, Aug 3—65
Ross, Robert	South Troy, Minn
Stiner, Jno	Rolla, July 25—65
Slade, Alphonzo, f	Stadesburg
Taylor, W B	Richmond

G

Name	Location
Capt Jas W Hubbard	Princeton
Lt H B Huntress	Elkhorn
Lt D K Sanford	
Lt H A Gaylord	
Lt J A Gillespie	
Barker, Cyrus	Rolla, July 3—65
Bass, Chas W	Delton
Bass, Silliman O	Delton
Brown, W O	Black Earth
Butterfield, Amos E	Fair Grove
Chase, H	LaCrosse
Dodge, Jno A	Hydes Mills
Drew Jno	Rolla, Mar 2—65
Eakins, Jos, corp	Rolla, July 5—65
Evans, Evan D	Jennietown
Hawes Jasper T	Madison
Mead, V R	Neillsville
Nicholson, M, f	Webster City, Ia
Rolfe, G H	West Depere
Tropp, Fred H	Millston
Wrightman, G	Mazomanie

H

Name	Location
Capt H O Price	
Lt W E Huntington, cl	Boston, Mass
Lt Jas J Babcock	Fall River
Armstrong, M E	Hebron, Neb
Bennett, Norrill	Hebron, Neb

Name	Location
Bover, Jno J	
Knapp, H S, pa	
Morrison, David	
Norton, Dan W	St Louis, Aug 19—65
Oharin, T	Jefferson
Park, Chas	Jefferson
Pierce, Albert, C	St Louis, Aug 14 65
Rosencrants, C S	Rolla, Mar 19—65
Smith, Henry	Madison, March 6—65
Southwick, C E	Rolla, Mar 30—65
Taylor, W R	Richmond
Wakefield, S P	Jefferson
Yost, P	Winneconne

I

Name	Location
Capt C C Miller	Tomah
Lt A A Pike	
Lt Jos M Bartholomew	
Lt R H Avery	
Bartholomew, M	Lodi
Bell, Richard	Sparta
Benedict, Jared, c	Howard, Neb
Benedict, J	Howard, Neb
Ensign, C S	St Louis, Aug 27—65
Haltz, Jno, f	Norwalk
LaDue, Edw	Rolla, Aug 1—65
McClun, Jno C	Rolla, April 11—65
Miller, Benj, f	Tomah
Palmer, Zerah, f	Sparta
Strauahan, R	Rolla, Mar 25—65
Taylor, E T	St Louis, Sept 12—65
Vincency, Ferdinand	Willou
Williams, Ed	St Louis, Mar 31—65
Young, Thos	Kendell

K

Name	Location
Capt A J Cheney	Chicago, Ill
Lt Jno A Smith	Geneva
Lt Frank Lawrence	
Lt Edw C Lawrence	
Brotherton, Perry	Racine
Campbell, Robt	Delavan
Fessender, C H	Rolla, Apr 19—65
Humphrey, W B, corp	St Louis, Apr 8—65
Lewis, Thos	Racine
Mary, Hobart W	Elkhorn
Pattick, Levi	St Louis, Sept 29—65
Pemberton, Jno	Delavan
Sheldon, E A	St Louis, Sept 30—65
Tubbs, H D	Rolla, June 30—63
Ward, Dostin	Rolla, Aug 29—65
Wood, Newton D	Ft Atkinson

UNASSIGNED.

Name	Location
Barber, G W	Manchester, Ia
Blanchard, C C	Delavan
Coon, Orson	Cedar Falls
Haynes, A D	Whitewater
Reed, A A, Q M, a	Sturgeon Bay
Sanford, D K	Hari Prairie
Torrey, Henry, f	Cambridge
Valentine, J J, m	Waukesha

FIFTIETH INFANTRY.

One year Organized March and April, 1865. Original strength, 912, gain by recruits, etc., 61. Total, 958. Death loss, 13—killed in action, 1, died of wounds, 0, of disease, 42. Other losses, '65—missing, 0, desertions, 141, transfers, 0, discharges, 127. Strength at muster-out, April, May and June, 1866, 647. Campaigns in Mo., Kan., Dak.

REGIMENTAL ROSTER.

Name	Location
Col Jno G Clark	
Lt Col Jno B Vliet	
Lt Col Edwin K Bryant	Madison
Lt Col Hugh McDermott	Kenosha

Name	Location
Brookville	
Whitewater	
Fort Atkinson	
Maj Arthur A Putnam	
Adj Geo H Myers	
Adj Rufus H Blodgett	
Q M Robt P Smith	
Surg Jno H Vivian	
A Surg David S Alexander	
A Surg Curtis P Fenn	
A Surg Chas G Crosse	
Chap Edw Morris	

A

Name	Location
Capt Jno C Spooner	St Croix
Lt Rufus H Blodgett	
Lt Sam'l S Tubbs	
Lt Wm F Fisher	
Lt Walter Baxter	
Brannan, Wm	Ft Rice, Jan 21 -65
Fisbeck, Chas	Rushford
Frederick, Aug	Stevensville
Kilmire, Wm	Beaver Dam
Manley, Orson	Madison, April 11—65
Moody, Wm	Russell, Kan
Mosly, Wm, f	Woodville, Kan
Neil, Alanson	Madison, Mar 24—65
Wolf, Jos	Ft Leavenworth, Sept 13—65

B

Name	Location
Capt Clayton E Rogers	
Capt Justin W Allen	
Lt Jas E Newell	
Lt Leonard Morley	
Lt Edw S Tuttle	Menominee
Abbott, A F	West Point
Fox, Jno O	Boonville, June 9—65
Gibbs, J S, f	Retreat
Halcomb, Miles D	Ontario
Hoverson, Peter, c	Soldiers Grove
Kyser, Peter	St Louis, Aug 3—65

C

Name	Location
Capt Oscar M Dering	
Lt Richard H Williams	
Lt Topping S Winchell	
Bannister, Wm	St Louis, Apr 6—65
Bliven, Pardon C	St Louis, Apr 25—65
Tinkham, Ervin W	St Louis, Apr 16—65

D

Name	Location
Capt Arthur A Putnam	
Capt Andrew Gasman	Weyauwega
Lt Jno J McKiernan	Chicago, Ill
Lt Harvey Shubert	
Lt Geo Strong	
Dreyer, Fred	Winchester
Faulks, J, corp	Ft Leavenworth, Aug 8-65
Hawes, Lester L	St Louis, May 19—65
Kregal, Jno	Fort Rice, Apr 3—65
Lyons, G M	Emmetsburg, Ia
Metzig, J G	Orihula
Metzig, Aug	Orihula
Metzig, Benj	Orihula
Pussett, Carl	Orihula
Stolyeg, Gotthelf I	Zour
Taves, Jno	Quincy, June 18—65
Ward, Lester	St Louis, May 12—65

E

Name	Location
Capt Philander Phinney	
Lt Jno O'Neil	
Lt Benj F Bailey	
Abbot, A H	West Point
Austin, Frank, c	Lodi
Bartholomew, Jos M, ex agt	Lodi
Buchanan, Jno, me	Lodi
Hamilton, G M	Emmetsburg, Ia
Hellickson, Hellick	Barker
Landphier, H B	Madison, Mar 25 -65
Langdon, Oliver	Madison, Apr 16—65

GAS FIXTURES.

Exclusive Agents For

RUNDLE & SPENCE,

PLUMBING, STEAM HEATING,

—AND—

VENTILATING, REBRONZING & REGILDING

MITCHELL, VANCE & COMPANY'S

Gas Fixtures

A SPECIALTY.

182 Grand Avenue, • MILWAUKEE.

MILWAUKEE STONE YARD.

COOK & HYDE,
Established in 1843.

Lime and Sand Stone

Yard, Erie and Milwaukee Streets, Milwaukee, Wis.

WISCONSIN SOLDIERS AND SAILORS REUNION ROSTER. 181

Meadowcraft, G R	Madison, Apr 8—65	Israelson, Jens G	Ft Rice, Feb 8—65	Spoher, Ernest	Shiocton
Schlosser, Henry	Lodi	Livesou, Nils	Menominee		
Smith, Wm E	Marinette	Post, Albert T	Leavenworth, Sep 4—62	**E**	
Webber, C A	Madison, Mar 28—65	Powell, Theopolus, f	Mineral Point	Capt Jno V Frost	
Willis, Jacob	Cambridge, May 30—65	Tyler, L A, f	Patch Grove	Lt Dan'l E Reilly	
				Lt Jas Croft	
F		UNASSIGNED.		Lt Geo Stewart	
		Crabtree, R	Rush River	Webster, Jas	Milwaukee, Apr 10—65
Capt Chas C Lovett		Follensbee, B	'sh River		
Lt Chas Plotenhauer		Jones, S	R h River	**F**	
Lt Frank T Brayton		Meyers, G H, n	Appleton		
Anderson, Andrew	Fontenoy	O'Thomas, Pedar	Rush ' er	Capt Geo W Gibson	Boscobel
Arveson, Arve	Fontenoy	Putnam, Theodore P*	Sept 6—65	Lt Sam'l Elmore	
Downing, Hugh	St Louis, May 10—65			Lt Henry G Klinefelter	Nora
Durocher, Michael	Green Bay			Brant, Aug	Nekimi
Flora, Jos	Weyauwega	## FIFTY-FIRST INFANTRY.		Fish, Spencer C	Reedsburg
Gardner, Henry	Ft Randall, Sept 22—65			Hepyer, Heary, me	Milwaukee
Harr, Jacob	Madison, Apr 3—65			Miller, Joe	Nekimi
Herman, G	Missouri River, Apr 10 65			Nightrup, Jno	Nekimi
Hesse, Franz	Fontenoy	One year. Organized Feb., March and April,		Peabody, Albert G	Baldwin
Hinsman, Chris, f	Big Suamico	1865. Original strength, 844; gain by recruits,		Raltes, Wm	Nekimi
Kuehn, Aug	Wrightstown	etc., 2; total, 843. Death loss, 16—killed in		Rhynehart, Frank	Nekimi
Krueger, Jno	Wayside	action, 0, died of wounds, 0, of disease, 16.		Sink, Aug	Nekimi
Lacount, Edw	Ft Rice, Apr 22—65	Other losses, 121—missing, 0, desertions, 87,		Smith, Christ	Nekimi
Latond, Michette	Two Rivers	transfers, 0, discharges, 31. Strength at muster-		Sheller, Henry	Nekimi
Lewis, Matt	Fontenoy	out, August, 1865, 706. Campaigns in Missouri.		Stall, Charley	Nekimi
Nelson, Peter	Ft Rice, Oct 16—65				
Nielson, Niel	New Denmark	## REGIMENTAL ROSTER.		**G**	
Rosenthal, Wm	Wayside				
Thompson, Large	St Louis, Apr 19—65	Col Leonard Martin		Capt Chester W Tuttle	
Thornton, F Leonard	Buck Creek	Lt Col Jno H Vliet		Capt Reuben R Wood	
		Maj Alf Taggart		Lt C Ardel Rogers	
G		Adj Andrew J Sutherland		Lt Edwin B Wood	
		Q M David S Ordway		Lt Jerome G Dockslater	
Capt Geo R Clements		Q M Henry G Klinefelter	Nroa	Lt Olans H Sukken	
Lt Mellville B Cowles		Surg Orestes H Wood		Degan, Jas	St Louis, Apr 24—65
Lt Reuben S Andrews		A Surg Reuse Bennett		Denison, Jno D	Clarion, Ia
Davis, David	Ft Rice, Jan 9—66	A Surg Sam'l Hall		Hantley, Wm	Neillsville
Fouks, G	Cylon	A Surg Erwin L Jones		Harris, Richard	St Joseph
Humphrey, Westly	Baldwin			Kelley, Jos	St Croix
Letscher, Jas, f	Branches	**A**		Locke, Jehiel	St Louis, May 15—65
Letscher, C	St Joseph			Milgram, Christian	Mishirott
O'Brien, Jno S	St Louis, May 7—65	Capt Loring J Edwards		Preno, O, i	Warrens Mills
		Lt Jas Flanagan		Piller, H	St Joseph
H		Lt Thos R Williams		Quennett, Alexauder	Madison, May 25—65
		Lt Elias H Webb		Ruff, Fred	Menominee
Capt Chas H Cox*	Missouri River, July 1—65	Wahterlin, F, sgt, f	Menominee Falls	Ruff, Fred	Two Rivers
Capt Jno C Cover		Bowman, I, i	Menominee Falls	Thompson, Robt	Madison, Mar 30—65
Lt Wm H Reed		Horn, J, f	Menominee Falls	Thompson, Thos W	Madison, Apr 10—65
Lt Jas W Raines		Hubenthal, M, f	Germantown	Wehe, Aug M	Milwaukee
Lt Jerome White		Shaefer, Frank, f	South Germantown		
Lt Anus Devoe		Such, W, ja	Menominee Falls	**H**	
Clay, Jno	Jefferson City, June 23—65	Thompson, Isaac, mc	Waupon		
Erickson, Peter	Ft Randall, Jan 5—66			Capt Silas W Clark	
Gotschall, C	Ft Leavenworth, July 29—65	**B**		Capt Rufus S Allen	
Motlimula, Joshua F	McGregor, Ia			Lt Geo E Nichols	Fond du Lac
Pearce, A	Adamsville	Capt J Clifford Sackett		Lt Benj F Williams	
Wilcox, Henry	Madison, Apr 24—65	Lt Geo Maxwell		Lt Edwin R Nichols	
		Lt Albert G Peabody		Lt Even H Bakke	
I		Lt Oliver A Keyes		Bartholomew, Ruben S	Rush
		Martin, Samindorf, sgt	Carondelet, June 6—65	Brown, Simon	Sparta
Capt Wm B Reed		Steffen, Frank, corp, f	South Germantown	Goff, Stephen D	Tomah
Lt Ira W Kainouse		Feukel, Jos	Newbury	Grant, A M	Beaver Dam
Lt Jos Tillotson				Hurd, Wm	Richmond
Lt Richard Mallock		**C**		Howe, T T	Beaver Dam
Barrett, Anthony	Erin Prairie			Preston, Levi	St Louis, Apr 11—65
Crain, A J	Eau Galle	Capt Chas R Williams		Stroule, Valentine	Scott
Davey, Geo	Mondovi	Lt Malcolm G Clark		Saller, S	Tunnel City
Keek, Jno	St Louis, Apr 23—65	Lt Morris R Rice		Tanner, Geo A	New Richmond
Muntner, Casper	St Kilian	Aner, Jno	Pleasant Hill, July 13—65	Walter, Theo, f	Newbury
Southwort, C O	St Louis, Apr 14—65	Dennison, J D, f	Clarion		
Smith, Sam'l W, sgt	St Louis, May 18—65	Dienner, Jno	Scott	**I**	
Stevens, Colt	St Louis, Apr 14—65	Fairund, Geo O	Milwaukee, Mar 27—65		
Warner, Geo A	St Louis, May 4—65	Hicks, Asa D	Milwaukee, Mar 27—65	Capt Albert G Peabody	
		Moll, C, f	Columbus	Capt Asa G Blake	
K		Pitzner, Chas	Columbus	Lt Jno Austin	
				Lt Dennis J F Murphy	
Capt Isaac N McKendry		**D**		Lt Chas A Johnson	
Lt Wm A Morgan				Lt Edgar Brown	
Lt Wm H Oettiker		Capt Ira B Warner		Briggs, L J	Richmond
Bliss, Sewall	Ft Sully, Oct 8—65	Lt Theo W Mason		Boardman, C A	Richmond
Gunderson, Nels	Ft Randall, Oct 7—65	Lt Orlando P Sowle		Crowley, Jno	Richmond
Hammel, Alfred, m	Des Moines, Ia	Jennerjohn	St Louis, Aug 3—65		

MILWAUKEE, WIS.

A. GUENTHER & CO., BOTTLERS.

Hawkins, S N	Richmond	
McNamara, Jas	Richmond	
Tanner, Geo A	Richmond	
Todd, Jacob	St Louis, Apr 24—65	
Thompson, Ole	Menomine	
Walthers, Theodore	Filmore	

K

Capt Hallock Surles
Capt Henry Bailey
Lt Sam'l Elmore
Lt Henry Rapka
Lt Geo S Garrity
Lt Jacob C K Lens
Lt Andrew J Hunting
Fisher, Jno
Manthy, Jas. 2d corp Good Thunder 1st, Mich
Hoar, Otto, mc — Milwaukee
Wash, Patrick — Chicago, Ill
Whitmore, Jno — Madison, Apr 25—65

UNASSIGNED.

Junk, Jos	Alaska
Killner, Leopold	Denmark
Ransom, L M	Elo
Warden, Martin	Beechwood

FIFTY-SECOND INFANTRY.

One year. Organized April, 1865. Original strength, 486, gain by recruits, etc., 25. Total, 511. Death loss, 6—killed in action, 0, died of wounds, 0, of disease, 6. Other losses, 99—missing, 0, desertions, 42, transfers, 16, discharges, 41. Strength at muster out, July 28, 1865, 406. Campaigns in Mo., Kan.

REGIMENTAL ROSTER.

Col Wm C Webb	Topeka, Kan
Lt Hiram J Lewis	
Maj Wm A Collins	Milwaukee
Maj Lucius A Kent	
Adj Norman A Keeler	
Adj Thomas A Conway	Milwaukee
Q M Chas C Graham	
Q M Allen A Grant	
Surg Lewis J Dixon	
Asst Surg Orville P B Right	
Asst Surg Cornelius Peal	

A

Capt Henry C Olney
Lt David M Bennett
Lt Allen A Grant
Lt Ezra G Warren
Armstrong, W J — Neillsville
Perry, Leander — Norwalk

B

Capt Roswell H Lee
Lt Dwight Jackson
Lt Andrew J Adams
DeMoe, Harry — Watertown Junction
Given, Henry — Madison, Apr27—65
Hazelton, Lyman — Madison, Apr 16—65
Towle, Jackson — Madison, Apr 12—65
Welsh, A — Neillsville

C

Capt Geo A Spurr — New London
Lt Roswell H Lee
Lt Geo Sexton — Wautoma
Lt Thos A Conway — Milwaukee
Lt Jas O Raymond — Stevens Point
Hill, V G — Dakota
Rutherford, J — Neillsville

Spees, Silas, f	
Swain, Al B	St Louis, Apr 28—65

D

Capt Sewall W Smith
Lt Alex McIntyre
Lt Jno J Coyle
Bronson, Isaac — St Louis May 17 - 65
Burgoner, Chris
Fuke, Aug
Hoffmeyer, Jno
J . P P f
l . . . . L. d

E

Capt W G Z Knesson
Lt Myron L Bowen
Lt Jno Budd
Werkle, Aaron — Holden, June 16—65
Meyer, Conrad, f — Kewaunee

F

Lt Jos M Copp

G

Lt Jno Ross
Lt Jas McCabe
Smith, Wm R — Lataberton, Minn

H

Lt Alton Stillwell

I

Lt Wm S Parr

K

Lt Jas Monahan
Lt Henry K Dodge
Zastrow, Walter — Pt Washington

FIFTY-THIRD INFANTRY.

One year. Organized spring of 1865. Original strength, 380, gain by recruits, etc., 9. Total, 389. Death loss, 8—killed in action, 0, died of wounds, 0, of disease, 8. Other losses, 65 missing, 1, transfers, 5, discharges, 47. Strength at muster-out, August 19, 1865, 315. Campaigns in Mo. and Kansas.

REGIMENTAL ROSTER.

Col Ole C Johnson	Beloit
Lt Col Robert T Pugh	Racine
Maj Tilson C Barden	
Adj S L Keith	
Adj Jas S Frisbie	
Q M Wm P Forsyth	
A Surg Irwin L Jones	
A Surg L M Benson	

A

Capt Reuben R Wood
Lt Edwin R Wood
Lt Olans H Lukkens

B

Capt Rufus S Allen
Lt Benj F Williams
Lt Evan H Bakke
Tan . . Geo A, l

Wautoma	
St Louis, Apr 28—65	

C

Capt Henry Bailey
Lt Geo L Garrity
Lt Andrew J Hunting
Streeter, J F — Oshkosh
Wettstein, Ulrich Tailor — Sparta

D

Capt X

t, dummies	
l. —	
Wabnabe, Fred	L.

Lt Duane Grout

G

Lt Lewis E Warren

H

Lt Stephen A Northrup

I

L Jno Y. . g

K

. . Clay Jess . . . .

FIRST CAVALRY.

Three years. Organized March 8th.... Original strength, 1021; gain by recruits, etc.,.... 118; total, 2205. Death loss, 358—died.... tion 54, died of wounds 5, of disease, 29, accidents, 8. Other losses, 583—missing 0 sertions, 9. transfers, 67, discharges, 6.... Strength at muster-out, July 9th, 18 6...... Campaigns in Te., Ark., Penn., Ala. Ga., G...

REGIMENTAL ROSTER.

Col Edw Daniels	Richmond, Va
Col O H LaGrange	San Francisco, Cal
Lt Col H Pomeroy	
Lt Col W H Torrey	Aug 2—61
Lt Col H Harnden	Madison
Maj H S Eggleston, 1st Bat	Milwaukee
Maj Thos H Mars	
Maj Nat Paine*	Campbelltown July 28—64
Maj S S Shipman	Chicago, Ill
Maj Newt J Jones, 2d Bat	
aj Levi Howland, 3d Bat	Fort Howard
Adj W Burbank	
Adj H S Town	Ripon
Adj C P Goodrich	Oakland
Q M J C Mann	
Q M J W Broughton	
Com H J Schneiris	
Com Jno McPherson	
Com A J Morehead	
Surg H N Gregory*	Arkansas, June 0—62
Surg E Kramer	Milwaukee
Surg S S Robinson	Neenah
A Surg C H Lord	
A Surg T P Russell	Oshkosh
A Surg E H Winston	Albany
A Surg H W Cansdell	
A Surg H J Young	
A Surg J H Turner	
Chap G W Dunmore+	Lake Auguile, Aug 3—64

BATTALION ADJUTANTS.

1—Richard L Grove
2—E F Brooks

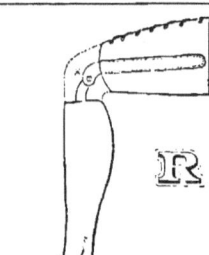

ARTIFICIAL LIMBS,

Manufactured By

ROBERT BATY,

ON GOVERNMENT ORDERS.

107 Wisconsin Street, Milwaukee, Wisconsin.

ALSO A FULL LINE OF

ORTHOPEDIC AND SURGICAL INSTRUMENTS,

FOR THE TREATMENT AND CURE OF ALL DEFORMITIES.

MANUFACTURES TO ORDER

Elevations for Shortened Limbs, Apparatuses for Hip Disease, Weak Ankles, Spinal Curvatures, Ladies' and Gentlemen's Shoulder Braces, Hard Rubber, Spring and Elastic Trusses, Abdominal Supporters, and Belts. Elastic Stockings. Suspensories, Etc.

Also, Surgical Elastic Hosiery for the Relief and Support of Varicose Veins, Weak, Swollen, or Ulcerated Limbs, Corpulency, Abdominal Weakness, and Tumors.

BATY'S ELEVATED FOOT,

For Elevation of the Pelvis, or Shortened Leg From Any Cause.

Catalogues Sent Free on Application.

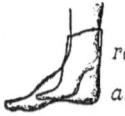 Any Soldier or Sailor ordering a limb of me, can receive transportation from their homes to Milwaukee and return, free of cost, from the Government.

WISCONSIN SOLDIERS AND SAILORS REUNION ROSTER. 185

BATTALION QUARTER MASTERS.
1—Jno Taylor
2—L H Rann

A

Capt T H Mars
Capt A Holcomb
Capt A B Hudson
Lt L Howland — Fort Howard
Lt Justus Williams — Fort Atkinson
Lt C M Leonard
Lt C L Hewitt
Lt W J Phillips* — Chalk Bluff, May 15—62
Lt Josiah Bent — Kenosha, Nov 9—64
Lt E E Vosburg* — Ft Tyler, Apr 16—65
Lt Frank Dolph
Ackley, Geo D, pa — Eau Claire
Brandt, Valentine* — West Point, Apr 16—65
Bilderback, Thos S — Potosi
Buttles, M M — LaCrosse
Bibsach, Wm — Lone Rock
Carpenter, Addison M — Cape Girardeau, Oct 3—62
Chase, Horace — Maple Works
Chase, H S — Neillsville
Chapman, Jonathan — St Louis, Dec 18—62
Colman, Elihu, a — Fond du Lac
Curtis, Geo — Jefferson—62
Coe, E D, ed — Whitewater
Daggett, Hillman G — St Louis, Nov 30—62
Delong, Robt — Shiocton
Edson, Henry A — Cape Girardeau, Oct 3—62
Edgarton, C F, l — Fond du Lac
Evans, Jas — St Louis, Dec 15—62
Farnam, E — Shiocton
Farnam, F — Stevensville
George, Gottfried* — West Point, Apr 16—65
Hamilton, J D — Lansing, Mich
Hart, Wm H — Ft Atkinson, July 13—62
Harrington, J — Shiocton
Hart, Frank J — Patterson, Nov 17—62
Holderness, Abraham — Fremont, Neb
Holmes, E — Nashville, Dec 23—63
Howland, A — Ft Howard
Helstab, Jno — New Albany, Feb 28—65
Hoxie, C J — New Tacoma, Wash
Jaussen, Antine — Kaukauna
Masters L T — Ft Atkinson
McCune, Jasper H — Helena, Aug 17—63
McCloughrey, Dan'l W+ — Chalk Bluff, Mar 22- 62
Moores, Edward P — Cape Girardeau Oct 3—62
Miner, Horace, m — Berlin
McQuinnan, Paul — Kingston, Aug 29—64
Noak, D C, m — Milwaukee
Ordway, Jno W — Nashville, July -64
Pickartz, Peter — Waterloo, Feb 1—65
Petran, August — Binghamton
Skinner, Chas M+ — Cape Girardeau, Oct 26—62
Schulter, Hubert — Barton
Swart, Jeremiah D — Knoxville, Feb 4—64
Shipley, Edwin — Mather
Smith, Wm K — Macon, May 5—65
Snyder, Geo — Oshkosh
Torrey, Sam'l — Shiocton
Van Vleck, Dors J — Louisville, Aug 22—63
Williams, L
Woltman, August — Memphis, Aug 18—62
Westover Carlos S — Nicodemus, Kan
Wendt, Fred'k — Louisville, Apr 16—64

B

Capt G O Clinton — Milwaukee
Capt E D Town — Washington, D C
Lt F T Hobbs — Prairie du Chien
Lt Geo Brown
Lt F P Esterly
Lt Olson P Clinton — Waukesha
Bushnell, Matthias J* — L'Anguille, Aug 3—62
Brown, Bradley* — L'Anguille, Aug 3—62
Banker, Sam'l W* — L'Anguille, Aug 3—62

Brown, Sidney R — Ripon, Apr 18—62
Buck, Sam'l, Jr — Ironton, Dec 3—62
Coates, H E — Neenah
Chapin, Henry L — St Louis, Nov 6—62
Clinton, Geo W, m — Milwaukee
Douglas, Harvey M — Ironton, Dec 3—62
Damp, Lafayet e — Clyman
Doyal, J — Troy
Eddy, Urial C — East Troy
Etchew, Jos — Cape Girardeau, Aug 15—62
Field, Walter O — Nashville, July 9—64
Franklin, Rowson P — Waupun
Gee, T W, m — Waupun
Guinn, Paul, f — Chippewa Falls
Hench, Edward W* — West Prairie, July 23—62
Hutchinson, C — Hutchinson
Hazzard, Frederick W* — L'Anguille, Aug 3—62
Hicks, E K — Troy
Hough, Chas W — St Louis, Dec 26—62
Hewitt, S T — Ishpeming, Mich
Hinkley, Orin D, f — Kiddis, D T
Hartford, M P — Loyal
Hinkley, D — Kiddis, D T
Knowlton, Harrison — Apr 8—62
Kilday, Abdal L — Cape Girardeau, Sept 20—62
Longstaff, Hugh — Minneapolis, Minn
Longstaff, Hugh — Fond du Lac
Medhery, J W — Troy
Miller, Ira — Bouldin Island, Cal
Mend, E F* — L'Anguille, Aug 3—62
Mason, Jos A — Stevens Point
Massey, S M — Alders, Ia
Northrup, Thos — Cape Girardeau, Mo
Osterhout, Cornelius R — Helena, Sept 10—62
Otly, Jas L — Olivet
Preston, Jas — Algoma, Ia
Preston, Jno B — Ft Atkinson
Putnam, H C — Brodhead
Russell, F T — Neenah
Rollo, Frederick C — Sept 26—64
Stabler, Jno, m — Hastings, Neb
Smith, Chester H — Apr 25—62
Shepherd, A A, broker — Fond du Lac
Stanley, Nathan L — St Louis, Feb 3—63
Seeber, Alfred W — Louisville, June 29—65
Stuart, E H — Hamilton
Trown, Peter, f — Chippewa Falls
Ware, Wm P* — L'Anguille, Aug 3—62
Wright, Frank R — Marinette
Westover, Geo — Prairie du Chien Jan 9—6,

C

Capt J W Decker
Lt L Howland — Ft Howard
Capt A a Chase
Lt A J Burrows
Lt J C Maun
Lt C C Townsend
Lt J A Atwood
Lt C F Hensford
Lt C A Pettibone — Juneau
Lt H L Palmer
O'Neil, Michael, sgt*Cape Girardeau, Apr 14—63
Parsons, Jno T, corp*Campbelltown, July 31—64
Brebner, Chas — Northwood, Ia
Brown, Ellis* — Campbelltown, July 30—64
Becker, Jno — Sep 20—62
Cornell, Isham — Patterson, Dec 15—62
Coburn, S W, me — Beaver Dam
Carpenter, Geo A — Bristol
Caswell, Wm H — Van Buren, Dec 11—62
Castle, Chas J — Andersonville, Aug 5—64
Crawford, Wm, pa — Fond du Lac
Denny, Jno — Stockbridge
Dewes, Chas H — Sep 16—62
Danney, Jno — Stockbridge
Duller, Fred — Waterford
Feder, Wm A — Nemo
Griffith, Wm — Sep 23—62

Griffith, Leonard — Spencer
Gowan, David — Nashville, Mar 5—65
Howland, A — Ft Howard
Howland, Ichabod — Georgia, May 9—65
Haight, Geo W, m — Chicago, Ill
Kalms, Fred — Apr 17—62
Longstaff, H C, e — Fond du Lac
Landers, Letter — Americus, Can
Miller, Curtis G — Andersonville Sep 20—61
Nelson, Elis — St Louis, Sep 29- 62
Prior, Geo W, f — Gentryville, Mo
Prior, E R, f — Gentryville, Mo
Reiter, Franz+
Rehtor, P R — Sep 14—64
Reinert, Gottfried — Brookside
Streeter, Gardner — Winchester
Sweet, Elbert E — Louisville, July 9—64
Stoddard, Corline — Stockbridge
Smith, Chas R — Louisville, Sep 14—62
Stewart, Stephen N — St Louis, Sep 22—62
Skinner, Ansel — Mound City, Oct 2—64
Swart, Wm M — Bowling Green, Jan 23—65
Turtle, J R — Nashville, July 8—63
Taylor, C R — Gentryville, Mo
Utley, D — Colby
Utley, A R — Sept 21—62
Williams Geo C — Clear Lake
White, Chas — Sept 24—62
Worley, Wm — St Louis, Sep 18—62
Ward, Alexis J — Kingston, July 10—64
Winters, Oleson G — Andersonville, Sep 9—64
— Pine Hill

D

Capt Nelson Bruett — Jefferson
Capt W W LaGrange+ — Dandridge, Jan 17—64
Capt Jno Baker
Capt L D Phelps
Lt F C Merrit
Lt G K McGunnegle
Lt Theron H Lane
Lt Oscar Barrett
Frederick, Geo W, 2d lt West Prairie, July 3—72
Patton, Thos, corp — Eddyville, June 4—63
Atwood, Jno, f — Berlin
Barrett, Oscar, m — Fargo, D T
Bassett, Chas H, elk — Berlin
Barnett, Andrew — Oct 28—62
Craig, A J, f — Ripon
Curtis, Elias — Wisconsin
Clayton, Geo W — Ludington, Mich
Chessemoore, Nathan R Bowling Green, Jan 10-65
Carlisle, J H — Stevens Point
Diezler, Jus — Binghamton
Foley, Jas — Seneca
Frisbee, Caleb — Helena, Sept 3—62
Ganes, Jno W — Falls City
Howard, Solomon R* — Chalk Bluff, Jan 3—62
Jansen, Lars — Cape Graham, 3—62
Kennedy, Moses — Wisconsin
McGregor, Jno — Pisquippi
McFarland, Wm C — St Louis, Oct 19—62
Palmer, Chas B — Lincoln, Neb
Peck, C S, f — Alexandria, Neb
Peck, Henry W — Monroe
Peck, Clement S, f — Berlin
Richter, Fred, m — St Paul, Minn
Ramsdell, Wm H — Helena, Aug 18—62
Rassmessinger, C+ — Knoxville, Jan 3—64
Speare, Jno — Binghamton
Soper, Myron F — St Louis, 3—62
Stewart, Robt L — St Louis
Widger, Theo — June 19—62
Winchell, Seth — Andersonville, Oct 8—64

E

Capt R H Chittenden
Capt A J Hunt
Capt S V Shipman — Chicago, Ill
Capt P C Stillman — Lima
C 1st C N Hoag — Little Rock, Sept 13—62

NATIONAL HOME
FOR
DISABLED VOLUNTEER SOLDIERS.

Gen. EDWARD W. HINCKS,
Commandant and Treasurer.

Capt. W. H. LOUGH,
Secretary.

Dr. A. F. J. HARE,
Surgeon.

The North-Western Branch

is beautifully situated, three miles from the City of Milwaukee. It is a capacious brick building containing accommodations for 1,000 inmates. In addition to this building which contains the main halls, eating apartment, offices, dormitory and engine room, are shops, granaries, stables and other out-buildings. The Home farm contains 425 acres, of which over one-half is cultivated. The remainder is a wooded park traversed by shaded walks and drives, beautifully undulating. The main line of the Chicago, Milwaukee and St. Paul Railway runs through the farm, and the track of the northern division passes beside it.

Who are Admitted and How.

Soldiers who were disabled in the service of the United States in the war of the rebellion, the Mexican war, or the war of 1812, and have been honorably discharged, are entitled to admission to the Soldiers' Home.

Admission is procured on a certificate, of which blank forms are furnished to every applicant, setting forth his enlistment, with date, rank, place of muster and the company, regiment or other organization to which he belonged, and the date and cause of discharge; and that he is receiving a pension. His identity is set forth in the same certificate, and a surgeon's statement of his disability and its nature.

Disabled soldiers, or their friends, county, city and town authorities, police officers, guardians of the poor and almshouses, trustees of benevolent institutions and public or private hospitals throughout the State and country, having knowledge of disabled soldiers, or such persons in their charge, are cordially invited to address the commandant by whom the necessary blanks and instructions will be sent by return mail.

Labor, Instruction and Amusement.

Such inmates as are able to do so, have the opportunity to practice various mechanical trades, or to work on the Home farm, for which they are paid a compensation of from $6 to $18 a month, averaging, all around, about 40 cents per day. Skilled laborers can earn more than these wages. The trades practiced are, boot and shoe making, carpenter and joiner work, tin-smithing, plastering and stone masonry, gas fitting, cigar making, broom making and basket making. Farming is largely carried on, and some of the finest products exhibited at the State fairs have been from the fields and gardens cultivated by the soldiers. All the labor of the institution, including care of the building, repairs which are found necessary, and farming operations, is done by the inmates.

The institution has an excellent library of 2,500 volumes, contributed by friends of the soldiers in various parts of the country. The reading room contains newspapers and magazines, all of which are in constant use and requisition by the inmates.

This institution is not a public charity, and the disabled soldiers of the country should understand it. The money that supports it has been forfeited by bad soldiers, and has been made by the law of congress, the absolute property of the disabled soldiers of the country. They do not place themselves in the list of paupers by becoming inmates of the Home.

No soldier or soldier's friend visiting Milwaukee will ever regret a call at the Home, where they are always made welcome by its efficient and worthy commandant.

CONSIN SOLDIERS AND SAILORS REUNION ROSTER.

Ripon	Berkley, Jno	Baraboo	Kobernick, Wm	Jeff Barracks, Mar 11—6
	Boundey, Geo	St Louis, Apr 20—62	Lammie, Geo	St Louis, Oct 11 -62
	Bacon, L C	Kenosha	Laurence, Wm	Windsor, Aug 26—62
	Bray, Henry	Macon, June 4—65	Lohmann, Henry	St Louis, Oct 19—62
	Bacon, C D	Kenosha	Long, Major J	Shannon, Feb 15—63
Madison	Blackman, Horace	Kenosha	Meehan, Jos	Fairfield, Neb
Apr 14 -65	Clark, Ira W	St Louis, Apr 29—62	Marton, Jas	Jeffersonville, July 29—64
Sparta	Cooper, A G	Baraboo	Miles, Edwin, f	Hewett
Aug 26—63	Crawford, Wm W	St Louis, Sept 30—62	McLean, Wm, f	Oak Centre
May 17 - 63	Carlisle, J H	Stevens Point	Miles, C	Neillsville
May 25—64	Combest, J as	Forest, Oct 22—64	Rice, Peter L	St Louis, Dec 17 - 63
May 18 —3	Fancer, S C	LaCrosse	Rolf, Columbus T	St Louis, Feb 9—63
l, Aug 7—62	Farmer, Jno	St Louis, Apr 13—62	Rowley, Geo	Bowling Green, Jan 9—65
Vinneconne	Foster, Chas R	Bloomfield, July—62	Rowney, Schubael G	Nashville, Oct 25—64
Apr 21—63	Fowler, Austin	Louisville, Dec 16 - 64	Schumacher, Louis, f	Naswaupee
leaver Dam	Fuller, Jonas	July 3—65	Shover, Frank, e	Schula, Ia
Apr 18—63	Greiber, Herman f	Roxbury	Spencer, Wm E	Sept 26—62
leaver Dam	Greiber, Henry J	Cartersville, Sept 22—64	Sanders, Josiah P	Weyauwega
lle, Aug -64	Gallaher, Michael B	Waterloo, Mar 4—64	Snyder, G W	Oshkosh
June 18 -63	Hetz, Jno	Des Arc, Aug 6—62	Sweeney, Martin	Chattanooga, June 18—65
a, Oct 9—62	Harris, Geo	Knoxville, Mar 4—64	Sprague, Oscar	Oak Centre
pring Creek	Knowles, Erastus H	St Louis, Apr 6—62	Town, H S	Ripon
Apr 16—65	Kimball, Chauncey C	Helena, Aug 24—62	Tennant, Arthur J	Evansville, Jan 1—65
Apr 24 - 63	Kimball, Chase P	Ironton, Dec 13 - 62	White, Josiah R	Mound City, Oct 29—62
Wild Rose	Lemler, Jno	Nashville, Feb 14—65	Wixen, Jesse, Jr	Richmond, Va
62	Leonard, Fernando F	Cape Girardeau June 2—62	Ward, David J	Louisville, Feb 7—65
Sept 11—62	Leslie, Josias	Nashotah	Willard, David A	Depere
t Atkinson	Moore, Erastus	Millsburg, Aug 2 -62		
r, Aug 3 - 63	McMillen, J Clifford	St Louis, Oct 13—62		H
Aug 29 —64	Moorehead, Jno M	Greenville, Oct 17—62		
Escanaba	Mounce, Squire	Louisville, Mar 3—61		
Colby	O'Brien, Pat	Winneconne	Capt L M B Smith	
Fox Lake	Oleson, Nels	St Louis, Oct 17—62	Capt Jas L Sprague	
July 39—62	Pease, Marcus A	Helena, Aug 21—62	Lt J M Comstock	
oomfield, Ia	Roberts, D Crawford	Cape Girardeau, Oct 15-62	Lt A D Hudson	
a, May 3—64	Sattler, Augustus	Cape Girardeau, May 9—62	Lt J Willard	
July, 8—63	Sanberly, Henry, f	Stevensville	Lt W S Cooper	Helena, Sept 3 - 62
Janesville	Swenson, Kittell	Nashville, Oct 13—64	Lt F A Blood	
le, Aug 3—64	Seager, Geo W	Jeffersonville, Apr 10—65	Lt N S Chambers	
Waupon	Vosburg, Jno	Cape Girardeau, June 25—62	Saunders, J H, 1st sgt	Cape Girardeau Oct 6—62
r, Aug 3 -62	Watz, H K	Des Moines, Ia	Greenwood, S M, sgt*	Varnells Station, Mar 9-64
e, Jan 19—61	Wilder, Jno W	Andersonville, May 10—64	Wilkins, Albert, sgt	Stevenson, Oct 18—63
ort Atkinson	Wurl, Ludwig	July 4—65	Hale, Jno, sgt	St Louis, Aug 25—62
Kentucky			Daniels, Chas D, sgt	Cincinnati, Apr—64
Colona		G	Fisk, Israel P, sgt	Andersonville, Aug 10—64
r, July 3—64			Fenton, Wm H, corp*	Bloomneld, Apr 29—63
July 10—62	Capt C F Robinson		Russell, Jas, corp	Cape Girardeau, Oct 7—62
Sparta	Capt H S Town		Ainsworth, Henry M	Memphis, Oct 2- 62
lle, Aug—64	Capt A S Downs		Bugby, Wm	Fairwater, June 3—62
Osseo	Lt S V Shipman	Chicago, Ill	Bock, Chas	Nashville, Feb 20—61
Linn Centre	Lt Wm Sandon	Whitestown	Brook, Edwin	Andersonville, June 22—61
Sparta	Lt J H Barnes		Bradford, Chas	Neillsville
Colfax	Lt E T Clark		Cole, Ezra	St Louis, May 20—65
a, Oct 13—62	Lt G W Chamberlain		Cooper, E H	LaCrosse
May 16—65	Lt Jos E Mosher		Curtis, Robert	St Louis, Oct 6—62
Ripon	Lt Geo G Seaton		Crouch, Hiram J	Madison, Apr 5—64
le, Feb 5—65	Ambrust, Nic, f	Sevastopol	Clute, Chas W	Nashville, July 9 - 64
May 13 - 65	Breitung, A A	Appleton	Carter, Thos N	Krokuk, Feb 16—65
lle, Apr 3 -65	Beuls, Chas W, corp	Greenville, Jan 10—61	Cavanaugh, Jno	Andersonville. Aug 2-64
amstown, Ia	Combs, Melvin R, corp	St Louis, Oct 20—62	Darling, Irvin C	Appleton, Apr 14— 62
Waupon	O'Reilly, Franklin corp	Louisville, Feb 6 -64	Dietrich, Gustav	Cape Girardeau, Nov 30— 62
lle, Aug—64	McLennan, Roderick, corp	Bridgeport, Mar 17 - 64	Darling, Jesus	Nashville, Oct 29—63
Harrison	Mossumann, Gottlieb, f		Dygart, Geo H	New Albany, June 13-64
le, Dec 24—63	Bjornseu, Christen	Cape Girardeau, May 18—63	Everson, Ole	Nashville, Dec 10—63
on, Jan 9—81	Breitung, Albert A	Appleton	Ferguson, Arvin*	West Point, Apr 16—65
ld, Aug 1—62	Bates, Geo P	Bloomfield, May 1—63	Frank, Jno	Helena, Sept 15—62
Fort Howard	Clark, E W	Neenah	Fuller, Lewis	Racine, Mar 18 _42
Fort Howard	Clark, Jas*	Dandridge, Jan 17 - 54	Flinn, Oscar	Andersonville, Aug 15- 64
	Chase, W	Chasburg	Fisk, Perry G	Andersonville
	Cole, Geo R	St Louis, Dec—62	Fisk, Alphonzo	Andersonville
	Campbell, Henry C, e	Milwaukee	Gordon, Edwin	Louisville, Dec 15—61
	Dausan, Aug	Chattanooga, Dec 12—45	Green, G L	South Haven, Mich
	Dollar, Peter	Nashville, Jan 16—65	Grover, Geo	Krokuk, Dec 25—64
	Ellis, Brasier R	Sun Prairie	Gordon, B, f	Waupon
	Gesser, Geo P	Poplar Springs, May 9- 64	Hezeltine, Jno F	Helena, Sept 14 -62
	Gerets, Wm*	Old Church, July 23—64	Holbrook, M	Lime Centre
	Hayes, Carroll	Cape Girardeau, Oct 7—62	Hunter, Wesley W	Andersonville, Aug 1—64
Sept 13—62	Hawes, Philander	Appleton, Jan 27 —63	Hanson, Thos	Cape Girardeau, Sept 14—63
	Heintz, Jacob	Alexandria, Nov 26—64	Kline, Jacob	Mukwanago
	Hodge, Geo P	Jeffersonville, Mar 29—63	Kurtz, Romanus	Patterson, Oct 26—62
le, Mar 19—64	James, Edw P	Pilot Knob, Feb 16—63	Knapp, E	Clarks Mills

187

HUNTER'S MAGNETIC SPRINGS

AND SUMMER RESORT.

MR. and MRS. JOHN E. GARVIN, late of Chicago, respectfully inform the public that they have leased the celebrated

HUNTER FOUNTAIN AND HOTEL,

and are now ready to receive guests. The house has been newly furnished throughout, and no finer suites of rooms can be found in the United States. Their table will be superior in every respect. The House is located on Lake Winnebago, near the Junction of the C. & N. W. Ry, and S. & F. du L. Ry, in the city of Fond du Lac, and has all the natural advantages offered by other resorts, besides the wonderful fountain, which is acknowledged to contain more medicinal properties than any spring in America. Bath Rooms have been added to the House and water from these springs will be used.

Medical advice can be obtained in the house. The price of board with rooms, at $10 and $12 per week, according to location. This celebrated water will be shipped to any point, delivered at depots in Fond du Lac. For further particulars address,

JOHN E. GARVIN, FOND DU LAC, WIS.

N. B.—A fine fleet of Yachts have been put upon the Lake this season, and row boats are in abundance. Good fishing and hunting may always be found.

Commercial Union Assurance Co
OF LONDON.

United States Branch, 37 and 39 Wall Street, New York.

NEW YORK BOARD OF DIRECTORS.

WM. ALLEN BUTLER, Chairman.   EUGENE DUTILH, Vice Chairman
G. S. BOWDOIN, Morton, Bliss & Co.   E. S. JAFFRAY, E. S. Jaffray & Co
DAVID A. WELLS.   JOHN T. TERRY, E. D. Morgan & Co.
S. VAN RENSSELAER CRUGER, Pres. Orient Ins. Co.

ALFRED PELL, Resident Manager.   CHARLES SEWELL, Ass't Man'r

United States Branch Statement.

Reserve for Total Liabilities, including Re-insurance in the
United States $981,393 13
Net Surplus, 1st January, 1879 .... 912,652 93
                                                        $1,494,046 06

London Office Statement.

Capital paid up in Cash, ... $1,250,000 00
Reserve for all Liabilities, including Re-insurance, ... 7,143,500 85
Net Fire Surplus, ... 2,296,106 55
                                                        $9,489,407 10
Subscribed Capital for which the Stockholders are personally liable, not yet called in,.................. $11,250,000 00

All Losses in the Western Department promptly paid through the Chicago office.

WESTERN DEPARTMENT, 164 La Salle St., Chicago

C. F. MULLENS, Resident Secretary.

H. A. BOND.   WM. H. HANCHETT.

BOND & HANCHETT.

MANUFACTURERS OF

Milwaukee Cream Colored, Common & Pressed

Yard, Foot of 13th Street.

MILWAUKEE,   -   WISCONSIN.

WISCONSIN SOLDIERS AND SAILORS REUNION ROSTER. 189

Name	Location/Date
Lobdell, Daniel	Nashville, Apr 9–64
Pillsbury, Adoniram J	Andersonville, Sept 11-64
Putnam, G S	Houghton, Mich
Posey, Erwin	Cleveland, Mar 20–64
Roseberry, Chas O	Andersonville
Stevenson, Herman H	Cape Girardeau, Oct 7–62
Slay, Jno	Nashville, July 3–64
Stanley, Lewis	Bowling Green, Feb 14–65
Somerville, Wm J	Andersonville
Smith, Wm H	Edgefield July 5–65
Talbot, Jasper*	Mossy Creek, Dec 24–63
Trexler, Henry J	Indianapolis, Sept 25–64
Toy, Thos	Andersonville
Van Valin, Henry+	Bloomfield, Sept 12–62
Van Vleck, Everett	Cape Girardeau, Jan 6–63
Vick, J	Andersonville, Sept 28–64
Walput, A H L	Rushford
Wyman, Edgar*	West Point, Apr 16–65
Winn, Stephen W	Bellevue, Feb 4–63
Winn, Jno H	North Clayton
Wittinger, Daniel W	Albauville

I

Name	Location
Capt W M Hoyt	
Capt O L Porter	
Capt O A Pettibone	Juneau
Capt A B Evarts	
Lt J J I Morrison	
Lt H S Schuyler	
Lt Jno Baker	
Lt M P Stone	
Lt J H Burnett	
Lt W G Cooper	
Lt W Hutchins	
Lt Jno Little	
Lt H P O'Connor	
Lt E D Town	Washington, D C
Lt s T Hewitt	
Lt H C Tarbox	
Abels, Wm H*	Scatterville, Aug 5–72
Alchen, Chris	Patterson, Jan 25–65
Atwood, Jno	St Louis, June 1–62
Barus, M, I	Menominee Falls
Barnes, D, I	Menominee Falls
Barnett, J R	Neenah
Brown, Lucius	Berudel
Bradfield, Geo	Cape Girardeau, Apr 20–63
Craig, Edw	Cape Girardeau, Oct 8–62
Collinson, Wm	Patterson, Dec 20–62
Decoudres, Jas D	Oct 6–62
Downes, Jno W	Nashville
Ferdhaus, Casper	Naugart
Goodrich, Delos	Stevenson, Feb 20–64
Goodrich, O Perry	Ft Atkinson
Horton, Adrian+	Arkansas, Aug 5–62
Heck, Jacob	Milwaukee
Horton, Eli D	Oakes
Mathews, Louis+	Stevenson, June 8–65
McKinney, Nicholas H	Nashville, May 7–66
Metiowan, J	Fond du Lac
McGowan, A J, I	Hamilton Mills
Newberg, Rich M	Helena, Sept 10–62
Oberinre, Frank*	Jonesboro, Aug 2–62
Nuttell, Benj*	Jonesboro, Aug 5–62
Mainspies, Fred	Cape Girardeau, Nov 16–63
Rogers, N	Nashville
Stanley, Edw*	Jonesboro, Aug 2–12
Sowerby, Jno*	Jonesboro, Aug 2–62
Schuck, Peter*	Jonesboro, Aug 2––
Sampey, Thos	Benton Barracks, Mar 2–62
Skinner, Nelson G	Barnsville, Jan 5–63
Williams, Geo R*	Jonesboro, Aug 2–62
Willis, Oscar F*	Jonesboro, Aug 2–62
Ware, Geo F	Oct 10–62
Walker, W II, ed	Peabody, Kan
Zimmer, Peter	Cape Girardeau, Dec 15–62

K

Capt A S Senton	

Name	Location/Date
Capt C N Wicks	
Lt G D Coyle	
Lt E S Chase	
Lt J C Atwater	
Lt C W Clinton	Murfreesboro, Mar 29–65
Lt P B Lameraux	
Allen, D A	Nellisville
Adams, Ira	Helena, Sept 23–62
Allen, Daniel	Loval
Baker, Russell W	Cape Girardeau, Sept 30–– 2
Brodzig, Gottlieb	Lomira
Bronson, Homer O	Cape Girardeau, Oct 10–65
Bohannan, Geo W	Raelia
Bissett, David F	Patterson, Dec 2–62
Butterfield, Lyman C	Nashville, July 7–64
Bush, Henry E	Louisville, May 12–65
Cushman, Jas	Etowah, Apr 14–64
Crapo, Wm	Louisville, Feb 22–64
Claron, DeWitt	Osage, Ia
Carey, Ernest D	Bowling Green. Jan 9–65
Clappo, Lester L	Milwaukee
Draper, T S	Eagle
Ellis, Brasier R	Sun Prairie
Edwards, Altaire H	Helena, Aug 16–62
Forbes, L D	Rivers, Minn
Gray, Orrin	West Fork, Ark
Garmon, Leander	Nashville, Mar 19–64
Griese, Wilhelm, me	Plymouth
Henderson, Jas, Jr	Ripon
Hoisapple, Rowland	St Louis, Oct 10–62
Hodgeman, Oliver	Brookfield Junction
Huntington, Almon S	Madison, May 14–64
Ingersoll, Jno S	St Louis, Nov 13–62
Jennings, Jno W	Cleveland, Apr 23–64
Kress, Louis	Beaver Dam
Kids, Chas	Sept 25–62
Longstaff, Thos	Nashville, Apr 29–64
LeFevre, Henry	May 1–62
Mitchell, Newell S	Memphis, Sept 2–62
Moore, Jas C	Oswego
Norton, Henry D	Macon, May 8–65
Arth, Peter	Lawrenceburg, Tenn
Platte, Chas M	Bloomfield, Sept 1–62
Ryan, Thos	Racine
Robinson, N	Winneconne
Savery, Frank	Sabula, Ia
Truesdell, Philander*	L'Auguille, Apr 2–64
Turner, Jno A	St Louis, Oct 10–62
Tillotson, S C	Nashville, July 3–64
Unger, W J	Nashville, May 29–64
Valentine, Geo	Winchester, July 23–63
Wright, Franklin W	Cape Girardeau, Oct 10–62

L

Name	Location/Date
Capt H Harnden	Madison
Capt T Bateman	Empire Prairie
Capt J L Steward	Rosedale
Lt H Hilliard	Chicago, Ill
Lt T B Roberts	
Lt J M Waterman	
Lt T C Ankeny	Johnsonville, Tenn
Ld J L Ackley	
Emerick, Jno, sgt	Cape Girardeau, Sept 26–63
Brandt, Andris, sgt	Madison, Dec 27–63
Richmond, Byron, corp	Andersonville, Dec 1–64
Brail, Eli+	Dandridge, Jan 17–64
Brager, Winslow	Hebron, Neb
Bohnauer, Jacob	Cape Girardeau, Oct 31–62
Brindley, Robt	Mount Ida
Briggs, Irving	Andersonville, Aug 8–64
Budson, Jno P	Andersonville, Aug 4–64
Cronk, Chatham*	Mossy Creek, Dec 29–63
Coats, N T	Neenah
Curtis, Jas E	Helena, Sep 16–62
Dagel Jno	Andersonville, Apr 3–64
Duffie, Edw	Andersonville, Apr 27–64
Davenport, Wm	Millen, Nov 5–64
Priddle, Nicholas*	Auguille, Aug 3–62

Name	Location/Date
Gifford, Harrison	Pilot Knob, Jan 1–63
Griffith, L	Nellisville
Huiman, Albert L ―	Cleveland, Apr 1–64
Halstead, Wm, me	Sturgeon Bay
Hanson, Hans C	Brownsville, Jan 4–63
Jones, Sam'l	Cape Girardeau, June–62
Jones, Evan E	Cape Girardeau, Oct 27–62
Klampe, L G	Janesville
Kellogg, T M	Kaukauna
Lee, Joseph K	Patterson, Aug 29–62
Lamberte, P J	Roxbury
Louis y. Jno	Andersonville, Aug 9–64
Mucklow, David	Wisconsin, Oct–63
McFadden, Hugh	Andersonville, Aug 9–64
McCormick, Ebenezer	Andersonville, July 6–64
Potter, Geo*	Georgia, May 2–64
Polter, Dany	Little Prairie
Peak, Fred	St Louis, Oct 24–62
Pagett, Mead R	Ft Atkinson
Pagett, Chas W	Mound City, Nov 15–62
Pagett, Mead R	Helena, Sep 16–62
Roberts, Jonas	Cape Girardeau, Oct 12–62
Redick, Royal	Nashville
Reynolds, W L	Jefferson
Rice, Anson P	Nashville
Rasmussen, Gorgen	Andersonville, Aug 15–64
Stevens, Jared L+	St Louis, July 12–64
Shafer, S	Weston
Slater, Wm+	Atlanta, Apr 14–64
Sharp, Jas H, sgt	Beaver Dam
Skinner, Eu	Cape Girardeau, Oct 31–62
Stney, Jno	Cape Girardeau, Nov–62
Slingerland, Jno	Andersonville, Aug 9–64
Thom Peter E	Andersonville, Aug 26–64
Tauton, Wm	Ek Mound
Tripp, David	Andersonville, July 2–64
Valive, Anthony	Andersonville, Sep 5–64
Volust, O H	Andersonville, July 6–64
Webb, Carey C*	L'Auguille, Aug 3–62
Weaver, Geo W*	Georgia, May 2–64
Wilson, Christopher	Cape Girardeau, Sept 15–62
Welcome, Edwin D	Andersonville, May 3–64
Welton, Moses	Andersonville, June 13–64
Walrath, Jno	Andersonville, Aug 16–64

M

Name	Location/Date
Capt Newton Jones	
Capt L J Davis	
Lt G W Barter	
Lt J A Owen	
Lt C Caldwell	Weyauwega
Lt J K Dening	
Lt W L Jacobs	
Lt Jno Ogden	
Lt H E Staples	
Lt C F Warner	
Dana, Wm M	Rushford
Suepard, Ed R, sgt	Nashville, Mar 25–64
Gray, Geo G, sgt	Florence, Sept 15–64
Taylor, Ed D	Chickasaw, Mar 5– 65
Brown, Chauncey*	Cape Girardeau, May 18–63
Brooks, Wesley J	Lind
Brooks, Martin	Lind
Brook, Judah	Lind
Bourne, Chas L	Kingston, Sept 26–64
Bust, Stephen	Milston
Chittenden, Thos	Cariton, Neb
Cooley, Ed	Patterson, Nov 13–62
Caldwell, C	Lind
Crawford, Jas	Cape Girardeau, May 8–63
Dumphy, Ansel W	Nashville, June 7–64
Harvey, Newton T	Cape Girardeau, Oct 8–62
Hicks, G H	Sextonville
Hawley, Newton T	
King, Geo H	Neenah
Lathrop, Stanley E, cl	Atlanta, Ga
McNitt, Jno H	Waterloo, Mar 5–64
Marsh, Homer*	Hopkinsville, Dec 17–61
Myers, Peter	Union Grove
Oakes, Harvey	Cape Girardeau, May 18–62

HUNTER'S
MAGNETIC FOUNTAIN OF HEALTH
AND SUMMER RESORT.

Recommending to the Invalid Portion of the Public the Extraordinary Curative Properties of the Magnetic Saline Waters of George Hunter's Artesian Fountain and Summer Resort.

There is no intention of advertising patent medicines, but to present to the public a thorough chemical analysis of the saline water, and a vast array of facts, and certificates, of wonderful cures by the use of it. Sufficient to convince the most skeptical that a very extraordinary discovery was accidentally made at Fond du Lac, by Mr. George Hunter, of a

GREAT NATURAL REMEDY

for many of the ills and diseases which poor frail humanity is subject to in this changeable climate. If the reader will have patience to read to the end he will be presented with evidence that must convince all rational minds that there is no intention to deceive or mislead the most credulous, and only a simple desire to

BENEFIT THE AFFLICTED.

Prof. Tyndall, F. R. S., of England, the most advanced scientist of the age, in his very popular illustrated lectures in Boston and New York, last year, said, that " the polarization of the ultimate molecules of matter by magnetic force surrounded each molecule with an intelligence that caused them to select their appropriate places in the formation of mineral compounds." The Saline waters of Mr. Hunter's Artesian Fountain are an evidence of the correctness of Prof. Tyndall's assertions,

These waters flow through and over mineral rock highly charged with magnetism, which polarizes the molecules of mineral salts and causes them to permeate the water in that proportion which makes it pleasant to the taste,

HEALTHFUL, AND CURATIVE

in an eminent degree.

Learned and eminent physicians may have an accurate knowledge of diseases that beset frail humanity, and may know well how to compound medicines proper for the cure of those diseases, but modern mercenary craft and cunning often defeat the best intentions and experienced knowledge of the ablest M. D.'s, by adulterating the drugs of which medicines are made. But in Nature's great chemical laboratory there are no mercenary motives to stimulate cunning devices in adulterating drugs; an honest intelligence selects the materials and compounds the medicines that will

CURE ALL DISEASES

that flesh is heir to, if we are wise and industrious enough to hunt up and make the proper selections of medicines which an All-Wise Power has placed all around us. The Magnetic Saline waters are made in the bowels of the earth, where the drugs are pure.

All statements made in these pages in regard to the extraordinary curative properties of the Magnetic Saline waters, will be sustained by the evidence of unimpeachable witnesses—ladies and gent'emen of respectability, who have been cured or much benefited by using the water, and know from actual experience the truth of their testimony.

OF MINERAL WATERS.

Mineral or medical veins of water are formed in the bowels of the earth by the percolation of fresh water through and over the deposits of soda, magnesia, potassa, and iron, (sometimes magnetic), and their compound salts—chlorides, carbonates, and sulphates, in greater or less proportions.

Anciently, only those veins that found their way to the surface through natural channels (called springs or pools) were used medicinally for the cure of diseases. Many of such springs or pools, found in all parts of the world

HAVE BEEN CELEBRATED,

in all ages, for their curative qualities. Some of them have a continuous flow, while others flow periodically, or intermittent like the hot springs in volcanic districts and the pools of Bethesda and Siloam in ancient Judea of which it is recorded that an

ANGEL CAME DOWN

at certain seasons and troubled the waters, when vast numbers of invalids, possessed of various diseases, went down to the pools, bathed in and drank of the waters, and were healed. But since the inauguration of artesian wells, many of these medicinal veins of water have been brought to the surface by drilling or boring deep into the earth, and these artesian fountains are generally found to possess much

MORE EFFECTIVE

curative properties than any natural springs or pools known to mankind. Such of Nature's simple substances as permeate the water which flows from Mr. Hunter's fountain, are now extensively used by the best physicians in compounding medicines for the cure of diseases, and the learned M. D. who is lucky enough to secure these materials unadulterated, will always be regarded as the most successful practitioner.

ACCIDENTAL DISCOVERY OF THE MINERAL WATER.

A thousand drafts upon the fountain head, or water supply to the ordinary fountains, considerably lessened the force of the flow of many of them, until in many parts of the city they ceased to rise above the surface of the ground.

Mr. Hunter, being in need of a greater supply of water than the ordinary fountains could furnish, and a purer quality, concluded to sink an artesian well into a lower strata of the limestone rock; believing that if he could strike a vein of water at a lower base, a sufficient quantity of pure water would be obtained adapted to his wants. Mr. Hunter, with a view of testing his theories in this regard, procured the services of John Dobyns, Esq., an experienced well-driller, who sunk a fountain until the

(Continued on page 192.)

WISCONSIN SOLDIERS AND SAILORS REUNION ROSTER.

Ogden, Jno, teacher — Ky and Tenn
Owens, Jno A, a — Chicago, Ill
Pool, Abe — Cartersville, Aug 15—62
Prekett, H S — Neillsville
Putney, J B — Lind
Robinson, Sam T, r r agt — Cassopolis, Mich
Rogers, David — South Haven, Mich
Shepard, Chester C — Woodworth
Scott, Rich I. — Cape Girardeau, Oct 5—62
Shepards, Chester C — Kenosha
Sonnerman, Aug — Nashville, Mar 8—64
Taggart, Geo W — Weyauwega
Van Horton, Jno M — Knoxville, Feb 1—64
Wheeler, Geo H — Beaver Dam
Whitney, Jno C — Weyauwega
Warren, Moses Scott — Helena, Sept 17—63
Wootsey, Rich J — Lind
Winters, Perry — Andersonville, May 5—65
White, N L — Lind
Walker, Abe E — Richmond, Feb 28—64
Williams, Lyman, c — Sacramento, Cal
Young, Enoch — L'Anguille, Aug 3—62

UNASSIGNED.

Anderson, Peter — Elk Mound
Arndt, P S, ph — Kenosha
Beutz, J, f — Taycheedah
Breed, Calvin — Whitehall
Church, Dan P — Leadville, Co
Clough, W — Oshkosh
Clemens, D C — Kiroy, O
Chambers, Nicholas — Racine
Diner, Henry — Shiocton
Downsy, Ed, r r shop — Minneapolis, Minn
Ertl, Jacob — Beaver Dam
Gill, Wm — Rock Grove, Ill
Gove, R L — Waukesha
Gone, R L — Waukesha
Hamilton, Jesse B — Lansing, Mich
Hankm, J — Blair
Hurd, C C, f — Waupun
Hamilton, G M — Emmetsburg, Ia
Howlund, L, m — Ft Howard
Horr, A M — Winneconne
Jensen, Louis — Kenosha
Jones, Newton — Geneva, O
Keyes, H W, sgt-maj — Beaver Dam
Kettler, A, f — Byron
Lisa, — — Plymouth
Maslick, Julius — East Claridon, O
Sharp, Jas H, f — Elo
Smith, J N, t — Oakfield
Stahl, Jonas —
Smith, Rich — Kewaunee
Stephan, Chris, f — N sewaupee

SECOND CAVALRY.

Three years. Organized March 12th, 1862. Original strength, 1127, gain by recruits, etc., 1343. Total, 2516. Death loss, 203—Killed in action, 16, died of wounds, 4, of disease, 263, of accidents, 8. Other losses, 676—missing, 5, desertions, 103, transfers, 31, discharges, 535. Strength at muster-out, November, 1865, 1541. Campaigns in Mo., Ark., Miss., La., Texas.

REGIMENTAL ROSTER.

Col C C Washburn — [Minneapolis, Minn
Col Thos Stephens
Col Nicholas H Dale
Lt Col Levi Sterling
Lt Col Wm H Miller
Lt Col H Eugene Eastman
Lt Col Wm Woods
Lt Col Newton De Forest
Maj Wm H Miller, 1st bat
Maj Myron W Wood, 1st bat
Maj Jno Whytock, 2d bat

Maj Edwin Skewes, 2d bat — Neosho, Nov
Maj Edw D Luxton, 3d bat
Maj Geo N Richmond, 3d bat
Maj Geo W Ring, 3d bat
Surg Clark G Pease — Janesville, June 27—64
Surg Moses P Hanson — Milwaukee
A Surg Alex McBean
A Surg Augustus H Guernsey
A Surg J Seaton Kelso — Ackley, Ia
Chap Wm H Brisbane
Chap Benj L Brisbane
Adj Wm H Morgan
Adj Jas P Scott — LaCrosse
Adj Jas H Woolfenden — Neosho, Mo
Q M Geo C Russell
Q M Henry P George
Q M Geo S Race
Com Jas B Bradford
Com Prosper L Knappen

BATTALION ADJUTANTS.

1—Horatio H Virgin
2—Oliver Gibbs
3—Jos E Scott

BATTALION QUARTERMASTERS.

1—Chas H Cox
2—Wm Bones
3—Sam Elmore Rundle

A

Capt Wm Woods
Capt Andrew J Palmer
Lt Napoleon Boardman
Lt Chas Adamson — Nov 15—63
Lt Henry Decker
Lt Geo T Williams
Lt Chas E Jonbert
Lt Erasus Moore
Lt Geo S Phelps, Co Judge — Medford
Stowe, Wm H, — Helena, Oct 8—62
Trowbridge, Dan'l P — LaCrosse, Feb 7—65
Huson, Wm S, — Helena, Aug 10—62
Adams, Dan'l J — Springfield, Feb 21—63
Anderson, Martin — Lamartine, May 26—65
Cook, S A, m — Unity
Dick, Jno W, f — Brothertown
Dick, O D, f — Brothertown
Fowler, Eaton, e — Brothertown
Garrity, Pat* — Lane's Prairie, May 20—34
Hammar, A H, t — Brothertown
Heidrudge, Geo C — Cairo, Nov 30—64
Hawley, Jno — Hempstead, Sept 25—65
Hopkins, H H, f — Nashua, Ia
Jenkins, E, mf — Rosendale
Lylle, Albert H — Sept 5—62
Marcy, Geo W, f — Nashua, Ia
Males, David* — Lanes Prairie, May 26—64
Munroe, B H, f — Lamartine
Pangborn, Henry — Wisconsin, Apr 5—65
Stringham, W H, f — Eldorado
Sigsby, Jas H, f — Vicksburg, July 13—64
Willis, Geo, I — Eldorado

B

Capt Albert W Bishop
Capt Jno Whytock
Capt Thos LaFlesh — Nevins
Lt Orin H Stone
Lt Jeremiah S McDaniel
L Purcell S Reppy
Lt Jno Steffens
Lafreniere, Chas B, corp — Redbone, Oct 10—63
McRea, Thos, corp — Redbone, Sept 25—61
Allen, Chas E — St Louis, Jan 26—65
Burton, David H — July 8—62
Bates, J A, f — Midland, Mich
Barlow, E — La Crosse
Dyke, Jos M — Helena, Sept 13—62
Fuller, Geo W — Vicksburg, Oct 14—64

Glover, Geo — Mound City, Sept 8—63
Gorder, Aulins — Helena, Oct 16—62
Grahon, Fred'k — Cairo, May 8—64
Godale, Jno M, mc — Goshen, Mich
Green, Walter — Bangor
Hanson, Jacob — Vicksburg, July 28—64
Johnson, Bennett — Clinton, July 22—63
Johnson, Elmore S — Vicksburg, Oct 26—64
Knudson, Geo — Memphis, May 20—63
Loach, Alfred J — La Crosse
Martin, Jas — Mound City, Sept 19—62
Miner, Isaac — Helena, Dec 26—62
Nellson, Neils, elk — Deadwood, D T
Reynolds, Alsop C — Helena, Sept 22—62
Staff, Frank, — Keokuk, Nov 1— 62
Schields, Chas H — Necedah
Sissin, O S — La Crosse
Thompson, Jos C — Mound City, Sept 19—52
Williams, Thos — Illnes Bluff, June 15—63
Wilbur, Cornellus — Mo River, May 17—62

C

Capt Reuben R Wood
Capt Myron W Wood — East Oakland, Cal
Capt Dan'l L Riley — Libbey, Ia
Lt Chauncey Blancher
Lt Jno Showalter — Beetown
Lt Francis A Toble
Blakesley, Geo W, sgt — Jefferson City, May 21—62
Wells, Henry K, sgt — Redbone, Nov 23—13
Jones, Jas W, corp — Mound City, Oct 8—62
Campbell, Jno. corp — St Louis, Feb 26—63
Shanley, Jas M, corp — Andersonville, Jan 27—65
Brandlin, Philip — Redbone, Feb 27—64
Cooper, Wm J — Vicksburg, July 27—64
Cook, Lynn B — Andersonville, July 7—64
Cook, Orson J — Vicksburg, July 27—64
Campbell, Chas C — Vicksburg, Aug 2—64
Dean, Elbanan W — Jeff Barracks, Jan 25—63
Davis, Joshua — Memphis, Jan 29—65
Graney, Wm — Chicago, Nov 27—64
Gulick, Edw D — Helena, Oct 8—62
Huson, Peter E — Helena, Sep 27—62
Hicks, Wm — Memphis, Jan 20—63
Holloway, Jas F — Vicksburg, Aug 2—64
Hoel, Jacob J — Vicksburg, Aug 10—64
Hezer, Auron E — Aug 15—61
Irish, H P, f — Hurricane Grove, Ia
Johnson, Jas — Florence, Feb 26—65
Kee, Lindsay — Helena, Sep 28—62
Knouse, Chas — Potosi, Sep 2—61
Kile, Geo — Helena, Jan 5—62
Lander, Isaac N — Keokuk, Oct 23—62
Murray, Wm G — Mo River, May 10—62
McKee, Jno E — Vicksburg, July 4—64
Mathews, Peter — Cairo, Sep 1—61
McIntosh, Jno L — Vicksburg, Oct 15—64
McCormick, Jno — Vicksburg, Oct 26—64
Pember, Francis L — Helena, Nov 11—62
Palmer, Horatio R — Vicksburg, Sep 19—64
Page Edwin J — Vicksburg, Oct 27—64
Runnion, Sam'l B — Potosi, Aug 31—64
Stonehouse, Edw — St Louis, May 13—62
Schlosser, Henry J — Vicksburg, Aug 1—64
Stewart, Martin V — Vicksburg, Aug 24—64
Sutton, Hugh — Ripley, Mar 9—65
Showalter, Levi — Beetown

D

Capt Geo F Hartwell
Capt Jos H Burnell
Capt Chas S Bentley — Dubuque, Ia
Capt Geo W Noble — Chicago, Ill
Lt Robt C Barrows
Lt Oscar Murphy
Lt Samuel L Barnell
Lt Dan'l Mears, f — Osceola Mills
Lt Chas H Cox
Lt L D Drummond — Missoula, Mont Ter

Continued from page 199

MINERAL ROCK

was reached, and drilled into twenty-seven feet, (in all, one hundred and eighty-seven feet deep) when a vein of water was reached with sufficient force to throw it far above the surface of the ground. A gentleman of some experience in mineral waters visiting the fountain, and noticing its sparkling effervescence, suggested that the water might be magnetic and medicinal, and to test it held an

ORDINARY JACK-KNIFE

in the stream as it flowed from the pipe. In a few moments the knife was highly charged with magnetism, so that eight and ten penny nails could be lifted with ease, by the attraction of the magnetized knife. These peculiarities of the water so on attracted attention, and awakened curiosity, and many rheumatic and other invalids in the neighborhood, who had tried various remedies without receiving only temporary relief, immediately began to use the mineral water, both for drinking and bathing purposes, and

ALL WHO DID USE IT

were materially benefited. Some were entirely cured in a few hours, while others, chronic cases, were somewhat slower. Some considerable time, however, elapsed after the water began to be used, before Mr. Hunter could be induced to believe that he had discovered mineral waters of such

EXTRAORDINARY

curative properties. But positive evidence of the fact accumulated so rapidly, that Mr Hunter was forced to fit up convenient bath-rooms near the fountain, for the accommodation of the hundreds of invalids who d ily visited his place. He likewise soon felt the necessity of inaugurating facilities for transporting the water away, to fill the accumulating orders coming from various parts of the country, in rapid succession.

After these arrangements had been made, and the public but partially advised of the extraordinary healing qualities of the mineral water,

THOUSANDS,

many of them from distant States, visited the bath-rooms, drank the water and bathed in it; and, as will be shown by the certificates of hundreds of respectable people, all wh gave the water a thorough trial, were materially benefited. Hundreds of persons living

HUNDREDS OF MILES AWAY

ordered casks of the water to be sent to their homes, and their letters and certificates are in evidence that the water, even when transported to distant places, loses none of its healing properties, but is just as effective in curing the diseases which the water advertised to cure, as if used in the bath-rooms or at the fountain.

ENLARGED.

The throng of visitors to the fountain was so great last year, during the bathing season, that Mr. Hunter found it necessary to enlarge the bathing establishment by fitting up several additional bath rooms, in elegant style, thereby doubling the capacity of his bathing facilities. Two of these additional bath-rooms, one in the ladies' and the other in the gentlemen's department, are fitted up and devoted to giving the

CELEBRATED TURKISH BATH,

which consists of places for four baths in each department. The Turkish bath lengthens human life, enlarges human happiness, and decreases human suffering. It being one of the safest and speediest eradicators of diseases from the human system now known to science; and as experience teaches is a hundred fold more efficacious when magnetic mineral waters are used.

The Turkish bath thoroughly opens the pores of the skin and lets in the oxygen of the air to purify the blood, and

STIMULATE THE CIRCULATION

of the fluids, by which impurities are forced to the surface of the body. The Turkish bath when scientifically administered, with magnetic mineral water, eradicates scrofula, cures consumption, annihilates rheumatism, neuralgia, headache, and general nervous debility. The pores of the skin, when in healthy action, assist the lungs in supplying the blood with pure oxygen. Without a continuous supply of oxygen to the blood, life ceases, and with diminished proportions health is impaired, hence the importance of always keeping the pores of the skin and lungs in a normal condition. The Turkish bath is scientifically arranged and inaugurated for this purpose. It was popular with Greeks and Romans of antiquity. But during the "dark ages" it was neglected and entirely forgotten in western Europe. The Turks in a later era, when in possession of Constantinople repaired the baths and revived their use, hence the name "Turkish Bath." In still later years these baths have become popular in all the large cities of Europe and in the United States. In some cities of Europe the Turkish bath is made efficient in curing insanity, and other brain and

NERVOUS DISORDERS.

The aristocratic Englishman however, still journeys to Constantinople to be cured of gout and other ailments brought on by high living, when intelligent Turks admit that the modern western Turkish bath is a vast improvement on the antique eastern one.

A physician of

EXTENSIVE EXPERIENCE

in attendance upon invalids in bathing establishments, for the past ten or twelve years, will always be present to give directions and advice as to the proper mode of using the water, both for bathing and drinking purposes, and also to administer the Turkish bath whenever it is desired by parties visiting the bath -rooms.

ANALYSIS.

The following analysis made by Prof. E. J. Gillett, President of the Medical College, Keokuk, Iowa, will show that the mineral water of George Hunter's artesian fountain is permeated with ample quantities and proportions of nature's simple elements, with their carbonates, chlorides and sulphates, which makes it more efficacious in healing man's physical infirmities than any other mineral water from any known spring or fountain.

Mr. Gillett, now professor of Chemistry and Toxology in the college of Physicians and Surgeons at Keokuk, Iowa, is a gentleman of extensive practical experience, as teacher of analytical chemistry for the last fifteen years, and has a reputation throughout the West for exact scientific knowledge in his particular branch of learning, and his analysis may be relied on. Still, to the mass of mankind, actual test and experience in the curative properties of the water, are much more satisfactory than the most thorough scientific analysis; and consequently he test and experience of many people who have used the water are given in the following pages.

George Hunter, Esq:—

*Dear Sir—*I have to-day completed the quantitative analysis of our mineral water, and with the following results. Out of one gallon of water, I obtained 19 grains as residuum.

The analysis is an approximate, leaving off decimals in calculating the proportions.

In 100 parts, the following are the

(Continued on page 194.)

WISCONSIN SOLDIERS AND SAILORS REUNION ROSTER.

Lt|Edmund Guy
Strong, Geo, q m sgt　　　　Baldwin
Anderson, Calvin, f　　　　Star Prairie
Allen, Andrew S　　Springfield, Oct 19 –62
Andrews, Jno　　　Milwaukee, Mar 16 –62
Brown, Jno, f　　　　Worthington, Minn
Baker, J H　　　　　　　　Clayton
Churchill, J B, town treas　St Croix Falls
Cox, G G, assemblyman　　Mineral Point
Downend, Robt, co treas　　Osceola Mills
Fish, Lewis D　　　Springfield, Nov 12 –62
Gay, R A　　　　　Walla Walla, Wash Ter
Gross, Geo　　　　　　　　Tomah
Graham, C E, ed　　　Janesville, Minn
Gillispee, A L, m　　　Stillwater, Minn
Green, Jas R　　　　Casseville, Oct 26 –62
Hale, Isaac, f　　　　　　Osceola Mills
Kent, Wm H　　　　Walla Walla, Wash Ter
Kent, W H, pa　　　　　New Richmond
Kent, J A　　　　　　　Osceola Mills
Kreiner, Michael, f　　　　Farmington
Kepp, Frank, bk　　　　Stillwater, Minn
Kinney, Philletus　　　Hudson, Aug 13 –61
Lane, Wm　　　　Mt Vernon, Sept 24 –62
Lane, M C　　　　　　　　Rock Falls
McCourt, Jno, ranchman,　　Montana, Ter
Mears, Chas E, ed　　　　Osceola Mills
Mason, Al, c　　　　　　Osceola Mills
Mann, W W　　　　　　Pines, June 11 –64
Nicholas, S A　　　　　　Chicago, Ill
Peterson, Ole　　　　Casseville, Oct 28 –62
Sparr, Andrew　　　　　　　Racine
Treadwell, E C, f　　　　Osceola Mills
Todd, Sam'l F　　　　Milwaukee, Feb 14 –62
Wood, G W, me　　　　　　Waupun
White, Robt B　　　　　Rolla, Nov 28 –63

E

Capt Geo N Richmond
Capt Carmi W Beach
Capt Stephen Woodward
Lt Wallace Smith
Lt Austin Cannon
Lt Zadoc Merrill
Lt Jos T Dean
Lt Jas H Waggoner
Lt Jas Myer, f　　　　　　　Plymouth
Riblett, Myron L　　　　St Louis, Apr 15 –63
Moore, Edw H, corp　　Madison, Mar 28 –65
Ames, Geo W　　　　　　Portage City
Atkinson, Wm　　　　Florence, Nov 19 –61
Bohoy, Alf　　　　　　　Portage City
Cook, Henry　　　　　　Portage City
Carpenter, H B, me　　Fredericksburg, la
Cannon, Fayette, me　　　　　Lodi
Chandler, Jas　　　　　Millen, Oct –64
Cook, Jos　　　　　Vicksburg, July 21 –64
Carr, Jno　　　　　Memphis, Apr 27 –65
Day, Thos　　　　　Helena, Nov 20 –62
Faller, Chas E　　　　Vicksburg, Aug 8 –64
Ferguson, Josephus　　　　　Apr 15 –65
Hale, Eben W　　　　Mound City, Aug 10 –62
Heath, Chas C　　　Memphis, Feb 27 –63
Herriman, Elonzo　　Marcellon, Aug 15 –65
Hewet, Geo　　　　　　　Portage City
Lee, Wm H　　　　　St Louis, Aug 6 –62
Mills, Hiram　　　　Pardeeville, Sept 10 –63
Murray, Robt　　　　　　　Jan 1 –65
McCarll, Jno　　　　Memphis, Feb 12 –65
Mathewson, Eugene　　Andersonville, Sept 1 –64
Payne, Wm*　　　　Redbone, Apr 21 –64
Parker, Washington　　St Louis, Nov 2 –62
Quiggle, Henry F, me　　　　　Lodi
Ross, Geo W　　　　Helena, Nov 29 –62
Race, Geo S　　　　　　Portage City
Stollman, Wm　　　　Cairo, Sept 1 –64
Sholes, Wm　　　　Vicksburg, Oct 13 –64
Singleton, Rich　　　Vicksburg, Oct 20 –64
Sliper, Sam S　　　　　Portage City

Taylor, Lorin
West, E C, f
Whiting, Robt

F

Capt Chas M Palmer
Capt Newton DeForest
Capt R R Hamilton, f　　　Richland Centre
Capt Francis M Poynter, f　Richland Centre
Lt H W Wadsworth
Lt Marquis F Catting
Lt Thos H Damon　　　　　Cairo, Aug 27 –65
Lt Geo H Sterner
Pelton, Nicholas W, sgt　　Madison, Jan 7 –65
Ripperdan, Jas, corp　　Vicksburg, Aug 23 –63
Logue, Jas, corp　　　Meridian, Aug 10 –65
Bsiee, Nathan L W　　　Clinton, July 15 –64
Bartle, Wm s　　　　La Grange, Dec 20 –62
Bowe, Walter　　　　Vicksburg Aug 24 –64
Birge, Wm D　　　　Marshall, Apr 8 – 62
Cody, Garrett　　　　Vicksburg, July 31 –64
Crasgo, Jos　　　　　　Yankeetown
Cringo, Jos M, f　　　　　Yankeetown
Decker, Harvey F*　　Redbone, Sept 13 –63
Davis, Lorain　　　　Vicksburg, Oct 9 –64
Goodwin, Alvardo　　Richland City, Oct 25 –83
Halstimson, Andrew　　Vicksburg, July 28 –64
Hewitt, Jno C　　　　Memphis, Jan 27 –65
Jeffrey, Jno J　　　　Helena, Sept 19 –62
Lilly, Bethel F　　　Hempstead, Oct 17 –65
Long, John M　　　　Vicksburg, Sept 12 –64
McDonald, Michael　　Helena, Dec 15 – 62
McKenzie, Geo　　　Helena, Aug 24 – 62
Maze, Willis　　　　Memphis, Apr 18 – 63
Moll, Henry　　　　　Alton, Oct 13 – 62
McGuire, Geo　　　Vicksburg, July 31 –64
McAllister, Archibald　　Memphis, Apr 23 –65
McFarlin, f　　　　　Richland Centre
Nelson, Jas　　　　　Arena, Oct 19 –65
Nobles, Wm, f　　　　　Fancy Creek
Pettet, Jos A　　　　Helena, Nov 7 –62
Palmer, Miles, f　　　　　　Baraboo
Squires, Jos　　　　　　Aug 28 –63
Sweep, Marshall B　　Memphis, May 6 –63
Sleep, Sam'l　　　　Vicksburg, Aug 27 –64
Shepherd, Thos P, f
Washburn, Geo W　　Memphis, May 13 –62

G

Capt Nicholas H Dale
Capt Chas S Bently
Capt Edwin Skewes
Capt Zolotes P Cogswell
Lt Jas P Walls
Lt Geo W Noble
Lt Edward S Miner
Lt Horace Vyse
Lt Edw B * ge　　　　　　　Racine
Lt Sidney H Nichols
Flint, Seneca R　　　Vicksburg, Oct 25 –61
Ammerman, David A　　Vicksburg, Nov 17 –64
Bacon, Chas N　　　　Vicksburg, Oct 31 –64
Brunette, Seraphim　　　St Louis, Aug 29 –65
Barrett, Geo　　　　　Galveston Nov 17 –65
Cocherns, Mathias, m　　　　Sturgeon Bay
Coller, Sam'l E　　　　Rolla, Apr 16 –62
Cyran, Nelson　　　　Memphis, Dec 14 –64
Carrells, Nicholas　　　　Wabasha, Minn
Dore, Jacob　　　　　Yorkville, Aug –62
Dorning, Sam'l　　　　Rolla, Aug 7 +3
Davis, Geo　　　　　　　　Plover
Harding, Geo　　　　Milwaukee, Feb 16 –62
Hartung, no　　　　　　Wabasha, Minn
Harris J C　　　　　　　　　Neosho
Kewes, Henry S　　　Sioux Falls, D T
Kine, Jno
LaGrow, Peter　　　　Alexandria, July 25 – 65
Leufesty, Dennis　　Hempstead, Oct 21 –65

Scott, Sept 16 –64
Bellefontaine
Helena, Sept 28 – 62

Mathews, Wm J　　　Springfield, Oct 10 –62
Mills, Chas　　　　　　　　　Racine
Morris, P H　　　　　　Waterman, Ia
Miner, E S　　　　　　　　Gibraltar
Mills, Chas C　　　　　　　Racine
Olds, Oney　　　　Springfield, Feb 28 – 63
Shepherd, Thos F　　　　　Racine
Shumway, Dwight L　　Wabasha, Minn
Strickland, Edw　　　　　　Racine

H

Capt Henry Von Heyde
Capt Ernest J Meyers
Lt Alvy Klaus
Lt Theo Georg　　　Vicksburg, Aug 29 –63
Lt Chas Doerflinger
Lt Gottfried Langstadt　　　　La Crosse
Lt Peter H Lantern
Lt Sam'l E Kundle
Lt Louis Stienstra
Lindemeyer, August, sgt　Milldale, July 18 –63
Wenntz, Ferdinand, sgt　　Memphis, Feb 14 –65
Behlke, Henry　　　　Memphis, Aug 18 –64
Eng, Jos　　　　　　Vicksburg, Aug 15 – 63
Brenner, Melchoir　　St Louis, Feb 1 –63
Buermann, Geo　　　　　　Oct 29 – 62
Becker, Henry　　　Snyders Bluff, July 12 –63
Bassak, Chas　　　　　　Young America
Gemudale, Philip　　　St Louis, Feb 8 –65
Gunderson, Andre　　St Louis, Sept 16 –65
Gassert, Martin　　　　　Aug 13 –65
Ja ger, Jno　　　　　Vicksburg, Jan 14 –63
Johnson, Nicholas　　La Crosse, Sept 10 –64
Johnson, E B　　　　　　　Neillsville
Karste, Jacob　　　　Milwaukee, Mar 14 –62
Kauffman, Julius
Milkowsky, Andreas　　Vicksburg, Aug 21 –64
Mueller, Rudolph　　　Vicksburg, Jan 29 –65
Nay, Adam　　　　　Vicksburg, Aug 28 –64
Newlning, Jacob　　Vicksburg, Aug 30 – 64
Newlung, Antonio　　Vicksburg, Sept 15 –64
Parr, Jno　　　　　Vicksburg, Aug 1 –64
Schmidt, Henry,　　　Helena, Mar 22 –65
St ecker, Chas　　Snyders Bluff, July 8 –63
Stein, Stra Dick　　　Memphis, Feb 4 +3
Schcomb, Wm　　　　　Illinois, Mar 23 – 62
Watson, Lyman　　　　　　　Fairchild

I

Capt Edw D Luxton
Capt Geo W King
Lt Benj L Brisbane
Lt Jno Larkin
Lt Wm H Brisbane
Lt Wm H Morgan
Lt Henry W Pinkham
McLead, Alex, 1st serg't　Vicksburg, June 3 –64
Davis, Chas W, serg't　　Helena, Nov 8 –62
Cressey, Marquis, serg't　Memphis, Mar 1 – 63
Cullen, Jas*　　　　Yazoo City, Dec 1 –64
Clark, Jas M　　　　Vicksburg, Aug 8 –63
Cullen, Jno M　　　Vicksburg, Aug 3 –64
Carr, LaFayette　　　Vicksburg, Aug 18 –64
Cutting, Chauncey C　　Vicksburg, Dec 1 –64
Cheney, F A　　　　　　　Janesville
Dunfy, Jno　　　　　Helena, Feb 5 –63
Dawning, Henry B　　Vicksburg, Aug 19 –64
Doty, Willard A　　　Vicksburg, Aug 30 –64
French, Chauncey　　Vicksburg, Oct 5 – 64
Fanning, Michael　　Vicksburg, Nov 9 –64
Faber, Luke　　　　　　　Darlington, Ia
Harris, Wm　　　　　　Illinois, Sep 7 –62
Hanson, Jas　　　　　　　Milwaukee
Hirsche, Christian　　Helena, Nov 17 –62
Hamlin, Andrew　　　Vicksburg, July 7 –64
Harwood, F W, clk　　　　Milwaukee
Hanrahan, Jas　　　　　　Beechwood
Heatleman, Squire E, f　Biff Pocahontia, Ia
Johnson, Jno　　　　Helena, Aug 29 –62

COMMANDANT'S HEADQUARTERS, SOLDIERS' HOME.

HUNTER'S MAGNETIC FOUNTAIN OF HEALTH AND SUMMER RESORT.

Continued from page 193

proportions of each ingredient:
1. (CaoCo) Carbonate of lime..... 5
2. (KoCo) Carbonate of Potash..... 4
3. (MgoCo) Carbonate of Magnesia. 6
4. (NaoCo) Carbonate of soda..... 4
5. (CaoSo) Sulphate of Lime . — 12
6. (KoSo) Sulphate of Potash..... 10
7. (MgoSo) Sulphate of Magnesium 17
8. (NaoSo) Sulphate of Soda....... 13
9. (NaCl) Chloride of Sodium...... 14
10. (KCl) Chloride of Potassium..... 8
11. (SiO) Silicic..................... 5

                  93
12. (EE) Traces of Iron............ —
13. Traces of Bromine............. —
14. Free Carbonic Acid.....
    Waste....................... 7
                         100

To my surprise, I found a trace of Bromine in it. I did not estimate the free Carbonic Acid. Very respectfully yours,   E. J. GILLETT.

HOW TO USE THE MAGNETIC WATER.

In rheumatic difficulties, kidney complaints, cutaneous eruptions, scalp d s cases, neuralgia, an ngdlervous disorders, the water should be warmed slightly above blood heat, and applied to the surface of the body, especially over the parts affected, with a large sponge, or coarse crash towel. A thorough bathing should be administered, and in a warm room, and in cold weather near a warm stove. After bathing, the surface of the body should be rubbed perfectly dry, and cold currents of air should be avoided for a time. In all cases, and especially in internal derangements of the system, the Magnetic Water should be drank regularly at night on retiring, and in the morning immediately after rising, and at other times, if necessary, to the exclusion of other water. With some delicate stomachs the Magnetic Water has the effect to produce slight nausea on first using it, but a continuous use for a short time in smaller quantities will soon make it agreeable to very sensitive stomachs.

Some persons have drank it hot as they do their tea, and with beneficial effects. So, also, have persons bathed in it when cold, and have been cured; but observation and experience teach that when the above rules are complied with, in using the water, it is the most effective in curing diseases.

In chronic cases, regularity in the habits of the invalid are essential, in order to give full effect to the curative properties of the water. All excesses should be avoided, if speedy relief is desired. The usual quantity of wholesome food may be indulged in, but much grease should be avoided in cases of dyspepsia, especially in warm weather.

The Magnetic Water is a pleasant, easy cathartic—a gentle laxative to most people, when first used, and in some instances too much so, if large quantities are drank. When this is the result, less should be used, until a normal condition of the bowels is effected. The results of one year's test and experience with the Magnetic Water from George Hunter's Saline Well, located in Fond du Lac, warrants the conclusion that it is the most effective cure in the following named diseases :

RHEUMATISM CONQUERED.

The Magnetic Saline Water of George Hunter's artesian fountain is a speedy and sure cure for that disagreeable and incomprehensible complaint known as rheumatism, which afflicts people at all ages, and in nearly every community throughout the whole country. Inflammatory rheumatism is entirely cured by a few applications of the water internally and externally, and sometimes, almost miraculously, by bathing once. In chronic cases, where the joints have been distorted, a longer and a more thorough course of treatment is required to effect a complete cure. But even in chronic cases pains are relieved in a very short time.

DYSPEPSIA CURED.

The Magnetic Water cures this uncomfortable affliction, and its consequent adjuncts, a sour stomach and a headache, in a short time, as many testimonials in the following pages will convince all rational people. No one
(Continued on page 196.)

WISCONSIN SOLDIERS AND SAILORS REUNION ROSTER.

Janes, Jas F — Redbone, Apr 26 -64
Kunrill, Pliny F, light house keeper — Bayfield
Lewis, Edw — Vicksburg, Aug 5--64
McManus, Michael — Vicksburg, Aug 5--61
Melvin, Oscar B — Vicksburg, Sep 2--64
Multee, Jacob N, l — Scott
Monah, Jno S, janitor — Chippewa Falls
O'Reilley, Thos — Whitecomne
Oleson, Andrew — Vicksburg, Aug 7--64
Owens, W T, mu — Belmont
Polley, Orrin D — Vicksburg, June 4--64
Sherman, Oliver P — Helena, Sep 15 62
Stolper, David, m — Scott
Woodworth, Watsou P — Memphis, May 22--63
White, Jno G — Vicksburg, July 28

K
Capt Fred W Hutchins — Delavan
Capt F Crocker
Capt Geo B Davidson
Lt Edson Williams
Lt David A Bennett
Lt Avery H Stone — Sioux Falls, D T
Lt Porter P Peck — Sioux Falls, D T
Lt Abe G Low — Mauston
Lt Porter M Roundy
Lt Jno M Vanderhoof, pa — Darien
Smith, Oliver H, sgt — Rolla, Mar 16--64
Carter, LeGrande, sgt*Lanes Prairie, May 26--64
Breed, Wm, corp — Springfield, June 12--62
Howe, Chas M — Vicksburg, Oct 21--64
Allen Jacob H — Vicksburg, Nov 2 64
Caldwell, Isaac — Memphis, May 8 -65
Enos, Emilus, pa — Racine
Fisher, E W — Racine
Fish, E W — Ravine
Greeman, J — Jefferson
Hines, Thos — Lake Spring, June 3--63
Hutchins, O C, rr agt — Bartlett, la
Hunneman, Jos, f — Lowden, la
Marlett, Peter — Lanes Prairie, May 26--64
Mosher, Jas H* — Lanes Prairie, May 26--64
Mills, Henry — St Louis, Apr 17--64
Manchester, Geo, quarryman — Menominee
Pounder, Jas T — Vicksburg, June 22--64
Powder, Geo H, me — Ft Atkinson
Smith, Thos — Memphis, May 1--65

L
Capt Arthur M Sherman
Capt Jas L LeRoy
Lt Israel B Burbank
Lt Thomas J Nary
Lt Geo E Grout
Lt Pierre Hartman
Lt Mile B Wyman
Lt L L Lancaster
Bush, Benj T, serg — Mound City, Oct 8-- 62
McNaughton, Alex E, sgt — Memphis, Feb 16--63
Bostwick, Bronco, sgt — Vicksburg, Aug 10--64
Ryan, Michael, sgt — Vicksburg, Aug 13--64
Dunbar, Oscar A, corp — Quincy, Dec 28 - 62
Hastings, Jno S, corp — Sparta, Aug 8- 63
Murphy, Geo, corp — Memphis, Mer 2-- 63
Tullman, M L, corp — Memphis, Mar 12 63
Dilworth, Olin, corp — Memphis, Mar 27-- 63
Lockwood, Benj T F, corp — St Louis, Sept 19--62
Au erus, Edwin L — Helena, Sept 18--62
A gust, David — Vicksburg, Oct 9--64
Bateman, Jno P — Helena, Aug 18--62
Bird, Wm H — Helena, Jan 18--63
Beeman, H — Rock Fa's
Dakin, Jno — Springfield, July 1--62
Fox, Jos A — Mound City, Oct 25--62
Fiddler, Geo A — St Louis, Dec 27--62
Gray, Geo W* — Yazoo City, Dec 1--64
Guthrie, Jus H — Vicksburg, July 31- 64
Halsted, Albert H+ — Vicksburg, Sept 14--63

Hartman, Henry
Johannes, Michael
Larabee, Hiram
Lang, Jno
Miller, Simon
McDonald, Christopher — Mound City, Sept 19--62
Morgan, Jas — Vicksburg, Aug 9--64
Mosher, Willard O — Memphis, Feb 12- 65
Manchester, Geo — Menominee
Olin, Orin O — Quincy, Dec 28--62
Paulin, Ernest — Cairo, June 15 -64
Root, Jas — Helena, Oct 9 62
Stevens, Marcellus — Downsville
Swan, Geo — Rock Falls
Stirling, F B, f — Clyde, Ia
Thompson, Joshua T* — Yazoo City, Dec 1--64
Vaughn, Jno — Helena, Sept 17- 62
Wells, Byron — Menominee

M
Capt Nathaniel Parker
Capt Freeman A Kimball
Lt John Baxter
Lt Geo W Walter
Lt John C Metcalf
Lt Geo W Taylor
Brooks, Perry L, sgt — Vicksburg, Aug 17--64
Alberty, Nelson — Helena, Sep 21--62
Belton, Jno — Janesville
Brown, Jas — Janesville
Cook, Henry C* — Helena, Jan 12--63
Crone, Jared — Helena, Aug 14--62
Cline, Wm P — Helena, Sep 18 62
Childs, Theodore R — Memphis, Apr 24 - 63
Coty, Henry — Vicksburg, Ju y 13- 64
Cooper, Thos — Vicksburg, Sep 17--64
Dresser, Geo, f — River Falls
Fuller, Sidney — Helena, Sep 23--62
Foster, Thos — Vicksburg, Nov 3--64
Hafer, Carl — Mound City, Nov 10--62
Howland, Levi H — St Louis, Aug 14--63
Hart, Ephraim H — Vicksburg, July 11--64
Hopkins, Melville — Vicksburg, Aug 16 -64
Hughes, Jas — Vicksburg, Aug 24 --64
Helms, Jno — Vicksburg, Oct 2--64
Herkelmer, Horace — Janesville
Hudson, E S, f — Magnolia
Jones, Henry A — Vicksburg, Sep 28--64
Jackson, W — Janesville
Kroenn, Alf — Helena, Aug 11--62
Lyon, Henry — St Louis, Feb--63
Morgan, EB — Helena, Nov 13--62
Meyer, Fred — Helena, Feb 1--63
O Conner, Jas — Vicksburg, Aug 17--64
Porter, Lester H — Memphis, Jan 31- 65
Schittenger, Jno — Helena, Aug 10 62
Smith, Adventure — Helena, Oct 20--62
Slocum, Jno — Vicksburg, Aug 10 64
Simerson, Jno E — Vicksburg, Oct 8--64
Thorn, E E — Vicksburg, Oct 18--64
Vandenborge, M A — Armstrong Grove, Ia
Van Patten, Minant — Vicksburg, Oct 9 - 64
Wallace, Wm H — Janesville, Mar 10--65
Webster, Rush B — Vicksburg, July 20--64
Wright, Jas B — Helena, Aug 13 62
Wisener, Smith — Vicksburg, July 28--64
Wells, Jno G — Chippewa Falls
Wright, Peter J, e — St Paul, Minn

UNASSIGNED.
Taylor, J B, lt — Millard
Veale, S E, sgt — Delavan
Smith, F, sgt — Sugar Creek
Parish, Ben, corp — Millard
Adamson, C, f — Colorado Mills
Amos, Geo W — Portage City
Boardman, N, engineer — Fond du Lac
Baxter, Jno — Chicago, Ill
Bohey, Alfred — Portage

Helena, Nov 13--62
Kewaskum
Helena, Sept 13--62
Helena, Feb 22 62
Vicksburg, Aug 5- 64

Carter, Louis — Sharon
Corbin, Alfred — Bradford
Cook, Henry — Portage
Cook, W T, me — Pipe Stone, Minn
Dolan, Henry, f — Fond du Lac
Eckhart, Chas — Darien
Flaherty, Michael — Darien
Goffy, Thos, f — Bradford
Gaffee, Thos — Darien
Guernsey, A H — Amherst
Gurnsey, Aug, d — Amherst
Halsted, D W — Sheboygan
Hare, Stephen — Darien
Hewett, Geo — Portage City
Holdman, Jacob — Milwaukee
Karl, Steven — Darien
Kullmann, Louis, m — Milwaukee
Kilmer, Ira F — Galesville
Kent, Wm H — Richmond
Longstaff, Gottfred — LaCrosse
Mansell, F B — Chicago, Ill
Mallory, Henry — Millard
Nelson, Andrew — Delavan
Owens, J H — Darien
Owens, Jno — Darien
Robeson, G — N-illsville
Race, Geo F — Portage
Stavin, O C — Darien
Seaver, Rodney — Darien
Siifer, Sam'l — Portage
Stearns, Warge — Darien
Walsh, Francis, f — Darlington

THIRD CAVALRY.

Three years, Organized Jan. 31, 1862. Original strength, 1186; gain by recruits, etc., 1337; total, 2523. Death loss, 210--killed in action, 56, died of wounds, 8, of disease, 123, of accidents, 24. Other losses, 832 --missing, 9, desertions, 126, transfers, 64, discharges, 443. Strength at muster-out, Sept , 1865, 1091. Campaigns in Kan., Mo., Ark., Cherokee Nation.

REGIMENTAL ROSTER.

Lt Col R H White
Lt Col E A Calkins, ed — Milwaukee
Maj L B Reed, 1st Bat — Oshkosh
Maj B S Henning, 2d Bat — Indianapolis, Ind
Maj Wm Culbertson,2d Bat
Maj J C Schroeling, 3d Bat — Port Washington
Maj J B Pond, 3d Bat — Boston, Mass
Adj Henry Sandes
Adj Wm H Hewitt
Adj W Knight — Poynette
Q M Asa W Farr* — Baxter Springs, Oct 6--63
Q M H M Taylor — New Orleans--65
Q M J W Hutchinson
Surg B O Reynolds — Geneva Lake
Surg Jos S Lane — Chicago, Ill
Surg W H Warner — Ft Scott, Kan
Chap H W Beers
Chap Jno S Baldwin

BATTALION ADJUTANTS.
2-- Wm H Thomas — Pewaukee
2-- M M Ehle
3-- C L Noggle
3 Julius Glesler* — 65

BATTALION QUARTERMASTERS.
1--Isaac Woodle — Apr 62
3--A O Hall

A
Capt J D Daumon
Capt Robt Carpenter
Capt Julius Glesler-j- — Clear Lake, Mar 12--65
Lt Jno Davis

ENTRANCE SOLDIERS' HOME.

HUNTER'S MAGNETIC FOUNTAIN AND SUMMER RESORT.

(Continued from page 194.)

need suffer tortures of indigestion, or its consequent inconveniences, if they are within reach of the water from Hunter's artesian fountain, as its steady use will invariably restore the stomach to a healthy condition.

CONSTIPATION DISPENSED WITH.

This disagreeable affliction loses its hold upon the bowels when the Magnetic Water is drank regularly, to the exclusion of other water. It is a pleasant, safe, easy cathartic, which regulates the bowels without inconvenience or trouble.

The liver is strongly sensitive to the peculiar properties of the Magnetic Water, and its effect in restoring that organ to a healthful condition, is truly wonderful. The liver is a very important organ in the internal arrangement of the human body. So much so, that when it is diseased the whole system is affected, and complicated troubles are the general consequences.

NEURALGIA ANNIHILATED.

This very disagreeable nervous complaint is relieved of its excruci.t ng pains at once by applications of the Magnetic Water to the parts affected. Persons afflicted with neuralgic torture need suffer no longer.

The Saline Water cures diseased scalps and prevents the hair from falling out. It has the effect also to make the hair soft and silky. Any one can be convinced of this fact by a few applications of the water.

In female complaints and physical weaknesses, the Magnetic Water is a effective remedy, acting speedily and surely in restoring the fragile female system to health and vigor.

The Magnetic Water cures gravel, it dissolves and forces the gravel out of the bladder.

Kidney complaints suddenly feel the curative effect of the Magnetic Water when properly used. Bright's disease and diabetes are also cured by close attention to the use of the water according to directions. In short the diseased urinary organs are more susceptible to the healing properties of the water than any others in the system.

REFERENCES.

The names of a number of gentlemen are here given for reference, by letter or otherwise. They are well known as gentlemen of truth and veracity, with no disposition to deceive others or to be deceived. They have all been materially benefited by using the Mineral Water from George Hunter's artesian fountain, and are willing that others should be helped, also. Most of them are old residents of Fond du Lac, but quite a number are residents of distant towns and cities :

A. G. Ruggles, Pres. First National Bank, Fond du Lac.
John S. McDonald, Manufacturer, Fond du Lac.
James B. Perry, Cashier First National Bank, Fond du Lac.
Hon. C. D. Mihills, Lumberman, Fond du Lac.
Capt. Alexander White, Union Iron Works, Waupun
Hon. E. W. Davis, Fond du Lac.
Rev. A. C. Barry, D. D., Delavan.
Geo. W. Sexsmith, Esq., lumberman, Fond du Lac.
Dr. E. C. Gray, Fond du Lac.
Byron Town, manufacturer, Fond du Lac.
R. W. Merriman, Esq , lumberman, Topeka, Kansas.
Prof. E. J. Gillett, President College of Physicians and Surgeons, Keokuk, Iowa.
Rev. H. G. Woodworth, Harvard, Ill.
Chas. W. Sweet, Revere House, Oshkosh.
Wm. A. Russell, Esq., Hub House, Plymouth.
Geo. A. Buckstaff, Esq., lumberman, Oshkosh.
James McGillan, Surveyor and Engineer, Appleton.
Joseph Gibson, Esq., Beaver Dam.
G. H. Stewart, Esq., Beaver Dam.

EVIDENCE FROM LIVING WITNESSES.

A few plain statements of facts— certificates, letters and tes imonials from respectable persons living in various States of the Union, who have seen and experienced the very beneficial effects of the use of the Magnetic Water from George Hunter's artesian fountain. MANY LETTERS have been re. ceived, varying in style and manner of expressing thoughts and facts. Besides, many people have what may be regarded as a false delicacy about publishing to the world, over their signatures, a description of their particular complaints, and the cures effected by the Magnetic Water. Especially is this the case with females. Therefore only a few of the letters, and a synopsis of others, will be published. Sufficient, however, of these letters and certificates will be given to satisfy all pe sons worthy of being convinced, that an almost MIRACULOUS REMEDY for many of the diseases which aff ct the human life has been discovered at Fond du Lac, and is now made known to the public through these pages.

The following note is from Rev. A.C. Barry, D. D. Mr. Barry is a gentleman of deep research and practical experience in science. He has filled various positions of public trust in this State, and is well known and appreciated as a gentleman of enlarged, liberal and patriotic views. His experience and observation, as regards the Magnetic Water, make his opinions very valuable :

HUNTER'S MAGNETIC FOUNTAIN.

To all whom it may concern : It is not
(Continued on page 198.)

WISCONSIN SOLDIERS AND SAILORS REUNION ROSTER.

Lt Jerome Nelson
Lt I Morley
Lt A W Farr*
Lt G M Ellis — Emmetsburg, Ia
Lt R T Fuchs — t8
Lt J L Prentice
Asa W Farr, Q M* — Baxter Springs, Oct 6—63
Isaac Woodle, Bat Q M — Janesville, Apr—62
Chas E Wiswell — Little Rock, Sept 2 61
Carr, Geo W, sgt — Sept 1—61
Palmer, Jas T — Illinois, Mar 26-62
Spencer, Jerome D, corp — Ft Scott, Nov 1—62
Moore, Jno, corp, f — La Valle
Case, H T, corp, f — Baraboo
Barker, Peter R — Parkers Prairie, Minn
Briggs, Chas — Illinois, Mar 26—62
Brandt, Fred, f — Sandusky
Bailey, Orson H — Ft Scott, Sept 26—61
Britters, Orio A — Alma Centre
Davis, Wm — Illinois, Mar 26—62
Davis, J* — Marais des Cross Road, Aug 31—63
Erflenger, C J H, f — Sandusky
Eddy, Ed, f — Sparta
Franklin, E R — Shiocton
Green, Moses — Ft Scott, Sept 16—64
Hatch, Chaa D — Illinois, Mar 26—62
Hathaway, Edw, f — Medley
Hubbard, W W — Sparta
Hooser, A D — Wilton
Hollinbeck, Francis M — Sparta
Hagerman, Chas — Mauston
Jordon, Jno, f — Medley
Johnson, Fred H — Tomah
Lee, Jno — Rolla, June 24—65
Long, S M, f — Ironton
Leusome, Jno B — Springfield, Apr 30—63
McWithy, S A, f — Sparta
Mallory, J P — Whitehall
McCarta, Jno — Illinois, Mar 26—62
Mason, Wm A, f — Appleton
Norris, Jas A, r r agt — Lans Centre, Minn
Niemand, Chris, f — Sandusky
Palmer, H H, f — Baraboo
Richardson, Jno, dep sheriff — Glendale
Rowe, David, f — Lime Ridge
Russell, Andrew, m — Viroqua
Rawson, Lucien M — Illinois, Mar 26—62
Stewart, Henry — Tomah
Stone, Caspar — Illinois, Mar 26—62
Warren, Harrison — Iola

B

Capt, A F David
Capt Wm Wagner — Oshkosh
Capt L B Reed — Oshkosh
Capt Wm Sharpe — Oshkosh
Lt H B Eastman — Fond du Lac
Lt A H Perkins
Bly, Cyrus K, 1st sgt* — Sept 1—64
Lull, Julius F, corp — St Louis, June 16—65
Busher, Narcissus — Jeff Barracks, Nov 22—61
Brainerd, A M — Oshkosh
Copeland, Wm* — Van Buren, Aug 4—61
Eastman, H B a — Fond du Lac
Gansen, Matthias — Little Rock, Sept 19—61
Hifant, Jas — Little Rock, Oct 7—64
Johnson Nelson — Ft Leavenworth, Dec6—62
Martin, Thos — Ft Leavenworth, Dec 17—62
McCarty, Jno — Ft Leavenworth, Feb 3—63
O'Connor, Patrick — Little Rock, Feb 6—65
Pierce, Alvin, I — Westh'ro
Polak, Fred'k — St Louis, Apr 10—62
Rogers, David H — Little Rock, Oct 3—64
Stevens, Edward P, me — Oshkosh
Teubner, August — Little Rock, Sept 28—64
Weitzel, Matthias, m — Oshkosh

C

Capt E R Stevens

Capt J B Poud — Boston, Mass
Capt Wm Culbertson
Capt A W Allyn
Lt J Daniels
Lt M M Ehle
Lt J C Lynch
Lt T V Dunn
Lt R W Smith
Lt H W Poud
Lt N Brayton
Bodman, Wm S — Ft Scott, Oct 31—61
Cass, Clarence W — Little Rock, Feb 5—65
Carrington, Chas H — June 10 -65
Davis, Jno* — Baxter Springs, Oct 6—63
Daniels, Jason — Montello
Eastman, H — Winneconne
Foster, Geo C+ — Ft Scott, Nov 21—64
Goodman, Robt+ — Ft Scott, Jan 13—63
Garber, J H — Dartford
Griffin, Ezra J — Cherokee Nation, July 19—65
Howard, Cyrus O* — Carthage, Dec 22—63
Hammond, T J, f — Mauston
Hunt, Eugene* — North Fork Creek, June 16—61
Jaycot, S M — Jefferson
Liegel, Wm* — Baxter Springs, Oct 6 - 63
Leach, Thos* — Baxter Springs, Oct 6—63
McNary, Dennis* — Baxter Springs, Oct 6—63
Martin, Henry H — Neosho, Mar 11—65
Murphy, Jas S — Little Rock, Apr 5—65
Mooney, T F — Springfield
Rockafellow, Abram A* — Baxter Springs, Oct 6—63
Stimpson, Philemon* — Baxter Springs, Oct 6—63
Southwick, Eli C — Busseyville
Spears, Byron, f — Deerfield, O
Stephen, Sept, c — Sturgeon Bay

D

Capt L J Shaw — Dry Wood, Mo
Capt F C Kaiser — Whitewater
Capt Jas Campbell — Ohio
Lt Jno Crites
Lt H D Bannister — Fond du Lac
Lt A Berkley
Lt B H Kilbourn — Milwaukee
Lt L W Robinson — Springfield, Feb 28—63
Lt Otis Titus
Lt Albert Berkley
Lt Thos Butler
Brewer, Newton, sgt, contractor — Baraboo
Ketcham, Austin, corp — Ft Scott, Oct 15—63
Brimmer, Wm H, f — Mukwonago
Blanchard, Hiram — Atchison, June 27—62
Brindler, C A — Cross Plaines
Bannister, H D — Fond du Lac
Cock, Harry — Leavenworth, Mar 16—62
Dewing, Nelson H — Fond du Lac
Duffy, Jas — Troy Centre
Hudson, Chas L — Elkhorn
Hooper, Daniel M+ — Clear Lake, Mar 11—65
Hunter, Geo M — Milwaukee
Hughes, Jno E, f — Delafield
Hughes, Jno E, f — Genesee
Metcalf, Wm — Herman, Jr, f
Mitchell, Jno — Ft Scott, July 20 63
Moses, Lyman — Mukwonago
Myers, A B, Ins Agt — Milwaukee
Perry, Oswin T — Merton, May 8—64
Richardson, Jas — Janesville, Feb 14—62
Schram, W J — Elkhorn
Whappie, Jas — Janesville, Jan 30—62
Wolfender, Jos L — Troy Centre
Yeaton, Robt — West Pensaukee

E

Capt Ira Justin — Leavenworth, June 29—62
Capt A M Pratt — Janesville
Capt De W C Brown
Lt L House
Lt A C Kent — Janesville

Lt Wm Culbertson
Lt T O Drinkall
Lt J C Lynch — Janesville
Lt Wm Ellis
Treat, Syrel, sgt — Little Rock, Sept 6—64
Armstrong, Robt+ — Fayetteville, Dec 10—62
Boylan, Robt W — Ft Scott, Nov 15—63
Brown, D C — Stevens Point
Bostwick, Geo L — Springfield, Feb 8—63
Briggs, Chas — Illinois, Mar 26—62
Bowen, Oscar — La Crosse
Jenks, Zenos — Fayetteville, Jan 15- 63
Jones, Owen — Columbus
Justin, Giles, f — Kingston
Krebs, Jno — Little Rock, Feb 15—65
Kent, A C, mf — Janesville
Looming, D H — Edgerton
Martin, Fred'k A* — Clarksville, Nov 8—63
Maxfield, A D — Janesville
Merrill, Albert G — Ft Scott, Feb 16—63
Miller, Eluart, mo — Braxton
Newhouse, Chas — Little Rock, Mar 19—65
O'Flarety, Wm — Little Rock, Sept 6—64
Robinson, Jno H* — Balltown, July 8—63
Russell, Jno S* — Clarksville, Nov 8—63
Rook, Jedediah — St Louis, July 7—64
Reed, Wm — Janesville, Mar 13—62
Schurtz, Ang — Winsted Lake, Minn
Singar, Henry — Van Buren, Oct 13—64
Spears, Byron, f — Deerfield, Ohio
Wing, Peter, m — Ft Atkinson
Williams, Jno — Madison, May 17—64
Walters, Chas — Little Rock, Mar 31—65

F

Capt C W Porter
Capt L P Luce
Lt Asa Wood
Lt W J Plows
Lt C H Wolsey — Chicago, Ill
Lt Q Loreland
Lt C O Ferris
Lt S H Craig
Lt E M Cooper
Lt H Southard
Borter, W, sgt, f — Baraboo
Ablenon, Wm — Ablemon Station
Allen, G W, f — Delton
Crawford, Jas, f — Baraboo
Dennis, Jno, f — Baraboo
Davis, C H, liveryman — Baraboo
Gardner, Wm H — Ft Scott, July 28—63
Hutchins, Jno C — Cane Hill, Dec 26—62
Hawes, Willis A — Muscoda
Hull, Ed R — Ohio, Apr 26—62
Jarvis, Stephen D — Mt Vernon, Apr 7—63
Johnson, Jno H — Balltown, Nov 16—63
Kelley, Geo R* — Balltown, Nov 8—63
Longley, P E, liveryman — Baraboo
Leee, L P — Hebron
Manke, Henry — Ft Scott, June 26—62
Perry, Lyman, f — Lime Ridge
Priest, Geo — Camp Bowen, Nov 6—64
Pryan, W, f — Baraboo
Prethero, J, musician — Baraboo
Russell, M, liveryman — Boulder, Col
Tinker, Chas M — Ft Scott, Nov 24—62
Turney, Henry, steward — Reedsburg
Wheeler, Stephen — Ft Smith, Ark
Wiggins, J, f — Baraboo
Whistance, A, me — Baraboo

G

Capt J P Moore
Capt B Fullagar
Lt Hugh Calhoun
Lt Henry Sander
Lt Jmius Giesler*
Lt H Goodsall

65

BAND STAND SOLDIERS' HOME.

HUNTER'S MAGNETIC FOUNTAIN AND SUMMER RESORT.

(Continued from page 106.)

possible for me to add anything in the way of description, or of statement to, what has already been said with reference to this fountain of healing. I can only bear testimony, which I most cheerfully do, to the correctness of what is set forth in these pages, in relation to the efficacy of the water of this fountain, in many forms of disease. With very many who have been helped by its use, and with many more who have found entire relief from rheumatic, nervous, and other diseases of long standing, when other remedies have failed, I am well acquainted, and know that their statements are true. That this water will work miracles is not claimed, but that it possesses a wonderful restorative and healing virtue, none can doubt. I do not hesitate therefore to recommend a trial of it to the afflicted. A. C. BARRY.

Mrs. L. H. Lyons, a lady residing on Sixth street, Fond du Lac, has been thought to be an almost incurable invalid. Her liver has been so affected that her countenance had become dark and discolored, her eyes weak, and the lids painfully inflamed. All of which, coupled with female weaknesses, rendered her life one of continual misery. She had been forced into a dropsical state, and her hands and feet had swollen exceedingly. The fame of the Magnetic Water reached her husband in San Francisco, and he wrote to her advising its use. She complied. To day she is a well woman. The swellings have entirely subsided. Her complexion is bright. Her eyes are free from trouble. Her friends who knew her previous condition are astonished. And she is willing to make affidavit that all this happy effect is attributable to the use of the Magnetic Saline Water for only a short time.

Miss Lizzie Malone, residing on Madison street, Fond du Lac, is now nearly 14 years of age. She has been afflicted twelve years with sore eyes, resulting from the measles. She bathed them with the water, is much better, and is rapidly progressing to a cure.

FROM MR. SAMUEL VAUX.

Mr. George Hunter:—

*Dea Sir—*I visited your city on the 13th inst., in very bad health. I was induced to come here by hearing of the Magnetic Water, at Waupun, and I determined to spend a few days, in hopes of benefiting myself by its use. I have been at the well daily, using the water both for drinking and bathing, and find that the benefit I have derived is very satisfactory.

I have been a great sufferer. My diseases have been phthisic and heart disease, and my case was pronounced incurable at the Charleston Infirmary, Charleston, Ill. After using the water, I find great relief, so far. The phthisic has left me, and the sensation about the heart is much improved.
SAMUEL VAUX,
Andrew, Mo.

MR. ALONZO RAYMOND,

of the late firm of Raymond & Smith, grocers, Fond du Lac, fell last summer and broke his leg, the fracture being a very serious and painful one. It had never healed, and Mr. Raymond has been a constant sufferer from sleeplessness and general debility. He has used the Magnetic Water, for three weeks, drinking it freely and bathing in it every morning. His general health is greatly improved thereby. He can now sleep, his appetite is better, and his bowels are now regular for the first time in a year.

This gentleman has long been identified with the business interests of Fond du Lac, and his statement as published herewith is entitled to and should command the most implicit credence. Mr. Nathan Parker is of the firm of N. Parker & Co., lumbermen, Fond du Lac. His case was one of disease of the kidneys complicated with other disorders. He had considered himself as incurable, but has become a healthy man. His mill is adjacent to Hunter's well, and as he is an intelligent and courteous gentleman it would be of great advantage to parties seeking relief to get the particulars of his case from himself. It is a very interesting one.

MRS. A. STEVELY.

She had been such a sufferer for *twenty-five years* that she was unable to eat anything but stale bread and crackers, and articles of similar diet. She drank the Magnetic Water but three weeks. Her health is restored. She can digest any description of food without the slightest trouble. We would request particular examination of this case by parties who are suffering similarly.

I hereby certify that I have been troubled with rheumatism for twelve years last past, and at times for months have been in great misery, unable to do any kind of business. I have used almost every variety of medicine, prescribed by almost all kinds of persons, from the best physicians to quacks and old women, and from all of these sources I have never received any permanent benefit, and only rarely any temporary relief, and at times was much discouraged, when a few days since I was induced by neighbors to use the mineral waters from George Hunter's artesian well, and found immediate relief, perfectly free from all rheumatic pains. LEROY GRAVES.

Mr. Graves is an old resident of Fond du Lac. He is a speculator in timber

(Continued on page 200.)

WISCONSIN SOLDIERS AND SAILORS REUNION ROSTER. 199

Lt J C Ellis
Lt T O Drinkall
Briggs, Isaac, corp — Ft Scott, Apr 27—63
Burgett, Rich, corp — Ft Scott, May 9—63
Busgen, Jacob — Little Rock, Sept 9—64
Bonus, Eli M — Illinois, Mar 26—63
Crandall, Benj F — Searcy, Sept 4—64
Case, W H — Illinois, Mar 26—62
Fuller, Wm, m — Baraboo
Gottfried, Adolph — Ft Scott, May 26—63
Hamilton, Jas — Kaukauna
Hamilton. Wm — Kaukauna
Jones, Wm — Janesville, Dec 27—61
Janney, Nat* — Van Buren, Sept 25—64
Long, Sam'l — Muscoda
Long, Leroy — Little Rock, Sept 8—64
Longstaff, Chas, m — Red River
Murphy, Jeremiah — Ft Scott, Nov 26—62
Moore, Volney, m — Baraboo
O'Connor, Rich — Kaukauna
Otwell, Jas A+ — Ft Scott, Jan 29—63
Primmer, Peter — Ft Scott, Oct 29—62
Ross, Jno — Little Rock, Nov 21—64
Rogers, Leroy S — Hopkins, Mo
Rawson, Lucien — Illinois, Mar 26—62
Rogers, Levi S — Hopkins, Mo
Snell, Walt H — Illinois, Mar 26—62
Tice, Geo W* — Baxter Springs, Oct 6—63
Wrenn, Tim — Little Rock, Nov 6—64
Wilson, David — Ft Scott, Dec 5—62

H

Capt N L Stout — Leavenworth, June 27—63
Capt W H Thomas — Pewaukee
Capt Julius Giesler* — 66
Capt Jas B Pond — Boston, Mass
Capt W T Brayton — Unity
Lt De W C Brown
Lt W W Griffith — Ouro
Lt J W Van Meyers — Watertown
Lt Jerome Nelson, mf — Nelsonville
Lt Ezra Bolion — Kansas
Bennett, Albert A, sgt — Baxter Springs, Oct 6—63
Page, Wm, corp — Ft Gibson, May 25—63
Henson, Wm A, corp — Ft Leavenworth, Jan 10—63
Beecham, Chas E — Little Rock, July 8—64
Buskirk, H D, f — Berlin
Brewer, Jas H — Leavenworth, Feb 13—64
Barry, Thos — Leavenworth, Feb 15—61
Cox, McClow — Ft Leavenworth, Dec 10—62
Coon, O N — Fulton
Dennison, Delos — Mississippi R, May 13—62
Jenkinson, J M, m — Ripon
Jones, Wm* — Clarksville, Sept 28—64
Metzner, Jno — Little Rock, Oct 12—64
Mann, Azro* — Ft Gibson, May 25—63
Nolan, Wm A — Leavenworth, Jan 24—63
Pitts, Geo M — Lexington, May 7—65
Richardson, Simeon S — Leavenworth, Jan 28—63
Robb, Daniel B — Mt Vernon, Sept 9—63
Sliman, Henry — Ft Scott, June 26—63
Shaver, Ormah* — Baxter Springs, Oct 6—63
Stockwell, Ezra — Kansas, July 3—63
Samphier, Peter, m — Omro
Stowell, Arnold — St Louis, Oct 23—61
Sanders, Wm E — Little Rock, Jan 3—65
Smith, Sidney S — White Cloud, Nov 4 -62
Smith, Robt H, teamster — Sturgeon Bay
Whitehead, Wm, f — Kingston
Wooden, Jas — Ft Atkinson

I

Capt J G Cavert — Independence, Kan
Capt Jno Crites
Capt M Rebstein
Lt H Bacon — Michigan
Lt C E Willett — New York City
Lt H D Bannister — Fond du Lac

Lt H E Baukson
Lt M M Ehle
Lt H B Eastman — Fond du Lac
Lt C Spooner
Burlingame, Jos, sgt* — Baxter Spa C N, Oct 6—63
Beans, David, corp* — Baxter Spa C N, Oct 6—63
Hopper, Wm E* — Baxter Spa C N, Oct 6—63
Hart, Sam'l P, corp* — Baxter Spa C N, Oct 6—63
Murphy, Robt R, corp* — Baxter Spa C N, Oct 6—63
Knight, West A, corp — Ft Scott, Dec 7—62
Allen, Ethan — Janesville
Alder, Jno W, m — Lawrence, Kan
Adams, Jno — Maisonville, Mich
Brewer, Henry* — Baxter Spa C N, Oct 6—63
Barker, Darius B, f — West Peusaukee
Bannister, H D — Fond du Lac
Carr, Wm, f — Sparta
Clark, Wm C* — Baxter Spa C N, Oct 6—63
Clark, R C — Shiocton
Cooley, F Frank, h — Plover
Dempsey, Jas* — Baxter Spa C N, Oct 6—63
Durkee, Timothy — Shiocton
Eastman, H B, a — Fond du Lac
Fraker, Pulaski — Brookside
Gallen, Stephen V* — Baxter Spa C N, Oct 6—63
Ganer, Jno* — Baxter Spa C N, Oct 6—63
Green, Alf B*
Gifford, Wm M
Gulvin, Frank
Gates, P J — Appleton
Henderson, Alex — Prairie du Chien, May 29—64
Hammond, Seneca E — Ft Scott—62
Metcalf, Wm — Herman, D T
Pond, Henry A* — Baxter Spa C N, Oct 6—63
Prickett, Jno — Ft Scott—62
Rice, Lincoln S* — Baxter Spa C N, Oct 6—63
Reeves, W H, m — Fond du Lac
Reckard, Marion* — Baxter Spa C N, Oct 6—63
Stillman, Riley H* — Dardanelles, Jan 14—65
Schapke, A — Bear Creek
Swartout, Barber, f — Milladore
Smith, Dennis* — Baxter Spa C N, Oct 6—63
Smith, D G — Mazomanie
Sprague, Wm H — Edgerton, Feb 9—64
Smith, Jacob — Stevensville
Stolte, Chas — Lawrence, May—65
Titus, O, me — East Troy
Titus, Willard — East Troy
VanCamp, Francis* — Baxter Spa C N, Oct 6—63
VanDuzee, Martin+ — Spring River, Jan 13—63
VanAlstine, Jas H — Shiocton
Woddall, Able* — Baxter Spa C N, Oct 6—63
Wright, Jno C* — Baxter Spa B N, Oct 6—63
Whittaker, Wm — Fond du Lac
Zahner, Jno* — Baxter Spa C N, Oct 6—63

K

Capt H Y Perry
Capt Benj Fullagar
Lt J P McDonald — Watertown
Lt F A Copeland
Lt S H Craig
Lt H L Nye
Lt W F McMillen — Cambridge
Ricket, J G, sgt, f — Arkansas, Apr 14—63
Bohnart, Jos* — Ft Scott, Sep 17—63
Chadwick, Wm A — La Crosse
Copeland, F A — Leavenworth, July 17—62
Howe, Preston M — Cottage Grove
Hustou, J W, f — Springfield, Mar 19—63
Hernel, Jno — Sparta
Hollenbeck, Henry D — Van Buren, Sep 10—64
Jones, Owen — Wabasha, Minn
Kaiser, Peter — Little Osage, Mo
Meadows, W H, me — Sparta
Meadows, Thos E, f — Black Creek
Marks, Theo, W, student — Oshkosh
Pierce, W F

Rivers, Jno — Lourden, Ia
Rappleye, Jasper — Richmond
Stegman, Conrad* — Arkansas, Apr 14—63
Van Hooy, Henry — Little Rock, May 2—64
Whittenbecker, Herman — Oct 18—64

L

Capt C A Perry — Chicago, Ill
Capt Robt Carpenter
Capt M M Ehle
Lt J D Welch
Lt Jas Campbell — Ohio
Lt Jesse Bermingham
Lt T B Parkinson — Dec 17—64
Lt C F King
Bartram, David E, sgt* — Ft Smith, Sept 8—63
Whitmore, Benel, sgt — Fayetteville, Feb 1—63
Austin, Dan'l — Fremont
Bull, Jas A, f — Lime Ridge
Bundell, Chas D — Ft Scott, Nov 1—62
Briscoe, Sam'l, me — Baraboo
Browning, Chas A — Salem, June 6—63
Brundier, C H, me — Cross Plaines
Castello, Sam'l B* — White Oak Creek, Aug 8—64
Hanson, Halvor* — Springfield, May 7—63
Hanson, Amund — Little Rock, Sept 19—64
Hummersly, Wm C — Lake Mills, Ia
Hull, J M, ph
Johnson, Andrew — July 29—63
Jones, Wm, me — Westport
Lavin, Thos — Little Rock, Nov 28—64
McClure, Lew A* — Van Buren, Sep 17—61
Meltzer, Wm, m — Black Earth
Nickel, Thos C, l — Fond du Lac
Perkins, Oscar W — Westport, Oct 8—62
Platts, Corliss I — Fayetteville, Feb 1—63
Parmelee, Ed A — Leavenworth, Sept 6—12
Shafer, Henry, me — Fond du Lac
Sharp, Elisha — Illinois, Mar 26—42
Thomas, Jno H — Janesville, Jan 8—62
Wilcox, Byron I. — Chicago, Apr 17—62
Workinbadge, Geo — Watertown
Warn H, f — Ableman

M

Capt H F Rouse — Marion Centre, Kan
Capt Jay Thompson — Ft Scott, Krn
Capt J M Bernard — Helena
Lt Wm Schmult
Lt Jas Armstrong — Leavenworth, Oct 2 - 62
Lt L A Dixon | — Independence, Oct 20—64
Lt H T Perry
Lt Olaf Meyer
Lt P P Rouse
Lt Wm Riley
Barber, Edgar — Osage Mission, Jan 21—65
Corby, Jno — Ft Scott, Mar 1—63
Classon, Martin L — Van Buren, Oct 9—63
Clossan, Wm S — Ft Scott, Sept 15—62
Free, Jas — Arkansas, Oct 23—63
Kirst, Conrad — Leavenworth, June 17—63
Lewis, Peter, W — Leavenworth, June 17—63
McCord, Andrew* — M Island, Mar 30—63
Mense, Albert — Milwaukee
May, Jno H* — Horney Springs, Aug 24—63
Montgomery, Benj A — Kansas, Sept 8—63
Odell, Robt — Ft Scott, Feb 11—63
Riley, Jno — Kansas, Sept 27—64
Raesver, C T, m — Milwaukee
Somers, Henry — Sheboygan
Tyler, Abel L — Ft Scott, Jan 24—63
Woolston, Wm — Columbus
Weeks, E J, f — Bloomer
Ward, W H — Richland Centre

UNASSIGNED.

Bliss, A J — Troy
Biss, Chas — Cambria

LAKE SOLDIERS' HOME.

HUNTER'S MAGNETIC FOUNTAIN AND SUMMER RESORT.

(continued from page 198.)

and other lands, and is well known throughout this part of the country.

Mr. John Bonnell, grocer, Forest st., Fond du Lac, has been for many years troubled with disease of his kidneys, and to such an extent that he had to a great degree lost control of his urine. He has been relieved by the use of the water, so that now he has seldom to arise during the night to pass his urine, and has every confidence that the cure will prove to be a permanent one.

Mr. John Musgat, harness-maker, doing business at 518 Main street, Fond du Lac, has had the rheumatism for some six years; has also had weak eyes and diseased kidneys. Has drank the water and bathed in it, and its effect has been to relieve him of rheumatic pains, strengthen his eyes, and cure his kidney complaint.

Mr. James Wilkins, of Lisbon, Waukesha county, Wisconsin, has been greatly troubled with the gravel for over twenty years. His urinary organs had become so weakened that he was compelled to leave his bed four or five times nightly for necessary purposes. Two days, use of the water has cured him! His son, Reuben Wilkins, is a resident of Fond du Lac, and works at his trade as blacksmith, on Third street.

Mr. Robert Longstaff is a citizen of Fond du Lac, living at the corner of Fifth and Ellis streets. He has used the Magnetic Water for but two weeks and it has had a most beneficial effect upon him. His case is one of gravel, of twenty years continuance. He had previously tried juniper berries, the best

gin, and spirits of nitre, without effect. Although not yet entirely cured he is so much improved that he has little doubt that his permanent cure is only a question of time.

Mr. James Graham, is a tinsmith in employ in Fond du Lac. He and his family board with Mrs. Edgell, on First street. His wife came to Fond du Lac a victim of the prevailing Michigan malaria—fever and ague. She had a chill every other day; now she is cured.

The above is simply a cure of fever and ague. Other medical waters, especially those of Michigan, have had some effect on rheumatism. In Michigan fever and ague prevails ; in Fond du Lac it is unknown, except when brought from abroad.

MR. S. W. VAN ARNAM,

Resides at No. 43 East Division St., Fond du Lac. He has for a great many years been severely afflicted with kidney disease. The use of the water has been a great benefit to him, and he is very much relieved. His wife has been cured of neuralgia, and an indescribably oppressive throat complaint, by the water. His daughter, Miss Lucy Van Arnam, has been entirely cured of neuralgia, with which she had been greatly troubled for a number of years, Such is the record of the water in a single family.

Mr. Jacob Avery, lives at No. 111 Amory street, Fond du Lac. Twenty-three years ago his wife after confinement, became afflicted with a "milk" leg. No doctor had been able to help her, and she had given up in despair.

Her limb had become so badly swollen that it was with the utmost difficulty she could get up and down stairs. She also had trouble with her kidneys. For this latter complaint she commenced using the water. After one week she observed a reduction in the swelling of her limb. Now the swelling has entirely disappeared, and the limb is assuming its natural shape, and she can use it freely and without pain. A constant pain in her side has entirely vanished. Her kidney troubles, which had lasted for ten years, are gone. This is one of the most remarkable cures yet developed.

The certificate of Mrs. Joseph Olmsted, an intelligent and affable lady living on Fourth street, in the First ward, will satisfy reasonable persons that she has been materially helped by using the Magnetic Water ;

This is to certify, That I have been troubled with rheumatism for thirteen years, at first through my whole system which finally settled in my shoulders and hands. I suffered great pain at times, and the joints of my hands were much distorted. I have drank and bathed in the Magnetic Water from Mr. Hunter's artesian fountain for two or three months, and am now entirely free from rheumatic pains.

MRS. JOSEPH OLMSTED,
Fond du Lac.

HERNIA CURED.

Mr. Stanchfield, lumberman, a quiet retiring gentleman, living on Fourth street, gives in testimony as to the efficacy of the Magnetic Water, in the following statement :

(Continued on page 202.)

WISCONSIN SOLDIERS AND SAILORS REUNION ROSTER.

Name	Location
Brown, Richard	Lind
Brown, Bitner	Lind
Butterfield, La Fayette, contractor	Sparta
Cunningham, Michael	Watertown
Colson, N L, f	Mill Centre
Cunningham, Michael	Milwaukee
Cooley, F F	Plover
Dyak, B B	Troy
Dye, Jas W	Merrillon
Foster, W H	Neosha
Fuller, Solomon	Pekin
Geese, S K, f	Tornado
Haus, Willis	Muscoda
Hutchins, J H	Sioux Falls, D T
Jas Enoch, miner	Osage City, Kan
Knight, Willard, me	Poynguette
Keyes, H W	Beaver Dam
Lobdell, Caleb, f	Council Grove, Kan
Mitchell, Sylvenieus, f	Neosho
Marsh, Sanford, me	Stone Banks
Mayhew, Jno, saddler	Chicago
Miller, Jacob, sr	Menominee
Parker, Jas M	Delavan
Robinson, J	Winneconne
Stout, Cornelius	Janesville
Serns, Theore, me	Cambridge
Shelden Jno, f	Council Grove, Kan
Stevens, E P	Oshkosh
Titus, Niles	Council Grove, Kan
Williams, Jno, f	Lime Springs, Iowa
Willard, W L, cd	Shelbyville, Mo
Worth, Dan	Baraboo

FOURTH CAVALRY.

Three years. Organized (as Infantry), June 6th, 1861. Original strength, 1047, gain by recruits, etc., 1258. Total, 2305. Death loss, 362—Killed in action, 72, died of wounds, 31, of disease, 261, of accidents, 18. Other losses 327—missing, 21, desertions, 76, transfers, 2, discharges, 471. By muster-out, Oct. 1st, 1865, 754 Strength at muster-out, May 28th, 1866, 506. Campaigns in Maryland, Miss., La., Ala., Ga., and Texas—Equipped as cavalry, Sept. 1st, 1863.

REGIMENTAL ROSTER.

Name	Location
Col H E Paine	Washington, D C
Col S A Beau*	Pt Hudson, May 29—63
Col F A Boardman*	Baton Rouge, May 3—64
Col W F Moore	Chicago, Ill
Col N F Craigne	
Lt Col G W Durgin	Indianapolis, Ind
Lt Col H B Baker	California
Maj O C Pierce, 1st Bat	Kilbourne City
Maj E A Ramsay, 1st Bat	
Maj E J Peck, 2d Bat	
Maj Jas Keefe, 2nd Bat, pa	Stillwater, Minn
Maj H Brooks, 2d Bat	Waupun
Maj Jas B Furnsworth, 3d Bat	Tomah
Adj L D Aldrich	Boston, May 21—62
Adj W S Payn	
Adj G Wintermeyer*	Pt Hudson, June 14—63
Adj N H Chittenden	
Q M A J McCoy	Beaver Dam
Q M C A Johns	Beaver Dam
Q M S C Watson	Illinois
Com T W Gilletto	Texas
Surg A H Van Nostrand	Green Bay
Surg S W Wilson	Milwaukee, Feb—61
A Surg J L Page	
A Surg D C Roundy	
A Surg S C Smith	
A Surg S W Wilson	
A Surg H R Merriman	Sept 18—64
A Surg W H Harrison	Texas
A Surg H D Horne	
Chap A C Harry,	Sauk
Chap G W Horney	Texas

A

Name	Location
Capt C W Steele, m	Whitewater
Capt J H Farnsworth,	
Capt G B Finch	Iowa
Lt P A Castle	
Lt A E Chaffee	Whitewater
Lt N H Chittenden	
Lt J E Williams*	Baton Rouge, Mar 8—64
Lt F N Thomas	Trempealeau
Lt N Bingham	
Criger, Jas J, sgt-maj	Whitewater
Nyer, Hiram S, 2d lt*	New York, Oct 7—63
Kenyon, Chas N, sgt*	Port Hudson, June 14—63
Ramsey, Moses, sgt+	Port Hudson, June 15—63
Perry, Henry A, corp*	Port Hudson, June 14—63
Duffee, Thos, corp+	Port Hudson, June 13—63
Ludeman, Wm T, corp+	Pt Hudson, June 17—63
Adams, Jas H	Baton Rouge, July 8—62
Berkhart, Amos H	Carrolton, Oct 11—62
Bates, Matthias,	Morganzia, July 25—64
Boswell, M E	Seymour
Carr, Nathan S	New Orleans, July 16—64
Cadmon Chas, I	Whitewater
Curr, J T, cd	Jefferson
Chamberlain, J A	Whitewater
Griffin, Welson O	Carrolton, Nov 27—62
Gardner, Winhehl I.	Baton Rouge, Aug 26—64
Green, Chas A, l	Janesville
Holden, Geo	Baton Rouge, June 18—62
Jackson, W	Kendall
Krets, Chas,	Vicksburg, July 20—62
Knight, Chas A	Whitewater, Nov 28—64
King, W M	Whitewater
Lewis, Chas H	Vicksburg, July 18—02
Lavejoy, Calvin S	Carrolton, Nov 3—63
Mallo, Wm W	Carrolton, Dec 11—62
Morrell, Jas P	Baton Rouge, Dec 30—64
Moody, Reuben	Springfield
Perry, Chas E	Delavan
Peters, Frank	Baton Rouge, Nov 20—64
Phillips, Jacob, l	Whitewater
Quick, H B	Waterloo
Sax. William O	Carrolton, Sept 26—62
Sabine, Irwin	Baton Rouge, July 8—64
Thompson, Wm	Jan 12—65
Tolles, Wm C	Ft Elwell, Oct 19—65
Vodre, Chas E	Mississippi R, Aug 6—62
Walker, Simon, f	Fond du Lac
Walsh, Edw P	New Orleans, Aug 16—64
Walden, Hubbard	Baton Rouge, Sept 28—64
Webb, Major P, c	Whitewater

B

Name	Location
Capt O H La Grange	California
Capt G W Carter	Waupun
Capt H B Baker	California
Capt E O Henry	Ontro
Lt A Medhurst	
Lt H O Gleason+	Baten Rouge, Mar 29—65
Lt O W Traynor	Juneau
Lt G F Clark	
Lt G W Pierce	Iowa
Lt M B Farr	
Shearer, John sgt+	Ft Hudson, May 29—63
Pygall, G F, sgt+	Baton Rouge, Oct 5—04
Alderman, Clark L+	Morganzia, Aug 1—64
Benedict, Wm H	Omaha, Neb
Brown, John A	Winona, Minn
Burt, James M	Bridge, Kan
Ocutey, Dennis+	Port Hudson, June 14—63
Cornwell, E D+	Port Hudson, June 14—63
Clark, Edward	Fortress Monroe, Apr 19—62
Crawford, William	Baton Rouge, Nov 16—64
Cross, Daniel S	Winneconne
Cross, A S, me	Ripon
Carter, Geo W, a	Fond du Lac
Davis, George H	Baton Rouge, July 18—64
Duane, Henry J	New Orleans, Sept 19—62

(continued)

Name	Location
Fordice, C F, f	West Rosendale
Folls, W R, vt surg	New Cassel
French, D O, clk	Ripon
Gunsolus, Abner	Ship Island, Apr 6—62
Henry, Charles	Baton Rouge, July 1—63
Harris, Asa O	La, Dec 2—62
Imus, Wallace C	Dec 22—64
Jenkins, Thomas	Carrolton, Jan 9—63
Kellorg, Reuben	Baton Rouge, Jan 18—65
Kleluhart, Frederick	Baton Rouge, July 26—62
Kuehke, Jno	Menominee
Lewis, A H, surg, m	Fond du Lac
Lynch, Jno L	Nov 2—61
Lamount, W M, f	Creston, Ill
McCollister, D	Carrolton, Oct 5—62
Noble, David A	Windom, Minn
Ostrom, Friend, clk	Brandon
Piper, Chester A—	Port Hudson, June 14—63
Phettyplace, Eli	Vicksburg, June 24—65
Russell, Jno	Berlin
Strong, DeWitt C—	Port Hudson, June 14—63
Saunders, Geo S	Baton Rouge, Dec 14—63
Sanders, Jas	Ship Island, Apr 7—62
Spencer, Wm H	Baton Rouge, July 8—62
Shoults, Cuyler A	Doniphan, Nev
Schults, Carl F	Fall Creek
Soper, Isaac, m	Berlin
Sleeper, Chas A, me	Northport
Stange, Fred	Fremont
Thompson, Jas	Madison, May 15—65
Thompson, J C	Manley June't, Ia
Turner, Jno S	Denver, Col
Vaughan, Jas	Waupaca
Wheeler, Solon	Menominee

C

Name	Location
Capt E D Gray	Chicago, Ill
Capt P Pauli	
Capt G W Duran	Waupun
Capt H Brooks	Waupun
Capt J O Stock	Madison
Lt J R Cole	
Lt G Wintermeyer	
Lt A C Bush	
Lt H H Bradford	
Lt F C Bartlett	Oascade
Lt T O Connor	
Lt Hugh Baker	
Clapp, Edw A, lt	Port Gibson, May 27—63
Guck, John W, corp	Bishard, Apr 13—63
Stewart, J L, bugler	Sheboygan Falls
Beechler, Jno S	Carrolton, Aug 28—62
Barnes, Edw H	Baton Rouge, May 8—64
Biewer, Adam	San Antonio, Oct 25—65
Baker, Hugh	Orient, Iowa
Bradford, Hiram, me	Plymouth
Brooks, Harry	Waupun
Bartlett, L C	Sheboygan Falls
Bump, Edwin, c	Waterloo
Cull, George H	Carrolton, Sept 21—62
Danforth, R B	New Orleans, Aug 24—62
Danforth, Q A, inf	Mecmee
Elmore, Andrew W	Baton Rouge, Nov 14—64
Esty, E A	Sheboygan Falls
Hansen, Marvin, f	Gibraltar
Higgins, Ingarans	Newport News, Mar 12—62
Hogan, Wm H	Manitowoc
Hamlin, S A	St Cloud
Huson, Alphonzo,	Sheboygan Falls
Hunt, Jno A, pa	Milwaukee
Harkins, Daniel	Hingham
Johnson, Sherman	Kelsg House, Nov 7—61
Jones, H B, collector	Chicago, Ill
Jackson, Nelson	Hingham
Kelly, Peter	Sheboygan Falls
Loeb, Jacob	New Orleans, Aug 30—62
Lacox, J B	Sheboygan Falls
McDonald, Emmett	Baton Rouge, Apr 7—62
Nare, George	Baton Rouge, Sept 16—61
Oliver, Wm H	Cairo, Nov 2—64

HUNTER'S MAGNETIC FOUNTAIN AND SUMMER RESORT.

(Continued on page 201.)

For the benefit of those who are afflicted as I have been, I will state my case in plain language. I hereby state that I had the misfortune to have a severe rupture twelve years ago. I have used various kinds of trusses, but never received any permanent benefit from their use. I often suffered severe pain and great inconvenience, so as often to be unfit for any kind of business. I have used the Magnetic Water from Mr. Hunter's fountain (not regularly, however), for two months, and am free from the pain and inconvenience heretofore caused by the breach. I have thrown aside trusses as useless and cumbersome.

I will further state that I had kidney complaint for several years, and now find myself benefited by the use of the Magnetic Water.

J. H. STANCHFIELD.

Mrs. Haines Hunter, an affable, intelligent lady living on Second street, gives in her testimony as to the good effects of Magnetic Water in cases of dyspepsia, in the following language:

This is to certify. That I have been troubled with dyspepsia for fifteen years, and have lately found great relief in using the Magnetic Water.

MRS. H. HUNTER.

I, John P. Hunter, formerly a resident of Beaver Dam, but now a resident of this city, certify that my wife was in bad health for two or three years previous to January, 1873, and during the winter of that year she was quite unable to do any kind of work, and often had to keep her bed. She was afflicted with physical female weaknesses and diseases. She also had dyspepsia and other complicated complaints, and among them cutaneous eruptions all over her body, so bad that some of her neighbors believed she had the small-pox. These complaints continued, with slight abatements, occasionally, till May, 1873. I employed four or five different physicians, who tried, but failed, to help her. In the latter part of May last I procured some of the Saline Water from George Hunter's artesian fountain, which she drank for ten or twelve days, and was entirely cured of all her complicated diseases and she is as well now as she ever was having gained forty pounds of flesh during the last summer. J. P. HUNTER.

Hon. C. D. Mihills, of the firm of Mihills & Son, late proprietors of an extensive lumbering establishment, and a large sash, door and blind factory, makes the following statement: This is to certify that I have had rheumatism in my arms and shoulders for eight or nine years past, and have tried a variety of remedies, and only found temporary relief, until last season, when I commenced bathing in and drinking the Magnetic Saline Water from George Hunter's artesian fountain. I used the water, occasionally, during the summer and fall of 1873, and am now entirely free from rheumatic troubles and can, at with utmost confidence recommend the Magnetic Water to all who are troubled as I have been, as a sure cure. I also know that the Magnetic Water is an excellent remedy for kidney complaints.

U. D. MIHILLS.

Statement of H G. Campbell, grocer on the corner of Scott and Brooke streets. Mr. Campbell's case is a peculiar one. To those who have known him for years, and have seen him going about daily, half bent, with his head and shoulders quite on a level with his hips, his cure is regarded as almost miraculous. Mr. Campbell's case was the first to attract public attention. But Mr. Campbell will speak for himself:

MR. HUNTER—*Sir:*—My statement is that I have had the rheumatism in its severest forms in all parts of my system for thirteen years—ever since I was thirteen years of age—so severely in my hips and back that I could not stand erect, but was forced to stand and walk a'out in a half-bent posture; that is my body was fixed at right angles with my legs. I suffered severe pains. The muscles of my body were sore and torpid, and apparently permanently contracted to my hips. During my thirteen years of suffering, I used great quantities of medicines prescribed by physicians and quacks, and found no permanent relief until last April, when I obtained some water from your artesian well, soon after it was discovered that the water possessed magnetic and medicinal properties. I immediately began to use the water, and have continued to do so ever since, and am now free from pain. My joints are limber, I can stand nearly erect, and feel as well as I did when I was a much younger boy. HUGH J. CAMPBELL.

The foregoing are but a few of the hundreds of exceptionally gratifying testimonials received weekly, lack of space precluding the publication of any more. It sufficeth to say, in conclusion, that language fails utterly in describing the beneficial effects of both the external and internal use of this celebrated water from the Hunter Fountain.

CLOTHING.

Foreseeing that the only result of the long continued boom in the prices of Wool would be a corresponding Boom in the price of Woolen Goods, while we could buy at old prices we laid in the

LARGEST STOCK OF WOOLENS

Ever brought to Fond du Lac. In SUITINGS ALONE we have over 250 Styles of NEW GOODS and a varied assortment enables us to suit the most exacting taste in style and quality.

OUR STOCK OF WORSTEDS

Is complete. Also in stock a large assortment of CLOTHS, DOESKINS, CASSIMERES, CHEVIOTS, YACHT CLOTHS, BLUE FLANNELS, Etc. Satisfaction guaranteed every time.

JOHN E. SULLIVAN & CO.,
FOREST STREET, - FOND DU LAC, WISCONSIN.

WISCONSIN SOLDIERS AND SAILORS REUNION ROSTER.

Phalin, Jno — Sheboygan Falls
Pierce, Harmon — Sheboygan Falls
Putnam, O S — Greenbush
Reed, Warren F — Milwaukee, June 26—61
Robbin, Windom — Baltimore, Dec 17—61
Seeger, Wm — Medford
Schumann, Christian+ — Baton Rouge, Mar 16—64
Sullivan, Dan'l — Baton Rouge, Oct 7—63
Steele, Thos — Neillsville
Steele, Thos — Greenwood
Turner, Wm J — Cedar Grove
Troub, Wm — Mazomanie
Windsor, Nathaniel* — Texas Feb 4—66
Wipprecht, Henry J — New Orleans, Aug 10—62
Wolff, Fred A — Carrollton, Sep 2—62
Wright, Orson D — Sheboygan Falls, Dec 23—61
Walsh, Henry — Sheboygan Falls

D

Capt Jos Bailey
Capt E R Herren
Capt C C Pierce — Kilbourn City
Capt A C Ketchum — Kilbourn City
Lt W S Payn
Lt I N Earl+ — Natchez, Dec 10—64
Lt W J Duffield+ — Baton Rouge, Oct 18—64
Lt A Boynton
Lt D C Freeland
Lt Myron Skinner
Martin, Geo M, sgt+ — Baton Rouge, Mar 13—65
Chase, Richard S, sgt — Baton Rouge, Mar 14—64
Niles, Amasa P, sgt — Baton Rouge, Aug 12—64
Wood, Milo, corp — Carrollton, Aug 24—62
McKinstry, Willie, corp — Rush, July 2—64
Austin, Isaiah L — Baton Rouge, Aug 16, 61
Brown, Michael* — Bisland, Apr 13—63
Baldwin, Jno W+ — Port Hudson, July 30—63
Brewster, Dan'l — Mound City, Nov 1—64
Boynton, Abraham — Maple Grove, D T
Boyle, J H — Hebron
Dawes, Frank* — Port Hudson July 4—63
Dike, Horace* — Port Hudson, June 14—63
Earl, Jos W — Ship Island, June 21—62
Early, David W — Baton Rouge, Nov 18—64
Ferris, Francis C* — Port Hudson, June 11—63
Foster, Otis S — Baton Rouge, Sept 2—64
Gibus, Jas S — Oconomowoc
Granuois, Stephen C+ — New Orleans, July 1—63
Geer, Jno J — Dec 22—64
George, Thos J — Menominee
Hubbard, Julius H — Relay House, Sept 23—61
Haughtelling, Aaron — Oxford
Holt, Jos — Downsville
Hollenbeck, Peter H — Tomah
Kerr, Jno* — Bisland, Apr 13—63
Lyons, Richard — Baton Rouge, Apr 1—61
McKune, Melvin W — Baltimore, Jan 25—62
McCarty, Michael — Baton Rouge, Nov 6—64
Meredith, Thos — New Orleans, Feb 26—65
Mains, Wm — Baton Rouge, Oct 23—62
Miller, Leonard — Quincy
Newell, Marshall — New Orleans, June 27—63
Needham, Jno H — Relay House, Aug 16—61
Olson, Chas — Ludington, Mich
Pickard, Chas S — Andersonville, Aug 18—64
Powers, J H — Baraboo
Rue, Chas A — Baton Rouge, June 27—61
Stellick, Wm P — Port Hudson, June 14—63
Shaffer, Chas W* — July 15—63
Stivers, Stephen — Southwest Pass, Apr 25—62
Smith, J D — Big Spring
Turner, Geo — Vermillion, Apr 28—63
Underwood, Geo W — Baton Rouge, Sept 29—63
White, Eaves O J — Port Hudson, July 1—63
Wilcox, D A — Springfield
Weiss, Lewis — Baton Rouge, Dec 20—65
West, Sam'l W S — New Orleans, Jan 29—65
White, N J — Colby
Wheeler, H W — Eldorado Mills

E

Capt W P Moore
Capt C D Wooster — Brodhead
Capt Lewis Jones
Capt Jos Hall — Decatur, Neb
Lt S H Tubbs
Lt H B Lighthizar
Lt D E Pixley — Sharon
Lt S C Watson
Lt G W Peck — Milwaukee
Sidney, A Benn, col* — Port Hudson, May 29—63
Fred A Beardman, col* Comite River, May 3—63
G Wintermeyer, wij — Port Hudson July 14—63
Lewis D Aldrich, adj — Boston May 21—62
H R Merryman, A Surg Baton Rouge, Sep 18—63
Geo M Chalfant — Baltimore, Dec 19—61
Slone, Chas A, sgt — Natchez, July 25—62
Whipple, Burton A, sgt Baton Rouge, Sep 16—64
Bell, Wesley J, sgt — San Antonio, Oct 23—64
Friedel, Martin, h — Cambridge
Frissell, Chas S, corp* Port Hudson, June 14—63
Mason, Arthur W, corp — Ship Island, Apr 3—62
Ames, Nathaniel — New Orleans, June 29—63
Allen, Gen
Allen, Wm H, a — San Francisco, Cal
Bartr m, David* — July 15—62
Brink, Nicholas — Baton Rouge, Feb 24—63
Banks, Geo — Baton Rouge, Sep 1—64
Basch, Peter, mail carrier — Burlington
Blodgett, Ben, f — Jefferson
Corey, Jos — Baton Rouge, Aug 11—62
Cameron, Wm — New Orleans, Sep 21—63
Duffie, Jas E* — Bisland, Apr 13—63
Duval, Francis — Plaquemine, Aug 6—64
Delile, Orlando — Carrollton, Oct 3—62
Doty, Wm H — Washington, Oct 30—62
Donaldson, Edw — Waukesha
Eberts, Peter — Cairo, Oct 6—64
Tichent, Jno — Manitowoc
Hall, S A, me — Unity
Hollenbeck, Peter H — Philadelphia, Pa
Hilzer, Luclus W — New Orleans, Oct 20—63
Hadley, Jno H — Carrollton, Oct 7—62
Hoard, W D — Ft Atkinson
Hubbard, Wm — Nashua, Ia
Hendee, S H, me — Beloit
Had, S A — Neillsville
Jinks, Orie S, f — Netherland, Kan
Kinney, Jas D* — Port Hudson, May 27—63
Knowlton, J F B* — Port Hudson, June 14—63
Leberer, Geo — New Orleans, May 21—63
Livingston, Thos J — Baton Rouge, Oct 6—61
Livournier, Camille — Camp Paraport, Oct 2—62
Neltzert, Andrew — New Orleans, June 18—63
Orendorff, L J, f — Oakland
O'Kelly, Wm H — Aug 1—62
Preston, Chas — Racine
Pott, Augu t — Carrollton, Sept 1—62
Piloti, Oscar F — Wausau
Ray, Milan E — Port Hudson, June 14—63
Ravenburg, Chas — Baton Rouge, Feb 24—64
Roehl, Christian — Baton Rouge, July 7—64
Spaulding, Robert E — Baton Rouge, May 5—64
Strapbarger, Peter, me — Milwaukee
Stone, A L — Marseilles, Ill
Taylor, Theo D W+ — Plaquemine, Aug 6—64
Terwilliger, Thos — Carrollton, Sep 28—61
Wright, Jeremiah N* Port Hudson, June 14—63
Whipple, Daniel, e — Owatonna, Minn
Westphall, Henry — Hebron
Leah, Jno W* — Port Hudson, June 14—63

F

Capt D C Roundy
Capt N F Craigue
Capt Milo Seeley
Capts S C Morver — Grand Haven, Mich

G

Lt G H Brown
Lt Harris Durkee
Lt D B Maxson+ — Clinton, June 3—63
Lt C A Johns
Lt J M Mead
Lt C C Coffee
Lt A J Weetherwax
Lt L W Davids
Lt G W Pierce — Iowa
Farnum, Ezra C, sgt* — Pt Hudson, May 26—63
Parks, Wm, sgt* — Pt Hudson, May 27—63
Carmichael, Rich D, sgt Vicksburg, July 26—64
Barry, M A — Lodi
Butters, Albert C* — Pt Hudson, May 27—63
Beardsley, Horace G New Orleans, Aug 10—62
Blake, Jos — New Orleans, Jan 14—65
Baker, Robt — Baton Rouge, Aug 24—64
Buel, Chas H — Vicksburg, June 15—65
Briggs, P T — Kenosha
Burdict, A R — Waterford
Campbell, Wm H — New Orleans, June 2—63
Carter, Chas L — Baton Rouge, Sept 2—64
Chappell, Turner H — Baton Rouge, Jan 4—65
Cronk, Reuben R — Elkhorn
Dyer, Wm H — Vicksburg, July 26—62
Dodge, Wm H — Relay House, Aug 24—61
Frederick, Jacob — Cairo, Oct 19—64
Fustenburg, Lorenzo — Lewiston, Minn
Gibbs, Jas S — Oconomowoc
Herrick, Wm S — Baton Rouge, Mar 12—64
Herriman, E Ive N — Edinburg, Apr 30—65
Hanson, Hans — Spring Brook, Jan 12—65
Hotchkiss, Jno, ed — Fox Lake
Hattle, Leander — Elkhorn
Lee, Wm* — Pt Hudson, June 14—63
Lyon, Chas W — Ingalls, Kan
Mettride, Allan B — Carrollton, Oct 36—62
Matthews, Jas — Baton Rouge, Aug 3—62
Marshall, Geo F — Baton Rouge, July 18—44
McFarlin, Jno C — Richland Centre
Putman, Henry — Geneva, Jan 1—66
Parker, Francis J — Baton Rouge, Oct 26—61
Parks, Jonathan, l — LaCrosse
Ross, Wm — Geneva
Sherman, A T — Baton Rouge, June 24—62
Smith, Jno — Baton Rouge, Aug 4—62
Smith, Henry — Baton Rouge, Aug 2—64
Squires, Jno H — Springfield, O S 22—64
Smith, Levi — Andersonville, Sept 8—64
Tabor, Wm W* — Pt Hudson, June 14—63
Tupper, Jos P* — Pt Hudson, June 14—63
Tuskey, Patrick* — Black Bayou, Mar 19—64
Tupper, A W — Geneva Lake
Utter, Cyrus E — Elkhorn
Vites, Gustavus G — Baton Rouge, June 15—63
Walker, Geo W — Relay House, Oct 30—61
Weeks, Theo — Springfield

G

Capt D M White
Capt Jas Keefe, pa — Stillwater, Minn
Capt W P Knowles — River Falls
Lt I H Wing
Lt Edw A Clapp* — Port Hudson, May 27—63
Lt J B Harrington — St Croix
Lt J E Felot, in — River Falls
Lt S H Briggs
Lt W H Nichols — River Falls
Dolly, Jesse, sgt, l — New Richmond
Vanmeter, Jno H, sgt — St Croix
Nutter, Jos, com sgt — Richmond
Dawley, Jesse N, sgt — Richmond
Briggs, Spencer, sgt — Hudson
Dexter, Wm E, corp — New Orleans, May 5—62
Allen, Gilbert — Carrollton, Nov 28—61
Adelson, P P, f — Clear Lake
Arno, Nelson — Clear Lake
Anderson, Mal — Baton Rouge, Jan 4—65
Boucher, Cyrelle, l — Osceola Mills

THE HARTFORD
Fire Insurance Co.,
HARTFORD, CONN.

CHARTERED, - - - - - 1810.

CASH CAPITAL,
$1,250,000.

CASH ASSETS, January, 1st 1880.
SEVENTIETH ANNUAL EXHIBIT,

$3,458,020.90.

Managed by Skilful Underwriters, and for Sixty-Nine Years one of the Leading Financial Institutions of the Country.

Cash Indemnity Disbursed to Patrons, Over

$23,000,000!

All Busines. Transacted on Principles of Commercial Honor.

MANUFACTURERS'
Fire & Marine Insurance Co.,
BOSTON, MASS.

NATIONAL STOCK.................$500,000.00
SURPLUS,................................. 660,805.57
TOTAL ASSETS,................. 1,160,805.57

ASSETS.
Capital Bank Stock.................. $203,130.00
Railroad Bonds....................... 198,410.00
Loans on Stocks and Mortgages, amply secured,.. 248,154.20
Real Estate............................ 83,700.00
Bills Receivable for Marine Premiums........... 37,247.62
Cash on hand and in Bank............... 300,601.09
Interest Accrued..................... 13,539.94
Premiums in course of collection............... 46,013.72
Bills Receivable,..................... 30,000.00
                                    $1,160,57805.

LIABILITIES.
Cash Capital, $500,000. 0
Reinsurance,
Reserve and 407,721.48
all Labilities,
                                $907,721.48
Net surplus, $253,084.09

SAMUEL GOULD, President.
JAMES J. GOODRICH, Secretary.
SAMUEL H. WISE, Ass't Secretary

Apply to Local Agent.

INCORPORATED 1825.
Firemen's Insurance Company,
OF BALTIMORE. Dec. 31, 1879.

CAPITAL STOCK PAID UP, - $378,000.00

Reserve for Reinsurance, $54,427 22
All other Indebtedness, 14,337 54
Surplus, as regards Policy-holders, 476,263 87
Assets, $545,033 63
Losses paid since organization, $2,271,785 56
Dividends paid since organization, $2,886,614 49

Insurance taken on Manufactories, Dwellings, Churches, Merchandise, Buildings, etc., etc.

APPLY TO NEAREST AGENCY.

THE
LONDON ASSURANCE
ASSOCIATION.

Gross Assets, Gold, $15,146,095 00
Gross Liabilities, including Capital $11,818,721 00
Net Fire Surplus, $3,327,374 00
Capital Paid up 2,241,375 00
Surplus to Policy Holders, $5,568,749 00

Agencies for writing acceptable risks at all principal points.

WISCONSIN SOLDIERS AND SAILORS REUNION ROSTER.

Name	Location/Notes
Brickley, Michael	Cylon
Bushnell, Alf, f	Hammond
Bushnell, Fred	Hammond
Butcher, S	Osceola Mills
Boggess, Jeptha	St Croix
Beeby S S	Cylon
Chamberlain, Henry N	Madison, Mar 17—61
Currier, Henry	Concord, Minn
Danforth, Anton F	Newport News, Mar 18—62
Dawley, Jesse N, c	Star Prairie
Densmore, Wm N	Richmond
Day, Ben	Hammond
Dodge, E F	Hammond
Davis, David, me	Brudman
Dinsmore, Wm, f	New Richmond
Davis, David	Richmond
Dwyer, Oliver P	Carrollton, Nov 2—62
Freeland, M A, m	Onawa, Ia
Foster, Wm, h	Batterum Lake
Finnegan P	Richmond
Folger, R J	Hammond
Flint, Geo W	Baton Rouge, Nov 23—61
Federly, Dan'l	Madison, Mar 30—64
Farnham, Henry J	New Orleans, Apr 25—65
Gilmar, Alex*	Baton Rouge, Sept 29—63
Gibson, W R	Cylon
Griffith, —	Cylon
Goodwin, Geo H D	New Orleans, July 13—64
Humphrey, Jno	Cylon
Hamilton, J S	Hammond
Henk, Chas	Watertown
Hoarning, F D	Hudson
Hardington, Jos H	Hudson
Hyslop, Thos*	Baton Rouge, Sept 8—63
Hand, Edw, f	New Richmond
Hatch, Wm W	New Orleans, Aug 23—64
Hays, Geo, sailor	Osceola Mills
Hawley, Jno D	Baton Rouge, Nov 24—61
Hughes, E M	St Joseph
Johnson Dan H*	Camp Beauregard, Nov 13—61
Jones, Dan	St Croix
Johnson, Wm F	Relay House, Nov 13—62
Knowles, C G	River Falls, Minn
Kenyon, M J, miller	Nebraska
Kidder, Alonzo	New Richmond
Kent, Wm, f	Osceola Mills
Law, Columbus, c	New Richmond
Law, Columbus, e	Star Prairie
Lalley, Patrick	Erin Prairie
Madison, Swan	Carrollton, Nov 22—62
Montague, F M	Sau Prairie
McAllister, Wilson	Camp Parapet, Oct 22—62
McGuire, Henry	Richmond
Netterfield, N, h	Taylor Falls, La
Nason, J W F, f	Osceola Mills
Nason, Jas, f	Osceola Mills
Nichols, Chas, f	River Falls
Nichols, Henry, f	River Falls
Noble, J S	Hammond
Nelson, Jas C	South Farming
Palmer, Albion P*	July 15—62
Philbrook, A	Richmond
Prospeck, Jos	New Orleans, Sept 9—63
Parrott, Sol	Richmond
Parrott, Sol	Boardman
Pittijohn, Robt R	Carrollton, Oct 2—62
Peabody, G W	Hammond
Rice, Geo, f	Osceola Mills
Randall, Bice T	Baton Rouge, Oct 23—62
Rodgers, Thos	New Richmond
Smith, Frank C	Baton Rouge, Nov 13—65
Sanceman, Jno	New Richmond
Silvertson, Ed C	Baton Rouge, Oct 2—62
Sussman, J	Richmond
Turnbull, Jno, f	St Croix Falls
Van Meter, Jno H	Hudson
Wade, Chas D	Carrollton, Sept 2—62

H

Capt Jos F Loy

Name	Location/Notes
Capt E J Peck	
Capt A St Ores	
Capt E A Ramsay	
Capt M V Marsh	
Lt W H Young	Oconto
Lt O H Hock	
Lt C B Pearsall	
Lt Jas O'Hare	
Lt Jas Marshal	
Lt F W Palmish	
O'Leary, Dan'l, sgt*	Port Hudson June 14—63
Coppers, Abraham, sgt+	Baton Rouge, Feb 24—64
Haskell, Wm H, sgt+	Port Hudson, June 8—63
Carpenter, Sidney L, corp*	Pt Hudson, May 23—63
Andrews, Rufus, corp*	Clinton, June 3—63
Lanning, Geo W, corp	New Orleans, June 12—62
Briggs, Wm*	Port Hudson, May 27—63
Brown, Jno	New Orleans, Aug 28—62
Cleary, Martin	Elkhorn
Dodge, Albert*	Risland, Apr 13—63
Houhkan, Cornelius*	Port Hudson, June 14—63
Hoffman, Jno	Dec 22—64
Hust, Jos	Baton Rouge, July 26—62
Layman, Valentine*	Port Hudson, May 27—63
Mullett, Franklin*	Port Hudson, June 14—63
Mluniek, Erastus D*	Port Hudson, June 29—63
McCabe, Henry*	Clint n, Mar 5—65
Mansel, Fred'k*	Clinton, Mar 5—65
Melmyre, Alexander	Baton Rouge, Apr 1—64
Marsh, C M	Black Earth
Mueller, August	Green Bay
Newman, Jas*	Port Hudson, June 14—63
Otto, Fred L*	Port Hudson, June 14—63
Perrigo, Wm*	Port Hudson, May 27—63
Spice, R A	Oconto
Tourtillotte, Jas A+	Briton Rouge, Jan 10—63
Thomas, Alexander	Baton Rouge, Nov 26—64
Young, Wm D	Menominee

I

Name	Location/Notes
Capt Jno W Lynn*	July 15—62
Capt Levi R Blake+	Baton Rouge, June 10—63
Capt D G Jewett	
Capt Jas B Farnsworth	
Lt M P Chase	
Lt A A West	
Lt F X Thomas	
Mattison, Jno P, sgt*	Pt Hudson, June 14—63
Leigh, Jno C, sgt	New Orleans, June 2—62
Bush, Wm J, sgt	Carrollton, Nov 8—62
Brist, Manley W, sgt	Pascagoula, Dec 25—64
Bailey, Geo P, sgt	Florence, Dec 1—64
Davidson, Jas H, corp*	Big Black R, June 2—65
Chandler, Jno S, corp+	New Orleans, July 10—63
Hall, Benj P, corp	Carrollton, Sept 10—62
Linsley, Nelson S, corp	Baton Rouge, Oct 10—64
Adolier, Jno	Loyal
Allen, F H, pension agt	Washington
Adams, Chas	Tomah
Brainard, Sam'l R	Relay House, Oct 31—61
Batcheider, Isaiah J	Carrollton, Oct 30—62
Burnet, Edw S	Baton Rouge, Mar 31—61
Coffey, Daniel	Baton Rouge, Aug 14—64
Cook, Walter D	Wilmington, Mar 18—65
Deal, Nicholas*	Pt Hudson, June 14—63
Dodge, Sidney	Menominee
Eaton, Arthur	Menominee
Grenzo, Jno*	Pt Hudson, May 27—63
Goodenough, Leonard*	Pt Hudson, June 14—63
Gailey, Thos S*	Pt Hudson, June 14—63
Gard, Jno R	Baltimore, Dec 11—61
Gillette, Theo	
Henderson, Wm H	Olean, Oct 28—64
Hanson, Brown	Baton Rouge, Sept 18—64
Hill, Jacob	Carrollton, Nov 8—62
Hoghkin, Edw J	Relay House, Aug 21—62
Jewell, Isaac	Rockland
McLane, E P, f	Carrollton, Sept 8—62
	Warrens Mills

Name	Location/Notes
McLain, Eleazer P	Tomah
Parsons, Wm H	New Orleans, Sept 20—62
Post, Sam'l D	Baton Rouge, Mar 26—64
Perry, J T	Neillsville
Read, Thos A	Tomah, Oct 12—61
Stockwell, Chas*	Big Bl ck R, June 2—65
Smith, Jas A	Relay House, Aug 25—61
Saunders, Geo	New Orleans, Aug 11—62
Seymour, Anton	Baton Rouge, June 19—64
Stevens, Alonzo	Baton Rouge, July 5—64
Stevens, Winslow	Hixton
Stanford, Miles	Florence, Dec 1—64
Smith, A B	Avalanche
Sherer, Alf	Tomah
Turner, J F, me	New Richmond
Turner, J F	Richmond
Walker, Solomon C	Baton Rouge, Sept 12—64
Walker, Walter B	Baton Rouge, Nov 19—64
Young, W H	Oconto

K

Name	Location/Notes
Capt H C Hobart	Milwaukee
Capt J B Reynolds	Chilton
Capt R J Needham	
Capt S C Mower	Grand Haven, Mich
Lt Jas Robinson	
Lt Legare Potter	Colby
Lt Stewart Newell	
Lt J W Hurlbart	
Lt Jerry Cunningham	
Breed, Norman F, sgt	New Orleans, Aug 13—62
Daskham, Wm H, sgt	New Orleans, Aug 17—62
Roehr, F Chas, corp*	Port Hudson, May 27—63
Dunlap, Andrew J, corp*	Pt Hudson, June 14—63
Sweet, Jno J, corp*	Port Hudson, June 14—63
Bedell, Marcus D L	Baton Rouge, Sept 3—64
Pettis, Hiram	Greenville, Apr 12—65
Acker, Perry A*	Port Hudson, June 14—63
Bloom, Chas L, f	Biothertown
Brewster, Chas L	New Orleans, Aug 18—64
Barber, Frank A	Baton Rouge, Aug 4—64
Brown, Jno	Beaver Dam
Carr, Hiram W	Jackson, June 3—62
Chicks, Andrew J	Relay House, Oct 22—61
Crouch, Geo	Baton Rouge, Oct 6—64
Craps, Edw	Ship Isl nd, Apr 2—62
Cullen, Jas	New Orleans, June 13—65
Chickering, Dan	Weston
Dutcher, Jas*	Port Hudson, May 27—63
Darling, Jno V	Baton Rouge, July 13—62
Dempsey, Jas	Baton Rouge, Dec 28—64
Dirk, C W	Quincey
Dillet, Jas	Ingalls Run
Forbes, Lorenzo	Ripon
Fowler, Orin	, Ship Island, Apr 3—62
Fendleson, Lexington D	Carrolton, Dec 16—62
Farnham, Wm B	Andersonville, Oct 21—64
Goodrich, Llewellyn D*	July 15—62
Gill, Luke*	Port Hudson, June 14—63
Harrington, Ebenezer J*	Port Hudson, June 14—63
Hart, Jas A	Relay House, Sept 23—61
Hardy, Henry A	Baltimore, Mar 14—62
Lawrence, Albert M	Baton Rouge, Aug 19—63
Laughlin, Robt	New Orleans, Apr 2—65
Lavehe, Fred'k	Baton Rouge, June 3—64
Miller, Wm M*	Pt Hudson, June 14—3
McGee, Chas*	Pt Hudson, June 14—63
McAllister, Jos	New Orleans, Sept 20—62
Maugan, Richard A	Baltimore, Nov 23—61
Morgan, Wm	Fond du Lac, Sept 25—63
McLaughlin, J	New Orleans, Apr 2—65
Marygold, Jas S	Memphis, Feb 20—64
Maloney, Wm, m	Chilton
Orlieb, Otto	New Orleans, May 3—63
Oleson, Tosten	Baton Rouge, June 23—64
Preston, Jno, me	Mazomanie
Plumb, Albert A	Andersonville, June 20—64
Palmer, Chester B	Baton Rouge, Aug 17—62

Thomas S. Allen.   *John Hicks.*

ALLEN & HICKS,

STATIONERS, BOOKSELLERS
AND
PRINTERS.

ARTISTIC

JOB PRINTING

A SPECIALTY.

WRAPPING PAPER,

Grocers' Bags,

Flour Sacks,

&c., &c.

PUBLISHERS OF THE

OSHKOSH NORTH-WESTERN

TERMS OF THE OSHKOSH NORTH-WESTERN:
Weekly, $2.00; Daily, 9.00---Postage Prepaid.

143 Main St., Oshkosh, Wis.

THE CHEAPEST AND BEST PAPER IN WISCONSIN.

SUBSCRIBE NOW!

THE

Wisconsin Farmer,

THE ONLY

Agricultural Paper in the State.

It is published for Wisconsin Farmers, and will stand by Wisconsin Farmers first, last and for all time. No farmer can afford to be without it. It will keep him posted on all subjects pertaining to Agriculture, Horticulture, Stock Raising, Dairying, Apiary, Household, General News and Markets. It is laboring to work a reform in the present system of taxation, a question which affects the farmer more than any other class.

Market Reports,

are unexcelled by any paper in the State. Special attention is given to this department, and can be relied upon as accurate. Send your name in at once and get a sample copy free, and we are confident that you will subscribe for it. Bear in mind that it is the only paper in the State that is not published in the interest of Parties, Cliques or Rings. No political or religious discussions are permitted in its columns.

ONE DOLLAR & FIFTY CENTS,

PAYS FOR THE FARMER.

THE

Saturday Reporter

FOND DU LAC, WIS.

{ J. L. THWING,   { THWING & PILLSBURY,
Editor and Publisher. }   Proprietors.

The REPORTER devotes an unusual amount of space and care, for a paper published outside the hundred thousand cities, to general literature, and verily it is having its reward. Its local columns contain faithful reports furnished by regular correspondents, from all parts of the county and vicinity, excellent general reading, have won for it an extensive home reading and it merits as a family journal have secured for it a wide circulation even where the local information is of comparatively little interest.

TERMS OF SUBSCRIPTION:

One Copy One Year - - $1 50
"   "   six months -   -   75
"   "   four months -   50

Try it for the great Campaign of 1880.

Sample copy sent free to any address on application.

Advertising Rates:

The REPORTER has been found an excellent advertising medium by the best advertisers in the State. Terms reasonable and promptly made known on applying to the publisher.

WISCONSIN SOLDIERS AND SAILORS REUNION ROSTER. 207

Name	Location
Bayles, Albert D	Andersonville, Dec 17—64
Scott, Norman F	Baltimore, Feb 6—62
Watrous, Henry O*	Pt Hudson, May 27—63
Wells, Nehemiah D	Baton Rouge, May 27—64

L

Name	Location
Capt H vonHeyde	
Capt Jos Hall	Decatur, Neb
Lt J G Stock	Madison
Lt A Gainokowsky	
Lt G W Peck, rd	Milwaukee
Haisch, Jno G, sgt	Baton Rouge, June 23—61
Magnussen, Theo, sgt	Fond du Lac
Gauser, Morize, sgt, f	Roxbury
Allmayer, Fred, m	Milwaukee
Gettle, Geo	Baton Rouge, Oct 29 -64
Gundy, Henry	Milwaukee, Nov 16—64
Gauver, Moritz	Sauk City
Holle, Edmund	Baton Rouge, June 24—61
Hober, Julius	Baton Rouge, Oct 21—64
Hanp, Xavier	Baton Rouge, Jan 18—63
Hartmann, Thos O, co clk	Milwaukee
Holstead, G W, f	Marshalltown, Ia
Krebs, Jos	Baton Rouge, Aug 8—61
Kellar, Isaac	Madison, July 15—65
Kumm, Lewis	Dec 22—64
Linzerhuber, Jos	Baton Rouge, Sept 24—65
Magnussen, Theo, sgt, l	Fond du Lac
Mayor, Leon	St Louis, June 18—61
Merhoff, Christopher	Milwaukee, Nov 14—64
Reuther, Anton	Baton Rouge, Oct 29—64
Richards, Arthur B	Baton Rouge, Nov 29—64
Rochon, Henry	Baton Rouge, May 9—61
Stalberg, Christopher E	Milwaukee Nov 5—64
Schoof, John	Baton Rouge Nov 4—64
Swemann, Henry	Milwaukee, Oct 20—64
Schiertz, Aug, c	Milwaukee
Toelle, Wm	Baton Rouge, Oct 23—61
Voigt, Julius,	Baton Rouge, Aug 20—64
Weinschenk, Chas	Baton Rouge, Oct 13—64

M

Name	Location
Capt M B Misner	
Lt Washington Hill	
Lt O W Traynor	
McLain, Jas, sgt	Baton Rouge, July 5—64
Witter, Robt W, corp	Baton Rouge, Jan 4—65
Carter, Wm E	Baton Rouge, Sept 1—62
Conar, Jerome S	Baton Rouge, Sept 25—65
Dougherty, The	Madison, Sept 25—64
Ewings, Jas C	Baton Rouge, Nov 6—64
Henderson, Wm	Madison, June 10—65
Heary, J	White Creek
Johnson, John	Baton Rouge, Aug 15—64
Johnson, John S	Wisconsin, Oct 4—64
Long, John	New Orleans, Nov 12—64
Land, Alpheus	Madison, Apr 2—64
McCord, Wm	Baton Rouge, Sept 2—64
Mahoney, Wm, m	Chilton
Parmelee, P, me	Ripon
Patton, John J	July, 1—65
Powers, John W	Baton Rouge, Apr 29—64
Stone, Emerson	Baton Rouge, Sept 4—64
Sparks, Eli	Carrollton, May 24—64
Trowbridge, Freeman	Baton Rouge, Sept 7—64
Vetter, Jno, f	Scott
Williams, Justus H	Vicksburg, June 30—65

UNASSIGNED.

Name	Location
All, John, f	Ripon
Boynton, Abraham	Maple Grove, D T
Benson, Harrison	Milwaukee
Balcom, D S	Chicago, Ill
Beadleston, Chas	Lind
Dexter, Ed	Waupaca
Foltz, W B	Campbellsport
George, T J, sheriff	Menominee
Gibson, Chas	Tomah
Giffey, Jno, f	Brandon

Name	Location
Giffey, Herman O, f	Brandon
Grey, E B	Chicago, Ill
Hatch, Wm B, Jr	Hudson
Hensey, Chas D	Jefferson
Hughs, Jno	Campbellsport
Heberd, L J	Waupaca
Hatch, Wm B, Jr, ar	St Croix
Kayser, Frank A	Madison
Karfe, Gustav, P M	Plymouth
Lehuen, P	LaCrosse
Lyman, Edwin	Morning Sun, Ia
Meiiner, Fred'k	Grand Rapids
Nells, Daniel D, f	Ripon
Pringle, Fred	Stockbridge
Parks, J H	LaCrosse
Phillips, Jacob	Whitewater
Parker, Calvin	Lind
Richards C	Packwaukee
Stahl, J S	Chicago, Ill
White, H J, Band	St Croix
Winn, Sidney	Cambridge

FIRST HEAVY ARTILLERY.

REGIMENTAL ROSTER.

Name	Location
Col C C Meservey	New York City, N Y
Lt Col J T Foster	Englewood, Ill
Maj A H Drury	Chicago, Ill
Maj it W Hubbell	
Maj D C Fulton	Hudson
Surg W H Borden	
A Surg Ambrose Jones	
A Surg M Waterhouse	
A Surg Ira Manley, Jr	Markesan

A

Three years. Organized June 11th, 1831. Original strength, 129; gain by recruits, etc., 232; total, 361. Death loss, 12—killed in action, 4, died of accidents, 2, of disease, 6. Other losses, 64—missing, 2, desertions, 37, transfers, 4, discharges, 22. Strength at muster-out, August 18, 1865, 286. Campaigns in Virginia.

Name	Location
Capt A J Langworthy, ed	Milwaukee
Capt C C Meservey	N Y City, N Y
Lt Caleb Hunt	Milton June, Jun 1—62
Lt Jno Jameson	Washington, D C
Lt E A Van Wie	St Louis, Mo
Lt P H Ray	U S Army
Lt W A Hopkins	
Lt F L Graves	
Lt G H Van Epps	
Baldwin, Theo*	Bull Run, July 21—61
Beebe, Ezra	Mar 17—64
Boyden, J L	Virginia, Apr 1—63
Calvert R	Battery Rodgers, Dec 14—64
Conn, O N	Fulton
Cooley, A, f	Hebron
Coulthard, Jas A	Troy
Crowley, Jno F	Clear Lake
Dutcher, Wm, f	Loyal
Draper, Francis	Eagle
Flanders, Martin V	Washington, Dec 11—64
Harris, Chas E	Palmyra
Hyde, Wm H*	Bull Run, July 21—61
Kanouse, E, ph	Columbus
Markley, Norman	Eagle
Oatman, Jacob F*	Bull Run, July 21—61
Olds, Jno	Little Prairie
Palmer, Jno	Ft Cass, Oct 29 62
Pond, Lulon	Westfield
Plugh, Byron T	Westfield
Reeves, Andrew J	Eagle
Rogers, Horace	Battery Rodgers, Jan 2—65
Scott, M L	Troy Centre
Short, Jno	Lagrange Centre

Name	Location
Stevens, Jerome	Jefferson
Ten Eyck, Andrew J	Fulton
Terwilliger, A, f	Adams
Trapp, Andrew	Waterloo
Tudder, A L	Whitewater
Tucker, Chas E*	Bull Run, July 21—61
Wade, G P	Battery Rodgers, Sept 21—64

B

Three years. Organized Aug 22, Sept 9, 1863. Original strength, 184; gain by recruits, etc., 59. Total, 183. Death loss, 7—Killed in action, 0, died of accidents, 1, of disease, 6. Other loss s, 73, missing, 0, desertions, 17, transfers, 16, discharges, 40. Strength at muster out Aug 30, 1865, 103. Campaigns in Ky., Va., Tenn.— "Morgan raid" June 8 and 10, 1864—Saltville, Va., and Cumberland Gap—Section of Battery took part in Gen Burbridge's raid after Morgan, in the mountains of eastern Kentucky, which resulted in the capture of Mt. Sterling and Cynthiana, Ky. At the latter place capturing 60 of Morgan's men, whom this battery guarded for several days at Fort Clay, Lexington, Ky.

Name	Location
Baker, H R L, corp, f	Menominee Falls
Bramley, Jno	Mumfordsville, Oct 28—63
Carpenter, M F	Fond du Lac
Cole, Judson R	Helena, Col
Cook, Jno H	Chippewa Falls
Fowle, Royal A	Louisville, Jan 14—64
Geb, Jacob	Racine
Gould, Levi, me	Chicago, Ill
Holmes, L O	Baraboo
Hasted, S H	Eagle Lake, Minn
Kellogg, O F, corp	Lexington, Mar 12—64
McLaughlin, I H	Trimbelle
Palmer, Chas B	Lincoln, Neb
Rice, Truman	Methd
Schultz, Gustave	Lexington, May 11—65
Sebastian, Herbert	Racine
Sherman, M S	Jeff Barracks, Apr 1—64
Sierns, E C	South Haven, Mich
Uth r, Dwight, f	Mission
Warner, S P, f	Mukwonago
Weeks, Chas H	Marshfield
Wood, A G	Camp Nelson, Aug 10—65

C

Three years. Organized October 1st, 1863. Original strength, 146; gain by recruits, etc., 25; total, 171. Death loss, 8—killed in action, 0, died of wounds, 0, of disease, 8. Other losses, 33—missing, 0, desertions, 7, transfers, 1, discharges, 31. Strength at muster-out Sept. 21st 1865, 124. Campaigns in Tenn.

Name	Location
Capt J R Davis	Milwaukee
Lt E R Lisk	
Lt Jno Silsby	
Lt B F Parker	
Lt Fred'k Ullmann	
Lt W S Tefft	
Lt E D Hewitt	
Aderhold, Aug	Nashville, Feb 1—64
Benedict, C, Jr	Buttes des Morts
Carpenter, Wm	Madison, Dec 25—64
Carro, Wm	Racine
Collins, Jno A	Janesville
Culver, H A, a	Richland Centre
Deitz, Jno, f	Rice Lake
Doughty, A	Winneconne
Ellis, Ed B	Chattanooga, Mar 21—65
Ferris, Elisha P	Omro
Fountain, Chas H	Lone Rock
James, W G	Eagle
Johnson, C A	Chattanooga, Apr 26—64
Judd, Pat	Barboo
Loomis, Geo	Chattanooga, Feb 16—64
Lum, Allen D	Racine

M. F. HOPPES, Pres't. SAM'L M. CRAFT, Vice-Pres't.
JOHN D. MACINTYRE, Sec'y.

Fire Insurance Co.,

113 BROADWAY, NEW YORK.

Assets,   -   -   - $338,778.08.
Liabilities,   -   - $84,242.00.

INSURANCE COMPANY
—OF—
NORTH AMERICA.
PHILADELPHIA, PA.

ORGANIZED 1794.

The History of the "OLD" INSURANCE CO. of NORTH AMERICA during the eventful 10 years just closed, is marked. Salient points in its History.

1—*Increase of Capital Stock from*..$ 500,000.00 to $2,000,000.00
2—*Increase of Assets from* .... 2,783,580.96 to 6,591,749.18
3—*Increase of Net Surplus from*.... 1,000,587.95 to 2,414,461.51
4—*Increase of Surplus as regards*
  Policy-Holders from............ 1,500,587.95 to 4,414,461.51
5—The prompt payment of the CHICAGO and BOSTON LOSSES of 1871-2, amounting to over $1,000,000, without impairing the Capital of the Company, or calling upon the Stockholders for a dollar!
6 —The paym'nt of Losses, in the 10 years, amounting to over $21,400,000—making Total Losses Paid since organization, over $17,500,000!
7—The remarkable fact that the Company's Stock is now worth over $7.00 for every $1.00 of par value!
Write to the Company or apply to nearest Agent.

Dr. J. A. SHERMAN—Is the Original and only Dr. SHERMAN known to the public for the past 35 years or more through his successful method of treating Rupture without the annoyance and injury trusses inflict. His system of cure is by local external application.

No man is safe who has a rupture, no matter how insignificant he may consider it, for every man who has died from it once flattered himself that it was but a trifling ailment; and every man who now suffers from it and the injury of trusses, to such an extent that life had no enjoyments, once regarded it as unworthy special attention. It is not a stand still addition; it is progressive, even unto death. References given to gentlemen in the city, who have been cured. During treatment no hindrance from labor. Patients from abroad can receive treatment and leave for home same day.

HIS BOOK ON RUPTURE

gives the most reliable proofs from distinguished professional gentlemen, clergymen and merchants his successful practice and popularity therefrom throughout this country and the West Indies.

The afflicted should read it and inform themselves of the certainty of being cured.

It is illustrated with photographic likenesses of extremely bad cases before and after cure, and mailed to those who send 10 cents. Save this, and remember in writing or calling the address is

DR. J. A. SHERMAN,
251 Broadway, Corner Murray Street, New York.

THE UNITED STATES
Life Insurance Co.,
IN THE CITY OF NEW YORK.

INCORPORATED 1850.

261, 262 AND 263 BROADWAY,   -   NEW YORK.

ASSETS,..............................$1,874,947.01
SURPLUS,............................. $820,883.09

JAMES BUELL, President.   C. P. FRALEIGH, Secretary.
T. H. BROSNAN, Supt. of Agencies.   GEO. H. BURFORD, Actuary.

All Forms of Life and Endowment Policies Issued.

THE CONVERTIBLE POLICY

Is issued by no other Company, and is considered by financiers and business men as the most desirable form of Life Insurance ever offered to the public.

The convertible plan avoids all the objections to Insurance as ordinarily offered for the following reasons:
First—All Premiums cease at the age of 65.
Second—If, on reaching that age, you still need Insurance, the policy continues in full force, the annual dividends increasing the amount of Insurance.
Third—If, at the age of 65, you no longer need Insurance, the Company will issue in lieu of the Policy an "Annuity Bond," stipulating that, annually, during the remainder of the life-time of the insured, the Company will pay to the policy-holder a sum equal to Seven per cent. per annum, upon the face of the Policy and its additions.
Send to company's Office for Circular giving full particulars.

WISCONSIN SOLDIERS AND SAILORS REUNION ROSTER.

Olesen, Dan'l — Davenport, June 30–65
Owens, Edw — Oshkosh
Phillips, Sam'l J — Keokuk, Aug 16–64
Mann, Jacob — Lime Rock
Miller, T O — Winneconne
Morey, Darius J — Racine
Raught, G M — Kaukauna
Rettman, A — Kenosha
Roberts, Griffith — Madison, Dec 29–64
Schneider, Frank — Racine
Schruder, Wm — Seymour
Sharp, Jno B — New Milford, Conn
Spencer, Chas D, f — Baraboo

D

Three years. Organized Nov. 7th, 1863. Original strength, 146, gain by recruits, etc., 64, Total, 230. Death loss, 39—Killed in action, 0, died of accidents, 3, of disease, 33, Other losses, 81—missing, 0, desertions, 9, transfers, 5, discharges, 67. Strength at muster-out, Aug 18th, 1865, 110. Campaigns in La. and Va.

Capt H W Peck
Capt C V Bridge
Lt J E Henry
Lt Isaiah Culver
Lt C M Ball
Lt W M Hanehett
Lt Richard Glennan
Lt J L Utley
Austin, S — Dec 22–64
Baker, Jno W — New Orleans, Dec 11 64
Bennett, C F — Cairo, Sept 28 - 64
Cadwell, S J — Mazomanie
Clemens, J N — Pedee
Cole, H F — Rock, Oct 17–64
Crocker, J B — Brashear City, Mar 8 65
Driscoll, Jer — Brashear City, Nov 24–64
Day, Sam'l W — Ft Jackson, Jan 21–64
Bley, Erastus — Feb 6–64
Filatrean, Paul — Ft Jackson, July 28–64
Gerity, Jas — Jefferson
Griffin, H E, f — South Haven, Mich
Hill, Geo S — Cairo, Oct 1–64
Huntley, R — Neillsville
Jones, Peter — Ft Berwick, Aug 22–64
Jones, Geo J — Brashear City, Dec 3–64
Kyle, Jno H — Ft Jackson, Mar 14 64
Loveland, H — Dec 22–64
Lovelace, Jos — Wicta
Mahan, Peter — Ft Berwick, Aug 23–64
McKinney, Alonzo — Ft Jackson, July 22–61
Macbam, W R — Ft Jackson, July 1–64
Mellor, Sam'l H — Brashear City, Nov 6–64
Miller, G W, sgt — Chicago, Aug 23–64
Ostrander, T S — Ft Berwick, Sept 1–64
Ostrander, Jno H, f — Oakley
Overacre, W H — Milwaukee, Feb 5–64
Perry, Dan'l W — New Orleans, Nov 14–64
Perry, Phil — Ft Jackson, June 1–64
Pierce, Otis — Ft Jackson, July 24–64
Rainboth, Jno — Ft Jackson, June 24–64
Resa, Chas — Ft Jackson, July 24–64
Sawin, Wm A — Ft Berwick, Oct 25–64
Seeley, Norman — New Orleans, Feb 21–61
Slaughtman, Aug — New Orleans, Feb 21–64
Sowles, Jas W — Ft Berwick, Oct 9–64
Spencer, A M — Libley, Ia
Spencer, T — Fargo, D T
Stolp, Jno — Fall River
Thomas, Wm H — Ft Berwick, Sept 29–64
Townsend, H W — Ft Berwick, Sept 13–64
Wagner, Bernard — Ft Berwick, Oct 23–64
Wardwell, E — Ft Berwick, Sept 9–64
Webb, DeWitt — Ft Jackson
Wells, David O — Madison, Mar 31–65
Williams, Geo D — New Orleans, Sept 15–64
Williams, Seth C — Oakley
Wilson, Jno — Ft Berwick, Aug 10–64

E

One year. Organized Oct 3d, 1864. Original strength, 151; gain by recruits, etc., 2. Total, 153. Death loss, 2—killed in action, 0, died of wounds, 0, of disease, 2. Other losses 1—miss ing, 0, desertions, 0, transfers, 0, discharges, 1 Strength at muster out, June 26, 1865, 150. Campaign in Va.

Capt N J H Potter — San Francisco, Cal
Lt A J Garrett — Chicago
Lt Elverton Bigelow — Maple Landing, Ia
Lt J J Gibbs
Lt H G Billings — Chicago
Beeden, Jno — Fort Lyon, Apr 12–65
Beoze, Marshall — Fort Berwick, Sept 10–64
Garrett, A J — Chicago, Ill
Goff, Sidney C — Elkhorn
Hicker, Jno, me — Sun Prairie
Henry, Russell — Fort Lyon, June 25–65
Hummel, Jno — Fort Atkinson
Jacynth, Phineas — Boltonville
Jobbins, Albert — Bedford, Ia
Johnson, Henry M, me — Milton
Knapp, Luke — Exira, Ia
Rockwell, A F — North Wells, Mich
Somhoff, Ang, m — Madison
Southoff, Wm, me — Madison

F

One Year. Organized Oct 3d, 1864. Original strength, 151; gain by recruits, etc., 2. Total, 151. Death loss, 0—killed in action, 0, died of wounds, 0, of disease, 0. Other losses, 7—miss ing, 0, desertions, 0, transfers, 1, discharges, 6. Strength at muster out June 26, 1865, 146. Campaign in Va.

Capt Erastus Cook
Capt J S W Pardee
Lt H Fenner
Lt A P Peck
Lt Thos Graham
Lt J H Anderson
Lt J C Blodget
Billington, B C — Arena
Burnett, Clarence — Black Earth
Carew, Jas — Little Wolf
Cutting, A J — Racine
Edwards, Jno — Racine
Finch, Chas F — Racine
Gallien, Abraham — Racine
Garrett, Jno G, m — Chicago, Ill
Haas, Jacob K — Racine
Hudson, Wm — Baraboo
Moorefield, Thos — Elkhorn
Morris, T W — Peterson, Ia
Moulton, F F — Mazomanie
Moulton, F S — Mazomanie
Neale, Robt M — Packwaukee
Nield, Henry — Racine
Peavy, M D — Arena
Peck, A C — Mazomanie
Quackenbush, Reuben W — Thayer, Neb
Randall, S F — Darien
Reeve, Geo C — Dodgeville
Robinson, B — Spring Green
Smith, Rufus B — Madison
Town, D H — Strongs Prairie
White, Marshall — Racine
White, A F, f — Delton

G

One Year. Organized November, 12th, 1864. Original strength, 152; gained by recruits, etc. 4. Total, 156. Death loss, 1 — Killed in action, 0; died of wounds, 0, of disease, 1. Other losses,—11 missing, 0, desertions, 0, transfers, 1, discharges, 10. Strength at muster-out, June 26, 1865, 144. Cam-

paigns in Va.
Capt H F Rouse
Lt M E Stevens
Lt S A Phoenix
Lt Wm Fallows
Lt Robt Bullen — Elba, Minn
Banks, Dan'l C — Kilbourn City
Chapin, E W — Neosho
Cooley, Frank C — Washington, Dec 9–64
Crites, Alex, f — Burlington
Dinwiddie, Clark — Scutt
Goodenough, W H — Paton, Ia
Fauder, Ben, f — Burlington
French, Jno D — Lamartine
Hambline, B, A. — Pickets Station
Hedding, Jas — Port Washington Wis.
Krakasky, Fred, f — Burlington
Lange, Wm, f — Plymouth
Marcellus, Jno — Boltonville
McCrendy, W C — Fond du Lac
Morefield, T W — Elkhorn
North, B f, — Mazomanie
Pease, Henry, f — Eldorado Mills
Powell, H — Eldorado Mil's
Schleler, Philip — Plymouth

H

One year. Organized October 7, 1864. Original strength, 151; gain by recruits, etc., 3. Total, 154. Death loss, 0—killed in action, 0, died of wounds, 0, of disease, 0. Other losses, 10, —missing, 0, desertions, 0, transfers, 0, discharges, 10. Strength at muster out, June 26th, 1865, 144. Campaigns in Va.

Capt Chas S Taylor
Lt A F Mattice
Lt Chas E Hoyt — Madison
Lt A E Blittimore — US Army
Lt J P Blakeslee
Lt Jno Corey — Madison
Ausburne, W J — Jacksonport
Austin, Nelson — Winchester
Benedict, Allen S — Seymour
Chalmer, Jno, sgt, f — Sun Prairie
Christiansen, Christian — Navarena
Cone, A E — Waterloo
Holdman, Jacob — Milwaukee
Hoyt, C E, p — Madison
Kittelson, Ole, Sr — Winchester
Kittelson, Ole, Jr — Winchester
Knudsen, Aug — Winchester
Ludington, Jas L. — Albany
Oleson, Johannes — Albaton, La
Parker, Jno, f — York
Pengilly, Henry L. — Mazeppa, Minn
Shepherd, S — Seymour
Souby, Ole — Winchester
Thompson, A E — Deansville
Thompson, Amos, corp, m — Marshall
Warner, Francis T, sgt — Deansville
Wentworth, W G — Ft Atkinson

I

One year. Organized Nov 12th, 1864. Original strength, 150; gain by recruits, etc., 13. Total 163. Death loss, 1—killed in action, 0, died of wounds, 0, of disease, 1. Other losses, 10—miss ing, 0, desertions, 0 transfers, 0, discharges, 10. Strength at muster out, 152. Campaigns in Va.

Capt D H Saxton — Charles City, Ia
Lt J S Daniels
Lt J H McLaughlin
Lt S S Johnston
Lt S S Leavitt
Lt G J Jarvis
Lt E A Gibbon
Lt S D Forbes
Alcox, J H, o — Whitewater

ESTABLISHED IN 1846.

DAILY AND WEEKLY.

The Fond du Lac Journal.

DEMOCRATIC BUT NOT PARTISAN.

As a Source of Reading.

Carefully compiled general news.

Full reports of county and state intelligence.

Complete and racy local pages.

Interesting Scientific and home departments.

Several columns of choice miscellaneous and humorous selections.

As an Advertising Medium.

Its circulation is as large as that of any paper in this section.

It is the only democractic paper in the county.

It is the official paper of the county and the recognized reference for all classes.

It circulates largely among farmers who read no other paper.

Its rates are reasonable.

Morning Journal

Is published every day in the year but Sunday, at fifteen cents per week.

JAS. RUSSELL, EDITOR & PROPRIETOR.

The Star Steam Printing House

Being the publication office of the Reunion Roster, and the largest and most complete Job Printing establishment in northern Wisconsin.

WISCONSIN SOLDIERS AND SAILORS REUNION ROSTER.

Dear, I, t — Menominee Falls
Brensman, Henry — Berlin
Chase, A E, me — Harrison
Gibson, Chas — Lind
Gibson, Wm, me — Lind
Hair, Wm — Lind
Huss, Jos M — Montello
Pope, Lester — Lind
Roberts, Thos H — Washington, Nov 2 —64
Selleck, Albert — Lind
Southoff, Wm — Mazomanie
Wilson, Chas — Waupaca

K

One year. Organized Oct 17th, 1864. Original strength, 164; gain by recruits, etc., 9. Total, 167. Death loss, 0—killed in action, 0, died of wounds, 0, of disease, 0. Other losses, 13—missing, 0, desertions, 3, transfers, 0, discharges, 10. Strength at muster out June 26, 1865, 144. Campaigns, in Va.
Capt W H Jennings
Lt Isaac U Jeunings
Lt A H Amos
Lt Chas Law
Lt Albert McNitt
Lt J E O'Neil
Bouchard, F J, justice — Milwaukee
David, Benj, f — Burlington
Davis, C A — Burlington
Goodwin, E O — Marshfield
TenEyck A G — Fulton
Walker, P, f — New London
Whitcomb, D H — Janesville

L

One year. Organized September 30th, 1864. Original strength, 155. Death loss, 0—Killed in action, 0, died of wounds, 0, of disease, 0. Other losses, 10—missing, 0, desertions, 0, transfers, r, discharges, 10. Strength at muster-out, June 26th, 1865, 145. Campaigns in Va.
Capt P H May — U S Army
Lt Edw Goodman
Lt O W Wallace — Chicago
Lt A S Trowbridge
Lt F O Ball
Lt S S Colton
Lt D W Cameron
Bailey, Nelson, f — San Prairie
Babcock, Caritou — Troy Centre
Cooley, A — Jefferson
Greenwood, Geo, f — Liberty Grove
Johnson, M — Jefferson
Minnette, Frank — Troy Centre
Morrow, Wm — Deansville
Pond, Henry — Fredericksburg, Ia
Rounds, C B — Mount Sterling
Vanderveort, Isaac — Tomah
Woodward, A S — Genoa

M

One year. Organized Sept 30th, 1864. Original strength, 152, gain by recruits, etc., 2. Total, 154. Death loss, 3—Killed in action, 0, died of wounds, 0, of disease, 3. Other losses, 6—missing, 0, desertions, 8, transfers, 0, discharges, 6. Strength at muster-out, June 26th, 1865, 145. Campaigns in Va.
Capt Ira H Ford
Lt Wm A Coleman
Lt O A Southmayd — Portage
Lt A J Close — Kansas City, Mo
Lt H R Lull
Maj C C Meservy — New York City
Bailey, Nelson R — Sun Prairie

Bray, Stephen R
Breese, J S
Dow, Joel C
Greenslit, Henry, f
Hovey, Jno W
Hubbard, O
Loveless, S S
Peevy, Wm H
Scott, J T, sheriff
Strong, W W, l
Scott, J H
Swan, R M, sgt, f
Trevett, E M

UNASSIGNED.

Behrend, Gustav
Bennett, Wm
Benedict, Cyrus
Billings, D D
Byron, Henry
Buck, Jno, M, me
Butterfield, H
Chambers, Isaac
Clements, Wm
Coulhard, Jas A
Daniel, Jno J, f
Davis, Jno
Dibble, H M, f
Day, O
Chambers, Isaac
Conrad, Aug
Ferney, Lewis
Gifford, F M, f
Huff, A J
Henry, T M
Jenkins, Wm H, sgt
Jenkins, Iran
Johnson, Andrew E, f
Kinder, David
LaLone, Jos, f
Libby, G A
Merkley, H
Miller, T G
Moore, Robt, f
Owens, Ed
Parks, Jno
Raethel, Martine, f
Rogers, E D
Rogers, Horea
Schulleder, Theo, cl
Schultz, Wm
Schwaris, Jno
Smith, H A
Voll, Jno, f
Webster, E H
Wesdman, Jno
Weston, Jno F, c

MILWAUKEE CAVALRY.

Three years. Organized Sept, 23d, 1861. Original strength 83. Gained by recruits, etc, 10. Total, 93. [No Report.] Body guard to Gen Fremont, afterwards incorporated as Co. M, Fourth Wis, Cavalry, with which regiment they served until the expiration of their term of service.
Capt E von Deutsch
Lt Chas Lehman
Lt P Iesi
Lt A Galoskowsky

FIRST ARMY CORPS IN-FANTRY.

[No Report.]

Ft Lyon, Dec 13—64
Wonewoc
Ft Lyon, May 27—65
Baraboo
Emmettsburg
Mazomanie
Neillsville
Ft Lyon, Nov 20—61
Bedford, Ia
Brandon
Cora, Kan
Sun Prairie
Pine Bluff

Oshkosh
Eau Claire
Butts des Mortes
Olin
Appleton
Rome
Baraboo
Racine
Shells Station
Troy
Rom
Racine
Rome
Buttes des Morts
Racine
LaGrange
Neenah
Rome
Randolf, Minn
Kenosha
Shells Station
Oshkosh
Moline, Neb
Sabula, Ia
Juneau
Janesville
Neenah
Winneconne
Rome
Oshkosh
Neenah
Rome
Necedah
Winneconne
Green Bay
Baraboo
Baraboo
Ft Atkinson
Rome
Greenbush
Oshkosh
Delmar Junction, Ia

LIGHT ARTILLERY.

FIRST BATTERY.

Three years. Organized Oct.30th, 1861. Original strength, 185, gain by recruits etc, 146. Total 303. Death loss, 27—Killed in action, 1. died of wounds, 3, of disease, 22, of accidents 1. Other losses, 64—missing, 0, desertions, 7, transfers, 14, discharges, 42. Strength at muster-out July 18th, 1865, 212. Campaigns, in Ky., Tenn., Miss., &c.
Capt J T Foster, Union Stock Yards Chicago, Ill
Capt Dan'l Webster
Lt O F Nutting — LaCrosse
Lt J D Anderson
Lt C B Kimball — San Francisco, Cal
Lt A W Bishop — Arkansas
Lt E L Hackett — LaCrosse
Lt E P Aylmer — New Orleans, July 13—64
Lt E E Stewart — Caledonia, Minn
Surg Wm Hobbins
Surg H W Causdell
Armstrong, C — St Louis, Aug 2—63
Barter, C K — Taylor
Basford, Wesley — New Orleans, Mar 29—64
Beal, Whitney A — Geneva Lake
Beckwith, Ed S — Elkhorn
Bigby, D — LaCrosse
Bigelow, W H — Maple Landing, Ia
Buforu, R O — Tayubeedah
Blake, L D, co treas — Black River Falls
Bradfield, N — LaCrosse
Bradfield, B — Eureka
Bardt, H H T — Neenah
Brass, Louis — Vicksburg—63
Bunn, F M — May 19—61
Burnton, Henry — LaCrosse
Bushwell, P — Louisville, Sep 14—62
Cameron, Silas
Cameron, D C, supt of schools — LaCrescent, Minn
Cameron, D C — LaCrosse
Carre, Wm — Chicago, Ill
Carson, Peter — LaCrosse
Chase, Sam'l I — New Orleans, Mar 9—64
Clark, E B — LaCrosse
Clark, D W — Millikens Bend, 11—64
Cotton, S S — Palmyra
Crawford, Jas B — Westfield
Crawford, Jno — Westfield
Dalton, G — LaCrosse
Dalton, J W — Canton, D T
Darrell, Ambrose, pa — East Troy
Davidson, J — LaCrosse
Delane, Jas — Neillsville
Dickerman, Joshua — Spencer
Dodge, J D — Hebron
Ernest, Michael — Kenosha
Finch, S, f — Whitewater
Foster, Wm — Millikens Bend, Apr 11 —64
Gale, Geo W, p m — Galesville
Garner, M — LaCrosse
Hall, Byron E — Bangor
Hargrave, M — LaCrosse
Harris, Edson J — Youngs Point, Feb 8—64
Hewn, O N — Canton, D T
Hayden, H — Rocky Springs, May 6—63
Hewitt, C — LaCrosse
Hewitt Edwin P — Lexington, Apr 16—62
Howard, W M — East Troy
Hoyt, Sam'l — Sparta
King, Chas E — Trempeleau, Jan 18—62
Kittleson, Ole — Neenah
Lange, Wm — Plymouth
Ledyard, N D, corp — Brashear City, Sep 17—63
Libenstern, Phillip — Scott
Longnan, Jos, f — Fond du Lac
Mugill, Jas A+ — Grand Gulf, May 5—63
Matesou, W+ — Chickasaw, Dec 29—62

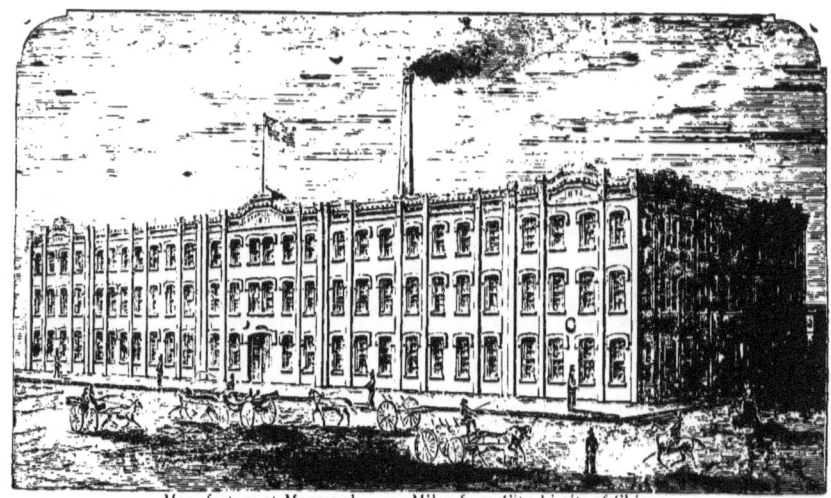

Manufactory at Maywood—5 1-2 Miles from City Limits of Chicago.

Patented Feb. 27, '79.   CHICAGO SCREW PULVERIZER, PULVERIZING THE GROUND AND SEEDING AT ONE OPERATION.
Address, MAYWOOD CO., Maywood, Ill.

WISCONSIN SOLDIERS AND SAILORS REUNION ROSTER.

McConnell, David — Youngs Point, Jan 29–63
McConnell, J — LaCrosse
McKeith, Wm, lumberman — Galesville
McKeith, Jno, f — Galesville
Meigs, Henry E — Youngs Point, June 5–63
Moulton, N H — Chicago, Ill
Murphy, Wm — Youngs Point, Feb 26–63
Owen, J J, sgt — Chicago, Ill
Peck, I — LaCrosse
Pier, Mike l — East Troy
Pierce, Nathaniel, butcher — Berlin
Pond, Simeon — Westfield
Ramsey, W D — New Orleans, Mar 31–64
Randless, Jas W — Youngs Point, Mar 9–63
Read, Jno, m — Neillsville
Reiley, W O D — Berlin
Reynolds, Jno — Mishicott
Richards, W F — Jeff Barracks, Feb 2–63
Rodman, Erasmus E* — Vicksburg, June 7–63
Scott, G W — LaCrosse
Smith, Gilbert — New Orleans, Aug 3–64
Snyder, Herman — New Orleans, July 26–64
Sowle, A W — LaCrosse
Stewart, E — LaCrosse
Stewart, E E — Caledonia, Minn
Summerfield, Wm J — Sparta
Thomas, Griff J — Berlin
Wable, L — LaCrosse
Walker, Wm H — Lexington, Mar 21–63
Waters, Chas L — Memphis, July 20–63
Webster, B — LaCrosse
Webster, Dan'l, p — Dennison, Texas
Whipple, Rufus — Olsville
Withee, Chas+ — Memphis, June 15–63

SECOND BATTERY.

Three years. Organized Oct 10, 1861. Original strength, 163; gain by recruits, etc., 90. Total, 243. Death loss, 12—killed in action, 0, died of wounds, 0, of disease, 12. Other losses, 13—missing 0, desertions, 6, transfers, 7, discharges, 30. Strength at muster out— 188. Campaigns in Va., Md.

Capt Ernst P Herzberg
Capt Chas Beger
Lt J C Her Von Schleu,
Lt Jno Belander
Lt Chas Schulz
Lt Chas Snipe
Lt C J Emil Stephen
Lt Jno Schabel
Lt Lewis Rabe
Lt August Bushwald
Lt Edw Hanson
Lt Geo Fischer
Ballus, Aug — Oct 26–62
Bergmiller, Max — Muscoda
Bettinger, Philip — Muscoda
Cress, Edw — Yorktown, Sept 14–63
Cuntant, Peter — Camp Hamilton, Oct 28–62
Droxler, Andreas — Ft Monroe, Aug 24–62
Engler, J J — Elmore
Fickler, Fred'k — Yorktown, Sept 29–63
Faellemier, Jos, l — Fond du Lac
Frey, Fred'k — Yorktown, Sept 14–63
Frohmonn, Aug — Scott
Haight, J H, m — Brothertown
Horn, Chas — Woodland
Kapha, Martin, me — Hingham
Kissel, Christian — Point Lookout. Sept 29–63
Kohn, Frank — Auburn
Krueger, Christian, — Ridgeway
Mann, Fred'k
Mueller, Wilhelm — Fort Monroe, Feb 26–62
Newdrok, Edw — Golden Colorado
Olson, A — Winneconne
Ranch, Geo, f — Elmore
Ranch, Elvir, c — Elmore
Reingruber, Thos — Yorktown, Oct 1–63
Richter, Chas F — Yorktown, Sept 19–63

Turk, Wm — YorktownJuly, 20–62

THIRD BATTERY.

Three years. Organized Oct 10, 1861. Original strength, 170; gain by recruits, etc., 100. Total, 270. Death loss, 26—killed in action, 2, died of wounds, 3, of disease, 21. Other losses 67—missing, 9, desertions, 3, transfers, 4, discharges 60. Strength at muster out, July 20th, 1945, 177. Campaigns in Ky., Tenn., Miss., Ala.

Capt Ira H Drury — Chicago, Ill
Lt Cortland Livingston — Boston, Mass
Lt Hiram F Hubbard — Ashland, O
Lt Jas P Purdy
Lt Henry Currier — Concord, Minn
Lt Albert Lestrun
Lt Webster J Colluro — Chattanooga, Tenn
Allen, Wm — Rushford
Armstrong, Gilbert S, f — Berlin
Bacon, Dan'l — Hamburg, May 7–62
Bates, Joel — Stevens Point
Best, Nathan — Nashville, Apr 8–62
Billings, F C, me — Madison
Bradt, H H G — Rushford
Bryant, Albert C — Stevenson, Sept 19–63
Burr, Eugene — Corinth, July 7–62
Carter, Jas W — Stevens Point
Chapin, Titus B — Andersonville–64
Clark, M A — Murfreesboro, Jan 28–63
Crimmings, Maurice
Delaney, Isaac — Rushford
Davis, Cassins M C — Madison, Aug 14–64
Decker, G E, sgt — Andersonville, Sept 11–64
Dibble, Morean W — Murfreesboro, May 13–63
Edgerton, S K — Savannah, Apr 11–62
Edgerton, W J — Corinth, June 25–61
Fessenden, T S — Spring Valley, D T
Frost, Ed — Plover Field
Galloway, Jno D, m — Berlin
Graham, Dan'l — Clifton
Hanley, Thomas — Andersonville, Aug–64
Harronn, Edw — Prineton
Harvay, E N, f — Lake Mills
Hays, Ansel — Dolceville
Hess, Henry E — Danville, Feb–64
Hoag, Hermin — Corinth, June 1–62
Hubbard, Chas W* — Chickamauga, Sept 20–63
Hunt, H F — Almond
Jarvis, Geo J, a — Richland Centre
Kanouse,Thos D — Watertown
Kanouse, A W — Columbus
Lambert, Thos. me — Ripon
Lewis, Jos H, c — Berlin
Livingston, Jas M — Stevens Point
McIntyre, Wm — Wisconsin, Jan 3–63
McMahon, Wm — Andersonville, July 1–64
Noble, Arza J l- — Chattanooga, Sept 27–63
Ostrander, Jno W, pr — Chicago, Ill
Palmer, Sam'l B+ — Chattanooga, Oct 8–63
Palmer, Herman B — Almond, Feb–64
Preston, Jas — Algona, Ia
Quimby, L — Plainfield
Randall, Dan'l S — Savannah, May 29–62
Scanlin, Michael — Buena Vista
Schyler, Abram — Shelbyville, Minn
Sheffield, Andrew M — Atica, O
Sickles, Chas* — Kenesaw Mt, June 26–64
Smith, Edgar — Columbus, Apr 15–62
Stevens, Hassell D+ — Chattanooga, Sept 24–63
Stilwell, R R — Port Byron, N Y
Terwilleger, Geo — Troy
Treet, L — Jefferson
Uline, Leonard J, corp — Oct 15–63
Van Slyke, Hiland — Lake Mills
Vedder, Chauncy, l — Berlin
Walker, L S — Plainfield
Washburn, Henry — Plainfield

FOURTH BATTERY.

Three years. Organized October 1st, 1865,

Original strength, 157, gain by recruits, etc., 143.
Total, 294. Death loss, 24—Killed in action, 2, died of wounds, 0, of disease. 21, of accidents, 1. Other losses, 99—missing, 1, desertions, 15, transfers, 1, discharges, 62. Strength at muster-out, July 3d, 1865, 171. Campaigns in Va.

Capt Jno F Vallee
Capt George D Easterly
Capt Dorman I. Noggle
Lt Martin H McDevitt
Lt Wm P Powers — LaCrosse
Lt Burr Maxwell
Lt Spencer S Hillier
Lt Robt Campbell
Lt Andrew H Hunt
Lt Chas A Rathbun
Lt Geo R Wright
Lt Delos H Cady
Lt Alexander See
Lt Levi Westinghouse
Lt Benj Brown
Abbott, Wm, me — Belvidere
Baker, C — Madison, Apr 5–64
Barry, D W — Yorktown, Sept 7–63
Bently, D — Ft Monroe, July 5–62
Bingham, W — Hampton, July 17–63
Boyington, H H — Chicago, Ill
Bullard, H D, ph — Delavan
Butler, Robt J — Beloit
Cavney, J — Pt Lookout, Sept 6–64
Chariott, E A — Monroe, Oct 30–63
Clark, A, corp — Hampton, Sept 13–63
Cobb, C W — Gloucester Pt, Sept 18–62
Collins, Alonzo — Dubuque, Ia
Dole, A P — Chicago
Dresser, A S — Portsmouth, July 29–64
Ellison, Wesley, f — Delavan
Graves, W I — Yorktown, July 30–63
Graves, J H, sgt* — Richmond, Sept 29–64
Guetzkow, Henry — Tuss Corners
Hall, E W — Jackson, Miss
Hellick, Ole — Yorktown, Aug 6–63
Hutchinson, John C, me — Necedah
Isaacson, L C+ — Darbytown Road, Oct 7–64
Jones, S J, m — Belvidere, Ill
Kelly, Thos — Beloit
Knell, S — Portsmouth, Apr 5–64
Latinon, Jos — Pensaukee
Lavine, P — Neillsville
McCalhran, Neil — Hampton, Sept 12–63
McDonald, Thos — Hampton, Apr 4–64
Oleson, C — Ft Monroe, May 27–62
Palmer, E M, sgt, me — Harrison
Parker, J E — LaCrosse
Pierce, A H — Menominee
Powers, W P — LaCrosse
Ries, J F — North Hudson
Russell, Henry C, pa — Detroit
Saner, Geo — Hampton, Aug 7–64
Lears, Dan'l A — Yorktown, May 3–64
Sins, Francis, B — Pensaukee
Smith, H D — Washington, Aug 7–63
Sparks, David — Reedsburg
Spencer, T P — Ft Monroe, Sep 12–62
Stevens, Chas A, c — Appleton
Stillman, B H — Albert Lee, Minn
Vandeventer, J W — Yorktown, Aug 22–64
Van Galder, Amos F — Portsmouth, Nov 10–63
Watson, B F, sgt — Yorktown, Aug 4–63
Whipple, E E — Racine

FIFTH BATTERY.

Three years. Organized October 1st, 1861. Original strength, 155, gain by recruits, etc., 149. Total, 304. Death loss, 24—Killed in action, 2, died of wounds, 3, of disease, 19. Other losses, 67—missing, 0, desertions, 1, transfers, 5, discharges, 61. Strength at muster-out, June 14th, 1865, 213. Campaigns in Tenn., Miss., Ala., Ga., S. C., N. C.

Scottish Commercial
INSURANCE COMPANY,
GLASGOW, - SCOTLAND.

CAPITAL AND ACCUMULATIONS
NEARLY
SEVEN MILLION DOLLARS.

United States Branch.
40 & 42 Pine St. New York.

Western Department.
CHAMBER COMMERCE, ST. LOUIS.

Agencies in all
Prominent Localities.

THE CONNECTICUTT MUTUAL
Life Insurance Co.,
—OF—
HARTFORD, CONN.

ORGANIZED, - 1846.

ASSETS, January 1, 1880................$48,792,334.48
Surplus by Conn. Standard................ 3,410,752.42
Surplus by N. Y. Standard................ 6,558,124.42
Ratio of expense of management to receipts in 1879,
0.54 per cent.

JACOB L. GREENE, President.
JOHN M. TAYLOR, Secretary.
D. H. WELLS, Assist. Secretary.

JOHN I. D. BRISTOL,
STATE AGENT FOR WISCONSIN.

406 Milwaukee Street.
MILWAUKEE, - WIS.

C. C. PRESTON, Pres. GEO W. LESTER, Sec

ORIENT
INSURANCE Co.
HARTFORD, CONN.
CASH CAPITAL, $500,000.

Experienced, Staunch, Always Reliable!

THE OLD

Pennsylvania Fire Ins. Co.,
OF PHILADELPHIA, PA.

With a successful BUSINESS EXPERIENCE OF FIFTY-FIVE Years, continues to offer strictly FIRST-CLASS INSURANCE on favorable terms.

Its reputation for FAIR and HONORABLE dealing has never been surpassed by any similar Institution!

It has always been equal to the emergency in every period of danger and disaster—in all of the "Ups and Downs" of Business in the last 50 odd years. If you want Reliable Insurance, ask for a policy in the

"OLD PENNSYLVANIA FIRE."

The company does not own a dollar's worth of real estate which is not worth more than it cost; and the stocks and bonds owned by the company are worth to-day in the market, nearly one hundred thousand dollars more than the par value.

JOHN DEVEREUX, President.
WM. G. CROWELL, Secretary.
JOHN L. THOMPSON, Ass't Secretary.

WISCONSIN SOLDIERS AND SAILORS REUNION ROSTER. 215

Capt Oscar F Pinney+	Feb 17—63	Campbell, Jno	Prairie du Sac	Clark O f.+	Parkers Cross Road, Jan 1–63
Capt Chas B Humphry		Clayton, A P	Richland Centre	Clark, J H	Jackson, Feb 10–63
Capt Geo Q Gardner		Colburn, Wm	Merrimac, July 16—63	Clow, A J	Memphis, Sep 10–63
Capt Jos McKnight		Davis, J W	Spring Green	Craig, Alex	Eagle
Lt Washington Hill		Dziewanouski, M	Muscoda	Criger, Wm, m	Milbrook, Mich
Lt Geo Lafferty		Eagan, J C	Wyoming	Dorward, I	Aug 27–62
Lt Dan'l Titus		Elbston, Al	Muscoda	Ernst, M D	Kenosha
Lt Elijah Booth, Jr		Fauches, J W	Prairie du Sac	Ferrey, Aaron G	Humbolt, July 31–62
Lt Almon Smith	Iuka, Aug 22—62	Gordon, W A	Etowah Bridge, Sept 4—64	Fox, Frank	Chilton
Lt Jno Dickson		Gould, S J	New Madrid, Apr 1—62	Gale, Chas	Eagle
Lt Chas M Wyman		Haskins, Jno G	Corinth, Oct 13—62	Gerrish, I	Trenton, July 1—62
Surg Wm H Smith		Hauxhurst, A	New Madrid, Apr 1—62	Gerrish, J	Trenton, July 12—62
Surg Robt G Jaines		Herdman, E J	Richland City	Graham, J, corp+	Jackson, Aug 8—63
Adair, Chas+	Stone River, Dec 31—62	Hill, Ed K	Baraboo	Gridley, A F	Milwaukee, May 12—62
Baldwin, O F, c	Wanpun	Hons, I B, corp*	Corinth, Oct 4—62	Griffin, W W	Memphis, Aug 21—64
Bluiliff, Alf, f	Monroe	Hungerford, E R	Corinth, Nov 9 –62	Hawkins, S W, sgt+	Memphis, Oct 21—64
Binuliff, A	Janesville	Johnson, Enoch	Huntsville, June 21—64	Higgins, Thos, me	Harrison
Brown, H A	Murfreesboro, Feb 16—63	Johnson, Jno I	Corinth, Oct 3—62	Hilditch, Wm, c	Harrison
Buck, Walter	Louisville, Aug 24—61	Jones, J L, el	Janesville	Hoffman, Jos	Kenosha
Ciarno, Andrew	Nashville, July 24—64	Jones, Jenk	Janesville	Kelley, Thos	Spring Valley, Minn
Foot, G N	Louisville, Mar 22, 63	Jones, T R	Richland City	Kelley, Jno	Spring Valley, Minn
Hamilton, G H	Madison, Aug 25—64	Jones, Geo D	Ottawa	Kinder, Sam'l, corp	Sebula
Jewett, Chas A	Chattanooga, Mar 20—64	Jones, Rich	Ottawa	Kinder, Jno W	Sabula, Ia
Johns, Morris	Big Shanty, June 26- 64	Keller, Jno	Prairie du Sac	Langworth, J W, m	Depere
King, Ben H, m	Coynga, Ill	King, F	Murfreesboro, June 29—65		
Kimnie, D L	Nashua, Ia	Lester, Jos	Taylor	Loomis, C R	Memphis, July, 9—64
Knapp, Jno D	Murfreesboro, Feb 21—63	Marden, J G	Chattanooga, May 18–65	Marsden, M I, sgt+	Parkins Cross R, Dec 31—62
Marden, Alf, Hosp Stew	Beaver Dam	Moore, Armstrong	Yankeetown	McBride, Jas	Kenosha
McDermid, Daniel	Northfield	Mory, Hiram	Muscoda	Morris, Asa	Racine
Miller, Morgan, H	Farmington, Sept 2—62	Moss, P B	Huntsville, Feb 28—64	Mower, A B, sgt	Memphis, Aug 21—64
Mitchell, Allen	Bowling Green, Dec 14—62	Murphy, M W	Huntsville, Mar 8—64	Mygatt, O C	Memphis, Apr 10—64
Morey, S H	Madison, Feb 4—64	Page, A B, corp*	Vicksburg, July 3—63	Palmer, B C	Milwaukee, June 20—62
Mycomber, Albert	Lookout Mt, July 25- 64	Parker, J E	LaCrosse	Patridge, Jas	Knowlton
Ross, Jno	Jacincto, July 12—62	Peele, C A	Woodstock	Phillips, H	Aug 6—62
Slawson, A C, f	Sylvester	Perry, E J D	Memphis, Oct 25—63	Putnam, S S, f	Berlin
Smith, Jno F*	Chaplin Hills, Oct 8—62	Phettepiace, Welcome	Lone Rock	Quick, Peter, o	Harrison
Spark, Jas W	Murfreesboro, Apr 1—63	Phillips, H B	Nashville, Aug—64	Riguette, Heinrich	Island No 10, May 30—62
Stewart, James	Annapolis, July 9—63	Piper, W N	Postville, Ia	Smith, L A	Dec 7—61
Strohm, C W	Nashua, Ia	Proctor, R	Cassels Prairie	Struthers, Cyrus F	Three Rivers
Sweet, Reuben	Nashville, Feb 22—63	Proctor, J W	Spring Green	Thompson, A D, f	Seymour
Thomas, Jno G+	Murfreesboro, Jan 25—63	Rodgers, J	St Louis, Jan 20—65	Thomas, J H	Memphis, Oct 21—64
Titus, Geo	Murfreesboro, Feb 9—63	Robson, J W	Mazomanie	Toynson, J	Aug 8—62
VanMater, Jas K	Wiota	Ryan, Thos	Berlin	Woggoner, A	St Louis, Mar 20—63
VanMatre, A P	Blair	Smity, Fred	Lone Rock	Wainwright, A, f	Bedford, Ia
Webster, Edwin A	Chattanooga, July 21—64	Stuart, Jno S	Muscoda	Walker, R	Memphis, Aug 21—64
Welty, W H	Dubuque, Ia	Sugar, Jno	Chicago, Ill	Wallwork, A, sgt Parkins Cross Road, Dec 31—62
Welty, David S+	Nashville, Feb 6—63	Tennant, M	Keokuk, Jan 11—63	Wells, Mathias N	Omro
		Thomas, G L	Corinth, Oct—62	Wheelock, A B	Eden, D T
SIXTH BATTERY.		Weaver, M	Cairo, Nov 28—63	White, E A	Chicago, Aug 4—64
		Woefe, J T	Orion	Willard, Chas, agt	Blair, Neb
Three years. Organized Oct. 2d, 1861. Original strength, 157; gain by recruits, etc., 119; total, 276. Death loss, 28—killed in action, 6, died of accidents, 2, of disease. 20. Other losses, 61—desertions, 6, transfers, 9, discharges, 37. Strength at muster-out, July 3d, 1865, 197. Campaigns in Tenn., Miss., La., Ala., Ga.		Weisman, W W	LaCrosse	Wright, Jos H	Wisconsin, Jan 20—64
		Wheeler, S F	Rienzi, Aug 2—62	Wright, A J	Rebel Prison—
		SEVENTH BATTERY.		EIGHTH BATTERY.	
		Three years. Organized, Oct. 4, 1861. Original strength 158, gain by recruits, etc, 183, Total. 311. Death loss, 29—Killed in action, 9, died of accidents, 1, of disease, 19. Other losses, 78, missing, 0, desertions, 3, transfers, 1, discharges, 68. Strength at muster-out, 237. Campaigns in Mo., Ky., Tenn., Miss.		Three years. Organized January 8th, 1862. Original strength, 101, gain by recruits, etc., 168. Total, 329. Death loss, 27—killed in action, 1, died of wounds, 4, of disease, 22. Other losses, 79—missing, 1, desertions, 12, transfers, 14, discharges, 53. Strength at muster-out, Aug., 10th, 1865, 223. Campaigns in Kan., Ky., Tenn., Miss., Ala., Ga.	
Capt Henry Dillon	Lone Rock				
Capt Thos R Hood*	May 4—67				
Capt Jas G Simpson	Steel City, Neb	Capt A D Wheelock	Eden, D T	Capt S J Carpenter*	Stone River, Dec 31—62
Capt Sam F Clark	Baraboo	L G E Larson	Jackson, Tenn	Capt H E Styles	Becker, Minn
Capt Jno Jenawein	Wonewoc	Lt J H Bridgeman	Kenosha	Lt J E Armstrong	Sac City, Ia
Capt A S Sweet*	66	Lt Moses Jerome	Evart, Mich	Lt Obediah German	
Capt J W Fancher	Prairie du Sac	Lt Sam'l Hays+	Jackson, Jan 21—63	Lt J J McLean	Stevens Point
Capt S E Sweet	Elkhorn	Lt Frank Fox	Regular Army	Lt H L Wheeler	Wausau
Capt Dan T Noyes*	Corinth, Oct 4—61	Lt J H Langworthy	Depere	Lt Azro Mann	
Capt L N Keeler		Surg L C Halstead	Waneeka	Lt S S Armstrong	Wausau
Surg Clarkson Miller	Libby Prison—64	Alvord, Geo W, sergt	Eagle	Lt W O D Reilly	Wautoma
Ashby, Henry	Stevens Point	Austin, E A, agt	Milwaukee	Surg A F St Sure Lindstelt	
Barney, G W*	Corinth, Oct 4—61	Avery, Edgar C	Minneapolis, Minn	Aldrich, G D	Amherst
Banks, R E	Chattanooga, Apr 14—65	Bramwell, J	Jackson, Apr 16—63	Allen, Charley	Fremont
Bennett, V A	Louisville, Dec 20—63	Brattz, R	Nellisville	Armstrong, R, m	Spencer, Ia
Benson, B	Nashville, Feb 22—65	Bridgeman, J H	Kenosha	Averill, Chith	Wausau
Booth, Wm R H	Emmetsburg, Ia	Brooks, A C	Sparta	Ballentine, T	Sept 4—62
Brown, G D*	Corinth, Oct 4—62	Brunson, Arthur B	Prairie du Chien	Bentley, D P	Stevens Point
Burdick, R J	Lone Rock	Burke, J	Memphis, Aug 7—61	Bremmer, Adolph	Muscoda
Durga, Christ	Prairie Du Sac	Chisholm, Wm, me	Fond du Lac	Buffum, A M, corp	Jacinto, Aug 8—61
Burnham, W A	Richland City				
Burnham, O J	Richland City				
Campbell, C	Vicksburg, Aug 16—64				

WISCONSIN SOLDIERS AND SAILORS REUNION ROSTER.

Calkins, Emerson R	Blackhawk	Wheeler, Henry L	Wausau	Lewis, Wm	Louisville, June 21—64
Callon, Jno T	Wausau			Laud, Swan	Chattanooga, Apr 23—64
Calvin, W H	Murfreesboro, Sept 23—64	**NINTH BATTERY.**		Malloy, S T	Waukesha
Cannon, S R, e	Neillsville			Maxey, Michael	Menominee
Case, Jno M, m	Minneapolis, Minn	Three years. Organized Jan 27th,1862. Original strength, 155; gain by recruits, etc. 141. Total, 296. Death loss,6—killed in action, 0, died of accidents, 1, of disease, 5. Other losses, 63—missing, 0, desertions, 6, transfers, 1, discharges, 56. Strength at muster out, Sept 30, 1865, 237. Campaigns in Kan., Col., New Mexico, Mo., Ark.		Miner, E	New Lisbon
Clark, Calvin	Murfreesboro, Feb 1—65			Miner, Jno	New Lisbon
Colwell, M	Louisville, Oct 18—63			Morehouse, H. sgt	Louisville, Nov 29—64
Crengon, Jack	Burlington, Ia			Mull, Fred	Milwaukee, Feb 14—68
Cross, Geo I.	Wautoma			Murry, Jno	Savannah, Jan 14—65
Daniels, J	Nashville, Apr 16—64			Netoll, W	Oakdale
Darling, Fritz H, f	Unity	Capt N C H Johnson	Milwaukee	Nuttall	Oakdale
Darling, Henry	Stevens Point	Capt H Dodge	Milwaukee	Nutting, Wm	Werner
Davis, R H	Neillsville	Capt W D Crocker	Sheboygan	Osock, Wm W	Harmony, Ill
Devoe, Wm	Wausau	Lt Jno A Edington		Reynolds, Wm, me	Chicago, Ill
Dodge, Jacob	Trippvil'e	Lt H A Hicks		Scott, Jno E, m	Chicago, Ill
Ellis, W	Jackson, Nov 1—62	Brown, S S, corp	Ft Lyon, Sept 9—64	Secor, Delos	New Lisbon
Ensign, Frank	Minnesota	Cole, Dwight H	Springfield	Stacks, Israel	Nashville, Apr 10—63
Ensign, Ed	Minnesota	Davis, J	Ft Lyon, July 19—63	Stanley, Jno	Nashville, Nov 30—62
Flemmings, Charley	Amherst	Finey, Mart	Burlington	Unsell, Jos	Ft Buford, D T
Frazer, Walter	Stevens Point	Fish, C Q	Delavan	Watts, Jno+	Salkehatchie River, Feb 5—65
German, Obadiah	Adams	Franklin, Luther, f	Waupun	Wells, A W	Johnstown
Gibbins, J H	Sun Prairie	Funk, C, corp	Ft Lyon, Sept 9—64	Wilcox, David, corp	Farmington, June 30—62
Gordon, Peter	Stevens Point	Granger, Josiah, me	Racine	Williams, Wm W	Alden, Oct 28—63
Gool, G W	Plainfield	Green, L	Camp Relief, Aug 7—62	Zottman, Fred F	Louisville, Nov 24—63
Green, Lon	Burlington, Ia	Haller, S O	Lyons		
Greed, N S	St Louis, Apr 13—62	Hicks, H A		**ELEVENTH BATTERY.**	
Harris, Anson	Murfreesboro Jan 28—65	Jones, Geo, sgt	Burlington		
Higgins, Melvin W	Corinth—68	Owens, C T, f	Waupun	Three years. Organized Apr 6, 1862. Original strength, 87; gain by recruits, etc., 47. Total, 134. Death loss, 3—killed in action, 0, died of wounds, 1, of disease. 2. Other losses, 23—missing, 0, desertions, 20, transfers, 2, discharges, 17. Strength at muster out, 1865, 108. Campaigns in Va., W. Va., Capt Jno Rourke	
Higgins, A	Nashville, July 28—63	Robinson, Oscar, pa	Burlington		
Hinckley, C G	Spring Creek	Waterbury, Newel J	Ft Lyon, Aug 2—62		
Hoffman, Francis E	Madison, Feb 20—64	Wood, W	Ft Lyon, Sept 19—62		
Howe, L T	New Albany, Dec 24—63				
Hubbard, I P	Mound City, Nov 7—63	**TENTH BATTERY.**			
Isherwood, Harry	Stevens Point				
Johnson, Jno R	Manston, May 10—64	Three years. Organized February 10th, 1862. Original strength, 47; gain by recruits, etc., 132; total, 179. Death loss, 27—killed in action, 2, died of disease, 25. Other losses, 64 —desertions, 4, discharges, 60. Strength at muster-out, April 20th, 1865, 88. Campaigns in Tenn., Miss., Ala, S. C., N. C.		Lt Jno McAfee	
Jones, C M, ms	Waupaca			Lt Chas Bagley	
Kuchen, Jimmy	Wausau			Lt W F McKenzie	
Lamb, S A	Tomah			Lt Michael Lantry	Chicago, Dec 18—63
Louison, Louis	Stevens Point			Lt M Cunningham	
Mann, Azro	Nebraska			Hastings, Jerome, me	Chicago, Ill
Marsh, Geo	Kansas			Humbolt, Jno	New Creek Jan 7—65
Matteson, Geo M, ed	New York City			Moran, Jas	Camp Douglas, June 6—62
McBride, A W •	Chardon, O	Capt Yates V Beebe	New Lisbon	Sanderson, Jno	Portage
McEwen, Joe	Wausau	Lt David C Platt		Wylie, Jno	Camp Jessie, Oct 6—62
McKennon, Aug, f	Portage	Lt P H M Groesbeck			
McLean, Henry	Wausau	Lt Eben W Stedson		**TWELVTH BATTERY**	
McLean, Jno D	Stevens Point	Lt Jas Tuner			
McMahon, Patrick	Stevens Point	Lt Elbert W Fowler		Three year. Organized, Feb, and Mar, 1862, Original strength, 90, gain by recruits, etc., 243, Total, 342. Death loss, 32—Killed in action, 4, died of wounds, 5, of disease, 22, of accidents, 1, Other losses, 185—missing, 1, desertions, 2, transfers, 81, discharges, 105 Strength at muster out, June 26, 1865, 121. Campaigns in Tenn., Miss., Ark., Ala., Ga., S C., N C., Capt Wm A Pile	
McMurphy, A	Jackson, Sept 26—63	Lt Henry A Hicks			
McMurphy, I.	Nashville, Jan 5—63	Lt Oscar A Clark			
Northrup, Eaton B, corp, ed	Milwaukee	Burg Geo Riddell			
Oleson, Jacob, corp	Jacinto—62	Alley, Chas H, sgt	Farmington, June 7—62		
Onit, Ole c	Iola	Bacon, Wm H	Racine, Mar 6—62		
Perry, A W	Racine, Jan 17—62	Beach, Aza	Georgia, Dec 8—64	Capt Wm Zickerick	Appleton
Persons, U	Murfreesboro, Apr 5—63	Belcher, Jno L	Camp Douglas	Lt Edw G Harlow	Janesville
Philbrick, W B, m	Milwaukee	Boyle, Jas	Farmington, June 17—62	Lt Wm Miles	
Pollbrick, W B, m	Milwaukee	Burbank, F E	New Lisbon	Lt L D Munson	
Pickle, Jno H	Fremont	Burbank, Geo E	Mt Olive, Mar 22—65	Lt M Amsden+	Allatoona, Oct 9—64
Reynolds, Wm	Mischicott	Cady, Byron H	Jackson, Sept 7—62	Lt S C Cheney	Monroe
Redlon, N K	Plainfield	Cash, W H, r creondctor	New Lisbon	Lt P H Cody	
Riley, Wm	Wautoma	Catlin, Auron	Chilton	Lt W H Hamilton	
Rose, Geo	San Francisco, Cal	Chase, Wm H	Neeenhah	Lt Sam'l E Jones	
Sanshove, Sergeon	Sheboygan	Clark, Chas F	Murfreesboro, Aug 29—63	Lt Henry Marks	
Sherwood, Simeon, f	Saratoga	Coltric, Oliver L	Nashville, Jan 22—63	Lt Henry Turner	
Sherwood, L D	Murfreesboro, Apr 13—65	Coltrie, Andrew J	Nashville, June 1—63	Ames, A C	Huntsville, Feb 5—64
Snider, R	Iuka, Aug 31—62	Cornell, David S	Eau Claire	Aron, Jno	Spring Green
Sparks, R D	Plainfield	Craig, Jno, i	Eau Claire	Baker, C C+	Allatoona, Oct 15—64
Spear, J A	East Oasis	Dyke, Jno C	Fountain City, May 1—65	Barlow, S, sgt*	Allatoona, Oct 6—64
Stiles, Henry E	Becker, Minn	Fye, David	Chattanooga, May 30—64	Bates, W R	Janesville
Stewart, T I	Louisville, Sept 11—63	Greenwood, E L	Nashville, Oct 8—62	Bowe, Fred	Live Ridge
Thurber, C D	May 27—62	Holt, M C	Ono	Bowen, W T, ed	Yankton, D T
Toner, Jno		James, H	New Lisbon	Brown, W S, ed	Yankton, D T
Walton, W H	Bowling Green, Nov 20—63	Johnson, Ole	Farmington, Aug 2—62	Burton, R W	Janesville
Warby, Jno	Jordan	Kellogg, Wm	Quincy	Carpenter, P E	Memphis, Jan 10—63
Washburne, Wm	Eau Plaine	Kewin, Jas*	Farmington, May 28—62	Chase, J W	Allatoona, Oct 6—64
Welch, H	Charleston, June 18—63	Kimble, J R	Stevens Point	Cleveland, J C	Mazomanie
Weigh, F	Janesville	Kittle, C B	Baltimore, Jan 17—65	Cook, Jno H	Chippewa Falls
Wells, Sam'l	Marinette	Lawrence, N L	New Lisbon		
Worsey, Jos	Iola	Lathrop, S D	Farmington, July 31—62		
Woodard, Jas A	Stevens Point	Lemon, Wm	Weston		

WISCONSIN SOLDIERS AND SAILORS REUNION ROSTER. 217

Name	Location	Name	Location	Name	Location
Croft, Jas	Janesville	Dennis, Geo J	Baton Rouge, Aug 19—64	Marstan, D W, C 16	LaCrosse
Croft, T T, druggist	Janesville	Field, Louis	Mishicolt	Myers, Thos, K 15	Neendah
Daniels, Lushton H	Ontario	Fizell, J	Horicon, Oct 23—64	Nutting, Isaac W, 1 art	
Davey, D C*	Allatooma, Oct 5—64	Green, Addison	Baton Rouge, July 19—64	Partman, Franklin B, I, 20	Sturgeon Bay
Doolittle, S H+	Allatooma, Oct 6—64	Ham, J H	Baton Rouge, June 18—64	Perkins, Eben, D 8	Stevens Point
Dransfield, I B	Annapolis, Mar 15—65	Harrison, A T, corp	Baton Rouge, June 29—64	Redmond, G K, F 20	Neillsville
Ellis, Fred W. mc	Jacksonville	Jones, Lafayette, mc	Whitewater	Royal, L M, 16	Somerset
Fish, E B	Racine	Lathrop, J H	Baton Rouge, June 17—64	Russel, H D, G 6	LaCrosse
Gray, J +	Cairo, July 22—63	Laurence, H	Baton Rouge, Oct 1—64	Smiley, H F, K 6	LaCrosse
Griffith, W H	Cairo, Nov 14—63	Morgan, Freeborn, f	Hebron	Stenson, M, m, A 20	Fond du Lac
Hass, J	Wilmington, Mar 19—63	Nelson, E R	Dec 26—4	Smith, Ebbin, 11	Peot
Harvey, W P, corp	Delton	Plain, Jno E	Baton Rouge, May 13—64	Smart, C, E 6	Colby
Haubelt, H F	New York City	Rowe, H M	Baton Rouge, May 23—64	Swan, Timothy, Capt H 7	New London
Hamilton, A P, corp*	Allatooma, Oct 5—64	West, N J	Clinton Junction	Southard, W A, K	Neillsville
Hockmar, H	Millikens Bend, Apr 19—63	Wickett, T	Baton Rouge, June 24—64	Valentine, Ed, U S Navy	Baldwin
Howland, Jerome	Janesville			*NEW HAMPSHIRE.*	
Jackman, C S	Janesville			Eaton, A S, capt, 10	Greenwood, H
Jewett, Jay M	Borgen	**BERDAN'S SHARP-**		Harwood, E O, pa, I 6	Fond du Lac
Kennedy, T H, sgt	Nashville, Apr 18—64	**SHOOTERS.**		Holmes, L O, E 7	Baraboo
Keyes, D H	Memphis, Mar 11—62			Palmer, Jno H, D 4	Baraboo
Kibbie, A, corp	Richmond			Parker, B F, D	Necoah
Kitterer, F	Champion Hills, May—63	Three years. Organized Sept, 1861. Original		Roberts, A J, B 2nd Inf, I cav	Baraboo
Lange, Michael, mc	Berlin	strength, 135; gain by recruits, etc., 89. Total,		Townsend, S W, m, 2d Lt E 5	Fond du Lac
Magwensen, Theo	Fond du Lac	154. Death loss, 34—killed in action, 12, died of		*VERMONT.*	
Mallory, L T	Waukesha	wounds, 9, of disease, 13. Other losses, 115—			
McCullock, Jno	Janesville	missing, 8 desertions, 4, transfers, 43,discharges,		Atkins, H A, I, E 15	Brandon
Mc Intyre, W J, f	Whitewater	58. Strength at muster out, Sept 23, 1864, 47.		Carleton, J F, E 15	Amherst
Merritt, Wm H	Milwaukee	Campaigns in Va., Md.		Cullum, Eli, D 5	City Point
Miler, Wm	Reedsburg	Capt F E Marble		Davis, E N, H 9	Baldwin
Morris, Saml	Oak Ceutre	Lt C F Shepard		Davis, M W, f, Maj 6	Sparta
Norantz, C	Lomira, Apr 29—64	Lt C A Stevens		Eldridge, Chas B, 1 cav	Tunah
Ocock, Wm W, f	Harmony, Ill	Lt E H Benson		Farnsworth, S E, Surg F 10	Baldwin
Palmer, M V	Clear Creek, June 16—62	Lt P C Judkins*	Todds Farm, May 8—64	Foster, H S, corp C 1	Baldwin
Parkham, W D	LaGrange, Jan 10—73	Baker, C W, G	Soldiers Grove	Fillmore, Jno H, G 6	Hortonville
Perry, Ellaklm	Logansville	Crane, M H, H	LaCrosse	Fillman, Jno H, G 6	Hortonville
Pierson, Ambrose	Janesville	Clemons, H H	Oshkosh	Fuller, Calvin, G 3	Kenosha
Pierson, F	Janesville	Fowler, H D	Elroy	Hilton, L J, B 7	Ezra, Ia
Plympton, J W*	Bentonville, Mar 22—65	Horton, S M, G	Eau Claire	Irish, Harley, B 5	Longwood
Libbie, Alouzo R	New Richmond	Lewis, G H, G	Jefferson	Irish, Harley, B 5	Neillsville
Sanders, K	Jeff Barracks, Oct 10—62	Luster, S, G	Jefferson	Knowlton, J O, K and C 9	Whitewater
Seefeld, G	Clear Creek, July 15—62	Price, A J, G		Lapage, Jos, H 9	Baldwin
Lexton, H B	Janesville	Roberts, H S, H	LaCrosse	McMahon, Jas, corp G 1 H	Fond du Lac
Shopbell, Hills	Janesville	Stannard, A C, 2d H, G	Milton	Morse, Jno O, A 8	Belle Centre
Sidow, C	Jeff Barracks, June 14—62	Schermerho, n, Jno P, H	Milwaukee	Marshall, C H, 1, 11 heav art	Racine
Sissein, G S	Janesville	Pounar, Geo, L	Menominee	Nichols, W T, mf, col 14	Maywood, Ill
Sleybaugh, J	Nashville, May 19—63			O'Donald, Wm, C I cav	LaCrosse
Stout, J	Corinth,—62			Pierce, A E, G I heav art	Omro
Trappman, Wm	Corinth, Oct 15—62	**RESIDENT SOLDIERS OF**		Roberts, J W, G	Whitewater
Walt, G	Eastport, Dec—63	**OTHER STATES.**		Robinson, Pearl, I, D 10	Fond du Lac
Wells, A	Johnstown			Stewart, Harp, C 11	Waterloo
West, Williamson	Memphis, July 20—63			Taylor, H M, I, 2d bat	Fond du Lac
White, Jno H	LaValle	Note—The company letter and number of		Thomas, Oscar, K 8	Ono
Whitman, J	Oxford, Dec 14—62	regiment to which soldier belonged follow the		Trupell, J E, C 11	Waterloo
Wilcox, Jno T	Janesville	initials of his name		Town, Jos C, H 9	Menominee
Wingate, H	Vicksburg, July 4—63	*MAINE.*		Williams, T A C 11	Waterloo
Zicherick, Wm, cl	Appleton	Austin, E S, U S Navy	Baldwin		
Zicherick, Wm, f	Fond du Lac	Atkinson, Jos S, 13	Bayfield	*MASSACHUSETTS.*	
Zicherick, A	Fond du Lac	Bishop, Jos, G 22	Emmet P O	Blood, P M, F 19	Milwaukee
		Ballard, J A, B 3	LaCrosse	Carlton, T V, C 1	Mexican war, Neillsville
THIRTEENTH BATTERY.		Bixby, H L, H D 9	Star Prairie	Clarke, Chas H. 5	Milwaukee
		Bussell, H D, G 19	LaCrosse	Grechen, J W, I, H 18	Milwaukee
Three years. Organized Nov. 14th. 1863.		Butterfield, J. 5	Neillsville	Hill, Chas H, A 3 heav art	Milwaukee
Original strength, 156, gain by recruits, etc., 32.		Chamberlain, E, E 1st heav art	LaCrosse	Howard, Sam't, 11 bat	Seymour
Total, 188. Death loss, 34—Killed in action, 0,		Champion, Geo, 31	Star Prairie	Larien, L D, sgt L 2 cav	Baldwin
died of accidents, 2, of disease, 12. Other losses,		Crommel, E B, K 31	Star Prairie	Martin, A W, me, corp, 12	Fond du Lac
68—missing, 1, desertions, 25, transfers, 3, dis-		Chapman, Frank P, sgt K 2	Richmond	Merrill, A F, E 44	Milwaukee
charges, 39. Strength at muster-out, 106.		Damon, J S, m, C 28	Spencer	Murray, Jas, corp C 9	St Joseph
Campaigns in La.		Elliot, J M, F 20	Neillsville	Moore, D E, E 2 bat	LaCrosse
Capt Richard R Griffith		Farnum, Wm, C 16	LaCrosse	McCarthy, P, H 350	LaCrosse
Lt Geo L Cross		Grove, W, 2nd cav	Neillsville	McNamara, Thos, E 3	Racine
Lt Alf E Chaffee		Henderson, G W, 1st heav art	Neillsville	Moulton, F B, C 1 cav	Oconomowoc
Lt Wm W Perrine		Harriman, A, G 5	Neillsville	Nodom, Benj, 2	Milwaukee
Lt Frank Fox		Heald, B F, m, F 9,	Sheboygan	Perry, J E, f, corp I 27	Sparta
Lt David Kinder	Sabula, Ia	Hansom, Wm H, 21	Iola	Remington, C W, F 19	Racine
Alrey, N	Clinton, May 14—65	Hart, S F, sgt, H 17	Milwaukee	Sawyer, Wesley C, H 23	Lawrence University
Barrett, J	Baton Rouge, Sept 11—64	Harris, Sam'l F, M 1 cav	Oshkosh	Shepard, L F, H 31	Milwaukee
Ballard, Jno C	Jefferson	Josslyn, E S, m, C 15,	Oshkosh	Staten, H H, 2	Baraboo
Bridges, M D, sgt	Milwaukee	McKinley, Jno, 9	Fremont	Staten, W H, F. 2	Baraboo
Clay, Wm, f	Hebron	Marston, D, C 16	LaCrosse	Sterns, I H, surg, 23	Milwaukee
Dainz, C L	Baton Rouge, Jan 14—65				
Dncey, G E, m	Palmyra				

PENSION, BOUNTY, ARREARS OF PAY:

Prize Money and Patent Bureau,

—BY—

W. F. C. FALBE,

U. S. Claim Agent.

Special attention to the settlement of Accounts and returns of OFFICERS of the ARMY and NAVY, and to

PENSION AND BOUNTY CLAIMS.

SOLDIERS AND SOLDIERS' WIDOWS

Your attention is called to the fact, that under the Act of Congress, approved January 25 1879, Pensions will commence

FROM THE DATE OF THE DISCHARGE OR DEATH OF A SOLDIER,

Provided the application is filed in the Pension Office before July 1, 1880; if not filed before that date, pension can only commence from the date of filing the application. Do not delay, and your case shall receive prompt and thorough attention at my hands.

Yours Respectfully,

W. F. C. FALBE.

OFFICE, ROOM 12, GRAND OPERA HOUSE.

MILWAUKEE, ▪ ▪ **WIS.**

WISCONSIN SOLDIERS AND SAILORS REUNION ROSTER. 219

Name	Location	Name	Location	Name	Location
Thompson, I, G, 42	Winneconne	Decker, J A, D 5 heav art	Menominee	Morgan, David, M 2 art	Racine
Weding, Fred, G, 25	Granville	Decker, David H, A 168	Menominee	Merriam, H P, H 106	Ferlin
Witherby, H F, B, 67	Amherst	Davis, S E, mf, K 114	Horicon	Munnig, Jno, C 66	De pere
RHODE ISLAND.		Dilenbach, Chas,l, D 106	Mukwonago	Myers, James, mc, corp, G 150	Fond du Lac
		Early, I' H, 1st bat	Milwaukee	Miller, J D, pa, C 1 art	Milwaukee
Bateman, H B, capt C 5th art		Fisk, D D, corp, 9 cav	Springfield	McCullock, Joseph, corp, E 124	Fond du Lac
Bowen, C T, capt 4th Infantry	Ashland	Ennis, J H, 97		McCourt, Geo, I, A 16	Cambridge
CONNECTICUT.		Ennis, Orin, —	Lind	McMahon, Jno, K 10 heav art	Friendship
		Fowler, Dan, me, 176	Whitewater	Moffat, W S, capt, B 243	Erin Prairie
Billings, J, C 28		Frank, L, L 2 art	Beaver Dam	Meyers, Martin, C 9	Racine
Clark, L W, asst surg 13	Beaver Dam	Fox, Jno, H heav art	Neillsville	Mead, D H, F 1	Lind
Cleveland, J J, K, 10	Cambridge	French, —, Q M S 118	Neillsville	McLean, Wm, G 76	Kaukauna
Estes, Jas, G, 1 cav	La Crosse Co	Ford, O C, 14	Rush Prairie	Manney, Jas, M 2 heav art	Lind
Morhouse, F T, light, art, 2 bat	Menominee	Frank, John D, capt, G 1st light art	Lamartine	Newman, M A, 155	Janesville
Riggs, G L, me, 1 A	Oconomowoc	Forbes, James A, D 10	Ripon	Normile, Michael, D 4 heav art	Fond du Lac
Shaw, Wm B, 1, 11	Ripon	Finch, J G, K 21	Ripon	Neill, Jas, H 60	Horicon
Stemple, Henry, D, 15	Milwaukee	Finn, J H, l E 26th cav	Fond du Lac	Nichols, B E, G 97	Reedsburg
Van Ness, J G, 2 light art	Oconomowoc	Fishlaw, Anb'o, baker, 150	Fond du Lac	Ober, H H, 13 cav	Neillsville
	Lind	Gilley, S A, L 6	Menominee	Olin, E E, grocer, E 121	Sparta
NEW YORK.		Grover, D H, G 130	Oconomowoc	Pabodie, G A, E 34	Baraboo
Adams, J T, me, F, 20	Lincoln Co	Gondey, E F, H 160	La Crosse	Parkinson, Winfield, H 20 cav	Brookside
Aruos, Jas, I, D, 153	Loyal	Gee, A A, M 9 cav		Parks, Silas, F 144	Stevens Point
Arms, Jas, I, D, 153	Neillsville	Griffes, S, E 60	Springfield	Peck, Geo, K 142	Little Rapids
Arnold, Thos, C, 11 cav	Milwaukee	Gates, C, 1 m't'd rifles	Neillsville	Pavy, W L, R C 24	Milwaukee
Atkins, J H, G, 80		Green, F R, sgt, D 180	Waupun	Porter, S D, M 10 heav art	Westfield
Baker, G C, B, 68	Soldiers Grove	Goodenow, Chas. 1 cav	Weyauwega	Parkill, En T, I 1	Colby
Briggs, G W, 11 cav	Oshkosh	Grebin, John, bat G 3	Stevens Point	Pavey, D C, ed, L 15	Milwaukee
Bailey, L S, F, 115	Oconto	Gorin, Frank,l, E 60,	Fond du Lac	Park, Jno, sgt, L 18	Minnesota Falls, Minn
Baker, Jas, sgt, L, 15	Watertown, D T	Hood, C L, M 1 cav	La Crosse	Panse, H B, 47	Madison
Borell, Wm M, D, 2d heav art	Janesville	Hunt, Jas B, I 187	Weyauwega	Pratt, J B, capt, K 8 ar.	Green Lake
Batchelder, Wm, I, 102	La Crosse	Hathaway, Wm, C 5 cav	Weyauwega	P.b dir, G A, L 20 cav	Baraboo
Burteh, N B, ed, B, 4	Richland Centre	Holly, A J, F 4 art	Waupaca	Perry, E H, B 156	Star Prairi •
Barry, M F, 1st bat	Hammond	Hewitt, C, 161h	Winneconne	Peebles, J E, 2d H, 186	Muscoda
Binnolys, J R, K, 97	Hammond	Hellwig, Philip, C 1 & 10 cav	Prairie du Chien	Parker, M W, G 8 heav art	Neillsv'e
Backus, J A, H, D, 181	Baldwin	Harvey, Oscar, E 139	Elmira, N Y	Phillips, Henry S, corp, K 10J	Little Rapis
Baker, Rolla, R, 186	Bayfield	Hall, J B, K 137	Racine	Palm r, H O, K 112	Lind
Bauer, Burgett, E, 3	Sharon	Howard, A 1, I 64	Omro	Perry, O H	Lind
Bersh. w, Martin, H, 110	Sturgeon Bay	Hamilton, W C, G 92	Chilton	Peters, Newton, C 93	
Burch, Newell, E, 154	Menominee	Hall, J W, F 14 heav art	Mauston	Pierson, H P, M 2 cav	Reedsburg
Blinn, W H, bugler, 9	Waupaca	Hoard, W D, A 1 light art	Ft. Atkinson	Underwood, C H, me L 10 cav	Fond du Lac
Brower, Andrew, J, H, 95	Kaukauna	Hubbard, Frank, sgt, D 181	Milwaukee	Beamer, R J, D 75	Waterloo
Bastine, E I, G, 98	Weyauwega	Haskell, J W, M 6 art	La Crosse	Roat, Lewis, F G	Two Creeks
Brower, Abraham, K, 118	Kaukauna	Hurlburt, J, pa, D 137	Milwaukee	Roe, Jno P, Chaplain, 97	Oshkosh
Baker, Henry H, C 14	Stevens Point	Hewitt, J, A 143	Winneconne	Rich, E C, C 118	Omro
Brown, Chas, G 19	Ripon	Hendy, H, m, 80	Whitewater	Rewell, A J, f, E 101	Eau Claire
Corey, Edwin R, E, 106	Rusk	Hayford, S S, I, I 13	Whitewater	Richards, T W, 92	Augusta
Chase, O H, vis, sgt maj, 20 cav	Portage	Haws, Otis, I 58	Sparta	R obeson, A F, A 49	Neillsville
Chase, J L, 3 cav	Janesville	Hunter, A, F 10 art	Springfield	R ssier, Henry, B 3 cav	Menominee
Carley. Wm, K, 64	Buena Vista	Hooper, J C, B 27	Winneconne	Rairdon, Dennis, G 2	Weyauwega
Cowing, Jas, F, 4	Menominee	Hoyt, J E, f, capt, C	Liberty Grove	Reynolds, J C, H, E 144	Waupun
Calkins, P H, G, 50	Augusta	Hammanton, A, 2 heav art	Neillsville	Richards, H T, sgt, K 12 cav	Milwaukee
Chesefere, Jerome, f, I 136	Eau Claire	Hermon, M B, L 18 heav art	Davis Corner,	Hunt, A, C 154	Hutchinson
Clark, C L, m 6, heav art	Whitewater	Horr, B J, E 10 A	Neillsville	Riley, Jerry, L A 8	Roseudale
Clark, C L, 10	Whitewater	Herrick, F M, me, 10 heav art	Bayfield	Stanley, Wm S, L 18 art	Milwaukee
Corthell, Jos, I 6	St Croix	Hendricks, H, E 64		Swain, W C, capt, B 93	Milwaukee
Cudney, J H, sgt, A 120	Star Prairie	Holmes, George, D 148	Fond du Lac	Soper, Oliver S, H 2 cav	Porters Mills
Conger, O P, I 187	Muscoda	Ingraham, C M, K 64	Oxford	Stevens, L M, N Y regulars	Sparta
Canfield, J C, D h av art	Neillsville	Ingraham, G C, K 64	Oxford	Stone, Festus, H 8 heavy art	Milwaukee
Carrol, G 106	Neillsville	Jenkins, B, C 117	La Crosse	Spoor, A L 1, D 130	Fond du Lac
Conklin, M D, me, E 94	Bayfield	Jones, Adelbert, I, B 97	Empire	Sutherland, G E, bat A 1st heavy art	Fond du Lac
Cady, Warren, A 13	Marshfield	Johns, S, K 126	Richmond	Sinath, John B, 2 cav	Omro
Cooper, Wm, K 122	Neillsville	Jordan, E L, f, 1 cav	Sparta	Smith, B, B 57	Tomah
Chapman, W D, H 13	St Joseph	Kraftt, Emil, C 20		Smith, Lewis C, E 14	Berlin
Culver, D P, 5	Waupaca	Kallenback, H, me, 41	Milwaukee	Stephens, E B, H 161	St Croix
Corrow, Nelson, A 98	Kaukauna	Klunn, Wm W, me, F 111	Whitewater	Shepard, Geo W, A 20 cav	Sparta
Copps, E M, K 98	Stevens Point	Knight, G N, C 112	Cylon	Sykes, Wm, I 9	Star Prairie
Crosby, D, Rev, sgt, 140	Ripon	Kuhart, Chas, F 27	Neillsville	Stratton, Chas, I 50	St Croix
Carpenter, W H, D 117		Kichl, Jacob, f, 2d bat	Lamartine	Sabine, J B, G 169	Beaver Dam
Diltenbach, Chas, D 106	Mukwonago	LaBarre, A J, G 110	Mukwonago	Stilters, Jno, A 98	Plover
Dickenson, Fred G, E 186	Kewaunee	LaBarre, A J, 109	Mukwonago	Smith, P W, H, capt, B 59	Bayfield
Durkee, H H, H 16	Geneva Lake	Lakin, Arad, H 1st cav	Plainfield	Spencer, T M, K 110	Stevens
Dooley, Daniel, 19 art	Rushford	Lawton, T S, me, B 81	Milwaukee	Snyder, J H, C 106	Neillsville
Donnelly, E F, me, K 50	Whitewater	Lee, Harry, 14 heav art	Tomah	Shafter, Jas W, me, I 49	Neillsville
Ducker, L P, C 9	Springfield	Lewis, S, I 8	Whitewater	Swain, Wm C, pr, capt B 93	Milwaukee
Durkee, A S, A 126	Seymour	Lincoln, W, G 35	Tomah	Scott, J O, capt D 34	Waupun
Dee, Jas, 112	Richmond	Ledsworth, J D, I 9 cav	Kenosha	Stickles, O C, e, G 1	Ripon
Denson, A B, 21 cav	Augusta	Lindsay, F D, E 116	Neillsville	Stickle, S H, e, I 1	Winneconne
Downs, R, sgt, B 80	Star Prairie	LaMouche, Nicholas, B 45	Fond du Lac	Snyder, Henry M, D 141	Stevens Point
Dolph, L, A 11 cav	Neillsville	Moody, Russell, G 168		Tebren, C L, K 107	Janesville
Duuwell, Geo W, E 4	Jefferson	Mossen, Dennis, 1 light art	Oconto	Thomas, S G, pa, 1 bat 2 light art	Star Prairie

HOWE.

If you want to see the lightest running, the most perfectly made, the easiest operated, the prettiest and the best machine in the world

CALL AT 410 MILWAUKEE ST.

AND SEE THE

New B Howe

THE late improvements on our NEW "B" MACHINE make it the wonder of all. Don't think of buying any other machine until you have seen the *New "B" Howe*. We cannot tell you its many good qualities; it must be seen to be fully appreciated. Special attention is also called to

OUR NEW "D" MACHINE

for manufacturing purposes of all kinds. It can be used either as a Cylinder or Platform machine.

IT STANDS
UNRIVALEED
AS A MANUFACTURING MACHINE.

The Howe Manufacturing Co.,
410 Milwaukee Street, MILWAUKEE, WISCONSIN.

T. W. WHITEHOUSE, Manager.

(Late Capt. 22d Maine Volunteers.)

WISCONSIN SOLDIERS AND SAILORS REUNION ROSTER.

Temple, Geo, f, G 12 — Eldorado Mills
Templeton, Alex, I, H 36 — Sevastopol
Townsend, H F, C 15 cav, — Neillsville
Thompson, L A. D 1 drag — Neillsville
Thomas, S G, I 3 — Star Prairie
Van Dusen, M H G 13 — Fond du Lac
Vernan, D, 14 2 E — Neillsville
Vroman, P, me, H 14 — Ripon
Van Wagoner, J, G 20 — Baldwin
Van Epps, Peter S, I 44 — Weyauwega
Vanderhoof, Nathan P, 51 — Menominee
Vincent, Hiruey, M 10 art — Weyauwega
Van Etten, Harlin, I 109 — Augusta
Wafler, David, I 27 — Weyauwega
Whitmore, J — Soldiers Grove
Waffle, Volney S, bat A 1 light art — Winona
Wilson, Samuel, C 16 H A — Sheboygan
Watterson, H, 26 ind bat — Ohio
Wooster, Geo B, livery, D 10 heavy art — Brodhead
Welsh, A, vol — Waterloo
Wicks, Geo C. L 15 — Paris Hill, N Y
Wilkins, G M, I — Whitewater
Weld, Jno W, f, 1 art — Little Prairie
Williams, A, 95 — Rush River
Wilson, Ruben, 24 — Neillsville
Wetherby, C E, F 77 — Troy
Welman, J L, J H 137 — Neillsville
Woodward, Wm F, A 64 — Neillsville
Wilcox, J, D 16 art — Neillsville
Wilson, Hiram, A 10 art — Neillsville
Walker, Gen, c, L 8 heavy art — Sturgeon Bay
White. Al, M 1 art — Neillsville
Wallace, Sylvester F, G 107 — Menomonee
Wilber, C R, I 151 — Omro
Way. A B F, 33 — Milwaukee
Whitsom, W R, A 144 — Buena Vista
Walker, Moses, f, A 166 — Berlin
Zork, Ed D, R 6 cav — Amherst

NEW JERSEY.

Hickey, J C, B 8 — St Croix
Kopper, Edward, f — Kaukauna
Tuthill, Wm H, R 2 — Lockley
Van Osman, Samuel, D 30 — Seymour
Young, D M, A and I 2 — North Bend

PENNSYLVANIA.

Adams, Joseph B, B 14 — Tomah
Andrews, J B, 148, — Appleton
Backhouse, Frederick, H 200 — Tomah
Bardenwerper, Robert C, K cav — Theisville
Blanchard, D J, H 2 — Colby
Bishop, J, 1 83 — Weston
Brooks, A S, C 2 heavy art — Reedsburg
Carpenter, Ira D, f 187 — Rushford
Campbell, S W, 1 199 — Star Prairie
Cassody, John H, B 81 — Verona
Cornmesser, A R, D 13 cav — Ono
Cole, —, Maj 28 — Kaukauna
Cape, C M, D 77 — Omro
Fuzer, Geo H, F 113 — Milwaukee
Fairbanks, John, E 61 — Milwaukee
Flihian, J D, corp H 29 — Hammond
Fertig, Hiram, 133 — Milwaukee
Fertig, J H, I art — Milwaukee
Field, Chas M, E 1 rifles — Milwaukee
Fuller, J W — Kilbourne
Gregoy, A S, m, R 22 cav — Whitewater
Gray, Aaron, H 46 — Richmond
Grinnell, R W, D 53 — Cornersville
Hart, J J, F 14 cav — Neillsville
Hisner, Hans, f, 149 — Lamartine
Hodge, A D, 109, A 14 — Lamartine
Jarrett, J H, D 7 cav — Sparta
Johnson, W F, 14 cav — Whitewater
Jordan, Foster, f 14 cav — Friendship
Kallock, F N, B 29 — Milwaukee
Lee, Henry, H 46 — Richmond
Longstaff, Robert M, G 5 cav —
McDonald, A, B 17 cav — La Crosse

McAdams, F, A 10 — La Crosse
McLean, Arthur, 28 — Harlan, Kan
McLean, John, 28 — Harlan, Kan
McMullen, Francis B, I, B 187 — Sturgeon Bay
Machen, A B, c, 45 — Sturgeon Bay
McIntyre, John, A 149 — Neillsville
Merrifield, Samuel, F 16 — Stevens Point
Neal, Jas A, H 100 — Grafton
Ormsbee, H M, C 16 cav — Westfield
Owen, John D, l, sgt L 12 — Ripon
Price, D J, C 6 and 7 — Bay View
Rodolf, Theo F, H 26 — La Crosse
Silverthorn, A C, D 145 — Emmet
Sanford, J, 1 76 — Neillsville
Smith, Ephraim, I 207 — Kaukauna
Sturdevant, H, F 51 — Neillsville
Thorence, Joseph, me, B 144 — Clay Banks
Vangarder, Samuel, H 207 — Stevens Point
Vanorsdale, Cornelius, F 58 — Blk River Falls
Weeks, L, A 79 — Neillsville
Wormer, J D, B 100 — Portage
Wasson, Daniel, E 16 — Troy
Whitman, J, B 177 — St Croix
Williams, John, C 58 — Stevens Point
Young, Edward, 2 bucktails — Whitewater

DISTRICT OF COLUMBIA.

Baker, J S, maj, 1 cav — St Croix Falls
Sterenes, Adam, 2d cav — Rock Falls

MARYLAND.

Anderson, Dr W A, 3 — La Crosse

VIRGINIA.

Schroedus, Christopher C, m, 2 cav — Alma

WEST VA.

Neal, James A, A 1 cav — Grafton, W Va
Baud, Phinas B, F 11 — Galesville

NORTH CAROLINA.

Smolk, William J, 2 — Stevensville

FLORIDA.

Richardson, W H, 1 cav — Milwaukee

ALABAMA.

Humphrey, Henry G, 13 — Atlanta, Ga

LOUISIANA.

Brent, N P, E 2 — St Croix

OHIO.

Allen, J D, D 7 — Colby
Adams, Richard, C 94 — Springfield
Adams, N C, J 11 — Menominee
Andrus, John, f, 14 — New Prospect
Arheger, George, f, A 103 — Van Dyne
Benjamin, Ass, B 2 cav — Tomah
Biller, C C, B 135 — Springfield
Birges, H c, e, 230 — Milwaukee
Bryant, B F, A 101 — La Crosse
Bernard, J L, K 29 — West Salem
Boorer, Henry, f, C 172 — Waupun
Beamer, K, C 125 — Menominee
Churchill, A, A 42 — Whitewater
Colton, Peter, F 61 — Stevens Point
Converse, F L, f, E 1 light art — Sparta
Dueschamb, William, ar, K 26 — Fond du Lac
Esterly, A B, f, C 2 cav — Whitewater
Filler, J S, G 46 — Kaukauna
Gallagher, Patrick, H 16 — Kenosha
Green, Albert, C 37 — Kaukauna
Gregg, L B, K 135 —
Gregg, Luther B, m, K 135 — Milwaukee
Higgins, C M, I, H 196 — Whitewater
Hinsin, J, 33 — Menasha
Ives, Frank, e, C 144 — Sturgeon Bay
Jordan, John, me, 2 H, C 34 — Fond du Lac
Judd, S S. 2 cav — Janesville

Logan, Wm. K 9 cav — Black Hawk
Lernis, P H, L 11 cav — Juneau
Lamb, Jas E, G 113 — Adams
Ludington, C A, H 30, — Neillsville
Miller, C M, H 43 — Neillsville
Merriam, C E, E 1 cav — Stevens Point
Melntosh, Jas, C — Kewaunee
McFarland, M, M 5 cav — Longwood
Neff, Henry, F 19 — Portage
Nelson, W V, C 177 — Portage
Putnam, W R, E 162 — La Crosse
Pinney, H A, f, G 23 — Sturgeon Bay
Pemberton, Alex, 23 — Brothertown
Possnis, Frank. G 6 — Stevens Point
Robbins, Burr, C 40 — Janesville
Randolph, Wm, C 147 — Springfield
Rockmer, Douglas, C — Menominee
Schallene, Ottmar, m, hosp st. 38 — Ripon
Stratton, Jos, E 31 — Menominee
Stratton, Harmon, E 31 — Downsville
Stafford, B G, C 174 — Neillsville
Shaw, Frank, K 3 cav — Bayfield
Spence. Jas A, 26 — Fond du Lac
Stacy, Wm, K 21 — Colby
Sehlong, H, B 84 — La Crosse
Stilson, C A, V 169 — Fond du Lac
Stutzman, W, A 88 — Buttes des Morts
Stultz, J, E 31 — Downsville
Sullan, A H, C 7 — Milwaukee
Truesdale, J C, E 2 cav — Viola
Travers, Tobias, F 20 — St Croix
Thatcher, Dan, D 74 — Springfield
Turner, T H, C 5 — St Croix
Thomas, Wm H, B 123 — Racine
Valentine, H A, H 14 — Milwaukee
Wells, Jacob, D 36 — Tomah
Wolcott, Geo H, m, K 155 — Milwaukee
Wilhelm, F, 2 — Rush River
Welsh, G, adj — Star Prairie
Welsh, D E, 2 cav — Baraboo

ILLINOIS.

Andrew, Leonard, E 52 — West Bend
Austin, G A, B 9, M 15 — Neillsville
Andrews, Jno, 60 — Janesville
Ambrose, M L, A 19 — Watertown
Atwood, Hiram H, — Richmond
Ambrose, Mortimer, A 19 — Watertown
Baldock, John, B 153 — Sharon
Boesevevelter, Otto, C 3 vet surg — West Bend
Bosseweetler, Otto, C 9 — West Bend
Baily, S J, G 6 cav — Jefferson
Bingenheimer, Val, H 104 — West Bend
Baxter, Jos, 45 — Marshfield
Berg, Frank, D 9 cav — Jefferson
Bechand, A, K 43 — Fond du Lac
Beechum, W E, 1 light art — Milwaukee
Baily, T W, G 132 — Belle Centre
Beal, Wm, 1 88 — Milwaukee
Brown, Isaac, m, sgt A — Ripon
Brown, Ben F, A 82 cav — Lochiel
Harrett, John, F 93 — Hammond
Buchand, Adolph, B cap 13 cav — Fond du Lac
Brown, J G. f 15 — La Crosse Co
Becker, J W. F 72 — Kenosha
Carpenter, A H, F sgt 20 — Fond du Lac
Cafftman, A, 13 — Fond du Lac
Calver, N, E 35 — Fond du Lac
Colby, W J, sgt maj 128 — Neillsville
Colson, E N, corp, A 76 — Fond du Lac
Carel, Edward, A 24 — Kewaunee
Curtis, James R, H 7 cav — Eau Claire
Cally, Hamilton N, 9 — Scotia, Neb
Conant, Jos, K 2 — Weyauwega
Culter, Frank W, maj 57 —
Curtis, R H, C 90 — Stevens Point
Dwyer, John, L 17 cav — Hammond
Drew, Thos, A 2 light art — Portage
Dowe, C, m 2 cav — Harrison
Erwin, C K, m, 45 — Tomah

WISCONSIN SOLDIERS AND SAILORS REUNION ROSTER.

Egan, Jno, sgt, D 49 — Beaver Dam
Ellsworth, W C, C 2 cav — New Richmond
Fradluburg, Geo, C 95 — Neillsville
Fiscott, D, 45 — Elkhorn
Glass, L J, II 61 — Neillsville
Greeble, L, G 25 — Milwaukee
Guilbault, H, inc, 72 — Bayfield
Grandy, Henry, I I 4 — Sevastopol
Gaylnart, Fred, H 68 — Brothertown
Gerhart, Fred, H 56 — Brothertown
Garrett Jacob, F 42 — Falls City
Gennug, W, G 13 — City Point
Gedgwick, Geo G, 132 — Kewaunee
Gingles, Jno, G 1 light art — Waterloo
Gaspard, W H, B 134 — LaCrosse
Helmenstine, A C, sgt C 7 cav West Blue Mounds
Hanks, Warren, I, F 6 cav — Sturgeon Bay
Haehmann, Jno, D 82 — Kirchhagu
Hutchinson, C, G 17 cav — Hutchinson
Hollinbank, Cornelius, C R K 43 — Knapp
Hull, H J, D 118 — Whitewater
Horlon, T W, G 1 light art — Friendship
Horn, Henry H, A 48 — St Croix
Hetherington, S H, I 10 — Richmond
Hurtley, F J, G 82
Haristony, Chas S
Hunt, R C, C 20 — Reedsburg
Johnson, R W, L 2 light art — Jefferson
Koch, Theo, A 16 cav — West Bend
Kensler, Miles, G 9 — Sturgeon Bay
Killnar, Leopold, 58 — Denmark
Kellogg, Harvey W, C 74 — Knapp
Kemp, N J, K 85 — Sparta
Lewis, G, I 15 — LaCrosse
Lesley, Alex, e, F 9 cav — Milwaukee
Leftingwell, Sam'l, H 9 cav — Wonewoc
LaIne, Isaac, ar, H — Waupun
Long, Jesse B, F 93 — Menominee
Marks, F C, corp, B 12
Murphy, Edw, L 6 cav — Janesville
Marsh, A G, D 13 — LaCrosse
McAlpin, A, 2 light art — Janesville
McCurdy. H, K 116 inf — Whitecome
McLaughlin, H, f, L sgt 17 — Hammond
Moberg, A, E 71 — Amherst
Morrison, J S — Richmond
Myrluh, J J, F 20 — Menominee
Munson, Geo S, L 8 cav — St Croix
Miner, C E, E 34 — Springfield
Merrit, C, K 7 — Stevens Point
Nye, E G, s, G 72 — Arcadia
Nichols, W F, 118 — Menominee
Noyes, G B, ph, C 146 — Winneconne
Odel, Eugene D, 36 cav — Richmond
Piers, Chas, Bridges Bat light art — Menominee
Palmer, C II, M 8 cav — LaCrosse
Painer, S R, l 4 — Menominee
Phillips, C, E 9 cav — Salem
Piper, Mahlin, C 95 — Sharon
Quinn, Frank D, A 72 — Milwaukee
Reynolds, Geo W, C 95 — Sharon
Rice, E J, K 78 — Neillsville
Reuschlein, Aug, sgt K 14 — Burlington
Ries, Ben, l, 14 — Burlington
Rogers, W H, I 15 — Ft Atkinson
Rogers, B F, Chaplain 15 — Whitewater
Rathburn, R A, 2 — Bush River
Rice, Horace K, I 7 — Little Chute
Salisbury, O A, C 58 — Sharon
Schilling, Alonzo, K 95 — Sharon
Smith, H A, capt 55 — Janesville
Slater, Wm, K 30 — Neillsville
Sister, G W, E 8 cav — Neillsville
Smith, J W, A 4 cav — Oconomowoc
Starr, Fred, K 46 — Muscoda
Sanner, Adam, G 69 — Janesville
Smith, Chas, A 13 — Janesville
Silck, Alonzo L, A 12 — Janesville
Strance, Henry — Osman
Steel, A J, L 8 cav — Memphis, Tenn

Spencer, Barzilla, C 137 — St Croix
Sutter, Jno B, C 127 — Stevens Point
Tuckwood, Jno, G 69 — Janesville
Tousley, W H, K 69 — Janesville
Tanner, W A, F 89 — Whitewater
Trash, Warren, H — Falls City
Truax, Robt, B 10 — Lincoln Co
Valentine, C L, Register of deeds. 1 — Janesville
Vetter, Ferd, policeman, I 11 — Fond du Lac
Volmer, Jacob, Chicago Battery — Kenosha
Wernen, Geo, I 150 — Oak Centre
Weber, Math, I 166 — Burlington
Wallace, C H, D 141 — Lincoln, Co
Wayman, Victor, M 17 cav — Madison
Wheeler, Henry. C 95 — Tomah
West, J C, corp H 15 — Muscoda
Young, G W, U 63 — Earaboo

INDIANA.

Amick, Jas, F 74 — Springfield
Archer, Isaac, 25 bat — Delton
Burns, Eli, K 29 — Menominee
Batley, Dan'l S, drum corps, 73 — Menominee
Cunningham, Jas, D, 34 — Springfield
Corral, Jno, f, G 144 — Bayfield
Crittenden, J D, Q M A 2 — Bayfield
Digen, Sam'l, C 97 — Neillsville
Dudley, W W, Gen 19 — Indianapolis, Ind
Dueschamb, Wm, me, M 34 cav — Fond du Lac
Fanning, Hiram M, K 44 — Tomah
Fillman, Jacob, C 27 — Menominee
Gibion, Jno, 19 — St Paul
Gerraughty M, me, f 80 Emerald — Erin Prairie
Green, Lucius L, A 27 — Menominee
Hotchkiss, Jno, B 146 — Fox Lake
Harvey, E, I 11 cav — Eagle Corners
Hurlburt, Jno, G 94 — Muscoda
Ketchum, Jerome D, K 7 — Racine
Kimball, M B, C 138 — Madison
Koerocr, Geo B, sgt M 1 cav — Fond du Lac
Lyons, Jas, C 46 — Springfield
Mahan, S E, ck, 1 R 149 — Bayfield
Mahan, J L R, A Q M A 118 — Bayfield
McCulloc, Jno, l 135 — Springfield
McDarmon, K F, art A 7 — Springfield
Parker, H J, me, F 68 — Brandon
Phellips, Geo W, F 11 — St Croix
Peabody, S V, A 128 — LaCrosse
Rapp, Antone, l, D 4 cav — Fond du Lac
Richards, J W, B 20 — Kenosha
Schoen, Chas, G 16 — Oconomowoc
Sutton, C C, H 48 — Stevens Point
Straitan, W, me, 11 bat — Milwaukee
Teller, F P, B 11 — Hortonville
Vaughn, T J, B 44 — Fond du Lac
Willer, Geo, 2 R D 9 — Burlington
Watts, L S, color sgt B 7 — Madison
Welch, Sidney, corp F 44 — Baldwin
Wallav, Jno J, M cav — Stevens Point

MICHIGAN.

Allen, Wm H. H, H 5 — Menominee
Atwood, A, E 3 cav — Seymour
Baker, L R, ph, B 20 — Lamartine
Batchelder, Carlos C, 1, 5 — Sevastopool
Bambrue, Vernon, 19 — Lind
Ballard, H D, K 1 — Oshkosh
Brown, O M, M 1 cav — Neillsville
Bhlopp, C, G 19 — Plover
Curtis, Aluren, C 1 — St Croix
Chape, E B, sgt maj, 24 — Milwaukee
Christmas, J H, G 12 — Neillsville
Doherty, Thos E, me, 5 — Bayfield
Ducut, H A, C 14 — Portage
Edwards, A M, col 24 — Detroit, Mich
Hardy, Ira M, E 26 — Oshkosh
Haller, Chas, m, 22 — Burlington
Harper, Andrew E — Kaukauna
Henderslut, Jas, 2 cav — Omro
Hilson, Frauk, 13 — Fond du Lac
Johnson, All P, c, L 1 — Rome

Keefe, Jno O, B 1 cav — Appleton
Kohl, Jno J — Negaunee, Mich
Kuchll, Henry, light-house keeper, 27 — Bayfield
Lambert, W E, E 2 — Racine
Livingstone, Jno, 6 cav — Janesville
Lambert, W S, E 2 — Racine
LaPointe, G W, col 37 — Springfield
Lewis, Solomon, I 7 — Friendship
McCarthy, W, G 14 — Colby
Michael, Jos I, fisherman, 29 — Bayfield
Palmer, G W, me, B 6 — Sturgeon Bay
Pike, R D, m, 1 lt, B 1 cav — Bayfield
Runsill, P, light-house keeper, 2 cav — Bayfield
Rottmann, Wm, G 22 — Milwaukee
Sherman, Wm, B 9 — Janesville
Snow, H, B G — Neillsville
Watson, H L, 17 — Adrian, Mich
Weaver, O F, 4 — Beaver Dam

IOWA.

Bolton, Jas, K 1 cav — Racine
Blair, Wm W, A 1 cav — Menominee
Brisboys, Jno W, A 3 — Portage
Cummings, Ed, H 29 — Neillsville
Clark, C D, 8 bat — La Crosse
Dougherty, Adolphus, I 29 — Tomae
Diedrich, Henry, 1 30 — Downsville
Diedrich. Fred, 6 cav — Menomineh
Dorr, D F, G 2 cav — Waupaca
Fay, Hiram, M 1 cav — Hammond
Forbes, Sam'l J, F 22 — Racine
Hill, E. A 7 — Ishpeming, Mich
Henrich, F W, D 8 — Janesville
Hoffman, E C, F 156 — Baldwin
Heller, Thos S, G 1 cav — Menominee
McLaugh'ln, D, 46 — Campbellsport
Milliman, C H, clerk, corp D 28 — Ripon
Oakley, P W G 9 — St Croix
Pipes, J E, 14 — Baraboo
Parker, A J, 17 — LaCrosse
Rodgers, Geo W, f, 7 cav — Ludoga
Ross, F J, B 94 — Springfield
Silvornall, Chas H, sgt G — Phillips
Soll, Jno, 1 lt, H 4 — Baldwin
Slytor, L T, K 5 — Superior
Snively J H, D 44 — Menominee
Siverson, J J, — Cambridge
Temple, W H, 1 3 — Knaph
Temple, Isaac N, B 6 cav — Knuph
Temple, Jas F, I 3 — Knaph
Trombles, H W, E 3 art — Neillsville
Van Wie, A C, I — LaCrosse
Woodruff, Alberius D, K 3 cav — Tomah
Wallace, Jno, E 6 cav — City Point
Woodard, Lysander, F 15 — Carlton
Wilson, C M, C 4 cav — Springfield
Wilsle, H, H 9 cav — LaCrosse
Whittle, H B, I, A 25 — Bayfield

MINNESOTA.

Burchadine, Richard, bat — St Croix
Butler, J C, A 2 — Madison
Brown, Ed, G 1 art — Weston
Bell, Alf H, I, K 5 — Bayfield
Brown, J, B 10 — LaCrosse
Crosby, Henry W, C 8 — St Croix
Corney, Martin, H 11 — Stevens Point
Davis, Jno H, G 10 — Springfield
Decker, Alonzo, 1 bat — Granger
DuCate, M H, D 9 — Spencer
Everts, K L, 2 cav — Falls City
Field, E B, corp L 1 cav — Star Prairie
Farnsworth, H J, C 3 cav — Neillsville
Ford, E W, O 5 — LaCrosse
Harris, Thos, a — Ripon
Hazen, G B, bugler B 1 — Waupun
Hoffman, Frank, D 4 — St Croix
Hunter, Jno, l 5 — Springfield
Hunter, W L, 1 1 cav — Springfield
Henstis, W G, K 5 — Star Prairie
Herbert, L. 10 — Rush River

WISCONSIN SOLDIERS AND SAILORS REUNION ROSTER.

Baunn, Conrad, M 2 cav — Kohlvill
Borvison, Aud, 1 bat — Weston
Jerome, Timothy, H 6 — Bangor
Kidder, L L, E — Star Prairie
Lake, Sidney, L — Merrimac
Marlett, Jno, C 2 — Tiffany
Meddaugh, Jno, pa, sgt C 11 — Waupun
Nordeen, P J, C 9 — Lind
Partridge, E C, B 3 — Warren
Pretell, II, G 7 — Rock Elm Centre
Patten, J, B 10 — LaCrosse
Patten, G, B 10 — LaCrosse
Perkins, E G, K 11 — LaCrosse
Scoville, J F, 1 mt rangers — Neillsville
Swan, B, B 10 — LaCrosse
Swanson, Anton — St Croix
Shehe, Owen, I 1 — Waupun
Shufelt, Sheldon, H 2 cav — Omro
Thompson, E J, K 1 — Cylon
Thoen, H A, 1 — Rush River
Washburn, Lewis, f, C 11 — Metomen
Wolf, Adam, F 1 — St Joseph
Welland, Dominick, f, D 4 — Sevastopol
Williamson, Jas, C 4 — Menominee
Wilcox, Heman, bus driver, H 11 — Waupun
Webster, C E, G 1 — Almond
Yoerg, Lewis, E 5 — St Croix

MISSOURI.

Austin, G O, F 10 cav — Waukesha
Allinger, Chas, m, D 20 — Fond du Lac
Berghardt, Gustave, sergt G 5 — Fond du Lac
Breneman, J, B 8 — La Crosse
Brickwell, Joseph, F 1 — Portage
Fischer, Henry, clk, F 2 — Milwaukee
Gaehler, Fredrick, sergt G 2 — Johnson's Creek
Gunn, A, E 11 cav — La Crosse
Gardner, G, B 8 — La Crosse
Goodman, Peter A, L 11 cav — Menomonee
Gray, Jno R, l, C 41 — Bayfield
Habermann, Jno, E 9 cav — Milwaukee
Haas, Andrew, corp, H 27 — Burlington
Ingman, J, B 8 — La Crosse
Langhoff, Jno, 27 — Mischicott
La Flesh, F J, capt, D 2 cav — Nevins
Mc Donald, D, maj, 2 — Louisville, Ky
Murphy, Wm, H 10 — Kenosha
Moddy, James, H 14 — Stevens Point
Noth, Frederick, E 2 — Tomah
Paulus, Jno, M 4 cav — Neillsville
Rogers, H C, 3 cav — La Crosse
Relph, C N, J 13 cav — Menomonee
Rooney, Thos, 32 — La Crosse
Spite, Thos J, H 18 — St Croix
Spencer, R C, A 3 — Milwaukee
Turner, W W D, a, Col, 20 — Ripon
Warner, A, B 15 — La Crosse
Wall, chas, l, A 2 — Milwaukee
Wright, H W, K 7 cav — Racine

KENTUCKY.

Burch, Isaac, 4 cav — Fond du Lac

NEBRASKA.

Stockman, Jno, 2 cav — Springfield

KANSAS.

Eastwood, Joe B, B 18 — Menominee
Noyes, Jno, f, capt E 7 cav — Sturgeon Bay

COLORADO.

Cate, Alden O, 2 cav — Appleton

NEW MEXICO.

Nevill, Jas, K 1 — Christie

CALIFORNIA.

Cleary, Sheldon, C 2 cav — Verona
Howley, Pat, h, E — Bayfield
Moore, l, W H, E 5 — Fond du Lac
Sharp, Jas H, 1 — Rio

REGULAR ARMY.

Austin, G O, F 10 cav — Waukesha
Erridge, H, Mexican vet H 13 — Oconomowoc
Garey, Peter V, sgt D 16 — Fond du Lac
Gilson, N S, a, lt col 58 U S C I — Fond du Lac
Heck, Jacob, 1]6 cav — Milwaukee
Hanson, Chas, 4 art bat B — Mauston
Maes, Alonzo B, G 20 art — Eau Claire
Rogers, Hugh, K 4 — Sharon
Reed, Morris, A 1 bat and inf — Seymour
Robinson, W W, 1 lt 9 — Port Potter, D T
Rees, Sam'l H, 16 — Portage
Smith, C W, mc, sgt A 3 cav — Fond du Lac
Skinner, C H, sgt 16 — Fond du Lac
Snowden, David H, field and staff — Sharon
South A J, B 3 — Amherst
Vaughn, M D, H 7 U S C I — Portage
Wood, Chas, E 13 cav — Oconomowoc

STATE NATIONAL GUARDS.

Evergreen City Guards.

Sheboygan, Wisconsin.

(ORGANIZED NOV. 4TH, 1874.)

Capt C A Born
1st Lt H W Trester
2nd Lt
Orderly Wm Schroeder
2nd Sgt Aug Warnecke
3d Sgt J C Schroeder
4th Sgt Wm Apel
5th Sgt F Jakubs
1st Corp A M Lausins
2nd Corp G Speekmann
3d Corp C Dern
4th Corp Jno Beisang
See O Geussenhaimer
Drum Maj H Ohde
Amanu, J
Buechle, Anton
Buechle, A
Behrens, J
Corson, S
Cary, C
Dean, A
Ewerhardt, J
Flemmig, E
Fuliner, G D
Gruebner, Aug
Gruebner, H
Gruebner, H
Gibbs, C
Gothard, E
Gunderman, E
Guyette, Wm
Horn, E
Hensel, C
Hoffman, R
Hammerslough, A
Haak, L
Hartsberg, Wm
Knocke, H
Kramme, A
Knoedler, J
Knoedler, F
Kulmer, H
Kohl, W
Kriegelstein, F
Leicht, M
Leuschel, Chas
Lind, A
Leighton, A J
Moser, A
Moser, Ad
Maas, H
Mohr, A
Maas, Fr
Mikels, P
Renewaud, R
Rose, H
Shinmeyer, L
Schreiber, H
Speckman, A
Schubert, P
Sym, R
Servis, C
Schnetz, G
Steuger, J
Thotp, F
Thorp, G
Thiernau, G
Vollmer, J
Wesnuth, Geo
Wright, Geo

Sheridan Guard.

Milwaukee. Wisconsin.

(ORGANIZED JUNE 23D, 1869.)

Capt H W White
Lt John Coogan
Lt T H Metiath
Orderly Jno E Pennefeather
2nd Sgt M A Seery
3rd Sgt W H Halsey
4th Sgt Wm Kane
5th Sgt John Foley
Q M Sgt T McManus
Anderson, H
Boyle, Wm
Campbell, Thos
Cunningham, E
Coffey, D
Connors, James
Coolidge, H E
Canning, Frank
Donnelly, P
Daggett, J T
Doyle, Charles
Deollu, James
Dunn, Joseph
Dunn, Michl
Dunn, Mert J
Dunner, Peter
Daley, James
Daley, John
Devitt, M
Driscoll, John
Duan, John T
Fitzgerald, H J
Flinn, Rich
Farrell, E
Foley, P
Fiskin, T A
Faran, P
Goldin, John
Graham, James
Grogan, H J
Grogan, John
Geishusch, Chas
Hess, Joseph
Lynch, John
Luneham, John
Lynch, John C
Linneham, P
McBride, Peter
McEvoy, Dan
McCann, Pat
McCaigne, Wm

WISCONSIN SOLDIERS AND SAILORS REUNION ROSTER.

Murphy, T
Magher, P
McGrath, P W
Mooney, L J
McCowell, J
Malone, Wm
Nicholls, J
O'Connor, Wm P
O'Connor, M J
O'Connor, Jere
O'Connell, Wm
O'Neil, J F
O'Connor, Phil
O'Neil, Joseph
Plunkett, Thomas
Peacock, Sam F
Quinn, Wm J
Riddy, Martin
Ryan, John
Reilly, John
Schumann, H
Schuipe, Andrew
Sullivan, M J
Sharr, C
Tice, Sam A
Voeyier, John
Ward, James P
Ulrich, Wm

Sherman Guards.

Neillsville, Wisconsin

(ORGANIZED MARCH 13TH, 1875.)

Capt J W Ferguson
1 Lt J C Canon
2 Lt G A Ludington,
Orderly Sam'l Dixon
2nd Sgt H Fuller
3d Sgt J B Rude
4th Sgt R McCaivey
5th Sgt L Soniac
1st Corp S Miner
2nd Corp W Ketel
3d Corp W A Southard
4th Corp Wm Poate
5th Corp G W Traguer
6th Corp R McAdams
7th Corp G K Redmond
8th Corp A Longren
Arnold, W C
Burgess, F
Blakeslee, Geo
Benedict, A
Carter, F M
Cummings, Ed
Carlton, E
Carlton, H
Cornwell, B
Case, J B
Churchill, T B
Darling, F C
Frantz, C
Ferguson, H T
Flint, F
Farnsworth, H J
Glass, L J
Gibson, S
Gates, C H
Gallaher, N E
Heaslet, Wm
Huntly, W M
Inham, Geo
Jones, W B
Johnson, Fred
Ketch, Herman
Ketch, Aug

King, H
King, F
Lynch, B D
Lawrence, H
Lawrence, E
Leo, F
Mead, E T
Markey, E H
Parker, H
Parker, M W
Poate, Henry
Payne, D
Reedll, F
Rowe, Wm
Rowe, Jos
Root, G A
Schuster, L
Schuster, H
Sprague, R L
Swan, Wm
Safford, D L
Stoker, Rich
Van Sickle, A
Widing, G
Wessenberge, W
Woods, J

La Crosse Light Guard.

LaCrosse, Wisconsin.

(ORGANIZED AUG. 13TH, 1878.)

Capt M T Moore
1st Lt J M Holley
2nd Lt F A Copeland
Orderly M J Pitkin
2nd Sgt W Rossiter
3d Sgt G L Lord
4th Sgt R L Spence
5th Sgt W B Webb
1st Corp A James
2nd Corp C B Friese
3d Corp C J Stevens
4th Corp A Metzgar
5th Corp D W VanBergh
6th Corp C U Hawley
7th Corp F H Hankerson
8th Corp W E Doane
Atkinson, Walter
Ansley, P T
Alter, C E
Benton, C
Brice, Harry
Burton, F A
Braddish, G
Berg, W H
Bacheller, N C
Blashek, H
Chamberlain, E
Chamberlain, C E
Cogswell, G H
Cramer, L H, musician
Corry, J W
Crosby, C S
Drake, Wm, musician
Eppinger, J A
Eckle, C F
Fahey, R
Fischer, C F
Grams, J
Hall, C G
Nell, F
Hanscom, S C
Hayes, M F
Hickson, F P
James, A
Junger, F
Kivin, J
Listman, C

Lewis, G
Langworthy, F E
Milton, W T
Meason, W E
Maxwell, J
Moran, Alex
Myers, H C
Norman, C
Nichols, L
Prentiss, A G
Powers, C F
Phelps, F I
Pamperin, O
Renehan, M F
Rand, J B
Rand, A R
Shove, B
Saupe, J
Stirneman, J
Smith, C A
Smith, L A
Snell, A T
Stockwell, C S
Swisley, J F
Shadbolt, G
Foeller, F
Thornley, A W
Torrance, W
Thurber, S G
Walker, R H
Warner, C
Weiks, M
Wilson, G E

Oshkosh Guards.

Oshkosh, Wisconsin.

(ORGANIZED MARCH 28TH, 1876.)

Capt Gabe Bouck
1st Lt W H Patten
2nd Lt J N Ruby
Orderly G O M Hasbrouck
2nd Sgt W S Wheeler
3d H W Leach
4th F N Snell
1st Corp F Cross
2nd Corp Wm Wall, Jr
Austin, E J
Allen, F
Anderson, W
Brainard, A M
Berkley, J J
Blake, C
Bremer, J
Bourke, D
Boyd, F
Buckstaff, M
Brow, O
Bennet, E E
Boynton, W D
Cameron, G W
Charbonneau, T
Clarke, C E
Damuth, S A
Ellis, E
Edwards, H
Fiell, J
Foster, G
Griffith, W L
Grlscoe, J
Hasbronek, S J
Hooper, A B
Hale, Chas
Kreuger, L
Koll, J
Larsen, S

Lewis, O E
Lichenberger, O
Leitz, F
Lang, I.
Laulis, O
Lane, N
Leuch, E
Mniva, J
Merritt, D
Meyer, R
Nudine, G
Osborne, R
Putney, G P
Raymond, M
Ransome, A
Service, A
Smith, L C
Steinfort, Wm
Strasser, H
Stroud, F
Schmidt, Jno
Traphagen, C
Williams, J R
Wheeler, G H
Ward, J P
Zenhisiorf, C
Bulb, Thos H, drum major
Brown, E, fifer
Crosby, F, fifer
Jones, A, drummer
LaQue, D, drummer
Perkins, F, drummer
Power, B, fifer
Schmidt, G, drummer
Spore, C B, bugler
Thomas, W R. fifer

Governor's Guard.

Madison, Wisconsin.

(ORGANIZED MARCH 24TH, 1875.)

Capt Ph Heinkel
1st Lt Jno Heyl
2nd Lt Geo Ueckermann
Orderly F Roessner
2nd Sgt Chas Renter
3d Sgt Aug Schmidt
4th Sgt J Ippel
5th Sgt H Baumgartner
1st Corp L Joachim
2nd Corp H Wiebur
3d Corp J Verbosen
4th Corp H Schmelzkopf
5th Corp W Sauthoff
6th Corp G Joachim
7th Corp H Behn
8th Corp F Schuckert
Trens W Holin
Anbrecht, H
Beyler, F
Blied, J
Boehmer, J
Eisig, L
Elsner, E
Fauerbach, L
Gehrke, E
Gartner, M
Gerfen, H
Gramm, A
Hank, A
Havermann, H
Helsig, H
Joachim, J
Kempf, J
Kineter, J
Knoch, G
Kupper, Th

Lange, A
Lane, H
Lueckensmeier, H
Marx, H
Mueller, E
Mueller, Ch
Nebel, G
Nebel, Ed
Nebel, Emil
Oldenberger, F
Ramthum, A
Reiner, E
Reuter, J
Suchs, J
Santhoff, F
Santhoff, A
Schenk, F
Schleicher, J
Schleibher, Chas
Schoen, T
Seidel, W
Singer, F
Scherer, Th
Stock, J
Trinkans, W
Wedelstaedt, W
Wirth, J
Wissler, A
Wolf, J
Zimmermann, A

Bayfield Rifles.

Bayfield Wisconsin.

(ORGANIZED FEBRUARY 5TH, 1873.)

Capt R D Pike
1st Lt J L Gouyon
2nd Lt F M Herrick
Orderly Thos Doherty
2nd Sgt S Bartin
3d W J Herbert
4th C E Herrick
5th L Bachand Jr
1st corp Jno Carroll
2nd F T Herbert
3d F Bartin, Jr
4th Geo Flemming
Atkinson, J S
Bachand, Nelson
Bouo, C A
Boutin, Jr, Edw
Boutin, Theo
Bowker, H C
Bruchner Jno
Coburn, Jos
Day, Jr, Geo
Dennis, H
Drouillard, Jno
Drouillard, W
Fisher, F
Godin, L
Godin, J
Guilbault, H S
Guilbault, C L
Herbert, F A
Herbert, J
Hofele, Geo
Hofele, Chas
Hofele, O
Hochdaner, M
Inglis, R
Larson, N
Leiby, Chas
Maban, S E
Morean, M
Morin, F
O'Kenson, P
Patrick, J F

Rhilly, J
Rabadowe, I
Sandgren, Jno
Smith, A B
Smith, James
Smith, N
Stofiles, J
Willey, N J

Janesville Guard.

Janesville, Wisconsin.

(ORGANIZED AUG. 5TH, 1876.)

Capt H A Smith
1st Lt M A Newman
2nd Lt C F Glass
Orderly W A Hand
2nd Sgt J B Doe, Jr
3d Sgt J W Bintliff
4th Sgt T Judd
5th Sgt G Woodruff
1st Corp F McLean
2nd Corp H P Chrlinger
3d Corp E D McGowan
4th Corp L D Libby
th Corp C C McLean
6th Corp S Smith
7th Corp W H Doe
8th Corp W Evenson
Arvis, W
Asheraft, W H, Jr
Bates, J W
Bump, L C
Bemis, O
Curtis, C E
Carter, H G
Coppin, J
Doty, E P
Dewey, F M
Decker, J
Eller, C
Grove, G F
Hudson, S H
Hogsboom, F D
Hemming, C
Hemming, W
Higgins, G W
Jackson, F D
Knox, L
King, L J
Lawrence, H
Lusk, O
Lane, E P
Mahoney, J A
Merrill, H E
McKenna, J E
McLean, R
Norton, W H
Palmer, W
Putnam, F
Putnam, C G
Rogan, R J
Ripley, O
Randall, C F
Stevens, O
Sykes, H D
Stone, F H
Scartliff, O
Shea, J E
Sutherland, C
Thomas, E G
Tracy, E
Taylor, F
Webster, F U
Wickham, A L
Woodruff, J J
Wintermute, C E
Williams, E E

Williams, W
Whitton, E V

Guppey Guard.

Portage, Wisconsin.

(ORGANIZED JUNE 26TH, 1877.)

Capt J D Womer
1st Lt W S Wentworth
2nd Lt W B Stevens
Orderly H W Orthman
2nd Sgt G C Cavnagic
3d Sgt J C Britt
4th Sgt J H Wells
5th Sgt C P Jeager
1st Corp I A Ridgway
2nd Corp T M Maine
3d Corp T J Wells
4th Corp R G Shackell
5th Corp J Dempsey
6th Corp B R Lewis
7th Corp J Sweenky
8th Corp W D McKinney
A Carnagie, colors
J B Wilts, drummer
Able, D H
Alverson, C L
Anderson, J C
Allen, L S
Barrett, T
Brandt, T
Bard, C M
Beattie, W D
Beattie, Rob I.
Bennett, G R
Beugel, Wm
Brandt, F
Cole, J F
Corning, W S
Cook, M E
Clark, H
Clark, A
Cleary, J
Dalton, D J
Dempsey, R
Edwards, F M
Edwards, W
Fathschild, W
Fyfe, G C
Frownfelter, E C
Gillman, W B
Goss, F F
Hemmenway, E H
Hardie, J L
Hoffman, F F
James, J E
Loomis, F W
Matue, D C
McDuffie, F S
Maely, H
Maloy, G M
Raundeau, L G
Ruthven, Jno
Richardson, Wm
Schulze, L
Swift, E J
Shackell, G T
Spain, Jno
Sherman, Wm I
Thompson, F B
Turner, F J
Tscharner, G
Williams, J E
Warren, F C
Witter, A L

Ripon Rifles.

Ripon, Wisconsin

(ORGANIZED MARCH 28TH, 1877.)

Capt Hugo Schultz
1st Lt F Thiel
2nd Lt E Kalk
Orderly Sgt Wm Marlwig
F Steinbring
A Steinbring
F Deguer
M Aruger
H Willroock
S Schmudlack
F Daniels
J Mailhofes
C Giese
Wm Nohl
Wm Reck
Birkholz, G
Bulzin, F
Denzin, G
Dreger, Wm
Drews, Wm
Eyyerl, C
Gartzke, C
Gelhsar, G
Grutzmacher, H
Grutzmacher, F
Haas, J
Hildebrandt, G
Hildebrandt, O
Hesse, J
Johnson, O
Kalk, Wm
Kohl, G
Litz, G
Lubitz, R
Lembert, T
Milahu, J
Marlwig, H
Maulhle, F
Marlen, H
Mielke, F
Otto, G
Pischke, J
Prulz, Louis
Prill, J
Rapp, Wm
Steinbring, E
Steinbring, T
Strelch, M
Schrandt, F
Schroder, H
Sauger, A
Tobalt, E
Tim, F
Tim, C
Tobalt, C
Teske, G
Weyner, Wm
Weishaar, A
Weinke, J
Wizinske, M
Zimmerman, Wm
Zimmerman, C
Zweiger, F
Zweiger, Wm
Zick, A
Ziehart, Wm
Qunst, Wm
Kohl, H

Bay City Light Guards.

Green Bay, Wisconsin.

Capt E C Kendall
1st Lt D Soper
2nd Lt O C Davidson
Orderly Sgt Chas Reisch
2nd Sgt A Lucas
3d Sgt A L Gray
4th Sgt J H Jansen
5th Sgt W P Greene
1st Corp J W Follett
2nd Corp G F Gaylord
3d Corp B F Sommers
4th Corp E J Colleffe
5th Corp W J Farnsworth
6th Corp W H Gray
7th Corp H O'Leary
8th Corp I. Hueffel
Color Sgt H Hagemeister
Q M F E Harris
Rosch, M
Martin, X
Elmore, J H
Libbey, O
Doyen, S L
Benson, M B
Lane, J D
Leddy, W D
White, C W
Last, J B
Nicholson, E
Spencer, H F
Lindley, S
Gilkey, A W
Greene, C F
Emeigh, J D
Bender, Louis
Harriman, L
Luas,e Dan
King, L A
McCormick, M J
Keir, Chas
Marshall, J W
Lucas, Jr, A
Chappie, J
Cooke, W D
Wilner, H D
Henderson, D F
Ranous, Geo
Collette, W E
Henderson, W P
Servis, J
Bugnelet, Geo
Lefebvre, Edw
Farnsworth, J
Roland, E
Wallwitz, C W
Masse, A G M
Griffith, E
Jacobs, A
Brire, J
Sager, Geo
King, D W, drum major

Kosciusko Guards.

Milwaukee, Wisconsin.

(ORGANIZED SEPT 2ND, 1874

Capt F J Jorhardt
Andczejesky, Jos
Andczejesky, Jos
Irneholz, Bernard
Besler, Jos
Biedwicky, Martin

WISCONSIN SOLDIERS AND SAILORS REUNION ROSTER.

Cyrmer, Alexander
Dombrowsky, Bernard
Fenig, Konstant
Heller, Jos
Janiszewsky, Lukas
Kloss, Michael
Kolodzy, Jno
Kolpacky, Seofil
Kolpacky, Bernard
Kubicky, Jos
Lukaszewsky, Valentine
Michalah, Albert
Matelsky, Jas
Muhulsky, Lukas
Markiewily, Alexander
Nowak, Jakob
Ploj, Jos
Grezel, Friderick
Casimir, Olszewsky
Powinsky, Fred
Piotrowsky, Valentine
Pormansky, Havier
Piechowsky, Jos
Korga, Michael
Kayskie, Ignatz
Koziaukowsky, Carol
Kozmarinowsky, Casimir
Kozansky, Theo
Kozmaryuowsko, Jacob
Kosinsky, Anton
Smolarz, Anton
Silbar, Himan
Wesolek, Frank
Wylepky, Albert
Walnek, Jos
Wojda, Matt
Wawzyniakowski, Jos
Zyburtowski, Martin
Zyburtowski, Peter
Halick, Jno
Osawsky, Jos
Besler, Anton
Trok, Frank
Broncell, Jno
Guarda, Sylvester
Halicky, Jos
Flanyrzewsky, Stanislaus
Bgeel, Andrew
Plafzek, Peter
Bzerwinsky, Iraman
Kozptoek, Jno
Kawulkowsky, Jacob
Gilinski, Alexander

Lake City Guards.

Madison, Wisconsin.

Capt C P Chapman
1st Lt S Proudfit
2nd Lt A B Burdick
Orderly Sergt E H Chase
Q M J E Davis
1st Sgt W D Curtis
2nd Sgt W J Hein
3d Sgt C L F Kellogg
4th Sgt Geo B Gilman
5th Sgt N A Nelson
1st Corp F R Norton
2d Corp J D Taylor
3d Corp A C Nelson
4th Corp A Proudfit
5th Corp O Norsman
6th Corp A B Morris
7th Corp M F Kain
8th Corp W Sullivan,
Aimers, G F
Beecroft, A B

Bruce, J H
Combs, E E
Corscott, G J
Crawford, J
Curtis, F W
Dean, I
Donnellan, W J
Esser, W B
Fitzpatrick, W D
Foresman, G A
Frenzil, W F
Gallagher, W H
Gleason, Jas
Gotterdam, E A
Grimm, J
Hallagan, Jno
Popkins, A A
Hyland, G
Hyland, J G
Jonas, F W
Kanouse, M
Kearnan, B M
Keenan, Geo
Kessenick, H
Knoerr, G
Lemmon, W D
Lyons, M
Main, E A
McArthur, P H
Membard, E
Moffett, F L
Nelson, C B
Nelson, Louis
Nelson, S A
Nelson, W B
Nichols, G
Park, A G
Pearson, W A
Pickarts, L J
Reesford, C E
Slighton, C F
Smith, F P
Smith, H A
Smith, T
Sorenson, O J
Sullivan, J
Taylor, J L
Van Bergen, A
Webster, B A
Welch, Victor
Zirkle, L J

Germania Light Guards.

Wausau, Wisconsin.

(ORGANIZED JANUARY 10TH, 1875,)

Capt Wm Krueger
1st Lt Ch Krueger
2d Lt Wm Abaham
Arnese, H
Benz, A
Benz, H
Benz, G
Bomann, C
Butzloff, W
Butzloff, H
Buttmhoff, G
Bohm, E
Dumke, W
Dudick, F
Demitz, E
Eggebrecht, A
Erdmana, H
Erdmann, F
Erdmann, Wm
Ereke, R
Ereke, A

Gruse, G
Goetset, R
Garske, C
Hahlke, F
Hahlke, G
Hahlke, Chas
Hass, A
Henning, H
Heling, H
Kopplin, Chas
Kickbusch, F
Kickbusch, Wm
Kickbusch, A
Kaatz, G
Kickhoefel, G
Lemke, A
Lambrecht, H
Miller, A
Mundt, H
Ohrmundt, A
Ruck, G
Stahl, J
Streck, J
Seidler, Wm
Schwranter, A
Schulz, F
Seipp, Chas
Treptou, F
Weiland, M
Weiland, F
Unacketty, L

Milwaukee Light Horse Squadron.

Milwaukee, Wisconsin.

Capt Robt Hill
1st Lt Albert Blatz
2nd Lt Geo W Peck
Adj W E Beecham
Q M J A Brown
Orderly Geo O Clinton
1st Sgt J P Rundle
2nd Sgt Geo J Schoeffel
3d Sgt F C G Brand
4th Sgt H Campbell
5th Sgt Jno Gregg
1st Corp G B Van Norman
2nd Corp C H M Toby
3d Corp Harry Sutter
4th Corp H S Stoltz
5th Corp G S Everingham
6th Corp A Mitchell, Jr
7th Corp C M Goucher
W S Stanley, Jr, treasurer
Dr C D Stanhope, surgeon
Rev G E Gordon, chaplain
Auer, Louis, Jr
Boyd, Jas G
Collins, W A
Cornes, F A
Clements, F M
Ellsworth, Lem
Falk, Frank
Falk, S W
French, S W
Halsey, S W
Huntington, C P
Hill, Jas
Hill, Jacob
Hart, Jesse
King, A R
Kiefer, F
Luscumbe, Robt
Lennox, R G
Larken, C D
Meyers, A B
Merrill, F A
Norris, C W

CARPETS AT WHOLESALE AND RETAIL.

GOLDSMITH & Co.,

355 and 357 East Water Street, Milwaukee, Wisconsin,

In our Retail Department we make a Specialty of Fine Goods in way of

CARPETS,

CURTAINS, SHADES,

Upholstery and Drapery Materials and Trimmings,

Bedding and all other Goods in this line. Have unsurpassed facilities for making up all kinds of

DRAPERY WORK,

Laying Wood Carpets, Parquettry Floors,

and give particular attention to fitting out

STEAMERS, HOTELS, CHURCHES, LODGES
and other Public Buildings.

Estimates and Designs Promptly Furnished.

We have endeavored by strictly fair dealing and close attention to business to merit the patronage of our customers, and should we be favored with your orders, feel confident of giving complete satisfaction. Correspondence solicited. Reliable Price-Lists and Samples sent on application.

WISCONSIN SOLDIERS AND SAILORS REUNION ROSTER.   229

Nowell, W A
Ormond, Wm
Quinn, E S
Swetland, T M
Shea, E A
Spener, Geo A
Spence, Wm
Scott, A H
Underwood, F D
Underwood, W J
Vance, Frank L
Webs, G E
Williams, W C
Wall, Jas C
Weller, Alfred

Randall Guard.

Darlington, Wisconsin

(ORGANIZED MAY 11TH, 1878.)

Capt S F Stewart
1st Lt E Stott
2nd Lt H E Maclellan
Orderly L L Dixon
2nd Sgt J Hanrahan
3d Sgt P VanHook
Brooks, H
Bowman, F
Bush, G
Breeze, G
Breeze, J
Burns, J
Cline, A
Crow, C
Cleary, J W
Curry, W
Chamberlain, J
Dunbar, C
Dunbar, J
Eckerson, L
Eckerson, W
Frinn, M
Fisher, P
Freeman, Geo
Fitzpatrick, J
Gibson, T
Gilman, I
Hough, W B
Hogan, J
Haggarty, F
Hopkins, F
Hanrahan, J
Harrold, S
Hayeh, J
Howe, E
Hanrahan, T
Ingraham, M D
Knight, A
Kitchen, C
Kearns, T
Laddy, E
Langford, J
Martin, J C
Miller, J
Moore, S
McDonald, J
Morrow, T
Morrow, J
Moore, J
Monihan, W R
Morgan, W
McDonald, J
Martin, C
Mahan, B
McDermott, J
Moore, R

Meylor, Jas
Marrs, R
Madlus, Wm
Newman, L
Nash, W E
Pratt, J
Russell, L
Rodgers, H
Smith, G
Stover, G
Stover, A
Sweeny, Ed
Sweeny, J
Sparrow, M
Smith, H
Shebron, G W
Stock, A
Smith, L
Strayer, G
Tennis, C
Tennis, H
Tennis, R
Taylor, F
Thomas, L
Thomas, W
VanHook, Joe
Westerman, J
Whalen, E
White, C
Welsh, J
Whalen, J
Wren, G
Young, M

Ludington Guard.

Menominee, Wisconsin

(ORGANIZED NOVEMBER 21ST, 1876.)

Capt T J George
1st Lt W D Young
2nd Lt G R Bremer
Orderly H T Cassidy
2nd Sgt H E Knapp
3d Sgt H A Wilcox
4th Sgt W W Blair
5th Sgt W P Kirkland
6th Sgt W D Brewer
7th Sgt W J Nott
1st corp M Coleman
2nd corp H A Anderson
3d Corp F L Wilcox
4th Corp H Lucas
5th Corp S A Peterson
6th Corp E Wiggin
7th Corp A S Ladd
8th Corp W Flood
Allen, W E
Bonnell, M
Bull, J
Brickley, J
Bundy, H
Dundy T
Coleman, H
Campbell, F
Curtiss, A O
Curtiss, A L
Curtiss, E
Curtiss, H H
Chapel, W
Cook, G
Diedrich, F
Doolittle, G S
Doolittle, M
Dodge, L
Flint, R J
Garret, W
Gesell, C A
Grover, A
Kelly, J

Lewton, F
Will, K A
Oleson, P E
Oleson, J
Phillips, J C
Reed, H W
Starrum, J
Strand, A
Tubbs, W
Tainter, L S
Schorem, J
Vespers, R
Whitcher, E
Whitcher, F
West, C
Watterson, H A
Webster, S F
Wright, W
Tales, W J
Young, G R
Grannis, E H, surg
Fincont, W, vet. surg
Arnold, W S, musician
Huber, F, musician
Williamson, J B, musician
Williamson, F, musician
Williamson, J, musician
Wright, S, musician
Miller, J, bugler
Wallace, C, bugler
Knoble, J, blacksmith

Bower City Rifles.

Janesville, Wisconsin.

Capt J D LaGrange
1st Lt W H Tonsley
2nd Lt J Andrews
Orderly C Brown
2nd Sgt R Skilley
3d Sgt J Bear
4th Sgt L Lee
5th Sgt A Bintliff
1st Corp J Smith
2nd Corp L Curler
3d Corp C Stout
4th Corp F Hendricks
5th Corp F Cheney
6th Corp F Davis
7th Corp Ch Blay
8th Corp J Murtaugh
Burns, J
Brown, G
Brooks, F
O'Brien, P
Collias, J
Collins, H
Curtis, H
Carlton, S
Decker, J
Delong, H
Darey, D
Eholinger, A
Fellows, F
Francis, F
Faley, J
Grampka, A
Heath, C
Houcland, J
Kelly, E
Kelly, W
Larson, N
Lee, C
Langley, M
Manning, M
Malone, M

Nolay, T
Phillips, C
Stringer, E
Stringer, J
Shaller, N
Smith, E
Truesdale, D
Tuckwood, C
Tuckwood, W
Thorn, J
Tracy, J
Van Buren, V
Wilson, G
Weaver, H, drum major
Wilson, G, fifer
Tobin, M, fifer
Van Kirk, F, fifer
Shaller, G, fifer
Watson, H, drummer
Macker, G, drummer
Mane, W, drummer
Goldsborough, W, drummer
Bronson, drummer

Delavan Guards.

Delavan, Wisconsin.

Capt Fred B Goodrich
1t Lt Chas T Isham
2d Lt Menson Vedder
1st Sgt E B Judson
2d Sgt N Washburne
3d Sgt C A Briggs
4th Sgt Frank D Hoag
5th Sgt David N Jacobs
1st Corp F D Goodrich
2d Corp Jay Seaver
3d Corp Wm Remey
4th Corp Wm Blanchard
5th Corp F C Devendorf
6th Corp Harry Hewes
7th Corp F H Young
8th Corp J S Parsons
Nelson, P A, drummer
Ware, E N, fifer
Reeder, L, waggoner
Austin, Wallace
Boynton, W
Briggs, W
Briggs, E
Belton, J H
Church, W C
Devendorf, S
Grove, G A
Gormley, E
Hoag, H S
Haines, W W
Johnson, A A
Jones, Harry
Leach, G E
McCoy, A
Menzie, S W
McPherson, P A
Martin, C T
McPherson, A C
Paddock, Wm D
Reeder, A H
Rice, Frank E
Reeder, J B
Smith, Fred B
Smith, W J
Spooner, C F
Trafford, H W
Tuttle, F W
Utley, H N
Washburne, F B
Waldrof, G A
Williams, W L

Williams, N C
Tallman, G B
Thomas, Fred
Sturtevant, Jno
Schultz, Chas H
Wildy, Ira W
Wilson, R J
Rice, Herbert K

Custer Rifles.

Whitewater, Wisconsin

(ORGANIZED JULY 7TH, 1877.)
Capt J E Bessett
1st Lt J D Hogan
2nd Lt J Rogers
Orderly Sgt J W Richardson
2nd Sgt J W Gruby
3d Sgt E Rosman
4th Sgt M Horen
5th Sgt M G Halverson
1st Corp D M Hayes
2nd Corp J Zimmerman
3d Corp W W Kinnie
4th Corp A F Culdwell
Aumon, J A
Abrahamson, L
Bridge, G
Bowen, W
Brady, G P
Caswell, A J
Cooper, J
Cappie, J A
Commerford, M
Carman, O L
Craine, E.
DeWolf, M
DeWolf, A
Drury, D
Esterly, P V G
Frazer, G
Fiedler, A
Fonda, E
Horen, J
Horten, E
Hughes, C F
Hughes, S
Hart, H L
Holmes, W D
Higgins, C
Inman, A
Johnson, J
Kraeplin, A
Kymaston, E
Kiser, F I
King, H H
Larsen, O
Mixer, H
Mills, A J
McBearth, R D
Noble, R H
O'Conner, B
Pearson, Ira
Partridge, J A
Prince, E D
Prince, W L
Patten, A
Richardson, W
Richmond, E D
Rhodes, Chas
Roseneraos, W
Salisbury, W M
Stearns, E A
White, R D
White, A C
Wells, W
Wintermute, F S

Fond du Lac Guards.

Capt Sumner L Brasted
1st Lt John C Keneally
2nd Lt Chas J Hunter
1st Sgt F A Dawes
2nd Sgt J D Radford
3d Sgt J Q Hans
4th Sgt E T Talmadge
5th Sgt A A Kelly
1st Corp F A Brasted
2nd Corp Jno L Martin
3d Corp Edw Foulkes
4th Corp C E Dickinson
5th Corp O H Peters
6th Corp J M Moore
7th Corp Geo S Burrows
8th Corp Waldo Sweet
Stowe, A F, drummer
Gibson, J B, fifer
Moore, W H, wagoner
Adams, E C
Boardman, C B
Button, J H
Carberry, J
Cooley, C M
Davis, O C
Duffy, F F
Estabrook, A L
Eyelshimer, Fred
French, Fred
Galland, C H
Galloway, E A
Haber, P B
Handt, C L
Hawes, J A
Hamilton, Jno
Hunter, Lemont
Kunze, Jno J
Kent, Jno E
Lange, E A
Little, E A
Little, J B
Lippitt, F S
Magnusen, Jno
Murphy, Jerre C
Noble, L W
Norman, M L
Olmsted, W H
O'Meara, B H
Parle, H F
Percell, R
Potter, H R
Robbins, W D
Shattuck, W H
Stowe, A W
Shepard, F H
Sullivan, Jno E
Sweet, Frank
Sweet, Geo B
Treleven, W T
Tripp, C C
Wallace, Frank
Waters, Jno E
Wiley, Geo H
Wiley, Frank S
Wilson, Robt H
Wilkner, Henry W

Unity Guards.

Unity, Wisconsin.

Capt J H Cook
1st Lt Jas Allen
2nd Lt Geo W Henderson
1st Sgt N C Ransom

2nd Corp E J Adams
3d Corp W R Hamlet
2nd Sgt Wm M Crawford
3d Sgt Allen W Stewart
4th Sgt Jos Rensimer
5th Sgt Miles Spring
Color Bearer F H Darling
1st Corp O M Brown
2nd Corp C T Haskin
3d Corp Francis Parrett
4th Corp Dimmick Marsh
5th Corp Benj Hammond
6th Corp C C Barber
7th Corp Frank Thompson
8th Corp R J Horr
Barber, Leonard, fifer
Roohr, Jacob, drummer
Wicker, Wm H H, wagoner
Petrie, Adam, treasurer
Bullman, E C
Brintnall, H N
Brewer, Jas
Barber, A H
Bixby, Wm H
Brown, Jas
Bowen, Geo
Brusewitz August C
Brusewitz, Fred
Becker, Frank D
Campbell, Alex
Christnagel, Jacob
Call, W S
Call, W W
Clark, Freeman
Craney, E P
Dygert, Jas
Dusenbery, Geo
English, C C
Flood, Chas
Falasha, Fred
Fermenich, Chas
Fairchilds, Thos I
Fuller, Geo H
Graham, C O
Garnett, W P
Hoffmaun, Peter
Horner, August
Hill, A B
Heintz, Peter
Hugel, Frank
Hall, Fred
Haffer, Paul
Horr, Frank J
Hacket, Theodore
Hepler, Geo
Jones, Dan'l

Ketler, Mathias
Kimbull, R C
Laboute, Zeph
Marsh, Henry
Marsh, Sidney
Marsh, Merrett
Marsh, Wm F
Nelson, Nels
Nichols, G W
O'Rourk, Geo A
Porter, Mouhford
Peep, Wm
Peterson, Geo W
Peterson, Marshall B
Peterson, Manley
Ritter, Jno
Rensimer, Corwin
Roohr, Geo C
Roohr, Chas A
Raymond, Israel
Remminger, Jacob
Stewart, Wm
Scott, A J
Shanks, Thos, Jr
Shigley, Geo W
Shigley, Henry
Shigley, Alonzo
Steiner, Louis
Sonnanstine, G F
Sheldon, D A
Smith, J B
Thompson, L A
Thompson, F W
Tripp, Everett
Wicker, J D, Jr
Wicker, Jos W
Wescott, Jno
Wescott, Chas
Woodruff, Stephen

Beloit City Guard.

Beloit Wisconsin.

Capt H H McLenegan
1st Lt C H Palmerly
2nd Lt E J Bending
1st Sgt W T Bois
2nd Sgt H C Powers
3d Sgt C A Smith
4th Sgt C R Hamlet
5th Sgt S B McLenegan
1st Corp F C Anderson

4th Corp H W Merrill
5th Corp S A Brown
6th Corp J Booth
7th Corp C M Corcoran
8th Corp L Rosenblatt
Anderson, H
Ayer, O L
Brand, O H
Bailey, F E C
Coats, Jno
Colt, M L
Carnian, C L
Cleavland, B
Craven,
Derbyshier, C H
Fredericks, Geo
Franz, Chas
Gaston, T R
Green, W H
Gillman, J C
Hendee, H S
Hamlet, J O
Hamlin, W
Hawkins, J
Johnson, H F
Johnson, K
Jones, Chas
Key, T B
Lewis, E A
Merriman, C C
Myers, J A W
McLenegan, Chas
McKinney, C
Morse, C F
Northrop, F H
Russell, B F
Raw, C F
Raw, J G
Royce, J
Stocking, Chas
Sharp, R H
Smith, E R
Smith, Chas
Scott, E D
Smith, G E
Stiles, Geo
Saxton, Frank
Searls, E E
Slyter, H L
Simmons, Chas
Truesdell, J A
Tasker, E W
Tripp, L W
Taltershall, C O
Vallee, A R
Venness, J W

THIRTY-FIVE YEARS' BUSINESS EXPERIENCE.
THE NEW YORK
LIFE INSURANCE CO.

PURELY MUTUAL. DIVIDENDS ANNUALLY.

| 140,000 Policies issued. | 45,000 Policies in Force. | $50,000,000 Paid to Policy-holders. |

ANNUAL INCOME, OVER
$8,000,000.

CASH ASSETS, OVER
$39,000,000.

SURPLUS, N. Y. STATE STANDARD, OVER $7,500,000.

CAREFUL MANAGEMENT.

AGE, STRENGTH,

THE COMPANY'S HOME OFFICE, 346 & 48 Broadway, New York

THE NEW-YORK LIFE INSURANCE COMPANY has been doing business for thirty-five years, and now offers to those desiring life insurance a combination of advantages which only long experience, a large and well established business and carefully perfected plans and methods can afford. Among these advantages are: (1) The absolute security of its policies. (2) Insurance at low cost. (3) Liberal and equitable dealing.

The large amount of Assets now held by the company, its large Surplus over and above all liabilities, the large number of policies in force, and the constant acceptance of new risks on carefully selected lives in the most healthful portions of North America and Europe, and the great experience of its officers and managers, render it one of the strongest, most prosperous, and most trustworthy companies in the world.

Having always been a purely mutual company, policy-holders receive their insurance at actual current cost, and its age, strength, prosperity and economical management combine to reduce that cost to the minimum. The company is conducted in the interests of policy-holders alone. In the decision of questions involving their rights the invariable rule is to consider not the technical legality of the claim alone, but its real justice.

The non-forfeiture system of policies originated with this company in 1860, and has since been adopted—though sometimes in questionable forms—by all other companies. This feature saves millions of dollars every year to policy-holders, and for this they are indebted to the New-York Life. The system as now perfected by the New-York Life secures safety to the company (without which all interests are jeopardized), and justice to the insured.

MORRIS FRANKLIN, Pres. WILLIAM H. BEERS, Vice-Pres. & Actuary.

THEODORE M. BANTA, Cashier.
D. O'DELL, Sup't of Agencies.
CHARLES WRIGHT, M. D., } Medical Examiners.
HENRY TUCK, M. D.

WALKER BUCKNER,
Manager for Wisconsin.

Office 416 Milwaukee Street, Milwaukee, Wisconsin.

...DIERS REUNION OF 1880.

...eir Measures Which Have Carried It Foward Towards With Anecdotes, Sketches and Reminiscences by Well-Known Contributors.

"RALLY ON THE COLORS!"

Comrades!
Now for a long pull,
A strong pull,
And a pull all together!
Rally for Reunion.
Organize by Towns or Counties.
Attend as Delegations.
Join old commands at Milwaukee.
Publish list of all soldiers in your county.
Correct and add to, until complete.
Send copy here.
The Association wants every Soldier's Name—Company—Regiment—Occupation and P. O. Address
In printed Roster by June 7.
Your local Papers are great helps.
Have them publish enclosed Announcement,
And "Boom" for the Soldiers until Reunion Day.
Railroads will give reduced rates—
We hope down to One Cent a mile.
Special rates at hotels and boarding houses.
Expect loan of five thousand tents from Government,
And other arrangements for Inexpensive subsistence,
So that (as one of the boys said at the last committee meeting,)
"It will be a darn sight cheaper to go than to stay at home."
It will be the occasion of a lifetime.
The "Badger State Centennial," as it were—for instance !
Think it up !
Write it up !   } Shake it up lively !
Talk it up !
Let us see what Wisconsin veterans can do When the battle cry is "Rally on the Colors!"
C. K. PIER,
President Reunion Association.
Fond du Lac, Wis,

The announcement of a proposed reunion of all Wisconsin soldiers at Milwaukee, having been published by the leading newspapers throughout the country, found in every state, comrades ripe and ready for the occasion. A few —a sample lot—of these responses will not be out of place in the columns of THE REUNION ROSTER.

Col. Dawes wants to Know.

Col. R. R. Dawes, of the Sixth regiment who step by step worked and won,

well merited promotion from corporal's chevrons to full spread eagle's, writes from Maritta, Ohio, where he resides and is engaged in business:

"I see you have suggested a re-union of the Iron Brigade. May I trouble you to let me know what steps, if any, have been taken in that direction. I am, as you see, where Wisconsin papers do not often come. There should, if possible, be at least one re-union of the old brigade. I doubt if our own or any other war affords a service record parallel with its history For the old Iron Brigade was literally destroyed on the field of battle. The gun-shot casualties up to, and including Gettysburg, amounted to over 3,000, fully one hundred per cent, after which came the terrible Grant campaign against Lee.
If there is to be a re-union, I wish to be there, and will do all that I can to further its interests and secure its success."

Gen. Bragg Assumes Command.

The wish expressed in the foregoing was fully reciprocated, as shown by the following circular notice and succeeding orders, duly promulgated :

SOLDIERS AND COMRADES :

At the request of the military and civic authorities, having in charge the success of the Grand Reunion of Soldiers to take place at Milwaukee, Wisconsin, on the 7th of June next and the week ensuing, and with your permission, I will resume my old command during that encampment.
EDW'D S. BRAGG,
Late Brig. Gen'l Vols.
March 5, 1880.

SPECIAL ORDER }
No. 1. }
HEADQUARTERS IRON BRIGADE,
CAMP REUNION, MILWAUKEE
The following named officers, absent on leave, will report to these headquarters June 7, 1880, at 10 A. M., for duty :
Capt. J. D. Wood, A. A. G.
Capt. Harry Holloway, A. C. S.
Sient. Lyman Upham, 6th Wis. Vols., A. A. Q. M.
Cabt. E. A. Andrews, 7th Wis. Vols., A. A. I. G.
Brevet Maj. Robt. Monteith, 7th Wis. Vols., A. D. C.
Brevet Capt. E. M. Rogers, 6th Wis. Vols., A D. C.
EDW'D S. BRAGG,
Brig. Gen. Vols. Comd'g

THE SOLDIERS REUNION OF 1880.

SPECIAL ORDER
No. 2.
HEADQUARTERS IRON BRIGADE.
CAMP REUNION, MILWAUKEE.

The following named officers will report at these headquarters June 7, 1880, at 12 o'clock M., with their respective commands, without arms, equipped for picnic duty:

Brevet Brig. Gen'l J. A. Kellogg, Col. 6th Wis. Vols.
Brevet Brig. Gen'l H. A. Richardson, Col. 7th Wis. Vols.
Major Geo. H. Otis, Com'd'g 2d Wis. Vols.
Brevet Brig. Gen'l W. W. Dudley, Com'd'g 19th Ind. Vols.
Brevet Col. E. M. Edwards, Com'd'g 24th Mich. Vols.

EDW'D S. BRAGG.
Brig. Gen'l Vols. Com'd'g.
(Wisconsin, Indiana and Michigan Papers please publish.)

General Bragg afterwards having been assigned to the 2d Division, comprising the Army of Potomac regiments, the following was issued:

THE SECOND DIVISION.

HEAD QUARTERS, SECOND DIVISION, REUNION.
MILWAUKEE, WIS, MAY 7th, 1880.

General Order, No 1.

The following named officers are hereby designated as the staff of the general, commanding the Second division, who will please report for duty, June 7th, 1880.

Capt. Robt. Monteith, Seventh Wisconsin, Asst. Adj't Genl.
Capt Otto Puhlman, Nineteenth Wisconsin, Asst. Insp. Genl.
Capt. Henry Curran, Fifth Wisconsin, A. Q. M.
Capt. J. G. Knight, Third Wisconsin, A. C. S.
Capt. E. M. Rogers, Sixth Wisconsin, A. D. C.
Capt. A. A. Kelly, Thirty-eighth Wisconsin, A. D. C.
Dr. A. J. Ward, Second Wisconsin, Division Surgeon.

EDW. S. BRAGG.
Brig. Genl.

The Way They Called.

How The Boys Heard of Reunion.

Regimental and company commanders issued calls to their old comrades, of which the following are samples:

FIRST REGIMENT WISCONSIN INFANTRY.

To the Members of the Old First.

(Three months and three years.) As well in cordial greeting of the living, as kindly memory of the dead: Surviving comrades of Wisconsin's first and favorite regiment—including both organizations—are hereby called to meet in regimental and company reunion, at Milwaukee, June 7-12, 1880, on the occasion of the general gathering of all Wisconsin soldiers.

Let each member strive to be present, as the event will undoubtedly be one of unparalleled importance and interest.

The three months fellows—including Gen. Lucius Fairchild, Co. K., and Col. C. K. Pier, Co, I—"may gather on the beautiful banks" of the Menomonee, while the rest of us will put up with a soldier's hard fare, at the Plankinton, or among the palaces on Grand Avenue in and about Old Camp Scott, as the weather and our pockets permit.

By order of
GEN. JOHN C. STARKWEATHER,
President First Regiment Reunion Society.
C. H. BENTON, Sec'y.

FIFTH WISCONSIN VOLUNTEERS.

The Old Fifth Wisconsin Volunteers will be assigned quarters as a regiment at the grand Reunion in Milwaukee. It is a matter of interest to all its members who feel a pride in the only Wisconsin regiment in the famous Sixth Corps, to come once more together, to revive old associations of the camp and field. Our comrades are scattered all over the State and all over the Northwest. Will they be kind enough to send their names, company and address to the undersigned, who would like to publish a complete list of all members of the regiment. Send the names of all you know in your several localities, directed to

T. S. ALLEN,
Late Col. 5th Wis. Vol Infantry.
Oshkosh, Wis.

The Second Wisconsin.

The following letter to the Sunday Telegraph explains itself:

McGREGOR, IA., March 17th.

A copy of your paper of the 7th, has reached me containing Gen. Bragg's order calling the Iron Brigade to the Reunion to be held in Milwaukee, June 7th. I write this more particularly to invite the members of the Second Wisconsin Volunteers, or such of them as will be present at the Reunion, to write me by postal card or by letter, addressed to this place, giving company in which they served, and rank at date of discharge. I shall be on hand at this Reunion, and hope to have the pleasure of meeting all of the surviving members of the Brigade. I know we shall enjoy a rally around the old battle flags and again renew friendships in the revival of the memories of the past. Especially let the members of the Second Wisconsin Infantry rally to a man, and once more march in column of fours with the tattered flags to the breeze. I will take pleasure in corresponding with all members of the regiment and impart such information in regard to the Reunion as I may possess. Very respectfully,

GEO. H. OTIS,
Brevet Lieut. Col. Commanding 2d Wis. Vol.

The Sixteenth Regiment.

The following Reunion call was issued to the Sixteenth Regiment:

To the Veterans of the Sixteenth Infantry:

The undersigned would rejoice to meet you at the Soldiers' Reunion in Milwaukee, in June next, and then go into camp with you. It permitted he will take with him the banners under which you so proudly marched to victory, that you may again have an opportunity of renewing your devotion to them, and your friendship for each other. The General under whose inspiring commands you so often "moved on the enemy's works" will be there to greet you. Fraternally yours,
THOS. REYNOLDS,
Late Col, of Sixteenth Wis. Infantry.
Madison, Wis., March 4, 1880.

ATTENTION, THE SEVENTEENTH.

The surviving members of the Seventeenth Wisconsin Infantry, known in Sherman's army as the Irish Brigade, are invited to attend the grand Reunion of Wisconsin veteran soldiers, to be held in Milwaukee, from the 7th to the 12th of June next, to celebrate the events of the war, and its great victories, and to honor anew the memories of our fellow-comrades. Headquarters will be provided, of which due notice will be given.
P. H. McCAULEY.

TWENTY-THIRD WISCONSIN.

Attention, Twenty-Third Wisconsin Infantry:

A Grand Reunion of Soldiers will be held at Milwaukee from the 7th to the 12th of June next, and it has been decided that the Twenty-Third shall have a Regimental Reunion on that occasion.

Let the members of our regiment join their local organizations and go with them to Milwaukee, to participate in the General Reunion, and while there we will camp as a regiment, and renew old and loved associations, and talk over the trying times in which so many of our number gave their lives, or their limbs, or the best of their health and strength to their country. All who intend to be present will please notify me by card before the 20th of May next, so that the necessary accommodations may be provided. Headquarters will be hereafter announced.

As soon as it can be done I intend to have prepared a complete regimental record, which will account for every man who belonged to our organization. And I request that each surviving member of the Twenty-Third who cannot attend the Reunion and report there, will write to me at the earliest day practicable, giving his residence, business and items of his history since discharge as well as matters of interest to comrades; also if a pensioner, to so state and on what account, and also to state the death of comrades since the war known to him, and the times and places thereof as near as possible. Each of our members residing in Wisconsin who knows the address of a comrade living outside of this State, will please send him a copy of this notice.
J. J. GUPPEY,
Late Col. 23d Wis. Infantry.
Portage, Wis., March 27th, 1880.

ATTENTION, TWENTY-FIFTH REGIMENT.

The undersigned has been requested to call upon the Twenty-Fifth Wisconsin Volunteers to be present at the great Soldiers' Reunion in Milwaukee, June 7th. Fall in line, boys, and bivouac in Milwaukee on the evening of the 7th of June.
J. M. RUSK.

ATTENTION, THE TWENTY-FIRST.

Comrades! You are cordially invited to attend the Grand Reunion of Wisconsin Soldiers to be held in Milwaukee on the 7th of June next. You who were at Chaplin Hills, Stone River, Hoover's Gap, Chicamauga, Mission Ridge, Resaca, Dallas, Kenesaw Mountain, Marietta, Chattahoochee, Peach Tree Creek, Atlanta and the March to the Sea, in the march through the Carolinas, at Bentonville, Raleigh, and the march to Richmond and Washington, rally once more to greet the living and revive the memories of the dead.

General Sherman, in his memoirs, says: "I remember that Wisconsin kept her regiments filled with recruits, whereas other States generally filled their quotas by new regiments, and the result was that we estimated a Wisconsin regiment equal to an ordinary brigade." With such a tribute from perhaps the greatest master among modern military men, Milwaukee may well be proud to welcome the defenders of the old flag.

WISCONSIN CENTRAL RAILROAD SUMMER RESORTS.

ELKHART LAKE.

GOVERNMENT OBSERVATORY.

BAYFIELD AND CHEQUEMACON BAY.

THE SOLDIERS REUNION OF 1880.

Report at the headquarters of the Twenty-First. HARRISON C HOBART.

Gen. Kellogg Leads Off.

All the officers and members of the old Iron Brigade joined heartily in co-operation. Republishing the foregoing Gen. Kellogg leads off.

MADISON, Wis., March 8.

REGIMENTAL ORDER No. 1 }
  NEW SERIES,   }

Comrades of the old Sixth, in accordance with the above, meet me in Milwaukee June 7th, and let us do honor, *if we can*, to the memories of those who gallantly fell, as well as to exchange hand clasps with those that remain.

J. A. KELLOGG,
Late Brev. Brig.-Gen. and Col. 6th Wis Vol.

Indiana Sounds the Long Roll.

The Indiana boys republished Gen. Bragg's circular in full and add to it the following call:

SPECIAL ORDER NO. 1.
HEADQUARTERS 19th Ind. Vols.

The late commanding officers of companies, and all survivors, of the 19th Regt. Ind. Vols., Iron Brigade, Army of the Potomac will take notice of the foregoing General and Special Orders, and will report with their respective commands, for the purposes therein set forth. This Regiment will as far as possible, rendezvous at Indianapolis, that we may move on Milwaukee with success, and at the lowest rate of transportation. In order that ample facilities and cheap transportation may be procured, it is desired that members of the Regiment who will report for duty should notify me at once by mail, at Indianapolis, Ind.

W. W. Dudley,
Lt. Col. and Brevet Brig. Gen'l Com'dg Regt.

NOTE—Only soft bread and fresh meat will be permitted, and the command will not be allowed to ride in box or cattle-cars; nor will walking be allowed unless personal notice is given Capt J A Coleman, R. Q. M., beforehand, a he will be expected to provide full rations of coffee, soft bread and fresh meat, and transport the command in Pullman cars.

Michigan.

The Michigan boys also spring forth at the trumpets sound, and the week following gave notice that their colors would be planted in Milwaukee for Reunion.

THE TENTH WISCONSIN.

HEADQUARTERS, TENTH WISCONSIN }
  INFANTRY VOLUNTEERS,   }
    MILWAUKEE, April 14th, 1880, }
To the surviving comrades of the old Tenth Wisconsin Infantry Volunteers;

You are hereby ordered to report to these headquarters, corner of Broadway and Huron streets, on the 7th day of June next, for duty during the Reunion.
Come one, come all.

J. W. RODY,
Colonel Commanding.

TWELFTH AND SIXTEENTH.

HEADQUARTERS, 1ST BRIGADE, 3D DIV., }
  11TH ARMY CORPS, CAMP RANDALL.   }

By order of Major M. D. Leggett, the undersigned assumes command of the Heroes, all who held the hill, that was the key, that enabled the dead MacPherson to win the battle of Atlanta.

The Twelfth Wisconsin Infantry, under the command of Col. James K. Proudfit, and the Sixteenth Wisconsin Infantry under command of Col. Thomas Reynolds, will form the front line, and as at break of day they charged Bold Hill and first saw the terrors of Atlanta, so at June 7th, 1880, they will move on Milwaukee.

Lieut. Frank H. Putney (in the absence of Lieutenant Nelson Chandler) will move the skirmish line forward from Waukesha, on the evening of the 9th and see that the campus is ready for the column.

Capt. Ed. Whitney will come up from Louisiana, with commissaries; Quartermaster Andrew Sexton will bring his mules (as at Kenesaw Monutain) close up to the line. He will be expected to provide stores when Whitney's are gobbled. As soon as rations can be provided (which will be promptly,) the Twelfth and Sixteenth are expected to entertain, in a hospitable way the Illinois men of their brigade. Chaplain Walker will pray for onions, and Surgeons Cary and Rogers will take care of the same. Any man who harms a hair of Geo. Leggett's cow will be shot on the spot! Pat Hogan, bring my horse!

Forward, then, comrades; let us spend a week in Milwaukee with our brothers of other Wisconsin regiments and make a green spot on the bill of time we are now toddling down.
Four flags will wave there!

GEO. E. BRYANT,
Late Colonel Twelfth Wis.
L. M. BREEZE, Lieut. and A. A. Gen.

THIRTY-EIGHTH WIS. VOL. INFANTRY.

"RALLY ROUND THE FLAG, BOYS, RALLY ONCE AGAIN."

In remembrance of our trials and triumphs the members of the Thirty-Eighth regiment Wisconsin Volunteers will assemble in camp at the Soldier's Reunion to be held in Milwaukee, commencing June 7th, to participate in the commemoration of the record Wisconsin soldiers made in the greatest war of history—a record which is cherished with a just degree of pride by every citizen of the State.

JAMES BINTLIFF,

THE THIRTY-SECOND REGIMENT.

FOND DU LAC, April 10.
To the Surviving Members of the Thirty-Second Wis. Vol. Inf:

Comrades, after due consultation with the officers of our organization, the committee of arrangements has deemed it advisable to change the time of our Reunion this year from October to June, and to change the place of meeting from Fond du Lac to Milwaukee, so as to join the great State Reunion which is to be held at Milwaukee, during the week commencing June 7th, 1880. Transportation will be cheap and accommodations will be furnished for all who attend, at little more than nominal prices. Let us rally and help make this the greatest gathering of soldiers since the war.

S. L. BRASTED,
Sec'y and Ch'n Com. of Arrangements.

Particular attention is called to the following order:

HEAD QUARTERS THIRTY-SECOND WIS- }
  CONSIN, FOND DU LAC, April 10th — }

Every survivor, of the Thirty-second Wisconsin, wherever he may be serving his country, is hereby relieved from duty at his present station during the week commencing June the 7th, 1880, and ordered to report to Col. C H DeGroat equipped with soup plates and silver forks, at Milwaukee, Wisconsin, June 7th, 1880, or immediately thereafter for special duty at the grandest Reunion of soldiers America ever saw. Quarters will be assigned and soup furnished. By order of

C. H. DEGROAT,
Col. Commanding.
S. L. BRASTED, Adj't

WISCONSIN PRISONERS OF WAR.

These and other soldiers who were in the enemy's hands during their military service, are requested to send their names, when and where captured and confined, to Gen. Kellogg, of Wausau, Wis., who has consented to take special charge of this interesting and impressive feature of the Soldiers' Reunion in June. Do this at once, as the information so gathered will be included in the Reunion Roster, now being prepared for publication

D. N. KASSON,
Secretary Executive Committee.

THE THIRTEENTH.

MADISON, May 5th.
To the members of the Thirteenth Regiment Wisconsin Volunteers:

You are cordially invited to attend the General Reunion of Soldiers and Sailors of the late war, to be held in Milwaukee, June 7–12 next. Many of you have expressed to me your intention to do so, and I earnestly hope that our regiment may be largely represented on that occasion.

A headquarters for the regiment will, doubtless, be designated by the local committee, of which timely notice will be given.

WM. P. LYON,
Late Colonel.

THE NINETEENTH.

Surviving members of the Nineteenth Regiment are invited to send their names to John Barry, of Co. K, Milwaukee, in order to make arrangements for a meeting, and to join in the Reunion. Col. R. M. Strong, of Racine, is the ranking officer of this regiment, so far as known.

TWENTY-FOURTH REGIMENT.

General Order No. 1.
Attention, Twenty-Fourth Regiment!

The Third Annual Reunion of the regiment will take place during the Soldiers' Reunion in June next. The day, and manner of observing it will be promulgated in future orders. A pleasant time may be anticipated, and every member of the regiment will be expected to answer to his name at that time.
By order of   WM. KENNEDY, President.
H. G. ROGERS, Secretary.

ATTENTION "E" COMPANY.

HEADQUARTERS "E" CO., FORTY- }
  SEVENTH,   }
    MILWAUKEE, WIS., April 10th.

General Order No. 1.
All members of Co. E, who propose attending the Reunion in June, will send their address to the undersigned, the organizer and first commander of the company, and report for duty at headquarters in camp, at Milwaukee, June 7.

Come on boys, and once again listen to the dulcet voices of Sergeants Scampton and Nut-

THE CHEQUAMEGON, AT ASHLAND
This Hotel is the property of the Wisconsin Central Railroad.

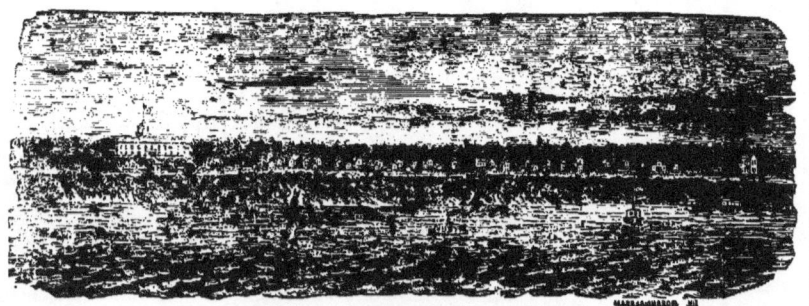

CHEQUAMEGON BAY, ASHLAND, LAKE SUPERIOR.

THE SOLDIERS REUNION OF 1880.

ting, ordering you to fall in for rations, and for guard duty.
WM. W. BIRD,
Late Captain Co. E., 47th Wis

ATTENTION, BATTERY.

You have no doubt heard of the Grand Reunion of Wisconsin Soldiers, to take place at Milwaukee, on June 7th, 1880. It may be the last opportunity with many of us to meet before the final muster-out by the Great Mustering-out Officer. At the request of many of the "boys" in this and adjoining counties, I write you to meet us in Milwaukee, on the above date.
GEO. W. GALE.
Galesville, Wis.

CAVALRY.

Camp Barstow will be established as headquarters of the Third Wisconsin Cavalry, at the Reunion encampment in Milwaukee, on the morning of June 7th next. The surviving members of the regiment are invited to be present and participate in the splendid celebration of the events of the war, and of its renowned victories, in which the veteran union soldiers of Wisconsin are then to engage.
E. A. CALKINS,
Late Lt Colonel 3rd Wisconsin Cavalry.

THE THIRTY-SEVENTH.

HEADQUARTERS, THIRTY-SEVENTH }
MADISON, APRIL 26TH, 1880. }
Special Order No, 1.
1. The members of the Thirty-Seventh regiment, without regard to rank, color or former condition of servitude; are respectfully requested to assemble at Milwaukee on the 7th of June, sharp.
2. A court of inquiry will be convened to find out how they have conducted themselves since July, 1866.
3. In the total absence of Adjt. Wittemore Hans D. Warner is hereby appointed Adjutant until Lieut. Wittemore can be run in and corralled, when said Warner will be reduced to the ranks (with loss) of all pay and allowances,
4. The rank of Adjt. Warner will for the present, be Brigadier General of volunteers. He will be respected and obeyed accordingly,
By command of,
SAM HARRIMAN,
Col. Thirty-Seventh Wis.

The Effect of the Calls.

The effect of these calls was to arouse the army spirit all over the state, and paragraphs like the following appeared thick and fast in the newspapers throughout not only Wisconsin, but the northwest generally:

The meeting of LaFayette County soldiers, held at the office of the county treasurer on Saturday last, was called to order by General Bluthiff, who offered the following resolution, which was adopted: Resolved, That we effect an organization for the purpose of obtaining the address of each soldier of the late war now residing in this county, and to make such arrangements as may be deemed necessary to enable all to attend, in a body, the Reunion of Wisconsin soldiers, to be held in Milwaukee, commencing June 7th.

Richland County will surprise the natives when her delegation of five hundred, or over, marches in solid column through the city of Milwaukee, headed by the Richland Center band. All we are bo hered about is that there will be no one left at hon. to run the printing offices, stores and other places of business.

A local committee, appointed to perfect the soldiers' Reunion roster for Fond du Lac county, has adopted a plan which can not fail of success. Lieut H. B. Eastman and Capt J. H. Hauser have made an arrangement by which the clerks at the polls in each of the election precincts of the county will be supplied with blanks upon which to record the name and address of each veteran who votes in April. It is urgently requested that at least one old soldier at each poll will make it his especial order of the day to see that the names are given in to the clerks. On Saturday the 10th of April, at one o'clock in the afternoon, there will be a meeting at the court house, in this city, of all those interested, for the purpose of organizing the vets of the county into a battalion to move upon the works of the Reunion. No stragglers should be allowed on this march.

The coming Reunion of soldiers will be in the interest of no political party. It will be as far removed from everything of a party character as it is possible for any gathering to be. Such democrats as Bragg, Hancock, Robinson, Hobart, Vilas and a host of others who will take an active part in the demonstration, would not be apt to do so if the Reunion was in the interest of the republican party. Such republicans as Allen, Hincks, Bintliff, Pier, Rusk and many others, would not be likely to engage in the enterprise if it was to be run in the interest of the democratic party.

Veterans of the Mexican war have written asking why they could not be included in the call.
"All soldiers in the State of Wisconsin and all Wisconsin soldiers wherever they may be." is the way the resolution of invitation reads.

The veterans held a rousing meeting at Janesville, Tuesday evening, and made arrangements for attending the Reunion in this city.

Wisconsin soldiers, write to D. N. Kasson, Secretary, Milwaukee, Wisconsin, for full information relative to the Soldiers' Reunion. Give name, number of regiment and company. Answer by return mail.

A few days ago a prominent gentleman, who is a republican and a friend of Hon. Robert G. Ingersoll, asked him who Illinois would be for in the contest for the republican presidential nomination.
"Grant," said Bob.
"But," says his friend, "I thought you were for Blaine?"

"So I was," said Bob, "four years ago and would be this year, if that would do any good ; but *this is going to be a soldier's year*, and Grant fills the popular eye in this character. I think Grant will be nominated at Chicago, and, if nominated, elected."

We wish a list of all the returned soldiers in every city, village and town in this county, with regiment and company in which they served, and postoffice address. We wish to publish a complete list preparatory to the grand Reunion commencing on the 7th of June.
Will some comrade in each town, or two or three together, get up and send us such a list. It will be of great interest to the people and to every old soldier, to know how many of us there are left, and where we are. We wish to arrange for a grand boom from Winnebago county to the Reunion, and to agree on a time for going down as nearly as possible together.
Railroad fare will probably be reduced to *one cent* a mile, which will enable all to go.
Send in the returns, directed to "Northwestern," Oshkosh, Wis.

Chairman Fischer has received a large list of names, from the town of Norway, of soldiers who will be present at the Reunion.

A grand gathering of Wisconsin soldiers was held last evening at the Grand Pacific Hotel in Chicago, for the purpose of making arrangements for attending the Reunion. It is understood from advices received from that city, that a large number of people will be present.

Eighty seven veterans have reported from Beloit for enrollment on the Reunion book.

Portage veterans held an enthusiastic meeting the other evening and resolved to organize, put on style and come to the grand Reunion in full force. It is said that every soldier in that county will attend, and one man up there has quit smoking long enough to save the necessary ducats.

The La Crosse Chronicle prints a list of names, numbering 192 soldiers of the late war, most of whom will attend the Reunion.

A county organization of survivors of the late "Unpleasantness" has been effected at Neillsville, and promises to show up strong at the June meeting.

Vernon County promises to send a large delegation to the Reunion, and Secretary Casson, of that county, in his call, says it is to be the largest gathering of ex-soldiers ever held in this country, exceeding any similar occasion of modern times

The coming Reunion of soldiers promises to constitute the largest gath-

VIEW OF THE WATER POWER AT APPLETON, WIS.

MIRROR LAKE WAUPACA, WIS.

THE NATIONAL HOTEL, MENASHA.

THE SOLDIERS REUNION OF 1880.

ering of people ever witnessed in the state. The managers, headed by Col. Pier, the president, of Fond du Lac, are leaving no thing undone to render the affair a success in all respects. The railroads will charge three cents a mile for round trip tickets.

The Reunion boom is the biggest thing out, in Wisconsin affairs. Not only the entire returned soldier element but the entire population of the state, is taking a warm and general interest in the movement, and nothing but bad weather can prevent the biggest crowd in Milwaukee, next June, that ever tested the capacity of any city in the United States.

The Reunion in Milwaukee next June will be the largest gathering of soldiers in America since the grand reviews in Washington, May 23 and 24, 1865.

Attention Soldiers! All soldiers of the war of the rebellion residing in Waupaca county, desiring to form a County Association, will please send their names and address to me, and if a sufficient number signifies their intention as favorable, a call for meeting and organization will be made.
Waupaca, Wis., March 1st, 1880.
JOE H. WOODSWORTH.
County papers please copy.

Distinguished ex-Union Generals, now living in remote parts of the country are arranging their affairs with the view of attending the Reunion So they write.

The veterans in charge of the Reunion arrangements report the daily receipt of letters from old soldiers in Nevada, Nebraska, and other portion of the far west, who are loaded to the muzzle with an enthusiasm which fire cannot destroy or water quench.

Veterans who served in New England regiments, who propose attending the Reunion, are respectfully requested to confer with Dr. I. H. Stearns, late surgeon Mass. Twenty-second; and if a suitable number respond, that quarters will be provided, that they may get together. Address Dr. I. H. Stearns, Milwaukee, Wis.

This evening about one hundred soldiers of the late war met at the court house, in the county clerk's office, for the purpose of making arrangements to attend the grand Reunion of soldiers and sailors to be held in Milwaukee on June 7, and it was agreed that the soldiers from the county towns should be invited to join and organize a county organization. A great deal of enthusiasm was manifested, and evidently about five hundred soldiers will attend the reunion. The meeting was adjourned to the 29th, when steps will be taken to form a permanent county organization.

Milwaukee and the Reunion.

How the Boom started in the Metropolis.

While the country was being so thoroughly aroused, Milwaukee (naturally a little slow to start, but strong when she does go) became alarmed as she beheld the mighty armies assembling to sweep down upon her, and in order that they might not be unprepared to welcome and properly care for their visitors a public meeting was called, and several soldiers and citizens outside invited in to report. Hon. John Johnson, cashier Wis. Mer. and Fire Ins. Bk., was president, and Mayor Black, D W. Dwall, Edward Sanderson, J. E. Mann. W. G. Roberts. C. H. Haskins, John Prizlaff, W. P. Lynde, C. B. Harger, Jas. G. Jenkins, Abner Kirby, J. M. Crombie, E Mariner, C. T. Bradley, G. C. Trumpff, E. R. Persons, D. L. Wells, C. Fernkes, O. P. Burt, W. Merrill, Auf. Uhlein, W. P. McLaren, A. Dohlman, V. Blatz, J. Dutcher, Franz Falk, William Al'en, C. D. Nash, T. L. Baker, C. M. Cottrill, F. Miller, H. H. Camp, B. Guerterboch, J. W. Exson, M. Kraus, E. P. Allis, C. J. Pratt, T. A. Chapman, Thomas Shea, C. H. Larkin, Elias Friend, J. A. Mallory, Edward O'Neill, J R. Goodrich, M. Bodden, John Plankinton, S. S. Merrill, James Kneeland, O. J. Hale, W. H. Jacobs, John Rugee, Fred. Kuehn, Dr. H. H. Butlow, C. E. Andrews, Fred Pabst, E. H. Broadhead. W. W. Coleman, Math. Keenan, Harrison Ludington, Ch. V. Baumbach, B. Leidersdorf, J. S. White, Horace Chase and J. F. Antisdel, were vice presidents. The morning papers gave the following report of the meeting:

BOOM!

FIRST GUNS OF THE GREAT REUNION FIRED AT TUESDAY'S EVENING'S MASS MEETING.

A VERY LARGE CROWD, A GREAT DEAL OF ENTHUSIASM AND A ROUSING OLD TIME.

ELOQUENT REMARKS BY COL. PIER, GEN. HINCKS, PRIVATE PECK, HANS WARNER, COL. JOHNSON, JUDGE MALLORY AND OTHERS.

LOADED TO THE MUZZLE.

The meeting at the academy of music, Tuesday evening, in the interest of the Soldier's Reunion was a splendid success. By the time the speaking was well under way the house was crowded and jammed, not less than 1,500 persons being present. At 7 o'clock Clauder's orchestra took a position in the street in front of the building, and for an hour discoursed music that stirred up a crowd chiefly characterized for its size and for the degree of enthusiasm manifest. Everybody appeared on the "enthuse," and the assembly was a happy conglomeration. At 8 o'clock, President Johnson and about 50 prominent citizens, not only of Milwaukee, but the state at large, were on the stage, and the band having taken a position back of the officers, first rendered a medley of patriotic, war time and peace prevailing melodies. President Johnson stepped forward and said:

"*Ladies and Gentlemen:—*
The executive committee of the Soldiers' Reunion have asked me to preside over this large and intelligent meeting, an honor which I highly appreciate and for which they have my most cordial thanks.

We have been invited to this hall to-night, to hear a number of distinguished speakers on the subject of the great Reunion which is to be held in this city, during the second week of June.

I fear the merchants, the manufacturers, the professional men and citizens of Milwaukee in general do not sufficiently estimate the importance of the proposed gathering, and that, as yet, we are far from being permeated with that inspiration and that enthusiasm which are worthy of the occasion, and are so necessary to insure its success.

Language cannot express the stirring memories which crowd in upon our minds, when we contemplate such a Reunion.

Think of it! To-morrow, nineteen years will have passed since the flag of the United States of America was lowered in derision before the assault of rebels at Fort Sumpter; and to-morrow, fifteen years will have passed since the selfsame flag was again raised in triumph over the battered walls of the old fort.

Before it fell, there was a dark stain upon its folds, for it was the flag beneath which the homes and blood of four millions of living men and women were bought and sold, but when it was again raised in triumph it could be said,

'This proud banner whose respleno nt fold
A fire waves wide above the young and old,
Is and shall be, without one star the less,
In triumph borne to unite and bless
These mighty states from farthest sea to sea,
With every man, whate'er his color, free!'

Who were the men who fought this fight, and achieved this glorious and lasting triumph?

They were the men who sweltered in the lagoons of Mississippi, and froze in the trenches at Stone River; who slaked their thirst in the waters of the Rappahannock, and slept for weeks in the swamps of the Chickahominy; the heroes of Vicksburg and Mission Ridge, of Antietam and Gettysburg; they are the men who are to be our guests next June, and shall we not give them an enthusiastic, a patriotic, aye an overwhelming welcome?

I have spoken of the stirring memories which the Reunion will call up in our minds, and so fleet are the footsteps of time, that to most of us the events of the war seem to have happened

WHITE RIVER VIADUCT.

HICKS' LAKE, ONE OF THE "CHAIN" AT WAUPACA.

but yesterday. Thousands, however, in our midst have no personal remembrance of the war. All the young men and young women, under twenty years of age, know of those dreadful days of sorrow and of sacrifice only what they have been told and what they have read.

Next June when they see nearly half of the ninety thousand men who followed the stand ards of Wisconsin to the war, marshal led in the streets of our fair city, the achievements and the sacrifices of the conflict will be brought home to their minds in a manner such as there could be in no other way.

The young men, the young women, and even the children of Wisconsin will tell in coming years th it although they do not remember the war, yet they well remember the great Reunion in Milwaukee in 1880, when thirty thousand veterans came together to fight their battles over again before meeting the last great enemy of all.

Ten thousand seven hundred and fifty of the brave men who went forth to the war from our beloved State never returned, and their names we have engraven on memory's most sacred tablets. In welcoming the living we bestow the highest possible tribute to the dead ; and be they living or dead their heroic deeds go down embalmed on the pages of history affording throughout all time the noblest incentive to patriotic devotion in the hearts of generations yet unborn.

In Roman history we are told of the brave Horatius, the captain of the gate, who kept at bay the whole Tuscan army, and saved the city. Centuries after, it was said

'Wives still pray to Juno
For boys with hearts as bold,
As his who kept the bridge so well,
In the brave days of old.'

And can we doubt, but that as long as the murmurs of Lake Michigan break upon the ears of a free people the mothers of Wisconsin will fire the patriotism of their boys by tales of the valor and self denial of the men who put down the rebellion in the brave days of old.

Ladies and gentlemen, as we are honored here to-night by the presence of many who are at the same time eloquent speakers and tried soldiers, I will detain you no longer, but I Invite for them your most earnest attention."

Mr. Johnson fairly outdid himself in the way of making a speech. He first introduced Col. Pier, of Fond du Lac, who said in the course of his remarks, that:

A little more than a year ago the surviving Wisconsin soldiers of the late rebellion, conceived the idea of having a Reunion in one of the centrally located cities of the state. The subject was talked up, a few postal cards were sent out, and eventually the newspapers took up the matter and gave it tangible shape. It was decided to hold the Reunion in Milwaukee, and June was decided upon as the month in which it would be held. Bushels of letters were being received daily, and had been for months past, and it was really suprising to know how the old Wisconsin soldiers had been scattered from one end of the world to the other, letters coming from every conceivable corner of the globe. The attendance at the Reunion could only be estimated by the capacity of the railroads and other transporting lines to bring them to the city. It was simply impossible to estimate the interest that was being manifested in this, the greatest Reunion of the times. Nothing less than an earthquake or a hundred earthquakes could keep them away. The most important question was: How are they to be fed and entertained when they get here? They expect to pay their way but where shall they, their wives and children be sheltered? The patriotic citizens will surely make some arrangement for them, for it would be better for us here at home to go into the streets and let the tired and dusty visitors abide in our homes, than to have them come up here and be disappointed. The visitors will find Milwaukee beer so good that it is feared that many of them will indulge unwittingly and the next morning will have to appear before the Blind Goddess—Judge Mallory, and beseech forgiveness. Many of you will doubtless appear for them and plead that they are such almighty good fellows that their sins might be forgiven, if he will just let them off this time. The speaker made several very happy local hits and told an anecdote that was, to use a common expression, "simply immense"

The speech fairly electrified, by its eloquence the audience, and at its close the applause was tremendous.

Gen. J. A. Kellogg, of Wausau, one of the "Pinery Boys," and during the war one of the commanders of the famous Iron Brigade, was next introduced and spoke as follows:

Mr President, Ladies and Gentlemen:

It is a pleasure to me to address so large and so intelligent a number of the citizens of Milwaukee. On looking over this sea of faces I do not see a single unkindly face and I assure you I have not the slightest animosity toward one of you and yet I pity you. Do you realize the fact that you are about to be charged upon by an army fifty thousand strong ; charged upon from all directions at once by this large army, armed to the teeth with giant appetites. A raid will be made upon your Comissary stores that it will require your utmost vigilance to defend. I assure you this will be the case and I am afraid you do not appreciate the situation. Why, you ought to commence now to instruct your chickens to roost high and teach your young pigs the art of self defense, for such a gathering of soldiers has never been seen in this state as will be with you on that occasion, and it is doubtful whether such a sight will ever be again seen in this state. From the letters I am receiving from all parts of the United States, from Maine to California, I am justified in saying that the attendance will be unprecedented. The object of the Reunion I understand primarily to be simply a gathering of the boys in blue for social enjoyment, that we may meet and compare notes, look ones more into each others faces and again clasp hands, I hope to see kind faces I now recollect as powder grimmed and distorted with pain or fixed with the frown of determination to do or die in their country's cause. I want to see kindly eyes which I recollect as flashing and glaring like the eyes of a wild beast as the battle raged around us. In fact we want a chance to light our battles over again as soldiers love to do, by memory's magic power, recall the lights and shades of a soldier's barren life. To those who have never been in the service it is hard, if not impossible, to appreciate the tenderness of the tie that binds soldiers together. Dangers mutually shared in the white heat of battle held them together and a still stronger tie binds together the hearts of those who suffered together the tortures of rebel prison. I see here tonight one with whom I formerly associated in Macon prison pen. We ate our part of corn meal together with the greatest pleasure we could experience. There is but one occasion when I remember of getting the better of him and that was by a meal of fresh meat acquired as follows : A cat by some means got into the prison yard—how or why I do not know for there was but few attractions for a cat—but it was there and caught a rat. The idea struck me that if Chinese could eat rats I could, so I raided the cat and took the rat away and immediately commenced skinning it. A hungry fellow at once took the hint and went for the cat, he ate one, I the other, while Collins I have no doubt envied both of us, for in rebel prison, starved as we were, all that was seld-h came to the surface and I say there is a tender tie binding all soldiers and especially prisoners second only to that binding us to wife and children, and sometimes I fear not second even to that. It was no holiday task to subdue a rebellion of the magnitude of that inaugurated by the Southern chiefs in 1861. No carpet knights were they who met and conquered the veteran troops of Lee, Longstreet and Johnson. It was a fight where Americans met Americans and it was only when it became a matter of endurance, of men, money and supplies that the North manifested its superiority over the South. The armies of the North met foemen worthy of their steel. It was a death grapple in which with equal numbers, equally supplied, it is hard to determine where or how the war would have ended.

Better men or better soldiers the world never saw than those who confronted each other on the battle fields of the South. It was a struggle which, when ended, left one of the combatants defeated and the other victorious but nearly exhausted by the struggle. In such a war as this an opportunity was given to display the metal of which our people was made, and in the fiery furnace of battle they proved pure gold. As an American I am proud to know that however wrong the cause for which they fought the people of the South were no poltroons and when the bitterness shall have passed away by the flight of time, while the scar may remain, the wound will be healed. The time will come when the people of the North will point with honest pride to the sterling traits of character and the true soldierly qualities of the boys in gray and I pray that the time may be hastened when the animosities engendered by the war may permanently pass away and when the blue and the gray may meet in a Reunion ; though perhaps few of the survivors may meet and clasp hands as ex-soldiers of one republic cemented all the more closely by the memories of the past. The brilliancy of the genius of such men as Lee, Longstreet, and Jackson made even treason respectable. I am proud of a victory gained over such soldiers. I trust that the Reunion may serve to bind even the American people more closely together in the bonds of friendship, and I hope no man will dare to say that it was inaugurated for a partisan purpose. On closing let me say I have never distrusted the ability or willingness of the people of Milwaukee to make the Reunion a success—such a success as shall leave Milwaukee associated in the minds of every visitor with the pleasantest recollection of their lives. From my own section you may expect a good delegation of the red shirted pinery boys some of whom will bring their tents with them. I believe that if a sufficient store of provisums is prepared the Attin and the Drinkin will in a great measure take care of themselves. Milwaukee, I know, will demonstrate its ability to take care of its invited guests, and that the Reunion will be a success.

Secretary of State Hans B. Warner

244　　WISCONSIN CENTRAL RAILROAD SUMMER RESORTS.

ISLAND CAMP, WISCONSIN CENTRAL RAILROAD.

THE OUTLOOK, NEAR BAYFIELD.

THE SOLDIERS REUNION OF 1880.

was introduced and made the usual remarks about not being present for the purpose of making a speech. He came as a private soldier, but supposed the privates would have to be taken care of in this matter as well as all of the rest. The magnitude of the great Reunion was well shown up, and he warned the citizens that soldiers would be here en masse. From one county he knew of 600 who would be present, and it was likely that at least 50,000 would be guests of the city during the week.

State Treasurer Guenther was called upon and said:

"*Mr. Chairman, Ladies and Gentlemen:*

Having received notice from the Reunion committee to be present on this occasion, and being informed by my military friends that a refusal would be an act of insubordination and subject me to a court martial, I am here ready to meet my fate, but hope to be dealt by with lenency.

Commendable as the spirit is, that prompted this demonstration, I am still of the opinion that so far as its object is to increase the attendance at the coming Reunion, you might as well have dispensed with it. Its grand success is already an assured fact as everybody can tell you who has kept his eyes and ears open for the last six months. I know that the soldiers will all rally around the old flag in June next. They have said so, and you know they always keep their word. You will have soldiers enough here to conquer the world, should the necessity arise.

And now, gentlemen, representing and speaking for the grand army of non-combatants, I herewith give you due notice, that it will not be within human power to keep us away. We are bound to be in this city during this grand gathering, whether you have room for us or not, and whether you wish us or not. You may cut off all railroad communications, and we will foot it; you may tie up all steamboats, and we will come in canoes or in bull ons; you may entrench yourselves and we will storm your fortifications; you may issue a proclamation to hang us—and we will risk that. We would rather hang here during these days than to sit on the sombre saw logs at Oshkosh or the lonely steps of the State House at Madison and read the dispatches of the glorious time you are enjoying here.

Gentlemen, we can stand, if necessary, the distant war and thunder of battle, we can face, without flinching, the enemy captured and disarmed; we can endure the hardships of civic life in time of war—we could see your soldiers crowned with the green laurels of victory without getting even a single leaf of that beautiful wreath ourselves. We could stand all this, but when you expect us to stay away from this peaceable engagement next June, you will have made the reckoning without your host. The soldier spirit is aroused in our hearts, and like Hannibal of ancient fame, we will cross the Alps of obstacles you may put in our way. And mind you, we'll not come alone. We will bring our wives, our children and those not blessed with those dear ones, their sweethearts.

And why, you may ask us, do you come? For them I will answer. Not merely for idle curiosity, not only because the railroad fare will be so cheap, not only because your beautiful Cream City offers so many attractions, not only because we are sure of a royal good time, not only for all this, but to help to pay off the debt of gratitude every loyal heart throughout this broad domain of freedom owes to the soldiers.

We want to greet the valiant men, we want to hail the brave defenders of our nation's honor, we want to cheer the surviving gallant patriots, we want to remember with grateful reverence the humblest of our immortal dead, who, with their own warm life blood sealed the declaration for time and eternity that the Union of the States is indissoluble, and forever.

We want to see, we want to show our children, the men, the heroes, the battle-scarred veterans, who in the dark hours of our nation's peril, in the great struggle for liberty and Union, forgetful of everything but their devotion to their native or adopted land, inspired by the loftiest patriotism, placed their all—their lives—upon the hallowed shrine of our common country.

We want to show them, not the soldiery of despotism, not soldiers by birth or profession, not soldiers for paltry gain, not soldiers who do the bidding of monarchs and kings for vain glory or brutal conquest, but the grand army of volunteer citizen soldiers of the Republic, led by the majestic, the divine, the American Goddess of Liberty, in the noble cause of right, of justice, and equality to all.

We want to take these brave men by the hand. We want once more to thank them for their heroic deeds, for their unfaltering love for our free institutions. We want to rejoice that through their efforts, through their valor, through their courageous perseverance, we are permitted to-day to so fully enjoy all the sweet boons of peace, prosperity and a united, free and powerful country, of which we, all of us, are proud to be sovereign citizens.

Gentlemen, we will all come, and my advice is : Prepare for the inevitable."

In noticing the speech the Milwaukee News said:

Mr. Guenther spoke in a vein of the richest and most irresistible humor, and his short speech was frequently interrupted by applause of the wildest kind. He ended by paying a tribute of the most lovable kind to the brave soldiers who upheld the union and saved the nation.

Loud calls were made by the audience for General Hincks, and upon his appearance the applause was so deafening and continuous that it was several minutes before he could be heard. He said that he had come to see how Milwaukeeans proposed to treat the soldiers. During the past few days he had experienced what it was to see a soldier stricken down. As to his management of the Home, every intelligent person in Milwaukee was conversant. He then gave a plain, sensible statement of what should be done by the citizens to help the Reunion along. There was a prospect of Milwaukee being eaten out of house and home. It was necessary for every family to take steps at once to help entertain some of the visiting soldiers, their cousins and their aunts. He dispel ed the idea of the Reunion being a political boom—indeed, if anyone wanted to turn it into politics, why let them do it; who cared—and if the men who carried the banners of this state from the lakes to the gulf didn't have a right to talk politics, if they wanted to, who did?

Gen. Bryant, adjutant general of the state, made a short but patriotic and telling speech. He said, among other good things, that the soldiers were anticipating the events of the Reunion with the greatest pleasure, and the event would indeed be one of the greatest in the annals of the northwest. He felt sure Milwaukee would hang out its latch string and dispense its hospitality as only the Cream city could. Every class of veterans would be present, the boys would lay down the ermine, would come from the work-shops, from the cities, towns and villages, from the fields and woods.

Col. Geo. B. Goodwin was called for. He said that in answer to all remarks about the chickens roosting high, he was delegated to pronounce them false. He understood that an order had been issued for the chickens not to go to roost at all. About the soldiers getting into Judge Mallory's court for drinking lager, that was also an egregious error, as it had long ago been decided in that popular tribunal that lager beer was not an intoxicating beverage. And the law was not dealt out by that official under the shadow of a blind goddess, but was dispensed with the bandage removed from the young lady's eyes. Col. Goodwin then spoke of the record made by Wisconsin soldiers, as the high st and best, and made a great hit in reiterating the almost forgotten fact that the then 18 year old state sent 80,000 soldiers to battle, who were noble volunteers. He concluded by offering a resolution inviting all soldiers to be present at the Reunion, and accept the hospitalities of the city. The resolution was unanimously adopted.

Judge Mallory was called for, and on appearing said it was too late to make a speech. He thought Milwaukee had been honored in being selected as the place of the Reunion, and every citizen felt the greatest interest in it. None need fear that they could not be well cared for. There was food in store for a million soldiers. There was millions of bushels of wheat and millions of pounds of pork, owners would be glad to dispose of. Later would come "2 for 5," and if any of the soldiers were so unfortunate as to appear before him, he would be glad to give 'em 3 for 5

At the conclusion of Judge Mallory's speech, loud calls were made for "Peck," and the strawberry blonde of an editor left his seat in the audience and clambered onto the stage. He simply said :

WISCONSIN CENTRAL RAILROAD SUMMER RESORTS.

RAPIDS OF THE TYLER FORK OF BAD RIVER.

ROBERTS' SUMMER RESORT, MENASHA.

", Ladies and gentlemen of Milwaukee, that is, not all of you but just enough of you. Many of those who are not present have sent their regrets. My friends there is an impression out that I crushed the late rebellion. I didn't do it. I have heretofore on various occasions admitted that I had, but as I spent most of my time, while soldiering, down in Louisiana, where they raise such awful liars, you will at once see that I am not responsible for it, and yet I know lots of men who crushed the rebellion. There are at least 20,000 in Wisconsin who squelched it. But the Reunion is to be a big thing. I have already received 35,601 letters from soldiers whom I owe, and they are all coming. Everything will be done to amuse, entertain and please them. I will lend them every cent I owe; all other citizens should do the same thing. Besides the beer and other good things, the Y. M. C. A. and The Sun, these two great moral institutions across the way, will be on tap every day from 7 A. M. to 10 P. M. There are facilities in the breweries and ice houses to sleep a million of 'em. There is no need of them coming here with a month full of straw to sleep on, for if there are any tents in these United States that aint filled with yellow fever, we are going to have them. Will get them by fair means if possible, and if not, by foul. Speaking of fowls reminds me. There is no danger of a scarcity of chickens. Gentlemen, the woods are full of them. Gen. Hincks and others have sold their game chickens in anticipation of this event, but they were bought in the same neighborhood and consequently can be relied on. There will be tents on hand to shelter the boys from the falling dews of heaven, or any other deuce. No outsiders can drink beer, the breweries and saloons will all be closed. But it is possible enough can be scared up to prevent a famine. New military companies are being formed on all sides to see that no guilty man escapes.— Thank you."

By the time this meeting was adjourned Milwaukee was fully alive to the exigencies of the case—the boom had started. A finance committee was at once organized, and $25,000 raised to meet contingent expenses of the occasion.

THE BADGERS IN BATTLE.

From Falling Waters to Appomattox.

How They Acted—A Proud Record.

(BY COL. ED. E. BRYANT.)

The Return.

When the war was over and peace, longed-for, prayed for, thrice blessed peace, returned, the soldiers of the Union looked forward to their discharge with profoundest joy. They were eager to resume those pursuits of civil life which they had reluctantly but promptly abandoned at the call of their country. They were impatient to leave the scene of their hardships and their triumphs, and return to "God's country," the better clime and more congenial atmosphere of home. And no happier mortals ever trod the earth than those gallant armies of the Union when their homeward march began. They were to lay aside the rough harness of war; they might engage once more in the avocations of peace, the blessed privileges of which they had learned to prize. The avenues of success in a quiet and prosperous land, opened to their ambition, and they felt the enthusiasm of those to whom the gateway of manhood had just appeared. Full of hope they were to begin life anew.

They felt, too, the loftiest, noblest pride that manliness can feel. Their valor had saved the nation. The destinies of a great people, the hopes of man kind for free government, had been committed to their charge, and they had proven faithful to the high trust. Their fortitude and devotion, their bravery and fidelity, had rescued their country from impending ruin. They were conquerors for the right. They were covered with honor and crowned with success; and life was clad with new light and dignity to them. And, above all, they were coming home; and amid toil and hardship, and in camp and march, in battle and in hospital, perchance in prison pens, God knows, they had learned how much of heaven is implied in the dear word "home!"

And in 1865, the armies of the Union passed off the stage of action to exist no more save in history's most thrilling annals, and in the memories of the host who composed that band of patriot heroes.

To their added honor be it said that no class of men ever devoted themselves with more alacrity and energy than did the returned soldiers, to the honorable avocations of peace. Comparatively but few of them were spoiled by the demoralizing influences of war; and in the walks of life the soldiers of the Union have, as civilians, taken the front rank for public spirit, for large hearted enterprise and for good citizenship.

Nearly half a generation of time has passed since those mighty armies dissolved back into civil life. The "Boys in Blue," then so full of life and the fire of youth, now find themselves approaching middle age. Grown more thoughtful as the years roll on, they love to turn from the business cares of life back to the eventful days in which they bore so active and glorious a part. They have to meet the comrades true and tried, of other days, and to recall those scenes, so vividly painted on their memories, and to enjoy the companionship of those choice spirits, whose recollections, like theirs, are stored with the rich historic experiences of the brave days of the war.

Hence it is, that annual reunions are becoming more general, and we look forward to them with deeper interest as the years wear away. On this occasion of your reunion it seems to me most fitting to choose as the theme for my address,

The Soldiers of Wisconsin.

Their service and their worth demand a better tribute than my gifts can bring. Their brave deeds can have but mere allusion, where time will not permit a full recital.

In no spirit of narrow state pride, nor invidious denomination, do I speak of them alone, for the brave men who maintained the honor of this state in the late war would resent any detraction from the merits of those valiant companions-in-arms who were enrolled in other states. Side by side with the brave men of every other loyal state, they bore their part in that war. Wisconsin's soldiers won for themselves, in every part of the great theatre of war the generous praise of other troops. They need not detract or belittle the services of others in order to give conspicuity to their own. Besides, the splendid material which made up Wisconsin's quota to the armies of the Union was in but small proportion native to the soil. Less than ten per cent. of her soldiers were born in her borders.

At the breaking out of the war, Wisconsin's population was composed mainly of immigrants from New York, New England, the Middle states, and from Ireland, Germany and Norway. It was composed mainly of young men and youths in their very prime; a sturdy, stalwart, self-reliant element such as push out to develop a new country.— Their superiority was noticeable.— Wherever a Wisconsin regiment appeared, the fine physique, the self reliant carriage of its men at once challenged attention; and division and brigade commanders were eager and proud to get Wisconsin regiments into their commands.

Wisconsin furnished, according to the very carefully collected returns prepared during the war, 91,397 men to the armies of the Union. In one respect her military history is peculiar. Her troops were sent to almost every part of the great theatre of war. It was a wise policy of the general government that suggested the brigading of the troops without regard to states. It put a check upon all state jealousies, and that mar-row and petty state pride, which, of all men, the soldiers who fought for the cause of national union, have learned to despise. It cemented in one great brotherhood the loyal armies. And Wisconsin's troops, I say, were not only studiously diffused among the various brigades, divisions and corps, but were put to service in nearly every prominent part of the seat of war. And wherever they were sent, they bore a conspicuous part in the events of all the principal campaigns. It can be truly said that a full record of Wisconsin troops and the part they bore and the events in which they participated, would not fall far short f a complete history of the war, so wide reaching was their war experience, and so fully diffused were they throughout the several armies and their several parts. Wisconsin stood side by side with the regiments of every loyal state, and faced in frequent battle the troops of every rebel state.

And history bears me out in the proud boast, if such it seems, that wherever they were sent, and with whatever troops distributed, they soon gained a name in army circles, as being among the very best of soldiers. Not only were they noted for courage and steadiness in the field, but for order and discipline, for intelligence and manly bearing, for cleanliness and orderly life in camp, for their careful military instruction, and for their quick appreciation of the duties and dignity of the character of the citizen soldier. They accepted the re stratum of discipline as a necessity of efficient service. They cheerfully obeyed men who were, in many cases, in every thing but the circumstance of rank, their inferiors, because they knew that of all evils in an army, insubordination is the worst; and that armed anarchy meant but shame, disgrace, defeat and ruin of armies and of the cause.

Another fact contributed largely to the efficiency of our fighting regiments, who served during the whole war. The state authorities, less ambitious to swell the number of regiments than to furnish good soldiers where most needed, adopted the policy of sending recruits to the old regiments. This was especially gratifying to army commanders. Says Gen. Sherman in his memoirs: "I remember that Wisconsin kept her regiments filled with recruits, whereas other states generally filled their quotas by new regiments, and the result was that we estimated a Wisconsin regiment equal to an ordinary brigade," as the recruits, mixed in with old soldiers and experienced officers, soon became veterans.

Time forbids more, than a passing glance at the panorama of those many and mighty campaigns, in which it is our pride that we shared. But on this occasion, which brings to mind the stirring events of those memorable days. I know my comrades will pardon me if I linger a few moments to refer to the great events in which Wisconsin soldiers covered themselves with imperishable renown.

The First Advance.

In the first advance into Northern Virginia, the first regiment was prominent, and at Falling Waters, July 2d, 1861. first met the enemy. The first bloodshed in the memorable and afterwards blood-drenched valley of the Shenandoah, flowed from the veins of Wisconsin boys. In the "On to Richmond" movement which culminated in the disastrous repulse at Bull Run, our state was represented by the second regiment in the brigade of then Col. W. T. Sherman, now general of the army. That they lost more than a seventh of the command in killed and wounded, and were among the last to leave that ill fated field, where troops all panic stricken were flying on either side of them, shows that even then, green and untried as they were, they gave promise of the mettle which in riper discipline made their fame world-wide. Sherman in his reports speaks of their steadiness.

Peninsular Campaign, 1862.

In this campaign, Wisconsin was represented by the gallant fifth regiment and by Co G, Berdan's sharpshooters. The Fifth at Williamsburg made the charge which turned in our favor the wavering scale of battle. For this they received the thanks of Gen McClellan. "My lads," said he, as he rode up to the regiment a day or two after, "I came to thank you for your gallant conduct the other day. You gained honor for your country, your state, and the army to which you belong. Through you we won the day." And telegraphing to the secretary of war the hasty report of the charge, he said it was "brilliant in the extreme."

The sharpshooters of Co. G, Berdan's regiment picketed, scouted and skirmished from York to the defences of Richmond; and what old soldier here does not know how much of hard, alert duty and danger are implied in that service. In many of the battles of that bloody campaign, their rifles at the front rang out the prelude to the volleyed thunder of the gr ral engagement.

The Battle of Winchester

In the campaign up the Shenandoah valley in 1862, the old Third Wiscon in bore a prominent part. When Gen. Banks, with his command stripped down to 4,000 fighting men, was pounced upon by the combined divisions of Ewell and Stonewall Jackson, the Third Wisconsin was in the little brigade which, in open field, manfully held in check the overpowering host for five hours.

The incidents of that battle have always a mournful interest to me. My most loved messmate and comrade, Capt. Moses O Brien, one of the bravest Irishmen who ever drew a sword in freedom's cause, fell at the head of the company. After having, earlier in the battle, been wounded severely, he refused to leave the field, and soon fell with a second and mortal wound. And, as the fight surged away from where he fell, with his dying breath, he begged of a stranger to draw the finger ring from his death-palsied hand, and bring it, as a token of his undying friendship, to me. Comrades, how many like him can you call to mind? Lion-hearted in action and in command; firm on duty as the iron and the oak; in companionship, gentle and loving as the child—now on the field of honor resting from their warfare!

Gainesville.

A few days after, the second, sixth and seventh regiments fought at Gainesville one of the sharpest, bloodiest minor battles of the war. The gallant behavior of the brigade elicited from Gen. Pope the encomium that it "consisted of some of the best troops in the service." Next, we hear of this gallant brigade at South Mountain, charging up the gap, pushing its way up the rocky crest, and dislodging an enemy having every advantage of position. Right gallantly it stormed the mountain gateway, paying dearly for its victory in Wisconsin's choicest blood; and gaining the immortal name of "The Iron Brigade of the west," a designation it bore unenvied and with honor.

Antietam

Then came Antietam, which Greeley calls "the bloodiest day that America ever saw." In that sanguinary battle, Wisconsin's honor was upborne by the third regiment standing bravely in line, in an exposed position, be ging for permission to charge, firing steadily and closing up the thinning ranks, until the fallen cartridge papers, for months afterwards, showed by a strange winrow its perfect line of battle—taking into battle 345 men, of whom 198 were killed or wounded—almost two-thirds. There was the fifth regiment, staunchly supporting a battery in the heart of the fight. There was the "Iron Brigade," winning by a fearful list of dead and wounded, the high praise of the commander of the army: "I have s en them under fire acting in a manner that reflected the greatest possible credit and honor upon themselves and their state. They are equal to the best troops in any army in the world."

Shiloh

The sixteenth and eighteenth regiments fought at Shiloh. Though but raw soldiers then, and receiving the command to load and fire for the first time, and that, too, after they had been surprised by an attack, "yet they held their position," says a war correspondent of the Cincinnati Gazette "with an obstinacy that adds new laurels to the character of 'American soldiers.'" Gov. Harvey wrote home just before his untimely death: "Many regiments of that fight may wel. covet the impression which the eighteenth Wisconsin left of personal bravery, heroic daring and determined endurance."

The Fourteenth Wisconsin came upon the field at midnight, took its place in line in mud, rain, and darkness, and waited for the morning; fought like veterans the next day; four times charged a battery; thrice repulsed, took it and kept it leaving a stack of 60 dead rebe's where it fell. Thus in their first fight, admiring witnesses of their soldierly valor gave them the merited name of the "Wisconsin Regulars."

Chaplin Hills, or Perryville.

When the tide of war rolled northward in the later summer of 1862, and Kirby Smith with a large army poured into Kentucky threatening Cincinnati, Gen. Buell left the Tennessee river to pursue. The two armies met in combat at Chaplin Hills. Here were Wisconsin's first regiment, the re-organized twenty-first, tenth, fifteenth, and twenty-fourth regiments and the third, fifth and eighth batteries. It is recorded of the first, that when one division of our forces had been driven back in disorder Gen. Rousseau, fearing the panic would become general, rode in front of the First Wisconsin shouting to the boys to "keep steady and we would whip them yet." The Wisconsin boys cried out with one voice: "Lead us to the front." Gen. Rousseau says: "They drove back the enemy several times with great loss, and until their ammunition gave out bravely maintained their position." They captured the colors of the rebel regiment.

The Tenth Wisconsin was under fire for seven hours that day. Rousseau says of their brigade, that, "Repeatedly assailed by overwhelming numbers, after exhausting its ammunition, it still held its position." He declared that these "brave men were entitled to the gratitude of the country."

The fifteenth regiment gained honorable mention here, capturing a large store of ammunition and many prisoners.

The fifth battery here gained renown. Three times they repulsed a rebel charge. Gen. McCook thanked them on the field saying: "They saved the division from a disgraceful defeat."

Corinth.

The siege of Corinth was participated in by the eighth, fourteenth, sixteenth seventeenth and eighteenth regiments of infantry, and the fifth, sixth, eleventh and twelfth batteries, and many of these commands shared in the pursuit after the evacuation. At the second battle of Corinth, these regiments came in f r a share of a very hard fight.

The fourteenth here won golden compliments. Hear the report of the brigade commander: "On Col. Hancock and his regiment, the fourteenth Wisconsin, there was no discount. This regiment was the one to rely upon in any emergency; always cool, steady and vigorous. Though suffering more loss than any of the regiments in the command, they maintained their lines and delivered their fire with all the precision and coolness which could have been maintained on drill." In this battle the Seventeenth Wisconsin made one of those sweeping, tearing charges which Irish soldiers the world over regard as their "best holt." "Boys," said the brigade commander, "boys of the seventeenth, you made the most glorious charge of the campaign."

The eighteenth was praised for "most effectual service." The eighth received high encomiums. The sixth battery did her duty and, says Gen. Hamilton, "did noble work." The twelfth battery was honored by Gen. Sullivan with the praise: "Boys, I am proud of you. You have done nobly. The dead in front of your battery show the work you have done."

Cedar Mountain.

In Pope's campaign in Virginia, the bloody battle of Cedar Mountain was opened by the Third Wisconsin Its fullest force fell on their part of the line. Greeley says, after explaining the situation, and the badly managed scheme of the attack on such a position, that "had victory been possible they would have won it." "The best blood of the Union was here poured out like water, but in vain."

Stone River.

The close of the year 1862 was signalized by the memorable fight at Stone River, Tenn. On this hard fought field Wisconsin reported with the first, tenth, fifteenth, twenty-first, and twenty-fourth regiments, and the third, fifth and eighth batteries, a l in battle array. On the 30th December the fifteenth regiment and the third and eighth batteries were in the hottest of the fight. The fifteenth Wiscon sin captured a gun as its trophy of the day. In his report of his share of the fight, Gen. Phil. Sheridan speaks of the "splendid conduct, bravery and efficiency of the twenty-fourth Wisconsin." Col. Scribner, their brigade commander, s ays: "The tenth Wisconsin would have suffered extermination rather than yield its ground without orders." Gen Rousseau reports that when, during the battle, Wheeler's cavalry attacked his supply trains, "the burden of the fight fell on the twenty-first Wisconsin who behaved like veterans. The commander of the brigade in which the eighth battery served speaks of the "determined bravery and chivalrous heroism of the officers and men." Gen Davis says the conduct of the fifth battery was "gallant and distinguished." Another commander says its "guns were splendidly handled.

Fierce, that battle raged on the 30th and 31st of December. Greeley tells the story of its conclusion. He says: "Night fell on our army successful at every point, notwithstanding every attempt which had been made to drive it, but with little reason for exultation. It had lost a fourth of its men and guns * * * But Rosencrans took stock of ammunition * * * he lay down with his army to await such a New Year's day as it pleased God to send them. * * * Rosencrans said: "T.is battle must be won. At 9 A. M. they, the rebels, had supposed our army in their hands; at sunset Bragg, the rebel commander, had enough to do to save his own.

Prairie Grove.

At Prairie Grove, Ark., the twentieth

WISCONSIN CENTRAL DOCK, ASHLAND, 1856 FEET LONG.

Wisconsin distinguished itself. Says Greeley; "The twentieth Wisconsin and the nineteenth Iowa were ordered to charge a rebel battery in their front. They did it most gallantly, hurling back its supports, but were unable to hold it. Their charge was at once returned with interest by the rebels, intent on the capture of our three batteries, and pushing within a hundred yards of our guns, they were likewise repulsed with great slaughter." Gen. Blunt reports the gallant charge of the twentieth Wisconsin, and says that "they did their duty nobly." Men of Iowa, Illinois, Kansas, Missouri and Wisconsin mingled their blood on the same field. He says: "For deeds of valor on the field of Prairie Grove, their native states may well be proud of them." Their brigade commander said: "They behaved nobly and stood fire like veterans." Gen Herron writes: "Their charge was a glorious sight." He says: "My two divisions (including the twentieth Wisconsin,) are invincible." "Better men never went up on the field. "But," he continues: "It is with a sad heart that I look upon the long rows of graves where lie my gallant soldiers, who have died, victims of this accursed rebellion. May the authors of it have a hot place in hell." These bitter words were wrung from the heart of one who looked upon the hundreds of graves of the boys in blue; and, if they come not up to the full measure of Christian charity, the recording angel will admit the grievous provocation and great sorrow that called them forth.

The second and third Wisconsin cavalry were present at this battle, and their efficiency and aid given on and near the field were highly commended by the commanding general; and Gen. Herron reports that they proved themselves "worthy of the name of American soldiers."

The third cavalry, under Major Calkins, elicited the admiration of both armies for its skillful maneuvers, and its sharp assaults on the rebels left wing which occurred in view of the entire field of action.

Fredericksburg and Chancellorville.

Turning our glance eastward, we find the Iron brigade, the fifth regiment and Berdan's sharpshooters in the battle of Fredericksburg. In the opening operations of 1863, came the battle of Chancellorville. Here were engaged the Wisconsin third. When Stonewall Jackson had crushed the eleventh corps, the third was in the division that was thrown in as a barrier to their victorious advance. Right gallantly that duty was done, and the victors were checked. Behind the third were gathered the forty pieces of artillery, which, through the night, belched their missiles into the woods over the heads of the lines. In the night attack made to c eck the rebel on et, this regiment took part; and on the morning at daybreak, the battle was resumed. While regiments on their flanks were retiring, the third, under an equally withering fire, was advancing, crowding the enemy before it, and supposed it was winning a victory.

The Fifth at Mary's Heights.

In this campaign, the fif h Wisconsin headed the famous charge which carried a part of the almost impregnable Mary's Heights at Fredericksburg. The position over which they charged was such, and the valor of the men who assailed it so heroic, that a correspondent of the London Times, southern sympathiser, writes from Lee's headquarters: "Never at Fontenoy, Altuera, nor at Waterloo, was more undaunted courage displayed * * * than during the six frantic dashes which they (Hancock's corps) directed against the almost impregnable position of their foe;" and Greeley says: "Braver men never smiled on death, than those who climbed Mary's Hill on that fatal day." The one gleam of success in that gallant but disastrous fight, was the capture by the fifth Wisconsin, of a rebel battery. All else was failure where "we had reason for sorrow but none for shame."

The Fall of Vicksburg.

The capture of Vicksburg, in 1863, was the crowning glory of the war in the Mississippi Valley. Wisconsin can proudly claim her full share in the laurels of that achievement. Twelve of her best regiments of infantry, one of cavalry, and three of her batteries were among the legion of heroes who closed around that stronghold. There were her eighth eleventh, twelfth, fourteenth, seventeenth, eighteenth, twentieth, twenty-third, twenty-fifth, twenty-seventh, twenty-ninth and thirty-third infantry; her second cavalry; her first, sixth and twelfth batteries.

In the preliminary operations, the capture of Arkansas Post was one of the brilliant series of valorous deeds. Here the twenty-third Wisconsin bore a noble part, Greeley records in his "American Conflict" how it charged the rebel right and dislodged the enemy.— This regiment was, for its gallantry here, highly complimented in general orders, and as a tribute to its gallant conduct, its brigade commander Gen. Burbridge, was appointed to plant the American flag upon the captured fort. In the battle of Port Gibson, which resulted in a victory which Grant, in his congratulatory order, declared "one of the most important of the war," the eleventh Wisconsin bore a part which was honorably mentioned in general orders. The twenty-third Wisconsin were there, too, capturing many prisoners

The twenty-ninth Wisconsin was in the hottest of the fight; and, in this, its first battle, its brigade commander testified that its brave men "fought like veterans."

In that sweeping advance to gain the rear of Vicksburg, the battle of Jackson was fought. The Eighth and Eighteenth Wisconsin were in the charge that carried the town. The eighth was one of the first regiments to enter, and was at once appointed provost guard, a compliment to efficiency and discipline that regiments were proud to receive. Then followed Champion Hills. Here the twenty-third regiment sustained a prominent part, rendering conspicuous and effective service on its part of the field. The twenty-ninth regiment was here in Hovey's division. Says Greeley: "The credit of this victory devolves on Hovey and his gallant division, which was for hours closely engaged with superior numbers strongly posted and well covered by dense forests, and who fought gallantly and repeatedly crowded back our line by the sheer weight of that which opposed it." An eye witness, the war correspondent of the Cincinnati Commercial, writes: "Shortly after the commencement of the general engagement, the rebels brought a battery of four to bear upon the first brigade of Hovey's division, and were inflicting severe punishment with it. Gen. McGinnis ordered it charged. The eleventh Indiana and twenty-n nth Wisconsin being in front, the hazardous task was assigned them. They marched cautiously up a high slope to within 75 yards of the guns, and then made a dash at the pieces. The rebel gunners performed their duty manfully, standing by their guns till they were driven away with bayonets or clubbed with muskets. The eleventh and twenty-ninth were not to be driven back, however, nor denied the object for which they started."

The twenty-ninth Wisconsin in this famous charge captured a battery of

GRAND ARCH, FISHING FOR ROCK TROUT.

VIEW OF ELK LAKE, PHILLIPS WIS.

brass pieces, a stand of colors and 306 prisoners. And Greeley exultingly records how Dillon's sixth Wisconsin battery strengthened Hovey's artillery on the right, "and opened on the advancing foe an enfilading fire that arrested and turned them back under a tempest of cheers from our men."

Next day our victorious army advanced on the Big Black, to find the enemy strongly posted there. Here the Thirteenth corps won the day. Here the First Wisconsin battery poured its effective shot into the rebel position, bravely disregarding the rebel shell which exploded its own caissons. Here the story of the intrepid charge of the Eleventh Wisconsin, and other regiments, is best told by the correspondent of the Cincinnati Commercial: "The order," he writes, "was given to the brigade command on the right to advance and charge the enemy's works. The order was received with shouts and cheers. The Twenty-first, Twenty-second and Twenty-third Iowa and Eleventh Wisconsin in Lawler's brigade, were the first to announce themselves in readiness. The order, Forward, was given, and steadily and valiantly the brave boys moved up to the assault. The enemy crouched down behind the breastworks. A portion of them stationed in a curtain on the right of the fort, whence they were able to get a cross fire upon the column, reserved their volley until we were within easy musket range, when they swept the advancing line with their terrible fire. The brave boys lost in that fearful volley 159 men, yet they faltered not nor turned their steps backward. They waded the bayou delivering their fire as they reached the other bank, and rushed on the enemy with fixed bayonets. So quickly was this accomplished that the enemy had not time to reload and was forced to surrender." Then came the investment of Vicksburg and the repeated assaults of May 19th and 22d. The eleven regiments of Wisconsin infantry, and three batteries above mentioned closed around the doomed city. The Eighth Wisconsin, under Sherman, on the right, in the assault of May 22d, reached the outer slope of the works, and staid there till ordered to retire. The Eleventh Wisconsin assaulted in the center and suffered heavily. The Fourteenth Wisconsin covered itself with glory at the cost of nearly half its men, advancing its line far beyond the regiments on either hand. So gallant was their conduct here that Gen. Rousseau, when his division entered the city, after the surrender, gave the Fourteenth Wisconsin the post of honor, saying in his order: "Every officer and man in the Fourteenth is a hero."

The Twenty-seventh Wisconsin took an honorable part in the assault of the 14th an l 23 l of May. The Twelfth and Eighteenth regiments did excellent service in the siege.

The Twenty-third Wisconsin, too, worn down to a squad, but with the courage and determination of heroes, pushed up to the base of the rebel forts. The flag of truce sent out by Pemberton proposing to surrender was received in its front by one of its officers. That their assaults were not successful, is not strange. Gen. Sherman, after seeing Sevastapol, says the position at Vicksburg was the more difficult of the two.

On the day of the surrender of Vicksburg, the battle of Helena, Arkansas, was fought. Here the Twenty-eighth Wisconsin participated, pouring its deadly fire into the assailants, and repulsing the flower of the rebel troops of Arkansas. A Wisconsin Brigadier Gen. F. Solomon, planned and constructed the defences, through the judicious location of which the victory was won.

Port Hudson.

Following Vicksburg, Port Hudson fell after a sturdy resistance.

The Fourth Wisconsin charged up into the ditch surrounding the fortification sustaining fearful loss. Greeley says of the assault in which they took part: "Never was fighting more heroic, * * * If valor could have triumphed over such odds, they would have carried the works."

Gettysburg.

That memorable July 4th, 1863, was a proud day for loyal hearts, for it carried all over the land the full details of the battle of Gettysburg, where the army of the Potomac rolled back the tide of rebel invasion from loyal soil. That battle, Swinton classes as one of the great battles of history, for here 45,000 men and more, engaged in combat, were killed or wounded. The Second, Third, Sixth, Seventh and Twenty-sixth Wisconsin regiments fought here. A prouder record than they made on that memorable field, no State can boast. In the first day's fight, "the Iron Brigade," says Gen. Doubleday, "charged with great gallantry, drove the enemy before them into a ravine, and there captured a large number of prisoners, including officers."

The Sixth regiment, temporarily serving in Cutler's brigade, participated in a charge which resulted in the capture of two rebel regiments. Braver fighting than theirs is rare in the annals of war. As a testimonial of their valor, I quote what was said of the Sixth Wisconsin, on the occasion of the presentation of the battle flag of the One Hundred and Forty-seventh New York to the City of Oswego, by the commander of that regiment. He says: "At this critical moment when, (on the first day at Gettysburg), the salvation of our regiment depended on immediate action, a little band of men was seen emerging from the woods at the left. They were what remained of the Sixth Wisconsin Volunteers, a regiment which had been two years in the service, and to whom the leaden rain and iron hail of battle had become as familiar as the showers of Heaven. Every man of that band was a host in himself. Steadily, swiftly, and furiously, they charged upon the enemy's flank. Northern courage was too much for Southern chivalry. The rebel columns wavered, broke and fled. Two entire rebel regiments were taken prisoners, all honor to the gallant Sixth Wisconsin! They saved what remained of the One Hundred and Forty-seventh on that day."

The Third Wisconsin on the second and third day's fight did their duty as become their fame, driving Ewell from Culp's Hill, they clung to their works, though the rebel shell tore through the woods which covered their position, and limbs and splinters rattled about and fell upon them; they repulsed all charges in front and gathered up thousands of rebel muskets which had been dropped before them. The mere accident of favorable position saved them from a fire that swept off full half of their brigade. They took part in the battle of the second day on our left and helped to check the advance on Gen. Sickles' corps.

The Twenty-sixth regiment here suffered a terrible baptism of fire—only four officers escaping unhurt. Berdan's sharpshooters, Co. G, bore their part bravely here, and were in the key of battle when the rebels tried to break our center in the final charge. When the rain of Heaven drenched that bloody field on the night of July 3d, it bathed the wounds of more than 500 of Wisconsin's sons. In the cemetery on that battle field, hundreds of Wisconsin's boys are sleeping the sleep of the soldier in their "windowless palaces of rest."

Chickamauga.

But we must linger by no field of glory, nor in our limited time can we even mention all.

At Chickamauga, the First, Tenth, Fifteenth, Twenty-first and Twenty-fourth Wisconsin infantry, and the third, fifth and eighth batteries fought and suffered heavily. Several of those regiments were under Gen. Thomas on the left, in that dogged and sturdy resistance of the rebel

Wisconsin Central R. R. and its Connections
WITH OTHER RAILROAD AND STEAMBOAT LINES.

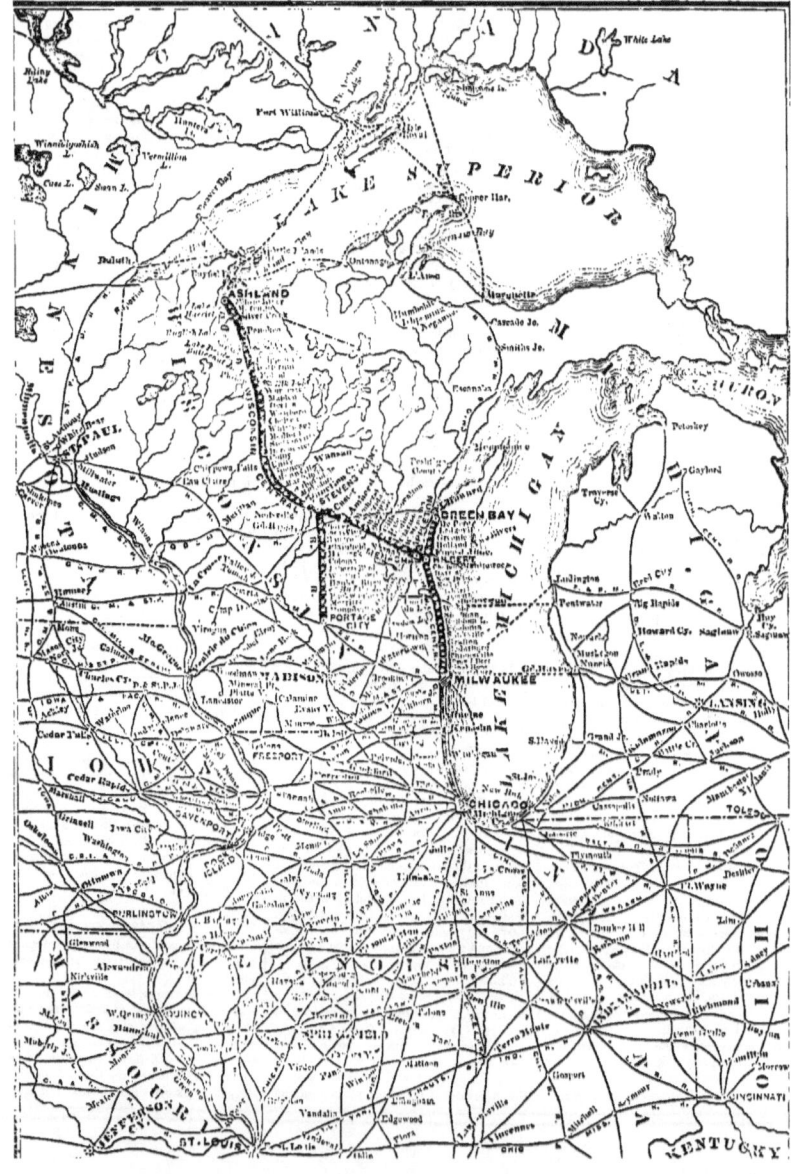

assaults which gave to Thomas the immortal name of the "Rock of Chickamauga." The rebels claimed this as a victory, but the prize for which they contended was Chattanooga. They squandered 1,000 men in the attempt, but thanks to Thomas and the brave boys who stayed with him at Chickamauga, that prize was never wrenched from our grasp.

Chattanooga.

And when Thomas, beleaguered in Chattanooga, telegraphed to Grant: "We will hold it till we starve," those same Wisconsin regiments and batteries were there and very near starved, they were, and the boys so hungry that they ate the oats the horses slobbered out of their nose-bags. And when Sherman marched up his Fifteenth corps, over the roughest roads ever known, to the relief of the besieged "Army of the Cumberland," at Chattanooga, the Eighteenth Wisconsin was in it. This regiment marched and fought in that corps of which Sherman said: "They have marched through mud and over rocks, sometimes barefooted, without a murmur. Without a moment's rest, after a march of 400 miles, without sleep for three successive nights, we crossed the Tennessee, fought our part of the battle of Chattanooga, and pursued the enemy out of Tennessee. * * I cannot speak of the Fifteenth army corps without a seeming vanity. * * * I assert that there is no better body of soldiers in America than it.

Mission Ridge.

In the assault which, carefully planned and executed under the eye of Gen. Grant, hurled Bragg back from Mission Ridge, driving his army from a position, which the rebel general himself says "ought to have been held by a line of skirmishers against any assaulting column." The First, Tenth, Fifteenth, Eighth, Twenty-first and Twenty-fourth and Twenty-sixth regiments from Wisconsin shared in that magnificent charge. Gen. Grant was writing of them with the rest, when he said: "They encountered a fearful volley of grape and canister from nearly thirty pieces of artillery, and musketry from well-filled rifle pits. Not a waver, however, was seen in all that long line of brave men. Their progress was steadily onward until the summit was in their possession." This victory relieved Chattanooga, resulting in the death, wounding or capture of 15,000 rebels and the taking of 35 guns.

Carrion Crow Bayou.

Turn where you will, Wisconsin boys were always at the front, always getting hard service, but always praised and beloved by their companions in arms. Away down in November, 1863, a column was sent out to Opelousas, merely as a feint to draw attention from a more important movement. On its return, near Carrion Crow Bayou, the rebels pounced up on it in the woods, taking it quite by surprise. The Twenty-third Wisconsin was there, holding in camp the election of state officers, when it was assailed, the only marked instance I ever heard of, of armed interference with an election, and one of which no confederate brigadier has ever been heard to complain. "This regiment," said Greeley in his American Conflict, "was speedily reduced from 226 to 98 men. Its colonel wounded and captured." "Our right," he continues, "was assailed in great force and with intense fury, was broken, and was saved from utter destruction by the devoted bravery of the Twenty-third Wisconsin, and the efficient service of Nim's battery."

Such, comrades, were the men of Wisconsin. Their praise was well sounded by the Second Massachusetts, who fought side by side through the war with the Third Wisconsin. In their farewell letter at parting at the close of the war, they said: "We always felt safe when you were beside us." It is related in a New York paper that Gen. Sherman, after the war, when beset by a newspaper reporter, and questioned in regard to the efficiency of the troops from the several states, replied that all, all did nobly, refusing to make any discrimination. But, after a pause, as his eye lighted up with the memory of the old struggles, said he: "But you ought to see the Wisconsin boys go in."

Turn we now for a moment, to the well planned, but sadly mismanaged,

Red River Expedition.

The Eighth Wisconsin was so patriotic that it joined this expedition when its men were entitled to their veteran furlough, but Gen. Sherman's desire was their law; and they bravely fought on the various fields of that expedition. The Fourteenth Wisconsin was there. At Fort De Russy, Pleasant Hill, Cloutierville, Markville and Yellow Bayon, it maintained its early renown. The Twenty-third Wisconsin, staunch and true as ever, was the last to leave the field at Sabine Cross Roads. When "crushed back in spite of desperate resistance," they covered the retreat with that steady valor for which they were ever famed. A part of the Twenty-ninth Wisconsin was engaged, and they can read with pride their record of that losing fight. The Thirty-third Wisconsin, too, fought from the transports repulsing the assailants along shore.—In a word, in all the gallant fighting of that advance and retreat, our troops were engaged and commended. But the crowning glory of that luckless expedition, the one star of success in its gloom of failure, was the building of the dam whereby the shoal waters of the river were raised and our fleet, worth millions, saved. That honor was reflected on Wisconsin by Col. Joseph Bailey, of the fourth regiment. He had learned his wisdom on our lumbering streams. His practical common sense was better than the science of the schools, and he convinced Banks, Franklin and Porter that he could pass the fleet. And when he felt the need of skillful men to aid in his gigantic work, he called for Wisconsin boys, and the Twenty-ninth Wisconsin toiled for him day and night with a will, and he "especially commended their faithfulness, energy and endurance;" and when the water rose and the great gun-boats floated safely down the deepened channel, Admiral Porter says " 30,0 0 voices rose in one deafening cheer; and universal joy seemed to pervade the face of every man!" All this in honor of the humble and patriotic lumbermen and mechanics of the Wisconsin pinery streams.

The Atlanta Campaign.

When the spring campaign of 1864 opened and Grant and Sherman, then the two great chieftains, had carefully planned their summer's work they laid out plenty of business for their armies and Wisconsin's boys had enough to do. Sherman gathered for his Atlanta campaign fourteen regiments of Wisconsin infantry The first, third, tenth, twelfth, thirteenth, sixteenth, nineteenth, twenty-first, twenty-second, twenty-fourth, twenty fifth, thirty first, thirty-second and our first cavalry and fifth and tenth batteries. He gathered all within his reach, for he started out as he said in his letter to Gen. Grant, to "knock Joe Johnston." The campaign from Chattanooga to Atlanta was a continued fight, in which strong skirmish lines steadily pushed their way. In these, our boys of these regiments were constantly under fire. In the leading battles, Wisconsin regiments invariably reported to the front. At Resaca, eight of them were hotly engaged; at Dallas, seven; at Kenesaw Mountain, nine. A volume could be written giving the wild, thrilling events of Wisconsin men in that advance. At Peach Tree Creek, seven Wisconsin regiments shared in the fight. Here the twenty-sixth regiment was specially commended as having "received the brunt of the battle on its brigade front, and repulsed it, and followed it by a spirited counter charge." Its brigade commander speaks of it in his report as "One of the finest organizations in the service." Old Jo. Hooker said of the Twenty-second Wisconsin, here, that "no regiment ever did better." The Tenth Wisconsin in this fight, also, by one of those skilful dispositions which only the cool regimental commander knows enough to execute in a battle, checked the enemy from piercing our line.

In this advance on Atlanta, the twelfth and sixteenth regiments were in McPherson's command, "the whip lash corps," which made those memorable flank movements that drove the rebels from their strongholds, and made their fortifications so much waste labor. And down in front of Atlanta, when the rebels dashed upon our left, the Twelfth and Sixteenth Wisconsin held their breastworks on Leggitt's or Bald Hill, which, shortly before they had carried by assault. Gen. Pat. Cleburne, "the rebel Stonewall Jackson of the West," tried to crush in our left, and attacked the flank and rear. The fight was most desperate. Sherman says in his "Memoirs" that our "men were skillful and brave, and fought for a time with their backs toward Atlanta," as the enemy had gone around to their rear and assailed them with fury. Soon after this rear attack, the rebels sallied out from Atlanta and these brave Wisconsin boys on Leggitt's Hill, were compelled to hop over their breastworks and face the fight the other way. They held one side of the breastworks and the rebels came up and held the other, till in the darkness the rebels crawled away. Logan spoke of their behavior thus: "The troops could not have displayed greater courage, nor greater determination not to give ground. Had they shown less, they would have been driven from the position;" and Howard adds, "I never saw better conduct in battle."

When that army, the victors of Atlanta, of whom Grant wrote, "that it had accomplished the most gigantic undertaking of the war," of whom Lincoln said, when he thanked them, that the "Battles, marches, sieges, and other military operations of the campaign, must render it famous in the annals of war," when this army was reorganized for the hi toric

March to the Sea.

Eleven Wisconsin regiments started out on that march, with a cheery look and a swinging pace, that made light of the thousand miles between them and Richmond, and singing "Old John Brown, his soul is marching on." The Fifth and Twelfth batteries, too, went clattering along over the Corduroy roads. And in their march we read how the old Third Wisconsin was provost guard at Milledgeville; how the boys held a session of the Georgia legislature in the State house, repealed the ordinance of secession, and passed other very sensible laws, while its regimental flag floated from the flag-staff of Georgia's capitol.

We read how the twelfth, the sixteenth, seventeenth and thirty-first, tore up mile upon mile of railroad track twisting up the rails like doughnuts, as they marched along, and how among all "Sherman's bummers," none could beat the detail from Wisconsin commands; how the Twenty-sixth Wisconsin got the name of putting down about as much Corduroy road in a day as any regiment cared to march over in two days.

In all the fights of that march, the siege of Savannah, and the march through the Carolinas, in which the infantry took part, it is noticeable that the Wisconsin regiments bore a part, and suffered loss, but not defeat.

Nashville.

In the battles of Franklin and Nashville, Wisconsin's good name was safe in the hands of the Twenty-fourth regiment. Their good conduct at the critical moment did much to save the day at Franklin. They were in Opdyke's brigade. Greeley tells the story of their valor, thus:

'The rebel charge was so impetuous, as well as heavy, that it was scarcely checked by the advance works, * * but swept over them like a torrent, hurling back our men in tumultuous rout. In an instant * * * the hill was lost, eight of our gunst aken, the rebel flag planted on our works. Caissons as well as men, streamed wildly to the bridge, supposing the day utterly lost. "First brigade forward to the works." rang out the steady voice of Opdyke, he riding rapidly forward, as the rabble and rout swept by, and, as the bayonets of his men came down to a charge, flashing the rays of the setting sun, swiftly steadily, grandly that brigade rashed upon the foe; a brief but bloody struggle ensued, and at the close no rebel remained upon or in our works but the dead and 500 prisoners." Our line was then re-established, and was not again broken, though assault, after assault battered against it. Thomas gave the credit of saving the day to Gen. Opdyke and he in turn attributed it largely to the Twenty-fourth Wisconsin.

At Nashville the Eighth, Fourteenth, and Twenty fourth, and Forty-fourth took part in that vigorous attack which finished all that was left of Hood's army.

The Army of the Potomac.

In the last year's work in Virginia, that bloody campaign from the Rappahannock to Richmond, the state of Wisconsin had eight regiments, the second, fifth, sixth, seventh, nineteenth, thirty-sixth, thirty-seventh, and th rty eighth. The blood of her sons drenched the fields of the Wilderness, The "Old Iron Brigade" crushed through two lines of the enemy in the first day's fight. At Spottsylvania they went to the aid of Hancock, and successfully resisted five desperate assaults of Lee. Constantly marching and fighting for four days and nights, it is recorded that these old veterans of a score of battles, sent by turns their fouled muskets to the rear to be washed, and stayed at the front, and slept under fire. Lee could not dislodge them nor Hancock from the position they had gained. Here, too, the fifth regiment showed a strong position and carried a battery after the front line of the charging column had given away. At the North Anna the old brigade by its intrepid behavior, turned the tide of repulse to their division and drove the assaulting brigade from the field. They received the compliments and thanks of their corps commander for their gallant behavior here. Thence they skirmished well nigh all the way to Petersburg. In front of Petersburg they repulsed assaults; and at the celebrated fight at Hatcher's Run, the old Seventh Wisconsin captured double its force of rebels.

In the same campaign, the bloody campaign of 1864, Wisconsin had put three new regiments into the army of the Potomac, the thirty-sixth, thirty-seventh, and thirty-eighth. Without training, with but little drill, green and raw, these regiments were to work in that advance and solid fighting which made the march and battle experience there the really hardest, perhaps, of any borne in a summer campaign during the war. This trying experience they bore remarkably well, and in the fall their soldierly conduct ranked them with the veterans of the war. Their division commander wrote to Gov. Lewis, telling of the valor of the Thirty-sixth Wisconsin, and how, at Hatcher's Run, they cut through a rebel line, crushed it, and captured, with arms, colors, and officers, a force three times greater than their own. Said he, "I now depend on them with my veterans." The same thirty-sixth, the following spring, took part in the final movement, and was present at Lee's surrender.

The Thirty-seventh Wisconsin was hurled into the fight at Petersburg, and put to veterans' work at the outset. In the first fight six companies engaged suffered a loss of 150 in killed and wounded. It was their misfortune to share in that terrible charge into the crater of Burnside's exploded mine, with a loss of 155 of a charging party of 250. The thirty-seventh and thirty-eighth were in charge on Fort Mahone before Petersburg, and did so with a gallantry that commanded the respect of older troops, and ranked them thereafter as veterans equal to any.

Mobile.

As Wisconsin soldiers took part in the first fights, so they were foremost in the last, both east and west. Around Mobile, on the same day that Lee surrendered, the Eleventh and Twenty-third Wisconsin were engaged in the famous assault which carried Fort Blakely. The valor of the assaulting party of the Eleventh was the glory of that army. The Twentieth was at the capture of Spanish Fort, and was the first to enter it on the same day.

The Wisconsin cavalry saw a varied experience of hard service, always seasoned with danger. The First cavalry regiment spent its first year of service in Missouri, scouting among rebel strongholds, dashing into, and dispersing guerrilla bands, and skirmishing. Their marches through bottomless swamps and regions barren of food and forage, their adventures by squads and squadrons, would read like romance. If written. In 1853 they reported for duty in Tennessee, where Wheeler's cavalry the best the rebels had in the west, put our cavalry to its mettle. The First Wisconsin cavalry soon gained reputation as being "by large odds the best in the division, for skirmishing." With a reputation for dash, and a dashing commander, they had varied luck. They fought and skirmished at Chickamauga, campaigned all the next winter, joined Sherman in the Atlanta campaign the next spring; were at Buzzard's Roost and Resaca; in hot fight at Dallas, Ackworth and Big Shanty, Pushing on to the Chattahoochee. they skirmished with the rebels across the stream; their and the rebel artillery slung shells at each other awhile, and then the foes fell to chatting, swapping coffee for tobacco; and finally, to cap the climax, Yankee and Johnnie went in swimming together without the red tape of a formal armistice. As our army closed around Atlanta, the First cavalry had hard work and constant activity in the numerous raids which Sherman sent out to tap railroads and cover his true movements. In McCook's raid, south of Atlanta, it shared and fought hard. Atlanta captured, they set out in pursuit of Hood's army, followed and hung about it, back to Nashville, then plunged back into the heart of the south in Wilson s expedition, that fought its way from city to city. At West Point they dismounted, and captured a fort. Sweeping on to Macon. they learned of Lee's surrender and of the flight of Jeff Davis. It was this regiment who pursued the flying President of the confederacy, and were the cause of his capture, though deprived by another command of the manual capture of Davis, yet thorough investigation accorded to them a full share in the honor and reward of the capture. Few, if any, mounted regiments in the service had wilder or more active service, covering so large an area as these dashing riders of Wisconsin. Maj. Gen. Stanley wrote of them: "The First Wisconsin cavalry, a most gallant regiment, with a colonel, La Grange, as dashing a trooper as ever Murat commanded. By the way, before the war, an impression existed that only southern men could ride well enough for dragoons, but, during my experience with cavalry, it became a fixed fact with us that the farther north the regiment was from, the more sure they were of being effectual and reliable cavalry."

The Second cavalry saw hard enough service in the low lands of the Mississippi, and participated in the siege of Vicksburg. They were in Grierson's raid; and their marches and skirmishes in Arkansas, Louisiana and Texas were constant.

The Third cavalry served its first year in Kansas, scouting, pursuing and fighting pestiferous bands of jayhawkers, bushwhackers and guerillas. Its companies often divided and scattered, and less is known of their movements. The regiment fought at Cane Hill, at Prairie Grove, and Honey Creek. In guarding trains it encountered much of excitement and danger, and fought Indians and Texans in the Cherokee nation. Their service was not sanguinary as some encountered, but they had a fair sprinkling of fighting, and it is the record that they invariably fought well, and no defeat suffered by them has ever been reported. They often fought the fiendish Quantrell. Their reputation in army circles is best expressed by the chief of cavalry department of Arkansas, as being "as high as it is possible for troops to stand." In relation to both the Second and the Third cavalry, at the battle of Prairie Grove, fought on Sunday, Dec. 7, 1862, Gen. Blunt's report of the battle says: "On coming up with Col. Wickersham I ordered him to proceed in the direction of Fayetteville with all of his cavalry, and endeavor to open communication with Gen. Herron. I also sent forward Maj. Calkins with the Third Wisconsin cavalry for the same purpose." * * * * *

After detailing the movements and opening of the battle, he says: "Observing that the enemy had now thrown a large force upon my center and right, * * * the first battery, and the Second Wisconsin cavalry, under Major Calkins, were ordered to proceed on my extreme right, to watch my flank movement of the enemy, * * and to guard the road leading to Rhue's Mills, and prevent communication being cut off with (Solomon's) first brigade."

Again he says: "Learning that a heavy force was massing on my right, with a view of turning my flank, I withdrew Tenny's battery and proceeded with it to an open field on the right, at the same time directing the infantry to withdraw from the woods. * * * Tenny wheeled his guns into position when his destructive fire of grape and canister sent the rebels back under cover of the woods. At the same time a fire from the two mountain howitzers attached to the Third Wisconsin cavalry was directed upon them, on my right, with good effect."

The fourth regiment, after making a brilliant record as infantry, was, in compliment to its efficiency, mounted as cavalry, became as dashing a regiment as any, and made a splendid record as cavalry in Louisiana and Texas. Its capture of prisoners several times exceeded the numbers of its command.

But from very weariness, I must close. The limits of this address will not permit even a mention of the actions and military operations in which Wisconsin troops took part. Such is the task of the historian. My object has been to glean up from various sources, testimonials to illustrate the fact that Wisconsin troops, everywhere, were regarded as among the best, and appreciated by commanders and comrades. The thousands of miles our infantry marched, the skirmishes, campaigns, expeditions, battles, sieges and movements in which they participated, deserve a fuller and completer record than has yet been made. Our infantry traversed every rebel State, save Florida, and saw service in Indian campaigns in Minnesota, Dakota, Indian Territory; and the twentieth regiment even went out and regulated the Mexicans on the Rio Grande.

When special service, calling for cool, judicious men, was wanted, it is noticeable how often Wisconsin regiments were detailed. When the rebel members of the Maryland legislature were plotting to take that State out of the union, and it was deemed, for the public safety, best to gobble them, the Third Wisconsin was sent to do it; and they slid the secession statesmen into the guard-house, and kept them there all day begging for whisky, in a way that the "My Marylanders" despised.

When the New York draft riots of 1863 threatened to, and did for a time, overthrow all law and order in that city, the president ordered some select regiments from the Potomac; and one morning the New Yorkers awoke and found the Third and Fifth Wisconsin bivouacked in the heart of the city, sun burned and war-stained, and ready to make short work of any mob, at the word of command. The orderly character of the men, and their excellent discipline, caused Wisconsin soldiers very frequently to be detailed as provost guards when our armies occupied large towns.

They had, too, their full share of that service which, Gen. Sherman says, "is the hardest in war, to lie in support of some position or battery under fire, without the privilege of returning it; or to guard some train left in the rear, within hearing, but out of danger."

The Fourth Wisconsin Captures a Railway Train.

(GEN. HARRISON C. HOBART).

The Fourth Wisconsin regiment struck their tents at camp Utley, Racine, on the 15th day of July, 1861, and steamed off to the war, to join Patterson's column, by the way of Harrisburg, Pa. The regiment reached Buffalo early on the morning of the 17th, and immediately moved forward by rail towards Harrisburg, arriving at Corning, N. Y., late in the afternoon. From that place to Elmira, it was necessary to pass over the New York & Dunkirk road, but the officers declined to take us that night, for the reason that we had gone round by the way of Buffalo, instead of taking their road at Dunkirk. Our cars, containing about twelve hundred men, were standing up in their track, and the crowd becoming excited, gathered around the depot, discussing the situation. While Col. Paine and others were with the railroad officials in the office of the company, laboring to obtain transportation, I met Major Boardman, of the regiment, and in conversation with him the idea was suggested to seize the first engine of the company that came over the road, and compel it to take us to Elmira. The major, who was the soul of bravery, immediately called Col. Paine out, and we laid the matter before him. He at first hesitated about taking the responsibility, but finally approved of the suggestion, and directed me, then captain of Co. K, to take a sufficient number of men, and seize the first train that came from Dunkirk. I requested Capt. Loy, of Co. H, to join me with a division of his company, and taking a division of Co. K, I placed them each side of the track where the engine would probably stop. In a very short time a passenger train came down the road, and halted between our lines. I immediately stepped aboard the engine, followed by Lieut. Brown, of Co. F, and Lieut. Newell, of Co. K; and our men instantly covered the wood-box. I explained briefly to the engineer, that we had seized the train, and that he could remain in charge of the engine, if he would run it under my direction; but if not, to step off instantly. Observing the strength of our force, he at once complied, and Lieut. Newell, who was a practical engineer, was directed to sit by and watch him. The conductor directly appeared upon the scene and desired to know "what all this meant?" It was explained to him, and taking in the situation, he at once consented to attach his train to ours, and take us over the road to Elmira. In the meantime, under the superintendence of Col. Paine, guards were stationed to prevent the cars from being uncoupled, which was once attempted by the tricky railroad employes, but they were emphatically warned against repeating the experiment. This seizure having become known to the people of the town, they turned out in force to witness the drama—their sympathies were with the soldiers. After taking wood and water, the cars were attached together, and a little after dark the long train moved out from the depot, and steamed off amid the shouts of the people, and cries of "bully for Wisconsin! Bully for Wisconsin!"

Dan the Cook.

(ADDIE L. BALLOU.)

I see by a late issue of your paper notice of the recent Reunion of the old thirty-second, which, had I understood in time, should not have passed by without at least one responsive recognition from the sunset border of the world.

In the report of its proceedings one name appears, often looked for in the soldiers' list, which brings vividly to mind many scenes of the old hospital days, and one in particular at the moment in which he became the central figure of interest in a little skirmish, the finale of which gave me the brief glory of once having—in the colonel's own words—out-generalled the commanding officer.

"Dannie" Morrison, besides being a "good boy" on general principles, was also proficient in the culinary art, a requisite much to be appreciated, in a sanitary sense, to a hospital department in the condition ours found itself after the march from the Holly Springs circuit, in its first installment at the navy yard barracks at Memphis.

We had had successive failures in preparing convalescent diet, until a happy fortune sent us "Dan," who "filled the bill" to satisfaction, and of course it was more after the order of women than of military—to expect his services secured forever.

It is an undisputed fact that the heads of departments, like the best regulated families, are not without their slight differences— not to say rivalries, and the departments were not, at the navy yard encampment, more amicably loving to each other than was strictly necessary—and so, one day, Dan was ordered to report and henceforth superintend the "mess" at headquarters

THE SOLDIERS REUNION OF 1880.

This was a loss not easily repaired, and threw our hospital department into a "mess" quite unprepared for. It was useless to urge upon the physicians the necessity of a remonstrance that had already proven of no avail, and they shook their heads at the suggestion of the "matron" that she would "b ing Dan back."

Doubtless Col. Smedley—the ever dignified—had an intimation of the errand as I approached, for he was on the defensive at once, tho' my demand was modestly and briefly worded, " Col., I want Dan!"

After a sharp and decisive review of reasons why he must deny the request, he urged as finale, that he had already refused the surgeons the same request and it would be unmilitary to surrender now.

"But, colonel, I insist that it is of the utmost importance that you do surrender, for we cannot at present do without Dan."

"But what will the surgeons think if, having denied him, I should conform to your request?"

"They will think in your after thought you are a good man, who, as a worthy commander, is willing to sacrifice personal pique, or his own comfort, to those of the sick and dying, and to the interest and health of the brave men under his care and command."

Dan cooked our next hospital rations San Francisco, Nov. 11, 1879.

["Dan the Cook" is now Hon. D. A. Morrison, Mayor of Rochester, Minnesota, an active business man of that beautiful state].

General John Gibbon.

(COL. J. A. WATROUS.)

It may not be generally known that the General's first brigade was largely composed of Wisconsin soldiers. It was also General Rufus King's first brigade General Lysander Cutler, another honored Milwaukee man, had h s first experience as a brigade commander in charge of the same body of men.

In the spring of 1862, Gibbon, who was then Capt. of battery B, fourth regular artillery, was made a brigadier general, and very soon afterward took command of the Second, Sixth and Seventh Wisconsin, and the Nineteenth Indiana. He was a most thorough disciplinarian, and the manner in which he put the brigade through drill while it was encamped opposite Fredericksburg, will never be forgotten by those who participated. There were early morning drills, before breakfast, forenoon drills, afternoon drills, evening and night drills, besides guard mountings and dress parades. Probably no brigade commander was more cordially hated by his men. He was all soldier, both in looks and deeds, and his adjutant-general, Capt. Frank Haskell, who went out as adjutant of the Sixth Wisconsin, and was killed while colonel of the thirty-six, was like in soldier qualities. When Gibbon's brigade marched there was straggling. His first fight as brigade commander, and the first fight, the brigade, except the Second Wisconsin, was engaged in, was the memorable b ttle of Gainesville, just before the second Bull Run. His brigade of four regiments fought and checked Elwell's fu l divison of picked troops. But the sacrifice was terrible. Eight hundred of his brave men were wanting at roll call next morning, and nearly all of them were dead on the field, or wounded; very few were taken prisoners. The brave little general was at all times in the thickest of the fight, cheering his men by word and example. How completely that litt'e battle removed all dislike for the strict disciplinarian, and how great became the admiration and love for him, only those who have witnessed similar changes can appreciate. The morning after the battle, when the regimental adjutants came in with their rep rts showing the frightful loss in killed and wounded, Gibbon dropped his head and wept most bitterly. H s sorrow was as sincere as that of the f ther who has been bereft of his children. For weeks after Gainesville whenever the losses were referred to, his eyes would fill with tears and he would ask that that subject be dropped. He never lost his love for the old brigade. It was at the battle of Sou'h Mountain, Sept. 14th, 1862, while Gibbon was in command, that the Western regiments earned and received the name of "Iron Brigade." The last t me he commanded the brigade in battle, was at Antietam, where his own brother, who commanded a confederate battery, fought him. When Gibbon left his old brigade to assume command of a division in the Third corps, he went with the love and hearty good wishes of every officer and soldier in the four regiments. In due time he was made a major-general, and when General Sickles was wounded at Gettysburg, Gibbon assumed command of the Third army corps, but was soon afterwards seriously wounded. His record throughout the war was such as any soldier may be proud of. Since the war he has been on the frontier most of the time. Two years ago he fought and severely punished the same band of Indians that Gen. Miles afterwards captured. He was wounded in this fight. At present Gen. Gibbon is stationed at St. Paul, in command of the department of Dakota. His response to the call for the names of honorably discharged soldiers, was in these words: "I was not a Wisconsin soldier, and have not been honorably discharged, but at the judgment day I want to be with Wisconsin soldiers."

Griff. J. Thomas

COL. J. A. WATROUS.

Went into the army when a boy of fifteen, making a good record and permanently injuring his health. He is commander of the Grand Army of the Republic for the Department of Wisconsin, an l one of the most active it has had. He is making a special eff rt to give the order a wider range in his department, and with fair prospects of success. About two years ago there was a vacancy in the Berlin postoffice. As is once in a while the case when a vacancy occurs in a nutritious office, several gentlemen made known their willingness to accept the Berlin postoffice, an l among them was modest Griff Thomas. The other applicants did not consider Thomas an obstacle in their way. One May afternoon while various anxious applicants were waiting in the telegraph offi e for dispatches announcing their appointment, the operator was called. It was still, very still. The words that lightning persuaded little instrument ticked off were full of weight. Eyes and ears were wide open. The operator was provokingly deliberate. Enclosing the precious words in an envelope, he asked, "is Griff Thomas in the office?" He wasn't; he was spading his garden. The messenger was directed to take the dispatch to Mr. Thomas. Be it known that Griff's faith that he would be appointed had never been well developed. Indeed, it may be sai l that he was a doubting Thomas all through the contest. He opened and read the dispatch and then read it again. Then he looked about him and seeing no audience to witness the performance, drew his sleeve across his cheek, and read again, as follows:

WASHINGTON, May 18, 1877.—The president has appointed you postmaster of Berlin.

A neighbor who saw Thomas receive the message and wipe away something from under his eye, wanted to know if he had bad news.

"Oh, no; its good news, to me."

"What did you weep for?"

"Me weep? I was only wiping away a rain drop."

"Why, man, it hasn't rained for a week."

"I know it ; that was a drop that lodged there at the time of the last shower."

In one respect Mr. Thomas is a light-weight, and only one. He weighs 113 pounds. A worthier gentleman could not have been given the appointment.

Our Little Matron.

Addie L Ballou.

Responding to the Reunion call, from away across the continent, Addie L. Ballou, who, during the war, was matron of one of the principal army hospitals at Memphis, and who, since 1865, has ranked among the best and brightest artists and writers on the Pacific Coast, gives modest notice of her whereabouts, and her continued interest in the "army boys," among wh m, the sick and wounded, she spent nearly four years.

Mention of her name brought Wisconsin men to their feet all over the country. Among these Capt. S. L. Brasted, of the 32nd, whose sentiments addressed to the Sunday Telegraph, a d harmonizing with the others, find expression as follows:

I noticed an extract from Miss Addie L, Ballou's letter. Why, the recollections which that paragraph brought back, are invaluable. I can never forget that woman's patience and kindness to all our boys, and to me, while sick and fretful with high fever at Memphis. She was as constant and tender as my mother could have been. My best wishes for her life's success and happiness.

S. L. BRASTED."

Miss Ballou having painted, in oil, a fine full ized picture of the war eagle "Ol'l Abe," and forwarded the same as a present to the Wisconsin Soldiers Reunion Association, writes in response to urgent invitations to contribute sketches of hospital experience for the soldier chapters, as follows:

No. 759 MARKET ST.,
SAN FRANCISCO, CAL., AUG. 6.

Pondering what among the thousand old reminiscences of hospital life in army days might be most worthy to appear as my tribute of respectful remembrance, and, with an incident shaping itself into form, my pen drops at a glance over the columns of the ever welcome Sunday Telegraph, bewildered at so touching a tribute of my own meek efforts to serve a country in her peril—over the signature of Summer L. Brasted.

What a train of recollections are flooding over the sands of the years bringing tears to my eyes, though I don't know why, for I didn't cry then.

"Why, boys, it was a privilege few women can boast, to have learned at your sick beds the heroism of men, and the cost of a nation's honor. Don't any more of you speak of "kindness,"

so feebly rendered on my part, while memory serves me as the recipient of so many.

Who was always remembered in choice bits of attention, all the way from the "confiscated" panel door that served as floor in my tent for my feet to rest on, the feathery pillow for my head, floral offerings without number, delicacies and good words, and every need anticipated? Why, the cup of goat's milk and cracked corn so often reserved for me at company A's headquarters, is still as sweet in memory as then, and then, when the night watch assumed his post in the hospital, and the camp was quiet, came the music of voices down the company streets, was not my tent often the centre of a serenading party, and all that?

That is a reminder of a never-to-be-forgotten incident of those days that comes back like the echo from the key note, long after the thunders of the psalm are hushed. Some of you will remember company A had been left at the old navy yard," on detach service, when the regiment, (the other companies of the Thirty-second,) were ordered to camp at North Memphis. After remaining some weeks away, company A also joined the camp, pitching their tents in line adjoining the long row of hospital tents, and at the other extremity of which were the tents of surgeons, hospital, four stores, mess tent "pations," etc., etc.,

Co. it was favored with the possession of a fine string band, consisting of three pieces, two violins and a guitar, the whether provided for in army transportations, or how obtained, was a somewhat vexed question never inquired into, so long as they were keeping time, at least by one individual.

The day they pitched their tents among us was a characteristic Tennessee spring day, and rounded off into the tenderest of twilights, sinking reluctantly into deeper shadows and night,

At the hour for taps, the tinting of sergeant Brasted's guitar and the attendant violins, were plaintively pleading to the moon and luring me to listen from my parted tent door for a few moments before retiring. Sleep is seldom tardy to the weary, and so usually came all came to me, with the opportunity. No sooner were my lids closed than the transit into dreamland began. My brain was just spanning that drowsy causeway in semi-unconsciousness, when an enchanted dream or a more enchanted reality, broke with subdued intensity upon my bewildered senses, and for a moment, like Paul, "Whether in the body or out, I could not tell," as just beyond my head, with only the partition of tent cloth and a small space of night air, the lowest notes of my favorite "fandango," were blended and vibrating from the strings of the instruments. It was so sudden, so unexpected, and almost noiselessly done, it was difficult to determine whether it was a delicious dream or a very clever reality until I recognized a familiar voice endeavoring to "bush" a still more successful silence.

Hastily robing, with a dispatch that would have done credit to a summons to assist in a piece of surgery (sans, shoes and hose,) a mammoth pitcher of lemonade was quickly hurried into existence, and so stealthily transferred to the serenading group as to take them by surprise, while they were still wandering through the wildnerness of their first tune. And half hour's music and pleasantry followed. And again it was still within the camp save the passing tread of the guards.

Something when all of the "boys" have told their more interesting stories, I may consent to tell of my own most serious encounters with the formidable foe, their unconditional surrender,

capture of arms and ammunition, how I came to be placed under guard on certain occasions, and several other funny things. Meanwhile, comrades of the Badger State, dear old Wisconsin, under promise to be heard from perhaps more acceptably at your next annual reunion, I am, loyally, as ever in remembrance of the soldier.

ADDIE L BALLOU.

On the 8th of June the oil portrait of Old Abe will be presented to the association.

On that occasion something may be said and done, not laid down in Jefferson's manual of parliamentary rules. The present is a most handsome one, reflecting the highest credit, not only to the generosity, but as well to the skill and artistic merits of the donor.

Rally Again, Boys!

Inscribed to the Wisconsin Soldiers' Reunion at Milwaukee, June 7th, 1880.

We'll rally again 'neath the standard we bore
On battle-fields crimson and gory ;
And we'd greet the brave men who in Freedom's fierce war
Have covered that banner with glory !

Then rally again ! Then rally again !
Every soldier, and sailor, and bummer ;
And the songs of the fight we'll sing once again,
As we clasp brave hands in the summer.

We'll rally again from the hill-side and glen,
But not to the conflict's fierce rattle ;
Yet they'll find us as true as we were to them then,
When we stood by their side in battle.

Then rally again, then rally again, &c.

We'll rally again 'neath the "Flag of the Free,"
With its folds waving peacefully o'er us,
While the land that we saved, united and free,
Shall join in the grand swelling chorus.

Then rally again, then rally again, &c

A cheer for the brave who that banner uphore
Who live to rejoice with us ever ;
And a dirge for the brave who will meet us no more
On this side of the dark flowing river.

Then rally again, then rally again, &c.

S. W. P.

The Record of Company " B."

(MRS. SARAH D. HOBART.)

At the open door of the cottage,
With a book upon her knee,
A fair-haired child sat reading
The record of company " B,"

"Father, the names are many,
And the list are long, she said ;
"But tell me ; who are the living
And, who were the wounded and dead?"

Then he took the ancient record
And laid it on his knee,
And he told in the purple twilight
The story of company " B."

THE SOLDIERS REUNION OF 1880.

"They came from the heart of the prairie,
These men so brave and true,
Who left their homes and dear ones
To march in the army-blue.

"One hundred stalwart yeomen,
Plowing in springtime sweet,
Gathering the sheaves in autumn,
Reaping the ripened wheat,

"They marched in storm and sunshine,
They fought in the battle-rain;
Ah, me! 'twas different labor
From gathering golden grain!

"In the wild Virginia mountains
Some rendered up their lives,
With prayers for the stricken country,
With prayers for mothers and wives.

"On the plains of sunny Georgia
Others were laid to rest, –
With Traitor soil around them
And its clods upon their breast,

"Some died on the dreary marches,
Hungry, weary, and worn,
And some in Southern prisons,
From friends and comrades torn.

"And when the crippled remnant
Came back, and peace was given,
Of the hundred who enlisted
The veterans were but seven,

"By many a blue-waved river,
And where old ocean's surge
Wakes through the solemn ages
An anthem and a dirge,–

"Unmoved by bugle's summons
Or drum's deep reveille,
While angels guard above them
Sleep the men of company 'B.'

"Ah, me!" she sighed; "The record
Is sad and filed with pain,
"Praise God! the war is over,
And the land's at rest again!

"But I'm proud that when the country
Was torn from sea to sea,
My father fought to save her
In the ranks of company 'B."
Fountain Prairie, Wis., 1879.

Maj. Phil Plummer's Death.

Gen. John Gibbon, U. S. A., formerly of the Iron Brigade, wrote the Reunion Association:

"Whilst you are hunting up Wisconsin Soldiers, will you please associate the circumstances attending the death of Major Philip Wilkinson Plummer, Sixth Wisconsin. He is supposed to have been killed in the Wilderness, May 4, 1864, and his friends have heard nothing of him since—not even positively that he is killed. I write at the instance of his sister who is here."

The foregoing having been published, received among others the following from Gen. Bragg:

"Poor Phil; he was a brave soldier, and a warm hearted gentleman. He went down with Capt. Rollin B. Converse, Co. B, 6th Wisconsin, which, by the way, taking it for all, was the best company of troops I ever saw, and Rollin was well worthy of his command, and Lieut. James Converse, Co. G., which was Phil's old command.

It all came about May 4th, something like this:

When the enemy was discovered by our wagon train, which happened to be moving up through the woods from the Lacey house in advance, als Red River campaign, the Sixth Wisconsin was given a roving commission to turn into the thicket on the right, and move on in support of a line of troops, said to be down in there somewhere.

The 6th was pretty reliable about obeying orders when there was a smell of gunpowder around, and away it went having no objective point, except the sound of irregular musketry in front, indicating where the hunt would be found. Presently wounded men met us; the woods became partially on fire in front; we staggered along half suffocated and stumbling now and then over dead bodies; some with some with grey, some with blue uniforms; but we fired never a shot, and held our cartridges for the hot work we were seeking, when, suddenly, as we passed out from a ball of smoke and fire in the timber, Little Halloway, of Co. K, who was a good marker, and who met his death by a railroad accident at the close of the war, after he had coolly faced death for four years without a scratch, called out, "See there, Colonel," when away at our right, passing up a hollow or part of ravine, at a double quick, was a line of Johnnies, moving by the flank and passing to our rear. The right wing of the regiment was refused at once to meet the movement, and at that instant a heavy volley of musketry was poured into the left wing by a rebel line that was making a corresponding movement, with the flank line on the right, but could not resist the temptation to fire as they passed.

The three officers named, fell here; the two Converses, I think, suffered amputation of a leg, each, and died at a rebel hospital improvised there in the woods and called "Locust Grove" or "Locust Hill" hospital. Plummer fell dead on the field and was spared the torture of the knife and saw.

I think this statement almost if not quite official. I did not see him fall; but I saw him just before and gave him orders. The volley came; I saw the command immediately after, but he was missing, and in the repertoire of my memory I have the statement of a wounded man, whose name escaped me, who fell at the same time and was taken up to the Locust Hill hospital,—if that was its name—which corroborates my story.

How the sixth got out of that scrape would make quite a little story.

Fond du Lac, July 14, 1879. E. S. BRAGG.

An officer of Co. C followed with this letter.

MILWAUKEE, July 31st.

EDITORS SUNDAY TELEGRAPH:—I have just read Gen. Bragg's letter describing the death of my old comrade, Major Phil. Plummer, and notice that he compliments company B, of the 6th, in a manner that is bound to awaken the least bit of envy from his own company, E, and the rest of the regiment. Not that I wish to detract, or can prove that his praise was not worthily bestowed, for I am not willing to be second to any one in my admiration of the brave, gallant company B, with their ever-to-be-remembered Captain Converse, but let me ask our little fighting General, how about company C? and remind him that Major Plummer, Lieut. Orrin D Chapman (killed at Gettysburg,) Adjutant Cuyler Babcock, (killed before Petersburg,) Major Ed. Whaley, (post master at Prairie du Chien, minus a leg,) Hawley Sprague, Lieut. Bull, Davidson, Hickok, Jack Bowman, (Devil Jack,) and many others who helped to make the record of the old sixth, were members of the Prairie du Chien company C. When in the service, Gen'l Bragg had no favorite, and it was this, added to his remarkable skill and fighting qualities that won for him the highest reputation as a colonel over the many who commanded regiments in the "Army of the Potomac." At the time the 6th re-enlisted for three years, hundreds of eastern soldiers refused to re-enlist in their own organizations, but were willing and did apply for permission to join the sixth under Bragg. You will excuse the length of this. There are but a few of us left, and I believe you will sustain me in the assertion that it is very rare to hear from any of the once famous sixth. GRAYSON.

And the chapter closed in this characteristic paragraph.

COLONEL: There is an old story about a Dutch justice (by the way all good jokes are laid to the Germans or Irish,) who exclaimed, when the defendant's lawyer closed his case, "Veil, you have got the case." The plaintiff's lawyer made his plea, and the old man scratched his head and said, "Mein Gott in himmel! you have got the case, too."

Just so with the boys of the old brigade! They all have won and are entitled to the case, when I sit as arbiter between them. So much for commendation what I said about Company B.

Colonel Tom Allen, who never shrank from danger of duty, but whose laurels are some of them worn by others, seems to be getting dyspeptic, and worries his honest soul about some comrade's talking to me about Bull Run when I was not there. Oh Lord Tom! Did you ever see anybody that was there, except you of course, who knew much about it, only that it was a wondrous skedaddle?

Please, Colonel Tom don't make me responsible for what anybody writes to the newspapers unless you see it signed.

July 28, 1879. E. S. BRAGG.

Where is Shooks?

(H. B. EASTMAN, 3D CAV.)

"Shooks!" cried the Orderly Sergeant at the roll call of Co. I, Third Wisconsin cavalry. "Yer!" was the prompt answer from a tall Arkansan who stood in the ranks.

All the boys of Co. I, would like to know what has become of William Shooks? He enlisted in Co. I in the fall of 1863, when that company was on provost duty at Fort Smith, Arkansas. We had never seen or heard of Shooks or his father until the latter produced the former at our camp one day, and declared that the boy wanted to enlist.

The old man said they lived "up on Mulberry"—a creek some twelve miles from Fort Smith—and that there "war a right smart of bushwhackers 'round thar" and he "reckoned Bill better be 'mong the Fed's, sorter like."

The boy didn't say much, and the old man didn't seem to be actuated by any particularly patriotic feeling in the promises. He wanted the boy well taken care of, and evidently thought him safer, and surer of rations among us than in a bush-

STANLEY & COMPANY,

WHOLESALE AND RETAIL

JEWELERS

108 Wisconsin St., Milwaukee, Wis.

OFFER AN ELEGANT LINE OF GOODS ESPECIALLY SELECTED FOR

BRIDAL GIFTS
Sterling Silver in Great Variety.
MARBLE CLOCKS
DIAMONDS,
UNSET and SET.

ELEGANT BRACELETS,
MOSAIC SETS,
GOLD CAMEO SETS.
THE LATEST STYLES
OF
SILVER PLATED
WARE.

THE ONLY FULL LINE
OF
Gorham Sterling Silver Ware
IN THE CITY.

whacking gang. So William Shooks was duly enlisted and invested with the army blue.

He was a curiosity to us; but a clique of the youngest and toughest boys, who styled themselves, "Tent Six," took kindly to him, and would not allow any fun to be made of him. He was eighteen years old, tall for his age, with straight, brown hair, and honest, light blue eyes. He was rather taciturn, had a quaint way of expressing himself and was very observing.

Some of us, at first, considered his demeanor a little suspicious, and it was hinted that Shooks would desert at the first opportunity and carry news to the rebs. But experience soon demonstrated that, whether or not Shooks had studied and understood the momentous questions at issue between the contending armies, he had cast his lot with us in good faith, and would be true to his oath.

He was a good shot, an elegant horseman and a fearless soldier. We all liked and respected him. The last we saw of Shooks was at Madison, when we were mustered out, in the fall of 1865. The boys were bidding each other good bye and preparing to start for their respective homes. All had a kind farewell for Shooks. Many of the boys wanted him to go home with them, knowing that his Arkansas home might be made unpleasant, if not unhealthy for him by his ex-rebel neighbors. But he refused all invitations, and in answer to the question, where he intended to go, said: "Gwine ter hell, I reckon." We want to know whether he went. In response to this, it would do us good to hear him once more answer "Yer!"

What we started to write, when we drifted into the martial history of Shooks, was an account of a little episode in which he took a prominent part, at Dardanelle, Arkansas. A small detachment of our regiment were sent as guard on a steamboat carrying supplies from Little Rock to Dardanelle, on Arkansas river, in the fall of 1864.

While at Dardanelle, the place was attacked by Col. Brooks, whose command consisted of mounted men and a battery. The garrison being weak, our boys were ordered to the front to help resist the attack, and were distributed in a thin line, in a zigzag trench with logs in front for breastworks. The rebs were much more numerous and kept up a pretty sharp fire, both from rifles and artillery. Our troops repelled several assaults, and finally held the field, the Johnnies retreating. During the action, Shooks banged away on his own hook, whenever he had a good shot, but said never a word. After awhile the boys noticed that Shooks was uncommonly interested in the vicinity of the rebel battery, some 500 yards distant. There were several prominent figures riding around near that battery, and among them a man on a white horse. Shooks, regardless of bullets and shells, peered well over his log and watched the white horse and its rider. Finally, the eager, determined look went out of his eyes, and an expression of disgust swept over his face, as he exclaimed: "Dog oned ef thet ain't dad!" Then, standing up so as to be fully exposed, and throwing up his hands with an impatient gesture, while he turned excitedly to the boys on each side of him, he yelled, loud enough to be heard above the din: "Say! don't nary one uv you uns shoot thet white hoss? Thet's my hoss! Wonder what'n hell dad brought thet hoss down yer fur—might a know'd he'd git shot. Don't none of you uns hit thet white hoss, now! what a dog-goned fool dad is, anyhow, to bring thet hoss down yet!"

You may be sure that none of the boys fired at "thet white hoss."

An Army Yarn.

(GEN. J. A. KELLOGG).

Almost everybody knows Col. Jerry (or more familiarly Jack) Watrous. I remember him as Lieut. Watrous. When I was cap——no. when I paid an involuntary visit to the rebs, on the 5th of May, 1864, he was ordnance sergeant of the division. When I returned in November, he was first lieutenant and adjutant of the regiment. and let me say right here, once for all, a more faithful officer never drew a sabre in his country's defense than Jerry Watrous. On the 25th of March he was acting as adjutant general of the Iron brigade temporarily commanded by himself, which became actively engaged in the battle known as Gravelly Run. Our forces, under command of Gen. Warren, became engaged with the enemy early in the morning. Our brigade happened to occupy a position of great importance, as subsequent events showed. Our line of battle consisted of the two divisions of Ayers and Griffin. with Crawford's division as a support. Just after the engagement opened. the first line was flanked by the enemy and compelled to retire. Our brigade, immediately upon the fact being realized, was in situation to deploy to meet the flanking line. which was promptly done. our orders being to then open fire, and to hold them as long as possible. For some little time it was impossible to comply with this order on account of the presence of scattered bodies of our own troops in our front, who were falling back in such disorder as always attends an attack on the flank.

As soon as possible. however. we opened fire, and checked the advance of the exultant foe; but soon our little brigade was also flanked, their line of battle overlapping ours at either end, and the Ninety-first New York, which was on our right. by some mischance became cut off. The rebels were in our rear and across both flanks, and the time had come when we must fall back. A portion of the ninety-first was got into position under the command of the gallant Col. Tarbell. and the rebs were all around us. Lieut. Watrous sat on his horse near me, viewing the scene. I said to him, "Mr. Watrous. we must get out of this. Do you think you can reach Tarbell?" Jerry surveyed the field, and saw that to do so he would be exposed to a fire from every quarter, especially as there was an open field which he would have to cross. All the danger of the situation was apparent. I shall never forget the reply, which was. "I can do it if any live man can." "Go, then." I replied, "and order Col. Tarbell to retire his regiment across the creek." Jerry started. I watched him with such anxiety as only those in like circumstances can appreciate—rebs in front of him. rebs in rear of him, and yet he rode on. A party threw themselves across his front: he wheeled to the right and dashed on. Again they crossed his front, and he wheeled to the left. How many times he was shot at, God only knows. I could see the gallant Tarbell and the remnants of his regiment holding their position. I knew he would stay until ordered to return, and I knew Jerry would carry that order if he could. But my God. what chances there were against him! Something attracted my attention for a moment. and when I again looked for Jerry. I saw him throw up his arms: his horse fell at the same time: the rebs were all around him by the score. Alas. I thought. poor Jerry is gone. But no. Tarbell had seen the movement, and heard Jerry's shout. His regiment about faced, and with the balance of the line. the glorious old sixth and seventh. we cut our way through. But here the campaign ended for Jerry. After the battle was over we searched the field for Jerry's body, all believing him dead, and it was several weeks before the gratifying news reached us of his safety. although a

THE SOLDIERS REUNION OF 1880.

prisoner, and, I think, wounded, yet alive. His deserved promotion followed news of his safety, and he was present for many a gallant fight on other fields, requiring moral courage; for peace has her victories as well as war, aye, and her battle fields, too.

How "Misery" Came, and Left us.
LIEUT. H. B. EASTMAN, 3RD CAV.

It was in the fall of 1862, and in the camp of company I, Third regiment Wisconsin cavalry, at Fort Scott, Kansas. People had begun to believe the war was in earnest, and must be fought out. So recruits were in order.

From an interior town in Wisconsin came to our company a squad of recruits among whom was one nick-named "Misery." His name was given him, by one of his fellow recruits, on the route to the regiments, and its appropriateness was recognized by the boys the moment "Misery" set foot in the camp, and thenceforward he was addressed by no other cognomen.

He was about eighteen years old, tall and ungainly. He had a shambling gait and the "image and superscription" of "slouch" was indelibly stamped upon him.

His eyes were sleepy looking, but he managed to use them effectively in finding the best of everything to eat. His mouth was drawn down at one corner as if in perpetual grievance, and turned up at the other in a continual leer. His hair was faded mule color and studiously worn ala "bang" in a manner to excite the envy of stylish girls of the present day. And he was the dirtiest critter who ever struck that camp. After a lapse of seventeen years, and a considerable experience with grimy men, I can, without any hesitation or secret evasion, assert that no hand so dirty as "Misery's" was ever raised, before or since, to protect the old flag. And his face was as dirty as his hands. No hints, expostulations of entreaties, though couched in the gentle language of a United States trooper, could induce "Misery" to wash his hands and face, until it was unanimously resolved he should not eat until he washed. He loved his rations more than he hated water, and so the boys forced him to the wash basin occasionally. He drawled his words, and closed each sentence with a whine. On the way to the regiment he seemed to be thirsting for rebel blood, and was loud in his declamations of a desire to kill. His only fear was, that the war would be over before his squad reached the field and he could take a scalp. It was noticed, however, the nearer he approached the regiment the less blood-thirsty he became. And when ushered into the presence of carbines, revolvers and sabres, with surroundings which indicated use for such weapons, he became as gentle a warrior as ever crawled under a wagon. So soon as it was announced in camp that a recruit had arrived who wanted to chew up the entire southern confederacy, the boys decided to have some fun.

There was no enemy, except irregular bands of "bushwhackers," within a few miles of the Fort, and scouting parties of Co. "I" were often exchanging compliments with these gentry. But the camp at Fort Scott was as safe a place, so far as casualties of war might be concerned, as even "a three month man" could wish for. "Misery" did not comprehend the exact state of affairs, but concluded that he was "at the front," "with all the name implies." The boys were not slow to impress upon him the gravity of the situation. In his presence the conversation invariably turned upon the nearness, the audacity and bloodthirstiness of the rebels. Terrible stories were told of the number of men nightly killed on guard. These night conflicts were particularly expatiated upon. In the day time, the boys said they could get along well enough, for they could look right in the mouth of the rebel cannon and see what they'd got to dodge; but this wholesale slaughter in the gloom, this losing ten or a dozen men every night—all shot full of bullets from an unseen foe—was calculated to make a man sick of service. It was painful one morning to see "Misery" put down his cup of coffee, when the boys came to breakfast and announced, "six more men killed last night," "heard about the Johnnies cutting off that recruit's head just before daylight?" "poor Bill got his wooden overcoat mighty sudden," "Well, none of us will ever see Wisconsin again," "wasn't it terrible the way Corporal Smith got his eyes slashed out with buckshot last evening?" "Gosh, boys, the whole picket line was just paved with the brains and in'ards of volunteers last night."—It was fair.y pitiful to see poor "Misery's" jaw drop when little corporal Bemis took Johnny Spencer one side, but within "Misery's" hearing, and with faltering voice said : "Johnny, m me and "Misery's" got to go on guard to-night, and—and—you know its not likely either of us will ever see the morning light. And I want you to—to—see that I have the old flag wrapped around me in good shape and my—my—my—spurs buried with m.. And when t e boys bring in "Misery's" body in the morning, please see that it is washed once real good, and bury us side by side, poor dirty cuss, for he was never killed before and he'll be lonesome."

When a sergeant came around soon after and detailed "Misery" for guard duty that night, the cold sweat started on him. But the boy had friends in his hour of need—veterans whose experience might yet be the means of saving his life. These kindly volunteered advice as to the necessary preparations for his perilous duty. Under their direction and with their assistance, he tremblingly reported for duty about 9 o'clock in the evening, arrayed as follows: A steel vest, weighing about seven pounds, buckled around his chest and another of equal weight strapped so as to protect his rear; the largest and heaviest sabre in camp fastened to his right side ; three cartridge boxes, all full; two revolvers which wouldn't revolve; a carbine, loaded with blank cartridges, and a pair of sharp spurs. "Misery" was informed that the rebels had made a considerable advance and were now in the immediate vicinity of the camp, so that the pickets would be stationed but a few rods out, and he might be sure of speedy support when attacked. As he was not used to managing a horse, it was considered best to have him stand picket dismounted. The camp was situated on the bank of the Marmaton river, a stream about four rods in width ard from one to three feet in depth. "Misery" was conducted to one end of the camp near the corn pile, instructed to blaze away at any one approaching and under no circumstances to desert his post, as the safety of the whole army depended on him.

After he had been alone a few minutes, four or five men could have been seen approaching through the gloom. Taking advantage of trees and bushes, they reached "Misery's" vicinity without his discovering them. When within twenty feet of him, they suddenly presented themselves and demanded his surrender. With a howl of terror he threw down his carbine and sped through the camp. He made straight for his tent, a big Sibley affair, holding twenty men, and every man in it was delightedly listening to the clatter of that running armory. His speed was accelerated by shots in his rear, and he burst into the tent and rolled into the middle of it, a rattling piece of disor-

THE SOLDIERS REUNION OF 1890.   267

ganized ordinance stores. "My stars!" he said, "boys, they drove me in!" The whole camp was now aroused, and everybody turned out to support the picket line. "Misery" was dragged out, soundly b rated for retreating before he had been wounded six or seven times, and pushed by his brave comrades back to his post, where they all declared they would die with him. Of course the attack was renewed, and with great vigor. Shots flashed through the darkness. Men tumbled around on the ground, wounded and in terrible agony. With three men to hold "Misery" and one to hold his carbine, they managed to make him discharge it at a mule. Then some one yelled, "we must retreat across the river!" all started, pell-mell for the stream. Down the bank they scooted with "Misery" well in advance, and he had waded nearly across the river wh n th terrified voice of "old Mac," the bugler was heard exclaiming: "Great Heavens! Just see those rebels on the other side!" Then another rush was made back up the bank and "Misery" was left in the middle of the stream He floundered back as best he could, falling down once in the deepest part and nearly drowning from the weight of his armor. As he was frantically clawing his way up the slippery bank, he was captured by a squad of rebels, who proposed to slay him at once, claiming that he was the fiend who had lately killed so many of their comrades. With streaming eyes, the poor wretch howled, "O, no, good Mr. Secesh. I never hurt none of your men. I'm a new recruit and never shot nobody." It was then decided to release him; the rebels retreated and "Misery" staggered, sadly demoralized, into his quarters, and announced to the boys that "these ere steel vests is awful heavy wh n they git wet."

The next day it was deemed necessary for the good of the service that "Misery" be court-martial'ed for deserting his post. The court-martial was composed of the cooks of the several messes, and after mature deliberation it was adjudged that "Misery" be excused from being shot, but that he be branded. That operation was successfully performed. "Misery" was blindfolded and led to the company's forge. While he was regaled with the furious pumping of the bellows and such exclamations as "ain't that a nice white heat?" "Golly, won't that make him jump?" A providential piece of ice, which had thinly formed the previous night, was being held on a belt plate.

When the proper temperature had been obtained the plate was smartly applied "as by the statute in such case. made and provided." "Misery" jumped and limped to his quarters.

The next d ty he applied to George Dunnett, who was a private, but who wore the best clothes of any man in the company, and whom "Misery" mistook for a Major General, for a pass. George wrote, "Guards and Pickets, pass this d——d fool right along."

And "Misery" took that pass. "passed right along," out of camp, out of sight, and we never saw nor heard of him again. But he can never pass out of our memory.

Ed. McCook's Luck.
(MAJ. LU DRURY.)

Having overcome that "funny feeling of modesty" to the extent of giving you an account of a scout that I once took in the Sequatchie Valley in Tennessee, it occurred to me to try what effect the narration of the adventure would have on a soldier who had seen service in the Valley before boring the balance of the boys with it,—so when an old friend, formerly of the First Wisconsin Cavalry, dropped in on me a few days ago. I placed him in a chair. filled a pipe for him, and was gently leading up to the point, when I mentioned "Sequatchie Valley," he broke in on me with "La, did I ever tell you about our charge in the Sequatchie?" It was no use for me to state that I had heard it a dozen times, besides seeing it illustrated in Harper's Weekly; the veteran trooper, slang himself into his old moth-eaten saddle, drew his rusty sabre, and went thundering up the valley, over riding my little yarn, and slashing the flying rebs as remorselessly as he did in October, 1863, and this is the way he did it:

"You see the boys struck a 'stalled' sutler's wagon early in the morning, and the colonel commanding the division, McCook—used to call him Horse-Ed, to distinguish him from his cousin Ed, who had an infantry command—halted right there, and with him stopped the newspaper correspondents, including the artist for Harper's: but the First Wisconsin, under Col. Hugh Lagrange, kept on up the valley, as we had sure news of the near proximity of the rebel cavalry under Gen. Martin. We struck the rear of their column about three miles from the sutler's wagon, and they faced about and formed to resist our advance. Just then an orderly rode up and handed Col. Lagrange a written order from Col. Mc-

Cook to halt the column. I think the colonel must have been a little confused when he read it. as he mildly remarked—that is. he remarked so you could have heard him a mile—'Now charge the———— , and give 'em h—l!' or words to that effect.

"You just ought to have been there, Lu. to see old Torry go. a rippin' and a rarin', a sweatin' and a swearin' up that valley and over such of the rebs as he could overhaul. He didn't use his sabre at all. He went into 'em like an ignuna vitæ ball among a lot of ten-pins, and with about the same result. In the field to the right of the pike charged a company under Capt. Levi Howland, who was under about the same pressure of perspiration and profanity as was Major Torry, but cutting and slashing with his sabre every reb that he came to. There was one chap, adjutant on Gen. Martin's staff, a dandy sort of a duck—lots of braid on his coat, mustache waxed 'a la Francois'—that Levi gave the cut St. George to, as he rode past him. It was a cruel blow and struck the reb across the face between the mustache and nose. The mustache dropped down like the band of a fatigue captain. Some of the boys consoled the poor fellow by telling him him his mustache wasn't hurt a bit.

One of the guiden bearers rode at the head of the column and couldn't handle his sabre and the gu den at the same time. so when he overtook a reb he would jab him in the back with the lance head in the top of his guiden staff. There were more rebs captured than there were men in the charging column, and that charge made Ed Mc-Cook a Brigadier General and subsequently governor of a territory.

The Future of the Association.
(LIEUT. D. C. PAVEY.)

Comrades. one and all. do you realize the magnitude of the unwritten history of the war, in its grand and imposing proportions. and that the day is already dawning when the survivors of Wisconsin's heroic citizen soldiers. may be counted by the score instead of by the thousand? This dual assertion and inquiry, if it may be so termed, constitute the preface of one of the most soul inspiring articles ever written by mortal, beside which the heroic strains of a Virgil or of a Cicero would rung with diminished tone. The future biographers of Wisconsin's gallant soldier boys. who sustained aloft, proudly, the starry emblem of the Republic from 1861 till the close of the civil war, will enter upon a field ripe for the sickle, and it behooves you comrades, one and all, to aid, so far as lies in your power, the compilation of the history which you largely helped to make. Each of you can, if you will, rescue from the remorseless waves of the great sea of oblivion, details with which you were respectively connected, which woven into book form by the skilled hands of the historian, would constitute one of the most entertaining and instructive works ever published in this country.

To thus set the ball in motion for the accurate transmission to posterity of the record of your patriotism, your patient self-denial and your terrible sacrifices beneath a southern sky, is the mainspring, it may be said of the Wisconsin Reunion Association. And in what manner can this object best be achieved; upon what general line ought the fight to be maintained? That of personal effort is the answer, and to-day that is both practical and practicable. Nearly every citizen of Wisconsin who shouldered a musket and went "to the front" during the dark days of the civil strife and who returned home in safety when the shriek of shell and the plunge of solid shot, the rattle of musketry and the roar of artillery, the shrill notes of the bugle and muffled drum had been silenced, let us hope, forever, has a history which can be summarized and which would be read with unbounded interest by his children, and children's children, through the ages yet in the shadowy future. It may seem a matter of but little consequence to you now but the time will surely come to each one of you, who responds cheerfully to this simple request, when the proudest exclamation from your lips will be: "I was a Union soldier." The state looks after the officers and the private soldiers also, who were killed in action or who died of disease or wounds during the war, the names appearing in the Adjutant General's report. Should any friend however, of a deceased officer or soldier desire to build more comprehensively upon the mere substructure afforded by the state, the Association would gladly receive the same, and give it a place in its archives. Independent of these, however, there are twenty or thirty thousand survivors of the "rank and file," whose valor was displayed on many a well fought field, and whose existence in an Andersonville or a Libby was a continual torture. In simple Anglo-Saxon, therefore, what is wanted is this: Let every soldier prepare, (or ask some friend to prepare for him), a condensed sketch of this army life. To the general public these will not be of equal interest, but if the sketch of Tom Brown's campaigning should be a trifle monotonous to the general reader—absolutely devoid, it may be, of thrilling incident, hence not at all comparable with that of John Smith, to Tom Brown's descendant's it will be evidence, if nothing more, of the fact that their ancestor "fought, bled, died and almost suffered," as the boys used to say, in the great cause of human freedom.

It is hoped and believed that the state, will ultimately take this matter in hand, or at all events lend valuable assistance to the Association in this collecting for permanent use the biographical sketches of surviving Wisconsin soldiers, but for the present, we must "go it alone," invoking the hearty and effective co-operation of the boys themselves, who in this connection will recall the favorite army maxim: "If a fellow don't look out for himself nobody else will."

Comrades, may we rely upon you to do your share of this work. It is a work in which we are mutually interested, and to postpone "till a more convenient season" is hazardous in the extreme. To be of value the work must be as complete as possible and "the files must be closed." No straggling, no shirking, should be the motto, but we shall expect a grand final rally under the fl g we love so well. Comrades ! To the front and center, every mother's son of you !

A Brave Captain Off His Feet.

Early and late the publisher of this the first book of the kind ever gotten up, has labored diligently to rescue from oblivion individual instances of heroism and daring which else had perished with the hero. With pleasure therefore, the following is given to our soldier friends to show that sometimes even a captain tried and true, may be taken "off his feet."

In June 1861 J. H. Marston, a sterling young Appletonian, united his fortunes with those of the gallant sixth Wisconsin as second lieutenant of E company, his commission dating from M ay 10th Gen. E. S. Bragg, of Fond du Lac, was captain. Subsequently Lieut. Marston was commissioned first lieutenant, with rank from Sept. 18, 1861, and afterward was honored with a captain's commission, to date from Sept. 18, 1862. He was with his regiment during Gen. Pope's retreat from the Rapidan to Upton's Hill in August, 1862, and took part in the following named engagements:

South Mountain, Sept. 14, 1862; Antietam, Sept. 17, 1862; Fitzhugh's Crossing, April 29, 1863; Chancellorsville, May 3 and 4, 1863; Gettysburg, July 1, 2 and 3, 1863. Was wounded at South Mountain by a shot in his left ear and at Antietam by a shot in left leg. In this battle a cannon shot (referred to in Love's "Wisconsin in the War" as killing and wounding thirteen men of the sixth Wisconsin, on the morning of the 17th) entered the ground under Capt. Marston's feet the result being that he "went up" with the explosion but landed all right. At Gettysburg his ankle was badly sprained in consequence of being tossed into the air for the second time by a cannon ball which plowed up the ground directly under his feet. July 1, 1863, he was taken prisoner but escaped the same day from his captors, finding a secure hiding place between the lines of battle until July 4, when he came into our lines, was honorably discharged March 25, 1864, on surgeon's certificate of disability, and to-day is of the flourishing manufacturing firm, at Appleton, of Marston & Deveridge, his involuntary ascensions in Virginia perhaps preparing him for aerial navigation hereafter. Captain Marston's military record is not only a most excellent one in every way but possesses a flavor of novelty which will be appreciated by every one of our soldier readers.

Old Pomposity.

Comrade Darwin C. Pavey of L Company 15th, N. Y. Vols. (Engineer Corps) tells a good story about a fellow soldier in the same company which for downright "rediculosity" as Charles Sumner would say, can't be beaten, This Soldier, whom we shall call Frank, was a fellow student with comrade Pavey in a well known eastern academy and was forever distinguishing (?) himself by the use of words of three and four syllables and as is usually the case with young men of his caliber, invariably get "the cart before the horse," as the phrase is, in his vain endeavor to convince the boys that his head was more level than heads would average. Frank enlisted some three months before comrade Pavey did, and when the latter joined his regiment at City Point, Va., the first person whom he encountered in the "Company Street" was his old school fellow Frank. Of course as he says he was right glad to see Frank, and considerately inquired after his health "since he'd been in the army." Upon this Frank straightened up proudly and in his most extinguishing tones replied: "I'm fond of the service excessively but I've been seriously ill for a great length of period."

Before the final muster out of the 15th occured at Fort Barrey, Va., June 13th 1865, the story of the man who had been "seriously ill for a great length of period" went the grand rounds of the brigade with the most agonizing Ohs and Ahs imaginable.

Our Future.

I

Equally in duty to Wisconsin's dead, and generations yet to come, the living soldiers of the late war have a work before them of a magnitude demanding prompt and untiring action.

This duty requires that the name and record of every man who went from Wisconsin to the war be truthfully made up and preserved, regardless of the rank he held, length of service or duties performed, or whether he died in the war, or since, or is still living. Without fear or favor, without romance, selfishness, or prompted by other sentiment than to make a straight, unpartisan, faithful record, the enterprise should be taken up and perfected. It is a large undertaking. It cannot be accomplished by any one man, or in any one year. The Wisconsin Reunion Association can do it if they try. No one else can do it as well, if indeed any other can attempt it with reasonable hope of success. Even though legislative appropriations be secured, it alone is not sufficient. This association must lend its efforts to the task or it will not succeed. United, harmonious and active, we may accomplish everything.

Think of this, comrades.

II

On the 30th of May a year ago, your executive committee issued to Wisconsin soldiers and their friends a circular on this subject, asking their co operation in making a record which should when complete, contain among other things,

1st—All the reports received from surviving soldiers and sailors, giving name, regiment, company, boat, present occupation, and re idence, together with historical facts, reminiscences, anecdotes and incidents personal and general, and which will make the most complete record of Wisconsin men in the war yet published.

2nd—Answers to all inquiries made in regard to Wisconsin veterans and their friends.

3rd—A complete list of all Wisconsin soldiers who were killed in Lattle, or who died of wounds or disease in the service, with residence at time of enrollment, and present place of burial. As Decoration Day becomes more and more observed this list will become invaluable.

4th—A description of all the engagements and battles and the part taken therein by Wisconsin men.

5th—A correct narration and statement of all Wisconsin men taken prisoners during the war, with full particulars of capture, rescue, imprisonment, escape or exchange.

6th—The Roster of the living, alphabetically arranged by regiment and company, P. O. address. &c.

The let'ers closed as follows:

To do this successfully the association asks and depends upon the co-operation of every soldier and sailor.

The association does not want your money, but does want your record, your history, your personal experiences, knowledge and information on the subject above mentioned.

Please give these in your own way (don't be afraid you can't write—we risk all that) at as early date as you can. Even a little at a time, a little more some other time, and so on until we get it all. Your comrades are interested in your doing this. Posterity is interested. It is proper that those who made history should take a hand in writing it.

Stir up the comrades who have not already done so, to send in their names, or send them yourself to the Association.

A little united action, when each does his part, yields most wonderful results. Try it.

The proposition was a new thing, its object uncertain, and your committee found their first task was to stir up an interest in the work, and establish a confidence that it was not a selfish scheme, for enhancing personal or political interests.

In no spirit of self-aggrandizement. but in compliment to the intelligence of the soldiers themselves, and the gratitude and patriotism of their friends all over the world who were not soldiers, it may here be recorded that so fast as the scope and objects of the association became known—with one single exception—none but kind words and acts of encouragement greeted the movement.

III.

The first object—to stir up the latent interest, and receive the names of the living, may be said to have reached a good beginning. The richest fields are beyond. Many comrades have sent in their valuable army experiences. Many more have not. When all shall have so done, when the record of every Wisconsin man shall have been made and published, and a harmonious unity of action organized, the association will have entered upon the widest fields of its usefulness.

IV.

The interest stirred up, the organization effected, the life imparted into this new movement is only partially reflected in these pages Subsequent volumes will show more of it. The association now has on hand a valuable accumulation of material, more than sufficient for another volume the size of this, and the "trouble" has only commenced. If each one will only do his share, most wonderful results will follow. Don't let up. Keep up the motion. No, one is sorry, for having done what they have, nor will they be, after doing ten times as much.

As a sample of company lists on hand to be published in a subsequent volume, we refer to the "Oshkosh Volunteers" by Col. John Hancock.

They are models. In the next Roster we hope to follow this system, except perhaps give more details of each comrade's service.

OSHKOSH VOLUNTEERS.

BY COL. JOHN HANCOCK.

April 12th, 1861, was made memorable in our annals as being the day Gen Beauregard trained his guns on Fort Sumpter; the sad and sickening news flashed through the North, palling cheeks and appalling the stoutest hearts, for then all hopes of averting the pending conflict were blasted. The Northern people did not believe that the feeling through the South was intense and bitter enough to sustain that people in resorting to such extreme measures. Previous to that the sentiment of the North had been to avert the storm by compromise, but at the receipt of that news, all thoughts of compromise vanished. Three days afterward Lincoln issued his call for 75,000 volunteers, and two days after the call was issued a public meeting was held at Oshkosh. At that meeting speeches were made, and then adjourned to meet at the same place the following Saturday evening. At the adjourned meeting the company then known as the Oshkosh volunteers was enlisted, which was afterwards known as company E. Second Wisconsin Regiment Volunteer Infantry. The next morning (Sunday), the company met and elected the following officers: Gabe Bouck, Captain, Jno. Hancock, First Lieutenant, H. B. Jackson, Second Lieutenant. The next morning the company met and elected non-commissioned officers, telegraphed Governor Randall for orders, and commenced drilling. May 4th the company took cars for Madison, where they arrived in safety, and were assigned quarters at Camp Randall. The following is a condensed history of each member while with the company :

Gabe Bouck, Captain, was at Blackburn's

Ford and Bull Run; promoted Colonel of the Eighteenth Wisconsin regiment, is now member of Congress; lives in Oshkosh.

John Hancock, First Lieutenant, was at Blackburn's Ford and Bull Run; promoted to Major of the Fourteenth Wisconsin regiment; is a lawyer at Oshkosh.

H. B. Jackson, Second Lieutenant, was at Blackburn's Ford, detached to duty on Gen. Sherman's staff as assistant quarter-master; is a lawyer at Oshkosh.

Lyman H. Smith was at Blackburn's Ford, Bull Run and Gainesville, where he was severely wounded; he held the position of Captain of the company when discharged; he is a collector of customs at Island Point, Vermont.

Melvin R. Baldwin was at Blackburn's Ford, Bull Run, Beverly Ford and Gainesville, where he was severely wounded, Fitzhugh Crossing, Chancellorsville and Gettysburg, where he was taken prisoner. When the company was mustered out he held the position of captain; is now general agent of the Grand Trunk line at Minneapolis.

Alanson M. Thomes was at Blackburn's Ford, Bull Run, Beverly Ford, Gainesville, Bull Run No 2, South Mountain, Antietam and Fredericksburg, held the position of First Lieutenant when discharged; is a lumberman now in Oshkosh.

Reuben Ash was at Blackburn's Ford, Bull Run, where he was wounded; Fitzhugh Crossing, Chancellorsville, Gettysburg, where he was taken prisoner; held the position of First Lieutenant when discharged; is now a grocer in Oshkosh.

Henry D. Harshaw was at Blackburn's Ford, Fitzhugh Crossing, Chancellorsville, Gettysburg; also was engaged May 5th, 6th, 7th and 8th, 1864, in the Virginia campaign on the last day was wounded in the left arm which had to be amputated; when mustered out he held the position of Second Lieutenant; he held the following different positions while in service: corporal, sergeant, major, chief of the brigade ambulance corps, aid-de-camp on brigade staff, second lieutenant of company; in all positions he demeaned himself as a soldier and gentleman, except on a single occasion while a corporal. One day he called the captain "cucky," or something else, and was reduced to the ranks; however the "fraction" still lives, and he is a lawyer and postmaster at Oshkosh.

N. N. Ruby was at Blackburn's Ford, Bull Run, promoted from sergeant of company to sergeant major of regiment; subsequently was promoted to captain of Co. F, same regiment, afterwards served as captain in the 34th Wisconsin regiment, also did duty as lieutenant in the 14th Wisconsin regiment; played poker on picket line, for which Capt. Gabe relieved him of his sword, but it was restored to him before returning to camp; a mechanic in Oshkosh.

Walker S. Rouse, sergeant, was at Blackburn's Ford, Bull Run, where wounded, Fitzhugh Crossing, Chancellorsville, Gettysburg, where he was wounded; died July 11, 1863 from wounds.

Wm., C. Bryant, sergeant, was at Blackburn's Ford, Bull Run, Beverly Ford, Gainesville, in color guard, and was wounded and paroled; was discharged to accept commission in a colored regiment; lives at Cedar Falls, Iowa.

Richard Lester, sergeant, was at Blackburn's Ford, Bull Run, where he was wounded, detached for duty as clerk at brigade headquarters; participated with the company on May 4, 5, 6, 7 and 8, 1864, in the campaign in Virgina; is now a lawyer at Appleton, Wis.

Jos. W. Roberts, sergeant, was in the engagement of Blackburn's Ford, Bull Run; was there wounded and discharged to accept a captain's commission in the 28th Wisconsin regiment; has a collection office in Michigamme, Mich.

John G. Sprague, sergeant, was on skirmish at Blackburn's Ford is now station agent on the M. L. S. & W. railroad in Oshkosh.

John B. Thompson, sergeant, was at Blackburn's Ford and Bull Run, appointed regimental commissary sergeant; lives at Longmont, Colorado.

Oscar F. Crary, sergeant, "participated in engagements at Blackburn's Ford and Bull Run. On the march to Bull Run, one evening, just as the regiment was going into camp, Crary was seen charging a fat turkey with the point of his bayonet close to the turkey's tail. One of his company officers yelled "sergeant Crary!" The sergeant straightened up, came to a present arms; he was ordered into the ranks. Crary insists that the same bird graced the colonel's table that night. At all events that was the only time Sergt. Crary was ever known to drop his gatue. He now travels for Gray Bros., Chicago, and lives in Oshkosh.

Geo. E. Smith, sergeant, clerk in regimental quartermaster's office; clerk in brigade quartermaster's department; took part in the following engagements: Blackburn's Ford, Bull Run, Beverly Ford, Gainesville, Bull Run No 2, South Mountain, Antietam and Fredericksburg; lives at Racine, Wis.

Norman H. Whittemore, sergeant, took part in the following engagements at Blackburn's Ford, Bull Run, Beverly Ford, Gainesville, Bull Run No. 2, promoted lieutenant, Co. D, thirty-second regiment; after the war he practiced law in Kansas, where he died.

John B. Davis, sergeant, was in the following engagements: Blackburn's Ford, Bull Run, Fitzhugh Crossing, Chancellorsville and Gettysburg; was in the latter battle taken prisoner; he is now surveyor at Vancouver, Oregon.

Edwin T. Ellsworth, sergeant, lives in Oshkosh.

Jos. M. Waite, sergeant, was at Blackburn's Ford, Bull Run, taken prisoner at Massaponax Run, Va., in Fitzhugh Crossing and Chancellorsville, was a participant also in Gettysburg, where he was wounded and then was transferred to V. R. C.; lives in Chicago, Illinois.

Chas. H. Montgomery, sergeant, was at Blackburn's Ford, Bull Run, Beverly Ford, Gainesville, Bull Run No. 2, South Mountain, Fredericksburg, residence unknown.

John Bunderob, sergeant, was in Blackburn's Ford, Bull Run, Beverly Ford, Gainesville. There wounded, taken prisoner and paroled; Chancellorsville; also took part in the spring campaign in Virginia in 1864; is now a manufacturer of boxes, etc., in Oshkosh.

Irwin W. Potter, corporal, was at Blackburn's Ford and Bull Run; was promoted to a lieutenancy in the sixteenth regiment U. S. A., Sept. 10, 1861. Died after the war, in Texas.

Charles Graves, corporal, engaged at Blackburn's Ford and Bull Run, where he was wounded and taken prisoner, residence unknown.

Louis Schlintz, corporal, engaged at Blackburn's Ford and Bull Run, clerk in quartermaster's department; discharged to accept commission; has abstract office in Appleton, Wisconsin.

Jas. C. Bartlett, corporal, was at Blackburn's Ford, Bull Run, Beaver Ford, Gainesville; died from wounds received in latter engagement.

Jas Spencer, corporal, was at Blackburn's Ford, Bull Run, Beaver Ford, Gainesville, Bull Run No 2, South Mountain, Antietam; died in Denver, Colorado, after the war.

Geo Carwardine, corporal, was at Blackburn's Ford, Bull Run, Beverly Ford, Gainesville, Bull Run No 2, South Mountain, Antietam, Fredericksburg, Fitzhugh Crossing, Chancellorsville, Gettysburg, where he was killed.

Wm A Boyd, corporal, engaged in Blackburn's Ford, Bull Run, Fredericksburg, Fitzhugh Crossing, Chancellorsville, Gettysburg, where he was wounded and discharged; is now commercial traveler, lives in Oshkosh.

Luke English, corporal, was at Blackburn's Ford, BullRun, Beverly Ford, Gainesville, Bull Run No 2, South Mountain, Antietam where wounded, Fitzhugh Crossing, Chancellorsville; died after the war, in Oshkosh.

Ebenezer P. Perry, corporal, engaged at Blackburn's Ford, Bull Run; promoted to second lieutenant Co. D, same regiment, Feb. 17, 1862; is a lawyer, in New London, Wis.

Edwin B. Wing, corporal, was at Blackburn's Ford, Bull Run, Beverly Ford, Gainesville, Bull Run No. 2, South Mountain, Antietam, where he was wounded and from which he was discharged, lives in Southern Illinois.

Gilman Cindinum, corporal, engaged in Blackburn's Ford, Bull Run, Beverly Ford, Gainesville, Bull Run No. 2, South Mountain, Antietam, Fredericksburg, Fitzhugh Crossing, Chancellorsville, Gettysburg where he was wounded, also engaged on May 5, 6, 7, 8, 9 and 10, 1864, in Virginia campaign; finally lost on the steamer Golden Gate.

Fr. ncis Dugie, recruit corporal, engaged in the Virginia campaign of 1864.

Geo. Abrams, was engaged at Blackburn's Ford and Bull Run; was detached on western gunboat service, had was blown up on gunboat "Mound City,"

Henry C. Adams, engaged at Blackburn's Ford, Bull Run, Beverly Ford, Gainesville, Bull Run No. 2, South Mountain, Antietam, Fitzhugh Crossing, Chancellorsville, Gettysburg; also in the memorable six days' Virginia campaign in May, 1864; is a mechanic in Oshkosh.

John Birch, was at Blackburn's Ford, Bull Run, Beverly Ford, Fitzhugh Crossing, Chancellorsville, and Gettysburg, were he was wounded; lives in Winneconne, Wis.

David T. Buswell, was at Blackburn's Ford and Bull Run.

Alvin N. Bugbee, was at Blackburn's Ford, Bull Run, wounded at the latter place; detailed in division engineer corps; discharged to accept commission as second lieutenant in colored regiment; runs a saw mill at Grantsburg, Burnett county, Wisconsin.

William Briene, was at Blackburn's Ford, Bull Run, Beverly Ford, Gainesville, Bull Run No 2, South Mountain, Antietam and Fredericksburg; finally was detailed for duty at division headquarters; he was a stalwart "Mick," always yelling "rashuns" while on guard duty, which meant a drop of the auld crathur; he lambers on B'ack River; P. O, LaCrosse.

Wellington Bridges was at Blackburn's Ford Bull Run, Beverly Ford, Gainesville, Bull Run No. 2, South Mountain, and was killed at Antietam; a chip of the old block, as his father was under the Iron Duke at Waterloo.

Edward L. Billings was at Blackburn's Ford, Bull Run, Beverly Ford, Gainesville, where he was wounded and discharged by reasons of wounds; lives at Peach Grove, Clay Co., Kan.

Horace Bedient was at Blackburn's Ford; is a hardware merchant, Oshkosh.

Geo. W. Bedient died in hospital at Georgetown, Jan. 22, 1862.

Lewis A. Briggs, fifer, appointed second prin-

THE SOLDIERS REUNION OF 1880.

cipal musician, May 1, 1863; is in nursery business at Appleton, Wis.

John Callahan discharged for disability and died after the war, in Missouri.

Augustus B. Clark was at Blackburn's Ford, Bull Run, where he was wounded and taken prisoner; was discharged on account of wounds.

Edwin Casper was at Beverly Ford and Gainesville where he was wounded, and died from effect of wounds.

Giles Carpenter was at Blackburn's Ford and Bull Run; detailed for western gun boat service killed when the "Mound City" blew up.

John Cary was at Blackburn's Ford and Bull Run now lives in Oshkosh.

Nicholas Caslow was at Blackburn's Ford,Bull Run, Beverly Ford and Gainesville where he was wounded and was discharged from effects of wound; died after the war, in Oshkosh.

Timothy O'Connor was at Blackburn's Ford, Bull Run, Beverly Ford, Gainesville, Bull Run No 2, South Mountain, and Antietam where he was killed.

Hiram J. Cusick was at Beverly Ford, Gainesville, Bull Run No. 2, South Mountain and Antietam; is a farmer in Minnesota; his address is Owatonna, Minn., care of J, C. Ellis.

Joe Dougherty was at Blackburn's Ford, Bull Run; detached on western gun boat service; killed when the gun boat "Mound City" blew up.

Louis Defoe did his duty as colonel's orderly; first one that brought the contraband question before the regiment; is a teamster in Oshkosh.

William Dillon was at Blackburn's Ford, Bull Run, Beverly Ford, and Gainesville, where he was killed.

Wm. G. Davis was at Blackburn's Ford, Bull Run, Beverly Ford, and Gainesville, where he was killed.

David J. Ellinwood was at Blackburn's Ford, and Bull Run; is now lumberman at Stevens Point, Wis.

John Eucking was at Blackburn's Ford and Bull Run, where he was wounded and taken prisoner, and finally discharged by reason of wounds, now lives at Fond du Lac, Wis.

Vincent Flannigan was at Blackburn's Ford, Bull Run, Beverly Ford, Gainesville, Bull Run No. 2, South Mountain and Antietam, where he was killed.

Elisha Ford was at Blackburn's Ford, afterwards did duty with ambulance corps; lives at New London, Wis

Edwin Finney played solos on the bass drum ; is now selling groceries in Oshkosh.

Allsworth Ford was at South Mountain, is now chief of police in Oshkosh.

Stephen Graham was at Blackburn's Ford and Bull Run, where he was wounded and taken prisoner.

Arthur T. Gallup was detailed with wagon trains during Gainesville; was at Bull Run No. 2, South Mountain, Fredericksburg, Fitzhugh Crossing, Chancellorsville and Gettysburg, missed after the battle of the Wilderness, supposed to have been killed.

Benjamin B Hart was in Blackburn's Ford, Bull Run, Antietam, Fredericksburg, Fitzhugh Crossing, Chancellorsville and Gettysburg; is a farmer, Waupaca, Wis.

Jas. Hanay was at Beverly Ford, Gainesville, Fredericksburg, Fitzhugh Crossing, Chancellorsville, Gettysburg; was in the 1864 spring campaign, 7th and 8th of May; lives at Oshkosh.

John Holland was in Blackburn's Ford Bull, Run, Beverly Ford, Gainesville, Bull Run No. 2, South Mountain, Antietam, detached to duty with battery B, fourth U. S. artillery; while with the battery, was in Fredericksburg, Chancellorsville and Gettysburg, where he was wounded; he returned to duty with his company to enable him to re-enlist as a veteran volunteer; re-enlisted March 9, 1865; lives in Oshkosh.

Thomas Hudson was in Blacksburn's Ford and Bull Run.

Samuel F. Sackett was in Blackburn's Ford, Bull Run, Beverly Ford, Gainesville, Bull Run No. 2, South Mountain, Antietam, Fitzhugh Crossing, Chancellorsville, and was finally killed at Gettysburg.

G. M Hasbrouck was in Blackburn's Ford, Bull Run, South Mountain; he is an artist and paints for the Oshkosh boys.

William Holland was at Blackburn's Ford and Bull Run, where he was wounded; subsequently he was detailed as butcher at division headquarters; finally was transferred to invalid corps.

Luther M. Hays was in Blackburn's Ford, Bull Run, Beverly Ford, Gainesville, Fredericksburg, Fitzhugh Crossing, Chancellorsville, Gettysburg; is now an auctioneer, New York city.

Chester M. Hugenin, was in Blackburn's Ford and Bull Run; is now railroad contractor, Clintonville, Wis.

Henry Hinth was in Blackburn's Ford, Beverly Ford, Bull Run, Gainesville, Bull Run No. 2, South Mountain and Antietam, where he was wounded, Fitzhugh Crossing, Chancellorsville and Gettysburg, where he was taken prisoner ; died in prison in Richmond, Va.

John A. Hamlin was at Blackburn's Ford and Bull Run ; is now selling Hall's safes at Kansas City.

Chas. Howe was at Blackburn's Ford and Bull Run ; then served on detailed duty at division headquarters; lives at Shawano, Wis.

Hiram J. Jacoby was at Blackburn's Ford, Bull Run, Beverly Ford, Gainesville and Bull Run No. 2

Sebastian Karbach was at Blackburn's Ford, Bull Run, Beverly Ford, Gainesville, Bull Run No. 2, South Mountain, Antietam, Fredericksburg; re-enlisted as a veteran, is in the regular army.

Jonah Leach was at Blackburn's Ford and Bull Run, where he was wounded, Beverly Ford, Gainesville, South Mountain; died in Oshkosh after the war.

Julius E. Loll was at Blackburn's Ford, Bull Run, Beverly Ford, Gainesville, where he was wounded ; discharged and subsequently served in Third Wisconsin cavalry ; while the latter regiment was in camp in St. Louis, after the close of the war on its return home, he was killed through the carelessness of the provost guard,

John L. Miller was at Beverly Ford, Gainesville, Bull Run No. 2 ; is a lumberman at Oshkosh.

Lachlin L. McIntosh was at Blackburn's Ford. Bull Run, Beverly Ford, Gainesville, Bull Run No. 2, South Mountain and Antietam, where he was killed.

Patrick Murty was at Blackburn's Ford, Bull Run, Beverly Ford, Gainesville, Bull Run No. 2, South Mountain, Antietam, Fredericksburg, Fitzburgh Crossing, Chancellorsville, Gettysburg, where he was taken prisoner ; he was one of Winnebago county's sturdy farmers ; P. O. Oshkosh.

Hiram Swings, drummer, army of the Potomac, was promoted for being a good boy to be second principal musician; is a telegraph operator, out west.

Harvey McDaniels was at Blackburn's Ford Bull Run, where he was wounded, Beverly Ford, where he was again wounded, South Mountain, Antietam, Fredericksburg, Fitzhugh Crossing, Chancellorsville, Gettysburg, where he was taken prisoner.

Patrick McDermott was at Blackburn's Ford, Bull Run ; was detailed as nurse in general hospital, Washington.

Edward Moscript was at Blackburn's Ford, Bull Run, Beverly Ford, Gainesville, Bull Run No. 2, South Mountain, Antietam, Fredericksburg, Fitzhugh Crossing, Chancellorsville, and Gettysburg, was also engaged in the Virginia campaign of 1864, on the 5th, 6th, 7th, 8th, 9th, and 10th of May, wounded on the last day.

Geo. Notter was at Blackburn's Ford, Bull Run, Beverly Ford, Gainesville, Bull Run No. 2 and South Mountain, where he was killed.

Sebastian Ostertag was at Blackburn's Ford, Bull Run, where he was wounded, Beverly Ford, Gainesville, where he was again wounded, Fitzhugh Crossing, Chancellorsville, Gettysburg, where the Johnnies perforated him the third time, when he was transferred to veteran reserve corps ; he still lives and is selling groceries and lager beer in Oshkosh.

Ole Oleson or Oleson Ole, have it which way you like, was sick with the measles during the engagements of July 18 and 21, 1861, spotted as a leopard ; he left the hospital and reported for duty but was peremptorily ordered back to hospital by Capt. Bouck ; subsequently was detached on duty in western gun boat service ; is now Captain of a tug and is principally engaged in hauling logs away from Bill Wall's boom, P. O. Oshkosh.

Isaac Oatman was at Blackburn's Ford, and Bull Run was detailed as a teamster at division headquarters ; is now a farmer at Spencer, Wis.

Sylvester D. Pitcher was at Blackburn's Ford, and Bull Run, where he was wounded and taken prisoner ; subsequently did duty with an ambulance corps, is now a butcher in Oshkosh.

Leslie J Perry was at Blackburn's Ford, and Bull Run, where he was wounded and taken prisoner ; paroled and sent to Lake Superior, to suppress insurrection ; re-enlisted as veteran.

Richard J. Ripley, was at Blackburn's Ford and B ill Run.

Horace Stroud was at Blackburn's Ford and Bull Run, where he was taken prisoner, was paroled and ordered to Lake Superior ; sells agricultural implements at Oshkosh.

Robt. Steevers was at Blackburn's Ford, Bull Run, Beverly Ford and Gainesville, where he was wounded ; was transferred to the Fourth U. S. heavy artillery, lives in Oshkosh.

Wells Steever, was at Blackburn's Ford, Bull Run, Beverly Ford and Gainesville ; died from wounds received at the latter place.

Jos W. Smith was at Beverly Ford and Gainesville, where he was killed.

Wm. Stickland participated in no engagements ; discharged for disability.

Henry Scovil, was at Blackburn's Ford, Bull Run ; died while in camp at Kalorama, Georgetown.

John Saxton was at Blackburn's Ford, Bull Run, Beverly Ford, Fitzburg Crossing, Chancellorsville, and Gettysburg died in Oshkosh after the war.

Prosper Stinson was at Blackburn's Ford,and Bull Run, when he was wounded and taken prisoner ; lives in New London, Wis.

Wm. Tilleck was at Blackburn's Ford, Bull Run, Beverly Ford and Gainesville, where he was wounded.

Stephen A. Turner was at Black burn's Ford, Bull Run and at Beverly Ford.

Osman B. Taplin was at Blackburn's Ford, Bull Run, Beverly Ford, Gainesville, Bull Run

No. 2, South Mountain and Antietam, died of wounds, received in latter battle.

Wm. P. Taylor, fifer, taken prisoner at Bull Run; was detached on duty in the Wisconsin sanitary office in Washington; died subsequent to the war, in Oshkosh.

Elmer Torrence was detached on western gun boat service; was blown up on gun boat "Mound City."

Jas. Vanscork, sick during engagements at Blackburn's Ford and Bull Run; subsequently was wounded by explosion of a gun while on drill; was sent to hospital and discharged.

H. C. Weed was at Blackburn's Ford and Bull Run, where he was taken prisoner. He was heard to remark on the march that he expected nothing else but that we should get into some d——d row or other before we got home; he is a carpenter and lives at Oshkosh.

Benjamin Whitney was at Blackburn's Ford, Bull Run, Beverly Ford, Gainesville, where he was killed.

Abram White was at Blackburn's Ford, Bull Run, Beverly Ford, Gainesville, Bull Run No. 2, South Mountain and Antietam; was wounded at Gainesville and also at Antietam.

Lanson Ward was at Blackburn's Ford, Bull Run, Beverly Ford, Gainesville, Bull Run No. 2, South Mountain, Antietam, Fredericksburg, Fitzhugh Crossing, Chancellorsville, and Gettysburg, where he was killed.

Fred O. Zahn was at Blackburn's Ford, Bull Run, where he was wounded, and again wounded, Fredericksburg, Fitzhugh Crossing, Chancellorsville and Gettysburg, where he was again wounded; is now a clerk in Cincinnati, O.

John Barton was at Blackburn's Ford and Bull Run, where he was killed.

John F. Miles discharged.

Abner P. H. Martin discharged.

Philip Smith was at Beverly Ford, Gainesville, where he was wounded, Fitzhugh Crossing, Chancellorsville, Gettysburg; was engaged in the spring campaign of 1864 in Virginia, on May 7th and 8th, and was wounded on the latter day; died after the war in Louisville, Ky.

LORING & BLAKE'S
CELEBRATED
PALACE ORGANS

ERNEST GABLER,

DUNHAM & SON,

AND

HALLET & CUMSTON

PIANOS.

INCORPORATED BY SPECIAL ACT OF CONGRESS.

Capital, $1,000,000!

HOME OFFICE
WASHINGTON,
D. C.

AGENCIES AT
PRINCIPAL POINTS.

Purchasers of Pianos or Organs should not fail to apply to JAMES B. BRADFORD, Gen'l Agt for the Northwest, for the prices of instruments in above list. The celebrated Chickering Upright stands WITHOUT A RIVAL in America and Europe. The Ernest Gabler is also acknowledged by the public as a FIRST-CLASS INSTRUMENT. The "Dunham" and Hallet & Cumston are well known and appreciated by purchasers of excellent medium priced instruments.

JAS. B. BRADFORD,
NO. 422 BROADWAY,   MILWAUKEE

PROGRAMME AND PLAN OF ORGANIZATION

OF THE

WISCONSIN SOLDIERS REUNION

AND

RECEPTION OF GENERAL U. S. GRANT AND OTHER DISTINGUISHED UNION GENERALS.

JUNE 7TH, 8TH, 9TH, 10TH, 11TH AND 12TH, 1880.

PROGRAMME.

MONDAY, JUNE 7TH.

Reception of comrades, and distribution of badges by the Reception Committee, and preparation of Camp. Evening: Local Reunions and social visits. Camp fires, etc., etc.

TUESDAY, JUNE 8TH.

Morning: Reception of comrades, distribution of badges and preparation of Camp continued. Afternoon: Meetings for local organizations, social reunions, etc. Evening: Election of officers of the Wisconsin Reunion Association; grand illumination of the Camp; Address of Welcome by General F. C. Winkler, Chairman of the Reception Committee; Response in behalf of the Wisconsin Reunion Association, by Colonel Wm. F. Vilas, of Madison; Songs, etc.

WEDNESDAY, JUNE 9TH.

GRAND PARADE.

Formation of Column, and Reception and Escort of General U. S. Grant and other distinguished Union Generals.

Composition of Column for the Grand Parade.

BAND.

It is expected that the Column will be escorted by the uniformed Militia of the State of Wisconsin, and visiting military companies from other States.

General Edw W Hincks, *Commander-in-Chief of Veteran's Reunion*
Chief of Staff: Gen Fred C Winkler, 26th Wis Vol's, of Milwaukee.
Adjutant General: Col W F Vilas, 23d Wis Vol's, of Madison.
Quartermaster General: Col Gabriel Bouck, 18th Wis Vol's, Oshkosh.
Chief Medical Officer: Surgeon Walter W Kempster, of Oshkosh.
Engineer: Henry C Koch, 24th Wis Vol's, of Milwaukee.
Chaplain: Gen Samuel Fallows, 40th Wis Vol's, of Chicago.
Aides: Col C K Pier; Capt Chas King, U S A; Capt Garth W James; Maj W A Collins; Capt J B Oliver; Maj Jas Sawyer; Col Jos McBell; Capt I M Bean; Col J L Hathaway; Capt E Ferguson; Col C D Robinson; Capt D W May; Col Jas H Howe; Col E C Hibbard; Surg Solon Marks; Gen J A Kellogg; Surg Sidney Fuller; Capt W F Angevine; Lieut F M Gove, U S Navy; Col Wm Chapman, U S A; Col H M Enos, U S A; Maj Wm J Clark; Lieut G W Peck; Lieut A Ross Houston; Lieut Byron H Kilbourn; Capt Robertson James; Lieut H B Harshaw; Lieut H B Jackson; Lieut F M Clemens; Capt A E Bauer; Lieut W M Root; Capt Jos Bankin.

FIRST DIVISION.

Major General C C Washburn, of Madison, Commanding.
Chief of Staff: Gen Amasa Cobb.
Adjutant General: Capt I M Bean.
Quartermaster: Capt S E Bundle.
Commissary: Col Chas J Martin.
Judge Advocate: Capt Henry Norcross.
Surgeons: Dr Alex McBean, Dr J H Vivian.
Aides: Gen Conrad Krez,Capt E E Woodman, Maj John Whytock.
Co M, 4th Mo. Cav (mounted), 3 years, original Capt, G Von Deutsch.

BAND.

1st Cavalry, 3 years, original Col, Edw Daniels.
2d Cavalry, 3 years, original Col, Cadw C Washburn.
3d Cavalry, 3 years, original Col, Wm A Barstow.
4th Cavalry, (formerly 4th Inf), 3 years, original Col, Halbert E Paine.
1st Battery Light Art, 3 years, original Capt, Jac T Foster.
2nd Battery Light Art, 3 years, original Capt, E F Herzberg.
3d Battery Light Art, 3 years, original Capt, Lucius H Drury.
4th Battery Light Art. 3 years, original Capt, John F Vallee.
5th Battery Light Art, 3 years, original Capt, Oscar F Pinney.
6th Battery Light Art, 3 years, original Capt, Henry Dillon.
7th Battery Light Art, 3 years, original Capt, R R Griffith.
8th Battery Light Art, 3 years, original Capt, Stephen J Carpenter.
9th Battery Light Art, 3 years, original Capt, Jas H Dodge.
10th Battery Light Art, 3 years, original Capt, Yates V Beebe.
11th Battery Light Art, (Battery "L," 1st Ill Light Art), 3 years, original Capt, John Rourke.
12th Battery Light Art, 3 years, original Capt, Wm Zickerick.
13th Battery Light Art, 3 years, original Capt, R R Griffith.
Co G, Berdan's Sharpshooters, 3 years, original Capt, Frank E Marble.

BAND.

Soldiers who served during the Rebellion in volunteer organizations other than those of the State of Wisconsin.
Inmates of the National Home, in uniform.
Soldiers of the Regular Army in the War of the Rebellion.
Veterans of the Mexican War.
Sailors who served during the war of the rebellion.

SECOND DIVISION.

General Edward S Bragg, of Fond du Lac, Commanding.

BAND.

2d Reg't Infantry, 3 years, original Col, S Park Coon.
3d Reg't Infantry, 3 years, original Col, Chas S Hamilton.
5th Reg't Infantry, 3 years, original Col, Amasa Cobb.
6th Reg't Infantry, 3 years, original Col, Lysander Cutler.
7th Reg't Infantry, 3 years, original Col, Jos Van Dor.
10th Reg't Infantry, 3 years, original Col, H T Sanders.

PROGRAMME FOR THE SOLDIERS REUNION OF 1880.

26th Reg't Infantry, 3 years, original Col, Wm H Jacobs.
36th Reg't Infantry, 3 years, original Col, Frank A Haskell.
37th Reg't Infantry, 3 years, original Col, Sam Harriman.
38th Reg't Infantry, 1 and 3 years, original Col, Jas Bintliff.
1st Reg't Heavy Artillery, 1 and 3 years, original Col, Chas C Meservey.

THIRD DIVISION.

General John C Starkweather, of Washington, D C, Commanding.

BAND.

1st Reg't Infantry, 3 years, original Col, John C Starkweather.
8th Reg't Infantry, 3 years, original Col, Rob C Murphy.
9th Reg't Infantry, 3 years, original Col, Fred Salomon.
10th Reg't Infantry, 3 years, original Col, Alfred R Chapin.
11th Reg't Infantry, 3 years, original Col, Chas L Harris.
12th Reg't Infantry, 3 years, original Col, Geo E Bryant.
13th Reg't Infantry, 3 years, original Col, Maurice Maloney.
14th Reg't Infantry, 3 years, original Col, Dav E Wood.
15th Reg't Infantry, 3 years, original Col, Hans C Heg.
16th Reg't Infantry, 3 years, original Col, Benj Allen.
17th Reg't Infantry, 3 years, original Col, John L Doran.
18th Reg't Infantry, 3 years, original Col, Jas S Alban.
20th Reg't Infantry, 3 years, original Col, Bertine Pinkney.
21st Reg't Infantry, 3 years, original Col, Benj J Sweet.
23d Reg't Infantry, 3 years, original Col, Wm L Utley.

FOURTH DIVISION.

General Jerre M Rusk, of Viroqua, Commanding.

BAND.

23d Reg't Infantry, 3 years, original Col, Joshua J Guppey.
24th Reg't Infantry, 3 years, original Col, Chas H Larrabee.
25th Reg't Infantry, 3 years, original Col, Milton Montgomery.
27th Reg't Infantry, 3 years, original Col, Conrad Krez.
28th Reg't Infantry, 3 years, original Col, Jas M Lewis.
29th Reg't Infantry, 3 years, original Col, Chas R Gill.
30th Reg't Infantry, 3 years, original Col, Daniel J Gill.
31st Reg't Infantry, 3 years, original Col, Isaac E Messmore.
32d Reg't Infantry, 3 years, original Col, Jas H Howe.
33d Reg't Infantry, 3 years, original Col, Jonathan B Moore.
35th Reg't Infantry, 3 years, original Col, Henry Orff.
34th Reg't Infantry, 9 months, original Col, Fritz Annecke.
39th Reg't Infantry, 100 days, original Col, Edwin L Buttrick.
40th Reg't Infantry, 100 days, original Col, W Augustus Ray.
41st Reg't Infantry, 100 days, original Col, Geo B Goodwin.
42d Reg't Infantry, 1 year, original Col, Ezra T Sprague.
43d Reg't Infantry, 1 year, original Col, Amasa Cobb.
44th Reg't Infantry, 1 year, original Col, Geo G Symes.
45th Reg't Infantry, 1 year, original Col, Henry F Belitz.
46th Reg't Infantry, 1 year, original Col, Fred S Lovell.
47th Reg't Infantry, 1 year, original Col, Geo C Ginty.
48th Reg't Infantry, 1 year, original Col, Uri B Pearsall.
49th Reg't Infantry, 1 year, original Col, Sam Fallows.
50th Reg't Infantry, 1 year, original Col, John G Clark.
51st Reg't Infantry, 1 year, original Col, Leonard Martin.
52d Reg't Infantry, 1 year, original Lieut Col, Hiram J Lewis.

FIFTH DIVISION.

(In carriages.)

General Halbert E Paine, of Washington, D C, Commanding.
A A G: Col G W Carter, Waupun.
A Com Subsist: Col A J McCoy, Beaver Dam.
A Q M: Maj C D Wooster, Brodhead.
A Surg: Maj A H Van Norstrand, Green Bay.
Chaplain: Capt A C Barry, Fond du Lac.
Aides: Maj G C Pierce, Lieut Eugene Fitzpatrick, Oconto, Capt O F Nims, Boston, Mass.

Committee of arrangements and distinguished military and Civic Guests, including His Excellency Wm. E. Smith, Governor of Wisconsin, and Staff; the War Governors of Wisconsin; Army Commanders; General Officers who commanded Wisconsin troops during the Rebellion; General Officers of Wisconsin; and Veterans of the War of 1812.

The places for the formation of the several Divisions for the Grand Parade and the route of march will hereafter be announced.

Officers who served in the War of the Rebellion on the General Staff, not otherwise assigned to duty during the Reunion, are cordially invited to attach themselves to the Staff of the Commander-in-Chief.

Organizations in Camp are requested to observe as far as practicable the order indicated for the column.

Soldiers who have formed county or city organizations, or Posts of the Grand Army of the Republic, and prefer to retain such organizations rather than to join their regiments, will on reporting such facts with the name of their commanding officer to General F C Winkler, Chief of Staff, be assigned a position in the First Division.

Wednesday evening in Camp : Grand Summer Night's Festival, Music. All the Musical Societies in Milwaukee are expected to participate in this Festival.

THURSDAY, JUNE 10TH.

FORENOON : Infantry Prize Drill, free to all uniformed Militia Companies, (of not less than 48 muskets), in the United States, participating in the Grand Parade of Wednesday.

For Best Drilled Company, - - $500.00 Prize.
For Second Best Drilled Company, $300.00 Prize.
For Third Best Drilled Company, $150.00 Prize.
For Fourth Best Drilled Company. $ 50.00 Prize.

Provided that not less than ten companies enter for competition. In case a less number than ten companies enter, each prize will be reduced pro rata, and no company will be awarded more than one prize.

AFTERNOON : Awarding of prizes to victorious companies. Introduction of distinguished guests, speeches, etc.

EVENING : Exhibition by the Milwaukee Turn Societies in Camp.

FRIDAY, JUNE 11TH.

MORNING : Memorial Services in commemoration of the honored dead, to be conducted by the Grand Army of the Republic ; Oration by———.
AFTERNOON : Visit to National Home and other points of interest.
EVENING : Camp fire and general jubilee.

SATURDAY, JUNE 12TH.

Breaking of Camp, Farewells. *"Home, Sweet Home."*

REUNION COMMITTEES.

The following is an official list of the various committees and sub-committees of the Soldiers Reunion :

GENERAL EXECUTIVE COMMITTEE.

Henry Fisher, Chairman ; D N Kasson, Secretary, S J Williams, Recording Secretary ; John Johnson, Treasurer, F Brocherdt, C S Rosser, Wm Shallock, H Herzer, G C Staff, John B Abert, Otto Horn, H C Burgess, C Woolett, Charles Perkins, E A Calkins, John S George, H C Hobart, F C Winkler, Phillip Gaubatz, H Fink, A J Langworthy, G W Peck, J B Oliver T M Babling, E W Hincks, John R Goodrich, J A Roundy, B Leidersdorf, D B Hopkins, W A Collins, M Bodden, Alexander Mitchell, Edward Sanderson, A K Shepherd, Benj M Weil, Wm P McLearn, H S Benjamin, and H C Koch, of Milwaukee ; C N Pier, Fond du Lac ; H S Town, Ripon ; G J Thomas, Berlin ; E D Henry, Omro ; E Ferguson, Milwaukee ; Geo W Carter, Waupun ; G C Pierce, Kilbourn City, and Wm Wall, Oshkosh.

SUB-COMMITTEES.

Plan of Organization—Henry Fisher, Chairman ; E A Calkins. A J Langworthy, C K Pier, C Woolett, Phillip Gaubatz, H C Hobart, E W Hincks and Geo C Staff.

Locating Encampment—H C Hobart, Chairman ; E W Hincks, C S Hamilton, H S Benjamin and John Black.

Subsistence and Quarters—Henry Fink, Chairman ; I M Bean, H G Rogers, T S Allen, E C Timme, P H McCauley and J C Iversen.

Invitation and Reception—Fred C Winckler, Chairman ; Chas A Hamilton, Jas H Howe, Wm F Vilas, and Hans B Warner.

Transportation— E A Calkins, Chairman ; E E Woodman, A A Arnold, W S Stanley, F W Cutler and Ed E Bryant.

Advertising—Geo W Peck, Chairman ; E A Calkins, C H Boynton, W W Coleman, Bernard Guesterbock, J S White, C D Harger, M Kraus and G C Bowsfield.

Decorations and Music—H C Koch, Chairman ; F A Lydston, H J Baumgaertner, H N Hempsted and G P Traumer.

PROGRAMME FOR THE SOLDIERS REUNION OF 1880.

Summer Nights Festival—B Liedersdorf, Chairman ; D N Kasson, and H N Hempsted.

Turn Exhibition—Henry Fischer, Chairman.

Soldiers from other States—President, W C Swain, Vice-presidents, H S Benjamin, R C Spencer, Capt J M Conine, Two Rivers ; Dr W Thorndyke, Secretary, W S Stanley.

Executive Committee—C H Clark G H Wolcott, C H Aason, A F Merrill, W H Richardson and F M Gove.

FINANCE COMMITTEE.

Chairman—Capt Wm A Collins, Secretary—Lieut Frank M Gove, Treasurer—Hon John Johnston.

On the Board of Trade—A K Shepard, M Bodden, J B Oliver, E Sanderson, T E Balding, E C Hibbard

Banks, Insurance Companies, Railroads, Etc—John Johnson, T L Baker, R Nunnemacher, Geo G Houghton, F G Bigelow, M Keenan, J A Hinsey.

Brewing Interests—C von Baumbach, Captain Fred Pabst, V Blatz. Frank Falk, Aug Uihlein, Fred Miller, G Stamm.

Rectifiers, Distillers and Wholesale Liquors—S G Herbst, Emil Kiewert, Lieut F M Clements, Major C P Huntington, Peter Barth, Lieut Chris Sarnow.

Merchants' Association—R Hill, J A Roundy, J R Goodrich, B B Hopkins, E P Mathews, Samuel Chandler.

Hotels—J F Antisdel, Wm Plankinton, Abner Kirby. C Vernekes.

Committee-at-large. South Side—C J Burnham, C W Milbrath, Dr H E Hasse, Maj C P Larkin, Horace Cheas, H F Fishedick, Selvester Stroug, Maj Wm Kennedy, Capt J A Langworthy, T H Wood, G F Porter, Peter Barth, Capt W Walter, Emil Durr, Thomas Shay, J W Coleman, Conrad Neiderman, Theodore Hartman.

West Side—Col J McBell, Capt Wm Steinmeyer, Col G H Walther, Maj. C P Huntington, Capt Geo Allanson, S C Herbst, Lieut Christian Sarnow, Capt Pius Dreher, Lieut Paul Binner, Phillip Schlosser, Fritz Comdohr, Jacob Koueroschild, Aug Kineger, Capt John C Mass, Col Wm H Jacobs, J C Boyd, Lieut Gottlieb Schweitzer, F W Hartman, Maj Chas Menzes, H Baumgariner, Wm Rauschenberger, C M Sanger, J P Rundle, Otto Zwietusch, Lieut F M Clements.

East Side—Lem Ellsworth, Hans Boebel, P Van Vechten, Jr., Dr S Marks, Dr E Kramer, Henry Baetz, Thos Tighe, Adam Dillman, A L Baynton, A Von Trott, Major Kempf, Lieut F M Gove, Emil Kiewert, K Miller, H C Payne, C H Haskins.

Bay View—D J Price, C Otjen.

CHAIRMEN OF SUB-COMMITTEES:

Committee on Plan of Organization: Henry Fischer
Committee on Locating Encampment: Gen H C Hobart
Committee on Subsistence and Quarters: Hon Henry Fink
Committee on Invitations: Gen F C Winkler
Committee on Transportation: Col E A Calkins
Committee on Volunteers from Other States: Col H S Benjamin
Committee on Advertising: Lieut Geo W Peck
Committee on Decoration and Music: H C Koch
Committee on Summer Night's Festival, Wednesday Evening, June 9th : B Liedersdorf
Committee on Turn Exhibition, Thursday Evening, June 10th : Henry Fischer

GENERAL NOTES.

The Commander-in-Chief, and the Commanders of the several Divisions have been elected by Joint Soldiers and Citizens Reunion Committee, which meets in Milwaukee on the last Tuesday of each month.

Commanding Officers will select and announce the members of their respective staffs.

Commanders of Divisions are requested to put themselves at once in communication with the several organizations assigned to their command, and to adopt such measures and take such action as they may deem proper to secure a full and well organized representation of their respective divisions at the Reunion ; and, if they deem it desirable, to divide their divisions into brigades and appoint brigade commanders.

All General, Field and Staff Officers are requested, as far as practicable, to appear, mounted and wearing side arms.

Regiments, batteries and companies will be commanded at the Reunion by the senior officer present, unless a different organization shall be effected for the occasion.

It is not expected that the men will appear in uniform, unless they desire to, but it is hoped that as many as conveniently can will wear dark clothes and slouched hats or fatigue caps.

Each regiment will carry the colors borne by it in the service, which will be found at the General Headquarters in Milwaukee. Let the storm tattered flags, riven by shot and shell on a hundred fields of battle, once more be unfolded to the breeze before they are forever laid away to moulder into dust.

Veterans are requested to provide themselves with blankets, tin cup, tin plate, knife, fork and spoon, prepared to go into Camp, as the committee will secure proper camp equipage, and consummate arrangements to provide good and wholesome rations at reasonable rates, not to exceed fifty cents per day ; but regimental commanders are requested, if they so desire, to make suitable arrangement for the quartering and subsistence of their respective commands.

The veterans will not be required to perform guard duty in Camp, nor to make any stated parade except the Grand Parade on Wednesday ; but commanders of regiments, etc., are requested to make proper details from their commands, to care for and protect public and personal property in their respective Camps, and to pitch and strike their tents.

Railroad fares will be at the rate of one and a half cents per mile, for soldiers and all others. Railroad tickets will be good for ten days, and if any want to remain longer an extension will be granted upon application to the executive committee.

Headquarters for the Commander-in-Chief, the Commanders of the several Divisons, and for the different committees, will be established during the Reunion at the County Court House, where staff officers and committee men will at all times be on duty to give information to visiting soldiers and sailors.

Members of regiments, companies and batteries are requested to confer with each other for purposes of organization, and as soon as possible to transmit the name of the officer who will command their respective organization during the Reunion to D N Kasson, Secretary of the General Committee, Milwaukee, Wisconsin.

All honorably discharged Soldiers who served in any Wisconsin organization at any time during the war of the rebellion and all honorably discharged Union Soldiers and Sailors who now are, or at any time have been residents of the State of Wisconsin, are requested to attend the Grand Reunion.

EXPERIENCED, STAUNCH, ALWAYS RELIABLE!

THE OLD
PENNSYLVANIA FIRE INS. CO.
OF PHILADELPHIA, PA.

With a Successful Business Experience of

FIFTY-FIVE YEARS,

Continues to Offer Strictly FIRST-CLASS INSURANCE on Favorable Terms.

THE average LIFE of Insurance Companies in the United States, has not exceeded 10 years! Hence the preference which Property-owners should give to a THOROUGHLY TESTED and TIME-HONORED Company like the

"OLD PENNSYLVANIA FIRE,"

☞ This Company during its existence of 55 years, has paid LOSSES amounting to an average of $100,000 per annum, or $5,500,000 for whole time !
☞ Its Reputation for FAIR and HONORABLE dealing has never been SURPASSED by any similar institution !
☞ It has always been equal to the emergency in every period of DANGER or DISASTER—in all of the "Ups and Downs" of Business in the last 50 odd years !
☞ During the last 10 years—from January 1, 1870, to January 1, 1880—a period of great disaster, to Insurance interests generally, the ASSETS and NET-SURPLUS of the Company were INCREASED nearly 100 per cent.—and this too, notwithstanding the payment of over $850,000 LOSSES by the great Boston fire of 1872! Such facts afford the best possible proof of CONSERVATIVE, SUCCESSFUL MANAGEMENT, as well as of the STRONG FAITH of the Public in the STABILITY of the Company!
☞ MORAL.—If you want Reliable Insurance, ask for a Policy in the

"OLD PENNSYLVANIA FIRE."

Agencies in all the Principal Cities and Towns in the United States.

THE ATTENTION OF PROPERTY OWNERS IS RESPECTFULLY DIRECTED TO THE OLD

INSURANCE CO. OF NORTH AMERICA,
OF THE CITY OF PHILADELPHIA.

"It is Wisdom and Economy to Insure in the Best Companies," and there is None Better than this Veteran of 86 Years Honorable Service, Firmly Established, Safe ! Reliable !

Over 350 Fire Insurance Companies in the United States, Failed or Retired from Business in 10 Years,
FROM JANUARY 1, 1870, TO JANUARY 1, 1880!
83 Were Ruined by the Great CHICAGO and BOSTON Fires of 1871-2.

The last Decade was a Period of Unexampled disaster to Insurance Companies—Millions of Dollars of Capital and Assets being swept away.

The History of the "OLD" INSURANCE CO. of NORTH AMERICA during the eventful 10 years just closed—January 1, 1870, to January 1, 1880—is in marked contrast with that of the 350 unfortunate Companies above alluded to. The Salient Points in the History of the "NORTH AMERICA," are:

1.—Increase of Capital Stock from..$ 500,000.00 to........$2,000,000.00
2.—Increase of Assets from..$2,783,580.96 to........$6,591,740.18
3.—Increase of Net Surplus from..$1,060,587.95 to........$2,414,461.51
4.—Increase of Surplus as Regards Policy-holders from.......................$1,560,587.05 to........$4,414,461.51
5.—The prompt payment of the CHICAGO and BOSTON losses of 1871-2, amounting to over $1,600,000, without impairing the Capital of the Company, or calling upon the Stockholders for a Dollar !
6.—The payment of losses in the 10 years, amounting to over $21,400,000—making Total Losses paid since organization, over $17,500,000.
7.—The remarkable fact that at no time during the past 10 years—either before or after the great Chicago and Boston Fires—was a single share of the Company's Stock offered for sale at less than 100 per cent. premium, and is now worth over $3.00 for every $1.00 of par value !
☞ The foregoing "Facts and Figures" fittingly illustrate the confidence of the Public in the STABILITY and SUCCESS of the

"OLD NORTH AMERICA."

Agencies in all the Principal Cities and Towns in the United States.

APPENDIX TO REUNION ROSTER

FIRST INFANTRY.

A

Mehl, Edw, lt	National Home, Milwaukee
Buden, A A	Oshkosh
Beardsley, J G, corp	Waupun
Bridges, M L	Milwaukee
McCurdy, C	Stevens Point
Newton, Isaac, f	Lamartine
Ross, Frank	Waupun

B

Collins, W A	Milwaukee
Franklin, Rawson, f	Waupun
Johnson, Newton S	Bloomfield, Iowa
McPartin, J A	Oshkosh
Orlem, Murray	Stevens Point
White, John s	Milwaukee

C

Appleton, J W	Black Creek
Austin, E E	Milwaukee
Bradshaw, Geo	Burlington
Fairbanks, Jno, f	Sparta
Parker, J G	Brandon
Smith, Geo	Fox River
Sorenson, Jno, f	Sturgeon Bay
Sorge, Henry	Kenosha
Timme, E G	Kenosha
Tubbs, J H	Menasha
Vanderbeck, F	Wheatland
Weyreagh, Jacob	Racine

D

Hughes, Wm K, lt, mo	Milwaukee
Baker, Wm B	New London
Bloomer, Henry	Delavan
Bernhardt, Carl	Milwaukee
Close, K D, sgt. f	Woodhull
Hartman, H S	Somerset
Stickney, A U	Janesville
Metz, Jacob	Rockford, Ia

E

Bird, Wm W	Milwaukee
Clark, A S, m	Waupun
Cobb, C B	Kenosha
Celter, Wm	Racine
De Diemer, B T	Kenosha
De Diemer, F	Kenosha
Gardner, J E	Kenosha
Gifford, J R C	Kenosha
Harmon, Philip	Kenosha
Harlem, Pat, f	Eden
Hoenm, A H	Kenosha
Huehting, F B, P O clk	Milwaukee
Irving, Jas	Kenosha
Miller, Jno M	Kenosha
Roberts, J C	Kenosha
Smith, Geo I, sgt	Fremont

F

Babcock, Geo W	Baldwin
Clark, D S	St Croix
Cowan, Wro	Baldwin
Craw, Jno	St Croix
Hass, Geo A	Racine
Humphrey, Thos	Ceylon
Olson, John	Baldwin
Peabody, F A	Hammond
Wyatt, Jno	St Croix

G

Bremmer, Jas A	Plover
Cole, Wallace, f	Waupun
Cobb, C E	Kenosha
Davis, Frank	Eau Claire
Oliver, Edw	Fall River
Trowbridge, D H, f	Waupun

H

Alverson, David, bugler, e	Coloma
Chamberlin, A C, mf	Waldo
Du Pons, A	Kenosha
Paine, Albert D	Grantsburg
Petevich, Aug	Harrisville
Riss, Jno	Grand Island Neb

I

Bates, Wm J	Anoka, Minn
Cole, E	Badger Hill, Ia
Eldridge, E A	Menasha
Goodwin, M	St Croix
Gretzer, Jno S	Milwaukee
Maguowen, Theo	Taychedah
Place, W H	La Crosse
Rogers, Earl M, m	Viroqua
Stanton, P G	Cobb
Tibbits, Arthur, sgt, e	Galesville

K

Beckman, F W	Kenosha
Boyer, David J	Brothertown
Billington, Frank	Sleepy Eye, Minn
Hile, Jas	Lamartine
Suber, Paul	Kenosha
Stewart, Geo F, clk	Fond du Lac
Walters, Herman, me	Fond du Lac
Walters, Thos	Lamartine
Wilson, D M, me	Eldorado Mills
Wyse, W A	Reedsburg

UNASSIGNED.

Babcock, Alonzo	Rush River
Babcock, Simeon	Rush River
Cady, Julius	Waupaca
Chamberlin, L M	Lyons, Kan
Hayford, M T	Taycheedah
Zemozis, G	Rush River

SECOND INFANTRY.

A

Bennett, A D, ord sgt	Milwaukee
Kinney, M L	Fort Atkinson
Morgan, Albert T	Washington, D C
Stringham, W H, sgt, f	Fond du Lac

B

Buller, Pitkin G	Norway Bridge
Fabry, K	LaCrosse
Harris, Wm H	LaCrosse
Huggins, Eri	St Joseph, Mo
Markle, E	La Crosse
Markle, J	La Crosse
Pitkin, Milo J	La Crosse
Phelps, F J	La Crosse
Rand, J B	La Crosse
Rand, T B	La Crosse
Scott, K A	La Crosse
Sherwood, W H	La Crosse
Webb, J B	La Crosse
Weeks, E F	La Crosse
Wenzel, G	La Crosse

C

Clough, Wm M	Ripon

D

Anderson, Calvin	Star Prairie
Atkinson, E	Carroll City, Ia
Catlin, Chas L	St Croix
Elliot, Sam'l, f	Rice Lake, Minn
Fisher, L	St Croix
Goodnoe, I E	Warren

E

Leister, Frank, sgt	St Croix
Montman, C	St Croix
Wilson, J	Warren
Bereh, Jno	Winneconne
Humor, Melcholr	Muscoda
Oatman, Geo J	Marshfield

F

Barry, M A	Lodi
Heyer, Frank	Waterford
Huggins, Jno C	Racine
Hughes, Isaac	Waterford
Rodman, F	Racine
Tapling, C W	Racine
White, W W	Cresco, Ia

G

Lt W S M Abbott, a	Minneapolis, Minn
Davis, W F	Grand Rapids
Ford, Elisha,	Waupaca
Hanson, Chas, me	Mauston
Lemarand, Jos, f	Red River
Linscott, Anson	Portage
Lupient, G A	Neillsville
Thompson, Clark	Baldwin

H

Beecham, R K	Litchfield, Minn
Chilente, Henry, me	Rosendale
Davis, O M, musician	Beaver Dam
Moore, C W	Cheteck
Williams, E J	Evansville

I

Dow, Wm H	Weyauwega
DeWolf, J H	Menasha
Goldthorp, Geo J	Mineral Point
Laboude, Peter	Milwaukee
Maloney, M	Des Moines, Ia
Mouser, Wm, sgt	Dubuque, Ia
Raymond, Jno N	Garrison, Ia

K

Gatfield, Geo	W U Junction
Goodenough, W H	Paton, Ia
Kinder, David	Sabula, Ia
Pioeger, Wm	Seymour
Zeutner, Rudolph	Point Bluff

UNASSIGNED.

Haight, J H, m	Brothertown
Peck Geo W, musician, f	Alma, Neb
Sanford, Henry	Manitowoc
Woldroff, A	Eden, D T

THIRD INFANTRY.

A

Benedict, S A, pa	Fond du Lac
Boughton, Orville	Weyauwega
Farmer, S C, corp, f	Fond du Lac
Marvin, Elias C	Springfield, Dakota
Newton, A H	LaCrosse
Redick, Albert A	Fond du Lac

B

Benty, Geo, f	Lomira
Durfee, Jno	Omro
Kline, Peter	Newfane
Terschbacker, J N, f	Kewaskum
Whitney, J K	Omro
Wright, Jeff	Stevens Point
Young, Jacob	Kaukauna

C

Brown Chas C	Rushford
Mury, Michael	Milwaukee
Besat, Alex	Gravesville

 The Oldest Insurance Agency in The City.

C. A. HANDT,
GENERAL FIRE AND LIFE
INSURANCE AGENT.

Represents the Oldest and Most Reliable Companies in the City.

Policies Issued in Any of His Companies on Reasonable Terms

OFFICE AT OLD STAND,

No. 428, - - MAIN STREET,

FOND DU LAC, WISCONSIN.

APPENDIX TO REUNION ROSTER.   277

Name	Location
Brown, Geo, f	Fond du Lac
Clark, J W, mc	Fond du Lac
Cane, Robt, f	Waupun
Converse, T W	Neillsville
Cook, Wm, f	Waupun
Corrigan, Andrew, f	Waupun
Cummings, Jas, f	Waupun
Oliver, R L, a	Waupun
Owens, G B, f	Waupun
Parsons, Wm H, me	Waupun
Smith, Barney, l	Waupun
Towle, Jno, corp	Appleton
Tibbits, Wm	Durand
Wells, R O	LaCrosse
Wells, Wm, f	Waupun
Wilkes, Jos, me	Waupun

E

Name	Location
Capt G Hammer	Beaver Dam
Bates, B H	Fond du Lac
Bullard, Henry	Lomira
DuBois, Jno B	Oshkosh
Martin Jerima	York, Neb
Reynolds, A P	Laverne, Minn
St John, Joe, me	Harrison

F

Name	Location
Doughty, Henry	Durand
Bartholomew, S	Boscobel
Graves, E V	Omro
Holm, A O	Friendship
Looker, G	Lind
May, David	Boscobel
Peterich, Aug	Harrisville
Perrine, Henry	Wisner, Neb
Wood, D S	Marshfield

G

Name	Location
Barney, Michael	Muscoda
Bentick, Hans	Waupaca
Beach, S H	Kaukauna
Dodge G W	Menasha
Clow, Chas C, sgt	Albaton
Goldsborough, J O	Menasha
Harris, W L	Symco
Knickerbocker, Chas	Iola
Myher, Ole	Neenah
Minude, L	Waukesha
Northam, W	Menasha
Pugent, Jno B	Menasha
Roby, Ben	Menasha
Schurin, J F	Stevens Point
Smith, Henry, me	Fond du Lac
Walch, Peter	Gravesville
Willard, V R	Jenny
Wood, T S	Winneconne
Warner, D W	Neenah

H

Name	Location
Capt Geo H Whitman, mf	Fond du Lac
Cutler, Geo H	Lexington, Mass
Dickenson, John, f	Nasewaupee
Smith, W B, dep sheriff	Belmont

I

Name	Location
Capt W W Freeman	Menasha
Bartholmew, S, sgt	Boscobel
Blenkhorn, Jno	Shullsburg
Bushby, W F	Argyle
Hillstrom, Dan'l	Amherst
Looney, Jas S	Aetna
Rickeman, Geo A, m	Racine

K

Name	Location
Daily, C F	Neillsville
Dunn, Jno W	Milwaukee
Kluesi, Fredolin, f	Lani, Ia
Thompson, D	Oconomowoc

UNASSIGNED.

Name	Location
Capt L B Balcom, nursery man	Waupun
Clark, David, f	Waupun
Close, Jeremiah, f	Lamartine
Hammelhel, Jacob	Galesville
Helbach, Jno	Menasha
Isbel, Henry C, sgt	Fremont
Nelson, Jerome	Amherst

FIFTH INFANTRY.

A

Name	Location
A Surg Ambrose Jones	Delton
Lt Frank Kelly	Menominee
Lt Thos Blair	Lochiel
Blair, Jas	Menominee
Harley, David	Menominee
Haveland, Richard	Menominee
Hill, Maine	Canton
Pease, Frank	Menominee
Rugler, Jno	Menominee
Scanlon, Jno	Menominee
Wagner, Arnold, brewer	Sturgeon Bay

B

Name	Location
Carvin, W J	Reedsburg
Conlon, J H	Beaver Dam
Johnson, Oscar, f	Brothertown
Keyes, Geo H, f	Empire
Kyle, Geo	Downsville
Ryle, Jno	Downsville
Smith, Jas	Menominee
Tiffany, P R	Taycheedah

C

Name	Location
Bonnell, Cornelius M	Rusk
Lias, F Aug, corp	Eagle
Perault, Peter	Menominee
Stover, Isaac	Knapp

D

Name	Location
Andrew, Paul	Stevens Point
Andrew, S W	Stevens Point
Blood, Calvin	Amherst
Blodgett, Phillip	Stevens Point
Campbell, J P	Stevens Point
Crane, E A, musician	Beaver Dam
Cromwell, Mason	Stevens Point
Cummings, Jno R	Lochiel
Delenh, L	Beaver Dam
Giles, Darius	Buena Vista
Hall, Geo	Beaver Dam
Hubbard, Jas K P	Stevens Point
King, Wesley	Stevens Point
Miller, J P	Stevens Point
Pellersels, Henry	Plainfield
Reading, Wm	Stevens Point
Richards, Edwin P	Stevens Point
Rossiter, L	LaCrosse
Samuels, David	Beaver Dam
Sinsar, Hiram	Linwood
Stultz, Geo L	Beaver Dam
Voyer, O	Junction City
Ward, J W, me	Fond du Lac
Ward, Herbert	Amherst
Webster, H S	Buena Vista
Wilmot, A C	Stevens Point
Young, R P, sgt	Beaver Dam
Young, Elijah	Beaver Dam

E

Name	Location
Lt John McCabe	Winneconne
Ashby, M	Winneconne
Bakiwin, B B, c	Waupun
Lansing, Willard	Neenah
Mietu, Eli, f	Neenah
Mattison, G D	Fairchild
Largood, Jno C	Menominee
Walker, Frank E	Stevens Point
Wagoner, Henry	Menominee

F

Name	Location
Brimhall, S	Amherst
Crane, G W	Belmont, Ia
Curran, J D	Stevens Point
Czesklebe, The	Amherst
Dwinell, Chester H	Amherst
Fancher, Orson	Amherst
Hunter, Luther	Custer
Lowe, Henry B, reg of deeds	Dartford
McGeen, Thos	Waukesha
Reubeche, Chas	Custer

G

Name	Location
Bayette, Wm	Longwood
Chamberlain, G M	Waupaca
Curran, Henry	Stevens Point
Murry, Frank	Waupaca
Welty, Henry	Stevens point

H

Name	Location
Bacon, M H	Kenosha
Butter, L M	Rushford
Crasgrove, Jos	Brothertown
Frost, Wallace, f	Fond du Lac
Galloway, Wm	Durand
Kinney, Jas, me	Richland Centre
Northrup, O H, m)	RichlandCentre
Pratt, E C	Beaver Dam
Vradenburg, Ellas	Durand
Walker, W B	Bowens Mills
Witherell, Halle, me	Fond du Lac

I

Name	Location
Lt N S Allen	Beaver Dam
Barnum, W H	Wausau
Goche, Franey	Inleseo
Foble, Jno, me	Gratiot
Oliver, Wm	Omro
Zimmerman, Wm C	Woodhull

K

Name	Location
Cummings, E R	Springfield
LeFevre, G H	Winneconne
Land, Haus	Menominee
Noulan, Jno, sgt	Menominee
Rehm, Geo	Menominee
Wiggins, G W	Weston
Wright, Chas	Durand

UNASSIGNED.

Name	Location
Lt M H Wilson	Menominee
Anson, f	Plover
Barker, N J	Lind
Downing, Geo	Plover
Esenhauch, Frank	Plover
Johnson, Francis, steward	Menomonee
Morrison, Jno	Plover
Otto, Gottlieb	Oconomowoc
Pierce, Jas	Plover

SIXTH INFANTRY.

A

Name	Location
Barker, Jas H	Milwaukee
Burbank, O O	Rochester, Minn
Clay, W H	Waupun
Johnson, A P	Baraboo
Maun, Jas R, f	Sevastopol
Thomas, T C	Baraboo
Foot C H	Delton

B

Name	Location
Lt Darwin W Kinne	Trimbelle
Marsegy, Simon	Menominee
Simons, Ed	Menominee

C

Name	Location
Dobson, Richard	Rochester
Darrow, W H	Point Bluff
Hildeman, Hy	Watertown
Schweitzer, Gottleib.	Fond du Lac

D

Name	Location
Blackburn, Wm, f	New Lisbon
Clark, Jas, f	Boltonville
Huffinan, Franz, f	Riceville
Hicken, David	Pewaukee
Minnett, Frank	Daeada
Rosenberg, Henry	Waukesha
Wetor. Jos	Dacada

THE
EQUITABLE LIFE ASSURANCE SOCIETY,
NO. 120 BROADWAY, NEW YORK.

GEO. I. BREWSTER,   H. W. HAMILTON,
GENERAL AGENT.   CASHIER.

406 MILWAUKEE STREET,   MILWAUKEE, WIS.

OF INTEREST
TO
LIFE INSURANCE AGENTS.

Men of experience in this business, who can show a successful record, will do well to correspond with Mr. E. W. Scott, Superintendent of Agencies of the EQUITABLE LIFE ASSURANCE SOCIETY, No. 120 Broadway, New York.

It is confidently believed that there is no company in the country for which an agent can work with more profit to himself.

1st. Because it makes liberal contracts, and always lives up to them.

2d. Because it is a firmly established and permanent institution. Its assets securely invested and its immense cash surplus guarantee to every agent who has renewal commissions running the security and permanence of his contract.

3d. Because its managers are constantly on the alert, and give their workers in the field ample material and every facility for the successful prosecution of their business.

4th. Because the agent can offer an incontestable policy, thus furnishing absolute indemnity to the insurer.

5th. Because he can offer a simple and concise policy, containing no unreasonable conditions.

6th. Because he can guarantee that every equitable claim will be settled promptly and in full. [The Society paid in 1879 nearly five million dollars in death claims, dividends, etc., and closed the year without a single contested claim on its books.]

7th. Because of the Society's Tontine Savings Fund policies, many of which are being settled in 1880, on a basis showing larger profits than any other company can exhibit on policies extending over the same period.

8th. Because the Equitable is a progressive company. Its new issues for 1879 amounted to $26,500,000, being an increase in one year of more than five million dollars.

9th. Because it is the most popular company in existence, and one with which the public are ready to insure.

EQUITABLE
Life Assurance Society.
120 BROADWAY, NEW YORK.

Total Assets, Dec. 31, 1879,	$37,366,841.75
Undivided Surplus,	$7,515,407.75

New Business, $26,802,511; an increase of more than FIVE MILLION DOLLARS over the previous year.

Policies Incontestable after 3 years.

On ordinary policies a liberal surrender value is given in paid up insurance, in case of forfeiture.

Contract clearly and concisely expressed, No technical conditions

The year closed without a single disputed death claim on the records All just claims p id promptly and in full.

Cash Returns on Tontine Policies.

The two following cases will serve as illustrations of settlements now being made by the society:—

Policy No. 43,563. Issued May 25, 1869. On the life of F. L., of Farmington, Conn

Amount of policy	$10,000 00
Annual Premium	508 00
Total premiums paid during eleven years	5,594 00
The policy holder, having decided to terminate the contract at the end of its Tontine period, draws in cash	6,155 00

Having had $10,000 of assurance for eleven years.

Policy No. 50,526. Issued Jan 8, 1870, on the life of A. G. C., of New York.

Amount of policy	$10,000.00
Annual premium	513 10
The total premiums during the entire period, ten years	5,441 00

On the eighth day of January, 1880, the policy holder had the privilege of terminating the contract and withdrawing $4,000 cash, or tak ng a paid-up p licy for $7,870. It decided, however, to continue the assurance, and his premium for 1881, less the annual dividend, will be under $150.

E		F		H	
Capt J D Marston	Appleton	Flaben, Wm	Racine	Wiegiel, E F	Janesville
Dillon, W A, sgt, bk	Ripon	Ludwig, Al	Chillou	K	
Haviland, E, f	Scott	Schwetzer, Henry	Roca, Neb	Chandler, Geo, me	Harrison
Hayford, Orlando	Weyauwega	G		French, A	Racine
Hamilton, Peter, f	Richland Centre	Bedell, Isaac	Stevens Point	Harrison, W H	Kenosha
Lawrence, Jas F, me	Fond du Lac	Crusey, Wm N	Plover	James, Jno F	Racine
Onker, Chris	Weyauwega	Evans, Hugh	Amherst	Pilmpton, Geo	Racine
Row, Louis, f	Scott	Puarlen, Moses	Plover	Smith, Thos	Racine
Rayner, Mathias, sgt	West Bend	Packer, Jno	Amherst	Smith, W	Racine
Tuttle, S D	Dorchester	Smart, Sam'l H	Plover	Smith, James	Racine
F		H		UNASSIGNED.	
Beltz, C F	Hastings, Minn	Capt Nick Hebes	Lake City, Minn	Capt Benj D Gano	Hartley, Ia
Bersch, Jacob, l	Milwaukee	Chandler, Curtis C	Orleans, Neb	Briggs, Abram	Menominee
Glaser, Michael, f	Berlin	Haus, Andrew	Racine	Downer, David	Waterville
Goermiller, Caspar	Milwaukee	Parsons, H D	Spencer, Ia	Entrikin, B F, clk of court	Clarion, Ia
Gaubatz, Philip, corp	Milwaukee	I		Humminston, Ed, eagle bearer	Rush
Huesler, Chas	Neillsville	Barnes, C B, f	West Bloomfield	Hawley, I I, reg of deeds	Wautoma
Miller, Jacob, a	Mankato, Minn	Barnes, B M, f	Pine River	Kinsman, Cyremus	Lind
Kaetz, U A	Independence	Bingham, Thos P, corp	Bury	Kirk, W G	Wanbeck
Sauke, Fred, f	Bloomfield	Crandall, Seeley K, f	Plainfield	Mills, C C	Neillsville
Zipp, Herman, musician, mo	Barton	Cooley, W W	Fredonia	Perry, Jas	Kirksville, Mo
G		Everett, Joel	Pine River	Phillips, Jno	Racine
Daggett, S S S	Rushford	Gould, A G	Oregon	West, Thos	Connorsville
Davis, W T	Grand Rapids	Powell, Benj F	Marshfield		
Guyer, G	Kilbourne	Wing, Noah	Roseville	NINTH INFANTRY.	
Weller, Alonzo	Amherst	Wilding, L H	Neillsville	A	
H		William, Hay	Fond du Lac	Dickmann, Claus	Stockbridge
Lt J D Lewis	Fountain City	K		Haas, Jacob	Lowell
Lt H B Merchant	Arcadia	Harrison J H	Friendship	Obst, Frank	Brillion
Cook, Atwall	Cumberland	Stowell, Frank, f	White Creek	Scheibe, August	Plymouth
Johnson, Jno O	Stevens Point	UNASSIGNED.		B	
Longyear, Sam'l J	Kapouee, Neb	Scott, Cockrell	Plover	Licterle, J	Sauk City
Shinne, Oliver, f	Burnion	Shelton, Chas	Ring	Promberger, J, mo	Milwaukee
Tucker, Isaac, ph	Spirit Lake, Ia	Sims, Jas	Ring	Puley, Albert	Collwer, Kansas
I		Thomas, David	Ring	Seidle, Wolfgang	Rellnerville
Kueehenmeister, Fred	West Bend	Workman, H M	Racine	Schutts, J	Lima
Newton, Thos	Coloma			C	
K		EIGHTH INFANTRY.		Annen, Peter	Kenosha
Benson, H	Stevens Point	A		Augustine. Robt	Racine
Juv, Soren H	Winchester	Devoine, T F	Sherman	Lenz, Michael	Kenosha
Spooner, Cyrus	Wouewoc	Farell, Thos	Royalton	Mueller, Jos	Kenosha
UNASSIGNED.		Horton, W H	Wuupaca	Moeuler, D	Kenosha
Yanke, Fred, f	Bloomfield	Sewerewright, A	Frankfort	Voerndt, Henry	Kenosha
		Bich, O A	Waupaca	D	
SEVENTH INFANTRY.		Rich, Truman	Waupaca	Abrecht, M	Baraboo
A		Rogers, W H	Buttes des Mortes	Giesen Jos	Pittsburg, W T
Capt Oley Grasley	Des Moines, Ia	B		Ostelback, Carl	Ripon
Ackerman, B	St Joseph	Coon, Thos	Kilbourne	Setzloff, Wm	Vivian, Minn
Chiland, Wm	Lodi	Stewart, S E	Elkhart Lake	Woltring, Hulbert	Grafton
Smith, David, l	Lincoln	Stoddard, S G	Juelson	Zundler, Wm	Brookfield Centre
B		Wade, S E, dentist	Fond du Lac	E	
Lt S I, Bachelder	Fall River	C		Beth, Jos	Green Bay
Bluwets, Jno J, f	White Creek	Hill, Julius A	Menominee	Engelbert, Hans	Plover
Batler, Al	Beaver Dam	Lane, David M	Menominee	Krakofsky, C A, me	Waterford
Butler, Antin	Beaver Dam	Lenz, Geo, me	Eau Claire	Kargus, Fred	Racine
Bronson, S H	Fall River	D		Lippert, Dionysius, f	Beloit
Cummins, G O	Oakwood, D T	Armitage, Ambrose	Neosha	Ehrhardt, Dan	Racine
Dean, E A	Fall River	Bartz, Edwin, f	Fall Creek	Willbolt, Fred, f	Racine
Frost, Isaac	Plain	Bowles, T J	Elo	F	
Handke, Chas, l	West Bend	Edwards, Robt, f	Berlin	Brill, Jno	St Joseph
Hilton, L J	Ft Collins, Col	Herman, Geo, f	Ripon	K'eberg, Ferd	Winchester
Henderson, D A	Iron Mountain	Houston, Walter	Elo	Nehring, Herman	Winchester
Russell, Z B	Fall River	Nuteman, J C, f	Luverne, Minn	G	
C		E		Capt Chas Frantz	Kenosha
Eubank, Thos, bk	Wautoma	Ash, Henry, f	Solder, In	Knubic, Andrew	New London
Washburn, Jas, me	Burton	Bell, Jno, f	Solder. Ia	Kern, Andrew	New London
D		F		Schmidt, Audrew, corp, reg of deeds	Barton
Huffron, Jas	Omro	Allison, J W, me	Sparta	H	
Pohl, Jos, f	Harrisville	G		Kakushke, Louis	Jefferson
Rase, Wm	Omro	Brown, W C	La Crosse	Hoxie, Wm	Baraboo
Shutelt, S A	Omro	Helue, E E	York, Neb	McKennan, H	Baraboo
Thomas, Frank	St Ansgar, Ia	Riker, Chas N, sgt	Janesville	I	
Tipple, O F	Stoughton	Morris, Hiram	Weyauwega	Gifford, Chris	Racine
Young, Isaac	Muscoda	Patterson, James, f	Brandon	Seefert, Wm	Portage
E		S'awson, G	Queen City, Mo	Willhoft, J	Burlington
Jones, J A	Neillsville	Watson, Wm	Janesville		

THE CONTINENTAL
Life Insurance Co.,
of HARTFORD, CONNECTICUT.

INCORPORATED 1862.   BEGAN BUSINESS 1864.

JAMES S. PARSONS, President.   *ROBERT E. BEECHER, Sec'y.*
H. R. MORLEY, Actuary.   *Wm. M. HUDSON,*
H. P. CLARTON, Supt. of Agencies.   *Medical Director.*

Assets, January 1st, '80 - - - $2,797,323.28
Income for '79 - - - - - 466,380.47
Surplus as to Policy-Holders - - - 421,465.28

Paid to Policy-Holders since organization of Company, in Dividends, Surrender Values, Endowments and Death Claims,

$5,215,621.83.

Policies issued, upon either Mutual or Stock Plan, at standard rates of premium.

All the Policies of this Company are definite in their terms, and liberal in their conditions.

Mutual Policies, non-forfeitable by their terms, after two premiums paid, by exchange for paid up insurance of equitable amount, upon condition only that the exchange shall be made within one year after lapse.

Wishing to meet all the legitimate wants of the insuring public, the Company offers a large variety of plans, among which are its

Life Rate Endowment or Accumulative Plan, its Guaranty Income Plan, its Long Term Plan, and its Single Payment Note Plan.

For explanatory Circulars, and full elucidation of the various plans, apply to any of the Company's Agents, or directly to the Home Office.

Reliable, active, persevering men, who wish to represent a popular and easy working Company, should apply for Agencies.

NORTHWESTERN DEPARTMENT,
No. 49 CLARK STREET, CHICAGO.

STEWART MARKS, Manager.   RUFUS CHENEY, Special Agent.

Office INSURANCE COMMISSIONER,
State of Connecticut.   *Hartford, May 7th, 1880.*

Robert E. Beecher, Esq., Sec'y Continental Life Insurance Co.:

My Dear Sir:--Having completed my examination of the affairs of your Company, as provided by law, it is due to you that I should say that I find it sound and solvent, and fully able to comply with all the requirements of law, and that the interests of its Policy-Holders are amply protected.   *Respectfully yours,*
JOHN W. STEADMAN, Ins. Com'r.

APPENDIX TO REUNION ROSTER.

K

Name	Location
Stacy, Peter	Sussex
Stacy, Fridolin	Sussex
Lambrecht, Adolph	Milwaukee

UNASSIGNED.

Name	Location
Fuss, Jacob, ord sgt	Waupun
Scheider, Bernhard	Kenosha
Seidel, W	Bellueville

TENTH INFANTRY.

A

Name	Location
Brabazon, Wm R, teamster	Jacksonport
Jokesh, Frank	Waukesha
Matison, Dave	Abaline, Kan
Shelden, J	Lima
Wood, Walter, corp, mc	Sparta
Wood, R B	Durand

B

Name	Location
De Barr, D	Menasha
Converse, L D	Neillsville
Fadden, Jas S	Spencer
Hull, Rosell J	Waukegan
Jalqriot, Jos	Mayville
Seaman, Thos, sgt, f	Eden
Watkins, Wm H, me	Ripon

C

Name	Location
Bixby, C C	Menasha
Conroy, Pat	Menasha
Collins, A W	Menasha
Catlon, W	Winneconne
Donaldson, C V	Menasha
Eldridge, H A	Menasha
France, A W	Menasha
Harvey, H B	Menasha
McCandles, Jno	Menasha
Plummer, H H	Menasha
Underwood, C	Menasha

D

Name	Location
Best, Edw	Granger
Best, Solon	Granger
Best, Jno	Granger
Burke, Juo, f	Sparta
Coleman, Chas	Durand
Dowd, Gilbert, sgt	Durand
Mason, H H	Friendship
Marsh, Geo W	Portage
Patchin, A E	Portage
Powers, Thos D	Mukawonago
Smith, H B	Kilbourn
Thompson, Wallace	Kilbourn
Webster, J E	Kilbourn

E

Name	Location
Baker, Alex, pa	Juneau
Babcock, S A	Beaver Dam
Dutcher, H B	Rock Island, Ill
Harrison, Thos W, sgt	Emmetsburg, Ia
Harrison, Wm M	Emmetsburg, Ia
Harrison, Francis	Emmetsburg, Ia

F

Name	Location
Boyle, Jack	Hebron, Neb
Eayers, Nelson P	Omaha, Ia
Eva, W	Omaha City, Ia

G

Name	Location
Cahill, J W	Hart, Mich
Hopkins, Jas	Stevens Point
Howard, Frank	Lima
Wright, Chas	Black River Falls

H

Name	Location
Feegler, Delos F	South Haven, Mich
Ingersoll, Geo	Vanceburg
Sallender, Fred	Retreat

I

Name	Location
Burkholder, David	Hurlbut Corners
Burns, A M, pa	Beaver Dam

K

Name	Location
Capt Edwin Hillyer	Waupun
Bierce, Austin O	Iola
Clark, Michael	Stevens Point
Rockwell, H	Neillsville
Owen, Nathaniel	Des Moines, Ia

UNASSIGNED.

Name	Location
Harris, William	Waupaca
Harris, Geo	Waupaca
Hammelehiel, Jacob, sgt	Galesville
Page, Wm	Durand

ELEVENTH INFANTRY.

REGIMENTAL ROSTER.

Name	Location
Col Chas L Harris	Myra, Neb
Maj Arthur Platt	Muzomanie
Maj Otis Remick	Ann Arbor, Mich
Adj Daniel Lincoln	St Louis, Mo
Adj Ira W Hunt	Menasha
A Surg C C Barnes	Manitowoc

A

Name	Location
Miner, Wm E	Hammond

B

Name	Location
Capt Jos H Hubbard	Oak Creek
Capt Otis Remick	Ann Arbor, Mich
Capt Wm Charlton	Madison
Lt Jas M Bull	Bismark, Dakota
Lt H J Luneburg	Schuyler, Neb
Taylor, Will, me	York, Neb
Thompson, R M, m	Sutton, Neb
Weber, J B	LaCrosse

C

Name	Location
Capt Jas Lang	Georgetown, Col
Lt M V B Hutchinson	Waterloo
Lt Azel Grover	Marshall
Lt Jno Seuright	Minneapolis, Minn
Lt Jas B Bonch	Milford
Beattie, Wm	Portage
Brown, Lindsley, ph	Madison
Klmber, Jesse, l	Sturgeon Bay
King, Geo, f	Sevastopol
Morrow, Carl	Lincoln
Meyer, Jno, f	Sevastopol
Simon, Nick, f	Nasewaupee
Wier, Jno B	Bangor
Wilcox, Geo	Ft Dodge, Ia
Wilcox, L C, f	Brushville

D

Name	Location
Lt A A Chamberlain	Orion
Lt W H Dawson	Orion
Lt Hiram Freeman	Richland Center
Lt Jas S Robinson	Stanton, Neb
Alderman, B	Boaz
Alling, C P, f	Orion
Albaugh, T, f	
Butler, Seth, sgt, f	Richland Center
Butler, Cyrus, f	
Briggs, D, corp, f	
Benton, D, corp, f	
Barrett, E, f	
Bailey, A T, f	Cromwell
Berry, L, f	Boaz
Beery, T, f	Boaz
Bowman, G, f	
Brown, A, f	
Cook, J, corp, f	Sylvan
Chamberlain, A A, p	Richland Center
Chesemore, D, f	Rockbridge
Collins, W, f	
Coates, W, f	
Conkle, J, f	Richland Center
Conkle, D, f	Richland Center
Conts, F M, f	
Dondna, J, f	Richland Center
Dary, J, f	Richland Center
Davis, L D, f	
Dicks, T, f	
Deford, J, f	
Davis, P A, f	
Davis, T, f	

Name	Location
Davis, W, f	
Davis, F, f	
Evans, H C, f	
Erving, J H, f	Richland Center
Fox, J W, drummer, f	
Fox, P P, sgt	
Fogo, D, sgt, f	Worthington, Minn
Fazel, J, f	
File, C, f	
Fowler, R J, f	
Freeman, H, sgt, f	Richland Center
Frult, J M	Richland Center
Fisher, W, f	
Favorite, W, f	
Guinn, J, sgt	
Grey, J, f	
Grimes, J, f	
Gustin, E T, f	
Gillingham, W, f	
Hoake, A	Loyd
Heckendorn, D, f	Woodstock
Huffman, J M, f	
Hanlin, C, f	Richland Center
Hankins, M D, f	Richland Center
Hebert, P, f	
Harris, S, f	
Hurd, H C, f	
Jagubsh, J M, sgt, f	
Kinney, A T, sgt	Richland Center
Kimbell, R E	
Kimbell, A, f	
Kramer, S, f	
Kitelinger, S, f	
Lyons, D, f	Rockbridge
Leach, L J	
Lindley, D T, f	
McClintic, A, f	
Maior, J, f	
Mathew, L, 8fer	
McCarthy, C, corp, f	
Miller, W H, f	
Mann, J, f	Spring Green
Mapes, W, f	
McGill, J S, f	
Morrison, F M, f	
Matoesin, D, f	
Mark, J, f	
Miller, J L, f	
McDermond, J, f	
McKey, J, f	Richland Center
Monn, W, f	Richland Center
March, J, f	Boaz
Mason, R, f	
Myers, C M, f	
Miles, J, f	
Manley, J, f	
Norman, G, f	
Newkirk, T B, f	
Owens, E W, f	Boaz
Parsons, W, corp, f	
Peters, L, f	
Pannell, J, f	
Ricsebeck, J C, f	
Robinson, R J, f	
Robinson, J T, f	
Robinson, J H, sgt, f	
Snyder, F, corp, f	
Snyder, A, f	
Slater, B F, f	
Stevens, A C, f	
Standish, A L, f	Boaz
Sutton, B F, f	
Southard, J W, f	Richland City
Sparling, L, f	
Sellers, M, f	
Sheafer, S, f	
Sallsbery, J, f	
Thompson, B F, corp, f	Richland Center
Thompson, J W, f	
Tadder, J, f	Richland Center

J. I. CASE THRESHING MACHINE CO.,
RACINE, WISCONSIN.

APRON, ECLIPSE, AGITATOR

IMPROVED! PERFECT! WARRANTED!

Apron, Eclipse, Agitator.

THESE POPULAR THRESHERS
ARE CONSTRUCTED

On True Scientific Principles

Thresh, Save and Clean More Grain, Flax, Grass Seed and Clover than any

Threshing Machine in Market.

8-10-15 HORSE
PORTABLE AND TRACTION

FARM ENGINES,
UNEQUALED IN THE MARKET FOR
Safety, Economy, Strength, Finish.

SPLENDID LIST OF HORSE POWERS.
4-Wheel Woodbury, 4-Wheel Pitts.
2-Wheel Woodbury, Down Pitts.
Climax and Tread Powers.

APPENDIX TO REUNION ROSTER.

Thomas, B H, corp
Tepler, E, f
Thomas, J, f
Vandusen, J, f
Williams, D F, sgt, f
Wilson, R J, f — Richland Center
Waddell, A G, f
Ward, P, f
Wood, W J
Wood, H H, f — Richland Center
Welton, W W, f — Richland Center
Widner, Martin, f
Wilfond, S, f
Woodman, E, f
Walsworth, R, f
Wildermuth, E C, f
Yeager, W, f
Zerving, C, f

E

Lt S E Shepard — Mineral Point
Lampka, Jno — Muscoda

F

Capt E R Chase — Dubuque, Ia
Capt P B Stone — Augusta
Capt R E Jackson — Hot Springs, Ark
Jackson, R E — Hot Springs, Ark
Harrow, Jas P, f — Eldorado Mills
Parsons, A S — Oregon
Priestly, Thos — Mineral Point

G

Capt W S McCready — Honey Creek
Stickle, Sam'l — Redwood Falls, Minn

H

Capt Alex Christie — Aplongton, Ia
Capt Jas O'Neal — Lynden, Wash Ter
Lt I J Wright — Muscoda
Camp, I P — Portage
Lavigne, J L — Neillsville

I

Capt N R Doan — Stoughton
Lt H C Welcome, m — Ripon
Benjamin, S C — Star Prairie
Cape, Wm — Cole Brook
Pierce, A D, f — Markesan
Pierce, Jonathan — Lincoln
Logue, Emery — Muscoda
Shaddock, Lester — Manchester

K

Capt Wm Chariton — Madison
Lt Ira W Hunt — Neenah
Lt Robt P House — Menasha
Kroeger, Aug — Orihula
Michelson, A — Neenah
McAllister, D — Neenah
Mark, J P, f — Centralia
Perry, J C
Small, Robt — Neenah
Vaughn, Morris — Marshfield

UNASSIGNED.

Allpress, W
Baker, George — Brothertown
Burrows, John, drover — Sparta
Grout, Enos — Fall River
Hicks, John — Fall River
Welker, H — Neenah

TWELFTH INFANTRY.

A

Richter, Aug — Grifford, Ill
Wallace, Kelsey, f — Cottage Grove, Minn

B

Armstrong, Geo G — Burnboo
Buelow, F — Reedsburg
Durward, Alex W — Neosho
Darling, Solon — Neillsville
Darn, Frank E — Edgerton
Kellogg, Lafayette — Reedsburg

C

Platta, Jno — Sharon
Seeley, M E — Reedsburg

Beisswanger, Gottlieb — Prairie Farm
Blodgett, A J, pr — Osage, Ia
Kolbow, Wm, f — Waterford
Molvey, Jno, sgt, l — Ripon

D

Holt, Geo R, el — Jackson, Mich
McHenry, Jas, l — West Bend
Meyers, W W — Stevens Point
Protest, Christopher, f — Boltonville
Senn, Andrew, teacher — Fond du Lac
Smith, Elias, l — West Bend
Venck, Edw — Cedar Creek
We-cott, A — Stevens Point
Wescott, E — Badger Hill, Ia
Willis, J C — Omro

E

Adams, G E, me — D Ron
Bonl, Robt, f — Red Willow, Neb
Bender, B — Sharon
Coleman, Chas — Reedsburg
Coleman, Arthur — Reedsburg
Clement, L D — Delton
Clement, Jas M — Kasson, Minn
Freer, Justice, — Delton
Hutchinson, A T — Planeville
Ingalls, Jno G — Menominee
Lawsha, Jacob — Delton
Lawsha, Geo — Reedsburg
Lawsha, Jacob — Reedsburg
Moshier, Wm L — Manston
Mentanye, J C, f — Delton
Rood, H W — Omro
Swain, S G, postal clk — Winona, Minn
Vanderpool, C C — West Mitchel, Ia
Vincent, Wm A — Kenosha

F

Brooks, G R, sgt — Peshtigo
Jones, J V — Canton
Keazar, L W — Canton
Lampka, F — Muscoda

G

Atchinson, H H, f — Cataraet
Bellanger, A — Meunsha
Butler, G H — Medford, Minn
McClaughry, Thos B — McGregor, Ia
Jones, Jno G — Planefield

H

Baptist, Arnold, l — Sturgeon Bay
Russell, Thos — Flintville
Cross, Jacob, f — Sevastopol
Falk, Jno, c — Sturgeon Bay
Harris, Jos, Jr — Baileys Harbor
Salvison, Ole, l — Sturgeon Bay
Peterson, Peter, f — Sturgeon Bay
Roe James T — Peshtigo
Rossiter, Wm — La Crosse
Wright, S M, a — Gibralter

I

Dixon, Nathan — Waubeck
Day, Geo W — Jefferson, Ia
Moran, Jos — Stevens Point
Murray, Jno A — Delton
Woodruff, W J, corp — Dell Rapids, D T

K

Chandler, D O — Lincoln
Platter, Jno — Sharon
Woodruff, W J — Dell Rapids, D T
Winchester, W W — Reedsburg

UNASSIGNED

Carpenter, Wm — Stevens Point
Granger, Francis, com sgt, me — Lamartine
Hurlburt, T H — Eau Claire
Winans, H — Plover

THIRTEENTH INFANTRY.
REGIMENTAL ROSTER.

Col Wm P Lyon — Madison
Col A H Kannard — Lawrence, —67
Lt Col Jas F Chapman — Venice, Ohio
Lt Col Thos O Bigney — Denver, Col
Lt Col Chas S Noyes — San Antonio, Texas
Adjt Wm Ruger — Janesville
Adjt A W Lownsbury — St Paul, Minn
Q M Platt Eyclesheimer — Chicago, Ill
Surg Jno Evans — Evansville
Surg Selden Cady — Kilbourn City
A Surg, C D Woodruff — Lima, N Y
A Surg S L Lord — Edgerton
A Surg Chas M Smith — Evansvil'e
Chap J I Foote — La Cygne, Kau

A

Capt Jno Auld — Kaukauna
Lt Milton Bowerman — Springfield, Mo
Lt Olney G Gibbs — Chicago, Ill
Campbell, A B — Albion
Hoskins, Geo, f — Washta, Ia

B

Lt D H Cheney — Phillipsburg, Kan
Lt Geo C Brown — Chicago, Ill
Lt Fred'k C Buten — Milton Junction
Capelle, Aug, l — Scott
McCarty, Jerry — Oconomowoc
Miller, L S, sgt — Wheatland, Neb
Monngan, Jno — Erin Prairie

C

Capt Jno T Fish — Racine
Lt D R Lamoreau — Mound City, Kan
Lt H G Bardwell — Philmore, Minn
Lt Wm Loucks — Philmore, Minn
Lt H N Moulton — Sharon
Alson, Levi E — Elkhorn
Bardwell, Henry — Sharon
Becker, Philip — Sharon
Eckerman, W D — Sharon
Grosbeck, E H — Sharon
Kline, C — Sharon
McDonald, David — Sharon
Merrill, Harvey — Sharon
Rodawalt, Jno W — Sharon
Story, Elliott — Sharon
Welch, Jno H — Sharon

D

Capt C E Patchin — Shellrock, Ia
Lt D B Lovejoy — Watertown, D T
Iveus, Chas — Chapin, Ia
Persch, Christian — Brillion
Sweet, Marion D — Weyauwega
Wurzbach, Henry — Weyauwega

E

Capt E H Hewitt — Cawker City, Kan
Capt Sam'l Parker — Manchester, Ia
Capt Simon Taylor — Depere
Lt E F Warren — Janesville
Lt A C Smith — Fort Lincoln, Neb
Lyon, Thos J, corp — Emmettsburg, Ia
McCall, Sanford — Cambria
Mulkins, Wm — Buena Vista

F

Capt J W Briggs — Shopiere
Lt J L Fowle — Ixona, Mich
Emerson, L D — Beloit

G

Capt Thos O Bigney — Denver, Col
Capt A N Randall — Broadhead
Lt C R Matson — Chicago, Ill
Lt S C Waggoner — Broadhead
Bates, Jno C — Orleans, Neb
Taylor, H M — McComb ee
Wood, H F, teamster — Ripon

H

Capt C N Noyes — San Antonio, Texas
Capt E J Pratt — Mt Ayr, Ia

Largest Threshing Machine Factory
IN THE WORLD.

Their use yields more Profit to Threshermen and Farmers than any Machine made.

Catalogue free for asking.

APPENDIX TO REUNION ROSTER.

Lt Robt Glover — Juneau
Lt A J Smith — Neosho
Lt C E Graham — Dubuque, Ia
Lt Ole Jacobson — Millard
Boylngton, Geo A — Valley Junction
Burham, J M — Jefferson
Case, G S — Jefferson
Clelshey, C — Jefferson
Morgan, Stephen — Orleans, Neb

I

Capt N H Kingman — Logansport, Ind
Lt H H Knox — Stoughton
Lt Jas Johnson — Mukwauago
Buckley, Dan'l — Oconomowoc
Foot, F — Jefferson
Hines, John — Oconomowoc
Hines, Geo — Oconomowoc
Mellean, Frank, sgt — Pewaukee
Soat, Joshua H — Baldwin
Smith, R W, f — Waukesha
Vaughn, Wm — Kendall

K

Capt Jno H Wemple — Norfolk, Va
Lt H C Carter — Juneau
Alder, Henry — Clairon, Ia
Deering, N W — Osceola, Ia
Stannard, A C — Milton
Weiss, N — Racine

UNASSIGNED.

Seldon, Cady, surg — Emmetsburg, Ia
Lindsley, Wm R, mc — Sturgeon Bay
Munigan, Mike — St Croix
Remmington, C N — Stevens Point
Stevens, D E — Milton
Weston, A H — Waukesha

FOURTEENTH INFANTRY.

A

Christjohn, John — Seymour
Drake, D M, e — Fond du Lac
Delaney, Ed, sgt, city clk — Fond du Lac
Giblin, Michael, f — Kewaskum
Israel, A, f — Fond du Lac
Louuire, F, f — Lamartine
Longstaff, H M, m — Chippewa Falls
Maseraft, E, bugler, pa — Fond du Lac
Pallant, O F, me — Fond du Lac
Pitcher, D — Fond du Lac
Spink, R A, ar — Oshkosh
Sanford, L N — Menasha
Barhen, Wm H — Stevens Point
Burk, Jacob — Weyauwega
Davis, Roswell C — Weyauwega
Derbrier, Leston — Stockton
Denny, A J — Weyauwega
Feherly, Patrick — Stockton
Fuller, P — Oconomowoc
Harkness, Orlande F — Marshfield
Haley, Michael — Weyauwega
Higgenson, Samuel — Lind
Jeffers, Albert A — Amherst
Larkie, Jno — Lind
Metlowan, Jno — Plover
Mack, Holmes — Weyauwega
Mack, John — Weyauwega
Smart, Elyer — Plover
O'Shay, J D — Brandon
Hoe, Hiram — Stevens Point
Wills, Wallace — Weyauwega

C

Burt, J R — Fond du Lac
Brick, Daniel W — Weyauwega
Johnson, C M — Winneconne
Miller, P C — Winneconne
Misner, Wm, me — Rosendale
Ottinger, Alvis, me — Barto

D

Dashner, Hank — Plover

Dasnel, Frank
Davis, Daniel
Driscoll, Jno
Fritz, Chas
Farrand, Daniel F, m
Hardson, L
Harrison, S A
Krueger, Christian
Martin, C D
McCoy, J F
McConnell
Sager, Peter
Waughs, H H
Weber, Jno

E

Lt H W Durand
Bacon, J W
Bacon, M A
Brown, C G, elk
Tennelson, Freeman, f
Hickaby, Geo M, f
Westcot, Geo P, f

G

Drentzer, C G, pr
Kuter, Samuel M, corp, mc
Mills, Calvin
Oleson, Ole
Wheeler, Arnold

H

Lt J F Prosser
Bradbury, Chas, f
Cudworth, Joel Z, real estate
Gibson, C W
Hamlin, S A
Nash, A D, f

I

Bel, Jno W, f
Cann, H
Habersetzer, L

K

Capt J J Postal
Bowman, Jos
Beames, W J, f
Lercher, Chas F

UNASSIGNED.

Capt H S Childs
McGowan, John
Prosser, Josiah, f
Prior, H D
Riley, Philip, f
Teal, Earnest

FIFTEENTH INFANTRY.

REGIMENTAL ROSTER.

Lt Col K K Jones — Quincy, Ill
Maj Chas M Reese — Chicago, Ill
Q M Ole Heg — Waterford
Q M Selah Mathews — Minneapolis, Minn
Surg S O Himoe — Lawrence, Kan
Surg A F St S Lindsfelt — Sheboygan
A Surg S J Hansen — Norway
A Surg G F Newell — Waterford
A Surg Sam'l Bell — Beloit
Chap C L Clansen — Blooming Prairie, Minn

A

Capt Andrew Torkildsen — Chicago, Ill

B

Lt Christian Heyer — Waupun
Booth A J — Stevens Point

C

Capt Jno T Rice — Waterford
Lt Jas Larson
Anderson, Peter — W U Jun ,tton
Branstad, Ole C, capt — Grantsburg
Carpenter, W L — Rochester
Davis, M L — Waterford
Elliot, Wm — Waterford

Stevens Point
La Crosse
Stevens Point
La Crosse
Onalaska
La Crosse
La Crosse
Ridgeway
La Crosse
La Crosse
La Crosse
La Crosse
Plover
La Crosse

Fond du Lac
Kenosha
Kenosha
Shelbina, Mo
Clay Banks
Clay Banks
Hilbert

Milwaukee
Eden
Christee
Mosinee
Lind

Oakfield
West Bloomfield
Fond du Lac
Grundy Centre, Ia
St Cloud
Lamartine

New Prospect
Neillsville
Neillsville

Muscoda
Baldwin
Rosendale
Whitewater, Kan

Beaver Dam
Plover
Brothertown
Waopaca
Gardner
Muscoda

Rolison, Lewis — Waterford

D

Capt Chas Campbell — Waupun
Lt C E Tomberg — Monroe
Lt Nels O Tuffe — Ashipun
Healverson, H O — Stevens Point

E

Capt T A Rossing — Lots Creek, Ia
Lt Wm Tientland — Moscow

F

Lt Thos Simonson — Christiania, Ill
Gill, M, f — Ripon
Gilbert, T G, m — Blair
Kekeberger, Ole — Eaton
Lavasson, Jos, f — Sturgeon Bay
Nilson, Carl, f — Gibraltar
Thompson, Eli A, f — Sturgeon Bay

G

Capt Jno A Gordon — Omaha, Neb
Gilbertson, Targer — Iola
Gregorson, Lars — Iola
Jenson, Johan — Zumbrota, Minn
Olson, John — Iola
Peterson, John — Iola

H

Capt K J Selm — Moorhead, Minn
Capt A A Brown — Alexandria, Minn

I

Capt Aug Gasman — Fargo, D T
Halverson, Heeloye — Stevens Point
Johnson, P A — Stockholm
Ingelburchtson, Andrew — Stockholm
Lind, P N — Stockholm
Long, P N — Stockholm
Nelson, Milkcher — Stockholm
Oleson, Chas — Stockholm

K

Capt Mons Grinager — Worthington, Minn
Lt Ole Peterson — Albert Lea, Minn
Lt Ellend Erickson, — Albert Lea, Minn
Lt Onus Solberg — Mankato, Minn
Lt J E Irgins — Albert Lea, Minn
Handeby, T K, sgt — Northwood, Ia

UNASSIGNED.

Kryer, W — Lima

SIXTEENTH INFANTRY.

A

Berry, Elisha B — Stevens Point
Evans, G E — Phillips
Russell, Ward — Clintonville
Keyes, Ezra A — Marshfield
Whipple, S A — Oconomowoc

B

Lt Sidney H Tullar — East Troy
Bolson, H — Oconomowoc
Cole, H B — Beaver Dam
Fike, Jno D — Oconomowoc
Jamieson, Geo — Millburn, Ill
Johnson, Jno, teamster — Fond du Lac
Quinn, W I — Oconomowoc
Shoenick, Henry — Weyauwega
Snell, James, f — Poyalppi
Waite, Gardner — Beaver Dam

C

Lt Thos M Macauley — Danville
Brown, Jerome — Beaver Dam
Carbet, Jno — Springfield
Carany, Tins — Beaver Dam
Dunn, Jas, f — Munston
Fairbanks, H W — Beaver Dam
Hampton, Jos — Beaver Dam
Manson, Jno — Beaver Dam
Winebrenner, Jos — Beaver Dam

SAM WORTHINGTON,

(Late Co. A, 11 Kansas Cav. Vols.

29 S. SIXTH STREET,

PHILADELPHIA, - PENN.

ANY WORKS

On the Rebellion,

BY MAIL,

AT PUBLISHERS' RATES

Sent to any Address.

AGENTS WANTED

FOR

Subscription Books,

BIBLES for Societies, Families, Pulpit and Private Devotion.

"ANDERSONVILLE"

A history of Prison Life in Richmond, Andersonville, Savannah, Millen, Blackshear and Florence, by McElroy, 654 pp., highly illustrated, large octavo.

MANTNER'S

"Book of Objects,"

2,000 Illustrations;—best book in the world for Children; they are agents, best helpers, send $1.00 for copy and territory.

Gen. J. MADISON DRAKE'S

'Fast and Loose in Dixie,'

JUST OUT.

Important to Book Canvassers.

Will shortly be published, a number of choice, standard, popular, illustrated works, specially designed as subscription books for Agents.

Experienced canvassers should immediately place themselves in direct communication with the undersigned.

Good Agents assigned exclusive territory in the nearest County or Counties, if untaken.

AGENTS' PUBLISHING HOUSE,
Philadelphia, Penn.

FROM WASHINGTON.

Washington, D. C., April 15th, 1886.
L. LUM SMITH, ESQ.

DEAR SIR :—I have received a copy of the AGENTS' HERALD and Official Supplement, and have no hesitation in commending your enterprise to the careful and continual attention, not only of every Postmaster and the clerks of every Post Office, but of the entire generally. The newspaper press can do and is doing much towards putting the ill-informed and unsuspecting on their guard against lottery and other kindred frauds; but your plan if fully carried out will do more than all the newspapers together in exposing this species of rascality. It is to be hoped that all Postmasters especially, will give their earnest aid to the enterprise.

Very Respectfully,
HORATIO KING, Ex-Postmaster General.

The AGENTS' HERALD of Philadelphia has had a new head put on it that is a beauty, it is expressive, artistic and just what was needed, the paper is certainly taking on new strength and is coming to the front strong. Laughable series of illustrated episodes, humorously picturing the lives and adventures of agents now occupy the whole of the last page of each issue of which over 100,000 copies are published. The new paper is highly endorsed by the press, and prominent officials in the employ of the U. S. Government. It contains a list of Frauds, carefully corrected by prominent officials in the Post Office Department at Washington, D. C. There is not a business man or woman in this community who can do without the HERALD, if they wish to keep out of the clutches of city advertising frauds.

For all of this success the energetic proprietor is entitled to the congratulations of all friends of the popular journal. It appears to be the one man created for the business.

Idleness is the curse of the Age and we would send for a copy of the AGENTS' HERALD, it is the sign of Harper's Weekly and annually outs thousands of deserving people in the way of making a good living.

The editor of the AGENTS' HERALD is the proprietor of the new and beautiful Imitation Stained Glass decoration.

99999 Agents Wanted
—BY—
999 ADVERTISERS
IN THE

A large well edited 16 page illustrated semi-monthly Journal. Rare chance for the unemployed to make money. Sample copies 10 cents. The HERALD contains special trade novelties, including 10,000 new and fast-selling Agents' goods, subscription books, etc., with beautiful cuts illustrating the same. Useful hints, Editorials, Gossip, and directory of "Notorious Humbugs," etc.

AGENTS' PUBLISHING CO.,
798 Sansom, St., Philadelphia, Pa.

Portraits, etc., drawn by machinery, with Pen, Pencil, or Crayon. Apparatus, with instructions, sent by mail only 25 cents. Complete outfit Painting, Crayoning and Shading, etc., $1.25.
SMITHOGRAPH MANF'G CO,
Philadelphia, Pa.

Adorn Your Window with the new Patent
STAINED New, elegant, cheap and durable. Is easily applied, temporarily or permanently, to glass in windows of churches
Imitation libraries, vestibule doors, transoms, bath rooms, stairways, &c., with the
GLASS full effect and brilliancy of variously colored stained glass, Curtains and Shades dispensed with. A new, neat, and fascinating occupation for ladies and gentlemen in tastefully beautifying their homes offices, &c. Samples of two styles, each 12x18, mailed with instructions on receipt of 50 cents. Circulars, large illustrated price lists, in colors, etc., free.

PHILA., PA. My windows maintain their beauty and brilliancy, and are as pretty as when decorated over a year ago. M. W. CASE, M. D.
PITTSBURG, PA. We have windows decorated with Imitation Stained Glass at Exposition Building; they look as well as real stained glass, and are much admired. J. P. DIEHL & SON.
FORT SCOTT, KANS. Material for the windows received to-day. I pasted it on the glass, and most confess that I am delighted and more than satisfied with the result. BENJ. HARTLEY,
Rector St. Andrews Church.
JERSEY CITY, N. J. I followed instructions and succeeded in making a very handsome window. Send on men and material sufficient to decorate all the windows in the church and Sunday-school room.
R. HARCOURT, Pastor Trinity M. E. Church
PADUCAH, KY. Finished the windows at Richmond House yesterday—owners are much pleased Captain David, of Uniontown, says he will guarantee me ten thousand feet at thirty cents per foot, large quantities with him and paste the material on the glass.
J. H. K. WILSON, Canvassing Agent
OCEAN GROVE, N. J., RECORD, L. Lum Smith Esq., of Phila., well sustained his reputation as one of the most enterprising men of the day, in finishing up the job he undertook on the Temple in a highly satisfactory manner on time. When determined by Rev. E. H. Stokes, President of the Ocean Grove Camp Meeting Association, to adopt this wonderful Imitation Stained Glass for the windows he had but a few days to execute the work and he ready for dedication. Twenty windows were quickly covered, and nothing could exceed the delight with which all the people hailed the effect. The rest was with it, comparatively, but the improvement is splendid. Nobody could tell the difference, either from the exterior or inside, between the finest stained glass and this excellent substitute.

AGENTS } L. LUM SMITH,
WANTED } 798 Sansom St., Philadelphia, Pa

APPENDIX TO REUNION ROSTER.

D

Bidwell, Loren — Friendship
Mayble, A F, f — Fond du Lac
McMartin, Jno — Menominee

E

Birkholz, Robt — Racine
Edwards, Jos, e — Waupun
Hopper, Wm — Friendship
Hammond, M F — Strongs Prairie
Keyes, I B — Friendship
Spark, R D — Plainfield
Smith, F B — Friendship
Shauks, Jas W — Friendship
Santong, Jas — Fall River

F

Aller, Jno O — Stacyville, Ia
Howe, E s — Waukesha
McMurtreyl Jos, m — Windom, Minn

G

Bradway, Myron, f — Poysippi
Green, De Fertis — Golden Gate, Minn
Halverson, Swinning — E roy
Long, Jackson P — Downsville
McCartie, D B — Frankfort
Macauley, Robt — Menominee
Rand, Jno — Waterville
Richardson, Chas — Waterville
Stratton, David — Downsville
Saddler, G F — Waterville
Stewart, Wm — Frankfort

H

Joerson, Sam'l — Rusk
King, Dwight A — Menominee
Londo, Henry — Sand Creek
Nelson, Guer — Menominee
Wood, C P — Oconomowoc

I

Bisset, A B — Grand Island, Neb
Dow, Thos W — Pacific
Green, Jos B — Janesville

K

Kann, R C — Pt Washington

UNASSIGNED.

Waterman, Chas F — New London

SEVENTEENTH INFANTRY.

A

2nd Lt Jas Brazoll — Beaver Dam
Clough, Chas, sgt — Beaver Dam
Ford, Jno, sgt — Kaukauna
Jenkins, J M — Benton Harbor, Mich
Kimball, W W — Rushford
Luthe, Sam — Beaver Dam
McNally, Myles — Emmetsburg
Nelson, Henry — Beaver Dam
Nelson, Lou — Deaver Dam
Taylor, Geo A — Beaver Dam

B

Breidenback, Jno — Eagle
Harding, Wm — Mcderville, Ia
Schulte, Anton, corp, m — Norwalk

C

Bernard, Jos, f — Barton
Dougherty, Dan'l, c — Eldorado Mills
Rogers, Felix, me
Scnurbrock, Victor — St Francis
Walsh, Lawrence, sgt, f — Eldorado Mills

D

Balch, Wm, f — Atwater
Feldler, Gottfried — Neillsville
Langdon, Dennis — Kenosha
Nice, Nicholas — Sharon
Faddleford, Sam'l T — Menominee
South, Peter — Sharon
Wescott, Geo — Kaukauna

E

Andrews, F E
Backhaus, W M, f — Kewaskum
Gueppe, Jno, me — New Cassel
Johnson, Henry — Plover
Luscomb, Francis — Omro
Rummel, H — Kewaskum
Welch, Anthony, f — Peebles Corners

F

Adams, T B, me — Richland Centre
Fraster, Geo — Beloit

G

Capt Wm Beaupree — Wausau
Lt Augustus Cantin — Sloan Tower
Croakes, Geo — McDillville
Gregware, Jno — Marshfield
Lafond Frank — Two Rivers
Lafond, Godfrey — Two Rivers

H

Blake, M T — Berlin
Birbank, J W — Marinette
Lawrence, T O, musician — Mellina
Ward, Jos — Marinette

I

Lt Jno Kane — Emmetsburg
Shourock, Fred — Caladonia
Woodworth, T S — Waupaca

K

Asphall, Alfred — Kaukauna
Laprary, Sanford, f — Brothertown
Murdock, Leander, f — Brothertown
Nell, Constautin — Stevens Point
Stiger, Jacob — Fremont
Shoepke, Chas — Dear Creek
Squres, W B — Watertown
Waffle, L H, f — Brothertown

UNASSIGNED.

Chaplin F Fasseder
Doern, Philip, f — Brothertown
Giffi, Jno, f — Rosendale
Salt, Fred, f — Brothertown
West, W K — Falls City

EIGHTEENTH INFANTRY.

A

Benedict, Adelman — Cazenovia
Brown, Anthony, f — Empire
Bailey, Dan'l C, l — Fond du Lac
Coffern, —— f — Peebles Corners
LaLonde, E — Volga, D T

B

Barber, Oscar B — Warren Mills
Robbins, Andrew — Oshkosh

C

Cleary, Henry, f — Springville
Metcalf, Jno C — Waterloo

D

Filentreau, Peter — Menasha
Muer, L H, R R man — Milwaukee
Newton, R H — Canton
Sprout, Cummings W — Emmetsburg, Ia

E

Andrews, Jeremiah — Stevens Point
Bacon, F G — Plainfield
Bates, A H — Stevens Point
Craig, Geo N — Plainfield
De Brien, Peter — Little Chute
Hietpas, Albert — Little Chute
Jackson, Benj J — Plover
Johnson, Henry — Wampun
Marshal, Dan — Depere
Olesen, Geo, el — Amherst
Packer, Chas

F

Cinderman, J — Winneconne
Dond, Free man D — Okaman, N no

Lamphier, 1 W — Omro
Mantor, M T — Winneconne
Pierce, A F, f — Fond du Lac
Yates, Jas W — Milwaukee

G

Mitzelee, Peter — Root Creek
Miller, Chas — LaCrosse
Mutkins, Jos — Duena Vista
Tennison, P — Portage

H

Dass, H H — Amherst
Buck, L O — Sherman
Hamilton, F B — Friendship
Hess, Jas — Rushford
Hickerman, Jno G — Fremont
Irish, H A — Plainfield
Merrill, A W — Alma Center
Palen, Jno, f — Poysippi
Vincent, Geo W, f — Poysippi

I

Shonrock, Fred'k — Caledonia

K

Chandler, H H — Lincoln
Danforth, Norman — Amherst
Green, Wm V, f — Sparta
Rice, Truman — Plover
Stempf, Jno — Stevens Point
Treiber, Aug, f — New Cassel

UNASSIGNED.

Alban, S C — Plover
Altenberg, Isaiah — Plover
Bremner, S O — Plover
Dell, A W — Plover
Berry, Jno — Plover
Halliday, C — Plover
Johnson, Henry — Plover
Jackson, Ben — Plover
Shepard, Wm — Plover
Shannon, Leary — Plover
Shannon, Mat — Plover
Schlimmelpfenulg, Jno, f — New Cassel
Smith, J H — Waupaca
Tade, Aug, f — New Cassel
Welton, A J — Plover
Whitaker, S — Plover

NINETEENTH INFANTRY.

REGIMENTAL ROSTER.

Chap A C Barry — Lodi

A

Lt A P Ellinwood — Reedsburg
Lt L H Cobson — Reedsburg
Lt Wm Sweetland — Reedsburg
Eser, Peter — Reedsburg
Fastnot, J C — Reedsburg
Fastnot, J H — Valley Junction
Groff, Ghes — Reedsburg
Pietzsch, W O — Reedsburg
Sheldon, C F — Reedsburg

B

Lt W W Gordon — LaCrosse
Wilson, H — Lima

C

Capt Jno A Chandler — St Paul, Minn
Capt Chas Caso — Minneapolis
Capt H B Nichols — Norfolk, Va
Lt A H Russell — Portage
Heneggen, Wm — St Marys
Levi, Peter — Racine
Woodliff, J, f — Melvina

D

Lt Edw O Emerson — Titusville, Pa
Lt Adam Christie — Albert Lea, Minn
Robinson, Thos — Hartford
Seward, Jos — Friendship

E

Capt Chas D Willard — Washington, D C

APPENDIX TO REUNION ROSTER.

Capt A P Ellinwood — Reedsburg
Allen, Cyrus — Racine
Chaffee, Geo W — Kingston
Webber, C L, m — Walnut Grove, Minn
Wood, Jos A, corp — Masonville

F

Capt Martin Scherff — Illinois
Lt Jos Standcuraus — Oshkosh
Lt Theodore Zeager — Winneconne
Darrow, Franz — Orihula
Hartman, F W
Leicher, J — Winneconne
Newman, Fred — Winchester
Remert, Fred — Winchester
Shedler, Christian — Winchester
Spegelburg, Fred — Winchester

G

Capt Otto Puhlman — Plymouth
Bulis, E C — Scranton
Blakesley, Chas L, sgt, f — Fond du Lac
Minaghan, M — Brothertown
Squires, Nelson D — Friendship

H

Capt Albert Graut — Washington, D C
Lt Cromwell Laithe — Waupun
Bricknell, H
Fuller, Homer P — Middleville, Minn
Seeley, David — Vinland

I

Capt Amos O Rowley — Minn
Lt C A Holley — Missouri

K

Capt Wm W Bates — Chicago, Ill
Capt Harmon Wentworth — Missouri
Lt Albert Harthman — River Falls
Gutman, Chas — Racine
Pierce, Wm, sgt, m — Hiawatha, Kan
Rodgers, A B — Friendship

UNASSIGNED.

Thornton, J — Menasha
Barry, A C, chap — Ludi
Howard, H H, B — Eau Claire
Springelburg, Wm, 1st lt — Orihula
Heek, Henry — Racine
Hoy, A H, ph — Racine
Latch, A G — Peshtigo

TWENTIETH INFANTRY.

A

Brownlee, Williamson — Stockholm

B

Rundle, J P — Milwaukee
Phetteplace, Delos — Spring Green
Van Warmer, E — Lynnville
Williams, Jas — Oconomowoc

C

Eiler, Adam — Racine
Thurber, L B, 2nd corp — Muscoda
Taylor, B W — Stevens Point
Koust, Louis — Racine

D

Gasenhauser, Jno G — W U Junction
Brad, Chas G — Geneva Lake

E

Capt Fred Kusel — Watertown
Conroe, Geo C — Racine
Bauman, G — Watertown
Eichel, Wm — Richmond
Miller, Henry — Watertown
Roth, F Chas — Watertown
Volkman, H L — Watertown
Wahl, Jno — Mitchell, Ia
Wegner, Chas — Watertown
Wenzel, Aug — Watertown

F

Foal, C H — Friendship
Krause, J H — Oconomowoc

G

Beach, A W
Caruelle, Ephraim A, corp, e — Oswego, N Y
Dailey, M — Milwaukee
Dean, Henry, l — West Bend
Foley, D — Milwaukee
Perkins, S R — Oconomowoc
Parkyn, Jno L, f — Vaughn, Neb
Penrely, Jas — Oconomowoc
Strong, S — Milwaukee
Young, Byron — Hebron, Neb
Zindson, H H — Iola

H

Fuller, Homer P — Middleville, Mich
Hyde, Lewis, f — West Roseudale
Martel, Prosper, f — Ripon
Plantz, Wm — Wausau
Perkins, E R, I — West Rosendale
Rawson, I C — Plainfield
Strong, H C — Baraboo
Turner, S W — Omro

I

Michael, Aaron — Durand
Quick, Wm F, sgt, f — Lamartine
Scott, W I — Racine
Wollitz, Chas, f — Ripon

K

Judd, Wm — Gibraltar
Southam, Wm — Dorchester
Wurwick, Geo — Two Rivers

UNASSIGNED.

Decanter, Amon, confectioner — Sturgeon Bay
Scott, Wm — Racine

TWENTY-FIRST INFANTRY.

REGIMENTAL ROSTER.

Col H C Hobart — Milwaukee
Lt Col M H Fitch — Pueblo, Col
Adj Jas H Jenkins — Oshkosh
Q M B J Van Valkenburg — Green Bay
Q M D H Fernandez — Oshkosh
Surg Jas T Reeve — Appleton
A Surg S S Tuller — Detroit, Mich
A Surg B C Britt — Green Bay
Chap O P Clinton — Menasha

A

Capt Alex White — Waupun
Lt K M Adams — Fond du Lac
Lt W H Cook — Stockbridge
Lt Sam'l Hotaling — Fond du Lac
Benedict, A — Neillsville
Demarra, Anthony, me — Fond du Lac
Dailey, J M — Neillsville
Halbhan, Jerry, l — Fond du Lac
Lichter, Peter, f — Brothertown

B

Capt Jas E Stuart, P O Dept — Washington
Lt Alex Peterson — Belle Plaine
Brown, Oscar A — Menasha
Benedict, M — Buttes des Mortes
Benedict, R P — Buttes des Mortes
Estey, Amos — Ash Creek, Minn
Grignon, N — Winneconne
Hoffman, H — Winneconne
Miller, C H — Waukau
Miller, L J — Elo
Otto, Rudolph — Fremont
Pollier, C — Buttes des Mortes
Scott, N H — S'evensville
Scott, Colt — Buttes des Mortes
Service, Dave — Winneconne
Spindler, Henry — Lind

C

Capt A S Godfrey — Denver, Col
Downing, Elijah — Oshkosh
Cowling, Jno, fireman — Oshkosh
Davis, E D — Oshkosh

Kinesley, B F
Morgan, Jno W

D

Capt Jno H Otto
Lt F W Borcherdt
Gurnee, D A
Stowe, F M

E

Capt Fernand Ostenfeldt
Lt Chas F Weston
Lt Aug Hanson
Beach, Emery
Friedler, Jno A, f
Howe, Geo W
Sampson, J J, f
Schooner, C W, f
Shelly, H J, f

F

Lt Martin L Clark
Lt Ambrose Delaware
Alya, J
Bills, Munroe
Carley
Carter, Jno
Dick, E M, me
Estabrook, C W, f
Hatch, Geo H, sgt
Hammond, Jno
McCain, Wm, corp, f
O'Reilley, Jas, l
Peterick, Aug
Potter, N W
Roberts, T D

G

Constance, C E
Damon, B F
Goodman, Amnison
Harris, J C
Horton, R A
Howlett, Geo
Lollin, Geo
Oleson, Ole R
Randall, F D
Sherwin, S R
Staufield, Jas
Stow, A K
Smith, J D

H

Brown, W K, me
Black, Jno B
Miner, J T

I

Capt A B Smith
Augustine, C F
Erb, J B
Ellight, D
Gates, Luke
Green, Chas C
Hercher, F
Marshall, Wm G
Morey, J H
Pierce, J G
Pierce, M L
Pierce, G L
Ryan, D J
Rheiner, J
Shipley, Elihu
Seely, Wm
Tritt, Wm

K

Bacon, H L
Boynton, Jno W
Button, C L
Hughes, H
Landon, Fred'k, f
Mason, Wesley
Noble, W H
Noble, Jas

Springfield
Embarrass

Appleton
Manitowoc
Lodi, Cal
Winneconne

Manitowoc
Webster City, Ia
Charleston
Dundas
Hayton
N Minneapolis, Minn
Brothertown
Brothertown
Brothertown

Neenah
Chicago, Ill
Winneconne
Omro
Rushford
Stevens Point
Brothertown
Fond du Lac
Omro
Omro
Lamartine
Brandon
Harrisville
Menasha
Nekim

Waupaca
Waupaca
Winchester
Wampaca
Waupaca
Waupaca
Lind
Waupaca
Waupaca
Waupaca
Waupaca
Waupaca
Hampton, Ia

Brandon
Benton Harbor, Mich
Brothertown

Green Bay
Waukesha
Winneconne
Menasha
Weyauwega
Kaukauna
Menasha
Brandon
Winneconne
Omro
Omro
Omro
Menasha
Menasha
Princeton
Durand
Omro

Kenosha
Amherst
Fond du Lac
Waupaca
Jacksonport
Cato
Reedsville
Reedsville

APPENDIX TO REUNION ROSTER.   289

UNASSIGNED.
Barnes, Henry L. pb — Ripon
Connon, A B — Waupaca
Chamberlain, L M — Lyons, Kan
Champton, Robt — Buttes des Mortes
Hubbard, W C — Oshkosh
Miner, T T, f — Brothertown

TWENTY-SECOND INFANTRY.

A
Adams, A H, 1st sgt — Racine
Burst, Leonard A. f — Independence, Ia
Bones, J R — Racine
Cadwell, Henry — Grand Rapids, Mich
Emerson, Wm 1, r r man — Racine
Ferdingburg, Larette — Union Grove
Morey, Harrison, f — Union Grove
Nichols, Geo C — Racine
Powels, Wm G — Union Grove
Rowbottom Abraham — Union Grove
Scott, Edwin B, c — Chesterfield, Ill
Taber, J Q — Union Grove

B
Edwards, Wm — Portage
Herring Benjamin, f — Maple Landing, Ia
Miller, S L — Reedsburg
Olmstead, C S — Browns Grove, Kan

C
Klaber, Christ — Winneconne
Redford, Robt — Oshkosh
Thompson, Wm — New York City

D
Ayers, B F — Sharon
Cutler, R H — Bartlett, Ill
Wheeler, Geo — Sharon

E
Osborn, Farin E — Milton
Peifer, J P — Waukesha

F
Coombs, Gilmore — Rochester
Foot, Jacob R — Waterford
Forbes, Sam'l — Racine
Hoffer, Jno — Waterford
Munzer, Aug — Racine
Pugh, R F — Racine
Shenkenberger, Jacob — Racine
Utley, Wm L — Racine
Williams, R W — Racine

G
Johnson, Jno — Otisville
Rottmann, Wm — Milwaukee

H
Baislee, Oscar — Waterford
Felton, M B — Delta, N Y
Herron, Peter — Burlington, Mich
Jones, Jas — Racine
Lythe, Andrew — Racine
Morris, Geo S — Carpenterville, Ill
Mahappy, A — Waterford
Near, Jacob H — Racine
Peterson, A — Waterford
Ryehl, Theo — Racine
Riel, H — Burlington, Mich
Schulzie, Chas — Racine
Underhill, Frank — Racine
Wells, F E — Burlington

I
House, A D — Jefferson, Ia
Parkhurst, E B — Durand
Parkhurst, L D — Durand

K
Bones, Thos A — W U Junction
Barrows, Chas — W U Junction
Carr, Ed — Salem, Neb
Carlin, Pat — W U Junction
Lytle, Henry — W U Junction

Nobles, Geo — W U Junction
Place, Luther — W U Junction
Reeds, Chas — W U Junction
Smith, Morris — W U Junction
Sears, G W — Salem, Neb
Treadwell, J G — W U Junction
Touse, Wm — W U Junction
Wilson, J G — Stevens Point

UNASSIGNED
Fowler, L P — Brothertown
Mead, Frank — Racine
Pulfer, Myron — Menasha
Slocum, Jos — W U Junction

TWENTY-THIRD INFANTRY.

A
Bennett, Jas, clk — Madison
Gray, H H — Baraboo

C
Blood, F A — Stevens Point
Culbert, D — Portage
Flint, R J — Menominee
Luther, H G — Rudd, Ia
Mountford, Geo — Portage
Northrup, Theo — Fayette Mills
Wilson, J E — LaCrosse

D
Seamonson, Wm — Stoughton
Seidmore, David P — Stevens Point

E
Lt Jno A Bull — Washington, Kan
Bullard, W W — Portage
Cramer, Jos — Grafton
Hine, O L — Omro
Learnerd, Porter D — Louisville, Col

F
Brill, Wm E — Floyd, Ia
Clark, Wm E — Merrimac
Moore, Chas — Baraboo
Snell, H P — Baraboo

G
Lt Wm H Dunham, pa — Ripon
Beaver, Henry — Fredericksburg, Ia
Swanger, Robt — Fredericksburg, Ia
Thomas, Allen — Fredericksburg, Ia
Wagoner, Jno — Fredericksburg, Ia

H
Church, Jos, f — Okee
Cleveland, Simon — Lodi
Scott, Jno R, f — Okee
Waffle, Byron S — Lodi

I
Curtis, C W — Neillsville
Keller, W J — Clay Centre, Neb

K
Render, Chas — Baraboo
Nettekoven, Peter, f — Darby
Stillwell, G W — Hannibal, Mo

UNASSIGNED.
Francher, Jacob B — Amherst

TWENTY-FOURTH INFANTRY.

A
Barron, W C S — Richland Center
Hubbard, S D — Mondovi
Jentsch, Chr — Waukesha
Mallory, J L, agt of express Co — Sheboygan

B
Jones, A J — Stewart, Minn

C
Gutheil, Bernhard — Kiel
Schmidt, Franz

D
Bloomfield, W R — Racine
Fellows, Victor, f — Vandyne

Gardner, J B — Stevens Point
Garvin, Jno E, prop Hunter's Hotel — Fond du Lac
Wilson, Jas J, town clk — Lakeville, Ill

E
Midinger, Peter — Oneida

F
Howard, Henry — LaCrosse
Peck, Wm — Evanston, Ill

G
Gngler, Godfrey — Bloomingdale
Lynch, R B — Washington

H
Carroll, A M — Milwaukee
Dalley, M — Oconomowoc
Johnson, Jno
Klopp, Jno B, me — Milwaukee
Rose, F W — Mancelona, Mich

K
Day, E T B — North East Md
Gabrielson, Otto D — Milwaukee
Guenther, Gottfried — Oakwood
Rodenbeck, Henry — Caledonia
Smith, Stephen Jr, bk — Milwaukee
Selond, Henry — W U Junction

UNASSIGNED.
Chamberlain, E K, sgt maj — Cleveland, O
Williams, Sanford J — Milwaukee
Nelson, Jno

TWENTY-FIFTH INFANTRY
REGIMENTAL ROSTER.

Col M Montgomery — Lincoln, Neb
Adj G G Symes — Montana
Adj Jno Fitzgerald — Ironton
Q M David C Hope — Sparta
A Surg C C Olmstead — Milwaukee
A Surg Dan'l L Downs — Richland Centre
A Surg Chas A Dalgairns — Mineral Point

A
Capt Cyrus M Butt — Viroqua
Capt Jno R Casson — Viroqua
Lt Warren G Davis — Viroqua
Gifford, D — Canton
Humphry, Henry, f — Sparta
Hurtley, Tom — Lima

B
Lt Edw E Houstain — Muscoda
Lt Edw B Wagoner — Whitehall
Logue, Scott — Muscoda

C
Capt H D Farguhgarson — Boscobel
Lt Joel A Barber — Lancaster

D
Lt Chas S Farnham — Sparta
Lt A J High — Monroe
Braman, R A, f — Tunnel City
Fettygrove, Walter — New Era, Neb
Wilcox, L, sgt, me — Sparta

E
Lt Jno W Smelker — Plattville
Lt Jas McCoy — Plattville
Lt B F Saltzman — Grovetown
Massey, Jas H — Washburn

F
Capt Geo G Symes — Montana
Lt Parker C Dunn — LaCrosse
Mott, Oscar — Benton Harbor, Mich
Janes, O A — Knapp
Travis, Jas — LaCrosse

G
Capt V W Darwin — Durand
Capt H J Whitteton — Harourel, Ill
Capt B B Gurley — Durand
Lt Jno W McKay — Mondovi
Delano, Columbus — Durand
Priddie, M D — Durand

⇥COME AND SEE.⇤

THE BEST PLACE IN MILWAUKEE TO BUY

CHOICE AND FRESH GROCERIES,

WARRANTED TO GIVE SATISFACTION, IS AT

C. J. RUSSELL'S,

117 WISCONSIN STREET, - MILWAUKEE.

A NEW, FRESH AND CAREFULLY SELECTED STOCK OF

Java, Mocha, Rio, Mancabo and Other Coffees,

GREEN, ROASTED OR GROUND.

⇥CHOICE STOCK OF⇤

Young Hyson, Old Hyson, Gunpowder, Oolong, Black Japan,

English Breakfast Teas, Pure Spices and Pure Sugars at Lowest Market Prices.

Raisins, Currants, Prunes and all Kinds of Dried Fruit.

All kinds of NUTS. GREAT Varieties of Plain, Sweet and Mixed Biscuits, Crackers and Wafers, FRUITS and VEGETABLES in Glass and Cans. Full Stock of Imported Goods, FRENCH, ENGLISH and GERMAN in Glass and Cans.

The Finest Store, Largest Stock and the Lowest Prices.

All orders from the COUNTRY filled and delivered at the Depot with Despatch and without any extra Charge.

REMEMBER TO CALL AND SEE US

⇥BEARING IN MIND THAT IT IS NO TROUBLE⇤

To SHOW GOODS and always PLEASED to give you Prices.

Remember the Place and Number,

APPENDIX TO REUNION ROSTER.

Willard, O W — Musood
Williard, O W — Moudovi

H

Capt Liba S Swan — Champion, Ill

I

Capt D N Smalley — Georgetown

K

Capt Chas A Hunt — Me'vina
Lt Jno R Cannon — Neillsville
Billington, A, I — Fond du Lac
Clapp, E O — Friendship
Clough, E B — Leeds Centre
Garthwait, G W — Friendship

UNASSIGNED.

Harris, Milo — Friendship
Jones, Edmund L — Plainville
Keesling, Fred
Perkins, Lew S — Friendship
Wallrath, Hamilton — Friendship

TWENTY-SIXTH INFANTRY.

B

Lt Adolph Hensel — Milwaukee
Yager, Chas — Oconomowoc
Yager, Wm — Oconomowoc

Hess, Lewis — Olivet
Sparr, Andrew — Racine

E

Zipp, Philip, f — Fond du Lac

F

Ludwig, Albert — Chilton

G

Blanker, Henry — Sherwood
Delmback, Peter, l — Nasewanpee
Dumas, Jno, f — Eden
Shattuck, Jas H — Omro

H

Lanerman, Jos — Muscoda

I

Baur, Chas — Oshkosh
Blanchard, Lee, l — Rosendale
Heilmann, Adam — Nasewanpee
Resak, Frank — Rochester
Stark, Jno — Lake City, Minn

K

Baumgarten, Henry — Milwaukee
Cleaver, Jno L, bk — Milwaukee
Cape, Jno — W U Junction
Kuchenmeister, F A — Milwaukee
Schneller, Peter — Black Hawk

UNASSIGNED

Krieger, Aug, f — Kiel

TWENTY-SEVENTH INFANTRY.

REGIMENTAL ROSTER.

Lt Col Jno J Brown — Sheboygan
Maj C H Cunningham — Lunenberg, Mass
Adj Chas Meyer — Milwaukee
Adj D L M ore — Hot Springs, Ark
Q M Wm N Shafter — Olena, Cal
Q M Jas F Kent — Sheboygan
Surg Robt Mitchell — Merrits Landing
A Surg Geo Hutchinson — Inrand
A Surg Geo Saltzmann — Whitewater
Chap Wm P Stowe — Milwaukee

A

Capt J J Borland — Chicago, Ill
Lt J C Saltzmann — Whitewater
Lt Edw Neil — Evanston, Ill
Boutin, Duffy, fisherman — Bayfield
Boutin, Sol D, fisherman — Bayfield
Conger, Lewis — Marshfield
Conrad, Martin — Milwaukee
Goynon, Jno S, corp, me — Bayfield

B

McNally, Jno

Capt Julius Schlaich
Lt Josiah Platt
Lt R H Tripp
Breitung, Wm
Helm, Aug
Koebel, Jacob

C

Capt Fred'k Schnellen
Capt Conrad F Smith
Lt C E W Struve
Lt Jno Gehring
Lt Julius Badenstab
Lt Philip C Enders
Baker, Fr'd
Decker, Henry
Friskly, Jno

Lt Peter Mulholland
Lt Niclulas Hanson
Hempke, Henry
Linden, Jus
Makee, Wm H, m
Oexly, Fred

Lt Jno A S Verdice
Lt Irwing V Bliss, mf
Linden, Jno
Lawrence, Horace A

F

Capt Josiah Platt
Lt Peter Daane, Jr
Smith, Geo W, corp, f
McGee, Edw, corp, f

G

Capt Wm Wigham
Capt Jas Gnun
Lt Amanzer Strong
Lt Jno C Brooker
Kramer, Jno
Schravle, Jno

H

Lt A L Land
Fraaser, S
Falk, O M, R, m

I

Platt, Stephen G
Howard, Aug
Loscombe, Chas

K

Lt M A McGuire
Oleson, Andras
Ortmayer, A
Schnittel, Jacob, fisherman
Wintwen, J P, county clk
Weber, Matthias

TWENTY-EIGHTH INFANTRY.

REGIMENTAL ROSTER.

Col Jas M Lewis
Col F B Gray
Lt Col Chas Whittaker
Maj Jno A Williams
Adj A S Kendrick
Adj J B Magill
Q M eo W Wylie
A Surg D M Miller
A Surg Chas W Frisbie

A

Capt Jno Williams
Capt Wm E Coates
Lt R F Hupper, m
Lt Elbam A Gage
Lt Lauren Barker
Butkin, Herman

Sandy Bay

Plymouth
Hingham
Hingham
Plymouth
Plymouth
Plymouth

Sheboygan
Trenton, Tenn
Madison
Young America
Howard's Grove
Brillion
Greenwood
Greenwood
Eagle River, Mich

Manitowoc
Edwards
Two Rivers
Menominee, Mich
Laporte, Ia
Edwards

Grand Rapids, Mich
Milwaukee
Charles City, Ia
Neillsville

Hingham
Oostburgh
Newlane
Lamartine

Iowa
Iowa
Iowa
Racine
Avoca
Highland

Cambridge
Jefferson
Stoughton

Colby
Neillsville
W U Junction

South America
Eaton
Stevens Point
Bayfield
Baraboo
Milwaukee

Oconomowoc
Chicago, Ill
Iowa
Pine Bluff, Ark
St Louis, Mo
Illinois
Elkhorn
Oconomowoc
Milwaukee

Pine Bluff, Ark
Milwaukee
Eatontown, N J
Geneva, Ohio
Brookfield Junction
Waukesha

Bentz, Geo — Oconomowoc
Bierke, Christian — Oconomowoc
Howard, Hiram — Menominee Falls
Hutchins, Jno A — Oconomowoc
Holmes, Geo W — Fremont
Kuntz, Louis — Oconomowoc
Price, David — Baldwin
Weaver, Alfred S — Milwaukee
Weaver, Fred — Milwaukee

D

Lt C K Davis — St Paul Minn
Lt F A Bennett, m — Janesville
Bordette, Peter — Tiffany
Devereaux, Thos — Eagle
Haverstine, Gottfried — Waukesha

C

Capt Thos N Stevens — Greenville, Mich
Lt Fred'k B Brown, Jr — Storm Lake, Ia
Brown, Henry — Oconomowoc
Cobb, C C, m — York, Neb
Glann, Albert — Oconomowoc
Hinze, Jno — Oconomowoc
Kinne, E G, f — Tomah
Pope, Wm — Oconomowoc

D

Capt Edw S Redington — Whitewater
Lt H H Watts — Whitewater
Hayes, A W — Doyceville
Hendrickson, C A, f — Harvard, Neb
Rusch, Henry — Milwaukee
Weiss, Jos — Depere

E

Capt J B Kenyon — Iowa
Brosdale, Mark — Oakdale
Cullier, C J — Jefferson
Dainton, Isaac — Oconomowoc
Haight, H P — Racine
Knowlton, F — Jefferson
Lange, L — Clifton
Phoenix, Jn. w — Emmetsburg, Ia

F

Lt H F Lyke — Oconomowoc
Lt J S Worthman — Baraboo
Devereaux, Nic — Eagle
Goodwin, G P — Hartland
Kipp, W D — New Hampton, Ia
Holt, Thos — Oconomowoc
Raymond, Horace, me — New Cassel
Stanton, Jas — Rushford
Williams, David — Waukesha
Wickman, Carl — Oconomowoc

G

Capt W V Tichnor — Cresco, Ia
Lt David Turner — Waukesha
Lt Seymour Gilbert — Minn
Lt Andrew McKee — Oconomowoc
Blum, Chas F, f — Pewaukee
Clark, Wm H — Waukesha
Goetzer, Jacob H, m — South Germantown
Hinkley, Edw P — Eagle
Jacobs, Christoff — Marshfield
McKee, Andrew — Oconomowoc
Smith, Nelson J — Waukesha
Schneider, Phillipp, sgt — South Germantown
Thomas, Edw — Cresco, Ia
Watson, J Q — Waukesha

H

Capt Jas Murray — Nebraska
Lt Thos Chandler — Oconomowoc
Lt J L O'Brien — Chicago
Lt Wallace Goff — Menominee
Lt J A Hurtgen — Duphneville
Downs, Jno — Waukesha
Stark, Aug — Waukesha

Capt Lyndsey J Smith — East Troy
Lt A T Seymour — Pine Bluff, Ark

ESTABLISHED 1860.
F. F. Riedel Manufacturing Company.

F. F. RIEDEL, President.   JOHN C. KEEFE, Sec'y & Treas.

STEAM MECHANICAL
CRACKER AND CANDY
MANUFACTURERS,

ALL KINDS OF CAKES AND CRACKERS.

Choice Confections of Every Description

ALL ORDERS BY MAIL RECEIVE PROMPT ATTENTION.

497, 499 and 501 BROADWAY,   -   MILWAUKEE, WISCONSIN.

GIANT FARM AND WAREHOUSE FANS,
Made by A. P. DICKEY, Racine, Wis.

Now having many late improvements, they are fully equal to every demand; cleaning all kinds of Grain, Peas, Beans, Castor Beans, Corn and Small Seed. They grade wheat perfectly by once handling. Separate Oats from Wheat, Barley and Rye. They have very perfect arrangements for cleaning Timothy, Clover, Flax Seed, Orchard Grass, and all other Small Seeds. They chaff perfectly, and combine every qualification required to do the best work in the shortest time.

Cut of Warehouse Mill No. 2, Capacity 200 to 300 Bushels per Hour. Hand and Power Machine.

Warehouse, as well as Farm Mills, are largely constructed, both kinds requiring nine sizes to accommodate the demand, and giving a capacity of from 50 to 80 bushels per hour, according to size of Mill. They are shipped boxed for Ocean transportation, and "set up" or "knocked down" for forwarding inland, as requested; and in all cases put free on board cars or steamer. Orders filled same day as received. Mills shipped "knock down" go for half the freight charged as when forwarded "Set up." Oleographs and circulars supplied on application. Prices will be quoted to v and on liberal terms. Correspondence solicited.

APPENDIX TO REUNION ROSTER. 293

Lt S A Hartwell — Colorado
Spoor, Chas — Lyons

K

Capt L J Billings — Green Bay
Bratsch, Ferdinand, f — Mountville, Minn
Gaylord, Jno D C — Oconomowoc
Hanson, A — Otter Creek

UNASSIGNED.

Sutherland, Frank — Plover

TWENTY-NINTH INFANTRY.

A

Surg J L Potter — Menasha
Green, L C — Whitewater
Halverson, Osmau — Stoughton
Nelson, Harvey — New Haven
Ray, O L — Jefferson
Weeks, E M — Baldwin

B

Bartlett, J N — Watertown
Brouson, R P — Marshfield
Gergenheimer, Michael — Watertown
Hill, Hector, f — Lamartine
Hilker, Fred — Jefferson
Jones, Alex — Racine
Martin, Thos — Jefferson
Tarrington, L H — LaCrosse
Robinson, Jno — Jefferson
Urtubees, Jno — Watertown

C

Capt W F Parsons — Kalamazoo, Mich
Alcox, Jerry, f — Harrison
Boson, Jno, f — Harrison
Bushhell, H, me — Harrison
Carey, Iran, f — Harrison
Dircheg, Chas, f — Harrison
Loop, David W — Waukau
Naven, T, l — Harrison
Quick, Jacob, l — Harrison
Ward, Charley, me — Harrison

D

Bemis, A J — Milford
Culver, H J — Kenosha
Miller, Christian — Aztalan
Fillible, W — Jefferson
Gorrow, Chas — White Hall
Peterson, Andrew — Alderby
Wilson, J J — Jefferson

E

Baldwin, Amos — Nordland, D T
Battles, J, me — Fairwater
Davis, Jas, f — Brandon
Dunning, G G, me — Brandon
Dibble, Chas A, x — Chicago, Ill

F

Inman, M M, f — Dry Lake, Ia
Kesu, Chas, corp — Lake Mills
Keso, L — Jefferson
Lang, A — Jefferson
Pirch, Jno — Jefferson
Stroetz, J N — Menasha
Smidif, Mishal — Jefferson
Smidif, Jno — Jefferson
Smith, J G — Jefferson
Veph, W P — Jefferson

G

Temberg, Andrew — Kingston
Rittenbush, J, p m — Neillsville
Smith, Jno — Spring Grove

H

Lt Wm Wilson — Watertown
Ferris, W H — Waupun
Hart, E — Jefferson
Hewitt, Clark, sgt, nursery — Waupun
Niverson, M, f — Waupun

I

Andrus, Mufton — Oconomowoc

Brewster, H C, sgt, h — Waupun
Calkins, Wm H — Tomah
Kero, G L — Neosho

K

Lt R Gray — Sparta
2nd Lt W V Perry — Beaver Dam
Bushuell, J V — Pond du Lac
Dinch, Julius, f — Waupun
Hambright, W D — Beaver Dam
James, R S, sgt, engineer — Harrison
Kendall, C M, com trav — Milwaukee
Page, Warren, f — Waupun

UNASSIGNED.

Bohn, H F — Falls City

THIRTIETH INFANTRY.

D

Bampton, R J — Rush River
Martell, Ambrose — Somerset
Nelson, Wm — Somerset
Thoen, H G — Rush River

E

Jones, Jno T, 1st lt, clk of court — Dodgeville
Truman, Wm A — Delton

F

Ford, J C — Ouro
Knight, Miletus, county clk — Durand

G

Capt J E Tilton, me — Hancock
Chamberlain, A A — Plainfield
Holmes, H — Plainfield
Parkins, J, drummer — Friendship

H

Allen, A — Plainfield
Baxter, Jas A — Waupaca
Brewster, L M, hunter — Dorchester
Daniels, A A, f — Auroraville
Eldred, Jerome B — Berlin
Matthews, J J — Winneconne
Rice, Warren — Weyauwega

I

Skinner, L — Menominee

K

Coleman, Ed H, city clk — Chippewa
Eastwood, Reuben — Sharon

UNASSIGNED.

Battram, Jas — Durand
Baker, E O, surgeon — Menominee
Bessy, Philip — Boyceville
Jamison, M M, ph — Muscoda

THIRTY-FIRST INFANTRY.

A

Canfield, D — Concordia, Kan

C

Capt I D Burdick — Janesville
Davis, C D — Oshkosh

D

Finegan, Patrick — Somerset
Putnam, David — Ouro
Rogers, Samuel C — Dowpsville

E

Matley, Josiah — Darlington

F

Brownell, B D, f — Loyd
Butty, J L — Richmond

G

Beaumont, Geo — Rochester
Dunnsen, Jno — Fountain City
Dickson, Wm — Argyle
Rowe, Luther T — Menominee

H

Bayette, J W — Badger Hill, Ia

I

Blockside, Jno J — Racine

Dent, Wm F — Canton, D T
Foote, Wm — Frankfort, Minn
Horner, Joel — Menominee
Morely, Richard — Racine
Schilling, Chas — Racine

K

Frederick, Theo — Kenosha

UNASSIGNED.

Noble, O W — Wakefield, Mass

THIRTY-SECOND INFANTRY.

A

Amandon, D P, f — Waupun
Beardsley, Leroy, f — Waupun
Brooks, Jas — Hortonville
Carey, Frank — Blooming Prairie
Chandler, Wm, l — Waupun
Euton, Jas K, f — Brandon
Foote, Washington — Alpaso
Foote, Jno — Waupun
Giebink, Jno, f — Waupun
Graues, David, corp, me — Waupun
Hart, Daniel — Dodge Center, Minn
Hilbert, J, f — Waupun
Lindsley, Geo, sgt, f — Waupun
Mosher, Robt, corp, f — Waupun
Morrison A D — Rochester, Minn
Phelps, Wm — Oronoco, Minn
Plumbley, Henry — Alpaso
Plumbley, Horace — Waupun
Sandner, Christoph — Milwaukee
Simond, O M — Plover
Sherer, Jas — Hebron, Neb
Van Houten, Henry, l — Waupun
Wood, L H, corp, pa — Fond du Lac

B

Connor, Jas, f — Brandon
Field, Alden, f — Brandon
Gee, Geo M, f — Brandon
Gee, Francis M, ord sgt — Brandon
Marsh, Canfield, f — Rosendale
Merry, E N — Lamartine
Messenger, F O — New London
O'Neil, Jas, f — Rosendale
Williams, Henry l — Cambria
Wood, Alanson, h — Ripon

C

Barrett, E S — Sharon
Briggs, Ed F — Markesan
Chapman, Jas — Cambria
Downs, Jno — Elo
Waldroo, Geo — Rochester, Minn

D

Brightman, Damon — Winchester
Buck, A C — Oshkosh
Dahlstrom, Jno — Winchester
O'Reilley, Alex — Winneconne
Potter, Henry — Brothertown
Putnum, David — Ouro
Shufelt, O H — Ouro

E

Bass, T W — Amherst
Bennett, Ben J — Buena Vista
Fancher, J B — Amherst
Fairbanks, J W — Waupun
Fargo, Matt, l — Fond du Lac
Morrison, Rolla — Amherst
Moss, Elisha — Amherst
Newby, Jno — Buena Vista
Nelson, Gardner — Amherst Junction
Peltiler, S — Amherst
Rice, Lemuel C — Plover
Schafer, Samuel — Barton
Shannon, Leroy — Plover
Washburn, R — Plover
Wilson, Rober — Wilson
White, Jonas, sgt — Plover

HEALTH IS ESSENTIAL TO HAPPINESS.

THE NEW YORK
MEDICAL AND SURGICAL INSTITUTE
147 FIFTEENTH STREET, N. Y. CITY.

Is a strictly private institution designed expressly for the treatment and cure of all CHRONIC and ACUTE DISEASES by the most approved methods known to modern s ience.

There are employed at this Institute FOUR PHYSICIANS, each of whom is a specialist and fully understands the diseases which he treats in all their several complications; hence patients coming under their care may rely on having the very best treatment that can be had in this city, and the benefit of the experience of all the physicians in extremely bad cases without extra charge.

We have, therefore, settled down upon the firm ground of experience, where *Every Step is Sure*; and for over a quarter of a century we have been engaged in the treatment of

Catarrh, Consumption, Asthma, Dyspepsia, Diseases of the Liver, Heart, Kidneys, Bladder, Nervous System, Etc., and Chronic Diseases Generally,

And all forms of disease whether requiring medical, surgical or mechanical treatment, some of the most obstinate and complicated cases, such as many other physicians have despaired of helping, have been fully and permanently cured at this Institute. We have made a searching investigation into the origin and cause of the various types of *NERVOUS DISEASES* that afflict mankind, and which arise from an exhausted state of the great nerve centres; and the special and individual influences the various nerve forces exert over every portion of the animal economy. Under this head we find Paralysis, Epilepsy, Brain Troubles, Nervous Debility, Loss of the Procreative Powers, with Organic Weakness, Dyspepsia and other functional disturbances, and we have determined that many obscure nervous diseases, and especially that nervous prostration and exhaustion which, in many cases, originates from imprudent habits in early life, can be speedily and permanently cured by remedies that remove the morbid influence and have specific control over the entire nervous system.

Stricture, Rupture, Bright's Disease of the Kidneys, Prolapsus Uteri, Spinal Disorders and Deformities, all have our attention and are speedily relieved.

We especially invite any who are suffering from any serious disease to send us a statement and we will advise them on the subject *free of charge* as treatment in most cases can be attended to by correspondence. Address

M. & S. INSTITUTE, 147 E. 15th STREET, NEW YORK.

APPENDIX TO REUNION ROSTER.

F

- Ash, Richard, f — Sevastopol
- Barrington, Jacob J, m — Egg Harbor
- Berg, Fred, f — Sturgeon Bay
- Claflin, Wm, f and fisherman — Gardiner
- Coyne, Luke, f — Sevastopol
- Christjohn, David — Seymour
- Gullickson, O'e, f — Clay Banks
- Knudson, Henry, f — Sturgeon Bay
- Morths, Rowland D — Cambria
- Odell, Benj — Wrightstown
- Phillips, Chas — Wrightstown
- Roberts, Jas — Cambria
- Wead, Sylvester, l — Gardiner
- Williams, David G — Cambria

G

- Bailey, Wm F — Portage
- French, Homer — Connorsville
- Stillmau, E N — Waterville
- Smith, Jno —
- Wight, S — Stevens Point

H

- Booth, Geo F — Marshfield
- Batterson, L, f — Eden
- Frederick, W — Rosendale
- Galland, Jos, f — Fond du Lac
- Henry, Fred'k, f — Lamartine
- Lawrence, J S, f — Fond du Lac
- McCain, Jos, f — Lamartine
- Muer, Jno, f — Brothertown
- O'Connor, Benj —
- Pyegan, Jno, f — Rosendale
- Seeley, Miles, l — Fond du Lac
- Vogt, Aug — Brothertown
- Wright, Wm A, f — Lamartine

I

- Lt Richard Beatrell — Medina
- Ackerman, Parmlee W, corp — Shawano
- Bushby, L P — Menasha
- Co-e, Chas M, sgt — Appleton
- Grant, Avery C — Kaukauna
- McMurdo, Jno H, sgt — Hortonville
- Parker, Henry — Seymour
- Robinson, Jno M, corp — Hortonville
- Schiveires, Fred'k — Shawano
- Welland, Nicholas — Appleton
- Wiley, Spencer, corp — Hortonville
- Young, Azro —
- Zerwas, Anthony — Shawano

K

- Lt J S Babcock — Fall River
- Lt Jno Walton — Easton
- Coon, F H — Fall River
- Foley, Timothy — Fall Creek
- Hawley, Chas — Fall River
- O'Brien, H S, sgt — Fall River
- Walton, Jno — Friendship

UNASSIGNED.

- Chap C D Pillsbury, cl — Ripon
- Phillips, B T, sgt maj, ph — Menominee, Mich
- Sisson, Henry, f — Waupun
- Rose, Henry — Princeton
- Wiley, Spencer — Lincoln

THIRTY-THIRD INFANTRY.

A

- Capt O C Deny — Muscoda
- McAllister N A — Muscoda
- Moty, Wm — Muscoda
- Reed, Chas — Falls Store, Idaho
- Solman, Jno — Muscoda

B

- Dremer, Jno — Kenosha
- Powell, Wm, f — Enterprise

D

- Cornish, B L — Oshkosh

E

- Rider, Brainerd — Osseo

- Quigley, Thos —

F

- Bartlett, Phoenix, — Washington, D C
- Day, Jesse — Rock Falls
- Fountain, Levi B — Stacyville, Ia
- Stichel, Jos H — Belvidere, Neb
- Wray, Jno M — Belvidere, Neb

H

- Lt Geo Hale — Kenosha
- Eddy, J M — Kenosha
- Gray, Alex — Kenosha
- King, Herman A — Kenosha
- Sherman, E R — Kenosha
- Wood, N C, f — Battle Creek, Ia

I

- Fellows, R M — Kenosha
- Gardiner, J G — Kenosha
- Smith, H P — Kenosha
- Vauderbeck, Theo, l — Egg Harbor

UNASSIGNED.

- Brig Gen J B Moore — Muscoda
- Maj G R Frank — Muscoda
- Thayer, C R, f — Clay Banks

THIRTY-FOURTH INFANTRY.

B

- Hanneman, August — Beaver Dam

C

- Spello, Fred — West Union, Ia

D

- Brown, Benj — W U Junction
- Fox, Peter — Flintville

F

- Capt Henry Keukel — Oconomowoc

I

- Darton, Wm — Neillsville
- Guest, Milton C — Rock Elm Centre
- Guest, Lewis — Rock Elm Centre

UNASSIGNED.

- Shields, Wm — Racine

THIRTY-FIFTH INFANTRY.

REGIMENTAL ROSTER.

- Col Henry Orff — Milwaukee
- Col Geo H Walther — Milwaukee
- Lt Col Robt Strohman — Detroit, Mich
- Maj Fred von Baumbach — St Paul, Minn
- Maj B S Schoeffel — Chicago, Ill
- Q M A J Cramer — Milwaukee

A

- Capt Robt Strohman — Detroit, Mich
- Lt A C Kuhn — Madison
- Lt Herman Schaub — Kansas City, Mo
- Newburgh, Chas — Beloit

B

- Capt Jasper Vosburg — Aurora, Ill
- Lt F R St John — Leavenworth, Kan
- Lt Jno McManinam — Aurora, Ill
- Barrington, Lewis — Muscoda
- Clapper, D A — New London
- Reinhardt, Wm C — Elmore

C

- Capt W E Fusien — New Orleans
- Capt N A Oleson — St Jac, Mich
- Lt Adolph Renter — Chicago, Ill
- Lt Geo Broshus — Milwaukee
- Lt Robt F Martini — Milwaukee
- Currier, S M, corp, m — Ripon
- Kranich, Henry — Waukesha

D

- Morrison, Jno R — Rochester

E

- Lt Jno L Derickson — Chicago, Ill
- Beller, Jno — Racine

- Phelps, Jas R — Kaukauna
- Shepley, Jas — Oakwood, D T
- White, J J, l — Harrison
- Wuss, Chas E — Okee

F

- Capt Jno W Johann — Cedarburgh
- Lt Paul Bluner — Milwaukee
- Alden, J H — Racine

G

- Capt A C Matthews — Mineral Point
- Lt Leonard Tregea — Des Moines, Ia
- Bernhardt, Carl — Madison
- Sterner, H D, m — Ripon

H

- Capt Cornelius Cuntz — Milwaukee
- Betsick, Andrew — Racine
- Gifli, Jno —
- Johnson, Fred — Racine
- Romes, Fred — Benton Harbor, Mich

I

- Capt Erhard Weber — Indiana
- Lt H E Ray — Delavan
- Lt Julius Lueck — Racine
- Keevil, Thos G — Brothertown
- Haas, Jno — Racine
- Glantz, Theodore, m — West Bend
- Shanks, Thos, f — Unity
- Shanks, Henry, f — Unity

K

- Capt Arch H Adams — Milwaukee
- Lt Herman Schaub — Kansas City
- Lt C J Walther — Milwaukee
- Lt Jno C Fink — Regular Army
- Ditter, Philip, corp, me — Fond du Lac
- Enlumer, Jacob, l — Fond du Lac
- Nehls, Jno — Racine
- Peck, J C, me — Peebles Corners

UNASSIGNED.

- Herrick, N D — Wautoma
- Keevil, Thos G, f — Brothertown

THIRTY-SIXTH INFANTRY.

A

- Vergin, Chas W, f — Poysippi

B

- Lt Wm H Parker — Lawler, Ia
- Cassiday, Jno — Verona

C

- Alcott, Jas — Seymour
- Carnahan, A D, f — Cataract
- Washburn, W H, f — Cataract
- Wright, W H —

D

- Herrick, J C — Plainfield
- Wild, W D — Friendship

E

- Rowe, O P, real estate — Fond du Lac
- Rowe, W H, real estate — Fond du Lac

F

- Fuller, Jas — Seymour
- Green, Franklin D — Sleepy Eye, Minn
- Howard, J B, me — Berlin
- Kanouse, D M, sgt — Sun Prairie
- Parsons, E M — Portage

G

- Jaques, D L — Brothertown
- Morehouse, R C — Breckinridge, Mo
- Pease, J F, f — Fond du Lac
- Phillips, T D — Menasha

H

- Allen, Uri T, corp, f — Lamartine

I

- Armstrong, J — LaCrosse
- Perry, C E — Canton
- Randall, J — Money Creek, Minn

APPENDIX TO REUNION ROSTER.

K

Badger, W D, com sgt	Seymour
Harvey, J D	Mondovi

THIRTY-SEVENTH INFANTRY.

A

Alger, Jos	Omro
Alger, Wesley	Omro
Kimberly, Benj A, f	Hudson
Penewell, Henry	Kendall
Parkin, Thos	Grand Island, Minn
Tritt, Z C, a	Steele City, Neb
Weed, Edw Z	Mapleton, Minn

B

Doty, Isaiah, f	Berlin
France, Aquilla, f	Waterman, Ia
Hewitt, Merrill, f	Brushville
Kissenger, Paul, f	Brushville
Lillicrack, E, f	Tustin
Parkin, W	Grand Island, Minn
Snell, Orange, f	Tustin

C

Averill, Wm	Jenny
Fitch, Victor	Waterville
French, Ed P	Elroy
Gunderson, Jno	Iola

D

Bahron, Fred	Orihula
Brown, Wm	Brookfield
Greenfield, C	Plainfield
Lane, David R	Oasis
Putman, Jacob	Nasacora
Woodward, J B	Wild Rose

E

Capt Wm W Buck, pen office	Washington, D C
Berry, B W, f	Terrills Corners
Thompson, Sam'l	Waubeck

F

Bradshaw, W F, corp	Waubeck
Graves, E V	Omro
Holberg, Christian	Sheboygan
Waldraff, M E	Standing Rock, D T

G

Lt A J Holmes, a	Boone, Ia
Bellinger, J B	Stevens Point
Lawrence, M E	Friendship
Pinckett, Jno A	Dorchester

H

Chisolm, Wm, l	Fond du Lac
Norton, Ed L	Pleasant Valley
Smith, W, f	Eldorado Mills
Thorp, Thos E	Custer

I

Brenner, Anton	Lima
Cady, B A, dist att'y	Poysippi
Loepeke, C	St Killian
Rosebgook, Jno, me	Osage, Ia

THIRTY-EIGHTH INFANTRY.

REGIMENTAL ROSTER.

Lt Col C L Ballard	California
Maj F A Hayward, mf	Omro
Adj A H McCracken	Waverly, Ia
Q M Anson Rood	Deer Creek, Ia
A Surg Hugh Russell	Dakota
A Surg C B Pierson	Spring Green
A Surg C Tochterman	Monroe
Chap J s M Walker	Waupaca

A

Capt C T Carpenter	Ithica, N Y
Capt C L Ballard	California
Capt Jas M Searles	Cedar Rapids, Ia
Lt Albert A Dye, m	Fond du Lac
Barrows, De Villier, f	Oakfield
McCormick, Jas, l	Black Earth
Taylor, Benejah, f	Fond du Lac

Taylor, N M, pa	Fond du Lac
Whitney, E J, me	Fond du Lac
Waters, E C, m	Fond du Lac
Wilcox, W W	Omro

B

Capt F A Hayward, mf	Omro
Capt Geo H Nichols	Iowa
Lt L B Waddington	Argyle
Lt S C Strickland	Scandanavia
Lt Thos Parks, f	Alexandria, Minn
Hayward, F A	Omro
Johnston, Wm H	Brodhead
Simcock, Isaac	Amherst

C

Capt L B Waddington	Darlington
Lt Wm N Wright	Iowa

D

Capt Wm H Foster	Southwest Missouri
Capt Benj S Kerr	Monroe
Austin, A E f	Brandon
Brown, Wm	Brookfield
French, L	Badger Hill, Ia
Gritzmaker, Christopher	Alma City, Minn

E

Lt F M Phelps	Depere
Bonnell, D P	Friendship
Carter, Jacob, f	Friendship
Flinn, E C	West Depere
Juslin, Thos P	Jefferson City

F

Capt E W Pride	Appleton
Lt Frank Glover	Iowa

G

Capt R F Beckwith	Chicago, Ill
Delano, Edgar	Oconto
Glynn, Jas A	Oconto

H

Capt D W Corey	Galena, Ill
Capt Benj M Frees	Chicago, Ill
Lt Jas Beth, Jr	Shakapee, Minn
Lt Wm Adams	Iowa
De Land, Geo	Brookside

I

Capt H H Coleman	Janesville
Mann, Jno	Quinney

K

Capt Thos B Maesden	Oil City
Lt Solon W Pierce, ed	Friendship
Bronn, Amos	Friendship
Burnham, T G	Friendship
Frazer, Lorenzo	Oxford
Gibbons, Wm E	Easton
Marble, N J	Friendship
Townsend, Jno	Friendship
Wright, W A	Friendship

UNASSIGNED.

Dildine, Al, f	Poysippi
Jewell, J B, mo	Fond du Lac
Mitchell, P, Jr	Plainfield
Lippitt, Isaac B	Fond du Lac
Osbourn, Edw	Amherst
Townsend, Jno	Plainville
Zettler, F T	Oconomowoc

THIRTY-NINTH INFANTRY.

A

Dousman, Jno P, m	Michigamme, Mich
Halvorsen, Martin	Janesville

B

Culver, O	Waukesha
Faulkner, E H, f	Brookfield Centre
Hartwell, Frank	Oconomowoc
Jones, J F	Oconomowoc

C

Lee, Leonard	Kenosha

D

Adams, Henry	Rochester
Belden, Albert	Racine
Everetts, Andrew	Rochester
Hoyt, Geo W	Rochester
Jackson, R S	Rochester
Soule, A	Rochester

F

Lt Geo Clark	Waukesha
Frayer, Cordealia	Owosso, Mich
Mohbecker, A	Racine

H

Chrysler, Wm, f	Flintville
Groat, E M	Racine
Harden, A	Waterford

I

Bischoff, W H, m	Fond du Lac

UNASSIGNED.

Craig, J S	Racine
Durand, Franklin, f	Fond du Lac

FORTIETH INFANTRY.

A

Brown, C E, m	Fond du Lac
Burdick, Edson A	Washington, D C
Lowis, W W	Lena, Ill

B

Coffin, Edwin D	Beloit

C

Burd'ck, F O	Utica
Phillips, Geo H	Fayette, Ia
Wilson, Jas B	Kansas City, Mo

D

Dodge, Maurice M	Albert Lea, Minn
Kegan, J M	Oconomowoc
Libby, C A	Evansville
Mitchell, Geo B	Richland Centre
Turner, Jas, ph	Brandon

E

Egelsien, Eugene, f	Fairwanter
Foster, E J	Wannakee
Long, Oscar	W Stewartstown, N H

F

Capt A J Cheeney	Oak Park, Ill
Bailey W C, a	Green Bay
Coary, B M	Sharon
Caraswell, O	Elkhorn

G

Everson, Geo	Jefferson
Keen, A A	Jefferson
Powers, Geo K	Red Oak, Ia
Teed, S R	Jefferson

K

Marble, F R	Hampton, Ia
Marsh, Austin, J	La Crosse
Weber, Edwin H, ed	Menominee

UNASSIGNED.

Towne, T Martin	Chicago

FORTY FIRST INFANTRY.

A

Chesebro, T R	Muscoda

B

Barnett, Jno, f	Nepseuskun
Butler, W F, me	Ripon
Cowan, Chas, sgt, m	Ripon
Hamley, Wm, me	Ripon
Osborn, C H, corp	Ripon
Rolf, Albert, me	Ripon

C

Sheldon, E T	Omro

D

Burt, Geo	Menasha
Bublitz, Wm	Menasha
Bates, M	Menasha

APPENDIX TO REUNION ROSTER.

DeShant, Frank	Menasha	
Jeffries, E	Menasha	
Jones, C H, m	Menominee	
Keyes, E E	Menasha	
Mossop, J C	Menasha	
Mitchell, T H	Seymour	
Olcott, L Q, sgt, p	Oshkosh	
Robinson, C A	Menasha	
Scott, L D	Menasha	
Ward, Andrew	Menasha	

G

Capt T M Moulton — Menasha

FORTY-SECOND INFANTRY.

A

Capt Duncan McGregor, teacher	Platteville
Austin, John	Amherst
Devan, C S	Sherman
Ludington, H	Oconomowoc
Smith, J L	Stevens Point

B

Lt C J Austin — Wh Creek

C

Church, Frank, f	Okee
Loos, Chas, m	Okee
Olson, Jno	Iola
Proper, Philip	Sibley, Ia

E

Church, Rufus H	Modena
Camp, Robt	Mauston
Grignon,	Winneconne
Hammond, L	Winneconne
LeClarni, Leonard B	Harvard, Neb
Schneider, H	Waukesha
Sullivan, Jerry	Winneconne

F

Latham, I L — Delavan
Loomis, R — Frankfort

G

Cartwright, L	Palmyra
Gray, G L	Jefferson
Higging, P E	Stevens Point

H

McCoy, G L — Magnolia
Tyler, Leonard — Janesville

K

Crandall, B F — Ripon
Cole, M L — Verona

UNASSIGNED.

Slover, Jas — Menasha

FORTY-THIRD INFANTRY.

A

Hanley, Patrick F — Delphos, Ohio
Moore, R C — Oconomowoc

C

Dibble, M Z — Oconomowoc

D

Curtis, Roland — Oconomowoc
Latson, A — Beloit

E

Capt I Stockwell — Yankton, D T
Ainnock, Philip — Starr
Cook, J S B — Charles City, Ia

F

Capt Jno S Wilson — Lawrence., Kan
Easthing, Cornelius — Bancroft
Everts, Jos B — Luverne, Minn
LaMay, Jos — Seymour
Potter, Jas — Plainfield

G

Cross, Wm	Racine
Delton, Jas	Rache
Gunter, Wm	Paris
Hagios, Martin	Racine

Hamilton, Thos	Racine
Hamlet, Thos	Racine
Lee, Frank	Neenan
Moore, Wm	Racine
Newbury, F E	Shell Rock, Ia
Patterson, David	Racine
Phillips, L H	Racine
Roberts, Cornelius	Racine
Shimway, W C	Racine
South, Bernhard	Milwaukee
Wilson, Alexander	

H

Crabtree, Edmund

I

Hary, Jno — St Nathan

K

Delap, Wm R — Viroqua
Locke, P W, m — Dartford

UNASSIGNED.

Comstock, S H	Racine
Hulce, E M	Menasha
Peek, Chas	Racine

FORTY-FOURTH INFANTRY.

A

Graves, Chas — Racine
Lane, C A — Lima

B

Gibson, D A	Red River
Jones, J R	Racine
Wilson, Robt	Amherst

C

Einson, Knut	Iola
Gunderson, Hans	Stevens Point
Himbale, J M	Amherst
Peterson, Andrew	Amherst

E

Ferry, W D — Oconomowoc
Hatch, Geo — Oconomowoc

H

Anderson, C, m — E dorado Mills

I

McKay, W J — Eau Claire

K

Burns, A M — Beaver Dam
Duescher, E H — Platteville

FORTY-FIFTH INFANTRY.

A

Laupp, Jno — Horicon
Ruppenthal, Peter — Brillion

C

Rosenberg, L — Milwaukee

E

Blitch, Jacob, m — Hartland

F

Barber, O B — Warren Mills
Rupp, Anton A — Madison

G

Harstard, Lars — Madison

K

Clauson, C — Waterford

FORTY-SIXTH INFANTRY.

A

Clinton, P H	Amherst
Fleming, Benj	Amherst
Holly, W C	Amherst
Grant, F B	Stevens Point
Grant, Horace	Stevens Point
Kheli, Valentine	Stevens Point
Peterson, Adam	Nelsonville
Santer, Philip	Stevens Point
Smart, Alonzo	Plover

D

Rice, Harry — Plover

G

Schilk, Herman	Garner, Ia
Wallace, Thos, f	Empire, Ia

H

St John, I Bovee — Brookside
Walker, F, f — Lime Ridge

K

Pickering, Jno — Trempeleau

UNASSIGNED.

Way, Hiram — Eagle

FORTY-SEVENTH INFANTRY.

REGIMENTAL ROSTER.

Col Geo C Ginty — Chippewa Falls
Lt Col Robt H Spencer — Iowa

A

Capt Wm Young — Medena
Schub, A, f — Outagamie

B

Capt R J O McGowan	Wautoma
Baker, Henry, f	Nepeushum
Boughton, Joel P	Watertown
Luker, Steven, f	Nepeuskum

C

Lt Chas D Haydam	Green Bay
Arndt, E W	Depere
Clark, Silas D	Plover
Lawton, C A	Depere

D

Lt Nels Anderson	Waupaca
Lt Julius A Jones	Waupaca
Boflin, Wm	Amherst

E

Capt Wm W Bird	Milwaukee
Capt Chas A Spencer	Sheboygan Falls
Lt D J Scrampton	Madison
Beckwith, S W	Richland City
Engelhart, Philip	Racine

F

Capt Geo R Wright	Milwaukee
Lt Jno P Dousman	Cedar River, Mich
Deran, Erastus A	Mauston
Huss, L E	Ripon

G

Lt Silas F Nice — Tomah
Chadbourn, H L, pa — Ripon

H

Capt Chas B Nelson — Beloit
Lt Jas Ginty — Racine
Duncan, Robt — Boscobel

I

Capt J D Weelock	Hartford
Lt W T Whiting	Ripon
Lt Jas Ginty	Racine
Lt Wesley G Curtis	Fond du Lac

K

Capt Chas H Roxter	Lancaster
Lt Jno Grindell	Lancaster
Blackner, D	Hanover

UNASSIGNED.

Bath, I	Portage
Huebner, Fred'k, musician	Milwaukee
Shute, Fred C, l	Ripon
Wheelock, L L	Stevens Point

FORTY-EIGHTH INFANTRY.

REGIMENTAL ROSTER.

Col U D Searsall	Ft Scott, Kan
Col Henry Shears	Milwaukee
Lt Col Cyrus M Butt	Viroq a
Maj Nathan Cole	Man towo ;
Adj A B Cady	Fair Point, Kan

·:·IT STANDS AT THE HEAD.·:·

~~·:·THE·:·~~

LIGHT RUNNING "DOMESTIC"

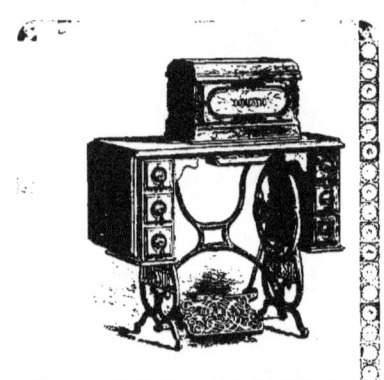

SEWING MACHINES.

The Pioneer in all Improvements.
  The Leader in the Progress of Invention.
    The Model of the Modern System.
      The Originators of the Approved Methods.

GENERAL OFFICE		FACTORIES.
Broadway and 14th Street, N. Y.		NEWARK, N. J.

·:·AGENTS WANTED.·:·

ADDRESS,

Domestic S. M. Co., 134 Grand Ave., Milwaukee, Wis.
Domestic S. M. Co., 180 State Street, Chicago, Ill.
Domestic S. M. Co., 187 Woodward Ave., Detroit, Mich.
Domestic S. M. Co., 35 Public Square, Cleveland, Ohio.

APPENDIX TO REUNION ROSTER.

Surg L O Armstrong — Baraboo
A Surg H E Tulley — Chilton

A

Capt C W Felker — Oshkosh
Lt Henry Felker — Nashua, Ia
Lt M J Briggs — Mazomanie
Darrow, E A — Omro
Fowler, I M — Omro
Graham, C L — Racine
Hamilton, B — Omro
Olin, C H — Omro
Reed, W R — Omro

B

Capt J J Roberts — Waupun
Everson, Jos — Fond du Lac

C

Fox, Stephen R — Stevens Point

D

Gunderson, Swaire — Waterford
Teslo, Wm — Grant City, Ia

E

Capt M V B Hutchinson — Waterloo
Capt David W Briggs — Milwaukee
Obenberger, Albert — Milwaukee

F

Martyn, Jas L — Flintville

G

Capt H M Stocking — Eau Claire

H

Capt Peter Trudell — Black River Falls
Benens, Jno, m — Waupun

I

Lt H C Sloan — Appleton
Burdick, Jared — Harvard, Neb
Kern, Geo G, m — Oconomowoc

K

Capt Jno D Lewis — LaCrosse

UNASSIGNED.

Lippert, Dionysius, l — Beloit
Noble, E H — Racine

FORTY-NINTH INFANTRY.

A

Arnson, Andrew — Barber
Vosler, Jay C — Delton

B

Richardson, Lewis, me — Berlin

C

Reilly, Hugh — Bellville, Nev

D

Willis Henry — Flintville
Willis, Wm — Flintville

E

Apple, Philip — Reedsburg
Evans, J D — Sutton, Neb
Green, Herman J, l — Okee
Hood, N B — Lone Rock

G

Mickleson, M A, f — Webster City, Ia
Rolfe, Lewis H — West Depere
Snita, C H — Seymour

I

Daggett, S M — Ft Howard

K

Hason, J L — Lyons
Wharry, Robt — Elkhorn

FIFTIETH INFANTRY.

B

Wright, A O — Fox Lake

D

Curtis, C, f — Waupun
Lyons, W J — Emmetsburg, Ia
Peterson, Ole — Amherst

Smith, Al, f — Fond du Lac
Tompson, E J, f — Brandon

I

Crain, Chas — Durand
Garvin, Adam — Durand
Hewitt, Henry — Plover
McCrystal, Thos A — Cottage Grove
Regan, Michael — Oconomowoc

K

Chadwick, Wm — Racine
Seaver, E F — Reedsburg

UNASSIGNED.

Hammer, Jno — Menasha

FIFTY-FIRST INFANTRY.

REGIMENTAL ROSTER.

Col Leonard Martin, pen office — Washington
Q M H G Kfluelcher — Nora

A

Lt Elias H Webb — Beloit

C

Gasper, Chas — Waukesha
Miller, Henry, l — Rockfield
Wasmuth, Henry — Rockfield

D

Davis, A E, mf — Appleton
Honey, Robt W — Ashippun
Keyes, O E — Menasha

E

Fitzhibbon, Henry — Menasha
Ray, Edw, f — Empire

F

Lt Sam'l Elmore — Milwaukee
Fratny, Fred — Fond du Lac

K

Capt Henry Bailey — Appleton
Ferris, D D, corp — Appleton
Phillipps, David S — Racine

UNASSIGNED.

Tolman, Anson — Sibley, Ia

FIFTY-SECOND INFANTRY

A

Tyler, Sam'l W — Planeville

B

Blodgett, E f — Berlin
Hill, Thos — Waterville
Stokes, Oliver — Waterville

C

Beech, L C — Plover
Jennings, Jno, f — Spring Lake
Kengs, E, f — Spring Lake
Marr, O B, f — Spring Lake
Morgan, Philip A — Wautomo
Sheldon, P W, f — Spring Lake

UNASSIGNED

Behuker, Fred E, f — Kewaskum

FIFTY-THIRD INFANTRY.

B

Miller, H S

I

Ladore, Crain — Durand

FIRST CAVALRY.

A

Lt Richard L Gove — Waukesha
Maj Newton Jones — Geneva, O
Decker, F — LaCrosse
Davis, C M — Merrillan
Foss, Goodsall — Oconomowoc
Gurner, D A — Lodi, Cal
Norris, Jas A — Sauk City, Minn

Stetson, Allen — Waterford
Woodruff, B — Oconomowoc
Wyatt, L D — Tomah

B

Baker, W J — Waseca
Brown, Volney, f — West Rosendale
Muzzy, Orlin B — Stevens Point
Reed, L E, a — Ripon
Spangler, W A, f — Woodstock, Ia
Stevens, W P, l — Ripon
Utley, A R — Clear Lake, Ia
Wright, Lynderman — Plainville

C

Lt J A Atwood — Ripon
Clemons, D A — Elroy
Castle, B N — Hadville
Callahan, Thos, sgt, f — Ripon
Cate, Geo E — Stevens Point
Culver, Ed, f — Ripon
Chase, Levi — Greenleaf
Kent, J J — Jefferson
Lyon, J F, clk — Cedar Forks. Mich
Meecher, Jno — Portage
Strong, Wm R — Wausau
Swett, C A, sgt, f — Fort Worth, Texas
Wagner, Jno — Sharon
White, C, f — Ripon

D

Lt Oscar Barnett, me — Fargo, D T
Larabee, Julius A — Berlin
Larabee, Doll, f — Ripon

E

Lt S Eggleston — Flintville
Lyman, A C — Oconomowoc
Morton, C C — Omro
O'Brien, J C — Cascade
O'Hearn, E H — Cascade
Queeman, J — Oconomowoc

F

Francisco, Orlando, m — Ripon
Irman, Lyman L — Havana, Minn
Hargraves, M, f — Ripon
Johnson, M C, f — Delton
Leslie, J — Oconomowoc
Thomas, W D — Racine
Woodward, Jno, l — Ft Worth, Texas
Wild, Jas — Oconomowoc

G

Lt E W Clark — Neenah
Coleman, Elihu, O M sgt, a — Fond du Lac
Haskins, J T — Stetsonville
Kuschke, Chas — Lounira
Miner, Ed S — Monroe
Miles, Calvin, f — Hewett
McLeod, David — Stevens Point
Morgan, Edwin A — Lincoln, Neb
Wolfenden, Jas — Racine

H

Treanor, E, l — Ripon

I

Lt J H Barnett, ph — Neenah
Calkins, W P — Waukesha
Ladkie, Chas, l — Brandon
Stephens, F — Jefferson
Wilding, Geo, Jr — Neillsville

K

Carr, Lester L, bk — Milwaukee
Daskum, Jno W — Chilton
Denning, B E, c — Ripon
Kvaris, Jno — Omro
Fero, C, f — Ripon
Homstead, S W — Stevens Point
Nelson, Wm, f — Waupun

L

Capt Jno L Stewart, f — Ripon
Brown, Lucius — Boscobel
Hilliard, W L — LaCrosse

NICOLL THE TAILOR.

620 Broadway and 139 to 151 Bowery, N. Y.

BRANCHES:

- 111 Nassau Street, New York.
- 707 Eighth Avenue, New York.
- 482 Fulton Avenue, Brooklyn.
- 315 Main Street, Buffalo, N. Y.
- 88 Fifth Avenue, Pittsburgh, Pa.
- 100 Market Street, Newark, N. J.
- Cor. E. Water and Wisconsin Sts., Milwaukee, Wis.
- 1 East Main Street, Rochester, N. Y.
- 99 W. Jefferson Street, Louisville, Ky.
- 9 South Illinois Street, Indianapolis, Ind.
- 1,031 Chestnut Street, Philadelphia, Pa.
- 617 Pennsylvania Avenue, Washington, D. C.
- 505 Montgomery Street, San Francisco, Cal.

BRANCHES:

- 727 Market Street, San Francisco, Cal.
- 853 Broadway, Oakland, Cal.
- 50 Asylum Street, Hartford, Conn.
- 369 State Street, New Haven, Conn.
- 87 W. Baltimore Street, Baltimore, Md.
- Lakeside Building, Chicago, Ill.
- 249 Washington Street, Boston, Mass.
- 72 Washington Street, Boston, Mass.
- 59 Fifth Street, Cincinnatti, Ohio.
- 145 Superior Street, Cleveland, Ohio.
- 9 Fourth Street, St. Louis, Mo.
- 708 Olive Street, St. Louis, Mo.
- Crescent Building, Canal Street, New Orleans.

Pants to Order, $5.00.   **Suits to Order, $20.00.**

THE LATEST STYLES OF
DOMESTIC AND FOREIGN WOOLENS

Of every Description, Cheviot Cloths, Diagonals, Overcoatings, Etc, always on hand.

The Public are cordially invited to visit our New York Stores, where the Electric Light is used, also Telephone, Steam Machinery, and all the latest modern improvements in Machinery, that can be used in the trade.

Samples and rules for Self-Measurement sent to any part of the Country on Application.

APPENDIX TO REUNION ROSTER. 301

Name	Location	Name	Location	Name	Location
Partridge, A W	Belle Centre	Shumway, D L, f	Castle Rock, Minn	Terry, Lyman	Lime Ridge
Whaley, C B	Jefferson			Wheeler, R A	Baraboo
M		**H**		**G**	
Haug, Jno	Montfort	Hegmann, Wm	LaCrosse	Seamans, G F	Stevens Point
Phelps, B H, d	Ripon	Hineman, Jos	Lowden, Ia		
Stoddard, Jno, f	Bowens Mills	Hiss, Jno	Grand Island	**H**	
Willes, Sylvester	Plainfield	Steinke, G	Canton	Allen, Edgar	Amherst
Wheeler, Gilbert	Reedsburg			Andrews, Nelson	Amherst
UNASSIGNED.		**I**		Groves, J K	Amherst Junction
		Blanchard, Levi, f	Rosendale	Hathaway, Edwin	Amherst
Bublitz, Alf	Menasha	Cole, M	Badger Hill, Ia	Lampbier, P	Omro
Bangs, E D, ar	Milwaukee	Davenport, Wm	Badger Hill, Ia	Scoville, J K	Edgerton
Benson, G	Badger Hill	Faber, Luke	Darlington, Ia	Sparling, Jno	Racine
Champlon, Robt	Buttes des Mortes	Goodrich, Wm	Waubeck	Sherman, A A	Keene
Draper, Seldon		Goodrich, Frank	Waubeck		
Gee, Hiram, m	Ripon	Raymond, Jno N	Garrison, Ia	**I**	
Hunt, G A	Durand	Rumsill, Pilty F, light-house keeper	Bayfield	Smith, D	Amherst
Morgan, Marvin	Eau Plaine	Sterling, N B	Clyde, Ia		
Nayler, E, me	Ripon	Stevens, W C	Friendship	**K**	
Pasha, Joe	Eau Plaine	Wescott, J C	Badger Hill, Ia	River, Jno	Lourdes, Ia
Sample, Jas	Pine Grove			Daniels, W O	Black Creek
Strong, Wm P	Metomen	**K**		Morrill, C C	Eau Plaine
		Capt B F Crocker	Wisconsin	Schilling, Julius	Plymouth
		Anderson, Stewart	Sharon		
SECOND CAVALRY.		Hillman, E E	Darien	**L**	
REGIMENTAL ROSTER.				Bowen, H	Sibley, Ia
Lt Col H E Eastman	Benton Harbor, Mich	**L**		Buel, Jas L, f	Lime Ridge
Maj M W Wood, 1st bat	East Oakland, Cal	Banister, Geo F, f	Eau Claire	Longley, P E	Baraboo
		Halsted, G W	Marshalltown, Ia	Moore, Volney	Baraboo
A		Loomis, Chas, sgt	Frankfort	Neikel, S R	New London
Lt N Boardman	Fond du Lac	Powell, Thos, m	Eau Claire	Quick, Shafer	Fond du Lac
Blanchard, Jas	New York City	Robbins, D	Lima	Swetland, Geo W	Reedsburg
Curran, Jas W, f	Fond du Lac	Stevens, Marcellus T	Durand	UNASSIGNED.	
Dolan, Henry, sgt, f	Fond du Lac	Wyman, Astald, f	Eau Claire	Farr, L B	Plover
Ferguson, Edwin P, f	Suamico			Halliday, W S	Plover
Halsted, D W	Sheboygan	**M**		Hall, A H	Chicago
Johnson, Loren M	Brothertown	Lt Jno Baxter	Chicago, Ill	Mortar, Jno, Jr, l	Okee
McGowan, Michael, f	New Berlin	Fink, Peter	Darboy	Reeves, W H, sgt	Fond du Lac
Monroe, E H	Blair, Neb	Malone, A	Beloit	Sidney, S	Plover
Mallet, German, f	Fond du Lac	Malone, G R	Beloit	Seboufeldt, Geo W	Reedsburg
Pasco, Quincy, bugler, l	Metomen	Parker, Isaac, sgt	Janesville	Smith, Jno	Caldwells Prairie
Phelps, Geo S	Medford	Zolkmen, Jno M	Janesville	Shannon, Norman	Plover
Sage, E B	Racine	UNASSIGNED.		Turney, H B	Reedsburg
Schnegan, Herman	Seymour	Lt J B Taylor	Millard	Tyler, Frank	Plover
Tompkins, Henry	Campbellsport	Brown, D J	Stevens Point	Vorly, J C	
Watson, Lyman	Fairchild	Mulroy, P	New London	Young, Simon	Plover
Watson, J D, f	Eldorado Mills	Parish, Ben	Millard		
Weyer, Fred, m	Fond du Lac	Smith, F	Sugar Creek		
		Stearns, Orange	Darien	**FOURTH CAVALRY.**	
B		Vearn, S E	Delavan	**A**	
Capt A W Bishop	Little Rock, Ark	Weaver, Frank	Millard	Maj G A Pierce	Olin
Capt Jno Whytock	Little Rock, Ark			Lt J H Wing, a	Bayfield
Brown, Jno A, sgt, f	Windom	**THIRD CAVALRY.**		Basler, Chris	Racine
Noble, David D, f	Windom			Farnham, Wm H	Milwaukee
		Lt Col R H White	Galena, Kan	Moody, Edw L, f	Geneva Lake
D		**A**			
Capt G W Noble	Racine	Capt Robt Carpenter	Lawrence, Kan	**B**	
Drummond, L D	Missula, M T	Capt J D Dammon	Ellensburg, W T	Capt G W Madison	Leavenworth, Kan
Olson, Chas, l	Ludington, Mich	Bawicy, H J	Stevens Point	Lee, Robt	Fond du Lac
Strong, Geo	Baldwin	Dunn, P	Stevens Point		
		Nelson, Jerome	Amherst	**C**	
E		Phillips, Jos P, corp	Waukesha	Lucas, J B	Plymouth
Albee, Wm C	Portage	Vaughn, D H	Stevens Point	Smalley, P J	Caledonia, Minn
Carpenter, H B	Fredericksburg, Ia	Wolverton, Martin	Oshkosh	Smith, Aug	Sheboygan Falls
Stevens, D B	Tonawanda, N Y			Schmidt, Aug	Plymouth
Klimer, Wilson	Weyauwega	**B**		Seeger, Wm	Medford
Price, Jas, sgt	Poysippi	Rice, J W	Omro		
Outsen, Jacob	Racine			**D**	
Williams, W E	Kingston	**C**		Harrison, J M	Friendship
		Allen, Eger	Amherst	Herren, E R	Stevens Point
F				Johnson, C H	Rock Rapids, Ia
Furstenberg, Lorenz	Leedston, Minn	**D**		Parkhurst, G A	Canton
Palmer, Walter, f	Durabo	2d Lt Byron Kilbourn, pb	North Lake	Rhodes, Jas	Durand
		Hockings, Wm	Racine		
G		Stokon, Tim	Durand	**E**	
Lt Geo W Noble	Racine	Whittaker, Wm	Fond du Lac	Carr, E S	Jefferson
Lt Edw S Minor	Fish Creek			Lyons, Christopher	Friendship
Lt S H Nichols	Chicago, Ill	**E**		McBeath, N	Waukesha
Bennett, Akem	Seymour	Lt Leonard House	Janesville	Parker, Wm B	Arborville, Neb
Burgess, C W, c	Fond du Lac	Dyer, Wayne B	Durand	Pixley, D	Sharon
Bullamore, Jno	Friendship			Tiebert, Jno	Manitowoc
French, C	Badger Hill, Ia	**F**			
McCall, Ira	Milwaukee	Lt L P Luce	Dryden, Neb	**F**	
Pengilly, Henry	Mazeppa, Minn	Adams, J J	Stevens Point	Brittain, Jno	Esbon, Ka
Pierce, W L	Sheboygan Falls	Bloom, Geo	Baraboo	Boesier, Christian	Racine
Sage, E B, sgt	Racine	Towler, Henry	Plover	Buttles, E C	Seymour
		House, David	Seymour		

FIRST-CLASS HOTELS OF WISCONSIN.

AMERICAN HOUSE,
FOND DU LAC, WIS.

H. SHATTUCK.

T. D. LAWRENCE.   W. H. LAWRENCE.

THE CLARK HOUSE,
LAWRENCE BROTHERS, Proprietors.

BEAVER DAM, WISCONSIN.

Corning House.
A. E. SMITH, Proprietor.

PORTAGE, WISCONSIN.

Huggins House,
RACINE, WIS.

AL. LEWIS, PROPRIETOR.

S. J. GOODWIN.   CHAS. L. GOODWIN.

Goodwin House,
BELOIT, WIS.

S. J. GOODWIN & SON, Proprietor.

FRANK SAXTON, Chief Clerk.   *$2.00 per day*   M. L. COLBY, Night Clerk.

First-Class in all its Appointments.

Free 'Bus to and from the House.

The Butter, Cream and Milk used at the Goodwin House is brought daily from Goodwin's celebrated Maplewood Farm.

DELIGHTFUL SUMMER RESORT,

AT THE DELLS OF THE WISCONSIN RIVER.

FINCH HOUSE.
W. H. FINCH, Proprietor,

Kilbourn City, - Wisconsin.

FREE 'BUS.

Also Part-owner of the "Dell Queen."

APPENDIX TO REUNION ROSTER.

Name	Location
Coffey, C C	Rock Creek, Ia
Gibbs, J F	Oconomowoc

G

Name	Location
Gabrielson, Otto D	Milwaukee
Harrington, Jos H	Hudson
Palmer, J W	Lincoln Centre

H

Name	Location
Groove, Henry	Bayfield
Hickox, Chas W	Lafarge
Newton, Origen	Oconomowoc
Quilty, Thos	Sun Prairie

I

Name	Location
Erickson, A, m	Black River Falls
Kinyon, D A	Seymour

K

Name	Location
Dutcher, Edgar	Volga, D T
Sutliff, Jas, f	Eldorado Mills
Wiggins, Jos W	Fall City

UNASSIGNED

Name	Location
Allen, Eugene	Stevens Point
Gunning, J W, bugler	Friendship
Henry, E D	Omro
Hicks, O C	River Falls
Monk, H C	
Parker, Geo	Menasha
Welch, Chas, ranchman	Dakota
Westphall, H C	Jefferson

HEAVY ARTILLERY.

A

Name	Location
Anthony, Jno	Jefferson
Henry, Antie	Rochester
Hullet, Geo	Waterford
Krakofiski Fred	
McKenzie, M	Waterford
Powers, W F, nf	LaCrosse
Sears, L C	Jefferson
Thompson, Wm	Thompsonville
VanLone, Jno	Hebron
Wheelock, Orville	Jefferson

B

Name	Location
Lt Chas B Palmer, teacher	Lincoln, Neb
Beal, Whitney A	Geneva Lake
Fitzgerald, Michael	Lake Forest, Ill
McKittrick, B H	Redwood Falls, Minn
McKinzie, R L	Waterford
Waddell, Wm	Racine
White W B	Plover

C

Name	Location
Crawford, Geo	Liberty Bluff
Langworthy, J A	Milwaukee
Wilson, Wm	Marquette

D

Name	Location
Lt C V Bridges	Spring Grove
Lt Wm M Hanchett	Albany
Lt C M Ball	Spring Grove
Burden, W H, ph	Miltou
Bohannan, S B	Bristol
Kildow, J P	Pedee
Vedder, E M, f	Korn

E

Name	Location
Lt J J Gibbs	Waukesha
Griffith, G W, f	Delton
Jaquith, Phineas, cl	Boltonville
Keinberger, Jos	Oconomowoc
Marshall	Racine
Medbury, M H	Reedsburg
Pelis, Jeremiah	Colona
Welty, W B	Dubuque, Ia

F

Name	Location
Bramow, C	Racine
Hall, J W	Mauston
Hanson, J P	Racice
Henry, Antell	Racine
Hume, Jas	Portage
Scranton, C M	Racine

G

Name	Location
Dodge, G D	
Robbins, J B, f	Lomira

H

Name	Location
Sharp, Peter	Seymour
Trapp, Andrew	Waterloo

I

Name	Location
Leatheard, Geo, f	Berlin
Mitchel, J B	Plainfield
Nichol, W H, l	Clarion, Ia
Smith, F R	Racine
Smith, B	Plainfield
Stone, G W	W U Junction
Stewart, I N, teacher	Berlin

K

Name	Location
Bush, Harvey	
Comple, Henry	
Coulan, Jas	Racine
Conlan, J A	Plainville
George, Samuel	W U Junction
Hunter, Jas	W U Junction
McCall, Irvin	Carson City, Mich
Sneizer, Stephen	W U Junction
Walker, Aus n	W U Junction

L

Name	Location
Lt Edwin Goodman, cl	Minnesota
Palmer, P P	Baraboo

M

Name	Location
Fowler, Benj	Racine
Gilmore, Hiram	Cambria
Hurd, A I	Plainfield
Putman, Geo W	Ash Ridge
Weeks, E J	Bloomer

UNASSIGNED.

Name	Location
Wise, Jno	Menasha

LIGHT ARTILLERY.

FIRST BATTERY.

Name	Location
Braymond, M	Ludington, Mich
Kusehke, Wm	Lomira
Lyman, Judson	Waterville
Wesson, Molthrope	Waterville
Watts, Jas	Watisford

SECOND BATTERY.

Name	Location
Brotz, Richard	Neilsville
Ickstadt, Jos M	Plymouth
Sebastion, Herbert	Racine
Williams, W R	Racine

THIRD BATTERY.

Name	Location
Lt J Albert Le Brun	Chicago, Ill
Currier, Henry	Concord, Minn
Hayes, A A	Boyceville
Canouse, Ira W	Cottage Grove
Kanouse, E M, corp	Columbus
Kanouse, A W, ph	Lancaster
Luce, J W H, me	Oshkosh

FORTH BATTERY.

Name	Location
Capt D L Noggle	
Capt Jno F Valier	Beloit
Lt M H McDervitt	Hampton Rhodes, Va
Austin, Wm L, sgt	Beloit
Jepson, N	Waterford
Smith, Jno S	Tiffany
Thom, W S	Clinton

FIFTH BATTERY.

Name	Location
Ross, J W	Galesburg, Ill

SIXTH BATTERY.

Name	Location
Burger, Christopher	Richland Centre
Hood, N B	Lone Rock
Dutchusou, Chas	Augusta

SEVENTH BATTERY.

Name	Location
Lt W O D Retley	Berlin
Conklin, Louis	Seymour
Dorwood, G B	Neosho
Hawn, J P	Neosho
Hawn, D B	Lincoln, Neb
McIntosh, C E	Seymour

Name	Location
Orville, Austin	Hope, Mich
Thompson, Elisha	Seymour

EIGHTH BATTERY.

Name	Location
Barker, Jno	Menasha
Hoyt, Wm	Durand
Lloyd, W C	Menasha

NINTH BATTERY.

Name	Location
Dodge, J H, f	M & St Paul Railroad
Haines, Sam'l	W U Junction
Sanford, E C, f	Delton
Todd, J H	Oshkosh
Waters, Jas	Waterford

TENTH BATTERY.

Name	Location
Reynolds, Elmer R, pen office	Washington, D C

TWELFTH BATTERY.

Name	Location
Capt T T Croft	Jamestown
Greenwold, J	Menasha
Greenwood, G	Menasha
Jacobs, W C	Menasha
Marks, Henry	Greenville
Mallory, Lucian T	Waukesha
Ribble, Aloazo R	New Richmond
Rome Fred, f	Lime Ridge

THIRTEENTH BATLERY.

Name	Location
James, G H	Black Creek
West, W J	Clinton Junction

UNASSIGNED.

Name	Location
Ebort, Edw	Menasha
Hubbs, Cyrus G	Spring Bluff
Littlefield, Geo	Racine
Plover, Wm	W U Junction
Weirnick, Wm	Racine

SHARP SHOOTERS.

Name	Location
Herrick, H H, f	Baraboo
McCaul, Thos	Tomah

OTHER STATES.

MAINE.

Name	Location
Hunter, Alvin, F t cav	Flintville
Ingalls, Isaac, war of 1812	Waterville
Scribner, S C, B 8 inf	Durand

NEW HAMPSHIRE.

Name	Location
Fiske, J B	Menasha
Kalliher, M M, 1st R B 7	Waukesha
Wakefield, G L, sgt G 9	Durand

VERMONT.

Name	Location
Brown, Joc, H 13	Waterville
Edwards, Wm, 10	Markesan
Jackson, A P	Menasha
Kelley, Henry	Waterville
Marshall, J J, K 1	Menasha
Martin, Joe	Waterville

MASSACHUSETTS.

Name	Location
Bonart, J, 1st R G 1	Waukesha
ForLush, Fred, G 35	Hales Corners
Hutchinson, J A, E 2	Racine
Porter, L C, G 4	Waterford
Willis, Atkins, G 6 inf	Durand
Workman, W M, K 7	Racine

NEW YORK.

Name	Location
Allen, Brenton, F 142	Waterville
Ainsworth, R C, 24 bat	
Allen, Henry R, D 154	Fond du Lac
Allen, Daun E, K 85	Trappe
Bashaw, Peter, I 60	Waterville
Bashaw, Joe, I 60	Waterville
Burger, J, I 107	Frankfort
Bennett, Fayette, E 164	Prospect Hill
Cataria, Frank, H 106	Waterville
Caturia, Louis, F 142	Waterville
Doam, Fred S, K 32	Waukesha
Dupree, Geo, E 98	Waterville
Fiske, W P, 1 bat	Fall River
Fartoole, J E, C 3	Racine
Haights, T W, H K 24	Waukesha
Irish, L C, 77	Beloit
Kruger, Andrew, K 85	Durand
Kenyon, A F, K 81	Lima

ALTHOUSE, WHEELER & CO.
WAUPUN, WIS.,
MANUFACTURERS OF THE ALTHOUSE & RAYMOND

WIND MILL,

And the Waupun Patent Premium Pump,
—AND WINDMILL—

FEED GRINDERS.

Our Wind Mills and Pumps wherever known, are recognized as the best in market. The Feed Grinders are comparatively new; but are rapidly making their way into notice, as a valuable machine for any farmer who has stock to feed. We make geared mills, capable of doing a larger amount of work and running a greater variety of machines than the pumping mills. Pumping mills of 8, 10, 12, 14, 16 and 25 feet diameter. Geared Mills of 12, 14, 16, and 18 feet. Send to

ALTHOUSE, WHEELER & CO.,
WAUPUN, WISCONSIN.

For Circulars and Prices of these valuable labor saving machines. Over 50,000 of our pumps in use in the Northwest. Over 3,000 wind mills in use.

Attention Comrades!

INTEREST YOURSELF

And Read the Advertisement of

C. J. RUSSELL,

Of 117 Wisconsin Street,

—ON—

ANOTHER PAGE,

—AND THEN—

CALL AND SEE HIM
—AND BE—

MADE HAPPY.

HEADQUARTERS

SOLDIERS REUNION

GEO. HECKMAN,

CIGARS &
TOBACCOS

(Successor to Heckman Bros.)

THE FINEST GOODS
AND LOWEST PRICES.

96 WISCONSIN STREET, MILWAUKEE, WISCONSIN.

APPENDIX TO REUNION ROSTER. 305

Knight, Henry, I 109 — Waterville
King, Jos, 60 — Waterville
Norvey, T W, 4 — Menasha
Parker, Wm, 17 — Menasha
Philler, Hugo, ph, surg 45 — Waukesha
Preston, A H, K 15 cav — Durand
Poquette, Jas, corp, I 60 — Waterville
Patrow, Joe, G 92 — Waterville
Patton, A B, B 112 — Frankfort
Patton, Jno. C 10 heavy art — Frankfort
Perkins H L, C it heavy art — Frankfort
Potts, L D, capt, 30 — Waterford
Raymond, N, M 9 cav — Durand
Robinson, Frank, K 14 artillery — Waterville
Robinson, F, 16 — Frankfort
Robinson, A M — Menasha
Smith, Jas, A 125 — Flintville
Smith, Nathan, B 118 — Durand
Sinkiwski, Joe, D 64 — Waterville
Taylor, Frank, K 60 — Waterville
Thompson, J M, B 187 — Canton
Taylor, Chas — Waterville
Wooster, Geo B, D 10 heavy art
Welch, David H, E 20 — Racine
Welton, Wm, 44 — Plover
White, Wm B, corp 5 bat — Plover
Wheeler, H C, H 14 heavy art — Flintville
York, Wm, A 80 — Waterville
York, W S, A 85 — Waterville

PENNSYLVANIA.
Ames, Milo, K 83 — Flintville
Bailey, Z K 1 — Frankfort
Gray, O A, H 58 — Waterville
Hardy, C H, com sgt 39 — Beloit
Hall, Chas, A 18 — Beloit
Hennessy, D J, I 23 — Beloit
Keiser, Hans, A 153 — Beloit
Moore, Thos, F 39 — Afton
Parmaly, C H, I 52 — Beloit
Reushlein, Aug, K 14 cav — Racine
Scott, H O, B 3 heavy art — Waterville
Wilson, A, F I cav — Lima
Zilley, Wm, A 153 — Beloit

LOUISIANA.
Hunstable, S L, capt, H 48 colored inf

OHIO.
Beardsley, Geo, G 7 — Durand
Graff, Jas, K 26 — Durand
Moulton, G H, el, F 2
Nuraberger, Fred W, C 21 — Stockbridge
Payson, O W, B 1 — Menasha

INDIANA.
Benton, S — Frankfort
Garrett, Anth — Waterville
Seppy, J M, 20 — Racine

ILLINOIS.
Frambach, H, A 6 — Menasha
Buettner, Henry, corp B #2 — Waukesha
Beth, Jno, K — Green Bay
Beal, Wm, f, I 156 — Racine
Crampton, Wm, C 142 — Durand
Cummings, Ben, A 72 — Menasha
Dixon, B, G 12 cav — Lima
Hight, J, G 4 — Waterville
Jung, F, A 91 — Jefferson
Kemerer, Adam, C 24 — Racine
Manore, Geo, A cav — Waterville
Morgan, Jno W, Chicago marine bat Embarrass
Pearsons, Jno, D 57 — Waubeck
Perkins, Chas, B — National Home
Stevens, J O, C 95 — Jefferson
Stage, J M, E 22 — Racine
Stickney, A L, A 19 — Janesville
Weber M, I 156 — Racine
Wettengel, Frank, C 24 — Racine

MICHIGAN.
Carr, J P, 6 — Neenah
Dopp, Cyrus, 10 — Plover
Ganoe, I P, G 1 — Frankfort
Granger, Alonzo, C 10 — Menasha

Henderhot, Jas, 2 cav — Menasha
Heckel, Ed — Menasha
Moore, D B, capt 27 — Plover
Papne, G M, 5 — Menasha
Schell, Henry, sgt H 1 — Durand
Williver, Peter, A 10 — Durand

IOWA.
Benton, Sol H, A 26 — Waterville
Cassell, Wm, H 21 — Waubeck
Dixon, Jno, C 4 — Racine
Downer, J L, C 38 — Beloit
Richie, C C, M 4 cav — Frankfort
Scott, S M, sgt B 4 cav — Durand

MINNESOTA.
Belden, N, I 1 inf — Lima
Crosby, S P, H 3 inf — Durand
Du Cate, Moses, D 9
Galloway, Wm, H 5 inf — Durand
Hunt, D W, 1 light art — Durand
Ingram, J A, M 2 cav — Frankfort
Krick, S G, G 3 inf — Durand
Kane, Jas, I B heavy art — Durand
Meyers, Chas, G 1 heavy art — Frankfort
Rundle, B P, E 11 inf — Frankfort
Story, C M, G 1 heavy art — Durand
Stokes, Nelson, 1 heavy art — Durand
Spooner, Albert, A 1 heavy art — Lima
Wallace, A J, 1 2 inf — Durand

MISSOURI.
Mack, Jno, F 3 cav — Frankfort
Shedd, Wm N, I 31 cav — Frankfort

KENTUCKY.
Flintzel, F, M 6 cav — Racine
Smith, J, J 23 — Waterville
Smith, David, H 37 mounted inf

U. S. REGULARS.
Anderson, Walter J, B 14 — Kaukauna
Almon, Jno, A 13 — Weynacwega
Andruss, C, K 3 — Kenosha
Briggs, Abram, D 8 — Menominee
Brug, F, A 1 — Neillsville
Brass, Jas, corp 7 — Star Prairie
Cornell, Jno O, 7 — Vandyne
Collins, Jno — Eden
Crippen, Amos, 2d lt U S colored — Baldwin
Coyu, Mich, 13 — Portage
Callenbrach, Gerhard, D cav — Richfield
Derline, W E, F 16 — Watertown
Dobb, S J, 3 8 8 — Stevens Point
Eadns, N G, F 16 — Racine
Flint, R J, sgt U S sig corp — Menominee
Fritzner, Amand, 3 musician
Goodletson, Goodlet, fisherman Washington Isle
Gritzner, Apand 3 inf band — Watertown
Grout, Le Roy, sgt B 16 — Emmetsburg, Ia
Hunting, G, 1st lt 3 art — Beaver Dam
Holland, Jno, A 22 — Neillsville
Hepler, Geo, K 3 cav — Neillsville
Hadley, H C, lt — Janesville
Hughes, Geo R, 2d lt D 99 colored — St Croix
Harding, Frank D, capt H 99 colored — St Croix
Haro, H C, teamster, C 13 — Milwaukee
Hase Henry me, E 13, — Milwaukee
Hepin, T H, C 21 — Buena Vista
Jnek, Jas, livery stable, K 4 — Waupaca
Johnson, T S, chap 3C coclored — Beaver Dam
Kimball, Henry, 2 cav — Kenosha
Knight, J H, a, capt 18 — Bayfield
Kelley, Jno, 2 — Janesville
Lee, Wm, 3 — La Crosse
Linton, F M, B 1 cav — Springfield
La Claire, Louis, D 7
Marshall, V R, k 4 — Egg Harbor
March, Wm S, C cav — Marshfield
McDermal, Jno A, A 14 — Little Rock, Ark
eCanl, Thos, G 1 8 8 — Tomah
Moore, C D, G 1 8 8 — Harvard, Neb
Mullen, Frank, ph — Sturgeon Bay

Mowon, Henry A, gen'l W S A, Iron Brigade, Ft
Klamath, W T
Noyes, Chas, detective service — Sturgeon Bay
Nichols, Wm F — Menominee
O'Connell, Jno, H 7 — Vandyne
Palmer, Henry, surgeon — Janesville
Proper, Peter C, D 6 cav — Davis
Richmond, F L, sgt maj 17 — Kenosha
Rhode, Jno I L, H 7 — Weganwega
Rich, Jas, me, col 8 colored — Sevastopol
Robinson, Jas, lcg colored troops — Whitewater
Stevenson, R S, 16 — Sturgeon Bay
Soper, J H, e corps ph, — Sturgeon Bay
Thorp, E A, a, G 4 — Bayfield
Thomas, W H, B 127 colored T — Racine
Thompson, Robt W, 4 cav — Menominee
Vaughn, Ira E, 17 U S I — Menasha
Van Styke N B, C 8 G M — Madison
Webster, F W, capt 8 U S C — Menasha
Wilson, Lyman, war of 1812 — Neillsville
Willis, Henry
Walker, E H, 29 C V — Fond du Lac
Wenk, Chas J deputy band, of Col — Watertown
Wing, N B, 69 cav — Janesville

UNITED STATES NAVY.
Allen, Edmund, Gunboat Juliette and Red River
Allen, Elias, Indianola — Nashun
Allison, Wm — Stevens Point
Boggs, Albert—Kickapoo, pa — Elkhorn
Bages, Omer, Monitor Kickapoo, West Gulf
Squadron — Elkhorn
Brown, G K — Waterville
Brown, J W, Gunboat — Port Edward
Bean, Frank J, Gunboat Paw Paw — Elo
Bigford, Walter, Enumerator — Quincy
Bruncie, Frank, Str Michigan — Ladoga
Clark, Cyral C, Keokuk, I — Winneiuka
Cole, M E, 2d Engineer Niaraga — Ripon
Caruthers, Hugh — W U Junction
Davrs, Irwin F, Gun Boat Sybil — Seymour
Duke, Jas, Crusader,Sailor — Milwaukee
Danbury, C M — LaCrosse
Edminster, W H, Crondit — Idain
Evans, David, A Johnson — Berlin
Felton, S K, General Pillow — Yankton, D P
Fowler, Dominic — Fremont
Godfrey, J W, Marine Gun Boat — Menasha
Graham, A F, Essex — Milwauke e
Gore, Frank M, sailor — Milwaukee
Gray, T R — Janesville
Hillman, E E, Montieello and Old N C — Darien
Hammer, Jno, Sunflower — Adell
Hasenfuss, Jacob B, Argosa — Manistee, Mich
Hayes, Jno, Kearsage — Basswood
Hunt, J W — Neenah
Harrison, S F — LaCrosse
Holly, J M — LaCrosse
Inglis, Robt, e — Bayfield
Jones, Daniel, U S Str Siren, me — Oshkosh
Johnson, Sam C, Surgeon in Navy — St Croix
Knudson, C, Proteur — Kenosha
Longworthy, A B, North Atlantic Squadron, m
Toronto, Canada
Lumb, Jas E, Flag Ship Benton — Adams
Locmis, E D — LaCrosse
Langdon, Phil — LaCrosse
Lindgraf, Andrew — Menasha
Murray, Jno, S Atlantic Squadron, under Du
pont — Nasewaupee
McElroy, Horace, 14 — Janesville
Mortimer, Patrick — Chicago, Ill
Neil, Cecil C, Shepperd Knapp and Sonama,
also Plato, Mayflower and Augusta, Aug, Ga
Nichols, G, U S Pittsburg, me — Fond du Lac
Nelson, Wm, U S Str Caromolelet — Kenosha
O'Regan, Timothy, Gunboats, Chillicothe, Es
sex and Reindeer — Fond du Lac
Purdy, A G, Miss Flotilla, mer — Fond du Lac

APPENDIX TO REUNION ROSTER.

Name	Location
Pock, E C	LaCrosse
Pavy, Wm L, Unens, Sachem, North Carolina, Michigan, E B Hale, Nipsic	Milwaukee
Roche, Thos, U S Str Sirou, me	Oshkosh
Sherman, Thad	Neenah
Stibbins, D W, Cincinnati, Mound City, U S S Portsmouth	Ahnapee
Spoor, J Ferris, U S Ram Avenger, Miss Squadron	Strong Prairie
Starin, Duane, Capt Geo W Peck, on Lake Koskomong	
Smith, Alex, Gulf Squadron, 1	Nasewaupee
Tneuzler, Jacob, B H 1st Mississippi, Marine, Briggid Str Baltic	Arnaton
Towers, Geo, U S Str General Pillow, Agt and Justice of Peace	Ellenwood, Kan
Treadway, Wm, DeSoto and Baltimore, Warren	
Thomas, Graf, John A Dix, f	Berlin
Van Buren, Chas, sailor, Marion Bat	Chicago
Wheeler, N A, Marmoria, me	Janesville
Wright, J B, Miami, me,	Milwaukee
Young's, King, Mich	Fremont

UNASSIGNED

Name	Location
Ayers, Riley, Mexican War	Waterville
Adams, J T, me	Jenny
Atherton, J, 1	Palmyra
Amos, A H	Racine
Abbott, Nat	LaCrosse
Anderson, D L, m	Lincoln
Alden, Isaac C	Weyauwega
Alcott, Jno	Waterville
Bailey, Robt	Plover
Baxter, Frank	LaCrosse
Blockridge, Jno J	Racine
Baxter, D E	LaCrosse
Barrow, D L, l	Plover
Bloom, Jno, l	Waupun
Bart, Jos	
Barker, Chas	Waupun
Barrows, Chas	
Brushel, Samuel, f	Brothertown
Bengley, N	
Bigiow, S M, teacher	Palmyra
Buzzoll, G H, m	Palmyra
Barlow, Horace	St Croix
Brisbin, Henry	Big Suamico
Buchan, Ed	Racine
Black Jas	Big Suamico
Brass, J	Richmond
Bailey, Henry	
Brown, Ed	
Brown, Leonard, me	Brandon
Bailey, Albert	
Barney, A N	Forth Worth, Texas
Clark, SD	Plover
Craig, D, elk	Palmyra
Cady, C H	
Cooley, R M	Stevens Point
Cooley, T F, paymaster	Plover
Chadwick, W S	
Cullier, Jubez	
Chamberlain, J H	
Carpenter, W H, me	Eldorado Mills
Carpenter, Al	
Cushing, Thos, l	Eldorado Mills
Cantwell, R	LaCrosse
Crocker, Geo	Plover
Crause, Jno	Muscoda
Comstock, F H	
Cheschro. Thos	Muscoda
Caborn, Richard	
Carter, A C	LaCrosse
Cullier, Joshua	
Crane, E F	LaCrosse
Clark, O A, lt	
Chesley, Jno	Plover
Courtney, Thos, f	Eden
Dog, Lieutenant	Augusta
Dushack, W	LaCrosse
David, J W, M D	Muscoda
Davis, Jno	Plover
Demarest, E L	Waupaca
Dolan, Jno, f	Eldorado
Durand, Wm	Waupun
Dolphis, Geo	LaCrosse
Dolphis, Wm	LaCrosse
Donald, Jno	Racine
Daniels, Ed	Big Suamico
Drew, Richard, S, f	Lincoln
Day, H	Warren
Dorothy, E B	St Croix
Dorgan, Michael K	StCroix
Edgerton, Chas	
Elfsey, L P	Warren
Empy, A J, D	Richmond
Elbert, L A	
Fowler, E W, lt	Stevens Point
Frantz, Henry	Chicago, Ill
Frost, Rd	Hammond
Finch, Abraham, f	Plover
Fulks, Sam'l	Whitewater
Fleming, Geo	Rippey
Foster, Wm C	Waupaca
Foster, Curil	
Farrand, D	LaCrosse
Fox, Jacob	
Full, l	LaCrosse
Frost, W J	Plover
Fishbeck, Thos	
Fishbeck, Iru	
Gintzer, M	LaCrosse
Gunkle, Conrad, lt	Chippewa Falls
Guy, R A	Richmond
Gibbon, Jno, 2, 6 and 7	St Paul, Minn
Gilbert, Jas L	Stones Prairie
Gilbert, Albert	
Gleason, Tom, l	Ripon
Griflin, H B	Waterford
Hall, Geo	Plover
Holliday, Davis	Richmond
Helms, Marvin H	Waseca, Minn
Holt, G	Warren
Heinrish, Heiner	Orihula
Hicks, W M	Springfield
Hilbach, Jno	
Hughes, H	Palmyra
Holmberger, C	
Hener, Heinrish	Orihula
Holmberger, C	
Hener, Heinrish	Orihula
Hatzenbuhter, J	LaCrosse
Hammond, A W, Army of Potomac	Durand
Hopkins, Thos	Weyauwega
Ives, S S	Lincoln
Jones, Jas H	Waupaca
Jeffries, Wm H	Muscoda
Jones, Thos	Nekimi
Kellogg, Roderick	Chardon, Ohio
Kertz, Henry	Muscoda
Kinsey, Lawrence	Kankauna
Kimball, J T	Plover
Koethe, G	LaCrosse
Koethe, L	LaCrosse
Killmner, O F	LaCrosse
Kennedamon, Jno	
King, Chas, mf	Palmyra
Krayne, Jno	Palmyra
Kaiser, M, me	Palmyra
Kelly, D A W	Palmyra
King, C F	St Croix
Kinsley, Geo	
Kapp, G A	Fond du Lac
Knight, Miletus	Durand
Largette, S	Fremont
Lee, G	Plover
Larson, T B	Rush River
Lathrop, Lucas	
Lamson, D	Warren
Liggins, J H, I 5 Cav	Springfield
McChesney, Jas P, 1st lt	Richmond
Mehan, Wm	Waterville
McArthur, J A	Palmyra
McDill, T H	Plover
Messersmidt, J B, h	Palmyra
Miles, A D	Palmyra
McClure	Big Suamico
Morris, Henry A	Durand
Murphy, Henry	
Murphy, Geo	Floyd Centre, Ia
McCarn, A J	Muscoda
Michael, Geo	Plover
Martin, J L	Emmetsburg, Ia
Moul, Fred, f	Waupun
Miller, C	LaCrosse
Morrison, Robt	Plover
Morrison, W F	LaCrosse
Morris, Sam'l A	Durand
Mabbott, J R	Muscoda
Martin, Henry	
Merritt, Jos	
Moody, Manly	
McClaughlin, Judd	
Maxon, D S	
Martin, Wm M	
Neveaux, Wm	
Newton, Chas	LaCrosse
Nothers, Felix	LaCrosse
Nobes, Robt N	
Nimocks, R J	LaCrosse
Nelsoo, W W, chaplain	Richmond
Oleson, Ole	Palmyra
Orlady, Jno G	Somerset
Olin, Clifford, lud	Waupaca
Orcutt, G W	LaCrosse
Platt, D B, lt	
Pruett, A	LaCrosse
Powles, Henry	Racine
Pollevs, D D	LaCrosse
Palmer, G W	
Page, A L	La Crosse
Powles, Wm	Racine
Pitt, Geo W	Fremont
Powell, B J	Richmond
Patterson, Alvin,	
Proudfit, J K	Wyandotte, Kan
Perry, M H	
Potter, Albert	
Prosser, Josiah	Brothertown
Richter, Jas	LaCrosse
Routh, Henry B	
Riddell, Geo, surg	
Rowly, Geo	Muscoda
Ross, W C, chaplain	Durand
Ratdka, Michael	Muscoda
Reifsnider, Jas lt, 1	Wanpun
Ratcliff, Jas	Waupaca
Roe, Peter	Palmyra
Rierstadt, Chas	Troy
Reed, Jno	Cylon
Reed, Chas	
Reten, Gildert A	Rush River
Sabin, Ezra	Lima
Stetson, E W	Newell, Ia
Spooner, W L	Springfield
Sanford, B F	Plover
Stevens, F F, maj and pay-master	Janesville
Simonds, M	Plover
Sheldon, C, R R	Iron Ridge
Severson, Jno L, f	Cambridge
Stone, J P, lt	Ripon
Sperbeck, R, f	Palmyra
Smith, Sam	Big Suamico
Stillman, Eugene G	Arkansas
Smith, H	
Spingleburg, Fred	Orihula
Stuart, Jno, f	Bayfield
Scott, Jos	
Stiles, Earl	Waupaca

Schelsser, Paul	Fremont	Thompson, J S	St Croix	Wilkes, Fred, 1	Eldorado
Sipher, Fred	Lind	Upham, C H	Ripon	Weinmouth, Al	Fremont
Shaughnessy, P H		VanEttre	Augusta	Williams, Lewis	Fremont
Simpson, Wm, 1	Waupun	Vandorn, P K	Winneconne	Whipple, Ed	Fremont
Summerton, Jas		Vanderhoof, J W		Wells, J M	Waupaca
Snyder, Jno, 1	Waupun	Vesey, Chas	Plover	Wilsey, H	LaCrosse
Smith, Jerry	Plover	Williams, J C		Walcott, E P	LaCrosse
Smith, Thos	Wevauwega	Woodworth, H N		Winters, A J	LaCrosse
Tuttle, Ransseller	Waupaca	Winters, J M, 7 cav	Neillsville	Wheelock, A B, p m	Eden, D T
Thompson, D R	LaCrosse	Wills, Geo W	St Croix	Wisemitter, C	Winneconne
Treadwell, Wisley		Walker, W M		Yankee, Louis	Waukesha
Taylor, G R, surg hosp service	Waupaca	Wells, J	Richmond	Young, Robt	Lincoln
Thatcher, Ed	Palmyra	Wheldon, E	LaCrosse	Young, Wm C	Wausera, Minn

G. D. NORRIS & CO.,
SHIP CHANDLERS

TENT AND SAIL MAKERS.

19 and 21 ERIE STREET,

Near North end E. Water Street Bridge,   MILWAUKEE WISCONSIN.

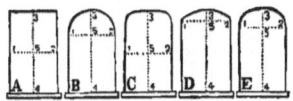

DEALERS IN

CORDAGE, CANVASS, NAVAL STORES, ETC.

INDEX.

ROSTER INDEX.
[SERIATIM, NOT ALPHABETICAL.]

First Infantry............................7, 275
Second Infantry........................11, 275
Third Infantry...........................17, 275
Fourth Infantry....................21, 261, 301
Fifth Infantry..........................21, 277
Sixth Infantry..........................29, 277
Seventh Infantry......................23, 279
Eighth Infantry........................39, 279
Ninth Infantry.........................45, 279
Tenth Infantry........................47, 281
Eleventh Infantry....................51, 281
Twelfth Infantry.....................57, 283
Thirteenth Infantry.................61, 283
Fourteenth Infantry................65, 283
Fifteenth Infantry...................71, 285
Sixteenth Infantry...................75, 285
Seventeenth Infantry...............81, 287
Eighteenth Infantry................85, 287
Nineteenth Infantry................89, 287
Twentieth Infantry.................91, 288
Twenty First Infantry..............95, 288
Twenty-Second Infantry..........99, 289
Twenty-Third Infantry...........103, 289
Twenty-Fourth Infantry.........107, 289
Twenty-Fifth Infantry............111, 289
Twenty-Sixth Infantry...........117, 291
Twenty-Seventh Infantry......121, 291
Twenty-Eighth Infantry.........125, 291
Twenty-Ninth Infantry..........129, 293
Thirtieth Infantry..................135, 293
Thirty-First Infantry.............137, 293
Thirty-Second Infantry.........139, 293
Thirty-Third Infantry............143, 295
Thirty-Fourth Infantry..........147, 295
Thirty-Fifth Infantry.............147, 295
Thirty-Sixth Infantry.............151, 295
Thirty-Seventh Infantry........155, 296
Thirty-Eighth Infantry..........159, 294
Thirty-Ninth Infantry............131, 296
Fortieth Infantry.................163, 296
Forty-First Infantry...............163, 296
Forty-Second Infantry...........165, 297
Forty-Third Infantry..............167, 297
Forty-Fourth Infantry...........169, 297
Forty-Fifth Infantry..............171, 297
Forty-Sixth Infantry..............171, 297
Forty-Seventh Infantry..........173, 297
Forty-Eighth Infantry............175, 299
Forty-Ninth Infantry..............177, 299
Fiftieth Infantry..................179, 299
Fifty-First Infantry...............181, 299
Fifty-Second Infantry............183, 299
Fifty-Third Infantry..............189, 299
First Cavalry.......................185, 299
Second Cavalry...................191, 301
Third Cavalry......................195, 301
Fourth Cavalry....................203, 301
First Heavy Artillery............207, 303
Milwaukee Cavalry..............211
Light Artillery....................211, 303
First Army Corps Infantry.....211
Berdan Sharp Shooters..........217
Resident Soldiers of other States...217, 303
Bay City Light Guards..........225
Bayfield Rifles....................226
Beloit City Guard................231
Bower City Rifles................229
Custer Rifles......................230

Delavan Guards....................230
Evergreen City Guards..........223
Fond du Lac Guards..............230
Germania Light Guards..........227
Governor's Guards................225
Guppey Guard......................226
Janesville Guards.................225
Kosciusko Guards.................226
La Crosse Light Guard..........224
Lake City Guards..................227
Ludington Guard..................229
Milwaukee Light Horse Squadron...227
Oshkosh Guards...................224
Randall Guard.....................229
Ripon Rifles.......................220
Sheridan Guard....................223
Sherman Guards..................224
Unity Guards......................230

ADVERTISERS' INDEX.
[ALPHABETICALLY ARRANGED.]

Adams, F F & Co...................126
Advertising Agents................160
Agents' Publishing House........286
Althouse, Wheeler & Co..........264
Allen & Hicks......................266
Andrews C E & Co.................172
"Andersonville"....................246
Appeal, The........................104
Appleton Chair and Bedstead Manufactory...36
Artificial Limbs....................184
Assurance Co., Commercial Union...184
Assurance Society, Equitable Life...178
Assurance Co., Western............80
Assurance Association, The London...201
Atkinson, D F.......................34
Ayer, N W & Son..................180
Baker, Robert.......................32
Baker & McKenney................96
Bakery, Excelsior Steam..........42
Baking Powder.....................172
Bass, James & Co..................141
Baty, Robert.......................184
Beer, Lager........................146
Belts, Electric....................102
Boots and Shoes...................112
Bond & Hunebert..................188
Bosworth, H & Sons..............130
Boylan & Co........................78
Bradford, Jas B.................120, 270
Brewing Co........................8, 170
Brewing Co., Best's...............148
Brewery, Bavaria..................182
Brick Manufacturers..............188
Bryan, Dr..........................102
Building Association, Fond du Lac...16, 58, 166
Buggies, Manufacturer of..........104
Calkins, E A......................110
Campbell, W G...................112
Cary, C J & Co....................86
Carbon Works, Michigan........106
Carpets, Curtains, etc...........114
Carpets, Drapery Work, etc....116, 228
Case, J I......................262, 264
Chapman, T A & Co..........100, 132
Chair and Bedstead Factory......
Cigars, Tobacco, etc.............264
Clark, James L..................138
Clement, C L.....................46

Cloaks, Suits
Clocks, Silv...
Clothing Ho...
Clothing, Mi...
Clothing ...
Clothing...
Connor, Miss
Cook & Hyde
Cracker and ...
Curtains, Dr...
Daniel & Gi...
Davis, Porte
Dentist...
Des Forges &
Dickey, A P.
Dixon, F J...
Doors, Blind
Domestic S...
Drapers, C...
Druggists, W
Drill, Monit...
Dutcher, Col
Dynamo Ma...
Engines, Bol...
Engines, Fa...
Eye and Ear
Falks, F...
Falbe, W F...
Fans, Ware...
Far o's Har...
Farmer, Th...
Fish Brothe...
Flints' Tob...
Flouring M...
Fond du La...
Fond du Ly...
Fond du La...
Fountain, A...
Galloway F...
Garvin, Joh...
Gas Fixtur...
Glass, Stain
Gluek's Ten
Godfrey &
Goldsmith ...
Goods, Mili
Goods, Mili
Goods, Lad...
Goods, Dry.
Goods, Dre...
Greene & N
Griffith, J ...
Groceries, ...
Groceries, ...
Groceries, ...
Gunther, ...
Hair Goods
Hair Store,
Hale, P C...
Handt, C A
Hamilton, ...
Harding, A
Harrow Co...
Haas Bros..
Haskins, C...
Hayes, Geo
Hats, Caps,
Heckman, ...
Hempsteds
Henry, T S

INDEX

Herald Agents.................................286
Hibbard & Vance...............................152
Home Ins Co., N Y.............................138
Home, Soldiers National....186, 194, 196, 198, 200
Hood Liquid...................................164
Hontaman Bros & Co............................88
Horgen, Jas A.................................120
Hotels of Wisconsin...........................362
Hotel, Woods..................................134
Houghman, Dr..................................142
How it commenced..............................5
Howe Machine..................................220
Hub and Spoke Factory.........................140
Hunters Magnetic Springs..................196-202
Institute, Medical and Surgical...............294
Instruments, Surgical.........................184
Insurance Co., N W Mutual Life..............2, 99
Insurance Society, N Y Life...................12
Insurance Co.'s, Hans Bros Agents.............14
Insurance Co., Commercial Fire................28
Insurance Co.'s, B C Baker, Agt...............32
Insurance Co., Washington Life................54
Insurance Agency, General.....................66
Insurance Co., Mass Mutual Life...............70
Insurance Co., The Travelers..................74
Insurance Co.'r, J L Martin, Agent............76
Insurance Co., Springfield....................82
Insurance Co., N Y Mutual Life................84
Insurance Agents, C J Cary & Co...............86
Insurance Co., The Merchants..................92
Insurance Co., N Y Mutual Benefit Life.......100
Insurance Co., Northwestern National.........100
Insurance & Loan Agency, H L Lawson's........124
Insurance Agents, Daniel & Gile..............126
Ins and Loan Agency, Green & Newton..........131
Insurance Co., N Y Home......................138
Insurance Co., The Queen Fire................140
Insurance Co., represented by J Bass & Co...144
Insurance Co's, Ed L Maloney, Agt............150
Ins and Vessel Agt's, Hibbard & Vance........152
Ins and Real Estate Agt., W McDermott........168
Insurance Co., The Miss Valley Mfrs Mutual..176
Insurance Co.'s, The Fireman's...............204
Insurance Co., The Hartford Fire.............204
Ins Co., Manufacturers' Fire and Marine......204
Insurance Co., Hoffman Fire..................208
Insurance Co of North America...........208, 274
Insurance Co., The U S Life..................208
Insurance Co., Scottish Commercial...........214
Insurance Co., The Orient....................214
Insurance Co., The Conn Mutual Life..........214
Insurance Co., The Old Penn Fire........214, 274
Insurance Co., The New York Life.............232
Insurance Co., The National Life.............270
Ins Agt, General Fire and Life, C A Haudt....276
Insurance Co., The Continental Life..........28
Insurance Co., Niagara.......................312
Jewelry, etc.................................120
Jeweler and engraver.........................166
Jewelry, etc............................124, 266
Journal, Morning.............................210
Kirby House..................................106
Knapp, W A...................................160
La Belle Wagon Works.........................6
Rake, Self Operating Wheel...................158

Lands, Pine..................................72
Lang, D C & J H..............................48
Lawson, H L..................................124
Leidersdorf, B...........................60, 178
Lime and Sand Stone..........................180
Limbs, Artificial............................184
Logs, Lumber, etc.........................50, 54
Lumber, etc...............................10, 14
Lumber, Sash, Doors, etc..................22, 52
Lusk, G W....................................60
Machinery and Supplies..................120, 136
Machine, Sewing..............................208
Machine, Sewing..............................152
Machine Co., Threshing..................283, 285
Malony, Ed L.................................150
Mann, I G....................................142
Map of Wisconsin Central R R.................285
Martin, J L..................................76
Marston and Beveridge........................140
Matches, Star................................138
Matthews Bros & Co...........................112
Maywood Manufactory..........................212
McDonald, Alex...............................52
McDermott, Wm................................164
Mendal, Henry M..........................60, 178
Menasha, Hub and Spoke Works.................140
Merrill & Ferguson...........................84
Millils......................................16
Millils Manufacturing Co.................22, 174
Miller, Miss E...............................124
Millinery....................................126
Milwaukee Sentinel, The......................68
Milwaukee Sunday Telegraph...................110
Moore & Galloway.............................10
Morawetz, Jacob..............................40
Morgan, Jas..................................192
Muller & Hharit.........................124, 142
Music, Temple of.............................26
National Home...........................186, 200
Naughten, Jno................................6
Newton, H W..................................174
News, Milwaukee Daily........................26
Nicoll, The Tailor...........................206
Nichols, H...................................100
Oil Co., Northwestern........................164
Oshkosh Northwestern.........................0
Packard, O L............................120, 136
Paper Hangings..........................124, 142
Peck's Sun...................................20
Pen, The Mac Kinnon..........................142
Pension and Claim Agt........................218
Perkins, A T.................................46
Perkins, Jas S...............................152
Pianos, Organs, etc...............129, 1,6, 270
Pier, P K..........................4, 10, 160, 166
Portraits, etc...............................296
Printer's Job................................166
Printing House, The Star Steam...............24
Pulverizing, Chicago Screw...................212
Queen, Insurance Co..........................140
Railroad, Fond du Lac, Amboy & Peoria....30, 92
Railroad, C R I & P..........................310
Railroad, Wisconsin Central.........38, 234, 254
Reinhard, Misses M & A.......................132
Reilly, Henry................................130

Reporter, The Saturday.......................206
Resorts, Summer...196, 204, 236, 238, 240, 242, 244, 246, 2,0, 251
Reunion of 1869, The Soldiers................233
Rich & Silber................................108
Riedel, F F..................................204
Rosenkrans, O L & Co.........................120
Roster, Regimental Reunion...................7
Rubber Co., Goodyear.........................98
Rundle & Spence..............................180
Rupture......................................206
Russell, Jas.................................210
Russell, C J............................290, 304
Saturday, Reporter The.......................206
Schiltz, Jos............................18, 170
Sentinel, The Milwaukee......................68
Sherman, Dr J A..............................208
Shoes and Slippers...........................142
Smith, L'Lum.................................266
Smith, Albert L..............................164
Smithograph Manufacturing Co.................286
Springs, Magnesic............................188
Stanley & Co............................124, 162
Stained Glass................................216
Stark, Brothers..............................114
Steenberg, O C...............................62
Stewart, Alex................................52
Stone Yard...................................180
Sullivan, Jno E & Co.........................202
Sun, Peck's..................................20
Superphosphate...............................106
Suydam, Jas..................................98
Tailor, Merchant.............................126
Tailor, Nicoll...............................206
Teas, etc....................................8
Telephone Co.................................24
Telegraph, Milwaukee Sunday..................110
Threshing Machine Factory....................284
Tilden, G A..................................106
Title Page...................................1
Tobacco Works, Western Steam.............60, 178
Tobacco Works, The Badger State..............126
Tobaccos.....................................178
Trunks.......................................48
VanBrunt & Davis.............................154
VanBrunt & Barber............................158
VanPelt......................................118
Wagon Works, LaBelle.........................6
Wagon Manufactory................94, 102, 150
Wagon Co., Spring............................46
Watrous, J A............................104, 110
Webster & Lawson.............................140
White, Jas S.................................26
Whitnal & Frank..............................102
White & VanPelt..............................118
Whitehouse, T W..............................120
Wild, B & Co.................................42
Willard, V R.................................72
Wisconsin Farmer, The........................200
Wind Mills...................................304
Window Blinds................................88
Wolcott & Gregg..............................152
Wood & Notholm...............................112
Wood, Lant...................................138
Worthington, Sam.............................286

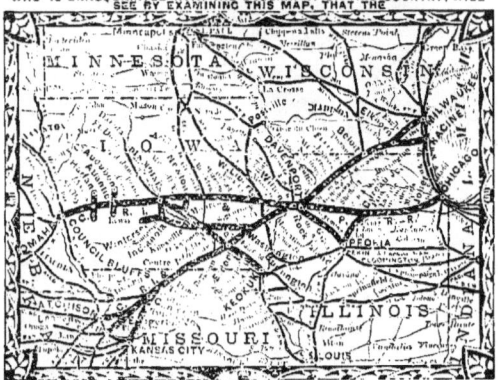

THE SOLDIERS REUNION ROSTER---CONCLUSION.

THE BUSINESS PART.

It seemed to your executive committee there was a very general demand for publication of a roster of your names.

To issue an edition of 5,000 volumes the size and contents of this, required an expenditure of money exceeding that number of dollars—the book paper alone costing in cash half that amount, while the preparing, printing, postage letters, cards, circulars, telegrams, express, freights, insurance, clerks, copyists, assistants, etc., cost more than as much again. We could not consent the book should cost you to exceed one dollar.

Many of you were in business, business that you advertised, and it was deemed best to break the expense of the book to you, by inviting business men favorable to the project to insert their announcements. This you will notice has been done, you have twice as large and twice as good a book and more of them, than you could have had without their aid, and at half the cost. Don't forget this. The men who have so aided you, are classed among the best business men of the country. If they find it pays to do this, they will lift again and again, and the road to future issues is open and comparatively clear to those of you who may succeed the present committee. This finance question is the important one in all projects. Fix this solid, and we can shake, hurrah, tip back in our chair, elevate our feet, and yarn it with clear conscience, and patriotic gusto.

Your present committee steps down and out on the eighth of June. Some of you will be elected to succeed us, and not only for their benefit especially, but for advantage of us all. We wish to make the following suggestions and impress upon you their importance:

When any of us want to buy anything, look within this roster and see if it is adve   . If so, patronize those who have in this way patronized us. It is not claimed that all the good, solid and patriotic business men or firms have advertised with us—the others when they find it pays will come in next time—nor is it at empted to make this an arbitrary classification; but it is a good rule, as a matter of sentiment, to remember those who remember u . In this, a matter of business, the business men wi 'gi   us unlimited patronage hereafter if we prove to th a' pays to do so. If we, as soldiers, will hitch our inter .ts to the business interests of the State, the success of our Association is guaranteed. Let us do this, not as begging for favors, but yielding value for value, and the published records of our Association will be standard, and spa   therein sought for far and near.

THE LAST WORD.

This is the *last* page of the book, hastily written after the others were in type and placed here for convenience. There are *two* different rosters, running in same regimental order. The first commences on page 7, ending on page 223 The other commencing on page 275. The index will be found conveniently arranged.

A name not found in its place in one or the other had not been received up to May 20th, 1889. Names and addresses received hereafter will be sent to the Milwaukee *Sunday Telegraph* for publication in its weekly Soldier Chapters, so that by noting in this roster any corrections or new addresses there given, the book can be maintained continuously complete and available.

No one can be more grieved at errors and omissions which will doubtless be found herein than the compiler.

Two serious unforeseen events rendered it impossible to put in some of the interesting sketches prepared and intended for the roster. Mr. Darwin C. Pavy, who has had the general supervision of the compilation, since adjournment of the legislature, was suddenly called away from his labors, the middle of May, and a disastrous fire in one of the manufacturing establishments in which the writer was largely interested occurring at the same time, threw more than double duty on the publishers, a duty they most heroically performed, regardless of hours or days, running continuously without intermission day and night and Sundays, to complete the work, and only omitting some sketches which would otherwise have been inserted.

On the whole, as one becomes acquainted with the volume, especially if he considers the brief space of time allowed to compile, he may draw consolation from Maud Muller's lament, "it might have been"—worse.

ESTABLISHED 1850.

NIAGARA

LOSSES PAID Over $6,000,000

FIRE INS. CO.,

OF NEW YORK

Cash Assets

JANUARY 1st, 1880.

$1,357,776.85.

of Which

OVER

$900,000.00

in

United States Bonds.

[From The New York Daily Bulletin, 10th Jan 1880.]

THE BANNER COMPANY.—The NIAGARA Fire Insurance Company is entitled to the credit of having made the largest relative gain in surplus of any of the New York fire companies last year. Its Annual statement shows that over and above all liabilities, the Company has a surplus in amount equal to its cash capital. In other words, the Niagara has not only $500,000 of capital, but another clear $500,000 besides, after providing for all policy liabilities. This indicates A GAIN IN SURPLUS of some $40,000 during 1879, in spite of all the fires and the prevalent demoralization in the business and conclusively proves that conservatism and skill are at the helm. The Niagara was *the first New York Fire Company to enter the agency field*, and at its present rate of progress gives promise of being one of the last that should leave that field. For such companies we have none too many.

Liabilities

JANUARY 1st, 1880.

Loss Claims, $42,757.0(
Reserve for
Re-Ins., 291,757.1;
All other Cl's, 235.5(

Total, $334,139.6

Capital St'k, $500,000.0
Net Surplus, 517,637.2

Total, $1,351,779.8

Surplus as to Policy Holders, — — — $1,017,637.3.

Agencies at all Prominent Points in This Nation

P. NOTMAN, Pres.   THOS. F. GOODRICH, Sec'y.

DAVID BEVERIDGE, Mang'r West'n Dep't.

THE CHICAGO & NORTHWESTERN R'Y.

TRANS-CONTINENTAL ROUTE,

Council Bluffs, Denver and California Route,

St. Paul and Minneapolis Line,	Milwaukee Line,
Lake Superior Route,	Elroy Route,
Winona and St. Peter Railroad,	Dubuque Route,
Sioux City and Yankton Line,	Freeport Line.

AND THE ROUTES, LINES AND BRANCHES OF THIS

PIONEER LINE,

RUNNING THROUGH FIVE GREAT STATES.

THE CHICAGO & NORTHWESTERN RAILWAY

OFFERS THE TRAVELING PUBLIC

GREATER ADVANTAGES

THAN ANY OTHER ROAD IN THE

WEST OR NORTHWEST,

AMONG WHICH MAY BE ENUMERATED:

1.—Its various lines reach more important business centers than any road in its territory.
2.—Its lines are the shortest, hence connections sure at terminal and junction points, and is not obliged to run trains at breakneck speed to make its connections.
3.—Its trains are invariably on time, in consequence of its lines being the shortest, and its system of moving trains the most perfect.
4.—The excellence of its road-bed and track has been tested by making the unequalled time of 11 hours and 11 minutes between Chicago and Council Bluffs, 488 miles, which is the fastest time ever made between these points.
5.—Its Steel Rail Tracks, Iron bridges, stone culverts, air brakes, &c., all conduce to render the "North-Western" absolutely safe, free from accident, and makes the traveler feel perfectly secure.
6.—Its equipment is the very best, being manufactured by the C. & N. W. Company, and contains all the modern appliances which add to the comfort and convenience of the passenger.
7.—Its trains are all equipped with the Patent Air Brakes, Couplers, Buffers, &c., which place the entire train under the direct control of the engineer.
8.—Hotel Cars.—It is the only road between Chicago and Council Bluffs running the Pullman Hotel and Sleeping Cars, which were constructed without regard to cost, and expressly for this line. They embrace all the Elegancies, Comforts and Luxuries of the best Hotels in the country, and present to the traveling public that which has so long been desired—a line of Hotels on Wheels. They run daily between Chicago and Council Bluffs on its Chicago, Council Bluffs and California line.
9.—It is the great Pullman Palace and Sleeping Car Road of the Northwest. The Pullman Cars are superior in every appointment to any other sleeping cars in use, preferred and patronized by all the best posted travelers. Passengers from all quarters may be safe of finding Pullman Cars on all night trains of the "North-Western," and should be particular in getting tickets over this road to get this advantage.
10.—It is the ONLY road running the Pullman Sleeping Cars between CHICAGO AND ST. PAUL, SPARTA, GREEN BAY, MILWAUKEE, CLINTON, WINONA, MADISON, OSHKOSH, FOND DU LAC, DUBUQUE, ROCHESTER, FREEPORT, MENASHA, SIOUX CITY, McGREGOR, MANKATO, OWATONNA, APPLETON, CEDAR RAPIDS, MARSHALLTOWN.
11.—It is the old "Lake Shore Route," between Chicago and Milwaukee, and the line passing through the beautiful suburbs of Ravenswood, Evanston, Lake Forest, Highland Park, Waukegan, Kenosha, Racine, on which is run

THE PARLOR EASY CHAIR CARS.

12.—It is the only road running four daily Express trains into Minnesota—two to St. Paul, and two via Winona, Rochester, Owatonna, Mankato, Marshall, New Ulm, and into Dakota.
13.—Is the only road having two lines from Chicago for the Lake Superior country; one via Milwaukee, Fond du Lac and Green Bay; one via Watertown, Fond du Lac, Oshkosh and Green Bay.

14.—It reaches, with its various lines, the pleasant "Summer Resorts," Fishing and Hunting Grounds of the great Northwest.
15.—It traverses six great States, affording with its many lines, the greatest variety of scenery, numerous points of interest and diversity of country, rendering a journey pleasant and profitable.
16.—It recognizes as identical with its interests those of its patrons, and has established Eating Houses at convenient points where meals are served at seasonable hours, at the liberal price of 50 cents each. These are reduced rates from prices of 75 cents.
17.—Through cars, of all classes, are run between important points, thus relieving the passenger from any anxiety of frequent changes of cars.
18.—The "Chicago, St. Paul & Minneapolis Line" is the only line from Chicago using, in connection with the St. Paul, Minneapolis & Manitoba R. R. and Northern Pacific R. R., a Union Depot at St. Paul. Remember this in buying Tickets to points beyond St. Paul.
19.—Rates.—It is prepared to ticket passengers to all important points, from any of its Coupon Ticket Offices, at the Lowest Current Rates.
20.—It runs no emigrant trains or cars. Passengers holding Second-class or Emigrant Tickets VIA THE "NORTHWESTERN" are CARRIED ON EXPRESS TRAINS, and in well ventilated cars with good upholstered seats, making same time as first-class passengers.
21.—It carries 150 POUNDS of baggage free on all classes of tickets for each full fare ticket, and 75 pounds on each half fare ticket.

GENERAL OFFICERS.

ALBERT KEEP	President	Chicago.
M. L. SYKES	Vice-Pres't, Sec. & Treas., 52 Wall St.	New York.
MARVIN HUGHITT	Gen'l Manager and Gen'l Sup't	Chicago
C. C. WHEELER	Ass't General Superintendent	"
H. C. WICKER	Freight Traffic Manager	"
C. G. FORD	General Freight Agent	"
W. S. MELLEN	Assistant General Agent	"
C. H. KNAPP	Division Freight Agent	"
C. V. McKINLAY		"
H. F. McCULLOUGH		W. & S. P. R.R Winona.
W. H. ST SNYFF	General Passenger Agent	Chicago.
W. A. THRALL	General Ticket Agent	"
E. H. JOHNSON	Chief Engineer	"
B. C. COOK	General Solicitor	"
M. M. KIRKMAN	Local Treas. and Gen'l Accountant	"
J. B. REDFIELD	Assistant Secretary and Auditor	"
R. W. HAMER	Purchasing Agent	"
S. A. PHILLIPS	General Baggage Agent	"
W. F. FITCH	General Claim Agent	"
G. H. THAYER	Superintendent of Telegraph	"
C. E. SIMMONS	Land Commissioner	"
F. P. CRANDON	Tax Commissioner	"
F. M. LACE	Car Accountant	"

www.ingramcontent.com/pod-product-compliance
Lightning Source LLC
Chambersburg PA
CBHW022046230426
43672CB00008B/1081